PENGUIN REFERENCE

THE QUICKWAY CROSSWORD DICTIONARY

9780723220190
W0027748

THE QUICKWAY CROSSWORD DICTIONARY

Twelfth edition

Compiled and revised by
Henry W. Hill and Rowland G. P. Hill

PENGUIN BOOKS

PENGUIN BOOKS

Published by the Penguin Group
Penguin Books Ltd, 80 Strand, London WC2R 0RL, England
Penguin Putnam Inc., 375 Hudson Street, New York, New York 10014, USA
Penguin Books Australia Ltd, Ringwood, Victoria, Australia
Penguin Books Canada Ltd, 10 Alcorn Avenue, Toronto, Ontario, Canada M4V 3B2
Penguin Books India (P) Ltd, 11 Community Centre, Panchsheel Park, New Delhi – 110 017, India
Penguin Books (NZ) Ltd, Cnr Rosedale and Airborne Roads, Albany, Auckland, New Zealand
Penguin Books (South Africa) (Pty) Ltd, 24 Sturdee Avenue, Rosebank 2196 South Africa

Penguin Books Ltd, Registered Offices: 80 Strand, London WC2R 0RL, England

www.penguin.com

First published by Frederick Warne & Co. Ltd 1953
Twelfth edition published by Penguin Books 1998
2

Copyright © Frederick Warne & Co. Ltd, 1998
All rights reserved

Set in 8/8½ Monotype Ehrhardt
Typeset by Rowland Phototypesetting Ltd, Bury St Edmunds, Suffolk
Printed in England by Clays Ltd, St Ives plc

Except in the United States of America, this book is sold subject
to the condition that it shall not, by way of trade or otherwise, be lent,
re-sold, hired out, or otherwise circulated without the publisher's
prior consent in any form of binding or cover other than that in
which it is published and without a similar condition including this
condition being imposed on the subsequent purchaser

CONTENTS

'Open Locks, Whoever Knocks'

PREFACE

This Dictionary has been specially compiled to meet the exacting needs of modern crossword enthusiasts. All the distinctive features of *The Quickway Key* – of which over 100,000 copies have been sold – have been retained; but notable additions have been made. These include a far greater number of CLUE words, a wide range of synonyms, and a complete vocabulary of the Eight-Letter Words.

The distinctive features are:

1. All CLUE words having the same number of letters are grouped together.
2. Every line begins with a possible CLUE word.
3. All CLUE words are printed in capital letters.
4. Classification code letters, such as *ar* = architecture, *md* = medicine, etc. are placed at the extreme right-hand edges of the lines, on the basis of the equivalents. A detailed list is given on page xi.
5. A very wide range of the latest words has been recorded, of which few may be found in any other one dictionary. Words in brackets indicate, not synonyms or equivalents, but areas in which the word in question is to be encountered.
6. Participles and past tenses of verbs have frequently been recorded, especially when in the passive they form adjectival phrases.

These distinctive features materially reduce the time that has to be spent in the search for interesting clues.

A large number of dictionaries have been consulted; these include *The Shorter Oxford Dictionary*, *The Century*, *Chambers's*, *Nuttall's*, *Webster's Collegiate Dictionary*; also etymological and classical dictionaries, Roget's *Thesaurus* and Nuttall's *Synonyms and Antonyms*. Clue words have been taken from encyclopaedias, *The Statesman's Year Book*, Dr Brewer's *Reader's Handbook*, and authoritative books on Glass, China, Pewter, Curios, etc.

Words such as **CRITH**, **HELITE**, **CHENAR**, **LIBIDO**, **ZYGOTE**, etc., have been collected from scientific books and reports dealing with Modern Chemistry, Electricity, Physics, Zoology, Botany, Engineering, Physiology, etc., also from books on Theosophy and New Thought. Store catalogues and the special catalogues referring to wireless apparatus, tools, seeds, drapery, and other trades have been ransacked. A wide range of terms dealing with sports and pastimes has been included, as for example: **SCRUM**, **CAPPED**, **STANCE**, **DORMY**, **ROQUET**, **BURNED**, **GOLD**, **HYPE**, **OXER**, **CRAPS**.

Australian, South African, Canadian, Indian, American, and foreign words, such as **COOEE**, **TREK**, **MUSH**, **BHYLE**, **PRONTO**, **DUCE**, **TCHEKA**, are represented.

The mythological names include many Greek, Roman, Norse, Egyptian, Chaldean, and Hindu Gods.

Nearly all English words have in the course of centuries passed through many variations in their spellings. For example, in Murray's *New English Dictionary* the spelling of the word 'POWDER' has between the thirteenth and seventeenth centuries passed through the following variations, *poudre*, *pudre*, *puder*, *powdre*, *powdir*, *powdyr*, *pouder*, *powdere*, *poudire*, *pouldre*, *pulder*, *poulder*, *powlder*; and to these might be added the Scots variations of *pouther* and *powther*. A number of variations in spelling have been collected, but the range of variations recorded in different dictionaries is so large that those now given should not be regarded as exhaustive.

The selection of suitable definitions or synonyms for the words of three or four letters seldom presents any difficulty; in fact, these short words often have so many completely different meanings that more than one line is required to indicate possible clue solutions. For example, **BOX** may refer to a receptacle, a shrub, a driver's seat, a box at the theatre, an affair of fisticuffs, or to some occult nautical rite in which a compass is involved.

The longer words are usually more definite in their meanings; but **BESTED** and **WORSTED** may in some cases be synonymous terms, whilst **CLEAVE** may imply either 'adhere to' or 'split asunder'. Crossword setters, however, have a somewhat similar outlook to that master of the English language, Humpty Dumpty, who declared that: 'When *I* use a word, it means just what I choose it to mean – neither more nor less'. And further, being bound by no inhibition of compunction in splitting up words to suit the nefarious purpose, the setter may insist that **BOOKS-HOP** is a voluminous dance in spite of any exact or meritorious definition while evolving his uncanny mystification.

Similarly, there are those who insist upon providing a clue such as 'five o'clock disappointment' for 'no tea' (spelt 'NO-T' i.e. 'NOT'), or 'up to his neck in the sea' for the philosopher Seneca (SE-NEC(K)-A) and, recently, that two auxiliaries acting correctly thus BE/HAVE.

This particular aspect of crosswords has been delightfully epitomized in the sonnet commemorating the 5,000th Crossword in *The Times*, reproduced on page xi by the kind permission of its author.

The various items enumerated under the heading *GENERAL INFORMATION* will frequently be found of special value in elucidating clues without the necessity of delving into a selection of reference books.

The compiler wishes to express his thanks to those numerous correspondents who so kindly forwarded valuable suggestions. It is his hope that this new volume will be found to fulfil the multifarious requirements of earnest crossword solvers and setters and so enhance the pleasures of the crossword hour.

H. W. HILL

Postscript

For this 12th edition, our fourth further revision, many more amplifications of definitions, meanings and usage, as well as new words have been added throughout this volume.

To the General Information section we have added the chronology of the founding and spread of the European Union, and the memberships within the Russian Commonwealth of Independent States (C.I.S.), the Länder of reunified Germany, communities in Federal Spain, as well as Metropolitan and older counties of England and Wales, and the Regions in Scotland. We are indebted to Dr David Hill for the much longer list of Chemical Elements.

The History of the Crossword Puzzle and our Miscellany of verses and quotations from letters and wordy articles is retained for your pleasure.

Once again we thank the generous-minded crossword enthusiasts for sending in words and suggestions, as well as corrections, welcomed and incorporated whenever possible.

R.G.P.H. and I.E.H.

Publisher's Note

The preparation of this, the 12th Edition has once again been undertaken by the author's son Rowland G. P. Hill and also Ingrid Hill for this fourth revision. Nevertheless, this resulting, greatly enlarged, volume remains substantially in the style of the 8 editions compiled (1923–51) by the late Col. H. W. Hill.

A HISTORY OF THE CROSSWORD PUZZLE

What is a fifteen-letter definition of one of the two or three most popular inventions of the twentieth century?

The answer, of course, is 'crossword puzzle'. On 21 December 1913, the first crossword puzzle ever set appeared in the *New York World* and the craze spread like wildfire. By 1925 it had crossed the Atlantic and Britain rapidly became a nation of crossword addicts. That bastion of dignity, *The Times*, however, was characteristically cautious. It was not until 1930, after a lively debate in the letters column, that it finally succumbed. The crossword was here to stay. Today 99 per cent of the world's daily newspapers and most Sunday papers carry a crossword and regular solvers are counted in multi-millions.

While the shape of the crossword puzzle derives from the word-square, with its repetition in both directions, the notion of differentiated verticals and horizontals probably derives from the acrostic: Greek 'akros' (at the end), and 'stichos' (line of verse). The sybils or prophetesses of ancient Greece used this form of riddle as fortune-telling devices and Cicero records this in De Divinatione. This led in due course to the double acrostic form favoured by our Queen Victoria.

However, it was in 1913 that Arthur Wynne of Liverpool, England, then with the *New York Sunday World*, was determined to introduce something fresh; so he began on a geometric shape – a diamond-shaped 'word-hanger' and gave it the name 'word-cross'.

Soon, the name was transposed to 'crossword', from the subtitle 'find the missing *cross words*', and the enthusiastic public began to send in their own creations; Wynne began to change a word here and there – the right of the crossword editor to suit the readers. It was the solvers, however, who insisted on rules: such as no obscure abbreviations; minimum use of (only well known) foreign words; definitions in dictionary form; that the grid pattern shall interlock all over; a set minimum of squares shall be black; a limit to the number of letters in isolation (unkeyed); and that the design be symmetrical.

This, in turn, led to a greater familiarity with all the shortest words; so much so that the **ZOO** was regarded as home for the **EMU** and animals from **AI** to **YAK**; the most important river was the **PO**, and Egypt was only famous for **IBIS** and **ISIS**, while **ERSE** was the celebrated language of all time!

Not long after this, the then editor of *The Bookman* found that the crossword had actually brought back many dying but acceptable words, to the extent that those previously unfamiliar with specific terms like **APSE** and **NAVE** in a cathedral, or more general words such as **AVER**, **IRE**, **NEE**, **EMIT**, **ERR**, **ELATE** etc. had now become aware of these words. Such was the comeback of vocabulary and usage that this new vehicle for wordpower had brought about, even if cliché use was a resultant hazard.

Reaction soon set in with the urge to discard 'limited vocabulary', make use of reference books, and for an undeniable educational value to bring the standard to a great art worthy of its exalted ancestors.

By 1925 there were about 10 million fans in America. Schools began to make use of them and university psychologists compared crossword ability with IQ tests and found parallel results. Further, a new national habit was revealed in changed situations, in everyday life.

To take one instance. The Baltimore and Ohio Railroad installed dictionaries in each carriage of commuter trains for the convenience of passengers, many of whom took crossword books when on long journeys; and one witness said that 'everyone is going about with knobs of knowledge sticking out on their foreheads like the buffers on a railway engine'.

One New York magistrate was faced with the frustrating task of distracting an intent group of twenty-one solvers; when one defendant pleaded innocent of failure to appear to the charge by explaining he had a longstanding engagement with a crossword, the judge promptly sentenced him to ten days in the workhouse!

Another incident related the effect on a would-be solver who was joined by two others in a noisy restaurant. When closing time had passed none of the three would budge, so the police had to threaten arrest of the first of the three. Thereupon that guilty party expressed delight at the prospect of further, uninterrupted, solitary solving being offered to him!

In the third printing of *The Times Crossword Puzzle Book* in 1925 – that vintage year for solvers – the following warning was given to solvers to alert readers to the possible two symptoms that might result once the contagion set in:

1. If you want to do any more work the rest of the day, put down this book now. If you insist on going ahead, say goodbye to everything else.
2. This is your problem: Do you want to own a book which will delight and distract you (and perhaps shatter the serenity of your home) for at least one hundred hours?

Again, a Broadway revue, 'Puzzles of 1925', included a skit on a Sanatorium for crossword fans seeking a cure, and in that year England reeled with horror as collectively 5 million working hours a day in America – most of them in office time – were spent on poring over a puzzle. 'But that couldn't happen here!'

However, Arthur Wynne had already sold six puzzles to the *Sunday Express*, and thereby earned the title of Crossword Originator and Constructor on both sides of the Atlantic. Soon, in that year, *The Times* was forced to eat its words. 'Who would have thought . . . that the crossword puzzle had come to stay? To most of us it looked like a transatlantic craze which could not be expected to take root in solid, unimaginative English minds.'

What a comeback for those, knowledgeable in the classics and such mysteries, to make use of a mine of 'irrelevance' and so-called 'useless information'.

It only remains to add that, just as everything stops for tea, so, even with newsprint rationing in wartime, the crossword remained a feature which many brains felt to be a necessity, for balance of mind and outlook.

Thus, in its inimitable, modest, way the crossword has invaded the international scene leaving a trail of possessed solvers in its wake.

Abridged and adapted from 'A History of the Crossword Puzzle' by Michelle Arnot; Papermac. This book also contains samples of not only the first, but other famous crosswords, as they originally appeared.

During the 1920s the first edition of this book – in pocket diary format, with a pencil – was already in evidence, especially among those travelling to and from the City. Later editions were enlarged to the present size.

R.G.P.H.

CROSSWORD MISCELLANY

To the Editor of The Times

SIR,

Much have I travelled in another life,
Taken the golden road to Samarkand,
Rolled down to Rio, wandered down the Strand
(Bananaless), asked after Laban's wife.
I swore, 'I will not cease from mental strife
Nor shall my pencil slumber in my hand
Till I have re-discovered Penguinland
And found a cricketer's Malayan knife.'

In vain; the tangled clues still tantalize
And synonyms elude, like runic rhymes.
So would-be solvers with lack-lustre eyes,
Confronted with the anagram for limes,
Look at each other with a wild surmise
Silent, upon a crossword in *The Times*.

Yours faithfully,
ELTON EDE

The Crossword Cure

To The Times *Crossword Editor*

O nameless coiner of the cryptic clue,
O master of delusive definition,
Embracing in your panoramic view
A world of miscellaneous erudition,
Once more I pay the homage due
To your wise conduct of your Inquisition,
Bringing a daily boon and breathing space
To the tired runners in a mad world's race.

You leave no fruitful avenues unexplored
That minister to innocent hilarity,
But never strike a harsh or jarring chord,
Or find a virtue in unveiled vulgarity.
Rumour and gossip are by you ignored;
You season ridicule with kindly charity,
Yet on occasion with unerring eyes
Transfix malicious folly as it flies.

You jog my memory with your mental jerks;
To you, in fine, I owe a double debt
For while the old machinery still works
And shows no sign of breaking down as yet –

Thanks to the stimulus of your quips and quirks –
  You teach me to remember, and forget.
For Hell's most grisly gangsters have no power
To crash the gate that guards the Crossword hour.

C. L. GRAVES

The above poem, which appeared in *The Times* of 23 July 1941, is reproduced by the kind permission of the author's son.

Wordy Might-have-beens

Many of us think that words mean what we can remember we thought they meant, in the manner that two famous historians described history as being not what we thought but what we can remember. We have done just that, as other methods are self-defeating.

Reader's Digest tells us that 'it pays to increase your word power' and this was clear to Sir Winston Churchill, who roused, cajoled, admonished and conciliated people of all nations during an era of unparalleled tribulation. He used strong words to convey his vigorous thoughts, such as imponderable, vitiate, ignoble, verbiage, juncture, brazen, subventions, and bemused.

We therefore dwell on the unknown weightlessness implicit in imponderable as a unit of slimming, as well as lack of seriousness or gravity in astronautical travel. Vitiate suggests a graduate of avoidance, according to the Boolean law of credibility, applied to hyper non-existensialism, or missing evidence.

Ignoble must rank as democratic in opposition to the Lords, and verbiage as a screen in the Dunsinane tradition of foliage rather than the modern smoke version. But then Shakespeare wrote all his plays on words, and depended on pitprops and malaprops to uphold his staging.

Likewise Brunel found himself in the position of King Lear's Gloucester in having his observant eyes outgauged at a juncture near Clapham Heath, and thereby losing his foresight together with his broad-minded, western, lines of development.

Further, while showing arrears or being topless may be the rule for nudists, these could be actionable matters for the Queen's Bench over which the royal motto proclaims 'My God, and I'm right', despite the questionable exposure of a thigh and a garter long ago at Court.

After the bronze age we find few brazen images or artifacts until horse brasses became popular, and top brass denoted support for an iron lady, and her generals. We hope that the discovery through scientific subventions encompassing nuclear magnetics will lead to chips with everything. How much can a polar bear?

Thus, in conclusion, we are bemused artistically by the Three Graces comprising Faith with Hope, and, as any vintner knows, the greatest of the three is Clarity.

E. & O.E.

---

50 years ago
From the Manchester Guardian Weekly, 12 December 1924

The world is a puzzling place, but man is not to be deterred from the delights of additional and self-inflicted bewilderment. At one time he found his pleasure in the manipulation of bits and pieces in a jig-saw. Then came the more intellectual diversion of acrostics. Now we are asked to revel in an import from America called 'cross words'. The acrostic in its time must have done valuable work for the Bible Society, since the more obscure names of the Old Testament have a knack of beginning and ending with the vowels that otherwise defy the puzzle-maker, while they are also fairly hard to remember. The new pastime must be a great comfort to the salesmen of dictionaries, glossaries, and the like, and the old complaint that the average man's vocabulary is limited to some five or six hundred words out of the treasury that is open to him may be dissipated by the present quest of verbal oddities. The complete 'cross word' enthusiast is led up hills of chemistry into dales of botany, he must even put his nose to the English grammar and be quite sure where the species 'adverb' begins and ends. The thing beneath the word need not excite him; it is the raiment of letters that he seeks, and he must be sure to get them in their proper order. The young lady who thought that to write was human but to spell divine might profit by the new pastime, but people who are more deeply interested in things than in words will wonder, like the charity boy confronted with the alphabet, whether it is worth going through so much to learn so little. However, the nominalists appear to be a large, happy, and busy faction, but this only increases one's fears as to the fate of a family in which there should be a lonely realist railing at all this quest of the shy noun or dim elusive epithet. May not the result of such a clash become upon occasion – cross words?

Our Mellifluous Bard

Together with his contemporaries (Chaucer,
Spencer, Dryden, Obs and Trad) our own
William Shakespeare once again appears
in this volume, introducing a unit of honeyed
sound/capacity. This arose from
the Tudor delight in gardens, leafy
bowers and walks, mells and malls –
a setting lending a counter point of interest to enhance
consorts of viols, recorders and gambas (and nightingales too).
While they were concerned to fill a mell
with melody, nowadays we would employ
garden orchestras and transistor radios.
This unit of pleasant sound bordering on the herbaceous,
appears as 'PHILOMEL' and, as
such, treads dainty a measure among the bulk of more weighty items.

THE ARDENT CHRONICLER

The Enthusiast – Christopher Robin

And finally, after dinner, almost a ritual, there was *The Times* crossword, with my mother (to give her a slight advantage) reading out the clues and my father trying not to be too quick with the answers.

My father had a passion for crosswords. We shared *The Times*: this was the rule. It was fairly easy. It took about half an hour and, though he would get most of the answers (including all the quotations), my mother and I would be able to manage a few contributions. On Sunday we took the *Observer* and so on Sunday evening we did the 'Everyman' crossword. This left my father free to wrestle single-handed with his favourite Torquemada.

How many Torquemada solvers survive today? Any that do will surely agree that his were the most difficult crosswords and he the most brilliant composer of them all; and that even Ximenes, good though he was, was never quite in the same class.

Solving crosswords is immensely satisfying. In a way it is the same sort of satisfaction you get from solving mathematical problems. Pencil, paper and brains: that's what you need. And you wrestle away until at last the answer comes. Or you can describe it as fitting words into an exact, interlocking pattern of squares. You can't alter the pattern: that is fixed. You juggle with the words, juggle with the letters, until at last it all fits, until the last letter falls neatly, satisfyingly into place. 'Got it!' and with a happy sigh you put your pencil back in your pocket. In this respect it resembles the writing of light verse.

from *The Enchanted Places* by CHRISTOPHER (ROBIN) MILNE

Breakfast Peace

From Mr and Mrs John Beeching

Sir, We were delighted this morning to find our crossword puzzles printed on separate sheets of paper, allowing a blissful return to the period of companionable silence after breakfast when we each apply ourselves to the puzzle most suited to our talents.

Thank you for your efforts in bringing this about.

JOHN BEECHING
CICELY BEECHING
The Times, 20 Feb 1987

Ready Solution

From Mr John Ruffle

Sir, On a recent visit to Egypt a friend purchased a copy of *The Times* for £E2.50 (approx. £1.25p) and was (I think) delighted to find that the crossword had been accurately completed.

I have tried asking my supplier what he will charge for this remarkable service. Mr and Mrs Beeching (20 February) might also be interested if you could provide details of how it can be arranged.

JOHN RUFFLE
The Times, 27 Feb 1987

Cryptic

5 March 1976

Sir, Returning home from my local **hammam** I was somewhat **esurient** and so visited our **spence** and set the table complete with **ortolan** but my fear was **adipose**, so I stopped eating and performed a quick **antiphon** with my wife, before retiring to bed.

All the words in bold appeared in this week's crossword puzzles, and if they are known and understood by your average reader I will eat my **zucchetta**.

W. L. FRASER,
GLASGOW

Royal Gravity

William Rufus was hunting one day in the New Forest, when William Tell (the memorable crackshot, inventor of the crossbow puzzle) took unerring aim at a reddish apple which had fallen on to the King's head, and shot him through the heart.

W. C. SELLAR and R. T. YEATMAN

Due to lack of space, Mary Poppin's favourite panegyric word will not appear in this edition. It has 34 letters and is 'Supercalifragilisticexpialidocious'. For a sample, please apply to your nearest chemist, with prescription.

(as printed on film posters)

'Open Locks, Whoever Knocks'

We wish to acknowledge with thanks and express our appreciation of kind and helpful letters suggesting the adoption of various new words or listings for the GENERAL INFORMATION section or items for our miscellany.

These are all welcomed and carefully considered as contributions to the worldwide community linked by crosswords and various word games and contents.

R. G. P. HILL and I. E. HILL

CATEGORY CLASSIFICATION

ac	acoustics	*fr*	forestry	*nv*	navigation
ae	aeronautics	*ga*	games	*oc*	oceanography
ag	agriculture	*gl*	geology	*pb*	plumbing
am	automation	*gn*	genetics	*pc*	psychology, psychiatry
ar	architecture	*go*	geography	*pg*	photography
as	astronomy	*gp*	geophysics	*pl*	physiology
au	automobiles	*gs*	glass	*pm*	pharmaceutics
ba	bacteriology	*hd*	heraldry	*pp*	paper
bc	biochemistry	*hr*	horology	*pr*	printing
bd	building	*hy*	hydraulics	*ps*	physics
bl	biology	*jn*	joinery	*pt*	paints, painting
br	brewing	*le*	leather-working	*rd*	radar
bt	botany	*lt*	light	*rl*	religion
ce	civil engineering	*lw*	law	*ro*	radio
cf	combining form	*ma*	mathematics	*rw*	railways
ch	chemistry	*md*	medicine and medical	*sp*	space
ck	cookery	*me*	measurements	*sv*	surveying
cn	cinema	*ml*	metallurgy	*tc*	telecommunications
cp	computers	*mn*	mining	*to*	tools
cr	carpentry	*mo*	mountaineering	*tv*	television
cy	cytology	*mt*	meteorology	*tx*	textiles
ec	ecology	*mu*	music	*vt*	veterinary
eg	engineering	*nc*	nuclear (physics)	*wv*	weaving
el	electrical, electronics	*nm*	numismatics, coins	*zo*	zoology
fd	foundry	*nt*	nautical		

Note: Language and nationality abbreviations are found closer to the definition, within parenthesis, but not in italic type, which is reserved for the above classifications.

Ass.	Assyrian	Hung.	Hungarian	Rus.	Russian
Aus.	Australian	Ind.	Indian	S. Am.	South American
Bab.	Babylonian	It.	Italian	Sc.	Scottish
C. Am.	Central American	Jap.	Japanese	Scand.	Scandinavian
Ch.	Chinese	Jew.	Jewish	Sem.	Semitic
Eg.	Egyptian	Lat.	Latin	Sp.	Spanish
Fin.	Finnish	N. Am.	North American	Sum.	Sumerian
Fr.	French	NZ	New Zealand	Turk.	Turkish, etc.
Ger.	German	Pers.	Persian		
Gr.	Greek	Rom.	Roman		

Various literary abbreviations are also given:

obs.	obselete
Shak.	Shakespeare
sl.	slang
Spens.	Spenser

GENERAL INFORMATION

Groups of a Kind

Terms of the Chase

3 **NAG** of colts
NYE of pheasants
POD of seals, whales
RAG of colts
4 **BEVY** of roes, quails
BITE of mites
CAST of hawks
CETE of badgers
CLAT of worms
COIL of teal
DOWN of hares
DULE of turtles
FALL of woodcock
GANG of elks
HERD of cranes, curlew, deer, cattle
HILL of ruffs
HIVE of bees
KNOB of wild duck
LEAP of leopards
NEST of rabbits
PACE of asses
PACK of hounds
ROUT of wolves
SEGE of herons
SORD of mallards
STUD of stallions
SUTE of mallards
TAKE of fish
TEAM of oxen
TRIP of goats
WISP of snipe
5 **BROOD** of hens
CHARM of goldfinches
COVFY of partridges
DOYLT of tame swine
DROVE of kine
FLOCK of sheep
HOVER of crows
PLUMP of wild fowl
PRIDE of lions
SEDGE of herons
SHOAL of fish
SIEGE of herons
SKEIN of geese (flying)
SKULK of foxes
5 **SLOTH** of bears
SWARM of bees
TRIBE of goats
TROOP of monkeys
WATCH of nightingales
WEDGE of geese (flying)
BARREN of mules
COLONY of gulls
COVERT of coots
DOGDOM of dogs
GAGGLE of geese
GAMBLE of lambs, casinos
HARRAS of horses
FLIGHT of doves
KENNEL of raches
KINDLE of kittens
LABOUR of moles
LITTER of whelps
MUSTER of peacocks
SCHOOL of porpoises, whales
SPRING of teal
TROGLE of snakes
UPPING of swans
7 **BUZZING** of bees
CLOWDER of cats
COMPANY of widgeon
DOPPING of sheldrake
FLITTER of bats
SOUNDER of swine
8 **BUILDING** of rooks
BUSINESS of ferrets, flies
DABBLING of ducks
FESNYING of ferrets
MUTATION of thrushes
RICHNESS of martens
SINGULAR of boars
STINGING of wasps
9 **BATTERING** of rams
BIRTHRATE of rabbits
COWARDICE of curs
10 **CHATTERING** of choughs
EXALTATION of larks
SHREWDNESS of apes
UNKINDNESS of ravens
11 **CONCOVATION** of eagles
LAMENTATION of swans
MURMURATION of starlings
12 **CONGREGATION** of plovers

Miscellaneous

3 **ACE** of spades, disaster
BAG of mail
BED of nails
BOX of delights
JAM of traffic
PIT of disgrace, miners
SEA of troubles
SEE of diocese

4 **AREA** of surfaces
BALE of hay
BANK of reserves, money
BEVY of buxom wenches
BODY of corporations, authorities
BUZZ of barflies
CAMP of allegations
CASK of beer, anglers
CREW of seamen
CURE of doctors
DISC of information
FOLD of highlanders
GANG of thieves, crooks
GIST of arguments
KNOT of sea-speeds, entanglements
LACK of principles
LAWN of grass
LEAP of lovers
LOAD of bricks
MASS of catholics
MESS of potage
MILE of distance
NEST of machineguns, pickpockets
NOOK of cookery
PACK of cards
PACT of agreements
PARK of artillery
PECK of popcorn
POOL of typists
REAM of paper
ROLE of supporters
ROPE of pearls
RUCK of stones
SACK of redundants, coals
SOLE of unitarians
STAB of bayonets
TALE of Two Cities
TANK of liquids
TEAM of players
TUFT of grass
WARD of patients
WIND of change
YARD of ships, ale, space
ZONE of influence

5 **BATCH** of mail
BENCH of bishops
BERRY of holes
BLAST of explosions, hunters
BLUSH of boys
BREAK of tea
BURKE of peers
CAPER of dancers
CASTE of ranks, religions, societies
CHAOS of regulations
CHOIR of choristers
CLUMP of trees
CROWD of people
DRIFT of fishers
DRUCK of people
FEAST of brewers
FIELD of interest
FLEET of cars, warships
HAREM of concubines
HORDE of insurgents, savages
HOUSE of cards, Commons, Lords, iniquities
LYING of pardoners
METER of consumption
ORBIT of spheres
PINCH of snuff
POINT of decimals
POSSE of police, savages
QUIRE of paper
RANGE of investments
ROUTE of knights
SCALE of wages, maps
SHEAF of corn, wheat
SKEIN of silk, wool
SLATE of candidates
SQUAT of daubers
STAND of arms, one night
STATE of princes
SYNOD of clergy
TRUSS of hay
TRUTH of barons
VAULT of architects
WINDS of uncertainties

6 **BABBLE** of barbers, brooks
BASKET of currencies
BORDER of the herbaceous
BOTTLE of drinks, hay
BOXING of compasses
BUDGET of exchequers, papers
BUMBLE of dignitaries
CELLAR of wines
CHARGE of entries, cavalry
COLUMN of gossip
COMEDY of errors
CONVOY of ships
CURACY of clerics
FLIGHT of angels, aeroplanes
GALAXY of beauty, stars
GARAGE of cars, buses
GIGGLE of comedians, schoolgirls
HATFUL of medals
LEAGUE of nations

6 LITTER of garbage
MARINA of pleasure craft
MEDLEY of tunes
MELODY of makers, harpers, songs
MOTION of meetings
NUDITY of naturists
PALATE of recipes
PAPACY of popes
PUNNET of strawberries
RECORD of events, LP music
SAVOUR of cookery
SPLASH of Baptists
TARTAN of Scots
THRAVE of threshers
THRONG of angels
TRIPOD of triangles
TROUPE of actors, vaudeville artistes
7 ACRONYM of organizations
BATTERY of guns
BLARNEY of bartenders
BOREDOM of briefs
BRIGADE of Guards, firemen
CABINET of curiosities, ministers
CLUSTER of stars
COMPANY of chairmen, actors
CONCERT of music
CONSORT of viols
DISCORD of tuners
DRAUGHT of beer
FRAUNCH of millers
HENPECK of husbands
HISTORY of remembrances
LIBRARY of books, information
PALETTE of artists
PEEPING of toms
POVERTY of beggars, pipers
SCUTTLE of coals
TABLOID of scandals
TOLLING of church-bells
WASSAIL of carollers
WORSHIP of writers
8 ALLIANCE of interests, nations
8 ALPHABET of indexes
BELCHING of drunks, smoke
CONCLAVE of cardinals
CREDENCE of sewers
EXCHANGE of stock, addresses, phones, ideas
FIGHTING of pugilists, beggars
FLATNESS of steppes
HATCHING of eggs, plots
LAUGHTER of ostlers
PLANNING of bureaucrats
REGIMENT of women, soldiers
SEQUENCE of events
SHOUTING of sergeants
SPECTRUM of light, politics, sex
SQUADRON of cavalry, aeroplanes
STRADDLE of athletes
STRIKING of clocks, off-rolls
SUBTILNE of sergeants
TERMINUS of trains, buses
TWANGING of harpists
9 ANTHOLOGY of verse, literature
BLOCKHEAD of dunces
CAVALCADE of horsemen, songs
COMMUNITY of saints
CONFUSION of initials
ELOQUENCE of lawyers
GATHERING of the clans
GEOGRAPHY of situations, surroundings
HASTINESS of cooks
MORBIDITY of majors
PORTFOLIO of shares
SAFEGUARD of policies, porters
SYMBIOSIS of life-styles
10 BLACKSLACK of handymen
CONFESSION of sins
DISCRETION of priests
IMPATIENCE of wives
INFIDELITY of boyfriends
SENTENCING of convicts
11 CONSPIRACY of authorities

The Chemical Elements

	Name	Atomic No.	Symbol
3	TIN	50	Sn
4	GOLD	79	Au
	IRON	26	Fe
	NEON	10	Ne
	LEAD	82	Pb
	ZINC	30	Zn
5	ARGON	18	A
	BORON	5	B
	RADON	86	Rn
	XENON	54	Xe
6	BARIUM	56	Ba
	CARBON	6	C
	CERIUM	58	Ce
	COBALT	27	Co
	COPPER	29	Cu
	CURIUM	96	Cm
	ERBIUM	68	Er
	HELIUM	2	He
	INDIUM	49	In
	IODINE	53	I
	NICKEL	28	Ni
	OSMIUM	76	Os
	OXYGEN	8	O
	RADIUM	88	Ra
	SILVER	47	Ag
	SODIUM	11	Na
7	ARSENIC	33	As
	BISMUTH	83	Bi
	BROMINE	35	Br
	CADMIUM	48	Cd
	CAESIUM	55	Cs
	CALCIUM	20	Ca
	FERMIUM	100	Fm
	GALLIUM	31	Ga
	HAFNIUM	72	Hf
	HOLMIUM	67	Ho
	IRIDIUM	77	Ir
	KRYPTON	36	Kr
	LITHIUM	3	Li
	MERCURY	80	Hg
	NIOBIUM	41	Nb
	RHENIUM	75	Re
	RHODIUM	45	Rh
	SILICON	14	Si
	SULPHUR	16	S
	TERBIUM	65	Tb
	THORIUM	90	Th
	THULIUM	69	Tm
	URANIUM	92	U
	YTTRIUM	39	Y
8	ACTINIUM	89	Ac
	ANTIMONY	51	Sb
	ASTATINE	85	At

	Name	Atomic No.	Symbol
8	CHLORINE	17	Cl
	CHROMIUM	24	Cr
	EUROPIUM	63	Eu
	FLUORINE	9	F
	FRANCIUM	87	Fr
	HYDROGEN	1	H
	LUTETIUM	71	Lu
	NITROGEN	7	N
	NOBELIUM	102	No
	PLATINUM	78	Pt
	POLONIUM	84	Po
	RUBIDIUM	37	Rb
	SAMARIUM	62	Sm
	SCANDIUM	21	Sc
	SELENIUM	34	Se
	TANTALUM	73	Ta
	THALLIUM	81	Tl
	TITANIUM	22	Ti
	TUNGSTEN	74	W
	VANADIUM	23	V
9	ALUMINIUM	13	Al
	AMERICIUM	95	Am
	BERKELIUM	97	Bk
	BERYLLIUM	4	Be
	GERMANIUM	32	Ge
	LANTHANUM	57	La
	MAGNESIUM	12	Mg
	MANGANESE	25	Mn
	NEODYMIUM	60	Nd
	NEPTUNIUM	93	Np
	PALLADIUM	46	Pd
	PLUTONIUM	94	Pu
	POTASSIUM	19	K
	RUTHENIUM	44	Ru
	STRONTIUM	38	Sr
	TELLURIUM	52	Te
	UNUNUNIUM	110	Uun
	YTTERBIUM	70	Yb
	ZIRCONIUM	40	Zr
10	DYSPROSIUM	66	Dy
	GADOLINIUM	64	Gd
	LAWRENCIUM	103	Lr
	MOLYBDENUM	42	Mo
	PHOSPHORUS	15	P
	PROMETHIUM	61	Pm
	TECHNETIUM	43	Tc
11	CALIFORNIUM	98	Cf
	EINSTEINIUM	99	Es
	MENDELEVIUM	101	Md
	UNNILENNIUM	109	Une
	UNNILHEXIUM	106	Unh
	UNNILOCTIUM	108	Uno
12	PRASEODYMIUM	59	Pr

	Name	Atomic No.	Symbol
12	**PROTACTINIUM**	91	Pa
	UNNILPENTIUM	105	Unp
12	**UNNILQUADIUM**	104	Unq
	UNNILSEPTIUM	107	Uns

Gaseous Emanations

5 NITON from Radium

6 IONIUM from Uranium

8 ACTINIUM from Thorium
POLONIUM from Radium

Weights and Measures

With some approximate English equivalents

1 A acre, ampere, electric current ***Int.***
B bel, power comparison unit ***Int.***
C colomb, charge ***Int.***
F farad, capacitance ***Int.***
G magnetic flux density, gram = 0.035 oz ***Int.***
H henry, inductance ***Int.***
J joule, energy ***Int.***
K kelvin, temperature ***Int.***
L litre = 1 qt (liq.) ***Int.***
M metre, length = 39.37 ins ***Int.***
N newton, force ***Int.***
S second, time, angle, lat., long. ***Int.***
T tesla, magnetic flux density, tonne, metric ton ***Int.***
V volt, voltage ***Int.***
W watt, power ***Int.***
2 AP apothecaries' measure ***Int.***
AV avoirdupois (avdp), weight ***Int.***
BU bushel, 4 pecks (2219.3 cu ins); 0.036 cu m (Br. Imp.) ***Britain***
BU TSUBO = 3.306 sq m (area) ***Japan***
CD candela, luminous intensity ***Int.***
CI curie, unit of activity of radioactive substance ***Int.***
CM centimetre = 0.394 ins ***Int.***
DB decibel (dB), unit of noise ***Int.***
DL decilitre (10 dl = 1 litre) ***Int.***
DR dram, 27.34 grains, 0.06 oz, 1.771 gram ***U.S.***
EL 1 metre (old EL = 27.08 ins) ***Netherlands***
FT foot = 12 ins, 0.33 yds, 30.48 cm ***Int.***
GB gilbert (Gb), magnetomotive force (magnetic potential) ***Int.***
GI gill (Br. Imp.), 5 fl oz, 8.66 cu ins, 142.06 cu cm ***Britain***
GI gill (liq.), 4 fl oz, 7.21 cu ins, 118.29 ml ***U.S.***
GO 0.18 litre ***Japan***
GR grain, 0.036 dram, 0.002 oz, 0.06 gram ***Int.***
2 HZ hertz (Hz), frequency ***Int.***
HU 51.77 litres ***China***
IN inch, $\frac{1}{12}$ foot, $\frac{1}{36}$ yard, 2.54 cm ***Int.***
KG kilogram, 2.2 lb ***Int.***
KM kilometre, 0.6 mile ***Int.***
KW kilowatt, 1.3 horsepower; kilowatt-hour/KWh. ***Int.***
LB pound, 16 oz, 7000 grains, 0.453 kg ***Int.***
LI ¾ mile = 360 pu ***China***
LM lumen, luminous flux ***Int.***
LX lux, illumination ***Int.***
MI mile, 5280 ft, 320 rods, 1760 yds, 1.609 km ***Int.***
ML millilitre ***Int.***
MM millimetre, 0.04 in ***Int.***
NT nit, luminance ***Int.***
OE oersted (Oe), magnetic field strength ***Int.***
OZ ounce, 28 grams, 16 drams, 437.5 grains ***Int.***
PE ¾ metre ***Portugal***
PK peck (dry), 8 qt, 537.605 cu in, 8.809 litres ***U.S.***
PK peck (Br. Imp.), 2 gals, 554.8385 cu ins, 0.009 cu m ***Britain***
PT pint (liq.), 4 gi, 28.875 cu ins, 0.473 litre ***U.S.***
PT pint (dry), ½ qt, 33.600 cu ins, 0.550 litre ***U.S.***
PT pint (Br. Imp.), 4 gi, 34.677 cu in, 568.26 cu cm ***Britain***
PU 70.5 ins = 5 ch'ih ***China***
QT quart (liq.), 2 pts, 57.75 cu ins, 0.946 litre ***U.S.***
QT quart (dry), 2 pts, 67.20 cu ins, 1.101 litres ***U.S.***
QT quart (Br. Imp.), 2 pts, 69.35 cu ins, 1.136 litres ***Britain***
RD rod, 5.50 yds, 16.5 ft, 5.029 m ***Int.***
RI 2.440 miles ***Japan***
SB stilb (Sb), unit of luminance ***Int.***
SE 118.615 sq yds (0.9918 are) ***Japan***
SR steradian, solid angle ***Int.***
ST stokes, kinematic viscosity ***Int.***
TO 18.03 litres = 4.77 U.S. gals ***Japan***

2 TU 100.142 miles = 250 li ***China***
WA WAH, 2 m ***Thailand***
WB weber, magnetic flux ***Int.***
YD yard, 3 ft, 36 ins, 0.914 m ***Int.***
3 AAM 30–35 gals ***E. Indies***
ARE 100 sq m, 119.6 yds ***Int.***
AUM 31 Imp. gal ***S. Africa***
BAT BAHT, TICAL, 15 grams (231.5 grains) ***Thailand***
BEL power comparison unit ***Int.***
CAB 3 pts ***Hebrew***
CHO 1815 sq ft (3000 bu/area; 360 shaku/length) ***Japan***
COR 8½ bushels ***Hebrew***
CWT hundredweight; 45.35 kg (short), 50.80 kg (long) ***Britain***
DWT pennyweight ***Britain***
ELL (Eng.) 45 ins, (Sc.) 37 ins, (Jersey) 4 ft ***Britain***
ERG unit of energy; 1 erg = 10^{-7} joules ***Int.***
FEN 5.76 grains (silver weight) ***China***
FOD 0.3138 m, 1.029 ft ***Denmark***
FOT 11.689 ins; 10 fot = 1 stäng ***Sweden***
FOU bushel ***Scotland***
FUT FOUTE 1 Eng. ft ***Russian Fed.***
GAL gallon (liq.), 4 qt (231 cu ins), 3.785 litres ***U.S.***
GAL gallon (Br. Imp.), 4 qt (277.4 cu ins), 4.545 litres ***Britain***
GIN KATI, CATTY 1¾ lb ***Malaysia***
GUZ GUDGE 27–36 ins ***E. Indies***
GUZ GUEZA, ZER 1 m (40.95 ins) ***Iran***
HIN 6 qts ***Hebrew***
KAN 1 litre; 1¾ lb (Hong Kong) ***Netherlands***
KEN 1.82 m, 5.96 ft ***Japan***
KIN 0.600 kg, 1.32 lb ***Japan***
KON CATTY 1¾ lb ***Korea***
KUP 10 ins ***Thailand***
LOG ¼ pt ***Hebrew***
LOT 10 grams (new), ½ oz (old) ***Germany***
LUX unit of light (lx); 1 1m over an area of 1m squared ***Int.***
MIL one thousandth of an inch ***U.S./G.B.***
MIL MILL 1.000 archins (new mil) ***Turkey***
MIN minim, $\frac{1}{60}$ fluidram, 0.0591 cu cm (Br. Imp.) ***Britain***
MIN minim, $\frac{1}{60}$ fluidram, 0.0616 cu cm ***U.S.***
MNA 1½ kg = 1.172 oke ***Greece***
MOU 806.65 sq yds (or 920.41 sq yds) ***China***
MUD 1 hectolitre ***Netherlands***
NIN $\frac{10}{12}$ in ***Thailand***
3 NIT (nt) luminance; 1 candela per m squared ***Int.***
NIU 1 in ***Thailand***
OCK 1 kg; (1881) 1 ock = 100 drachmas; new batman = 10 ocks, kantar = 10 batmans ***Turkey***
OHM resistance V/A ***Int.***
OKA 3 lb ***Egypt***
OKE 1.28 l (liq.); 1.28 kg (old); 2.8 lb ***Bulgaria***
OKE 400 drams ***Cyprus***
ONS 100 grams ***Netherlands***
PIC PIk 2 ft (Greece picki 0.64 m) ***Cyprus***
PIE 11.73 in ***Rome***
PIK DIRAA 0.58 m ***U.A.R.***
PIN half a firkin ***Britain***
POT 0.966 litre ***Denmark***
RAD radian, plane angle; radiation absorbed dose, 0.01 joule/kg (100 ergs/gramme) ***Int.***
RAI ¾ acre ***Thailand***
REM roentgen equivalent man; 1 rem = 1 rad Q.F. ***Int.***
RIO ounce ***Japan***
ROD 5.50 yds, 16.5 ft, 5.029 m ***Int.***
SEN 40.6 m, 44 yds ***Thailand***
SHO 1.804 litres ***Japan***
SUN 1 in ***Japan***
TAN 133 lb ***China***
TOD 2 stone ***Britain***
TON 20 cwt, 0.907 m/tons (short), 1.016 m/tons (long) ***Int.***
TOU 10 litres ***China***
TUN 252 gals ***Britain***
VAT 1 hectolitre ***Netherlands***
WAH WA 2 m ***Thailand***
WEY 13 stone ***Britain***
ZAK 1 hectolitre ***Netherlands***
ZAR 1 m ***Iran***
ZER GUZ, GUEZA 1 m (40.95 ins) ***Iran***
4 ACRE 4840 sq yds, 0.405 hectare, 4046 sq m ***Britain***
ATTO (a) 10^{-18} ***Int.***
AUNE 1 m, (France 1.18 m), (Jersey 4 ft) ***Belgium***
BAHT BAT, TICAL, 15 grams (231.5 grains) ***Thailand***
BALE 10 reams ***Britain***
BATH 6 gals ***Hebrew***
BUTT 108 gals ***Britain***
CHEE TAHIL 1¾ oz = 10 chee = 100 hoon ***Malaysia***
CHEK 14⅜ ins ***Hong Kong***
CH'IH 14.1 ins (customs), 5 ch'ih = 1 pu ***China***
CHIN CATTY 1¾ lb (customs) ***China***

4 **CHUO** 1.815 sq ft (customs) ***China***
COSS 1.82 km, 1¾ miles ***India***
CRAN ca. 750 herrings ***Britain***
CU CM 0.06 cu in ***Int.***
CU FT 1728 cu ins, 0.0370 cu yd, 0.028 cu m ***Int.***
CU IN 0.00058 cu ft, 16.387 cu cm ***Int.***
DECI (d) 10^{-1}; 1 dm = 0.1 m ***Int.***
DEKA DECA (da) 10; 1 dekametre = 10 metres ***Int.***
DITO 1 cm ***Italy***
DOLA DOLIA, 96 doli = 1 zolotnick ***Russian Fed.***
DOSE quantity of radiation (absorbed energy), see rad, rem
DRAH 22 ins ***Morocco***
DRAM 27.343 grams, 0.0625 oz, 1.7718452 grains ***Int.***
DUIM 1 in ***Russian Fed./Netherlands***
DYNE unit of force; 1 dyne = 10^{-5} newton ***Int.***
ELLA 1 yd ***Sabah/N. Borneo***
ELLE 60 cm; (Latvia) 0.53 m ***Switzerland***
EPHA bushel ***Hebrew***
FL DR fluidram, 60 minims (0.22 cu in), 29.572 ml ***U.S.***
FL DR fluidram, 60 minims (0.21 cu in), 3.5516 cu cm ***Britain***
FL OZ fluid ounce (Br. Imp.), 8 fluidrams, 28.413 cu cm ***Britain***
FOOT 12 ins, 0.333 yd, 30.48 cm ***Int.***
FUNT FOUNTE 0.90 lb (U.S.S.R.), 405.5 grams ***Poland***
FUSZ 12 zolls = 1.037 ft (Vienna), 1¾ fusz = 1 m ***Switzerland***
GIGA (G) 10^9; 1 GHz = 10^9 hertz ***Int.***
GILL 4 fl oz (7.218 cu ins), 118.29 ml ***U.S.***
GILL 5 fl oz (Br. Imp.), 8.669 cu in, 142.0652 cu cm ***Britain***
GRAM 0.035 oz ***Int.***
GRAO 0.769 gr, 0.18 in ***Portugal***
HAND (horses) 4 in ***Britain***
HAT'H MOOLUM, CUBIT, 18 ins ***India***
HIDE 120 acres ***Britain***
HOON TAHIL, CHEE, 1¾ oz = 10 chee = 100 hoon ***Malaysia***
IMMI 1.5 litres ***Switzerland***
INCH 0.083 ft, 0.027 yd, 2.540 cm, 25 mm ***Int.***
JOCH 57.55 ares = 1.422 acres ***Austria***
KATI CATTY, GIN 1¾ lb ***Malaysia***
KELA ½ bushel ***Egypt***
KHAT 1 cm ***Turkey***
KILO (k) 10^3; 1 km = 1000 m; comput.: 2^{10} = 1 kilobyte = 1024 bytes ***Int.***
KILO kilogram, 2.2 lb ***Int.***

4 **KNOT** 6.080 ft; 1 nt mile/hour = 0.514 4444 m/s ***Britain***
KOKU 180.39 litres (see TO) ***Japan***
KOSS 2000 yds ***India***
KUNG 78.96 ins (customs) ***China***
KWAN KUWAN, 3.75 kg, 8.26 lb ***Japan***
KYAT 16.33 grams ***Burma***
LAST 30 hectolitres ***Netherlands***
LINE LIGNE, 2.26 mm ***Paris***
LINK 7.92 in ***U.S./G.B.***
MACE 93¾ gr (Sabah/N. Borneo), 58¾ gr ***China***
MARC MARK 0.2448 kg (old) ***France***
MEGA (M) 10^6; 2^{20} 1 megabyte = 1048576 bytes ***Int.***
MIJL 1 int. nautical mile ***Netherlands***
MILE 5280 ft, 320 rods, 1760 yds, 1.609 km ***Int.***
MILE nautical, 6080.20 ft (formerly) ***U.S.***
MILE nautical/admiralty, 6080 ft ***Britain***
MILE nautical/international, 1853 m ***Int.***
MILE postal, 4714 ft ***Austria***
MOIO 2¾ qts ***Portugal***
MUDD 1 bushel ***Morocco***
NAIL 2¼ ins ***Britain***
NANO (n) 10^{-9}; 1 nm = 10^{-9} m ***Int.***
NATR 2 lb ***Ethiopia***
OKET 1 oz avoirdupois (av) ***Ethiopia***
ONCA 28.68 grams ***Portugal***
ONCE 30.59 grams (old) ***France***
PAAL 1½ m ***Indonesia***
PACK 240 lb ***Britain***
PALM 1 decimetre (dm) ***Netherlands***
PARA 90 lb ***Sabah/N. Borneo***
PECK 2 gals ***Britain***
PHOT intensity of illumination (1 lm/sq cm), 1 phot = 104 lux ***Int.***
PICO (p) 10^{-12}; 1 pF = 10^{12} farad ***Int.***
PIED 11.81 ins = 10 pouces (Belgium), 12.79 ins ***Canada***
PIED de roi 0.3248 m ***Paris***
PINT (liquid) 28.875 cu ins, 0.473 litre ***U.S.***
PINT (dry) ½ qt (33.67 cu ins), 568.260 cu cm ***Britain***
PINT (Br. Imp.) 4 gi (34.67 cu ins), 568.260 cu cm ***Britain***
PIPA 500 litres, 429 litres (old) ***Portugal***
PIPE 126 gals ***Britain***
POLE 16½ ft ***Britain***
POND ½ kilogram ***Netherlands***
POOD 36.113 lb ***Russian/Fed.***
PUND 500 grams, (Sweden 425.1 grams) ***Scandinavia***
REAM 20 quires (of 24 sheets: paper) ***Britain***

4 REED 152 ins ***Hebrew***
RODE 3.138 m ***Denmark***
ROOD 40 perches, ¼ acre ***Britain***
ROTL ROTTOLA, RATEL, 0.9905 lb (customs) ***U.A.R.***
SACK 2 weys ***Britain***
SAWK 20 in ***Thailand***
SEAH 14 pts ***Hebrew***
SEAM (glass) 24 stone ***Britain***
SEER 1.061 lb (Sri Lanka), 2.057 lb (government) ***India***
SIHR 16 miseals, 1136 gr weight ***Iran***
SHIH 157.89 lb ***China***
SKOT low-intensity lighting ***Int.***
SQ IN 0.007 sq ft, 6.4516 sq cm ***Int.***
SQ MI 640 acres, 102 400 sq rods, 2.589 sq km ***Int.***
SQ RD 30.25 sq yds, 0.006 acre, 25.293 sq m ***Int.***
SQ YD 1296 sq ins, 9 sq ft, 0.836 sq m ***Int.***
STAB 1 m (3¾ old fuss) ***Germany***
TAEL 1¾ oz (Hong Kong), 936¼ grams ***Thailand***
TAEL 10 momme (Japan), 1¾ oz (silver weight) ***China***
TANK 68.1 grams (72 tanks = 1 seer) ***Bombay***
TENG (basket) 2218.2 cu ins (varies) ***Burma***
TERA (T) 10^{12}; 1 Tm = 10^{12} m ***Int.***
TOLA 180 grains; legal weight of rupee ***India***
TORR unit of pressure (vacuum), 133.322 newtons/sq m ***Int.***
T'SUN 1.41 ins ***China***
VARA 83.5 cm–1 m, 33–43 ins (varies) ***S. America/U.S.***
VISS 3.60 lbs (3.65 old) ***Burma***
VOLT (V) W/A voltage ***Int.***
WATT kilowatt, 1.3 horsepower ***Int.***
X-RAY unit of length, 1.002×10^{-13} m ***Int.***
YARD 3 ft, 36 ins, 0.9144 m ***Int.***
YLEM hypothetical density (10^{16} kg m^{-3}) ***Int.***
ZOLL 3 cm (ca. 1 in. old) ***Switzerland***

5 ANKER 7½ gals ***S. Africa***
ANKER 38.25 litres (or 30 stoof) ***Latvia***
ARDEB 5.61 bushels = 100 sq m = 119.6 sq yds ***Egypt***
ASSAY ton, 29.16 grams ***U.S.***
BAHAR BEHAR 450 lb ***Arabian Peninsula***
BARYE unit of pressure (old); 1 barye = 0.1 pascal ***Int.***
BERRI 1.67 km, 1.04 miles (old) ***Turkey***
BRACA 2.20 m ***Portugal***
BRAZA 1.732 m ***Argentina***
CABLE 100 fathoms ***Britain***
CABOT 10 pots (19.75 litres) ***Jersey***
CANCH 6 cubits ***Hebrew***
CANDY 500 lb (560 lb Bombay) ***India***
CANNA 2 yds ***Malta***
CARAT metric, 200 milligrams ***Int.***
CATTY 1¾ lb ***China***
CAWNY 1 acre ***India***
CENTI (c) 10^{-2} ***Int.***
CHAIN 66 ft, 22 yds ***Britain***
CHANG 10 ch'ih = 11 ft 9 ins (1200 grams/3 lb Thailand) ***China***
CHEKI 509 lb ***Turkey***
CH'IEN (1 lb), 58¾ grains (silver weight) ***China***
CHING 121 sq ft ***China***
CH'ING 72 600 sq ft ***China***
CLOVE 7 lb ***Britain***
COOMB 4 bushels ***Britain***
COVID CUBIT 18–21 ins (Tamil Nadu/Madras) ***India***
CUBIT 18 ins ***Britain***
CURIE (Ci) unit of activity of radioactive substance ***Int.***
DEBYE 10^{-18} e.s.u.; 1 d = $3.335\,64 \times 10^{-30}$ coulomb metre ***Int.***
DIRAA PIK 0.58 m ***Egypt***
DOLIA DOLA 96 doli = 1 zolotnick ***Russian Fed.***
DUCAT 58.873 grains (gold weight) ***Vienna***
EIMER 29–30.7 litres ***Germany***
EPHAH bushel ***Hebrew***
FADEN 4.077 steres ***Latvia***
FANAN THANAN 1 litre ***Thailand***
FARAD (F) capacitance ***Int.***
FEMTO (f) 10^{-15} ***Int.***
FOUTE FUT, 1 Eng. ft ***Russian Fed.***
GAUSS (G) magnetic flux density; 1 G = 10^{-4} tesla ***Int.***
GISLA 360 lb of rice (Tanzania) ***Zanzibar***
GRAIN 0.0365 dram, 0.002 oz, 0.06 grams, $\frac{1}{24}$ pennyweight ***Britain***
GRANO 0.757 grain ***Rome***
GREIN 0.065 gram ***Netherlands***
GROSS 12 dozen ***Britain***
GUDGE GUZ, 27–36 in ***India***
GUEZA GUZ, ZER, 24–44 ins; 1 m (government) ***Iran***
HECTO (h) 10^2 ***Int.***
HENRY (H) inductance ***Int.***
HERTZ (Hz) frequency ***Int.***
HOMER 8 bushels ***Hebrew***
JOULE heat, energy (1 joule = 1 watt second) ***Int.***
KANEH 6 cubits ***Hebrew***

5 KANNA 2.62 litres ***Sweden***
KANNE 1 litre (formerly 1.06 liq./ 0.91 dry qt U.S.) ***Germany***
KERAT 1⅛ ins (old), 3.09 grains weight (old) ***Turkey***
KETTE CHAIN 10 m ***Germany***
KIKEH ca. 1 bushel (varies) ***Turkey***
KODDI 7.58 litres ***Arabian Peninsula***
KOUZA 9 Br. Imp. qts ***Cyprus***
KOYAN 5333¾ lb ***Malaysia***
KRINA 20 litres ***Bulgaria***
KUWAN KWAN, 3.75 kg = 8.267 lb ***Japan***
LATRO 1.917 m ***Czech Rep.***
LIANG LEANG, 1¾ oz, 16 liang = 1 chin = ¾ lb ***China***
LIBRA ca. 1 lb ***S. America/Malta***
LIBRA ARRATEL, 1.012 lb ***Portugal***
LIGNE 2.26 mm ***Paris***
LIPPY ½ gal ***Scotland***
LITRE 1.057 liq./0.908 dry qt ***U.S.***
LITRE 2 pts (1 qt/liq.) Br. Imp. ***Britain***
LIVRE 1 kg (Greece 1 lb) ***Belgium***
LOKETca. 0.59 m ***Czech Rep.***
LUMEN (lm) luminous flux; 1 lm = (¼ pi) cd. ***Int.***
MAAS 1.837 litres (Switzerland 1.5 l) ***Germany***
MAHND 2.04 lb ***Arabian Peninsula***
MARCO 8 oncas, 229.5 grams ***Portugal***
MARCO 3550 grains ***Spain***
MAUND 82.286 lb (government) ***India***
METRE 3.3 ft, 1.1 yds ***Int.***
METZE 61.5 litres ***Austria***
MICRO (μ) 10^{-6} ***Int.***
MILHA 1.297 miles ***Portugal***
MILLI (m) 10^{-3}; 1 mm = 10^{-3} m ***Int.***
MINIM (min) $^{1}/_{60}$ fl. drams (0.003 cu ins), 0.061 mm ***Int.***
MKONO 45.72 cm ***E. Africa***
MOMME $^{1}/_{1000}$ kwan = 10 fun, 3.75 grams ***Japan***
OBOLE 10–12 grams ***Greece***
OCQUE 3 lb ***Greece***
OKIEH 1 oz ***Egypt***
ONCIA 436.165 grains ***Rome***
PALMO 0.22 m (Spain 0.20 m) ***Portugal***
PARAH 25.4 litres, (China 15 gals) ***Sri Lanka***
PECUL 133 lb ***China***
PERCH POLE, 1 rod (U.S.); 30¼ sq yds (5½ yds) ***Britain***
PIEDE 11 ins ***Malta***
PFUND 500 grams (zollpfund) Switzerland, Austria ***Germany***
PFUND 419 grams ***Latvia***
PICKI PIK, PIC, 0.64–0.67 m ***Greece***

5 PICUL 132.3–133 lb (ca.) Malaysia, Hong Kong ***Japan***
PICUL 180 lb weight of water ***Sabah/ N. Borneo***
PINTE 0.931 litre ***France***
POIDE de marc 0.2448 kg = 8 oz ***France***
POISE dynamic viscosity; 1 poise = 0.1 pascal second ***Int.***
POUCE 27.07 mm, 1.066 ins (old) ***France***
POUND 0.45 kg, 16 oz, 7000 grains ***Int.***
QIRAT 209 sq yds ***Egypt***
QUART (Br. Imp.) 2 pts (69.35 cu ins), 1.136 litres ***Britain***
QUART (liq.) 2 pts, 57.75 cu in, 0.946 litre ***U.S.***
QUART (dry) 2 pts, 67.20 cu in, 1.101 litres ***U.S.***
QUIRE 24 sheets of paper ***Britain***
RATEL 1.014 lb ***Iran***
RATEL ROTL, ROTTOLO, 0.9905 lb (customs) ***Egypt***
ROEDE 1 dekametre ***Netherlands***
SAJEN 7 ft ***Russian Fed.***
SHAKU $^{10}/_{33}$ m, 12 ins, 3.306 sq dm, 18.039 cu cm ***Japan***
SHENG 1.035 litres ***China***
STERE 1 cu m ***Netherlands/France***
STILB (sb) luminance; 1 candela/ sq cm; 1 sb = 10^{4} nits ***Int.***
STONE 14 lb ***Britain***
STOPA 0.288 m ***Poland***
TAHIL 1¾ oz = 10 chee = 100 hoon ***Malaysia***
TESLA (T) magnetic flux density (1 weber per m squared) ***Int.***
THERM unit of heat (gas), 100.000 btu ***Int.***
TOISE 1.949 m ***France***
TONDE 131.4 litres (liq.), 139.1 litres (dry) ***Denmark***
TONNE (t) metric ton = 1000 kg (Br. Imp. ton = 1016 kg) ***Int.***
TONOS 3307 lb ***Greece***
TOVAR 128.2 kg ***Bulgaria***
TSUBO 4 sq yds ***Japan***
UNGUL 1 in ***India***
VEDRO 10 schtoffs, 12.3 litres (Bulgaria 10 l), 3 gals ***Russian Fed.***
VERST VERSTA 0.66288 mile, 1166 yds ***Russian Fed.***
WISSE 1 stere ***Netherlands***
YOJAN ca. 5 miles ***E. Indies***

6 ALMUDE 16.7 litres ***Portugal***
AMPERE electric current, force = 2×10^{-7} newton/m of length ***Int.***
ANOMAN AMMOMAM, AMOMAM, 5.77 U.S. bushels ***Sri Lanka***

6 ARCHIN ARSHIN, ARSIN, (cloth) 27 ins; 1 m (39.37 ins) ***Turkey***
ARPENT 100 sq perches, 51.07 m.ares (Quebec 180 Fr. ft) ***France***
ARROBA 14.68–15 kg, 32 lb ***Portugal/ Brazil***
ARSHIN 28 ins, 0.7112 m ***Russian Fed.***
ARTABA 66 litres ***Iran***
BANDLE 2 ft ***Eire***
BARILE 58.34 litres ***Rome***
BARREL 36 gal cask ***Britain***
BATMAN 6½ lb (varies) ***Iran***
BRASSE 1.62 m ***France***
BUNDER 1 hectare ***Netherlands***
BUNDLE 2 reams ***Britain***
BUSHEL 8 gals ***Britain***
CANTAR KANTAR, 124.45 lb (old weight) ***Turkey***
CAWNIE 1.322 acres (Tamil Nadu) ***India***
CENTAL 100 lb ***U.S.***
CHAPAH 1.8 lb ***Sabah/N. Borneo***
CHARKA 0.123 litre ***Russian Fed.***
CHOPIN quart ***Scotland***
CHUPAH 3.125 lb of water at 62°F (as a measure of capacity) ***Singapore***
CHUPAH 36 oz of water ***Malacca***
COVADO 0.66 m ***Arabian Peninsula***
COVIDO 19 ins ***Arabian Peninsula***
DECARE 1000 sq m ***France***
DENARO 1 gram; (old/Rome 18.17 grams) ***Italy***
DIRHEM 1.761 dr (customs); (Cairo 3.12 grams) ***Egypt***
DJERIB 1 hectare, 2½ acres ***Turkey***
DOENUM DONUM, 25 acres ***Turkey***
DRACHM (fluid) 0.961 U.S. fluid dram ***Britain***
ENDAZE 25½ ins ***Turkey***
FANEGA ca. 55.5 litres (Argentina 137 litres) (Costa Rica 11 bu) ***S. America/ Portugal***
FATHOM 6 ft ***Britain***
FEDDAN 1.038 acres ***Egypt***
FIRKIN 9 gals ***Britain***
FOUNTE 0.90282 lb ***Russian Fed.***
FRASCO 2⅜ litres ***Argentina***
GALLON (gal) 0.004 cu m ***U.S./Britain***
KANTAR CANTARO, 99.049 lb = 100 rotls; 45 kg/cotton ***Egypt***
KANTAR 100 lb ***Ethiopia***
KARWAR 100 batmans ***Iran***
KEDDAH 2.0625 litres ***Egypt***
KELVIN (K) temperature, 1 K = 1°C ***Int.***
KOILON 33.12 litres ***Greece***
KORREL 0.1 gram ***Netherlands***
KULMET 10.93 litres ***Latvia***
KWARTA 1 litre ***Poland***
LIBBRA 1 kg; 339 grams (old) ***Italy***

6 LINIYA 0.1 in; 1 archine = 280 liniyas ***Russian Fed.***
MAATJE 0.1 litre, 1 dl ***Netherlands***
MICRON millionth part of a metre ***France***
MIGLIO 0.925 mile ***Rome***
MISCAL 10 grams; 71 grains (old) ***Iran***
MUSCAL 1½ drams ***Turkey***
NEWTON (N) force; 1 kg with acceleration of 1 m/s per s. ***Int.***
NOGGIN small cup, ¼ pt ***Britain***
PARMAK 1 arsin (1 m) = 10 parmak = 100 khats (cm) ***Turkey***
PARSEC (astron.) 3.2616 light years ***Int.***
PASCAL (Pa) 1 newton per sq m (air pressure) ***Int.***
POTTLE 4 pts ***Britain***
RADIAN (rad) plane angle; (1 rad = 57.296° = 57°17'45" ***Int.***
RATTEL ROTLLE, 1.02 lb ***Arabian Peninsula***
ROTOLO 1¾ lb ***Malta***
ROTTOL 1.6 ltres (old) ***Turkey***
SAGENE 7 ft ***Russian Fed.***
SCHENE 7½ miles ***Egypt***
SECOND (s) second 60th of an hour ($\frac{1}{60}$ of a min.) ***Int.***
SEIDEL 0.354 litre ***Austria***
SHTOFF 1 qt ***Russian Fed.***
SKEPPE 17.39 litres ***Denmark***
STOKES (St) kinematic viscosity; 1 St = 10^{-4} m squared/s ***Int.***
STREEP 1 mm ***Netherlands***
STRICH 1 mm ***Germany***
STUNDE 4.8 km ***Switzerland***
TALBOT luminous energy ***Int.***
THANAN FANAN, 1 litre ***Thailand***
TIERCE 42 gals ***Britain***
TOMAND 187.17 lb of rice ***Arabian Peninsula***
VERSTA VERST, 0.66288 mile, 1166 yds ***Russian Fed.***
VISHAN 3 lb ***India***
YOJANA ca. 5 miles ***India***

7 BRACCIO d'ara, 0.7 m (a cubit) ***Italy***
CALORIE unit of heat; 1 calorie = 4.1868 joules ***Int.***
CANDELA (cd) luminous intensity ***Int.***
CANTARA 1 arroba ***Spain***
CANTARO KANTAR, 99.0492 lb = 100 rotls; 44.5 kg ***Egypt***
CAPICHA 263 litres ***Iran***
CELSIUS thermometer, 0°C = 32F (30°C = 85F, 100°C = 212F) ***Int.***
CENTNER 50 kg ***C. Europe/Denmark***
CENTRAD $\frac{1}{100}$ of a radian (rad) plane angle ***Int.***

7 **CHALDER** 96 bushels ***Britain***
CHENICA 1.359 litres ***Iran***
COULOMB (C) electric unit of charge ***Int.***
DARIBAH 15.84 hectolitres ***Egypt***
DECIARE $\frac{1}{10}$ are ***France***
DECIBEL (dB) unit of noise; $\frac{1}{10}$ of a bel (B) ***Int.***
DIOPTER optical measure ***Greece***
DRACHMA 3.906 grams approx (Netherlands); 3.21 (Turkey) 3.2 grams ***Greece***
ESTADIO 258 m (old) ***Portugal***
FALTCHE 143.22 ares ***Moldavia***
FURLONG 220 yds ***U.S./Britain***
HECTARE 2.5 acres ***Int.***
GANTANG 1 Br. Imp. gal (Malaysia); 144 oz weight of water as measure of capacity ***Sabah/N. Borneo***
GARNETZ 3.28 litres ***Russian Fed.***
GILBERT (Gb) magnetomotive force; 1 Gb = 10/4π ampere-turns ***Int.***
KLAFTER 2.0740 yds; (Switzerland 1.9685 yards) ***Austria***
KULIMET 11.48 litres ***Estonia***
LAMBERT unit of brightness (obs.) ***Int.***
MEGA-ERG a million ergs ***Greece***
MILLIER 1000 kg ***France***
OERSTED (Oe) magnetic field strength; 1 Oe = $10^3/4\pi$ Am^{-1} ***Int.***
PECHEUS 0.648 m ***Greece***
PERSAKH 6000 guz, 3.88 miles ***Iran***
POUNDAL unit of force ***Int.***
PULGADA 0.914 in ***Spain***
QUANTAR 99 lb ***Egypt***
QUARTER 28 lb; 8 Br. Imp. bu (8.257 U.S. bu) ***Britain***
QUINTAL 100 libras, 101.4 lb (France 1 cwt) ***Spain***
QUINTAL 58.752 kg, 129.5 lb ***Portugal***
QUINTAL (metric) 100 kg = 220.46 lb ***Int.***
ROTTOLO ROTH, RATEL, 0.9905 lb (customs) ***Egypt***
SCHEPEL 1 decalitre ***Netherlands***
SCRUPLE (s ap) 20 grains, 0.3333 dram, 1.295 grams ***Int.***
SIEMENS (s) electric conductance ***Int.***
SKJEPPE 17.37 litres ***Norway***
STREMMA 10 ares ***Greece***
THERMIE unit of heat/calory ***France***
VERCHOK 1.75 ins ***Russian Fed.***
VIERTEL 7.73 litres (Switzerland 15 litres) ***Denmark***
VIRGATE a quarter of a hide ***Britain***
WICHTJE 1 gram ***Netherlands***

8 **ANGSTROM** unit, 1 angstrom = 10^{-10} m ***Int.***
APOSTILB unit of luminance, 10^{-4} lambert ***Int.***
ASSAY-TON 29.167 grams ***U.S.***
BOISSEAU 15 litres ***Belgium***
BOUTYLKA 1.625 U.S. liquid pints ***Russian Fed.***
CENTIARE a square metre ***France***
CENTIBAR meteorological measure ***France***
CHALDRON 25 cwt of coal ***France***
CHITTACK 5 tolas, 900 grains ***Bengal***
DAKTYLOS 25.4 mm ***Greece***
DECAGRAM 10 grams ***Int.***
DECIGRAM $\frac{1}{10}$ gram ***Int.***
FLUIDRAM 60 minim (0.2255 cu in) 29.572 ml ***U.S.***
FLUIDRAM (Br. Imp.) 60 minim (0.2167 cu in) 3.55 cu cm ***Britain***
FOOT-RULE a 12 in measure ***Britain***
HIYAKA-ME 5 797 198 grains ***Japan***
HIYAK-KIN 132½ lb ***Japan***
HOGSHEAD a large cask ***France***
KASSABAH 3.8824 yds ***Egypt***
KILODYNE 1000 dynes ***France***
KILOGRAM 1000 grams; 2.2 lb ***Int.***
KILOWATT 1000 watts; 1.3 horsepower (1 h.p. = 0.75 kw) ***Int.***
KORTONDE 138.97 litres ***Norway***
MUTCHKIN about a pint ***Scotland***
NEUTRINO 7×10^{-32} grams, beam without mass ***Int.***
PARASANG PERSAKH, 6000 guz, 3.99 miles ***Iran***
PASSEREE 5 seers ***Bengal***
PHAROAGH 10 mills (10 000 km); 2 hours' journey (old) ***Turkey***
PHILOMEL unit of sound capacity (Shakespeare) ***Britain***
POLEGADA 27.77 mm ***Portugal***
PUNCHEON a large cask ***France***
QUADRANT an arc of 90° ***France***
QUARTERN a gill; 4 lb ***Britain***
SCHEFFEL 50 litres (old 16 metzen/Prussia) ***Germany***
SCHOPPEN ½ litre (Switzerland 0.375 litre) ***Germany***
SERPLATH 80 stone ***Scotland***
SKALPUND (skaal-pund) ½ kg (Sweden 425 grams/0.937 lb) ***Norway***
SULTCHEK cu m (whose sides equal a parmak/dm) ***Turkey***
THANGSAT 21.3 litres ***Thailand***
THORLAND unit of illumination ***Int.***
TONELADA 793.15 kg ***Portugal***
YARDLAND usually 30 acres ***Britain***
ZOLOTNIK 65.8306 grains, 96 doli ***Russian Fed.***

Coins and Monies: Ancient and Modern

2 **AS** Roman bronze coin
AT Laotian monetary unit (1 kip = 100 at)
BU 17/18 cent. Japanese (¼ of a ryo)
LI old Chinese monetary unit (1/100 of a tael)
PU ancient Chinese currency
XU Vietnamese monetary unit (1 dong = 100 xu)

3 **AES** Roman money (Grave, Rude, Signatum)
AKA Ceylonese gold piece (Sri Lanka)
ATT Siamese (Thailand) copper coin (1/64 of the tical)
BAT BAHT, TICAL Thai monetary unit (100 satangs = 1 baht)
BIT West Indian money of a/c
BOB British shilling (obs.)
BUN penny, British late 19 cent.
COB Spanish monetary unit
DAM DAWM, Indian copper coin
DUA Malayan 19 cent. hat money (2 ampat)
ECU French five-franc piece
FEI Oceanian monetary unit, see YAP
FEN Chinese monetary unit (100 fen = 1 yuan)
FIL Iraqi monetary unit (1000 fils = 1 ID); Jordanian; Yemeni (Aden); Bahraini; Kuwaiti
FUN Korean copper coin, late 19 cent.
HAO Vietnamese monetary unit (10 hao = 1 dong)
HAT money, coinage of Pahang/Malay, 19 cent.
JOE Portuguese Joao (in English)
JON North Korean monetary unit (100 jon = 1 won)
KAS 17 cent. copper coin for Tranquebar/India (Danish col.)
KIP Laotian monetary unit (1 kip = 100 at)
LAT Latvian monetary unit; 17/19 cent. Siamese (Thailand) silver tongue money
LEK Albanian monetary unit (1 lek = 100 qindars)
LIS French 17 cent. gold and silver coin
LEU Romanian monetary unit, pl. LEI (1 leu = 100 bani)
LEV Bulgarian monetary unit, pl. LEVA (1 lev = 100 stotinki)

3 **MAS** Indonesian (Sumatra) 13/18 cent. small gold coin
MIL proposed coin, 1/1000
ORE Scandinavian monetary unit (100 öre = 1 krona)
PIE Indian monetary unit (1/12 of the anna)
PUL Russian and Georgian copper coin 15/19 cent.
PYA Burmese monetary unit (100 pyas = 1 kyat)
REE REI, Portuguese money of a/c
RIX 19 cent. Ceylonese dollar
RYO Japanese monetary unit (10 ryos = 1 oban)
SEN Japanese monetary unit (100 sen/ 1 yen); Indonesian (100/1 rupiah); Cambodian (100/1 riel)
SHU old Japanese coin (1/16 of a ryo)
SOL Peruvian monetary unit (1 sol = 100 centavos); old French halfpenny
SOU French five-centime piece
WON N and S Korean monetary unit (1 won = 100 jon/chon)
YAP Micronesian (Caroline I.) stone discs used as currency (Fei)
YEN Japanese monetary unit (1 yen = 100 sen)

4 **ADLI** ADLEA, old Indian silver coin, Tripoli (20 cent.)
AKÇE AKÇA (OTMANI), first Ottoman silver coin (¾ of a para)
ANGE D'OR, French 14 cent. gold coin
ANNA Indian copper coin (1/16 of a rupee) from 17 cent. onwards
ATIA 18 cent. copper coin of Portuguese India (6⅛ Port. reis)
AURA Icelandic monetary unit (100 aurar = 1 krona)
BAHT Thai monetary unit (1 baht = 100 satangs)
BANU Romanian monetary unit, pl. BANI (100 bani = 1 leu)
BEKA Hebrew monetary unit (½ shekel)
BELL money: Chinese copper coinage; French Revolution
BIRR Ethiopian monetary unit (1 birr = 100 cents)
BONK colloq. for Javanese old copper coins (½ stuiver, 8 stuivers)
BUCK the US dollar (colloq.)
CASH 2000 years old Chinese bronze currency (1/1000 of a tael)
CEDI Ghanian monetary unit (1 cedi = 100 pesewas)

4 CENT decimal coinage of various countries
CHIP a counter; a sovereign
CHON South Korean monetary unit (100 chon = 1 won)
DALA late 19 cent. Hawaiian silver coin
DAWM DAM, Indian copper coin
DEKA 10 cent. small Ceylonese (Sri Lanka) gold coin
DEMY late 14 cent. half-piece of Scottish gold coin
DIME US 10-cent piece
DOIT Dutch half-farthing 16–19 cent.
DONG Vietnamese monetary unit (old 60 dong = 1 tien/tael)
DURO Spanish monetary unit (5 pesetas)
EURO common European unit
FALS copper coin of Persia and Umayad and Abbasid caliphates
FYRK Swedish monetary unit (¼ of an öre)
GANI Italian 14 cent. token currency (dodkin)
GELD ancient tribute; Ger. for money
GROS French 13 cent. silver coinage (gros tournois)
HVID 15 cent. Danish silver coin
HWAN WON Korean monetary unit
ISAR other name for 17–19 cent. German river gold ducats (Flussgelddukaten)
JOAO 18–19 cent. Portuguese gold coin (6400 reis)
JOEY 4d. piece (Joseph Hume); later 3d. piece
KASU 18 cent. Indian (Mysore) copper coins
KINA Papuan (New Guinea) monetary unit; (Australian dollar)
KOBO Nigerian monetary unit (1 naira = 100 kobo)
KRAN 19 cent. Persian silver coin (1000 dinar)
KYAT Burmese monetary unit (100 pyas = 1 kyat)
LAKH Indian monetary unit, 100 000 rupees
LARI Indian/Maldive Islands monetary unit (100 lari = 1 rupee); old Persian silver wire money
LIRA Italian monetary unit (pl. LIRE); Turkish monetary unit (100 kurus = 1 lira)
MAHE BICHE, French for pice
MARK German monetary unit (100 Pfennige = 1 Mark)
4 MERK Scottish 13s. 4d. (thistle merk); money of a/c
MITE a very small coin
MOCO late 18 cent. San Domingo coin; centre piece of Sp. dollar
OBAN Japanese oval gold coin (1 oban = 10 ryos)
OBOL B.C. Greek silver coin (⅙ of a drachm); Charon's ferry fee, 1½d.
ONZA Sp. and Latin American 8 escudos gold piece
PALA Ceylonese (Sri Lanka) deka
PARA Yugoslavian monetary unit (1 dinar = 100 paras); money in Turkish and old coin (1/40 of the piastre)
PEÇA PEZA, 18 cent. Portuguese gold coin (4 escudos)
PESO Filipino monetary unit (1 peso = 100 centavos); monetary unit of Mexico, Cuba, and various S. American countries; former piece of eight
PICE Indian monetary unit, Nepalese monetary unit (100 pice = 1 rupee) (¼ of an anna)
PITI old Indonesian tin coin (1 Spanish real = 4000 piti)
POGH ancient Armenian copper coin
POND S. African pound (Eng. gold sovereign)
PULS Afghani monetary unit (1 afghani – 100 puli)
PUNT Irish monetary unit
QUID a sovereign; a pound (colloq.)
RAND monetary unit of S. Africa and various nearby countries
REAL old Spanish (¼ of a peseta) and Portuguese monetary unit; Dominican Rep. monetary unit (8 reales = 1 peso)
REIS plural of REAL
RIAL Persian monetary unit (1 rial = 100 dinars); Moroccan (old)
RIEL Cambodian monetary unit (1 riel = 100 sen)
RING money, first coins of Australia
RUBA 10 cent. Sicilian monetary unit (¼ dinar)
RYAL gold coin; the rose noble
SALT money, primitive African currency
SENT Estonian monetary unit (100 sent = 1 kroon)
SKAR Tibetan copper coin
SPUR RYAL, colloq. for ½ ryal

4 SYLI Guinean monetary unit (1 syli = 100 cauris)
TAEL old Chinese monetary unit (1000 bronze cash = 1 tael)
TAKA Bangladeshi monetary unit (1 taka = 100 paisa)
TARO 16–18 cent. Maltese silver coin (12 tari = 1 scudo); early Sicilian gold coin
VELD POND, S. African (Boer) gold coin
WARK Ethiopian 19 cent. gold coin
WIRE money, Persian Lari (thin bars of silver)
YANG 19 cent. Korean silver coin
YUAN Chinese monetary unit (Yuan Shi Kai)
5 ABBEY CROWN, 16 cent. 20 shillings gold piece
ACKEY 18/19 cent. silver coin (Gold Coast)
ADLEA ADLI, old Indian silver coin; Tripoli (20 cent.)
AGNEL 13 cent. French gold coin (mouton d'or)
ALBUS German 'Weisspfennig' (grossus albus/white groat) 14/15 cent.
ALTUN Turkish 15 cent. gold coin
ALTYN Russian (Tartar) silver coin 17 cent. (3 kopeks)
AMANI early 20 cent. Afghani gold coin (1 amani = 30 afghani)
AMPAT Malay hat money
ANGEL old English gold coin
ASPER 13/15 cent. Middle Eastern base silver coin
AUREI Roman gold coins
BAIZA Omani monetary unit (1000 baizas = 1 rial/R.O.)
BELGA Belgian coin
BETSO small Venetian coin
BICHE French for 18 cent. pice
BRASS money (colloq.)
BRICK TEA, ancient Chinese and Tibetan currency (2½ lb = 1 tael)
BRIOT CROWN for Charles I
BUTUT Gambian monetary unit (100 butut = 1 dalasi)
CANOE DOLLAR, Canadian silver dollar
COLON Costa Rican monetary unit (1 colon = 100 centimos); El Salvadorian monetary unit
CROWN five-shilling piece
DALER Scandinavian Thaler (riksdaler)
5 DARIC gold coin of Darius (Persia) (1 daric = 20 sigloi)
DENGA 14/15 cent. Russian coin (silver penny)
DINAR Yugoslavian monetary unit (1 dinar = 100 paras); various Moslem countries; ancient Arab gold coin
DOBLA a number of old gold coins; 16 cent. double scudo
DOBRA 14 cent. Portuguese gold coin
DUCAT Italian old gold coin
EAGLE former US gold coin (10 dollars)
FANAM Indian monetary unit, gold (ancient), silver (modern) (⅛ of a rupee)
FUANG 19 cent. Siamese (Thai) monetary unit (⅛ of a Baht)
FUGIO CENT, first US coin
FRANC monetary unit of various countries
GERSH Ethiopian monetary unit, silver ($^1/_{10}$ of a talari)
GIGOT 16 cent. Brabantian copper coin (Flemish negenmanneke)
GRAMO late 19 cent. Spanish private gold coin
GRANO Maltese monetary unit; old copper coin of Naples and Sicily
GROAT silver 4d. piece
GROOT 13 cent. Dutch silver gros
HARDI 14 cent. gold and silver piece of England and dominion of France
HECTE Greek monetary unit ($^1/_6$ of the statar)
HENRI D'OR French gold coin, 16 cent.
HOLEY DOLLARS, ring money
HUSUM DALER, 16 cent. Danish daler
IMADI Yemeni precursor to the riyal
JUSTO 15 cent. Portuguese gold coin (= 2 cruzados)
KAIKI SHOHO, ancient Japanese gold coin
KAKIM ancient Siamese (Thai) bars currency
KARAN KRAN, Persian silver piece
KNIFE money, simple B.C. Chinese bronze coinage
KOBAN 16/19 cent. Japanese gold coin ($^1/_{10}$ of the oban)
KOPEK Russian monetary unit (100 kopeks = 1 rouble)
KRONA Scandinavian monetary unit (1 krona = 100 öre)
KRONE Austrian monetary unit, gold or silver

5 KROON Estonian monetary unit
LEONE 17 cent. Venetian silver coin (= 10 lire)
LEPTA Greek monetary unit
LIARD old French farthing
LIBRA 19 cent. Peruvian monetary unit; Roman pound
LITAS Lithuanian monetary unit, pl. LITU
LITRA 6 cent. B.C. Sicilian monetary unit
LIVRE old French franc (20 sols = 1 livre)
LOCHO Venezuelan monetary unit
LOUIS D'OR, 20-franc piece
MASSE D'OR, 14 cent. French gold coins
MEDIO Venezuelan monetary unit
MINIM tiny Roman bronze coins
MOHUR 15-rupee gold coin
MOKKO East Indian islands drum currency
MONGO Mongolian monetary unit (100 mongos = 1 tugrik)
NAIRA Nigerian monetary unit (1 naira = 100 kobo)
NGWEE Zambian monetary unit (100 ngwee = 1 kwacha)
NOBLE old English coin, 6s. 8d.
ONCIA 14 cent. Italian money of a/c; gold coin
ONLIK old Turkish silver coin (= 10 paras)
ORTUG old Swedish silver coin
PADMA TANKA, S. Indian B.C. gold coin
PAISA PICE, Indian monetary unit (100 paisa = 1 rupee); Bangladeshi monetary unit (100 paisa = 1 taka); Bhutani monetary unit
PAOLO Italian cities
PENCE plural of penny, British
PENGO Hungarian silver unit
PENNI Finnish monetary unit (100 penniä = 1 markka)
PENNY British copper coin
PIECE OF EIGHT = peso
PLACK Scottish 15/16 cent. billion coin
PLATE money, Swedish copper plates (platmynt)
POUND monetary unit of Britain and various countries
QUART D'ECU, French silver coin (= 15 sols)
RIYAL Sudanese monetary unit (1 Sud. pound = 10 riyals); monetary unit of Arabian Peninsula

5 ROYAL D'OR, French Louis IX gold coin
RUPEE Indian monetary unit (1 rupee = 100 paisa); Nepalese, Pakistani, Mauritian monetary unit
RUPIA Portuguese rupee (Goa and Diu)
SAIGA 7 cent. Merovingian coin
SALUT D'OR European medieval gold coin
SAUDI Arabian gold sovereign
SCEAT SCEATT 7 cent. English coin, base silver or copper
SCUDO old Italian 'shield' currency, gold or silver; pl. SCUDI
SEMIS half a Roman as
SENGI Zairean monetary unit (10 000 sengi = 1 zaire)
SHAKI Persian silver coin (= 10 kazbegi)
SICCA RUPEE, colloq. for E. India Co. rupee
SOLDI old Italian gold coin; pl. of soldo
SOLDO Italian sol or sou (halfpenny)
SPADE money, Chinese B.C. coinage
SRANG early 20 cent. Tibetan silver currency
STICA STYCA, small Saxon coin
SUCRE Ecuadorian monetary unit (1 sucre = 100 centavos)
SWORD DOLLAR, 16 cent. Scottish silver ryal
SYCEE boat-shaped Far Eastern silver ingot
TAKOE ⅛ of an ackey (Gold Coast)
TALAR a special 19 cent. thaler
TANGA 17 cent. Portuguese East Indian coin
TARIN old Sicilian silver coin
THIRD GUINEA, old English gold coin
THREE PENCE, British coin from 16 cent. (obs.)
TICAL Thai monetary unit (bar or baht); old Burmese monetary unit
TICCY S. African 3d. piece
TIGER tongue money, old weight-related silver bar currency of Indochina
TILLA old Afghani and Turkestani gold coin
TOMAN Persian gold unit
TRIME US 3-cent silver piece
UNCIA ancient Roman monastery unit ($\frac{1}{12}$ of the as)
UNITE English/Scottish 17 cent. gold piece; 'Faciam Eos in Gentem Unam'

5 VLIES old Dutch gold or silver coin
WITTE special 14 cent. albus
ZAIRE Zairean monetary unit (1 zaire = 100 makuta = 10 000 sengi)
ZLOTY Polish monetary unit (1 zloty = 100 groszy)
6 ABACIS old Portuguese Indian and E. African silver coin
ABBASI old Persian coin (base metal) and Georgian coin (silver)
ABDERA ancient Thracian coins
ADOLFS D'OR, Swedish 5-thaler coin, gold
AGOROT Israeli monetary unit (100 agorot = 1 Israeli pound)
AMANIA Afghani monetary unit
ANCHOR money, 19 cent. British silver coins
AUREUS Roman precursor of the solidus, gold
BALBAO Panamanian monetary unit (1 balboa = 100 centesimos)
BAMBOO money, inscribed Chinese 'stick' currency
BAUBEE BAWBEE, Scottish billion coin
BEZANT Byzantine gold coin (Nomisma)
BONNET PIECE, Scottish 16 cent. gold coin
BULLET money, 14/19 cent. Siamese (Thail) monetary unit, gold or silver
BUKSHA old Yemeni monetary unit
CANOPY type penny, William the Conqueror era
CARLIN 13 cent. Sicilian monetary unit, gold or silver
CARLIN D'OR, old English monetary unit, pure gold (salute)
CAURIS Guinean monetary unit (100 cauris = 1 syli)
CEITIL old Portuguese copper coin
CHO-GIN 18 cent. Japanese silver bar
CONDOR old Chilean monetary unit
COPANG Japanese gold coin
COPPER old penny (colloq.)
COWRIE shell money, Far East and Africa
CUARTO old Bolivian half-peso; ¼ of a Real
DALASI Gambian monetary unit (1 dalasi = 100 butut)
DECIME S. American 10-centavos
DENARO Italian denier, 8 cent.
DENIER Carolingian silver penny (12 deniers = 1 solidus)
6 DINERO old Spanish silver penny; Peruvian 10-centavo coin; Spanish for money
DIOBOL ancient Greek silver coin (¾ of a drachma)
DIRHAM Moroccan monetary unit (1 dirham = 100 M. francs); Iraqi (20 dirhams = 1 dinar); monetary unit Arab Emirates
DIRHEM ancient Arab and Ottoman coin
DIZAIN old French decimal coin (10 deniers)
DOBLON old Uruguayan coin, gold
DODKIN old coin of poor metal
DOLLAR monetary unit of the USA and various countries
DOPPIA 18 cent. Sardinian gold unit
DRACHM DRACHMA, Greek monetary unit, both ancient and modern
EIRAKU SEN, cash-type Japanese bronze coins
ESCUDO Portuguese monetary unit (1 escudo = 100 centavos); Chilean monetary unit (100 centesimos); old Spanish monetary unit
FALUCE Ceylonese (Sri Lanka) monetary unit, ¼ of a fanam
FILLER Hungarian monetary unit (100 filler = 1 forint)
FLORIN silver 2-shilling piece
FOLLIS Byzantine bronze coin
FORINT Hungarian monetary unit (1 forint = 100 filler)
GADHYA PAISA, old Indian base silver coin
GEORGE D'OR, 18 cent. five thaler coin, gold
GEORGE NOBLE, 16 cent. English gold coin (6s. 8d.)
GIULIO papal 'grosso largo'
GOTHIC CROWN, Victorian
GOTHIC FLORIN, superseded godless florin, 19 cent.
GOURDE Haitian 19 cent. silver coin
GRINNA Russian monetary unit, silver (= 10 kopeks); money of a/c
GROSSO Italian monetary unit, pl. GROSSI
GROSZY Polish monetary unit (100 groszy = 1 zloty)
GUINEA 21 shillings
GULDEN Dutch monetary unit, German (old) monetary unit
GYLLEN 16 cent. Swedish gulden

6 HALALA Yemeni monetary unit, bronze and copper (obs.)
HALERU Czechoslovakian monetary unit (100 haleru = 1 koruna), (Heller)
HALLER HELLER
HEAUME D'OR and d'argent, 14 cent. Flemish
HELLER German, Austrian, Swiss monetary unit (penny)
ICHIBU GIN, 19 cent. Japanese coin (= 1 bu)
JAITIL Indian 14 cent. (50 jaitils = 1 tankah)
KAPANG KEPING
KENGEN DAIHO, ancient Japanese bronze sen
KEPING 18/19 cent. Malay & Sumatran copper coins
KHOUMS Mauritian monetary unit (5 khoums = 1 ouguiya)
KORONA Hungarian monetary unit, silver (Austrian krone)
KORUNA Czechoslovakian monetary unit (1 koruna = 100 haleru)
KURUSH Turkish monetary unit (100 kurus = 1 lira)
KWACHA Zambian monetary unit (1 kwacha = 100 ngwee); Malawi monetary unit (1 k. = 100 tambala)
LAUREL 17 cent. twenty-shilling piece
LEPTON Greek coin, copper ($\frac{1}{7}$ of an obol)
MACATA old Guatemalan monetary unit
MACUTA Portuguese African monetary unit 18/19 cent. (= 50 reis)
MAKUTA Zairean monetary unit (100 makuta = 1 zaire)
MANCUS European designation of old Arab gold dinar
MARKKA Finnish monetary unit (1 markka = 100 penniä)
MATONA Ethiopian monetary unit, copper or nickel
MAUNDY money, British royal 'give aways'
MAZUNA Moroccan monetary unit, 19 cent.
MISCAL 18 cent. Spanish silver piastre; monetary unit of Chinese Turkestan
NICKEL US 5-cent piece
OCTAVO OCHAVO, old Spanish silver coin; Mexican copper coin
OSELLA 16 cent. Venetian gift coin

6 OTMANI Ottoman monetary unit, silver (see AKÇE)
OBOLUS OBOL, ancient Greek coin
PAGODA Indian gold coin
PAHANG Malay hat money
PARDAO Portuguese Indian monetary unit, xeraphim
PATACA 17 cent. Arab silver and money of a/c; old Brazilian monetary unit
PATACA 18 cent. Brabantian and Westphalian monetary unit, silver
PATACA 18 cent. Algerian money of a/c; African name for Maria Theresa thaler
PATACA Macauan monetary unit (1 pataca = 100 avos)
PATARD 15 cent. Dutch silver piece
PERPER early 20 cent. Montenegran silver unit; old Ragusan monetary unit
PESETA Spanish monetary unit
PLAQUE old Dutch billion coin
PRAGER GROSCHEN, late 13 cent. Bohemian coin, silver
PRUTAH old Indonesian monetary unit
QINDAR Albanian monetary unit (100 qindars = 1 lek)
QUARTO old Spanish monetary unit (¼ real)
QUIRSH Saudi Arabian monetary unit (20 quirsh = 1 Saudi riyal)
RAPPEN Swiss monetary unit (100 rappen = 1 Swiss francs)
ROUBLE Russian monetary unit (1 rouble = 100 kopek)
RUPIAH Indonesian monetary unit (1 rupiah = 100 sen)
SANESE D'ORO, 14 cent. North Italian (Sienna) coin, gold
SATANG Thai monetary unit
SEQUIN Venetian gold coin (Zecchino); Ottoman monetary unit
SESINO 18 cent. Italian copper or billon coin (½ soldo)
SHEKEL Jewish half crown
SIERRA LEONE, late 18 cent. silver coin
SIGLOS ancient Persian silver piece ($\frac{1}{20}$ of a gold daric)
SIXAIN old French monetary unit (= 6 deniers)
SOMALO old Somali monetary unit
SOOKOO SUKU, old Malayan coin, silver
SOVRAN poetical sovereign
STATER ancient Greek gold or silver coin

6 STIVER West Indian Dutch Stuiver
SUELDO 19 cent. Bolivian coin, silver (8 sueldi = 1 peso)
TALARI Abyssinian coin, silver
TALBOT 15 cent. Anglian, gold
TALENT old Hebrew monetary unit; ancient weight unit
TANGKA 18 cent. Tibetan monetary unit, base silver
TANKAH various old Indian coins
TANNER British sixpence (obs.)
TESTER Henry VIII shilling
TESTON TESTONE/TESTOON, 16 cent. shilling; Italian silver coin
THALER 15/20 cent. German monetary unit, silver (Guldengroschen)
TICKEY S. African 3d. piece
TOMAUN Persian gold coin
TORNEZ 14 cent. Portuguese coin, silver (French gros tornois)
TOSTAO 16 cent. Portuguese coin, headless
TRIENS small Byzantine gold coin (¾ of a solidus)
TRIPLE UNIT, largest English Civil War gold coin, 17 cent.
TUGRIK Mongolian monetary unit (1 tugrik = 100 mongos)
UNGARO Italian for the Hungarian 17 cent. ducat
VIERER old Swiss coin, silver (2 vierer = 2 rappen)
VINTEM 15 cent. Portuguese silver coin (= 20 reis); old Brazilian copper coin
WOLSEY GROAT, English, 16 cent. special coin
YUZLIK large, old Turkish silver coin equal to 100 paras
ZECHIN SEQUIN, Venetian monetary unit

7 ACRAGAS ancient Greek monetary unit (Sicily)
AFGHANI Afghani monetary unit (1 afghani = 100 puli)
ALTILIK 19 cent. Ottoman 6-piastre piece, base silver
ANGELET half an angel, 17 cent.
ANGELOT a Louis XI gold coin
ANGOLAR Angolan escudo
ANGSTER 14/19 cent. Swiss coin, silver or copper
ASHRAFI 15/18 cent. Persian coin, gold (replaced by the toman)
BAIOCCO Italian papal coin ($^1/_{100}$ of the scudo)

7 BARHINA Portuguese coin, gold (1 bahrina = 400 reis)
BOLIVAR Venezuelan monetary unit (1 bolivar = 2 reales = 100 centimes)
BRILLEN DUKAT, 17 cent. Danish coin, gold
BRILLEN THALER, 16 cent. German monetary unit
BRIQUET French for Dutch vuurijzer, 15 cent. silver coin
BULLION pieces, gold or silver objects valued on carat-mass content
BUQSHAH (Sana) Yemeni monetary unit (40 buqshahs = 1 riyal)
CADIERE late 15 cent. gold piece; silver coin of Charles V and VI
CAROLIN old Swedish coin, gold or silver
CAROLUS gold coin of Charles V (Spanish) Habsburg Emperor
CAVALLO 15 cent. Sicilian copper coin ($^1/_{200}$ of a ducat)
CENTAVO S. American monetary unit, various countries
CENTIME one-hundredth of a franc (various countries)
CHALKOS Greek monetary unit (Alexander the Great), copper ($^1/_{48}$ of the drachm)
CORDOBA Nicaraguan monetary unit (1 cordoba = 100 centavos)
CORONAT KWARTNIK, 14/15 cent. Polish monetary unit (½ groschen)
CRUSADO old Portuguese monetary unit
CRUZADO 15 cent. Portuguese gold coin; new Brazilian monetary unit
DAALDER Dutch thaler; Charles V silver coin
DENARII pence
DENNING 17 cent. Danish equivalent of Russian denga
DHARANA Indian old punch-marked coins (Ceylonese purana)
DOBLONE Italian 4 or 8 scudi gold pieces
DOUZAIN old French shilling (12 deniers)
DRACHMA Greek monetary unit (1 drachma = 100 lepta), ancient and modern
DUPLONE 18/19 cent. Swiss gold coin (16 francs)
ENRIQUE 15 cent. Spanish gold coin
ESCALIN 17 cent. Dutch silver coin
ESPADIN 15 cent. Portuguese ½ justo
ESPHERA Goan (Portuguese) 16 cent. gold coin

7 EKPWELE Equatorial Guinean peseta (1 ekpwele = 100 centimos)

FERDING Swedish silver farthing, 16 cent.

FILIPPO 16/18 cent. Spanish coin, silver

FOLLARO Italian Byzantine copper coin

GAZETTA old Venetian copper coin

GODLESS FLORIN (Victoria/Britain) omitting 'Dei Gratia', not valid in heaven

GUARANI Paraguayan monetary unit (1 guarani = 100 centimos)

GUERCHE 19 cent. Ethiopian coin, silver ($\frac{1}{6}$ of the talari)

GUILDER Dutch florin

HIBERNO Viking coin, Ireland

JACOBUS gold coin of James I

KAZBEGI Persian Safavid copper coin

LEMPIRA Honduran monetary unit (100 centavos); old Brazilian monetary unit

LEOPARD 14 cent. English 3-shilling gold coin

MANCHIR first Ottoman copper coin, 14 cent.

MANILLA W. African copper coin

MARENGO Napoleonic 20 franc gold piece

MATAPAN 13 cent. Venetian grosso

MILREIS old Brazilian and Portuguese coin

MOIDORE Portuguese 4-cruzado piece (= 4000 reis); 18 cent. Brazilian monetary unit

NOMISMA Byzantine gold coins; Greek for money

NONSUNT 16 cent. Scottish 12-penny groat; Northumberland shillings

NOVODEL Russian coins (or imitations)

NUMMIUM Byzantine bronze unit, pl. nummia

ORMONDE money, minted in Ireland 1643

OUGUIYA Mauritanian monetary unit (1 ouguiya = 5 khoums)

PAHLEVI former Persian gold unit, superseded the toman

PAOLINO Italian silver scudo, 15/16 cent.

PARISIS D'OR, 11 cent. French gold coins

PATAGON Dutch early 17 cent., silver (= 48 stuivers)

7 PEACOCK RUPEE, 19 cent. Burmese coin, gold or silver

PESEWAS Ghanaian monetary unit (100 pesewas = 1 new cadi)

PFENNIG German copper coin

PHOENIX 18 cent. Sicilian gold coin; 19 cent. Greek silver coin (= 100 lepta)

PIASTRE PIASTER, Egyptian monetary unit (100 piasters = 1 E. pound); Sudanese monetary unit; old European name for Spanish peso and variations

PISTOLE DOUBLOON, old Spanish double escudo, gold

POLTINA Russian ½ rouble

QUARTER US quarter of a dollar

QUETZAL Guatemalan monetary unit (1 quetzal = 100 centavos)

QUINTAR QINDAR, Albanian monetary unit

ROYALIN 18 cent. Danish colonial monetary unit (Tranquebar/India); silver

RUSPONE 18 cent. Florentine monetary unit, gold (= 3 ducats)

SANTIMS early 20 cent. Latvian (100 santims = 1 lats)

SAN TOME THOME, Portuguese Indian 16 cent. gold piece

SAPEQUE Indochinese dong

SESTINO 15 cent. Neapolitan billion piece

SEXTANS ancient Roman bronze coin

SILIQUA Byzantine silver coin ($\frac{1}{24}$ of a solidus)

SOLIDUS old Roman gold coin (= 72 Roman libra)

SOSLING 15 cent. Danish six-penny coin, silver

SOVRANO SOUVERAIN D'OR, old Dutch gold coin

STAMPEE French W. Indies 18 cent. sous

STOOTER 16 cent. Dutch coin, base silver ($\frac{1}{20}$ of a daalder)

STUIVER 15 cent. Dutch coin, base silver

TALLERO old Italian thaler; 20 cent. It. Eritrean

TAMBALA Malawian monetary unit (100 tambala = 1 kwacha)

TAMPANG Malay hat money

TESTOON old Italian silver coin

TESTRIL tester; a sixpence

THISTLE crown, dollar, merk, British 16/17 cent.

7 **THISTLE** NOBLE, 16 cent. British large gold piece
THRYMSA 6 cent. Anglo-Saxon monetary unit (¾ of a solidus)
TRIBUTE penny, Judaean Roman denarius
TRIOBOL day-money for a judge in ancient Greece (½ drachm)
UGORSKY Russian name for Hungarian 15 cent. gold coin
UNICORN Scottish 15 cent. gold piece
ZLATNIK first Russian gold coins
ZOLOTYE Russian gold coins; Crimean campaign reward, 17 cent.

8 **ADELAIDE** TOKENS, Australian one pound gold tokens
AGNUS DEI type of penny of Aethelred II
ALBERTIN 16 cent. Dutch (Spanish) gold coin
AMBROSIN Milanese coin
ASSIGNAT paper currency, French Revolution
BAZARUCO Portuguese Indian 16 cent. coin, base metal
CAROLOUS KAROLUS, French dizain
CENTIMOS Equatorial Guinean monetary unit (100 centimos = 1 ekpwele)
CHUCKRAM Indian 18/20 cent. (4 chuckrams = 1 gold fanam)
CLEMENTI papal silver coin (15 baiocchi)
CROSAZZO Genoese 17 cent. silver coin
CRUZEIRO Brazilian monetary unit (1 cruzeiro = 100 centavos)
DENARIUS main silver coin of the Roman Empire
DIDRACHM ancient Greek 2-drachma
DINHEIRO 12/14 cent. Portuguese billon denier
DOHOZARI 19 cent. tiny Persian gold coin
DOUBLOON Spanish monetary unit (2 pistoles)
DREILING 15 cent. German 3 pfennig. billon
DUCATONE Italian 16/18 cent. silver coin
DUCATOON Venetian silver coin
FARTHING a quarter of a penny
FLORENCE Edward III gold florin
FLORETTE variations of French 15 cent. gros
FREDERIK D'OR, Danish 19 cent. gold coin

8 **GENOVINO** 12 cent. Genoese gold coin
GIGLIATO 14 cent. silver coin of Charles II of Naples
GIUSTINA 16 cent. Venetian silver coin (8 lire)
GORY-OBAN 19 cent. Japanese ½ oban gold coin
GROSCHEN Austrian monetary unit (100 groschen = 1 schilling); monetary unit of Holy Roman Empire, silver
GROSSONE papal 14/18 cent. silver coin
GULDINER GULDENGROSCHEN, 15 cent. European silver coin (before thaler)
HALFMARK old English coin, 6s. 8d.
HATPIECE 16 cent. English monetary unit, gold (80s.)
HEMIOBOL ancient Athenian and Corinthian ½ obol
HEXAGRAM Byzantine silver coin
IMPERIAL Russian 10-rouble gold coin, 18 cent.
JOHANNES old Portuguese coin
KAHAVANU 9 cent. Ceylonese (Sri Lanka) gold coin
KREUTZER old Austrian copper coin
KWARTNIK Polish 14/15 cent. ½ groschen
MAGDALON Provençal 15 cent. gold florin
MARAVEDI MARABOTINO, old Spanish copper coin
MILLIMES Tunisian monetary unit (1000 millimes = 1 dinar)
MOCENIGO a kind of 15 cent. Italian lira
MURAJOLA Italian billon coins of low silver content
NAPOLEON French 20-franc gold coin
NGULTRUM Bhutani monetary unit (1 ngultrum = 2 tikchung = 100 paisa)
PAVILLON D'OR, 14 cent. French gold coin
PHILIPPI 4 cent. B.C. Macedonian (Black Sea) currency
PICCIOLO old Maltese copper coin
PLAPPART 14 cent. Swiss billon coin (15 Heller)
QUADRANS Roman copper coin (temncius), ¼ as
QUATRUNX Roman 4 oz coin (triens)
QUINCUNX Roman 5 oz coin
ROSE-RYAL English gold coin of James I (30s.)
SCELLINO Somalian monetary unit

8 SCYPHATE Byzantine monetary unit
SEMUNCIA Roman ½ uncia
SEQUENCE marks, Roman B.C. denarii
SESTERCE Roman silver coin
SHILLING old English 12 pence; monetary unit of Austria and various other countries
SIXPENCE old English silver coin
SKILLING old Scandinavian shilling
SPINTRIA old porno tokens (tesserae)
SREBENIK 10 cent. Russian silver coins
STAMENON Byzantine solidus
STERLING gold or silver purity of British coinage

8 STOTINKA Bulgarian (100 stotinki = 1 lev)
TESSERAE old Roman tickets or tokens
TIKCHUNG Bhutani monetary unit (2 tikchung = 1 ngultrum)
VIRGINIA Virginian 18 cent. copper coin
XERAPHIM Portuguese Indian silver coin
ZECCHINO old Italian ducat
ZERMABUB early 18 cent. Ottoman gold coin

Alphabets

Greek

ALPHA
BETA
GAMMA
DELTA
EPSILON
ZETA
ETA
THETA
IOTA
KAPPA
LAMBDA
MU
NU
XI
OMICROM
PI
RHO
SIGMA
TAU
UPSILON
PHI
CHI
PSI
OMEGA

Hebrew

ALEPH
BETH
GIMEL
DALETH
HE
VAU
ZAIN or **ZAYIN**
CHETH or **HETH**
TETH
JOD or **YOD**
CAPH or **KAPH**
LAMED
MEM
NUN
SAMECH or **SAMEKH**
AIN or **AYIN**
PE
TZADDI or **ZADE**
KOPH
RESH
SCHIN or **SHIN**
TAU

French Revolutionary Calendar

French Republic 1794

VENDEMIAIRE Vintage ***Sept.***
BRUMAIRE Fog ***Oct.***
FRIMAIRE Sleet ***Nov.***
NIVOSE Snow ***Dec.***
PLUVIOSE Rain ***Jan.***
VENTOSE Wind ***Feb.***
GERMINAL Seed ***Mar.***
FLOREAL Blossom ***Apr.***
PRAIRAL Pasture ***May***
MESSIDOR Harvest ***June***
THERMIDOR, FERVIDOR Heat ***July***
FRUCTIDOR Fruit ***Aug.***

The 12 Signs of the Zodiac

Spring

ARIES Ram
TAURUS Bull
GEMINI Twins

Summer

CANCER Crab
LEO Lion
VIRGO Virgin

Autumn

LIBRA Balance
SCORPIO Scorpion
SAGITTARIUS Archer

Winter

CAPRICORNUS Goat
AQUARIUS Water Carrier
PISCES Fishes

The 9 Planets and their Satellites

MARS Deimos, Phobos
EARTH Luna
VENUS
NEPTUNE Triton, Nereid
SATURN Rhea, Dione, Mimas, Titan, Phoebe, Tethys, Janus, Iapetus, Hyperion, Enceladus
PLUTO
URANUS Ariel, Titania, Oberon, Umbriel, Miranda
JUPITER Io, Europa, Callisto, Ganymede
MERCURY

Constellations in the Heavens

3 ARA
LEO
4 CRUS
CRUX
LYRA
URSA MAJOR
URSA MINOR
5 ARIES
CETUS
DRACO
HYDRA
INDUS
LEPUS
LIBRA
LUPOS
MUSCA
ORION
VIRGO
AQUILA
AURIGA
BOOTES
CANCER
CARINA
CORONA
CORVUS
CRATER
CYGNUS
DORADO
FORNAX
GEMINI
6 PUPPIS
TAURUS
TUCANA
7 CENTAUR
CEPHEUS
COLUMBA
PEACOCK
PEGASUS
PHOENIX
PERSEUS
SCORPIO
SERPENS
8 AQUARIUS
ERIDANUS
HERCULES
PLEIADES
9 ANDROMEDA
CENTAURUS (Alpha & Beta Centauri)
DELPHINUS
OPHIUCHUS
10 CANIS MAJOR
CANIS MINOR
CASSIOPEIA
TRIANGULUM
URSUS MAJOR
URSUS MINOR
11 CAPRICORNUS
SAGITTARIUS

CANES VENATICI
CORONA BOREALIS
PISCIS AUSTRALIS
TRIANGULUM AUSTRALIS

Major Stars

4 **BETA** Centaurus
ENIF Pegasus
KAUS Sagittarius
MIRA Cetus
VEGA Lyra
5 **ACRUX** Crux
ALGOL Perseus
ALPHA Centaurus
ANKAA Phoenix
AVIOR Triangle
DENEB Cygnus
DUBHE Ursus Major
HADAR Centaurus
HAMAL Aries
MIZAR Ursus Major
NUNKI Sagitarrius
RIGIL (KENT) Centaurus
SABIK Ophiuchi
SPICA Virgo
6 **ACAMAR** Eridanus
ADHARA Canis Major
ALIOTH Ursa Major
ALKAID Ursa Minor
ALNAIR Crux
ALTAIR Aquila
CASTOR Gemini
DIPHDA Cetus
ELNATH Taurus
GACRUX Crux
GEINAH Corvus
HYADES Taurus
6 **KOCHAB** Ursa Minor
MARKAB Pegasus
MENKAR Cetus
MIMOSA Crux
MIRFAK Perseus
POLLUX Gemini
SHAUFA Scorpio
SIRIUS Canis Major
SUHAIL Velori
7 **AINILAM** Orion
ALPHARD Hydra
ANTARES Scorpio
CANOPUS Carina
CAPELLA Aurga
ELTANIN Draco
MENKENT Centaurus
POLARIS Ursa Minor
PROCYON Ursa Minor
REGULUS Leo
SCHEDAR Cassiopeia
8 **ACHERNAR** Eridanus
ALPHECCA Corona Borealis
ARCTURUS Bootes
DENEBOLA Leo
ZUBENUBI Libra
9 **ALDEBARAN** Taurus
ALPHERATZ Andromedra
BELLATRIX Orion
FOMALHAUF Pisces
10 **RASALHAGUE** Ophiuchi
11 **BETELGEUSE** Orion
MIAPLACIDUS Carina

Months of the Jewish Year

TISHRI
HESHVAN
KISLEV
TEBET
SHEBAT
ADAR or **VEADAR**
NISAN or **ABIB**
IYAR
SIVAN
TAMMUS
AB
ELUL

Books of the Bible

Old Testament (39)

GENESIS
EXODUS
LEVITICUS
NUMBERS
DEUTERONOMY
JOSHUA
JUDGES
RUTH
1st SAMUEL
2nd SAMUEL
1st KINGS
2nd KINGS
1st CHRONICLES
2nd CHRONICLES
EZRA
NEHEMIAH
ESTHER
JOB
PSALMS
PROVERBS
ECCLESIASTES
SONG OF SOLOMON (SONG OF SONGS)
ISAIAH
JEREMIAH
LAMENTATIONS
EZEKIEL
DANIEL
HOSEA
JOEL
AMOS
OBADIAH
JONAH
MICAH
NAHUM
HABAKKUK
ZEPHANIAH
HAGGAI
ZACHARIAS
MALACHI

The Apocrypha (13)

ESDRAS
TOBIT
JUDITH
ESTHER
THE WISDOM OF SOLOMON
ECCLESIASTICUS
BARUCH
EPISTLE OF JEREMY
SONG OF THE THREE HOLY CHILDREN
HISTORY OF SUSANNA
BEL AND THE DRAGON
THE PRAYER OF MANASSES
MACCABEES

New Testament (27)

GOSPEL OF ST MATTHEW
GOSPEL OF ST MARK
GOSPEL OF ST LUKE
GOSPEL OF ST JOHN
ACTS OF THE APOSTLES
EPISTLE FO THE ROMANS
1st EPISTLE TO THE CORINTHIANS
2nd EPISTLE TO THE CORINTHIANS
EPISTLE TO THE GALATIANS
EPISTLE TO THE EPHESIANS
EPISTLE TO THE PHILIPPIANS
EPISTLE TO THE COLOSSIANS
1st EPISTLE TO THE THESSALONIANS
2nd EPISTLE TO THE THESSALONIANS
1st EPISTLE TO TIMOTHY
2nd EPISTLE TO TIMOTHY
EPISTLE TO TITUS
EPISTLE TO PHILEMON
EPISTLE TO THE HEBREWS
1st PETER
2nd PETER
1st JOHN
2nd JOHN
3rd JOHN
JAMES
JUDE
THE REVELATION

The 7 Major Ecumenical Councils (in Asia Minor)

NICEA (Iznik) ***A.D. 325***
CONSTANTINOPLE (Istanbul) ***A.D. 381***
EPHESUS (Efes) ***A.D. 431***
CHALCEDON (Kadikoy) ***A.D. 451***
CONSTANTINOPLE (Istanbul) ***A.D. 533***
ISTANBUL ***A.D. 680–681***
NICEA (Iznik) ***A.D. 787***

British Prime Ministers

From 1770

Lord NORTH
Lord ROCKINGHAM
Lord SHELBURNE
Duke of PORTLAND
William PITT
Henry ADDINGTON
William PITT
Lord GRENVILLE
Spencer PERCEVAL
Lord LIVERPOOL
George CANNING
Lord GODERICH
Duke of WELLINGTON
Lord GREY
Lord MELBOURNE
Sir Robert PEEL
Lord MELBOURNE
Sir Robert PEEL
Lord John RUSSELL
Lord DERBY
Lord ABERDEEN
Lord PALMERSTON
Lord DERBY
Lord PALMERSTON
Lord John RUSSELL
Lord DERBY
Benjamin DISRAELI
W. E. GLADSTONE
Benjamin DISRAELI
Lord BEACONSFIELD
W. E. GLADSTONE
Lord SALISBURY
W. E. GLADSTONE
Lord SALISBURY
W. E. GLADSTONE
Lord ROSEBERY
Lord SALISBURY
A. L. BALFOUR
Sir H. CAMPBELL-BANNERMAN
H. H. ASQUITH**
David LLOYD GEORGE
A. BONAR LAW
Stanley BALDWIN
J. R. MACDONALD
Stanley BALDWIN
J. R. MACDONALD**
Stanley BALDWIN
Neville CHAMBERLAIN**
W. Spencer CHURCHILL**
Clement ATTLEE**
Sir W. CHURCHILL
Sir Anthony EDEN
Harold MACMILLAN**
Sir Alec DOUGLAS-HOME
Harold WILSON**
Edward HEATH
Harold WILSON**
James CALLAGHAN
Margaret THATCHER***
John MAJOR**
Tony BLAIR

** and *** signify the number of consecutive terms of office

Presidents of the United States

George WASHINGTON
John ADAMS
Thomas JEFFERSON
James MADISON
James MONROE
John Quincy ADAMS
Andrew JACKSON
Martin van BUREN
William HARRISON
John TYLER
James Knox POLK
Zachary TAYLOR
Millard FILLMORE
Franklin PIERCE
James BUCHANAN
Abraham LINCOLN
Andrew JOHNSON
Ulysses GRANT
Rutherford HAYES
James GARFIELD
Chester ARTHUR
Grover CLEVELAND
Benjamin HARRISON
Grover CLEVELAND
William McKINLEY
Theodore ROOSEVELT
William TAFT
Woodrow WILSON
Warren HARDING
Calvin COOLIDGE
Herbert HOOVER
F. D. ROOSEVELT
Harry TRUMAN
Dwight D. EISENHOWER
John F. KENNEDY
Lyndon B. JOHNSON
Richard M. NIXON
Gerald R. FORD
James E. CARTER
Ronald REAGAN
George BUSH
Bill CLINTON

Nobel Prize Winners in Literature

Since 1901

1901 **Sully PRUDHOMME** *Fr.*
1902 **Theodor MOMMSEN** *Ger.*
1903 **B. BJORNSON** *Nor.*
1904 **Frédéric MISTRAL & J. ECHEGARAY y EIZAGUIRRE** *Fr. & Spain*
1905 **H. SIENKIEWICZ** *Pol.*
1906 **Giosue CARDUCCI** *Italy*
1907 **Rudyard KIPLING** *Brit.*
1908 **Rudolf EUKEN** *Ger.*
1909 **Selma LAGERLOF** *Sweden*
1910 **Paul von HEYSE** *Ger.*
1911 **Maurice MAETERLINCK** *Belg.*
1912 **Gerhart HAUPTMANN** *Ger.*
1913 **Sir R. TAGORE** *India*
1914 **no award**
1915 **Romain ROLLAND** *Fr.*
1916 **V. von HEIDENSTAM** *Sweden*
1917 **Karl GJELLERUP & H. PONTOPPIDAN** *Den.*
1918 **no award**
1919 **Carl SPITTELER** *Switz.*
1920 **Knut HAMSUN** *Nor.*
1921 **Anatole FRANCE** *Fr.*
1922 **J. BENAVENTE y MARTINEZ** *Spain*
1923 **William Butler YEATS** *Ire.*
1924 **Wladyslaw REYMONT** *Pol.*
1925 **George Bernard SHAW** *Ire.*
1926 **Grazia DELEDDA** *Italy*
1927 **Henri BERGSON** *Fr.*
1928 **Sigrid UNDSET** *Nor.*
1929 **Thomas MANN** *Ger.*
1930 **Sinclair LEWIS** *U.S.*
1931 **Erik Axel KARLFELDT** *Sweden*
1932 **John GALSWORTHY** *Brit.*
1933 **Ivan BUNIN** *U.S.S.R.*
1934 **Luigi PIRANDELLO** *Italy*
1935 **no award**
1936 **Eugene O'NEILL** *U.S.*
1937 **Roger MARTIN du GARD** *Fr.*
1938 **Pearl BUCK** *U.S.*
1939 **Frans Eemil SILLANPAA** *Fin.*
1940–
1943 **no awards**
1944 **J. V. JENSEN** *Den.*
1945 **Gabriela MISTRAL** *Chile*
1946 **Hermann HESSE** *Switz.*
1947 **André GIDE** *Fr.*
1948 **T. S. ELIOT** *Brit.*
1949 **William FAULKNER** *U.S.*
1950 **Bertrand RUSSELL** *Brit.*
1951 **Pär LAGERKVIST** *Sweden*
1952 **François MAURIAC** *Fr.*
1953 **Sir Winston CHURCHILL** *Brit.*
1954 **Ernest HEMINGWAY** *U.S.*
1955 **Halldor LAXNESS** *Ice.*
1956 **Juan Ramon JIMENEZ** *Spain*
1957 **Albert CAMUS** *Fr.*
1958 **Boris PASTERNAK (declined award)** *U.S.S.R.*
1959 **Salvatore QUASIMODO** *Italy*
1960 **Saint-John PERSE** *Fr.*
1961 **Ivo ANDRIC** *Yugos.*
1962 **John STEINBECK** *U.S.*
1963 **George SEFERIS** *Gr.*
1964 **Jean-Paul SARTRE** *Fr.*
1965 **Mikhail SHOLOKHOV** *U.S.S.R.*
1966 **Shmuel Yosef AGNON & Nelly SACHS** *Isr. & Sweden*
1967 **Miguel Angel ASTURIAS** *Guat.*
1968 **Kawabata YASUNARI** *Japan*
1969 **Samuel BECKETT** *Ire.*
1970 **Aleksandr SOLZHENITSYN** *U.S.S.R.*
1971 **Pablo NERUDA** *Chile*
1972 **Heinrich BOLL** *Ger.*
1973 **Patrick WHITE** *Austr.*
1974 **Eyvind JOHNSON & Harry MARTINSON** *Sweden*
1975 **Eugenio MONTALE** *Italy*
1976 **Saul BELLOW** *U.S.*
1977 **Vicente ALEIXANDRE** *Spain*
1978 **Isaac Bashevis SINGER** *U.S.*
1979 **Odysseus ELYTIS** *Gr.*
1980 **Czeslaw MILOSZ** *U.S.*
1981 **Elias CANETTI** *Bulg.*
1982 **Gabriel Garcia MARQUEZ** *Colombia*
1983 **William GOLDING** *Brit.*
1984 **Jaroslav SEIFERT** *Czech.*
1985 **Claude SIMON** *Fr.*
1986 **Elie WIESEL** *U.S.*
1987 **Joseph BRODSKY** *U.S./U.S.S.R.*
1988 **Negbeh MAHFOUZ** *Egypt*
1989 **Camilo José CELA** *Spain*
1990 **Octavio PAZ** *Mexico*
1991 **Nadine GORDIMER** *S.A.*
1992 **Derek WALCOTT** *St Lucia*
1993 **Toni MORRISON** *U.S.*
1994 **Kenzaburo OE** *Japan*
1995 **Seamus HEANEY** *Ire.*
1996 **Wislawa SZYMBORSKA** *Poland*
1997 **Dario FO** *Italy*

Counties of the British Isles

England and Wales

Metropolitan Counties

GREATER MANCHESTER
MERSEYSIDE
SOUTH YORKSHIRE
TYNE & WEAR
WEST MIDLANDS
WEST YORKS

Non-Metropolitan Counties

3 MON* is **GWENT**
4 AVON
BEDS
CAMS
GLAM* now **S. GLAM, W. GLAM**
GLOS
KENT
OXON
TYNE & WEAR
5 BERKS
BUCKS
CARDS* in **DYFED**
CARMS* in **DYFED**
CLWYD
DERBY
DEVON
DYFED
ESSEX
FLINT* in **CLWYD**
GWENT
HANTS
HERTS
HUNTS*
LANCS
LEICS
LINCS
NOTTS
PEMBS* in **CLWYD**
POWYS
SALOP** now **SHROPSHIRE**
WILTS
WORCS in **HEREFORDSHIRE & WORCS**
YORKS
6 BRECON* in **POWYS**
DORSET
DURHAM
LONDON
OXFORD
RADNOR* in **POWYS**
STAFFS
SURREY
SUSSEX now **E. SUSSEX, W. SUSSEX**
7 BEDFORD
CUMBRIA
DENBIGH* in **CLWYD**
GWYNEDD
LINCOLN
NORFOLK
RUTLAND in **LEICESTERSHIRE**
SUFFOLK
WARWICK
8 ANGLESEY* in **GWYNEDD**
CARDIGAN* in **DYFED**
CHESHIRE
CORNWALL and **SCILLY**
HEREFORD in **HEREFORD & WORCS**
HERTFORD
MONMOUTH* is **GWENT**
PEMBROKE* in **DYFED**
SOMERSET
STAFFORD -shire
9 CAMBRIDGE -shire
CLEVELAND formerly North Yorkshire
NORTHANTS NORTHAMPTON-shire
WILTSHIRE
YORKSHIRE
10 GLOUCESTER -shire
HUMBERSIDE SOUTH RIDING YORKS
+ part of **NORTH LINCOLNSHIRE**
HUNTINGDON in **CAMBRIDGE**
LANCASHIRE
NOTTINGHAM -shire
12 LINCOLNSHIRE
14 NORTHUMBERLAND

Scotland

9 Regions (53 districts)

3 AYR*
4 BUTE*
FIFE
ROSS*
5 ANGUS*
BANFF*
ELGIN*
MORAY*
NAIRN*
PERTH*
6 ARGYLL*
FORFAR*
LANARK*
7 BERWICK*
BORDERS
CENTRAL
ISLANDS (Orkney, Shetland, Western)
KINROSS*
LOTHIAN
PEEBLES*
RENFREW*
SELKIRK*
TAYSIDE

7 **WIGTOWN***
8 **ABERDEEN***
AYRSHIRE*
CROMARTY*
DUMFRIES
GALLOWAY
GRAMPIAN
HIGHLAND
ROXBURGH*
STIRLING*
11 **STRATHCLYDE**

Ireland

4 **CORK†**
DOWN
LEIX†
MAYO†
5 **CAVAN†**
CLARE†
KERRY†
LOUTH†
MEATH†
SLIGO†
6 **ANTRIM**
ARMAGH
CARLOW†
DUBLIN†
GALWAY†
OFFALY†
TYRONE
ULSTER (P)
7 **DONEGAL†**
KILDARE†
LEITRIM†
MUNSTER (P)†
WEXFORD†
WICKLOW†
8 **KILKENNY†**
LAOIGHIS
LEINSTER (P)†
LIMERICK†
LONGFORD†
MONAGHAN†
9 **FERMANAGH**
11 **LONDONDERRY**

* Counties which no longer exist after local government reorganization in 1974.
** Name for Shropshire from 1974 to 1980.
† Counties of the Republic of Ireland.

The 50 United States of America

	State/Abbreviation	*Joined/no.*	*Approx. Population*	*Capital*
4	**IOWA** ***Ia.***	1846/29th	2.8 mill.	DES MOINES
	OHIO ***O.***	1803/17th	10.8 mill.	COLUMBUS
	UTAH ***Uh.***	1896/45th	1.5 mill.	SALT LAKE CITY
5	**IDAHO** ***Id., Ida.***	1890/43rd	1.0 mill.	BOISE
	MAINE ***Me.***	1820/23rd	1.2 mill.	AUGUSTA
	TEXAS ***Tex.***	1845/28th	17.0 mill.	AUSTIN
6	**ALASKA** ***Alas.***	1959/49th	0.5 mill.	JUNEAU
	HAWAII	1959/50th	1.1 mill.	HONOLULU
	KANSAS ***Kan.***	1861/34th	2.4 mill.	TOPEKA
	NEVADA ***Nev.***	1864/36th	1.2 mill.	CARSON CITY
	OREGON ***Ore., Oreg.***	1859/33rd	2.8 mill.	SALEM
7	**ALABAMA** ***Ala.***	1819/17th	4.0 mill.	MONTGOMERY
	ARIZONA ***Ariz.***	1912/48th	3.6 mill.	PHOENIX
	FLORIDA ***Fla.***	1845/27th	13.0 mill.	TALLAHASSEE
	GEORGIA ***Ga.***	orig. 13	6.5 mill.	ATLANTA
	INDIANA ***Ind.***	1816/19th	5.5 mill.	INDIANAPOLIS
	MONTANA ***Mont.***	1889/41st	0.8 mill.	HELENA
	NEW YORK ***N.Y.***	orig. 13	18.0 mill.	ALBANY
	VERMONT ***Vt.***	1791/14th	0.6 mill.	MONTPELIER
	WYOMING ***Wyo.***	1890/44th	0.5 mill.	CHEYENNE
8	**ARKANSAS** ***Ark.***	1836/25th	2.3 mill.	LITTLE ROCK
	COLORADO ***Colo.***	1876/38th	3.3 mill.	DENVER
	DELAWARE ***Del.***	orig. 13	0.6 mill.	DOVER
	ILLINOIS ***Ill.***	1818/21st	11.5 mill.	SPRINGFIELD
	KENTUCKY ***Ky., Ken.***	1792/15th	3.7 mill.	FRANKFORT
	MARYLAND ***Md.***	orig. 13	4.8 mill.	ANNAPOLIS
	MICHIGAN ***Mich.***	1837/26th	9.3 mill.	LANSING
	MISSOURI ***Mo.***	1821/24th	5.1 mill.	JEFFERSON CITY

	State/Abbreviation	*Joined/no.*	*Approx. Population*	*Capital*
8	**NEBRASKA** ***Neb.***	1867/37th	1.6 mill.	LINCOLN
	OKLAHOMA ***Okla.***	1907/46th	3.1 mill.	OKLAHOMA CITY
	VIRGINIA ***Va.***	orig. 13	6.2 mill.	RICHMOND
9	**LOUISIANA** ***La.***	1812/18th	4.2 mill.	BATON ROUGE
	MINNESOTA ***Minn.***	1858/32nd	4.4 mill.	ST PAUL
	NEW JERSEY ***N.J.***	orig. 13	7.7 mill.	TRENTON
	NEW MEXICO ***N.M.***	1912/47th	1.5 mill.	SANTA FE
	TENNESSEE ***Tenn.***	1796/16th	4.9 mill.	NASHVILLE
	WISCONSIN ***Wis.***	1848/30th	4.8 mill.	MADISON
10	**CALIFORNIA** ***Cal.***	1850/31st	29.7 mill.	SACRAMENTO
	WASHINGTON ***Wash.***	1889/42nd	4.9 mill.	OLYMPIA
11	**CONNECTICUT** ***Conn.***	orig. 13	3.2 mill.	HARTFORD
	MISSISSIPPI ***Miss.***	1817/20th	2.6 mill.	JACKSON
	NORTH DAKOTA ***N.D., N.Dak.***	1889/39th	0.7 mill.	BISMARCK
	SOUTH DAKOTA ***S.Dak., S.D.***	1889/40th	0.7 mill.	PIERRE
	RHODE ISLAND ***R.I.***	orig. 13	1.0 mill.	PROVIDENCE
12	**NEW HAMPSHIRE** ***N.H.***	orig. 13	1.1 mill.	CONCORD
	PENNSYLVANIA ***Penn.***	orig. 13	12.0 mill.	HARRISBURG
	WEST VIRGINIA ***W.Va.***	1863/35th	1.8 mill.	CHARLESTON
13	**MASSACHUSETTS** ***Mass.***	orig. 13	6.0 mill.	BOSTON
	NORTH CAROLINA ***N.C.***	orig. 13	6.6 mill.	RALEIGH
	SOUTH CAROLINA ***S.C.***	orig. 13	3.5 mill.	COLUMBIA
	COLUMBIA ***(District) D.C. (site of the capital of the U.S.)***			WASHINGTON D.C.

The 12 Provinces of Canada

State	*Population*	*Capital*
YUKON Territory	ca. 30,000	WHITEHORSE
QUEBEC	ca. 7.3 mill.	QUEBEC
ALBERTA	ca. 2.7 mill.	EDMONTON
ONTARIO	ca. 11.1 mill.	TORONTO
MANITOBA	ca. 1.1 mill.	WINNIPEG
NOVA SCOTIA	ca. 0.9 mill.	HALIFAX
NEW BRUNSWICK	ca. 0.7 mill.	FREDERICTON
NEWFOUNDLAND	ca. 0.6 mill.	ST JOHN'S
SASKATCHEWAN	ca. 1.0 mill.	REGINA
BRITISH COLUMBIA	ca. 3.8 mill.	VICTORIA
PRINCE EDWARD ISLAND	ca. 0.2 mill.	CHARLOTTETOWN
NORTHWEST TERRITORIES	ca. 65,000	YELLOWKNIFE
District of Franklin		
District of Keewatin		
District of Mackenzie		

The 15 Union Republics of the Former Soviet Union

State	*Population*	*Capital*
UZBEC S.S.R* (Uzbekistan)	ca. 12 mill.	TASHKENT
KAZAKH S.S.R. (Kazakhstan)	ca. 14.5 mill.	ALMA-ATA
KIRGIZ S.S.R. (Kirgizstan, Kirghiz/Kirgiziya)	ca. 3 mill.	FRUNZE
LATVIAN S.S.R.	ca. 2.4 mill.	RIGA
RUSSIAN SOVIET FEDERATED S.R.	ca. 134 mill.	MOSCOW

State	*Population*	*Capital*
TADZHIK S.S.R. (Tajikistan, Tadzhikstan)	ca. 3.5 mill.	DUSHANBE
TURKMEN S.S.R. (Turkmenistan, Turkmeniya)	ca. 2.5 mill.	ASHKHABAD
ARMENIAN S.S.R.	ca. 3.1 mill.	YEREVAN
ESTONIAN S.S.R.	ca. 1.4 mill.	TALLINN
GEORGIAN S.S.R. (Sakartvelo, Gruziya)	ca. 5 mill.	TBILISI (Tiflis)
MOLDAVIAN S.S.R.	ca. 3.9 mill.	KISHINYOV
UKRAINIAN S.S.R. (Ukraine)	ca. 50 mill.	KIEV
AZERBAIJAN S.S.R. (Azerbaydzhan)	ca. 5.8 mill.	BAKU
LITHUANIAN S.S.R.	ca. 3.3 mill.	VILNIUS
BELORUSSIAN S.S.R. (Byelorussia, Belorussia/White Russia)	ca. 9.1 mill.	MINSK

* S.S.R. = Soviet Socialist Republic

C.I.S. The Commonwealth of Independent States

(formerly the Soviet Union) now is comprised of the founders and 9 other Republics

State	*Population*	*Capital*
BYELORUSSIA	ca. 10 mill.	MINSK
UKRAINE	ca. 51.5 mill.	KIEV
***THE RUSSIAN FEDERATION**	ca. 148 mill.	MOSCOW
and 9 other Republics:		
ARMENIA	ca. 3.8 mill.	YEREVAN
AZERBAIJAN	ca. 7.5 mill.	BAKU
GEORGIA	ca. 5.5 mill.	TBILISI
KAZAKHSTAN	ca. 17 mill.	ALMA-ATA
KYRGYZSTAN	ca. 4.4 mill.	BISHKEK
MOLDAVIA	ca. 4.4 mill.	KISHINEV
TAJIKISTAN	ca. 5.1 mill.	DUSHANBE
TURKMENISTAN	ca. 4.5 mill.	ASHKHABAD
UZBEKISTAN	ca. 21.2 mill.	TASHKENT

* Divided into 2 cities of Federal Status (MOSCOW and St Petersburg), 21 Republics, 6 Territories (Krai), 49 Provinces (Oblast), 10 Autonomous Areas + 1 Jewish Autonomous Region. CHECHENIA is within the Russian Federation.
The 3 Baltic Republics ESTONIA, LATVIA, LITHUANIA were recognized as Independent in 1991.

The Former 6 Socialist Republics of Yugoslavia (Jugoslavia)

State	*Population*	*Capital*
SERBIA (Srbija) (includes the 2 Autonomous Provinces of Vojvodina and Kosovo/Kosmet)	ca. 9.3 mill.	BELGRADE
CROATIA (Hrvatska)	ca. 4.8 mill.	ZAGREB
SLOVENIA (Slovenija)	ca. 2.0 mill.	LLUBLJANA
MACEDONIA (Makedonija)	ca. 1.9 mill.	SKOPJE
MONTENEGRO (Crna Gora)	ca. 0.6 mill.	TITOGRAD
BOSNIA AND HERZEGOVINA (Bosna i Hercegovina)	ca. 2.9 mill.	SARAJEVO

SERBIA & MONTENEGRO are now one State
CROATIA – Independent
BOSNIA & HERZEGOVINA is divided into Independent BOSNIA (capital SARAJEVO)
SERBIAN BOSNIA (SRPSKA) (temporary capital PALE)
MACEDONIA – Independent

Germany (Reunited 1991)

The 15 Länder, semi-autonomous provinces (incl. 3 cities)

Länder	*Population*	*Capital*
BADEN-WÜRTTEMBERG	ca. 10.2 mill.	STUTTGART
BAYERN (Bavaria)	ca. 11.8 mill.	MÜNCHEN (Munich)
BERLIN	ca. 3.5 mill.	BERLIN, the city
BRANDENBURG	ca. 2.5 mill.	POTSDAM
BREMEN, Freie Hansestadt	ca. 683,000	BREMEN, the city
HAMBURG, Freie Hansestaat	ca. 1.7 mill.	HAMBURG, the city
HESSEN	ca. 5.9 mill.	WIESBADEN
NIEDER SACHSEN (Lower Saxony)	ca. 7.6 mill.	HANNOVER
MECKLENBURG-POMMERN (Pomerania)	ca. 1.8 mill.	SCHWERIN
NORDRHEIN-WESTFALEN	ca. 17.6 mill.	DÜSSELDORF
RHEINLAND-PFALZ (Rhineland-Palatinate)	ca. 3.9 mill.	MAINZ
SAARLAND	ca. 1 mill.	SAARBRÜCKEN
FREISTAAT SACHSEN (Saxony)	ca. 4.6 mill.	DRESDEN
SACHSEN-ANHALT (Saxony)	ca. 2.7 mill.	MAGDEBURG
SCHLESWIG-HOLSTEIN	ca. 2.7 mill.	KIEL
THURINGEN (Thuringia)	ca. 2.5 mill.	ERFURT

Spain

Autonomous Communities and Provinces

Province	*Population*	*Capital*
ANDALUCÍA	ca. 6.9 mill.	SEVILLA
ARAGÓN	ca. 1.2 mill.	ZARAGOZA
ASTURIAS	ca. 1 mill.	OVIEDO
BALEARES (Balearic Islands)	ca. 709,000	PALMA de MALLORCA
BASQUE	ca. 2.1 mill.	VITORIA
Islas CANARIAS (Canary Isles) 2	ca. 1.5 mill.	1) LAS PALMAS 2) SANTA CRUZ de TENERIFE
CANTABRIA	ca. 527,000	SANTANDER
CASTILLA-La MANCHA	ca. 1.6 mill.	TOLEDO
CASTILLA-LEÓN	ca. 2.5 mill.	VALLADOLID
CATALUÑA	ca. 6 mill.	BARCELONA
EXTREMADURA	ca. 100,000	MÉRIDA
GALICIA	ca. 2.7 mill.	SANTIAGO de COMPOSTELLA
MADRID	ca. 5 mill.	MADRID
MURCIA	ca. 1 mill.	MURCIA & CARTAGENA (jointly)
NAVARRA	ca. 520,000	PAMPLONA
La RIOJA	ca. 263,000	LAGRONO
VALENCIA	ca. 3.8 mill.	VALENCIA

Enclaves in North Africa (Morocco)

CEUTA	3750
MELILLA	4054

European Union (EU)

(from the Iron & Steel Union: France, Germany & Luxembourg)

1950 **BELGIUM, FRANCE, W. GERMANY, ITALY, LUXEMBOURG, NETHERLANDS** (The Six)
1973 **DENMARK, IRELAND, UNITED KINGDOM** joined
1981 **GREECE** joined
1985 **GREENLAND** autonomously opted out of Denmark's membership of the EEC
1986 **SPAIN** and **PORTUGAL** joined
1995 **AUSTRIA, FINLAND** and **SWEDEN** joined

Association Agreements (for future membership)

1991 **CZECHOSLOVAKIA, HUNGARY, POLAND**
1992 **CZECH REPUBLIC, ROMANIA, SLOVAKIA**

Applicants for Membership

1987 **TURKEY**
1991 **CYPRUS**
1994 **POLAND, HUNGARY**

European Free Trade Association (EFTA)

(Prior to these countries entering the European Union)

1960 **AUSTRIA, DENMARK, FINLAND, ICELAND, LICHTENSTEIN, NORWAY, SWEDEN, UNITED KINGDOM** – also **SWITZERLAND** (not in EU)

African Countries

With Present & Former Names

	Country	*Capital*
4	**CHAD/TSCHAD**	N'DJAMENA (Fort-Lamy)
	MALI (col. French Soudan)	BAMAKO
	TOGO (col. Togoland)	LOME
5	**BENIN** (col. Dahomay)	PORTO-NOVO
	CONGO (Brazzaville)	BRAZZAVILLE
	CONGO (Kinshasa) (Zaire)	KINSHASA (Leopoldville)
	EGYPT (Arab Republic of Egypt)	CAIRO
	GABON (col. part of French Equatorial Africa)	LIBREVILLE (Freetown)
	GHANA (col. Gold Coast & part of Togoland)	ACCRA
	KENYA	NAIROBI
	LIBYA	TRIPOLI
	NIGER	NIAMEY (Zinder/Damagaram)
	SUDAN, The	KHARTOUM
6	**ANGOLA** (col. Portuguese West Africa)	LUANDA
	GAMBIA, The	BANJUL (Bathurst)
	GUINEA	CONAKRY
	MALAWI (col. Nyasaland)	LILONGWE (Zomba)
	RWANDA (Kinyarwanda) (col. Ruanda)	KIGALI
	UGANDA	KAMPALA
	ZAMBIA (col. Northern Rhodesia)	LUSAKA
7	**ALGERIA**	ALGIERS
	BURUNDI (Kirundi) (col. Ruanda & Urundi)	BUJUMBURA
	COMOROS islands (Grande Comore & Moheli & Anjouan)	MOCONI (Moheli & Anjouan)
	ERITREA	ASMARA
	LESOTHO Kingdom (Sesotho) (col. Basutoland)	MASERU
	LIBERIA	MONROVIA
	MOROCCO	RABAT
	NAMIBIA (col. South West Africa)	WINDHOEK (national) SWAKOPMUND (summer)
	NIGERIA Federal Republic (col. British protectorates of Northern & Southern Nigeria)	ABUJA
	SENEGAL (together with Gambia: Senegambia)	DAKAR
	SOMALIA (col. Br. & It. Somaliland)	MOGADISCIO
	TUNISIA	TUNIS
8	**BOTSWANA** (col. Bechuanaland)	GABORONE
	CAMEROON (Col. Kamerun)	YAOUNDE
	DJIBOUTI (col. Afars & Issas, Fr. Somaliland)	DJIBOUTI
	ETHIOPIA (ancient Abyssinia)	ADDIS ABABA
	MALAGASY/MADAGASIKARA (col. Madagascar)	ANTANANARIVO
	TANZANIA (col. Tanganyika & Zanzibar)	DAR ES SALAAM
	ZIMBABWE (col. Southern Rhodesia)	HARARE (Salisbury)
9	**CAPE VERDE islands** (Windward & Leeward groups)	PRAIA

9	**MAURITIUS** (in the Indian Ocean, incl. islands of Rodrigues, Cargados Carajos Shoals, Agalega)	PORT LOUIS
	SWAZILAND Kingdom	MBABANE (administrative) LOBAMBA (royal & legislative)
10	**BOKINA FASO** (col. Upper Volta)	OUAGADOUGOU
	IVORY COAST	ABIDJAN
	MAURITANIA	NOUAKCHOTT
	MOZAMBIQUE (col. Portuguese East Africa)	MAPUTO
	SEYCHELLES (archipelago of ca. 85 islands)	VICTORIA
11	**SIERRA LEONE**	FREETOWN
	SOUTH AFRICA	CAPETOWN (legislative) PRETORIA (administrative) BLOEMFONTEIN (judicial)
	GUINEA-BISSAU (col. Portuguese Guinea)	BISSAU
	WESTERN SAHARA (col. Spanish Sahara, divided 1976 between Morocco and Mauritania; Southern region: Rio de Oro; Northern region: Saguia el Hamra)	EL AAIUN (chief town, formerly capital)
	EQUATORIAL GUINEA (col. Spanish Guinea) incl. Macias Nguema Biyogo (Fernando Po/Poo) and Pagolu islands	MALABO (Santa Isabel)
	SAO TOME E PRINCIPE (islands)	SAO TOME
	CENTRAL AFRICAN REPUBLIC (col. Oubangui-Chari)	BANGUI

Note: French-speaking Central Africa today comprises the territories of Central African Republic, Congo/Brazzaville, Gabon and Congo/Kinshasa

Other Recent Changes of Name

	Country	*Status*	*Capital*
5	**YEMEN** (formerly South Yemen)	People's Democratic Republic	ADEN
	YEMEN (Yemen P.D.R. & Yemen (San'a) formed the Yemen Republic 1972)	Republic	SAN'A
6	**BELIZE/BELICE** (formerly British Honduras)	self-governing	BELMOPAN
	BRUNEI (Negeri Brunei) (formerly Sarawak)	British protected sultanate (N. Borneo)	BANDAR SERI BEGAWAN
	GUYANA (col. British Guiana)	Republic	GEORGETOWN
	TAIWAN (formerly Formosa)	Republic	TAIPEI
7	**MYANMAR** (formerly Burma)	Republic	YANGON/Rangoon
8	**SRI LANKA** (formerly Ceylon)	Republic	COLOMBO
	SURINAME (col. Dutch Guiana)	Republic	PARAMARIBO
9	**IRIAN JAYA** (Irian Barat, West Irian or West New Guinea) (formerly part of Dutch East Indies)	Province of Indonesia	DJAJAPURA
10	**BANGLADESH** (formerly East Pakistan)		DHAKA

Country	Status	Capital
10 **KALIMANTAN** (Indonesian name for Borneo) divided into West, Central, South & East Kalimantan	Provinces of Indonesia	PONTIANAK (W) PALANGKARAJA (C) BANDJARMASIN (S) SAMARINDRA (E)
PAPUA NEW GUINEA (formerly Australian Papua & UN Territory of New Guinea)	Australian territory admin. as part of Territory of Papua & New Guinea	PORT MORESBY
SARAWAK & SABAH	States of E. Malaysia on N. Borneo	KUCHING KOTA KINABULU
THE UNITED ARAB EMIRATES (formerly Trucial States or Trucial Oman) include:		
OMAN (Sultanat Uman) (formerly Muscat and Oman)	Sultanate	MUSCAT
DUBAI (Dubayy) (incl. exclave Hajarayn)	Emirate	DUBAYY (Dubai)
QATAR (Dawlat Qatar)	State of Qatar	ad-DAWHAH (Doha)
SHARJAH (Ash-Shariqah) (incl. exclaves Dibbah, Khwar al-Fakkan, Khwar al-Kalba)	Emirate	ash-SHARIQAH (Sharjah)
ABU DHABI (Abu Zaby)	Sultanate	ABU ZABY

Polynesia

Islands	Status	Capital or admin. headquarters
4 **FIJI** (borders on Melanesia) main islands: Viti Levu, Vanua Levu, Lau group	Independent	SUVA (on Viti Levu)
5 **SAMOA** main islands: Tutuila, Manu'a, Rose Island	Dependency of US	PAGO PAGO (on Tutuila)
TONGA or PULE'ANGA TONGA (Kingdom of Tonga, also called Friendly Islands) main islands: Tongatapu/Tongatabu, Vavau, Haapai	Independent 1970	NUKUALOFA (on Tongatapu/ Tongatabu)
6 **HAWAII** includes Mauna Kea, highest island in Polynesia	50th state of US	HONOLULU
TAHITI or OTAHEITE includes Tahiti Nui & Tahiti Iti; largest island of the Windward Group (Society Islands)	French Polynesia	PAPEETE (on Tahiti, capital of French Polynesia)
TUBUAI ISLANDS (Austral Islands) main islands: Tubuai, Rurutu Raevavae, Rimatara, Rapa	French Polynesia	MATAURA (on Tubuai)
TUVALU (col. Ellice Islands) (formerly part of the British crown colony of Gilbert & Ellice islands) largest island: Vaitupu	Independent 1978, constitutional monarchy	FUNAFUTI (on Funafuti)
7 **EASTER ISLAND – RAPANUI** (Great Rapa) or **TE PITO TE HENUA** (Navel of the World) main islets: Motu-Nui, Motu-Iti, Motu-Kaokao	Dependency of Chile	HANGA-ROA (on Easter Island)
TOKELAU ISLANDS (Union Group) main islands: Nukunono, Atafu, Fakaofu	New Zealand territory	NUKUNONO (unofficial capital)

TUAMOTU ARCHIPELAGO or **PAUMOTU** main islands: NW = Rangiroa, Makemo, Raroia (Kon-Tiki!), centre: Anaa, Amanu, Hao, SE = Mururoa, Fagataufa, Tureia	French Polynesia	APATAKI (on Apataki)
MANGAREVA/MAGAREVA ISLANDS (Gambier Islands) main islands: Mangareva/Magareva, Taravai, Aukeua, Akamaru	French Polynesia	RIKITEA (on Mangareva/ Magareva)
CLIPPERTON ISLANDS (uninhabited)	French Polynesia	
NEW ZEALAND (North & South)	Independent	WELLINGTON (on North Island)
COOK ISLANDS S (Lower) Cooks: Rarotonga, Atiu Takutea, Mauke, Mitiaro, Manuae, N (Manuhiki) Cooks: Penrhyn, Manihiki, Danger (Pukapuka), Palmerston, Rakakanga, Suvorov, Nassau	Dependency of New Zealand	AVARUA (on Rarotonga)
WESTERN SAMOA main islands: Savaii, Upolu	Independent 1962	APIA (on Upolu)
SOCIETY ISLANDS Windward group: Tahiti, Moorea, Leeward group: Bora-Bora, Raiatea Motu-Iti, Huahine	French Polynesia	PAPEETE (on Tahiti)
MARQUESAS ISLANDS main islands: Hiva Ova (largest), Tahuata, Nuku Hiva/ Nukahiva, Hatutu	French Polynesia	HAKAPEHI (TAI-O-HAE) (on Nuku Hiva/ Nukahiva)

Melanesia

Islands	*Status*	*Capital or admin. headquarters*
FIJI – see Polynesia		
LOYALTY ISLANDS main islands: Mare, Uvea, Lifou	French New Caledonia	TADINOU (on Mare)
VANUATU (col. New Hebrides) main islands: Espiritu Santo (largest), Efate, Banks, Ambrim	Republic	VILA (on Efate)
BISMARCK ARCHIPELAGO main islands: New Britain, New Ireland, the Admiralties, Mussau, Lavongai (New Hanover), Duke & York Islands, Vitu Islands	Papua New Guinea	RABAUL (on New Britain)
ADMIRALTY ISLANDS main islands: Manus (largest), Hermit & Ninigo groups	extension of Bismarck Archipelago	LORENGAU (on Manus)
NEW CALEDONIA main islands: New Caledonia, Belep, Pins, Walpole, Hunter, Huon	French Overseas Territory	NOUMEA (on New Caledonia)
D'ENTRECASTEAUX ISLANDS main islands: Normanby, Fergusson, Goodenough (Morata), Sanaroa (Welle), Dobu	Papua New Guinea	VIVIGANI (on Goodenough)

Micronesia

Islands	*Status*	*Capital or admin. headquarters*
GUAM – (largest & southernmost of the Mariana Islands)	self-governing territory of US	AGANA
***BANABA** (col. Ocean Island)	Republic	Tapawa?
NAOERO/NAURU (col. Ger. Marschall Islands protectorate: UN Trust Territory under Australia)	Republic	YAREN (on Naoero/Nauru)
MARIANA ISLANDS (North) main islands: Saipan, Tinian Agrihan (highest), Rota	UN Trust Territory under US jurisdiction	SAIPAN (on Saipan – also territory capital)
CAROLINE ISLANDS main islands: Ponape, Yap, Truk, Kusaie, Nukuoro, Kapingamarangi	UN Trust Territory under US jurisdiction	SAIPAN
KIRIBATI (col. Gilbert Islands, or Kingsmill) stretching from Washington to Flint Islands & Christmas atoll to Banaba; main islands: Tarawa Butaritari (Makin), Abemama, Abaiang (the former British crown colony included Ocean Island, Central & Southern Line Islands, Phoenix I.)	Independent 1979	TARAWA (on Tarawa)
MARSHALL ISLANDS main islands: Radak Chain (Sunrise): Mili, Majuro, Bikar, Utirik Ralik Chain (Sunset): Kwajalein, Jaluit, Bikini, Wotho, Eniwetok	UN Trust Territory under US jurisdiction	SAIPANTHE
TRUST TERRITORY OF THE UN under US jurisdiction includes: Mariana & Caroline Islands, Marshall Islands, the Federated States of Micronesia (Ponape, Kusaie, Truk & Yap) and the district of Palau	under US jurisdiction	

* Population resettled on Rambi/Fiji

The 12 Caesars and later Roman Emperors

Name	*Manner of death*	*Born*	*Rule*
Gaius **JULIUS CAESAR** (wife **CORNELIA**)	Murdered 15/3	12/7 100 B.C.	60–44 B.C.
Caesar **AUGUSTUS** (Octavian/ Gaius Octavius/Gaius Julius Caesar Octavius) (wife **LIVIA**)	Old age (77) on 19/8	23/9 63 B.C.	27 B.C.–A.D. 14
TIBERIUS (Claudius Nero Caesar Augustus) (wife **JULIA**)	Natural 16/3 on Capri	23/9 63 B.C.	A.D. 14–37
CALIGULA (Gaius Caesar) (wife **CAESONIA**)	Murdered 24/1	31/8 12 B.C. in Antium/ Anzio/Italy	37–41
CLAUDIUS I (Tiberius Claudius Drusus Nero Germanicus) (wife & niece **AGRIPPINA**)	Poisoned 13/10	1/8 10 B.C. in Lugdunum/Lyon	41–54

Name	*Manner of death*	*Born*	*Rule*
NERO (Lucius Domitius Achenobarbus) (wife: a) **OCTAVIA**, b) **POPPAEA SABINA**, first wife of Otho)	Suicide	15/12 37 in Rome	54–68
End of Caesar's line			
GALBA (Servius Sulpicius)	Murdered 15/1	24/12 3 B.C.	68–69
OTHO (Marcus Salvius Otho) (wife **POPPAEA SABINA**)	Suicide 16/4	A.D. 28/4 32	69–69
VITTELLIUS (Aulus)	Murdered 20/12	A.D. 15	69–69
Flavian House			
VESPASIAN (Titus Flavius Vespasianus)	Natural 24/6	A.D. 9	69–79
TITUS (Titus Flavius Vespasianus) (wife **AGRIPPA II BERENICE**, wife of Herod)	Murdered? 13/9	A.D. 30/12 39	79–81
DOMITIAN (Titus Flavius Domitianus)	Murdered 18/9	A.D. 24/10 51	81–96
End of Flavian line & the 12 Caesars			
Five Good Emperors			
NERVA (Marcus Cocceius Nerva)	Natural	A.D. *c.* 30	96–98
TRAJAN (Marcus Ulpius Traianus, Germanicus) (wife **PLOTINA**)	Natural 8/8 in Selinus/Selindi (TR)	15/9 53 in Italica (Santiponce/Spain)	98–117
HADRIAN (Publius Aelius Hadrianus) (wife **VIBIA SABINA**)	Natural 10/7	24/1 76 in Rome?	117–138
ANTONINUS PIUS (Titus Aurelius Fulvius Boinonius Arrius Antoninus) (wife **FAUSTINA**)	Natural 7/3	19/9 86 Lanuvium	138–161
LUCIUS VERUS (Lucius Aurelius)	Natural	15/12 130	161–169
Roman Emperors			
MARCUS AURELIUS (Antoninus) (co-ruler with Antoninus Pius & Lucius Verus 140s–169)	Natural 17/3	A.D. 26/4 121	169–180
COMMODUS (Lucius Aelius Aurelius) (mistress **MARCIA**)	Murdered 31/12	31/8 161 in Rome	180–192
PERTINAX (Publius Helvius)	Murdered 28/3	1/8 126 (Liguria)	193–193
MARCUS DIDIUS (Julianus)	Murdered 1/6	*c.* 135 in Milan	193–193
***SEPTIMIUS SEVERUS** (Severus Lucius Septimius) (wife **JULIA DOMNA**)	Illness Febr. in Eburacum/York, Engl.	146 in Leptis Magna, Libya	193–211

* 198–211 Septimius Severus ruled with his son Caracalla

Name	*Manner of death*	*Born*	*Rule*
GETA (Publius Septimius) (together with his father Septimius Severus & brother Caracalla)	Murdered Febr.	189 in Milan	209–212
CARACALLA (Marcus Aurelius Antoninus) sole ruler 212–217 (wife **FULVIA PLAUTILLA**)	Murdered 8/4 in Carrhae (Harran/TR)	4/4 188 in Lugdunum/ Lyon	198–217
MACRINUS (Marcus Opellius)	Executed June (TR)	*c.* 164 (Caesarea/ Algeria)	217–218
ELAGABALUS (HELIOGABALLUS) (Varius Avitus Bassianus)	Murdered	204 (Emesa/Homs)	218–222
SEVERUS ALEXANDER (Marcus Aurelius Severus Alexander)	Murdered in Gaul	208 (Phoenicia/ Lebanon)	222–235
MAXIMINUS/MAXIMIN (Caius Julius Verus Maximinius)	Murdered March		235–238
GORDIAN I (Marcus Antonius Gordianus) together with	Suicide Apr.	*c.* 157	238 for 3 weeks
his son **GORDIAN II**	Killed in battle		
***GORDIAN III** (Marcus Antonius Gordianus)	Murdered in Zaitha	225	238–244
* May 238–Aug. 238 GORDIAN III ruled with the elderly senators Maximus and Balbinus, both murdered			
PHILIP THE ARABIAN (Marcus Julius Philippus)	Murdered		244–249
DECIUS (Gaius Messius Quintus Trajanus)	Killed in battle	*c.* 201 (Budalia/ Pannonia/Yu)	249–251
GALLUS (Gaius Vibius Trebonianus) co-rulers: Hostilian (son of Decius, died early) & Volusianus (his own son)	Murdered		251–253
AEMILIAN (Marcus Aemilius Aemilianus) ruled 3 months	Murdered	Mauretania/Africa	253–253
VALERIAN (Publius Licinus Valerianus); his son Gallienus ruled the West	In Persian captivity		253–260
***GALLIENUS** (Italy & the Balkans only); fought usurper **AUREOLUS**	Murdered		260–268
* While GALLIENUS ruled Italy & the Balkans POSTUMUS (258–268) was independent emperor in Gaul; he was succeeded by VICTORINUS			
CLAUDIUS II GOTHICUS (Marcus Aurelius Claudius)	Of plague	May 214 (Dardania Yu)	268–270

Name	*Manner of death*	*Born*	*Rule*
QUINTILLUS (brother of Claudius II)	Murdered?		270 for 3 months
***AURELIAN** (Lucius Domitius Aurelianus)	Murdered in Caenophrurium (TR)	*c.* 215	270–275
* **TETRICUS** ruled Spain, Gaul & Britain, but went over to Aurelian's side			
ULPIA SEVERINA (Widow of Aurelian)	Natural		275 for 6 months
TACITUS (Marcus Claudius)	Murdered Apr. in Tyana/Cappadocia	*c.* 200	275–276
FLORIAN (Florianus) half-brother of Tacitus	Murdered June		276–276
PROBUS (Marcus Aurelius Probus)	Murdered Nov.		276–282
DIOCLETIAN (Gaius Aurelius Valerius Diocletianus) in the East; co-emperor in the West:	Abdicated 1/5; died 313 or 316	245 (Dalmatia)	284–305
MAXIMIAN (Marcus Aurelius Valerius Maximanus)	Abdicated 1/5; murdered or suicide 308		286–305
CONSTANTIUS I CHLORIUS (Aurelius Valerius Constantius) of the West (wife: a) **HELEN** b) **THEODORA**, stepdaughter of Maximian), father of Constantine the Great	Natural		305–306
GALERIUS (Gaius Valerius Maximianus) of the East	Disease	Sardica/Sofia	305–311
FLAVIUS VALERIUS SEVERUS declared emperor in West by Galerius (his friend)	Murdered by Maxentius, son of Maximian		306–306
MAXENTIUS (Marcus Aurelius Valerius) proclaimed Augustus of the West 28/10 306	Killed by Constantine in battle		306–312
MAXIMINUS (Gaius Galerius Valerius) nephew & friend of Galerius who proclaimed him Augustus of the East 308; died in Tarsus/TR shortly after having invaded dominion of Licinius & been defeated	Disease		308–313

Name	*Manner of death*	*Born*	*Rule*
LICINIUS (Valerius Licinianus Licinius) 11/11 308 Galerius declared Maxentius a usurper & appointed Licinius Augustus of the West; Constantine defeated Licinius at Adrinople 324	Executed 325		308–324
CONSTANTINE THE GREAT (emperor of the West from 312; Licinius emperor of the East 308–324); declared Constantinople the capital of the East Roman Empire (wife **FAUSTA**, daughter of Maximian)	Natural 22/5	27/2 late 280s	324–337
CONSTANTIUS II (Flavius Julius Constantius) co-emperor with his brothers, **CONSTANTINE II** (murdered 340) and **CONSTANT I** (murdered 350); sole ruler 353–361	Illness	7/8 317 (Sirmium, Yu)	337–361
JULIAN THE APOSTATE (Flavius Claudius Julianus)	Died in battle June	331/332	361–363
JOVIAN (Flavius Jovianus)	Natural 17/2	*c.* 331 (Singidunum/ Belgrade)	363–364
VALENTINIAN I (Flavius Valentinianus) (wife/2nd **JUSTINA**) 28/3 he appointed his younger brother Valens as co-ruler (East)	Illness March	321	364–375 (West)
***VALENS** (uncle of Gratian)	Killed in battle 9/8	*c.* 328	364–378 (East)
* The pagan PROCOPIUS proclaimed himself Emperor in Constantinople in September 365, but he was killed by Valens on 27/5 366			
GRATIAN (Flavius Gratianus) proclaimed co-emperor on 24/8 367 by his father Valentinian I and from that date also shared his office with his uncle Valens till 378		359 (Sirmium, Yu)	367–383 (West)
VALENTINIAN II (Flavius Valentinianus) half-brother of Gratian and son of **JUSTINA & VALENTINIAN I**; recognized as co-ruler of West (Italy, Africa, Illyrium) by Gratian; 387–388 in exile in Thessalonica; a caesar compared to Theodosius I	Murdered?	371 (Treveri/Trier)	375–392 (West)

Name	*Manner of death*	*Born*	*Rule*
THEODOSIUS (I) THE GREAT (son of Valentinian I's general Theodosius) one of the last to reign over both East & West Roman Empire; appointed his sons Honorius (West) & Arcadius (East) to succeed him	Illness 17/1	11/1 347 (Cauca/Coca/ Spain	379–395 (East & West)
MAGNUS MAXIMUS Spanish usurper who ruled Britain, Gaul & Spain; he and his son **FLAVIUS VICTOR** as co-ruler recognized for a short time as co-emperor by Theodosius I & Valentinian II	Executed by Theodosius		383–388 (West)
***HONORIUS FLAVIUS**, co-ruler with his father Theodosius I 23/1 393–17/1 395 then sole ruler until 409 and again from 411–423 (wives: 1) **MARIA**, 2) her sister **THERMANTIA**)	Natural	9/9 384	393–423 (West)
* ATTALUS (Priscus Attalus), a usurper elevated to emperor by the Visigothic leaders Alaric & Ataulphus (409–410 & 414), was exiled by Honorius			
ARCADIUS, ruled jointly with his father Theodosius I 383–395, solely 395–402, together with his son Theodosius II 402–408 (wife **EUDOXIA**)	Natural	377	383–408 (East)
CONSTANTINE III (Flavius Claudius Constantinus) usurping emperor of Britain & Gaul, recognized by Honorius 409 as joint ruler but threatened Italy; had made his son **CONSTANS** caesar 407	Executed by Honorius' generals		407–411
CONSTANTIUS III, Honorius' master of the soldiers who helped to overthrow Constantine III; in 417 married **PLACIDIA**, half-sister of Honorius; appointed co-emperor 8/2 421 but died soon afterwards, still unrecognized by the Eastern Emperor	Natural		421–421 (West)

Name	*Manner of death*	*Born*	*Rule*
***VALENTINIAN III** (Flavius Valentinianus) son of Constantius III and Placidia who controlled the government till 437; married **LICINIA EUDOXIA** 29/10 437 (daughter of Theodosius II)	Murdered 16/3	2/7 419 in Ravenna	425–455 (West)
* JOHN, a usurper, ruled briefly in the West (423–425) on death of Honorius			
MAXIMUS PETRONIUS, proclaimed Western Emperor 17/3 455 and forced Valentinian's widow **EUDOXIA** to marry him	Killed by the people 31/5	396	455–455 (West)
THEODOSIUS II, son of Arcadius who made him co-emperor 402 (wife: **EUDOCIA**)	Of injuries from hunting accident	10/4 401	408–450 (East)
MARCIAN, ruled together with his nominal wife Empress **PULCHERIA** (d. 453), sister of Theodosius II	Natural	396	450–457 (East)
AVITUS (Eparchius Aritus) proclaimed Emperor by the Goths of Toulouse, but forced to abdicate by the 'kingmaker' Ricimer on 17/10 456			455–456 (West)
MAJORIAN (Julius Majorianus) helped to overthrow emperor Avitus (455–456)	Executed 7/8		457–461 (West)
LEO I, a Thracian who recognized Majorian in the West 457, but not his successor Libius Severus in 461; vacant throne in the West for 2 years until he installed Anthemius 467 as West Roman Emperor	Natural		457–474 (East)
LIBIUS SEVERUS, installed by the 'kingmaker' Ricimer, but never recognized by Leo I	Natural 15/8		461–465 (West)
ANTHEMIUS, son-in-law of Eastern Emperor Marcian (wife **EUPHEMIA**); his daughter **ALYPIA** married to Ricimer	Beheaded 11/7		467–472 (West)

OLYBRIUS, installed by Ricimer and emperor from April to Nov. (wife **PLACIDIA**, daughter of Valentinian III)	Natural 2/11		472–472 (West)
GLYCERIUS, installed as emperor 5/3 472 by Gundobad (nephew of Ricimer); never recognized by Leo I who sent a fleet commanded by **JULIUS NEPOS** against him	Natural		473–474 (West)
JULIUS NEPOS, proclaimed himself emperor on landing in Italy; Glycerius surrendered without a struggle	Murdered		474–475 (West)
ZENO, father of Leo II (474–474 who died 7 years old); in exile 475–Aug. 476 when **BASILISCUS** (brother-in-law of Leo I) ruled in Constantinople; appointed Theodoric to replace Odoacer as king of Italy (489)	Natural	Isauria	475–491 (East)
ROMULUS AUGUSTULUS, usurper and last of the Western Roman Emperors; installed on the throne 31/10 475 after his father Orestes (who ruled Italy in his young son's name) had deposed Julius Nepos; German warrior **ODOACER** captured & executed Orestes 28/8 476	Unknown		475–476

End of Western Roman Empire

The Sevens

The seven against Thebes

The seven military leaders in the civil war between Oedipus' twin sons Eteocles and Polyneices

6 TYDEUS
8 CAPANEUS
ETEOCLUS
10 AMPHIBRAUS
POLYNEICES (or ADRASTUS)
HIPPOMEDON (or ADRASTUS)
13 PARTHENOPAEUS

The seven deadly sins

4 ENVY
LUST
5 ANGER
PRIDE
SLOTH
8 GLUTTONY
12 COVETOUSNESS

The seven Epigoni

The seven sons of the seven chieftains against Thebes

8 ALCMAEON
DIOMEDES
EURYALUS
9 AEGIALEUS
PROMACHOS
STHENELUS
11 AMPHILOCHUS

The seven hills of Rome

7 CAELIAN
VIMINAL
8 AVENTINE
PALATINE
9 ESQUILINE
QUITRINAL
10 CAPITOLINE

The seven Pleiades

(stars)

Daughters of Atlas & Pleione

4 MAIA
6 MEROPE
7 TAYGETE
ALCYONE (brightest)
CELAENO
ELECTRA
8 ASTEROPE (faintest)

The seven senses

5 SIGHT
SMELL
TASTE
6 SPEECH
7 FEELING
HEARING
13 UNDERSTANDING

The seven sleepers of Ephesus

Western tradition

4 JOHN
5 DENIS
7 MALCHUS
MARCIAN
8 MAXIMIAN
SERAPION
11 CONSTANTINE

Eastern tradition

4 JOHN
6 MARTIN
8 ANTONIUS
9 DIONYSIUS
10 JAMBLICHUS
MAXIMILIAN
11 CONSTANTINE

The seven wise men

(according to Plato)

4 BIAS
5 MYSON
SOLON
6 CHILON
THALES
8 PITTACUS
9 CLEOBOLUS

The Seven Wonders of the World

1 The **PYRAMIDS** of Egypt
2 The **TOMB of MAUSOLOS in Bodrum**
3 The **COLOSSUS** at Rhodes
4 The **HANGING GARDENS** of Babylon
5 The **TEMPLE OF ARTEMIS** at Ephesus
6 The **STATUE OF ZEUS** by Phidias
7 The **PHAROS of Alexandria** or
The **PALACE OF CYRUS** cemented with gold

The Threes

The Cyclops

Three round-eyed sons of Uranus & Gaia who forged the thunderbolts for Zeus; one-eyed cannibal giants (Homer) who built walls of ancient cities.

5 ARGES Bright
7 BRONTES Thunderous
8 STEROPES Lightener

The Furies

Avenging deities – ERINYES or EUMENIDES – sent from Tartarus to avenge wrong and punish crime.

6 ALECTO Unceasing in Anger
7 MEGAERA Jealous
9 TISIPHONE Avenger of Murder

The three Gorgons

Winged female creatures with hair of snakes; daughters of Phorcys and his sister-wife Ceto who were children of Gaia and Pontus, the sea.

6 MEDUSA The Queen
7 EURYALE The Far Springer
STHENNO The Mighty

The three Gorgon sisters

with only one eye between them

4 DINO
ENYO
9 PEMPHREDO

The three Graces

Goddesses of fertility and charm, associated with Aphrodite; daughters of Zeus by Hera or Eurynome (daughter of Oceanus) or of Helios and Aegle.

6 AGLAIA Brightness
THALIA Bloom
10 EUPHROSYNE Joyfulness

The Greek fates

6 CLOTHO spins the thread of life
The Spinner
7 ATROPOS cuts it off
The Inflexible One
8 LACHESIS controls its destiny
The Disposer of Lots

The Hecatoncheires

Hundred-handed giants, children of Uranus and Gaia/Ge.

4 GYES
6 COTTUS
8 BRIAREUS

The Seasons (Horae)

Three daughters of Zeus and Themis or of Helios (sun) and Selene (moon)

4 DIKE Justice
6 EIRENE Peace
7 EUNOMIA Good Order

The Fours

The Harpies

Malignant monsters with birds' wings and claws who snatched away the souls of the dead.

5 AELLO Stormswift
7 OCYPETE Swiftwing
CELAENO Dark one
PODARGE Swiftfoot

The four primary divine beings

From whom Erebus (the dark void) and Night were born.

4 EROS Love
4/6 GAIA/GE Earth
5 CHAOS Space
8 TARTARUS Hell

The pyramids of Egypt

5 ZOSER
6 CHEOPS
KHAFRE
8 HENKAURA

Some Others

Sixteen nymphs

4 ECHO repulses Pan
5 THETIS mother of Achilles
6 AEGINA wife of Zeus
CALYCE mother of Endymion
DAPHNE of a mountain
MEROPE wife of river god Asopos
RHODAS mated with the sun Helios
THOOSA mother of Polyphemus
7 ASTERIA mother of Hecate
CLYMENE wife of Helios, mother of Phaethon
GALATEA of the sea
8 ARETHUSA one of the Hesperides
CASTALIA excited Apollo
ECHENAIS loved by Daphnis
PENELOPE mother of Pan, wife of Odysseus, wife of Hermes
PERIBOCA mother of Penelope

Groups of nymphs by habitat

6 DRYADS of the trees
NAIADS of caves and springs
7 NEREIDS of the sea
10 HAMADRYADS of trees

The six wives of Hermes

5 HERSE son Cephalus, a hero
6 CHIONE son Autolycus
8 AGLAUCUS son Ceryx, first high priest of Eleusis
PENELOPE son Pan
DEIANIRA
10 PERSEPHONE son Eleusis, eponymous hero

The nine Muses

4 CLIO History
5 ERATO Erotic Poetry
6 THALIA Comedy
URANIA Astronomy
7 EUTERPE Lyric Poetry
8 CALLIOPE Epic Song
9 MELPOMENE Tragedy
10 POLYHMNIA Hymns
11 TERPSICHORE Dance

The twelve Titans

(Children of Heaven/Uranus & Earth/Ge/Gaia)

4 RHEA
THEA
5 COIUS
CRIUS
6 CRONUS
PHOEBE
TETHYS
THEM1S
7 IAPETUS
OCEANUS
8 HYPERION
9 MNEMOSYNE

The Hesperides

Guardians of Golden Apples; variously daughters of Erebus & night, Atlas & Hesperis, or Phorcys & Ceto

5 AEGLE
8 ARETHUSA
ERYTHEIA
HESPERIS or
12 HESPERETHUSA

Offspring of Zeus

(the son of Cronus & Rhea)

3 ATE (d) evil; evicted from Olympus by Zeus
ARES (s) god of war; warlike spirit; mother: Hera
4 HEBE (d) mother: Hera; goddess of youth; married Heracles
5 AEGLE (d) wife of Helios (sun god); sometimes claimed as mother of the Three Graces
ARCAS (s) mother: Callisto; ancestor of the Arcadians
BELUS (s) mother: Io; father of Danaus & Aegyptus
5 HELEN (d) mother: Leda of Sparta; wife of Tyndareus
MINOS (s) mother: Europa; King of Crete
6 AEACUS (s) mother: nymph of Aegina
AGLAIA (d) one of the Three Graces
APOLLO (s) mother: Leto; god of divine distance, crops & herds; Averter of Evil (Alexikakos); common to Greece & Rome
ATHENE (d) mother: Metis; virgin goddess of war & good counsel
CLOTHO (d) one of the Three Fates
HERMES (s) mother: Maia; fertility & messenger god born in a cave
POLLUX (s) mother: Leda; twin-brother of Castor (the Dioscuri)

6 THALIA (d) one of the Three Graces
ZETHUS (s) mother: Antiope
7 AMPHION (s) mother: Antiope
ARTEMIS (d) mother: Leto; goddess of wild nature; sister of Apollo
PERSEUS (s) mother: Danae; founder of Mycenae; King of Argos
ZAGREUS (s) mother: Persephone; killed as a child by the Titans
8 DARDANUS (s) mother: Electra; founder of Troy; grandfather of Tros
DIONYSUS (s) mother: Semele; wine god
ENDYMION (s) mother: nymph Calyce; King of Elis
HERACLES (s) mother: Alcmene; of the 12 Labours
8 LACHESIS (d) one of the Three Fates
SARPEDON (s) mother: Europa; leader of Lycian forces in Trojan War
TANTALUS (s) punished by eternal thirst & hunger; ancestor of Pelopids
10 HEPHAESTUS (s) mother: Hera; smith god
PERSEPHONE (d) mother: Demeter; wife of Hades; as Kore, grain goddess
11 EUPHROSYNE (d) one of the Three Graces
12 RHADAMANTHUS (s) mother: Europa; King of the Cyclades islands

Consorts of Zeus

2 IO daughter of Inachus (river god of Argos); priestess Callithyia
4 HERA sister & wife of Zeus; Queen of Heaven; as Eileithyia, birth goddess
LEDA daughter of Thestius (King of Aetolia); Zeus swanned around and so she leda-'n-egg hatching Helen & Pollux
LETO daughter of Coeus & Phoebe (Titans); goddess of fertility
MAIA eldest of the 7 daughters of Titan Atlas (the Pleiades) by Pleione
5 DANAE daughter of Acrisius, King of Argos
METIS (wise counsel); Zeus mated with Metis by mouth and Athene was his brainchild
6 AEGINA daughter of river god Asopus & nymph Merope
CALYCE a nymph; mother of Endymion who was loved by moon goddess Selene
EUROPA daughter of Phoenix who rose from the ashes to take Zeus, the bull, by the horns to Crete
SEMELE daughter of Cadmus (founder of Thebes) and Harmonia; niece of Europa
SELENE moon goddess; daughter of Eos
THEMIS steadfast daughter of Gaia; prophetess; mother of the Seasons & the Fates
7 ALCMENE daughter of Electryon, king of Mycenae; wife of Amphitryon who killed his uncle Electryon
7 *ANTIOPE daughter of Nycteus (one of the Spartoi) raped by Zeus in the guise of a satyr
DEMETER sister & consort of Zeus; goddess of agriculture, health, birth & marriage & divinity of the underworld
****ELECTRA** daughter of Atlas & pleione; mother of the Cabeiri (Cabiri), protectors of seafarers & promoters of fertility
8 CALLISTO handmaiden of Artemis who changed her into a she-bear; later, by courtesy of Zeus, she stars as Ursa Major and her son (Arcas) as Arcturus
EURYNOME daughter of Oceanus; together with Hera & Aegle variously regarded as mother of the Three Graces
GANYMEDE son of Tros (or Laomedon), King of Troy; Latin Catamitus; kidnapped by Zeus in the guise of an eagle
10 PERSEPHONE daughter & consort of Zeus; as Persephassa goddess of the dead

* not to be confused with the daughter of Ares, god of war, or a queen of the Amazones.
** not to be confused with the mother of the Harpies Aello & Okypete, or the daughter of Agamemnon and Clytemnestra

Brothers & Sisters of Zeus

4 HERA Queen of Olympus; mother of Ares (god of war), Hebe (goddess of youth & cupbearer to the gods), Hephaestus

5 HADES ruled the underworld together with his queen Persephone

7 DEMETER goddess of agriculture; bore Plutus (Wealth) by her consort Iason, and Persephone by Zeus; also known as Ioulo

8 POSEIDON god of sea, water, earthquakes; also worshipped as 'Hippios' (of horses); divine ancestor of rulers of Thessaly & Messenia

Offspring of Poseidon

(brother of Zeus)

5 ARION/AREION by DEMETER; swift horse who saved the life of Adrastus, King of Argos

ORION son of EURYALE, one of the Gorgons

6 NELEUS son of TYRO; father of Nestor, Pero, etc.

PELIAS brother of Neleus

TRITON son by AMPHITRITE; minor sea god

7 ANCAEUS son by TEGEA; King of the Leleges of Samos

ANTAEUS son by GAIA; wrestling giant of Libya, crushed by Heracles

BUSIRIS son by LYSSIANASSA; King of Egypt (Usire/Osiris); killed by Heracles

***GLAUCUS** gleaming son, in love with sea god Melicertes; merman covered with shells and seaweed; sea god

PEGASUS by the monster MEDUSA; winged horse

8 EUMOLPUS sweet-singing son by CHIONE, daughter of Boreas (North Wind); King of Thrace

NAUPLIUS son by AMYMONE, one of Danaus' 50 daughters

10 AMPHIMARUS son; father by Linus (the musician killed by Apollo) by the Muse Urania

POLYPHEMUS son by the nymph THOOSA; sea god and one of the Cyclopes; made Odysseus his prisoner

* not to be confused with a) son of Sisyphus (King of Corinth) by Merope: father of Bellerophon; b) the honeyed son of King Minos (Crete) and Pasiphae; c) 'gold for bronze' Lycian prince, ally of Priam in the Trojan War; grandson of Bellerophon

Trojan War

Besiegers of Troy and ancestors & offspring

4 AJAX colossal son of Telamon (king of Salamis); took on Hector single-handed; rescued body of Achilles from the Trojans

AJAX small son of Oileus (king of Locri); violated Cassandra; drowned by Poseidon

5 CREON father of Lycomedes of Scyros who hosted Achilles, and killed Theseus, Attic hero

6 ATREUS father of Agamemnon & Menelaus by Aerope; son of Pelops; later married Pelopia, daughter & wife of Thyestes

DANAOI besiegers of Troy

MOPSUS seer and son of Manto by Carian king Rhacius (or Apollo); challenged Calchas after fall of Troy

NESTOR son of Neleus (brother of Pelias, son of Poseidon by Tyro); Achaean leader; sailed home after the war

PELEUS father of Achilles; husband of Thetis (one of the Nereids)

TEUCER half-brother of Ajax; famous archer; defended Achaean camp; founded city of Salamis on Cyprus

7 ARGEIOI besiegers of Troy

CALCHAS seer of the Achaean forces; son of Thestor; priest of Apollo

ORESTES son of Agamemnon & Clytemnestra

PROTEUS helped Menelaus to reach Sparta; assistant to Poseidon

8 ACHAEANS besieged Troy together with the Danaoi & Argeioi

ACHILLES son of Peleus (king of the Myrmidons) & Thetis; handsome warrior of Agamemnon's army; killed Hector

8 DIOMEDES commander of 80 Argive ships and important leader; son of Tydeus (one of seven against Thebes); wounded Aphrodite; took the Trojan Palladium

MENELAUS brother of Agamemnon; husband of Helen

ODYSSEUS (also known as ULYSSES) captured Troy by means of the wooden horse; suitor of Helen; king of Ithaca and son of Laertes & Anticleia; father by Penelope of Telemachus

TELEPHUS wounded by Achilles; guided Achaean fleet to Troy; son of Heracles & Ange

9 AGAMEMNON commander-in-chief of the forces against Troy; brother of Menelaus; kin of Mycenae or Argos and son of Atreus and Aerope; husband of Clytemnestra (daughter of Tyndareus, king of Sparta); murdered by their son Orestes; his daughters: Iphigeneia/Iphianassa (sacrificed to Artemis), Electra/Laodice, Chrysothemis

PATROCLUS cousin of Achilles and allowed to impersonate him; killed by Hector

10 ANTILOCHUS son of Nestor; killed by Memnon

TELEMACHUS son of Odysseus by Penelope; welcomed by Nestor when searching for his father

Defenders of Troy and ancestors & offspring

4 ILUS ancestor of Priam; one of the three sons of Tros

TROS grandson of Dardanus; father of Ilus, Ganymede & Arsaracus

5 HELEN daughter of Zeus by Leda or Nemesis; sister of Clytemnestra; wife of Menelaus of Sparta; after death of Paris wife of his brother Deiphobus whom she betrayed; indirect cause of the war

PARIS son of Priam; stole Helen and caused the Trojan War

5 PRIAM King of troy (VII) son of Laomedon; also known as Podarces; father of Hector, Paris, Cassandra, Polyxena, Helenus, Polydorus, Troilus

6 AENEAS cousin of Hector; leader of Trojan survivors; founder of Rome; son of Trojan Anchises by Aphrodite

HECTOR chief Trojan warrior; eldest son of Priam

HECUBA wife of Priam

MEMNON hero and brother of Priam; son of Eos (dawn); King of Ethiopia; killed Antilochus and was killed by Achilles

7 ANTENOR elder of the city of troy; advised the Trojans to return Helen to Menelaus, and Agamemnon to give up girl he stole from Achilles

GLAUCUS ally of Troy; leader of the Lycian forces

HELENUS son of Priam and Hecuba

HESIONE daughter of Laomedon

TROILUS son of Priam; killed early by Achilles

8 ANCHISES father of Aeneas by Aphrodite; king of Dardanus on Mt Ida

ASTYANAX son of Hector

DARDANUS founder of Troy; grandfather of Tros; son of Zeus & Electra; father of Erichtonius

GANYMEDE one of the three sons of Tros

LAOMEDON father of Priam and Hesione; refused to pay Apollo and Poseidon for building the walls of Troy; he and all his sons (except Priam) killed by Heracles

POLYXENA daughter of Priam and Hecuba

SARPEDON ally of Priam; leader of the Lycian forces

TITHONUS son of Laomedon, king of Troy, and brother of Priam; father of Memnon by Eos; made immortal but not ageless by Zeus

9 ARSARACUS one of the three sons of Tros

POLYDORUS son of Priam and Hecuba

ANDROMACHE wife of Hector

Argonautica, on Board and Ashore

3 INO second wife of ATHAMAS who hated his children by NEPHELE and wanted PHRIXUS sacrificed

5 AESON father of JASON deprived of the throne of Iolcos by his half-brother PELIAS

5 **CIRCE** witch-goddess & sister of the king of Colchis (or daughter of HELIOS, the sun god, & nymph PERSE); freed MEDEA & JASON from the guilt of murdering ABSYRTUS

CREON king of Corinth whose daughter caught JASON's fancy and drove MEDEA mad with rage

HELLE daughter of JASON's uncle ATHAMAS by NEPHELE, the cloud goddess; tried to escape by sea with her brother PHRIXUS on the ram with the golden fleece; drowned in the Hellespont

JASON son of AESON who had been told by his uncle PELIAS to fetch the Golden Fleece of Colchis if he wanted to regain the throne of Iolcos, his rightful inheritance; assembled fifty heroes on board 'Argo' and set sail to find this fleece washed in a gold-carrying stream of the Caucasus; met MEDEA and married her on the return voyage

MEDEA enchantress of JASON who escaped with him and the Golden Fleece from Colchis; killed PELIAS on their return and turned murderous in jealousy towards the daughter of CREON, killing both, and her own children by JASON; later became Queen to AEGEUS of Athens and when attempting to poison her stepson THESEUS was exiled; eventually reached Colchis and restored her father AEETES as king; by some accounts her Athenian son MEDUS later gave his name to the country of the Medes (Media) who later joined with the Persians

TALOS rock-throwing bronze giant; a creation of the god Hephaestus; invulnerable to fire, but made drunk by MEDEA who by prising out the bronze nail in his foot killed him

6 **AEETES** King of Colchis and father of MEDEA; refused to give up the Golden Fleece and placed many obstacles in the way of JASON & MEDEA

AEGEUS king of Athens who received the refugee MEDEA and married her

AMYCUS ruler in Bithynia of the savage Bebryces; killed by POLYDEUCES

6 **CHIRON** king of the CENTAURS (half man half horse); educator of JASON, ACHILLES & ASCLEPIUS (god of medicine, son of APOLLO and the nymph CORONIS)

MOPSUS seer (one of two); sailed on 'Argo'; died of snake bite in Libya

PELIAS king of Iolcos and uncle of JASON; usurper

SIRENS daughters of the river god ARCHELOUS; spurned by the Argonauts

TIPHYS navigator of the Argonauts

TRITON minor sea god, son of POSEIDON by AMPHITRITE; assisted JASON

7 **ANCAEUS** navigator of the Argonauts after TIPHYS

ATHAMAS uncle of JASON; king of the MINYANS in Boeotian city of Orchomenus; father of PHRIXUS & HELLE by NEPHELE; later consort of jealous INO

CYANEAN ROCKS (the Symplegades) two moving cliffs at the mouth of the Bosphorus that crushed whatever sought to pass

CYZICUS king of the DOLIONES who was killed by JASON

HARPIES supernatural winged beings; tormentors of king PHINEUS

MINYANS the tribe of JASON whose most prominent members took part in the expedition

NEPHELE first wife and cloud goddess of ATHAMAS who bore him HELLE and PHRIXUS

ORPHEUS musician and husband of EURYDICE, a dryad

PHINEUS aged and blind king whose food was spoilt by the HARPIES; he told the Argonauts the course to Colchis and how to clear the CYANEAN ROCKS

PHRIXUS son of ATHAMAS and brother of HELLE who escaped to Colchis on the ram with the Golden Fleece; on arrival he killed the ram and hung up the fleece in the grove of ARES there to be guarded by a dragon which MEDEA later put to sleep

8 **ABSYRTUS** son of AEETES and younger brother of MEDEA

ALCIMEDE perhaps the wife of AESON and mother of JASON

DOLIONES the tribe ruled by CYZICUS

10 **POLYDEUCES** one of the Argonauts who defeated the Bithynian king AMYCUS in a fist fight

A Sweep around the World in Mythology

Ass. Assyrian Fin. Finnish Jap. Japanese S.Am. South American Bab. Babylonian Ger. German N.Am. North American Scan. Scandinavian C.Am. Central American Gr. Greek N.Z. New Zealand Sem. Semitic Ch. Chinese Hung. Hungarian Pers. Persian Sum. Sumerian Eg. Egyptian It. Italian Rom. Roman

1 **I** (Ch.) the Excellent Archer; husband of **CH'ANG-O**, Moon goddess

2 **AN ANU** (Sum/Sem.) supreme sky god; see **BEL/BAAL/MARDUK & EA**

AN (Brazil/Tupinamba Indian) the Soul

BA (Eg.) 'soul', immortal element (**KA**)

DA (Africa/Benin) assistant to the creator-god **MAWU** of the Fon people

EA ENKI (Sum./Sem.) 'House of the Water', god of the **APSU** & supreme wisdom; see **BEL/BAAL**

EC (Siberia) Yeniseian high god who swallowed souls

EL Creator & chief god of the Sem./Ugaritic pantheon; see **BEL/BAAL, ALEYIN & MOT**

FU SHEN (Ch.) 'the bat', dispenser of Happiness; see **SHOU HSING & TS'AI-SHEN**

GE GAEA/GAIA (Gr.) Mother Earth born of **CHAOS**; mother of **URANUS** & the 12 **TITANS**

HU (Ch.) deity of creative will; emperor/god of the North Sea

HU (Eg.) crew member, with **SHIA**, of the solar barque of **RE**

IO (Gr.) mistress of cloud-disguised **ZEUS** who turned her into a white heifer; equated with Eg. **ISIS**

IO (N.Z./Maori) supreme being with eternal abode in the highest of 12 heavens

JE (Ch.) the Sun

KA (Eg.) 'spirit', immortal element (**BA**)

KA (India) Who? Indefinable Absolute (Brahma)

LI (Ch.) the Earth

LU HSING (Ch.) deer-mounted god of prosperity

MA Hittite/Hurrian **HEBAT**, goddess of war (Rom. **BELLONA**)

NU (Eg.) frog-headed male or female aquatic god, waist-high in water; see **NUN**

NU & KUA (Ch.) incestuous couple whose relationship resulted in the human race

OM sacred syllable; eternal soul; penetrator & cause of the universe (India/Brahman)

OT Mongolian Queen of fire

PO (Polynesia) the Void (Chaos) from which the world evolved; place of the dead; see **HINA**

RA RE/PHRA (Eg.) supreme celestial & solar god & creator; son of **GEB** (Earth) and **NUT** (Sky); see **HAPI & MAAT**

SA (Eg.) hieroglyphic sign & magic, vital fluid of every divine 'Lord of the City'

TU (Polynesia) chief warrior god

UL (Oceania) lord of the moon and spirit of night

UO (C.Am.) trusted frog-mates of Mayan rain gods **CHAAC**

VE (Norse) son of **BOR & BESTLA**; brother of **ODIN**; (Ger.) sacred places

WO (Africa/Cameroon) the chimpanzee son of **ZAMBA** (God)

YU (Ch.) monster & great tamer of the flood

ZU (Sum./Sem.) thieving storm-bird from whom **MARDUK** recovered the Tablets of Fate, token of the all-powerful supreme gods

3 **AER** Air, pure intelligence, born of Desire & Darkness (Phoenician cosmology); begat cosmic Egg with **AURA** (breath)

AHI IHI (Eg.) sistrum-playing son of Hethor & Horus of Edfu

AHU (Polynesia) raised shrine for offerings within the marae

AMA (Jap.) Japan-like Heaven linked to Earth by a heavenly bridge

AMA TSU-KAMI gods of the Earth (Jap.)

ANU (Sem.) see **AN, ANSHAR**

ANU Celtic mother-goddess (**ANA/DANU**)

APO (India) 'the Water' (Vedic apas); see **APSU**

ASK ASH/ASKR (Norse) forefather of man by his wife **EMBLA**; son of **ODIN**

ASO holy mountain in S. Japan

ATE (Gr.) malevolent daughter of **ERIS** or **ZEUS** who led gods & men astray; exiled by **HERACLES** & followed by her limping sisters, the **LITAE**

AYA (Ass./Bab.) wife of **SHAMASH**, sun-god & soothsayer who revealed the future

AZI (Altaic) forest and mountain spirit

BAU (Sum.) she gave the kiss of life to

man; daughter of **AN/ANU** & wife of **NINGURSU/NINURTA**

BEL (Sum.) **BAAL** ('Lord', a title conferred on a number of gods by the Phoenicians) god of War & Rain; son of **EL**; see **MARDUK, ENLIL**

BES BISU (Eg.) large-headed dwarf with bushy tail; god of recreation

BOR (Norse) father of **ODIN** by **BESTLA**; see **MIDGARD, VILI, VE**

COU CU CHULAINN (Ulster Cycle) tribal hero; father of **FINN**

DIA (Gr.) was seduced by **ZEUS** disguised as a horse; wife of **IXION** (king of the Lapiths) who, as punishment for casting eyes on **HERA**, was bound to a fiery wheel rolling ceaselessly through the sky

DIS Roman **HADES**, divinity of the Netherworld

DON DANU (Welsh/Irish) god of fertility & the forge; fiend of the Children of Darkness (**LLYR**); father of **GWYDION**

EOS (Gr.) the Dawn & mother of the winds **ZEPHYRUS, NOTUS, BOREAS** and **HESPERUS** (the evening star) & all stars, and **PHAETHON** by **CEPHALUS**; sister of **HELIOS & SELENE**; daughter of **HYPERION & THEIA** (Titans) (Rom. **AURORA**)

FAL (Irish/Celtic) stone of Fal which gave a cry when stepped on by the rightful king of Ireland; one of 4 magical treasures (**DAGDA**/cauldron; **LUG**/spear; **NUADA**/sword) possessed by the chieftain gods of the Irish Tuatha De Danann

FAM (Africa/Bantu) an Adam, created by an invisible father; see **NZAME**

GEB KEB/SEB (Eg.) goose or male with head surmounted by a goose (ideogram of his name); earth god

HAP (Eg.) see **HAPI**

HEH NEHEH (Eg.) Infinity, Happiness & Long Life; husband of **HEHET**

HEL (Norse) Queen of Niflheim (nine worlds of Darkness); goddess of death and daughter of **ODIN**'s rogue **LOKI**

HAP HEP (Eg.) see **HAPI**

HOD (Norse) killer of **BALDR**; see **HODUR**

IAB (Samoyed) spirit of nature

IDA mountain on Crete & birthplace of **ZEUS**; Mt in Asia Minor near Troy; ancient Germanic temples

IFA (Nigeria/Yoruba) the Great Truth

INO (Gr.) mother of Melicertes who was carried by a dolphin to Corinth; sister of **SEMELE** whose baby, **DIONYSUS**, she had cared for, much to the annoyance of **HERA**; nymph Leucothes

ION (Gr.) forefather of the Ionian people; prince of Athens; son of **CREUSA & APOLLO**

ITI (Oceania) the Moon; see **VATEA**

KEB GEB/SEB separated from his sister & spouse **NUT** by their father **SHU**

KUA see **NU**

KUL (Siberia/Ostyaks) genie that haunted big lakes & deep waters

KUU (Fin.) father of Kuutar; 'moon' in Finnish

LAR LARES (plur.) (Rom.; Etruscan 'chief' or 'prince') the juvenile family guardian of the household whose altar was the hearth

LHA (gods) & **DRE** (demons) Tibetan supernatural beings; Buddhist deities

LIR Irish sea god; father of **MANANNAN**

LOA (Oceania/Marshall I.) creator of the world

LUG (Irish/Celtic) **LAMFOTA** intellectual father of Ulster hero **CU CHULAINN/COU**; Welsh **LLEU/LLAW/GYFFES**, uncle of **GWYDION** & son of virgin **ARANRHOD**; also Lugnasad fertility feast (1 August)

MAH MAO (Pers.) moon god and assistant of **VOHU MANAH**

MAO MAHOU (Africa/Dahomey) superior being

MEN Hittite/Hurrian mounted lunar god associated with **ATTIS** and Thracian **SABAZIUS**; (Pers. **MAH/MAO**)

MIN AKHMIN (Eg.) son of **RA**; ithyphallic Pan-god of fertility & travellers

MOT (Sem.) god of the Dead, harvest deity; son of **EL**; killed by **BAAL** (who was helped by his sister/wife **ANATH/ANAT**)

MUT (Eg.) as **HERA**, wife of **AMON-RA**, becoming Queen of the Gods; also appears as **BAST/BASTET** or cat or lioness-headed goddess **TEFNUT** or Pekhet, patron of music and festivals

NIO (Jap.) Herculean spirits

NUM (Siberia) sky god, like **TORUM** and **EC**

NUN (Eg.) primordial ocean; see **NU**

NUT NUIT/NEUTH (Eg.) mother of **OSIRIS, HORUS, SETH, NEPHTHYS, ISIS**; goddess of the sky; (Gr. **RHEA**)

NYX (Gr.) (Night) son of **CHAOS**; brother of **EREBUS** (shadows)

ONI (Jap.) malevolent forces/devils;

Oni of Hell have red or green bodies & heads of oxen or horses
OPS Roman goddess of crops; wife of **SATURN**
ORO Tahitian deity who rules the Underworld
PAN (Gr.) son of **HERMES & PENELOPE** & part of the cult of **DIONYSUS**; shepherd god of woods & pastures, worshipped as phallic he-goat (Satyr) in grottoes by Arcadians; great nymph chaser, one, Syrinx, became a reed so he cut several to make Pan-pipes; also surprised lone travellers causing 'panics'; known as Priapus in Asia Minor.
PAN NYAMIA (Africa) son of the Earth; god of the sky and cultivation
QAT (Siberia) spirits residing on high mountain tops
QAT QUAT (Australia/New Hebrides) chief god, hero or spirit; rel. **TANGAROA**
RAM (Eg.) most sacred Ram Ba Neb Djedet (see **BANADED**); (Celtic) cult animal associated with ram-headed serpent god Cernunnos
RAN (Norse) 'the ravisher' wife of **AEGIR** who used a (drag)net to capture men; her 9 daughters were also temptresses
ROT Lappish deity of the Netherworld
SEB KEB/GEB father of the Osirian gods
SET SETH (Eg.) brother or son of **OSIRIS** whom he killed & rival of **HORUS**; incarnation of evil & the arid desert
SHU (Eg.) god of light & air, supporter of the sky; unisexually created by **RA**; brother & husband of **TEFNUT** (1st couple of the Ennead) who bore him **GEB & NUT**
SIF (Norse) Thor's faithful wife
SIN NANNA (Bab./Sum.) moon god and Lord of the Second Cosmic Triad; see **ISHTAR**
SOL INDIGES Rom. sun god (Gr. **HELIOS**)
SUN Hittite weather god; father of **TELEPINU**
TYR TIW (Norse) an **AESIR** and one-handed god whose other hand was severed by the hideous wolf **FENRIR**; (Rom. **MARS**); (Tuesday)
ULL (Norse) **AESIR** enchanter & stepson of **THOR**; patron of snowshoes
UNO (Hung.) female deer/heifer; ancestor of the Hungarians
UTU (Sum.) god of sun & justice with head of buffalo; son of **NANNA/SIN & NINGAL**; see **ISHTAR**
YIN (Ch.) the Earth, moon being the essence of **YIN**; **YIN**/fem.–**YANG**/masc., theory of opposite & complementary forces in nature
YUE (Ch.) the Moon and the lunar month

4 **ABUK** (Africa/S.Sudan) spirit & fem. name of one of the first Dinka; see **DENG**
ACIS (Gr.) Sicilian shepherd crushed under a rock by jealous Polyphemus, the main Cyclops, blinded by **ODYSSEUS**; see **GALATEA**
ADAD (Bab.) see **HADAD**
ADAM Persian-Mazdean first man, after **JINNS**; also Gayomart-Adam
ADAT (N.Borneo) governs the Cosmos acc. to Dayak/Iban belief; 'custom' in Arabic
AEON ancestor of the first inhabitants of Phoenicia, Genos & Genea; see **BAAU**
AGNI (India/Hindu) two-faced, many-tongued mouthpiece of the gods; god of fire & lightning (Gr. Hephaestus); see **RUDRA**
AHTO AHTI (Fin.) chief water god; husband of **VELLAMO** (Kalevala)
AJAX (Gr.) see Trojan War, besiegers
AKKA RAUNI (Fin.) sacred mountain ash; 'old woman' in Finnish; see **UKKO**
AKNA (C.Am.) divinity of childbirth; wife of **AKANCHOB**
AMMA (Bokina Faso/Dogon) chief god & creator among 8 sacred pairs; (Sudan) father of Yurugu & Nommo
AMON AMMON, AMEN, AMANA, AMON-RA, AMOM (Eg.) King of the Gods, 18th-dynasty conqueror of Thebes; the phallic, or Ram, **AMON** represented regeneration, fertility, harvests & was patron of the Pharaoh; husband of **MUT** (mother) with adopted son **KHONS**
ANAT ANATH (Sem.) sister & wife of **BAAL**
ANPU (Eg.) see **ANUBIS**
APEP APEPI (Eg.) swallower of solar barque
APET OPET/TAUERET (Eg.) hippopotamus deity of maternity & household
APSU (Ass./Bab.) earth-encircling sweet water; united with **TIAMAT**, salt water, to bring forth all beings (Gr. **OCEANUS**); see **EA, APO & MARDUK**

ARES (Gr.) spear-brandishing warrior from Thrace; companions: **ERIS, ENYO, DEIMOS, PHOBOS**
ASET ISIS (Eg.) member of the Osirian Triad
ASHA (Persia) 'universal law', born of **AHURU MAZDA**, king of Nature
ASIA (Gr.) rivals Oceanid Clymene as mother of **ATLAS**; (Africa/Guinea) Earth goddess; (Siberia) see **MAMALDI**
ATAR (Persia) Mazdean-Zoroastrian **FIRE**, comforting & wise; accompanies the Sun's chariot
ATEA (Oceania/Marquesas I.) creator & father of Dawn/**ATANUA**; rel. **RANGI**, sky-god (N.Z.)
ATEN ATON (Eg.) solar disk whose rays end in hands; Atenism introduced by Akhenaten/Amenophis **IV**, married to Nefertiti
ATRI (India) son of **BRAHMA**; father of **SOMA**
ATUA (Polynesia) the gods
ATUM ATUM-RA/RE/TUM (Eg.) mongoose-headed, self-fertilizing creator (ichneumon) god; the setting Sun, father of **SHU & TEENUT**
AUGE priestess of **ATHENE** seduced by **HERCULES**
AURA (Phoenicia) 'breath'; see **AER**
BAAL (Sem./Rom. Jupiter) Lord of the Earth & chief Ugaritic warrior, rain & fertility god; son of **EL**; husband of **ISHTAR**/Asherat; see **BEL, MARDUK, MOT**
BAAU (Sem.) wife of Kolpia & mother of **AEON**
BADB war goddess in the Celtic Triad of 'Valkyries'; see **MORRIGAN & MACKA**
BAST BASTET (Eg.) cat-headed goddess in Bubastis of music & dance & spouse of Ptah of Memphis
BIAS (Gr.) brother of **MELAMPUS**, seer & descendant of **AEOLUS** (son of **HELLEN**)
BISU (Eg.) see **BES**
BOUS (Norse) son of **ODIN & RINDA** who killed the blind **HODUR/HOD**
BRAN (Celtic) the blessed giant & poet who waded across the Irish Sea; child of **LLYR**
BRES (Celtic/Irish) King of the Tuatha Dé Dannan (people of goddess **DANU**) who married **BRIGIT**, daughter of the chieftain **DAGDA**; forced to abdicate which resulted in a war fought with magical weapons between the Tuatha & the Fomorians
BULL Universal symbol of power & strength (**EL**/Canaan); (Persia) Gosh/Bull & Gayomart/first man, the animal/human pair which produced all life; Bull of Mithraism; emblem of the Great God (Crete)
BUNI (Siberia) chief of the Netherworld
BURI (Norse) grandfather of **ODIN, VILI & VE**, the 3 brothers who killed **YMIR** and formed the earth, named Midgard, from his body; see **AUDUMLA**
BUTO (Eg.) nurse of **HORUS**; cobra-goddess; she & **NEKHEBET**, the **NEBTI**, appeared on royal documents or on Pharoah's forehead
CAGN (Africa) omnipotent creator and chief Bushman deity whose abode is known only to antelopes; husband of Coti
CETO (Gr.) daughter of Pontus & Gaia with a heart of steel; mother of the Gorgons, the dragon Ladon (father of Syrinx & **DAPHNE**) & perhaps also of the Hesperides
CEYX (Gr.) & wife Alcyone turned into birds for comparing themselves to **ZEUS & HERA**; changed by **APOLLO** into a sparrow-hawk
CHIN (C.Am./Yucatan) Mayan god of Vice
CLIO (Gr.) Muse of History, with trumpet & clepsydra
DANU Irish Celtic mother goddess
DENG (Africa/S.Sudan) weather god; with **ABUK** & Garang founder of the Dinka religion
DEUS Latin for divinity; Sanskrit Dyaus (Zeus)
DEVA happy Buddhist heavenly being; Devas are opposed to Asuras who encourage evil
DEVS (Persia) Mithratic demons
DJOL (Samoyed) spirit of nature
DWYN DWYNWEN Welsh god of love; son of **DAGDA**
ECHO (Gr.) a nymph; mother of **IAMBE** by **PAN**; (N.Am.) with Thunder (Hino) & Wind (Ga-oh/a) member of Iroquois Triad of giants & magicians
ENKI (Sum./Sem.) **EA** god of liquid elements, revered in Eridu, holy city at the mouth of **APSU**. See **MARDUK**
ERIS (Gr.) 'Strike', daughter of Night & sister of **ARES**; mother of **ATE**
EROS (Gr.) god of love; son of **HERMES** & Aphrodite; beloved of Psyche ('soul')

ESUS wood-cutter & part of Celtic Triad acc. to Lucan

FINN (Celtic) mac Cumal, of the Ossianic Cycle; hero, warrior & poet of the fiana band; see **COU**

FREY see **FREYR**

GAEA **GAIA** (Gr.) see **GE** and **RHEA**

GARM **GARMR** (Norse) wolf destined to kill and be killed by **TYR** in Ragnarök; son of **ODIN** (or a giant)

GERD **GERDA/GERDR** (Norse) of the Netherworld & giant **GYMIR**'s daughter; wife of **FREY/FREYR**

HAPI **HAP/HEP** (Eg.) bearded fertility god of the Nile & consort of **NEKHBET**; as a bull, reincarnation of **PTAH**

HELL (Ch.) 18 hells, reserved for torture & dispersed among 10 law-courts, each ruled by a king; (Jap.) underground kingdom of the dead with soldiers; deep land (Soko no Kuni) home of ugly female & male demons

HARE (Ch.) producer of the drug Immortality; stopped I, who shot down 9 suns, from punishing his wife, the moon goddess **CH'ANG-O/** Heng-o

HEBE (Gr.) **DIA** goddess of eternal youth; a female Ganymede, dispenser of nectar to the gods; married **HERCULES** on his deathbed

HERA (Gr.) Olympian Queen of the sky, jealous of other goddesses; much deceived by brother & husband **ZEUS**; see **MUT**

HERO (Gr.) priestess of Aphrodite and beloved of **LEANDER**

HINA **HINE** (Polyn.) guardian of **PO** & women; see **TANE**

HIRO Tahitian chief of the Netherworld

IDUN (Norse) wife of divine poet **BRAGI**; keeper of apple trees for longevity; see **AESIR**

ILMA (Fin.) weather god whose daughter Luonnotar (Nature), mother of Väinämöinen, was associated with creation

INTI **APU-PUNCHAU** Inca sun god & ancestor of the Incas with the face of a disk of gold

IREJ (Persia) inherited Iran from his father **FERIDUN**; murdered by his brothers Selm (of Rum) & Tur (of Turkestan)

IRIS (Gr.) winged water-carrier for the gods; messenger & rainbow goddess

ISIS **ASET/ESET** (Eg.) Queen of the gods & the Osirian Triad; wife of **OSIRIS** & mother of **HORUS** & great mother goddess; see **IO**

JADE (Ch.) 'Jade Emperor Lord on High', 2nd in supreme Triad whose heavenly court was modelled on that of earthly Emperors

JORD **FJORGYN** (Norse) mother of **THOR**; beloved of **ODIN**; see **AESIR**

JOVE (Gr./Rom.) one of the 12 chief gods of Gr./Rom. pantheon: **JUNO, VESTA, MINERVA, CERES, DIANA, VENUS, MARS, MERCURIUS, NEPTUNUS, VOLCANUS, APOLLO**

JUNO (Rom.) deity of state & protectress of women (a female **JUPITER**)

JUOK (Africa/Nile) supreme being; creator of all men on earth

KADI (Ass./Bab.) symbol of the creative earth & goddess of justice

KALA (India) weather, an epithet of **YAMA**

KAMI (Jap.) Shinto deities

KAPO (Hawaii) deity of fertility and abortion

KARA (Norse/Iceland) a sweet-singing swan-maiden Valkyrie; beloved of warrior Helgi who wounded her in flight

KINK (C.Am./Maya) 'Time', worship of; also 'sun' or 'day'; a 260-day calendar was intermeshed with a 365-day one & renewed every 52 years; end of Universe set for year A.D. 2011

KORE (Gr.) **DEMETER**'s beloved flower-gathering daughter abducted by **HADES** near Nysa, or, as Persephone, by Enna in Sicily

KUSA (India) the plant from which **RAMA** made his bed & rested when **HANUMAN** brought him news of his wife **SITA**, abducted to the kingdom of Lanka

LARA (Rom.) talkative nymph (Mania); mother of the **LARES & MANES**; lost her tongue to **JUPITER** (hence 'Muta')

LEDA (Gr.) conçeived **POLLUX & HELEN** by the seducer **ZEUS**, & **CASTOR** & Clytemnestra by husband Tyndareus in the same night!

LETO (Gr.) another of **ZEUS**'s conquests; jealous **HERA** made sure she underwent many misadventures before giving birth to **APOLLO & ARTEMIS**

LEZA LESA (Africa/Zambia) God & Creator to many people, including Bantu tribes
LLEW LLAW GYFFES (Celtic/Welsh) 'Llew of the strong hand', wielding a spear & a sling; see Irish **LUG**
LLYR (Welsh) children of Llyr, deities of the underworld as opposed to the children of **DON**, sky deities; god of fertility & craftsmanship; brother of **BRAN** the Blessed (Bendegeit Bran)
LOKI (Norse) the evil flame, son of giant **FARBAUTI** (fire raiser) & Laufey (tinder wood); the mischief-maker among the gods, causing also the death of **BALDR** using the blind **HOD/HODUR** (of the shadows); Loki was bound to a rock, but escaped to fight the **AESIR** gods at **RAGNARÖK**, being killed by **HEIMDALL**; father of **ANGRBODA** (Anguish) & 3 evil offspring: **HEL**/Death, **JORMUNGUND**/evil serpent surrounding the world & **FENRIR**/wolf; see **HOENIR**
LOTA (Tahiti) divine bird; (burbot fish)
LUNG WANG (Ch.) dragon kings
MAAT MAYET (Eg.) patroness of law & order & counterweight on a divine scale to the hearts of the dead; daughter of **RA**; wife of **THOTH**
MAIA (Rom.) wife of **VULCAN**, oldest of gods; pre-Jupiter goddess of the waters & earth mother (as also **VESTA**)
MAMI (Ass./Bab.) goddess of child-labour thus mankind; see **NINTUD**
MANA (Polynesia) all-penetrating dynamic force
MANU (India) ancestor of mankind; see **SURYA**
MARA (India) demon defeated by **BUDDHA**
MARS MASPITER/MARSPITER/MAMAR/MAVORS Rom. spirit of plants who grew to become god of war, subordinate only to **JUPITER**, receiving woodpeckers & wolves as sacrifice
MAUI (Polynesia) fished for the Earth and lifted up the Sky and made it his tutor; gave fire to mankind
MAWU (Africa) see **DA**
MENG (Ch.) guardian of exit from Hell; gave compulsory soup of Oblivion & Forgetfulness to souls en route to Transmigration
MILK Altaic satans
MIRU (Polynesia) ruler of the Netherworld
MO-LI (Ch.) 4 brother gods, guardians of Buddhist temples
MONT MENTHU (Eg.) Thebes, sun god, of war, deposed by his son **AMON** (later, King of Gods)
NAGA Buddhist serpent deities
NIKE (Gr.) as **ATHENA** a portable, wingless owl, but as herself a winged goddess of victory & daughter of **PALLAS** (Giant) & **STYX**; (Rom. **VICTORIA**)
NINA fire god of the Incas
NUIT (Eg.) see **NUT**
ODIN WODEN/WOTAN (Norse) sovereign & magician of the gods; also Lord of wisdom, poetry, heroism, fate, war, victory, and husband of **FRIGG/FRIJA**, father of Volsungs; helped by his brothers **VILI & VE** he killed **YMIR**, first of all living beings & father of all giants; dwelled in **VALHALLA**; made an Adam & Eve (**ASKR & EMBLA**) out of trees & lifted the earth from the sea; grandson of **BURI** & son of **BOR** by **BESTLA**; see **YMIR**
OGUN (Africa/Nigeria) god of the Yoruba tribe
OPET (Eg.) see **TAURT**
PAHA (Fin. 'bad') one of 3 evil spirits, with **HIISI & LEMPO** (Kalevala)
PAPA (N.Z.) the Earth; see **RINGI & VATEA**
PASI or **VARUNA** (India) the all-seeing god regulating oaths, civil order, movements of the heavens, rains, waters; also King of the Dead, father of **AGASTYA**, the ascetic, & brother of partner **MITRA**
PTAH PHTHAH (Eg.) of Memphis, mummified maker of things, incl. the universe; god of fertility; patron of fine arts; husband of **SEKHMET**; father of **NEFERTUM**; see **BAST & HAPI**
PENG (Ch.) gigantic bird causing huge waves when rising from the sea
POIA (N.Am./Indian) the Scar-face & orphaned son of disobedient **SOATSAKI**, who found a way to his grandfather, the Sun, and was relieved of his scar as reward for slaying 7 monstrous birds threatening his father, the Morning Star
P'O-P'O (Ch.) Mrs Wind riding a tiger in the clouds; once male **FENG PO**
PURA (Oceania) originally sky god, later minor hero
QUAT (Polynesia) celestial deity

RAKI (Maori) the Heaven in Polynesia and New Zealand

RAMA (India/Hindu) popular deity and a model of reason, with a devoted monkey **HANUMAN**; husband of **SITA**; as **RAMACANDRA** 7th incarnation of **VISHNU**

RHEA (Gr.) mother goddess (Phrygian **CYBELE**); daughter of **URANUS & GAEA**; sister and consort of **CRONUS** and mother of **ZEUS**; see **NUT**

RIGI (Polynesia) butterfly who separated the earth from the sea

RIGR (Norse) another name for **HEIMDALL** as father of three classes (bond-man, free citizen, royal) by three women

RITA (India) guardian of fire

ROHE (N.Z.) ruler of the middle world

RONA (N.Z./Maori) mother of **TANE** who ate the moon

SATI (Eg.) goddess of the Cataracts of the Nile & the archer who released its flood force; together with **ANUKET** she was a wife of **KHNUM**

SATI (India) wife of **SIVA** & daughter of **DAKSA** (Sage); places of pilgrimage sprung up where bits of her body, murdered by divine hands, fell

SETH see **SET**

SHEN (Ch.) gods

SHOU HSING (Ch.) patron of longevity

SIGI (Norse) son of **ODIN?**; founder of the **VOLSUNG** tribe

SITA (India) see **RAMA & HANUMAN**

SIVA SHIVA (India) three-eyed ambiguous lord of Saiva sects; Vedic **RUDRA** (destruction), Agni (fire) & Prajapati (creator) absorbed by him; father of six-headed **SKANDA** & elephant-headed **GANESA**; bull **NANDI** was the mount for this half male, half female; husband of **SATI**; see **BRAHMA**

SOMA (India) Vedic holy plant & ambrosia conferring immortality; the golden nectar of the gods assuming many different forms; **HAOMA** of the **AVESTA**

SPOR Slav deity guarding stables and fields

STYX River of Death; see **CHARON**, **NIKE & TETHYS**

T'AI-I (Ch.) took the place of **SHANG TI** as Supreme god

TANE (Polynesia) coloured Heaven red and separated it from the Earth; mixed sand & clay to create **HINA/HINE**, an Eve, and then married her; creator of **TIKI**, messenger & guardian spirits; son of **RONA**

TARA (Himalayas/Mongolia) multi-eyed, multi-coloured Buddhist divinity dispensing relief from suffering and protecting travellers both on their earthly journeys and spiritual explorations

THAT (India/Hindu) the Absolute; Brahman

THOR THUNOR/DONAR (Norse) thunder & war god (armed with the 'boomerang' hammer **MJÖLLNIR**), the most worshipped of all (Rom. **JUPITER**), with very ornate temples & travelling in chariot drawn by goats; his mother was **JORD** (earth), his faithful wife **SIF** & sons Magni (strength) & Modi (anger); he fell at **RAGNARÖK** having slain the undersea evil serpent of **MIDGARD** but dying of its venom

TIKI Polynesian protective spirits; see **TANE & HINA**

TILO (Mozambique) god of the sky, thunder & rain

TI-MU (Ch.) Earth, Mother

T'U-TI (Ch.) divine old couple & popular gods of Place

TYRO (Gr.) nymph & mother of **NELEUS & PELIAS** (enemy of **JASON**) by **POSEIDON**

UKKO (Fin.) sky god who supported the world and ruled the heavens; controlled rainfall & fertility; husband of **AKKA/RAUNI**

UMAI (Siberia/Orkhon) goddess of cradles and the hearth

VALI VELI/VILE (Norse) unkept son of **ODIN** waiting for his battle

VELA Lithuanian realm of the Dead

VILI (Norse) son of **BOR**; brother of **ODIN & VE**

YAMA (India) red-eyed inventor of mortality astride a buffalo, with many-eyed dogs protecting his realm of the Dead; first of eight steps to full concentration, with him as judge; see **SURYA**

YAMM YAM (Sem.) hydra-like serpent ruler of the waters of the earth who was killed by **BAAL**

YANG (Ch.) Sky, and square (hence royal domain square); active masculine principles that permeate all being

YIMA (Pers.) son of the Sun; first man and father of the human race; accused by Zoroaster of causing the end of the golden age; replaced as first man by **GAYOMART**

YMIR AURGELMIR (Norse) first living being; father of all the giants & dwarfs emanating from his corpse; great-grandfather of **ODIN** who killed him; see **MIDGARD & AUDUMLA**

YOMI (Jap.) the Netherworld to which **IZANAGI** descended to look for his wife **IZANAMI**

ZEUS (Gr.) was the omnipotent lord of the skies & of wisdom, and protector; son of **CRONUS** (the cannibal, later exiled) & he overcame the revolts of the **TITANS** (see Classical Miscellany) & **GIANTS & GAEA**; he married Metis (wisdom), Themis (law), **HERA**, & seduced many more

5 **AEGIR** (Ger./Scan.) giant monster of the sea

AESIR (Norse) family of gods, enemies of the **VANIR**; together with **BALDER, BRAZI/BRAGI, IDUN, JORD, HEIMDALL, LOKI**, etc. the gods of battle **ODIN, FRIGG, TYR, THOR** inhabited **ASGARD/VALHALLA**, the top celestial abode

AESON (Gr.) son of **TYRO** and father of **JASON**; see **ENIPEUS**

AGAVE (Gr.) aunt of **DIONYSUS** who, escaping from **PENTHEUS'** prison, struck her & the other women of Thebes with madness; as the Maenads they held orgies on Mount Cithaeron; her father **PENTHEUS**, in pursuit, was riven apart by her (Euripides' drama Bacchae)

AHURA MAZDA/AURAMAZDA (Pers.) Zoroastrian creator of the universe and the twin spirits of evil and good fighting it out on Earth

AMANA (Eg.) see **AMON**

AMMON (Eg.) see **AMON**

ANATH ANAT (Sem.) sister & consort of **BAAL** whom she rescued from the Netherworld; goddess of war and patron of love who later merged with **ASTARTE** and was called Atargatis; see **MOT**

ANNWN (Celtic) the Netherworld; see **PRYDERI**

ANSUD (Sum.) **NINURTA** as a thunderbird

ARTIO (Celtic/Helvetii) bear-goddess of the Bern region

ARURU (Sum.) mother-goddess & wife of **ENKI**

APEPI APEP/APOPHIS/REREK (Eg.) huge serpent; god of darkness & evil; enemy of **RA**

ARION (Gr.) swift horse, son of **POSEIDON & DEMETER**

ASHUR ASSHUR (Ass.) Lord of the gods of Assyria and its capital Ashur; similar to **ANSHAR** (father of **AN**) or Sum. **ENLIL**

ASIAQ (Eskimo) protectress of the weather and the atmosphere

ATIRA (N.Am.) held court in heaven together with husband **TIRAWA**

ATLAS (Gr.) a Titan condemned by **ZEUS** to support the pillars that separated Heaven & Earth; turned into a rocky mountain by **PERSEUS**; son of **ASIA?**

ATTIS ATTS (Gr.) Phrygian husband of **CYBELE** (Magna Mater); son of twin-sexed **AGDISTIS** who killed him; solar divinity of the Roman Empire; see **MEN & LYCUS**

AYWIL (Africa) father of **DENG**

BALDR BALDER (Norse), the Sun god killed by **LOKI**

BALOR Irish divinity with an evil eye

BENNU (Eg.) heron-like sacred bird; soul of **OSIRIS**; (Gr. **PHOENIX**)

BINGO (Africa/Bantu) son of **NZAME**

BRAGI (Norse) like **ODIN**, a poet & scald; husband of **IDUN**

BRESS (Celtic) husband of **BRIGIT/BRIDGET**, pastoral poetic goddess

CACUS Roman cattle-thief and bandit who was killed by Hercules; son of fire god **VULCAN** and brother of **CACA**

CHAAC (C.Am.) Mayan rain god; see **UO & TLALOC**

CHONS see **KHONS & MUT**

CERES Roman goddess of crops associated with Gr. **DEMETER**

CH'UNG (Ch.) celestial administrator

CIRCE (Gr.) goddess of debased love, enchantments & evil spells who poisoned her husband & transformed whoever landed on her island into an animal

CREON (Gr.) King of Thebes whose city **OEDIPUS** freed from a monster, the **SPHINX**

CUNTI (India) mother of seven hundred thousand Buddhas

CUPID Roman arrow-shooting son of **VENUS**; roguish good spirit; (Gr. **EROS**)

DAGDA DAGDE/EOCHAID (Irish/Celtic) all-knowing pot-bellied father-figure, with a wheel-mounted outsize club;

with one end he could crush the enemies of his people, with the other restore them to life – hence master of life & death, & symbol of fertility & owner of a magic cauldron that never became empty; see **DWYN & BRIGIT**

DAITI (Pers.) river which flows from the centre of the world

DAKSA DAKSHA (India) father-in-law of **SIVA** & husband of 27 lunar stations

DANAË (Gr.) **ACRISIUS**, king of Argos, was father of **DANAË**, whose future son, said the oracle, would cause the king's death; so **ACRISIUS** built an underground prison for **DANAË** & her nurse; but **ZEUS**, already attracted by the charms of **DANAË**, entered as a shower of gold to become her lover; the result was **PERSEUS**, and the fulfilment of the fate as foretold

DATAN a Polish god of the fields

DEIVA Lithuanian werevolves

DELKA Lithuanian divine baby-minder

DIANA Roman huntress and helper of women; sister of **APOLLO**; (Gr. **ARTEMIS**)

DIEVS Baltic sky god

DOMFE (Sudan) aquatic spirit

DONAR (Ger.) see **THOR**

DURGA (India) another of the characters assumed by **SIVA**'s wife when called on to annihilate a demon; she mounts a lion & has 10 arms, each with a weapon, to overcome the monster; see **GANESA**

DYAUS (India) Vedic father in the sky; (Gr. **ZEUS**/Rom. **JUPITER**)

DYLAN (Celtic) divinity of darkness and the sea; son of **GWYDION** and **ARANRHOD**

ECHUA (C.Am.) god of travellers

ELVES ALFAR (Ger./Scan.) water (wood & mountain) creatures

EMBLA (Norse) wife of **ASK/ASH** and thus mother of mankind

EMMA-O (Jap.) (Indian **YAMA**) King of Hell from which only the supplication of the living could release you; left the judgement of female souls to his sister

ENECH (Hung.) see **HUNOR**

ENLIL BEL (Sum.) god of sky & wind; second in the divine assembly of **AN/ANU**; husband of **NINLIL**, grain goddess; see **ASHUR**

EPONA AUGUSTA (Celtic/Rom.) mounted goddess connected with horses & donkeys; patroness of riders; see **MACHA**

ERLIK (Siberia/Altaic) father figure and an Adam; master of Death; sometimes in bird disguise

FATUA FAUNA, see **FAUNUS**

FAUNS (It.) see **SATYRS**

FLORA FERONIA Roman divinity of flowers

FREYR YNGRI (Norse/Swedish) a **VANIR** and son of **NJORD** and divine forefather of the Ynglingar kings of Sweden; bestower of fertility and guardian of crops; husband of **GERD** (daughter of giant **GYMIR**)

FRIGG FRIJA/FREA ('Friday') (Norse/Ger.) beloved wife of **ODIN/WODAN**; mother of **BALDR/BALDER**

FU-HSI (Ch.) with serpent's tail, one of 3 legendary emperors & in Triad of medicine gods

GAMAB (Africa) vicious divinity

GANAS (India) attendants of **SIVA**

GARMR (Norse) see **GARM**

GAUNA (Africa/Bushmen) vicious divinity

GANGA GANGES (India) sacred river & deity

GYMIR (Norse) see **GERD & FREYR**

HADAD ADAD (Ass./Bab.) controlled rainfalls & tempest; withheld rains on orders of **ENKI**, causing famine

HADES (Rom. **PLUTO**, Gr. **TARTARUS**) son of **CRONUS & RHEA**; King of the Netherworld with queen Persephone; 3-headed **CERBERUS**, guardian dog, stolen from him by **HERCULES**; allowed the Furies (Erinyes) to torment the wicked

HAKEA (Hawaii) chief of the Netherworld

HAOMA (Pers.) see **SOMA**

HALDI chief Urartian god depicted standing on a lion

HEBAT Hurrian Queen of gods; see **MA**

HEHET (Eg.) see **HEH**

HEKET (Eg.) frog-headed goddess

HELEN (Gr.) wife of **MENELAUS** won by shepherd **PARIS**; see Trojan War

HIISI (Fin.) vicious spirits

HODUR HODER/HOD (Norse) blind son of **ODIN**, tricked by **LOKI** into slaying **BALDR**; see **BOUS**

HORON (Sem.) god of the Netherworld

HORUS HOR (Eg.) falcon-like sky god with solar & lunar vision & son of **ISIS**; each Pharaoh a **HORUS** incarnate; **HORUS** succeeded **OSIRIS** by defeating **SETH**

HOU T'U (Ch.) supreme Earth

HSI-HO (Ch.) wife of **TI CHUN/SHANG TI**; gave birth to ten suns whom she polished by bathing them every morning
HUACA Incan mystic forces and guardian spirits
HUNOR ENECH (Hung.) horned forefather of the Hungarians
HYLAS (Gr.) a partner of **HERCULES** who was drowned by a naiad
IAMBE (Gr.) inventor of iambic verse; see **ECHO**
INARI (Jap.) rice god
INDRA (India) storm, rain & sky god who gained mastery over the sun and killed the monsoon-preventing dragon **VRTRA**; chief thousand-eyed Vedic warlike god, rival of **KRISHNA**; husband of **INDRANI**; father of **ARJUNA**
INNUA (Eskimo) **SILAP INNUA**, master of the air; powers of the Universe/Yua
INUAT (Eskimo) souls and spirits
IRENE EIRENE (Gr.) goddess of peace and one of the Horae (Seasons)
IXION (Gr.) see **CENTAURS & DIA**
JANUS (Rom.) keeper of the universe and all beginnings who faced both the future and the past
JASON (Gr.) leader of the Argonauts in the quest for the Golden Fleece; see **TYRO**
JINNS (Oriental) genii spirits
JUMNA YAMUNA (India) river sacred to Hindus at its confluence with the Ganges
KALKI (India) giant with horse's head; **AVATAR/VISHNU** incarnation still to come
KALMA (Fin.) goddess of death; see **SURMA**
KAMSA (India) see **KRISHNA**
KARMA (India) see **SURYA**
KAU-FU (Ch.) giant or composite animal; son of **KUNG-KUNG** (horned monster)
KENOS (S.Am.) great forefather; an Adam
KHNUM KHNEMU (Eg.) elephantine lord of the cataracts and potter-god; shaped and gave life to his god models; husband of the sisters **SATI** (fertility) and **ANUKET**
KHONS (Eg.) moon god and adopted son of **MUT** and AMON-RA
KINGU (Sum.) husband of **TIAMAT** from whose blood **ENKI/EA** made Man; see **MARDUK**
KINTU (Mozambique) initially the only man on earth
KISIN (C.Am./Maya) the 'earthquake' who assisted evil Usukun & his brother **HAPIKERN**, all enemies of mankind locked in eternal war with the god of creation
KURKE Baltic divinity of the crops
KWOTH (Sudan) supreme god
LADON (Gr.) river god & father of **SYRINX** whom he transformed into a reed; dragon who guarded the entrance to the garden of the Hesperides & was killed by **HERCULES**; see **PAN**
LAHMU & LAHAMU/Lakhmu & Lakhamu (Sum.) a pair of hideous serpents & parents of **ANSHAR**
LAIUS (Gr.) ruler of Thebes and father of **OEDIPUS** by **IOCASTE/JOCASTA**, sister of **CREON**
LARES Roman household genii; see **LAR & PENATES**
LAUME Baltic protective goddesses
LEMPO (Fin.) vicious spirit; see **HIISI**
LESKY Slav sylvan spirit and guardian of flocks & herds
LETHE (Gr.) river and spring of oblivion in the Netherworld; daughter of **ERIS** (Strife); sister **MNEMONYME** (Spring of Memory)
LIBER (It.) divinity of rural settlements, vines & fertility who, on his festival day **LIBERARIA**, presided over boys entering manhood
LINUS (Gr.) may have invented melody & rhythm; killed by **APOLLO** after challenging him to a song contest; music-teacher to **HERCULES** who killed him in anger
LITAE (Gr.) daughters of **ZEUS**; old, limping Prayers who blessed those showing them respect
LODUR (Norse) fellow-traveller with **ODIN, LOKI & HODUR** on an unpopulated earth; gave warmth & colour of life to trees
LOTAN LEVIATHAN (Sem.) primeval serpent
LOUHI (Fin.) goddess in the land of the dead, **MAAN-ALA (MANALA)**
LUGUS LUG (Irish/Celtic) see **NUADU**
MACHA MORRIGAN/BADB/NEMAIN (Celtic) three war goddesses: a) mother of twins and guardian of **MACHA**'s fortress (Emain Macha/ Ulster), b) wife of **NEMHED**, c) similar to Gallic **EPONA** (mare goddess)
MADER ATCHA (father) & **MADER AKKA** (mother) Lappish gods of Creation

MAHOU (Africa) see **MAO**
MAIRA (Brazil) Indian paradise, a land with no evil
MANES (Rom.) good, protective objects of a popular cult culminating in the festivals of Parentalia & Feralia; see **LARA**
MANNA Lappish Earth Mother
MAYET (Eg.) see **MAAT & THOTH**
MBOIA (Africa/Bantu) see **NZAME**
MEDEA (Gr.) murderous enchantress who helped **JASON** to overcome the obstacles to secure the Golden Fleece placed in their way by her father, king **AEETES** of Colchis; see **AEGEUS**
MIDAS (Gr.) son of **GORDIUS & CYBELE**, wished for the touch of gold, was granted it & repented; he was later asked to choose between **APOLLO** & Marsyas on lyre or flute playing; **APOLLO**, not being chosen, gave him the ears of an ass, whereupon **MIDAS** ended his life by consuming the blood of a bull
MIMIR (Norse) giant wise water spirit of **AESIR** tribe; guardian of the fountain of knowledge (Mimisbrunnar); often consulted by **ODIN** whose eye lay in **MIMIR**'s well; also a smith
MINOS (Gr.) lover of **SCYLLA** who drowned; enemy of the Athenians who killed his son Androgeus; son of **ZEUS** and **EUROPA**
MITRA (India) maintains universal order together with **VARUNA**, a dyad; see **PASI**; (Pers. Mithra)
MOIRA (Gr.) Fate that supersedes the gods
MOMUS (Gr.) symbol of guilt and son of Night
MONJU BOSATSU (Jap.) guide of all Buddhas; supreme wisdom
MUMMU (Sum.) male attendant of **APSU**
MUSUN (Samoyed) spirit of nature
NANDI (India) divine bull; mount of **SIVA**
NANNA (Sum.) see **SIN & ISHTAR**
NEBTI (Eg.) vulture and cobra goddess
NEHEH see **HEH**
NIOBE (Gr.) wife of **AMPHION** (Thebes) and sad mother of a dozen; see **SIPYLON**
NJORD (Norse) a **VANIR** and father of fertility deities **FREYR & FREYJA**
NUADU (Irish) came before **LUG** as King of the gods; fisherman
NUSKU (Sum.) lunar god of fire & light who wards off the demons of night; shows himself when the Moon (**SIN**), his father, is new
NZAME (Africa/Bantu) invisible divinity who made **FAM**, an Adam; husband of **MBOIA** and father of **BINGO**
OMARA (Africa/Nile) descended from the sky & became the first man; ancestral god of the Shilluks tribe
OPHIS (Eg.) see **OPHOIS**
ORION (Gr.) a giant, son of **POSEIDON** who could walk on the seabed; went hunting with **ARTEMIS** & then swam far out to sea; **APOLLO** challenged his sister to hit this target on the waves & she killed **ORION**; alternatively, set a scorpion on **ORION** who was then tended by Asclepius, struck by a thunderbolt from Zeus & ended up as a bright constellation in the heavens
OTAVA (Fin.) or **TAPIO**, sky god as a Great Bear
PAIVA (Fin.) the sun and mother of Päivätär; 'day' in Finnish
PALES (Rom.) rural festival spirits (Parilia)
PARIS (Gr.) awarded **ERIS**'s golden apple to Aphrodite on Mt. Ida, much to the annoyance of **HERA & ATHENE**; see **HELEN**
PEMBA (Sudan) created all beasts & plants on earth and made the first woman
PERUN PERKUNAS (Slav/Lithuanian) spirit of the sky governing lightning; Russian war god; see **VARPULIS**
PICUS (Rom.) woodpecker god of agriculture sacred to **MARS**; as myth. king, son of **SATURN**; father of **FAUNUS** and unwilling husband of sorceress **CIRCE**
PINGA (Eskimo) protectress of game
PLUTO (Gr.) see **HADES**
PWYLL (Celtic) see **PRYDERI**
RADHA (India) beloved of **KRISHNA**
RANGI (N.Z./Maori) sky god
RAUNI (Fin.) see **UKKO**
RAVEN (N.AM./Indian) important hero associated with **COYOTE**
REMUS founder of Rome with his twin brother **ROMULUS**; later killed by him; adventurous sons of **MARS** and the vestal virgin **RHEA SILVIA**, daughter of the ruler **NUMITOR** whose brother **AMULIUS** wanted **ROMULUS & REMUS** drowned in the Tiber
REREX (Eg.) see **APEPI**

RERIR (Norse) husband of **FREYJA**; see **VOLSUNG**
RINDA RENDI (Norse) mother of **BOUS** who was raped by **ODIN**
RINGI (N.Z.) the Sky, in love with **PAPA**, the Earth
ROBUR Gallic divinity of the oak tree
RUDRA (India) destructive ancestor of **SIVA**, causing death & disease with his arrows; father of the storm gods **MARUTS/RUDRAS**
SAKTI (India) chief Hindu goddess and wife of **SIVA**
SATYR (Gr.) wood genii; monkey/he goat, sensual companions of **DIONYSUS** at his orgy festivals
SEBEK SEBEQ/SEBEK-RE/SOBK-RE/SUCHOS (Eg.) crocodile or crocodile-headed man; protector of reptiles
SEIDA SAITI/SEJDA is found in the mountains as the head-like rock resembling some animal, and as such was worshipped & sacrificed to by the Lapps (Saami people)
SEDMA (Eskimo) goddess of marine animals
SEKER SOKAR/SOKARIS (Eg.) hawk or hawk-headed mummy; god of Darkness and Decay
SHAIT (Eg.) goddess of destiny
SHEDU (Ass./Bab.) good demons
SHEOL Hebrew Hell
SHERI KHURRI, the bulls of the Hurrite storm-god **TESHUP**
SIBYL one of ten Roman female prophets
SILAP INUA (Eskimo) master of the air
SKADI (Norse) wife of **NJORD** after his defection to the **AESIRS**
SUANU (Africa) deity of sudden death
SURMA (Fin.) monster guarding the abode of **KALMA**; personification of Death
SURYA (India) important Hindu solar divinity and dissipator of Darkness who fathered the Aswin twins (heavenly horsemen), **SURGIVA** (ruler of monkeys), **KARMA** (fighter), **YAMA** (god of Death) and **MANU** (ancestor of mankind)
TAGES (Rom./Etruscan) self-appointed grandson of **JUPITER** who possessed magic and wisdom
TAPIO (Fin.) dark-bearded, with cloak of moss; spirit of the woods together with his family; see **OTAVA**
TAURT APET/OPET/TAWERET/THOUERIS (Eg.) pregnant hippopotamus standing on his hind legs; deity of maternity & household
TELLA Hittite bull
THEIA (Gr.) mother of **SELENE**
THOTH DJHOWTEY (Eg.) ibis-headed god of the moon & learning; created the languages and was the scribe of the gods; protector of **ISIS**; husband of **MA'AT/MAYET**; representative of **RA** on earth; (Gr. **HERMES**)
TORUM (Siberia) Ugrian sky god (like **NUM & EC**)
TUONI (Fin.) hellish river god and resident of **TUONELA**; husband of **TUONETAR** and father of **LOVIATAR**
TUPAN (S.Am.) spirit of lightning & thunder who rejects prayers
TYCHE (Gr.) goddess of fortune & abundance (Rom. **FORTUNA**)
VANIR (Norse) family of gods (**NJORD, FREYR, FREIJA**, etc.), enemies of the **AESIR**; associated with fertility & riches
VARUA (Polynesia) the spirits
VATEA (Oceania) perhaps father of **PAPA**; from his eyes emerged the Sun (**TONGA**) and the Moon (**ITI**)
VELNS Baltic/Teutonic devil
VENUS charming Roman goddess of gardens associated with Gr. **APHRODITE**; divine ancestor of the Roman Caesars through **AENEAS** (son of Aphrodite); beloved of **ADONIS**
VESTA Roman goddess of the hearth fire & patroness of bakers; her assistants, the six Vestal Virgins (priestesses)
VIDAR (Norse) son of **ODIN** who killed the monstrous wolf **FENRIR**
VOLKH VOLGA (Slav) werewolf; white bull with golden horns
VOLOS VYELYES (Slav) divinity of cattle
VRTRA (India) see **INDRA**
WEN-TI WEN CH'ANG (Ch.) god of literature
WODAN WODEN/WOTAN (Ger.) see **ODIN**; (Wednesday)
YAKSA (India) tree demon
YU-TZU (Ch.) rain maker with a magic sword
ZAMBA (Cameroon) god and creator, father of the Learned (**N'KOKON**), the Idiot (**OTUKUT**), the Gorilla (**NGI**) and the Chimpanzee (**WO**)
ZEMIS Haitian heroes and spirits
ZETES (Gr.) Argonaut & son of **BOREAS**, the North Wind

ZORYA (Slav) female triad of protectors of the whole universe
ZOSIM (Slav) patron of bee-keepers
6 **ABNOBA** Gallic goddess of hunting (Black Forest)
ADONIS (Gr.) beautiful lover of **APHRODITE/VENUS (ATARGATIS/ ASTARTE)** and son of **SMYRNA (MYRRHA)** by her father **THEIAS**, ruler of Syria; claimed also by Persephone; originally associated with plant life and the Babylonian couple **TAMMUZ & ISHTAR**
AEGEUS (Gr.) King of Athens; like **POSEIDON**, claimant to fatherhood of **THESEUS** (Attic hero) by **AETHRA** from Argolis; husband of exorcist **MEDEA** of Colchis who tried to poison his son **THESEUS**
AEOLUS (Gr.) wind god (Aeolian harp) who tried to help **ODYSSEUS**; eponymous ancestor of Aeolis; see **BIAS, ALCYONE, MELAMPUS**
AEROPE (Gr.) see **ATREUS**
AESHMA (Pers.) incarnation of rage & devastation; Asmodeus in Book of Tobit
AETHER (Gr.) see **EREBUS**
AETHRA (Gr.) suicidal mother of **THESEUS** and guardian & slave of **HELEN**; see **AEGEUS**
AGENOR (Gr.) see **CADMUS & PERSES**
AH-PUCH (C.Am./Maya) god of Death & the ninth hell; skeleton-like
AKHMIN MIN (Eg.) Pan-god of fertility, travellers
ALEYIN (Sem.) son of **BAAL**
ANANDA (India) favourite disciple of **BUDDHA**
ANANTA VASUKI (India) serpent; as 'infinite' another name for **VISHNU**
ANSHAR (Bab.) supreme ruler of heaven above (an-), twin brother and husband of earth below (Ki-shar); both children of **APSU** (the waters around the earth) & **TIAMAT** (the sea) or their twins **LAHMU & LAHAMI**; each a parent of **AN/ANU**
ANUBIS ANPU (Eg.) son of **RA** or **OSIRIS**; god of the dead, funerals etc.; Lord of the mummy; black-skinned, with head of jackal or dog
ANUKET ANQET/ANQUET (Eg.) goddess of the Nile and the Cataracts; second wife of **KHNUM**; sister of **SATI**, his first wife
APOLLO (Gr. & Rom.) deity of light and later sun god; also associated with healing & prophecy & herds; see **DIANA, IASO, ION, LINUS, MIDAS**
ARAWAN (Gr.) see **PRYDERI**
AREMHA (Polynesia) spirits of ancestors, as gods
ARJUNA (India) see **INDRA**
ASGARD (Norse) the abode of the **AESIR** gods
ASHMAN (Sum.) grain goddess
ASHTAR Phoenician patron goddess of Carthage, as Venus
ASOPUS (Gr.) river god; husband of nymph **MEROPE**; father of **AEGINA**
ASSHUR (Ass.) see **ASHUR**
ATABEI (Haiti) father of **JOCA-HUVA**, god in heaven
ATANUA (Oceania) see **ATEA**
ATHENA ATHENE (Gr.) unmarried & childless goddess of war; protectress of Athens and wise counsellor; see **NIKE, CECROPS**
ATREUS (Gr.) son of **PELOPS** of Mycenae & Hippodamia; father of Agamemnon & **MENELAUS**; his son Pleisthenes by **AEROPE** was killed by **ATREUS'** younger brother **THYESTES**, father of **PELOPIA**
ATUGAN Mongolian mother goddess
AUGEAS (Gr.) King of Elis whose manure-filled stables were cleaned in one day – one of the labours of **HERCULES** who directed the rivers Alpheus & Peneius to flush out these stables for him
AURORA (Rom.) the dawn wind; see **EOS**
AVATAR (India) bestial or human incarnation on earth of a god (**VISHNU**)
BACABS (Yucatán/Maya) four wind gods and brothers, placed by their supreme god at the four points of the compass to support the sky; patrons of bee-keepers
BAIAME (Australia) omnipotent father & hero
BALDER (Norse) see **BALDR**
BANNIK (Slav) spirit of the baths
BASTET see **BAST**
BENDIS (Gr.) moon-goddess wife of **DIONYSUS**
BESTLA (Norse) wife of **BOR**; see **ODIN**
BICUDO (Brazil/Indian) fish with beaklike jaw
BOREAS (Gr.) winged North Wind who kidnapped Oreithyia (daugher of the King of Athens) and had two sons by her, **CALAIS & ZETES**; see **EOS**
BRIGIT BRIGANTIA (Celtic) poetic

goddess of arts & crafts (confused with **DANU**) who had three namesakes, daughters of **DAGDA** (Rom. **MINERVA**)
BRIXIA (Celtic) wife of **LUXOVIUS**
BRAHMA (India) Hindu four-faced creator god who emerged from a lotus of **VISHNU**'s navel (or from a golden egg) to become part of the trinity after **SIVA**; identified with Vedic Prajapati (creator); married to **SAVITRI** and **SARASVATI** (or **SATARUPA**)
BROMIO (Gr.) **DIONYSUS** when roaring
BUDDHA Bodhisattva (India) whose mother, Queen Maya, dreamt he entered her womb as a little white elephant; founder of Buddhism
CADMUS (Gr.) son of **AGENOR** (King of Tyre) who founded Thebes and married **HARMONIA**, and brought writing to Greece
CALAIS & ZETES, sons of **BOREAS**, later slain by **HERCULES** & changed into **NE** winds 'Prodromes' (ahead of the rising Dog Star); an **ARGONAUT**
CASIUS (Gr.) mountain abode of myth. Khazzi people; near Antioch/Antakya
CASTOR & POLLUX (Rom.) (Etruscan Kastur & Pultuke) prominent deities of the Roman cavalry & protectors of sailors & travellers
CAUTES (Pers.) symbol of dawn
CH'ANG-O (Ch.) the Moon
CHARON ferryman for the underworld
CHASCA Inca male page to the Sun
CH'IH YU CHI-YOU (Ch.) monster with iron head
CHI-LIN (Ch.) friendly unicorn and, like the stork, herald of babies; patron of the saintly and wise
CONSUS Italian deity of agriculture whose festival days spelt a holiday for horses & mules; colleague of **OPS**
COYOTE (N.Am.) greatest hero of N.Am. Indian tribes; clever trickster; see **RAVEN**
CREUSA (Gr.) see **ION**
CRONUS (Gr.) son of **URANUS & GAIA** and father of **ZEUS**; see **RHEA & HADES**
CURCHE (Baltic) see **KURKE**
CUYCHA Inca rainbow god
CYBELE (Gr.) goddess of caverns & earth; married **ATTIS**, then **GORDIUS** (of the knot); their son **MIDAS** succeeded
DAEMON (Gr.) supernatural evil power
DAEVAS (Pers.) evil power, as devil
DANAUS (Gr.) father of fifty murderous daughters & twin brother of **AEGYPTUS**; see **AMYMONE**
DAPHNE (Gr.) nymph, daughter of river Peneius; desired by **APOLLO**, she barely escaped, called for help from **GAEA** & disappeared into a new chasm from which a laurel soon grew; **APOLLO** made this sacred to her memory
DEIMOS Fear; see **ARES**
DEVANA a Czech **DIANA**
DOGODA (Slav) the West Wind
DUMUZI (Sum.) presided over fertility & regeneration in many forms; as wild bull, son of **NINSUN**; as **DUMUZI-ABZU**, god of the marshland
EREBUS (Gr.) Darkness born of Chaos and incestuous brother of **NYX** (Night), fathering Day and **AETHER** (Sky)
EUROPA (Gr.) daughter of **PHOENIX** or of **AGENOR**, King of Phoenicia (Lebanon) & Telephasso; captivated & captured by new bull in her herd, **ZEUS**, who when she climbed onto him plunged into the sea to reach southern Crete where she gave birth to **MINOS**, Rhadamanthus & Sarpedon, each adopted by **EUROPA**'s new husband, King Asterius
FAUNUS (It.) prophetic divinity of the countryside; father or husband of **FAUNA/FATUA**; (Gr. **PAN**); see **MAIA**, **PICUS**
FENG-PO (Ch.) releaser of winds from goatskin sack; transformed into female **P'O-P'O**
FENRIR (Norse) wolf-giant son of **LOKI**, once chained but escaped for **RAGNARÖK** (Armageddon) where he swallowed **ODIN**, whose son **VIDAR** in turn killed **FENRIR**
FREYJA (Norse) many-sided goddess with magic powers presiding over fertility, wealth, love & death; produced golden tears; wife of hammer-snatcher **THRYM**; daughter of **NJORD**
GANESA (India) elephant-headed son of **SIVA** and **PARVATI**; ejects barriers
GARUDA (India) god and bird; mount of **VISHNU**
GAUNAB (Africa) Hottentot vicious demon
GEFION (Norse) fertility goddess & patroness of virgins whose sons were cloaked as oxen & ploughed out (Danish) Zealand (as an island) from Sweden, leaving empty lake Vänern
GRAIAE (Gr.) the three grey sisters of

the Gorgons with only one eye to share – taken from them by Perseus (**DINO, ENYO, PEMPHREDO**)

GRI-GRI (Sudan) clan spirit

GURUHI (Africa) vicious god able to poison humans

HAEMUS (Gr.) one of the mountain abodes (Thrace) of the hundred-headed monster **TYPHON**, son of **TARTARUS & GAIA**

HARITI KISHI-MOJIN (Jap.) Buddha changed her from child-eating monster to protectress of children; female counterpart of **KAN-NON**

HATHOR ATHYR (Eg.) mother goddess with cow's horns in attendance at the birth of a pharaoh; associated with festivity & love; daughter of **NUT** (Sky) and **RE**; linked with Aphrodite, **ARTEMIS, DIANA, JUNO** and Sem. **ASTARTE**

HECATE (Gr.) Carian divinity of fertility & witchcraft; daughter of **PERSES** (Titan) & **ASTERIA** (nymph); promoter of wealth & influential over heaven, earth and the sea; famous for her pillars (Hecataea) and protection of doorways & crossroads; see **SCYLLA**

HELIOS (Gr.) the Sun god who sailed to Rhodes in a crescent moon bowl where he mated with the nymph **RHODAS** and became the ancestor of the Rhodosians; see **EOS**

HELLEN (Gr.) ancestor of all the Greeks (named after his sons **AEOLUS & DORUS**, and grandsons **ION & ACHAEUS**); King of Phthia and grandson of **PROMETHEUS**

HEPATU Hittite Queen of gods standing on a panther; Hurrian **HEBAT**

HERMES (Gr.) bearded messenger and fertility god from Arcadia, linked with the Cabeiri and Roman **MERCURY**

HOENIR (Norse) fellow-traveller with **ODIN, LOKI** and **LODUR** who gave a soul to the trees

HUN-TUN (Ch.) Chaos, depicted as long-haired dog

ICARUS (Gr.) flew too high on homemade wings and drowned near Icaria island; son of **DAEDALUS**, sculptor and architect (Labyrinth/Crete)

IKTOMA (N.Am./Sioux) invisible being who formed the world

INANNA (Sum.) goddess of the Netherworld

INTOTA (N.Am.) Sun god

IOLAUS (Gr.) helped his labouring uncle **HERCULES** with the killing of the Hydra

ISHTAR (Ass./Bab.) (Sum. **INANNA**) variously described as goddess of the morning & evening star **VENUS**, as a warrior & as goddess of love, harlots & courtesans; daughter of **ANU** or **SIN**; as the 'star of lamentation' stirring up quarrels & breaking friendships; threatened the release of the dead back to earth if thwarted; left her lovers worse off, but was revered as the omnipotence of love; see **ASTARTE**

ITZANA (N.Am.) the Great God of the Lacandones Indians

IXCHEL (N.Am.) moon goddess and vicious woman

JUMALA (Fin.) ancestor of **UKKO**; 'god' in Finnish

KAN-NON (Jap.) protective deity

KAUKIS Baltic dwarfs and guardians of homes

KEELUT (Eskimo) dog-like vicious earth demon

KHEPAT Hurrian wife of **TESHUP**

KHEPER KHEPRI (Eg.) sun-pushing scarab or man with a scarab on his head; the rising sun **RA**

KHNEMU (Eg.) see **KHNUM**

KHONSU (Eg.) see **KHONS**

KHURRI (Hurrian) see **SHERI**

KOSHAR KOTHAR (Bab.) divinity of arts & crafts; palace-builder to **BAAL**

KRICCO (Slav) guardian of orchards

KRIMBA Bohemian house divinity

KUBABA Hittite **CYBELE**

KUPALA (Slav) associated with herbs & trees

KVASIR (Norse) a man of surpassing wisdom created by the saliva of the **AESIR** & the **VANIR**; killed by 2 dwarfs who mixed his blood with honey; this became the mead of the gods, hydromel, dispensed by **ODIN** to poets in favour

LAKSMI SRI (India) wife of **VISHNU**

LAUFEY (Norse) see **LOKI**

LOTHIA (Fiji) ruler of the Netherworld

LYCAON (Gr.) Mountain and king of Arcadia whose family was turned into wolves by **ZEUS**

MANALA TUONELA/POHJOLA (Fin.) home of **LOUHI**, goddess of the dead – like **TUONELA** of **TUONI**; entered over bridge or by boat

MANNUS (Ger.) son of giant **TUISTO**; sired the forefathers of 3 main Germanic tribes

MARAWA (Australia) strong, forceful spirit
MARDUK (Ass.) oldest son of **EA & APSU**; personified creation & fertility & the growth of Babylon, becoming leading god; he defeated **TIAMAT**, goddess of the sea, floods & primitive chaos & organized the world, regulating the heaven & the stars; see **LAHMU**
MARICI MARISHI-TEN Buddhist and Tibetan three-headed sunrise god
MARUTS RUDRAS (India) young storm gods of the clouds; rain-givers
MASAYA Nicaraguan lord of volcanoes
MEDUSA (Gr.) one of the 3 Gorgons; seduced by **POSEIDON** in the temple of Athene who revenged herself by turning **MEDUSA**'s hair into snakes; decapitated by **PERSEUS**, her blood gave birth to the horse **PEGASUS**
MEGARA (Gr.) wife of **HERCULES**
MEIDEN Baltic hare god
MEMNON (Gr.) Lord of Ethiopia; son of Tithonus & **EOS**, supporter of Priam; killed Antilochus, son of Nestor, but in turn died by the hand of Achilles at Troy
MENTHU (Eg.) see **MONT & BUKHE**
MERWER (Eg.) bull sacred to Ra-Atum (Gr. **MNEVIS**)
METION (Gr.) see **DAEDALUS**
MEULER (Chile) god of waterspout (and whirlwinds & typhoons)
MINEPA (Mozambique) evil spirit
MITHRA (Pers.) Creator who killed the bull from whose blood life sprang; trusted helper of **AHURA MAZDA**; bestower of rain and patron god of the Roman army; sun god; see **RASHNU**
MNEVIS (Eg.) see **MERWER**
MOKADI (Cameroon) a spirit
MOKOSH (Slav) divinity of domesticated animals
MOTRES MATRONAE (Gaul) Mother Goddess
MULUKU (Mozambique) the highest being
MYRRHA (Gr.) see **ADONIS**
NAREAU (Oceania/Gilbert I.) maker of Heaven & Earth
NANSHE (Ass./Bab.) goddess of springs & canals; daughter of **ENKI/EA**
NEMHED (Celtic) see **MACHA**
NEREUS (Gr.) old Aegean sea god, son of **PONTUS**; father of the sea nymphs **NEREIDS**
NERGAL (Sum.) ruled the Kingdom of the Dead, whom he could recall to life, with his consort Allatum
NGAHUE (N.Z.) Lord of the dead & thunder
NINHAR (Sum.) rain & weather god & roaring bull responsible for the greening of the desert; son of **NANNA & NINGAL** (or **ENKI & NINHURSAG**); husband of **NINIGARA**
NINIGI (Jap.) divine ancestor of the emperors of Japan whose grandmother was Amaterasu (sun goddess); her gifts, the jewel, mirror and sword, are Imperial emblems
NINLIL BELTIS (Ass./Bab.) fertility goddess; see **ASHUR/ASSHUR, ENLIL & BEL**
NINSUN (Ass./Bab.) all-knowing mother of all-seeing Gilgamesh, the hero of the Babylonian 'national' poem
NINTUD (Sum.) see **MAMI**
NOMIOS (Gr.) **APOLLO** as lord of herdsmen
NYAMIA (Guinea) supreme god
OENEUS (Gr.) King of Calydon, Aetolia who neglected to make **ARTEMIS** a due offering of his fruit harvest & therefore saw his domains ransacked & his family perish by the fury of a monster bull; see **ALTHAEA & DEIANIRA**
OENGUS (Irish) son of **DAGDA**; an Irish **EROS**
OILEUS (Gr.) see **AJAX**
OLOFAD (Micronesia) ascended to Heaven; divides his time between it & the Earth
ONATHA (N.Am./Iroquois) goddess of Wheat, for ever sacred of searching for the Dew after being kidnapped by the evil spirit
OPHOIS Wepwawet (Eg.) see **UPUAUT**
ORENDA (N.Am./Iroquois) divine force and vigour in Nature
ORMAZD OHRMAZD (Pers.) omnipotent first man who sprang from **ZURVAN**
OSIRIS (Eg.) father of **HORUS**; supreme god & ruler of the Dead; son of **NUT & GEB**; see **ISIS, UPUAUT & BENNU**
PADURI (Siberia/Altaic) lord of the reinder
PALLAS (Gr.) four namesakes: a) son of **EVANDER**; b) a giant killed by **ATHENE**; c) a Titan; d) Attic idol, brother of **AEGEUS**; (Pallantids, his sons)
PANDIA (Gr.) beautiful daughter of **SELENE**
PELEUS (Gr.) father of **ACHILLES** by

nereid Thetis; he inadvertently killed his father-in-law & caused his wife **ANTIGONE** to hang herself believing she had been deceived

PELOPS (Gr.) son of **TANTALUS** whom Poseidon befriended; uncle of Agamemnon

PERSES (Gr.) son of **PERSEUS** (King of Argos) & Andromeda; perhaps myth. founder of Persia

PHANES (Gr.) first divinity, born from an egg; married Night and begat Heaven & Earth

PHOBOS (Gr.) see **ARES & DEIMOS**

PHOEBE (Gr.) bright titaness & daughter of **URANUS & GAIA**; mother of **LETO**; associated with the moon

PILLAN (Chile/Araucanians) thunderbolt

PLUTUS (Gr.) wealthy son of **DEMETER** & the Titan **IASION**

POLLUX (Rom.) see **CASTOR**

POMONA Roman divinity of orchards

PONTUS (Gr.) most ancient divine embodiment of the sea (Black Sea) and waters; incestuous son of **GAIA**; father of **NEREUS, EURYBIA, THAUMAS, PHORCYS** and **CETO**

PURUSA (India) primal man from whose body the universe emerged

RAGANA Lithuanian werevolves

RASHNU (Pers.) one of a trio of judges (Mithra, Sraosha) deciding the fates of the souls of the deceased

RESHEF (Eg.) god of war with head of gazelle

RHODAS (Gr.) see **HELIOS**

RUDRAS (India) storm gods; see **RUDRA & MARUTS**

SATURN SATURNUS Roman grain god and patron of sowing; colleague of **OPS** and **CONSUS**; (Gr. **CRONUS**); see **LUA & PICUS**

SATYRS (Gr.) creatures of the wild, part man, part goat; male counterparts of nymphs; (It. **FAUNS**)

SCYLLA (with Charybdis) female monster of Straits of Messina, devoured sailors; though killed by **HERCULES**, she was revived by Phorcys, her father

SEKHET (Eg.) see **SEKHMET**

SEKUME (Africa) second after **FAM**, the first man; made **MBONGWE**, his wife from a tree

SELENE (Gr.) moon goddess whom **PAN** lured into the forest with white fleece; wife of **ZEUS**; mother of **PANDIA**; daughter of **HYPERION & THEIA** (Titans); sister/daughter of **HELIOS & EOS**; (Rom. **LUNA**)

SEMELE (Gr.) daughter of **CADMUS** immolated when forced to witness her lover **ZEUS** in all his glory by jealous **HERA**; **ZEUS** carried her child **DIONYSUS** until the destined time of birth

SHAKAN (Sum.) see **UTU**

SILENI Phrygian river genii, waterhorse beings, including Marsyas; see **SATYRS**

SIRENS (Gr.) 2 female-faced hawks, sometimes mermaids, on the rocks of Straits of Messina, sang to lure seamen into shipwreck & massacre; Ulysses/**ODYSSEUS** was warned by **CIRCE**, stopped the ears of his crew while he was tied to the mast to listen to Alerta and Alclara, and so his ship passed unharmed; see **ACHELOUS**

SKANDA (India) see **SIVA**

SMYRNA (Gr.) see **ADONIS**; now modern Izmir, port of Turkey

SPHINX (eg.) body of lion (or ram or goat), head of lion, later replaced by that of Pharaoh; (Gr.) a monster; lion with female's face & breast & bird's wings, guarded the way to Thebes, famous for challenging wayfarers with tricky questions, with death for failure; **OEDIPUS** solved the riddle 'what has 4 legs, then 2 legs & finally 3 legs?' as man (infancy, maturity, old age); thereupon the **SPHINX** jumped to death into the sea

SVAROG (Slav) god of the sky; father of Svarogich, a fire god

TAATOA (Oceania/Society I.) made the earth and the sea

TAKARO (New Hebrides) he organized cosmos

TAMMUZ TAMMUZI (Sum.) forerunner of **DUMUZI**; pastoral grain god & shepherd with a large following; son of **ENKI & DUTTUR**; husband of **INANNA/ISHTAR**; see **ADONIS**

TARHUN TARHUND (Hittite) see **TELEPINU & WURUSEMU**

TAWALS Polish divinity in charge of the welfare of fields

TEFNUT TEFNET (Eg.) lioness or lion-headed woman with solar disc; diety of dew & moisture; sister and wife of **SHU**

TELLUS Roman earth divinity receiving pregnant cow as sacrifice

TENGRI (Siberia) both good and bad demons
TESHUB TESHUP Hittite weather god victorious over **KUMARBI**; see **SHERI**
TETHYS (Gr.) incestuous mother of the Oceanids & **STYX**; sister & wife of **OCEANUS**; daughter of **URANUS & GAIA**; see **TYCHE**
THEIAS (Gr.) see **ADONIS**
THEMIS (Gr.) consort of **ZEUS**; mother of the Seasons & the Fates; daughter of **GAIA**; prophetess
TIAMAT (Sum.) primeval salt water & sea who gave birth to the gods; wife and mother of **KINGU** (or **APSU**); killed by **MARDUK**
T'IEN-MU (Ch.) goddess of lightning with blazing mirrors
TINNIT Carthaginian chief goddess of fertility; consort of **BAAL HAMMON**; Sem. **ASTARTE**
TIRAWA (N.Am.) the Great Chief; see **ATIRA**
TITYUS (Gr.) son of **GAIA** by a giant; tried to assail **LETO** and was killed by her children **APOLLO & ARTEMIS** (or **ZEUS**); ended as a square meal of liver for vultures
TLALOC (C.Am./Aztec) god of rain, thunder & lightning
TODOTE Samoyed divinity of Death and illwill
TORANN (Irish) Thunder; (Gallo-Roman **TORANIS/TARASUS**)
TRITON (Gr.) sea-god, son of **POSEIDON** & Amphitrite; a merman with crayfish claws who lived near Libya & enjoyed blowing his conch (shell) trumpet to terrify enemies; **TRITON** also appeared in a sea-chariot drawn by Centaurs with crawfish claws; he also lasciviously ravished women on shore
TUISTO (Ger.) giant father of **MANNUS**, the hermaphrodite first man
TUNGAT TUMRAT (Eskimo) spirits of locality
TUWATA (Hittite) see **KAL**
TYDEUS (Gr.) brain-eater & brother of Melanippus; father of **DIOMEDES**
TYPHON (Gr.) hundred-headed winged monster, half man, half serpent, with thunderous voice who threw **ZEUS** (later rescued by **HERMES & PAN**) into a cave in Cilicia; fled to Sicily and was crushed under Mt Etna by **ZEUS**; son of **GAIA & TARTARUS**; husband of **ECHIDNA**; see **HAEMUS**
UPUAUT (Eg.) wolf- or jackal-headed conqueror of the world together with **OSIRIS & ANUBIS**; he was at the head of the procession at Osirian festivals
URANUS (Gr.) god of an incestuous heaven; made his chaotic wife and mother **GAIA** fertile with rain; she gave birth to the Titans, Ceclopes and hundred-handed Hecatoncheires; attacked and overthrown by his son **CRONUS**; the giants and ash-tree nymphs arose from the blood of **URANUS'** testicles, and from the genital foam in the sea came Aphrodite, goddess of love; see **RHEA & PHOEBE**
USUKUN (C.Am./Maya) hater of humans & brother of **HAPIKERN**
VAHRAM (Pers.) bull, white horse, camel, ram, bird, wild goat; also youth and a warrior
VARUNA (India) Sky, one supreme being
VASUKI (India) see **ANANTA**
VISHNU (India) Hindu guardian of the world known through **RAMA, KRISHNA** and other incarnations (avatars); renewer of moral order; husband of **LAKSMI/SRI** and Bhumidevi; see **ANANTA & GARUDA**
VULCAN VULCANUS (Rom.) one of earliest gods (pre-dating Jupiter); married **JUNO**, earth goddess **MAIA**, & **VESTA**, father of **CACUS**, a **SATYR** killed by **HERCULES**, & in turn Servius Tullus, King of Rome; **VULCAN** was sun god, the thunderbolt & power of fire, later warmth, heating
VU-NUNA (Ugric/Votyak) water deity
VU-VOLO (Ugric/Votyak) water deity
XOLOTL (C.Am./Aztec) dog-headed god who created present mankind out of bloodied dried bones; twin of chief deity the Feathered Snake (Quetzalcoatl)
YANTHO (C.Am./Maya) brother of **USUKUN & HAPIKERN**
YARILO (Slav) deity of love and happiness
YASODA (India) mother of **KRISHNA** by adoption
ZETHUS & Amphion (Gr.) twins born in a thicket to **ZEUS** & Antiope & for a while cared for by shepherds; attacked Thebes & killed Lycus & his wife Dirce; see **NIOBE**

7 **ABELLIO** Gallic divinity of the apple tree

ACHERON (Gr.) river of Woe in **HADES** near Epirus
ADMETUS (Gr.) **ZEUS** punished **APOLLO** for the murder of the Cyclopses, makers of the thunderbolt that had killed **APOLLO**'s son Asclepius (father of medicine), by sending **APOLLO** to serve at the court of **ADMETUS**; there **APOLLO** (Nomios) played the lyre & looked after the king's mares & ewes
AHRIMAN (Pers.) evil spirit; see **GAYOMART**
ALCYONE (Gr.) one of the 7 Pleiades & daughter of **AEOLUS**, god of the winds
ALTHAEA (Gr.) mother of **MELEAGER** & wife of **OENEUS**, King of Calydon
AMYMONE (Gr.) fountain & spring; mother of **NAUPLIUS** by **POSEIDON**; one of fifty murderous daughters of **DANAUS**
ANDARTA ANDRASTA (Celtic) warrior goddess
APOPHIS (Eg.) see **APEPI**
ARIADNE (Gr.) daughter of King Minos of Crete; took pity on **THESEUS**, sent by Athens to kill the cannibal **MINOTAUR**; she, with **DAEDALUS**, gave **THESEUS** the thread-spinning spider that showed **THESEUS** the way out of the Labyrinth by retracing his steps; when he had killed the **MINOTAUR**, she escaped with **THESEUS** to Naxos where he left her; later **DIONYSUS** claimed her, resulting in the sons Oenopion, Euanthes & Staphylus
ASTARTE (Sem.) great goddess of fertility associated with **ISHTAR/ ATHTAR, ARTEMIS, DIANA, JUNO** & Aphrodite, and also Hebrew **ASHTORETH**, and Atargatis; see **ANATH** and **ADONIS**
ASTERIA (Gr.) see **HECATE**
ATAKSAK (Eskimo) joyful spirit living in Heaven
AUDUMLA (Norse) cow and wet-nurse (made of molten hoar frost) of the giant **AURGELMIR**'s (**YMIR**'s) six-headed son; she formed **BURI** (grandfather of **ODIN** and his brothers who later killed Aurgelmir) by passing her tongue over stones; created the sky and the earth from his corpse
AUGUSTA (Celtic/Rom.) see **EPONA**
AUMANIL (Eskimo) land-based guide of whales
BACCHUS Roman wine god; (It. **LIBER**) (Gr. **DIONYSUS**)
BALANZA (Africa) lord of the trees
BANADED (Eg.) ram, incarnation of the soul of **OSIRIS**; (Gr. **MENDES**)
BELENUS (Celtic) connected with the sun & fire; widely revered pastoral god; (Gr. **APOLLO**)
BELLONA DUELLONA Roman goddess of war; perhaps sister or wife of **MARS**; see **MA**
BHARATA (India) see **RAMA**
BRIDGET (Celtic) see **BRESS & BRIGHT**
BUXENUS Gallic divinity of the box-tree
CABEIRI (Gr.) major divinities of Samothrace
CALYPSO (Gr.) daughter of **ATLAS & TETHYS**, who was told by **ZEUS** to let **ODYSSEUS/ULYSSES** go after her 7 years of bliss with him on her isle of Ortygia where he had been cast ashore by a storm
CAMENAE (Rom.) prophetic nymphs, a.o. Antevorta (the past), Postvorta (the future) & Carmenta, mother of Evander by Mercury
CAMILLA (Rom.) huntress taught by her father **METABUS**; warrior and friend of **DIANA**
CAMULON (Celtic) see **COU**
CECROPS (Gr.) cultured, dragon-like arbitrator between **ATHENA & POSEIDON** and first King of Attica
CHU-LUNG CHU-YING (Ch.) reptile with human face whose eyes when open brought daylight and, when shut, made night fall, and whose changing breath brought on the seasons
CLYMENE (Gr.) Oceanid & mother of Prometheus & perhaps **ATLAS**; see **ASIA**
COCYTUS (Gr.) tributary of **ACHERON** (NW Gr.) & one of the rivers of **HADES**
CORONIS (Gr.) mother of Asclepius (god of healing) who was shot by **ARTEMIS**
CUMHALL (Celtic) see **COU**
CURETES (Gr.) young protectors of the baby **ZEUS**
CYLLENE (Gr.) sacred mountain in Arcadia where **HERMES** was born in a cave to **ZEUS & MAIA**
DAPHNIS (Gr.) shepherd son of **HERMES** born near Etna
DAZBORG DAZHBOG Russian sun god
DEMETER (Gr.) daughter of **CRONUS & RHEA**; corn maiden & goddess of fertility, harvests, marriage & laws; her Megara temples in the forest were centres of orgies: Eleusinian

mysteries; **POSEIDON**, as a stallion, seduced her & she bore the speaking horse **ARION** & daughter Despoena; after the kidnap of her daughter **KORE** by **HADES**, all natural growth on earth ceased until her parents **RHEA & ZEUS** made a compromise, claiming her daughter's presence 2/3 of the year, granting **HADES** 1/3 – hence the seasons

DIIWICA Serbian **DIANA**

DOMOVOI (Slav) hairy spirit of the house in human shape, sometimes with horn & tail; silky fur even on palms of hands

DWYNWEN (Welsh) see **DWYN**

ECHIDNA (Gr.) half woman, half snake; wife of **TYPHON**; mother of **CERBERUS**, the Hydra, the **CHIMAERA** & the Nemean lion

EK-CHUAH (C.Am./Maya) divine patron of cacao growers & traders; also connected with war and death

EMAKONG (Australia) a traveller in the Netherworld of ophidian men who took back fire and the night

ENIPEUS (Gr.) river god of Elis; loved by **TYRO**; mother of **AESON**

ERIGONE (Gr.) suicidal daughter of the Athenian **ICARIUS**

EURYALE (Gr.) see **ORION**

EURYBIA (Gr.) with heart of steel; daughter of **PONTUS**

EVANDER (Gr.) son of **HERMES** associated with **PAN**; see **CAMENAE**

FERIDUN (Pers.) see **IREJ**

FERONIA Roman/Etruscan divinity of springs and fertility

FJORGYN (Norse) see **JORD**

FORTUNA Roman **TYCHE** (Gr.)

FU-HSING (Ch.) see **FU**

FYLGJUR female Germanic protective spirit

GALATEA (Gr.) sea nymph who preferred **ACIS** (son of **FAUNUS**) to large one-eyed Polyphemus

GLAUCUS (Gr.) a) son of King **MINOS** by **PASIPHAË** & brother of **ARIADNE**; b) sea god, son of **POSEIDON**

GOIBNIU Irish smith; (Welsh **GOFANNON**)

GORDIUS (Gr.) Phrygian king who tied the Gordian knot (cut by Alexander the Great); father of **MIDAS**

GUMONGO (N.Am./Guacure Indians) rules the northern half of the sky

GWYDION (Welsh) cultured son of the sky god **DON** and brother & husband of **ARANRHOD** (Fertility); father of the twins **DYLAN** (Sea) and **LLEU** (Irish **LUG**) for whom he made a wife out of flowers

HANUMAN (India/Jap.) red-faced monkey in human shape, born of the wind and a nymph; adventurous – on solo flight to the Himalayas to collect healing herbs; giant jumper across to Ceylon, or clever spy to retrieve **RAMA**'s wife **SITA** from the clutches of the demon **RAVANA**

HARPIES (Gr.) these tempest-goddesses, Podarge, the ravisher, Aello & Ocypete were winged & as fast as the wind; later these appear as monsters, birds with bear's ears, old hags & as birds with strong claws stealing food from the table; attacked & defeated by the Argonauts, they finally fled

HELICON (Gr.) highest mountain in Boeotia (Gulf of Corinth); favoured place of the Muses where **PEGASUS** gave them a fountain by stamping with his hoof

HIPPIOS (Gr.) **POSEIDON** when associated with horses

HUNAB-KU (C.Am./Maya) father of **ITZAMNA**

HURAKAN (C.Am./Maya) divinity of thunder and tornado

IACCHUS (Gr.) son of **ZEUS & DEMETER** (or **DIONYSUS & KORE**/Persephone) welcomed at the Eleusinian Mysteries)

IAPETUS (Gr.) a Titan and son of **URANUS & GAIA**; father of **ATLAS**, Prometheus, Epimetheus and Menoetius

ICARIUS (Gr.) king of Attica & host to **DIONYSUS**; murdered by his intoxicated shepherds; father of **ERIGONE** who found his grave

INDRANI (India) wife of **INDRA**

INTONAN (C.Am.) Aztec Earth goddess

IOCASTE JOCASTA (Gr.) wife of **LAIUS**

ITZAMNA (C.Am./Maya) four-fold cultured lord of heaven who introduced writing and the calendar to mankind and patronized medicine; decided the points of the compass were Red in the East, White/North, Black/West and Yellow/South, and had a skilful female colleague in the moon goddess **IXCHEL**; married to Ix Chebel Yax (Weaving)

IZANAGI & **IZANAMI** (Jap.) eighth incestuous couple after the separation of Heaven & Earth who used a gem-studded spear to stir the primordial soup to create terra firma to stand on instead of their drifting bridge of heaven; on taking a bath, the sun (Amaterasu) sprang from **IZANAGI**'s left eye, the moon from his right one and out of his nose came the storm god **SUSANOVO**; see **YOMI**

JOCASTA IOCASTE (Gr.) mother of **OEDIPUS**; sister of **CREON**

JUPITER JOVIS Roman protector of the state & war god; chief of the triad with **JUNO & MINERVA**; also sky god (Gr. **ZEUS**) whose divine presence was welcomed at harvest & wine festivals; called **FULGUR** as master of the thunderbolt and **LATIARIS** when lording it over the Latin League; often busy with oaths & treaties; god of light & weather & of the Roman Games, chariot races, athletic contests; see **TAGES**

KANTAKA (India) the horse of **BUDDHA**

KIVUTAR (Fin.) divinity of illness and pain

KHOVAKI SAVAKI (Siberia) creator and protective spirits of the shaman

KRISHNA (India) born of **VASUDEVA & DEVAKI** (sister of **KAMSA**, vicious king of **MATHURA**) but cared for by a cowherd (**NANDA**) and his wife **YASODA**; this eighth incarnation of **VISHNU** humiliated the storm god **INDRA**; in love with **RADHA**, but married **RUKMINI**

KUEI-HIU (Ch.) unfathomable crater into which all the waters of the world flow or emerge from

KUKUKAN (C.Am./Maya) feathered serpent divinity

KUMARBI Hurrian heir to **ANU** who was defeated by **TESHUB**; fathered monstrous stone **ULLIKUMMI**; depicted standing on the shoulders of **UPELBURI** (Atlas)

LAELAPS (Gr.) hound of **CEPHALUS**

LAMASSU or **SHEDU** (Ass./Bab.) good, protective genii, often depicted as winged bulls with human heads

LAPITHS (Gr.) see **CENTAURS**

LEANDER (Gr.) see **HERO**

LEI-KUNG (Ch.) lord of thunder and Taoist gruesome divinity who punishes men guilty of hidden crimes

LIBANZA (Congo) God of the Upotos, who gave immortality & 2 days' rest each month to the moon

LOPEMAT Latvian protectress of cattle

LYNCEUS (Gr.) see **AEGYPTUS**

MAAN-ENO Estonian fertility deity and consort of **UKKO**

MAMALDI (Siberia/Amur) wife of **KHADAU** with whom, as the first human couple, she brought **ASIA & SAKHALIN** into existence before he killed her; shamans

MAMMITU (Ass./Bab.) bestower of Destiny on the new-born; see **MAMI**

MANITOU MANITOUS (N.Am./Algonquins) mystical & clever forces of nature

MARSABA (Oceania) divinity of the Netherworld and vile spirit

MARSYAS (Gr.) river god & satyr; defeated **APOLLO** in flute contest and was flayed alive by him; (tributary of the Meander river)

MELQART most important god of Tyre and chief of the Carthagean pantheon; (Rom **HERCULES**)

MERCURY Roman patron of traders; son of **MAIA**; (Gr. **HERMES**)

METABUS Roman; see **CAMILLA**

MEZAMAT Latvian protectress of wood

MICHABO (N.Am./Algonquin) the Great Hare spirit

MICTLAN (C.Am.) Aztec Netherworld with 9 rivers that the souls of the dead must negotiate, & 9 hells

MIDGARD (Norse) the middle abode where humanity dwelt, situated halfway between Niflheim (for the dead) & Muspellsheim (for the giants); made by the sons of **BOR** from **YMIR**'s body

MINERVA Roman divinity of the arts, war & victory; (Gr. **ATHENA/NIKE**)

MODEINA Polish god of the forest

MORRIGU (Celtic) see **MORRIGAN**

NEKHBET NEKHEBET (Eg.) vulture or vulture-headed goddess of childbirth; winged serpent protecting the pharaoh; daughter of **RE**; wife of **HAPI**; associated with **MUT**; counterpart of **BUTCE**/Lower Egypt

NEPTUNE (Rom.) god of water and the sea, perhaps of Etruscan origin

NEREIDS see nymphs and daughters of **NEREUS**

NERTHUS Germanic peaceloving island-based mother goddess revered by several tribes, including invaders of England, the Angles

NINMAKH NINTUR/ARURU/NINHURSAG (Sum.) guardian of animal birth & bestower of desert wildlife
NINURTA NINGURSU/IMDUGUD/ANZU (Sum.) god of rain, floods & thunder; son of ENLIL & NINLIL and husband of BAU/NINNIBRU
NYIAMIA NYAMIA (Guinea) chief god
NYIKANG (Africa/Nile) his grandfather OMARA came from Heaven as the first man – or his ancestry traced to the first cow
OCEANUS (Gr.) the river surrounding the flat earth and forefather of the gods as son of URANUS & GAIA; husband of TETHYS (Titaness) & father of thousands of stream spirits & sea nymphs; see STYX
OEDIPUS (Gr.) incestuous son of LAIUS (King of Thebes) & JOCASTA who unknowingly killed his father & married his mother; see SPHINX
OGYRVAN Arthurian giant; father of Guinevere
OHDOVAS (N.Am.) midgets below the earth who control poisonous monsters
OHRMAZD (Pers.) see ORMAZD
OLUKSAK (Eskimo) divinity of lakes
OLYMPUS (Gr.) site of the throne of ZEUS; abode of gods; highest mountain in Greece (2917 m/ 9370 ft); one of many namesakes in Greece & Asia Minor
ONUPHIS (Eg./Gr.) together with Mneuis/Merwer (Ra Atum) & Buchis/Bukhe (Menthu) sacred bull & soul incarnate of OSIRIS
ORPHEUS (Gr.) skilful musician and son of CALLIOPE (a Muse) and OEAGRUS, Thracian river god (or APOLLO); joined the Argonauts; killed by Thracian women; see EURYDICE
PARVATI (India) the charming lover wife GANESA of SIVA enjoying discoursing metaphysics when so required
PEGASUS (Gr.) winged horse born of dying MEDUSA; see HELICON & SISYPHUS
PELOPIA (Gr.) wife of ATREUS
PENATES (Rom.) the guardian deities of the household, as images, normally 2 to look after the food & wine; shared a place on the hearth by the altar of VESTA. At every meal the first helping was offered to them, see LARES
PERSEUS (Gr.) son of ZEUS & DANAË; he cut off the head of the Gorgon MEDUSA & later rescued Andromeda from being sacrificed to a monster & took her as his wife, retiring to Mycenae; forefather of the Perseids; see ATLAS
PHEBELE (Congo) divine father who by MEBELI begat MAN, a son
PHOENIX (Eg./Gr.) as a sun-eagle immolates itself in fire & flies upwards with life renewed
PHORCYS (Gr.) see PONTUS
POLEVOI POLEVIK (Slav) grass-covered, black lord of the field
POUNTAN (Micronesia) ingenious divinity of cool, light winds
PRIAPUS (Gr.) son of DIONYSUS & Aphrodite, a satyr variation of PAN, with superphallus to fertilize both animals & plants; guardian of seafarers & garden gnome
PROCRIS (Gr.) see CEPHALUS
PROTEUS (Gr.) a prophetic, aged sea-god, son of OCEANUS & TETHYS, was the protector of POSEIDON's seals; (Eg.) king of Egypt who gave protection to Paris & Helen (of Troy)
PRYDERI (Celtic) song of RHIANNON and PWYLL, king of Dyfed (myth. land of abundance) who swopped home with his friend ARAWAN, the ruler of ANNWN (Netherworld)
PYRAMUS & THISBE, Babylonian couple who killed themselves under a mulberry tree (referred to in *Midsummer Night's Dream*/ mechanicals' play)
ROBIGUS Roman divinity of corn rust and mildew
ROMULUS twin brother of REMUS and co-founder of Rome
RUKMINI (India) see KRISHNA
RUSALKA (Slav) aquatic & sylvan divinity; drowned maiden
SAVITRI (India) see BRAHMA
SEKHMET SEKHET (Eg.) lioness or lion-headed goddess of war; wife of PTAH and mother of NEFERTUM, lotus deity; see BAST
SEMARGL (Russia) wind god
SHAMASH (Sem.) (Sum. UTU) a bestower of life and mounted sun god who belonged to the second cosmic triad together with his father SIN and sister & wife ISHTAR/AIA; sirened Justice & Right
SHANG-TI TI CHUN (Ch.) husband of HSI-HO and father of ten suns
SHIKOME (Jap.) demons

SHIVENI Urartian sun god with winged solar disc
SIGMUND (Ger./Scan.) son of **VOLSUNG** with magic weapon
SIPYLON (Gr.) Lydian mountain on which **NIOBE** (daughter of **TANTALUS**) turned into rock after **APOLLO & ARTEMIS** had killed her children
SOKARIS (Eg.) see **SEKER**
SRAOSHA (Pers.) see **RASHNU**
STRIBOG STRIBORG Russian wind god
SURGIVA (India) see **SURYA**
T'AISHAN FUCHUN (Ch.) ruler of Mt T'ai where sacrificial ritual ceremonies and prayers for good crops were held; spiritual fountain of life
TARANIS Welsh thunder & sky god; (Rom. **JUPITER**)
TARHUND TARHUN Hittite weather god; see **TELEPINU & WURUSEMU**
TAUERET APET/OPET (Eg.) divinity of childbirth
TELAMON (Gr.) father of **AJAX**
TELAVEL Baltic heavenly smith who made the sun and the skies
T'EN-LUNG (Ch.) heavenly dragon who may have produced the Universe and all life
TESHEBA bull-mounted Urartian weather god
THAUMAS (Gr.) see **PONTUS**
THAUNAS (Gr.) see **PONTUS**
THESEUS (Gr.) Attic hero & son of **AEGEUS**, ruler of Athens, and **AETHRA** (or of **POSEIDON & AETHRA**); assailed the fire-breathing bull **MARATHON** & the Cretan **MINOTAUR**; fathered Hippolytus (partaker in the Argonautic expedition) by captured Amazon **ANTIOPE**; see **ARIADNE**
TOOTEGA (Eskimo) little woman on island who can walk on water
TORTALI (New Hebrides) ruler of the sun and mate of mortal **AVIN**
TUONELA (Fin.) the Netherworld and home of **TUONI & TUONETAR**, his wife
TUPURAN (N.Am.) killed by **NIPARAYA**; his disciples, absorbed with witchery & magic, were imprisoned in a subterranean cave
VEJAMAT Latvian patroness of the wind
VELLAMO (Fin.) wife of **AHTO/AHTI**
VIZ-ANYA (Hung.) water mother
VIZETOT Nicaraguan divinity of famine
VOLSUNG (Ger./Scan.) saga dynasty of the line of **ODIN**, through 2 generations (Sigi & Rerir) to **VOLSUNG**; thence Sigmund & his son Sigurd/Siegfried are the heroes in Wagner's Ring Cycle
VOSEGUS protective divinity of the forest-covered Vosges
WAKONDA (N.Am./Sioux) great life force and father figure in the sky
YEN-WANG YEN-LO-WANG (Ch.) highest judge in hell; (Indian **YAMA**)
YU-HUANG (Ch.) divine Jade Emperor
YUM-KAAX (C.Am./Maya) god of the forests and maize
YUN T'UNG (Ch.) a youth stirring up the clouds
ZIPACNA (C.Am./Maya) twin brother of **CAPAKRAN**

8 **ACHELOUS** (Gr.) river god; father of the **SIRENS** (killers, deceptive birds)
ACHILLES (Gr.) son of **PELEUS** & the nereid Thetis, a sea nymph, who bathed him in fire for invulnerability but omitted the heel – later the cause of his death in the fall of Troy where he had already killed Hector
AEGYPTUS (Gr.) twin brother of **DANAUS** whose daughters killed all their cousins except **LYNCEUS**
AGDISTIS (Gr./Rom.) great mother goddess; see **CYBELE**
AGLOOLIK (Eskimo) lives under ice; good spirit of the seal cave
AITVARAI Baltic winged spirits
ALCESTIS (Gr.) wife of **ADMETUS**
AMAETHON (Welsh) god of agriculture and third son of **DON**
AMALTHEA AMALTHEA (Gr.) she-goat (or nymph) and foster-mother of **ZEUS** whom she suckled in a cave on Crete
ANGRBODA (Norse) daughter of **LOKI**
ANTICLEA (Gr.) mother of **ODYSSEUS**
ANTIGONE (Gr.) daughter of **JOCASTA** by her son & husband **OEDIPUS**
ARDUINNA Gallic goddess of hunting; **DIANA** of the Ardennes
ARICONTE Brazilian divinity blamed for the deluge
ASTRAEUS (Gr.) see **ZEPHYRUS**
AULANERK (Eskimo) lives nude in the sea; cause for gladness
AWIKWAME North American Indian sacred mountain
BAGBARTU BAGMASHTU Urartian gods
BALARAMA (India) wine-loving, strong serpent-like (Sesa) incarnation of **VISHNU**; half-brother of **KRISHNA**
BHUSANDI (India) crow which flew into **RAMA**'s mouth

CAPAKRAN (C.Am./Maya) divinity of earthquakes and mountains; twin brother of **ZIPACNA**

CATEQUIL Inca deity of thunder & lightning

CENTAURS (Gr.) part man, part horse anarchic mountain denizens and children of **IXION**, king of the **LAPITHS**; chariot-pullers for **DIONYSUS**; mounts for **EROS**

CENTEOTL (C.Am./Aztec) young maize gods

CEPHALUS (Gr.) beloved of **EOS** who made him kill his wife **PROCRIS**, who had given him a magic spear and the hound **LAELAPS**

CERBERUS (Gr.) venomous watchdog of **HADES**, son of the giant Typhoeus & **ECHIDNA**, had 3 heads & welcomed all the dead to **HADES**, to enter but not leave; however, **HERMES** with his flute & **ORPHEUS** with his lyre charmed him, as did also honeycakes; as a labour **HERCULES** lifted him up to earth to make a show of him

CERCOPES (Gr.) twin sons of **OCEANUS & THEIA**; thieves of Ephesus

CHIMAERA CHIMERA (Gr.) fire-breathing female monster (part lion, part goat, part dragon) of Caria & Lycia, killed by **BELLEROPHON**; see **ECHIDNA**

CIPACTLI (C.Am./Aztec) alligator-like divinity

CUKULCAN (Yucatán) the bird-snake & law-giver who came from the West with 19 followers and, after 10 years, sailed away again into the rising sun

DAEDALUS (Gr.) father of **ICARUS**; son of **METION** & descendant of Hephaestus; sculptor, & architect of the Labyrinth in Crete

DARZAMAT Latvian protectress of the garden

DEIANIRA (Gr.) 2nd wife of **HERCULES** who caused his death; sister of **MELEAGER** & daughter of **OENEUS**

DIOMEDES (Gr.) Thracian king whose horses fed on human flesh; see **TYDEUS**

DIONYSUS (Gr.) son of **ZEUS & SELENE**; married **ARIADNE** on Naxos; as god of fecundity, warmth & lust, herds, fruits & wine, often in love with nymphs, he was much associated with Bacchantes, rustic Satyrs, goat-god **PAN, PRIAPUS** & the **CENTAURS** in the woods

DIVIRIKS Baltic rainbow deity

DZIEWONA Polish **DIANA**

ECALCHOT Nicaraguan wind god

ENDYMION (Gr.) shepherd son of **ZEUS** & nymph **CALYCE** (or of **AETHLIUS**, ruler of Elis) fathering fifty daughters in his sleep in a cave on Mt Latmus (Caria) with the mood goddess **SELENE**

EURYDICE (Gr.) wife of **ORPHEUS** killed by a snake bite

FARBAUTI (Norse) giant father of **LOKI**

GAHONGAS (N.Am./Iroquois) dwarfs who live in water rocks

GAYOMART (Pers.) creative force dormant for three thousand years whose golden sperm became mankind after his losing battle with the evil spirit **AHRIMAN**; see **YIMA**

GLUS-KABE GLUS-KAP (N.Am./ Algonquin/Micmac) unselfish killer of a frog monster

GOFANNON Welsh smith; (Irish **GOIBNIU**)

GUCUMATZ (Guatemala) a plumose snake and maker of life who can take the form of different animals as he pleases

HAPIKERN (C.Am./Maya) fiend of the human race; see **YANTHO & USUKUN**

HARMONIA (Gr.) married **CADMUS** with all the gods in attendance; daughter of **ARES** and Aphrodite

HEIMDALL (Norse) an **AESIR** god, guarded the Bifrost (Rainbow bridge) that linked the Asgard gods to mankind & sounded the last trumpet call commencing the final battle of **RAGNARÖK** (Twilight of the Gods) in which he killed **LOKI**, although he died too; born of 9 mothers!

HELLOTIS (Gr.) see **EUROPA**

HERACLES (Gr.) strong son of **ZEUS & ALCMENE** (grandchild of **PERSEUS**) who had to labour for his half-brother Eurystheus; husband of **MEGARA** whom he killed together with their children

HERCULES (Rom.) 12 Labours: 1. to kill the Nemean Lion & obtain the skin of invulnerability; 2. the destruction of the 9-headed Lernaean Hydra; 3. capturing the wild boar of Erymanthus; 4. dispersing the Stymphalian Birds; 5. the Ceryncian Hind; 6. cleaning the Augeian Stables; 7. the Cretan Bull; 8. the mares of **DIOMEDES**; 9. Girdle of

Hippolete; 10. the cattle of Geryon; 11. the golden apples of the Hesperides; 12. the journey to the Underworld

HESPERUS (Gr.) he & his brother Phosphorus appear (as sons of **EOS**) jointly as **VENUS** the morning or evening star; he was also perhaps a son of **ATLAS**; his sons were Daedelion & Ceyx & his daughters (3 or 4) were the **HESPERIDES** (see Classical Miscellany); they were the clouds, or celestial flocks, in the West, near the setting sun, who lived in their garden, watching over the Golden Apples

HUECUVUS (Chile) demon readily able to assume any other form

HYPERION (Gr.) a Titan, ancestor of man; father (with **THEIA**) of **HELIOS** (the Sun) **SELENE** (the Moon), **CIRCE** (debased love) & **EOS** (Dawn/Aurora)

IPHICLES (Gr.) father of **IOLAUS** and mortal half-brother of **HERACLES**

ISMENIUS (Gr.) river god; his son **LINUS** killed by **HERCULES** for trying to teach him how to play the lyre

JELPIN-JA (Ugric/Vogul) sacred rivers and lakes

JOCA-HUVA (Haiti) lord in heaven; see **ATABEI**

JURASMAT Latvian mother of the sea

JUVENTAS Roman goddess of youth; (Gr. **HEBE**)

KAKA-GUIA (Guinea) bull-headed deliverer of the souls of the dead to the chief deity **NYAMIA**

K'RACOCHA Inca high god

KULLERVO (Fin.) shepherd and evil spirit

KUMARBIS Hurrite father of the gods; see **KUMARBI & ANUS**

KUNG-KUNG (Ch.) horned monster whose power-struggle with **SHANG-TI** put heaven askew; see **KAM-FU**

KUSANAGI (Jap.) the sword **SUSANOO** found in the snake-god's tail & which later became one of the 3 emblems of Imperial power

LATIARIS (Rom.) see **JUPITER**

LAUKAMAT Latvian protectress of the field

LOMPSALO Lappish wizard

LOVIATAR (Fin.) black-faced creature with horrible skin, goddess of illness, who gave birth to nine monsters; see **TUONI**

LUKELONG (Oceania) female creator of heaven and earth

LUXOVIUS (Celtic) god of the baths and healing married to **BRIXIA**

MAMA-QORA Inca sea mother

MANANNAN MANAWYDAN (Celtic/Welsh) deity of the sea; see **LLYR & LER**

MARATHON (Gr.) fire-breathing bull assailed by **THESEUS** (son of **AEGEUS**)

MARZANNA Polish patron of orchards

MELAMPUS (Gr.) seer who could understand the talk of animals; descendant of **AEOLUS** (son of **HELLEN**); see **BIAS**

MELEAGER (Gr.) descendant of **AEOLUS** who killed his uncles; see **ALTHAEA**

MENELAUS (Gr.) son of **ATREUS & AEROPE**; brother of **AGAMEMNON**; see **PROTEUS**

MESHKENT (eg.) brick-shaped goddess with human head sprouting long palm shoots & symbol of crouching mothers-to-be

METSABOK (C.Am./Lacandones) divine master of rain and clouds

MEZAVIRS Latvian divinity of forest

MINOTAUR (Gr.) half human, half bull monster of Crete; offspring of **PASIPHAE & POSEIDON**'s white bull; killed by **THESEUS & ARIADNE**

MORPHEUS (Gr.) patron of dreams about humans; see **PHOBETOR**

MORRIGAN MORRIGU (Celtic) war goddess & consort of Irish **DAGDA**; see **MACHA**

MYRTILUS (Gr.) charioteer of **OENOMAUS** (King of Pisa killed by his son-in-law **PELOPS**) and thrown into the Myrtoan sea by **PELOPS**

NAUPLIUS (Gr.) see **AMYMONE**

NEFERTUM NEFERTEM/NEFERTEMU (Eg.) lion-headed man; lotus god; son of **PTAH & SEKHMET** (or **BAST**)

NEKHEBET (Eg.) see **BUTO, NEKHBET**

NINGURSU NINURTA/IMDUGUD/ANZU (Sum.) as a rain cloud huge lion-headed bird with a thunderous roar; deity of tilling & ploughing

NINIGARA (Sum.) cream and butter goddess and spouse of **NINHAR**

NIPARAYA (California/Indian) bodyless omnipotent god of heaven & earth; dispenser of food to all beings; father of **QUAAYAYP**

NYALITCH NYALIC (Africa/Nile) chief god of the Dinka people

ODYSSEUS ULYSSES (Gr./Rom.) the hero of a great wandering saga tale of the victor of the siege of Troy, interlaced with connections with the Greek gods, magic, Cyclops etc.; son of Laertes & Anticleia (or of **SISYPHUS**); King of Ithaca; brave & wise wanderer married to **PENELOPE**; consort of **CIRCE**, **CALYPSO** etc.

OENONAUS (Gr.) see **MYRTILUS**

ORAMATUA Tahitian 'forefathers'; spirits

OSSIANIC Cycle (Celtic) tells about the superhuman exploits of a band of young heroes (the fiana); named after Ossian, their greatest poet & son of **FINN**

PACA-MAMA Inca Earth Mother

PASIPHAË (Gr.) see **GLAUCUS & MINOTAUR**

PELOPIDS (Gr.) see **TANTALUS**

PENELOPE (Gr.) mother of **PAN**; wife of **ODYSSEUS** or Telegonus, his son by the sorceress **CIRCE**; daughter of **ICARIUS** of Sparta and nymph **PERIBOCA**

PENTHEUS (Gr.) King of Thebes, from whose prison **DIONYSUS** escaped, to strike Pentheus' mother, **AGAVE**, & all the other women of Thebes with madness

PHAETHON (Gr.) killed by a thunderbolt (**ZEUS**) while searching for his father **HELIOS**; son of nymph **CLEMENE**; see **EOS**

PHILEMON & **BAUCIS** senior hospitable Phrygian couple who received **ZEUS** and **HERMES**

PHOBETOR (Gr.) provider of dreams about animals; see **MORPHEUS**

PORTUNUS Roman god of harbours (and city gates)

POSEIDON (Gr.) major sea god; brother of **ZEUS**; see **TYRO**

QUAAYAYP see **NIPARAYA**

QUIATEOR Nicaraguan rain god

QUIRINUS Roman war and state god

RAGNARÖK (Norse, 'the final fate of the powers'); the final battle between the **AESIR** gods & the Giants when the Sun will be devoured & a terrifying winter spread over the earth (Götterdämmerung)

RHIANNON (Welsh) Gallic mare goddess **EPONA**; Irish **MACHA**; wife of king **PWYLL**; mother of **PRYDERI** whom she killed

ROSMERTA (Celtic) goddess of abundance; (Rom. **MERCURY**)

SABAZIUS (Thrace) see **MEN**

SAKHALIN (Siberia) see **MAMALDI**

SATARUPA (India) see **BRAHMA**

SHARRUMA son of **HEBAT**, Hurrian Queen of gods

SILVANUS Roman god of untilled earth associated with **PAN**

SISYPHUS (Gr.) trickster husband of **MEROPE** and son of **AEOLUS**; grandfather of Bellerophon, the hero who fought the **CHIMAERA** with **PEGASUS**

SLEIPNIR (Norse) magical, eight-legged horse of **ODIN**, born of trickster **LOKI** (as a mare) and swift & clever Svadilfari

SOATSAKI (N.Am.) beloved wife of Morning Star (a heavenly power & daughter of the Sun & Moon) whose disobedience relating to a turnip caused the Sun to expel her from heaven; see **POIA**

STRIBORG STRIBOG Russian wind god

SUCELLUS Dis Pater (Celtic) often depicted with wooden hammer (mallet) & drinking cup

SUSANOWO SUSANOO (Jap.) who sired 8 children, revered as princes, with his sister Amaterasu; their first-born male child was the ancestor of the Emperors; on one of his exploits he killed the man-eating 8-headed snake & thunder god with his sword; see **KUSANAGI**

TANGAROA (Polynesia, N.Z.) made the earth and lesser gods and mated with **HINE**, but sprouted mankind from himself

TANTALUS (Gr.) son of **ZEUS** (or **TIMOLUS** of Lydia) and ruler of Sipylus in Lydia/Phrygia who abused his friendship with the gods and suffers never-ending hunger and thirst in **HADES** as a result; cursed ancestor of the **PELOPIDS**; father of **PELOPS & NIOBE**

TARTARUS (Gr.) see **HAEMUS**

TELEPINU son of Hittite weather god **TARHUNT/TARHUND**; his disappearance caused life on earth to retreat but the sting of a bee made him reappear & life resumed

TEUTATES (Celtic) god of the clan & messenger; (Rom. **MARS**, **MERCURY**/ Gr. **ARES**, **HERMES**); see **ESUS & TARANIS**

THOUERIS (Eg.) see **TAURT**

THUNNUPA (Chile/Aymara) bearded white puritan from the North who said No to polygamy and chica (popular drink)

THYESTES see **AEGISTHUS**
TONATIUH (C.Am.) Aztec sun god of the fifth age connected with the eagle
TPEREAKL (Micronesia) with his wife Latmikaik (who emerged from a sea-lashed rock) they rule the world & are the source of life
T'SAI-SHEN (Ch.) divine lords of wealth
T'SAO-SHEN (Ch.) divine lords of the kitchen
UPELBURI (Hurrian) see **KUMARBI**
VAMMATAR (Fin.) diety of illness and pain
VARPULIS (Slav) wind god and follower of **PERUN**
VASUDEVA (India) father of **KRISHNA**
VODYANOI (Slav) huge fish and fearsome water deity covered with moss
WURUSEMU Hattic sun goddess (Hittite Arinnitti) and wife of **TARHUN/TARHUND**, the weather god
YUNCEMIL (C.Am.) death deity; see **ECHUA & BACABS**
ZEPHYRUS (Gr.) the West Wind, suitor of Hyacinthus; son of **EOS** by **ASTRAEUS**
ZUTTIBUR (Slav) sylvan god

TWO-LETTER WORDS

A

gl, go **AA** volcanic lava; river (Scand.)
AB, AV a Hebrew month
AB- as prefix (from; away; off)
el, ch **AC** alternating current; Actinium
AD a short advertisement; Anno Domini
ch **AG** silver (Argentum)
AH exclamation of Satisfaction
zo **AI** South American three-toed sloth
cp **AI** Artificial Intelligence
ch, pc **AL** Aluminium; adaptation level
AL AZ, 'The' in Arabic
ch **AM** 1st person sing. to be; Americium
ps **AM** Anno Mundi; amplitude modulation
AN if; ornate box; Actinium; Acton
rl **AN** indefinite article; deity (Anu)
AO any other; essential (alpha & omega)
bt **AP** son of (Welsh); arboreal pollen
pm, me **AP** apothecaries' measure
ch **AR** Argon, inert gas
me, nm **AS** Roman pound & bronze coin
ma, ch **AS** integer; Arsenic
nm **AT** preposition of location, scale; coin
ch **AT** Astatine, radioactive element
ch, mn, as **AU** gold; element; astronomical unit
me **AV, AB** Jewish month; (avdp) weight
AW interjection
to **AX** axe
AY, AYE yes, yeah; more so
AZ, AL 'the' in Arabic

B

ch, rl **BA** Barium; the soul (Egypt)
BE 2nd letter; exist; Chinese language
ch **BE** Beryllium; Japanese bread-winner
ch **BI** Bismuth
BI- bisexual; both of; double
ch **BK** Berkelium
bt **BO** sacred tree of Buddha
ch **BR** Bromine
me **BU** bushel; tsubo, Jap. measure
BY preposition of agent

C

ch **CA** Calcium; ca' canny (Sc.); alert
me **CC** cubic centimetre (liquid)
ch, me **CD** Cadmium; candela (luminance)
CD corps diplomatique
ch **CE** Cerium; letter 'C'
ch **CF** Californium
me **CI** curie (radioactivity)
me **CL** chlorine; centilitre
me **CM** centimetre
ch **CO** Cobalt; company
ch **CR** Chromium; credit
ch **CS** Caesium
md **CT** computer (axial) tomography (CT)
ch **CU** Copper

D

DA father; knife; yes (Rus.)
me **DB** decibel
el **DC** direct current
mu **DE** musical note; Liberian tribe (KRU)
DE letter 'D'
mu **DI-** of both; pair; musical note (di)
me **DL** decilitre
mu **DO** act; ditto, perform; 1st note (doh)
me **DR** dram; debit; doctor
ch, ec **DY** Dysprosium; plant detritus (lake)

E

go **EA** inlet; drainage canal in Fens
rl **EA** Chaldean fish god (Enki)
me **EB** Epstein-Barr virus
rl **EC** Yeniseian (Siberia) deity
EE eye (Sc.); letter 'E'
EF letter 'F'
EG for example; ancient pyramid
EH exclamation
EL 'the' (masc.) in Sp.; letter 'L'
el, me, rl **EL** electricity; Dutch metre; deity
'EM them (colloquial); letter 'M'
pr **EM** printing unit of space
pr **EN** half the width of an em
cf **EP-** outside; extra; above

ER interjection
rl **ES** letter 'S'; soul (Finno-Ugric & Hung.)
ch **ES** Einsteinium, element
as **ET** Ephemeris Time (celestial mechanics)
ch **EU** Europium, element; European Union
EX late; out of
cf **EX-** formerly

F

mu **FA** 4th note (major key)
ch, mu **FE** Iron; 4th note (minor key)
mu **FI** musical note
rl **FO** Chinese Buddha
ch **FR** Francium, element
me **FT** foot
rl **FU** Ch. lit. form; prefecture; pot; god
FY, FIE denoting disgust

G

ch **GA** Gallium; people (S. Ghana)
me **GB** Gilbert; Great Britain
ch **GD** Gadolinium, element
ch, rl **GE** Germanium; Mother Earth, Gaea (Gr.)
GE S.Am. Indian tribe & language
tx **GI** judo, karate garment
GO proceed; depart; fare
me, ga **GO** Japanese measure & board game (i-go)
mu **GU** violin; rainy season (Somalia)

H

ch **HA** Hahnium; exclamation
ch **HE** Helium; male pronoun
ch **HF** Hafnium, element
ch **HG** Mercury
HI exclamation; North Am. greeting
HM, HUM perhaps; disbelief
ch, tx **HO** Holmium; exclamation; Jap. dress
HO, HUO Chinese wine storage vessel
HO tribe & language of Bihar (India)
rl **HU** ancient invaders of China; vessels; gods
me **HZ** hertz, radio wave frequency

I

pc **ID, IDE** fish (carp); instinctive impulses; hedonist (Fr.)
rl **ID** (Syriac ida), Arabic festival
IE that is; pine tree
IF supposing that
IL male pronoun, definite article (lit.)
I'M I am
me **IN** prep. within, inside; inch
rl **IO** beloved of Jupiter; Zeus' beloved heifer
ch **IR** Iridium, element
rl **IS** being; existing; soul (ES)
cf **-IS** of abnormal condition, disease (Gr.)
IT personality, a thing; sex appeal

J

rl **JE** the Sun (China)
rl **JI** Japanese Buddhist sect ('times')
JO a sweetheart (Sc.)

K

zo, bt **KA** jackdaw (Sc.); tropical tree
rl, me **KA** spirit; Babylonian measure, Qa
me **KG** kilogram
me **KM** kilometre
KO knock out; Jap. floral art school
ch **KR** Krypton
KU ancient Chinese wine beaker
me **KW** kilowatt
zo **KY, KYE** kine, cattle (Sc.)

L

LA 'the' (Fr., It., Sp.: fem.)
mu, ch **LA, LAH** 6th note; Lanthanum
LE 'the' (Fr. Masc.)
mu **LE** musical note
md **LH** luteinizing hormone
me **LI** Ch. character; mile; food vessel
nm **LI** coin; Hainan island people (Ch.)
rl, ch, mu **LI** Ch. 'the Earth'; Lithium; note
lt, me **LM** lumen (light)
LO and behold!'; look – a surprise for you!
ch **LR** Lawrencium, element
ps **LS** -coupling (nuclear physics)
ch, rl **LU** Lutetium; Chinese deity
lt, me **LX** lux (luminance)

M

rl, eg **MA** mother; goddess; mechanical advantage
MC son of (Sc., Irish)
mu **ME** 1st-person pronoun; musical note
ch **MG** Magnesium
mu, me **MI** 3rd note (sol-fa scale); mile
me **ML** millilitre
me **MM** millimetre
md **MO** moment; Medical Officer
ch **MO** Molybdenum; Modus Operandi
MO -ho, Tungus tribe in Manchuria
MP Member of Parliament; legislator
md **MS** abbr. for Mrs or Miss; multiple sclerosis
MU letter of Greek alphabet
MY of me, mine

N

ch **NA** Sodium (Natrium); negative reply
ch **NB** Niobium, element
ch **ND** Neodymium, element
ch **NE** Neon; negative reply
ch **NO** Nobelium; negative reply
ch **NP** Neptunium, element
lt, me **NT** nit (luminance)
NU Gr. letter; minority population (Ch.)
rl **NU** Nun, Kua, deities (Eg., Ch.)

O

lw **OB** objection
OD magnetic force
me **OE** grandchild; oersted (magnetic)
OF preposition of possession; af (Sc.)
OG King of Basan (Old Test.)
OH exclamation; surprise
OK all correct (Americanism)
mu, ri **OM** Hindu mantra chant
ON preposition of location
mu **OP** opus (musical or artistic work)
hd **OR** alternatively; heraldic gold
pl, ch **OS** bone; mouth; Osmium
cf, rl **OT-, OTO-** (Gr.) of the ear; deity Ot
OU OW, exclamation of pain
zo **OX** a bull (cattle)
me **OZ** ounce; (Australia)

P

ch **PA** Protactinium; Maori fort
ch **PD** Palladium, element
me **PE** Portuguese measure
PH acid/alkaline content value
pr **PI** mixed type (circle); Gr. letter
PI ritual jade (China)
me **PK** peck
ch **PM** Promethium; afternoon; Prime Minister
ch **PO** Polonium; people (Min-chia)
rl **PO** chamber-pot; Ch. earthly soul
rl **PO** Maori 'night'; the Void (Polynesia)
ch **PR** Praseodynium; public relations
me **PT** pint
ch, nm, me **PU** Plutonium; Ch. money & measure

Q

me **QA, KA** Mesopotamian liquid measure
me **QT** quart

R

ch, rl **RA** Radium; Eg. sun god (Re, Phra)
ch **RB** Rubidium, element
me **RD** rod
mu, rl **RE** 2nd note; concerning; (Ra, Phra)
ch **RE** Rhenium, element
md **RH** rhesus blood type
me **RI** Japanese miles
ch **RN** Radon, element
ch **RU** Ruthenium, element

S

me **SB** stilb
ch **SC** Scandium, element
ch, mu, me **SE** Selenium; musical note; Jap. me
ch, mu **SI** Silicon; 5th note (minor)
me, rl **SI** Intern. System of Units; Inca Moon
ch **SM** Samarium, element
ch **SN** Tin, element
mu **SO** thus, therefore, then, 5th note (sol)
SO language (Laos, Thailand)
ch, me **SR** Strontium; steradian
me **ST** street; saint (abbreviation); stokes

T

ch **TA** thanks; Tantalum, element
ch, md **TB** Terbium; element; tuberculosis
ch **TC** Technetium, element
ch, mu **TE** Tellurium; 7th musical note (ti)
ch **TH** Thorium, radioactive element
bt **TI** tree-lily (Asia, Polynesia)
ch, mu **TI** Titanium; Ch. flute; 7th note (te)
rl **TI** Ch. people, concept & deity (T'ien)
ch, md **TM** Thulium; me of glucose in man
me **TO** prep. of direction; Jap. liquid me
me, rl **TU** Ch. miles; chief warrior (Polynesia)
TV (television)

U

mu **UD, OUD** Islamic stringed instrument
UG UH, ugh, exclamation of horror, disgust
rl **UL** Lord of the moon (Oceania)
UM sound of pensive understanding
cf **UN-** negative, not
rl **UO** Mayan 2nd month; rain god acolytes
UP preposition, adverb (above)
rl **UR** of the Chaldees
cf **UR-** prehistoric; original; primitive (Ger.)
US objective of 'we'
mu **UT** 1st note; Universal Time

V

mu **VA** go on
rl **VE** sacred place; brother of Odin
go **VO, VOE,** vae, firth; creek

W

me **WA** exclamation; unit of length (wah)
nt **WA** Pacific outrigger canoe
me **WB** weber
WC toilet; (bog)
WE plural pronoun
WO WHOA! stop!
WU Ch. dialect; -chin, Ch. pottery glaze
rl **WU** deepest contemplative Buddhist experience (Ch.)

X

ch **XE** Xenon, element
nm **XU** Vietnamese monetary unit

Y

YA yes, exclamation
ch **YB** Ytterbium, element
me **YD** yard
YE you (plural, obs.); the (obs.)
YI Chinese philosophy
YO exclamation of surprise
mu **YO** basic Japanese scale
rl **YU** precious jade; wine vessel; monster (Ch.)

Z

ZA abbr. of pizza (N. Am.)
ZA guilds of feudal Japan
ch **ZN** zinc, element
zo **ZO** Himalayan cattle; Jap. image
ch **ZR** Zirconium, element
ZZ slumber (cartoon indication)

THREE-LETTER WORDS

A

rl **AAH** the Moon-God of Egypt
me **A-AK** Dutch liquid measure
ABA Eastern camel-hair fabric
ABB yarn for the warp
ABC a railway guide; alphabet
ABP abbr. for Archbishop
ABS anti-lock braking system (cars)
ABU father (Arabic)
ABY atone; pay penalty; retribution
ACE aviator; particle; (cards); great, terrific
lw, pc **ACT** deed in writing; do; perform
ADD join; tag; annex; append; tot
ADO stir; fuss; commotion; hubbub
ADS advertisements
to, ag **ADZ** adze; wood-shaping; tilling
nm **AES** Roman money
nt **AFT** abaft; astern
rl **AGA, AGHA** oriental title; (Khan) Ismaili spiritual leader
AGE era; period; epoch; senility
AGO past; gone
AHA! exclamation of discovery
rl **AIA** Sumerian god
AID succour; help; subsidy; assistant (-fatigue, -burn out)
-AID funds, events for charity
AIL suffer; pain; peak; pine
AIM object; direct; intend; purpose
AIR mien; ventilate; display; tune
AIT river or lake islet; eyot
bt **ALA** wing or side petal of blossom
rl **ALB** white linen clerical vestment
ALE mead; beer
ALK resin from turpentine tree
ALL entirely; whole
go **ALP** pasture land; (high mountain)
md **ALS** serum
mu **ALT** high notes in the scale
rl **AMA** holy wine or vessel
me **AMP** electrical unit (abbr. for ampère)
rl **ANA** Celtic goddess; equal parts
cp **ANA-** prefix; up; back; again
cp **ANA-** without-; interference
pr **AND** the ampersand, &
cp **AND** logic element; binaries
lw **ANN** annat (Sc.)
zo **ANT** emmet; pismire; termite
ANU Celtic goddess; Babylonian sea-god
ANY some (in questions, negatives)
zo **APE** imitate; copy. mimic; monkey
APT appropriate; pertinent; prone
ARB dealer in take-over bids (Am.)
el, ma **ARC** luminous bridge; curve; (lamp)
me **ARE** hectare (2.5 acres)
ARG abbreviation for chemical silver
rl, nt **ARK** chest; coffer; place of refuge; floating zoo
ARM equip; limb; estuary
bt **ARN** elder tree
ART skill; dexterity; craft
md **ARV** Aids related virus
bt, rl **ASA** gum; Norse God (Valhalla)
pg **ASA** colour system
ASE Peer Gynt's mother
bt, gl, go **ASH** cinder, forest tree; wood; volcanic
ASK interrogate; invite; sue
zo **ASP** viper; snake (Cleopatra)
zo **ASS** moke; burro; donkey
ATE Goddess of Mischief; eaten
AUF fool; oaf; simpleton
zo **AUK** flightless sea bird; garefowl
me **AUM** Afrikaans liquid measure
AVA kava; Hawaiian palm-lily drink
rl **AVE** prayer; hail
AWE reverential veneration
to **AWL** the cobbler's tool; bradawl
bt **AWN** beard in chaff
to **AXE** to cut down; hatchet
cf **AXO-** of nerve fibre projection (Gr.)
AYE yea; for ever
rl **AZI** Altaic spirit

B

zo **BAA** to bleat (sheep)
BAB fishing bob
BAC ferry; brewing tub
BAD evil; depraved; detrimental; baneful
ga **BAG** hand-; sack; steal; score
BAH! a derogatory exclamation
BAM bamboozle; hoax
BAN muslin; bar; interdict; outlaw
ck **BAP** small soft bread loaf (Scotland)
lw **BAR** pub; ban; except; hinder; law
mu, hd **BAR** musical notation division; fess
go, nv **BAR** (sand-); rod; glazing; window
BAR ingot (gold); (prison, zoo)

cf **BAR-** of weight, pressure (Gr.)
BAT spree; batsman; vampire
bed **BAT** striker; brick-; lead wedge
me, nm **BAT** Thai measure and monetary unit
bt **BAY** bark; laurel; (sick-)
go, bd **BAY** cove; bight; wing; mill-dam
gl, bt **BED** -rock; couch; berth; layer; plant-
zo, hd **BEE** insect; emblem of Fr. Empire
BEG crave; implore; entreat; petition
BEG BEY, Ottoman title
rl, tc **BEL, BAAL** god; circuit amplifier
ma **BEL** logarithmic unit
bt **BEN** winged seed of ben-tree
BET lay; wager; stake; gamble
BEY, BEG Ottoman title
BIB sip; tipple; baby's napkin
zo, ga **BIB** whiting pout; (fencing)
BID order; direct; invite
BID tender, offer (auction)
BIG huge; swollen; pregnant
BIN receptacle (wine, corn, bread, litter-)
cf, bl **BIO-** organic, of life (Gr.)
BIS encore
to **BIT** piece; fragment (lathe); cutter
cp, nm **BIT** harness; binary digit; account
zo **BOA** snake; fur collar
nm **BOB** style of hairdressing; Br. shilling
ga **BOB** dog-sleigh; (racing)
BOG sog; morass; swamp; marsh; (WC)
zo **BOK, BUCK** a South African deer
zo **BOM, BOMA** snake (anaconda)
BOO cry down; decry; hoot; execrate
zo **BOT** the larva of the bot-fly
nt **BOW** tie; prow; knot; bend, defer (squash)
ga, mu **BOW** arc; archery; (violin stick)
el **BOX** encase; chest; container; (TV)
cp, rw **BOX** flowchart; signal; connection
bt **BOX** seat (theatre; driver); shrub
ga, nt **BOX** cuff; fight; spar
ga **BOX** close-rank (cycling); rugby scrum)
ga **BOX** abdomen protector (cricket, baseball)
BOY lad; page; stripling; Champagne
BOZ Charles Dickens' non-de-plume
BRA woman's garment; brassière
me **BTU** Br. Thermal Unit as joules
BUB yeast; strong drink; boy (USA. Ger.)
bt **BUD** sprout; blossom; graft; chum (Am.)
zo **BUG** -bear; insect; secret mike
BUM bailiff; loafer; backside
ct, nm **BUN** coiffure style; penny; (baker's-)
BUR, BURR rough edge
bt, to **BUR** chestnut shell; drill bit (lathe)
cp, el **BUS** omnibus; trunk route for signals; -bar
BUT yet; except; nevertheless; unless
BUY purchase; bribe; corrupt
ga **BYE** (cricket); (golf); (tournament draw)

C

me **CAB** cabriolet; taxi-; Heb. 3 pints
cf **CAC-** degenerate and diseased; (cacaphony)
CAD vulgar rascal; cheat; deceiver
cp **CAL** Conversational Algebraic Language
CAM oval wheel; (machinery)
CAN able to; preserve (food); pannikin
ar **CAP** out-do; headgear; roof of windmill
CAP explosive; cover
CAR vehicle
nt, zo **CAT** tackle; whip; rig; puss; mouser
mt **CAT** clear-air turbulence (aviation)
md **CAT** computerised axial tomography, X-ray, CT
CAW KAW, bird sound
CAY kay; key; shoal; reef; islet
CEE a shape of spring
rl **CER, KER** Gr. destructive spirit
ma, rl **CHI** Gr. letter; -square; Ch. breath of life
me **CHO** Jap. unit of length; commodity of tax
CID (el-), Spanish warrior
CIG cigarette (fag)
CIT citizen
CLY to steal
bl **CNS** Central Nervous System
zo **COB** pony; male swan; spider
bt, ck **COB** a head; spike of maize; nut
nm **COB** harbour; clay; basket; dollar
zo **COD** pod; husk; deceive; codfish
COG toothed wheel; humble status
bd **COG** rib (roof tile); wooden bowl
cr, nt **COG** tenon (locking joint); small boat
COG coax; cajole; cheat; wheedle
go, gl **COL** mountain pass; neck; arête (Fr.)
nv, mu **CON** (pro and con); steer; swindle; with
CON study; memorize; a convict

cf **CON-** prefix: conjoint
COO dove's voice of peace
ga **COP** hill; head; tuft
COP policeman; arrest; (ice hockey)
mu, me **COR** heart; horn; Hebrew bushels
bt **COS** lettuce
nt **COT** cottage; crib; small boat
zo **COW** bovine; browbeat; intimidate; depress
rl **COU** Celtic and Gallic god
ga **COX** coxswain; steersman (rowers)
COY shy; bashful; demure; diffident
COZ cousin (obs.)
CRI the crackle of pewter
ck **CRU** yield; produce; wine/ champagne (Fr.)
CRY sob; yell; bawl; blazon
zo **CUB** enclosure for cattle; young animal
CUB scout
CUD food for re-chewing (bovine)
CUE signal; stimulus; shuffleboard
ga **CUE** (billiards); (acting)
CUP bleed; succeed anew; prize; (drink)
bd **CUP** a beverage; warp in plank
zo **CUR** mongrel; pariah; dog
CUT incision; gash; wound; channel
CUT chop; sever; carve; avoid; shorten
go **CWM, CWYM** steep rounded hollow (Welsh)
CWT a hundredweight (50kg)
cf **-CYT, -CYTE** of the cells

D

zo, ck, ga **DAB** fish; expert; trial effort; touch ground (motorcycling); apply paint
DAD a blow; to thrash; to scatter; father
DAG shred; cut; dagger; pistol
to **DAH, DHAR** Burmese curved knife
ar **DAK** post; bungalow (Ind.)
bt **DAL** lentil
bd, zo, nm **DAM** barrier; brood mare with foals; Indian coin (dawm)
DAN tub; a title; Israeli tribe (Danites); martial arts expert
DAP to fish with a may-fly
zo **DAR** dace (fish)
DAW idiot; jackdaw
DAY epoch; era; 24 hours
ch **DDT** pesticide
DEB a debutante
el **DEE** die (Sc.); electrodes
nc, me **DEL** nabla; differential operator
DEN cave; lair; haunt; snuggery
DEW an aqueous precipitation
DEY dairymaid
DIB dip; make holes
DID diddled; performed
pr **DIE** embossed metal block; (dice); dee (Sc.)
ar **DIE** perish (death); pedestal dado
ga **DIG** excavate; delve; appreciate (slang); scoop; (volleyball)
zo **DIK** -dik, small African antelope; trouble
DIM obscure; vague; tarnish
pt, me **DIN** clamour; row; paper size
pg **DIN** colour system
DIP dop; duck; douse; souse; swim
ce, ck **DIP** descent; magnetic angle; (fondue)
gl **DIP** (strike); (pole); lower; immerse
cf, md **DIS-** neg. prefix; disjoint (disease); fail
rl **DIS** Pluto, the underworld (Gr.)
DIT a ditty (Spenser); (verse)
rl **DIV** (dividend); evil spirit (Persia)
ga **DIX** lowest trump (card game)
nv, me **DME** distance measuring equipment
bl **DNA** deoxyribonucleic acid; genetic heredity code
md **DOC** doctor
DOD clip; poll; lop
zo **DOE** female of fallow-deer, hare, rabbit
zo, ml, to **DOG** canine; (firedogs); to trail; spike; dressing iron; nippers
zo **DOG** -day cicada; (-winkle, a snail)
mu **DOH** first note of tonic sol-fa scale
me **DOL** pain intensity unit
DOM Portuguese title (lord, prince)
rl **DON** put on; assume; Sp. title; Danu (a god)
DOP to dip; duck; Cape brandy
DOR befool; mock; mockery; bedim
zo **DOR, DORR** dung-beetle; drone
mu **DOT** decimal point; full stop; speck; lengthened note
DOW fit and able
mt **DRY** parch; desiccate; (freeze-)
go, tx **DRY** (forest); (gas); (spinning)
nm **DUA** Malaysian money
cn **DUB** to name; substitute sound track
DUB to smooth; rub; confer knighthood
DUD worthless; defective
DUE owing; proper; becoming; (tax)
mu **DUE** expected; two parts shared
DUG udder; nudged; exhumed; excavated

md, nt **DUM** dum fever; Dutch fishing boat
DUN mound; sand-brown; gloomy
DUN to cure fish; to demand payment
bl **DUN** mayfly development; pupa of imago
mu **DUO** song in two parts; partnership
DUP to open
mu **DUR** major key (Ger.)
DUX a leader (Lat.); (duke)
me **DWT** pennyweight
DYE colour; tinge; stain
md, cf **DYS-** (dysfunction), failure

E

ma, me, ps **EAN** to produce; effective atomic number
ag, pl **EAR** plough; till; lug; heed; hearing organ
EAT chew; consume; devour; erode
EAU -de-Cologne, anti-odour water
EBB recede (tide); wane; subside
el **ECM** electronic counter measures apparatus
el, md **ECT** electroconvulsive (shock) therapy
nm **ECU** 5-franc coin; European currency unit
EDO last trad. Jap. period (Tokugawa)
EEC European Economic Community
md **EEG** electroencephalography (neurology)
zo **EEL** snake-like fish
pl **EEN** eyes (Sc.)
E'EN even
E'ER ever
EFE a Pygmy people
zo **EFT** a newt; forthwith (obs.)
bl, ck **EGG** ovum; (hen's, new laid-); incite
ar **EGG** oval (-shape); -and dart; esteem
pc **EGO** I, the self; conscious subject
pc **EGO-** -tism; -centric; self-centred aspect
vt **EIA** equine infectious anaemia
ma **EIK, EKE** add; addition (Sc.)
EKE increase; likewise; extra income
ELD old age; olden times; decrepitude
rl **ELF** sprite; gnome; imp; pixy/pixie
zo **ELK** moose; the whooper swan
me **ELL** cloth length; elbow; pipe-fitting
bt **ELM** stately tree
ELO mask and show of Nupe tribe (Nigeria)
el **EMF** electromotive force
zo **EMU** Australian bird, cassowary type
ps, me **EMU** electromagnetic unit
END conclude; finality; terminate; death
mu **END** aim; -s and means; -piece (encore)
gl, bl **END** moraine; -plate (illustration)
ENE once (Sc.)
fr **ENG** durable dark Burmese wood
ENS entity; (realissimum, perfect being)
EON, AEON an age; eternity
rl **EOS** dawn goddess (Aurora) (Gr.)
cf **EPI-** outer-; skin (-dermis); epicentre
bl **EPP** end-plate potential
ps **EPR** electron paramagnetic resonance
ERA age; period; epoch; cycle; time
ERE before; sooner than
ERF small garden in S. Africa
me, pc, go **ERG** unit of work; 1 dyne; force; purpose; sand dune desert (Arab)
me, md **ERG** electroretinogram (retina)
zo **ERN** sea eagle
ERR offend; sin; wander; tresspass
bt **ERS** vetch
ESS the letter 'S'
ps, me **ESU** electrostatic system of units
ETC et cetera, and so forth
vt **EVA** equine viral arteritis (disease)
rl **EVE** evening (ere an event); Adam's mate
zo **EWE** fem. sheep; people (SE Ghana, Toto)
cf, ar **EXO-** exterior of; (exogamy); (exonarthex)
pl, mt **EYE** visual organ; (needle); (cyclone)
EYE observe; watch; view; bud; island

F

FAD whim; craze; crochet; hobby
bl **FAD** flavinco enzyme 'D'
FAG knot; -end (cigarette)
FAG drudge; fatigue; a bore; pupil servant
mu **FAH** spoken sol-fa note (4th)
rl **FAM** the hand (slang); Bantu god (Africa)
FAN air cooler; flutter; blower
ae **FAN** admirer; agitate; inflame; -jet
go, ag **FAN** alluvial; spread out; thresher
ag, ga **FAN** belt; winnower; (Am. football)
FAP drunk; fuddled (Shak.)

pc **FAP** fixed action pattern (ethology)
bt, ck **FAR** distant; remote; buck-wheat
ck, pr **FAT** obese; grease; vat; printing term
lw **FAS** free alongside ship (commerce)
FAW gypsy
tc **FAX** electronic facsimile transmission
FAY, FEY clean out; fairy; elf; fit closely
FEB the shortest month, February
FED ate; subsisted; supplied (means)
FEE remuneration; pay; reward; toll
nm **FEI** yap, Micronesian monetary unit
go, nm **FEN** marsh lands; Ch. weight and money
FET get; fetch (obs.)
lw **FEU** tenure; lease; tax (Sc.)
FEW scant; rare; scarce
FEY, FAY spiritual exaltation; fated
tx **FEZ** cap with tassel (Moslem)
FIB petty falsehood; white lie
FIE add; insult (obs.)
bt **FIG** fruit; excrescence; tobacco
FIG costume (obs.); small trifle
nm **FIL** Middle Eastern monetary unit
zo, mu **FIN** organ of locomotion (fishes); end
ae **FIN** metal piece; rudder; tail-
bt **FIR** cone-bearing tree, conifer
FIT appropriate; qualified; suitable
md **FIT** spasm; healthy; adjust; befit
FIX repair; correct; quandary; dilemma
ce, nv **FIX** hitch; tie; ground control
md **FLU** influenza
FLY coach (obs.); sly; observant
nt **FLY** abscond; flee; Dutch coastal sailboat
pr, ae, zo **FLY** pr. term; decamp; winged insect
FOB watch pocket; impose; delude
lw **FOB** free on board (commerce)
me **FOD** Danish unit of measure (foot)
FOE antagonist; opponent; enemy
bt, mt **FOG** moss; rank grass; thick mist
FOH Buddha (Chinese)
FON people (Dahomey, Nigeria)
FOP a dandy; a 'nut'; beau; coxcomb
FOR dative prep., direction; purpose
FOR on this account, reason
me **FOT** Swedish unit of measure (foot)
me **FOU** tipsy; full; a bushel (Sc.)
zo **FOX** deceive; baffle; reynard
FOX N. Am. Indian tribe (Mesquakie)
nt **FOY** parting feast; assistance boat
rl **FRA** brother; friar
FRO from; away; (to and fro)
ck, zo **FRY** cook; swarm; small-; smolt (fish)
FUB fat man; cheat
zo **FUD** hare's tail
FUG frowsty warmth; un-aired room
rl **FUM** Chinese phoenix
nm **FUN** merriment; enjoyment; Korean coin
FUR incrustation; a pelt, winter wear
FUR people (Sudan)
me **FUT** foute; Russian unit of measure

G

GAB talk; gas; mouth (gam); hook
GAD rod; goad
rl **GAD** to rove; prophet, OT; Israeli tribe
GAE go (Sc.)
GAG wheeze; to silence; (reflex)
ps, me **GAL** girl; unit of gravity; gallon
GAM gossip; talk; mouth; leg
zo **GAM** school of whales
gl **GAP** fissure; opening; gat; interval
zo **GAR** to compel (Sc.); a fish (bowfin)
ch **GAS** chat; gab; poison-; gasoline
mu **GAT** pistol; strait; gap; Ind. music form
GAU ancient Ger. community (Lat. *pagus*)
rl **G'AU** Tibetan reliquary
GAY, GEY lively; merry; homosexual
rl **GEB** Keb, Seb, Egyptian god
zo **GED** pike or luce (fish)
GEE surprise cry (Am.); (-up, hasten) (horse)
GEG Albanian dialect
GEL viscous colloidal; lubricant
bt **GEM** jewel; precious (stone); a leaf-bud
GEN detailed information; manna (Heb.)
ge, gl **GEO** gio; creek; voe; vae; firth; frith
cf, ps **GEO-** ge-, earth-related (geophysics)
rl, ga **GET** obtain; fet; breed; divorce (Jew.); return of ball
GEY GAY; fairly; rather (Sc.)
zo, cr **GIB** cat; the Rock; iron or steel packing band; cotters'-
GID sheep-disease; sturdy
GIE give (Sc.)
GIF if (Sc.)
GIG whirl; cloth machine; vehicle
GIM neat
bt, ck **GIN** machine; snare; juniper-flavoured spirits
me **GIN** Malaysian measure

ck, zo **GIP** cleaned herring
zo **GIR** Indian cattle breed
GMT Greenwich Mean Time
zo **GNU** bovine-like antelope (S. Africa)
zo **GOA** Tibetan antelope
GOB mouthful; coal (left-overs)
GOB worked out mine; mouth (sl.)
GOD Deity; idol; image
rl **GOG** and Magog; evil force (Bible)
GOT seized; procured; achieved
rl **GOY** gentile, Christian (Jew.)
GRU ice
mu **GUE** Shetland violin
mn **GUF, GUFA, GOPHER** reed ships
mn **GUG** inclined mine tunnel
nt **GUL** sail; outrigger; dugout (Papua)
bt **GUM** stick; mucilage; resin; -tree
rl **GUN** artillery; pistol; African god
GUP idle chatter; rumour
me **GUR, KOR, COR** Mesopotamian measure
pl **GUT** narrow channel; intestine; (intuition)
nt **GUY** rope; effigy; burlesque; man
me **GUZ** a measure (E. Indies and Iran)
G'WI Kalahari bushmen
ga **GYM** gymnastics-hall (gymnasium)
fr **GYN** timber-loading device
md **GYN-** of woman; (gynaecology)
GYP college servant; bedmaker
GYR- rotate; gyrate; revolve

H

HAD befooled; caught; kept; owned
HAE have (Sc.)
HAG parasite fish; virago; beldam; witch
HAH! exclamation
rl **HAL** Sufi Moslem state of mind (ahwal)
rl, ck **HAM** a heavy actor; amateur radio operator; meat (pork)
ar **HAN** Ottoman inn (Turkish)
HAN -jen, CH. people; Jap. fief
nm **HAO** Vietnamese money
rl **HAP** chance; luck; accident; fortuity; god
HAS (he) owns, possesses; (have)
rl, nm **HAT** dignity of Cardinal; bonnet; coin
bt **HAW** hawthorn berry; hedge; boundary
bt **HAY** hedge; fence; harvested grass
rl **HEH** Neheh, Hu, Sia, Eg. god
rl **HEL** Norse goddess of death
HEM a cough; to sew (edge); confine
zo **HEN** a fowl
bt **HEP** hip; berry of the dog-rose
rl **HEP** Hapi, Hap, Eg. god
HER 'she' as object
bl **HET** hot and bothered; heterosexual
HEW chop; hack; fell; cut rocks
cf, me **HEX-** a group of six (Gr.); magic spell; (hexameter)
HEY! exclamation to call attention
mu **HEY** English country dance (traditional)
HIC! a small hiccup
HID secreted; concealed
HIE to hasten; a cry; greeting (Am.)
HIM 'he' as object
me **HIN** 6 quarts (6.8 litres) (Heb.)
pl, bt **HIP** -hurray; -joint; rafter; berry; hep
HIS belonging to him
cp **HIT** computer answer; data record
mu **HIT** strike; success; pop song
HOB part of grate; hub; peg or stake, target for quoits
HOB a rustic; a fairy
rl **HOD** a coal scuttle; Hoder, Hodur, a god
to **HOE** a promontory; to weed; cutter
zo **HOG** boar; pig; glutton; scrubbing broom
HOG act selfishly; monopolize road-; trim horses' manes
HOO! hold! stop!
bt, ga **HOP** plant; tree; dance; step; jump
rl **HOR** Horus, Egyptian god
ck **HOT** violent; acrid; fervid; ardent; spicy
pc **HOT** heated; highly radioactive
go **HOW** glen; dell; low hill
HOW in what manner, condition?
HOX to hamstring
HOY ahoy, hoa! sailor's cry; (exclamation)
nt **HOY** sailing coaster; smack; sloop
rl **HSI** Ch. deity; Ch. Imperial seal
rl **HSU** of Chinese and Japanese faiths (Tao)
ga **HUB** centre; wheel cap; (quoits)
HUB plug socket; cover; hilt (sword)
HUE and cry; tint, colour shade
HUG embrace; enfold; clasp
HUH! exclamation (surprise or contempt)
HUI hui-hui, Moslems of NW China
mu **HUM** bee-sound; Pooh song; wordless sound (tune); workshop sound
el **HUM** extraneous elements from other circuits in amplifier
gl **HUM** limestone outcrops (karst)

HUN nomadic pastoral Cossack
rl **HUN** Taoist superior soul
HUP! a horse hastener; hiccup
HUT hovel; shed; cabin; cot
HUX method of fishing
HYP depression; hip

I

rl **IAB** spirit of nature (Samoyed)
cp **IAL** International Algebraic Language
IAT International Atomic Time (TAI)
IBN son of (Arabic) title
IBO native and lang. (Igbo), E. Nigeria
ICA Indian people of Colombia (Arhuaco)
go, ck **ICE** frozen water; gru; coat with sugar
hd **ICH** (Ich Dien) 'I serve' (Prince of Wales)
ICY cold; frigid; chilling; frosty
rl **IDA** birthplace of Zeus (Crete)
zo **IDE** kind of carp (orfe)
IDO artificial language
rl **IFA** the Great Truth (Nigeria)
ILK clan; category; that same (Sc.)
ILK each, every (Sc.); (OE: gaelic)
ILK ailing; evil; bad; sick
IMP extend; strengthen; graft; sprite
INK writing, printing fluid
INN caravanserai; tavern; hostelry
el **ION** electrically charged particle
rl **ION** forefather of the Ionians
I.O.U. (I owe you) debt agreement; note of hand
IPA International Phonetic Alphabet
IRE rage; fury; resentment; passion
IRK make weary or bored; (irksome)
ISE I shall (Sc.)
cf **ISH** exit; issue (Sc.); -ish (-like, adj.)
cf **ISM** ideological preference
cf, mt **ISO-** equal; same (Gr.); -bar (pressure)
ISO new colour system
ITS belonging to it
md **IVP** intravenous pyelogram
bt **IVY** a creeper sacred to Bacchus

J

ga **JAB** prod; poke; stab; a thrust; injection; punch (boxing); stroke (hockey)
JAD a quarrying cut
JAG a notch; a binge; to stab
JAH Jehovah
bt **JAK** bread-fruit tree
ck, tx, ro **JAM** A conserve; child's garment; radio block; non-function
ga **JAM** tightly packed, congested (traffic); pitch inside (baseball)
mu, ga **JAM** jazz-session; impede (Am. football)
JAP Japanese
JAR discord; jolt; jangle; pot (glass)
JAT Indo-Aryan
pl, go, ga **JAW** the mouth; gossip; entrance; corner (billiards); to splash
zo **JAY** bird; nitwit; (-walker)
JEE to move; to budge (Sc.)
rl **JEN** Confucian supreme virtue
mn, ae **JET** spray; black lignite; -propel
ga **JEU** a game (Fr.); (gambling call)
JEW A Hebrew, Israeli (yehudi)
nt **JIB** to baulk; shy; a sail; lifting arm, boom (crane); insult; sly remark
to **JIG** tune; dance; apparatus
cp **JOB** stab; profession; work; unit of runs
nm **JOE** a sweetheart (Sc.); Port. 'joao' coin
JOG push; nudge; -trot; rog; run slowly (memory); (cattle driving)
nm **JON** N. Korean monetary unit
JOT an iota; to note briefly
JOW to toll; a stroke of a bell (Sc.)
JOY rapture; ecstasy; delight; (-ride)
me **JUD** a mass of coal
ck **JUG** ewer; pot (drinks); to stew; prison
bt **JUR** earth-nut
JUT protrude; extend
rl **JUZ** the 30 sections of the Koran (Quran)

K

zo **KAA** (jungle) rock python (Kipling)
zo **KAE** jackdaw (Sc.)
KAF fountain conferring immortality
pr **K'AI** shu, standard Ch. script and print model
KAM crooked (Shak.)
me **KAN** Dutch and Hong Kong measure
nm **KAS, KAST** Dutch wardrobe, chest; Ind. coin
me **KAT** Egyptian weight
KAW, CAW bird sound
go, gl **KAY, CAY, KEY** shoal; reef (bed)

zo **KEA** parrot that kills sheep (NZ)
zo, rl **KEB** ewe; sheep louse, Eg. god (Geb)
KEF drugged stupor
KEG small cask or barrel
bt **KEI** an apple (Indian plum)
me **KEN** know; recognize; knowledge; Jap. unit of length
KEP shaft-hoist stop; to catch (Sc.)
rl **KER** destructive spirit (Gr.)
KET carrion; matted wool; a fleece (Sc.)
me **KEV** 1000 electron-volts
bt **KEX** fool's parsley; dried stalks
mu **KEY** code; (crib); solution; legend; wedge; clamp; (lock); -board (music); opener; reef
rw, cp, ga **KEY** signal; identification digit; penalty area (baseball)
le **KID** faggot; bundle of sticks; tub; deceive; hoax; pliable leather
zo **KID** young goat; a boy; infant
bt **KIF** Indian hemp; drug (cannabis)
KIN relationship. affinity; kindred
me **KIN** Japanese unit of weight
rl **K'IN** Mayan Sun god (C. America)
eg **KIP** nap; unit of force (1000lb/ 454kg)
le **KIP** small untanned hide; (sleep)
mu **KIT** tub; (army-); violin; gear; accessories
bt **KOA** acacia (Sandwich Islands)
zo **KOB** water antelope; target (quoits)
KON catty, Korean unit of weight
go **KOP** hill (S. Africa)
me **KOR, COR, GUR** Mesopotamian measure
KRI Hebrew marginal direction
KRU KRoo; a Liberian
KRU, KROO De, Liberian Kawa-speaking people
rl **KUA** Nu, progenitors of humanity (Ch.)
KUL, KULA the family (India)
rl **KUL** water-haunting genie (Siberia)
KUN Turkic nomads (Cumans)
rl **KUN** soil magician; whale monster (Ch.)
me **KUP** Thai unit of length (10 ins)
rl **KUU** (moon), father of Kuutar (Finland)
KWA subgroup of Niger-Congo language
KYA native hut (S. Africa)
zo **KYE, KY, KINE** cattle (Sc.)

L

mn **LAC** dye; shellac; transparent resin
LAD youngster; stripling; boy; kid
LAG convict; dawdle; loiter; dally
LAG delay; insulate; cover; wrap
mu **LAH** spoken sol-fa 6th note
mu **LAI, LAY** ballad, poem (Sd.)
LAM to thrash; weaving device; Arabic letter
LAO Thai people
LAP fold; wrap; polish; circuit; drink
zo **LAR** white-handed gibbon
rl **LAR** Roman household god
LAT inscribed pillar (India)
nm **LAT** Latvian and Thai money
LAV wash; (toilet); lavage
lw, ps **LAW** statute; canon; rule; (gravity)
LAX slack; loose; remiss; careless
LAY, LAI ballad; put down; (egg) (table)
LAY person; non-professional egghead
LAZ, LAS E. Black Sea people and language
ga **LBW** leg before wicket (cricket)
me, go **LEA** measure of yarn; meadow; lee; lay; open land; pasture
LED induced; helped; conducted
go **LEE** sheltered (wind); lea; meadow
nt, nv **LEG** lower limb; stage, tack in sailing
cp, ga **LEG** section of route; path in routine walk; square- (cricket); gam
ga **LEG** division of turns (skittles)
nm **LEI** garland (Hawaii); Romanian leu
nm **LEK** bird courtship; Albanian coin
as **LEO** lion; 5th sign of Zodiac
rl **LER, LIR** Irish sea god
ga **LET** permit; allow; lease; hire; (badminton, tennis)
LET hindrance; prevent; delay
nm **LEU** Romanian money (plur. lei)
nm **LEV** Bulgarian money (ley)
LEW luke-warm; tepid
lw **LEX** an enactment
nm **LEY** lev; lea; pasture; common pewter
rl **LHA** -mo, city goddess of Lhasa (Tibet)
LIB ad lib.; extemporize (acting)
LID top; cover; coverlet
LIE falsehood; rest; recline; repose
ga **LIE** shape of landscape; (golf)
rl **LIF** male survivor of chaos (Norse)
rl **LIL** lelek, 'soul' (Finno-Ugric)
go, nt **LIN** pool, port (Celtic); to cease
LIP touch the edge; rim; mouth
rl **LIR, LER** Irish sea god

lw **LIS** litigation
bt, hd **LIS** fleur-de-lis; heraldic lily (Fr.)
LIT lighted; kindled; ignited
rl **LOA** creator, ritual drama (Guatemala)
ga **LOB** worm; clumsy throw (underarm) (cricket) (badminton)
cp, nt **LOG** record; diary; tree-trunk
ma **LOG** Hebrew pint; (logarithm tables)
ga **LOO** toilet; card game
LOP truncate; amputate; dock (tails)
me **LOT** to catalogue; fate; portion; (choose); unit of weight (Ger.)
LOW base; vile; abject; depressed
LOW bellow; moo; to flame; to blaze (Sc.)
LOW first of group (jump) (parachuting)
LOY narrow spade
LSD money (Libra; Solidus; Denarius)
md **LSD** hallucinatory drug
rl **LUA** Roman deity
LUD King Lud patron of anti-automation
rl **LUD** sacred fir tree grove (Votyaks)
LUE to sift
nt **LUG** ear; tug; haul; drag; handle; (sail)
rl **LUG** Celtic deity
rl **LUL** 'soul', lelek (Finno-Ugric)
LUM chimney (Sc.)
LUO kavironda, people (Kenya, Uganda)
mu **LUR** Scand. prehistoric bronze horn
LUR native mountain people (Iran, Luristan)
me **LUX** unit of light
LUZ a legendary bone
ch **LYE** alkaline solution
zo **LYM** dog on leash
go **LYN** waterfall (Celtic)

M

MAB the queen of the fairies
as **MAC** son of (Sc.); 13th month, Mayan cal.
MAD crazy; demented; raving; insane (angry)
zo **MAG** chatter; steal; magpie
nm **MAG** halfpenny; magazine (journal)
rl **MAH** Mao, Persian moon god
cf **MAL-** faulty; wrong; imperfect
MAM Madame, ma'am (respected lady); (brothel)
MAN mankind; husband; employee; male human
MAN Bantu people (Yao), Africa
zo, rl **MAO** the peacock; Persian god Mah
go **MAP** delineate; chart; plan
MAR spoil; deface; impair; disfigure
nm **MAS** Indonesian gold coin
pg, wv **MAT** dull surface; weave; interlace
ar, wv, ga **MAT** carpet; raft; slab; foundation floor (boxing) (wrestling)
zo **MAW** craw; crop; (stomach)
MAX a kind of gin; (trap); maximum
MAY have permission, possibility
bt **MAY** hawthorn blossom; 5th month
me, mu **MEL, Mell, Mall** honey; unit of pitch; leafy bower; promenade
MEL language group (Sierra Leone)
rl **MEN** humanity; lunar god (Asia Minor)
MEO Miao, mountain dwellers, SE Asia, Ch.
me **MET METROPOLITAN**; bushel; came together
me **MEV** million electron-volts
zo **MEW** sea-gull; moult
MEW cage; confine; cat-speech
me **MHO** electrical unit of conductivity
MID central; amid; middle
me, nm **MIL** unit of measure; thousand
MIM prim; demure; precise
me, rl **MIN** liquid measure; Eg. fertility god
MIR Russian commune; space station
cf **MIS-** hatred of (Gr.); wrong act (mistake)
MIX blend; combine; jumble; mingle
nm **MNA** mina; 50 shekels
zo **MOA** extinct bird, emu type (N.Z.)
MOB cap; rabble; populace; crowd
MOD assembly; meeting; (mod con)
mu **MOD** modern; Gaelic choral contest
MOE mow; grimace; mop
MOG move away
as **MOL** 8th month of Mayan calendar
MOM, MUM, BAMUM people (Cameroon, Africa)
nt **MON** canoe (Solomon Islands, Pacific)
MON people (Talaing) and lang., SE Asia
MOO when a cow lows
MOP swab; grimace; moe; -of hair
fr **MOR** type of humus layer
rl **MOT** bon mot; witticism; god of ME
me **MOU** Chinese unit of area
MOW stack; pile of hay; cut down (lawn)

MOW facial expression; moe
MRS married woman; (mistress)
MUD mire; sludge; slime; Dutch measure
MUG fool; face; cup; assault; injure
MUM mother (Mom); silence; beer brew
MUN man (dialect)
rl **MUT** Egyptian goddess
MUX to spoil; a mess
zo **MYA** shellfish

N

nt **NAB** seize; grab; knoll; shoal
NAE none (Sc.)
NAF unfashionable; unsuitable
zo **NAG** harass; pester; horse
lw **NAM** distraint (obs.)
bt, ga **NAP** doze; forty winks; cherry; card; game
bt, ga **NAP** non-aubacial pollen; racing tip
NAY contrariwise; vote against; no (obs.)
N.C.O. non-commissioned officer (army)
NEB beak; nose; nib; a point
NEE born (Fr.) (maiden name)
nt **NEF** silver model ship; cadenas; casket; salt cellar
go **NEK** a pass (S. Africa); a col
cf, ar **NEO** old style revived (Gr.)
bt **NEP** catmint; knot in cotton fibre
rl **NER** tamid, Hebrew holy lamp (synagogue)
NET neat; nett; snare; capture; (fishing-)
NEW novel; recent; fresh; modern
NIB beak; point; neb; (pen)
NIL nihil; zero; nothing
NIM steal; (nick)
me **NIN** Thai inches (Niu)
rl **NIO** Japanese herculean spirits
NIP squeeze; pinch; bite; sip; a dram
NIS not so; imp; hobgoblin; mix
zo, me **NIT** egg of louse; light unit
me **NIU** Thai inches
rl **NIX** nothing; water elf; nixy (Ger.)
NOB aristocrat; knave at cribbage; head
NOD head gesture; assent; -off (doze); on the -(auction, bid)
me **NOG** small pot; tree nail; peg; wooden brick; noggin, ale cup
NOK ancient Nigerian culture
NOM de plume (Fr.), writer's pseudonym
cf **NON-** negative; not; without (Lat.)
NOR logic; not (neither here nor there)
cp **NOT** negating; Boolean logic of false and true
NOW at this time or instant; the present
lt, me **NOX** measure of illumination
rl **NOX** Nyx; personification of night
ac, me **NOY** unit of perceived noise
NUB shove; hang; knob; gist
rl **NUM** sky god (Siberia)
rl **NUN** a religieuse; a sister; -Nu, Eg. god
NUR knot in wood
rl **NUT** dandy; eccentric person; sky goddess; screwed bolt end
mu **NUT** boss on anchor; bridge (holding strings above soundbox – violin)
bt **NUT** single-seeded fruit in shell
md, bt **NUX** (vomica)
zo **NYE** brood of pheasants
rl **NYX, NOX** night goddess (Erebus) (Gr.)

O

OAF fool; idiot; dolt; changeling; oof
OAK outer door (university)
bt **OAK** hardwood tree; heart of-(seaman)
OAR narrow paddle; to row; an oarsman
bt, mu **OAT** a grain; pan-pipe; (wild-s)
OBI, OBY magic; a fetish (West Indies)
OBI Japanese sash; karate belt
OBO annual Mongolian festival (5th month)
bt **OCA** potato (South Africa)
OCA pal-leaf book (Sri Lanka)
OCH! oh! or ah! (Sc. & Ir.)
me **OCK** unit of weight (Turkey)
ODD singular; peculiar; quaint; droll
ODE celebratory poem
O'ER poetical over
OES Os; circlets
OFF away; gone (switched-)
OFT often; frequently; repeatedly
el, me **OHM** unit of electrical resistance
OHO! exclamation
cf **-OID** of resemblance, similarity (Gr.)
OIL anoint; lubricate; petroleum
zo, bt, ck **OIL** (plant-) (fish-) (blubber-)
me **OKA** 3lb in Egypt
me **OKE** unit of dry and liquid weight
OLD antique; archaic; pristine; aged

OLI Buli, African people (Congo)
zo **OLM** a blind lizard
ONA S. Am. Indians (Tierra del Fuego)
ma **ONE** indivisible number; pronoun; single ae, ane (one and own) (Sc.)
me **ONS** 100 grams in Netherland
OOF, OAF silly fellow
OOM uncle (Afrikaans)
OPE open (obs.)
cf, bt, ck **OPO-** derived from juice
OPS Goddess of Wealth; wife of Saturn
OPT to choose; elect; pick
cf **-OPY, -OPIA** of visual defect (Gr.)
pl **ORA** mouths, orifices (Lat.)
ORB globe; -weaver (spider); emblem of royal power; 'Imperial apple'
zo **ORC** killer whale; ogre; eagle
ORD edge; beginning
mn **ORE** metal-bearing earth; (iron-)
nm **ORE** Scand. coin (öre, øre)
rl **ORO** Tahitian deity
ORT a bit; refuse; a crumb
OSH oblost, admin. region (Russian)
mu **OUD, UD** Islamic lute
OUR ¾ of an –; belongs to us
OUT outside; expose; get out!
zo, ck **OVA** eggs; cod's roe; (caviare)
OWE run up an account; to be in debt
zo **OWL** night bird; to smuggle (by night)
OWN possess; admit; concede
ch **OXO** organic compound radical
me **OZS** ounces

P

zo, tc **PAD** cushion; stuff; paw; data; packet; (factory-); (floor); spare bed
el **PAD** attenuator; electrical network
PAH! exclamation of disgust; stockade (NZ)
PAI Po (Min-chia), people of Yunnan, Ch.
PAL staunch friend; mate; palooka
ga **PAM** knave of clubs at loo (card game)
ck **PAN** small pool; (frying); (-gold); Ch. bowl
rl **PAN** goat-like god; African sky god
ga, go, zo, mu **PAN** film camera motion; Mexican card game; saline flats; ape; -pipes
PAN- all-embracing unity (Gr.)
PAO authorized court circular; gazette (Ch.)
go, pl, ck **PAP** conical hill; nipple; mushy food
zo, ga **PAR, PARR** young salmon; equality (golf)
PAS pace, ballet step
PAT dab; tap; rap; caress; aptly
zo **PAU** bustard (S. Africa)
zo **PAW** fury foot; handle roughly
rl **PAX** kiss of peace; era of -; hold! osculatory (marriage)
PAY expend money; (wages) (compliment) (respects); (stipend); (debts)
bt, ck **PEA** flower; pod vegetable
mu **PED** pack-saddle; basket; pedal; organ
PEE to urinate; (piss)
ga **PEG** short drink; spigot; wooden nail; rod; dowel; spike; (croquet)
PEG secure; fasten; (tent) (violin); (prices); a scale
to, zo **PEN** impound. write (quill-); indite; female swan; squid shell
go **PEN** mountain; headland (Celtic)
PEP energy; drive (USA)
PER by means of; (price – amount)
PES hind-limb equestrian pedestal
zo **PET** fondle; favourite; kept animal
rl **PEW** row of seats in church
ma **PHI** binary listing
bt **PIA** arrowroot (Polynesian)
me **PIC, PIK** picki, diraa, units of length
ma, ck **PIE, PI, PYE** pastry-covered flan; tart
pr, nm **PIE** mixed print; Rom. inches; Ind. money
zo, ml **PIG** hog; (savings) (-gy bank); to guzzle; (-lead); (-iron)
me **PIK, PIC** picki, diraa, inches (Medit.)
ga **-PIK** high lob (pelota, Sp.)
me, ga **PIN** half a firkin; transfix; wedge; pile; (point); (-down, wrestling)
jn **PIN** peg; nail; to fasten; dowel; dovetail; tenon; (tailoring)
ga **PIP** to black-ball; overtake (racing)
bt, vt **PIP** fruit seed; fowl disease; depression; code signal; dice spots; chirp
mn **PIT** mine; abyss; oppose; (theatre)
ga **PIT** set; match (tennis); (cock-); (motor racing-)
mu **PIU** little more (or less) (It.)
rl **PIX** holy box; coin box; pyx
md **PKU** gene disorder (phenylketonuria)
fr, nt, tx **PLY** fold; layer; veneer; roofing felt; to ferry; yarn; (career)
bt **POA** a genus of grass

bt **POD** husk; to swell; group unit; room
zo **POD** a shoal of whales or seals
zo **POE** parson bird (NZ)
POH! exclamation
bt, ck **POI** Polynesian fermented taro starch
zo **POM** Pomeranian dog; Briton in Australia
mu **POP** sound burst; explode; (weasel)
as **POP** 1st month of Yucatán Mayan year
POT vessel (flower-); (tea-); tankard
ga **POT** random shot (billiards) (bowls)
POT (home-distilled) (poteen) (drugs)
me **POT** Danish litre
POW Prisoner of War
md **POX** disease; small-; cow-; syphilis
POY balancing-pole; a grant
POZ positive; certain
cf **PRE-** before (pre-war) (Lat.)
PRO for (argument); professional
cf **PRO-** in favour of (on account of) (Gr.)
PRY peer; snoop; examine
PSI Greek letter
md **PSP** test of blood flow through kidney
md **PTH** parathyroid hormone
PUB licensed public drinking house
zo **PUD** paw; pad; pudding
zo **PUG** dog; fox or monkey
nm **PUL** Russian and Georgian coin
PUN same-sound words; (humour); homophone; paronomasia
zo **PUP** whelp; young dog or seal
zo **PUR, PURR,** curr, hoot (cat or owl sounds)
md **PUS** septic discharge (infection)
PUT game at cards; rustic; (throwing the weight/shot)
PUT place; -down; demote; quell; install; -off; delay, evade; -through; connect
PUT -up; construct; -up with, tolerate; -up for (election)
PUT -and call (Stock Exchange)
gl **PUY** volcanic formation
ch **PVC** synthetic resin, polyvinyl chloride
nm **PYA** Burmese money
rl **PYE** rule for determining Easter date
zo **PYE** pie; magpie; thief
PYO Burmese verse, type
rl, nm **PYX, PIX** holy box; coin box at the Mint

Q

rl **QAT** mountain spirits (Siberia); Melanesian and Australian deities
QUA as (Lat.)
QUI who (Lat.)
QUO whither (Lat.); status quo; as it is

R

me **RAD** radical; afraid (Sc.); radiation dose
mu **RAG** worn garment; (-paper) (-stone); (-time jazz); prank; (-week) (student's-)
mu **RAG** torment; tease; Hindi scale
me **RAI** Thai acre; ethnic group (orig. Nepal)
RAJ British power (India)
bt **RAK, Arak** Ar. desert shrub; (toothbrush)
zo, nt **RAM** male sheep; butt; (prow); (power-press); cram; engine
RAN raced; scurried; flowed; melted
mu **RAP** snatch; tap; music; reprimand
nm **RAP** counterfeit Irish halfpenny
RAS vizier (Abyssinia/Ethiopia)
zo **RAT** to desert; rodent; betray
cp **RAW** bleak; crude; uncooked; painful; unprocessed data; (-deal)
RAX reach; strain (Sc.)
zo, mu **RAY** the skate; spoken sol-fa note (re)
vt, zo **RAY** sheep scab; (-spider) (light-) (X-)
RED disentangle; revolutionary; colour
nm **REE** hen-bird of ruff; riddle; tipsy; Portuguese unit of account; rei
md **REF** reference; a hormone factor (renal)
go **REG** gravel, desert plain (Arabia)
go **REH** saline efflorescence (India)
nm **REI** Portuguese unit of account, ree
me **REM** ionizing radiation dosage (roentgen)
cf, md **REN-** of the kidney (renal)
REP debauchee; rip; fabric; agent; repetition; repertory (theatre)
lw **RES** a thing; a point
RET to rot flax; hemp or jute
rl **REV** to speed up; Reverend; increase revolutions, accelerate
REV revise, revision; revert, reverse
zo **REX** a king; cat breed
go **RIA** inlet of the sea (funnel-shaped)

ck **RIB** bone (-cut, spare); border band
go, bd, bt **RIB** ridge; petiole; frame; watercress
RID to free; clear; expel; destroy
bt **RIE, RYE** a grain; (-whisky)
RIF, RIFF riffi, riffians, Berber tribe
nt **RIG** wanton; manipulate; fit out; sail
go **RIM** brim; border; edge; lip
me **RIO** a tael; ounce (Japan)
RIP tear; rend; -saw, -cord (safety); (speed); lose control
ga **RIP** rest in peace; famous sleeper; seaward current (surfing)
RIP fish-basket; a Lothario
mu **RIT** strike; tear (Sc.); ritardando, repeat
nm **RIX** Ceylonese (Sri Lankan) dollar
ch **RNA** ribonucleic acid (genetic code)
ROB rook; fleece; strip; fruit syrup
zo **ROC, ROK** fabulous bird (Sinbad)
me **ROD** pole or perch; cane; twig; gad
nc, ga, md **ROD** metal bar (piston); (fishing-); retinal nerve; gun (Am.)
zo **ROE** deer; fish ova (caviare)
ROG to jog; to shake
zo **ROK** roc; fabulous bird
ROM gipsy; a Romany
RON King Arthur's ebony spear
zo **ROO** a kangaroo
rl **ROT** to decay; putrefy; nonsense; Same god
ROW line; brawl; din; (oars); quarrel
cp **ROW** cards; punched cards
ROY a king (obs.)
rl **RTA, RITA** Hindu cosmic order (Vedas)
RUA storage pit (NZ); 'street' (Port.)
RUB chafe; abrade; dilemma
zo **RUC** rok; roc; a fabulous bird
RUD rub; polish; flush; ochre
RUE lament; regret; suffer; sorrow
bt **RUE** herb of grace
RUG mat; coverlet; a drink; shaggy dog
RUM Rummy card game; Moslem term for Roman Empire and its people
RUN hurry on foot; race; (-away), escape; manage; propel; trip; long- (theatre)
ga **RUN** score (cricket, baseball etc.)
cp **RUN** route; series (track); chicken coop; sequence; performances
RUT wheel track; groove; desire
ga **RUT** (mating season); deep piste (skiing); monotony of routine
RYA a wall-rug
vt **RYE, RIE** (-bread); a bird disease
RYE rie; (whisky)
me **RYO** Japanese monetary unit

S

SAB sob (Sc.)
md **SAC** bag, often fluid-containing; N. Am. Indian tribe (Sauk)
SAD sorry; downcast; gloomy; dismal
SAE so (Sc.); stamped addressed envelope
SAG droop; settle; bend
zo **SAI** Brazilian monkey
bt, ch **SAL** Indian timber tree; salt
SAM together; to collect; to curdle
bt, zo **SAP** undermine; juice; egghead; moisture; (stone); (-beetle)
SAT seated; perched; settled
to **SAW** a saying; adage; seen; toothed cutter
to, mu **SAX** knife; slate-cutter's hammer; (o-phone)
SAY tell; declare; utter; allege
SAZ guitar (Turk.)
go **SEA** basin; ocean; wave surge
rl **SEB, KEB, GEB** Egyptian deity
SEC dry (flavour)
SED (fish-hook); a fillet
rl **SEE** watch; heed; holy- (Vatican)
bt, zo **SEG** sedge; bullock
SEL self (Sc.)
me, nm **SEN SE** Asian unit of length and money
bt **SEP** sepal, outer leaf of flower (calyx)
ma, zo **SET** group; clique; fix; prepare; (-out); (-sail); badgers' den
nt **SET** wave flow (surfing) (tennis); (-sail) (hair-) (stage-)
rl **SET, SETH** god of darkness (Eg.)
SEW stitch; hem; baste
SEX gender
zo **SHA** shapo; wild sheep
SHE female pronoun
SHE Miao-Yao speaking people (Ch.)
mu, me **SHO** Jap. mouth organ; unit of capacity
nm, rl **SHU** old Jap. coin; god of Eg. and Ch.
SHY coy; bashful; jib; wary
SIB, SYB akin to (sibling), brother, sister
SIC as written (Lat.)
SIK to seek (Sc.)

SIL ochre pigment
rl **SIM** a Simeonite; low churchman
SIN transgress; wickedness; inquity; err
rl, ma **SIN** Nanna, moon god; (trig. sine)
SIP, SUP taste
SIR sire; master; knight
SIS girl; sweetheart; sister
cf **-SIS** (analy-sis); abstract results
SIT brood; incubate; rest; repose
SIX sax (Sc.)
ga **SKI** gliding on snow; winter sport
ga **SKY** the heavens (weather); rowing fault
SLY artful; wily; astute; fly
SNY upward curve
SOB cry; blubber; weep; snivel
lw **SOC** privilege; sac; society
SOD turf; lawn; grass; pervert
go **SOG** morass; marsh; to saturate; bog
mu **SOH** spoken 5th note of sol-fa scale
nm, mu **SOL** old Fr. halfpenny; 5th note (so, soh); monetary unit (Peru)
rl **SOL** Indiges, Roman sun god; gold
mu **SON** male offspring; disciple; Fr. sound
SOP to soak; to steep; a bribe
SOS help! Save our Souls!
SOT drunkard
nm **SOU** French mite; sol
ag, zo **SOW** disseminate; plant; seed; fem. pig
tx **SOX, SOCKS** stockings; hose
bt, ck **SOY** bean, sauce; oriental footwear
SPA spring; health resort; hydro
SPY espy; behold; detect; observe
md **STY, STYE** pig pen; eye ailment
SUB subscription; money gift; substitute; junior officer
cf **SUB-** beneath, inferior, under (Lat.)
rl **SUD** Mesopotamian goddess (Ninlil)
lw **SUE** prosecute; plead
zo **SUG** a kind of worm
SUK Nilotic language
ma, cp **SUM** total; amount; addend and augend
as, rl **SUN** centre of solar system; -gods
me **SUN** Japanese inches
SUP to take super; imbibe
lw **SUS** arrest on suspicion
zo **SUS** silicon unilateral switch; wild pig
SYB, SIB akin to; (sibling)
SYN syne; since (Sc.)
cf **SYN-** joined, together, along with (Gr.)

T

TAB flap; tally; check; pull-strip
TAB protector for bow (archery) (theatre)
TAD a little (USA); street boy (USA)
ga **TAG** catchword; touch; label; game; wedge; append
cp, ga **TAG** identification symbols; digits; expel (baseball)
zo **TAI** Japanese bream; Thai people
ar, tx **TAJ** Mahal; headdress (Ind.)
TAN to beat; brown colour
me **TAN** boat people (Tanka); a weight (Ch.)
rl **TAO** 'heavenly way' (Ch.)
to, pb **TAP** rap; pat; knock; broach; exploit; faucet; (screw) (stopcock)
nt **TAR** pitch; bitumen; sailor
tx, zo **TAT** needlework; native cloth; pony
zo **TAU** bug; toad-fish
rl **TAU** Egyptian or St Anthony's cross
TAW a marble; game
TAY SE Asian people
lw **TAX** levy; tariff; (accuse); strain
bt, ck **TEA** beverage; bohea; (cannabis)
TEC teck; detective
TED spread
mu **TEE** (golf); hinge; 7th note (te, ti)
zo **TEG** deer; sheep; tag
ch **TEL** tetraethyl lead
rl **TEM, ATUM** Egyptian god
TEN a net drawn up; number
TER thrice
TEW gear; iron chain; scourge
me **TEX** weight in grams of 1000m of yarn
THE definite article
THO' though; SE Asian people
THY of thee; thine
zo **TIB** a courtesan; gib; cat
me **TIC** nervous twitch; spasm
TIE dead-heat; bind; unite; (neck-)
ga **TIG** game; cup; equal scores (games)
mn, ga **TIN** can; preserve; receptacle; money; metal; wall strip (squash)
rl **TIN** Tinia, Tina, Etruscan and Gr. gods
TIP gratuity; vails; cant; tilt; incline
TIR Transport International Routing
'TIS it is
zo, pl **TIT** small bird; pony; teat or nipple
TIV N. Nigerian farming people
rl **TIW, TYR** Germanic god
me, bt, zo **TOD** 28lb of wool; bush; fox
pl **TOE** foot-finger; on -s; readiness
tx **TOG** to dress; garment

zo **TOK** nesting place of capercaillies (Sc.)
TOL take away; Bengali school of humanities
TOM male cat; -boy (girl)
me **TON** measure of weight (2240lb/ 1000kg)
me **TON** 20 cwt; (displacement) (cargo space)
ga **TON** hundred runs (century, cricket)
TOO also; as well; – much; – many (overdone)
TOP toy; vertex; zenith; acme; excel; lid
gl, ar **TOR** granite outcrop on a hill; (tower)
TOT child; to total
me **TOU** Ch. unit of capacity (10 litres)
bt **TOW** haul; flax, hemp, jute, bast fibres
mu **TOY** trifle; plaything; (instrument); lute
cf **TRI-** of three together (Gr.); (-angle)
TRY test; essay; attempt; endeavour
ga **TRY** rugby football score
nt **TUB** basin; container; boat; kit; kid
TUG tow; (-ship); pull; (-of war); gliding (aircraft)
zo **TUI** parson-bird (NZ)
me **TUN** barrel; large cask; 252 gals
zo, to **TUP** ram; to mate (of sheep); hammer
zo **TUR** Caucasian goat
TUT! deprecating exclamation
TUT piece-work; a hassock
TWA two (Sc.); Pygmy people
TWI Niger-Congo lang. subgroup (Kwa)
TWO a pair; brace; couple; deuce (cards)
TYE ore washing buddle; tie
TYG tall china cup; mug
TYO Teke, Bateke, Ato, Bantu people (Congo/Kinshasa)
rl **TYR** Norse (Engl. Tiw), one-handed war god
mu **TZ'U** speech-like trad. songs (Ch.)

U

zo **UCA** fiddler crab
UDA purplish brown glaze
bt **UDO** Jap. vegetable; universal language
UGH! UG, UH, exclamation of disgust
bt **ULE** gum (Mexico)
ULL Norse patron of snow-shoes
ULT ultimo, the latest
rl **UMA** Parvati, wife of Siva/Shiva (Ind.)
nt **UNA** gat-boat with centreboard for deltas
cf **UNI-** treat as one, singular (Lat.)
rl **UNO** United Nations Organization; ancestor of the Hungarians
UPS peak occasion; (– and downs)
zo **URE** wild ox; aurochs
URF stunted child (Sc.)
URN jar; vase; receptacle
URU S. Am. Indians (Lake Titicaca)
USE usage; avail; employ; apply; usury
zo **UTA** American lizard
UTO Aztecan languages
UTU blood-money; requital (NZ); sun god
bt **UVA** a bunch (of grapes)

V

VAC vacation; holiday
VAD Voluntary Aid Detachment (Women's); war worker
go **VAE, VOE** gio; creek; firth; fjord
VAG peat (Sc.)
VAI, VEI tribe (Liberia and Sierra Leone)
VAN fan; forefront; vehicle; wind vane
el, me **VAR** unit of reactive power of A/C
pl **VAS** blood vessel; vesicle, glandular tubes
me **VAT** fat; vessel; tank; value-added tax; Dutch liquid measure
VEI, VAI Mande-speaking African tribe
me **VEL** (wind) velocity; speed + force (of impact)
vt **VET** animal doctor; examine; check
VEX harass; fret; chafe; make angry
VIA by way of; route detail
VIE strive; contend; contest
mu **VIF** lively (Fr.)
VIM force; (vim and vigour)
VIS -a-, facing; comparison
VIZ namely
go **VLY** vlei, pool (S. Africa)
VOE vae; geo; gio; fiord; estuary; firth
hd **VOL** two wings coinjoined at base; crest
VON in names of nobility (of) (Ger.)
nv **VOR** navigational ranging system

VOW promise; dedicate; oath
mu **VOX** voice; song part; public opinion
gl **VUG** rock cavity (Cornish)
VUM boom (cannon noise) (USA)

W

mn **WAD** manganese ore; stuffing; pile of paper; (cottonwool)
WAE woe (Sc.)
WAG vibrate; wit; humorist; (tailing)
me **WAH, WA** Thai unit of length
WAN pale; sickly; languid
WAP whop; a bundle; swat; wrap; copulate; beat
WAR strife; enmity; hostilities; (price-)
WAS past of 'be' (sing.)
zo **WAT** hare; drunken (Sc.)
WAX increase; grow; beeswax (seal)
WAY route; method; track
WEB a textile fabric; cobweb
WED a pledge; to marry; unite
WEE diminutive; urinate (sl.)
ga **WEI** chi-go board game (Ch.)
md **WEN** tumour; wart; metropolis
WET humid; watery; drench; moisten
me **WEY** various weights, salt, corn, etc
WHO which person?
WHY for what reason (purpose?)
WIG vallancy; toupee; periwig; peruke
WIG berate; scold; lecture; upbraid
ga **WIN** gain; acquire; achievement
WIS, WIT know (obs.)
WIT wag; quick thinker; humorist; (half-)
WOE affliction; sorrow; grief; anguish
nm **WON** to dwell; abode and money (Korea)
WON came first (race); earned; got; swayed; persuaded
WOO to court (for marriage or gain)
WOP, WHOP whip; (Sc.)
WOT known (obs.)
WOW event; sound change
WRY awry; askew; crooked; distorted
WUM aghem, African tribe (Cameroon); vum
pb **WYE** a person (Sc.); Y-branched pipe

Y

YAB jabber (Sc.); confused chattering
YAH! exclamation of derision
zo **YAK** Tibetan ox
rl, bt, ck **YAM** sweet potato; Semitic deity
YAO pottery ware and Ch. legendary emperor
YAO mountain people of Ch. and SE Asia
nm **YAP** yell; cry; bark; money (fei) Pacific stone-disc currency
nt **YAW** deviate; sideways heaving; head movement of horse (gliding)
YEA, AY, AYE yes; verily
nm **YEN** a gold or silver Japanese coin
YEP yeh; yes (Amer.)
YES yea; aye; ay
YET a gate (Sc.)
YET still; further; besides; however
bt **YEW** wood for the bow; (cemetree)
YEX hiccough
rl **YIN** -yang, life's complementary forces (Ch.)
YIP pert forward girl (Sc.)
YOD phonetic sound 'y' (yon)
YON yonder
YOU 2nd-person pronoun
zo **YOW** ewe (Sc.)
rl **YUE** Moon and lunar month (Ch.)
YUG an age of the world (Hind.)

Z

nt, me **ZAK** Kashmir raft; Dutch measure
rl **ZAM** Persian earth spirit (djin)
me **ZAR** Iranian 1 metre
to **ZAX** slate cutter; sax
ZED, ZEE letter 'Z' (Engl., USA)
mu **ZEL** cymbal
rl **ZEN** sect and school of Buddhism (Jap.)
me **ZER** guz, gueza, gudge, measure (Iran)
zo **ZHO** zobo; hybrid yak and cow
ZIP liveliness; fastener (trousers); a ping sound; postcode
zo **ZOO** zoological garden
cf **ZOO-** of animal classification (Gr.)
nm **ZUZ** an ancient Jewish coin

FOUR-LETTER WORDS

A

rl **ABBA** Chaldean or Coptic divine; father
rl **ABBE** French abbot; priest
ABED in bed
ABER river mouth (Celtic)
ABET aid; incite; favour; countenance
ABIB 1st month of the Jewish year
ABLE skilful; adroit; expert; competent
ABLY masterly; powerfully; cleverly
nt **A-BOX** opposite bracing of yards
ABUT **ABUTT**; adjoining; terminate
bt **ACER** the maple-tree
ACES (spot); dice game
ACHE pain; pang; agony; anguish
ch **ACID** vitriolic; sour; tart; (-rain) (-drop, sweet)
ACME zenith; apex; pinnacle; pitch
md **ACNE** a skin disease
md **ACOR** acidity
me **ACRE** area of space (land)
cf **ACRO-** topmost; first (Gr.)
lw **ACTA** proceedings in a court
ch **ACYL** carboxylic acid radical
ADAM the first man; a gaoler
ADAR 12th month of the Jewish year
bd **ADDS** overall quantities, extras
ADIT opening or passage; entrance
to **ADZE** adz; a mattock
AEON an age; era; cycle; period; eon
cf **AERO-** air or gas
AERY ethereal; visionary
AFAR away; distant; remote; aloof
AFER the South-West wind
AGAR ploughman of playing fields, Eton
bl, ck, md **AGAR** seaweed; mucilage; gel
AGED elderly; ancient; antiquated
rl **AGHA** **AGA**, ruler of sect, estates owner
AGIO premium; discount; brokerage
AGNI Hindu fire-god and protector
AGOG astir; eager; excited
ck **AGON** sardine-like Alpine fish
ga **AGON** contest; struggle; (antagonist) (Gr.)
zo **AGUA** South American toad
md **AGUE** malarial fever; chilliness
AHEM! exclamation
nt **AHOY!** exclamation (nautical)
AIDE helper; assistant; coadjutor
md **AIDS** acquired immune deficiency syndrome
ga **AIDS** last three fingers of sword hand (fencing)
AIN'T (am not, are not)
AINU aboriginal (Jap.)
bt **AIRA** hair-grass
AIRE an altar; Irish freeman
AIRY blythe; breezy; ethereal; spacious
AJAR slightly opened
bt **AKEE** West Indian fruit tree
AKIN sib; agnate; similar; related
ALAR winged, pertaining to wings
ALAS alack; welladay
zo **ALCA** sea-auk genus
nt **ALEE** on the lee-side
bt **ALFA** esparto grass
bt **ALGA** seaweed
cf, md **ALGO-** pain
pr **ALIF** 1st letter Arabic alphabet
ALLY **ALLEY**; a marble of real alabaster
ALLY unite; marry; confederate; friend
ALMS oblations; gifts; bounty
ALOD allod; freehold
bt **ALOE** a large genus of bitter herbs
go **ALPS** mountain range; (-pastures)
ALSO in like manner; further
mu **ALTO** male voice of highest pitch
ch **ALUM** mordant mineral salt
AMAH ayah; Indian nurse
md **AMBE** ancient surgical instrument
AMBO high reading desk
rl **AMEN** prayer affirmation (Hebrew)
zo **AMIA** bow-fin or mud-fish (N. Amer.)
ch **AMIC** ammoniac; friend
AMID betwixt; between; amongst
ch **AMIN** ammoniate (acid)
AMIR **EMIR**; Arab ruler
rl **AMMA** a truss; Syrian abbess
AMMO ammunition
AMOK **AMUCK**; in a frenzy; berserk
AMOR Roman cupid; Eros
AMOY language (Formosa)
ch **AMYL** a tar product
ANAK a giant of Palestine
pl, zo **ANAL** of the anus

zo **ANER** male ant
ANEW again; freshly; repeatedly
cf, md **ANGI-** of blood vessels
bt **ANIL** the indigo plant; dye
ANKH life symbol (Egypt)
nm **ANNA** 16 annas to the rupee
zo **ANOA** wild ox of Celebes
ANON unknown; hidden; at once; again
ANSA decorated vase-handle
ar **ANTA** a pilaster
ANTE a stake at poker
cf **ANTE-** before
pl **ANUS** excremental orifice
APED copied; imitated; mimicked
APER an impersonator
APEX acme; zenith; pinnacle; ticket
APIS sacred bull (Egypt)
zo **APOD** fish without ventral fins
ar, rl **APSE** polygonal recess; behind altar
rl **AQUA** water; solution
ARAB Saracen; Moor
ARAF Mohammedan purgatory
bt **ARAK** oriental palm sap spirit; areca nut
bt **ARAR** North African timber tree
ARBA covered wagon (Tartar)
rl **ARCA** chest or coffer
ar **ARCH** roguish; cunning; portal
mu **ARCO** bow of stringed instrument
cp, me **AREA** of space; zone; yard; topic
ARES Mars, the God of War
nt **ARGO** the Argonauts' ship
mu **ARIA** air; tune; melody (opera)
ARID dry; parched; sterile; barren
bt **ARIL** outer seed cover
ARMS armorial emblems
ARMY host; array; throng; force
mu **ARPA** harp (It.)
'ARRY **HARRY**; Cockney names
nt **ARSE** backside; tail of block
ARTS crafts; guiles
ARTY spuriously aesthetic
bt **ARUM** lily genus
ch **ARYL** aromatic hydrocarbon radical
ASAR eskar; gravel ridges
bt **ASCI** bags of spores
ASHY ashen; wan; pallid; hueless
ASIA largest continent
zo **ATKA** type of mackerel
ATLI a Norse king (Atle)
ATOM jot; tittle; whit; particle
ATOP acop; on top (obs.)
cp, ma **ATTO** one million million millionth 10^{-18}
cf **AUDI-** of hearing
AULA a hall; a court
AUNT (Aunt Sally)
nm **AURA** a zephyr; emanation
rl **AUTO** da fé, act of faith (burning of heretics)
cf **AUTO-** (-car) (-matic)
AVAL an endorsement on a bill
bt **AVEL** an awn of barley
go, gl **AVEN** subterranean; sinkhole
AVER avouch; confirm; authenticate
zo **AVES** birds, collectively
AVID eager; greedy; voracious
AVON river (Celt.)
AVOW own; aver; admit; confess
AWAY afar; distant; abroad; absent
AWED inspired by reverence, cowed
bt **AWNY** bearded
AWRY askew; oblique; crooked
AXED discharged; sacked; cut down
AXEL freestyle jump (ice skating); (optional)
bt **AXIL** angle between branch and trunk
AXIN cochineal ointment
zo **AXIS** the chital; Indian spotted deer
AXLE axis; spindle; shaft
zo **AXON** nerve cell impulse-carrying process
AYES supporting votes (Parliament)
mu **AYRE** **AIR**; old English verse song
AZAN polychrome microanalytical
AZER **AZERI**; Azerbaijani (Asian)

B

BAAL Phoenician god; false god; idol
BAAS the boss; master (Cape Dutch)
rl, ck **BABA** **PAPA**, Pope, Patriarch; (rum-, cake)
BABE infant; suckling
BABU Hindu clerk
BACK help; support; posterior; wager; trim sails to windward; reverse; retreat
nt, ga, ar **BACK** (-pay); fall-; (wrestling) (football); extrados of arch; (-sail)
BADE (bid); commanded
BAFF **BIFF**, **BUFF**; smite
BAFT abalt; an oriental fabric
nm **BAHT** Thai monetary unit
lw **BAIL** (cricket); hoop; handle; surety
BAIT worry; badger; a lure; refreshment
go **BAIU** plum rains; Japan
BAKE harden; parch
BALD bare; hairless; prosaic; unadorned
ag **BALE** **BANE**; harm; misery; bundle; hay

ga, nt **BALK** **BAUK**, **BAULK**, impede; refuse; timber; (baseball) (-head)
BALL party; rout; globe; bullet
BALM salve; unguent; fragrance; soothing
BANC bench; office place (obs.)
lw, mu, bd **BAND** **BOND**, unite; a troupe; a coterie; musicians; brace; (elastic-)
cp, ro **BAND** magnetic; zone; wavelength
ch, bt, zo **BANE** poison; ruin; sheep-rot
BANG explosion; a fringe of hair
BANG bhang; the assassin's drug
ck **BANG** a drink (beer, cider, nutmeg, ginger)
nm **BANI** Romanian monetary unit
go, cp **BANK** bench of rowers; deposit and loan office; tilt ridge; obstacle; layer; (river-)
BANT adopt a slimming diet
BARB to shave; thorn; spike; (fish-hook)
zo **BARB** horse
BARD a poet, playwright; minstrel
BARE naked; nude; exposed; bleak
cf **BARI-** **BARY-**; low (baritone) (Gr.)
bt, nt **BARK** cortex; yelp; yap; a ship; cork
BARM yeast; ferment; leaven
BARN granary; store; out-building; (-dance)
me **BARN** nuclear cross-section unit 10^{-18} metres
cf **BARO-** of weight, pressure (barometer)
BART Bartholomew, baronet
bt **BARU** fluffy fibre
cp **BASE** basis; abject; vile; sordid; starting point; foundation; data; radix
nt, ga **BASE** (naval-); (baseball)
BASH smite; baff; wallop; buffet; attempt
cf **BASI-** **BASO-**; depth (bassoon) (Gr.)
BASK luxuriate; revel; yap; (sunbathing)
mu **BASS** low voice; deep, grave
bt, zo **BASS** American linden tree; perch
bl **BAST** bass; fibre of that tree
ri **BAST** cat-headed Egyptian goddess
BATE abate; decrease; lessen; tease
BATH basin; pool; (mud-)
me **BATH** Jewish liquid measure
me, cp, tc, rd **BAUD** telegraphic transmission; pulse rate (modulation)
BAUK **BAULK**, **BALK**, beam; ridge; hinder
zo **BAWD** whore; hare
BAWL howl; yawl; yell; shout
BAWN fort; cattle-pen
zo **BAYA** the Indian weaver bird
bt **BAYS** laurels of distinction
cp **BEAD** bubble; globule; a moulding; module
BEAK magistrate; prow; bill; mandible
nt, ga **BEAM** rafter; ray; shine; emit; smile; plank (gymn.) (fencing) (baseball)
nt **BEAM** radio directional system; width
bt **BEAN** leguminous plant
zo **BEAR** carry; uphold; suffer; produce
ck, pl, mu **BEAT** spent; exhausted; batter; throb; (heart-); rhythm; notation
nt **BEAT** a policeman's walk; patrol route; sail to windward; punish (corporal)
BEAU fop; dandy; gallant; coxcomb
BECK beckon; a small stream
ck **BEEF** meat of cattle; grumble (USA), strength
mu **BEEN** the vina; Indian guitar
BEEP telephone signal
BEER ale; lager; swipes
bt **BEET** the beetroot
BEIN comfortable; well-found (Sc.)
BEJA tribe (Africa)
nm **BEKA** Hebrew monetary unit
mu **BELL** model of soundness; to bellow; alarm-; telephone-; resonant musical peals
mu **BELL** (church-s)
nm **BELL** monetary unit (Fr. Revolution); Ch. coin
BELT zone; girdle; band; thrash
rl **BEMA** judge's seat; pulpit
BEND stoop; incline; a spree; sag; curve
hd, ga **BEND** diagonal band on a shield; ball to swerve in flight (soccer)
bt **BENE** the oil-plant
bt **BENT** curved; crooked; withered grass
bt **BERE** bear; barley (Sc.)
mo **BERG** mountain; iceberg
BERM a ledge; slanting bank
BEST worst; defeat; overcome
nc **BETA** ray; function; 2nd ltr of Gr. alphabet
BEVY swarm; flock; throng
bt **BHEL** Bengal quince
BHIL a Dravidian race (Ind.)
cp **BIAS** prejudice; (bowls); error; partiality
el, ps **BIAS** voltage applied to determine characteristics of device
tx **BIBS** uniform for babies and netballers

ga **BICE** pale blue or green
BIDE await; tarry; stay; dwell
BIER a conveyance for the dead; hearse
BIFF **BAFF**; **BUFF**; smite; crash
BIGA two-horsed Roman chariot
BIGG bere; a kind of barley (Sc.)
zo **BIKE** bicycle; wasp's nest; a swarm
md **BILE** bitter liver secretion; ill-humour
BILK balk; cheat; decieve; thwart
lw, zo **BILL** fondle; account; placard; poster; invoice; law; beak; -hook
go **BILL** narrow headland; peninsula
BIND tie; fasten; restrain; secure
ga, lw **BIND** seizing prey in flight (falconry); (fencing) agree; hindrance
bt **BINE** hop-stems; (wood-)
BING a heap of corn or alum
BINK bench; bank; shelf (Sc.)
BINT a girl (Arabic)
bt **BION** plant capable of separate life
ch **BIOS** yeast-growth promoter
zo, ga **BIRD** a fowl; shuttlecock (badminton); prison term; magistrate; girl
bt **BIRK** the birch-tree
BIRL spin; whirl (Sc.)
BIRR impetus; violent thrust; a whirr
nm **BIRR** Ethiopian monetary unit
zo **BIRT** the turbot
BISE cold dry wind (Swiss)
ck **BISK** bisque; soup; pottery style
BITE a nibble; etch; nip; grip; grasp
nt, cp **BITT** (to bitt a cable)
BLAB divulge; disclose; tell tales
BLAD fragment; lump; stain; batter (Sc.)
bt **BLAE** blue (Sc.); (-berry)
zo **BLAY** **BLEY**, a river fish; the bleak
bt **BLEA** inner bark of tree
md **BLEB** transparent blister; bubble
BLED past tense of bleed
BLEE complexion; colour
bt **BLET** spot on decayed fruit; to rot
BLEW sounded, puffed; panted; past of to blow
rd **BLIP** radar reflection spot
BLOB viscous globule
BLOC political/economic grouping
BLOT blur; mar; tarnish; erase
ga, mu **BLOW** sound (horn); puff; pant; (baseball); (bowling); strike (boxing)
bd **BLUB** sob; cry; blubber; blistering (**USA**); hole in plastercast
BLUE navy; azure; sapphire; (Oxford)
mu **BLUE** cobalt-; ultramarine; glum; jazz
BLUR dim; sully; obscure; blot
zo **BOAR** male hog
nt **BOAT** craft; bark; skiff; vessel
BOCK light beer
BODE portend; presage; augur
BODY corpse; carcass; substance; torso; horse (gymn.)
BOER Afrikaaner (ex-Dutch)
ga **BOGU** kendo armour of Kendoka
BOGY bogey; bugbear; hobgoblin
pr **BOIL** seethe; rage; fume
BOKO nasal organ (sl.)
pr **BOLD** brave; valiant; daring; strong
bt **BOLE** a tree-trunk; recess
bt **BOLL** pod; capsule
ga **BOLO** Filipino knife; uppercut blow (boxing)
BOLT abscond; flee; gulp; missile; fasten; sift; lock (door); (nuts and —s); (-hole)
zo **BOMA** boa; anaconda
BOMB petard; block-buster; bombard; charged explosive; success
ga **BOMB** (basketball); (lacrosse); surfing)
BOND link; band; chain; contract; (bricks)
zo **BONE** steal; (china); skeletal
sp **BONK** knock; extreme fatigue (cycling); sexual intercourse
BONT many-coloured (S. Africa)
BONY full of bones; strong; stout
BOOB **BOOBY**, blockhead; dune; mistake
BOOH! a derisive interjection; sadness
BOOK tome; volume; manual; reserve
nt **BOOM** boost; resound; barrier; vum (Am.); spar attached to mast; dhow; economic upthrust
BOON benefit; merry; jovial
BOOR clodhopper; lout; lubber
ga **BOOT** gain; to eject; luggage recess; footwear; kick; dismiss
ar **BOOT** facing brickwork base
BORA cold Adriatic wind
BORD coal face (mining)
to, mu **BORE** tidal wave; tire; drill; calibre, North Wind
BORN née; begotten
to **BORT** **BOART**, low-quality diamond for drills

BOSA a Persian liquor
BOSH tosh; inane chatter; bunkum
BOSK bosket; thicket; grove
pb, gl **BOSS** foreman; stud; protuberance; keystone; boxwood cone; hole plug; rock dome
ga **BOSS** (archery, butt)
lw **BOTE** compensation; reparation
BOTH all of two
zo **BOTS** botts; the larvae of the botfly
zo **BOUD** insect in grain; weevil
BOUN to dress; prepare; set out (Sc.)
rl **BOUS** Norse deity, son of Odin and Rinda
BOUT contest; conflict; turn
nt **BOVO** Genoese fishing boat
mn **BOWK** large iron barrel; kibble
BOWL beaker; goblet; dish; (pipe); heavy ball; stadium, show centre
ga **BOWL** throw (cricket); (Am. football)
nt **BOWS** the fore-end of a ship; fancy knots
BRAD small nail
go **BRAE** hill overlooking valley (Sc.)
BRAG boast; vaunt; a game of cards
bt, rl **BRAN** husk of grain; Celtic deity
BRAT urchin; gamin; child
BRAW fine; brave; showy (Sc.)
BRAY braise; pound; clamour; blare; donkey talk
BRED reared; raised; nurtured
BREE eyebrow; liquor
BREN sub-machine gun
BRER brother; (brer-rabbit)
zo **BRET** a fish of the turbot kind
BREW concoct (beer); devise; plot
ck **BRIE** a creamy cheese
nt **BRIG** two-masted sailing ship; bridge (Sc.)
me **BRIL** unit of brightness
BRIM verge; marge; border; to coast
BRIN a fan-stick
mu **BRIO** vivacity
zo **BRIT** whitebait (fish); a citizen of UK
BROB a wooden wedge
BROC pewter wine measure
to **BROG** an awl; to pierce
BROW rim; edge; brink; forehead
zo **BUBO** the eagle owl
zo, nm **BUCK** talk; jump; deer (bok); dollar
BUDE a gas burner
BUFF baff; biff; strike; yellow; devotee
BUFF pliant leather; the bare skin
BUHL brass and tortoiseshell inlay
mn **BUHR** burr-stone; a millstone
bt **BULB** (electric); corm; tuber
cp **BULK** mass; volume; magnitude; storage
zo, ga, rl **BULL** male animal (deer) (walrus); deck game; centre of target; papal decree
zo, ga **BUMP** fall; the call of the bittern; noise of rocks; volleyball pass
BUND league; association
BUNG barrel-stopper; large cork
rl **BUNI** chief of the Netherworld (Siberia)
rl **BURI** Odin's grandfather (Norse)
nt **BUNK** sleeping berth; run away
nt, ga **BUNT** butt; part of a sail; (baseball)
nt **BUOY** cheer; sustain; floating mooring; (light-)
ar **BURG** borough; burgh; bury; castle
BURK burke; murder; smother; hush up
BURL a knot in thread or wood
ps, md **BURN** a brook; char; glow; set on fire; combustion; (sun-)
ga, md **BURN** (bowls) (Am. football); injury
BURR rough edge; the burdock; dialect tone
bt **BURR** growth on tree-trunk, root
zo **BURT** flat-fish, turbot type
BURY burgh; clump of trees; inter
bt, zo **BUSH** thimble; (bearings); a shrub; (-baby)
go **BUSH** outback; wild scrubland
BUSK to entertain in the street
nt **BUSS** to kiss; a fishing boat
BUST bosom; sculpture; broken; bankrupt
BUSY sedulous; officious; industrious; engaged
rl **BUTO** nursing deity (Eg.)
BUTT log end; meet exactly; abut
BUTT thrust; a mound; bottom; fag-end; (rifle); bum
BUZZ rumour; a whispered report; wasp noise
BYRE a cow-house
cp **BYTE** data or data transfer unit

C

CABA cabas; work-basket; pannier
cf **CACO-** degenerate; diseased; (cacophony)
zo **CADE** cask of herrings; pet lamb
CADI **CAID**, **KADI**, Ottoman ruler; judge; (alcaide, mayor)
CAER camp; fort (Welsh)
ck **CAFE** coffee-house; snackbar

CAGE confine; cabin; lift (mine); road crossing
nt **CAIC CAIQUE**, Turkish coastboat
lw, zo **CAIN** rent (in kind); a weasel
ck **CAKE** (baked); solidify; piece of soap
zo, pl **CALF** young of cow; part of leg
nt **CALK CAULK**; spike; calkin
CALL (name); summon; visit; (-girl)
me, cp, tc **CALL** conversation time unit
CALM tranquil; still; windless
mn **CALP** shale bed (Irish)
mn **CALX** chalk or lime
zo **CAMA** South African hartebeest
bd **CAME** arrived; reached; attained; lead for lights fixing
CAMP pitch a tent; outdoor living place
CAMP exaggeratedly stylized; gay
bt **CANE** rattan; bamboo; beat
CANG Chinese pillory
CANT incline; thieves' patter; hypocrisy; tilt
bd **CANT** to cut waste from a log
CANY made of cane
CAPA Spanish cloak
tx, go **CAPE CAPA, COPE**, cloak; headland
mu **CAPO** (da-); device on guitar fingerboard
tx, ga, cp **CARD** woolcomb; personality; game; (wool); (credit); (punched); (score)
lw **CARE** tend; concern; worry; heed
cr **CARF** groove made by a carpenter
CARK care; trouble; fret; anxiety
CARL churl; clown
zo **CARP** cavil; censure; goldfish
CARR reclaimed bog land
CART van; wagon; transport
bd, md, lw **CASE** box; enclose; plight; facing (brick); patient; law
nm **CASH** ready money; Chinese coin
CASK casque; helmet; barrel; tub; cade
CAST mien; shed; toss; mould; tint; throw; direct, arrange, performers; (eye); (angling)
ga **CAST** swift, clean-shooting bow (archery)
cf **CATA- KATA-**, from; against (catapult)
CATE dainty food
CAUF live-fish box
mn **CAUK** sulphate of baryta
bd **CAUL** net; membrane; aluminium or plywood sheet
gl **CAVE** cavern; grotto; den; beware!
zo **CAVY** genus of rodents; guinea-pig
mn **CAWK** heavy spar
CEDE yield; relinquish; apportion; forego
bd **CEIL** ciel; roof; ceiling
el, bl **CELL** cavity; dungeon; nucleus + protoplasm
me **CELO** unit of acceleration
CELT Kelt; early Aryan
nm **CENT** 10 cents make one dime
CERE to wax; to wrap in cerecloth
CERT alleged certainty; a snip
CEST cestus; a belt or girdle
rl **CHAC CHAAC**, C. Am. (Mayan) rain gods
zo, cp **CHAD** shad; sea-bream; punched hole
CHAI gipsy girl
CHAL gipsy man
CHAM CHAMOIS, -leather (cleaning)
CHAP jaw; cleft; fellow; guy; chapman
zo, ck **CHAR** a lake fish; tea; to scorch; to burn
zo **CHAT** talk; gossip; warbler; wheatear
CHEF expert cook
CHEW ruminate; munch
CHIC charmingly correct
CHID scolded; rated; rebuked
pl **CHIN** part of lower jaw
ga **CHIP** fruit basket; cut; to chaff; stake; golf shot
ck, cp **CHIP** (potato); semi-conductor; (microchip data)
cf **CHIR-** the hand (chiromancy, palmistry)
CHOP the jaw; veer; vary; change
ga **CHOP** cut; meat; strike; (cricket); (table tennis)
CHOU ornamental ribbon
zo **CHOW** Chinese dog
zo **CHUB** the cheven; a freshwater carp
CHUG throb of motor
CHUI Judo referee's rebuke
CHUM pal; palooka; buddy; messmate
CHUT a peevish cry
bd **CIEL** ceil; plaster; wainscot
bd **CILL SILL**, wall window frame base
ar **CIMA CYMA**, ogee moulding of cornice
CIRC prehistoric stone circle
tx **CIRE** polished silk fabric (Fr.)
zo **CIRL** a species of bunting
CIST CYST, stone chest; tomb
lw **CITE** quote; summon; adduce
CITY cathedral town
CLAD garbed; dressed; clothed
nt **CLAG** smokescreen (naval)
zo **CLAM** bivalve shellfish; to clog

CLAN family; coterie; clique; set
zo **CLAP** beak of hawk; applaud; cheer
cr **CLAW** tear; scratch; lacerate; talon; nail extractor
mn **CLAY** alumina; fine grained earth; (ceramics)
mu **CLEF** key; (treble; bass); score
zo **CLEG** horse-fly
CLEM to starve
nt **CLEW** clue; trace; brail; truss; aft corner of windsail
zo **CLIO** Muse of History; molluscs
CLIP cut; trim; prune; curtail; embrace
ga **CLIP** fasten; (film); speed; club; (Am. football)
CLIP coloured marker (croquet)
CLOD sod; turf; lump; yokel; rustic
CLOG obstruct; hamper; trammel
md **CLOT** curdle; thicken; coagulate; idiot
CLOY glut; pall; satiate; surfeit
CLUB cudgel; bludgeon; combine; set
CLUE clew; hint; guide; ball of string
COAK a dowel-pin; metal bush
mn **COAL** fossil fuel
COAT cover; lay; spread; vesture
COAX cajole; allure; wheedle
bt **COCA** the cocaine plant (Peru)
zo, pl **COCK** rooster; cockerel; penis
bd **COCK** (hay-) (stop-) (-a pistol) (-a snoot)
bt **COCO** coconut palm (fruit)
mu **CODA** finale
lw, cp **CODE** digest of laws, rules; cypher; (genetic)
CODY trampoline somersault
CO-ED mixed school
lw **COIF** hairstyle; judge's black cap
el **COIL** wind up; (dynamo)
nm **COIN** of currency; invent; counterfeit
nv **COIR** cordage; coconut fibre
bt **COIX** a grass; Job's tears
COKE processed coal; (Coca-Cola)
COLD icy; polar; gelid; passionless
bt **COLE** kale; cabbages generally
COLL fondle; embrace
zo **COLT** young horse; camel or ass
COLT gun; young cricketer
md **COMA** stupor; drowsiness
bt **COMA** tuft of follicles; (comet)
COMB cock's comb; crest; wave; (bees) (hair-dressing)
COMB combe; coomb; dell; valley
COME reach; attain; ensue; arrive
mu **COME** as, like; (come prima); as at first
COMS malt-dust
nt **COND** to navigate
bt, nt **CONE** (fir-cone); buoy; navigation mark; doubles badminton
CONK the nose
nt **CONN** con; cond; steer; navigate
CONS arguments again; cf. pros
zo **CONY** **CONEY**, hyrax; rock-rabbit
ck, lw **COOK** chef; to falsify accounts etc.
COOL calm; collected; allay; indifferent
COOM soot; axle dirt; coal-dust
zo **COON** sly fellow; raccoon
CO-OP co-operative, idealistic stores
CO-OP add to governing board
COOP hen-coop; cask; cage; confine
zo **COOT** old idiot, a water-fowl
tx, rl, ar **COPE** manage matters; cloak; wall mouldings
rl **COPT** Egyptian Christian
COPY model; ape; mimic; transcribe
CORB **CORF**, iron, coal, (alms)-basket
CORD line; rope; braid; cut wood
pl **CORD** (vocal); (spinal); (umbilical)
bd **CORE** centre; heart; kernel; (solid) base; (steel, brick)
bt **CORK** a stopper; bung; bark of cork oak
bt **CORM** a kind of bulb
bt **CORN** preserve; an excrescence; grain
COSH police baton; to slug
me **COSS** about 1¾ miles (2.8 km) (Ind.)
COST price; charge; outlay; detriment
COSY tea-pot cover; cozy; snug
COTE (sheep-); enclosure
COUP (-d'état); overturn; gain
bd **COVE** bay; bight; harbour; a fellow; moulding
COWL a monk's hood; chimney-pot
pl, zo **COXA** the hip-joint; leg of insect
COZY **COSY**, snug; comfortable
bt **CRAB** bitter apple; peevish person
zo **CRAB** a portable winch; crustacean
gl, mo **CRAG** steep, ragged, rockface
CRAM ram; stuff; glut; study
me **CRAN** about 750 herrings
CRAW maw; crop; fowl's stomach
zo **CRAX** S. American bird; curassow
CREE to soften grain
nt **CREW** mob; gang; crowd; crowed
bt **CREX** the white bullace
ce, rl **CRIB** manger; cot; coop; copy; grillage; (Xmas)
CRIS creese; Malay knife; kris
CROP reap; an ox-hide; whip; craw

zo **CROW** brag; vaunt; crowbar; croak
CROY embankment; fish-trap
CRUD hardening crust of snow (skiing)
CRUP the buttocks; brittle
bt **CRUT** a dwarf; shaggy oak-bark
mo **CRUX** the crucial point; mountaineering
ma **CUBE** shape of dice; the third power
CUFF sleeve-end; buffet; slap; a stroke
lc **CUIR** leather
CULL reduce numbers (of herds)
bt **CULM** coal-dust; corn or grass stalk; peak
CULT ritual; worship; system; ism
CURB check; restraint; kerb
ck **CURD** (lemon-); coagulated milk
CURE remedy; antidote; panacea; heal
rl **CURE** care of souls; priest (Fr.)
ga **CURL** wind; wave; ringlet; ripple; (Am. football); wave-top (surfing)
CURT abrupt; terse; brief; laconic
zo **CUSK** burbot, an eel-like fish
as **CUSP** point of change (curves) (moon) (zodiac)
CUSS a curse; cross-grained fellow
CUTE shrewd; clever; adroit; chic
CWYM steep rounded hollow (Welsh)
pl **CYAR** the ear-hole
CYMA moulding of a cornice; ogee
bt **CYME** young; shoot; inflorescence
pl **CYST** water-bag; bladder; growth
cy **-CYTE CYTO-**, of cells (cytology
CZAR TSAR, TZAR, ruler (caesar) (Russia)

D

zo **DACE** small river fish; dare; dart
DADA anarchic artistic non-style
DADE hold child by leading-strings
DADO decorative skirting
DAFT idiotic; absurd; ridiculous
nt **DAGO** felucca; lateen-rig vessel
DAIL Irish Parliament
DAIS raised platform; a canopy
DALE vale; valley; dingle
bt **DALI** Brazilian timber-tree
DALL incised tile; cow-dung fuel
DALT a foster-child
DAME the wife of a baronet
DAMN doom; condemn; ruin
DAMP dank; humid; depress; discourage
zo **DANE** man of Denmark; (great-) dog
DANK moist; clammy; humid; damp
pl **DANT** soft or fine coal
DARE defy; venture; challenge; presume
bt **DARI** Indian millet
DARK ebon; murky; Cimmerian
DARN to mend by stitching; curse (damn)
DART rush; run; hurl; a missile
DASH throw; onset; elan; frustrate
DATA accepted inferences; premises; facts
cp, tc **DATA** available coded information
bt **DATE** period; epoch; age; a fruit
DAUB smear; sully; smirch; plaster
lw **DAVY** safety-lamp; affidavit
nm **DAWM** a fortieth of a rupee (Ind.)
DAWN cock-crow; dayspring; gleam
DAZE stun; amaze; astound; confuse
D-DAY invasion day (6 June 1944)
DEAD exactly; directly; defunct; late
DEAF heedless; inattentive; (no kernel)
DEAL pinewood; allot; treat; bargain
rl **DEAN** guild president; church dignitary
DEAR beloved; costly; expensive
DEBT liability; arrears; obligation
cf **DECA-** ten times (decade)
cf **DECI-** one tenth (decilitre)
nt, cp, tc **DECK** adorn; array; (cards); floor, sound centre; (surfing)
lw **DEED** feat; exploit; document
DEEM opine; judge; imagine; believe
DEEP the ocean; profound; recondite
zo **DEER** a solid-horned ungulate
DEEV devil; (spirit) (Persia)
DEFT dextrous; adroit; handy; skilful
DEFY flout; spurn; brave; dare
ck **DELI** (delicatessen) food shop
DELL dale; dene; dingle; vale
bl **DEME** possible interbreeders
DEME Greek township; tribal division
DEMO demonstration (political)
DEMY a size of paper
DENE dell; dune; sandhill
DENT niche; notch; dint; indentation
DENY contradict; gainsay; refute
md **DERM** the skin
DERN durn; secret; dreadful; gatepost
DERV diesel oil
ga **DESI** (designated) baseball hitter
DESK writing table; a lectern
rl **DEVA** a benign spirit (Hindu)
rl **DEVI** the wife of Siva (Hindu)

DEWY spangled with dew
nt **DHOW** Arab ship; lateen sail
ch **DIAD** divalent atom; social (dyad)
DIAL (telephone); face; indicator disc
DICE game; sometimes loaded
lw **DICK** sworn declaration; detective
DIDO antic; caper; queen of Carthage
zo **DIEB** North African jackal
DIED perished; expired; departed
to **DIES** days; screwtaps
DIET assembly; viands; sustenance
DIGS lodgings
bt **DIKA** West African mango
DIKE ditch; rine; rhine; mortarless wall; lesbian
bt, md, ck **DILL** medicinal herb; condiment
nm **DIME** a ten-cent piece (USA)
DINE give a dinner to; eat
DING ring; urge; enforce; dash; sea-damage to surfboard
ga **DINK** a hit (tennis) (volleyball)
DINT in skilled manner
DIRE awful; disastrous; calamitous
DIRK dagger; poniard (Sc.)
DIRT mud; mire, dust; muck; grime; soil
bt **DISA** S. African orchid
cp, tc **DISC** disk; record; flat round plate; recording plate (gramophone)
DISH a culinary conception; frustrate
bt, cp **DISK** disc; any flat round token; magnetic computer storage device
bt **DISS** an Algerian grass
mu **DIVA** a prima donna
DIVE plunge; descent; a gambling hell
DOAB alluvial land (India)
bt **DOCK** curtail; lessen; deduct; a weed
nv, lw **DOCK** basin for shipping; (law court)
zo **DODO** extinct bird (Mauritius)
DOER agent; executive; performer
DOFF daff; take off; divest
DOGE Duke of Venice
bt **DOHL** pulse; (dried peas)
nm **DOIT** Dutch or Scotch half-farthing
DOJO martial arts centre
DOKE a dint; a dimple
DOLE an allowance; dispense; share
DOLL to dress up; a toy
DOLT dunce; booby; dullard
gl **DOME** a cupola; round roof; similar rock formation
DONE ended; finished; transacted
nm **DONG** Vietnamese monetary unit
DON'T prelude to a prohibition
bt **DOOB** an Indian grass
zo **DOOD** camel or dromedary
DOOM kismet; condemn; last judgment; fate
DOOR portal; entrance; access; egress
ch **DOPO** source of adrenalin
DOPE drug; narcotic; doctor; varnish
mu **DOPA** after(wards)
DORA Defence of the Realm Act
zo **DORN** the thorn-back skate
DORP burg; town; village
zo **DORR** the dor-beetle
zo, nt **DORY** golden-coloured fish; skiff; dinghy
DOSE draught; drench; physic
DOSS a shake-down; a hassock
DOST thou doest
DOTE love tenderly; talk trash; (infatuation)
DOTH a poetical 'do'
DOTS grains, insulting material
DOTY decayed; half-rotten
zo **DOUC** a highly coloured monkey
bt **DOUM** the doom-palm
tx **DOUP** weaving half-haeld
DOUR stem; grim; relentless; obstinate
DOUT extinguish
mu **DOUX** sweet (Fr.); also billet doux love notes
zo **DOVE** emblem of peace
DOWD woman's nightcap; scruffy
DOWN fluff; pasture; hill; prone
DOXY loose woman; moll
DOZE nap; slumber; forty winks
DOZY drowsy; sleepy; dreamy; date; timber; decay
DRAB khaki colour; a cloth; a trull
ga **DRAG** (billiards); (snooker); (coaching); (net)
bd **DRAG** a hunt; haul; pull; steel plate smoother; linger
DRAG uneven painting; men got up as women
me **DRAM** drachm; a tot of spirits
DRAT a mild expletive
DRAW depict; attract; raffle; lottery
nt **DRAW** tie; (curling); taking in sails
DRAW iron; chimney draught
DRAY strong cart for heavy goods
DREW drafted; depicted; extracted
zo **DREY** a squirrel's nest
DRIB purloin small pieces; inveigle
ar **DRIP** ooze; dribble; trickle; percolate; cornice projection
ar **DROP** globule; bead; sink; quit; lower newel stair-post projection; overtake; discontinue

DROW trow; troll; cave elf (Shetland)
DRUB maul; thrash; beat; pound
md **DRUG** medicinal; narcotic etc.
mu **DRUM** ridge of hills; tambour
cf **DRUM** base of dome; recording centre
DUAD union of two
DUAL twofold
DUAN a division of a poem; a canto
DUCE leather, dictator (It.)
zo, ga **DUCK** cloth; dive; dip; underplay; bird; zero score (cricket)
DUCT tube; canal; pipe; conduit
DUDE a dandy; fop; nut
DUDS clothing; rags; useless ones
DUEL single combat (of honour)
mu **DUET** composition for two voices
mn **DUFF** low-calory fine-grain coal
DUFF muff; a pudding; refurbish; useless
DUKE (strawberry leaves); peer
DUKW amphibious army vehicle
DULL benumb; blunt; abate; stolid
DULY properly; regularly; exactly
DUMA Russian Parliament
nt **DUMB** mute; inarticulate; soundless; lighter
ga **DUMP** (bawling); (drag racing); (trotting); (ice hockey); (Am. football)
DUMP unload; rubbish-heap; storage program; slovenly place
DUNE dene; sandy ridge
DUNG manure; droppings
ck **DUNK** dipping bread into soup, etc.
DUNT staggering affection; heavy blow
DUPE gull; delude; outwit; hoodwink
bt **DURA** an Indian grass
DURE endure; harden; severe
DURN dern; a door-post
DUSE deuce; demon; evil spirit
DUSK eventide; twilight; eve
DUST pulverulence; a disturbance
DUTY obligation; excise; tariff
ch **DYAD** cf. monad; pair (team of 2)
DYAK a native of Borneo
DYED stained; tinted; tinged
DYER dye-worker
bd **DYKE** **DIKE**, ditch; fosse; lesbian
me **DYNE** the unit of force

E

EACH both; every one
EARL **JARL**, lord; peer
EARN win; gain; merit; acquire
EASE allay; still; assuage; relief
EAST a cardinal point
EASY facile; affluent; flowing
ar **EAVE** roof overhang; (-s dropping) listening
EBON of ebony; black
bt **ECAD** habitat-adapted plant form
ECHO repeat; resound; reverberate
tc **ECHO** delayed reflected sound
ECRU pale yellowish brown
cf **ECTO-** external
EDAM spherical Dutch cheese
EDDA Scandinavian saga
EDDY ripple; swirl; vortex
EDEN garden of delight
EDGE brink; fringe; zest; sharpness
EDGY on edge; nervous
cp **EDIT** revise; annotate; arrange data; (newspaper)
EGAD a refined expletive
EGIS **AEGIS**, patronage; shield
EIRE Republic of Ireland
bt **EJOO** the sago palm
EKED existed on small pittance
ELAN dash; impetuosity; vivacity
ELIA Charles Lamb
ELMO Elmo's fire; electrical flame
bt **ELMY** abounding with elms
ELSE other; otherwise; besides
ELUL 12th month of the Jewish year
EMIR amir; Eastern title
EMIT vent; eject; exhale; discharge
zo **EMYS** terrapin genus
cf **ENDO-** internal (Gr.)
ENTE heraldic engraftment
cf **ENTO** internal (Gr.)
ENVY ill-will; malice; covet; grudge
EOAN dawning; eastern
ga **EPEE** sharp-pointed duelling sword (Fr.) (fencing)
me **EPHA** ephah; Hebrew bushel
EPIC heroic; historic; saga-like
EPOS epic poem (Homeric)
ERGO therefore
cf **ERGO-** of work (Gr.)
ERIC eriach; blood-money (Irish Law)
ERIN the Green Isle, Ireland
zo **ERNE** the sea-eagle
EROS God of Love; Cupid
ERSE the Gaelic language
bt **ERSH** stubble
ERST formerly; whilom

zo **ESOX** the pike
ESPY discover; observe; perceive; notice
ESSE mere existence
ETCH engrave; draw; cropped ground
ETNA volcano (Sicily)
ETON a returnable note
ETUI needle case; container; etwee
EVEN level; uniform; steady; impartial
EVER aye; always; eternity
zo **EVET** eft; newt; ewft
EVIL harm; malice; baneful; malign
EVOE a Bacchanalian cry
EWER pitcher; jug with handle
EWRY scullery; place of ewers, pots
EXAM examination
EXES expenses
EXIT way out; a stage departure
EXON an officer; Yeoman of the Guard
EXPO exposition; exhibition
zo **EYAS** nyas; young hawk
EYED observed; watched; espied
EYER a watcher
EYES visual organs; discs on bowls
EYOT ait; river or lake islet
zo **EYRA** S. American cat
lw **EYRE** journey; circuit; court

F

bt **FAAM** Indian orchid
zo **FAAP** the garfish
bt, ck **FABA** broad Windsor soup bean
ga **FACE** defy; dare; surface; confront; dial; forward side of stick; wave; (hockey); (surfing)
FACT incident; actuality; truth
FACY impudent
FADE wither; dwindle; insipid; ball off course; lose colour
mu **FADO** lament of the heart (Port.)
FAEX dregs
FAIL wane; flag; decline; neglect
FAIN willingly; gladly; readily
FAIR market; just; equitable; blond
FAIX by my faith
ga **FAJA** coloured sash (pelota)
FAKE a cable coil; counterfeit; pretence
mu **FALA** old madrigal
nt **FALL** autumn; the Fall; drop; cascade; part of halyard sail
md **FALX** a membrane
FAMA the goddess of rumour
FAME renown; repute; lustre; celebrity
rl **FANE** vane; temple; church
FANG tooth; claw; talon
FARE manage; victuals; passenger (ticket)
ck **FARL** Scottish oatcake
FARM ferm; till; cultivate; lease
ck **FARO** card game; sour beer
FART puff of wind; flatus
ga **FAST** astain from solid food; firm; rapid; (stand-); stop (archery)
FATA Morgana; a mirage; perfect knight
FATE kismet; doom; destiny; lot
FAUN woodland deity; Pan
FAUX pas; offensive false step
ck **FAVA** faba; bean puree
zo **FAWN** cringe; a colour; fallow-deer
FAZE disconcert; worry
FEAL faithful; constant; loyal
FEAR awe; alarm; dread; anxiety
FEAT exploit; deed; trick
FEED cater; sustain; provender
FEED thickening paint; (-pipe); consume; (cattle-)
FEEL sense; touch; experience
FEET paws, hoofs
FELL hew; cut; tumbled; barren hill
FELL cruel; deadly; spirited; skin
lw **FELO** de se; suicide
lw **FELT** fabric; sensed; handled; touched
FEME a woman
FEND parry; ward off, make shift
bt **FERN** vascular cryptogamous plant
hd **FESS** **FESSE**, broad heraldic band
FETE gala; festival; carnival; holiday
FEUD clan warfare; strife; a fief
lw **FIAR** freeholder, not a life-renter
lw **FIAT** decree; command; ukase
bt **FICO** a snap of the fingers; a fig
lw **FIEF** land held on fuedal tenure
mu **FIFE** a variety of flute
FIFF dress required to play pipes
FIKE fidget; trivial detail
cp **FILE** list; dossier; smoothing tool; data set to
tc **FILE** arrange in order; available stored information
bd **FILL** sate; glut; replenish; earthwork
FILM thin skin; scum; thread; pellicle; cine
FIND discover; discovery; decide
mu **FINE** forfeit; delicate; tenuous; exact; end (It.)
FINN a Finlander

FINS stabilizers on ships, aircraft (surfing)
FIRE discharge; kindle; ignite; blaze
FIRM fast; tight; compact; a company
FIRN nerve; granular glacier snow
FISC state treasury; revenue; purse
zo **FISH** to angle; search by sweeping
FIST neif; the clenched hand; to punch
FIST calligraphy
FITZ son of
FIVE the pentad
FIZZ hiss; champagne
nt **FLAG** banner; ensign; to signal
bt **FLAG** droop; weary; a stone; a plant
FLAK anti-aircraft gunfire (German)
FLAM 2-note side-drum flourish
ck **FLAN** open tart; savoury quiche
ck **FLAP** flop; wave; vibrate; cover; pastry
FLAT smooth; level; insipid; residence
mu **FLAT** level; (platform); sandbar; lowered pitch
FLAW blemish; defect; crevice
bt **FLAX** linum; the linen plant
FLAY skin; excoriate; strip; criticise
zo **FLEA** pulex irritans
FLED ran; bolted; retreated
FLEE escape; abscond; decamp
FLEW fled; the chap of a hound
FLEX to bend; an electric lead
FLEY flay; frighten; cause to fly
FLIP a joy ride; (egg-flip)
FLIT fly; dart; flicker; migrate
zo **FLIX** fur; beaver-down
FLOC accumulation of solids in liquid
FLOE floating arctic ice
FLOG lash; scourge; whip
FLOP flap; a failure; a fiasco; high jump
FLOT stratified ore
FLOW run; emanate; abound; circulate
FLUE smoke pipe; light down; fluff
FLUX flow; mutation; change; (soldering)
zo **FOAL** colt or filly
bd **FOAM** spume; froth; spray; rage; lightweight concrete
FOHN warm mountain wind (N. Alpine)
FOIE liver (Fr.)
ga **FOIL** track of game; baffle; outwit; (table tennis)
ga **FOIL** thin metal; fencing rapier
FOIN a thrust with spear or sword
gl **FOLD** lap; wrap; furl; double; envelop; bend in rock strata; (sheep)
FOLK kindred; relations; people
pr **FOND** loving; attached; archive unit
rl, pr **FONT** fount; source; spring; type
FOOD viands; victuals; rations
FOOL gull; beguile; hoodwink; ninny
pl, me, mu **FOOT** pay; discharge; settle; walking base of body; lower edge; measure of pitch
FORD wade; a river crossing
FORE a warning cry at golf
FORK branch; divide; divaricate
FORM bench; formula; mould; fashion
FORM bed of hare; mode; ceremony
FORS force; fortitude; fortune (Ruskin)
FORT keep; citadel; fastness
FOSS ditch or moat
FOUD magistrate or bailiff (Orkney)
FOUL noisome; ribald; unfair; sullied
ga **FOUL** infringement of rules in games, sports
ga, ck **FOUR** 4; cricket boundary worth four runs score; (petit)
zo **FOWL** poultry; game birds
FOXY sly; wily; sour; a colour
FRAP to bind; to strike
FRAU a German married woman
FRAY rub; brush; quarrel; skirmish
nv **FREE** rid; loose; clear; informal; wind from the beam or abaft; available, unmarked player (netball)
FRET fray; fume; chafe; abrade; grieve
cr, mu **FRET** (swa); (work); geometrical ornament; wood slats for fingers on guitar-like instruments
zo **FRIT** glass material; a wheat-fly
FRIZ frizz; to curl; to crisp
to **FROE** woodcutter's cleaver
zo, rw **FROG** a batrachian; horse's foot; rail crossings
bd **FROG** cloak or coat button or tassel; brick indentation
FROM preposition of source
to **FROW** tool or lathe splitting
FUEL combustibles
mu **FUGA** **FUGUE**, contrapuntal composition
FUGH exclamation of abhorrence
FULL replete; copious; ample; thicken
FUME smoke; vapour; exhalation; reek

FUMY vaporous; fumous; fussy
FUND reserve; store; supply; capital
zo **FUNG** mythical Chinese pheasant
FUNK terror; fear; shirk; touchwood
cr **FUOR** decayed-rafter strengthener
FURL fold; roll; stow; wrap
FURY frenzy; rage; turbulence; shrew
FUSE melt; liquefy; blend
FUSE electric safety cut-off
FUSS ado; stir; fume; fidget; fret
FUST shaft of column; musty smell
FUZE quickmatch; a timing device
FUZZ fluff; light particles; police
FYKE bagnet for fishing
FYRD pre-Conquest Saxon military array

G

GABY a simpleton; nitwit
to **GADE** gaid; gad; goad; graver
GAEL Celtic
nt **GAFF** low theatre; a hook; a spar
bt **GAGE** a pledge; stake; wager; plum
to **GAID** gade; gad; spike on gauntlet
GAIN get; win; acquire; profit
tc, cr **GAIN** increase of message signal power; mortise; notch
GAIR field of lush grass
GAIT walk; bearing; step; pace
bt **GAIT** pasturage; charge; sheaf of corn
GALA festival; festivity; pomp; show
bt **GALE** high wind; rent; a bog plant
GALL vex; torment; provoke; rancour
GALL bile; malignity; glass scum
GALT gault; clay; marl; brick-earth
mu **GAMB** leg; shank; (viol de-) cello
GAME lame; plucky; dauntless; pastime
cf **GAMO-** marital, sexual union
GAMP an umbrella
GAMY high in flavour
hd **GANG** crew; band; horde; coterie
ga **GANT** sports glove; basket pelota
GAOL jail; prison; objective
GAPE stare; to yawn
GARB dress; costume; heraldic sheaf
GASH slash; score; slit; wound
GASP pant; puff
zo **GATA** tropical Atlantic shark
ga **GATE** (slalom); (canoeing); (skiing); (water skiing)
GATE entrance; barrier; attendance; ban
ga, cp **GATE** goal; portal; electrical switch
GATE (flood-); valve); (lock)
bt, nt **GAUB** an Indian tree; guy-rope
GAUD a gewgaw; showy ornament; gawd
pt **GAUL** old France; hollow in a finishing coat
GAUM to smear; to daub
GAUP gawp; gape
zo **GAUR** a wild Indian ox
GAVE presented; granted; yielded
GAWD gaud; a piece of finery
zo **GAWK** gowk; simpleton; a cuckoo
GAWN small tub; a ladle
GAZE stare; view; regard; contemplate
GEAL to congeal; pert. to earth
bt **GEAN** wild cherry
GEAR tackle; harness; dress; mechanism
GEAT hole for metal casting
GECK dupe; mock; simpleton
zo **GEDD** the pike
GEED went faster
GEEZ archaic Semitic dialect
GELD gold; tribute; castrate; spay
GELT geld; gilt; money; emasculated
md **GENA** the cheek
md **GENE** heredity factor
GENS Roman class; patrilineal kin, sib
GENT a would-be gentleman
GENU nerve-tract bend
cf, bl **-GENY** of origin; cause; generation
md **GERM** ovule; nucleus; a bacillus
GEST an exploit; feat; bearing
bt **GEUM** avens and herb-bennet genus
GHAT Indian mountain; landing-stair; funeral pyre
GHEE Indian oil or butter
nt **GIBE** jibe; sneer; deride; taunt
GIFT boon; bounty; gratuity; faculty
ma, mu **GIGA** one thousand million 10^9; jig (It.), folkloric dance form
cp **GIGO** garbage in, garbage out; data unreliability
GILD guild; trade's union; add lustre
bt, go **GILL** a flirt; a ravine; ground ivy; mountain stream
zo, me **GILL** breathing organ; ¼ pint
zo **GILT** gilded; aureate; a young sow
GIMP smart; spruce; a trimming
GING gang or company
GINN jinn; djinn; demon; spirit
GIRD bind; reproach; gibe; spasm
zo **GIRL** young roe-buck; young woman
GIRO payment transfer system
nt **GIRT** tightly moored; bound; girth

cr **GIRT** surround rail; beam
GIST essential point; pith
ga **GITE** bed or an abode (Fr.); (mountaineering)
GIVE yield; confer; grant; present
GLAD (eye); joyous; elated; delectable
GLEE hilarity; merriment; mirth
mu **GLEE** squint; part song
GLEN vale; dale; dell; dingle; valley
bl **GLIA** supportive cells (neuroglia)
GLIB voluble; fluent; ready; facile
GLIM a light; a glimmer
GLOW fervour; shine; burn; gleam
GLUE cement; an adhesive
GLUM grum; crestfallen; downcast
GLUT surfeit; surplus; cloy; satiate
G-MAN gun-man; bandit
GNAR knar; yarr; snarl
zo **GNAT** insect (mosquito)
GNAW bite; corrode; erode; champ
GOAD spur; rouse; incite; an ankus
GOAF worked-out mine; slag
ga **GOAL** end; aim; ambition; object; score-portal
GOAN Indian; E. African Indian
zo **GOAT** Capricornus; horned animal
cn **GOBO** sound-absorbing panel
GO-BY evasion
zo **GOBY** fish having nests of seaweed
GODS lofty theatrical supporters
GOEL an avenger of blood (Heb.)
GOER a mover; a go-between
GOLA a cyma; cyme; a moulding
GOLD or; money wealth; bull at archery
ga **GOLF** goff; gowf; for 9, 18, or 19 holes
GOME black cart-grease
bl **GONA- GONO-**, of genitals; offspring; seed
GONE hied; wended; fared; left; parted
cy **GONE** group of 4 nuclei or cells
mu **GONG** prelude to a meal; percussion instrument, oriental
GOOD weal; virtuous; upright; proper
GOOF simpleton; silly cuckoo
GOOR coarse sugar from the date-palm
GORE clotted blood; wedge of cloth
GORM sheen; shine of varnish
GORY sanguinary; ensanguined
GOSH an ejaculation
GOTH Teutonic barbarian
GOUL GOWL, howl; yowl
GOUM native Algerian soldier (Fr.)
GOUT a drop; taste; relish
md **GOUT** paroxysmal form of arthritis
zo **GOWK** gouk; simpleton; oaf; cuckoo
GOWN robe; garment
GRAB snatch; seize; grip; a card game
nt **GRAB** two-masted vessel (Malabar)
GRAF German title; a count
bt, me **GRAM** misery; chick pea; weight
cf **-GRAM** written; drawn; result
GRAY grey; ash-coloured
GREE a step; degree; goodwill
GREW thrived; raised; progressed
GREY gray; a neutral tint
el **GRID** frame; network; box layout of crossing lines
zo **GRIG** sand-eel; grasshopper; cricket
GRIM stern; dire; hideous; grisly
GRIN girn; smirk; a snare
GRIP clutch; handbag; small ditch
gl **GRIT** endurance; courage; quartz-rock (sand)
GROG rum and water
GROS silken fabric
GROT a grotto
GROW wax; develop; expand; raise
zo **GRUB** caterpillar; food; (cricket); root out
GRUM glum; surly; morose; guttural
mn **GUAG** space left by mineral extraction
zo **GUAN** Brazilian game bird
nt **GUFA** Tigris ferry boat
mn **GUHR** loose earth found in rocks
zo **GUIB** the harnessed antelope
GULF chasm; abyss; bight; bay
zo **GULL** beguile; hoax; deceive; sea-bird
cp **GULP** as many bytes as digits; swallow; choke
hd **GULY** coloured red in heraldry
GUNK semi-solid material from synthesis
GURU Hindu teacher
GUSH rush; spout; stream; an outburst
pc **GUST** squall; burst of passion; relish; taste unit
zo **GYAL GAYAL**, E. Indian ox
nt **GYBE** gibe; sneer
GYLE to ferment; a brew
zo **GYNE** ant
cf, pl **GYNE- GYNO-, -GYNY**, of females
GYRA embroidered border
GYRE a circular motion
GYRO a gyroscope
GYVE fetter; shackle; handcuff; bond

H

HAAF deep-sea fishing ground (Shetland)
HAAK sailing lighter (North sea)
HAAR harr; a cold sea mist
to **HACK** notch; gash; kick; chopper
zo **HACK** literary drudge; sorry; jade (horse)
ga **HACK** mattock; blow; foothold (curling)
HADE slope of mineral vein or fault; hole in the ice
rl **HADJ HAJI**, a pilgrimage to Mecca
md **HAEM** iron pigment in haemoglobin
HAFF river mouth, lagoon (Ger.)
HAFT heft; hilt; handle; to haggle
HA-HA haw-haw; sunken fence; laughter
HAIK hyke; haick; an Arab wrap
HAIL health; greeting; frozen rain
HAIR jot; iota; quality; character
HAKA native dance (NZ)
zo **HAKE** a pot-hook; loiter; sea fish
HALE haul; drag; healthy; robust
ga **HALF** a moiety; a half-back; draw (tie); golf; term (netball)
ar **HALL** manor house; a college; aula
ag **HALM HAUM, HAULM**, cornstalk at harvest time
rl, as **HALO** a saintly aura; solar, lunar ring of light
HALT to stop; to limp; crippled; waver
HAME bar for trace attachment
HAND manual labour; assistance
me **HAND** proffer; (cards); 4 in (horses); serve (badminton)
HANG suspend; hover; slope; drift; long jump technique
nt **HANK** skein; coil; hoop; ring
HARD firm; compact; arduous
zo **HARE** to speed; puss
HARK hear; listen; attend (nostalgia)
HARM hurt; scathe; wrong; injury
lw **HARO** an appeal (Channel Islands)
mu **HARP** reiterate; lyre, plucked instrument
HARR haar; a storm; an eagre
zo **HART** male red-deer
ck, cp **HASH** chop; mangle; mince; a jumble; mess-up; unwanted data
jn **HASP** clasp or fastening; staple; clip
HAST (thou) havest
HATE abhor; loathe; enmity; odium
HATH has
HAUL tug; pull; drag; draw; heave
HAVE own; possess; hold; contain
zo **HAWK** rapacious bird or person
HAWK intentional cough; to peddle
to **HAWK** plasterer's mortar board
HAWM to lounge about
HAZE fog; mist; pall; miasma; to bully
HAZY vague; obscure; indistinct; murky
HEAD top; chief; steer; (bowls); (beer)
cp, tc **HEAD** acme; (black-); electromagnetic
HEAL cure; remedy; assuage; compose
HEAP pile; mound; amass; collect; jack and live bowls
lw **HEAR** heed; hark; try judicially
ga **HEAT** rage; passion; ardour; excite; qualifying round in sports; to warm
HEBE an Olympian cup-bearer
HECK fish-weir; a rack; river bend
HEED mind; mark; obey; regard; caution
jn **HEEL** submit; low fellow; twerp; underfoot; spur
HEFT hilt; handle; heaved
HEIR inheritor; offspring
HELD grasped; adhered; restrained
HELL Hades, Gehenna; gambling house
nt **HELM** tiller; steering gear; steer
HELM helmet; crown; top; guide; direct
HELP aid; abet; back; second; relieve
cf, pl **HEMA- HEMO-**, of blood (Gr.)
bt **HEMP** rope-fibre; a plant
HEND to seize; to apprehend (obs.)
HERA (Juno), wife of Zeus
bt **HERB** a simple; an annual plant
HERD drove; rabble; tend; collect
HERE at this place
HERL harl; barb of feather
ar, rl **HERM** (Hermes') head or bust on decorative pillar
zo **HERN** heron (obs.)
HERO a priestess of Aphrodite
HERR German gent
HERS HERN, of her
HEST behest; command (Shak.)
HEWN cut; felled; chiselled
HICK bucolic; country cousin (USA)
me **HIDE** about 100 acres (41 hectares)
HIDE a skin; pelt; secrete; cache
HIED set off
HI-FI high-fidelity sound
HIGH eminent; lofty; arrogant; shrill; pressure; drug-induced state

HIKE to carry; to ramble; long distance walk; (price rise) (Am. football)
bt **HILA** the eyes of beans
bt, go **HILL** to earth up plants; midget mountain; (mole-)
HILT haft; heft; handle
zo **HIND** a rustic; backward; a deer
to **HINK** a reaping hook
HINT imply; insinuate; innuendo
HIRE rent; charter; lease; salary
HISK to breathe with difficulty
HISS also **HISH** and **HIZZ**
HIST! hush!
HIVE to collect; store up; a skep
HOAR hoary; rime; venerable
HOAX gammon; spoof; dupe; delude
HOBO a tramp; a vagrant (USA)
HOCK Rhenish wine; a joint; the hough
HOED weeded
HOER manipulator of a hoe
zo **HOGG** hog; a two-year old sheep
HOIK hike; an upward turn
HOIT to leap; to caper
cp, nt **HOLD** grasp; contain; keep; cargo space; order a halt
HOLE cavity; lair; burrow; pierce; (golf)
cp **HOLE** orifice; punched-card system
bt **HOLM** evergreen oak; holly
HOLM flat land; an islet (Scand.)
HOLT woodland; a copse; a burrow
HOLY sanctified; consecrated; divine
HOME habitat; seat; institution; residence
cf **HOMO-** of same; alike; (homosexual) (Gr.)
HOMY homelike
HONE to pine; to moan; a whetstone
HONG Chinese factory
HONK to hoot
HOOD cowl; cover; to blind
zo **HOOF** horse's foot; to walk
HOOK promontory; snare; sickle
to **HOOK** to bend; to steal; seize; connect; strike; curved device; to hit (boxing) (bowls) (baseball) (rugby) (football) (cricket); (rug making); hold
HOOP a whoop; a band; a toy; (baseball)
HOOP the basket and its rim (basketball)
HOOT honk; boo; decry; execrate
HOPE expect; anticipate; confidence
bt **HOPS** beer flavouring
go, pl, zo, mu **HORN** cornucopia; drinking cup; wind instrument; antler; phallus; pyramidal moutain peak
ck **HORS** out of; beyond (hors-de-combat); (-d'oeuvres)
HOSE stockings; hosiery; to sprinkle
HOSH courtyard of Arab house
HOST multitude; consecrated wafer
HOUR always passing
HOVA a Malagasi; from Madagascar
HOVE past tense of heave; raised
HOWL growl; yowl; wail; yell; squall
HOYA genus of climbing plants
rl **HUAN** jade Chinese ritual object
zo **HUCK** a German trout
HUED coloured; tinted
HUEL a wheal; a Cornish mine
HUER fish-scout watching for shoals
HUFF swell; bluster; anger; (draughts)
HUGE vast; colossal; gigantic; immense
zo **HUIA** New Zealand starling
nt **HULK** old ship used as store, prison, etc.
bt, nt **HULL** husk; pod; to pierce; ship
pc **HUMP** hillock; to carry; depression
HUNG dangled; draped; hovered
HUNK chunk; lump; large slice
HUNT pursue; hound; search; chase
HURL cast; pitch; fling; whirl
HURT pain; offend; mar; an injury
HUSH quiet; calm; still; silence
bt **HUSK** hull; rind; coating
zo **HUSO** the great sturgeon
HUTO native of Rwanda (Africa)
nm **HWAN** (Korea) monetary unit
HWYC emotional fervour; intonation (Welsh)
HYKE haik; loose Arab garment
mu **HYMN** panegyric; paean; song of praise
HYPE a wrestling throw
ch, md **HYPO** diluted; syringe (sl.); injection
cf **HYPO-** of lesser, smaller (Gr.)

I

zo **IBEX** mountain wild goat
IBID in the same place (Lat.)
zo **IBIS** a wading bird, sacred in Egypt
ICED frozen; congealed
rl **ICON** **IKON**, sacred picture; image
IDEA notion; fantasy; conceit; insight; scheme; plan; vision
lw **IDEM** the same
cf **IDEO-** of mental image; idea
IDES Roman date

cf **IDIO-** personal; self produced; distinct
IDLE inert; lazy; inactive; unused
IDLY indolently
IDOL hero; pet; image
IDYL idyll; pastoral poem
IEIE Hawaiian palm tree
IGEL squat tumbler glass (Ger.)
wv **IKAT** pattern dye and wave technique (Indonesia)
bt **ILEX** evergreen oak
rl **IMAM** Mohammedan priest
rl **IMAN** Moslem faith
IMPI Zulu regiment
INBY inbye; inwards (Sc.)
INCA ancient king or prince of Peru
INCA an Indian of Peru area
me **INCH** measure of short length; creep
INCH creep forward
INFO information (centre)
INKY black; blotted
INLY inward; secret
INRO Japanese comfit box
INTO preposition of direction
IOTA a jot; tittle; whit; particle
cf **IPSA- IPSO-**, one's own, of self (Gr.)
pl **IRIS** Rainbow Goddess, messenger of Zeus; eye membrane
mn **IRON** golf club; metal; to smoothe
IRON gyve, fetter; strength
bt **ISCA** excrescence on oak or hazel
ISIS Moon Goddess; mother of Horus
ISLE ait; eyot; islet
md **ITCH** constant teasing desire
ITEM detail; entry; innuendo
zo **ITER** canal or duct
md **ITIS** undiagnosed disease
ar **IWAN** Islamic vaulted hall
IWIS ywis; certainly
bt **IXIA** South African iridaceous plants
IBZA Russian arctic log hut

J

bt **JACA** the bread-fruit tree
zo, nt **JACK** (cards); flag; lifter (car); pike
nt, cp **JACK** appliance; sailor; (bowls); plug
mu **JACK** harpsichord plucking device
zo **JADE** sorry nag; mean woman
mn **JADE** to fatigue; Chinese gemstone
JAIL gaol; to imprison
JAIN Indian religious sect
JAMB a door-post; to wedge; stick
nm **JANE** jean; twilled cloth; Genoese
JANN jinn; Moslem demon
JANT jaunt; ramble
JAPE jibe; joke; jest; quip
JARL earl (Norse)
JAWY with jaws
mu **JAZZ** rag-time music
JEAN jane; twilled cloth
JEEP American general purposes vehicle
JEER mock; scoff; taunt; deride
JEFF dicing with quadrants; circus rope
JEHU a coachman
JERK yerk; jolt; pluck; twitch; a good-for-nothing; (weight-lifting)
JESS a leg-strap in falconry
JEST jape; quirk; raillery; banter
JETE leap from one foot to another (gymn.)
bt **JHOW** Indian grass
JIAO Chinese coin
JIFF a jiffy; a moment
JILL a flirt; Jack's girl friend
JILT deceive; delude; to discard
JINK a sharp turn; to dodge
JINN ginn; djinn; Moslem spirit
JINX bad joss
JIVE jazz dance (swing)
JOCK a Scotsman; college athlete (USA); -strap (genital support)
zo **JOEY** small kangaroo
nm **JOEY** small drinking glass; 4d. piece
bt **JOHN** a variety of pink
JOIN link together; associate
JOKE jest; banter; witticism
JOLE jowl; jaw; jolt
JOLT jar; jog; jerk; shake
JOSH to rag; ridicule
JOSS Chinese idol; luck; incense; perfume (wooden stick)
JOTA (Sp.) dance, with castanets
JOUK jook; duck; dodge; bow (Sc.); perched hawk (falconry)
JOVE Jupiter; alchemist's tin
JOWL dewlap; the cheek
JUBA negro dance
rl **JUBE** rood-loft
JUDO advanced form of Jap. wrestling
JUDY Mr Punch's wife
bt **JUGA** leaflets in a pinnate leaf
JU-JU W. African black magic
JUKE a head movement; -box (gramophone); feint (Am. football)
JULY seventh month
JUMP leap; skip; bound; purloin; escape; recoil of guns; sprint (cycling)
JUNE sixth month

nt **JUNK** scrap-metal; trash; Chinese ship
JUNO Queen of Heaven
lw **JURY** twelve persons; makeshift
JUST true; exact; impartial; barely
bt **JUTE** sack and twine fibre

K

rl **KABA** sacred stone of Mecca and all Islam
KADI cadi; Moslem judge
nt **KAEP** dugout canoe (sail) (Philippines)
KAGO Japanese palanquin
zo **KAGU** crane of New Caledonia
KAIF **KEIF**, drugged stupor
nt **KAIK** **CAIQUE**, sailing vessel (Med.)
KAIL a ninepin
KAIN cain; tribute in kind
zo **KAKA** New Zealand parrot
bt, ck **KAKI** the Chinese date-plum; persimmon fruit
KALA time; destiny; death (Sanskrit)
bt **KALE** kail; colewort; curly cabbage
bt **KALI** prickly saltwort or glasswort
KALI wife of Siva; goddess of destruction
KAMA Hindu cupid
gl **KAME** glacier-outwash mound
KAMI Japanese god or title
KANA Japanese handwriting
KANG Chinese water-jar
bt **KANS** Indian sugar-cane grass
KAON 1 of class of mesons
KART midget racing car
KAST **KAS**, Dutch wardrobe
tx **KATA** Tibetan cloth or scarf
cf **KATA-** **CATA–**, against; down (Gr.)
bt **KAVA** ava; Polynesian drink; plant
bt **KECK** to retch; dried hemlock; type of grass
KEEL ruddle; flat-bottomed barge (coal) (-over, to capsize)
nt **KEEL** undermost part of ship; projecting fin; main frame of airship; (balancer)
KEEN acute; eager; sharp
mu **KEEN** funeral song (Irish)
KEEP stronghold; provender; retain
KEIF kaif; drugged stupor
KEIR bleaching-vat
KELK a blow; to beat; large stone
KELL caul; cobweb; film; network
KELP kilp; seaweed; wrack
zo, tx **KELT** Celt; salmon; woollen cloth
KEMB to comb
KEMP coarse rough hairs of wool
mu **KENT** pole; pike; bugle with keys
KEPI military cap (Fr.)
KEPT held; stored; retained; endured
KERB curb; edge of pavement
KERF a saw-cut; a swath
to **KERN** **QUERN**, a hand-mill for grain
KERN **KIRN**, Irish footsoldier
zo **KETA** a caviare fish
KHAN Oriental ruler
KHEL a clan (Afghanistan)
KHOR wadi-like riverbed (Sudan)
KHUD Indian ravine
md **KIBE** chilblain
KIBY affected with chilblains
KICK resist; rebel; spurn; boot; punt
KIEF keif; kef; stupor; drowsiness
KIER keir; bleaching-vat
KILL slay; destroy; despatch; consume
KILN furnace; oven
me **KILO** unit of 1000 (metric system) 10^3
KILP kelp; calcined ashes of seaweed
KILT a philbeg; pleated skirt; tuck up
KIND class; type; genus; benign; gentle
zo **KINE** cows
cf **KINE-** of moving; movies; cinema (Gr.)
KING monarch; sovereign; ruler; a card
KINK bend; knot; curl; loop; whim
KINO a mixture of gums; catechu
KIPE basket for catching fish
KIRI knobkerrie; Kaffir throwing stick
rl **KIRK** a church (Sc.)
KIRN kern; last sheaf; harvest image
KISH wicker turf basket; impure graphite
KISS buss; touch gently; (billiards)
KIST chest; coffer
zo **KITE** accommodation bill; a toy; a bird
KITH kindred; acquaintances; friends
KIVE a mashing vat
zo, bt **KIWI** apteryx, NZ flightless bird; fruit
KNAB to bite; to gnaw
KNAG knot in wood; peg; a wart
KNAP to snap; a swelling; a hillock
KNAR gnar; snarl; growl; a knarl
pl, ma **KNEE** leg-joint; graphic curve
KNEW understood; perceived
KNIT draw together; weave; wrinkle
KNOB a bunch; boss; door-handle

KNOP knob; hilltop (S.A.); button
go, nv, zo **KNOT** knag; small sandpiper; 1 sea mile (200 yards, 1.85 km) per hour
KNOW comprehend; discern; be familiar with
KNUB knob; a small lump
KNUR knar; gnarl; wooden ball
KNUT a nut; a dandy
zo **KOBA** kob; African water antelope
zo **KOEL** Indian cuckoo
nt **KOFF** Dutch sailing vessel
KOHL black antimony eye pigment
bt **KOLA** African nut tree; a beverage
KOOK novice surfer; inept person
pc **KORO** fear of penis retraction
mn **KOTH** volcanic mud (S. America)
mu **KOTO** Japanese stringed instrument
KRIS creese; Malay dagger
KROO an African race
zo **KUDU** a large African antelope
KUEI food vessel; bronze age; (China)
KUFI calligraphy (Mid. East)
KUNA Panamanian Indian
KURD native of Near East
ck **KVAS** rye beer (Rus.)
nm **KYAT** (Burma) monetary unit
KYLE narrow strait or sound (Sc.)

L

LACE tie; fasten; (boot-); intermix
LACE intricate thread tracery
LACK need; deficiency
LACY **LACEY**, lace-like texture
LADE load; burden; ladle; bale
LADY gentlewoman
LAIC layman
LAID deposited; ribbed; prostrate
LAIN rested; reclined; reposed
LAIR den; form; burrow; quagmire
LAIS a courtesan
pt **LAKE** mere; pool; crimson colour; inland water
nm **LAKH** lac; 100,000 rupees
LAMA Tibetan priest
zo **LAMB** baby sheep
LAME halt; crippled; feeble; imperfect
LAME gold- or silver-threaded material
LAMP lantern; shine
bt **LANA** the genipap tree of Demerara
ae **LAND** realm; tract; disembark; (fish); (bowls)
LANE narrow way; passage; by-road; subdivision of track (running); (traffic)
LANG long (Sc.)
LANK lax; loose; drooping; thin
LANX Roman platter
LAPP a Laplander; Saami
LARD bacon fat; smear; flatter
rl **LARE** Roman household god
zo **LARK** frolic; prank; spree; skylark
LASH whip; scourge; satirize; (eye-)
LASS girl; a sweetheart
to **LAST** final; boot-maker's anvil
LAST continue; endure; a cargo
LATE overdue; past; recent; deceased
LATH a narrow strip of wood; batten
LAUD extol; praise; eulogy; panegyric
mn, gl **LAVA** plutonic rock matter; magma
LAVE to wash; bathe; bath
LAWN fine linen or cambric; greensward
LAZE to idle; relax
LAZY torpid; slothful; sluggish
el, pb, nt **LEAD** surpass; guide; precede; plummet; conductor, plumbing metal; bullets; (swing the —)
bt **LEAF** thin plate; lamina; page of book; leaf foliage
LEAK ooze; drip; percolate
LEAL loyal; true; faithful (Sc.)
LEAN rest; rely; depend; incline; lank
LEAP spring across; (-clear); caper; (-year)
LEAR an unlucky king
LEAT watercourse to a mill
rl **LEDA** beloved of Zeus (disguised as swan)
hd, bt **LEEK** an emblem of Wales; onion genus
LEER ogle; smirk; smile with contempt
LEES the dregs; open lands (park)
lw **LEET** court of record; list of candidates
LEFT sinister; abandoned; bequeathed
LEHR glass annealing oven (King Lear)
LEND (loan); furnish; grant an advance
LENE unaspirated
tx **LENO** a fabric like muslin
pg **LENS** optical glass (camera) (spectacles) (tele-, microscope)
rl, mu **LENT** loaned; inclined; a fast; slow music pace (It.)
LESS smaller; inferior; minor; fewer
LEST for fear that
LETO mother of Apollo and Artemis

LETT Baltic people of Latvia, Lettland
LEUD Frankish vassal
LEVY tribute; exact; muster; impose
LEWD licentious; rude; pornographic
LIAR an economizer of truth
mn **LIAS** argillaceous limestone
zo **LICE** insect carriers of typhus; bedbugs; skin, hair parasites
LICH **LYCH**, corpse; (funeral gate)
LICK to tongue; to lap; defeat; overcome
LIDO a bathing pool with sunbathing area
LIED stated falsely; German ballad
LIEF gladly; willingly; beloved
lw **LIEN** right of retention; cylindrical bronze vessel (China)
LIEU place; stead
LIFE vitality; duration; existence; (memoir); -style; -sentence
ga **LIFT** exalt; raise; elevate; steal; underarm stroke (badminton); drug-serenity
LIFT thermal current (gliding); hitchhiking
LIKE prefer; enjoy; cognate; match
mu **LILT** cheerful song or air; ditty
hd, bt **LILY** fleur-de-lis; (water-)
pl, zo **LIMB** extension to torso; edge; border; branch; an imp
bt **LIME** to ensnare; citrus fruit
LIMN to paint; draw; illuminate
LIMP walk lamely; slack; flaccid
LIMY glutinous; viscous
LINE link; ancestry; (business-); rope; (air-); (life-); note; row
LING small bronze bell (China)
zo, bt **LING** sea-fish; common heather
me **LINK** connect; chain; torch; nexus; circuit; (route); (missing-); 7.92 in/20cm
LINN pool; waterfall
LINO linoleum floor covering; (-cuts)
md **LINT** surgical linen; loose fibre dust
LINY streaky; wrinkled
zo **LION** cat; predator; King of Jungle
zo **LIPP** a crimson fish
nm **LIRA** **LIRE**, Italian, Turkish money
mu **LIRE** **LYRE**, harp
LIRK a fold; to hang in creases (Sc.)
nt **LISI** canoe, S. Pacific
LISP make th of s
LIST register; roll; elect; (catalogue)
LITH joint; segment
LIVE exist; survive; active; alive; dwell; appearing in person; mortal
rl **LLEW** **LLEU**, **LLAW**, Gyffes, Irish/Celtic deity
rl **LLYR** (Irish **LIR**), Celtic deity
LOAD lade; charge; encumbrance; burden
LOAF lounge; dawdle; (bread)
ag **LOAM** rich mould; soil
pl, bt, ga **LOBE** projecting part of ear; a cotyledon; arc of skating
LOCH lake; arm of the sea (Sc.)
cp **LOCK** close; seal; bolt; hug; ringlet (hair); entwine
rw, mu **LOCO** locomotive; stand-in; playing at a certain pitch (It.)
LODE vein in ore; drain; open ditch
LO-FI opp. of Hi-Fi
ga **LOFT** upper room; attic; striking angle (golf)
LOGE a box in a theatre
LOGO symbol for services, organizations
cf **-LOGY** science of, knowledge; speech
pl **LOIN** pubic, genital zone; groin; crutch; (-cloth)
LOKE grassy road (East Anglia); cul-de-sac
rl **LOKI** Norse Aesir deity, enemy of Odin
LOLL sprawl; lounge
LOLO **SW** China aboriginal tribe
LOMA lobe; fringe
zo **LOMP** the lump fish
LONE isolated; solitary; secluded
LONG prolix; lengthy; crave; aspire
tx **LONK** north-Engl. mountain wool
LOOF the palm of the hand
LOOK scan; gaze; peer; seem; mien
LOOM approach menacingly; weaving device; lighthouse rays; midpoint of oar (rowing)
zo **LOON** Great Northern Diver (water bird); rascal, loafer
cp, zo **LOOP** bight; bend; loophole; closed circuit feedback; continuous tape; flank of horse
LOOT booty; plunder; sack; ransack
LOPE run with easy strides
zo **LOPH** molar cusp crest
LORD dominate; master; ruler; a peer
LORE wisdom; erudition; doctrine
LORN forlorn; lost; forsaken; undone
zo **LORY** Australian parrot
LOSE mislay; waste; squander; fail
cp, el, tc **LOSS** defeat; reverse; deprivation; reduction of power; lose out; bereavement
LOST missing; astray; vicious; dreamy

bt **LOTE** lotus; water-lily
LOTH averse; unwilling; allergic
ga **LOTO** lotto; a game (now lottery)
LOUD clamorous; noisy; stentorian
LOUP loop; to leap
LOUR scowl; frown; glower
LOUT boor; clod; booby; yokel
LOVE adore; affection; courtship (-birds); zero score (lawn tennis)
LOWN sheltered; tranquil (Sc.)
ck **LUAU** traditional roast-pig feast (Hawaii)
zo **LUCE** full grown pike
LUCK hap; fate; hazard; fortune; chance
ga **LUDI** **LUDUS**, public games (Rome)
ga **LUDO** a game (dice and counters)
LUES poison; plague; disease
nt **LUFF** the weather-gauge; leading edge of a sail
LUGE toboggan
LULL calm; assuage; an interim
LUMP chunk; projection; hunk
hd **LUNA** the moon; heraldic argent
LUNE half-moon shape
pl, rl **LUNG** respiratory organ; Ch. deity
LUNT a light; a slow-match
LURE entice; decoy; bait; recall (falconry)
LURE dummy bird (falconry); mechanical hare, rabbit (greyhounds)
LURK skulk; lie in wait
bt **LUSH** juicy; luscious; richly verdant
LUSK a sluggard; to laze
LUST desire; cupidity; covet
mu **LUTE** tenacious composition; guitar
mu **LUTH** lute (Fr.)
LUTZ jump (ice-skating) technique
LUXE luxuriousness (Fr.)
LYAM leam; dog-leash
bt **LYME** a coarse grass
zo **LYNX** sharp-eyed cat
hd **LYON** Heraldic Court (Sc.)
LYRA a constellation
zo **LYRA** brain psalterium in mammals
mu **LYRE** **LYRA**, early harp (It.)
md **LYSE** make undergo lysis

M

MA'AM marm; madame (the Queen)
gl **MAAR** a crater
bt **MACE** staff of authority; spice
MACH supersonic speed
MACK **MAIK**, make (Sc.)
MADE formed; fashioned; compelled
rl **MAGI** wise men of the East; (magicians)
nm **MAHE** biche, French pice
rl **MAIA** Roman deity
MAID lass; damsel; virgin
MAIL the post; chain-armour (-order)
MAIM cripple; mutilate; disable
MAIN at dice or cockfighting; essential
pb **MAIN** the ocean; might; power; (pipe)
MAKE do; gain; form; cause; reach
zo **MAKI** a Malagasy lemur
zo **MAKO** Australasian shark
zo **MALA** -lobe in insects
bl **MALE** masculine gender; virile
MALL mallet; to bruise; public walk
mn **MALM** calcareous loam
bt, ck **MALT** steeped grain
MAMA **MAMMA**, mammy; mother
rl **MANA** magical influence (Maori); Polynesian divine force
zo **MANE** neck hair on lions, horses
rl **MANU** mankind's ancestor (India)
MANX curtailed (cat); of Isle of Man
MANY sundry; divers; manifold
me **MARC** oil-cake refuse; old Fr. measure
zo **MARE** female horse
nm **MARK** (letters of); brand; stigma; coin (Ger.); catch (football); strike (bowls)
cp **MARK** (post); symbol; character; code pulse; signature
MARL mixture of clay, sand and lime
MARM ma'am; madame (the Queen)
MARS God of War; a planet
MART market; bazaar; emporium; hammer (Sc.)
MASH mix; crush; knead; compound
MASK veil; cloak; revel; disguise; visor
cp **MASK** (gas-); conceal; isolating bits
rl **MASS** bulk; whole; heap; (church)
ae, bt, nt **MAST** beech-nuts, etc.; supporter of sails, aerials, airships
bt, ck **MATE** comrade; checkmate; tea plant
MATH a mowing
pg, pt **MATT** roughened; glass; non-glossy photographs, paint
tx **MAUD** shepherd's woollen plaid (Sc.)
rl **MAUI** Polynesian divine fire maker
to **MAUL** mall; hammer; to molest; melée (rugby football); tear (flesh)
zo **MAWK** a maggot

MAXI larger than standard
MAYA people and language of C. Am.
MAZE daze; bewilder; a labyrinth
MAZY winding; intricate
ck, go **MEAD** fermented honey; meadow; field
bt, ck **MEAL** a repast; ground grain; flour
MEAN middle; average; intend; signify
MEAT food; flesh
MEDE native of Media (Medes and Persians)
MEED reward; recompense
MEEK mild; lowly; pacific; unassuming
MEER mere; pool; lake (obs.)
MEET fit; proper; encounter; join; competition (athletics); (hunting)
cf, ma, me **MEGA-** one million times
cf **MEIO-** decrease in size or numbers (Gr.)
MELD fuse; merge; face-up (cards)
MELT dissolve; fuse; thaw; soften
MEMO memorandum; note; jotting
MEND repair; patch; amend; correct
mu **MENO** less tempo; slower (It.)
ck, cp **MENU** bill of fare; optional facilities
MERE pool; lake; marsh; boundary
MERE unmixed; simply; alone; only
MERI Maori war club
nm **MERK** an old Scots silver coin
tx **MERV** silk dress material
MESA broad; flat; rocky; tableland (Sp.)
MESH net-work; brewery grains; ensnare
cf **MESO-** middle; intermediate secondary (Gr.)
ck **MESS** muddle; jumble; dish of food; eat; (-table) military
mu **META** Roman racing pylon; half-speed (tempo) (It.)
cf **META-** between; beyond; change (Gr.)
METE measure; limit; boundary
rl **MEUM** and tuum (liturgical me or thee)
MEWL to squall
MEWS stables; cages for hawks
MEZE hors d'oeuvres (Gr.)
MIAN Ind. title of respect
MIAU a cat-call
mn **MICA** a silicate used as glass
zo **MICE** small rodents
MICH lie hid; skulk; sneak; play truant
zo **MIDA** the larva of the bean-fly
MIEN air; bearing; deportment; aspect
MIFF annoyance; resentment
MIKE shirk; loiter; microphone; tease; (take the –)
MILD suave; bland; placid; soothing
me **MILE** 1760 yards (1.609 km)
rl **MILK** cat-lap; (dairy); Altaic devils
nm **MILL** grind; factory; fight
zo **MILT** the spleen; roe; spawn
MIME mimic; ape; copy
zo **MINA** 50 shekels; Indian bird
MIND mark; heed; dislike; intention; (brain)
MINE pit; colliery; sap; of me
MING Chinese porcelain; (dynasty)
cf **MINI-** small; of compact size
zo **MINK** furry animal, weasel type
MINO Japanese raincoat
nm **MINT** coin factory; unused, fresh
bt **MINT** aromatic plant; to invent
zo **MINX** pert selfish girl; she-puppy
MINY subterraneous
go **MIRE** mud; swampy ground; bog
MIRK **MURK**, gloom; darkness
rl **MIRU** Polynesian ruler of Netherworld
MIRY muddy; marshy
lw **MISE** cost; expense; a treaty
MISS fail; want; need; (spinster)
MIST fog; haze; obscurity
mn **MISY** **MYSY**, impure iron ore
nm, zo **MITE** widow's donation; (cheese-)
MITT mitten; a covering for the wrist
MIXT mixed; mingled; blended
MOAN bewail; lament; deplore
MOAT protective ditch; (– in the eye)
MOCK taunt; flaunt; deride; imitate
zo, nm **MOCO** rock cavy; coin (San Domingo)
MODE style; form; way; vogue
el, mu **MODE** method; wave frequency; (scales)
MODI methods; (modus)
mu **MODO** style of playing required (It.)
mu **MODO** system of major, minor scales
MODS first B.A. examination, Oxford
tx **MOFF** Caucasian silk fabric
cf **MOGI-** effort, difficulty, defect (Gr.)
gl, go **MOHO** earth crust/mantle boundary
zo **MOHR** West African gazelle
MOIL toil; soil; daub
me **MOIO** Portuguese measure
zo **MOKE** burro; ass; donkey
MOKO Maori tattooing

MOLD MOULD, shape
MOLE jetty; artificial harbour; skin blemish
zo **MOLE** the gentleman in velveteens
MOLE unit of substance, betrayer of secrets; birthmark
mu **MOLL** courtesan; gangster's sweetheart; minor key (Ger.)
bt **MOLY** a countercharm; garlic
MOME a dullard; buffoon
rl, pr **MONK** friar; ink-stain in printing
el **MONO** single; transmission path
rl **MONT** Mentu, Mont-Re, war god (Upper Eg.)
MOOD humour; temper; vein; disposition
MOON wander aimlessly; a satellite
MOOP to nibble; to browse (Sc.)
MOOR fasten; berth; heath; (Othello)
MOOT an assembly; debate; discuss
MOPE to be dull and listless
zo **MOPS** a pug-dog
MOPY downcast; dejected; sad
bt **MORA** finger game; tree; short syllable
MORE additional; further; again
MORN morning; tomorrow
MORT death tune; a quantity
bt **MOSS** a cryptogamic plant
MOST more than more; superlative
MOTE particle; speck; blemish
MOTE moot; assembly; to debate (obs.)
zo **MOTH** large-winged insect
mu, cf **MOTO-** of creating movement (Gr./It.)
MOUL MOOL, mouldy (Sc.)
MOVE shift; stir; budge; propose
MOWN scythed; cut
bt, md **MOXA** a cauterizer
mn **MOYA** volcanic mud
MOZE to raise the nap on cloth
MUCH plenteous; greatly; largely
MUCK refuse; dirt
me **MUDD** Moroccan measure
MUFF a duffer; hand-warmer; spoil
me **MUID** hogshead; dry measure for corn
MUIR moor (Sc.)
zo **MULE** machine; slipper; a hybrid
go **MULL** snuff-box; headland; mistake
MULL to heat wine, punch; to ponder; err
pr **MULL** cotton book-cover
MULT multure; fee for grinding corn
MUMM to mask; act; masquerade
MUMP nibble; grin; deceive; beg
nc **MUON** heaviest known lepton
MURE immure; a wall
MURK mirk; darkness; obscurity
bt **MUSA** banana genus
MUSE meditate; ponder; contemplate
MUSE poets (source of inspiration)
MUSH pulp; dog-sled command
zo **MUSK** a scent; a deer
MUSS a mess; scramble; disarrange
MUST obliged; necessitated
MUST mould; unfermented grape juice
MUST elephant frenzy
mu **MUTA** change; (style of playing) (It.)
mu **MUTE** dumb; still; a sordine
MUTT a fool
zo **MYNA** the Indian starling
MYTH legend; fable; invention
zo **MYXA** beak extremities

N

bt **NABK** a petal in the crown of thorns
rl, zo **NAGA** sacred Hindu and Buddhist snakes
NAIF naive; artless; ingenuous
me **NAIL** spike; secure; pin; 2¼ inches (57 mm)
zo **NAJA** venomous snake; a cobra
NAME term; nominate; renown; (called)
NANA benteak skill
cp **NAND** logic; **NOT-AND** (Boolean)
ma **NANO-** one thousand millionth 10^{-9}
me **NANO-** second and light advances one foot
NAOS a shrine (Greek)
NAPE the back of the neck
NAPO (ne plus); finish
zo **NAPU** the musk-deer of Java
nt, md, ga **NARD** spikenard; an unguent; Arab backgammon
zo **NARE** nostril
NARK police spy; a squealer
NARY neither; nor any
cf **NASO-** nasal, of the nose
pl **NATE** buttock
me **NATR** Ethiopian measure
rl **NAVE** (wheel); hub; main aisle
nt **NAVY** fleet of ships
NAZE cape; mull; headland; ness
NAZI German national socialist
NEAL anneal; to temper (metal)
nv **NEAP** a small-measure tide
NEAR nigh; close by; stingy; miserly
zo **NEAT** trim; tidy; gim; simple; cattle
NECK col; an isthmus

NEED want; lack; require; poverty
bt, md **NEEM** (medicinal) shrub; (margosa oil)
bt **NEEP** a turnip
NE'ER never (poetic)
NEMO nobody
ch **NEON** an inert gas; (lighting)
NEPE flannel footwear
NERD untidy, good-for-nothing, person
NERF car bump (motor racing)
NERO a tyrant; imperial fiddler (Rome)
NESH soft; crumbly; tender
NESS naze; cape; promontory
NEST abode; resort; store (-egg)
NETT **NET**, without discount; price after tax
mu **NEUM** **NEUME**, a musical phrase
NEVE firm, dry glacial snow
NEWS tidings; word; report
zo **NEWT** an eft; amphibian
NEXT close to; bordering; adjacent (of kin)
zo **NIAS** nyas; eyas; a young hawk
NIBS His Nibs; home ruler
NICE precise; fine; finical; pleasant
NICK notch; reckoning; winning throw
ga **NICK** steal; prison; Satan; shot (squash)
zo **NIDE** a brood of pheasants
NIGH near; impending; almost
rl **NIKE** winged goddess of victory (Gr.)
nc **NILE** reactivity unit
ma **NILL** unwilling; incandescent sparks
rl **NINA** fire god of the Incas
NINE one over the eight (drunk)
bt **NIPA** Indian palm tree; toddy
lw **NISI** prius; unless previously
NIXY nixie; malignant water-spirit
NIZY dunce; simpleton
NOCK the notch of an arrow
bt, cp **NODE** knot; knob; information site; junction (stem)
tc, mu **NODE** drama plot; difficulty; retransmission; border-point of second
rl **NOEL** Xmas; Yule
NOES opposition votes
NOIL a knot of combed wool
NOLL **NOUL**, **NOWL**, the head; poll; crown
md **NOMA** mouth gangrene
NONE not one
NOOK cranny; corner; recess; arbour
NOON mid-day; meridional
cp **NO-OP** do nothing instruction
NOPE American negation
NORM rule; model; standard behaviour; output
rl **NORN** one of the three Norse fates
pl **NOSE** sagacity; scent; pry; projection; beak
NOSY **NOSEY**, inquisitive; (busy body)
NOTE heed; mark; record; letter; fame
NOTE single musical sound; ultimatum
NOUN a substantive
NOUS talent, sharp wit, intellect
zo **NOUT** neat; cattle (Sc.)
as **NOVA** a newly exploding star
NOWT nothing (slang)
hd **NOWY** knotted
NUDE bare; naked; undraped; stark
NULL void; invalid; nugatory
cp **NULL** ineffectual; no-op
NUMB torpid; deadened; paralysed
NUNG a bale of cloves
NURL to mill; to indent
zo **NYAS** nias; eyas; young hawk

O

OAKS a race for fillies at Epsom
OAKY hard; tough; strong
OAST hop-kiln; (-house)
OATH vow; pledge; curse; expletive
nm **OBAN** Japanese gold coin
OBEX a barrier; an obstacle
OBEY heed; mind; comply; submit
rl **OBIT** R. C. funeral service
mu **OBOE** the hautboy
nm **OBOL** Charon's ferry fee over Styx
lw **ODAL** udal; absolute tenure in land
ODDS chances; probabilities
ODIC odylic force
rl **ODIN** Norse father of heaven
ODOR **ODOUR**, stink; smell
ps **ODYL** magnetic force
OFFA King of Mercia; (–'s dyke); (trench fortification)
OGAM ogham; ancient Irish writing
ar **OGEE** a double curve in architecture
OGLE side glance; leer; smicker
rl **OGMA** Ogmios, Irish/Celtic deity
OGPU Soviet secret police
rl **OGRE** monster; giant
rl **OGUN** Yoruba deity (Nigeria)
OILY greasy; unctuous; oleaginous
OKAY perfectly correct
me **OKET** Ethiopian measure

bt, ck **OKRA** gumbo vegetable; mallow
mt **OKTA** ⅛ of sky area
cf **OLEO** oleomargarine; oleograph
OLID evil-smelling
ck **OLIO** mess; medley; mixture; stew
OLLA olio; jar; urn; cooking pot
OLPE Grecian jug
OMAR Arab title
OMEN sign; portent; presage; augury
me **OMER** a Hebrew unit of capacity
OMIT miss; skip; exclude; neglect
me **ONCA** Portuguese measure
me **ONCE** **ONST**, old Fr. measure; ene (Sc.)
cf **ONCO-** of mass; swelling; tumour (Gr.)
tx **ONDE** fabric using shades for effect
hd **ONDY** wavy; ondine
ONER singular; a single; an adept
ONLY sole; alone; singly; barely; but
ONST once
cf **ONTO-** of origin; development (Gr.)
ONUS burden; load; responsibility
zo **ONYM** special or zoological group
ONYX agate streaked with chalcedony
nm **ONZA** old Spanish-Latin Am. gold piece
OOCH illegal mooring method (yachting)
OOFY wealthy; opulent; plutocratic
OOID egg-shaped
OOZE slime; mire; exude; leak; drip
OOZY viscous; slimy
zo **OPAH** the king-fish or sunfish
mn **OPAL** iridescent precious stone
OPEN access; overt; candid; undo; commence
rl **OPET** **APET**, Taweret, Thoueris, deity (Eg.)
cf, md **-OPIA** **-OPY**, sight defect (Gr.)
O-PIP observing station
mu **OPUS** a composition; a work
ORAL by word of mouth
zo **ORCA** the whale genus
zo **ORFE** a gold fish; ide
ORGE drunken revelry
ORGY sensual, sexual excess
ar **ORLE** fillet under an ovolo
nt **OROU** trading vessel; canoe (Papua)
ORRA odd; worthless (Sc.)
zo **ORYX** antelope; legendary unicorn
cf, md **-OSIS** of pathology; diseased (Gr.)
cf **OSMO-** liquid balance pressures
mu **OTEZ** remove! (usually the mutes) (Fr.)
pl **OTIC** receptor cells in ear
OTTI attar; an essential oil; perfume (It.)
OUFE phonetic word for 'woof'
OURS **OURN**, belonging to us
OUSE bark for tanning
OUST evict; eject; expel; dislodge
OUZO aniseed spirits (Gr.)
OVAL elliptical
OVEN kiln; heated container
ga **OVER** above; besides; very; (cricket)
zo **OVID** horned ruminant; Roman poet
md, zo **OVUM** egg, female reproductive cell
OWED due; outstanding; indebted
zo **OWRE** the wild ox
OWSE tan vat liquor
zo **OXEN** kine; cattle; neat
OXER a stiff fence
lw **OYER** authority to hold courts (hearings)
OYES **OYEZ**, Hear! (call of the public crier)

P

me **PAAL** Indonesian metric measure
zo **PACA** South American rodent
PACE speed; step; walk; peace
PACK stow; crowd; bale; load; (cards)
cp **PACK** group (cubs, wolves); store data; secret influence
me, ga **PACK** forwards (rugby); bringing in supporters; 240 lb (Br.)
zo **PACO** the alpaca; Peruvian camel
PACT bond; agreement; contract
PADS body protection (cricket)
PAFF piff-paff; jargon
ce, cp, tc **PAGE** bell-hop; attendant (boy); wooden wedge; leaf (books); screen display; paginate
PAID requited; defrayed; settled; (– a visit)
PAIK a beating (Sc.)
PAIL bucket
PAIN vex; fret; ache; rack; torment; injure
PAIR two; twain; brace; couple
lw **PAIS** a jury list
zo **PALA** South African antelope
PALE wan; sallow; paling; district
hd **PALE** vertical division; frontier; (beyond the –)
rl **PALI** Buddhist sacred language
PALL mantle; cloak; cloy; sate; surfeit; funerary cloth cover
bt **PALM** to conceal; a token of victory
zo **PALP** jointed feeler (insects)

PALT rubbish (Dutch)
hd **PALY** ashen; divided vertically
PAND narrow curtain over a bed (Sc.)
PANE window glass; a patch
PANG throe; paroxysm; to cram
PANT gasp; puff
rl **PAPA** Gr. parish priest; a bishop
rl **PAPA** the Earth (NZ)
nm **PARA** paragraph; monetary unit of Turkey and former Yugoslavia
me **PARA** measure of weight (Sabah/ Indonesia)
bt **PARA** Brazilian rubber
cf **PARA-** irregular; beyond (Gr.)
cf **-PARA** bring forth; (parent) (Gr.)
zo **PARD** leopard; panther
PARE cut; peel; lessen; diminish
PARK train of artillery; an enclosure; (cars); public garden; sportsfield (Sc.)
zo **PARR** young salmon
PART sever; divide; quit
PASS exceed; overstep; enact; (time); discharge; satisfy examiners
ga **PASS** length of inviting gesture; water-ski course; (football)
go **PASS** narrow mountain route (via col)
PAST gone; done; over; former; bygone
PATE top of head; pie, patty, meat paste
PATH way; track; trail; access
cp **PATH** route (transmission); sequence
nt **PAUL** **PAWL**, a check stop; gadget
zo **PAUW** the South African bustard
PAVE smooth; prepare; facilitate
PAVE the cobbled roads, of stone
zo **PAVO** peacock; southern constellation
PAWK trick; a cunning device (Sc.)
ga **PAWN** pledge; a chessman
PAYA Honduran Indian
PAYE pay as you earn
mo **PEAK** top; acme; apex; zenith; upper aft corner (sail)
PEAL clang (bells); echo; resound; thunder
mu **PEAN** **PAEAN** song of triumph
bt **PEAR** juicy cousin of apple
bt **PEAS** vegetables in a pod; sweet- (flowers)
PEAS fine gravel for parachuters' landings
PEAT turf used for fuel
zo **PEBA** armadillo; the black tatou
nm **PECA** **PEZA**, Portuguese gold coin
PECH **PEGH**, to pant (Sc.)
me **PECK** strike with beak; 2 gal. (9 litres)
cf, md **PEDI-** of the feet (Gr.)
cf **PEDO-** **PAEDO-**, of children, infants (Gr.)
PEEK to peep (Sc.)
mo **PEEL** skin; pare; rind; bark; flay; fall; (croquet) (jumping)
PEEL a shovel; a fort; to pillage
to **PEEN** mason's hammer with cutting face
PEEP sly look; cry of a chicken; (-show)
PEER to peep; to appear; a nobleman; equal status group
zo **PEKE** a Pekinese dog
PELA white wax from a scale-insect
PELF money; riches; filthy lucre
PELL skin; hide; parchment
PELT raw hide; throw; rain heavily
PEND hang; impend; an enclosure
rl **PENG** gigantic bird (Ch.)
PENT enclosed; confined; shut up
PEON day-labourer; bondsman; police
PEON foot-soldier; serf (Mex.); messenger
bt **PEPO** a fruit of the gourd type
rl **PERI** fairy (jinn); peeress (Iolanthe)
PERK smarten up; trim; spruce
PERM a permanent wave
zo **PERN** the honey-buzzard
PERT saucy; forward; impertinent
nm **PESO** monetary unit (Latin Am., Philippines)
PEST plague; pestilence; scourge
PHEW! exclamation of exertion
PHIZ face; visage; physiognomy
me **PHON** a decibel; unit of loudness
me **PHOT** unit of illumination
rl **PHRA** **RE**, **RA**, supreme deity (Eg.)
PHUT broken; out of order; (go-)
pl **PIAL** spinal cord membrane
PIAT anti-tank gun
pr **PICA** magpie; size of type
md **PICA** depraved appetite
nm **PICE** Indian and Nepalese monetary unit
to **PICK** cull; select; choice; peck; charge forward (basketball)
cf, ma **PICO-** one million millionth 10^{-12}
PICT early Scottish race
ck **PIDE** unleavened bread (Turk.)
PIED spotted
PIER jetty; mole; sea promenade
zo **PIET** the magpie; dipper; water-ousel

mu **PIFA** piffero; rustic shawm (It.)
zo **PIKA** small rodent; guinea-pig type
zo **PIKE** peak; a turnpike; a weapon; fish; posture
bd **PILA** Roman javelin; pile column
el, wv **PILE** nap; heap; mass; stake; projecting carpet threads (velvet, knots)
zo **PILI** hairs on bacteria
md **PILL** to rod; plunder; blackball
cf **PILO-** of body hair (Gr.)
PIMP procurer for immoral purposes
bt **PINE** to wilt; pine-apple; fir-tree
PING the noise of a bullet
bt, nt **PINK** rose colour; a flower; to pierce; to knock; mast-carrying sail ship
me **PINT** measure of capacity; 4 gills (0.5 l)
bt **PINY** full of pines
me **PIPA** Portuguese measure
pb **PIPE** long tube; (hose-) (drain-); calumet
mu **PIPE** to call; cask; bosun's whistle
me **PIPE** exchequer roll; 126 gallons
le **PIPI** pods for tanning
PIPY tubular
PIRN reel; bobbin; thread on a reel
PISE rammed clay
PISH exclamation of contempt
PISS to pee; urinate
bt **PITH** quintessence; gist; marrow
cy **PITS** (coal mines); cell cavities; scars
ga **PITS** despair; (arm-); (auto racing)
PITY ruth; condolence; compassion
PIXY pixie; a small fairy
PIZE term used in execration
PLAN plot; scheme; design; sketch
PLAP plop; plash; splash
PLAT to plait; piece of ground; dish
zo **PLAX** flat platelike structure
ga **PLAY** act; romp; game; frolic; farce; (match); umpire's command; theatre
PLEA excuse; prayer; claim; argument
PLED pleaded; argued; disputed
PLIM to swell
PLOD jog along; toil; moil; drudge
PLOP to fall into water
PLOT plan; conspiracy; outline; allotment
PLOW a plough; to plough
PLOY employment; a frolic (Sc.)
PLUG a stopple; stop; plod; peg; pipe-fitting; promote; (angling)
bt **PLUM** £100,000; a fruit
PLUS in addition; more
PNYX Athenian meeting place
ga **POCH** card game (half pack) (4 persons)
md **POCK** a pustule; pox-scar mark
mu, md **POCO** little; rather (It.); slightly
POEM ode; lyric; elegy; lay
POET bard; balladmonger
nm **POGH** ancient American copper coin
POKE bag; bonnet; nudge; prod; jab
POKY POKEY, small; cramped; confined; stupid
nt, me, ps **POLE** a mast; 5½ yds (5m/16½ ft); native of Poland; (magnetic-)
zo **POLL** clip; lop; election; head; parrot
ga, mu **POLO** 4-a-side mounted game (ball and sticks); Sp. dance with song
POLT a blow; a hard knock; a club; (bolt)
cf **POLY-** of many (Gr.)
bt **POME** an apple; a ball of dominion; orb
POMP pageantry; ceremony; display
POND pool; mere; to ponder
me **POND** Dutch ½ kg; S. African pound
ck **PONE** bread made from Indian corn
ga **PONE** who cuts dealt cards
md **PONS** medical link or bridge
zo **PONY** £25; nag; tit; palfrey
me **POOD** Russian weight, 36 lb (16 kg)
POOH exclamation of contempt; (bear)
ga **POOL** mere; pond; tarn; merge; combine; billiards
bt **POON** East Indian tree; wood for spars
nt **POOP** nincompoop (idiot); stern of ship; a push
POOR scant; meagre; sterile; needy
rl **POPE** the Bishop of Rome
nt **POPO** outrigger; sail dugout
rl **POPO** Po'po, tiger riding wind (Ch.)
md **PORE** con; study; small orifice
PORK swine flesh
PORN pornography
ck **PORT** haven; gate; entry; (-wine)
nt, mu **PORT** larboard (bearing); bagpipe music
mu **PORT** bagpipe music; mien; bearing
cp, tc **PORT** gateway for information retrieval
PORY porous; pervious
POSE puzzle; nonplus; feign; a posture
POSH very superior
cp **POST** mail; (-station); appoint (job); pillar; record
ga **POST** passing (football) (basketball)
cf **POST-** after, after, behind; (-war)

bt **POSY** motto or verse; nosegay
pp **POTT** size of hand-cut paper
POUF pouffe; large cushion; gauze
POUR gush; flow; emit; stream; rush
zo **POUT** to register pique; whiting
PRAD a horse (slang)
nt **PRAM** perambulator; Baltic coasting vessel; dinghy with transoms
nt **PRAO PRAU**, vessel of East Indies
PRAY beg; crave; implore; entreat
PREE to prove; to taste (Sc.)
cf **PREP-** preparation; prepatory; (-school)
PREX college president (USA)
PREY despoil; pillage; devour; quarry
PRIG pilfer; a coxcomb; a fop
bt **PRIM** formal; precise; mim; privet shrub
nt **PROA** Malay sailing canoe
PROD goad; poke; nudge; prick
PROG proctor; (university police)
mu **PROM** promenade concert
PROP support; uphold; buttress
PROS arguments for; cf. cons
nt **PROW** the cutwater; ram; bow
PROX proximo; next month
PSHA! pshaw
rl **PTAH** Phthah, god of fertility, creation (Eg.)
PUCE pink colour
PUCK ice hockey ball; an imp
zo **PUDU** a small deer of the Andes
PUFF fuff; pant; blow; flatter; (smoke)
PUGH interjection of disgust
PUJA Hindu ritual; obeisance
PUKE to vomit
zo **PUKU** Central African antelope
PULE to whine; to cry
PULK Laplander's sledge
PULL draw; drag; haul; pluck; pick; handle (sash lift) sidestroke (polo)
PULP any soft uniform mass
nm **PULS** Afghan monetary unit
PULT Germ. orchestral music stand
bt **PULU** Haaiian tree-fern fibre
zo **PUMA** mountain lion
ga **PUMP** raise water; inflate; compressor; dance shoe; interrogate; (angling)
nm **PUMY** pumice-stone
PUNA Andean plateau
me **PUND** Dutch pound; weight
PUNK tinder; dud; worthless
nt, nm **PUNT** gamble; kick; flat-boat; Irish money
PUNY tiny; weak; petty; Lilliputian
zo **PUPA** a chrysalis, dormant stage
PURE chaste; unsullied; unmixed; neat
rl **PURE** Oceanian deity
PURL knit; row; ripple; mulled ale; fine wire worked round silk thread
PURR curr (cat or pigeon noise)
ga **PUSH** a gang; urge; jostle; press; (badminton); jog
zo **PUSS** cat or hare
ga **PUTT** to hole the ball (golf)
zo **PUXI** North Amer. edible caterpillar
rl **PYES** calendar for calculating Easter
md **PYIC** discharging plus
rl **PYRE** a funeral pile (for cremation)
ch **PYRO** pyrogallic acid

Q

ar, zo, pr **QUAD** quadrangle; quadruped; prison
go **QUAG** quagmire; morass; swamp
QUAT **TWAT**, **TWERP**, a nonentity; a nobody
nt **QUAY** wharf; landing place; jetty
QUIB jibe; quibble
nm **QUID** chew of tobacco; sterling pound
zo **QUIN** a kind of scallop; (quintuplet)
QUIP sally; retort; taunt; joke
QUIT leave; desert; retire
QUIZ puzzle; chaff; an enquiry
QUOB quab; tremble
QUOD prison
QUOP quap; throb

R

RAAD South African parliament
bt **RABI** the grain crop of Hindustan
RACA a term of contempt
nv, mt **RACE** tidal high seas by headlands; current (mill) rapids; human
ga **RACE** compete; run (horse); groove (ball)
zo **RACH** dog; pointer or setter
RACK torture; stretch; anguish; harass
RACK a grating; wrack; cloud; to amble
RACK toothed rail (cog); shelf
RACY spirited; piquant; pungent
RAFF riff-raff; rabble; rubbish
nt **RAFT** a floating framework; (mat)
RAGE fume; fury; craze; ire
mn **RAGG** ragstone; siliceous sandstone

bt **RAGI** species of millet
rl **RAHU** the dark planet in Hindu Myth
RAID foray; inroad; invasion; irruption
zo **RAIL** fence; scold; genus of birds
rw **RAIL** sleeping on sleepers
mt **RAIN** pitter-patter; a downpour
RAIS Arab chief, captain
RAJA **RAJAH**, Indian ruler
to, nt **RAKE** roué; inclination; gardening; streamline angle of mast (funnel)
rl **RAKI** aniseed brandy (Turkey); heaven (NZ)
RAKU tea ceremony pottery Japan
md **RALE** rattling sound in the lungs
mu **RALL** rallentando, slow down (It.)
rl **RAMA** heroic incarnation of Vishnu
zo **RAMI** appendage ends in collembola
RAMP a slope; a swindle; climb; spring
zo **RANA** amphibian genus, frogs, etc.
RANA a Rajput prince or chief
nm **RAND** mountain; S. African monetary unit
RAND edge; border; margin; inner sole
RANG past tense of ring
RANI ranee; the wife of a rajah
RANK row; grade; foul; musty; nasty; set of organ pipes
RANT rave; orate; spout; declaim
mu **RANT** corranto, dances
mu **RANZ** alphorn for cowherds (Swiss)
bt **RAPE** land division in Sussex; oil seed
RAPE ravish; violate; outrage
RAPT enthralled; absorbed; fascinated
ck **RARE** choice; unusual; precious; part-raw
RASE erase; expunge; level
md **RASH** hasty; headlong; skin eruption; to slice
to, bt, ck **RASP** to file; abrade; (-berry)
bt **RATA** ironwood (NZ); instalment
RATE scold; assess; appraise; speed
RATH Burmese state carriage
RATH **RATHE**, early; soon; Irish fort
RAVE rant; enthuse wildly
RAZE **RASE**, gut; demolish; overthrow
READ peruse; decipher; study; understand (radio); evaluate conditions; (curling)
lw **REAL** true; genuine; (-estate)
nm **REAL** a monetary unit
me **REAM** expand a hole; 20 quires (paper)
REAP gain; crop; gather; harvest
REAR raise; breed; erect; end; behind
RECK to care for; regard; heed
REDD to tidy; to arrange; to clear
REDE counsel; advise; advice
bt, me **REED** rush; watergrass; inches (Isr.)
mu **REED** to thatch; a pipe
go, nt **REEF** rocky ledge; shoal; lode
REEK smoke; vapour; fume; stink
to **REEL** sway; whirl; totter; a bobbin
mu **REEL** a quick folkdance pattern
zo **REEM** unicorn of the Bible (oryx)
REFT bereft; left destitute
REIN govern; restrain; check
nm **REIS** plural of real (coins)
RELY depend; lean; confide; trust
REND rip; tear; sunder; sever; rupture
tx **RENT** hire; let; lease; schism; torn
tx **REPP** ribbed fabric
vt **RESP** a sheep disease
REST repose; lean; recline; sit; respite
bl **RETE** a plexus; network of vessels
lw **REUS** a defendant; debtor
zo **RHEA** the South American ostrich
rl **RHEA** mother of Zeus; nature-goddess (Gr.)
bt **RHEA** the ramie plant or fibre
cf, md **-RHEA** **-RHEO**, flowing, fluidity (Gr.)
RHOM parellelogram; brick
bt **RHUS** cashew-nut genus
nm **RIAL** **RYAL** (Iran) (Morocco); English gold
bt **RICE** a cereal
RICH opulent; wealthy; fertile; luscious
ag **RICK** stack; wrench; sprain
RIDE domineer; control; mount (horses)
nm **RIEL** Cambodian monetary unit
le **RIEM** **REIM**, leather strap (S. Africa)
RIFE prevalent; current; abundant
mu **RIFF** a Moroccan (mountain Berber); jazz
gl **RIFT** fissure; cleft; gap; split
go **RIFT** rif, a Berber tribe; valley
RIFT disagreement
bt **RIGA** deal; balsam; (-hemp)
rl **RIGI** Polynesian butterfly deity
rl **RIGR** Heimdall, Norse deity
RILE vex; anger; provoke; irritate
go **RILL** rivulet; brook; streamlet
bl **RIMA** narrow cleft
RIME hoar-frost; rhyme; poem
bt **RIND** peel; bark; external cover
go **RINE** rone; rune; rean; water-course

RING encircle; hoop; arena; siege
nm **RING** (old) Australian coin; (wedding-)
ga **RINK** a sheet of ice for curling; ice hockey, skating
RIOT orgy; broil; uproar; tumult
RIPE mature; ready; mellow; fit
RISE soar; mount; tower; rebel
RISK chance; hazard; peril; speculate
bt **RISP** to rasp; branch of green stalks
rl **RITA** guardian of fire (India)
rl **RITE** form; usage; observance
RIVA rift; cleft
gl **RIVE** tear apart; rend; pierce
zo **RIXY** quarrelsome; the sea-swallow
ROAD route; thoroughfare; highway
ROAM rove; ramble; meander; saunter
ROAN a colour; sheepskin binding
ROAR yell; shout; bellow; howl
ROBE clothe; invest; drape; dress
ROCK a distaff; oscillate; sweetmeat
gl, mu **ROCK** hard earth-crust; (-'n roll)
me **RODE** travelled; a roadstead; Danish me
pl, nc **RODS** retinal receptors (eye); (reactors)
ROER elephant gun
rl **ROHE** ruler of the middle world (NZ)
ROIL rile; to stir up; to vex
ROKY foggy; reeky; smokey
ROLE part; function; character
nt, ga mu **ROLL** reel; lurch; enfold; scroll; tilting movement (gliding); mini-loaf sandwich; stroke (croquet); linked drum notes
rl **ROME** Holy See (Rome)
ROMP sport; frisk; caper; gambol
pl **RONA** Maori (NZ) deity
RONE rine; rune; rean; gutter
RONT **RUNT**, stunted; a stump
rl **ROOD** The Cross; church screen
me **ROOD** a quarter of an acre
ar, mo **ROOF** cover; canopy; shelter; overhang
zo **ROOK** cheat; defraud; gregarious bird; chariot (Arab); castle (chess)
ROOL to ruffle; to raggle
ROOM chamber; accommodation; space
ROOM roum; a deep-blue dye
bt **ROOT** fix; implant; origin; radix
mu, ma, cr **ROOT** lowest note of a chord; tenon; (square-) (cubic-)
nt **ROPE** tie; secure; bind; tether; (guy)
ROPY stringy; viscous; adhesive
bt, mu **ROSE** arose; colour; (ceiling); flower; sound vent of lute
bt **ROSS** the refuse of plants
ROSY roseate; blooming; blushing
rl, mu **ROTA** roster; R.C. court; wheel of life; perpetual musical round; canon
ROTE mechanical repetition; order of work
ck **ROTI** the joint (Fr.)
me **ROTL** rottola, ratel, Arab measure
ROUE rake; debauchee; libertine
bt **ROUM** a deep-blue dye; pod
ROUT vanquish; defeat; disorder; cut a groove
ck **ROUX** sauce of melted butter, flour
ROVE roam; ramble; stray; range
nm **RUBA** Sicilian monetary unit
RUBE a rustic (USA)
mn **RUBY** a size of type; a gem
ga **RUCK** wrinkle; fold; crease; sprain; 3 players in football
zo **RUDD** freshwater fish; the red-eye
RUDE boorish; churlish; rough; raw
RUED regretted; repented
zo **RUFF** a frill; to trump; a bird
RUGA fold; corrugation
RUIN wreck; demolish; subvert
go **RUKH** the jungle (India)
RULE control; sway; precept; custom; regime
pl **RUMP** survivors of previous parliament; behind
RUNE incised writing of the Norsemen
RUNG ladder step; toiled
go **RUNN** low-lying land in India
zo **RUNT** dwarf; stump; a pigeon
zo **RUSA** Indian deer; the sambar
bt **RUSA** Indian grass; (geranium oil)
RUSE wile; trick; artifice; stratagem
bt **RUSH** dash; fly; career; sally; a reed
ck **RUSK** a biscuit
RUSS a Russian (slang)
RUST fust; must; corrosion
bt **RUTA** genus of plants; rue
RUTH mercy; pity; sorrow; misery
nm **RYAL** **RIAL**, rose-noble, old English coin
RYND iron millstone support
RYOT Indian cultivator

S

ck **SACK** sherry; container; pillage; pouch
me **SACK** dismiss; container (wool); 2 ways
bt **SADR** the lote-bush

SAFE sure; secure; reliable; certain
SAFE strongbox; guaranteed secure
SAGA heroic Norse history
bt **SAGE** a Solomon; genus salvia
bt **SAGO** edible palm pith
SAGY seasoned with sage
nt **SAIC** Levantine ketch
SAID stated; declared; alleged
nt **SAIL** cruise; glide; depart; jib (rig)
SAKE cause; regard; reason
ck **SAKI** Japanese wine from rice
zo **SAKI** South American monkey genus
SALE market; vending; auction
zo **SALP** swimming tunicate
SALT mariner; wit; pungent; salacious
ch, nm **SALT** (sea-); primitive African currency
SAME ditto; identical; exactly similar
ck **SAMP** porridge made from Indian corn
mn **SAND** grit; (seashore)
SANE rational; sound; normal; lucid
hd **SANG** chanted; blood red
SANK foundered; subsided; dug
SANS without (Fr.)
zo **SAPO** the toad-fish
mn **SARD** a precious stone; agate
ga **SARE** pelota game
tx **SARI** Indian garment; scarf
tx **SARK** a shirt or chemise
SARN a pavement
tx **SASH** window frame; ribbon for order
SASS impudence; sauce
SATE cloy; glut; surfeit
rl **SATI** suttee (self-immolation); deity (Ind.)
bt, mu **SAUL** Indian tree; an oratorio
SAVE except; rescue; to husband; retain
me **SAWK** 20 inches (Thailand)
SAWN cut with a saw
SAXE a kind of paper; light blue
md **SCAB** a blackleg; a sore-scar
zo **SCAD** horse-mackerel
SCAN view; examine; scrutinize; poetic metre
cp **SCAN** check records; test communication channels
gl **SCAR** mark; blemish; steep rock
SCAT a tax; scare away; be off
zo **SCAT** animal waste
go **SCAW** **SKAW**, a promontory
SCON **SCUN**, skim; skip
SCOT a Scotsman; a tax
nt **SCOW** flat-bottomed boat; dumb-barge
SCUD wrack; hasten; bustle
mt **SCUD** small low clouds
SCUG skug; shelter; expiate
SCUM dross; froth; refuse; scoria
SCUN **SCON**, skim
zo **SCUP** a swing; the porgy fish
SCUT a short tail
tx **SCYE** armhole of a garment
me **SEAH** Jewish dry measure 14 pt
zo, pb **SEAL** fasten; a pinniped; drainwater; seadog
me **SEAM** joint; vein; stratum; 24 stone
SEAN **SEINE**, a drag-net
SEAR burn; scorch; a pawl; dry
SEAT chair; residence; abode; See
SEAX Celtic sword
SECT faction; schism; party
bt, zo **SEED** sow; germ; embryo; progeny; selected player (tennis)
SEEK try; ask; hunt; search; court
SEEL to close the eyelids; good fortune
SEEM appear; look; pretend
SEEN observed; regarded; perceived
SEEP to ooze; to trickle; to sipe
SEER augur; prophet; soothsayer
me **SEER** Sri Lankan and Indian measure (kg)
bt **SEGO** an American plant
SEID a descendant of Mohammed
SEIL sile; strain; a sieve (Sc.)
cf **SELF-** of ego (-centred) (-ish) (DIY)
SELL vend; barter; hawk; betray
pr, hd **SEME** heraldic printing design detail; strewn with stars, etc.
cf **SEMI-** (demi-) (hemi-); a prefix of half
SEND transmit; propel; eject
SENT forwarded; despatched; flung
nm **SENT** Estonian coin
zo **SEPS** reptile genus; lizards
SEPT a clan in Ireland; (one of 7)
md **SERA** a lock of any kind; pl. of serum
SERB native of Serbia
bt **SERE** succession of plant communities
SERF thrall; villein; slave
SESS **CESS**, tax
SETA bristle; prickle
rl **SETH** **SET**, Setekh, Setesh, god of death (Eg.)
SETT squared block; packing piece; pile driving
SETT badger's home, (mining)
SEVE wine's distinctive bouquet (Fr.)

SEWN stitched
mu **SEXT** musical interval
zo **SHAD** a fish of the herring type
zo **SHAG** tobacco; green cormorant; rape
SHAG coarse hair; roughen; deform
SHAH Persian monarch
SHAM deceive; substitute
SHAN Burmese borderer
go **SHAP** a steep hill
SHAW a grove; a thicket
bt **SHEA** African butter-tree
SHED emit; cot; shack
rl **SHEN** Chinese gods
SHEW show; exhibit; parade
me **SHIH** Chinese measure
SHIM brake-plate; to wedge up; packing tool
rw **SHIN** to climb; tramp; trudge; fishplate (track)
nt **SHIP** to export; seagoing vessel
SHIR **SHIRR**, to pucker
SHIT to defecate; faeces; nonsense; insult
SHOD provided with shoes
el, rw **SHOE** footwear; fitting; (-horn); socket; pick-up
SHOO be gone! scare away
SHOP emporium; store; jargon
ga **SHOT** (marksman); pellets; report; injection; dose; attempt; winner (bowls)
SHOT putting the weight/shot (throwing)
rl **SHOU** Hsing, patron of longevity (Ch.)
SHOW flaunt; blazon; expound; pomp
SHUG to crawl
SHUN avoid; evade; eschew; elude
SHUT lock; bar; close; slam; secure
gl **SIAL** granitic earth shell
SICE the six at dice
SICE **SYCE**; groom (India)
SICK poorly; ailing; disgusted; ill
bt **SIDA** genus of mallows
SIDE verge; border; cause; behalf; facet
SIDI Afr. Moslem title of respect
SIDY aloof and pretentious
SIFT separate; sort; search out
pc **SIGH** a heavy sad breath
rl **SIGI** Norse deity
SIGN beckon; endorse; emblem; portent
cp, ms **SIGN** arithmetical or instructional pointer
go **SIKE** **SYKE**, Arctic stream
rl **SIKH** sect; a Punjabi military tribe
SILE sieve; colander
tx, lw, pt **SILK** coccoon thread; Queen's Counsel; eggshell gloss
bd, gl **SILL** doorstep; window frame (lock) igneous rock plate
SILO fodder storage; ensilage
gl, go **SILT** sediment; ooze; mud
gl **SIMA** basaltic earth shell
SIMP a simpleton; a mutt
SINE **SYNE**, since; then (Sc.)
mu, rl **SING** relate in verse; chant; (hymn)
SINK flag; droop; subside; founder; descending air mass (gliding)
mu, rl **SINK** point where lines of flux end; (kitchen-); (geology)
SINN Fein (Irish party)
SIPE ooze; to seep; percolate
SIRE progenitor; father; 'My Lord' (liege)
lw **SIST** summon; delay; stay (Sc.)
rl **SITA** wife of Rama (India)
SITE location; place; position
bt **SIUM** the water parsnip
rl **SIVA** **SHIVA**, the Destroyer (India)
SIZE glue; varnish; bulk; volume
SIZY sticky; viscous
nm **SKAR** Tibetan copper coin
go **SKAT** a card game
go **SKAW** **SCAW**, a promontory
bt **SKEG** stump; branch; wild plum
SKEG fin-keel of surfboard; rudder fastening (yachting)
SKEP beehive; wicker basket
SKEW **SKUE**, awry; oblique; a squint
SKID heavy timber; drag shoe; side-slip
SKIM graze; touch; skirt; brush
SKIN peel; pare; flay; hide; pelt; veneer; film
SKIO **SKEO**, a hut in the Orkneys
SKIP skipper; large tub; omit; leap; kibble
cp **SKIP** (-rope); jump to next instruction
SKIP captain of team; rink (ice sports)
SKIT a lampoon; burlesque
lt, me **SKOT** unit of low-intensity lighting
zo **SKUA** the pirate gull
zo **SKUG** **SCUG**, shelter; expiate; squirrel
zo **SKYE** terrier
SKYR curds (Iceland)
SLAB chunk; block; mat; thick; mud
gl, ga **SLAB** flat rock shelf; pitcher's mound (baseball)
bt **SLAE** sloe (Sc.); blackthorn
SLAG scoria; debris; mine waste

SLAM bang; shut with violence
ga **SLAM** illegal lift (wrestling) (bridge)
SLAP spank; a cleft; a gap in a fence
SLAT strip; lath; slate; sharp blow
SLAV European ethnic grouping
SLAW sliced cabbage used as salad
SLAY kill; destroy; despatch; murder
SLED sledge; sleigh; snow vehicle on runners
SLEW to twist; turn round; killed
wv **SLEY** the reed of a weaver's loom
cp **SLIC** Selecting Listing in Combination
SLID slipped; skidded; glided; tripped
SLIM slight; slender; lithe
SLIP trip; fall; slide
rw, el, pa **SLIP** (-carriage); ring; escape; let go; garment; mistake
nt **SLIP** launch (way); (factor); (scraper); paint
ga **SLIP** ceramic decor base; fielding position (cricket)
SLIT rip; rend; tear; slash; sever
SLOB muddy ground
bt **SLOE** **SLAE**, blackthorn
SLOG smite; swipe; work doggedly
SLOP a policeman; night soil; a spill
SLOT track of deer; slit; groove; fixture
rw, ga **SLOT** reserved future; tackle; (timetable); (-machine); position on wave (surfing) (Am. football)
cp **SLOW** tardy; dilatory; dull; (-down)
SLUB to twist whilst spinning
SLUD sludge; ooze; mud
SLUE to revolve
SLUG a pellet; homeless snail
me, pr, nm **SLUG** pound; unit of acceleration of mass; typecast; strike; token coin
SLUM a purlieu; squalid neighbourhood
mu **SLUR** stigma; stain; aspersion; sully
SLUT a slattern; a jade; prostitute
SMEE widgeon; pintail
SMEW migratory sea duck
SMIT to infect; a stain; infection
SMOG chemicals as fog
SMUG self-satisfied; to confiscate
SMUT soot; a plant disease
SNAG projecting stump; a hindrance
SNAP bite; nip; snip; crack; break
bt, ga **SNAP** a snap-shot (photo); (cards); break; grab; sudden action; (-dragon)
SNEE a large knife (Dutch)
zo **SNIG** to cut; an eel
ga **SNIP** clip; piece; snippet; a certainty (racing)
SNOB proud social climber
mt **SNOW** frozen vapour flakes; (cocaine)
SNUB slight; give offence; (of tickets)
SNUG cosy; compact; sheltered; pub
SOAK steep; drench; saturate
SOAP to flatter; washing agent; (box); (opera)
SOAR rise; mount; tower; aspire
SOCK plough-share; hose
ch **SODA** an alkali
SOFA couch; divan; ottoman
rl **SOFI** **SUFI**, Moslem mystic; dervish
SOFT pliable; plastic; yielding; dulcet
SOHO London quarter
SOIL loam; stain; sully; tarnish
lw **SOKE** privilege; (East Anglian)
bt **SOLA** hat-plant; sponge-wood; pith
SOLD retailed; paddled; deceived
zo **SOLE** a fish; unique; solitary; only; under-surface of shoe
ga **SOLE** ski, golf club; curling stone
ga, mu **SOLO** card game; lone performer
ck **SOMA** an intoxicating drink
zo **SOMA** animal body
cf **SOMA-** some-, somatic of the body (Gr.)
SOME several; indefinite; (much, slang)
ac, me **SONE** unit of loudness
mu **SONG** lay; carol; ballad; lullaby
SOON anon; early; willingly; lief
SOOT grime (coal-smoke)
SOPH sophomore; a student
zo **SORA** Carolina rail
bt **SORB** mountain ash; service tree
SORE raw; tender; grievous; painful
bt **SORI** fern spore-cases
SORN to cadge board and lodgings
SORT arrange; classify; kind; race; character
ch **SORY** sulphate of iron
SO-SO indifferent; moderate
SOSS a mess; a puddle; plump
SOUK bazaar; Eastern market stall
SOUL spirit; fervour; essence
ch **SOUP** broth; consommé; muddle; mix-up; laboratory medium for cultures
ga **SOUP** broken wave foam (surfing)
SOUR tart; acid; rancid; caustic; bitter
SOWN disseminated; scattered; strewn

bt, ck **SOYA** Korean protein bean
bt **SPAD** **SPUD**, potato; surveyor's nail (USA)
ck **SPAM** spiced ham
me **SPAN** yoke; to bridge; wholly; (spick and –)
mu, cp **SPAN** interval; difference in value range
nt, mn **SPAR** to box; rafter; pole
zo **SPAT** the spawn of shellfish; a slap
SPAY to render unfertile; geld; castrate
SPEC on speculation (slang)
SPED fled; hurried; hastened
SPEW vomit; eject violently
SPIN turn; twist; twirl; prolong
go **SPIT** eject saliva; tongue of land (shoal)
ck **SPIT** rod for impaling meat over fire (barbecue); (-and polish) (-image)
SPIT express contempt; spittle; froth
SPIV felonious speculating parasite
SPOT blot; stain; patch; mark; site
SPOT hand punch (cards); treated carbon paper
SPOT aiming point; billiard balls; (leopard); observe
SPRY alert; brisk; nimble; lively
bt, jn **SPUD** narrow spade; potato; plumb bob nail; weight; dowel
tx **SPUN** whirled; woven; extended; told
rw **SPUR** goad; urge; impel; prick; siding
SPUR wing dam; griffe (decor); (dyke)
me **STAB** pierce; spear; gore; Ger. measure
me **STAG** male deer; share pusher; (-party, men only)
STAM to confound; confusion
STAR an asterisk; a heavenly body
lw **STAY** stop; check; curb; tarry; abide
nt **STAY** support (rope, wire); remain; (put); stamina
bt **STEM** dam; hold; resist; stock; stalk
nt **STEM** bowsprit (-rudder bearing)
STEN a tommy-gun
STEP pace; tread; rung; stage; -dance
nt **STEP** fixture for securing base of movable mast
STET let it stand (Lat.), instruction to printers
ck **STEW** ragout; simmer; jug; fishpond
STIR spur; stimulate; tumult; prison
ar **STOA** covered colonnade
STOB stub; stump; wedge
STOG to stir up mud
STOP block; impede; cease; desist
zo **STOT** young ox; steer
STOW pack; arrange; place
bt **STUB** fag-end; counterfoil record; tree stump
bd **STUC** stucco; stone-like plaster coat
ck **STUD** knob; nail; breeding place; collar fastener; headless bolt (gun) weld)
STUM unfermented wine; must
STUN bewilder; amaze; dumbfound
md **STYE** an inflamed eyelid
rl **STYX** river to Hades
SUCH so; like; similar; sic
SUCK imbibe; chew; absorb; engulf
SUDD flood debris; dense mat of aquatic vegetation (Nile)
nt **SUDS** soapsuds; the wash
SUED entreated; prosecuted; high and dry
lw **SUER** a plaintiff
ck **SUET** meat fat for cooking
SUEZ canal; (Lesseps, the engineer)
SUFI Islamic mystic; Moslem sect
SUIT gratify; beseem; action; case
SULK glower; be sullen; silent anger
SUMA Nicaraguan Indian
SUMO Japanese wrestling and martial art
SUMP pit; morass; tank for remainders
SUNG chanted
SUNK immersed; engulfed; dug
bt **SUNN** Indian plant; its fibre
SUPE a supernumerary; a toady
SURA a chapter of the Koran
bt **SURA** the sap of the coco-palm
SURD an irrational number; (ab surdum)
SURE certain; secure; reliable; safe
SURF foaming waters
SWAB swob; mop up
SWAD pod; podgy person; clump
SWAG plunder; festoon
SWAM swim (past tense)
zo **SWAN** the Swan of Avon, Shakespeare
SWAP **SWOP**, to barter; exchange
SWAT a fly-killer; a smart blow
bd **SWAY** rock; roll; reel; influence; power; (thatching)
SWIG gulp down; pulley gear
SWIM float; overflow; be dizzy
SWIN sea river or channel
SWOB **SWAB**, mop
SWOP **SWAP**, exchange; barter
SWOT **SWAT**, an earnest student

SWUM swim (past participle)
SYBO cibol; onion
nm **SYLI** Guinean monetary unit
SYNE SINE, syn (Sc.); since

T

TABI Japanese sock (with separate toe)
TABU TABOO, ban; veto; (against mores)
mu **TACE** be silent
nt **TACK** a nail; navy food; hasten; change course; (zigzag) sailing
ck **TACO** fried tortilla/salad dish (Mex.)
TACT diplomacy; finesse
nm, me **TAEL** money of account, weight (Asia)
TA'EN taken
TAFT a plumbing joint
zo **TAHA** African weaver-bird
zo **TAHR** Himalayan goat
TAIC THAIC, Indo-Chinese lang. group
rl **TAI'I** supreme deity (China)
TAIL extremity; queue; trail; entail
nm **TAKA** Bangladeshi monetary unit
TAIN mirror silver
TAKE grasp; seize; adopt; carry
mn, md **TALC** mica; baby powder
TALE story; fable; narration
TALK parley; speech; lecture; (small-)
TALL towering; elevated
TAME docile; dull; domesticate
TAMP pack earth solidly; thump
rl **TANE** Polynesian deity
me **TANK** cistern; reservoir; refuel; armoured vehicle; weight (Ind.)
cp **TANK** mercury delay line
zo **TANT** small scarlet spider
tx **TAPA** Polynesian fibre cloth
TAPE to bind; ribbon; to measure; (red)
cp **TAPE** magnetic strip for recording data
TARA old Irish Convocation
bt, rl **TARA** edible NZ fern; Buddhist deity
bt **TARE** gross weight; a weed
go **TARN** mountain pool; a marsh
bt **TARO** edible plant of the arum type
nm **TARO** Maltese, Sicilian coin
TART sharp; small pie; call girl
TASH Indian silk fabric with gold thread
TASK toil; drudgery; labour
TASS pouch; thigh-armour
TA-TA good-bye; a short walk
TATE a London art gallery
TATH cattle dung; to manure
zo **TATU** tatou; peba; armadillo
TAUT tense; strained; stressed
TAWA N. Zealand hardwood
ae **TAXI** motor-cab; move on runway
TAYO apronlike garment (S. Am.)
T-BAR drag ski-lift
bt **TEAK** hardwood tree; (wood)
zo **TEAL** small waterfowl; a duck
TEAM group; harnessed animals
TEAR rip; rend; lacerate; sob
TEAT a nipple
TEDE tead; torch; flambeau
TEED ball mounted for driving off (golf)
TEEM swarm; to abound; be prolific
gs **TEEM** pour molten glass
TEEN grief; affliction; allot (obs.)
TEER to stir; to sieve
bt **TEFF** Abyssinian cereal grass
bt **TEIL** the lime tree
bl **TELA** weblike tissue
cf, tc **TELE-** of wired communications
TELL recite; divulge; reckon
TEND incline; verge; nurture; minding
me **TENG** Burmese measure of weight
TENT probe; a pavilion, canvas, bivouac
me **TERA** International unity of quantity
ar **TERM HERM**, dub; entitle; phrase; period; a pedestal supporting a bust
zo **TERN** sea-bird (gull-type)
ch, md **TEST** essay; assay; try; (-tube)
TEST attest; proof; ordeal; criterion
cp **TEST** probe; examine; check data element; competition
TETE head; (-a-), secret
TEXT writing; (-book); theme; sermon
tc **TEXT** the message for transmission
THAI (Siamese); language; people
THAN conjunction of comparison
zo **THAR** goat-antelope of Nepal
THAT pronoun (demonstrative)
mt **THAW** melt; liquefy in heat
THEE objective of thou
THEM objective of they
THEN adverb of past time
THEY Kipling's pronoun; the bosses who decide
THIN lean; fine; lank; sparse
THIS pronoun (demonstrative)

THOR the God of Thunder (Norse)
rl **THOU** familiar pronoun; (God)
THUD a dull sound
THUG violent criminal
THUS like this; as a result
bt **THUS** Frankincense, form of resin
nm **TIAO** Chinese money of account
TIBU Saharan tribe
zo **TICK** credit; mark; (clock); bug
zo **TICK** blood-sucker, cattle disease carrier
nt **TIDE** season; course; sea movement
TIDY neat; spruce; trim; orderly
TIED united; constrained; fastened
nt **TIER** row; rank; mainsail to boom canvas link
TIFF quarrel; peevishness
ar **TIGE** the shaft of a column
rl **TIKI** Maori charm or amulet; spirits
bd **TILE** roof brick; a hat
mn, gl **TILL** cash drawer; cultivate; tillite; boulder clay; moraine boulders; until
rl **TILO** god of the sky (Mozambique)
TILT incline; lean; slant
TIME era; term; date; (-switch)
cp **TIME** single channel with multiplex signals
rl **TI'MU** Earth Mother (Ch.)
TINE point of antler; spike; to enclose
TING ring; tinkle; food vessel (Ch.)
TINT hue; dye; stain; tinge
TINY pygmy; wee; puny; minute
TIRE tyre; iron hoop; attire
TIRE weary; harass; vex; fatigue
zo **TITI** South Amer. squirrel monkey
TIVY with speed; tantivy (bugle/ call)
zo **TOAD** an amphibious batrachian
cr **TOAT** handle of bench plane
zo **TOBY** beer-mug; Punch's pet dog
TO-DO ado; bustle; excitement
zo **TODY** green humming bird
cr **TOED** of obliquely fastened timber
pl **TOED** having toes; (-the line)
TOFF fop; dandy; swell
lw **TOFT** grove
ck **TOFU** soya curd (China)
tx **TOGA** Roman garment
tx **TOGS** garments for a purpose
TOIL snare; travail; pains; strive
TOIT a cushion
TOLA Indian weight; 180 grains troy
TOLD narrated; related; recounted
TOLL tribute; road fee; (funeral bell)
bt **TOLU** oleo-resin; balsam
TOMB grave; sepulchre; mausoleum
TOME book; volume; work
cf, md **-TOMY** of surgery, removal (Gr.)
TONE cadence; inflection; tint
nt **TONY** a simpleton; genteel; posh
TOOK grabbed; gained; captured
nt **TONY** Indian sailing canoe
to **TOOL** cat's paw; utensil (artisan's)
bt **TOON** Indian cedar
TOOT a wastrel; the devil; honk
zo **TOPE** shark known as the penny-dog
TOPE Buddhist monument
TOPE clump of trees; to booze
TOPO fishing boat, (Venice)
cf **-TOPY** of location, habitat (Gr.)
TORE rent; split; a moulding
ar **TORI** mouldings at the base of columns
TORN lacerated; ripped
me, ps **TORR** unit of low pressure
lw **TORT** redress of wrongs
TORY a Conservative
TOSH bosh; twaddle; boloney
TOSS pitch; hurl; cast; throw of coin (matches/sport)
TOTE to carry; totalizator
TOUR trip; round; jaunt; ramble
TOUT paid agent; tipster
TOWY like tow; hempen
TOYE lute music
TOZE to pluck; pull by the ears
TRAM a beam; tramcar
gl, mn **TRAP** U-shaped bend (pipe); igneous rock; (-door)
el **TRAP** adorn; ambush; ensnare; pony carriage; switch
cp **TRAP** automatic branch switch for emergencies
TRAY salver; carrying board
TREE the Cross; decoder; (family-)
TREK travel by ox-wagons (S. Africa)
TREK blue, black outlines on tin-glazed earthenware (Holland)
TRET a trade allowance
TREY a three at cards or dice
TREZ third; the third tine of antler
TRIG trim; tight; secure; a dandy
TRIG wedge; skid; boundary line
bd **TRIM** neat; tidy; clip; adjust; edging, skirtings
TRIM correct level of vessel in water; speeds of surfing; balance (gliding)
mu **TRIO** composition for 3 instruments
TRIP tour; err; slip; stumble; dance; 'high' period of drug influence
TROD trampled; walked
TROT to run; gait of a horse
TROW to trust; believe; suppose

me **TROY** weights used for gold, etc.
TRUE loyal; staunch; straight; exact
TRUG hod for mortar; gardening basket
TSAR Czar; Ksar; Tzar; Zsar; ruler of Russia
me **TSUN** Chinese inch; ritual jade (Ch.)
TUAN title of respect (China and Malay)
mu **TUBA** bass trumpet; transmitter
rw **TUBE** pipe; telescope; Underground; cathode (television); (follicle); hollow part of wave (surfing)
TUCK fold; net; thrust
TUCK beat of drum; food; to cram; body posture (athletic)
mn, gl **TUFA** calcareous deposit; volcanic dust
mn **TUFF** volcanic rock-debris
TUFT knot; bunch; clump; tuffet
bt **TULE** Californian bulrush
TUMP hillock; to earth up
bt, zo **TUNA** prickly pear; great tunny fish
mu **TUNE** air; melody; strain
TURF sod; sward; earth; peat; (racing track)
TURK citizen of Turkey; Ottoman; (young-)
cp **TURN** spin; bend; divert; curdle; hinge; act; output
mu **TURR** three-stringed Burmese violin
zo **TUSK** pointed tooth; sea-fish cod type
bt **TUTU** short ballet skirt; shrub (NZ)
rl **TUUM** (meum and tuum); thine (Latin)
zo **TUZA** tucan; Mexican pouched rat
TWAS it was
TWEE precious; overly cute
bt **TWIG** observe; understand; sprig
TWIN double; duplex
TWIT taunt; ridicule; upbraid; ass
zo **TYKE TIKE**, dog; cur
TYMP mouth of blast furnace's hearth
TYPE kind; sort; class; species; emblem
TYPO a compositor; (typographer)
TYRE rubber outer wheel of vehicle
TYRE tire; attire; dress
TYRO tiro; novice; recruit; neophyte
TZAR Tsar; Czar; Ksar; Zsar (Rus.)

U

nt **UCHE** 2 mast, passenger vessel
lw **UDAL ODAL**, freehold estate
UGLY hideous; unsightly; hateful
bt **ULEX** furze genus
md **ULNA** an arm-bone
UMBO boss of a shield; a knob
zo **UMBO** the point of a bivalve shell
zo **UNAU** S. American two-toed sloth
UNDO open; untie; nullify
zo **UNIO** genus of freshwater mussels
UNIT a standard quantity; measure
UNTO preposition of direction
bt **UPAS** the deadly antiar tree
UPON on, preposition of situation
hd **URDE** pointed, variated
URDU a language (India, Pakistan)
md **UREA** a crystalline compound, or gas
URGE push; drive; impel; incite; spur
zo **URIA** a genus of sea-birds, guillemots
ch, md **URIC** the acid (of urea)
mn **URRY** blue clay near a coal seam
as **URSA** a constellation (Great Bear)
zo **URUS** the European wild ox
zo **URVA** an ichneumon (India)
USED habituated; employed
cp, tc **USER** consumer; spender; subscriber
lw **USUS** act, right of making use of something
UTIE wall tie (USA)
UVAE grapes, raisins, etc
pl **UVEA** part of the iris of the eye

V

VAIN empty; conceited; unavailing
hd **VAIR** heraldic fur
nt **VAKA** outrigger, sailing canoe
VALE dale; valley; farewell
VALI provincial governor (Turk)
VAMP boot-uppers; to patch
VAMP cinema character (parody)
mu **VAMP** improvise accompaniment
VANE weathercock; nag; blade; fane; feather-fletching of arrow (archery)
nt **VANG** mast-peak steadying brace
me **VARA** S. Amer. yd of 33 in (84 cm)
zo **VARI** monkey (Madagascar)
VARY alter; change; alternate; differ
VASE urn (flowers)
cf, md **VASO-** of canal, duct, blood-vessel
VAST huge; spacious; colossal

ce **V-CUT** wedge cut, tunnelling technique
ck **VEAL** dinner for prodigal son; (calf)
rl **VEDA** sacred Hindu books
nv **VEER** vary; turn; shift (of wind)
as **VEGA** star
tx **VEIL** mask; cloak; screen; cover
gl, pc **VEIN** lode; seam; ledge; mood; humour
bt, pl **VEIN** blood vessel; (vascular) bundle (leaf)
nm **VELD** Boer gold coin (S. Africa)
ag **VELL** rennet; to cut turf
me **VELO** speed of 1 ft (30 cm) per sec.
VEND sell; hawk; peddle
VENT utter; discharge; orifice; wind
VERB part of speech denoting action
lw **VERT** the greenery of the forest
hd **VERT** heraldic green
nt **VERY** a signal light; (-much)
lw, tx **VEST** endow; endue; clothe; a garment
VETO ban; forbid; embargo
hd **VETU** lozenge
VIAL phial; ampulla; level tube; bubble
to **VICE** vise; a screw-press
VICE sin; iniquity; in place of
VIDE see (Lat.)
VIED contested; competed; strove
VIEW eye; scan; survey; prospect; opinion
lw **VILE** base; ignoble; paltry; cheap
mu **VINA** East Indian banjo
bt **VINE** climbing grape plant
VINT Russian card game, to make wine
VINY producing grapes or vines
mu **VIOL** antique violin
hd **VIRE** crossbow bolt; heraldic amulet
VISA permit; authorization
me **VISS** 3.60 lb (Burma and India)
VIVA long live! (It.) (Sp.) (Ptg.)
VIVE long live! (Fr.)
mu **VIVO** lively; with animation
go **VLEI** artificial lake (S. Africa)
VOCE the voice; (sotto-voce) (It.)
VOID null; invalid; empty; vacant; emit
mu **VOLA** rapid series of notes
zo **VOLE** genus of rodents; water-rats, etc.
me **VOLT** electrical unit
VOLT a turn; sudden leap; (fencing)
VOTE suffrage; ballot; elect; poll
nt **VOYA** anchor cable
hd **VULN** to wound (heraldic)
ar, bd **VYSE** spiral staircase

W

mn **WADD** manganese ore
WADE to ford
go **WADI** desert river bed (often dry)
WAFT float; convey; beckon
nt **WAGA** outrigger sail canoe (Papua)
WAGE pay; hire; stipend; salary
WAIF a stray vagabond; (ownerless)
WAIL cry; weep; deplore
as **WAIN** wagon; constellation
mu **WAIT** bide; tarry; linger; serve; minister; carol singer; shawm
nt **WAKA** Maori canoe
WAKE funeral vigil; rouse; trail; wash
WALE weal; raised streak; ridge; bruise
ga **WALK** hike; saunter; gait; career; (police beat); (baseball)
bd **WALL** dividing construction; rock face; alignment of players (soccer); obstacle (jumping)
ga **WAND** rod; staff; baton; (magic); target (archery)
bt **WANE** ebb; fail; decline; droop; (moon)
WANT need; crave; wish; penury
nt **WAPP** shroud-tightener; yachting
lw **WARD** fend; repel; custody; a minor
ar **WARD** hospital dormitory; bailey, courtyard
bt **WARE** a caution; seaweed
nm **WARK** bulwark; Ethopian coin
WARM ardent; fervid; keen; zealous
WARN caution; admonish; notify
nt, tx **WARP** twist; haul; carpet thread base
md **WART** a verruca; body blemish; (character)
WARY canny; cautious; vigilant
WASE straw head-pad
nt **WASH** lave; rinse; cleanse; wake
zo **WASP** stinging insect
rl **WAST** preterite of 'to be' (thou-)
me **WATT** unit of electrical horsepower
WAVE sway; beckon; brandish; ripple
WAVE swell; billow; comber; roller
WAVY curly; sinuous; billowy
WAXY pliant; yielding; wrathful
WEAK frail; insipid; watery; fragile
WEAL prosperity; state; stripe (beating)
WEAN alienate; detach; grow up
WEAR bear; don; sport; impair
nv **WEAR** alter course stern to wind
bt **WEED** a cigar; to root out; eradicate; hoe

WEEK unit of time (7 days)
WEEN to think; consider; guess; judge
WEEP sob; bewail; lament
tx **WEFT** threads crossing warp
WEIR a low dam across a river
zo **WEKA** Maori hen
bt **WELD** join together; mignonette
ar, bd **WELL** fount; source; origin; hale; staircase area
bd **WELT** shoe-edging; to flog; metal roofing seam
WEND wander; a Slavonic race
WENT left; departed; decamped
WEPT cried; lamented; sobbed
WERE past of 'to be'
rl **WERT** 'thou' form
WEST cardinal direction
WHAP **WHOP**, **WHIP**, chastise
WHAT interrogative pronoun
WHEN adverb of time
WHET sharpen; heighten; rouse
WHEW exclamation of exertion
WHEY skimmed milk
WHIG Liberal; sour whey
WHIM caprice; notion; idea
gl **WHIN** doleritic igneous rock
bt **WHIN** gorse, furze
mu **WHIP** quirt; flog; driver; coachman; V-shaped woodwind instrument
WHIP official controlling group (MPs) (cyclists)
WHIR whirl; spin; revolving rapidly
WHIT jot; iota; speck; scintilla
WHIZ **WHIZZ**, a noise of speed
WHOA! exclamation 'to halt'
WHOM object of who
WHOP **WHAP**, **WHIP**, wop; chastise
WICK (candle); creek; quick; alive
ga **WICK** stone against stone (curling)
ga **WIDE** broad; rife; distant; (cricket)
WIEP fascine; part of Dutch mattress
WIFE spouse; to marry
WILD rash; disorderly; savage; untamed
WILE ruse; stratagem; dodge; chicanery
WILL wish; desire; bequeath; testament
rl **WILT** to droop; to wither (thou of to be)
WILY sly; artful; crafty; insidious
WIND coil; twist; turn; breeze; blow
bt, ck **WINE** fermented grape or other juice
WING to fly; aerofoil; (stage); (chair); flank
ga, bd **WING** flanker (football) fielder (baseball, lacrosse); annexe
WINK an eye signal
WINO an excessive alcohol drinker
WINY having the flavour of wine
WIPE rub; clean; polishing rag
tc, nm **WIRE** bind; snare; telegram; Persian money
WIRY flexible and strong, but thin
WISE sagacious; sage; sapient
WISH will; want; desire; behest
rl **WISP** (of snipe); small broom; a whisk
WIST knew (thou)
WITH in company (preposition)
bt **WOAD** plant yielding a blue dye (Druids)
fr **WOLD** wood; a weald downland (forested)
zo **WOLF** devour; wild canine; jarring howl
WOMB uterus
WONT habit; custom; practice; use
bt **WOOD** timber; grove; forest
tx **WOOF** the weft
tx **WOOL** fleece; a staple product
WOOM beaver fur
WORD term; news; advice; pledge; (pass-)
cp **WORD** remark; rumour; data units
WORE bore; sported; donned; lasted
WORK toil; operate; endeavour; a job
zo **WORM** a groveller; to insinuate; creature
WORN rather the worse for wear
bt **WORT** malt after mashing a plant genus
wv **WOVE** intertwined; matted; knitted
WRAP wind; swathe; enfold; muffle
WREN member of **WRNS** (Women's Royal Naval Service, 2nd World War
zo **WREN** a bird
rl **WRIT** summons; formal document; (holy-)
me **WROT** wrought timber abbrev.
WYND a lane; narrow alley (ancient)

X

zo **XEMA** genus of gulls
cf **XERO-** of being dry (Gr.)
rl **XMAS** Christmas; Noel; Yule
md **X-RAY** Roentgen ray
XYST gymnasium

Y

YAFF **WAFF**, to bark (Sc.)
YALD **YAULD**, active; supple (Sc.)
rl **YAMA** Hindu underworld god
nm **YANG** Korean silver coin
YANK an American; to heave; hoik; extract with a twist
le **YAPP** limp leather binding
me **YARD** 36 in/91 cm
YARD (court-); (Scotland-)
nt **YARD** (lan-) rope; lugsail; (-arm)
YARE dexterous; quick; prompt
tx **YARN** spun thread; sailor's story
bt **YARR** to snarl; the spurrey plant
zo **YAUP** yelp; hungry; blue titmouse
nt **YAWL** yowl; howl; fishing-boat
YAWN gape
md **YAWS** tropical disease
YEAH yes (USA) (slang)
zo **YEAN** **YEEN**, to lamb; to produce
YEAR 12 months
YEEN **WEEN**, to know (suspect) something
YEGG hobo; cracksman; safe-breaker
YELD barren, not giving milk
YELL bawl; scream; screech
YELP yap; cry of pain; bark
YERK jerk; rouse; excite
YEST yeast
zo **YETI** abominable snowman
YILL ale (Sc.)
YIPS nervousness (golf)
zo **YITE** the yellow bunting
nc **YLEM** theoretical neutron substance
YMIR the Frost Giant (Scand.)
YOGA Hindu philosophy and exercises
YOGI ascetic yoga practitioner (Ind.)
YO-HO exclamation (piratical)
zo **YOIT** the yellow bunting
YOKE team together; enslave; restrain
YOKE shoulder crosspiece harness, also of rudder
YOKO Japanese wood block
ck **YOLK** heart of egg; wool oil
YOOP an onomatopoeic sob
YORE in olden times (former ages)
YOTE board-game (West Africa)
YOUR of you
YOWL howl; yawl; gowl; bawl
YO-YO a toy; a bandalore
nm **YUAN** Chinese monetary unit
YUCK to itch; the itch
rl **YUGA** one of the Hindu ages of the world
YUKO score in judo
rl **YULE** Xmas; Noel; winter solstice
ga **YUMP** bump or collision (motor racing)
zo **YUNX** the wryneck bird
YURT a Siberian house or tent

Z

ZANY buffoon; merry-andrew; mimic
ZARF zurf; metal coffee-cup holder
zo **ZATI** an Indian parrot
gl **ZAWN** cavern
bd **Z-BAR** building fixture
ZEAL fervour; intensity; enthusiasm
zo **ZEBU** humped domestic ox (India)
bt **ZEIN** zeine; a protein found in maize
ZEND a Persian dialect
ZENO- of strangeness, foreign (Gr.)
ae **ZEPP** zeppelin; airship
nm **ZERO** cipher; nought; nothing; nil
ZEST peel-flavouring; gusto; relish
ZETA the Greek Z
ar **ZETA** sexton's room over porch
rl **ZEUS** Olympian deity
zo **ZIMB** Abyssinian tse-tse fly
ch **ZINC** a metallic element
ZING pep (USA)
mo **ZION** **SION**, a hill (mount) in Jerusalem
ZOAR a place of refuge
zo **ZOBO** zhobo; dsomo; hybrid yak-cow
gl, bl **-ZOIC** pertaining to life; (mesozoic)
me **ZOLL** Swiss measure; toll; customs-duty (Ger.)
ZONA zone; belt
zo **ZONA** patch; strip; area
cp **ZONE** belt; girdle; district; (category)
pg **ZOOM** aerobatic manoeuvre; change focal length
bl **ZOON** the product of a fertilized ovum
ac **ZOOP** extraneous noise
ZOOT fashionable; gaudy
ZSAR **TZAR**, **TSAR**, **CZAR**, ruler (Russia)
ZULU native people of Kwa-Natal, S. Africa
zo **ZUNA** Angola sheep
ZUNI Mexican Indians
ZUPA Serbian village confederation
ZURF zarf; metal coffee-pot holder
bl, md **ZYME** (en-) a ferment; a disease germ

FIVE-LETTER WORDS

A

AAZIZ Queen of Sheba; also Balkis
bt **ABACA** Manila hemp
ar **ABACI** counting frames; column crowns
nt **ABACK** aft; behind; backwards; (taken-)
nv **ABACK** sails set for wrong side wind
ABADA rhino (15th cent.)
nt **ABAFT** aft; astern
ABASE lower; reduce; disgrace
ABASH awe; confound; disconcert
ABATE wane; diminish; lessen
rl **ABBEY** a monastery
rl **ABBOT** the head of an abbey
ABCEE an abc; an alphabet
nt **ABEAM** abreast; on the beam
bt **ABELE** the hoary poplar
bt **ABHAL** the fruit of the cypress
ABHOR hate; loathe; abominate; detest
ABIDE lodge; tarry; tolerate; sojourn
bt **ABIES** the fir genus
zo **ABLEN** a freshwater fish; the bleak
ABLER more competent; more expert
zo **ABLET** ablen; the bleak
ABODE house; dwelling; home; lived
me **ABOHM** electro-magnetic unit
ABOIL on the boil; boiling
zo **ABOMA** boa-constrictor (S. Amer.)
A-BOMB nuclear weapon
cp, md **ABORT** to miscarry; sterile; break off
ABOUT almost; around; near
ABOVE aloft; over; before; exceeding
ch **ABRIN** toxic protein
ABUSE misuse; defame; traduce; revile
ABUZZ buzzing; humming
ABYSS **ABYSM**, chasm; bottomless pit; gulf
zo **ACARI** mites and ticks
ck **ACCRA** Caribbean batter fritters
zo **ACERA** bubble-shell genus
ACERB sour; bitter; acid; harsh
ck **ACHAR** acid pickles; salt relishes (Pers.)
ACHED pained; sorrowed; grieved
md **ACHOR** dandruff
md, bt **ACINI** granulations; berries
bt **ACKEE** Jamaican fruit
ACLIS spiked club; javelin
zo **ACONE** insects' coneless compound eyes
bt **ACORN** oak seed; cord-end
ACRED lavishly landed
ACRID sour; pungent; bitter; mordant
zo **ACRON** head of embryonic insect
ACTED performed; simulated; deputized
bl **ACTIN** muscle protein
ACTON padded jerkin
ACTOR player; trouper; histrion
md **ACUTE** keen; sharp; accent (illness)
ma **ACUTE** closed geometrical angle
ADAGE proverb; dictum; maxim; saw
ADAPT adjust; accommodate
ma **ADDED** summed; combined; appended
cp, zo **ADDER** viper; snake; asp; calculator
ADDLE confuse; putrid; muddled
lw **ADEEM** to revoke a legacy
md **ADEPS** fatty tissue
ADEPT adroit; expert; proficient
AD-HOC for a set purpose
ADIEU farewell; goodbye
ADIOS farewell (Sp.)
md, mu **AD-LIB** extemporize; natural body weight
ADMAN advertising pundit
ADMIT acknowledge; concede; own
ADMIX infuse; blend; mingle
ADOBE sun-dried brick
ck **ADOBO** braised stew (Philippines)
ADOPT accept; assume; espouse; father
ADORE worship; revere; idolize; love
ADORN decorate; deck; enrich; garnish
ADSUM (present at a roll-call)
ADULT a grown-up; mature; ripe
rl **AEGIS** Minerva's shield; protection
AESOP a fabulist; parable teller
AFFIX add; fasten; subjoin; attach
AFOOT astir; happening
AFTER later; in imitation of
AGAIN anew; afresh; moreover
zo **AGAMA** genus of lizards; saurians
zo, ck **AGAMI** game bird, edible when young (S. Am.)

AGATA shaded coloured glass (N. Am.)
mn **AGATE** a quartz; ruby type
pr **AGATE** type printing measure
AGATY like an agate
bt **AGAVE** aloe; cactus drink; drug
rl **AGAVE** daughter of Cadmus
lw **AGENT** doer; factor; deputy; proxy
AGGER a mound
AGILE nimble; spry; alert; brisk
AGING AGEING, growing old
lw **AGIST** pasture rate
AGLOW glowing; gleaming; shining
nm **AGNEL** French gold coin (lamb)
rl, zo **AGNUS** Dei; pascal lamb
AGONY pangs; anguish; torment; throe
AGORA Greek, Roman market place
AGRAS sweet Algerian drink
AGREE accede; engage; conform; concur
AHEAD leading; onward; in front
nt **AHOLD** close to the wind
nt **AHULL** hove to
AIDED abetted; seconded; succoured
AIDER helper; assistant; acolyte
AILED afflicted; peaked; pined
AIMED directed; pointed; trained
AIMER purposeful person
AIRED ventilated; spread abroad
AIRER dryer; ventilator
rl **AISLE** passage; walk
AITCH (H); aitch-bone
bt **AJUGA** bugle genus of plants
AKALI Sikh fanatic
zo **AKELA** Kipling's lone wolf
ALACK alas; lackaday; woe is me
ALALA Anc. Gk. battle cry
hd **ALANT** heraldic mastiff
ALARM fear; scare; dismay; a tocsin
zo **ALARY** alar; having wings
ALATE winged; of late; lately
mn **ALBIN** an opaque white mineral
ALBUM book for photos or stamps
zo **ALCES** the elk; moose (N. Am.)
bt **ALDER** a hardwood tree
ALERT wary; watchful; vigilant
bt **ALGAE** the seaweeds
md **ALGID** cold; chilly
ALGIN seaweed extract for iodine
cp **ALGOL** a star; language-data
md **ALGOR** unusual coldness
bt **ALGUM** almug; sandalwood
ALIAS otherwise; an assumed name
lw **ALIBI** proof of absence
ALIEN strange; exotic; remote; foreign
ALIGN ALINE, adjust; rectify; arrange; regulate; conform
ALIKE similar; analogous; equal
ALISH resembling beer
ch **ALITE** ground clinker from sintering
ALIVE vital; quick; alert; brisk
ALKYD glyptal resins; polyesters
ch **ALKYL** aliphatic radicals
rl **ALLAH** Moslem word for the Deity
ALLAY lull; calm; relieve; repress
ALLEY large marble; taw; passage
ALL-IN exhausted; insurance policy; inclusive
zo **ALLIS** the allice shad; a fish
ALLOD freehold estate
ALLOO halloo
ALLOT distribute; apportion; assign
ALLOW admit; own; concede; grant
ALLOY a base admixture
ch **ALLYL** organic radicle
bt **ALMUG** algum; sandal-wood
bt **ALOED ALOID, ALOIN**, aloes bitter fruit
bt **ALOES** bitter purgative drug
ALOFT above; overhead; skyward
ALONE only; sole; single; isolated
ALONG by; beside; together
ALOOF apart; away; distant
zo **ALOSE** allis; shad-fish
ALOUD audibly; loudly; clamorously
ALPHA the first or beginning (Gr. letter)
bt **ALPIA** bird-seed
nt, rl **ALTAR** shrine; sanctuary; receding step in drydock
ALTER vary; change; turn; transform
zo **ALULA** bastard wing
AMASS heap; gather; accumulate; pile
mu **AMATI** violin (Cremona)
AMAZE daze; astound; perplex
mn **AMBER** fossilized resin
AMBIT precinct; extent; compass
AMBLE dawdle; saunter; stroll
cf, md **AMBLY-** dysfunction (Gr.)
rl **AMBON** lectern; pulpit
rl **AMBRY** alms-box; niche; almonry
AMEND emend; better; rectify; correct
bt **AMENT** a catkin
tx, rl **AMICE AMICT**, pilgrim's linen cloak
ch **AMIDE AMINE**, ammonia compounds
AMISS wrong; faulty; erroneously
AMITY friendship; fellowship; harmony
zo **AMMON** Tibetan sheep
AMONG emong; amidst; amongst
AMORT halfdead; dejected; spiritless

AMOUR an affair; a love intrigue
cf **AMPHI-** of double function
AMPLE ointment-box; wide; capacious
AMPLY plentifully; bountifully
AMPUL ample; oil-jar; flask
zo **AMSEL** **AMZEL**, blackbird
AMUCK madly; in murderous frenzy
AMUSE entertain; cheer; charm; divert
bt **ANANA** the pineapple
md **ANCON** the elbow; a console
cf **ANDRO-** of the male
rl **ANEAL** **ANELE**, anoint; unction
zo, nm **ANGEL** divine messenger; fish; old English coin
ANGER ire; rage; choler; passion
cf **ANGIO-** of blood vessels
ga **ANGLE** a corner; to entice; to fish; (tennis)
ANGOR acute pain or anxiety
ANGRY irate; wroth; piqued; riled
pc **ANGST** anxiety; anguish; pain (Ge.)
pc **ANIMA** living personality; soul
bt **ANIME** resine; fiery
ANION electro-negative ion
bt **ANISE** plant furnishing aniseed
ANISO unequal
me **ANKER** European liquid measure
pl **ANKLE** foot-leg joint
ANKUS elephant goad
ri **ANNAL** a Mass
rl **ANNAT** an Ecclesiastical levy
zo **ANNET** the kittiwake
ANNEX add; append; join; unite
ANNOY badger; worry; affront; molest
ANNUL cancel; quash; revoke
el **ANODE** positive electrical pole
pc **ANOIA** idiocy; anoesia
pc **ANOMY** urban isolation syndrome
ANOMY lawlessness; miracle
bt **ANONA** custard-apple genus
ANTIC prank; lark; caper
ANTRE a cave; a cavern
zo **ANURA** frogs; toads; batrachians
zo, md **ANVIL** ossicle, ear bone for sound
mu **ANVIL** blacksmith's forge block; operatic percussion
ANZAC Australian, NZ Army Corps
AOGAI lacquer inlaid with mother-of-pearl (Haliotis), Japan
pl **AORTA** the great artery; coronary
APACE rapidly; swiftly; at speed
APART aloof; asunder; separately
zo **APERY** monkey-house
zo **APHID** **APHIS**, green-fly; ant-cows
zo **APIAN** relating to bees
APING copying; mimicking; imitating
zo **APISH** ape-like
bt **APIUM** the celery genus
md **APNEA** cessation of breathing
zo **APODA** eels, etc.
zo **APODE** limbless creature
ce **A-POLE** wooden A frame
nt **APOOP** astern
nt **APORT** to port
APPAL scare; daunt; shock; astound
ga **APPEL** stop-call (fencing); appeal
bt, ga **APPLE** the award of Paris; fruit; (Adam's); ball (baseball); orb; big city
APPLY bestow; use; employ; refer
APPUI **APPUY**, support; reciprocal action
APRIL 4th month
rl **APRON** short cassock; protective garment
to **APRON** wedge; lathe; sea defence
APRON aircraft parking area
ar **APRON** lead sheet dam slope; panel
APSIS extreme point in an orbit
APTLY fittingly; appositely; apropos
go **ARABY** Arabia
bt, ck **ARACK** **ARRACK**, fermented palm juice
bt **ARBOR** tree; bower; spindle; axis
zo **ARDEA** the heron genus
me **ARDES** 5½ bushels, Egyptian
bt **ARDIL** fibre from groundnuts
bt **ARECA** betal-nut palm
AREFY dry up; shrivel; wither
ARENA ring; stage; battlefield
bt **ARENG** the sago palm
ARETE knife-edge mountain ridge (Swiss)
ch **ARGAL** crude tartar
mn **ARGIL** potter's earth
ch **ARGOL** argal; crude tartar
ch **ARGON** a light gas
ARGUE plead; dispute; reason; debate
zo **ARGUS** watchful; a pheasant
rl **ARIAN** heretic sect (Christian)
zo **ARIEL** a sprite; a gazelle
ARIES the Ram of the Zodiac
ARISE ascend; soar; emerge; rebel
ARLES earnest money on engagement
ARMED equipped protected
ARMET medieval helmet
ARMIL insignia of royalty
ARNEE Indian buffalo
bt **ARNOT** pig-nut; earth-nut
bt **AROID** a plant allied to the sun

AROMA scent; perfume; fragrance; odour
AROSE got up; began; sprang; revolted
bt, ck **ARRAH** Indian lentil; Irish expletive
ARRAS tapestry; hangings
cp **ARRAY** range; marshal; contents
lw **ARRET** decree; arrest
ARRIS sharp edge; arete
ARROW bolt; shaft; dart; reed
ARSIS vocal inflection; emphasis
lw **ARSON** fire-raising; pyromania
ARTEL a Russian guild
ARYAN Indo-European
ck **ASADO** saddle (meat) (Sp.)
ASCII dwellers on the equator; computer code
ASCOT fashionable race meeting
bt **ASCUS** spore case
nt **ASDIC** submarine-detector
ASHEN wan; pale; hueless; pallid
ga **ASHES** results of cricket on the hearth
ASHUR Assyrian god
ASIAN Asiatic
ASIDE apart; away; aloof; laterally
ASKED invited; demanded; requested
zo **ASKER** a newt; petitioner; suitor
ASKEW awry; aslant; askance; oblique
bt **ASPEN** the trembling poplar
nm **ASPER** a small silver Turkish coin
ck **ASPIC** savoury meat jelly; sap
bt **ASPIC** 12-pounder cannon; lavender
mu **ASSAI** enough; very
ASSAY essay; test; try; analysis
ASSER rafter; thin lath
ASSES mokes; donkeys; burros
ASSET a possession
ASTEL a dam; a splinter
bt **ASTER** flowering plant
ASTIR alert; awake; agog; excited
md **ATAXY** functional disorder; (Ataxia)
zo **ATCHI** Caucasian ibex
cf **ATELO-** incomplete; imperfect
ATILT on edge; slanting
ATIMY dishonour; disgrace
zo **ATLAS** a Titan; a moth; a bound collection of maps
ATMAN the Buddhist ego
ATOLL coral island
ATOMY atom; skeleton; a pygmy
ATONE expiate; satisfy; propitiate
md **ATONY** debility; off colour
nt **ATRIP** anchor clear; aweigh
ATTAR otto; fragrant rose oil
ATTIC Athenian; (salt); garret; loft
ATTLE refuse from mines; rubbish
AUBIN Canterbury gallop
cf, tc **AUDIO-** related to hearing
cp **AUDIT** examine accounts; review of patients; record
ga **AUFIN** bishop (chess)
to **AUGER** a drill
AUGET explosive charge for mines
AUGHT zero; ought; naught; 0
AUGUR seer; soothsayer; portend
AULAE Roman halls or courts
AULIC (royal court)
mu **AULOS** ancient Gr. oboe-like instrument
AUNTY auntie
AURAL of the ear
AURIC golden
ch **AURIN** golden red dye
ch **AURUM** gold; chemical element
ch **AUXIN** growth-affecting substance
AVAIL benefit; help; suffice; use
nt **AVAST** stop; stay; cease
bt **AVENS** the herb bennet
AVERT avoid; divert; forfend; parry
zo **AVIAN AVINE**, of birds
AVION air (by air) aircraft (Fr.)
nt **AVISO** a dispatch boat (Sp.)
AVOID shun; elude; forsake; eschew
lw **AVOUE** French lawyer, advocate
AWAIT tarry; bide; stay; pause
AWAKE alert; ready; alive; vigilant
AWARD give; grant; adjudge; prize
AWARE mindful; conscious
nt **AWASH** nearly submerged
AWFUL dire; dread; fearful; imposing
bt **AWNED** bearded like barley
AWNER grain separator
AWOKE bestirred; roused; incited
AXIAL AXILE, sharing same axis
AXIOM truism; assumed truth
pl **AXION** brain/spinal cord
AXITE a propellant
AXLED having a spindle
AXMAN chainman (USA)
AXOID axoidean
ch **AZIDE** hydrazoic acid salt
AZOIC devoid of life
ch **AZOTE** nitrogen
AZOTH the alchemist cure-all; panacea
ch **AZOXY** potash/nitro-affected
AZTEC extinct Mexican-Indian
AZURE AZURN, sky-blue; the sky; vault of heaven
AZURY blue; cerulean
ro **AZUSA** missile tracking system
AZYME unleavened bread

B

BAARD transport ship
BABEL (tower), multilingual confusion
bt BABUL gum-arabic tree
bt BACCA a berry
pl, ga BACKS dorsals; defence (football)
ar BACKS riverside of colleges (Cambridge)
ck BACON gammon; to be saved
hd BADGE emblem (for recognition)
BADLY corruptly; wickedly; imperfectly
BAFFY an old golf club
ck BAGEL hard glazed doughnut roll (Jew.)
BAGGY loose fitting; bulging
me BAHAR 3½ cwt (197 kg), East Indian
tx BAIZE BAYZE, coarse (curtain/billiard) cloth
ck BAKED oven-cooked (sundried)
BAKED parched; hardened; dried up
ck BAKER bread/pastry maker
mn BALAS orange ruby
ae BALED in bundles
nt BALER a bowl; scoop (small boats)
BALKY apt to stop suddenly
mt BALMY relaxing air, climate; soothing
as BALOO the Bear; (hulla-)
bt, nt BALSA Peruvian raft; a tree
tc BALUN balance/unbalance transformer
zo BAMBI faun
bt BANAK American tree
BANAL commonplace; trivial; trite
BANAT Transylvanian district
nt BANCA outrigger sail canoe (Philippines)
lw BANCO bench; bank money
ga BANDY ice hockey; crooked; dispute
mu BANJO job an octaroon would like; 5-string fretted, plucked stringed instrument
lw, rl BANNS public notice of marriage
zo BANNY a minnow
BANTU African tribe
BARBE war-horse armour; nun's kerchief
zo BARBS jagged tip of feathers
BARED naked; unadorned; stripped
rl BARET BIRETTA, cardinal's cap
BARGE shove; jostle
nt BARGE cargo craft
mn BARIA BARYTA
mt, ch BARIC of weight/pressure (barometer); barium
bt BARKY pertaining to tree bark
BARMY foolish; dotty
ck BARON lord; (-of beef) sirloin
mu BARRE single finger chord on guitar
hd BARRY divided by horizontal bars
me BARYE unit of pressure dynes
BASAL basic; fundamental source
BASED founded on
le BASEL tanned skin
cp BASIC basal; fundamental source
bt, ck BASIL chisel edge; a herb
ga, pl BASIN pond; dock; reservoir; bowl; trough
BASIS ground work; first principle
BASON a basin
zo BASSE bass; fish like a perch
mu BASSO a bass singer (It.)
mu BASTA stop! enough (It.)
BASTE cook; sew; stitch; thrash
ga BASTO ace of clubs (cards)
BATAK Mayo-Polynesian language
BATAK people in Sumatra
cp BATCH lot; amount; crowd; series
BATED restrained; repressed; reduced
BATEY gold and silver embroidery
BATHE immerse
cf BATHY- deep (bathysphere)
tx BATIK method of dyeing (Ind.)
zo BATIS wattle-eye flycatcher
mu, ck, ga BATON staff; wand; sceptre; rod; (relay) athletics; truncheon; bread
BATTA Indian grant
BATTY bat-like; dotty
tx BAUGE cloth; drugget
ga BAULK deliberate fault (badminton); hinder; refuse (horse-jumping)
ga BAULK timber beams; thwart (billiards)
nt BAULK (-head) ship's watertight section walls
bt, nt BAVIN faggot of brushwood
BAWDY lewd; immoral (-house)
BAYED recessed; howled like a dog
BAYOU channel, outlet of river/lake
BAZAR bazaar; mart; souk; exchange
BEACH shore; strand; sands; margin
rl BEADS necklace rosary, (prayer-)
BEADY small and bright; (-eyed)
BE-ALL sum and substance; ultimate
BEAMY shining; radiant; broad; smile
BEANO jamboree; beanfeast; spree
BEARD defy; oppose; confront
BEAST brute; ruffian; animal
mu, pl, ps BEATS (heart); (drum); fluctuations in sound intensity; strokes
BEAUX gallants (Fr.)

mu **BEBOP** dissonant jazz
to **BECHE** drill extractor
lt **BECKE** of microscope juncture light
BEDAD! Irish interjection
bt **BEECH** a hardwood tree
BEEFY stolid; powerful
to **BEELE** pickaxe
BEERY maudlin; fuddled
BEFIT suit; become
BEGAD! exclamation of surprise
BEGAN started; initiated; originated
BEGAT bred; sired; engendered
BEGET sire; become father
BEGIN start; initiate; commence
BEGOT procreated; gave rise to
BEGUM Moslem princess
BEGUN originated; opened
bt **BEHEN** sea-lavender
BEIGE fabric; yellowish grey
BEING existence; actually
zo **BEISA** oryx; unicorn
nm **BEKAH** half shekel (Hebrew)
nt **BELAY** make fast (rope) (sails)
BELCH a report (from stomach)
nm **BELGA** Belgian currency
BELIE prove an accusation was wrongly held
BELLE beauty queen
BELLY stomach; abdomen; (-laugh)
mu,ga **BELLY** (-flop) flat dive; to swell; topside of string instrument; bottom of surfboard
BELOW under; beneath; Hades
ce **BENCH** seat; form; court; tribunal; form of quarry
md **BENDS** cramps, pains (deepsea divers)
hd **BENDY** divided into bends
bt **BENNE BENE** an oil plant
bt **BENTH** ground ivy
tx **BERET** round (Basque) cap
bt **BERRY** fruit; barrow; mound
nt **BERTH** cabin bed; ship at quay; situation
mn **BERYL** a gem
zo **BERYX** perch-like sea fish
ck **BESAN** Indian lentil flour
BESET assail; encircle; surround
ga **BESOM** a broom of twigs (ice curling)
BESOT assot; get fuddled, or drunk
bt **BETEL** nut of the areca palm
BETON a kind of concrete
nm **BETSO** a small Venetian coin
ck **BETTY** flask; jemmy; sweet pastry
BEVEL BEZEL, glass ornamentation groove
BEWIT leather strap in falconry
tx **BEZAN** Bengali cotton cloth
BEZIL metal groove for glass
BEZIL clock gem
bt **BHANG** hashish; Indian hemp
zo **BHYLE** Indian ox
nt **BIBBS** wooden brackets
rl **BIBLE** The Scriptures
zo **BIDDY** a fowl; a chicken; farm girl
zo **BIDET** genitals bath; small horse
me **BIDON** about 5 qt (5.6 litres)
BIDRI Indian metal-ware
BIELD shelter; protection
bt **BIFER** twice-yearly flowering/fruiting
BIFID two-clefted
nt **BIGHT** cove; bay; coil; loop
BIGLY ostentatiously
BIGOT zealot; fanatic; dogmatist
BIJOU pretty trinket (gift)
BILBO Spanish rapier
nt **BILGE** waste-space between deck and hull
nt **BILGE** underwater curve of hull; nonsense
BILIN BILE, intestinal enzyme; anger
cp **BILLI** giga; one thousand million 10^9
zo **BILLY** Australian cooking can, goat (male)
BINAC Binary Automatic Computer
BINAL twin; double
BINGE a carousal
BINGO brandy; gambling pastime
zo **BINNY** a Nile fish
ec **BIOME** largest land community area
ec **BIOTA** a region's fauna/flora
zo **BIPED** two-footed animal
BIPOD (cf. tripod) two-legged
bt **BIRCH** to flog; forest tree
BIRTH genesis; nativity; origin
zo **BISON** American buffalo
ce **BITCH** female dog; wolf; disagreeable woman; spike
BITER wild dog; insect; cheat
nt **BITTS** a cable attachment
BITTY incomplete; fragmentary
mu **BIWAR** Japanese lute-form
ch **BIXIN** annatto
BLACK ebon; inky; dusky; sombre
bt **BLADE** roisterer; leaf; flat edge (bat, club, (golf), knife, oar, sword)
mn **BLAES** hardened shale
md **BLAIN** blister, blotch
BLAME chide; rebuke; reproach
BLAND soft; suave; mild; benign
BLANK lacuna; vacant; empty; void; (cartridge); no score
BLARE blazon; proclaim; clangour
BLASE cloyed; surfeited (Fr.).

BLASE immune to novelty or impressions
BLAST gust; explode; (shrivel); cell; noise
cp **BLAST** release memory areas
BLAZE horse mark; flame; proclaim
BLAZE path mark (trees)
zo **BLEAK** drear; desolate; river-fish
BLEAR dim; rheumy; watery
BLEAT the cry of a sheep
zo **BLECK** coal-fish
BLEED exude; secrete; impoverish
BLEEP radio signal
BLEND mix; unite; knead; coalesce
BLENT blended; amalgamated
BLESS laud; exalt; praise; extol
BLEST endowed with blessings
BLIMP small airship; (reactionary Colonel)
BLIND ruse; feint; curtain; sightless
BLINK glance; flicker; ignore
nt **BLIRT** blore; squall; gust
BLISS ecstasy; rapture; felicity
bt **BLITE** the plant Good King Henry
BLITZ sudden total bombardment; lightning war (Ge.)
ck **BLOAT BLOTE**, cure by smoke; dilate
cr, nt **BLOCK** bar; obstruct; mass; (tackle) building; hoist
cp, me, tc **BLOCK** unit of data
ga **BLOCK** foul (badminton); (Am. football); (basketball)
BLOKE a fellow; a man
BLOND fair; flaxen
BLOOD cruor; gore; kindred; lineage
ce, bt, pt **BLOOM** bud; blossom; prime; thrive; film on old paint, iron, steel block
cn **BLOOP** sound-track joint thud
BLORE blirt; violent gust
BLOWN winded; trumpeted; exposed
BLOWY breezy; gusty; windy
BLUED tempered; squandered
BLUER more blue; gloomier
mu **BLUES** Royal Horse Guards; sad American-negro songs
BLUEY blanket; bundle (Australia)
go **BLUFF** sheer; brusque; spoof; headland; cliff
BLUNT blont; dull; abrupt
BLURB recommendation; description (bk. cover)
BLURT utter hastily
BLUSH flush; colour; redden
BOARD embark; victuals; council; non-gem diamond drill
to **BOART BORT**, square-sawn timber; pressed wood; (squash) platform; stage; plank
ga **BOAST** brag; crow; vaunt; angle stroke (squash)
BOBBY policeman
BOCAL glass beaker
BOCHE a Hun, also a German
BODED portended; presaged; augured
BODGE BOTCH, bungle; fail
bt **BODHI** Buddhist sacred tree
nm **BODLE** farthing (Sc.)
ga **BOGEY** min. golf score; hobgoblin
BOGGY soggy; swampy; marshy
rw **BOGIE** railway axle; truck
BOGLE bugbear; scarecrow
BOGUS sham; spurious; false
bt **BOHEA** inferior tea
BOIAR BOYAR, Slavonic nobleman
BOITE night-club, disco
BOLAR pertaining to clay
BOLAS S. American missile
nt **BOLIN** bowline
me **BOLUS** large pill
BOMBE swollen Rococo style decor
ga **BONCE** marble game; head (slang)
BONED seized; stole; purloined
bl **BONER** sharp blow; erection
tx **BONES** of skeletons; bobbins (lace)
mu **BONGO** African antelope; percussion single small drum; head injury from fall (skateboarding)
BONNE French nurse
ml **BONNY** bonnie; ore pocket
BONUS award; premium; subsidy
rl **BONZE** Buddhist priest
BOOBY looby; dunce; simpleton
zo **BOOBY** water bird
BOOED hooted; noisily objected
BOOER vociferous interrupter
zo **BOOPS** humpbacked whale
BOORT (diamond polishing)
BOOST boom; push; eulogize
BOOTH market stall; voting cubicle; (toilet)
BOOTS last joined; shoe cleaner
BOOTY loot; spoil; plunder
BOOZE BOOZY, alcoholic drink; tipsy
BORAK banter; chaff (Australia)
ch **BORAX** tincal; borate of soda
BORED drilled; wearied
BOREE French peasants' dance
zo **BORER** an insect; seaworm
ch **BORIC** boracic
BORNE narrow-minded; carried
ch **BORON** a non-metallic element
BOSKY busky; shady; thickly wooded
BOSOM breast; confidential

nc **BOSON** elementary particle (photons, mesons)
nt **BOS'UN** boatswain (leader)
BOSSY dictatorial; domineering
BOTCH to patch; worthless
BOTHY hut; cottage (Sc.)
zo **BOTTS** larvae; worms
BOUCH to bush; to debouch
bt **BOUGH** branch; limb; offshoot
BOULE (buhl); inlay work; hardwood log
ga **BOULE** Greek Parliament; roulette; French bowls
BOUND limit; pale; leap; spring
BOURG a town; burgh; borough
BOURN **BURN**, stream; border
BOUSE **BOWZE**, **BOWSY**, drunk; tipsy
mn **BOVEY** a kind of coal
BOWED bent; curved; subdued
pl **BOWEL** rectum
nt **BOWER** arbour; shelter; anchor
ga **BOWER** the knave at euchre (cards)
BOWIE a large knife
ga **BOWLS** skittles; a game
nt **BOWSE** to heave; bouse
nt **BOW-TO** to face the wind
BOXED crated
BOXEN made of boxwood
BOXER a pugilist
pr **BOX-IN** surrounding type with rule
ck **BOXTY** Halloween dish (Ir.)
BOX-UP mistake; error
BOYAR boiar; Russian nobleman
BOYAU ditch; trench (Fr.)
nt **BOYER** Flemish sloop
ga, to **BRACE** pair; couple; stiffen; anti-capsize stroke (canoeing); stirrup-stand (polo); support; tauten; string a bow (archery)
zo **BRACH** bitch-hound
tx **BRACK** a flaw in cloth
bt **BRACT** specialized leaf
cf, go **BRADY-** of slow (river)
tx **BRAID** brede; broid; weave; entwine
ga, nt **BRAIL** (falconry); to furl sails
BRAIN cerebellum; intellect
mn **BRAIT** rough diamond
BRAKE thicket; harrow; wagonette
bt **BRAKY** overgrown with ferns
BRAND brond; stigma; mark; torch
bt **BRANK** buckwheat
BRANK bridle for scolds
zo **BRANT** a goose
BRASH hasty; brittle; loose rock
ml, mu **BRASS** (top) money; impudence; effrontery; alloy of copper and zinc; metal wind instrument
tx **BRAUL** striped cloth
BRAVE to dare; heroic; valiant
BRAVO well done!; an assassin (It.)
BRAWL struggle; fight; quarrel (drunk)
BRAWN muscular strength
BRAXY splenetic sheep disease
BRAZE to solder
ck **BREAD** food; fare; aliment
mu **BREAK** interval; smash; shatter; successful sequence; separate; sprint; voice-change; tone quality; short solo
zo **BREAM** a fish; to clean
go **BREDE** slow river
BREED farm; beget; race
BRERE brother (-Rabbit: Mark Twain)
zo **BRENT** lofty; smooth; a goose
mu **BREVE** a long note
bt **BRIAR** a pipe; wild rose
BRIBE pass money (inducement); graft
BRICK building unit; a loyal friend
BRIDE (betrothed) banned but beloved
lw **BRIEF** short; concise; a writ
bt **BRIER** briar; wild rose
zo **BRILL** prill; type of turbot
BRINE salt water; the sea; tears
BRING fetch; convey; produce
BRINK brim; brow; verge; margin
BRINY the sea; salty
BRISK agile; alert; nimble
BRITE over-ripe
bt **BRIZA** totter-grass
zo **BRIZE** the gadfly
go **BROAD** wide; spacious; liberal; stretch of fresh water (inland); woman
BROCH early stone hut
zo **BROCK** badger; a brocket
ck **BROIL** quarrel; affray; roast
BROKE broken; ruined; penniless
BROOD incubate; progeny; meditate
BROOK beck; rill; tolerate; allow
BROOL a deep murmur
bt **BROOM** brush; gorse (plantagenet)
BROSE Scottish porridge
ck **BROTH** soup; a concoction
BROWN tan; ecru; russet; sorrel
zo **BRUIN** a bear
BRUIT to noise abroad; a rumour
BRUME fog; mist; vapour
BRUNT shock; impulse
BRUSH skirmish; scrap; sweep; conductor; grooming; touch lightly
BRUTE savage; senseless; rough
zo **BUCCO** puff-bird genus

bt **BUCHU** African medicinal plant
BUCKO a bully (USA)
BUDDY a partner; blooming
BUDGE lambskin fur; pompous; to stir
mu **BUFFA** comic opera (It.)
BUFFO comic actor
BUFFS a famous regiment
BUFFY buff colour
BUGGY a gig; a vehicle
mu **BUGLE** jet bead; horn
bt **BUGLE** genus of flowering plants
BUILD erect; construct; raise
BUILT fabricated; established
BULGE swell; belly
BULGY protuberant
BULKY vast; massive; voluminous
rl, zo **BULLA** Papal seal; edict; mollusc
pl **BULLA** bone cover of ear
ga **BULLY** hector; intimidate; splendid; salt beef; race off (hockey)
BULSE a bag of diamonds
BUMBO rumbo; a drink
BUMPS Cambridge and Oxford rowing event
BUMPY uneven
BUNCH set; lot; lump; batch; group of people (associated interest)
zo **BUNNY** a rabbit
BUNTY wheat disease; purge
mt **BURAN** or **purga** westerly tundra wind (Siberia)
BURGH town; borough
to **BURIN** engraving tool
BURKE murder; hush up
BURLY stout; lusty; portly
BURNT charred; parched; tanned
zo **BURRO** donkey; moke
bt **BURRY** having burs; prickly
md **BURSA** a sac; a pouch
BURSE **BOURSE**, **PURSE**, money container; treasury
BURST split; exploded; rent asunder
BUSBY bearskin headdress
BUSES vehicles
BUSHI kerido; samurai (Japanese knight)
BUSHY overgrown; bosky (tail)
BUSKY bosky; woody; shady
go **BUTTE** hill with flat top; ridge
BUTTS rifle range
BUTTY mining partner; deputy; barge
BUXOM (of females) comely; lively; jolly
BUYER purchaser; shopper
BUZZY muzzy; dazed
BWANA master; boss (Swahili)
BYARD miner's hauling strap
ce **BYATT** walkway; timber support
BY-END subsidiary aim
lw **BY-LAW** municipal bye-law
lw **BY-WAY** (indirect route) by-path

C

CABAL clique; junto; set
CABAS rush-basket
CABBY coach or taxi-driver
ga **CABER** tossing a treetrunk (Scots)
nt **CABIN** hut; shed; room in ship
CABIR nature worship (Lemnos)
me, nt **CABLE** wire; 100 fathoms
CABRE aero-stunt
bt **CACAO** the chocolate-tree
CACHE a hide; store
CADDY porter (golf); tea container
CADET younger son; trainee
CADGE peddle; sponge; portable perch (falconry)
CADGY frolicsome; wanton
CADRE nucleus; framework
CAGED captive; mewed
CAGEY cautious; irritable; secretive
CAGOT Pyrenees pariah race
CAIRD tinker; gipsy
zo **CAIRN** heap of stones; terrier
CAKED clotted; plastered
CALID hot; fiery; ardent; glowing
rl **CALIF** **CALIPH**, **KALIF**, Moslem governor
CALIN a Chinese alloy
bt **CALIX** calyx; cup
bt **CALLA** bog-arum
zo **CALVE** give birth
bt **CALYX** flower's outer whorl, calix
zo, nt **CAMEL** ship of the desert; caisson
CAMEO small relief carving in colour-layered gem stone
tx **CAMIS** **CAMISE**, **CHEMISE**, loose garment (Fr.)
go **CAMPO** Savanna (Brazil)
CANAL channel; duct; waterway
ga **CANAS** form of jousting
CANDY a sweetmeat; to crystalize
CANED thrashed; tanned
fr **CANEY** with unduly narrow growth rings
bt, ck **CANNA** arrowroot; thickening starch
CANNE walking cane; quarter staff (fencing)
CANNY shrewd; cautious; knowing
nt **CANOE** dug out, river vessel (N. America)
rl **CANON** precept; rule; church dignitary

mu **CANON** repetitive part song
mu **CANTO** sung contrapuntal poem
CANTY cheerful; talkative
rl **CAPEL CAPLE**, composite stone; church (Welsh)
zo **CAPEL CAPUL**, a horse
bt **CAPER** dance; gambol; a plant
nt **CAPER** Dutch privateer
zo **CAPLE** capel; capul; a horse
bt **CAPOC** kapok; Indian cotton
zo **CAPON** fish; letter; fowl
ga **CAPOT** to win all tricks at piquet
zo **CAPRA** she-goat
md **CAPUT** head; distal-end swelling; broken
bt, me **CARAT** gold weight (carob seed)
CARED heeded; recked; minded
CARET the mark ⁄
bt **CAREX** sedge; reed; grass
nt **CARGO** load; freight
CARIB a Caribbean
CARLE rude strong man
CARNY blarney; flattery
bt **CAROB** locust or algaroba tree, bean
mu **CAROL** lay; ditty; warble; hymn
ga **CAROM** cannon in French billiards
CARRY convey; urge; accomplish; transfer (sound, golf); sustain
go **CARSE** low-lying land
ga **CARTE** (fencing score); card
md **CARUS** unconsciousness
CARVE cut; hack; slice; engrave
bt **CARVY** caraway plant
CASAL belonging to a case (grammar)
nt **CASCO** Manila barge
CASED boxed; packed; enveloped
CASSE broken paper
CASTE class; rank; lineage
mu **CATCH** latch; clutch; ensnare; seize; crab (rowing); a round (song); canon
CATER provide food, etc
CATES viands; dainties
CATTY feline; spiteful
nt **CAULK** make water-tight
CAUSE reason; object; source
CAVED CAVERNOUS, (-in), fallen; collapsed
gl, go **CAVES** grottoes; caverns
CAVES darts; table quoits (East Anglia)
CAVIE hen-coop or cage
CAVIL carp; censure; criticize
CAVIN covered approach
CAWED crowed
ch **CAWKY** of baryta; of barium oxide
CAXON hairy wig
CEASE cesse; end; stop; desist
zo **CEBUS** S. American monkey
bt **CEDAR** a Lebanon tree
CEDED granted; allotted; yielded
mu **CEDEZ** restrain the tempo (Fr.)
CELLA central body of temple
mu **CELLO** violoncello
rl **CENSE** burn incense
cf **CENTI-** 100th; (centimetre)
mu **CENTO** a medley
CEORL churl; a freeman
CERED covered with wax
rl **CERES** harvest goddess
rl **CERGE** altar candle
CERIC wax-like
ch **CERIN** a constituent of wax
ga **CESTA** curved basket (pelota)
zo **CETIC** (spermaceti)
CETYL a radical in spermaceti
CHACK the toss of a horse's head
CHAFE rub; heat; vex; gall
CHAFF husks; deride; raillery
go **CHAIN** line of mountains, of islands
me **CHAIN** necklace; tether; fetter; measure of distance; (-stores)
rw **CHAIR** seat of profession; preside; rail-track binding
ga **CHALK** white limestone pencil; record; touch-mark (bowls)
zo **CHAMA** large oyster
CHAMP (horses); chew; crunch
CHAMP potato dish (N. Ire.)
zo **CHANK** species of conch-shell
mu **CHANT** intone; carol
CHAOS anarchy; disorder; confusion
CHAPE the catch of a buckle
ck, md **CHAPS** the jaws; chops; cold-sores
CHAPS cowboy's leather leg overalls
bt, ck **CHARD** kale-like vegetable
CHARE chore; daily work
CHARE narrow street or court
CHARK char; charcoal
CHARM spell; allure; amulet
CHARM nuclear behaviour
zo **CHARR** char; (trout)
nt **CHART** sea-map; weather map, graph, diagram
CHARY frugal; circumspect; wary
ga **CHASE** pursue; hunt; follow; race; forest; (baseball)
CHASE engrave; frame; type-case
CHASM gap; cleft; rift; abyss
zo **CHAUS** Ind./Afr. wild cat
CHEAP mean; common; paltry
lw, ga **CHEAT** dupe; fraud; swindle; deceive; (iceskating) (surfing)
ga **CHECK** curb; stay; control (of king) chess

pl, bd, cr **CHEEK** insolence; sauce; jaw; mortise; tenon lock; dormer side
CHEEP pipe; bird song
CHEER gaiety; hearten; encourage
zo **CHELA** lobster claw
rl **CHELA** a Buddhist disciple
cf **CHEMO-** chemical action
mu **CHENG** Chinese reed instrument
CHERI darling (masc., Fr.)
nt **CHERT** flint; hornstone
ga **CHESS** a matey game
mu **CHEST** coffer; coffin; breast; set of 6 viols
CHEVY chivy; chase; scamper
CHIAN of Chios
ck **CHICA** orange-red dye; liquor; girl (Sp.)
zo, bt, ck **CHICK** to sprout; child; chicken; (-peas)
CHICO youth (Sp.)
CHIDE scold; rebuke; reprove
CHIEF boss; head; prime; principal
CHILD babe; nursling; offspring
bt, ck, mt **CHILI** pod of cayenne pepper; hot southerly sirocco wind (Tunisia)
CHILL cold; frigid; depress
CHIMB edge of cask
CHIME harmonize; strike; agree
CHINA porcelain; Celestial Empire
md, go **CHINE** cleft; ravine; backbone
CHINK gap, rift; cranny; clink
ck **CHIPS** a carpenter (potato) software
CHIRK chirp; cheep; cheerful
CHIRM bird noises
cf **CHIRO-** hand; (chiromancy, palmistry)
CHIRP chirr; chirl; to trill; bird call
CHIRT to squeeze
bt, ck **CHIVE** a type of onion
CHIVY chevy; chase; pursue
CHOCK wedge; block; a log
ar, rl, mu **CHOIR** the chancel; a group of singers
CHOKE gag; stifle; burke; strangle; stutter
el **CHOKE** (carburettor); waveguide groove; inductor
pl, ck **CHOPS** chaps; the jaws; cutlets
mu **CHORD** harmonious sound combination; wing-width (hang-gliding)
CHORE chare; household toil
CHOSE selected; picked; culled
mo **CHOSS** scree or shale climb
pg, mu **CHROM- CHROMATIC** colours; scale
to **CHUCK** jerk; throw; cluck; instrument
CHUFF to feel better
ga **CHULA** rebound from wall (pelota)
CHUMP lump of wood; blockhead
ck **CHUNK** lump or bit (marmalade)
CHURL ceorl; freeman; clodhopper
CHURN stir strongly (milk-)
go **CHUTE** waterfall; sloping channel
bt **CIBOL** variety of onion; shallot
bt **CICER** chick-pea
ck **CIDER** cyder; fermented apple-juice
CIGAR a Havana
md **CILIA** filaments; eye-lashes
CIMAR cymar; simar; scarf
zo **CIMEX** bed-bug
CINCH girth; a certainty
CIRCA about, approximately (Lat.)
rl **CIRCE** a glamorous witch (Ulysses)
CIRRI tendrils; clouds
zo **CISCO** American char
CISSY effeminate youth
lw **CITAL** summons; accusation
CITED quoted; adduced; mentioned
CIVET cat; perfume; fur
CIVIC municipal; corporate
CIVIL polite; courteous; suave
CIVVY a civilian
CLACK click; clink; clatter; prate
zo **CLAIK** the barnacle goose
CLAIM right; privilege; usurp
cr, to **CLAMP** vice; fasten; joining device
to, zo, ck **CLAMS** pincers; seafood
mu **CLANG** (characteristic) sound of church bells
CLANK clatter; clangour
rl **CLARE** a nun of St Clare
CLARO milk in taste (cigars)
bt **CLARY** sweet-herb
CLASH jar; differ; contend; collide
CLASP hasp; catch; grip
CLASS set; grade; category
zo, bt **CLAVA** club-shaped swelling; fungi
CLAVE clove; cleft; clung
CLEAN immaculate; pure; scour; innocent; penalty free (contests, events)
cp **CLEAR** serene; free; lucid; to empty
nt **CLEAT** a wedge; slat; T-shaped fitting for rope
CLEEK golf club; hook; peg
CLEFT clift; split; rift; cranny
CLERK scribe; scrivener; recorder
CLEVE a cliff; a valley
CLEVY draught-iron of a plough
CLICK klick; tick; a latch
bt **CLIDE CLITE**, burweed
CLIFF crag; headland; precipice
CLIMB scale; ascend; surmount
CLIME region; place; climate
bt, zo **CLINE** ecological life assessment

CLING hold; cleave; embrace
CLINK prison; chink; jingle
gl **CLINT KLINT**, limestone ridge
CLOAK cape; cover; pretext; (-room)
nt **CLOCK** chronometer; horologe; timepiece
CLOFF cleft; a weight allowance
CLONE asexual; duplicated life
bt **CLONE** plant stock; pure line
rl, mu **CLOSE** estop; end; grapple; cadence; shut; near; familiar
ga **CLOSH** skittles
rl, tx **CLOTH** woven fabric; the clergy
CLOUD haze; vapour; obscure; billowy aerial mass; gloom
CLOUR to knock; a bump
CLOUT dish-cloth; nail; buffet; clothing; influence
bt, me **CLOVE** a spice; a weight
CLOWN jester; fool; buffoon; dunce
ga **CLUBS** suit (cards); (juggling); apparatus (gymnastics)
CLUCK the call of a hen
CLUMP cluster; group; patch
CLUNG clasped; adhered; held
CLUNK a gurgle
CLUNY pillow-lace
go **CLUSE** gorge, Jura mountains (Fr.)
COACH teach; trainer; vehicle
CO-ACT co-operate; aid; abet
CO-AID helper; assistant
COALY resembling coal
rl **COARB** bishop or abbot
COAST shore; strand; seaside
zo **COATI** American racoon
COBBY stout; brisk
nt **COBLE** fishing boat
zo **COBRA** hamadryad snake
COCKY conceited
bt, ck **COCOA** beverage from cacao
bt **COCUS** green ebony
CODAN carrier-operated-device-anti-noise
CODED in code; in cipher
CODEX ancient manuscript
md, pl **CODON** triplet DNA bases fixing genetic codes
ar **COIGN QUOIN**, corner-stone; (wedge)
COKED coal converted in gasworks
md **COLIC** flatulence
zo **COLIN** American partridge
COLLY coal-smut
COLON punctuation; money
pl **COLON** large intestine
bt **COLZA** cabbage; rape oil
go **COMBE COOMB**, hollow in hillside
COMBO small jazz/dance band
COMER an arrival; (new-)
as, ga **COMET** card game; nebulous body
COMFY comfortable
COMIC droll; farcical; ludicrous
zo **COMMA** a butterfly; punctuation mark; posture (skiing)
ar, ck **COMPO** (-site); stucco; soldier's ration
COMUS God of Revelry; a masque
mu, rl, ar **CONCH** seashell; trumpet; semicircular niche
CONED tapering
CONES fine flour; retina; pigments (eye)
zo **CONEY CONY**, hamster
mu **CONGA** dance (Afro-Cuban)
CONGE leave; dismissal (Fr.)
bt **CONGO** black tea
bt **CONIA** hemlock
CONIC conical; tapering
bt **CONIN CONINE**, hemlock
CONTO KONTO, money account
COOED (doves) made love
COOEE cooey; Australian bush-call
ck **COOKY** a cook; a small cake
CO-OPT to select extra committee
rl **COPAL** a resin; a varnish
nm **COPEC** kopeck; a Russian copper
COPED vied; contended; overcame
COPER dealer
COPOS lassitude
bt **COPRA** dried coconut kernels
COPSE coppice; grove; thicket
zo, cp **CORAL** lobster roe; language
bt, mn **CORAL** marine growth reef; gem
mu **CORDA** string; soft pedal (It.)
CORED centre removed, bored
CORER fruit/earth-sample cutting device
zo **CORGI** small breed of dog (Wales)
CORKY lively; skittish
mu, zo **CORNO CORNU**, Fr. horn; deer
CORNY horny; (humour) trite (slang)
CORPS staff; contingent; troops
mn **CORVE** tram used in mines
COSEY COSY, snug; teapot-cover
lw **COSTS** expenses; prices; fees
rl **COTTA** a surplice
bt **COUCH** sofa; divan; squat; grass
pl **COUGH** to clear throat, lungs
COULD was able (past of can)
ga **COULE** a thrust (fencing)
COUNT compute; number; reckon; lord
COUPE car with adjustable roof
lw **COURT** woo; (homage); tribunal
COURT (-yard); enclosed area; cards
ga **COURT** of palace; (-favour) (tennis-)
COVEN group of witches

COVER wrap; cloak; shroud; invest
COVET desire; hanker after
zo **COVEY** a brood; a bevy
lw **COVIN** collusive fraudulence
COWAN uninitiated freemason
COWED daunted; overawed; abashed
COWER fawn; quail; cringe; shrink
COWLE written agreement (Ang.-Ind.)
COWRY small shell used as money
md **COXAE** hip-joints
COXED commanded; steered
COYLY bashfully; demurely; shyly
zo **COYPU** nutria; S. American rodent
COZEN cheat; deceive; sponge
CRACK gap; rift; rent; crevice
nt **CRAFT** skill; dexterity; guile; vessel
gl **CRAIG CRAG**, rocky outcrop
zo **CRAKE** the corncrake
CRAME booth; covered stall
bd **CRAMP** a spasm; hinder; impede; joining device; metal; tool
zo **CRANE** hoisting machine; wader
CRANK handle; bend; twist; quirk
CRAPE transparent gauze; to curl
ga **CRAPS** a dice game (gambling)
CRASH (-course); shatter; smash
CRASS gross; dense; stupid
CRATE hamper; packing case
CRAVE beg; yearn; implore
CRAWL fish-pen; creep; abase
CRAZE mania; insane passion; fad
CRAZY mad; idiotic; rickety
CREAK grate
CREAM to mantle; top of milk
zo **CRECK** the corncrake
rl **CREDO CREED**, belief; tenet; dogma
CREEK bay; cove inlet; bight
CREEL fish-basket
ce **CREEP** crawl; cringe; grovel; heat stress expansion/shrinkage of steel/concrete
hd **CREME** cream-like substance
CRENA a furrow; a notch
ck **CREPE** wrinkled fabric; rubber; pancake (Fr.)
CREPT crawled; fawned; glided
bt **CRESS** watercress, etc.
ht **CREST** top; apex; summit; device
CREWE CRUSE, earthenware pot
CRICK cramp; spasm; convulsion
CRIED wept; sobbed; lamented
CRIER proclaimer; howler
CRIES yells; shrieks; shouts
CRIME felony; enormity; misdeed
CRIMP corrugated surface; decoy
ck **CRISP** curl; brittle; friable; (potato-)
me **CRITH** unit weight of a gas
CROAK throaty speech; (raven) (frog)
CROAT inhabitant of Dalmatia, Croatia
CROCK antique; invalid; earthenware plate
CROFT a small farm; a pasture; small writing table
mu **CROMA CROME**, a quaver; cromb; crook; hook
CROME cromb; crook; hook
CRONE old woman; a ewe
CRONY familiar friend
rl, mu **CROOK** crome; bend; crosier; detachable section of horn
CROOL to mutter
to **CROOM** a pitchfork
CROON chromatic singing
nm **CRORE** 100 lacs of rupees
CROSS crusty; sullen; thwart
rl **CROSS** hybrid; symbol; burden
mu **CROUD** Welsh violin
md **CROUP** rump; throat disease
CROUP pommel or side-horse (gymn)
ck **CROUT** (sauer-) pickled cabbage (Ger.)
CROWD mob; throng; herd; swarm
nm **CROWN** diadem; garland; 5 shillings (25p)
to **CROZE** cooper's tool; groove
ar **CRUCK** medieval oaken roof; crossbeam
CRUDE raw; rough; immature
CRUEL fell; dire; brutal; inhuman
ck, rl **CRUET** pepper; salt; eucharistic flagon
ck **CRUMB** soft part of a loaf
CRUMP crooked; wrinkled; a bang
CRUSE vial; small bottle
CRUSH squeeze; subdue; pulverize
CRUST incrustation; coating
mu **CRWTH** Welsh violin
rl **CRYPT** vault; tomb; catacomb
cf **CRYPT-** secret; hidden (cryptic, coded)
CUBAN a native of Cuba
bt, ck **CUBEB** dried pepper-berry
CUBED raised to third power
me **CUBIC** volumetric
me **CUBIT** length of 18 or 22 in (45 or 55 cm)
zo **CUDDY** cabin; rent; donkey
CUFIC an Arabic script
CUISH cuisse; thigh-armour
CULCH rubbish
CULET lower facet of a diamond
zo **CULEX** a gnat genus

CULLS brick or timber rejects (USA)
CULLY silly dupe; to deceive
me **CUMEN** a cubic metre per sec. (flow)
bt, ck **CUMIN** **CUMMIN**, caraway; spice
CUPEL assaying vessel
CUPID Eros; the god of love
tx **CURCH** **KERCHIEF**, scarf; hankie
ck **CURDY** coagulated; (lemon-, tofu curd)
CURED healed; remedied; preserved
CURER healer; (fish, ham) (smoker)
rl **CURIA** Vatican papal court
me **CURIE** unit of radiation
CURIO rare bric-à-brac
CURLY wavy; sinous; twisty
zo **CURRE** golden-eye duck
CURRY to dress leather; thrash
ck **CURRY** Indian spiced dish
CURSE anathema; execrate; maledict
CURST tormented; plagued
CURVE turn; bend; inflict
me **CUSEC** cubic flow per second
CUSHY easy and well-paid
bt **CUTCH** catechu; couch grass
CUTER more cunning; sharper
bt **CUTIN** in plant cuticle
ga **CUT-IN** football; motoring; intrude
md **CUTIS** true skin
to **CUTTO** cuttoe; large knife
CUTTY short; curtailed; clay pipe
CUT-UP carved out; criticized adversely; distressed; (rough); high spin-shot (golf)
CUVEE blend of wine (Fr.)
bt **CYCAD** a palm
CYCLE period; age; era; circle
cp **CYCLE** series of repeating sequences
CYMAR **CIMAR**, **SIMAR**, scarf; loose dress
CYMRY Cymric; Welsh
CYNIC misanthrope; captious; morose
CZECH Bohemian; of Czech Republic

D

DACHA weekend villa (Rus.)
DADDY dadda; papa; father; (sugar-)
DAFFY stunt riding; aerial skiing; crazy
DAGON Philistine Fish-God
DAILY diurnal; quotidian
DAIRI (Japan) Mikado's palace
DAIRY milkshop; creamery
bt **DAISY** sometimes ox-eyed
zo **DAKER** corncrake; crake
DAKIR daker; dicker; half-a-score
rl **DALAI** Lama; Tibetan Priest-King
nm **DALER** a dalesman; coin dollar (Sw.)
DALLY sport; wanton; toy; dawdle
zo **DAMAN** coney; Syrian hyrax
bt **DAMAR** dammar; resin
DAMON and Pythias
DAMPS exhalations; humidity
DAMPY dejected; moist; humid
DANCE hop; caper; prance; pirouette
nt **DANDY** fop; beau; swell; coxcomb; ketch or yawl; sailship
mn **DANTY** broken coal
mu **DANZA** dance (It., Sp.)
el **DARAF** elastance unit
to **DARBY** plasterer's float
me **DARCY** permeability coefficients unit
DARED braved; ventured; presumed
nm **DARIC** gold coin of Darius
bt **DAROO** sycamore
ga **DARTS** target game (mini-javelins) (blow)
DASHY showy; ostentatious; gaudy
DATED of an era
cp **DATUM** something given
ck **DAUBE** braised meat in wine (Fr.)
DAUBY sticky; viscous; glutinous
DAUNT cow; appal; scare; intimidate
nt **DAVIT** ship's crane for lifeboats
DAYAK **DYAK**, river people (Borneo)
DAZED mazed; dazzled; bewildered
DEADS ore débris
DEALT (cards); trafficked; traded
DEARN mournful; lonely; solitary
DEARY a dear
DEATH demise; decease
DEBAG remove trousers forcibly
DEBAR ban; deny; prevent; stop
DEBIT due; arrears; liability
cp **DEBUG** de-program; error removal
cp **DEBUG** cleansing of vermin, microphone
DEBUS get off a bus
DEBUT first appearance
me, ps **DEBYE** unit of dipole moment
DECAY rot; putrify; wither
DECAY decline, decompose, disintegrate
cp **DECAY** decrease of voltage
nc **DECAY** transformation of radioactive nuclide
cf **DECEM-** **DECIM**, **DECEN**, of ten (prefixes)
DECOR of decorative effect
DECOY lure; ensnare; inveigle
DECRY censure; vilify; disparage
DEDAL daedal; intricate
DEEDE Devil (17th cent.)

DEEDY illustrious; active
DEFER delay; adjourn; postpone
DEIFY idolize; apotheosize
DEIGN condescend; vouchsafe
rl **DEISM** belief in a god
DEIST a free-thinking believer
rl **DEITY** god; divine providence
DEKKO reconnoitring inspection
DELAY dally; retard; impede
DELFT glazed earthenware (from Holland)
DELPH delf; pottery
go **DELTA** multiple river mouth; 4th letter (Gr.)
ae, gl **DELTA** (wing) alluvial deposits
DELVE dig; scoop; excavate
DEMIT release; resign
DEMOB demobilize
DEMON imp; goblin; devil; troll
DEMOS the common people
DEMUR pause; object; waver
DENIM twilled cotton goods
DENSE compact; close; solid
DEPOT depository; storehouse
DEPTH profundity; abyss
DERAY to disarrange
DERBY a race; a hat
DERIC pertaining to skin
cf, md, pl **DERMA-** of the skin
DERRY a prejudice (Aust.)
DETER prevent; restrain; dissuade
ga **DEUCE** the Devil; score; two; (cards) (tennis)
DEVIL imp; to drudge; Lucifer
DIAMB 2-iamb verse foot
rl **DIANA** moon-goddess; Artemis
DIARY journal; chronicle; record
pr **DIAZO** reproduction process paper
tc **DIBIT** 2 binary units of information
ck **DICED** cut in cubes; bookbinding decoration
DICER dice-player
cf, bt, pl **DICHO-** combining in two parts (-tomy)
DICKY open back-seat; apron; shirt-front
DICTA pronouncements
go **DIDOT** typographical measurement
DIDST (thou) did
zo **DIDUS** the dodo genus
ch, ps **DIENE** unsaturated hydrocarbons
DIGHT adorned; arrayed
cp, ma, pl **DIGIT** finger; toe; integer; data symbol
DIGUE water-advance-prevention seawall
DIKED banked; ditched
DILDO artificial penis
DILLY native bag (Aus.)
bt **DILLY** diligence; the daffodil
mn **DILSH** inferior-coal layer
ch **DIMER** 2-like-molecule-based species
DIMLY obscurely; vaguely
nm **DINAR** coin (Iran, Jordan, Yugoslavia)
DINED and wined, replete
rw **DINER** restaurant car
zo **DINGO** Australian dog
DINGY dull; sullied; squalid
DINIC dizzy; vertiginous
DINKY elegant; miniature
el **DIODE** thermionic valve; one-way circuit
DIOTA two-handled jar
DIPPY a little insane
DIPUS the jerboa
DIRGE elegy; requiem; lament
DIRTY foul; sordid; mean; paltry
DISCO recorded-music dancehall, discothèque
DISME a tithe; a tenth; a dime
mu **DITAL** guitar tuning key
DITCH moat; trench; rine; drain
DITTO the same again
DITTY refrain; sonnet; ode; lilt
DIVAN council; saloon; sofa; couch
DIVED plunged; fathomed; explored
zo **DIVER** a sea-bird; underwater descendant
DIVES the rich man in the Bible
DIVOT a piece of turf
DIVVY dividend; share; divide
DIXIE camp-kettle; Southern USA
DIZEN to dress gaudily
DJINN genie; demon; afrit
DO-ALL factorum
DOBBY a dotard; part of a loom
zo **DODDY** hornless cow
DODGE evade; avoid; shuffle
DODGY artful; tricky; risky
DOGAL of the Doge of Venice
DOGGO to be hidden; concealed
DOGGY fond of dogs
DOGMA tenet; doctrine; maxim
tx **DOILY** ornamented cake cloth
DOING performing; swindling
DOLCE softly, sweetly
DOLED (-out) (benefit money)
tv, ce **DOLLY** camera carriage; grommet (washer); hardwood block; corn-; tee marker (curling)
ck **DOLMA** rice-filled leaf
DOLOR dolour; grief; sorrow
ar **DOMAL DOMED**, upper vaulting
mu **DOMRA** Russian plucked instrument

ar **DOMUS** patrician's house (Roman)
DONAH coster's sweetheart
DONAT donet; grammar-book; primer
DONEE the recipient
DONNA my lady in Spain
ps **DONOR** giver; bestower; (blood); semi-conductor
DOPED drugged; covered with varnish
DOPER dauber; horse-doper
DOPEY slow-witted; dull
rd **DORAN** missile-tracking system
zo **DOREE** dory; golden-yellow fish
ar **DORIC** Greek architecture
DORMY unbeatable at golf
zo **DORSE** Baltic cod; coal-fish
DORSE reverse side
DOSED physicked; drenched
tx **DOSEL DOSER**, tapestry cloths
DOTAL referring to a dowry
DOTED loved; drivelled
DOTTY barmy; silly; deranged
DOUAR dowar; Arab camp
DOUAY a Bible edition
DOUBT distrust; indecision; demur
DOUCE dulce; sweet
DOUGH money; the kneadful
bt **DOURA** millet
DOUSE dowse; slacken suddenly; drench
DOWDY slovenly; untidy; slatternly
bd **DOWEL** a wooden pin; steel rod (stairs); slate; cramp
lw **DOWER** bequest (-house)
DOWLE fluff; downfibre
DOWNY feathery; filamentous; knowing
DOWRY wedding endowment for bride
DOWSE water-divining art
DOYEN senior member
DOZED snoozed; drowsed; slumbered
DOZEN apostolic number
DOZER nap taker
DOZER (bull-), earth mover, tractor
DRACO a constellation
DRAFF dregs; residue
DRAFT outline; sketch; prepare
DRAIL to trail; to draggle
el **DRAIN** empty; tap; a gutter; sewer; (brain-); transistor electrode
zo **DRAKE** male duck
DRAMA histrionic art; play
DRANK quaffed; caroused; imbibed
DRANT to drone; to drawl
DRAPE cover; array; deck
DRAWL lag; drag; drone
DRAWN hauled; sketched; eviscerated
DREAD awe; fear; apprehension
DREAM reverie; hallucination
DREAR bleak; dismal; gloomy
DREGS lees; draff; sediment
DRESS garb; guise; apparel
DREST DRESSED
DRIED aerified; parched; desiccated
DRIER desiccator; dryer
to, ga, gl, go **DRIFT** wander; intention; surface water; glacial; continental; meaning; float; (archery) (motor-racing)
zo, to **DRILL** cloth; ape; bore
DRILY dryly; sarcastically
to **D-RING** 'D'-shaped ring
DRINK potion; draught; absorb
DRIVE urge; impel; coerce; motivate; private access road; hit
cp **DRIVE** operate; pulsating circuit
DRIVE mechanical power transmitter
lw, hd **DROIT** ancient right; title
DROLL odd; rummy; whimsical
DROME racecourse; aerodrome
DRONE idler; hum; dawdle
mu, zo **DRONE** bagpipes' tone; male bee
DROOL salivate before eating; drivel (pleasure)
DROOP sag; fade; wilt; languish
md, ae **DROPS** small doses; gouts; pastilles (sweets); (rain) (ear/eye); guttae carvings; globular earrings
DROSS scum; dregs; scoria
DROVE has driven; led cattle
DROWN flood; drench; lose life
rl **DRUID** Celtic priest; bard
DRUNK crapulous; tipsy; quaffed
bt **DRUPE** a stone fruit
mn, rl **DRUSE** mining cavity; a sect
mn **DRUSY** having cavities
DRUXY partly decayed timber
DRYAD wood-nymph
bt **DRYAS** mountain avens
DRYER drier
DRYLY drily; insipidly; aridly
zo **DSOMO** zhomo; a hybrid
DUCAL with strawberry leaves; duke's
nm **DUCAT** Italian gold or silver
DUCHY a dukedom of land
DUDDY ragged; in tatters
DUKEY wheeled platform; inclined-road train
DULCE soft; sweet; douce
rl **DULIA** angel adoration (RC)
DULLY stupidly; inertly; languidly

bt **DULSE** edible seaweed
zo **DUMBA** fat-tailed sheep
mu **DUMKA** **DUMKY**, laments; songs (Rus., Cz.)
cp **DUMMY** doll; (bridge); model for practice
pb, to **DUMMY** mallet head; mason's hammer
DUMPS low spirits; dejection
DUMPY short and thick
DUNCE dolt; dullard; booby
DUNCH punch; jolt; to gore
zo **DUNNE** the knot-sandpiper
DUNNY deaf; dull of apprehension
rl, ar **DUOMO** Italian cathedral
DUPED deluded; gulled; hoaxed
DUPER trickster; dodger; sharper
DUPLE double; twofold
rl **DURGA** wife of Siva
DURGY undersized; dwarf
bt **DURIO** Malay tree; (durian fruit)
DUROY corduroy; figured serge
bt **DURRA** molasses/sugar-source sorghum grass
bt **DURRA** semi-tropical grain sorghum
DURST dared
bt, ck **DURUM** hard wheat for pasta
DUSKY swarthy; shady; dark; dim
DUSTY powdery
DUTCH of Holland; (go-) share
DUVET eiderdown; for bed or jacket
hd **DWALE** heretic; heraldic sable
bt **DWALE** the deadly nightshade
DWARF imp; pygmy; midget; stunted
DWELL abide; reside; linger
DWELT stayed; tarried; sojourned
DWINE to pine; to fade
DYING moribund; expiring; demise
me **DYNAM** work unit

E

EAGER keen; ardent; avid; zealous
nm **EAGLE** (golf); 10-dollar; gold piece
zo **EAGLE** lectern; standard; erne; bird
EAGRE **AIGRE**, tidal bore (wave)
EARED having lugs (ears)
EARLY betimes; before usual
EARST **ERST**, formerly
el **EARTH** world; soil; humus; ground; base; end of flow
EASED allayed; soothed; assuaged
EASEL canvas carrier
EASLE hot ashes (Sc.)
EATEN masticated; corroded
EATER consumer; devourer
ar **EAVES** overhanging roof-edges
EBBED waned; receded; declined
EBLIS a djinn; evil spirit
bt **EBONY** black wood
rl **ECHAL** synagogue cupboard for ark, law
ECLAT splendour; brilliance; panache
ECTAL ectad; outer; external
EDDER top binding of a hedge
md **EDEMA** **OEDEMA**, dropsy; waterlogged body
EDGED keen; bordered; fringed
EDGES curving; skating technique
EDICT ukase; decree; order
EDIFY uplift; enlighten; instruct
EDILE Roman magistrate
EDUCE elicit; draw; extract
EDUCT deduction
EERIE eirie; uncanny; weird
EGEST throw out; eject; cast
zo **EGGAR** egger; silkworm moth
EGGED incited; urged; impelled
EGGER an egg collector; inciter
zo **EGRET** heron
zo **EIDER** sea-duck
EIGHT twice four; figurative (ice-skating)
EIGNE eldest son; first born (Sc.)
lw **EIGNE** entailed and inalienable
EIRIE eerie; weird; unaccountable
EJECT evict; expel; oust; emit
EKING prolonging
EKKER exercise (an old word)
ELAIN clarified oil or fat
zo **ELAND** antelope (S. Africa)
zo **ELAPS** venomous coral snake
ELATE exult; rouse; animate
pb **ELBOW** jostle; nudge; a bend; pipe-fitting, gate-joint
ELCHI Turkish envoy
bt **ELDER** older; ancestor
ELECT cull; select; chosen
ELEGY dirge; threnody; lament
ELEVE pupil (Fr.)
ELFIN small elf; puckish; pixy
ELGIN (marbles)
ELIDE contract; curtail
ELITE the elect; very select
bt **ELMEN** made of elm
ELOGY **EULOGY**, funeral speech; panegyric
ELOPE run away; abscond; decamp
ELUDE evade; baffle; escape
ELUTE cleanse; purify by washing
mn **ELVAN** Cornish rock; elvish
bt **ELVAS** prune; plum (Port.)
zo **ELVER** young eel

EMAGE area of text block in square ems
EMBAR prevent; bar; shut; stop
EMBAY to shelter; to landlock
EMBED to plant; enclose
EMBER glowing fuel
EMBOG engulf
EMBOW to arch; to vault
EMBOX encase; pack
EMBUS to put in a bus
EMEER Ameer; Emir
EMEND amend; rectify; correct
mn **EMERY** carborundum
EMOTE register emotion
EMPTY void; vacant; vacuous; inane
ENACT ordain; decree; authorize
ENATE growing out
ENDED finished; concluded; ceased
ENDER a finale; a cropper
END-ON abutting
ENDOR home of a witch
ENDOW endue; indue; endew
ENDUE grant; endow; invest
md **ENEMA** a clyster; rectal douche
ENEMY foe; rival; antagonist
ENGLE **ANGLE**, early English people
ENJOY relish; appreciate
ENMEW to put into; contain; cage
ENNUI weariness; boredom (Fr.)
ENODE jointless; knotless
ENROL list; enlist; chronicle
tx **ENSOR** levers net
ENSUE pursue; result; follow
ENTER invade; record; insert
ENTRY adit; inlet; portal; note
ENURE inure; accustom
ENVOY diplomat; postscript
ch **ENZYM** **ENZYME**, ferment yeast
rl **EOLIC** **EOLUS**, **EOLIAN**, **AEOLIAN**, god of the Winds
ch **EOSIN** red dye or ink
EPACT moon's age at new year
me **EPHAH** Hebrew bushel
rl **EPHOD** vestment; surplice
EPHOR Greek magistrate
EPOCH era; cycle; remarkable period
EPODE part of an ode
EPOPT an Eleusinian initiate
EPOXY oxygen fixed to 2 different atoms; epoxide resin
md **EPSOM** salts
EQUAL peer; competent; equable
EQUES Roman Knight
EQUIP rig; arm; accoutre; array
zo **EQUUS** the horse genus
cp **ERASE** delete; cancel; use null data
ERATO Muse of lyric poetry
ERECT build; upright; vertical
cf,pc **-ERGIC** of work, function, purpose
pc **-ERGIC** purposive; of innate drive
el **ERGON** quantum of oscillator energy
bt **ERGOT** parasitical fungus
bt **ERICA** the heath genus
lw **ERICK** a blood-fine (Irish)
ERODE eat away; corrode; consume
bt **EROSE** gnawed-looking (of leaves)
cf **EROTO-** of sexual love
ERRED strayed; sinned; wandered
cp **ERROR** mistake; fault; fallacy
bt,zo **ERUCA** the salad plant; a larva
ERUPT eject; eruct; burst forth
bt,ck **ERVUM** the lentil
gl **ESCAR** **ESKER**, glacial gravel ridge
ESCOT scot; an ancient tax
ESSAY discussion paper
ch **ESTER** ethereal salt
ESTOC short cavalry sword (Fr.)
lw **ESTOP** stop; bar; impede
go **ETANG** lake amid sanddunes (Fr.)
ETAPE stage point, esp. cycle races
ch **ETHER** upper air; volatile gas
ETHIC ethical; moral
ETHOS guiding spirit of a group or nation
ch **ETHYL** alcohol radical
mu **ETUDE** a composition (Fr.)
ETWEE étui; pocket-case
ga **EULER** jump (ice-skating); card-game
mt **EURUS** the East wind
EVADE elude; avoid; foil; dodge
EVENS fifty-fifty
cp **EVENT** incident; outcome; occurrence
EVERT turn inside out
EVERY all; each
EVICT eject; dislodge; dispossess
EVITE evade; avoid; shun
EVOKE arouse; excite; summon
EXACT precise; extort; mulct
EXALT raise; extol; magnify
EXCEL outvie; surpass; exceed
EXEAT a short leave
EXERT strive; try; endeavour
EXILE refugee; banish; proscribe
bt **EXINE** outer pollen-grain wall layer
EXIST be; live; endure; last
zo **EXITE** limb-lobe in arthropoda
lw **EX-LEX** outlaw
EXODE dramatic climax
EXPEL eject; dislodge; oust
EXTOL exalt; laud; glorify
EXTRA supernumeracy; additional
EXTRA- **EXTRO-**, outside of the usual
EXUDE ooze; percolate; sweat
EXULT crow; gloat; triumph

EYING watching; observing
EYRIE eagle's nest

F

FABLE myth; legend; allegory
bd **FACED** defied; confronted; covered
FACER opponent; a blow
FACET small polished surface
FACIA control panel; shop name-board
FADDY crotchety; particular
rl **FAERY FAIRY**, elf
FAGIN beech mast; (Oliver Twist) (Dickens)
mu **FAGOT FAGGOT**, bundle of sticks; bassoon (It.)
bt **FAGUS** the beech tree
bt **FAHAM** Indian orchid
FAINT swoon; dim; indistinct
FAIRY FAERY, peri; elf; pixie
FAITH tenet; dogma; belief
FAKED spurious; counterfeit
FAKER forger; cheat; swindler
FAKIR monkish mendicant; magician
FALSE sham; erroneous; untrue
FAMED illustrious; renowned
FANCY whim; idea; caprice
md **FANGO** radioactive mud
el **FAN-IN** convergence; inputs to circuit
nt **FANNY** messdeck kettle; underparts (female)
rl **FANON** napkin; scarf
el, me **FARAD** unit of electrical capacity
ck **FARCE** hilarious comedy; parody; travesty
ck **FARCE FARCI**, forcemeat; stuffed; filled
FARCY glanders; equine malady
FARED fed; travelled; prospered
FARLE oatcake (Sc.)
rl **FARSE** biblical extract
FARSI PARSI (Persian) language
FASTI Roman calendar of festivals
FATAL lethal; baneful; ruinous
FATED doomed; destined
FATES Clotho, Lachesis & Atropos
FATTY adipose; pudgy; plump
rl **FATWA** Islamic edict
cp, el, ga, gl **FAULT** blemish; mistake; (blame) misfunction (electric); tectonic crust break; infringement of rules; tennis; badminton
zo **FAUNA** animal life
FAUST a drama by Goethe
md **FAVUS** scalp disease

FEAST banquet; carousel; delight
FEAZE TEAZE, unravel (knots)
FECIT FACIT, maker (signature) (arts)
FED-UP disgruntled; browned off
FEEZE to twist; worry
FEIGN pretend; simulate; assume
ga **FEINT** stratagem; artifice; trick; pretence; capillary break (fencing)
zo **FELID** one of the cat tribe
zo **FELIS** the cat tribe
FELIX the cartoon cat
FELLY felloe; part of rim of wheel
FELON criminal; miscreant; outlaw
FEMTO one thousand million millionth 10^{-15}
md, pl **FEMUR** thigh bone
bd **FENCE** receiver of stolen goods, border; palisade; duel
FENDY shifty
FENKS finks; blubber refuse
FENNY marshy; swamp; boggy
lw **FEOFF** a fief; grant of land
zo **FERAE** wild animals
FERAL wild; deadly; funereal
me **FERMI** very short length unit
bt **FERNY** fernlike, covered with fern
nt **FERRY** river-crossing craft; transport
hd **FESSE** heraldic band
FESTA FIESTA, festival (Saint's day)
FETAL FOETAL, of the unborn; embryonic
nv, mt **FETCH** bring; carry; storm distance; wind
FETED partied; honoured; lionized
FETID noxious; stinking; noisome
FETOR offensive odour
lw, rl **FETWA FATWA**, judgement; sentence (Arab)
lw **FEUAR** a lease-holder (Sc.)
md **FEVER** ardour; passion; (heated)
FEWER rather less
pl **FIBER** neuron; nerve tissue
FIBRE staple; cellulose; filament; toughness
FICHE chit, official note form
FICHU small lace or muslin shawl
bt **FICUS** the fig
FIELD glebe; arable acre, (sports) (racing)
cp **FIELD** (magnetic) stored data
FIEND imp; demon; monster; wretch
lw **FIERI** facias; a writ
FIERY ardent; fierce; igneous
mu **FIFED** fluted
FIFER fife-player
mu **FIFTH** ordinal of 5; harmonic interval
FIFTY L

FIGHT fray; brawl; combat; contest
FILAR threadlike; filamentous
FILCH steal; pilfer; purloin
to **FILED FILER** (smoothed) (archivist)
zo **FILLY** girl-foal
FILMY diaphanous; see through
FILTH dirt; muck; impurity
FINAL last; ultimate; terminal
zo **FINCH** a passerine
FINED mulcted; amersed
FINER refiner; keener; smaller
lw **FINES** penalty payments; mechanical particles
FINIS the end; conclusion
FINOS merino wool
go **FIORD FJORD**, arm of the sea (Scand.)
FIRED discharged; kindled; sacked
FIRER an incendiary; igniter
bt **FIRRY** full of pines
FIRST chief; premier; primeval
go **FIRTH FRITH**, wide inlet, estuary
FISHY questionable; unreliable
FISTY of fisticuffs (fight)
zo **FITCH** pole-cat; fur-brush
bt **FITCH** vetch; chick-pea
FITLY aptly; properly; seemly
FITTE FYTTE, verse of a ballad
cp **FIT-UP** casing shutter, form work
nm **FIVER** £5 bank note
ga, vt **FIVES** wall ball game; horse disease
FIXED secured; placed; settled
FIXER builder, mason, fraudster
FLAFF flutter; be fussy
to **FLAIL** threshing whip; to skin (an animal)
FLAIR natural aptitude
FLAKE hurdle; hanging platform
nt **FLAKE** scale; lamina; to peel off (corn-); (snow-) hook bait (angling); coil a rope serpentine fashion
FLAKY FLAKEY, fissile
FLAME ardour; blaze; flare; lover
FLAMY FLAMEY, lambent
to **FLANG** miner's pick
FLANK side; border; touch (Am. football)
FLARE a signal light; glare
FLARE flame; dress spread; talent
FLARY flaming; flickering
el **FLASH** glint; sparkle; showy; mark; display (electric)
FLASK ampulla; vial; phial
ck **FLAWN** custard; pancake
FLAXY FLAXEN, hemp linen colour
FLEAD pork fat for lard
FLEAK a small lock
md **FLEAM** surgical knife
FLECK dapple; speckle; variegate
zo **FLECK** the flounder
nt **FLEET** a creek; swift; flotilla
FLESH mankind; to accustom
FLEWS bloodhound's chaps
ga **FLICK** flip; fleece; wound; lifting stroke (hockey); silent movie
bd **FLIER FLYER**, aeronaut; poster; shoring post
ga **FLIER FLYER**, fast mover; (high-); ball out of play
zo **FLIES** stage screens; (angling); (trouser fastening); insects
FLING hurl; dance; escapade
mn **FLINT** variety of quartz
FLIRT philander; coquet; flip
FLISK FRISK, comb; hand search; caper
nt, tx **FLOAT** drift; raft; buoy; weaving technique
bd **FLOAT** (procession); (cash); memory; WC ball valve
zo, wv **FLOCK** herd; multitude; unspun wool
FLONG stereotyping paper; brick made with moist paper and glue
FLOOD spate; downpour; deluge
FLOOK FLUKE, lucky shot
FLOOR stumping ground; nonplus; throw down
bt **FLORA** flowers collectively
bd, nt **FLORY** fleury; boat
FLOSS silklike; slag; dental debris
FLOUR ground grain meal
FLOUT scoff; mock; taunt; jeer
FLOWN flew; (high-) insolence; rotted
FLUFF make mistake; lint; unspun wool; girl
FLUID liquid; unsettled; gaseous
zo **FLUKE** parasite worm; (whale)
nt **FLUKE** (anchor); fortunate shot
FLUKE unaverage
FLUKY FLUKEY, accidentally fortunate
FLUME a water-chute
FLUMP plump down
FLUNG tossed; hurled; pitched
mn **FLUOR** calcium spar
pr **FLUSH** blush; poker term; level, even; margin
FLUSH chase out, surge; (hot-); (toilet)
nt, mu **FLUTE** kind of boat; wind instrument
FLYER FLIER, aviator; bird
FOAMY frothy; spumy

FOCAL converging
FOCUS point of convergence
mt **FOEHN** a hot wind in the Alps
FOGEY old-fashioned person
FOGGY obscure; hazy; indistinct
FOGLE silk handkerchief (slang)
rl **FOISM** Chinese Buddhism
FOIST impose; thrust; palm
md **FOLIC** acid in vitamin-B complex
FOLIO a sheet of paper; play; edition
FOLLY inanity; absurdity; fatuity
FOMES absorbent substance
tx **FONDU** colour blending in calico
ck **FONDU** cheese and wine dip (Swiss)
FORAY raid; inroad; sally; invasion
FORBY adjacent
cp **FORCE** power; energy; army; coerce; intervene
gl, go **FORCE** fors; foss; waterfall (Scand.)
FORDO undo; ruin; destroy
pr **FOREL** heavy parchment book cover
to **FORET** a drill
FORGE smithy; falsify; fabricate
FORGO renounce; go without
FORKY branching
pr **FORME** bed of type
mu, ga **FORTE** outstanding skill; loud; handguard of sword (fencing)
FORTH forward; onward; ahead
FORTY two score
FORUM tribunal; court; market-place
FORUM open discussion; public-speaking
zo **FOSSA** Malagasy civet cat
FOSSE ditch; moat; canal
FOUND to cast; establish; start
pr, cp **FOUNT** spring; well; source; type
md **FOVEA** pit; a pock mark; centre of vision in retina
FOXED baffled; deluded; yellow; damp stain
FOYER lobby; fire grate; (theatre interval)
FRACK **FRECK**, eager; bold; hale
FRAIL weak; infirm; rush basket
FRAME fashion; concoct; mood
ga, lw **FRAME** a game of snooker; unit of film; tv; display; (snooker) chassis surround; conspire; entrap; falsify
nm **FRANC** 100 centimes
zo **FRANK** candid; open; gannet
rl **FRATE** **FRATER**, brother; friar
rl **FRATI** friars; brethren
FRAUD guilt; imposture; deception
FREAK monstrosity; quirk; vagary
FREED emancipated; exempted
FREER deliverer; more lavish
FREMD strange; a stranger (Sc.)
FRESH novel; recent; unsalted; bold
FRETT ore refuse
rl **FREYA** wife of Odin
rl **FRIAR** **FRIER**, **FRATE**, wandering monk
ck **FRIED** simmered in fat
FRILL ruffle; border; mannerism
FRISK romp; search
FRITH **FIRTH**, estuary
ck **FRITO** **FRITES**, crisp potato (tortilla) mix
FRITZ a German
FRIZZ to curl; to crisp
FROCK smock; costume
bt **FROND** fern leaf
md **FRONS** part of skull
mt **FRONT** van; face; assurance; weather; cover; (war)
ag **FROST** (hoar-); rime; iciness; a failure
FROTH spume; foam; effervesce
FROWN glower; scowl
FROWY rank; musty
FROZE became ice; stopped still; acted coldly
bt, ck **FRUIT** produce; crop; issue (ripeness); offspring; edible plant seed flesh coating
FRUMP a joke; dowdy woman
FRUSH brittle; broken; thrush
FRYER a frying pan
bt **FUCUS** dye; disguise; seaweed
FUDER large wine cask (Moselle)
ck **FUDGE** fake; nonsense; sweetmeat
mu **FUGAL** like a fugue
mu, pc **FUGUE** polyphonic composition; escape from sanity
FULLY amply; entirely; completely
ck **FUMET** bone/veg. essence for sauce; deer dung
FUMID smoky; vaporous
bt **FUNDI** a West African grain
bt **FUNGI** mushrooms; toadstools, etc.
md **FUNIS** umbilical cord
FUNKY nervous; timid; cowardly
nt **FUNNY** droll; comical; boat
mu **FUOCO** with fire (It.)
zo **FURCA** forked structure
FUROR wave of enthusiasm
FURRY incrusted
FURZE gorse; whin
FURZY whinny; horse-call
FUSED melted; merged; blended
FUSEE vesuvian; firelock fuzee
FUSIL fusible; a musket
FUSSY fidgety; bustling
FUSTY musty; rank; mouldy
FUZED provided with a fuze

FUZEE fusee
FUZZY wooly; shaggy; blurred
FYTTE **FITTE**, verse of a ballad

G

ar **GABLE** roof/window construction
GADGE instrument of torture
zo **GADUS** the cod genus
GAFFE a social solecism
GAGED pledged; pawned; engaged
GAGER one who pawns his goods
GAILY gayly; blithely; lively
bd **GAIZE** friable sandstone
zo **GALAH** Australian cockatoo
ar **GALBE** elegant sweep; contour
bt **GALEA** helmet-shaped
tx **GALON** scalloped-edge narrow lace
mu **GALOP** lively round dance
mu **GAMBA** ancient cello
GAMMA letter (Gr.); radioactive ray
mu **GAMUT** range; scope; entire series; notes and scales
GANAT **KANAT**, **QANAT**, tunnelled cliff irrigation (Oman, Iran)
GANCH execution by throttling (Turk.)
mn **GANIL** limestone
GANJA Indian drink made of hemp
zo **GANZA** a wild goose
GAPED wide open; yawned
GAPPY crannied
ck **GARNI** **GARNISH**, addition of vegetables to a dish
GARNI bed and breakfast only (hotel)
GARTH Celtic fort; yard; fish-weir
mt, go **GARUA** winter precipitation mist in W. Peru
GARUM fish sauce
GASSY gaseous; aerated
GATED confined (school)
GAUDY garish; tawdry; flashy
rw, to **GAUGE** estimate; measure; track width; (rain)
mn **GAULT** clay
GAUMY dauby; smeary
GAUNT lean; lanky; emaciated
me **GAUSS** unit of magnetic intensity
tx **GAUZE** transparent fabric; bandage; mesh
GAUZY filmy
to **GAVEL** mason's hammer; mallet
GAVEL sheaf of corn
GAWKY awkward; ungainly; clumsy
zo **GAYAL** wild ox
GAYER merrier; brighter
GAZED looked intently
GAZER starer; rubber-neck
GEBUR neighbour (Ang. Sax.)
zo **GECKO** lizard
cp **GECOM** automatic computer code
zo **GEESE** plural of goose
gl, go **GEEST** heath; sandy region (glaciated)
GEIST ghost; (polter-) mental phantom
GELID cold to freezing
GEMEL twin; coupled vessels/bottles
bt **GEMMA** leaf-bud
GEMMY **JEMMY**, glittering; wood-pole
GENET civet-cat fur
cf **-GENIC** genetic; caused by genes; focus or origin
rl **GENIE** **GINIE**, Arabian apparition
GENII men of genius
ck, nt **GENOA** a cake; large jib-sail
gn **GENOM** gamete nucleus chromosome content
GENRE speciality (artistic)
zo **GENUS** group of a species
zo **GENYS** lower jaw in vertebrates
mn **GEODE** crystalline cavity
GEOID globe; shape of this earth
nm **GERAH** twentieth of a shekel
GESTE generous act of honour
GET-UP style of dress
GHAZI Arab fanatic; conqueror
GHOST spook; spectre; phantom
GHOUL a gruesome fiend
GHYLL goyal; ravine; gully
GIANT Cyclops; colossus; huge
ce **GIANT** monitor; nozzle; water gun
GIBED **JIBED**, taunted; jeered
GIBER **JIBER**, scoffer; joker; derider
bo, mt **GIBLI** hot sirocco wind (Libya)
GIBUS an opera hat
GIDDY dizzy; fickle; mutable
GIGOT leg of mutton (Fr.)
mu **GIMEL** **GYMEL**, vocal music
ga **GIMME** very short putt (golf)
GIPSY gypsy; zingaro; a Romany
GIRTH girdle; thong; cinch; tummy belt of horse; holds on saddle
GIVEN **GIVER**, conceded; bestowed; donor; granter
ck **GLACE** polished; sugar-surfaced
GLADE woodland avenue
GLAIR eggwhite; varnish
pl, pb **GLAND** a secretory organ; seal
pl **GLANS** the acorn of the penis
GLARE glower; frown; glitter
GLARY dazzling; lustrous
GLASS mirror; telescope; tumbler

GLAVE keylike halberd
GLAZE GLAZY lustre; burnish; shiny
zo **GLEAD GLEDE**, buzzard; kite
GLEAM ray; beam; glimmer; shine
GLEAN cull; collect; harvest
bt **GLEBA** spore-bearing tissue in truffles
rl **GLEBE** sod; church land
GLEED glowing ember
ga **GLEEK** three-handed card game
ga **GLIMA** ancient Icelandic wrestling
GLINT gleam in the eye, or in a gem
GLOAM dusk; darkening
GLOAT exult; crow; revel
GLOBE orb; sphere; ball; earth
ck **GLOGG GLUGG**, spiced, mulled wine (Scan.)
bt **GLOME** globular head of flowers
GLOOM sadness; depression; darkness
GLORY exult; honour; renown
GLOSS comment; polish; veil
gl **GLOUP** subterranean blowhole; cave
GLOUT to be sulky
GLOVE gauntlet; mitten
GLOZE wheedle; flattery; adulation
GLUED stuck together; adhered
GLUER a user of mucilage
GLUEY adhesive; viscous; glutinous
bt **GLUME** husks
el **GLUON** hypothetical particle binding two quarks
ar **GLYPH** vertical fluting
GNARL snarl; growl; grumble
GNARR a knot in wood; a snag
GNASH to grind the teeth
GNOME dwarf; a maxim
bt **GOBBO** okra; a fruit
tx **GODET** dress gusset (flare); open cup
rl **GODLY** holy; pious; devout
GOETY black magic
GOFER gauffre; wafer; errand boy
GOING wending; faring; elapsing; road conditions
GOING horizontal nosings (stairs); departure
zo **GOLDY** goldfish
GOLLY exclamation
pl **GONAD** reproductive gland
zo **GONAL** forming a gonad
GONER irretrievably lost
GOODS chattels; effects
GOODY a sweet
GOOFY crazy stunt; goofy foot on skateboard (Disney dog)
to, zo **GOOSE** tailor's iron; poultry bird
GO-OUT sluice in embankment
GORAL indian antelope
GORED run through (bull-fighting); (tailoring)
go **GORGE** gulch; defile; gulp; cram; narrow canyon
bt **GORSE GORSEY**, ginst shrub
ck **GOUDA** a Dutch cheese
to **GOUGE** to scoop out; circular chisel
bt, ck **GOURD** pumpkin (as container)
md **GOUTY** acidic; oedemic swelling
bt **GOWAN** a daisy
GOYAL ghyll; kloof; coombe
GRACE adorn; embellish; favour
GRADE step; rank; slope; degree
GRAFF graft; ditch; moat
GRAFT intrigue; swindle; engraft
rl **GRAIL** Holy Grail; sacred chalice
bt, me **GRAIN** corn; response; flow; grist
to **GRAIP** dung-fork
go **GRAMA** pasture land (USA)
GRAME gram; misery
nm **GRAND** lordly; £1,000
GRAND granolithic screed; jointless cement floor
GRANT cede; confer; gift; largesse
bt **GRAPE** fruit of the vine
ma **GRAPH** a diagram showing related factors
GRASP clasp; clutch; hold; scope
bt **GRASS** herbage; pasture; to turf; to betray others
GRATE abrade; rasp; jar; fireplace
mu **GRAVE** solemn; engrave; tomb; slow tempo
ck **GRAVY** meat juice
ga **GRAZE** skim; browse; touch lightly; pre-attack (fencing)
GREAT eminent; bulky; huge
zo **GREBE** web-footed bird
GREED voracity; avidity; gluttony
GREEK Attic; Doric; Hellenic
ga **GREEN** raw; fresh; inexperienced; outdoor range (archery)
ga **GREEN** verdant; (village); (golf); (bowls); unbroken wave (surfing); ecology party supporter
GREET hail; welcome; greit (Sc.)
GREYS cavalry regiment
bt **GRIAS** species of pear
zo **GRICE** young wild boar
GRIDE GRYDE, to grate
GRIEF woe; anguish; mishap
gl **GRIKE** limestone-rock fissure
GRILL broil; grid-iron; question
GRIME dirt; soil; sully; befoul
GRIMY filthy; smutty; unclean
GRIND abrade; pulverize; sharpen
GRIPE grasp; squeeze; ditch
GRIST corn for milling; provision

ck **GRITS** coarse oatmeal porridge
GRIZE grece; grees; staircase
GROAN moan; complain; grumble
nm **GROAT** Joey; fourpenny piece
GROCK a kindly clown
ar, ce **GROIN** breakwater; under abdomen; intersection edge (vault)
GROOM syce; equerry; bridegroom
GROPE search by feeling
me **GROSS** coarse; 12 dozen
cp **GROUP** clump; cluster; arrange; index reference
tc **GROUP** multiple channels on one path
cp **GROUP** sequence of data storage stations
GROUT coarse meal; mortar
GROVE wood; thicket; spinney
GROWL snarl; grumble; complain
GROWN raised; waxed; extended
ck **GRUEL** thin porridge
GRUFF surly; rude; churlish
GRUNT snort like a pig
GRYDE gride; grate
bt **GUACO** plant; snake-bite antidote
GUANO bird's manure
GUARD shield; watch; bulwark
cp **GUARD** fire-; safety barrier between circuits; protect; soldier; linesmen; vigilante
bt **GUAVA** pear-shaped fruit
GUESS surmise; conjecture; divine
GUEST visitor; lodger
nt **GUFAH** **GOPHER**, reeds for Ra ships
cp **GUIDE** pilot; signpost; control; -line; edge; information
GUILD trade's union; fraternity
GUILE craft; duplicity; cunning
lw **GUILT** proof or sense of wrong
mu **GUIRD** Cuban instrument
GUISE garb; aspect; manner
GULCH gully; gorge; ravine
hd **GULES** heraldic red
GULFY full of whirlpools
GULIX fine linen (Dutch)
GULLY water-worn channel; (cricket); rift between rocks (mountaineering)
ck, ga **GUMBO** a stew; okra soup; muddy course; (horse racing)
GUMMY viscous, sticky
GURRY fish offal; Indian fortress
mu **GUSLA** **GUSLI**, Slavonic zither
GUSTO zest; relish; enjoyment
GUSTY squally; stormy; puffy
GUTSY deep voice; of the intestine; greedy
ar **GUTTA** Doric ornament; drop
GUTTY old type golf ball
GUYED mocked; ridiculed; derided
gl, go **GUYOT** submarine mountain
zo **GYALL** gayal; jungle bull
nt **GYBED** (a sailing manoeuvre)
zo **GYGIS** tern genus (water birds)
mu **GYMEL** **GIMEL**, 14th C. vocal music
GYPSY **GIPSY**, zingaro; Romany
GYRAL revolving; whirling
hd **GYRON** heraldic device
md **GYRUS** convolution of the brain

H

HABIT dress; usage; wont; custom
rl **HADES** the abode of the dead
rl **HADJI** **HAJJI**, pilgrim (Arab)
cf, pl **HAEMA-** **HAEMO-**, concerning the blood (Gr.)
HAFIZ knowledge of the Koran
HAIRY furry
HAJIB Moslem court chamberlain
HAKIM wise man; physician (Arab)
HALED hauled; dragged along
bt **HALFA** esparto grass
HALLO! hello! hillo!
HALMA a board game of leapfrogging
ck **HALVA** ground sesame sweetmeat
HALVE bisect; divide
HAMAL porter (Turk.)
HAMAM Turkish bath
HANAP pewter goblet
HANDY near; dexterous; adroit
HANIF orthodox Moslem
HANKY handkerchief
HANSA of North German mercantile league, Hanseatic
cf **HAPLO-** single; simple (Gr.)
HAPLY perchance; peradventure
HAPPY joyous; lucky; opportune
rl **HARAM** the inviolable, Islam
HARDS **HURDS**, refuse of flax, cornstems etc.
HARDY bold; intrepid; robust
HARED sprinted; sped; ran
bd **HAREM** seraglio; zenana; ladies' quarters
bt, tx **HARLE** **HARL**, flax fibre
zo **HARPY** fabulous monster; vulture
zo **HARPY** golden eagle; extortioner
HARRY harass; ravage; raid
HARSH raucous; strident; caustic
HASTE alacrity; speed; hustle
HASTY swift; reckless; headlong
HATCH to plot; doorway; to shade
HATED loathed; abominated

HATER abhorrer; detester
zo **HATHI** wild Indian elephants
HATTO bishop eaten by rats
bt **HAULM** halm; stubble (harvest); stem
HAUNT frequent; importune; resort
HAURL harl; rough-cast
HAUSA Northern Nigerian
HAVEN port; refuge; asylum
HAVER to drivel; blather
HAVOC waste; carnage; devastation
nt **HAWSE** bow anchor pipe
bt, ck **HAZEL** a colour; nut-tree; nut
ga **HAZER** steer riding, wrestling for cowboys (rodeo)
nt **HEADS** or tails; toilets (bows); chief; source; foam; endpoint; tool edge
HEADY rash; hasty; wilful; intoxicating
HEALD warp guide in a loom
HEARD listened to; tried
HEART core; centre; spirit
go **HEATH** heather- or ling-covered acid soil or scrubland
ga **HEATS** preliminary qualifying races
nt, gl **HEAVE** to raise; push; haul; (rock strata)
HEAVY weighty, serious, ponderous, of gravity, massive
cf, me **HECTO-** multiplied by 100; of units (Gr.)
HEDGE lay off; enclose; fence
pc **HEDGE** guarded reservation (speech)
HEFTY heavy; strong; powerful
HEIGH! exclamation
HEKIM judge (Arab.)
HELIO a heliograph
zo **HELIX** screwthread form; snail
HELLO! hallo! hillo! hollo!
HELOT Spartan slave; serf
ag **HELVE** axe-handle; haft; shaft
HEMAL **HAEMAL**, concerning blood
HE-MAN virile; butch
HEMPY like hemp
HENCE henceforth; away; therefore
bd **HENCH** chimney shaft side
bt **HENNA** a dye; a shrub
me **HENRY** electrical induction unit
ch **HEPAR** a sulphur compound
HERBY herbaceous; herbous
HEROD a tyrant
zo **HERON** a wading bird
HERSE a portcullis
me, tc **HERTZ** unit of signals frequency
HERUT political party (Israel)
HET-UP hot and bothered, aroused
bt **HEVEA** rubber-tree
HEWED axed; hacked; fashioned
HEWER cutter; sculptor; miner
HIDER one who conceals
HIKED **HIKER**, tramped as rambler
go **HILLY** undulating
bt **HILUM** the eye of a bean
HINDI Indian dialect
rl **HINDU** practiser of Ind. religion
HINGE depend; turn; hang
zo **HINNY** whinny; a mule; mule call
cf, zo, go **HIPPO-** (horse) (of rivers) (-potamus)
HIRED chartered; leased; rented
HIRER an employer of labour
cf, pl **HISTO-** of tissue (Gr.)
HITCH fasten; catch; obstacle; knot; (baseball)
HITHE **HYTHE**, haven; port
HIVED bees accommodated; stored
HIVER a bee keeper, apiarist
md **HIVES** bee homes; nettle-rash; croup
HOARD amass; garner; save; secrete
HOARY venerable; ancient; silvery
zo **HOBBY** recreation; horse; falcon
HOBIT mortar; short gun
mu **HOBOY** **HAUTBOIS**, the oboe; (high) woodwind
HOCUS (-pocus); to cheat; drug; conjure
HODGE codged; a rustic
HOGAN hooch; a strong liquor
to **HOIST** heave; elevate; pulley
HOLEY holed; riddled
bt **HOLLY** an evergreen
cf **HOMEO-** of sameness (Gr.) (-pathy)
zo **HOMER** homing pigeon; boomerang
HOMER guide signal arrangement; home run (baseball)
mu **HONDO** sad Andalusian song (Sp.)
HONED whetted; sharpened
HONEY sweetness
HOOCH fire-water
HOOEY **HOO HA**, balderdash; nonsense
HOOKA hookah; narghile; hubble-bubble pipe
HOOKY full of barbs
ck **HOOSH** a stew; a mixture
vt **HOOVE** a cattle disease
HOPED desired; anticipated
HOPPY flavoured with hops
HORAL horary; hourly
HORDE clan; throng; gang; crew
HORNY callous; spikey; lustful
zo **HORSE** steed; palfrey; nag; cob
HORSE cavalry; flogging frame
HORSY **HORSEY**, equuscentric
HORUS son of Osiris (Egypt)
HOSED drenched; watered

HOTEL inn; tavern; hostel
HOTLY eagerly; ardently; fervidly
HOUGH hamstring; the ham
zo **HOUND** pursue; chase; hunting dog
HOURI a nymph of paradise; peri
HOUSE mansion; domicile; lineage; (curling)
HOVEL shelter; hut; cabin; shed
HOVER hang; vacillate; wave
to **HOWEL** barrel maker's tool
HOWSO howsoever; although
HUBBY husband
HUFFY petulant; irritable
HULCH hunch; bump; bunch
HULKY unwieldy; clumsy
HULLO! hallo!
HULLY husky
HUMAN mortal; cosmic; rational
hd **HUMET** abbreviated fesse
HUMIC wet; dank; mouldy
HUMID damp; moist
md **HUMOR** bodily fluid (eye)
HUMPH! exclamation of dissatisfaction
HUMPY Australian native hut
HUMUS decomposed organic soil enrichment
ck **HUMUS** chick pea/garlic puree
HUNCH presentiment; hump; lump
HUNKS miser; niggard
HUNKY rugged masculine physique
zo **HUNYA** fighting rams
HURDS hards; flax refuse
HURLY confusion; flurry (-burly)
HURRY hasten; expedite; speed
HURST a grove; a wood
zo **HUSKY** Canadian sled-dog
HUSKY hoarse; raucous; guttural
HUSSY housewife; brazen girl
HUTCH coop; (chicken-); bin
HUZZA Bravo; Hurrah!
as **HYADS** **HYADES**, cluster of stars
HYDRA water monster; source of trouble
HYDRO a spa; a hotel
cf, md **HYDRO-** of water; spa (Gr.)
zo **HYENA** a carnivore (2nd hand)
nt **HYLAM** form of junk (Thailand)
HYLEG ruling planet in horoscope
HYLIC materialistic
rl **HYMEN** God of Marriage
pl **HYMEN** maidenhead; vaginal membrane
md **HYOID** tongue-bone
cf **HYPER-** above normal; excessive (Gr.)
HYPHA a fungus filament
zo **HYRAX** rock-rabbit; cony
bt **HYSON** green tea (China)
HYTHE **HITHE**, haven; port

I

cf, md **-IASIS** abnormal; diseased (Gr.)
cf, pc, md **-IATRO** **-IATRY**, of healing (Gr.)
ICENI Ancient British tribe
md **ICHOR** a god's blood; a fluid
ICIER **ICILY**, colder; frostily; frigidly
ck **ICING** a sugar-coating
cf, pc **ICTAL-** of transitory emotions (Gr.)
ICTIC abrupt; sudden
ICTUS a stroke; accentuation
IDEAL Utopian; fanciful; visionary
cf, pc **ID-EGO-** single but divided entity (Gr.)
IDIOM lingo; peculiar phraseology
IDIOT moron; subnormal; foolish person
IDIST Ido linguist
IDLED **IDLER**, slacked; lounger; drone
IDOLA fantasies; apparitions
IDOSE monosaccharide
IDRIS mythical Welsh giant; (water)
IDYLL pastoral poem of ideal dreams
IGLOO Eskimo snow-hut
md **ILEAC** **ILEUM**, **ILEUS**, of intestine; colic
md **ILEUM** (intestine)
md **ILEUS** intestinal obstruction, colic
ILIAC pertaining to loins
ILIAD epic poem; (siege of Troy)
md **ILIUM** part of hip-bone
gl **ILLAM** gem-bearing Sri L. gravel
cp **IMAGE** ikon; idol; copy; likeness (mirror) stored (public relations)
zo **IMAGO** perfect state of insect
mt **IMBAT** cool Near-Eastern wind
zo **IMBER** the great northern diver
IMBOW to arch
IMBUE dye; steep; stain; permeate
ch **IMIDE** acid anhydride compound
IMPEL urge; drive; incite; actuate
IMPEN to pen; to write
IMPLY mean; hint; signify; involve
bt **INAJA** Brazilian palm
INANE fatuous; empty; void; vapid
INAPT unfit; inapposite; clumsy
INARM to encircle
mn **INBYE** mine direction
INCOG incognito; disguised
lw **INCUR** (debt); become liable for; arouse
md **INCUS** ear-bone like an anvil
pr **INCUT** inset; side note let into text
INDEX pointer; forefinger; exponent

INDRA Hindu God of Rain
zo **INDRI** babakoto; large lemur
INEPT inane; futile; pointless
bt **INERM** without prickles
INERT slack; dull; torpid; inactive
INEYE to graft
INFER deduce; gather; surmise
cp **INFIX** implant; ingraft; instil; notational graft
cf **INFRA-** below; inferior; (-red); (Gr.)
ar, bd **INGLE** fireside; (nook); (seat)
mn **INGOT** lump of gold, metal
md, pl **INION** the nape of the neck; occiput
INKER recording device
INKLE broad linen tape
INKOS Zulu chief
lw **IN-LAW** of spouse's relatives
INLAY (buhl) tesselate
cp, el, go, ro **INLET** bay; bight; creek; entrance; intake opening; valve
INNER interior; within; (mind); (soul); central
tc, el **INPUT** capital investment; charge; work done
cp **INPUT** program; data signal fed in
ga **IN-RUN** pre ski-jump start
INSET an insertion; implant
INTER bury; inhume; entomb
cf **INTER-** (-national) (-racial) combined
INUIT an Eskimo
bt **INULA** herb
INURE harden; toughen; train
INURN bury; entomb
zo **INUUS** Barbary ape (Gibraltar)
INVAR an alloy of nickel and steel
INWIT intuition; conscience
ch, md **IODAL** **IODIC**, containing iodine
ar **IONIC** of **IONIA** (Asia Minor)
lw **IRADE** Turkish written decree
IRAQI **IRAKI**, dwellers in Iraq
IRATE wroth; ireful; angry; incensed
IRENE Roman goddess of peace
md **IRIAN** relating to the iris
IRISH Hibernian
mn **IRITE** an iridium compound
IRKED bored; wearied; jaded
fr **IROKO** African utility timber
ch **IRONE** smell constituent of violets
IRONS prisoners' chains; golf clubs
IRONY satire; sarcasm; mockery
ISIAC referring to Isis
rl **ISLAM** (Mohammedanism) submission to Allah
ISLET isle; eyot; atoll
pr **ISSUE** outcome; result; publication; vent
bt **ISTLE** **IXTLE**, aloe fibre
ITCHY scratchy; desirous; uneasy
zo **IVORY** dentine; elephant tusk
IVRIT modernized Hebrew (language)
IXION wheel-bound king; (Hell)
zo **IZARD** Pyrenean ibex or chamois

J

go **JABAL** **JEBAL**, **JIBAL** (Arab) mountain, Gibraltar (Jabal Tariq)
JABOT lace frill; neck ruffle
JACKS wooden wedges
JADED weary; tired; fagged; exhausted
tx **JADOO** artificial silk
bt, ck **JAFFA** orange (type)
zo **JAGER** the great skua; pirate gull
JAGGY uneven; serrated; notched
bt, md **JALAP** a cathartic root
JAMBE a part of leg armour
bt **JAMBU** rose-apple tree
JAMES a flunkey
JAMMY smothered in jam
JANTU Indian water-raising device
JANTY jaunty; airy; showy
JANUS god of doorways
JAPAN varnish; lacquer; enamel
vt **JARDE** tumour on a horse's leg
JASEY worsted wig
mn **JASPE** veined jaspar
JAUNT trip; outing; excursion
JAWED talked; lectured
tx **JEANS** overalls; denim trousers
rl **JEHAD** **JIHAD**, Islamic Holy War
ck **JELLY** gelatin; aspic (-fish) (wobble)
to **JEMMY** gemmy; spruce; lever
JENNY spinning machine; billiard shot
JERID Turkish javelin
JERKY spasmodic; convulsive; irregular
ck **JERKY** beef biltong
JERRY a German; (chamber) -night-pot
rl **JESSE** candlestick; stained window
nt **JETTY** jut; projection; a pier
JEWEL gem; trinket
JEWRY Judaea; the Jews
go **JHEEL** Indian marsh
JHOOM jungle cultivation
nt **JIBED** gibed; sneered; taunted
JIFFY a moment; an instant
to **JIMMY** jemmy; a lever for break-ins
rw **JINTY** locomotive type
JINGO ultra-militarist; nationalist
JINKS high jinks; merry-making

JIPPO jupon; vest
zo **JOCKO** a chimpanzee
cp **JOINT** splice; seam; united; concerted
ck **JOINT** meat roast; marijuana 'cigarette'
bd **JOIST** log or plank supporting floor/roof
JOKED **JOKER**, jested; wag; humanist
nt **JOLLY** mirthful; cheerful; (-boat)
JONAH bad luck bringer
tx **JORIA** East Indian wool
JOTUN Norse giant
JOUGS iron neck-ring; pillory
me **JOULE** electrical unit of work
JOUST tilt; encounter; tournament (knights)
bt **JUDAS** traitor; spy-hole; tree
lw **JUDGE** decide; arbiter; critic
pl **JUGAL** malar; (cheek-bone)
bt **JUGUM** pair of opposite leaves
JUICE sap; fluid extract; petrol
JUICY succulent; moist; lush
ck **JULAP** **JULEP**, cordial cocktail (Am.)
zo **JULIS** a wrasse; a small fish
zo, bt **JULUS** **IULUS**, catkin; wire-worm
mo **JUMAR** movable clamp on rope
zo **JUMBO** elephant; locomotive; airliner (jet); drill carriage
JUMPS nervous apprehension; obstacle (horse racing)
zo **JUNCO** North American snow-bird
JUNTA cabal; govt. by rebel clique
JUNTO coterie; clique; faction
JUPON jippo; surcoat; petticoat
lw **JURAL** legal; lawful
lw **JURAT** an alderman; (affidavit)
lw **JUROR** a juryman
tx **JUSSI** Manila textile fabric
JUTES people of Jutland (Danes)
cf **JUXTA-** (-position) (in front or behind)

K

rl **KAABA** sacred stone in Mecca
zo **KAAMA** hartebeest; S. Afr. antelope
KADIR (cup for pig-sticking)
nt **KAFIR** Turkish/Greek lateen ship
zo **KALAN** sea otter of North Pacific
rl **KALIF** Calif; Caliph; ruler of Islam
rl **KALPA** calpa; a day of Brahma
mn, go, gl **KAMES** glacial deposits
KAMIS Eastern tunic
KANAT ancient tunnel network (irrigation) (Oman)
me **KANDY** S. Indian weight
me **KANEH** **CANEH**, 6 cubits (Hebrew)
bt, ck **KANYA** Afr. shea tree; its butter
bt, tx **KAPOK** fibre of silk-cotton tree
fr **KAPUR** Indonesian wood
KARMA destiny based on each incarnation
me **KAROB** 24th part of a grain
go **KAROO** South African plateau
fr **KARRI** dense Australian wood; tree
gl, go **KARST** limestone caves (Yugoslavia)
cf, pl **KARYO-** nucleus (Gr.)
tx **KASHA** dress material
ck **KASHA** cracked-buckwheat meal (Rus.)
KASHI enamelled Islamic tiles (Persia, India)
bt, ck **KASSA** catechu made from betel-nut
bt **KAURI** New Zealand fir tree
nt **KAYAK** covered seal-skin canoe (Eskimo)
ga **KAYLE** ninepin; skittle
mu **KAZOO** children's 'hum' instrument
ck **KEBAB** meat dish (Turk.)
bt **KECKS** fool's parsley
nt **KEDGE** small anchor; using anchor rope to move boat (sailing)
KEDGE **KEDGY**, brisk; lively; happy
KEEPS permanent possession
mn **KEESH** carburet of iron
ck **KEEVE** vat; fermenting tub
ck **KEFIR** fermented milk
tx **KELAT** short springy Asian wool
mn **KELLY** top pipe of drill string; Manxman
KEMPO martial art (China)
KEMPS the plantain
KENDO swordsmanship (Japan)
ps, nc **KERMA** kinetic movement energy released in matter
KERNE Irish foot-soldier; boor
nt **KETCH** two-masted vessel
ch **KETEN** colourless gas
nt **KEVEL** belaying pin
zo **KEVEL** young gazelle
cr, jn **KEYED** wedged; beam; (typewriter); solvable; tensed
tc **KEYER** frequency-change device
KHAKI olive-drab; army uniform colour
KHEDA elephant enclosure
KHMER people and language (Cambodia)
zo **KIANG** Tibetan wild horse
KIBED chapped with cold
zo **KIDDY** youngster; goatling
KIDEL **KIDDLE**, fish-trap
KIDGE brisk; pot bellied
KILEY **KYLEY**, boomerang

KILIM woven carpet without pile (Turk.)
KINGS two biblical books; monarchs
KINKY crotchety; entangled; bizarre; unconventional
to **KINSH** stone-mason's lever
ar **KIOSK** covered stall; booth (telephone); open pavilion (Moslem)
zo, ga **KITTY** kitten; common cash; jack (bowls)
mu **KLANG** complex musical tone
KLICK click
KLONG canal; waterway; floating market (Thai)
go **KLOOF** S. African ravine
KLOPS German meatballs
KNACK skill; dexterity; faculty
KNARL gnarl; a knot in wood
bt **KNAUR** swollen tree-trunk outgrowth
KNAVE rascal; rogue; caitiff
KNEAD mix; blend; incorporate
KNEED (baggy-); (knock-)
KNEEL bend knee, submit; (prayer)
KNELL toll; ring; sound; (bells)
KNEPH an Egyptian deity
to **KNIFE** to stab; to lance; blade (cut)
KNOCK rap; beat; buffet
KNOLL knell; hillock; mound
KNOSP ornamental flower-bud
KNOTE (rope-making)
zo **KNOUD** the grey gurnard
KNOUT Russian whip
KNOWN understood; recognized
tx **KNUBS** waste silk
KNURL knob; milled edge
KNURR knot in wood
zo **KOALA** Australian bear
nt **KOBIL** cobble; small boat
ck **KOFTE** **KOFTA**, meat rissole
zo **KOKOB** venomous serpent
bt **KOKRA** wood used for flutes
nt **KOLEH** racing canoe (Malay)
KONDO bronze-gilt finish
nm **KOPEC** **KOPEK**, Russian farthing
go **KOPJE** S. African hillock
KORAN Moslem Sacred Book
nt **KOTIA** Indian dhow
KOWTOW kow-tow; make obeisance
KRAAL native village
zo **KRAIT** venomous snake
KRANG **KRENG**, whale flesh
zo **KRILL** plankton; whale food
nm **KRONA** **KRONE**, Scandinavian coin
KUDOS credit; prestige; fame
KUFIC early Arab alphabet
KUKRI Gurkha knife
KULAK Russian peasant proprietor
bt **KUNDA** lawyer-vine
KVASS Russian beer
KWELA tin whistle (African)
KYACK American pack saddle
KYLEY kiley; boomerang
KYLIN Chinese or Japanese dragon
KYLIX Greek drinking vessel
zo **KYLOE** Hebridean cattle
KYOTO Japanese pottery
bt **KYPOO** extract of catechu; (couch grass)
rl, mu **KYRIE** orthodox Mass (response)
KYUDO mounted archers (Japan)

L

LABBA S. Am. guinea-pig
hd **LABEL** badge. adhesive sticker; address tag
cp **LABEL** coded information signal
bt, pl **LABIA** lips of orifice
rl **LABIS** cochlear; eucharistic spoon
LACED twined; stiffened; (straight)
cp **LACED** fortified drink; final punched card
tx **LACET** lace-work
LACIS filet lace; network
LADAS a classic runner
LADED **LADEN**, loaded; burdened (freight)
LADIN Swiss Latin
LADLE scoop; bale; dole
lw **LAGAN** **LIGAN**, (flotsam)
ck **LAGER** light beer; storage area
gl **LAHAR** volcanic mud avalanche
tx **LAINE** woollen fabric
LAIRD Scottish landowner
LAITY laymen
LAKIN ladykin; small damsel
LAMED crippled
LAMIA sorceress; witch
LAMMY sailor's quilted jumper
LANCE lancet; spear; pierce
go **LANDE** sterile tract (Fr.)
LANKY lean; tall; gaunt
nt **LANTY** lightbuoy to aid navigation
LAPEL upper folds on face of a coat
mn, tx **LAPIS** stone; (calico-printing)
LAPSE slip; slide; indiscretion
bt **LARCH** genus of trees; softwood; tamarack (USA)
ck **LARDY** full of lard; (-cake)
LARES Roman household gods
mu **LARGE** massive; bulky; copious; longest note
mu **LARGO** slowly

LARKY sportive; frolicsome
to **LARRY** mortar-mixing tool
LARUM alarm
LARUS aquatic bird
zo **LARVA** caterpillar; grub; maggot
md **LASER** resin; searing ray
LASSO rope with running noose
mu **LASSU** slow section of a csardas Hung. dance
jn **LATCH** catch; fasten (door); attach oneself; comprehend
LATER tardier; more recent
bt **LATEX** sap; untreated rubber
to **LATHE** county division; machine
LATHI bamboo cudgel
LATHY thin; long and slender
LATIN Roman; of Latinium; tongue
rl, mu **LAUDA LAUDE**, religious praise, concert poems
rl **LAUDS** liturgical office after matins; praises
LAUGH guffaw with mirth; (-at) deride
LAUTA royal Inca badge
LAVED washed; bathed
LAVER brazen washing basin
bt **LAVER** edible seaweed
LAXLY loosely; slackly; remissly
LAY-BY halting place beside road
zo **LAYER** seam; stratum; bed; hen
LAY-IN maternity; extended sleep
ga **LAY-UP** shot near basket (b-ball)
LAZAR leper
LAZED idled; reposed
LEACH to wash by percolation
LEADY leaden
LEAFY leavy; full of leaves
LEAKY not watertight; tattling
LEANT inclined; reposed; trusted
LEAPT jumped; sprang
LEARN acquire; hear; memorize
LEARY old mine-shaft
LEASE let; hire; tenure
LEASH three; bind; thong
LEAST smallest; minutest
LEAVE forsake; quit; depart
LEAVY leafy
LEDGE shelf; ridge; layer
LEDGY full of ridges
nt, zo **LEECH** blood-sucker; hanger-on; (limpet); leecher (doctor); sail
nt **LEECH** edge of a sail
LEERY sly
lw **LEGAL** lawful; licit; proper; correct
LEGER a race; light; small
LEGGY lanky
LEG-IT proceed on foot; walk; hike
mu **LEGNO** wood (It.), drumstick

LEMAN lover; gallant; paramour
bt, ma **LEMMA** grass glume; subsidiary theorem
LEMMA summary preceding a tome
cf **-LEMMA-** of subsidiary theorem; (true data logic)
bt, ck **LEMON** citrus fruit; the answer
zo **LEMUR** ghost; nocturnal monkey
LENCA Honduran Indian
mu **LENTO** slowly
LEPER lazar
LEPID jocose; pleasant
zo **LEPIS** a scale
md **LEPRA** leprosy
cf, md **-LEPSI** of seizure, collapse (Gr.)
nm **LEPTA** (Greece)
cf, md **LEPTO-** small, thin, fine, weak (Gr.)
mt **LESTE** dry African South wind
LETCH to separate by percolation
LETHE the river of oblivion
LET-IN admission; note added to text
LET-UP an alleviation
cf, md **LEUKO-** white; (blood); colourless
ch **LEVAN** polymerized grass fructose
LEVEE embankment; reception
LEVEL raze; plane; even; flush; grade
to **LEVER** a jemmy; prise
LEWIS masonry grip; machine gun
bt **LIANA LIANE**, tropical climbing plant
me **LIANG** Chinese ounce
LIART LIARD, LYART, dapple-grey
lw **LIBEL** slander; defame; traduce
LIBER bast; inner bark; a book
LIBRA the Balance (Zodiac)
LICIT lawful; permissible
mt **LIDAR** cloud pattern detector
LIEGE one bound by oath
LIFER prisoner sentenced for life
lw **LIGAN** lagan; (flotsam)
mu **LIGHT** kindle; illume; buoyant; easy; featherweight; music
hr **LIGNE** watch-movement measure unit
LIKED enjoyed; relished
LIKEN to compare
LIKIN Chinese transport duty
bt **LILAC** a colour; a shrub
LIMBO hell; paradise of fools
LIMED cemented; ensnared; treated
pc **LIMEN** threshold
LIMER fibre brush for limewashing
LIMIT restraint; bound; border
mu **LIMMA** a semitone
LINCH ledge; projection; cliff
LINED care-worn; with lines
tx **LINEN** flax cloth; underwear; bed sheets

nt **LINER** a shim; a vessel; layer of paint
LINGO speech; language
wv **LINGO** jacquard harness weight
LINGY active; limber; heathery
LININ (cell nucleus)
ga **LINKS** (cuff); golf course; chains; shackles; connections; back players (hockey)
ch, md **LIPID** living-tissue fat/wax
tx **LISLE** thread
LISSE warp threads in tapestry
LISTS the combat-ground
nm **LITAS** Lithuanian currency unit
LITHE blithe; active; supple
LITHY pliable; bendable; limber
pr **LITHO-** (-graph), printed picture technique
me **LITRE** nearly 1¾ pints
LIVED dwelt; abode; survived
LIVEN enliven; animate; vivify
md **LIVER** internal organ
LIVID ghastly pale
nm **LIVRE** old French franc
LLAMA S. American camel
go **LLANO** S. American plain
zo **LOACH** loche; a river-fish
LOAMY of sand-clay mix tilth; soil
LOATH reluctant; unwilling
LOBAR **LOBATE**, **LOBED**, rounded projection
ar, bd **LOBBY** pasage; to seek votes; pressure group; tambour entry hall
LOCAL an inn; topical; regional
zo **LOCHE** a loach; a river-fish
md **LOCUM** locum tenens; a deputy
LOCUS locality; position; area
nv **LODAR** special loran system, radar
LODGE reside; sojourn; deposit; dwelling; masons' workshop
gl **LOESS** alluvial deposits
LOFTY stately; imposing; towering
bt **LOGAN** poised rock; a berry
zo **LOGGE** miller's thumb; small fish
LOGIA oracles; dicta
cf **-LOGIA** of speech
LOGIC reasoning; dialectics
LOGIE sham jewels
LOGON provision for new group to be added
cp, tc **LOG-ON** check-in for new users of computers
LOGOS the Divine Word
LOKAL tavern, club, assembly place
ck **LOKUM** Turkish delight (sweetmeat)
LOLLY lollipop; a lump; money
LOLOS aboriginal race (China)
bt **LOOFA** luffa; flesh-brush
LOONY mad; lunatic
LOOPY kinky; dotty
ga **LOOSE** liberate; slack; vague; lax; free; puck, ball (ice hockey); let fly (archery)
LOPED ran with easy strides
nt, nv **LORAN** radio-navigation system
LORDS cricket ground
LORIC corset (13th cent.)
zo **LORIS** Cingalese monkey
LORRY larry; truck; vehicle
zo **LORUM** mandibular plates in hemiptera
LOSEL worthless; scoundrel; ne'er-do-well
LOSER also ran; (billiards)
LOSSY of energy-dissipating equipment
ec **LOTIC** of running water
ga **LOTTO** a game
bt **LOTUS** water lily
go **LOUGH** loch; an arm of the sea; ria; or inland lake
nm **LOUIS** obsolete French gold coin
mu **LOURE** French bagpipe; dance; technique applied to violin playing
zo **LOUSE** parasitic insect
LOUSY mean; louse-infected
tx **LOVAT** close tweed
LOVED adored; liked; esteemed
LOVER a Romeo; admirer; swain
LOWER depress; degrade; frown; (under)
LOWLY meek; humble; modest
zo **LOXIA** cross-bill birds
LOYAL leal; true; devoted
LUBBA coarse grass in Orkneys
LUCID clear; limpid; sane; pure
LUCKY fortunate; auspicious
LUCRE gain; profit; wealth; (gold)
cf, pc **LUDIC-** amusing play; (-rous) absurd (Gr.)
LUGER automatic pistol; sleigh driver
me **LUMEN** unit of luminous flux
LUMPY coagulated
LUNAR of the moon
ck **LUNCH** luncheon; midday repast
mu **LUNGA** **LONGO**, prolonged sounds (It.)
ga **LUNGE** thrust forward (fencing); equitation
LUNIK artificial moon satellite
bt **LUPIN** a flower
tx **LUPPA** cloth of gold or silver
md **LUPUS** skin disease
LURCH stagger; sway; roll; toss
LURED enticed; decoyed; inveigled
LURID glowing; sensational

zo, ... (left column)

LUSHY tipsy
LUSTY robust; vigorous; sturdy
LUSUS a freak; an exception
LUTED sealed with luting
mu **LUTER** lute-player
LYART liart; liard; dapple-grey
LYASE double-bonding enzyme
LYCEE high school (Fr.)
LYING mendacious; recumbent
md **LYMPH** a fluid; vaccine
LYNCH mob law; kill
LYRIC a short poem; tuneful
LYRID meteor from Lyra
zo **LYRIE** Manx shearwater gull
md **LYSIN** disintegratory antibody
md **LYSIS** recovery
LYSSA hydrophobia; rabies
zo **LYTHE** the pollack
LYTHE **LITHE**, flexible; agile
cf, pc, md **LYTIC** **-LYTTIC**, pertaining to lysis; opposing action (drugs) (Gr.)
zo **LYTTA** rod of tongue cartilage

M

zo, bt **MACAW** parrot; palm
lw **MACER** a court usher
MACHE materials for papier mâché
mn **MACLE** double crystal
cf **MACRO-** of major, large (Gr.)
MADAM **MADAME**, lady; manageress (boss) (bordel)
zo **MADGE** leaden hammer; magpie
bt **MADIA** the tar-weed; oil-plant
MADLY deliriously; insanely
MAFIA Sicilian secret society
gl **MAFIC** non-felsic strata in igneous rock
zo **MAGAR** Indian crocodile
mu **MAGAS** stringed-instrument bridge
MAGIC witchery; sorcery; charm
mn **MAGMA** plutonic rock
rl **MAGOG** legendary giant (and Gog)
rl **MAGOT** Barbary ape (as oriental monster)
rl **MAHDI** Moslem prophet (dervish)
bt **MAHWA** butter-tree
bt **MAIZE** Indian corn
MAJOR a rank; greater
MAKER creator; manufacturer
MAKWA Chinese jacket
md **MALAR** cheek-bone
MALAX soften by kneading/diluting
MALAY of Malaysia
bt **MALIC** (apples)
MALIK village headman (Ind.)
MALTY malt-flavoured
zo **MAMBA** S. African snake
mu **MAMBO** dance
pl **MAMMA** mother; mammary gland (lactation)
MAMMY negro nurse
MANAL pertaining to the hand
ch **MANEB** chemical fungicide
MANED having a mane
nm **MANEH** mina; 50 shekels
MANES ghosts; departed souls
MANET stage direction 'remain'
MANGA covering for a cross
vt **MANGE** **MANGY**, scabrous; parasitic
bt **MANGO** tropical fruit
MANGY scabrous
MANIA frenzy; delirium; craziness
zo **MANIS** the scaly ant-eater
MANLY hardy; intrepid; bold
bt **MANNA** food; a form of sap
MANOR freehold estate
MANSE priest's house
zo, rl **MANTA** ox ray; a sea fish; prayer chant
zo **MANUS** mane; of the hand
MAORI first colonizers (New Zealand)
MAPES ice skating jump
bt **MAPLE** sugar-tree
bt **MAQUI** Chilean evergreen shrub
MARCH advance; walk; border land; 3rd month
MARDY spoilt; naughty
pr **MARGE** margin; verge; edge
rl, as **MARIA** virgin; lunar seas
MARID powerful jinn
MARLY clay-like
MARRY unite; wed; espouse; join
go **MARSH** bog; swamp; fen; morass
MASAI African tribe
el **MASER** microwave amplifier
MASHY mashie; a golf club
MASON stone-worker
MASSA master
ga **MASSE** a billiard stroke
MASSY massive; bulky
bt **MASTY** full of beech-mast
cp, ga **MATCH** suit; tally; agree; lucifer; equivalence; contest; best of 3 games (tennis)
MATED (chess); married; matched
MATER mother
MATEY be friendly, chummy
MATIN morning (Fr.)
mn **MATTE** crude black copper
ck **MATZO** thin unleavened Passover bread
bt **MAULS** marsh mallow
me **MAUND** an Eastern weight

MAUVE a mallow colour
zo **MAVIS** the thrush
MAWKY crotchety; maudlin
MAXIM gun; adage; saw; precept
MAYAN native of Honduras, Mexico
MAYBE perhaps
MAYOR town chief
rl **MAZDA** Supreme Deity (Zend-Avesta)
MAZER goblet; bowl
ck **MEALY** farinaceous; flour mix
MEANS mode; agency; method; wealth
MEANT signified; purposed
me **MEASE** a group of 500
MEATY fleshy
ck **MEBOS** salted apricots (S. Africa)
rl **MECCA** desired objective; heart of Islam
MEDAL decoration; award of honour
MEDIA communications (TV, radio, press etc.)
md, bt **MEDIC** doctor; clover lucerne etc.
MELEE fray; brawl; scuffle; mixture
zo **MELES** badger genus
bt **MELIC** lyric; a grass
ck **MELLA** honey mixtures
bt **MELON** a gourd
pl, pc **MENSA** of brain genius; table; tooth surface
MERCY pity; lenity; clemency; grace
MERGE coalesce; immerse; submerge
MERIT desert; worth; credit; earn
zo **MERLE** the blackbird
zo **MERON** posterior of certain insects
ar **MEROS** triglyph channel surfaces
bt **MERRY** the English wild cherry
ga **MERRY** blithe; jocund; lively; too strong a stroke (golf) (bowls)
ma **MESAL** of geometric measures
bd **MESHY** netted; reticulated; structure
lw **MESNE** intermediate
MESON cosmic ray constituent
rl **MESSA** **MISSA, MASS, MESSE** (musical setting) (liturgy)
MESSY untidied; disordered; unclean
mu **MESTO** sadly (It.)
ch, mn **METAL** bullion; ore; (element)
METAL broken stone for roads
METED measured; apportioned
bt **METEL** thorn apple
ma **METER** counting instrument; (taxi-)
cf **-METIC** alien; (cos-) make-up (Gr.)
METIF **METIS**, person of mixed race
ch, pg **METOL** 4-methylaminophenol
ma **METRA** a measuring instrument
me **METRE** measured rhythm (prosody, verse, music)
me **METRE** 39.37 inches per metric system base unit
rw **METRO** metropolitan underground railway
mu **METRO-** of regular beat; (-nome)
MEUTE **MEW**, cage for hawks, falcons
mu, ar **MEZZO** middle voice; storey
MIAOW miaul; caterwaul
md **MIASM** miasma; effluvia
zo **MICKY** Irish lad; young bull; microphone
cf, ma **MICRO-** tiny; one millionth 10^{-6}
MIDAS had a golden touch
nt **MIDDY** a midshipman
zo **MIDGE** dwarf; gnat
ga **MID-ON** (cricket) fielding position
MIDST among; middle
MIGHT indefinite subjunctive of verb
zo, ag **MILCH** milk-cow
MILER relative to mile (high, run in a minute etc.)
as **MILKY** lacteal; (-way) heavenly dairy
cf, ma **MILLI-** one thousandth 10^{-3}
MIMED mimicked; acted
MIMIC ape; copy; mime; mock
MINCE chop fine; palliate
MINED dug; undermined
MINER sapper; (coal-)
mu **MINIM** dwarf; single drop; note
MINIM down-stroke of pen
mu **MINIM** 2 crochets of ½ semi-breve
MINOR pretty; lesser; under-age
MINOS King of Crete
MINUS less; lacking; wanting
me **MIRED** bogged; unit of colour temperature
MIRTH glee; gaiety; hilarity
MIRZA a Persian title
MIS-DO sin; do wrong
to **MISER** skinflint; hoarder; stingy niggard
cr **MISER** hand-auger; marline spike for drilling holes
MISSY young lady
MISTY dim; obscure; cloudy
rl **MITRA** **MITHRA**, god of Persians, Gr., Romans
rl **MITRE** bishop's hat; 45 degrees
tx **MITTS** **MITTENS**, fingerless gloves
MIXED blended; mingled; confused; atypical
MIXEN **MIDDEN**, dunghill
ro **MIXER** a good companion; kitchen; compatible; frequency changer
MIX-UP mêlée; scuffle; brawl; muddle

MIZZY bog; swamp; quagmire
pc **MNEME** effect of memory persistence
ck **MOCCA** chocolate/coffee mixture
mn **MOCHA** agate; gem
tx **MOCHE** packet of spun silk
mu **MODAL** logic; music; grammar general structure
MODEL example; pattern; copy; miniature; design; art
tc **MODEM** varying speed links to tranmission lines
nv **MODER** matrix of astrolabe
lv **MODUS** style; a method
rw **MOGUL** ex-Mongolian empire builder in India; type of steam locomotive; mound on ski slope
nm **MOHUR** Indian gold coin
tx **MOIRE** watered silk
MOIST dark; clammy; humid
MOLAR grinding; tooth; holistic phenomena
pc **MOLAR** purposive behaviour; learning situations
nc, ps **MOLAR** volume of unit of substance
bd **MOLER** diatomaceous earth
zo **MOLLY** the wagtail bird; she-man
mu **MOLTO** very; much (It.)
rl **MOMUS** God of Ridicule
zo **MONAD** primitive organism; minimal matter units
zo **MONAL** a pheasant
MONDE MONDANE, worldly society (Fr.)
MONEL an alloy
nm **MONEY** cash; coin; currency; wealth
bt **MONOX** the crowberry
ga **MONTE** gambling game like faro
MONTH lunar cycle
MOOCH slouch; loiter
MOODY sullen; morose; glum; captious
MOOED lowed (cow-speak)
MOONY dreamy; distraight
MOORE movement in gymnastics
MOORY sterile; boggy
zo **MOOSE** the elk
MOPED pined; motorized bicycle
MOPPY tipsy; fuddled
MOPSY mopsey; untidy woman
MORAL ethical; virtuous; 'right-minded'
MORAT mulberry juice
zo **MORAY MURAY**, variety of tropical eel
bt **MOREL** cherry; nightshade
MORES social norms, behaviour, standards
bt **MORIL** morel; mushroom
MORMOR bugbear
MORNE blunt head of a lance
MORON mental defective; retarded; stupid
ro, zo, rl **MORSE** signalling (code); the walrus; cope or cloak clasp (metal)
bt **MORUS** mulberry
MOSES a law-giver
mu **MOSSO** (It.) moving; animated; lively
bt **MOSSY** cryptogamous; lichenous
MOTED of dust particles
MOTEL motorists' hotel
mu **MOTET** sacred melody
MOTHY moth-eaten
mu, ar, **MOTIF** theme; feature
hd, wv, le,
cr
MOTIF repeated pattern in art, music
eg **MOTOR** automobile; engine; prime mover
pl **MOTOR** stimulator of movement
ar **MOTTE MOTE**, castle mound (keep)
MOTTO pithy maxim; slogan; theme
MOUCH mooch; skulk; slouch
bl **MOULD** shape (in form); create; fungus blight
MOULT to cast feathers
MOUND knoll; tumulus; hillock
MOUNT climb; scale; ascend; tower
MOURN bewail; lament; deplore
MOUSE MOUSY, of small quiet rodents
MOUTH opening; orifice; declaim; (river); (utterance); pompous speech
MOVED shifted; budged; roused
MOVER proposer
MOWED scythed; cut
MOWER grass-cutting machine
MOYEN means; influence
MPRET Albanian ruler
nt **MTEPI** canoe dugout, sail (East Africa)
ch **MUCIC** an acid
MUCID musty; mouldy; slimy
MUCIN viscous proteins/carbohydrates
MUCKY dirty; filthy; muddy
bt **MUCOR** mould; fungus
bt **MUCRO** stiff sharp point
pl **MUCUS** slime (nasal)
bt **MUDAR MADAR**, medicinal herb
MUDDY impure; without clarity (of water, ideas)
rl **MUFTI** Moslem high authority
MUFTI civilian clothing

MUGGY damp and warm
zo **MUGIL** the mullet fish
MULCH soil condition; manure
lw **MULCT** fine; penalize
MULSE mulled wine
MULSH mulch; litter; manure
cf **MULTI-** many-sided; of uses; much (Lat.)
MUMMY embalmed corpse (Eg.); mother
md **MUMPS** glandular epidemic
MUNCH chew; crunch; masticate
tx **MUNGO** shoddy; inferior cloth
MURAL fixed to a wall
zo **MURAY** cf. moray; murry
MURED walled in; immured; pent
zo **MUREX** Tyrian dye; molluscs
MURID Moslem disciple
MURKY lurid; dark; lowering
mn **MURRA** fluorspar
zo **MURRE** razorbill or guillemot
MURUT language of N. Borneo
MUSAL pert. to poetry/Muses
zo **MUSCA** fly genus
bt **MUSCI** the mosses
MUSED pondered; contemplated
MUSER ruminator; non-active thinker
MUSHY pulpy
mu **MUSIC** melody; harmony
MUSKY fragrant like musk
MUSTY mucid; fusty; mouldy
mu **MUTED** muffled; pianissimo
gn **MUTON** smallest mutable gene element
MUZZY dazed; confused
bt **MYALL** Australian hard-wood tree
md **MYOID** like muscle
md **MYOMA** muscle-fibre tumour
MYOPE **MYOPS**, of short-sightedness
MYOPY **MYOPIA**, of short-sightedness
bt **MYRRH** labdanum with aromatic gum (scent)
zo **MYSIS** the opossum shrimp
zo **MYXON** fish of mullet family

N

NABIT crushed candy
NABOB Indian ruler (wealthy)
NACRE mother-of-pearl
NADIR opposite to zenith
md **NAEVE** a birthmark
NAGGY querulous; quarrelsome
zo **NAGOR** Senegal antelope
NAIAD water-nymph
NAIVE artless; ingenuous; candid
NAKED stark; open; bare; denuded
mu **NAKER** a kettle-drum
NAKIR examiner of the dead (Koran)
NAMED yclept; specified; dubbed
NAMER nominator; god-parent
zo **NANDU** rhea; American ostrich
zo **NANNY** children's nurse; female goat
gl **NAPPE** mountain-chain structure
ce **NAPPE** normal surface overflow of dam
NAPPY drowsy; a dish
NAPPY napkin; baby's diaper; horse refusing orders
cf **NARCO-** of sleep, numbness, stupor (Gr.)
pl **NARES** **NARIS**, of the nostrils
md **NASAL** of the nose, phonetics, errhine
NASIL conflict-inhibiting social signal
NASTY foul; loathsome; ribald
NATAL nascent; initial
NATTY neat; spruce; matching; trim
NAVAL nautical; maritime; marine
pl **NAVEL** centre (meditation); belly-button
bt **NAVEW** wild turnip
NAWAB Indian governor, nobleman
NAZIR Indian bailiff
nt **NEAPS** shortfall tides
NEATH beneath
mu **NEBEL** the Jew's harp
cf **NECRO-** of the dead (Gr.)
zo **NEDDY** donkey; moke; burro
NEEDS perforce; necessarily
NEEDY poor; indigent; penniless
NEELE **NEELD**, needle; sharp point
NEESE neeze; sneeze
NEGRE **NEGRO**, black
NEGUS Abyssinian King
NEGUS a drink; hot punch
NEIGH to whinny
me **NEPER** power ratio unit
md, pl **NERVE** pluck; hardihood; neural; fibres
pc **NERVY** anxious; apprehensive; excitable
NETTY meshy; reticulated
mu **NEUME** a musical phrase (Gr.)
pc **NEURO-** of the nerves; nervosity (Gr.)
NEVER not at any time
pl **NEVUS** birthmark; discolouration of skin
NEWEL finial of a staircase
NEWLY recently; freshly
NEWSY chatty; gossipy

lw, tc **NEXUS** interconnecting series; ideas; bonds
NICER more pleasant; more exact
ar, bd **NICHE** nook; corner; recess
NICOL (polarizing light)
NIDGE to dress stones
NIDOR odour of cooking
md **NIDUS** nest; a breeding place
NIECE daughter of brother or sister
NIFFY smelly
NIFTY classy; stylish
NIGHT darkness; obscurity
NIHIL nil; zero; nothing
bt **NIKAU** New Zealand palm
NINES elaborate party clothes
cp **NINES** complement representing negative values
NINNY simpleton; nitwit; coward
NINON dress material
mu **NINTH** ordinal number 9th; chord
NIOBE a weeper
NIPPY a waitress; alert; parsimonious
NISAN Jewish April
NISUS an effort; an endeavour
NITID gleaming; shining
ch **NITON** gaseous element
ch **NITRE** saltpetre
zo **NITTY** full of nits; lice eggs
NIVAL nivose; niveous; snowy
NIXIE water-elf
NIZAM Indian prince
NOBBY smart; ornate; snobby
NOBEL invented dynamite; prize
nm **NOBLE** patrician; obsolete gold coin
NOBLY grandly; splendidly
mu **NODAL** knotty
zo **NODDY** fool; sea-mew
NODUS knotty point
ga **NO-HIT** noscore for striking games
NO-HOW in no way
mu **NOIRE** quarter note; crotchet (Fr.)
cp, mu **NOISE** din; clamour; uproar; digit mode fixed
NOISY blatant; vociferous; riotous
NOMAD migrant herder (seasonal)
NOMEN name title description (Lat.)
NOMIC customary
NOMOS Greek province
NONCE the present; time; now
NONES (Roman calendar)
mu **NONET** piece for 9 singles
bt **NOOPS** the cloudberry
NOOSE loop; lasso; lariat
bt **NOPAL** Mexican cactus
NORIA Persian water-wheel
NORMA NORM, fixed rule; model style
NORNS Scandinavian Fates
NORSE Viking; early Scandinavian
mt **NORTE** northerly wind in Central America (Sp.)
NORTH (to Polestar); septentrion (Shak.)
NOSED advanced carefully; snooped
NOSEY inquisitive
md, pl **NOTAL** dorsal; of the back
NOTCH natch; dent; nick; incision
NOTED famous; recorded; remarked
zo **NOTUM** back of a bug
mt **NOTUS** southerly wind
NOVEL recent; new; book of fiction
NO-WAY in no manner; no-how
hd **NOWED** coiled; in knot
fd **NOWEL** foundry loam
ck **NOYAU** almond cordial
pl **NUCHA NUQUE**, nape; back of neck
NUDGE jog; jostle; elbow
ga **NULLO** a game
NURSE tend; sickbed attendant
ck **NUTTY** nut-like; -flavoured
zo **NYALA** African antelope
tx **NYLON** artificial fibre
zo **NYMPH** maiden; development stage of insect
zo **NYULA** parasite insect

O

bt **OAKEN** made of oak
nt **OAKUM** picked tarred rope
nt **OARED** rowed; oar-bearing
OASIS fertile spot in desert
ck **OATEN** made of oats
OAVES (OAFS), idiots; changelings
nm **OBANG** old Japanese gold coin
OBEAH obi; West African magic
OBESE abnormally fat; corpulent
me **OBOLE** weight of 10 or 12 g
OCCUR happen; befall; chance
go **OCEAN** the broad sea; main
OCHER OCHRE, OCHRY, browny yellow pigment
bt, zo **OCREA** armoured shin-guard
OCTAD series of eight
OCTAL notation system based on 8
OCTAN happening every 8 days
mu, tc **OCTET** group of eight; packet signal
ch **OCTYL** organic radical
bt **OCUBA** vegetable wax
cl, pl **OCULO-** of the eye (Gr.)
ODDLY queerly; quaintly
mu **ODEON ODEUM**, ancient Grecian music hall
ODIUM obloquy; hatred; enmity

ck **ODOUR** smell; stench
ODYLE mesmerism
bt **OFBIT** devil's bit; a scabious
OFFAL edible entrails; garbage
OFFER bid; tender; proposal
OFTEN oft; frequently; repeatedly
cf **OGAMY** of marital relationship
OGGLE to quiver
OGHAM Irish alphabet
ar **OGIVE** pointed arch (Gothic)
OGLED OGLER, leered; voyeur (contempt)
OILED OILER, lubricated; oil can; oil man
zo **OKAPI** animal related to giraffe
OLDEN OLDER, ancient times; more elderly
ch **OLEIC OLEIN**, **OLEON**, fatty acid; (glycerine)
ch **OLEUM** fuming sulphuric acid
cf **OLIGA- OLIGO-**, of the clique (Gr.)
bt **OLIVE** (branch), emblem of peace
OLLAM Irish doctor
cf **-OLOGY** study, science of (Gr.)
OMAHA a Sioux Indian of Nebraska
OMATI a Mexican Indian
ga **OMBRE** a card game
tx **OMBRE** colour-shaded woven stripes
OMEGA last letter of Greek alphabet
OMLAH N. Ind. court officers
OMRAH Moslem court lord
ONCER he did not do it again
bt **ONION** a shallot
ON-OFF control and keying electron
ONSET assault; attack; storm
ONTAL pert, to reality/noumena
cf **-ONYMY** group nomenclature (Gr.)
OOMPH magnetic personality
OOPAK black pea
OOZED seeped; percolated
go **OPACO OPAC**, shadow side of mountain slope (It.)
mu **OPERA** drama set to music, voices; works
zo **OPHIC** pertaining to snakes, serpents
OPIHI Hawaiian limpets
OPINE suppose; surmise; ween
bt, md **OPIUM** a narcotic drug
bc **OPSIN** rhodopsin protein
OPTED chosen; elected
md **OPTIC** optical; the eye
bt **ORACH** a kind of spinach
rl **ORALE** Papal veil
zo **ORANG -UTAN**, primate (Indonesia)
ORANT worshipper
ORATE declaim; harangue
ORBED globular; spherical
ORBIT ambit; heavenly path; circuit
md **ORBIT** the eye-socket
zo **ORCIN** killer whale
ORDER group; decoration; bid; decree; enact; ukase
ORDER rank; (working); (purchasing); (tall) purpose
OREAD mountain nymph
ch **ORGAL** argal; crude tartar
mu **ORGAN** medium; means; instrument (govt); keyboard instrument with bellows
bl **ORGAN** differentiated, function structure
zo **ORIBI** South African antelope
ORIEL mullioned window
as **ORION** a constellation
ORIYA (Orissa, India) language
tx **ORLON** artificial textile fabric
nt **ORLOP** a ship's deck
zo **ORMER** ear-shell
zo **ORNIS** avifauna; a bird
ORPIN yellow pigment
ORRIS gold or silver lace
bt **ORRIS** astringent root
cf **ORTHO-** correct, straight (Gr.)
zo **ORTYX** American quail
bt **ORVAL** the herb clary
bt **ORYZA** grass genus; rice
OSCAN early Italic tribe
OSCAR film award
bt **OSHAC** gum-plant
bt **OSIER** a willow
OSMIC relating to smell
ch **OSONE** oxidation product of osazone
ch **OSRAM** osmium and wolfram
mu **OSSIA** alternative version (It.)
zo **OTARY** genus of seals
OTHER different
OTTAR attar; aromatic oil
zo **OTTER** fishing device; water weasel
OUGHT aught; nought; a cipher
zo, me **OUNCE** small snow-leopard; weight
OUNDY ONDY, of the waves; scalloped
zo **OUSEL OUZEL**, blackbird
OUTDO exceed; surpass; eclipse
OUTED exposed as gay; expelled
OUTER exterior; external; outside
OUTRE odd; bizarre; strange
bt, pl **OVARY** seed-vessel; (of female)
OVATE OVAL, **OVOID**, eggshaped
lw **OVERT** open to view; apparent
zo **OVINE** sheep-like
gn **OVISM** ovum germ theory
ar **OVOLO** a moulding; wide & convex
bt **OVULE** small seed
OWCHE ouch; jewel socket
OWING due; outstanding

OWLER smuggler (by night)
zo **OWLET** young owl
OWNED admitted; confessed; allowed
nt **OWNER** the captain
zo **OWSEN** oxen
OWSER tan vat liquor
zo **OX-BOT** bot-fly
OXBOW part of yoke
go, gl **OX-BOW** lake; former meander of river
bt **OX-EYE** daisy; marguerite
zo **OX-FLY** bot-fly
ch **OXIDE** oxygen compound
ch **OXIME** aldehyde/ketone compound
ch **OXINE** metal analysis reagent
bt **OXLIP** species of primrose
md **OZENA** an ulcer
OZONE doubled oxygen (surrounds Earth)

P

PACED stepped; walked; hurried
ga **PACER** speed setter; (heart ticker); runner; trotting horse; (bowls)
ck **PADAR** coarse flour meal
bt **PADDY** Irishman; temper; rice
bt **PADMA** lotus
bt **PADRA** black tea (China)
rl **PADRE** army chaplain; priest
PAEAN chant of praise, joy, triumph
cf **PAEDO-** of children, infants (Gr.)
PAEON a poetical foot
PAGAN paynim; heathen idolator
PAGED found by the bell-hop
bt **PAGLE PAIGLE**, cowslip
md **PAINS** meticulous care; discomfort
pt **PAINT** depict; portray; pigment; colour medium (art)
ga **PAIRS** couples; 2-person teams (tennis) (rowing) etc.
bt **PALEA** inner husk; chaff
PALED blanched; encompassed
cf, zo **PALEO-** of ancient; prehistoric life (Gr.)
PALES Goddess of cattle
cf **PALIN-** of repetitive, reverse (Gr.)
PALMY of oasis; flourishing; thriving
zo **PALPI** jointed feelers
md **PALSY** oedema; waterlogging
go **PAMPA PAMPAS**, grazing land S. America
bt **PANAX** ginseng; medicinal plant
nt **PANCH** thick mat; fender
zo **PANDA** giant (bear) and lesser (raccoon)
PANDY a slap on the open hand
PANED variegated; glazed
lw **PANEL** list; board; schedule; wall carving
PANIC fear; fright; terror; alarm
bt **PANSY** flower; effeminate man
cf **PANTO-** of all, everything (pantomime) (Gr.)
PANTS undershorts; short breaths (panting)
rl **PAPAL** popish; pontifical
bt, ck **PAPAW PAWPAW**, fruit (S. Am.)
PAPER journal; sheet; essay
PAPPY succulent; juicy; easy
PARCH dry; scorch; shrivel
PARED PARER, cut (nails); trimmer
tx **PAREU** Polynesian wrap
PARGE to apply plaster; whitewash
PARKA Alaskan fur coat with hood
PARKY cold; chilly
PAROL oral; by word of mouth
PARRY avert; evade; prevent; move (fencing)
PARSE analyse grammatically
PARSI Parsee; Indo-Persian
PARTS abilities; talents; (spare-)
lw **PARTY** eligible suitor; (3rd-)
PARTY faction; clique; (political-)
PARTY social occasion; feast
PASCH Passover (Hebrew); Easter
PASEO promenade (Sp.)
PASHA Turkish governor
PASHM under-fur of Cashmere goat
PASSE faded; out of date; old-fashioned (Fr.)
ga **PASSE** 17 to 36 at roulette
PASTE to stick; an adhesive
ck **PASTY** glutinous; patty; a pie
PATCH cobble; botch; mend; small area; (eye) (ice-skating)
cp **PATCH** routine for correcting mistakes
rl **PATEN** eucharistic plate
PATER father
cf **PATHO-** suffering; diseased; abnormal (Gr.)
-PATHY ditto; also treatment
PATIO courtyard
tx **PATTE** ash-band (Fr.)
ck **PATTY** a small pie; dumpling-shaped concoction
PAUSE rest; hesitate; interval (concert)
mu **PAUSA** break in music (It.)
PAVAN a dance (Sp.); a dream; fantasy
PAVED tesselated
PAVER pavier; pavement layer
PAVID timid

PAVON lance pennon
PAWED fingered; scraped
PAWKY sly; crafty; shrewd
PAYED moored (by ropes) (covered with pitch)
PAYED remunerated; paid (in cash)
PAYEE receiver of payments
PAYER rewarder; liquidator
pr **PAYNE** decorative floral printing style
PEACE harmony; concord; repose
bt **PEACH** to divulge
bt **PEACH** fruit; sweetheart
PEAKY sickly
pr **PEARL** a gem (oyster); mother (shell); fall; wave for surfing; a size of type
PEASE peas as pudding
PEATY like peat
to **PEAVY** lumberman's hook
bt **PECAN** American nut
me **PECUL** Chinese weight, 133 lb (60 kg)
PEDAL to cycle
cf **PEDIA-** concerning children, infants (Gr.)
PEDUM shepherd's crook
ga, mu **PEELS** equal shots (curling); rounds of bells
PEERY peg top
zo **PEGGY** a warbler; bird
zo **PEKAN** the fisher-marten
PEKOE black tea (China)
PELLS records; rolls of parchment
md **PELMA** sole of foot
PELTA light shield or buckler
PENAL punitive; disciplinary
nm **PENCE** pennies; (Peter)
pl **PENIS** male reproductive organ; phallus
zo **PENNA** a feather
nm **PENNY** a denarius
bt **PEONY** piony; a plant
me **PERCH** pole; 5½ yd (5 m)
zo, bt, pc **PERCH** fish, roost; seat; fixation pause
PERIL risk; hazard; danger; jeopardy
PERKY smart; lively; brisk
PERMA- Siberian/Arctic continuous -frost
tx **PERMO** lustre; dress fabric
PERRY fermented pear juice
tx, wv **PERSE** dark blue; a cloth
PESKY irksome; trying; vexatious
bt **PETAL** a flower leaf
nt, rl, ga **PETER** blue flag; rock (cards)
PETIT mignon; petty; trivial
ch **PETRE** saltpetre
nt **PETTY** trivial; unimportant; -officer
PHARO **FARO**, a game of chance
cp, el **PHASE** stage of development; (moon); aspect; guise; periodic operation quantity; electrical cyclic motion; conduct a planned series on scheduled basis
PHEON the broad arrow
PHIAL **VIAL**, ampulla (flask for a potion)
PHILO- **-PHILE**, fond of; loving; freindly towards (Gr.)
bt **PHLOX** flowering plant
cf **-PHOBE** hater of; averse to; anti- (Gr.)
zo **PHOCA** genus of seals (seadogs)
tc, cf **-PHONE** speech, sound (telephone); lingual factor (Gr.)
cf **PHONO-** science of sound, speech, word phonetics (Gr.)
cf **-PHOTO** **PHOTO-**, of light reactions, pictures, transmission (Gr.)
pl **PHREN** the head, brain, mind; mentality; psychology
cf **PHYLA** **PHYLO-**, classifications of kind, genus (Gr.)
md **PHYMA** tubercle
mu **PIANO** softly; keyboard
bt **PICEA** spruce genus
PICOT little lace loop
md **PICRA** powdered aloes
me **PICUL** pecul; Chinese weight
zo **PICUS** woodpecker
ck **PIDAN** preserved duck egg
zo **PI-DOG** Indian pariah dog; stray; scavenger
PIECE part of (theatre, music etc.) (-together)
mu **PIENO** all performing (It.)
rl **PIETA** holy picture
PIETY holiness; sanctity
me **PIEZE** pressure unit
PIGMY small race (Africa)
PIKED armed with pikes
ck **PILAV** **PILAU**, **PILAFF**, savoury rice dish
PILCH fur or flannel gown
PILED amassed; heaped; erected
PILER gatherer
nt, nv, ga, cp **PILOT** guide; steer; direct; (-boat); croquet; experimental; effort; processing representative; sample
PILUM heavy javelin
bt **PILUS** a botanical hair
ck **PINCH** squeeze; grasp; (-of salt)
PINED languished; drooped
go, gl **PINGO** frozen hill (tundra) (Eskimo)
ch **PINIC** an acid

nt **PINKY** small boat; dinghy
zo **PINNA** wing-like structure
md **PINNA** bone in ear/nose
PINNY pinafore
md **PINTA** tropical Amer. skin disease
zo **PINTO** spotted American bean; piebald horse
PIN-UP cut-out romantic wall picture
PIOUS devout; godly; religious
PIPED canalized; shouted
mu **PIPER** (bagpipes)
zo **PIPIT** tit-lark
PIQUE vexation
PISTE track; footprint; ski-way
mu **PITCH** toss; hurl; locate; tar; emphasis; acoustics; voice
gl **PITCH** angle of inclination of axis in fold
nt **PITCH** heaving of ship in storm; camping
ga **PITCH** play area; sports ground (baseball); position of ball (croquet, fencing)
PITHY terse; concise; laconic
mo **PITON** iron spike for ropes (climbing); peak tapering to a point
PITOT tube recording air speed
PIVOT hinge; axle; axis; centre
PIXIE pixy; a fairy; elf
ck **PIZZA** Italian savoury 'pie'
cp **PLACE** site; scene; post; assign; digit position in ordered set
as **PLAGE** spectroheliogram spot
PLAGE continental seaside resort
tx, wv **PLAID** a tartan; a maud; clothing (Sc.)
go **PLAIN** prairie; obvious; simple; grass lands; steppes; unelaborate
PLAIT weave; twine; braid
to, bt **PLANE** level; flat; smooth; a tree; slide specimen
PLANK sawn timber; lay down
bt **PLANT** inculcate; sow; machinery; place in reserve; evidence (frame-up)
PLASH plesh; pool; weave; splash
PLASM mould or matrix
ch **PLATE** silver ware; to overlay; wrought silver & gold; electro-plated silver
PLATE accumulator electrode; ceramic; window glass; dish
PLATE competition prize (money); (quantity plateful)
PLATO Greek philosopher
PLATT ore dump
cf **PLATY-** of broad, flat shape (platypus) (Gr.)
go **PLAYA** beach; dryable wetlands (Sp.)
PLAZA public square; market place
PLEAD argue; reason; entreat
PLEAT fold
PLEBS common people; proletariat
mu **PLEIN** full organ stops mixed max (Fr.)
cf **PLEIO-** of more; increase
zo **PLEON** abdominal region in crustacea
PLIED folded; carried on; ferried
PLIES (plural) ply, laminate (wood)
PLUCK pick; cull
PLUCK valour; daring; mettle; courage
PLUFF to puff
PLUMB vertical; to fathom level
PLUME feather; crest; to pride (nom de)
PLUMP stout; chubby; corpulent
PLUMY feathered
wv, tx **PLUSH** a material long-pile cut velvet
PLYER transport worker
me **PMEST** formula; personality; matter; energy; space; time
ck **POACH** coddle (eggs); steal animals (game)
POCKY pitted
zo **PODEX** anal region
PODGE a fat man; a puddle
PODGY short and fat; pudgy
POESY poetry; a posy
zo **POGGE** armed bull-head fish
POILU French soldier; unshaven
lw **POIND** distrain
cp, mu **POINT** aim; tip; apex; sharpen; remark; fixed; floating; decimal; identify; pedal; organ; score
me **POISE** deportment; balance; viscosity
POKAL a drinking cup; prize (Ger.)
POKED thrust; jabbed; prodded
POKER cards; (red hot-)
el **POLAR** opposite (magnetic) (current flow)
md **POLIO** infantile paralysis
gl **POIJE** large limestone depression
mu **POLKA** a dance (Polish); (Bohemian)
zo **POLLY** parrot
md, zo **POLYP** coral; sea; anemone; a growth in humans
zo **PONGO** orang-utan, primate of Indonesia
gl **PONOR** vertical downshaft in karst sink-hole caves

rl **POOJA** Hindu ritual; obeisance
go **POORT** col or pass (S. Africa)
bt **POPPY** (opium) flower
PORCH portico; entrance; stoa
PORED examined diligently
PORER student
pl, gl **PORES** sweat excretion glands (skin); granular soil cavities
zo **PORGY** porgie; a sea-fish (Bess)
PORKY fat (super piglet)
md **PORTA** transverse fissure; liver
PORTE (sublime) Ottoman government
POSED perplexed; masqueraded
POSER an attitudinizer
POSIT to affirm; postulate
POSSE power; force of constables
zo **POTTO** West African sloth
POTTY petty; small; dotty
POUCHE cortex particles in flax roughing
POUCH bag; wallet; sack; steal
zo **POULP** a cephalopod
ck **POULT** **POULTRY**, fowl (edible)
zo, nm, me **POUND** to crush; strike repeatedly; enclosure; money; unit of weight
POUZE refuse of crushed apples
zo **POWAN** Loch Lomond fish
zo **POWER** force; faculty; control
zo **POYOU** armadillo
nt **PRAAM** a barge; small cargo coaster, Northern Europe
PRADO art gallery, Madrid
nt **PRAHU** Malay boat
PRANG a crash landing; destroy
PRANK practical joke; caper; frolic
mn **PRASE** green quartz
PRATE babble; chatter; jabber
zo **PRAWN** a crustacean
nt **PREDY** ready for action
PREEN to clean the feathers
PRESS crush; urge; crowd; hurry; burden; newspapers; linen; juice extractor; press-ups (gymn) (fencing) basketball
PREXY college president (USA)
PRICE cost; charge; rate; reward
pl **PRICK** perforate; mark; penis
PRIDE arrogance; hauteur; conceit
PRIED peeped; spied; snooped
PRIER pryer; a nosey parker
PRIMA first; leading; (-donna)
pr **PRIMA** repeated, resumption mark
pt, ps **PRIME** chief; principal; zenith; first quality; prepare by charging (oil stoves, explosives, gas lamps); pre-paint coating; prize cycling
mu **PRIMO** leading part
PRINT stamp; brand; impress
rl **PRIOR** previous; earlier; cf. abbot
PRISE to lever
PRISM refracting glass
PRIVY private; outdoor toilet; parts (genitals); councillor
PRIZE esteem; reward; booty (ship, -money); salvage; premium; sports cup; (boxing) (racing)
PROBE scrutinize; examine; prove
PRONE face downwards; apt to; rifleman's firing position; with tendency to
to **PRONG** the tine of a fork
lw, ck, cp, pr **PROOF** test; ordeal; impenetrable; evidence (whisky); (water-); study; first print; control
PROPS theatrical properties (scenery etc.)
PROSE non verse writing
cf **PROSO-** of matters ahead; future (Gr.)
PROSY prolix; tedious; vapid
cf **PROTO-** of beginning, original, primitive (Gr.)
PROUD vain; imperious; stately
PROVE evince; verify; examine
PROWL prey; stalk; rove; slink
PROXY substitute; deputy; agent
PRUDE person of intolerant modesty
ck **PRUNE** dried plum
gs **PRUNT** applied glass badge mass
mn **PRYAN** felspathic clay
PRYER prier; snooper
mu **PSALM** sacred song sung to a harp
PSHAW! belittling exclamation
md **PSOAS** tenderloin
md **PSORA** the itch
zo **PTERE** a wing (-dactyl)
pl **PUBES** genital zone of abdomen
pl **PUBIC** of genital/loin region
md **PUBIS** pelvic bones
PUDGY podgy; fat; fleshy
PUFFY tumid; swollen; bombastic
PUGIL a pinch of
PUKKA veritable; genuine (Hindu)
PULED whined
PULER a whimperer
zo **PULEX** the flea
PULKA Lapland sledge
PULPY soft; succulent
ck, md, bt, ps, el **PULSE** a lentil; to throb; beat; transient disturbance
PUMPS evening shoes (dancing) (men's)
PUNCH pummel; pierce; horse; chisel; (Mr puppet)
nt **PUNGY** Chesapeake Bay schooner

PUNIC Carthaginian; faithless
PUNKA punkah; Indian fan
mu **PUNTA** with the point of the bow of violin (It.)
ga, mu **PUNTO** fencing; Cuban dance
to **PUNTY** glass blower's iron
zo **PUPAL** in the chrysalis state
pl **PUPIL** learner; tyro; alumni; (eye); alumnus
zo **PUPPY** whelp; novice
ck **PUREE** thick soup; strained pulp
PURER cleaner; more chaste
mt **PURGA BURAN, NW** tundra wind (Siberia)
PURGE cleanse; absolve; shrive
PURIM Jewish feast
zo **PURRE** the dunlin bird
PURSE to wrinkle; money-bag
PURSY fat and asthmatic
bt, zo **PUSSY** willow catkin; tame cat
PUTID putrid; worthless
ck **PUTOO** nut-meal
PUTTI chubby Baroque child image
PUTTY cement with linseed oil
PUT-UP preconcerted
ga **PUTZI** Chinese game
go **PUZTA** Pannonian plain (Hungary)
PYGAL related to backsides
PYGMY pigmy; midget; Lilliputian
PYLON gateway; turning mark; tower; tow-rope hitch (water-skiing)
md **PYOID** pus-like
PYRAL (funeral pyre)
ch **PYRAN** cyclic carbon/oxygen compound
bt **PYRUS** apple or pear genus
rl **PYXIS** pyx; sacred box

Q

QANAT GANAT, KANAT, underground irrigation system (Oman)
nt **Q-BOAT** disguised armed ship
ar **QIBLA** mihrab wall, mosque
QUACK charlatan; humbug; empiric; cry
QUADS quadruplets
QUAFF gulp; swallow; drink deep
mu, zo **QUAIL** cower; flinch; small bird; toy musical instrument with birdsong
gl **QUAKE QUAKY,** tremble; quiver; unstable; shaky; (earth-)
QUALE having independent existence
QUALM scruple; pang; throe
QUANK sound a rhino makes
QUANT punt or jumping pole
QUARK hypothetical sub-atomic entity
ck **QUARK** curd cheese (Ger.)
QUARL a segment of fireclay
zo **QUARL** jellyfish
me **QUART** (cards); 2 pints (1.13 litres)
QUASH nullify; annul; override
QUASI as it were; virtually; pretence; false
cp **QUASI** excess data
cf **QUASI-** seemingly; resembling (Gr.)
QUASS KVASS, Russian beer
QUEAN transvestite; gay
ga **QUEEN** (cards); (chess); (royal); (bee); gay
QUEER odd; rummy; curious; strange; gay
QUELL suppress; crush; quench
QUERK to throttle; to grunt
QUERL to twirl; a coil
QUERN primitive stone handmill
QUERY question; dispute; ask
QUEST search; pursuit; inquiry
QUEUE a hopeful tail
QUICK fleet; agile; brisk; alive
QUIET still; calm; lull; pacify
QUIFF a curly lock
QUI-HI Anglo–Indian
zo **QUILL** a feather; a pen
QUILP a hideous dwarf
QUILT twilt; counterpane
md **QUINA** quinne
QUINS quintuplets
mu **QUINT** sequence of five; organ stop
QUIPO QUIPU, mnemonic Inca language; coloured and knotted cords
me **QUIRE** choir; 24 sheets
QUIRK twist; subterfuge; evasion
QUIRT riding whip
QUITE fully; exactly; entirely
QUITS acquittance; clear of debt
QUOAD as far as
QUOIT discus
QUOTA share; portion; allotment
QUOTE cite; mention; adduce
QUOTH spake; said; remarked
rl **QURAN KORAN,** Moslem Holy Book

R

rl **RABBI** Jewish religious teacher
md, zo **RABID** furious; violent; result of rabies bite
RABOT marble polisher
RACED ran; hurried; competed
RACER that races; competes

RACON remote-object identifying beacon
RADAR radio-location
zo **RADGE** rodge; grey duck; gadwall
RADII plural of radius
nc, ro **RADIO** telegram; wireless (-active)
ma, bt **RADIX** (logarithms); a root
ch **RADON** radioactive element
nt **RAFFE** three-cornered sail
RAFTY damp; musty
RAGED raved; fumed; stormed
rw **RAILS** safety fence; iron road; surrounds (surfing)
RAINY showery
RAISE erect; uplift; exalt; breed
RAJAH Indian prince
RAKED enfiladed; searched; combed
RAKER ransacker; scraper
bd **RAKER** inclined tubular scaffolding
RALLY arouse; recover; (tennis); banter
RALLY mass meeting (motor sports; party)
zo **RALPH** a mischievous raven
RAMAL branching
nt **RAMED** framed on the stocks
RAMET asexual offspring of clone
md **RAMEX** hernia; rupture
nt **RAMIE** ramee; rope fibre
tx **RAMIE** Chinese grass for banknotes, textiles
RAMMY strongly scented
bt **RAMUS** branch; twig; spray
RANCE a rocket trough
RANCH stock-farm; (dude); estate
RANDY sexually rampant
RANDY a virago; a romp; a beggar
RANEE rani; Indian queen
RANGE array; align; scope; roam; distance; habitat
RANGE variation limits; mountain chains; (kitchen)
RANGY long-limbed and slender
RANTY boisterous; vociferous
RAPED violated; outraged; ravished
RAPID fast; fleet; swift; hasty
hd **RAPIN** devouring animal
RARER scarcer; more uncommon
mu **RASCH** (Ger.) rushed/rushing/in a rush
RASED **RAZED**, erased; effaced; demolished; blotted out
RASPY rough; scratchy; abrasive
zo **RASSE** small civet
RATAL rate value
zo **RATAN** rattan; cane
RATCH pawl; ratchet; rack
RATED assessed; chid; scolded; valued
RATEE a person being rated
zo **RATEL** honey-badger
nt **RATER** assessor; (yachting)
RATIO proportion; rate; quota
RATTY irascible; irate; angry
RAVED raged; ranted; drivelled
RAVEL entangle; twist together
zo **RAVEN** large crow-like bird
RAVER a maniac
RAVIN raven; prey; plunder; rapine
RAWLY unskilfully; immaturely
RAYAH Ottoman non-Moslem
RAYED shone; arrayed
tx **RAYON** artificial silk
RAZOR shaving device
REACH expanse; stretch; scope
REACT recoil; resist; repeat
READY prompt; alert; willing
REALM kingdom; domain
tx **REAMY** novely yarn
RE-ARM re-equip (defence)
mu **REBEC** **REBECK**, Moorish fiddle (violin)
REBEL revolt; rise; insurgent
REBID (auction)
REBUS a pictorial puzzle
REBUT confute; disprove; rebuff
RECAP redescribe briefly
RECCE reconnaissance
go, nv **RECIF** reef or bar (S. Africa)
mu **RECIT** swell of organ
RECTO right-hand page
RECUR reappear; revert; resort
REDAN earthwork; redoubt
mu **REEDY** a thin tone (woodwind)
nv **REEFY** full of rocks
REEKY smoky; vaporous
lw **REEVE** steward; sheriff; rope
zo **REEVE** the female ruff; a bird
REFER submit; relate; advert
REFIT repair; re-equip
mu **REGAL** royal; kingly; princely; a reed-organ portable, for churches
REGET regain; recover
REGIE government monopoly; control
bt **REGMA** botanical capsule
REICH German realm
REIFY to materialize
REIGN rule; govern; control
REIVE **REAVE**, to ravage
RELAX abate; slacken; loosen
RELAY team race; pass on
RELET to offer on hire again
RELIC memento; souvenir; keepsake; survival from past

RELIT rekindled; re-illuminated
ae, nt **REMAN** get a fresh crew
REMIT send by post; release; postpone
pl, md **RENAL RENES**, of the kidneys
RENEW renovate; refurbish, restore
REPAY refund; recompense; avenge
REPEL repulse; parry; withstand
md **REPET** repeat; the same again
REPLY echo; answer; respond
REPOT transplant
cp **RE-RUN** repeat; commence again; restart after error or fiasco
RESAW saw again; revisualized
pr **RESET** reprint with alterations; adjust
bt **RESIN** rosin; confier gum
ch **RESOL** synthetic resin
ag **RE-SOW** to sow again
md **RETCH** attempt to vomit; strain
cf **RETRO-** predated, from the past (Gr.)
lw **RE-TRY** try again; new trial
REVEL feast; carouse; luxuriate
mu **REVUE** variety entertainment
REWET part of a wheel-lock
REWIN regain
cf, md **-RHAGE** of bleeding; discharge (Gr.)
bt **RHEIC** (rhubarb)
ch **RHEIN** chrysophanic acid
RHEMA word, verb (Gr.)
md **RHEUM** water mucous discharge
RHINE wine; ditch; (-stone) gem
cf, pl, zo **RHINO-** of the nose (Gr.)
ma **RHOMB** a rhombohedron; geometrical shape
bd **RHONE RONE**, eaves gutter
nt, as **RHUMB** sky compass; (stars)
RHYME rime; poetry; metre
bt **RHYNE** Russian hemp
bt **RIBES** currant genus
ck **RICER** machine for mincing food
ch **RICEN** castor bean albumin
RIDER horseman; added clause
go **RIDGE** ledge; crest; weal; range
RIDGY furrowed; corrugated
RIFLE ransack; strip; to groove
RIGEL a star in Orion
RIGHT due; equity; privilege
RIGID staunch; unbending; strict
RIGOL a diadem; crown; coronet
md **RIGOR** rigour; rigidity
md **RIGOR** shivering, chill (of death)
RILED angered; annoyed
RILLE lunar valley
RIMED frosted
to **RIMER** an enlarging tool
RINGE heather whisk
RINGS pair for hanging gymnasts
ga **RINKS** fours (bowls); ice floors (skating)
RINSE lave; clean; wash
RIOJA Spanish wine
RIPEN mature; develop; perfect
RIPER further advanced
RIPON a spur
RISEL support for a vine
RISEN ascended; mounted; revolted
RISER rebel; stair-board; handle, centre of bow (archery); early bird
RISHI poet; Vedic seer
RISKY hazardous; speculative
zo **RISSA** kittiwake genus
go **RITHE** small stream
RITZY luxurious; presumptuously; sham
RIVAL vie; emulate; match; equal
RIVEL to wrinkle; shrivel
RIVEN rived; rent; split
RIVER stream; torrent; tributary
RIVET fasten; metal bolt
nm **RIYAL** Sudanese coin
bt **RIZOM** head of corn or oats
nt, zo **ROACH** part of sail; a fish
ROAST parch; chaff outrageously
ROBED garbed; attired; arrayed
zo **ROBIN** national bird; circular appeal
bt **ROBLE** Californian white oak
ROBOT an automaton
ROCKY stony; shaky; unsteady
mu **ROCTA** ancient violin
RODEO cattle round-up; competitive spectacle
zo **RODGE** radge; grey duck; gadwell
ro **ROGER** wireless call – over
ROGUE knave; rascal; scamp
bl, pc **ROGUE** genetic variant/exception (-elephant, wild, dangerous mood)
bt **ROHAN** red-wood mahogany tree
ROIST to bluster; to swagger
zo **ROKER** thornback; ray; skate
ROMAL kerchief; raw hide whip
ROMAN citizen of Rome; (-Empire)
ROMEO a lover
ROMER (Rhineland) broad wine glass
ROMIC a phonetic notation
hd **ROMPU** heraldic fracture
pr **ROMPY** rampageous
RONDE round-hand type (Fr.)
mu **RONDE RONDO**, dance; music in several strains
ROOKY new recruit
ROOMY spacious
ROOST a fowl support; to perch
ck **ROOTY** radical; bread (India)

ROPED tied; lashed; bound
ga **ROQUE** a form of corquet (Fr.)
RORAL RORIC, ROSCID, moist with dew
bt, ck **ROSIN RESIN** (conifer gum) (wine)
ROTAL according to roster
ps **ROTON** quantum of rotational energy
ROTOR a machine; airfoil; wind turbulence (aeronautics)
ga **ROUGE** (Eton wall gamc); cosmetic; point for Can. football
ROUGH rugged; crude; coarse; long grass areas on golf course
mu **ROUND** convex; rotund; period (tour); canon; (visits); (a table)
ROUND shot; in a circle; (drinks); (contest); cut; series
ROUSE awaken; annoy; disturb
ROUTE way; course; itinerary
ROVED roamed; wandered; rambled
ga **ROVER** nomad; pirate; (croquet); (Australian football)
bt **ROWAN** mountain ash
ROWDY ruffian; rough; boisterous; drunk and disorderly; noisy
ROWED sculled; upbraided
ROWEL spurwheel (riding)
ROWEN second hay crop
ROWER oarsman
ROYAL regal; superb; august
ROYLE to rile; to salt fish
RUADE parallel turn (skiing)
nt **RUATA** junklike craft (Siam)
bt **RUBIA** madder genus
nm **RUBLE ROUBLE,** Russian monetary unit
bt **RUBUS** bramble genus
RUCHE plaited trimming
RUDDY rubicund; red
RUDER coarser; cruder
zo **RUDGE** a partridge
zo **RUFFE** ruff; freshwater perch
ga **RUGBY** (football); (school)
RUING regretting; lamenting
RULED lined; governed; decided
RULER monarch; regent; dictator
RUMAL -romal; shawl (Hindu)
mu **RUMBA** Cuban dance
RUMBO rum punch
RUMEN paunch of ruminant
bt **RUMEX** sorrel genus
ga **RUMMY** odd; queer; card game
bt **RUNCH** crunch; the wild charlock
RUNER bard
RUNIC ancient Scandinavian script
me, lw, pr **RUN-IN** the finish in racing; to train a new motor; arrest (police); merge paragraphs
RUNNY liquid
pr **RUN-ON** process of continuing; unbroken
pr **RUN-UP** gold band, binding; approach run (jump); last preparations before event; sew a garment rapidly; hoist a flag; accumulate debts
nm **RUPEE** 16 annas
md **RUPIA** skin disease
RURAL Arcadian; sylvan; pastoral
RUSHY full of rushes
RUSTY corroded; out of practice
RUTTY uneven; furrowed; grooved

S

bt **SABAL** a fan palm genus
SABER cavalry sword (USA)
ac **SABIN** unit of acoustic absorption
zo **SABLE** antelope; marten; fur
hd **SABLE** black; dusty; sombre
SABOT wooden shoe; (-age)
SABRA SABRE, native of Israel; cavalry sword
SADHU Hindu ascetic
SADLY gloomily; dismally; mournfully
SAFER surer; more secure
rl **SAGAN** Jewish priest
SAGER wiser; cleverer
zo **SAGRA** bettle genus
SAGUM Roman cloak
SAHIB boss (white) (India)
zo **SAIGA** puff-nosed antelope
rl **SAINT** to canonize; one venerated
rl **SAITH SAYS,** Biblical usage
rl **SAIVA** votary of Siva
zo **SAJOU** American monkey
SAKIA Persian water-wheel
ck **SALAD** mixed cold dish
bt **SALAL** evergreen shrub
zo **SALDA** a bug genus
bt, ck **SALEP SALOP,** orchis root beverage
lw **SALIC** male succession; law
ch **SALIN** saline; a salt
bt **SALIX** willow genus
SALLE salon; hall (Fr.)
pr **SALLE** paper-sorting room
SALLY bell-rope tufting, outburst; wit
zo **SALLY** a stone-fly; a wren
ck **SALMI** hashed game
zo **SALMO** salmon genus
SALON saloon; hall
zo **SALPA** genus of sea-squirts
gl, go **SALSE** volcanic mud

md **SALTS** saline draughts
SALTY witty; briny; saline
SALVE save; rescue; heal; a remedy
SALVO an exception; a volley
mu **SAMBA** dance (S. American)
ga **SAMBO** official Fila-style (wrestling)
zo **SAMIA** silk-worms genus
SAMMY American Tommy; G.I., footsoldier (N. Amer.)
SANDY yellowish red
SANER less idiotic; more normal
mu **SANSA** tambourine
SAPID savoury; affected; palatable
SAPOR **SAVOUR**, flavour; taste
SAPPY juicy; succulent; weak
zo **SARDA** mackerel; tunny genus
mu **SAROD** **SAROH**, Indian guitar
as **SAROS** an astronomical cycle
SARSE a fine sieve
SARUM Salisbury; (rotten borough)
zo **SASIA** pigmy woodpeckers (Ind.)
zo **SASIN** antelope; Indian blackbuck
SASSE Dutch weir with flood-gates
rl **SATAN** Devil; Lucifer; Beelzebub
SATED replete; surfeited; cloyed
tx **SATIN** glossy fabric
SATIS enough (Latin)
rl **SATYR** goat-like sylvan deity; Pan
SAUCE impudence; a condiment; relish
SAUCY pert; bold; malapert; flippant
nm **SAUDI** gold sovereign (Arabia)
go **SAULT** a rapid (Canadian)
SAUNA Finnish steam-bath
zo **SAURY** skipper-fish
ck **SAUTE** boiled, then fried
SAVED rescued; freed; redeemed; kept
SAVER a hoarder; an economist
bt **SAVIN** evergreen conifer
SAVOR savour; taste; odour; relish
bt **SAVOY** curly cabbage
SAVVY commonsense; nous; gumption
SAWED cut with a saw; sawn
SAXON of Saxony
SAYER a speaker; an assayer
SAYON medieval peasant's jacket
SAY-SO a dictum
md **SCALA** a surgical instrument
bt **SCALD** the dodder-plant; a burn
SCALD skald; Scandinavian bard
zo, mu **SCALE** climb; balance; flake; lamina; (fish-); proportion and size; exact drawing; sol-fa application
md **SCALL** leprosy; a scab; mean
SCALP skin + hair of the head; trophy
SCALY encrusted; shabby; mean
SCAMP rogue; knave; stint
SCANT to stint; scarcely sufficient
bt **SCAPE** leafless peduncle bearing flowers
SCAPE shaft; stem; fault
SCARD shard; sherd; fragment
SCARE alarm; appal; dismay; daunt
SCARF neckerchief; a carpenter's joint
zo **SCARF** cormorant; scart; skart
hd **SCARP** heraldic scarf; rampart slope
SCART to scratch; scrape; a niggard
SCARY timid; frightening; windy
SCATT **SCAT**, tax; (-free)
zo **SCAUP** a sea-duck
go **SCAUR** river bank; rocky cliffs; scar
mu **SCENA** stage of an ancient theatre; operatic unit of aria; duet etc
SCENE show; pageant; sight; view
SCENT perfume; odour; redolence; trail
SCHUT cattle-pound (South Africa)
SCION offshoot; branch; descendant
SCOAT scote; to scotch; to wedge
SCOBS shavings; sawdust; dross
zo **SCOBY** **SCOBBY**, the chaffinch
SCOFF sneer; mock; deride
SCOLD rate; upbraid; censure; chide
ck **SCONE** coronation stone; a confection
SCOON skim along the water
SCOOP dig; hollow; excavate; ladle
pr **SCOOP** gliding singing; journalists' (–)
SCOOT decamp; bolt; run
zo **SCOPA** stiff hairs of moths
SCOPE room; space; liberty; object
cf **-SCOPE** viewing instrument (Gr.)
zo **SCOPS** screech-owl
cf **-SCOPI** **-SCOPY**, viewing scrutiny (Gr.)
mu **SCORE** record; mark; furrow; scratch; music in parts form; printed
SCORN spurn; deride; mock; disdain
cf **SCOTO-** of darkness (Gr.)
SCOTS of Scotland; Scottish
SCOUR scrub; scrape; purge
SCOUT to explore; reconnoitre
zo **SCOUT** the guillemot; razor-bill
SCOVE to tamp; to poise
SCOVY smeared; blotched
SCOWL frown; lower; glower
bt **SCRAB** crab-apple; to scratch; scrape
SCRAG to throttle; odd lean bit
SCRAM! clear off! get out!
nc **SCRAM** emergency plant shutdown

SCRAN skran; scraps of food
SCRAP bit; atom; particle; tussle
SCRAT a devil; a goblin; monster
SCRAW a turf; a sod (Irish)
zo **SCRAY** sea-swallow
gl, mo **SCREE** slope of loose rock face (talus)
SCREW twist; copulate
tx **SCRIM** strong muslin lining for walls
SCRIP wallet; purse; satchel
lw **SCRIP** (receipt for) share certificates
zo **SCROD** to shed; young codfish
go **SCROG** stunted bush; thicket
bt, go **SCRUB** clean; scour; maquis; stunted growth land
SCRUM (rugby football)
SCUBA underwater breathing apparatus
nm **SCUDO** Italian silver dollar
SCUFF scurf; a scale; to shuffle
SCUFT **SCRUFF**, the nape of the neck
nt **SCULL** an oar; a cockboat; to row
zo **SCULL** skua-gull; a shoal of fish
SCULP to carve; to engrave; to flay
zo **SCURF** dandruff; scum; bull-trout
zo **SCUTE** a shield; scale of fish
SEAMY dark; sordid; nasty
zo **SEA-OX** the walrus
SEAVE a wick made of a rush
bt **SEAVY** overgrown with rushes
SEBAT 5th month of the Jewish year
zo **SEBUM** sebaceous gland excretion
mu **SECCO** a fresco; unaccompanied
SEDAN carrying chair
bt **SEDGE** **SEDGY**, reeds; overgrown grass; flock of herons
SEEDY shabby; run to seed; unwell
ga **SEEGA** board game (Egypt, Somalia)
mu **SEGNO** repetition
mu **SEGUE** follow on at once (It.)
SEINE large fishing net
SEISM an earthquake
SEITY personality; selfhood
SEIZE grasp; clutch; grapple; impound
SEKOS Greek sanctuary
SELAH a pause in the Psalms
go **SELVA** tropical rainforest (Brazil)
zo **SEMEN** fluid containing spermatozoa
SEMIC pertaining to a sign
nm **SEMIS** Roman bronze coin, half an as
SENAL a landmark (South America)
SENCH to cause to founder
zo **SENEX** S. American hawk; a swift
md **SENNA** dried cassia leaves
SENOR Spanish title of address
pc **SENSE** wisdom; reason; receptive perception; detect; notice
cp **SENSE** (common); (intuition); perception system
mu **SENZA** without
bt **SEPAL** calyx segment
zo **SEPIA** genus of cuttlefish; pigment
SEPIC done in sepia
SEPOY native Indian soldier
gl, go **SERAC** glacial ice
SERAI caravanserai; Seljuk Turkish inn
tx **SERGE** twilled fabric
SERIC Chinese; silken
pr **SERIF** short cross-line in typography
zo **SERIN** song-bird; canary
gl **SERIR** gravel desert (reg), Libya
SERON bale of exotic produce
zo **SEROW** Asiatic goat
gl **SERRA** **SIERRA**, saw (serrated) mountain ridge
mu **SERRE** tightened, with tension, speed
SERRY to crowd together
md **SERUM** antibody for inoculation
SERVE do; act; suit; aid; obey; attend
ga **SERVE** put ball into play (court games)
au, cp **SERVO** braking system; difference minimizer
rl **SESHA** Serpent-King (Hindu)
zo **SESIA** clear-wing moths
SESSA hurry!
bt, zo **SETAE** bristles; cat's whiskers
md **SETON** a dressing
SET-TO an affray
SET-UP scheme; plot; locate; unit
SEVEN cardinal number
SEVER cut; part; sunder; detach
SEWED stitched; threaded
SEWEL a scarecrow
zo **SEWEN** sewin; salmon type
SEWER drain
rl **SEXTE** sixth hour service
SEXTO a size of book
S'FOOT by Jesus' foot! an imprecation
SHACK a shed; to tramp; a vagabond
SHADE hue; tint; veil; cover; screen
SHADY shadowy; obscure; doubtful
SHAFT arrow; missile; handle; pit
nm **SHAHI** Persian copper coin
mu **SHAKE** jar; jolt; agitate; quiver; dance; shudder; trill (ornamental)
SHAKO chako; military cap
SHAKY tottering; unstable; loose
mn **SHALE** shaly clay; husk

SHALL future auxiliary verb
SHALT future auxiliary verb
SHALY laminated and friable
zo, bt **SHAMA** Indian song-bird; cereal
SHAME abash; mortify; infamy
SHAND shame; base coin; worthless
pl **SHANK** (golf); the tibia
SHAPE mould; fashion; form; image
zo **SHAPO** wild sheep of Tibet
SHARD **SHERD**, fragment; wing case
SHARE divide; quota; (stocks & –s)
SHARK predatory fish or financier; cheat
mu **SHARP** fine; thin; keen; caustic
SHAVE pare; clip; shear; skim; graze
SHAWL a wrap
mu **SHAWM** **SHALM**, proto-oboe
ag **SHEAF** bundle of harvested wheat
SHEAL to shell; to husk
SHEAR clip; cut; fleece; strip; force; retreat
SHEEN gloss; lustre; shine; polish
zo **SHEEP** a woolly ruminant
SHEER absolute; precipitous; turn aside
tx **SHEET** a bed-cloth; wide expanse; rope
SHEIK Arab chief
SHELF ledge; shoal; sandbank
nt **SHELL** case; husk; projectile; bombard; racing rowing boat (universities)
SHETH part of plough
SHEVA (Hebrew vowel point)
SHEWN **SHOWN**, displayed; revealed; taught
rl **SHIAH** Moslem sect
ga **SHIAI** tournament (judo)
SHIED (coconuts); (horses)
SHIEL **SHIELING**, sheep shelter
ma, cp, ga **SHIFT** chemise; vary; alter; trick; wile; change place; working hours; flexible arithmetic; realignment of forwards (Amer. football)
rl **SHIKO** prostrate veneration (Burma)
SHINE **SHINY**, radiate; glitter; polished
SHIRE county; draught-horse
SHIRK evade; avoid; neglect; malinger
SHIRL to slide
SHIRR to pucker; to wrinkle
SHIRT a blouse; distinctive garment
SHIVE a slice; a wooden bung
mn **SHOAD** fragments of ore
nv, nt, zo **SHOAL** swarm; throng; bank; bar; fishes
zo **SHOAT** young hog
ag **SHOCK** **STOOK**, pile of corn sheaves
SHOCK onset; disturbance; to disgust
SHOER a farrier; blacksmith
ga **SHOGI** chess variant (Japan)
SHOLA a wood; a thicket (Ind.)
SHOLE ground plank
SHONE radiated; sparkled; flashed
SHOOK cask staves; trembled; quaked
bt **SHOOT** emit; dart; fire; spout
go **SHORE** prop; brace; strand; beach
mn **SHORL** tourmaline
SHORN shaven; fleeced; clipped
SHORT terse; abrupt; laconic; pithy; wee
go **SHOTT** seasonal salt lake
SHOUT cry; cheer; call; bellow
SHOVE jostle; push; press; elbow
SHOWN presented; paraded; revealed
SHOWY gay; garish; loud; gaudy
ck **SHRED** cut into small pieces; scrap
SHREW dormouse; virago; scold
bt **SHRUB** a cordial; dwarf tree
SHRUG to draw up; contract
bt **SHUCK** a husk; shell or pod
el, rw **SHUNT** electrical diversion; sort a train
SHYLY shily; coyly; bashfully
SIBBE sibling; close of kin
SIBYL prophetess; witch; sorceress
nm **SICCA** newly coined; a rupee
SIDED flattened; biased
SIDER partisan; protagonist
SIDLE to go crabwise
SIEGE besiege; invest; city
SIEUR **SIRE**, title of respect
SIEVE to sift; to strain; a temse
cp **SIGHT** see; view; observe; scene; visual scan check
SIGIL signature; occult mark; seal
SIGMA a Greek letter; reactor circuit
ml **SILAL** high-silica cast iron
mn **SILEX** silica
SILKY silken
SILLY inane; inept; unwise; stupid
bt, fr **SILVA** **SYLVA**, forest area
tx **SIMAR** **CYMAR**, **CIMAR**, scarf; loose dress
zo **SIMIA** genus of apes
pl **SINAL** pertaining to sinus
SINCE after; subsequently; because
md, pl **SINEW** a tendon
SINGE sear; burn; scorch
SINIC Seric; Chinese
rl **SINTO** shinto; ancestor-worship (Jap.)
pl **SINUS** a cavity; a bay; nasal duct
SIOUX Dakota Indian

SIPED oozed; exuded; percolated
SIRED fathered; generated
SIREN syren; seducer; hooter
bt **SIRIH** betel-leaf (Malay)
bt **SISAL** fibrous plant, (ropemaking)
bt **SISON** stone parsley
SISSY sweetheart; a weakling
mu **SITAR** Indian long-necked lute
SITED placed, situated
SIT-IN demonstration by occupying premises
zo **SITTA** the nut-hatch
SIVAN Jewish month
mu **SIXTH** ordinal number; harmonic interval
SIXTY cardinal number
SIZED SIZER, graded; cut to size (-machine)
SIZEL SCISSEL, metal clipping
SKALD SCALD, Scandinavian bard
gl **SKARN** silicate-gangue mineral
zo **SKATE** scate; the ray; a roller-skate
zo **SKEET** the pollack; a long scoop
zo **SKEIN** coil of yarn; group of geese
bd **SKIDS** short planks; load-taking rail; unsinkable tube
SKIED SKIER, skied in the crowd; tourer on skis
SKIES the firmarment
nt **SKIFF** a light boat; to skim; sculling (university) boat
SKILL knack; address; art; facility
SKIMP stint; scamp; scanty
zo **SKINK** African lizard; a shin-bone
SKIRL a shrill cry or sound
SKIRR scurry; hasten; scour
SKIRT hem; border; skim; edge; part of target (archery); garment (ladies'); canvas cover of canoe; feathers on shuttle (badminton)
SKISH competiton (angling)
zo **SKITE** the yellow bunting
SKOAL Hail! a toast! (Scand.)
SKULK lurk; slink; cower; sneak
SKULL the sconce; the noddle
SLACK lax; loose; lazy; sluggish
SLACK shallow dell; small coal
SLADE valley; spade
SLAIE weaver's reed
SLAIN killed; despatched; murdered
SLAKE quench; extinguish; allay
SLANG argot; to scole; to abuse
SLANT tilt; list; lean; slope
SLASH cut; gash; slit; swipe
SLATE SLATY, roofing stone; reprimand
SLAVE serf; thrall; drudge; menial
ro, tc **SLAVE** (-stations of signal network)
SLEEK smooth; soft; glossy; silken
SLEEP doze; slumber; nap; siesta
SLEET snow mingled with rain
SLEPT drowsed; slumbered; rested
SLICE fire-shovel; cut; sever; piece; dip oar too deep; cause a ball to spin (golf) (cricket); (bread-)
nt **SLICK** plausible; efficient; oil spill
SLIDE skid; glide; transparency
mu **SLIDE** grace notes; trombone
SLIDE sliding seat (rower); microscope
S'LIFE God's Life imprecation
SLIME SLIMEY, ooze; mire; viscous; clammy
SLING hang; hurl; drink
SLINK move away secretly; lurk
SLIPE SLYPE, mining skip
SLIPS men's bathing trunks
SLIPS (theatre); (shipbuilding)
mn **SLOAM** clay between coal-beds
SLOAT slot; bar; bolt
nt **SLOOP** escort ship, yacht
SLOPE slant; shelve; grade; a ramp; (ski-); sneak off
SLOPS ready-made clothes; nightsoil (prison)
SLOSH slush; sludge; sentimentality
zo **SLOTH** torpor; tree bear; laziness
SLOYD Swedish handicrafts training
SLUED turned round; tipsy
SLUGS half-roasted ore
SLUMP collapse; sudden fall; marsh
SLUNG flung; thrown; suspended; cast
SLUNK lurked; cowered; skulked
SLUSH slosh; sludge; mire; bathos
SLYLY SLYER, more craftily; artfully
gl **SLYNE** face of a jointed rock
SLYPE narrow passage
nt **SMACK** coastal fishing vessel
SMALL tiny; petty; trivial; minute
SMALT blue glass; blue pigment
SMART rankle; pungent; trim; witty
SMASH crash; crack; disrupt; ruin
ga **SMASH** hard strokes (in ball games)
SMAZE smog and haze (N. Am. & Aus.)
SMEAR daub; plaster; sully begrime
SMELL scent; aroma; odour; perfume
zo **SMELT** stank; melt ore; small fish
SMIFT a fuse
SMILE smirk; grin; simper
SMIRK an affected smile
SMITE hit; buffet; knock; chasten
SMITH a metal worker; blacksmith
SMOCK a chemise; pastoral garment

ck **SMOKE** fume; (fire-); cure; tobacco-
zo **SMOLT** young river salmon
SMOTE struck (in battle)
zo **SMOUT** speckled trout
zo **SMUCK** a crowd of jellyfish
SNACK hasty light repast; a share
zo **SNAIL** spiral cam; mollusc
zo **SNAKE** serpent; reptile; currency link-up
SNAPE to bevel
SNARE gin; net; toil; wile; trap
SNARL gnarl; growl at; entangle
SNATH SNEAD, crooked
SNEAK lurk; slink; skulk; blab
SNEER gibe; mock; jeer; scoff
SNIDE spurious; dishonest; counterfeit
SNIFF to smell; inhale; scent; snuff
zo **SNIPE** to shoot from ambush; bird
zo **SNOEK** S. African fish; barracouta
SNOOD hairnet; a fillet
SNOOK lurk; snoop; derisive action
SNOOP to pry
SNORE loud breathing during sleep
SNORT loud exhalation through nostrils
gl **SNOUT** nose; nozzle; proboscis; glacial valley
SNOWY pure; unblemished; niveous
SNUFF sniff; (tobacco)
SOAPY unctuous; emollient; flattering
mu **SOAVE** sweetly
SOBER staid; sedate; steady; grave
zo **SOBOL** the Russian sable
cf **SOCIO-** of social; societal nature
SOCKS a drubbing; foot covers
SOCLE plinth
SODDY covered with sod; turfy
nv **SOFAR** underwater navigation system
SOFTA Moslem student
SOGGY boggy; marshy; wet; saturated
SOKEN socage district
bt **SOLAH** solar; sola; sponge-wood
as **SOLAR** concerning the sun (light, heat)
ar, bd **SOLAR** sunshine parlour; solarium
nm **SOLDO** Italian copper coin
ar **SOLEA** raised pathway
SOLED (boots)
zo **SOLEN** razor-fish genus
mu **SOL-FA** the major octave as sung
SOLID hard; dense; stout; stable
cp, bd **SOLID** (-state) electronic devices; door; floor, etc.
SOLON wise legislator; wiseacre
SOLUM piece of ground; soil
lw **SOLUS** alone; sole right, agreement
SOLVE elucidate; unravel; interpret
mu **SOMMA SOMMO**, highest; utmost
nt, nv **SONAR** underwater sound ranging
SONDE upper atmospheric probe; long tube
ae **SONIC** relating to sound; (super-)
cp **SONIC** acoustic delay line
SONNY term of endearment to son
SOOTH truth; reality; true; indeed
SOOTY begrimed
SOPOR deep sleep; moral lethargy
SOPPY moist; wet; silly; weak-minded
mu **SOPRA** above
SORAL pertaining to sorus
SORBO porous rubber
mu **SORDA** damped with a mute
md **SORDE** lips/teeth crust during fever
zo **SOREL** a buck of the third year
SORER more grieved; tenderer
zo **SOREX** a genus including shrew-mice
SORRY sad; dejected; regretful; abject
bt **SORUS** cluster of capsules on ferns
SOUGH low moan; whine; drain
SOUND probe; fathom; hale; valid
tc **SOUND** (music) audible waves, ethereally sent
go, nt **SOUND** narrow sea passage; inlet
SOUPY like soup
SOUSE pickle; sauce; douse; swoop
SOUTH the Southern regions
SOWED strewn; spread; cast
SOWER propagator; disseminator
cp **SPACE** extent; capacity; duration; (universe); a blank
cp **SPACE** area; line conditions in a spiral
to, ga **SPADE** for a dig; (suit of cards)
SPADO spade; eunuch; a sword
SPAHI Algerian cavalryman
SPAKE discoursed; declared; told
SPALL break; split; clip
SPALT a flux; brittle
SPANK a blow; a slap on the bottom
SPARE save; hoard; store; frugal
ga **SPARE** full-pins score on 2 balls (bowling)
SPARK to flash; bright lad
SPASM tic; throe; twitch; paroxysm
SPATE a sudden flood
zo **SPAWN** offspring; ova; sperm
SPEAK express; declare; talk
SPEAR a lance; to pierce
hd **SPEAR** male descent (cf. **DISTAFF**)

SPECK stain; blemish; blubber; lard
SPECS spectacles; reading glasses
SPEED haste; urge; celerity; rate
SPELD chip; splinter
SPELK rod; switch
SPELL write correctly; charm; period
bt **SPELT** spelled; German wheat
SPEND lavish; disburse; exhaust
SPENT consumed; worn; wasted
ar **SPERE** screen of open hall
zo **SPERM** spawn; semen
SPEWY wet; boggy
zo **SPHEX** the wasp genus
md **SPICA** spur; spike; bandage
SPICE to season; flavour; relish
SPICK spike; nail; tidy; fresh
ck **SPICY** aromatic; piquant; racy
SPIED observed; beheld
SPIES secret agents
bt **SPIKE** large nail; lavender; disarm (gun); impale; peak; (fence); volleyball
SPIKY spiny; sharp; pointed
SPILL (woodpile) (wood shed)
SPILL upset (liquid); shed; matchstick
SPILT diffused; scattered; dropped
md **SPINE** spina; spike; back-bone; thickness of arrow (archery); axis of book
zo, bt **SPINK** chaffinch; primrose
SPINY thorny; spiky; difficult
bt **SPIRE** steeple; a curl; sedge
SPIRT spurt; spout; gush; jet
SPIRY spiral
SPITE gall; pique; hatred; malice
zo **SPITZ** Pomeranian dog
zo **SPIZA** a finch genus
SPLAT part of a chair-back
SPLAY to widen; spreak out
SPLIT divulge; rent; cleave
SPODE china-ware
zo **SPOIL** mar; booty; snake's skin
SPOKE orated; spouted; said
SPOOF hoax; humbug; bamboozle
SPOOK phantom; ghost; spectre
cp **SPOOL** reel; bobbin; small wheel (tape); (film)
nv **SPOOM** to scud down wind (sailing)
SPOON ladle; to court; metal lure (angling); golf club
SPOOR track or trail of an animal
SPORE reproductive cell
SPORT play; gambol; romp; frolic
zo **SPOTS** blemishes; markings (leopard)
SPOUT gush; issue; nozzle
bd **SPRAG** a check-stop; young salmon; pipe or timber wedge
zo **SPRAT** small sea-fish
SPRAY foam; spring; diffuse
SPREE a carousal
SPRIG shoot; twig; a brad
nt **SPRIT** a sprout; boom; spar
zo **SPROD** a second year salmon
md **SPRUE** a disease
SPUME froth; spray
SPUMY foaming
SPUNK pluck; courage; tinder; semen
SPURN scorn; scout; slight; disdain
SPURT spout; sprint; rush; speed; sudden increase; spray
SQUAD band; gang; crew; bevy
SQUAT crouch; cower; dumpy; stocky; occupy empty house; technique (weight-lifting)
SQUAW Native American woman
SQUIB firework; skit; lampoon
zo **SQUID** cuttlefish; a calamary
SRUTI Hindu tradition
cp, mo **STACK** to pile; chimney; (cards); store; (hay); data; rock (sea)
STADE stadium; arena
mu **STAFF** rod; pole; stick; personnel; (stave) notation system
STAGE produce; present; platform; set up; so far; rig; (motor race)
STAID steady; grave; sedate
STAIN sully; taint; tarnish; soil
STAIR a step; a stairway
STAKE picket; wager; risk; hazard; target (horse-shoe pitching)
nv **STAKE** pole; sea mark; share
STALE dried out; unappetizing; out of date
bt, ag **STALK** hunt; strut; stride; stem; haulm
rl **STALL** (flying); stop; halt; booth; carved seat (church)
STAMP impress; brand; (postage-)
STAND sustain; tolerate; arena seating; fair; defence; upright
ga **STAND** cricket partnership; lacrosse etc.
STANK **STUNK**, reeked corruption
zo **STARE** gape; gaze; the starling
STARK (naked); scared; severe
lw, rl **STARR** Jewish deed; bond
START begin; entry point (races)
STATE nation; officialdom; condition; (control); status; declare; (of war, alert) period of time; (circumstances)

ar, mu **STAVE** staff; stick; ladder rung; musical notation; (–church; Scand); -dance
md, ae, nt **STAYS** abdominal supports; visits; struts (aircraft); guy ropes (sails, masts, boats)
STEAD substitution; bed frame; use; help
ck **STEAK** thick slice of meat
STEAL (hearts); (shows); quick scores (cricket); rob; move silently; seize; gain
rw, ck, ps **STEAM** (power); (engines); light cookery; water vapour
STEED warhorse; palfrey; mount
STEEL blade; metal; braze; nerve; strength; hardness; determination; resolution
STEEP imbue; dip; soak; excessive; uphill gradient
zo **STEER** guide; pilot; bullock
STEIN earthenware beer tankard (Ger.)
STELA STELE inscribed column; tablet; sap system
STEPS ladders; grades; stages; (dance-) (ice)
nt **STERE** cubic metre
nt **STERN** dour; grim; rigorous
STEVE to stow
nm **STICA** Saxon farthing
mu **STICH** stave; a verse
STICH a row of trees
STICK adhere; attach (loyal); stab; endure
STICK (parachutist); punishment; (walking-)
STIED penned like pigs
STIFF stark; erect; prim; starchy
STIFF not easy; also-ran (horse-racing); corpse
me **STILB** unit of luminance
STILE the gnomon of a sundial
STILE steps in wall or fence (footpath)
STILL not sparkling; calm; distil
zo **STILT** a pole (pole-walking); a snipe
STING prick; wound; hurt; afflict
STINK stench; odour; smell
STINT allotted task; limit; scrimp
zo **STINT** sandpiper; dunlin
bt **STIPA** the feather grasses
bt **STIPE** stalk; stem
zo **STIRK** young ox or cow
STIRP line of descent
ck **STIVE** to stew
STIVY stuffy; close
me **STOAK** to stop; to choke
zo **STOAT** ermine; weasel
STOCK cravat; store; gamer; fund
STOCK log (-house); ski-stick; (-in trade); seat (live-); (-anchor); procure
STOCK wooden chest; stocks (penalty)
ar **STOEP** stoop; verandah (S. Afr.)
STOIC Zenonist; suffers silently (Gr.)
STOKE replenish; refuel
STOLA Roman lady's dress; shawl
bt **STOLE** peculated; plagiarized; a sucker
STOLE robbed; priest's vestment
bt **STOMA** breathing pore
STOMP move importantly (heavily)
STONE boulder; weight 14lb/6.3kg
STONY hard; flinty; obdurate; broke
STOOD allowed; brooked; bore
bt **STOOK STOUK**, 12 sheaves (of corn)
STOOL a seat without a back; ramify
STOOM stum; renew fermentation
STOOP flagon; condescend; yield
STOOR stour; dust; commotion
STOPE mining ledge; to excavate
bd, mu, lw **STOPS** projecting stones; (organ); delays, hindrances
cp **STORE** hoard; garner; stock; supply
zo **STORK** infant conveyor; bird
mt **STORM** fume; rage; scold; turmoil
pr **STORY** narrative; novel; (news-)
STOUP stoop; flagon; tankard
md **STOUR** tumult; paroxysm
ck **STOUT** wide-girthed; robust; a drink (porter)
STOVE oven; kiln; to heat; (-in) smashed
mu **STRAD** a Stradivarius violin
STRAP belt; binding; (safety-)
bt, bd **STRAW** dried cereal stalk; thatch; trifle; (last-)
STRAY err; rove; wander; deviate; lost
STREW scatter; spread; broadcast
STRIA stripe; streak; small channel
bt **STRIG** stalk; footstalk
STRIP peel; divest; dismantle; shred
STRIP (air-); marked line; ribbon
zo **STRIX** screech-owl
STROB measure of angular velocity
le, nt **STROP** sharpening leather; rope
mu **STRUM** thrum; (guitar)
STRUT support; brace; walk; swagger
STUCK set; fixed; adhered; stabbed
STUDS wall timber; collar fasteners; men

STUDY con; scan; reflect; learning; den
STUFF cram; pack; cloth; fabric
mn **STULL** cross-timber in a mine
mn **STULM** shaft used to drain a mine
STULP a stump (cricket)
ga **STUMP** log; block; stub; (cricket)
STUNG pricked; afflicted; deceived
STUNK **STANK**, of ill odour
STUNT to dwarf; (arrested); breakneck risks
cp **STUNT** box in teleprinter controlling operation
STUPA Buddhist monument; a dagoba
md **STUPE** hot bandage; fomentation
STURT strife; wrath; vexation
ga **STUTZ** parallel bars swing (gymn.)
nm **STYCA** Saxon half-farthing
STYLE pen; dub; entitle; mode; distinction; (life-)
cp **STYLE** constant; recognization script for viewing
STYLO a pen; a stylograph
SUAVE bland; pleasant; polite
SUBAH province; viceroyship (Ind.)
zo **SUDAK** the pike-perch
SUDRA the lowest Hindu caste
le **SUEDE** unglazed leather
SUENT neaty and tidy
ck **SUETY** of suet fat
rl **SUFIC** Islamic mysticism
ck **SUGAR** sweetening; flattery
lw **SUING** legal prosecution
SUITE retinue; series; train; apartment
cp **SUITE** sequence of interrelated programs
SULKS **SULKY**, grumpiness; morose
ga **SULKY** chariot for trotting races
SULLY soil; taint; stain; defame
bt, ck **SUMAC** **SUMACH**, plant used in dyeing
SUNCK female chief of Native American tribe
rl **SUNNA** **SUNNI**, of Moslem traditions; orthodox sect
SUNNY bright; brilliant; unclouded
SUN-UP sunrise; dawn; cock-crow
SUPER a supernumerary; extra special
cf **SUPER-** superior; above; (-market)
cf **SUPRA-** transcending; (supra-national)
tx, rl **SURAH** Indian silk; chapter of Koran
md **SURAL** (calf of the leg)
tx **SURAT** coarse Indian cotton
SURER more certain; safer
SURGE roll; swell; heave; a billow; advance
SURLY churlish; morose; crusty; gruff
SURMA Ind. eyeshadow
rl **SURYA** Hindu suŋ-god
ck **SUSHI** bean-curd rice dish (Jap.)
SUTOR a cobbler
rl **SUTRA** Bralımin exercises
SWAGE drill-bit shaping tool
SWAIN a peasant; a country lover
SWALE shady spot; vale; channel
rl **SWAMI** religious instructor (Hindu)
SWAMP flood; inundate; fen; slough
SWANG swamp greensward
SWANK brag; swagger
SWAPE handle; oar; sconce
SWARD turf; bacon rind
SWARE testified; deposed; cursed
SWARF to faint; to swoon; grit
zo **SWARM** throng; teem; cluster; bevy; (bees)
SWAZI of Swaziland (S. Africa)
SWEAR affirm; vow; vouch; blaspheme
SWEAT exude; ooze; perspire; (toil)
bt, ck **SWEDE** a turnip
SWEEP (chimney); brush; lottery
nt **SWEEP** a blend; scope; curve; oar
SWEET luscious; honeyed; dulcet
mu, nt **SWELL** expand; dilate; amplify; bulge; undulating sea
SWEPT brushed
zo **SWIFT** fleet; quick; sudden; prompt
SWILL quaff; wash; rinse
zo **SWINE** pig; evil-doer; (foul); deceiver
SWING sway; dangle; hang; turn round
mu **SWING** movement; pendulum; 1930s' easy music
ga **SWING** of golf; oar (strokes); punch (boxing)
SWIPE smite; slog; steal
go **SWIRE** a col; a hollow between 2 hills
SWIRL whirl; gyrate; eddy
SWISH to birch; thrash; posh; fine
SWISS of Switzerland; Helvetian
md **SWOON** to faint (with shock)
SWOOP rush; stoop (eagle); descent
SWORD (-blade); rapier; cutlass
SWORE oaths; blasphemies
lw **SWORN** under oath; affirmed
SWUNG rocked; vacillated; dangled
SYCEE silver in small ingots (China)
rl **SYLPH** **SYLPHIDE**, an airy fairy; (Pope); Cupid's beloved

fr **SYLVI** (-culture) forestry management
rl **SYNOD** ecclesiastical Council
mu **SYREN SIREN**, alarm hooter; love songs; enticer
ck **SYRUP** strongly sweetened liquid

T

TABAC snuff-colour; (tobacco)
tx, zo, wv **TABBY** brindled; watered silk; a cat; earliest plain weave
md **TABES** emaciation; atrophy
md **TABID** consumptive; phthisical
cp **TABLE** index; list; schedule; board; array of data
TABOO ban; bar; prohibit; interdict
mu **TABOR** camp; laager; small drum
bt **TACCA** tropical plant genus
mu **TACET** be silent!
TACHE moustache; catch; freckle; loop
cf **TACHY-** rapidity, speed (Gr.)
TACIT silent; implicit; inferred
TACKY viscous; gummy; sticky
TAFFY a Welshman; toffy; blarney
TAFIA Malay rum
TAGAL Filipino
zo **TAGMA** region of metameric animal
TAHLI Hindu gold ornament
go **TAIGA** coniferous region (Siberia)
tx **TAILS** men's evening dress; (heads or–)
TAINT stain; tarnish; sully; defile
zo **TAIPO** taepo; vicious animal (NZ)
TAKEN seized; captured; won; assumed
TAKER grasper; acceptor
ro **TALBE** air/sea rescue system
TALES stories; equals in kind; (jurors)
TALLY agree; correspond; match; count; score; (wag)
cp **TALLY** printout from adding machine
TALMA loose cloak
TALON claw; concave; moulding
zo, md **TALPA** on the mole genus; a wen
TALUK Indian subdistrict
gl, md **TALUS** steep scree slope; knuckle bone, dice; earthwork; ankle bone
TAMED docile; domesticated; curbed
TAMER subjugator; subduer
TAMIL a Dravidian language (Sri Lanka)
TAMIN glazed worsted stuff
TAMIS tammy; straining cloth
TAMMY tamis; a tam-o'-shanter (Scots hero)
bt **TAMUS** black bryony
mu **TANGO** Argentine dance
TANGY piquant; sharp in taste
bt **TANIA** African farinaceous tuber
TANKA Canton boat population
TANNA tana; Indian police station
ck, bt **TANSY** Easter cake; bitter herb
mu **TANTO** so; so much
TAPAS side-snacks in a bar (Sp.)
TAPED measured; sized up; bound together; (red-)
TAPER wax-candle; slender and conical
TAPET tapestry; tapis
zo **TAPIR** related to pig (South Amer.)
TAPIS TAPET, of tapestry; wall decoration
TAPIS hidden; under consideration
bt **TAPPA** tapa; fibre for mats
mu **TARDO** slowly
TARDY late; sluggish; dilatory
TARED macadamized (road); freight weighed
bt **TARFA** tamarisk; (exudes manna)
zo **TARIN** the siskin
TAROT divining cards (78)
TARRY stay; linger; sojourn; loiter
md **TARSE** the tarsus; foot; ankle
zo **TARSI** feet of insects
TARUS projection between roof surfaces
TASSE thigh armour; drinking cup (Fr./Ger.)
TASTE savour; experience; preference
mu **TASTO** It. finger board of stringed or keyboard instrument
TASTY piquant; savoury; appetising
TATAR Turkic native within CIS
zo **TATOU** tatu; peba; armadillo
TAT-TA goodbye; a stroll
bt **TATTA** Indian screen; of cuscus grass
TATTY tattered; worn out; shabby
nt **TAUNT** deride; revile; high-masted
TAWED treated with alum
TAWER a leather-dresser
TAWNY fulvid; brown; tanned
TAWSE taws; leather strap (Sc.)
TAXED burdened; accused
zo **TAXEL** N. American badger
TAXER inspector of taxes
bt **TAXIN** yew extract
TAXIS taxi-cabs (hired cars)
-TAXIS tropism; species responses
bt **TAXUS** yew genus

TAZZA wine cup with shallow bowl
TEACH coach; edify; instruct
TEASE vex; annoy; plague; harass
ar, rl **TEBAM** dais; rostrum in synagogue
zo **TEDDY** a bear; Pooh's cousin
TEENS thirteen to nineteen
TEENY wee; tiny; minute
TEETH dentures; snowcomb (curling)
TE-HEE titter; snigger
TEIAN Ionian, (Anacreon)
TELAR web-like; woven; spun
cf **TELEO-** far, distant, end (Gr.)
tc **TELEX** teleprinter universal system
TELIC final; conclusive
zo **TELUM** last abdominal somite in insects
rl **TEMPE** the Gods' amusement park, Thessaly
mu **TEMPO** (cards); relative rapidity
TEMPT allure; lure; decoy; entice
TEMSE sieve; to sift
zo **TENCH** a fish
TENET rigid doctrine; dogma; belief
ar **TENIA** moulding on architrave
TENNE an orange-brown colour
TENON of mortise lock (doors)
mu **TENOR** purport; trend; course; high male voice
TENSE taut; tight; intent; strained
TENTH a tithe; ordinal number
TENTY attentive; alert; (tenter hooks)
TEPAL a perianth leaf
TEPID **TEPOR**, lukewarm; moderate
me **TERCE** about 42 gal (191 litres)
zo **TEREK** a sandpiper
md **TERES** a muscle
bt **TERFA** edible fruit-body of terferia
md **TERMA** terminal lamina of brain
TERNE inferior tin-plate
TERRA earth
tx **TERRY** a fabric
TERSE abrupt
me **TESLA** magnetic-flux density
bt **TESTA** husk; integument
TESTY techy; fretful; irritable
cf **TETRA-** of four parts (Gr.)
TEWEL chimney flue
THANE Scottish baron
THANK express gratitude
THAWY inclined to thaw
bt **THECA** seed or spore case
THEFT larceny; robbery; pilfering
THEIC tea-pot devotee
bt **THEIN** tea
THEIR of them
THEMA subject for discussion
mu **THEME** melodic/topical motif repeated
THERE at that place
me **THERM** thermal unit of gas
THESE pl. of this
THETA a Greek letter
THEWY muscular; strong
THICK dense; solid; stupid; friendly
THIEF pickpocket; an Autolycus
pl **THIGH** upper part of leg; (hams)
THILL shaft of a cart; fire-clay
rl **THINE** of Thee, Thy, of God
THING object; article; entity
THING **TING**, Scandinavian Parliament
THINK deem; muse; cogitate
mu **THIRD** ordinal number, 3rd; melodic interval
mn **THIRL** to cut through workings
THIRL a restriction; to pierce
THOFT a rowing bench
nt **THOLE** **THOWL**, rowlock
le **THONG** length of leather; lash; whip
bt **THORN** prickle; spine; (in flesh)
THORP homestead; hamlet; dorp
THOSE pl. of that
THOTH Egyptian god of wisdom
zo **THOUS** African jackal genus
nt **THOWL** thole; pin for an oar
THRAP to fasten
THREE cardinal number; a leash
THREW flung; hurled; projected
md **THROB** regular beat; palpitation
THROE pang; agony; anguish
THROW cast; toss; fell; pitch; (dice); (fit); (party)
mu **THRUM** yarn; fringe; to strum
THULE Ultima Thule; (Greenland)
THUMB that odd large finger; turn pages
THUMP knock; bang; punch; pommel
THURL thirl; passage in a mine
bt **THUYA** arbor vitae
bt, ck **THYME** fragrant savoury plant
cf **THYMO-** of emotion; temper; soul (Gr.)
THYMY fragrant
TIARA ornamental head-dress
zo **TIBBY** cat
tx **TIBET** heavy goat-hair fabric
md **TIBIA** the large shinbone
nm **TICAL** Siamese rupee
nt **TIDAL** of ebb and flood
zo **TIDDY** the wren
TIDED surmounted; managed to survive

TIE-IN tubular scaffolding; interior grip
nt **TIFFY** an artifer
zo **TIGER** jungle cat; diminutive groom
TIGHT taut; tense; close; compact; tipsy
ga **TIGNA** forward somersault (gym.)
bt **TIKUL** Indian tree
TILDE diacritical mark
TILED tesselated
TILER Masonic doorkeeper
bt **TILIA** lime-tree
TILKA Hindu caste mark
ag **TILTH** good soil condition for cultivation
TIMED measured, finite
cp **TIMER** time-fixed, -ing device
TIMES the newspaper
TIMES durations
TIMID shy; fearful; diffident
TIMON Athenian misanthrope
zo, md **TINEA** moth genus; ringworm
TINED pronged
TINGE hue; tint; stain; dye
bt **TINGI** Brazilian soap-tree
TINNY like tin; sharp in sound
TINTY crudely tinted
TIPSY tight; drunk; fuddled
tx **TIRAZ** Moorish silk fabric
TIRED weary; harassed; attired
T'IRON a webbed bar
TISRI Hebrew month
TITAN giant; Cyclops; Goliath
rl **TITHE** a tenth; a tax
lw **TITLE** claim; right; (due); ownership; deeds; rank
ba **TITRE** quantity of antibody
TITUP tittup; skip; canter
TIVER ochre sheep dye
nm **TIZZY** a sixpence
TOADY a sycophant
TOAST scorch; health proposal
TOBAS S. American native race
TOBIT Apocryphal book
TODAY this day
me **TODDE** 28 lb weight (obs.)
TODDY a cordial; mixed drink (India)
au **TOE-IN** front-wheels adjustment
TOGGY arctic coat made from beaver
TOGED arrayed in a toga
zo **TOGUE** mackinaw; lake-trout
tx **TOILE** twill; linen-silk mixture
TOILS a snare
me **TOISE** old French linear unit
TOKAY Hungarian wine
TOKEN sign; symbol; mark; badge
nm **TOMAN** Persian gold coin
me **TOMIN** a weight of 12 grains
to **TOMMY** Atkins; soldier; lever
mu **TONAL** accented; harmonious notes
TONDO circular relief sculpture
TONED moderated; shaded; tinted
pt **TONER** organic dye
TONGA Eastern cart
ck **TONIC** strengthening; bracing; quinine drink
mu **TONIC** keynote of octave
bt **TONKA** tree whose seeds contain coumarin
mu **TONUS** state of persistent excitation; minor scale; Gregorian tone
bt, ar, pl **TOOTH** prong; fang; tusk (cog) (comb) (dog-)
zo **TOPAU** rhinoceros-bird
mn **TOPAZ** a gem
TOPEE sun helmet
TOPER toss-pot; sot; tippler
zo **TOPET** crested titmouse
zo **TOPHI** ear cartilage nodules
TOPIA Roman mural decoration
md **TOPIC** theme; subject; a remedy
TOPOS cliché description
tx **TOQUE** Canadian knitted cap
TOQUE woman's twisted silk turban
lw **TORAH** the Mosaic law
rl **TORAN** Buddhist porch
TORCH flambeau; link; fire-brand
TORIC type of lens
ar **TORII** Jap. gateway
hd **TORSE** heraldic wreath
zo **TORSK** a cod
md **TORSO** body trunk
ar **TORUS** an architectural moulding
TOSSY contemptuous
TOTAL all; sum; whole; gross
TOTED carried; borne; transported
TOTEM symbol of local guardian spirits (from 'ototeman') N. Am.
TOUCH contact; handle; concern; effect
TOUGH tenacious; strength
TOUSE tousle; haul; tease
nt **TOWED** hauled; dragged; tugged
tx **TOWEL** an altar or drying cloth (bathroom)
TOWER soar; mount; turret
TOWNY a townsman
TOXIC TOXIN
TOYED played with (idea) (ball) etc.
TOYER dilettante; trifler
TRACE vestige; remains; copy; sketch
TRACE trail; elements; figures
TRACK spoor; (rail-); (racing-); follow

pr **TRACT** region; pamphlet; homily
pl **TRACT** bundle of nerve fibres
go **TRADE** exchange; barter; swap; (-winds)
TRAIL path; route; tow; haul; follow
rw **TRAIN** drill; school; retinue
TRAIT characteristic
bt **TRAMA** agaric-gill hyphae
nt **TRAMP** hike; vagrant; hobo; (-ship)
TRAPE **TRAIPSE**, move around vaguely
TRAPS snares; luggage etc.
TRASH worthless refuse; poor whites (USA)
mn **TRASS** volcanic earth
TRAVE beam; wooden frame
TRAWL a drag-net
TREAD trample; step; press
TREAT offer; occasion; cure; deal
fr **TREED** up-a-tree; in refuge (cornered); forested
TREEN wooden; collectors' term for household objects
TREND popular fashion; (inclined to)
TRESS ringlet; lock of hair
tx **TREWS** Scottish trousers
el, ps **TRIAC** silicon-controlled rectifier
tv, mu **TRIAD** a trinity; 3-colour phosphor dot pictures; chord
cp **TRIAD** 3 binary digits, symbols, data units
lw **TRIAL** test; ordeal; case; (court)
mn **TRIAS** sandstone
TRIBE clan; race; class; order
nt **TRICE** an instant; to haul
TRICK dupe; cheat; artifice; (cards); duty turn; device
lw **TRIED** essayed; attempted
TRIER experimentalist
ga **TRIES** (Rugby football, 3 or 4 points)
mu **TRILL** warble; quaver; shake
as **TRINE** triple; threefold; a triad; astrology
as **TRINE** favourable planet aspect
lw **TRIOR** an examiner
ck **TRIPE** stomach offal; nonsense
TRIST sorrowful; sad
TRITE hackneyed; obvious; worn
ga **TROCO** a ball game
TROIC Trojan
TROLL to fish; sing; cave-elf (Scand.)
mn **TRONA** Egyptian soda
TRONC distribution of pooled tips
me **TRONE** steelyard; a drain
TROOP march (army); throng; crowd
TROPE metaphor; figure of speech
mu **TROPE** 12-note technique
TROTH to plight; confidence; faith
zo **TROUT** fish of Salmo genus
TROVE something found; (treasure-)
TRUCE lull; respite; armistice
TRUCK a wheel; barter; a vehicle
nt **TRUCK** wagon; mast-head
TRUER more worthy of belief
TRULL vagrant; a drab
TRULY verily; exactly; veritably
ga **TRUMP** (the last trump); to ruff; leading suit (cards) (bridge)
mu **TRUMP** a trumpet; Jew's harp
TRUNK torso; butt; stem; saratoga
cp **TRUNK** highway; interface channel
md, ar **TRUSS** bind; fasten; framework of timbers
TRUST credit; reliance; merger
ma **TRUTH** probity; fact; honesty; reality; (Boolean)
bt **TRYMA** a stone fruit; a drupe
TRY-ON a bluff
mu, rl **TRYST** rendezvous: (Lutheran carol)
TSUBA Japanese sword hilt
rl **TSUNG** ritual jade (China)
mu **TUBAL** of tuba; tubular construction
TUBBY fat; obese; dull
TUBED piped
bt **TUBER** bulbous growth
zo **TUCAN** Mexican pouched rat
bt **TUCUM** S. American palm
TUDEH political party (Iran)
TUDOR a royal house
TUFTY feathery
TUILE **TUILLE**, **TUILLERY**, armour plating
TUISM a curious theory
bt **TULIP** showy flower
tx **TULLE** a delicate fabric
mu **TUMBA** instrument S. Domingo
TUMID swollen; bombastic
TUMPY lumpy; uneven
TUNED attuned; harmonized; adapted
mu, ro, tv **TUNER** sound adjuster; channel selector
md **TUNIC** surcoat; a membrane
zo **TUNNY** large fish, mackerel type
mu **TURBA** chorus of the people in opera
zo **TURBO** whelk and winkle genus
ae **TURBO-** jet engine
TURCO Ottoman soldier
TURFY swardy; grassy; cespitose
TURNS rotation; artistes' acts; pirouettes; virtuoso tricks (ice skating) (water-skiing)
TURPS turpentine

zo, pl **TUSKS** **TUSKY, TUSSES,** elephant's ivory; teeth
TUSKY with long teeth
bd **TUSSE** wall-face projecting stone
TUTOR coach; instruct; guardian
TUTSI native of Burundi (Africa)
mu **TUTTI** all in (It.)
ch **TUTTY** impure oxide of zinc
TUZZY tuft; tuffet; cluster
TWAIN a couple; brace; pair
zo **TWAIT** species of shad
TWANG tang; flavour
TWEAK pinch; twist; twitch
tx, wv **TWEED** twilled cloth
TWEEN between; twixt
TWEER **TWIER** blast-furnace
TWERP nasty nitwit
TWICE twofold; doubly; encore
wv, tx **TWILL** **TWEEL,** woven fabric
TWINE **ENTWINE,** bind together; cord; winding
TWIRL whirl; rotate; revolve
TWIST writhe; hunger; (tobacco)
zo **TWITE** mountain linnet
TWIXT betwixt; between
pr **TWO-ON** doing 2 jobs at once
pr **TWO-UP** printing, processing twin series
TWYER **TWEER,** blast furnace; jet
rl **TYCHE** Greek goddess of fortune
TYING fastening; shacking
TYLER tiler; Masonic doorkeeper
fr **TYLER** tight-line gorge system
TYPAL typical; representative
pr **TYPED** typewritten; given a classification
bt **TYPHA** bulrush
TYPIC emblematic; symbolic
TYRED wheeled, pneumatic
rl **TYTHE** tithe; a tenth; church tax

U

nt **U-BOAT** a submarine
UBYKH language
zo **UDDER** mammary gland
bd **U-DUCT** gas heater ventilator
UGRIC Finns, Magyars, Turks, etc.
UHLAN Prussian cavalryman
UHURU freedom (Swahili)
UKASE Russian decree
md **ULCER** open sore
ULEMA Turkish hierarchy
bt **ULMIC** **ULMUS,** of elms; (exudations)
ULMIN humus; a brown pigment
bt **ULMUS** elm genus
pl **ULNAD** **ULNAR,** of the forearm bone
md **ULOID** like a scar
cf **-ULOUS** of tendency towards
el **ULTOR** anode
ULTRA extreme
cf **-ULTRA** of extreme, beyond excessive
bt **UMBEL** inflorescent flower
UMBER brown pigment
as **UMBRA** a shadow; (total solar eclipse)
zo **UMBRE** the grayling
nt **UMIAK** Eskimo boat
pc **UMWEG** detour to goal, round about (Ger.)
UNAPT inept; irrelevant
UNARM disarm
ch, cp **UNARY** consisting of 1 component; monadic operation
UNBAR open; permit
UNBAY to open up
UNBED arouse
UNBID uninvited; spontaneous
UNBIT not bitten
ar **UNBOW** to unbend
UNBOX uncase; unpack
UNCAP unhat; uncover; open
UNCLE pawnbroker; relation
UNCLE Sam; Tom; Remus
zo **UNCUS** hook or claw
UNCUT untrimmed; book before guillotine process
UNDAM release
UNDER below; lower; subject to
UNDID untied; nullified
UNDUE excessive; inordinate
UNFIT unqualified; improper
UNFIX detach; undo; loosen
UNGUM unstick
UNHAT uncover; uncap
rl **UNIAT** Russian Christian
UNIFY unite; combine
lw **UNION** linked; marital; coalition; guild
pb **UNION** league; joint organization; junction (pipes, el., gas)
UNITE bind together; federate; (concerted)
UNITY concord; harmony; accord
UNLAP unfold
UNLAY untwist; unravel
UNLED without guidance
UNLET vacant; tenantless
UNMAN dishearten; unnerve
UNMEW release from confinement
ma **UNODE** a geometric conception
UNSAY retract; disavow; (cancel previous pacts)
ck, bd **UNSET** unmounted; still liquid or sticky; virgin

cp **UNSET** for computers as reset
md, vt **UNSEX** geld; castrate; spay
lw **UNTAX** declare free from tax
UNTIE undo; unbind; unknot
UNTIL till; to such time as
UNWED not yet married
UNZIP undo patent fastening
mu **UP-BOW** violin bow position in play
UP-END tilt; place in vertical position
nt **UPPER** superior; higher; part of shoe above sole; (-works of ship)
md **UPSET** capsize; overturn; disconcert; spill; (stomach)
zo **UPUPA** hoopoe genus
ch **URATE UREIC**, of uric acid
URBAN of the city
bt **UREDO** fungus genus
UREIC pertaining to urea
bt **URENA** Indian mallow
URGED URGER, pleaded; impelled; prompter; agitator
zo **URIAL** Asiatic wild sheep
zo **URILE** cormorant
md **URINE** liquid body waste
URNAL URNED, of the urn (cremation)
zo **URSON** Canadian porcupine
zo **URSUS** the bear genus
zo **URUBU** American turkey-buzzard
USAGE habit; wont; custom
lw **USHER** court official; precede
USING applying; employing
USUAL normal; ordinary; habitual
USURP arrogate; assume; seize
USURY exoribitant; interest
UTTER declare; enunciate; total
md **UVULA** (soft palate)
UZBEG UZBEK, Turkish Tatar; of Uzbekistan region

V

VAGAL of the vagus nerves
VAGUE dim; indistinct; indefinite
md **VAGUS** a cranial nerve
hd **VAIRE VAIRY**, charged with heraldic fur
VALET gentleman's gentleman
VALID cogent; substantial; strong
mu **VALSE** waltz; dance
VALUE worth; price; cost; utility
el, pl, mu, rw **VALVE** electron tube; regulator device; (heart); (horn); steam
VANED having vanes or blades
VANIR three Norse deities
VAPID insipid; feeble; jejune
VAPOR vapour; miasma; steam
bt **VAREC** seaweed; kelp
VARIA miscellany
md **VARIX** uneven dilation
md **VARUS** pigeon-toed
gl, go **VARVE** clay; silt sediments in lake or sea
md **VASAL** (blood-vessel)
rl **VATIC** prophetic; oracular; (Vatican)
VAULT leap; cell; tomb; crypt
VAUNT boast; exult; swagger
rl **VEDAS VEDIC**, of Hindu sacred writings
zo **VEERY** American thrush
VEGAN total vegetarian
VEINY full of veins
ar **VELAR** cupola or dome
VELDT grass lands (S. Africa)
zo **VELIA** water-bugs
md **VELUM** soft palate
VENAL mercenary; corrupt; sordid
ga **VENEW VENEY**, fencing thrust
VENOM virus; poison; rancour; gall
VENUE location of an event
VENUS Aphrodite
VEREY signal light
cp, rl **VERGE** edge; staff; mace; margin (punched card)
VERSE poetry; stanza; stich; stave
pr **VERSO** left-hand page
me **VERST** Russian; ⅔ of a mile (1 km)
VERTU VIRTU, rarity in art
VERVE energy; vigour; inspiration
zo **VESPA** wasp genus
VESTA goddess of the hearth
bt **VETCH** ers; the tare
VEXED VEXER, annoyed; bothered; provoker
bt **VEXIL** a banner; a petal
VIAND food
md **VIBEX** a blood spot
rl **VICAR** parish parson
cp **VIDEO** recorded television film; visual display unit
ck **VIFDA VIVDA**, dried meat
VIGIL watch; wake; eve
VILER more degraded
ar **VILLA** country residence (Roman)
md, bt **VILLI** small fibres
bt **VIMEN** slender shoot
bt **VINCA** periwinkle
VINED with tendrils
VINIC of wine making; alcoholic
VINYL plastic fibre
bt, mu **VIOLA** plant genus; stringed instrument
zo **VIPER** adder; asp
zo **VIREO** American song-birds

as **VIRGO** (Zodiac); a constellation; the Maiden
md **VIRUS** mini-transmitter of infection
VISIT frequent; call; drop in
zo **VISON** American mink
VISOR VIZOR, movable part of a helmet; a mask
VISTA view; scene; prospect
VITAL essential; animate; living
bt **VITEX** verbena
bt **VITIS** the vine
VITTA a headband; garland
bt **VITTA** stripe; oil cavity
VIVAT (applause)
ck **VIVDA VIFDA** dried meat
vt **VIVES** a disease of horses
VIVID intense; brilliant; graphic
zo **VIXEN** female fox; hussie
zo **VIZEN** scold; shrew; termagant
VIZIR vizier; vezir; minister (Ottoman)
VLACH a Wallachian; (Romanian)
VOCAL articulate
tc **VODAS** echo-suppression device
ac **VODER** synthetic-speech device
ck **VODKA** Russian spirits; drink
VOGAD telephony
VOGUE fashion; mode; practice
mu **VOICE** express; declare; utter; sound production; (vocal)
tc **VOICE** human speech as electrical signals
VOIDS ratio of solids to spaces occupied by air or water
tx **VOILE** gauzy material
md **VOLAR** (palm of the hand)
mu **VOLEE** rapid phrase
VOLET part of triptych
mu **VOLTA VOLTE**, old dance turn; repeat
VOLTE 2-legged turn (horsemanship)
mu **VOLTI** turn over
md **VOMER** ploughshare; nose-bone
VOMIT spew; eject; disgorge
VOTED VOTER, polled; balloted; elector
VOUCH VOWED, VOWER, swore; dedicated; pledger
VOWED swore; pledged; dedicated
VOWEL open speech sound
VOWER pledger; promiser; swearer
VROUW woman; wife (Dutch)
VULGO VULGATE, in popular style (language)
pl **VULVA** female genitals; orifice
mu **VUOTA VUOTO**, pause, interval (It.)
VYING striving; competing

W

mn **WACKE** basalt; trap-rock
WADDY Australian war club
WADED forded
zo **WADER** long-legged bird
WADEX word/author index for computers
ck **WAFER** crisp cake
WAGED pledged; conducted; salaried
zo **WAGEL** black gull
WAGER bet; hazard; stake; gamble
WAGES stipend; remuneration
WAGON wain; lorry; truck
md, bt **WAHOO** cascara sagrada
pl **WAIST** narrows above hips
WAITS Yule minstrels
WAIVE remit; forego; relinquish
WAKED kept vigil; stimulated
WAKEN awaken; excite; animate
bt **WALAN** amboyna tree
nt **WALAP** outrigger sail canoe (S. Pacific)
zo **WALER** Australian horse
nt, rd **WALTY** unstable; radar
mu **WALTZ** valse; dance
WANED ebbed; decreased; declined
WANLY sickly; languidly
WANTY a loading strap
WARES merchandist; commodities
WARTY with excrescencs; blemishes
WASHY watery; thin; feeble
WASTE dissipate; squander; fritter away
WASTE industrial-; household-; rubbish (-paper)
WASTE infertile; unusable area; (-land)
nt **WATCH** guard; tend; mark
WATCH small timepiece; (wrist-)
ch, go **WATER** liquid of life; (rain-) (drinking-)
WATER irrigate; flood; sprinkle; moisten
WAVED fluctuated; brandished; hand-greeted
WAVER sway; totter; vacillate
zo **WAVEY** rough sea; (design); snow-goose
WAXED cered; sealed; grew; increased (moon)
WAXEN of ceruminous secretion; (bees-); images
fr, go **WEALD WOLD**, woodland
WEARY jaded; spent; fatigue; tire
wv **WEAVE** plait; mat; entwine; interlace
ga **WEAVE** figure of 8 movement (basketball) (lacrosse) (football)

WEBBY filmy; reticulated
me **WEBER** magnetic flux
ga **WEDGE** tapered wood blocker; golf club
bt, tx **WEEDS** unwanted plants in garden, crops, lawns; widow's mourning costume
bt **WEEDY** weak and lanky
WEELY wicker fish trap
WEEPY lacrimose; oozy
nt **WEIGH** balance; ponder; (anchor)
WEIRD eerie; uncanny; supernatural
WEISM excessive use of 'we'
WELCH WELSH, people of Cymru; of Wales
WELCH WELSH, fail a promise
WENCH maid; damsel
WHACK THWACK, beat; smite; defeat
zo **WHALE** the orc; a cetacean
WHALL wall-eye
zo **WHAME** the burrel-fly
WHARE Maori hut
WHARF quay; dock; pier
zo **WHAUP** curlew
WHEAL weal; bruise mark after blow
mn **WHEAL** mine (Cornish)
bt **WHEAT** a cereal
WHEEL a revolving frame; to turn; whirl
WHEEL of tactics (– & deal) (roulette) (fate)
zo, ck **WHELK** edible gastropod; seafood
zo **WHELP** puppy; cub; pup; to litter
WHERE the place concerned
WHICH the item concerned
nt, ga **WHIFF** puff; outrigger boat; strike-out (baseball); smell; cigarette
WHIFT a breath; a snatch; glimpse
WHILE at concurrent time; pass the time
zo **WHILK** the scoter; sea duck
WHINE whimper; snivel; cry
WHIRL twirl; spin; gyrate; eddy
WHISK a brush; stir; hasten; rush
WHIST keep silence; (cards)
WHITE pale; wan; pallid; chalky
WHIZZ whiz; rush past; flash by; of fireworks (-king)
WHOLE entire; intact; total
WHOOP a shout of joy
WHORL convolution; spiral; medieval furniture motif
bt **WHORT** whortleberry
WHOSE the owner of item concerned
WHOSO he who
bt **WICKY** mountain ash
WIDEN extend; enlarge
WIDER broader; more remote
zo **WIDOW** a bereaved wife; (black-, spider)
WIDTH span; amplitude; beam
WIELD control; exert; ply; brandish
tx **WIGAN** stiff canvas
WIGHT a creature; strong; nimble
WILED beguiled; let time pass
WILLY wool cleaning machine; penis
WINCE flinch; blench; shrink
WINCH hoisting machine
WINDY stormy; breezy; pneumatic (Sc.); afraid
WINED drank wine
ga **WINGS** boundary players (football) (bowls) (flying) (theatre)
WINGY rapid
WINZE ventilating shaft; a curse
WIPED rubbed; mopped; cleansed
WIPER cleaner-dryer; (windscreen-)
el **WIRED** telegraphed; snared; connected
WISER sager; more expedient
WISPY flocculent; nebulous
WITAN Witenagemot (Anglo-Saxon); moot; council
WITCH hag; crone; sibyl
bt **WITHE** willow twig
bt **WITHY** species of willow
WITTY droll; facetious; humorous
WIVES spouses
WIZEN shrivelled; dried up
rl **WODEN** Odin; Wotan
WOMAN female human
WOMEN pl. of woman
zo **WONGA** Australian pigeon
fr **WOODS** tree area; wooden-head clubs (golf)
WOODY of tree products; sylvan
WOOED WOOER, courted; lover; swain
WOOER a lover; a swain
ga **WOOFS** variation in handicapping (golf)
WOOFY dense; close in texture
bt **WOOLD** twist; dyer's weed
zo **WOONT** the mole
WORDY verbose; prolix; garrulous
WORLD universe; globe; earth
zo **WORMY** vermigerous
WORRY fret; chafe; fidget; badger
WORSE comparative of bad
WORST the most bad; to defeat; conquer
WORTH value; cost; merit; desert
rl **WOTAN** Odin; Woden
WOULD conditional auxil. verb
WOUND harm; hurt; lacerate
wv, tx **WOVEN** plaited; interlaced

bt **WRACK** (– and ruin); seaweed
tx **WRANG WRUNG**, twisted to squeeze water out
WRATH ire; rage; fury; passion
WREAK avenge; inflict havoc
nt **WRECK** ruin; blight; shatter; (ship-)
WREST to twist; obtain by violence
WRICK to sprain
WRING extort; wrest; writhe
WRIST hand/arm joint
cp **WRITE** indite; scrawl; scribble; (pen); transcribe data
WRONG injure; falsify; error; tort
WROTE inscribed; penned; engrossed
WROTH wrathful; angry; furious
WRUNG tormented; racked
WRYLY in a distorted manner
bt **WYTHE** willow twig

X

nt **XEBEC ZEBEC**, Algerian pirate ship
bt **XENIA** pollen effect on young plant
ch **XENON** a gas
ec **XERIC** adapted to dry conditions
cr **X-MARK** face-mark
X-RING innermost target (shooting)
md **X-UNIT** X-ray unit
XYLEM woody tissue
ch **XYLIC** benzoic acid
XYLOL aromatic fluid
ch **XYLYL** xylene

Y

bt **YACCA** Jamaican tree
nt **YACHT** pleasure ship
zo **YACOU** guan, a game bird
ga **YAGLI** traditional oiled wrestling (Turkey)
YAHOO hooligan
YAMEN YAMUN, mandarin's office, house (Ch.)
zo **YAPOK** S. American water-opposum
bt **YAPON** evergreen shrub; cassino
YAQUI Mexican Indians
rl **YASHT** Zend-Avesta prayer book
nt **YAWED** slithered in rough sea
YEARN crave; hanker; desire
YEAST leaven; balm; ferment
YELEK a long vest (Turk.)
bt **YERBA** Paraguay tea
bt **YEWEN** made of yew
YEXED hiccupped
YIELD submit; render; supply
YODEL yodle; Tyrolese singing
YOICK encourage; Lappish chants
me **YOJAN** about 5 miles (8 km) (E. Ind.)
YOKED coupled; linked; paired
YOKEL rustic; churl; clodhopper
YOLKY egg-yolk consistency
mn, bd **YORKY** slate with curved cleave
YOSHI order to continue judo contest
YOUNG boyish; juvenile; recent
YOURS of you; ending of a letter
YOUTH lad; stripling; heyday of life
el, me **YRNEH** unit of reciprocal inductance
bt **YUCCA** lily genus
YUCKY itchy
bt **YULAN** Chinese magnolia
nt **YULOH** aft-oar for sculling
YUSHO Chinese rice disease

Z

nt **ZABRA** Spanish coasting vessel
ZAMBO cross-bred Indian
bt **ZAMIA** a palm genus
ZANJE irrigation canal (S. Amer.)
bt **ZANTE** satin-wood
nt **ZARUG ZARUK** Yemeni dhow
ZAYAT Burmese inn
nt **ZEBEC XEBEC**, Algerian ship
zo **ZEBRA** a horse in pyjamas
zo **ZEBUS** Abyssinian tsetse-fly
bt **ZEINE** the gluten of maize
zo **ZEMNI** the blind mole-rat
ZENER semi-conductor current
ZERDA African fox
zo **ZHOBO ZHOMO**, yak and cow hybrid
rl **ZIARA** Moslem shrine
zo **ZIBET** Asiatic civet
ga **ZIMBA** Am. Indian and Eskimo game
zo **ZIMBI** cowry used as money
ZINCO zincograph
mu **ZINKE** old type of comet
zo **ZIZEL** marmot; ground-squirrel
nm **ZLOTY** Polish money
ar, ma **ZOCCO ZOCLE**, square base
zo **ZOEAL** early crustacean life
zo **ZOFRA** Moorish carpet
ZOGAN Japanese inlay work
rl **ZOHAR** sacred Jewish book
ZOISM theory of life origin
ZOIST a believer in zoism
ZONAL ZONAR, of regional areas
ZONIC ZONES, of girdle divisions, 5 belts
ZONDA the dry wind of the Andes
zo **ZOOID** polyp; polypide

ZOOKS gadzooks; exclamation
mu **ZOPPA** limping syncopation
zo **ZORIL** African skunk
zo **ZORRA** American skunk
zo **ZORRO** S. American fox-wolf
ZUPAN Serbian rural council
ZYGAL like an 'H'
ZYGON connecting bar
ZYMIC relating to fermentation
zo **ZYMIN** ex-enzyme

SIX-LETTER WORDS

A

ABACOT bycoket; hat of state (15th cent.)
ma, ar **ABACUS** ancient hand computer; sandstone (capital)
ABALYN synthetic resin; lacquer
ABASED demoted; humbled; put down
md **ABASIA** uncoordination in walking
lw **ABATED ABATER**, tension; moderated nuisance
ABATIS abattis; obstacles
ck **ABATTE** heavy meat-flattening knife
rl **ABBACY** office of abbot
rl **ABBATE** a title
rl **ABBESS** head of nuns' abbey
ABDALS Moslem fanatics (Pers.)
ABDEST Mohammedan rite
ABESSE thin, long pastry
rl **ABDIEL** seraph; 6-winged angel
ABDUCE separate; retract
ABDUCT remove; kidnap
ABIDED ABIDER, sojourned; dweller; accepted decision
pc **ABIENT** avoidance reflex
ABJECT servile; base; ignoble
ABJURE renounce; recant; repudiate
ABLAUT vowel pronunciation mark
ABLAZE on fire; flaming; excited
ABLEST most competent; cleverest
bt **ABLOOM** thriving; flowering
ABLUSH blushing; flushing
nt **ABOARD** on/within a ship; (transport)
ABOLLA black cloak in Anc. Rome
pl **ABORAL** remote from the mouth
ABOUND verb of plentifulness (abundance)
ABRADE erode; scrape a surface
ABROAD overseas; far and wide
ABRUPT steep; hasty; brusque; curt
mo **ABSEIL** rapid twin-rope descent technique
pc **ABSENT** not present; evading; (-minded)
ABSORB assimilate; engulf; merge
ABSURD irrational; asinine
md, pc **ABULIA** atrophy of reasoning
ABUSED ABUSER, violated; ravager
bt **ACACIA** flowering tree
bt **ACACIO ACAJOU**, cashew nut
ACADIA Nova Scotia
bt **ACAJOU** gum; acacio
zo **ACARUS** insect genus
ck **ACATES** food; nourishment
ACCEDE assent; agree; comply
ACCENT tone; stress; cadence
ACCEPT take; receive; admit
cp **ACCESS** entry; approach; retrieval
ACCITE to cite
ACCLOY to cloy; satiate; surfeit
ACCORD mutual agreement; text guide
ACCOST confront; hail; greet
ck **ACCOUB** edible thistle
ACCREW ACCRUE, accumulate; bank interest; result
ACCUSE charge; cite; censure
md, zo **ACEDIA** torpor; fish
ACERIC (Maple)
ch **ACETAL** plastic; cosmetic base
ck **ACETIC ACETYL**, the acid in olive oil
bt **ACHENE** seeded fruit
ACHING continued pain; sorrowing
ck, bt **ACHIRA** edible canna; ginger, america herbs
mu **ACHTEL** eighth note; quaver
bt, mn **ACICLE** bristle; sharp crystal
ch **ACIDIC** containing acid
bt **ACINUS** berry
ACK-ACK anti-aircraft guns; (defence)
mn **ACLIDE** spiked club
mn **ACMITE** pyroxene rock
ma **ACNODE** in double point tangets
md **ACOPIC** curative of fatigue
md **ACORIA** morbid appetite for food
bt **ACORUS** sweet flag; calamus root
ACQUIT absolve; release; exonerate
ACRACY anarchy
ACRISY poor judgement
zo **ACRITA** sponges
ACROSS athwart; transversely
ACTING performing; pretending
lw, md **ACTION** doing; function; deed; (legal-)
cp **ACTIVE** operator; busy; self-adjusting
cp **ACTUAL** real; true; definite; topical
ACUATE ACUITY, pointed; sharp (perception)
bt, zo **ACULEI** prickles; thorns
ACUMEN keenness of perception

mu **ADAGIO** leisurely
ADAMIC pertaining to Adam
ADDEEM judge
cp, ma **ADDEND** an increase
ADDICT habituate (hooked) (drugs) (hobby)
ADDING totting; summing
ADDLED deranged; rotten; (eggs)
ADDUCE offer proof; analysis
ch **ADDUCT** product of molecular reaction
md **ADENIA** enlargement of glands
ADHERE cohere; cling; cleave
ADIENT tending to expose to stimulus
ADIEUS ADIEUX, farewells
ADIPIC fatty; adipose
ADJECT to add to; extend
ADJOIN abut; annex; link
ADJURE exhort; urge; beg; pray
ADJUST arrange; trim; rectify; fit
ADMASS common consumers; the masses
ADMIRE esteem; prize; revere; respect
ADNATE joined to another organ
zo **ADNEXA** appendages; close structures
ADNOUN noun derived from adjective
ADONAI lord (Hebrew)
ADONIC species of short verse
zo **ADONIS** perfect boy; eye of bird
zo **ADORAL** adjacent to the mouth
ADORED ADORER, worshipped (lover)
cf **ADRENO-** of adrenalin
ADRIFT afloat; distracted; loose
ADROIT expert; skilful; masterly
ADSORB to condense a gas
ADVENE come to agreement
rl **ADVENT** arrival; approach; coming; (Xmas)
ADVERB manner; time of an action
ADVERT to notice; printed offer; (notice) (ad.)
ADVICE ADVISE, ADVISO, recommend; bulletin
ar, rl **ADYTUM** chancel; in a church
ck **ADZUKI** red Japanese bean
bt **AECIAL** spore-producing part of fungi
AEDILE Roman magistrate
rl **AENEAD AENEID**, epic of Aeneas (Lat.)
AEOLIC Aeolian dialect (Gr.)
rl, mu **AEOLUS** god of the wind (aeolian harp); wind operated
AERATE expose to air action
ro, tv **AERIAL** etherial; empyreal; airy; transits (leaps); antenna
AERIFY aerate
md **AEROBE** an organic growth
AEROSE coppery; brassy
AERUGO verdigris; patina
AFFAIR incident; concern; skirmish; (love-)
AFFEAR to be terrified
AFFECT assume; feign; influence; mood
lw **AFFEER** settle a price
ma **AFFINE** similar curves of variables
AFFIRM vouch; endorse; allege; oath
AFFLUX incoming flow; influx
AFFORD produce; impart; confer; spare
AFFRAY onset; brawl; strife; fracas
AFFRET effray; broil; startle; frighten
AFFUSE sprinkle; pour upon
zo **AFGHAN** native of Afghanistan; (-hound)
AFIELD in the open; away from base
AFLAME blazing; on fire; (set –)
nt **AFLOAT** on the sea; drifting; unfixed; lost
pg **AFOCAL** without focal length
AFRAID timid; fearful; anxious; scared
ce **A-FRAME** two sloping legs joined at top
AFREET evil spirit (Arab.)
AFRESH anew; again
AFRIDI Afghan tribe NW Frontier
AFSHAR rug-making nomadic tribe
ck **AFTERS** sweet or dessert course
AGALMA impression of a seal
bt **AGAMAE** cryptogamic plants
AGAMIC assexual
bt **AGARIC** fungus; mushroom
AGEING maturing; mellowing (process)
AGEISM discrimination against elderly people
pc **AGENCY** trading office; go-between
AGENDA items of business
AGHAST appalled; astounded
md **AGNAIL** a whitlow
AGNAME nickname
AGNATE (relationship) akin; allied
AGNISE acknowledge; confess
AGNOSY ignorance
AGOING going on; current; topical
AGONIC zero declination
zo **AGOUTA** Haitian rat
zo **AGOUTI AGOUTY**, guinea-pig; S. American rodent

ck **AGRAFA** Greek cheese
AGRAIL narrow-gauge railway
AGREED consented; (same aim)
md **AGUISH** shivering; chilly
AHIMSA sacredness of life (Hindu, Jain)
AIDING assisting; succouring
zo **AIGLET AGLET**, young eagle; pendant
zo **AIGRET AIGRETTE-EGRET**, white plume
AIKIDO ancient Japanese martial art
AILING sick; unwell; indisposed
AIMING pointing (gun); endeavouring
AINHUM chronic disease causing digit loss
AIR-ACE super-airman
AIR-BED inflated mattress
AIRDOX coal-mining process using air
AIR-DRY dry to parity with atmosphere
AIR-GUN air-operated weapon
AIRILY buoyantly; gaily
AIRING stroll; ventilation
AIR-LOG linear travel recorder
AIRMAN aeronaut
AIR-SAC air-cell
AIRWAY AIRLINE, route; transport company
ar, rl **AISLED** having (processional) corridors; (church; hall)
AJOURE perforated metalwork
AKIMBO arched; bent arms
md **ALALIA** loss of speech
ALALIA decorative script (Sp.); Moresque ceramic wares
ALARUM ALARM, danger signal; panic; (-clock)
zo **ALATED ALATE**, winged (birds, insects, aircraft etc.)
ALBATA an alloy
ALBEDO light reflective power
ALBEIT although; despite all; even though
ALBERT a watch chain
gl **ALBIAN** cretaceous rock stage
zo **ALBINO** white (genetic exception)
ALBION England (Morte D'Arthur)
mn **ALBITE** (felspar)
md, bt **ALBUGO** eye-trouble; fungus
ALCADE ALCAID, judge; mayor (Sp.)
ALCAIC poetic metre
zo **ALCEDO ALCYON**, kingfisher
ALCLAD an aluminium alloy
ALCOVE a bower; arbour; recess tree
bt **ALDERN** wood of alder tree
ALDINE 16th-century books printed by Aldus
ALECTO a Fury
ALEGAR sour ale
ALEGER lively; cheerful
bt **ALERCE** cedar wood
ar **ALETTE** pilaster
zo **ALEVIN** salmon fry
md **ALEXIA** inability to read
md **ALEXIN** defensive protein
ALGATE always; nevertheless
bt **ALGOID** (seaweeds)
bt **ALGOUS** (algoid)
ALIBLE nourishing
ALIGHT descend; ignited; flaming
ar, pr **ALINED ALIGNED**, brought into line; layout
ALIPED having winged feet
ch **ALKALI** opposite to acid
ch **ALKANE** methane series
ch **ALKENE** ethylene series
ALLEGE assert; maintain
gn **ALLELE** alternative form of gene
zo **ALLICE** Severn shad; fish
ALLIED united; related; cognate; akin
ALLIES affinities; associates
ALL-OUT top speed
ALLUDE refer; imply; hint; insinuate
ALLURE tempt; decoy; seduce; cajole
mu **ALMAIN ALMAND-ALLEMANDE**, Ger. dance form
ALMIRA storage furniture (Ind.)
ALMOIN alms; alms-chest (tenure)
bt, ck **ALMOND** dessert nut; (oil)
ALMOST nearly; approximately
ALMUCE amice or furred hood
me **ALNAGE** measuring by the ell
ALNICO permanent magnet alloy
ALOGIA mental deficiency speech defect
tx, zo **ALPACA** llama; Peruvian camel (mohair)
md **ALPHUS** leprosy; psoriasis
ALPINE of the Alps
ALPINI Italian mountain troops
bt **ALPIST** bird-seed
bt **ALSIKE** Swedish clover
ALTERN alternata
bt **ALTHEA** rose of Sharon
ch **ALUDEL** distilling apparatus
ALUMNA a woman graduate
ALUMNI collegiates; pupils; scholars
md **ALVINE** pert. to belly, intestines
ALWAYS continually; eternally
AMADOU dried fungus; tinder
ch **AMATOL** explosive
AMAZED astounded, nonplussed

md **AMAZIA** mammary non-development
AMAZON female warrior; virago; shrew
AMBAGE circumlocution; subterfuge
mn **AMBERY** stone-like Baltic resin (gem)
ga **AMBIGU** French version of poker
AMBLED AMBLER, sauntered; casual walker
bt **AMBURY ANBURY**, turnip disease
AMBUSH surprise trap attack
md **AMELIA** congenital limb absence
AMENDS recompensate; apology; adjustment; (make-)
AMENED ratified
md **AMENIA** menstrual disorders
bt **AMENTA** catkins
AMERCE to fine arbitrarily
ch **AMIDIN** starch solution
pg **AMIDOL** developing agent
pc, md **AMIMIA** loss of sign ability
ch **AMINOL** an explosive
md, zo **AMNION** embryonic habitat
md **AMNOIS** membrane
zo **AMOEBA** protozoa
bt **AMOMUM** cardamom; aromatic shrub; seeds as spice
AMORAL against customary mores
AMORCE toy detonator; percussion cap
AMORET sweetheart; love knot
ar **AMORPH** altogether shapeless
AMOUNT sum; total; aggregate; attain
el, me **AMPERE** unit of current intensity
AMPLER more copious; fuller; richer
AMREET water of immortality
AMRITA nectar; ambrosia
AMULET charm; talisman; safeguard
AMURCA olive-oil extract
AMUSED diverted; beguiled; enlivened
md, pc **AMUSIA** loss of musicality
ch **AMYLIC AMYLUM**, of starch
md **AMYOUS** lacking muscle; muscular weakening
zo **ANABAS** tree-climbing fish
ANADEM garland; chaplet
ANALET précis of an analysis
cp **ANALOG** system behaviour comparison
bt **ANANAS** pineapple
ANANYM name written backwards
ANARCH ANARCHIST, against all forms of government
ck **ANNATO ANOTTO**, orange dye in cheeses
nt **ANCHOR** ship's brake; (sheet-) (-bolt)
md **ANCOME** a boil; a whitlow
zo **ANCONA** a fowl
go **ANDEAN** of the Andes (S. Am.)
cf, pc **ANDRON ANDROS-**, men's meeting room; of males (Gr.)
ANELED anointed (extreme unction)
md **ANEPIA** loss of power of speech
ANERGY failure of energy; immunity
mu **ANESIS** tuning to lower pitch
md **ANESIS** abatement of symptoms
ANGARY angaria; war-rights
md **ANGINA** quinsy (pectoris)
zo **ANGLED ANGLER**, fished; schemed; fisher; frog
ANGLES corners; aspects; (– and Saxons)
tx **ANGORA** cloth (mohair) of camel, goat, cat
zo **ANHIMA** horned screamer bird
ANICUT dam for irrigation (Ind.)
ANIGHT at night; nocturnal
ch, tx, md **ANILIC** of dyes (anil/indigo)
zo **ANIMAL** creature; beast; carnal
ANIMUS spirit; soul; animosity (ill will)
ANKLED having ankles
ANKLET ornament or fetter
cf, md **ANKYLO** fusion; bent
ANLACE dagger
ANNALS historical records
rl **ANNATE ANNATS**, first fruits
ml **ANNEAL** to temper; strengthen metal
ANNONA year's produce
pr, bt **ANNUAL** yearly (book) (occasion) (plants)
bt **ANODAL** genetic spiral upward
ANODIC anodal; positively polar
ANOINT anele; consecrate
zo **ANOLIS** lizard genus (Amer.)
pc **ANOMIA ANOMIC**, inability to recall names
pc **ANOMIE** crash of social values
ANONYM purposely without signature
md **ANOPIA** defective vision
ANORAK hooded windproofer
ANOTIA absence of ears
zo **ANOURA** frog genus
md **ANOXIA** deficiency of oxygen
ANSATE handled
ANSWER reply; response; refute
zo **ANT-COW** arphis (fly)
ANTERO before; previously; prior to
ANTHEM ANTIPHON, church (national) hymn
bt **ANTHER** part of stamen

ANTHUS meadow pipit
bt **ANTIAR** upas tree
zo **ANTLER** sheddable deer horn
zo **ANTLIA** proboscis of insects
md **ANTRUM** cavity; cave; den
rl **ANUBIS** jackal-headed Egyptian deity
md **ANULUS** ring-shaped structure
zo **ANURAL** tailless
md **ANURIA** absence of urine secretion
ANYHOW in any case; in any way
ANYWAY anyhow
AONIAN (Muses)
AORIST a past tense (Gr.)
pl **AORTAL AORTIC**, of great heart artery
AOSMIC free from odour
APACHE Parisian assassin; American Indian
APATHY show of disinterest; torpor
APEDOM apishness
md **APEPSY** poor digestion
APERCU a précis; a summary
md **APHONY** loss of voice; dumbness
md **APHTHA** thrush disease
APIARY art of beekeeping
APICAL topmost
APICES culminations; highest points
APIECE to each
APINCH pinching
gl **APLITE** quartz-feldspar microgranite
APLOMB self-possession; poise
mn **APLOME** garnet
pl, md **APNOEA** breaks in breathing rhythm
zo **APODAL APODEL**, footless, 'fin-less'
as **APOGEE** furthest distance of other orbit from earth
APONIA painlessness
APORIA rhetorical doubt
md **APOSIA** absence of thirst feeling
bt **APOZEM** a decoction
lw **APPEAL** entreat; implore; invoke
APPEAR seem; emerge; dawn; look
APPEND add; fasten; subjoin
APPORT object produced by medium
APPOSE to seal; superimpose
zo **APTERA** wingless insects
APTOTE indeclinable noun
APULSE pulsing
zo, rl **AQUILA** eagle; bird of pray (lectern, bible holder)
mt **AQUILO** N, N-E wind (Lat.)
ARABIC language; race
bt **ARABIN** gum arabic
bt **ARABIS** rock-cress
ARABLE tillable; cultivable
mn **ARANGO** cornelian
ARBOUR bower; garden; retreat
bt **ARBUTE ARBUTUS**, strawberry tree
ar **ARCADE** arched gallery; (shopping passage)
rl **ARCADY** mythical pastoral paradise (Gr.)
rl **ARCANA ARCANE** (astrological) mysteries
ar **ARCATE ARCHED**, bow-shaped; vaulted; concave
as **ARCHER** bowman; (Zodiac Sagittarius)
bt **ARCHIL** violet dye
ARCHLY roguishly; merrily; shrewdly
ARCHON Greek magistrate
el **ARCING** electrical leap; diversion; sparking
ARCTIC northern; boreal; cold
ARDENT fiery; fervent; intense
ARDOUR warmth; heat; passion; zeal
bt, md **AREOLE AREAOLA**, cell nucleus; minimal space
zo **ARGALA** adjutant bird (Hindu)
zo **ARGALI** wild sheep of Asia
ARGAND (burner); (diagram)
md **ARGEMA** optical ulcer
hd **ARGENT** silver
ARGIVE (Argos); Greek
nt **ARGOSY** richly laden vessel
ARGUED reasoned; implied; mooted
ARGUER disputed; debated; pleaded
ARGUFY wrangle
ARGUTE subtle; ingenious
tx **ARIDAS** East African taffeta
ARIGHT correctly; properly
mu **ARIOSE ARIOSO**, melodious, aria-recitation
ARISEN reappeared; origin; arose (cropped up)
bt **ARISTA** beard of corn
ARKITE Noachian
nt **ARMADA** invasion fleet
ARMING preparing for war
go, hd **ARMLET ARMULET**, arm decoration; creek; armour
ar **ARMOUR** metal wear (knight's); foundation protection
md **ARMPIT** the axilla
tx **ARMURE** embossed-appearing cloth
ARNAUT Albanian mountaineer
bt **ARNICA** a plant genus
AROINT AROYNT, be gone from here!
AROUND about; encompassing
ma **AROURA** 100 square feet (Egyptian)
AROUSE excite; stir; provoke
me **ARPENT** 100 square perches
bt, ck **ARRACH ARRACK**, orache herb; fermented toddy

ARRANT errant; unmitigated
ARREAR **ARREARS**, unfinished; overdue (debts)
ARRECT erect; intent; alert
ARREST stem; curb; detain; capture
ARRIDE to please; to laugh at
ARRIVE reach; attain; land; come
me **ARROBA** Spanish 25 lb (11 kg) weight
ARROWY like an arrow
go **ARROYO** ravine; gully (Sp.)
me **ARSHIN** 30 in (76 cm) (Rus.)
ch **ARSINE** poison gas
md **ARTERY** blood vessel
ARTFUL sly; wily; subtle; astute
cf, md **ARTHRO-** joint; articulation
pt **ARTIST** painter; master; adept
bt **ARUNDO** reed genus
ASALTO assault (fox & geese game) (It.)
ASCEND climb; scale; mount
ASCENT rise; elevation; eminence
ASCIAN equator dweller
ASEITY self-origination
pc **ASEMIA** symbol comprehension inability
ASGARD abode of Norse gods
ASHAKE ashiver; aquake
ASHAME to feel shame (obs.)
ASHERY ash-heap
ASHIER more ashen; pale grey
ar **ASHLAR** **ASHLER**, hewn stone (building)
nt **ASHORE** stranded; aground; on land
ASH-PAN dust-pan; trash pan
rw **ASH-PIT** fire-refuse tip (locomotive)
md **ASITIA** off one's oats
ASKANT askance; obliquely
ASKARI African soldier
ASKING requesting; begging; inviting
ASLAKE to slake; to mitigate
ASLANT **ASLOPE**, obliquely; askew; awry
ASLEEP dormant; slumbering
ASNORT snorting
mu **ASONIA** inability to distinguish pitch
ASPECT facial expression; view; outlook
bt, zo **ASPICK** lavender; asp
ASPIRE aim; seek to attain; yearn for
zo **ASPOUT** blowing-off (whales)
ASQUAT squatting
ASSAIL attack; defame; asperse
ASSART to grub up trees, etc
nm **ASSARY** ancient Roman coin
ASSENT concur; agree; accord
ASSERT declare; maintain; allege; aver
ASSESS compute; tax; rate; value
ASSETS possessions; effects
lw **ASSIGN** allot; appoint; adduce; transfer
ASSIST aid; help; succour; abet
lw **ASSIZE** county court
ASSORT group; arrange; classify
ASSUME to take as fact; feign; take office
ASSURE aver; guarantee; warrant
ASTARE staring
ASTART suddenly
nt **ASTERN** aft; abaft; in reverse
ASTERT astart; suddenly (Spens.)
md **ASTHMA** breathing disorder
ASTRAL starry; stellar; sidereal
ASTRAY erring; wandering; missing
ASTRUT puffed up (obs.)
ASTUTE artful; subtle; wily
ASWARM swarming
ASWING asway
ASWOON in a swoon
ASYLUM a sanctuary; refuge
mu **ATABAL** Moorish drum
ATAMAN Cossack chief
ATAVIC inherent; heriditary
ATAVUS remote ancestor
md **ATAXIA** paralysis
md **ATAXIC** irregular
pc **ATELIA** retaining childish traits
rl **ATHENE** goddess of wisdom and war
AT-HOME a reception; open house
ATHROB throbbing
ATHYMY melancholy
ATKINS British private soldier (Tommy)
md **ATOCIA** female sterility
ch, ps **ATOMIC** of minimal particle (energy)
mu **ATONAL** lacking tone
ATONED reconciled; propitiated
ATONER an expiator
md **ATONIC** unaccented; debilitated
md **ATOPIC** allergic; misplaced
ATRIAL pertaining to atrium
ar **ATRIUM** Roman hall; (patio)
zo **ATRIUM** cavity (sinus); fish gills
ATROUS jet black
ATTACH annex; adhere; cement
ATTACK storm; charge; assail; impugn
ATTACK sudden onset of battle or disease
ATTAIN acquire; achieve; reach; grasp
ATTASK to task
ATTEND serve; guard; hearken; heed
ATTENT intention; attentive (Spens.)

ATTEST ratify; confirm; endorse
ATTIRE garb; rig; accoutre; outfit
lw **ATTORN** transfer (homage) (property)
ATTRAP array; adorn
ATTUNE harmonize; accord; adapt
ATWAIN in sunder
ATWEEM between
ATWIXT betwixt
md **ATYPIC** unclassified; unusual
AUBADE dawn; concert; morning song
AUBURN carroty; Titian; hair (colour)
AUDILE who prefers auditory images to visuals
ro **AUDION** wireless amplifier
AUGEAN foul; arduous (stables) (Hercules)
cp, ma **AUGEND** sum to be added to
mn **AUGITE** volcanic rock
AUGURY omen; portent; sign; presage
AUGUST majestic; venerable; imposing
mu **AULETE** flautist
rl **AUMBRY** ambry; cupboard
AUMUCE amice; furred hood
AUNTIE aunty; prude
ar **AURATE** having ears; gilded (design)
AUREAT gilded; golden; auric
nm **AUREUS** Roman gold coin
AURIFY change into gold
AURIGA a constellation; the Charioteer
AURINE dye-acid
md **AURIST** ear specialist
AURORA goddess of dawn; northern lights
AUROUS golden; aureate
AUSPEX seer; diviner; prophet
AUSSIE an Australian
mt **AUSTER** South wind
AUSTIN Augustine
AUTHOR writer; creator; cause; agent
AUTISM self-absorption
AUTUMN the fall
AVALON a western legendary isle
bt **AVANCE** avens; herb bennet
AVANTI forward (It.)
rl **AVATAR** incarnation of Brahma
AVAUNT be off with you!
AVAUNT AVENER, AVENOR, feudal master of the Horse
AVENGE retaliate; to take revenge
AVENUE entry; access; approach; fine road
AVERSE loath; allergic; reluctant
zo **AVIARY** a large bird-cage
AVIATE to fly (aircraft pilot)
ch **AVIDIN** protein in egg
AVIDLY voraciously; greedily; eagerly
AVISED hue; complexion
AVITAL hereditary; ancestral
lw **AVOCAT** advocate (Fr.)
zo **AVOCET AVOSET**, wading bird
AVOUCH maintain; guarantee
AVOURE confession; justification (Spens.)
lw **AVOWAL AVOWED**, open admission; on oath
lw **AVOWEE** (advowson)
lw **AVOWRY** (replevin)
AVULSE to grab
AWAKEN rouse; stir up; kindle
AWASTE wasting
AWATCH watching; alert
AWEARY tired; faded; spent
nt **AWEIGH** atrip; apeak (raise anchors)
AWHEEL cycling; motoring
AWHILE sometime; briefly; soon
ar **AWNING** tent-like shelter; canopy
md **AXENIC** free from parasites
ar, nt **AXICLE** pulley wheel in sheave; (tackle)
md **AXILLA** armpit
AXUNGE hog's lard; wheel-grease
zo **AYE-AYE** squirrel-like lemur
bt **AZALEA** plant, rhododendron type
ch **AZARIN** brilliant crimson dye
AZAZEL Satan's standard-bearer
tx **AZMURE** semi-embossed cloth
AZONAL recent formation (soil)
AZONIC not local
AZOTIC lifeless
AZRAEL destroying angel
AZURED coloured light blue; (sea)
ch **AZURIN** blue dye
AZYGOS occurring singly

B

BAAING bleating; (sheep & lambs)
BAALIM false gods (Baal)
BABBIT Babbit metal
BABBLE noise (babies) (crowds) (chatter)
BABBLE (Eco-, Euro-) etc. jargon
BABIES newborn, of human & wildlife
bt **BABLAH** acacia-rind
zo **BABOON** dog-like herd monkeys
BACKED BACKER, reversed (cars); aided (finance); abetted

BACKET coal box; hod; coal scuttle
cp **BACK-UP** supporting service; assistance
zo, to **BADGER** animal (-teasing; -baiting) tool; pester
bt **BADIAN** tree with anise-flavoured fruit
bd, ce **BAFFLE** balk; thwart; acoustics; slat; plate
tx **BAFTAS** cotton; muslin
BAGFUL contents; capacity of a bag
BAGGED obtained (first); stolen; shot (wildlife)
zo **BAGGIT** salmon after spawning
BAGMAN commercial traveller; tramp
bd **BAGNIO** bath-house (It.)
mt **BAGUIO** tropical cyclone; Philippines
BAGWIG an 18th-century wig
go **BAHADA BAJADA**, alluvial plain (Piedmont)
lw **BAILED BAILEE**, obtains pre-trial freedom
lw **BAILER BAILOR**, deposits securities as bail, on trust
nt, ce **BAILER** who pumps out water (sump); sand pump
ar **BAILEY** courtyard in castle
lw **BAILIE** alderman in council (Scots)
BAITED teased; provoked; (bear-) (badger-)
bt **BAJREE** Indian grass
BAKERY bake-house
ck **BAKING** cooking in oven; heat drying
BALAAM unimportant newsprint
mn **BALASS** a ruby
bt **BALATA** rubberlike gum
nm **BALBOA** coin of Panama
rl **BALDER** less hirsute; Nordic sungod
BADLY inelegantly; plainly
zo **BALEEN** whalebone
BALING bundling; emptying
nt **BALIZE** sea mark
go **BALKAN** of S.E. Europe (peninsula)
BALKED refused; frustrated
BALKER fish-spotter
BALKIS Queen of Sheba; also Aaziz
mu **BALLAD** narrative poem; epic song
BALLED clogged; ill done; (black-); vetoed
BALLET art dance
BALLOT voting; (election); rote paper
bt **BALSAM** aromatic balm
go, nt, lw **BALTIC** European sea; (-shipping exchange)
bt **BAMBOO** tree-like grass
ck **BAMMIE** Caribbean cassava cake
bt, ck **BANANA** fruit; (republic); (can split)
nm **BANCOR** monetary unit
BANDED united; bound
BANDIT outlaw; brigand; footpad
me **BANDLE** 2 ft (60 cm) (Irish)
zo **BANDOG** ferocious (banned) dog
BANGED with hair cut square
ck **BANGER** a cooked sausage
BANGHY Ind. porter's shoulder-yoke
BANGLE bracelet; armlet; ring
BANGUE bhang; a narcotic
BANG-UP slap-up; stylish
bt **BANIAN** Hindu caste; fig-tree
BANISH exile; expel; eject
bd, rw **BANKED** deposited; road; rail; dyke
ga **BANKER** lender; pushing locomotive; cards
BANKER mason's table; fishing boat; (gambling)
gl **BANKET** auriferous rock (Transvaal)
BANNED barred; tabooed; vetoed
bt **BANNER** petal; flag; standard
zo **BANTAM** carved work; small hen; (boxing)
BANTER cheerful; witty repartee; bandy
bt **BANYAN** Indian fig; banian
ga **BANZAI!** Japanese hurrah; drag-racing
bt **BAOBAB** African tree
ga **BARANI BARONI**, gymnast's somersault (It.)
BARBED bearded; hooked; pointed
zo **BARBEL** carp
BARBER hairdresser (men)
zo **BARBET** bird; dog
bt **BARCOO** grass (Aust.)
BARDIC poetic; epic
tx **BAREGE** fabric
BARELY only just
ga **BAREME** rules for show-jumping
BAREST bleakest; baldest; shoved
BARGED charged into; shoved
BARGEE bargeman
BARING uncovering; (-teeth)
BARISH rather bare
ch **BARIUM** metallic element
BARKED grazed (shins); helped
BARKEN to become like bark
BARKER shop-tout
bt, ag, ck **BARLEY** a cereal for beer
BARMAN pot-man; bar-tender
BARNED stored
BARNEY humbug; prize fight
BARONY a baron's holding
nt **BARQUE BARQUA-BARK**, three-masted sailing ship

bt **BARRAS** resin
BARRED barricaded; forbidden; ostracized
me, ck **BARREL** cask for beer, wine, oil; 36 gal.
ar **BARREL** part of a gun; vaulting
BARREN bare; sterile; unfertile
rl **BARRET** beret; cap
BARROW street seller's cart; ancient mound
BARTER trade; exchange; traffic
BARTON domain lands; farmhouse
ps **BARYON** heavy subatomic particle
ch **BARYTA** barium oxide
mn **BASALT** igneous rock
BASELY spuriously; corruptly
BASIAL osculatory
BASIFY make into a salifiable salt
BASING founding; establishing
BASKED warmed by the sun
BASKET pannier; creal; punnet; trug; goal (basketball)
BASNET helmet; bassinet
BASQUE Biscayan
zo **BASSET** outcrop; (cards); hound
BASTED oiled while roasting; patched; thrashed
hd **BASTON** heraldic baton
BASUCO BAZUCO, crack; cocaine waste (S. Am.)
BASUTO African
ch **BASYLE** radicle
bt, ck **BATATA** sweet potato; yam
nt **BATEAU** boat (French)
nt **BATELO** small dhow (Arabian coasts)
BATHED laved; suffused
BATHER swimmer; laver
BATHIC pertaining to sea depths
BATHOS anti-climax; bombast
BATING except; abating; deducting
BATLET linen-beater
BATMAN an officer's servant (valet)
BATOON baston; bar; staff; truncheon
ga **BATTED** (cricket)
BATTEL Oxford kitchen account
nt, bd **BATTEN** slat used for sails, tarpaulins; hatches
BATTEN BATTON on someone (become dependent) (parasitic)
ck, ar **BATTER** pancake mix; beat to destroy; sloping wall; player with striker (cricket, baseball)
BATTLE military encounter (armies); contest; fight
BATTUE a beat; slaughter
nm **BAUBEE BAWBEE**, halfpenny (Sc.)
BAUBLE showy trinket (gee-gaw); jester's wand
nt **BAURUA** rapid outrigger canoe (Polyn.)
zo **BAVIAN** poetaster; baboon
BAWLED clamoured; shouted; yelled
BAWLER a howler
nt **BAWLEY** Thames fishing-boat
zo **BAWSON BAWSIN**, a badger
zo **BAWTIE** a hare; a dog
BAYING in full cry; sound of foxhounds (hunting); wolves
BAYRAM Mohammedan festival
BAZAAR mart; emporium; exchange
gl **BEACHY** pebbly (of shoreline)
nt **BEACON** signal-fire; lighthouse; sea mark
rl **BEADED** strung together; (necklace) (prayer-s)
BEADLE public order officer
ro, zo **BEAGLE** a hound; jammer
nt **BEAKED** of birds; of ships; rammer bow
BEAKER drinking cup, mug
ar, bd, nt **BEAMED** smiled; (lighthouse); supported (wood); guided by radar
ga **BEAMER** head line bowling (cricket) (foul)
BEARER porter; joist; (cheque) (funerals)
ck **BEATEN** punished (bodily); defeated; whisked (eggs); hammered
BEATER striker; whisker; knocker; (fire-) (gamebirds-)
BEAUTY grace; comeliness; fairness
zo **BEAVER** water rodent; (-dam); hard worker; (-hat)
BECAME grew into; graced
nt **BECKET** an eye in a knot
BECKON call; wave; signal; invite
BECOME BECAME, suit; changed; grown into
zo **BED-BUG** cimex; (bed-louse)
bt **BEDDED** planted out; (hotel room); (laid)
bt **BEDDER** millstone; a plant; bedmaker
BEDECK array; gild; adorn
to **BED-KEY** bedstead tightener
BEDLAM mad-house; uproar
BEDLOCK WEDLOCK, matrimony; marriage
BEDUIN BEDOUIN, nomadic Arab
ae **BEEPER** remote-controlled aircraft
zo **BEETLE** insect; maul; heavy mallet; (to speed)
BEFALL betide; happen; chance
BEFANA Epiphany present; a fairy

BEFORE formerly; above (texts); in front of
BEGGAR pauper; to bankrupt; beyond imagination
BEGGED implored; entreated; cadged
BEGONE! go away; avaunt!
BEGUNK piece of deception
BEHALF benefit; interest; advantage
BEHAVE act; comport; demean
BEHEAD decapitate; execute
BEHELD saw; surveyed; contemplated
BEHEST command; mandate; order
pl **BEHIND** abaft; following; buttocks
BEHOLD regard; discern; look
BEHOOF profit; advantage; benefit
BEHOVE befit; suit; beseem
BEHUNG draped; well-endowed
BELACE adorn with lace; beat
BELATE delay; retard; hinder
BELAUD overpraise; bepuff
BELDAM a hag; beldame
BELFRY bat habitat; bell-tower
BELGIC Belgian; of Belgium
BELIAL a low and profligate devil
BELIED falsified; counterfeited
BELIEF faith; creed; dogma; tenet
BELIER confidence criminal; liar
BELIKE likely; perhaps; maybe
BELIVE speedily; ere long (Sc.)
BELLED bellowed
bt **BELLIS** the daisy
md **BELLOW** lead colic
BELLOW roar; bawl; clamour
nt **BELLUM** Iraqi long canoe
BELOCK to fasten; to lock
zo **BELONE** garfish
BELONG to appertain
BELTED girt; zoned; girdled
zo, ck **BELUGA** sturgeon; source of caviare
BEMASK to conceal
zo **BEMBEX** genus of sand-wasps
BEMOAN lament; bewail; mourn
BEMUSE daze; bewilder
BENDER spree; a stretcher
tx **BENGAL** fabric; (Lancer)
BENIGN kindly; amiable; friendly
nv **BENITO** navigation system
bt **BENNET** herb
bt **BEN-NUT** oil-nut of horse-radish tree
rl **BENSHI** **BANSHEE**, Irish fairy; house ghost
BENUMB stupefy; deaden; blunt
ch **BENZOL** benzene
BERATE rate; scold; chide; reprove
BERBER Moroccans of Atlas mountains
BERBER a Barbary language
BEREAN extinct Scottish sect
BEREFT stripped; deprived; destitute
BERLIN a vehicle; wool
BERTHA big Hun gun (1st World War)
hd, nm **BESANT** **BEZANT**, Byzantine gold; circlet
BESIDE near; close by; alongside
BESTED overwhelmed; worsted
BESTIR hasten; rouse; strive
BESTOW confer; grant; give; award
BESTUD to stud
BETAKE **BETOOK**, remove oneself; go away; leave
BETEEM produce; shed
rl **BETHEL** a chapel; sect
BETIDE befall; happen; chance
BETIME betide; befall
BETISE stupid act (Fr.)
bt **BETONY** a plant
BETRAY divulge; reveal; entrap
BETTED wagered
BETTER superior; amend; rectify; gambler
BETTOR punter; wagerer
BEVIES flocks; crowds
hd **BEVILE** heraldic device
BEWAIL moan; lament; grieve; deplore
BEWARE achtung! heed; mind
zo **BEWTER** bittern
BEYLIK a Bey's province
BEYOND over; past; farther
nt **BEZAAN** **BEZAN**, Dutch ketch
nt **BEZANT** **BESANT**, Dutch sailing vessel
BEZOAR a stony concretion
zo **BHARAL** wild sheep (Tibet)
BHISTI Indian water-carrier
ch **BIACID** of a base
BIASED prejudiced
BIAXAL **BIAZAL**, having two optical axes
BIBBER wine-bibber; toper
bt **BIBLUS** papyrus; paper-reed
pl **BICEPS** upper arm muscle
BICKER bowl; quarrel; nipple
hd, zo **BICORN** having 2 horns (ungulates)
BIDALE a benefit
BIDDED (auction) offered
BIDDER tenderer
BIDENT two-pronged
BIDING waiting; sojourning
BIDOUS lasting 2 days
BIFFED coshed; bashed
BIFFIN apple pie; dried apple
BIFLEX double curve
bt **BIFOIL** two-blade plant

BIFOLD two-fold; double
BIFORM having two shapes
BI-FUEL propelled with two fuels
BIGAMY plural marriage
BIG-END crank end of connecting rod
BIGGEN BIGGIN, child's cap; small wooden bowl
BIGGER larger; greater; bulkier
el **BIGRID** double-control-grid thermionic
BIG-WIG important person
BIKING cycling
BIKINI minimal 1- or 2-piece bathing-suit
BILBAO wall mirror (N. Amer.)
BILDAR Indian camp servant
nt **BILGED** double-bottomed (broad) boat
BILKED BILKER, defrauded; absconder
BILLED advertised; debited
ar **BILLET** a log; note; lodgings; ticket; romanesque moulding; thumbpiece on a tankard
zo **BILLIE** tin can; billy; male goat
BILLON an alloy
BILLOT gold or silver bar
BILLOW rolling, heaving (waves); glider wing fullness
BIMANA BIMANE, both handed
BIMBOY male bimbo
ma, cp **BINARY** mathematical system; 2 digits
mu **BINARY** sonata form in 2 keys
BINATE double; in pairs; twosome; twin
pr, bd, ce **BINDER** loose cover; bandage; (book); cement
BINGHI Australian aborigine
BINGLE base hit (baseball)
ga **BINGLE** base hit (baseball)
el **BINODE** 2-electrode thermionic tube
BINOUS binate; double
md **BIOPSY** tissue examination
zo **BIOSIS** life; distinguishing organisms
md **BIOTIC** biological
BIOTIN B vitamin
BIPACK two-film colour photography
pr **BIPONT** bipontine
BIRDED snared
BIRDER bird catcher
ga **BIRDIE** one under bogey at golf
nt **BIREME** cf. trireme; 2-banked oared galley (Mediterranean)
BIRKEN made of birch-wood
BIRKIE BIRSIE, lively lad (Sc.)
BIRLER a carouser
BIRSLE to scorch; to toast (Sc.)
BISECT to halve
rl, ga **BISHOP** church dignitary; chess; (horse-faking)
BISQUE croquet handicap; glazeless firing
ck, ga **BISQUE** lobster soup; extra stroke (golf)
BISTER BISTRE, sombre brown pigment
BISTRO small eating house (Fr.)
BITING mordant; champing
BITTED (horse's bit)
BITTEN tricked; corroded; (once-)
BITTER acrimonious; sour; tart; (beer); severe; (grief); (pill)
BITTLE flat club; beetle
zo **BITTOR** the bittern
ch **BIURET** urea product
BIZARD carnation
BLADED having a blade
BLAGUE blarney; swagger
BLAMED reproached; censured
BLANCH bleach; whiten; fade
BLARED trumpeted; pealed
BLASHY watery
BLAZED proclaimed; (trees)
BLAZER bright-coloured sports jacket
hd **BLAZON BLASON**, to display; blare; bear (crest); (mark)
BLEACH blanch; whiten
BLEAKY bleak; cheerless
BLEARY blear-eyed; tired-looking
BLEBBY blubby; blistered
BLENCH blink; shrink; flinch
mn **BLENDE** an ore of zinc
zo **BLENNY** fish
bt **BLEWIT** mushroom
bt **BLEYME** inflammation
bt **BLIGHT** mildew; disease; shrivel
BLINDS camouflage; screens; deceit
bt **BLINKS** chickweed
BLINKY blink-eyed
BLITHE merry; vivacious; joyous
BLONDE silk lace; fair lady
BLOODY sanguinary
BLOOMY blooming
BLOTCH a blemish; pustule; (ink-)
BLOTTO fuddled
BLOUSE loose outer garment
au **BLOW-BY** piston-leakage gas
BLOWED blasted; confounded
zo **BLOWER** a whale; telephone; voice pipe
BLOWTH bloom; blossoms

BLOWZE coarse woman
BLOWZY fat; tawdry; unkempt
BLUISH of blue colour
BLUEST most blue; gloomiest; (films)
BLUFFY an act of deceit (bluffing)
BLUING tempering steel
BLUISM (blue-stocking); female intellectual
BLUNGE (clay mixing)
BOARDS theatre stage; ice rink wall
BOATEL botel; boating hotel afloat
BOATER straw hat
BOBBED short hairstyle; moved up & down
cp **BOBBIN** spool; reel; magnetic core
BOBBLE bauble; trinket; ripple; decoration
BOBBLE regain lost balance (water-skiing); fumble (baseball)
ga **BOBLET** 2-man bob; sled
BOBWIG wig of short hair
bt, ag **BOCAGE** boscage; leafy underwood; small fields and large hedges (Fr.)
BOCKEY bowl made from a gourd
BODEGA wine-shop (Sp.)
BODGER pedlar; botcher
BODICE woman's upper body garment
BODIED real, live persons; (able-)
pl **BODIES** organizations; corpses; torsos
BODILY corporeally
BODING an omen; portending
BODKIN dagger; needle for tape
BODKIN three people crowded up
BOECKL figure skating, jump and turn
nt **BOEIER** Dutch merchantman
BOFFIN back-room scientist
BOGGLE to be amazed, stupified
BOGLET a small bog
bt **BOG-OAK** near-fossil wood
mn **BOG-ORE** limonite found in marshes
BOILED heated to evaporation point
BOILER hot-water heater
zo **BOIOBI** green snake
BOLARY clay-like
BOLDER more daring; saucier
BOLDLY confidently; valiantly
mu **BOLERO** Spanish dance; rhythm
BOLIDE meteor
BOLLED BOLLEN, swollen; podded
BOLTED barred; escaped; ate rapidly
BOLTER bran shredder
bt **BOMBAX** cotton-tree
BOMBED blitzed
zo **BOMBIC BOMBYX**, silkworm
BON-BON sugar-plum; Xmas cracker
BONDED warehoused (customs-free)
BONDER binding stone or brick
zo **BONGAR** poisonous Indian snake
mu **BONGOS** Conga twin drums
BONING levelling; removing bones
zo **BONITO** (tunny) (Sp.)
BONKED BONKER, performed sexual intercourse
BON-MOT witticism
nt, ar, bd **BONNET** women's cap; car casing; sail; bay window roofing; chimney cowl
BONNIE blithe; fair; joyous; pretty
tx **BONTEN** woolen stuff
BON-TON chic; good style; fashionable
zo **BONXIE** skua-gull
BONZER lucky strike (Aust.)
BOODLE loot; stolen money; as bribe
BOOHOO weep aloud
BOOING noisily disapproving; hooting
BOOKED entered; recorded; reserved; (copped)
BOOKIE bookmaker (betting)
BOOMED advertised; resounded
zo **BOOMER** born in baby boom; surfwave; kangaroo
BOOSED BOOZED, drank lustily
BOOTED wearing boots; dismissed
BOOTEE short boot
BOOTES constellation
BO-PEEP (sheep) hide and seek; (game)
bt **BORAGE** a plant
ch **BORATE** boric oxide
to **BORCER** rock-drill
BORDAR cottage
BORDEL sex-workers' den; bawdy-house
BORDER margin; boundary; edge
mt **BOREAL BOREAS**, of North wind
BOREEN Irish lane or track
BORING tedious; drilling
nt **BORLEY BAWLEY**, Thames barge
ma **BORROW** copy; assume; feign; obtain a loan; linguistic absorption; (arithmetical device)
ck **BORSCH** beetroot soup (Rus.)
zo **BORZOI** Russian hound
go **BOSCHE** wood; bush (S. Afr.)
bt **BOSKET** a grove; small wood
BOSSED controlled; dominated
BOSSED ornamented with round knobs
zo **BOSSET** rudimentary antler
BOSTAL hill road

mu **BOSTON** a dance
tx, bt **BOTANY** Australian wool; of plants
BOTCHY of ineptly bungled repair
zo **BOT-FLY** gad-fly
BOTHER pother; pester; worry
BOTHIE a house; a hut (Sc.)
hd **BOTONE** heraldic budding
bt **BO-TREE** sacred tree; pipal
nt **BOTTER** sea yacht
BOTTLE container; (-bank); courage; (-out, funk)
nt, pl **BOTTOM** basis; foot; foundation; buttocks; dell; (sea-); ship's; lowest rank; alluvial plain
ga **BOTTOM** unjumpable ditch (horse riding); last innings (baseball)
BOTTOM time a diver spends under water
BOUCAN dried meat
BOUCHE metal plug
wv, tx **BOUCLE** billowy woven cloth
BOUFFE farcical (Fr.)
BOUGHT purchased; bribed; bond deals (N. Am.)
mu **BOUGIE BOOGY**, form of jazz music
BOULET sloping pastern
zo, ga **BOUNCE** dog-fish; rebound (bad cheque); of ball games
BOUNDS (out of bounds)
BOUNTY gift; reward; liberality
go **BOURNE** destination; burn (Sc.); intermittent stream (often dry)
BOURSE Stock Exchange (Fr.)
cy **BOUTON** axon arborization end
me **BOVATE** peasant holding (20 acres; 8 hectares)
BOVINE cow-like (character); dull
BOW-BOY Cupid; Eros
BOW-CAP an extreme bow of airship
BOW-DYE scarlet
pl **BOWELS** colon & rectum, undermost parts
BOWERY shady; (New York)
zo **BOWESS** a young hawk
zo **BOWFIN** mudfish (N. Am.)
BOWING fiddling; submitting (respect)
ga **BOWLED** ball cast (cricket; bowls)
pl **BOW-LEG** crooked leg (knock-kneed)
ga **BOWLER** hard hat; cricketer (thrower)
BOWMAN archer
BOW-NET lobster-pot
BOW-OAR No. 1 of a racing crew
BOW-PEN a drawing instrument
to **BOW-SAW** narrow saw
nt **BOWSIE** cleat; knot on wood
tx **BOW-TIE** male neckwear
zo **BOW-WOW** jocular word for dog
cp, rw **BOXCAR** data converter; goods truck
ce **BOX-DAM** surrounding coffer-dam
lw **BOX-DAY** day for lodging papers
BOXING pugilism; packaging; cased frame (in window)
ce, bd **BOXING** (Christmas box); stone ballast under/between sleepers; boarding
BOYISH youthful; puerile; young
zo **BOYUNA** serpent
BRACED supported; propped
BRACER pick-me-up; support; protector; arm guard (archery)
cf **BRACHY-** short
BRAINY intellectual; clever
bt **BRAIRD** germination
ck **BRAISE** to stew
zo **BRAIZE** red pandora fish
BRAKED put on the brake; halted
BRANCH bough; off-shoot; agency; division
cp **BRANCH** change of direction; sequence
BRANDY strong distilled spirit
BRANKS scold's bridle
BRANKY showy (Sc.)
mu **BRANLE BRANSLE**, dance movement (Fr.); gavotte
BRANNY like bran
BRASEN BRAZEN, made of brass; impudent
BRASHY fragmentary
bt **BRASIL BRAZIL**, Brazil wood; sappan tree
zo **BRASSE** perch
BRASSY brassie; a golf club
BRAVED dared; defied; challenged
BRAVER nobler; more daring
BRAWLY bravely; excellently
BRAWNY hefty; lusty; sturdy; robust
BRAYED ground in a mortar
to **BRAYER** (printing) roller
BRAYLE hawk leash
BRAZED soldered
BREACH rupture; crack; rift; quarrel
ga **BREAST** chest; bosom; (-plate); oppose; (-high); -stroke; riser of stairway (-wall)
pl **BREATH** air for lungs; -of life; (-less)
BREECH the hinder part of a gun (loader)
BREEKS trousers
bd, zo **BREESE BREEZE**, soft wind; even pace (horses); cinder-brick; gad fly
BREEZY gusty; windy; hearty
md **BREGMA** part of skull
lw **BREHON** Irish judge

BRETON of Brittany
ck **BREVET** a patent; nominal rank
mu, rl **BREVIS** short; mass setting
ck **BREWED** plotted; concocted
ck **BREWER** a brewster; maltster (beer)
bt **BRIARY BRIERY**, set with brambles
BRIBED paid for wrong doing
BRIBER a corrupter
bd **BRICKY** of brick
BRIDAL nuptial; conjugal
ce, ga, mu **BRIDGE** card game; span; surmount; loan; violin; billiards; (bowls); (gym); (wrestling); transition; convert; link between passages
BRIDLE curb; control; restrain; check; harness; track; path (horses)
BRIGHT vivid; shining; gay; merry
BRIGUE intrigue; cabal; strife
BRILLS eye-lashes (horse)
bt **BRIONY** bryony; a plant
BRISKY brisk; effervescing
BRITON ancient British inhabitant
to **BROACH** hint; suggest; tap; clasp; pointed chisel
go, nv **BROADS** waterways
BROCHE brocade; embroider
BROGAN leather shoe
BROGUE decorated shoe; Irish accent
BROKEN fractured; snapped; smashed
BROKER dealer
BROLLY umbrella
ch **BROMAL** oily fluid
ch **BROMIC** containing bromide
zo **BRONCO** unbroken horse (Amer.)
BRONZE an alloy of copper and tin
BRONZY bronze-like
BROOCH ornamental clasp
BROODY pensive; hen
BROOKY abounding with streams
bt **BROOMY** full of broom (gorse)
BROUGH town; burgh; borough
BROWNY of brown colour
BROWSE nibble; crop; feed
zo **BRUANG** Malayan bear
md **BRUCIA** a poison
BRUISE batter; crush; contuse; wale
zo **BRUMBY** unbroken horse
ck **BRUNCH** combined breakfast-lunch
BRUSHY rough; shaggy
BRUTAL inhuman; ruthless; savage
BRUTUS a kind of wig
to **BRUZZE** V-shaped woodturning tool
bt **BRYONY BRIONY**, a plant
BUBBLE trapped air; (blowing–s) (-bath); (S. Sea-); gurgle
BUBBLY champagne; effervescent
pl **BUCCAL** (cheek); cavity; mouth
ck **BUCCAN** dried meat
BUCKED bleached; exhilerated
ce, cp **BUCKET** water pail; container; (seat); (mill wheel); goal
zo **BUCKIE** large whelk
BUCKLE thatcher's spar; bootclasp; wrinkle
BUCKRA white man
BUDDED grafted
rl **BUDDHA** founder of religion
BUDDLE (ore-washing)
BUDGER a stirrer; a mover
BUDGET package (finance); tiler's pocket
bt **BUDLET** a little bud
BUFFED buffeted; polished
zo **BUFFEL** an American duck
BUFFER concussion absorber; old fool
cp **BUFFER** limited memory storage
BUFFET cuff; smite; sideboard
BUFFET self-service meal
cn, nt **BUG-EYE** wide-angle; N. Am. fishing boat
BUGGER active sodomite
tc **BUG-KEY** faster transmission key
mu **BUGLER** horn blower
BUGLET a small glass bead
zo **BUGONG** a moth
nm **BUKSHA** Yemeni coin
BUKSHI tip; percentage (Ind.)
bt **BULBED BULBAR**, bulbi form
bt **BULBIL** bud developing into a plant
ck, zo **BULBUL** nightingale; Turkish sweet
bt **BULBUS** a corm; a bulb
ck **BULGAR** Bulgarian
BULGED protruded
BULGER a golf club
ck **BULGUR** cracket wheat (Levant)
md **BULIMY** morbid appetite; voracity
BULKED in bulk
BULKER street thief
BULLED (Stock Exchange)
BULLER torrential turmoil
BULLET projectile; slug
BUM-BAG hip pouch on waist belt
nt **BUMKIN** short broom
BUMMED loafed; idled around
BUMMEL meander; cycle seat
BUMMER camp follower; man of trade
BUMMLE to blunder; an idler
ga **BUMPED** knocked into; (-off); (oarsman's race)
BUMPER buffer; full; generous; bouncer; (cricket)
BUNCHY clustered; tufty
BUNDLE parcel; package; packet; roll

BUNGED blocked up; (pipes)
BUNGLE miss; fail; botch
md **BUNION** a swelling
BUNKED bedded in tiers; decamped; gone away
ga **BUNKER** defence shelter; coal depot; (golf)
BUNKUM blather; nonsense
ch **BUNSEN** laboratory gas burner
BUNTED butted
mn **BUNTER** mottled sandstone
BUOYED moored; sustained (-up); uphold
BUPPIE black urban Yuppie
BURBLE confusion; trouble
zo **BURBOT** eel-pout; fish
BURDEN load; incubus; onus
BUREAU office; department
nt, mn **BURGEE** pennant; flag; coal
BURGLE rob premises
ck **BURGOO** savoury mess
zo **BURHEL** Asiatic goat
BURIAL BURIED, interment; hidden; (funeral)
BURKED hesitated; hushed up; avoided (-issue)
BURLAP coarse canvas
BURLED with knots removed
BURLER cloth-dresser
BURMAN native of Burma; Burmese
BURN-BAG container for disposal of scandal
BURNED BURNT, scorched; charred; (sun-)
BURNER controlled flame; (balloon); (welding)
bt, zo **BURNET** plant; moth
BURN-UP damage by excess; nuclear combustion
BURRED roughened surface
BURROW tunnel; mine; excavate
md **BURSAL BURSAE**, cavity
BURSAR treasurer; cashier; (college)
BURSCH German student
nt **BURTON** a tackle
BURYAT Central Asian Turkmens
el **BUS-BAR** metallic rod link; contact
BUSHED lost in the bush
me **BUSHEL** 8 gallons (36 litres)
BUSIED actively employed
BUSIES detectives (sl.)
BUSILY diligently; assiduously
BUSKED wearing a busk; corseted
BUSKER tragedian; street entertainer
BUSKIN kind of boot; cothurnus
BUSMEN transport workers
BUSSED transported; osculated; kissed
BUSTED gone bust (sl.); bankrupt; caught
BUSTER frolic; a roisterer
BUSTLE busy street crowd; stir; tumult
BUST-UP violent quarrel
ch **BUTANE** bottled gas for households
BUTLER male household steward
BUTTED trammed; bunted
ck **BUTTER** milk fat spread (bread and –)
ck **BUTTIE** sandwich
el **BUTTON** switch; (press-); fastening; (-mushroom)
ch **BUXINE** (alkaloid)
BUYING purshasing; bribing; corrupting
BUYOUT obtaining control of shareholdings
BUZZED spread abroad; bruited
el **BUZZER** electric sound signal (intercom, phone)
BYE-BYE (golf); adieu
BYE-LAW subsidiary law
BY-FORM a variant
BYGONE past; of yore
BY-LANE BYROAD, side road
mu **BYLINA** Rusian poem; song
ga **BY-LINE** goal area line (soccer)
BYNAME nickname
md **BY-PASS** a shunt (heart etc.); major ring road
BY-PATH hidden path
BY-PLAY significant acting in dumb show
BY-PLOT subsidiary plot
BY-ROAD secondary road
BY-ROOM small ante-chamber
tx **BYSSUS** fine linen cloth
zo **BYSSUS** a tuft of filaments
BYWORD maxim; proverb
BY-WORK by-time work
nm **BYZANT BEZANT**, gold coin (Byzantine)

C

rl **CABALA** Jewish traditional doctrine
CABANA beach house; shack
ae **CABANE** pyramidal strut system
CABBLE smash into small pieces
tx **CABECA** Indian silk
CABIRI ancient Semitic divinities
el, ro, tc **CABLED** telegraphed
CABLET tow-rope
CABMAN cabby (taxi-driver)

zo **CABRIE CABRIT**, prong-horn antelope
CABURN spun-yarn
mu **CACCIA** the chase, hunt (It.); oboe form
CACHED hidden; concealed; (stores depot)
CACHET seal of prestige; distinctive merit
bt, ck **CACHOU** a sweetmeat; cashew nut
pl **CACKIE** faeces (human waste)
zo **CACKLE** of hens' egglaying chorus
bt **CACOON** bean
bt **CACTAL** of a cactus plant
bt **CACTUS** prickly plant
CADDIE caddy (golf); porter
zo **CADDIS** tape; a worm
mu **CADENT** falling tones; speech inflection
CADGED sponged; begged; importuned
CADGER huckster; beggar; mendicant
ch **CADION** chemical detection reagent
ch **CADMIA** sulphide of cadmium
md **CAECUM** a blind sac
CAESAR an autocrat; tsar; shah
go **CAFARD** Algerian desert; melancholia
zo **CAFFRE** Caffrarian; wild tabby cat
CAFTAN kaftan; Persian vest
CAGING confining (zoos); frame work; enclosing
CAGMAG meat unfit for food
CAHIER notebook (reports)
CAHOOT partnership
zo **CAIMAN** alligator (S. Am.)
nt **CAIQUE KAIK**, skiff
CAJOLE persuade; coax; wheedle
CAKING clotting; precipitating; coagulating
ps **CAKRAS CHAKRAS**, psychic body centre (Asia)
CALADE fairground horseshow circus
CALASH vehicle; hood
CALCAR glass furnace
CALCED wearing shoes; shod
ch **CALCIC** containing calcium
ga **CALCIO** 17th-century football, Florence
tx **CALICO** cotton cloth
md **CALIGO** dimness of sight
mt **CALINA** dusty haze in Med. region
rl **CALIPH CALIF**, sheik of Islam
nt **CALKED CAULKED**, hull made watertight; refitting
nt **CALKER CALKING**, ship's bottom painter
CALLED visited; named; shouted for; phoned
CALLER representative; referee; ringer
CALLID skilled; expert; shrewd
CALL-IN transfer control; main to sub
CALLOW immature (of character, growth)
CALL-UP military induction
pl, bt **CALLUS CALLOUS**, wart; hardening (skin, bark)
CALMED lulled; soothed; sedated; allayed
CALMLY sedately; serenely; placidly
me **CALORY CALORIE** thermal energy unit
CALPAC Eastern cap
bt **CALTHA** king-cup
CALVER iceberg beginning to break up
zo, go **CALVES** pl. of calf; give birth to (deer) (icebergs)
bd **CALYON** wall construction stone
CAMAIL chain-mail
bt **CAMASS** lily (edible bulbs)
bt **CAMATA** acorns
ar, ga **CAMBER** cross-slope; tie-beam; convexity; ski-flexibility; arching position
lw, pg **CAMERA** closed courtroom; image-recorder
tx **CAMESE CAMISE-CAMISOLE**, woman's blouse (or bodice)
CAMION motor truck; waggon
tx, wv **CAMLET** Angora goat hair fabric
CAMPER tent dweller; lives rough
el **CAMP-ON** electronic telephone connector
go **CAMPOS** Savannah (Brazil)
CAMPUS college grounds
ck **CANAPE** cocktail delicacy; sofa or settee
CANARD hoax; news spoof
zo, ck **CANARY** caged finch; dance; wine
CANCAN a dance
CANCEL quash; annul; blot
as, md **CANCER** the Crab (Zodiac); malignant cell growth
ga **CANCHA** court for playing pelota
CANDID frank; honest; sincere
me **CANDIE** 500 lb (226 kg) (Ind.)
CANDLE light; taper
CANGUE Chinese criminal yoke
CANINE doggy
CANING thrashing

CANKER corrupt; infection/infestation
mu **CANNED** preserved; pre-recorded (ro, tv)
mn **CANNEL** bituminous coal
CANNON (artillery); (billiards); (croquet)
CANNOT unable to
ar **CANOPY** awning; umbrella/shade; cover (firmament) (parachute); ceiling décor
CANTAB Cambridge; university; (degree)
me **CANTAR** about 1 cwt (50 kg) (Syrian)
CANTED cross-sloped; tilted; oblique
CANTER slow relaxed gallop (horses)
md **CANTHI** corners of the eye
CANTLE (saddle); fragment
go **CANTON** autonomous province (Swiss)
mu, rl **CANTOR** Precentor; leading church singer
mu **CANTUS** chant
CANUCK Canadian
nt, ga **CANVAS** sails; tent covering (linen); winning length (rowing)
CANVAS **CANVASS**, list voting intentions
CANYON deep ravine; gulch; rift
me **CAPFUL** the quantity to fill a cap
lw **CAPIAS** writ
lw **CAPITE** royal tenant, feudal
md **CAPIVI** balsam; copaiva
zo **CAPLIN** small smelt
eg **CAP-NUT** end-sealed nut
CAPOTE long cloak (Fr.)
CAPPED covered; limited (finances); decorated; exceeded (record)
ch **CAPRIC** acid
zo **CAPRID** of goats
CAPRIN an acid found in butter
CAPTOR capturer
nt **CARACK** **CARRACK**, sailing vessel (of the Discoveries)
CARACT mark; sign; character
CARAFE glass water-jug
zo **CARANX** mackerel
bt **CARAPA** crab-wood tree (S. Am.)
ch **CARBOL** (carbolic)
ch **CARBON** charcoal
CARBOY glass jar
pg **CARBRO** carbon/bromide printing
lt **CARCEL** French luminous-flux unit
CARDED combed (wool); indexed
cf, md **CARDIO-** of the heart
ck **CARDOL** cashew-nut oil
nt **CAREEN** heel over; trim; nit picking
CAREER move swiftly; professional lifestyle
CARESS embrace lovingly; fondle
CARFAX **CARFOX**, crossroads, four forked
bt **CARICA** paw-paw tree
pl, md **CARIES** dental decay
bt, zo **CARINA** keel-like structure
CARING tending; nursing; feeling; committed concern
CARKED worried; perplexed
CARLOT churl; peasant
CARMAN van driver
CARMEN carriers; an opera
CARNAL of the flesh; sensual; sexual
CARNET motorcar passport
CARNEY horse-disease
eg **CARNOT** thermal-efficiency unit
pl **CARPAL** of the wrist
CARPED cavilled; grumbled
bt **CARPEL** seed vessel
CARPER censurer; critic
CARPET floor fabric
md **CARPUS** the wrist
me **CARRAT** **CARAT**, gold measure
CARREL cross-bow arrow; quarry
bt, ck **CARROT** root vegetable; incentive; (donkeys)
CARTED removed (by transport)
CARTEL price fixers' ring; league; cabal
CARTER wagoner
CARTON strengthened cardboard box
ga **CAR-TOW** automobile rescue (police station); glider-launching method
CARVED **CARVEN**, cut, shaped, engraved
CARVEL **CARAVEL**, the Discoverer's sailing vessel; jelly fish
CARVER sculptor; a knife
bt **CASABA** yellow winter melon
ck **CASEIC** **CASEIN-CASEUM**, of cheese (protein)
CASERN army barracks
CASHED converted into money (specie)
bt **CASHEW** tropical nut
bt **CASHOO** **CATECHU**, an astringent
bd **CASING** cover; packing; box; lining
ga **CASINO** gaming saloon; 15th-century card game
CASKET jewel case; reliquary
CASQUE a helmet; morion
bt **CASSIA** **CASSIS**, the black currant
zo **CASSIN** snail's helmet shell
pr, cp **CASTER** cruet; furniture wheel; type casting
ar **CASTLE** citadel; fortress; stronghold

ga **CASTLE** (chess move); wicket (stumps) (cricket); (home)
md **CASTOR** beaver gland scent; purgative oil
pr **CAST-UP** vomit; job content
CASUAL chance; informal; (-partner)
rl **CASULA** a chasuble; vestment
CATCHY deceptive; infectious
CATENA a chain; a series
CATENA doctrinal writings
zo **CATGUT** cord; violin string
CATHAY China; (Marco Polo)
el **CATION** electro-positive element cathode
bt **CATKIN** pendulous inflorescence
CAT-LAP tame tipple
CATLOG catalogue
CATNAP forty winks; doze
bt **CATNIP** mint; catmint
ck **CATSUP** a relish; ketchup
nt **CATTED** the anchor well slung
zo **CATTLE** kine; oxen
CAUCUS powerful, inner political group
zo **CAUDAD** towards the tail
zo **CAUDAL** tail-like; inferior
bt **CAUDEX** palm-stem
CAUDLE hot spice wine
CAUGHT trapped; entangled
CAUKED CAWKED, hull made water tight
CAUKER CAWKER, oakum picker's yarn; drink
bt **CAULIS** stem
CAUSAL producing; resulting
CAUSED occasioned; created; effected
CAUSER instigator; prime mover
CAUSEY pavée; causeway (obs.)
CAUTEL craft; wariness (obs.)
CAUTER searing-iron
lw **CAVEAT** suspension of court hearting
CAVERN cave; grotto; den
zo **CAVIAR** fish-roe of the sturgeon
zo **CAVIES** guinea-pig
ce **CAVING** exploring caves; (-in); collapse quarrying & mining method
CAVITY void; empty hole; (teeth)
CAVORT prance; buck; leap
pr **CAXTON** a book in block letters
zo **CAYMAN** alligator; caiman
zo **CAYUSE** Wild West bronco; nag
CEASED stopped; desisted; terminated
mu **CEBELL** old English gavotte
ck **CECILS** rissoles
md **CECITY** blindness
bt **CEDARN CEDARY**, cedar wood; colour
CEDING yielding; giving way
CEDRAT CEDRATE, citrous
lw **CEDULA** S. American mortgage
bt **CELERY** crisp vegetable
md **CELIAC** coeliac; abdominal
CELLAR underground cold storage; low purchase prices
CELLED honeycombed; alveolate
CELTIC KELTIC, Gaelic language; culture
CELURE decorated route; wagon roof
bd, md **CEMENT** cohese; adhere; concrete; hold together (friendship) (teeth)
CENSED redolent with incense
rl **CENSER** urn for burning incense
CENSOR to control secrecy, morals etc.; official who vets books, films
CENSUS official counting (population)
me **CENTAL** 100 lb (45 kg)
ga **CENTRE CENTER**, middle point; official head office; (-forward)
cf **CEPHAL-** of the brain (Gr. pl)
zo **CEPOLA** snake-fish
bt **CERAGO** pollen
md **CERATE** an ointment
CERCAL caudal, of the tail
bt **CEREAL** grain; corn
bt **CEREUS** a cactus genus
mn **CERINE** an ore of cerium
CERING covering with wax
pr **CERIPH SERIF**, style of lettering
CERISE cherry-colour
ch **CERITE** cerium silicate
ch **CERIUM** metallic element
ml **CERMET** metal-ceramic alloy
CEROON seroon; a bale
bt **CERRIS** the bitter oak
ch **CERUSE** white-lead
zo **CERVID** with antlers (deer)
md **CERVIX** neck of womb
zo **CERVUS** the stag genus
lw **CESSIO** an assignment
lw **CESTUI** a beneficiary
CESTUS a girdle; boxing glove
mu **CESURA CESURE**, pause interruption
zo **CETINE** spermaceti
zo **CHACMA** baboon
CHAFED fretted by rubbing; galled
zo **CHAFER** a beetle; cockchafer
CHAFFY light; worthless; jovial
CHAGAN a Khan; oriental ruler
CHAISE horse drawn vehicle
CHALET Swiss cottage
CHALKA Zulu king
CHALKY of chalk, pasty

CHANCE happen; betide; fortune
CHANCY hazardous; risky; fortuitous
cp **CHANGE** alter; vary; shift; veer; printout
nt, mu **CHANTY SHANTY**, sea songs
rl **CHAPEL** a printer's association; (church)
CHAPPY cleft; chinky
el, lw **CHARGE** fee; trust; command; (cavalry-); (electrical-); indict
CHARKA small cup with silver handle (Rus.)
CHARON ferryman of Styx
CHARRY like charcoal
CHASED followed; tracked; engraved
CHASER hunter; pursuer; a neutralizing drink; steeple-chasing horse
CHASMY gaping; yawning
CHASSE a liqueur; dance step (ice skating); (badminton)
CHASTE pure; virginal; incorrupt
CHATON the head of a ring (Fr.)
ar **CHATRI** umbrella-shaped dome (Hindu)
CHATTA umbrella (Ind.)
CHATTY talkative; gossipy
CHAWED CHEWED, gnawed; crunched; masticated
CHECKY chequered (chess-board)
CHEEKY insolent; impudent
CHEERY buoyant; merry; blithe
CHEESE CHEESEY, of milk, fatty
CHEESY tacky
mn **CHEKOA** porcelain-clay
CHEQUE order to pay (banking); (bouncer)
bt **CHERRY** a tree fruit; ruddy colour
mn **CHERTY** flinty
CHERUB angel; child
CHERUP chirp; to urge
mn **CHESIL CHISIL**, gravel; shingle
pl **CHESTY** of bronchials; low-pitched voice
ga **CHEUCA** Argentine Indian's game like hockey
CHEVAL a frame
zo **CHEVAN** chevin; chub
ar **CHEVET** an apse
zo **CHEWET** chough (bird); chatterer
md **CHIASM** (optic nerve)
ck **CHICHA** liquor from maize (S. Am.)
CHICHI 'precious'; over-decorated
bt **CHICLE** chewing gum
CHICLY fashionably; modishly
CHICOT jester to Henri III
CHILDE chylde; nobleman's son (Harold)
bt **CHILLI CHILLY-CHILI**, cayenne pepper
CHILLY bleak; frigid; cold
mu, rl **CHIMED CHIMES**, clock music; church bells; (-in)
rl **CHIMER** bishop's robe
mu **CHIMES** bell tunes (clocks)
zo **CHINCH** grain insect; bed-bug; cimex
go **CHINED** ravined; cleft to the backbone
CHINEE a Chinaman
CHINKY gaping; chappy
nt **CHINSE** to caulk
tx **CHINTZ** floral cotton cloth
CHIPPY off colour
pl **CHIRAL** pertaining to the hand
CHIRPY chatty; cheerful; cheery; (bird)
to **CHISEL** carpenter's planing tool; to cheat
mn **CHISIL** chesil; gravel
zo **CHITAL** spotted deer
zo **CHITIN** horny material
zo **CHITON** a mollusc; Greek tunic
CHITTY disrespectful; infantile; order note
mu **CHIUSO** closed horn notes (It.)
bt, ck **CHIVES** onion-like salad plant
CHIVVY hasten; nag; pester
CHOICE select; dainty; option; election
CHOKED stifled; throttled; suppressed
CHOKER a tie; a neckerchief
CHOKEY prison
CHOKRA office boy (Ind.)
CHOLER anger; ire; spleen; rage
md **CHOLIC** (bile); bilious
CHOOSE pick; elect; adopt; prefer
CHOOSY pernickety; fastidious
CHOPPY irregular; of sea waves
mu **CHORAL** chanted; sung
md **CHOREA** St Vitus' dance; the shakes
cf **CHOREA-** dance; (choreography)
CHOREE trochee; poetic metre
bt **CHORIA** external membranes
mu **CHORIC** of a choir
mu **CHORUS** group of voices
CHOSEN elected; selected; picked
CHOUAN Breton guerilla
zo **CHOUGH** cliff bird
CHOUSE to cheat; a trick
rl **CHRISM** Holy oil
cf, mu **CHROMA- CHROMATIC**, highly coloured all-note scale
ml **CHROME** pigment of chromium metal
bc, cf, md **CHROMO** -somes, genes in **DNA** protein

cf **CHRONO-** -meter (time)
CHUBBY plump; buxom
CHUFFY puffy; surly
ga **CHUKKA** period of play at polo
CHUMMY sociable; matey
mn **CHUNAM** lime; stucco (Ind.)
CHUNKY with lumps (marmalade)
rl **CHURCH** temple; kirk
CHURLY churlish; surly; sullen
ck **CHUTNY CHUTNEY**, fruity pickle (India)
CHYLDE churlish; sullen; surly
ch **CHYMIC** chemical
CHYPRE a perfume
zo **CICADA CICALA, CIGALA**, a chirping insect
bt **CICELY** a genus of plants; myrrh
pr **CICERO** type fount; guide; (orator)
bt **CICUTA** hemlock; cow-bane
rl **CIERGE** wax candle
zo **CIGALE** cigala; cicada
ar **CILERY** carving; carved foliage
CILICE hair-cloth
bt, zo **CILIUM** whip-like hair
zo **CIMBEX** the saw-fly
ar **CIMBIA** a fillet
CIMIER crest of helmet (Fr.)
zo **CIMISE** bed-bug; cimex
CIMNEL simnel; saffron cake
CINDER ember; ash
CINEMA kinema; movies; talkies
CINGLE surcingle; girth; cinch
ga **CINQUE** five (cards) (dice) (ports); (-foil)
ar **CINTRE** centering
ma **CIPHER CYPHER**, the zero; secret writing system
CIPHER an unimportant person
CIPIER Swiss jailer
CIPPUS funereal column
CIRCAR district (Hindu)
CIRCLE ring; compass; circuit; set
cf **CIRCUM-** around; (circumference)
CIRCUS round; (acrobatics, riding etc.)
gl, go **CIRQUE CORRIE, COOMBE**, deep, rounded glacier hollow
bt **CIRRUS** tendril; cloud
CISLEU a Jewish month
bt **CISSUS** wild vine
CISTIL pewter box
bt **CISTUS** rock-rose
mu **CITHER** zither (guitar)
CITIED with many cities
CITING quoting; summoning
mu **CITOLE** a dulcimer; psaltery
ch **CITRIC** (lemons)
zo **CITRIL** song bird; a finch
CITRIN vitamin P
bt **CITRON** a fruit; lemon
bt **CITRUL** the pumpkin
bt **CITRUS** plant genus
CIVICS science of citizenship
CIVIES mufti; civilian clothes
CIVISM good citizenship
CLAGGY sticky; cloggy; cledgy
CLAMMY dank; viscous; sticky
CLAQUE hired applause (theatre)
ck **CLARET** dark red wine colour
CLARTY miry; muddy
CLASSY superior; (upper-); high-toned
CLATCH botch; daub
CLAUSE paragraph; proviso; condition
mu **CLAVES** Cuban percussion
CLAVIS a translation; a key
md **CLAVUS** toga stripe; corn; callus
CLAWED lacerated; torn; extorted
CLAYES hurdles; wattles
CLAYEY like clay; cledgy
nt **CLEATS** herb coltsfoot; rope holders
CLEAVE cling; cohere; split; rend
hd **CLECHE** a cross voided
mn **CLEDGE** fuller's earth (clay)
CLEDGY clayey; tenacious
CLENCH clinch; secure; fasten; grapple
rl **CLERGY** the cloth; priesthood
rl **CLERIC** clerical; a clerk; church officer
CLEVER able; adroit; gifted; dexterous
CLEVIS draught-iron of plough
nt **CLEWED** coiled; trussed
CLICHE artist's proof; trite phrase
CLIENT customer; dependant
gl **CLIFFY CLIFTY**, craggy; (broken)
ec, bl **CLIMAX** acme; culmination; orgasm
ga **CLINCH** clench; grasp; (agreement); (boxing) (fencing)
CLINGY adhesive; sticky
md **CLINIC** health centre; hospital
zo **CLIONE** 'whales' food'; small fish
CLIQUE coterie; junto; cabal; set
zo **CLOACA** a sewer; reproductive canal
CLOCHE bell-glass; (hat)
CLOCHE protective glass cover for plants
CLODDY clodly; earthy; gross; boorish
CLOGGY adhesive; clingy
CLOKED cloaked; concealed; disguised
CLONIC convulsive
md **CLONUS** muscular spasm

ar **CLOSED** united; grappled; shut
CLOSER nearer; tighter
ar **CLOSET** small room; wardrobe; (WC)
CLOTHE attire; drape; invest; robe
ck **CLOTTY** like thick cream; curd
CLOUDY dim; overcast; gloomy; murky
CLOUGH ravine; cleft; chine
CLOUGH trade allowance
zo **CLOVEN** cleft; hooved (ungulates); split asunder
bt **CLOVER** trifolium
CLOYED satiated; cumbered; surfeited
CLUMPS a numskull; nitwit; dullard
CLUMPY massive; shapeless
CLUMSY awkward; heavy-handed
mn **CLUNCH** marl; clay
zo **CLUPEA** sprat genus
CLUTCH (of eggs); grasp; clench; grip
CLUTCH (motoring); (in the –es of); critical situation
COACHY a coachman
md **COAGEL** gel made by coagulation
zo **COAITA** S. American monkey; coati
COALED stoked (stocked with coal)
COARSE crude; impure; rough; rude
COATED spread; covered
COATEE coat with short tails
COAXED persuaded; allured; seduced
COAXER cajoler; flatterer; wheedler
mn **COBALT** element; blue
mn **COBBLE** a stone; to repair (shoes)
COBCAL sandal
bt **COBNUT** hazel-nut
bt **COBRES** S. American indigo
zo **COBRIC** cobra-type
tx **COBURG** a twilled fabric
COBWEB flimsy fly-trap; spider's web
md, bt **COCCUS** seed-vessel; microbe
md **COCCYX** terminal bone of spine
zo **COCHIN** a fowl
COCKAL the game of knuckle-bones
COCKED erect; drunked; (-hat); (gun)
zo **COCKER** a spaniel
COCKET customs seal; a certificate
bt **COCKLE** a weed
zo **COCKLE** shellfish; to pucker
COCKSY bumptious; conceited
COCK-UP blunder; mistake; fiasco
zo, tx **COCOON** silk casing; to isolate
CODBER pillow-slip
CODDED in a pod; hoaxed
CODDER a gatherer of peas
ck **CODDLE** pamper; humour; indulge; (eggs)
CODGER an eccentric old man
lw **CODIFY** regulate; reorganize; systematize (law making)
cp **CODING** sorting; putting into cipher
cp **CODIST** summarist; programmer
bt **CODLIN** an apple
md **COELOM** the body cavity
COERCE force; impel; constrain
COEVAL contemporaneous
ck **COFFEE** beverage; of Kaffe, Ethiopia
ce, nt **COFFER** chest; box; lock chamber (-dam)
pr **COFFIN** burial case; printing frame
COFFLE a slave gang
COGENT potent; urgent; forcible; convincing; persuasive
COGGED toothed; cheated
COGGIE small bowl
nt **COGGLE** small boat
COGNAC brandy from that district
COHEIR joint heir
COHERE cleave; unite; join; stick
COHORN obsolete trench-mortar
COHORT tenth part of a legion; group (army)
bt **COHUNE** palm
COIGNE enforced billeting (Irish)
COILED spiral; wound
COINED invented; minted
COINER counterfeiter; inventor
COITUS sexual intercourse; copulation
CO-JOIN join together; unite
COKING making coke from coal (gas)
COLDER chillier
COLDLY frigidly
ar **COLLAR** neckband; (clothing); harness; pipe joint cover; tie beam
COLLED embraced; hugged
COLLET collar; setting of a jewel
zo **COLLIE** colley; sheep-dog
ck **COLLOP** a slice of meat
bt **COLLUM** lowest part of stem
bt **COLMAR** pear
zo **COLMEY** the coal-fish
COLONY a settlement (dominion)
COLOUR tint; hue; dye; shade
COLTER ploughshare
zo **COLUGO** flying lemur
pr **COLUMN** pillar; (army movement); file; (agony-) (newspaper-)
as **COLURE** intersecting celestial circle
rl **COMARB** abbot; coarb
COMART an agreement
COMATE comose; hairy; hirsute
COMBAT contest; war; resist; oppose
COMBED brushed; carded; straightened

COMBER foaming billow; searcher (beach)
md **COMEDO** a blackhead
COMEDY a light play (theatre)
COMELY seemly; graceful; shapely
ck **COMFIT** sweetmeat; confit
bt **COMFRY** comfrey; wild plant
COMING approach; future; expected
COMITY courtesy; civility
COMMIT entrust; enact; consign
COMMIX to mix; mingle
COMMON shared; (-land); usual; vulgar
mu **COMODO** easily flowing, leisurely (It.)
COMOPT cine-film with optical soundtrack
COMOSE hairy; downy; comate
COMPEL coerce; force; oblige
COMPLY agree; submit; yield; conform
ck **COMPOT** a preserve
pl, zo **CONCHA CONCH**, ear cavity; sea shell (spiralled)
CONCHY conscientious objector
CONCUR agree; harmonize; help
CONNED navigated; steered
CONDER pilot; fish-scout
md **CONDOM** safe-sex sheath
zo **CONDOR** vulture
CONFAB pow-wow; conference
CONFER bestow; grant; consult
ck **CONFIT** comfit; sweetmeat
CONFIX fasten; attach; append
CONGEE confee; dismissal; farewell
zo **CONGER** eel
bt **CONGOU** black tea
CONICS geometry of the cone
zo **CONIES CONEYS**, rabbits; pikas; hyrax genus
bt, ch **CONIIN CONIUM**, hemlock extract
bt **CONIMA** gum resin
ch **CONINE** an alkaloid
ck **CONJEE CONGEE**, rice-water
CONKED petered out
bt **CONKER** chestnut
CON-MAN trickster; swindler
nt **CONNED CONNER**, studied; deceiver; steered; (-ing tower)
pl **CONOID** pineal gland; a paraboloid
nv **CONSOL** Government bond; long-range navigational system
CONSUL Government official (abroad)
CONTRA against; opposite; contrasting; guerrilla in Nicaragua
cf, mu **CONTRA** -lower in pitch; anti

CONVEX protuberant lens; (mirror) (shape)
CONVEY carry; transport; transfer
nt **CONVOY** an escorted group (ships) (motorcade)
bt **CONYZA** fleabane
COOING (and billing); dovetalk
ck **COOKED** heated food; falsified accounts (books)
ck **COOKER** stove; range; processor (factory)
ck **COOKIE** super-heavy bomb; a bun
COOLED calmed; allayed; moderated
COOLER a drink; colder; (jail)
COOLIE labourer (China)
COOLLY calmly; placidly; impudently
COOMBE combe; rounded valley
bt **COONTY** arrowroot (Florida)
COOPED cabined and confined
COOPER a mixed drink; cask-maker; casked
COOTIE feathered legs (Sc.)
nm **COPANG** Japanese gold coin
nm **COPECK KOPEK**, 1/100th part of rouble
COPIED transcribed; aped
COPIER copyer; scribe; plagiarist
COPIES reduplications; imitations
COPING top course of a wall; striving
COPPED caught; run in; arrested
mn, nm **COPPER** metal; penny; policeman; laundry bowl
COPPIN ball of thread
COPTIC (Egyptian Christianity)
COPULA a link
COQUET to flirt
ar **CORBEL** stone bracket
zo **CORBIE** a raven; carrion crow
bt **CORCLE** embryo seed
CORCUR purple dye
CORDED ribbed; furrowed
CORDON a ribbon of honour; a guard
COREAN KOREAN, of Korea
to **CORERS** geological specimen collectors (oil)
to **CORING** boring; drilling (oil-fields)
md **CORIUM** true skin
CORKED sealed (bottle)
CORKER a poser; a finisher
CORKIR red or purple lichen dye
bt **CORMUS** stem
md **CORNEA** eye-membrane
CORNED preserved; granulated; salted
bt **CORNEL** dog-wood
ga **CORNER** angle; bend; nook; monopolize; (football)

mu **CORNET** an officer; trumpet
zo **CORNUA** horns
CORODY an allowance; a pension
el **CORONA** a crown; (solar); (aura); discharge
bt **COROZO** vegetable ivory
md **CORPSE** carcass; cadaver; dead body
CORPUS governing body; association
CORRAL cattle-pen; to round up
go **CORRIE** **CIRQUE**, a hollow; a valley
zo **CORSAC** **CORSAK**, fox (Central Asia)
CORSET a bodice; stays
CORTES Spanish Parliament
pl, bt **CORTEX** skin tissue; treebark; covering
pm **CORTIN** extract of adrenalin
CORVET **CURVET**, leap; frolic; jump about
zo, nt **CORVUS** a crow; grappling iron
bt **CORYMB** a panicle; a raceme
md **CORYZA** snuffly cold
COSHED bashed; mugged; set upon
COSHER to pamper; to chat
COSIER more cosy; a botcher; cobbler
COSILY snugly; comfortably
ma **COSINE** sine of complement of angle
COSMIC cosmical; orderly
COSMOS universe; order
rl **COSSAS** Indian Muslims
zo **COSSET** a pet lamb; to pet
md **COSTAL** (rib)
CO-STAR actors cast together
COSTER costermonger; apple-seller
COSTLY dear; sumptuous; rich
hd **COTISE** a bendlet
COTTAR **COTTER**, a cottager
COTTER wedge; pin
bt, tx **COTTON** yarn; oil; (-on, learn)
zo **COTYLA** a sucker
md **COTYLE** bone-cavity; cup
zo **COUGAR** puma
COULEE ravine; couloir
COUPED bartered for; cut off
COUPEE an antic; a salute
COUPER a dealer
COUPLE pair; brace; connect; mate
COUPON a voucher
md **COURAP** disease (E. Ind.)
COURSE circuit; orbit; series (lecture-)
COURSE (river-); flow; direction; hunt
COUSIN a kinsman
nm **COUTER** £1 (sl.)
tx **COUTIL** strong cotton fabric
rl **COVENT** **COVEN**, **CONVENT**, ladies' home
COVERT concealed; secret; thicket
COVESS female cove or chap
bd **COVING** (fireplace); moulding
bt **COWAGE** a leguminous plant
COWARD craven; dastard; recreant
COW-BOY cattle herder; erratic cyclist
bt **COWDIE** cowrie-pine
COWING intimidating; browbeating
COWISH like a cow
COWLED hooded
COW-MAN cow-herd
bt **COWPEA** herb, source of black-eye peas
vt **COW-POX** cow-teat disease
zo **COWRIE** sea-shell; cowry
COYISH coy; rather reserved
zo **COYOTE** prairie wolf
zo **COYPOU** coypu; rodent (S. Am.)
COZIER tramp; cosier
CRABBY perplexing; peevish; nit-ridden
zo **CRABER** water-vole
zo **CRABRO** hornet genus
ga **CRADLE** crib; holder; (cats'-); (lacrosse) (wrestling)
CRAFTY artful; deceitful; cunning
CRAGGE the neck
CRAGGY rugged; rough; jagged
ga **CRAMBO** a game; a rhyme
CRAMPY affected with cramp
CRANCH crunch; chew
CRANED with neck out-stretched
md **CRANIA** skulls (cranium)
CRANKY eccentric; crotchety
CRANNY chink; fissure; cleft; rift
nt **CRANSE** boom iron to take stay-sails
CRANTS funeral garlands
CRAPED curled
md **CRASIS** temperament
CRATCH hay-rack; manger
CRATED boxed; encased
gl **CRATER** bomb-hole; funnel of volcano
CRAVAT necktie; neckscarf
CRAVED entreated; desired
CRAVEN coward; recreant; dastard
CRAVER beggar; an addict
nt **CRAYER** small trading ship
CRAYON coloured pencil; blackboard chalk
CRAZED decrepit; loony; deranged
CREAKY crepitative, groaning voice; (wood)
CREAMY like cream
CREANT forming; creative
CREASE Malay dagger; creese; kris

ga **CREASE** a fold; wicket limit (cricket); goal area (ice hockey)
CREASY crumpled
CREATE cause; fashion; invent
CRECHE a day-nursery
CREDIT trust; loan; merit; belief
CREEKY winding
CREEPY **CREEPS**, eerie; horrific
CREESE Malay dagger; crease; kris
CREESH grease (Sc.)
CREMOR creamy juice
CRENEL loophole or notch
ck **CRENIC** acid
ck **CREOLE** descendant of people of mixed races; West Indies cookery
tx **CREPON** crêpe fabric
ch **CRESOL** tar product (creosote)
ch **CRESOL** resin/plastic phenols
bt **CRESSY** like water-cress
CRESTA the ice-run at St Moritz
me **CRETIC** a metric foot
CRETIN deformed; idiot; moron
CREVET goldsmith; crucible
CREWEL embroidery
CRIKEY exclamation of surprise
lw **CRIMED** charged with (framed)
CRIMPY frizzy, waved
CRINAL comate; hirsute; hairy
CRINGE fawn; stoop; cower
CRISES decisive moments
CRISIS emergency; turning point
ck **CRISPY** crisp
pl **CRISTA** a crest; balance organ in ear
CRITIC arbiter; reviewer; judge
CROAKY harsh; guttural (voice)
CROATS Croatia (Yugoslavia)
mu **CROCHE** eighth note, quaver (Fr.)
bt **CROCUS** the saffron
ga **CROISE** attack on blade; cross-swords (fencing)
CRONET horse-hoof hair
mu **CROOKS** tubular devices
CROPPY crop-eared
CROSSE lacrosse stick
pl **CROTCH** a crutch; a fork; the groin
CROTON oil plant
CROUCH cringe; stoop; cower
md **CROUPY** affected with croup
CROUSE lively; pert (Sc.)
ck **CROWDY** gruel (Sc.); thin porridge
CROWED exulted; boasted; (cocks)
ar **CRUCKS** tree-trunk framework
CRUDER rougher; coarse; harsher
CRUISE ocean travel; economical speed; patrol
CRUISE search for partner; (street patrol)
CRUIVE fish trap
CRUMBY in crumbs; crummy
zo **CRUMMY** cow with crumpled horn
CRUNCH cranch; munch; bite
pl **CRURAL** of the thighs
CRUSET crucible; crevet
CRUSIE lamp with rush wick (Sc.)
CRUSTA engraved gem; a shell
ck **CRUSTY** of bread; surly; morose
pl **CRUTCH** walking support; the groin
CRYING weeping; calling out; notorious; clamour
cf **CRYPTO-** hidden; secret; (cryptogram); coded
CUBAGE solid content
tx **CUBICA** shallon cloth
CUBING raising to third power
CUBISM modern artistic geometry
CUBIST geometrical daubist
CUBOID (cubical)
CUBSHA Indian drug
zo, mu **CUCKOO** migratory bird; simpleton; (clock); toy (instrument)
zo **CUDDIE** a donkey; a silly ass
CUDDLE hug; embrace; fondle
CUDDLY easily fondled; lovable
to, ga **CUDGEL** heavy club; bludgeon; batter
ga **CUE-BID** (contact bridge)
zo **CUE-OWL** scops-owl; a migrant owl
gl **CUESTA** gently sloping ridge (Sp.)
CUISSE thigh-armour
CUITER fondle; pamper
rl **CULDEE** order of monks
CULLED numbers reduced selectively; altered
CULLER group reducer
CULLET scrap-glass
ck **CULLIS** broth; jelly; gutter; groove
go **CULMEN** summit; highest point
zo **CULTCH** oyster-spawn
CULTUS a cult
zo **CULVER** pigeon; wood-pigeon
CUMBER encumber; impede; clog
tx **CUMBLY** harsh woollen cloth (Ind.)
CUMMER **KIMMER**, godmother; gossip
bt, ck **CUMMIN** **CUMIN**, spice (seed); anti-colic
CUNEAL wedge-shaped
nt **CUNNER** Chesapeake oyster boat
me **CUPFUL** filling a cup
CUP-MAN boon companion
ar, ml **CUPOLA** dome; furnace
md **CUPPED** hollowed; bleeding process
CUPPER cup-bearer
ch, ml **CUPRIC** of copper
CUP-TIE annual football competition

bt **CUPULA CUPULE**, acorn-cup; husk; crusta body
rl **CURACY CURATE**, vicar's assistant
bt **CURARE CURARI-CURARA**, arrow poison used by S. Am. Indians
rl **CURATE** assistant to parish priest
CURBED restrained; held back
bt **CURCAS** a nut
ck **CURDLE** coagulate; congeal; (curds)
lw **CURFEW** general prohibition to leave house
md **CURING** healing; preserving (leather); (food)
CURLED wavey; twisted; (hairstyle)
CURLER ice skating technique; hair-holder
zo **CURLEW** wading bird
CURRED purred; cooed
bt, ck **CURRIE CURRY**, hot spice mix (Asia); horse comb
CURSED CUSSED, sworn at; damned as evil
CURSER vituperator
cp **CURSOR** a slide-rule adjunct; space indicator
mu **CURTAL** early bassoon
CURTER CURTLY, in more brusque style; briefly
CURTSY CURTSEY, a woman's courtesy knee bow
CURULE Roman chair
CURVED arched; bent; bowed
CURVET CORVET, leap; frolic; jump about
ck **CUSCUS COUSCOUS**, millet dish (N. Africa)
zo, bt **CUSCUS** flying squirrel; cereal fibre
zo **CUSHAT** ring dove
md **CUSPID** a canine tooth
CUSTOM habit; usage; wont; tax
CUSTOS university official
CUTEST most alluring; cunning; slyest
CUTLER a dealer in knives etc.
ck **CUTLET** meat sliced wtih bone; chop
go, el **CUT-OFF** end process; cessation of power
el **CUT-OUT** automatic process or power stoppage
tx, nt, bd **CUTTER** tailor; fast yacht; rubbed brick
pr **CUTTER** author's abbreviation marks
zo **CUTTLE** squid
CUTTOE large knife (US)
bt **CYANIN** colouring of rose/cornflower
CYCLED repeated sequence of operations
cp **CYCLIC** periodic; closed-loop data
CYCLUS a bicycle or tricycle
CYESIS pregnancy
zo **CYGNET** young swan
zo **CYGNUS** swan genus
mu **CYMBAL** metal clashing instrument
md **CYMENE** (camphor)
CYMOID having a waving profile
CYMOSE CYMOUS, inflorescence quality
CYMRIC Welsh
bt **CYNARA** artichoke genus
CYNICS Athenian philosophical sect
CYNOID dog-like
bt **CYPHEL** flowering shrub
ma, pr **CYPHER CIPHER**, zero; non-entity; code
zo **CYPRIS** shrimp species
tx **CYPRUS** black fabric
md **CYSTIC CYSTIS**, of bladder; cyst (body capsule)
md **CYTASE** an enzyme
CYTOID cell-like
zo **CYTULA ZYGOTE**, fertilized ovum

D

DABBED touched repeatedly; daubed
bd **DABBER** dome-shaped brush; inking ball
DABBLE mix; meddle; sprinkle
zo **DABOIA** venomous snake
fr **DABREY** latex collection tray
DACOIT pirate; robber (Burma)
tx **DACRON** polyester fibre
DACTYL finger or toe
DADDLE walk totteringly
DAEDAL intricate; mazy; complex
DAFTLY idiotically; crazily
DAGGED cut into slips
pr **DAGGER** dirk; stiletto; poniard († mark)
DAGGLE bedraggle; defile; sully
rl **DAGOBA** Buddhist shrine
bt **DAHLIA** a flower genus
bt **DAIKON** Japanese radish
DAIMIO Japanese noble
DAINTY choice; exquisite; tasty; chic
ch, me **DALTON** of oxygen (atomic mass)
DAMAGE mar; hurt; impair; injury
tx **DAMASK** patterned linen fabric
DAMIER large-squared pattern
DAMINE like a fallow deer
bt **DAMMAR** resin; damar
ce **DAMMED** embanked; blocked; (rivers)
DAMNED condemned; doomed

DAMPED moderated; deadened
DAMPEN moisten; discourage; depress
DAMPER (ironing); a regulator
pr **DAMPER** printing roller (lithography)
DAMPLY unenthusiastically
DAMSEL lass; maiden; girl
bt **DAMSON** small plum
DANCED capered; frisked; hopped
DANCER ballerina; rhythmic artist
DANDER saunter; anger
zo **DANDIE** terrier (dog)
DANDLE pet; fondle; caress
DANGER risk; peril; hazard; jeopardy
DANGLE to fondle; swing; suspend
DANISH of Denmark
DANITE (Mormon sect)
DANTON to daunt; to subdue (Sc.)
bt **DAPHNE** evergreens
DAPPED fished with a mayfly
DAPPER neat; nimble; sprightly
pt **DAPPLE** to variegate with spots (horse)
DARING lark snaring; audacious
DARKEN darkle; cloud
DARKEN obscure; perplex
DARKER blacker; duskier
DARKLY opaquely; mysteriously
tx **DARNED** repaired; mended; accursed
bt **DARNEL** rye grass; tares
tx **DARNER** special thread; needle; sewing machine
DARTED sprang out; shot; flew
zo **DARTER** Brazilian pelican
md **DARTRE** skin-disease; herpes
DASHED cast; sped; rushed; shattered
tx **DASHER** gadabout; (haber-) (clothing)
zo **DASSIE** badger; hyrax
DATARY papal officer
ps **DATING** courting; (post); age estimate
DATION act of giving
DATIVE prepositions of giving; for, to
bt **DATURA** thorn-apple
DAUBED smeared; plastered; stained
DAUBER inferior painter
bt **DAUCUS** the carrot
mn **DAVINA** volcanic substance
DAWDLE amble slowly; idle; dally
DAWISH like a jackdaw
DAWNED sunrise; began to appear; (ideas)
DAY-BED a sofa; couch
DAY-BOY non-resident schoolboy
zo **DAY-FLY** an ephemeral insect
DAZING sunshine direct into eyes
DAZZLE daze; confuse; bewilder
rl **DEACON** church official
DEADEN benumb; blunt; obtund
DEADLY fatal; mortal; baneful; lethal
DEAFEN overwhelm with loud noise
DEAFLY unhearingly
DEALER vendor; monger; trader
DEARER costlier; fonder
DEARIE term of endearment
DEARLY affectionately; expensively
DEARTH scarcity; lack; shortage
DEBASE degrade; lower; humble
DEBATE dispute; contest; argue
DEBRIS broken bits & pieces
DEBTED indebted; owed
lw **DEBTEE** the lender
lw **DEBTOR** the borrower
DEBUNK expose; unmask; reveal
cp **DECADE** ten of (years); data locations
DECAMP abscond; bolt; fly
ar, rl, mu **DECANI** deans-side; southside (choir) of cathedral
DECANT to pour gently
me **DECARE** 1000 sq. metres
DECEIT guile; fraud; chicanery
DECENT proper; seemly; suitable (clean)
DECERN to judge; to decree
DECIDE settle; determine; resolve
ma, as **DECILE** aspect; deci-intervals
mu, nm **DECIMA** **DECIME**, a tenth
nt **DECKED** **DECKER**, with floors (double bus); adorned
pr **DECKLE** paper (-frame; -edge; -gauge)
ck **DECOCT** boil; concentrate the essence
DECODE decipher; translate; solve
DECREE ordain; ukase; fiat; edict
DECURY squad of ten (Roman)
ga **DEDANS** gallery (tennis)
DEDUCE infer; gather; conclude
DEDUCT subtract; withdraw
lw **DEEDED** conveyed by deed
DEEMED believed; determined; judged
DEEPEN darken; dredge; make obscure
DEEPER **DEEPLY**, further down; profoundly
DEESHY very small (Irish)
DEFACE disfigure; injure; sully
DEFAME asperse; vilify; traduce
DEFEAT rout; frustrate; overwhelm
DEFECT flaw; blemish; faul (traitor)

DEFEND ward; protect; guard
DEFIED challenged; braved
DEFIER scorner; challenger (opponent)
DEFILE violate; taint; vitiate; a gorge
DEFINE specify; explain; limit
pl **DEFLEX** unflex; relax (muscles)
md **DEFLUX** a discharge
DEFORM distort; deface; spoil
DEFRAY pay; meet; liquidate; bear
DEFTLY adroitly; skilfully
me **DEGREE** grade; rank; class; order; units of measurements
DEHORN remove horns from cattle
ch **DE-ICER** windscreen, wing-ice remover
DEIFIC divine; godlike
DEIXIS linguistic context limits
DEJECT cast down; depress; dishearten
DELETE erase; obliterate; efface
DELICE **DELOUSE**, remove louse invasion
DELUDE dupe; beguile; trick
DELUGE flood; cataclysm; inundate
DELVED dug; excavated; searched
DELVER a digger; miner
lw **DEMAIN** **DEMESNE, DOMAIN**, private land
cp **DEMAND** claim; exact; require; request
DEMEAN behave; lower; degrade
DEMENT madden; derange
DEMISE a death; to bequeath
DEMODE not fashionable; out of date
DEMOTH take out of storage (armaments)
DEMURE modest; grave; discreet
DENARY ten
DENIAL dementi; refutation; refusal
DENIED refused; contradicted; refuted
wv, tx **DENIER** disowner; gainsayer; silk; nylon quality
DENNET light two-wheeled carriage
DENOTE signify; imply; indicate
DENSER more compact; thicker; closer
DENTAL of teeth
DENTED **DINTED**, bent after bumping
ar **DENTEL** **DENTIL**, dogtooth pattern (arches)
zo **DENTEX** sea perch
pl **DENTIN** **DENTINE**, tooth ivory
DENUDE strip; bare; divest
DEODAR sacred tree
DEPART start; vanish; retire; die
DEPEND rely; hang; hinge; rest
DEPICT sketch; limn; portray; draw
DEPLOY open; expand; extend; unfold
lw **DEPONE** to testify under oath
DEPORT banish; expel; behave
DEPOSE oust; divest of office; depone
DEPUTE delegate; authorize; change
DEPUTY envoy; proxy; agent
rw **DERAIL** upset; leave rail track
DERAIN vindicate; prove; justify
DERATE reduce; devalue; demote
zo **DERBIO** a green sea-fish
nm **DERHAM** dirhem; Moroccan coin
DERIDE ridicule; mock; lampoon; scorn
DERIVE obtain; draw; trace; receive
pl **DERMAL** dermic; relating to skin
pl **DERMIS** **DERMIC**, of layer of skin
DESCRY to espy; detect; discern
DESERT quit; abandon; forsake; merit
ck **DESERT** a Sahara; fruit, etc
ar **DESIGN** plan; devise; scheme
DESIRE covet; crave; want; passion
DESIST stay; stop; forbear; pause
zo **DESMAN** musk-rat
bt **DESMID** river-weed
DESPOT dictator; tyrant; autocrat
DETACH sever; divide; part; disengage
DETAIL delineate; recount; relate; item
DETAIN retain; keep; hold; confine
DETECT discover; reveal; unmask
DETEST hate; abhor; loathe
lw **DETORT** to pervert
DETOUR deviation; circumambulation
ro **DETUNE** adjust resonant circuit
DEUCED devilish; confounded
rl **DEUNME** Jew turned Moslem
DEVICE gadget; ruse; bomb; emblem
lw **DEVISE** scheme; plan; bequeath
DEVOID lacking; vacant; empty
DEVOIR politeness; duty
DEVOTE dedicate; give; resign
DEVOUR gorge; gobble; consume
DEVOUT pious; saintly; sincere
mt **DEWING** morning precipitation
DEWLAP pendulous neck-flesh
DEXTER on the right-hand side
ch **DEZINK** (zinc extraction)
rl **DHARMA** law of Buddha
DHOBIE Indian washerman
DIADEM crown; coronet; tiara
tx **DIAPER** a napkin for incontinent babies

bt **DIATOM** algae with silica shells
zo **DIAXON** with 2 axes, in sponges
to **DIBBED DIBBER**, pointed tool (garden)
DIBBLE dibber; to make holes
DICING gaming
DICKER ten; to barter
DICTUM maxim; precept; wise words
lw **DICTUM** precept; award
DIDDER to shiver
DIDDLE cheat; totter; dodder
DIESEL heavy oil (motor)
pr **DIESIS** printing mark
ck **DIETAL DIETED-DIETER**, of food regime
DIFFER deviate; vary; wrangle
DIGAMY second marriage
DIGENY sexual reproduction
DIGEST assimilate (summarized material)
DIGGED delved; dug; mined
DIGGER Australian
DIGRAM double picture
DIKAST diecast; Athenian judge
zo **DIK-DIK** S. African antelope
bd **DIKING** making floor barriers (dikes)
DIKKAH tribune in a mosque
zo **DIKKOP** bustard (S. African)
DIKTAT enforced settlement
md **DILATE** amplify; expand; enlarge
DILOGY double-entendre
DILUTE water down; weaken a solution
tx **DIMITY** figured cloth; strong cotton
DIMMED obscured; clouded; dulled
DIMMER light-fading device (cars)
DIMMER fainter; darker
DIMOUT partial black-out
DIMPLE cheek depression
DIMWIT fool; weak-minded
mu **DIN-DIN** Indian cymbals
DINGED hurled; enforced; urged
DINGER home-run (baseball)
DINGES what's its name (S. African)
nt **DINGHY** dingey; open, ballasted sailing craft
DINGLE dell; dale; vale; glen
DINGUS gadget; contraption
DINKUM honest; genuine (Aust.)
DINNED persistently repeated
DINNER principal meal
DIONYM name containing 2 terms
md **DIOTIC** affecting both ears
DIPLEX simultaneous tranmission
md **DIPLOE** skull tissue
zo **DIPNOI** fish with lungs and gills
pl **DIPODY** two-footed
el, ro **DIPOLE** type of radio aerial
DIPPED immersed; doused; soused
zo **DIPPER** waterbird; ousel; ladle
me **DIP-ROD** oil gauge
me **DIPSAS** serpent
mn **DIPYRE** a silicate of alumina
DIRECT straight; bid; order; address
DIREST most calamitous; cruellest
nm, me **DIRHAM DIRHEM**, coinage (Morocco); ancient weight (silver)
DIRKED stabbed by dagger
DISARM to remove guns, weapons etc.
lw **DISBAR DEBAR**, expel a professional from practice
bt **DISBUD** remove buds (gardening)
mu **DISCAL** of discs
bt **DISCUS** flower centre; quoit
ga **DISCUS** a thrown weight
DISEUR DISEUSE, raconteur (Fr.)
DISHED frustrated; thwarted
DISMAL dull; doleful; lugubrious
DISMAN to castrate; render impotent
DISMAY appal; scare; daunt; alarm
DISOWN deny; disclaim; reject
DISPEL banish; scatter; dismiss
bt **DISTAL** terminal; furthest from axis
DISTIL vaporize; drip; emanate
DISUSE desuetude; neglect
DITHER didder; tremble; hesitate
mu **DITONE** notation interval
zo **DIURNA** insects; ephemerae (of a day)
DIVERS diverse; different; sundry
DIVERT distract; amuse; relax; deflect
DIVEST divest; strip; denude; bare
DIVIDE separate into parts; share; sever
go **DIVIDE** watershed; continental-; cleave
DIVINE sacred; angelic; defect
rl **DIVINE** (water); augur
DIVING plunging; penetrating; swooping
mu **DIVISI** separation of strings for part playing (It.)
mu **DIVOTO** solemnly; in devotion (It.)
DIZAIN poem in ten stanzas
zo **DIZOIC** with 2 sporozoites
DJIBBA Eastern garment
DOABLE practical
DOBBIE a dotard; a brownie
zo **DOBBIN** old horse
DOCENT reader/teacher in University
DOCILE pliant; amenable; compliant
nt, sp, vt **DOCKED** without tail; safe in harbour
DOCKER dock-labourer; stevedore

lw **DOCKET** doquet; a summary
zo **DOCTOR** a fish; medico; to falsify
vt, zo **DODDED** de-horned
bt **DODDER** parasitic plant; didder; shake
bt, zo **DODDLE** a pollard
DODGED evaded; quibbled; avoided
DODGER trickster; shifter; evader
nm **DODKIN** a doit
zo **DODMAN** a snail
DOFFED removed; took off (cap)
DOFFER carding mechanism (wool)
DOGANA DOUANE, customs house (It/Fr.)
zo **DOG-BEE** a drone
DOG-BOX enclosure for dogs
DOG-EAR broken/damaged book corner
zo **DOG-FOX** renard
mn **DOGGAR** ironstone
DOGGED sullen; obstinate; determined
nt **DOGGER** fishing boat (North Sea)
DOG-LEG crooked hole shot (golf)
DOG-MAD rabid; crazy; insane
DOIGTE finger play (fencing)
DOINGS multifarious activities
DOITED crazy; stupid
DOLING distributing (to needy)
DOLING (small portions)
zo **DOLIUM** molluscs
nm **DOLLAR** 100 cents
DOLLED prinked up; overdressed
ck **DOLLOP** viscous mass; helping
DOLMAN hussar's jacket
DOLMEN ancient grave; cromlech
DOLOSE fraudulent; deceitful
DOLOUR anguish; sorrow; pain
lw **DOMAIN** demesne; dominion; sway
ps **DOMAIN** borders of strong magnetic force on ferromagnetic crystals
DOM-BOC Saxon book (judgments)
tx **DOMETT** shroud fabric
ga, rl **DOMINO** priest's cape; cloak; game
mn **DOMITE** variety of trachyte
DONARY DONATE, gift; give (money etc.)
ar **DONJON** castle keep (above dungeon)
zo **DONKEY** burro; moke; ass
DONZEL budding knight; a page
DOODLE a simpleton; a trifler; drawing
DOOMED destined; condemned
DOONGA flat-bottomed house-boat (Indian)
DOPING administering drugs
DOPING sniffing varnish
mu **DOPPIO** increase speed to double (It.)
as, zo **DORADO** constellation; a dolphin
zo **DORBIE** heath bird; dunlin
DORCAS charitable society
ar **DORIAN** Doric scroll motif (capitals) (Gr.)
DORING lark-catching
DORISM Doricism
ar **DORMER** window in the roof
DORMIE dormy; unbeatable at golf
bt **DORMIN** hormone controlling dormancy
tx **DORNIC** figured linen
pl **DORSAL** nerves of touch; limbs
pl, zo **DORSAL** spinal, back fin
DORSEL pannier
rl **DORTER** dormitory
md **DOSAGE DOSING**, medicine amount prescribed
rl **DOSSAL DOSSEL**, altar cloth in church
md **DOSSIL** pledget; slug
DOTAGE DOTANT, DOTART, DOTISH, senility
DOTERY drivel spoken by senile
DOTING infatuated; madly fond of
DOTTED stippled; speckled
pt **DOTTER** birds'-eyes graining brush
DOTTLE pipe-ash
DOUANE custom-house (Fr.)
mu, ga **DOUBLE** twofold; dual; score; trill
DOUCHE shower (bath)
ck **DOUGHY** soft consistency like dough
zo **DOUKAR** dabchick
DOURLY grimly; sternly; obstinately
DOUSED drenched; extinguished (fire)
DOWSED DOWSER, water found by diviner
DOUTER extinguisher
ar **DOWELL** metal pin; cramp
lw **DOWERY DOWER**, widow's share of assets
tx **DOWLAS** coarse cloth
DOWNED floored
DOWSER water-diviner
tx **DOYLEY DOILY**, lacement (dining room)
DOZING somnolent; drowsy
DRABBY sluttish; unkempt
nm **DRACHM** drachma; a dram
DRAFFY dreggy; waste; worthless
DRAFTS preliminary texts
DRAFTS cheques (bank-); recruits
DRAGEE sweetmeat
zo **DRAGON** monstrous saurian
DRAPED dressed; robed; clothed

DRAPER haberdasher
DRAPET coverlet
DRAPPY a wee drop (Sc.)
DRAWEE (Bill of Exchange) payee
DRAWER cheque-payer; (chest of); artist
DRAZEL a slut
DREAMT **DREAMY**, imagined visions
DREARY dismal; lonely; dull; gloomy
DREDGE use dragnet; deepen a channel
lw **DRENCH** (tenure); soak; imbrue
DRESSY dapper; dandified
DRIEST very dry
DRIVEL prate; twaddle; balderdash
DRIVEN urged; compelled; overworked
DRIVER chauffeur (taxi-); (pile-)
ga **DRIVER** club (golf)
nt **DROGER** a coaster; drogher; (Irish Sea)
DROGUE sea anchor; wind sleeve; target
DROMIC **DROMOS**, of aerodrome; racecourse
nt **DROMON** medieval warship; galley
DROMOS Greek race-course
DRONED buzzed; drawled; idled
zo **DRONGO** king crow
cp **DROP-IN** computer error; visit; party
md **DROPSY** condition of retention of fluids
DROSKY Russian horse-cab
DROSSY impure; foul; worthless
DROUGE harpoon drag
DROUTH **DROUGHT**, dryness (climate)
DROVER cattle-driver
DROWSE nap; slumber; doze
DROWSY lethargic; comatose; soporific
DRUDGE menial; scullion; toil; slave
rl **DRUIDS** a sacred order
bt **DRUPEL** a stone-fruit; a drupe
DRUSED crystalline
rl **DRUSES** Moslem sect (Lebanon, Syria)
DRY-BOB non-rower (Eton)
DRY-FLY (fishing) (angling)
DRYING parching; desiccating
DRYISH rather dry; very dull; sarcastic
mn **DRYITE** fossil wood
DRY-ROT wood decay
DRY-RUB massage; rub down
DUBBED **DUBBER**, sound film translator
DUBBED greased
DUBBIN a leather grease; dubbing
DUCKED bobbed; immersed
zo **DUCKER** a plunger; bird
DUDDER to shake; to deafen
DUDEEN Irish clay pipe
DUELLO duelling (It.)
DUENNA chaperone
mu **DUETTO** a duet
DUFFED stole cattle (Aust.)
tx **DUFFEL** **DUFFLE**, coarse felt cloth coat
DUFFER a pedlar; muff; stupid person
zo **DUGONG** sea-cow; halicore; manatee
ga, nt **DUG-OUT** canoe; shelter; (baseball)
DUG-OUT retired officer
zo **DUIKER** duyker; cormorant
DUKERY seat of a duke
mu **DULCET** melodious; honeyed (sounds)
DULLED blunted; assuaged; softened
DULLER more listless
DUMBLY silently; mutely
DUM-DUM soft-nosed bullet
DUMPED unloaded; deposited; corpse
ga **DUMPED** surfer (Australia)
DUMPER track with unloading chute
ga **DUMPER** mighty wave surfing
DUMPLE to cook a dumpling
zo **DUN-COW** species of ray
gl **DUNITE** olivine igneous rock
DUNKER tunker; baptist; dipper
zo **DUNLIN** sandpiper
ck **DUNLOP** a cheese; –type
DUNNED importuned
DUNNER debt-collector
bd **DUNTER** monumental mason or polisher
DUPERY deception; gulling
DUPING confidence tricks
zo **DUPION** double cocoon
ps **DUPLET** electrons bonding atoms
mu **DUPLET** of equal time notes
el **DUPLEX** two-room flat; two-way flow
DUPLEX double-sided emulsified photo paper
mn **DURAIN** type of coal
DURANT glazed fabric
mu **DURATE** harsh to the ear
DURBAR Grand Audience; festival (Ind.)
DURDEN a thicket; a copse
DURDUM dirdum; an uproar
DURESS restraint; imprisonment
rl **DURGAH** Moslem saint's shine (Ind.)
DURGAN dwarf
zo **DURHAM** breed of cattle

bt **DURIAN** Malay fruit
DURING throughout; pending
bt **DURION** see durian
DURITY hardness; firmness
tx **DURRIE** Indian cotton fabric
DUSKEN to grow dark
DUSKLY duskily; gloomily
tx **DUSTER** dry house cloth (cleaning)
DUST-UP quarrel; fisticuffs; fight; brawl
DUTIED posted to other duties (army)
DUTIED charged; taxed (excise)
DUTIES obligations (work) (excise)
zo **DUYKER** duiker; African antelope
ch **DYADIC** (two); characteristic of things paired
cp **DYADIC** binary operation
DYEING colouring; staining
el **DYNAMO** energy converter
DYNAST ruler (in family line)
el **DYNODE** valve
zo **DZEREN DZERON**, Mongolian antelope

E

EADISH aftermath; second crop
zo **EAGLET** a young eagle
EAR-BOB an earring
EAR-CAP ear-muff
EARFUL a diatribe; (explosion of anger)
nt **EARING** ploughing; rope
md **EARLAP** tip of ear
EARNED merited; won; deserved
EARNER wage taker; breadwinner
EARTHY material; gross; unrefined
EAR-WAX cerumen
zo **EAR-WIG** informer; insect
ce **EASERS** relief holes (prior to tunnelling)
EASIER more tranquil; more pliant
EASILY tranquilly; calmly
EASING relieving; calming; soothing
rl **EASTER** Resurrection
rl **EASTER EOSTRE** (goddess); Saxon Spring
EATAGE cattle food
EATING food intake; devouring; eroding
EBBING waning; declining; subsiding
ga **ECARTE** card game
bl **ECESIS** unviable-species invasion
bt **ECHARD** non-usable soil water
ECHOED repeated sound
ECHOES resounded reverberations
ECHOIC aural copycat; mimic
ECLAIR a cream-filled pastry
md **ECLEGM** oil and syrup
cf, md **-ECTOMY** (surgical) removal
ar **ECTYPE** a cast; a copy
md **ECZEMA** a skin disease
EDDIED swirled; rippled; whirlpool
EDDISH eadish; aftermath
bt **EDDOES** W. Indian potatoes
rl **EDENIC** of the garden of Eden
EDGING border; frill; rim; nearing
EDIBLE eatable; esculent
pr **EDITED** prepared for publication
EDITOR corrector; reviser; annotator
EDUCED extracted; elicited; derived
EEL-POT an eel-trap
EERILY wierdly; uncannily
EFFACE erase; expunge; delete
EFFECT achieve; cause; create
EFFETE spent; worn; barren; abortive
rl **EFFIGY** image; statue; likeness
EFFLUX flow; effusion; discharge
EFFORT essay; trial; striving; strain
EFFUSE emanate; issue; pour; spill
EGENCE exigence
mn **EGERAN** garnet
EGERIA spiritual adviser
ck **EGG-CUP** container for boiled egg
EGGERY nesting-place
EGGING inciting
EGGLER an egg-dealer
ck **EGG-NOG** a drink; egg and rum
pc **EGOISM** conceit; vanity; self-praise
EGOIST egoist; not an altruist
EGOITY identity
pc **EGOTIC** essence of personality
EGRESS emergence from shade; exit
bt **EGROIT** a sour cherry
EIDOLA apparitions
mu **EIGHTH** a quaver ⅛ note
ga **EIGHTS** carmanship; (the boat race)
EIGHTY four-score
zo **EIRACK** young hen (Sc.)
EITHER one of two
EKEING ekeing; adding; stretching
bt **ELAEIS** African oil palm
ELAINE the lily-maid of Astolat
ELANCE throw out; launch
zo **ELANET** insectivorous kite
ELAPSE intervene; pass; slip
ELATED exalted; proud; excited
zo **ELATER** click-beetle genus
ELATOR a rouser
ELDEST oldest
lw **ELEGIT** writ
ELEMIN oil from resin
ELEVEN a cricket team

ae **ELEVON** hinged wing-control surface
ELFISH puckish; impish; mischievous
ELICIT deduce; evoke; extract
ELIDED cut off a syllable
lw **ELISOR** (jury selection)
ELIXIR a cordial; quintessence; (potion)
bt **ELK-NUT** oil-nut
zo **ELLECK** red gurnet
md **ELODES** sweating sickness
rl **ELOHIM** the Creator (Hebrew)
ELOIGN to carry away
ELOPED bolted; absconded; disappeared
ELUDED evaded; dodged; foiled
mn **ELVANS** felspar veins
ELVISH elfish; elf-like; tricksy; –pixie
me **ELWAND** an ellwand
ELYTRA chitinized forewings in coleoptera
EMBALE to pack; to bundle
EMBALL encircle; ensphere
EMBALM perfume; to preserve
EMBANK confine by banks
nt **EMBARK** start; enter; board
EMBERS live cinders
EMBLEM badge; token; device; symbol
EMBODY imbody; incorporate; include
zo **EMBOLY** pushing or growing in
EMBOSS cover with raised decoration (gems)
pl **EMBRYO** fertilized ovum; rudiment
EMERGE emanate; appear; issue
md **EMESIS EMETIC**, vomiting (causing this)
EMEUTE riot; disorder; insurrection
EMIGRE French royalist abroad
EMMESH immesh; enmesh; entrap
EMPALE EMPARK, enclose with a fence
EMPAWN pawn; impawn; pledge
EMPERY empire; power
EMPIRE commercial, financial dominions
EMPLOY make use of (workers, methods etc.)
rl **EMPUSA EMPUSE**, ghost or goblin (Hecate)
EMUCID mouldy
ENABLE allow; permit; empower
md **ENAMEL** durable paint; crown cover (teeth)
ENCAGE hold captive (hen coop) (zoo)
ENCAMP camp; pitch; settle
ENCASE pack in box; (set jewels)
ENCASH convert from cheque to cash
ENCAVE to cache; to store away
cp, tc **ENCODE** convert into cyphers or symbols
cp **ENCODE** data as digits for processing
md **ENCOPE** an incision
ENCORE call for repeat (threatre)
pl, md **ENCYST** form capsule in living body
END-ALL finish; conclusion; ultimate
ENDEAR captivate; charm; win
ENDING finale; closing; finis
zo **ENDITE** phyllopodium lobe in crustacea
bt **ENDIVE** species of chicory
ENDOSS ENDORSE, sanction; ratify
nt **ENDROL** dugout canoe sailing outrigger (S.W. Pacific)
END-SAC coelomic vesicle in arthropoda
ENDUED indued; endowed; supplied
ENDURE tolerate (pain, disaster, hunger)
md **ENECIA** fever
me **ENERGY** vigour; power; (Joule)
md **ENESIS** vomiting
ar **ENFACE** decorate a surface (art)
ENFOLD wrap up; cover (protective)
ENGAGE contend; agree; promise
ENGINE machine; device; method
ENGLYN 4-line stanza (Welsh)
ENGOBE ceramic technique
ENGULF surround; overwhelm
ENIGMA mystery; puzzle; code; rebus
ENJOIN bid; direct; command
mu **ENKOMO** small Cuban drum
ENLACE enfold; entwine
ENLIST engage; enrol; secure (ally) (army) (association)
ENMESH entrap (in net); (involved)
ENMITY animus; hatred; aversion
ENNEAD group of nine
zo, bt **ENODAL** without joints, knobs
ENOSIS political fusion (Cyprus) (Gr.)
ENOUGH ample; adequate; sufficient
ENRAGE incense; infuriate; madden
rw **ENRAIL** to transport by train
ENRAPT in an ecstasy
ENRICH fertilize; endow; adorn
ENROLL enlist
ENROOT enrace; implant
bt **ENSATE** sword-shaped
lw **ENSEAL** (documents, laws etc.); legalize

ENSIGN National Flag (ships)
ENSIGN officer (US Army)
ag **ENSILE** fodder storage (silage)
ENSPAN to yoke up (S. Africa)
ENSUED followed; resulted; accrued
ENSURE guarantee; secure; fix
lw **ENTAIL** leave; bequeath; involve
md **ENTERA** intestines
ENTICE seduce; allure; decoy; cajole
ENTIRE complete; perfect
ga **ENTIRE** stallion (racing)
ENTITY being; essence; existence; unit
ENTOMB bury; inter; inhume
ENTRAP inveigle; ensnare; entangle
ck, mu **ENTREE** dish; menu; arrival (theatre)
ENVIED grudged; coveted
ENVIER rival
bt, ch **ENZYME** ferment; catalyst; leavening
EOCENE a geological period
mu **EOLIAN** **AEOLIAN**, **EOLIC**, Aegean harp (Gr.)
to **EOLITH** prehistoric flint implement
pc **EONISM** transvestism (d'Eon)
EOSTRE Saxon goddess; (Easter)
EOTHEN from the East
gl, mn **EOZOIC** **EOZOON**, rock containing fossilized foraminifera
EPACME vigorous period in a life-history
EPARCH Greek governor
ar **EPAULE** bastion-shoulder
zo **EPEIRA** genus of spiders
EPHEBE young Athenian
EPHORI Spartan magistrates
as **EPIGEE** **APOGEE**, furthest point of orbit from Earth
zo **EPIZOA** parasites
EPODIC lyric
EPONYM name derived from a person
EPOPEE epic poem
md **EPULIS** gum disease
EQUANT imaginary circle
EQUATE to equalize; to average
EQUINE horsey
EQUITY impartial justice
ERASED expunged; cancelled; deleted
ERASER a scraper; a mark remover
ml **ERBIUM** rare metal
EREBUS darkness; son of Chaos
EREMIC pertaining to sandy desert
ERENOW before this time
zo **ERGATE** sterile female ant, worker
lw **ERIACH** a fine; blood-money (Irish)
bt **ERINGO** **ERYNGO**, sea-holly
ERINYS one of the Furies
tc, me **ERLANG** unit of telephone traffic flow
ERMINE the stoat's winter coat
gl **ERODED** worn away (by climate, water)
EROTIC amatory; sexual; libidinous
ERRAND mission; change; message
ERRANT roving; rambling; wandering
ERRATA errors; mistakes
ERRING straying; mistaking
ERSATZ substitute (food etc.) (Ger.)
bt **ERYNGO** sea-holly genus
ga **ESCAPE** break free; flee; wrestling
bt **ESCAPE** (fire-); a non-weed in wild
ESCARP steep slope
ESCARS gravel ridges
md **ESCHAR** burnt wounds; scab
ESCHEW to shun; avoid; miss
ESCORT protect; guard; convoy
hd **ESCROL** **ESCROW**, deed; heraldic scroll
nm **ESCUDO** Porguguese coin
ESKIMO an Inuit; arctic dweller
lw **ESNECY** privilege of choice
ESPADA bull-fighting sword (Sp.)
ESPIED discovered unexpectedly
ESPRIT wit; sprightliness; (de corps)
rl **ESSENE** ascetic Hebrew
md **ESSERA** skin eruption
lw **ESSOIN** excuse for absence
ml **ESTAIN** French pewter
lw **ESTATE** condition; rank; property; (landed)
ESTEEM deem; consider; value
ESTRAY to stray; a stray; lost
bl **ESTRUS** (oestrus) heat; rut
lt **ETALON** an interferometer
er **ETCHED** engraved; corroded by acid
pr **ETCHER** an engraver
ch **ETHANE** odourless paraffin gas
ETHICS moral science; philosophy; code
ETHIOP an Ethiopian
mu **ETHNIC** racial
mo **ETRIER** portable stirrup
ETYMON derivation; meaning
ETYPIC unique
md **EUCAIN** drug similar to cocaine
ga **EUCHRE** card game
ma **EUCLID** geometer (laws)
zo **EUCONE** of insect compound eyes
mn **EULITE** an orthopyroxene
EULOGY panegyric; encomium
EUNOMY good government
EUNUCH a castrated man
EUONYM a suitable name
bt **EUPION** vegetable oil

zo **EUPODA** beetles
EUREKA Found! (Archimedes)
mn **EURITE** a granite
EUTAXY regularity
EUTONY pleasantness of wood sound
EVADED eluded; dodged; avoided
EVADER sidestepper of law, tax, etc.
EVANID faint; evanescent
to, cr **EVENER** leveller; roller; plane
EVENLY smoothly; fairly; uniformly
EVILLY wickedly; maliciously
EVINCE display; show; exhibit
EVOKED reminded; recalled; reroused
EVOLVE unfold; unroll; develop
EXAMEN a disquisition; an enquiry
rl **EXARCH** a title; viceroy; Gr. bishop
EXCEED cap; outdo; surpass; transcend
EXCEPT bar; ban; exclude; omit
EXCESS surplus; glut; balance
md **EXCIDE** **EXCISION**, to cut off
EXCISE duty; impost; tax; (Walpole)
EXCITE rouse; incite; kindle
EXCUSE acquit; pardon; exempt
EXCUSS to decipher; shake off
lw **EXCUSS** to seize
ar, bd **EXEDRA** a hall; a recess
EXEMPT free; released; immune
EXEQUY **OBSEQUY**, funeral rites; gifts
EXEUNT all quit the stage
EXHALE breathe out; emanate; emit
EXHORT urge; encourage; counsel
EXHUME unearth; disinter
EXILED banished; outlawed
EXILIC (Jewish) exile
lw **EXITUS** yearly rent; issue
EXODIC (Exodus); migratory
EXODUS departure
bt **EXOGEN** a class of plant
EXOMIS Greek sleeveless tunic
EXOTIC not native; extraneous; foreign
EXPAND spread; dilate; swell; extend
EXPECT hope; await; forecast
EXPEND disburse; consume; exert
EXPERT apt; adroit; skilful; able
EXPIRE end; die; stop; finish
EXPIRY conclusion; extinction
EXPORT sell & send goods abroad (ship)
EXPOSE an exposure; reveal; unmask
EXPUGN take by assault; conquer
EXSECT to cut away; cut out
zo **EXSULE** apterous life-cycle form in hemiptera
EXTANT existent; current
EXTASY ecstasy; rapture; trance
EXTEND stretch; reach; expand
EXTENT amount; scope; range; field
EXTERN day-boy (non resident)
EXTERN not inherent
bt **EXTINE** (pollen grain)
EXTORT exact; extract; wrench; elicit
EXUDED sweated; oozed; percolated
zo **EXUVIA** cast-off skins, shells
md **EYE-CUP** (used for eye lotion)
EYEFUL a glance
EYEING watching
EYELET loop-hole
pl **EYELID** eye skin cover
zo **EYRANT** bird of prey on nest

F

FABIAN policy of patiently waiting for opportune moment
FABLED renowned; fictionalized
FABLER an Aesop; parable teller
FABRIC structure; texture; web
ar **FACADE** front view; face; masking
cp **FACE-UP** confront; position of printing
md **FACIAL** frontal; of the face
lw **FACIES** external appearance; the face
FACILE easy; dexterous; plaint
ar, ce **FACING** confronting; opposing; covering; forward looking; surface finish
FACTOR broker; middleman
FACTOR agent or manager of estate
ma **FACTOR** causal influence; component
lw **FACTUM** memorandum; deed; point of controversy
as **FACULA** sun-spot
FADDLE to trifle; to play
FADGED suited; prospered
ro **FADING** diminishing; withering; reducing speed at end of race
FAECES human excrement
FAERIE fairy; fairyland; (Spens.)
FAFFLE to stammer
FAG-END butt (cigarette)
FAGGED tired
bd, mu **FAGGOT** **FAGOT**, bundle of sticks; fascine bassoon; facing brick
mn **FAIKES** shaly sandstone
FAILED did not succeed; missed (fiasco)
FAILLE nun's veiling
FAINTY feeble; languid
FAIRER more equitable; beautiful; blonde
FAIRLY moderately; passably
FAITOR rogue; imposter; evil-doer

FAKEER Indian beggar
FAKING forging; doctoring; feinting
ga **FAKING** pretending; (badminton etc.)
zo **FALCON** hawk; missile
wv, tx **FALLAL** finery; streamer
FALLEN cast down; disgraced; lapsed
FALLOW untilled; idle; dormant
FALSER more fallacious
FALTER totter; waver; vacillate
gl **FALUNS** Miocene deposits
pl **FAMBLE** the hand (sl.)
FAMILY household; race; lineage
FAMINE dearth; scarcity; starvation
FAMOUS renowned; eminent
FANGED toothed; taloned
FANGLE a contraption; (new-); novelty
FANGOT a quantity of wares
FANNED inflamed
FANNEL FANNON, flag; banner; splint
FANNER winnower
ps, el **FAN-OUT** multiple outputs (circuit)
ga **FAN-OUT** fanlike scattering (football)
ga **FANTAN** Chinese gambling game
FANTOM phantom; spook; ghost
FAQUIR religious mendicant
FARCIN glanders; farcy
FARDEL a bundle; burden; load
ck **FARFEL** kosher dumplings; doughy grains
ck **FARINA** flour; cereal meal; polenta
FARING experiencing; feeding
FARMED leased
FARMER tiller; cultivator
FARROW litter of pigs
FASCES Roman badge
ar, pl **FASCIA** a band; name-board; connective tissue
FASHED vexed; worried (Sc.)
FASTED abstained from food
FASTEN bind; secure; tie; latch
FASTER quicker; speedier
FASTLY firmly
bt **FAT-HEN** goose-foot
FATHER adopt; beget; sire
nt **FATHOM** 6ft (1.8 m); comprehend
FATTED fattened
FATTEN grow plump
FATTER more obese
FAUCAL throaty; guttural
md **FAUCES** (mouth)
FAUCET a tap; fosset
FAULTY defective; blameworthy
zo **FAUNAL** relating to animals
FAUNUS Pan
FAUTOR a supporter
FAVOSE honeycombed; cellular
FAVOUR gift; patronize; bias
FAWNER sycophant; clinger; parasite
nt **FAYING** fitting closely
FEALTY fidelity; loyalty; homage
FEARED apprehended; dreaded
FEATLY neatly; dexterously; adroitly
FEAZED untwisted; unravelled
rl **FECIAL** Roman priest; fetial
FECKET waistcoat (18th cent.)
bt, ck **FECULA** (plants); starch
FECUND prolific; fertile; fruitful
FEDARY a confederate
FEDORA trilby hat (USA)
FEEBLE faint; frail; weak; without strength
FEEBLY languidly; without strength
FEEDER a bib; inflow channel
cp **FEED-IN** programming data
FEEING hiring; recompensing
zo **FEELER** antenna; tentacle
zo **FEELER** organ of touch; (put out a-)
FEELER tentative suggestion
zo **FELINE** catlike; catty
FELLAH a peasant; worker (Arab)
FELLER wood-cutter
md **FELLIC** (bile)
FELLOE felly; rim of wheel
FELLOW peer; mate; equal
lw **FELONY** crime; misdemeanour
FELTED covered with felt
FELTER to mat together
FELTRE cuirass
FEMALE feminine
FENCED walled; equivocated
FENCER hedger; dealer in stolen goods
ga **FENCER** swordsman
nt **FENDER** protective rope mat; firescreen
FENIAN an Irish conspirator
FEN-MAN fen-lander; (East Anglian)
zo **FENNEC** African fox
bt, ck **FENNEL** vegetable
FEODAL feudal
FERASH lowly servant (Ind.)
FERGIE double-side kick (skiing)
FERIAE Roman holidays
FERIAL (holidays)
FERINE wild; savage; untamed; fierce
FERITY wildness
zo **FERRET** polecat; silk ribbon
FERRIC (iron)
FERULA fennel
FERULE a rod; cane
FERVID fervent; eager; ardent
bt **FESCUE** a pointer; a grass
FESTAL joyous; gay
FESTER rankle; rot; putrefy

rl **FETIAL** **FECIAL**, Roman priest
FETISH talisman; amulet; charm
FETISH idol; object of sexual fantasy
el **FETRON** junction; field-effect transistor
FETTER manacle; shackle; bond; gyve
FETTLE good condition; fitness
FEUDAL vassal-lord polity
FIACRE French cab
FIANCE betrothed man
FIASCO total failure, breakdown; flask
FIBBER a liar
FIBRED having fibres
FIBRID synthetic fibrous bonding particle
FIBRIL small fibre; slender thread
bt, md **FIBRIN** gluten; clot formative
md **FIBULA** ancient brooch; leg bone
FICKLE volatile; mercurial; unstable
FICTOR a modeller
mu **FIDDLE** a railing; violin; ruse; touch
FIDGET nervous movement; fret; worry
FIERCE savage; cruel; violent
rl **FIESTA** carnival; Mardi Gras (S. Am.)
FIGARO a barber; schemer
FIGGED all dressed up
cp **FIGURE** reckon; digit; (father-); ground
bd, mu **FIGURE** diagram; timber markings
FIJIAN (Fiji Islands)
FIKERY fuss (Sc.)
bt **FILAGO** cudweed
FILFOT fylfot; a swastika; (Nazis)
FILIAL dutiful, as a son; branch office
FILING particle; documents; rasping
FILLED replete
nm **FILLER** Hungarian coin; (complete)
bd **FILLER** extenders; (stopgap); paste
ck **FILLET** hair-ribbon; boneless fish/meat
to **FILLET** band; plain lines on book; tool
pg **FILL-IN** shadow technique
FILLIP to flip; an incitement
FILOSE thread-like
tc **FILTER** strain; selective process
el **FILTER** limited band network output
FILTHY foul; dirty; corrupt
ck **FILTRE** coffee-brewing method (Fr.)
bt **FIMBLE** hemp
mu **FINALE** climax; conclusion; finis; last movement
FINDER discoverer
ck **FINDON** dried haddock
FINEER (fraudulent credit)
FINELY excellently; delicately
tx **FINERY** splendour; trappings; fallals
FINEST keenest; sharpest; purest; best
FINGER digit; pilfer; touch
ar **FINIAL** a pinnacle; decorative acorn, knob
FINING refining
FINISH end; terminate; accomplish
bt **FINISH** final coat of paint; fixed joinery
FINITE limited; restricted
zo **FINLET** small fin
zo **FINNAN** Findon haddock
FINNED bearing fins
zo **FINNER** fin-back whale; torqual
FINNIC Finnish-related (peoples etc.)
zo **FINNOC** white trout
bt **FIORIN** bent-grass
mu **FIPPLE** wood block in recorder mouthpiece
FIRING igniting; kindling; expelling
me **FIRKIN** 9 imperial gallons
me **FIRLOT** a quarter boll
FIRMAN Ottoman decree; licence (Turk.)
FIRMED confirmed; established
FIRMLY steadily; compactly; strongly
lw **FISCAL** monetary; financial
nt **FISHED** strengthened; caught (angled) (compliments)
FISHER (-man); (weasel; black fox)
zo **FISHES** alternative pl. of fish
FISSLE rustle; whistle (Sc.)
FISTED struck with the fist
ga **FISTIC** (-cuffs); fight; (boxing)
hd **FITCHE** **FITCHY**, pointed
FITFUL off and on; irregular; unreliable
FITTED apt; seemly; adjusted
ce **FITTER** an artificer; more seemly; engine assembler
FIXING repairing; deciding; settling
FIXITY permanence; fastness
FIXIVE gummy; adhesive; glutinous
FIZGIG fisgig; a flirt; damp squib
FIZZED hissed; effervesced
ga **FIZZER** a fast one; ball
FIZZLE a fiasco; (-out); splutter
FLABBY lacking body firmness; flaccid
FLACON scent-bottle; small flask (Fr.)
FLAGGY drooping; weak

FLAGON a flask; later beer tankard
FLAITH Anc. Irish chief
FLAKED peeled off
ck **FLAMBE** ignited brandy dish; uneven pottery glaze (Fr.)
FLAMED on fire; excited; glazed
FLAMEN Roman official of rites
FLANCH a flange
rw, ce **FLANGE** projecting rim (wheel); pipe disc; chord (girder)
bd **FLANKS** haunches (horse); sides; intrados of arch
FLARED burnt unsteadily
FLASHE a sluice
FLASHY gaudy; impulsive; vapid
FLATLY positively; plainly
FLATTY puncture (tyre)
FLATUS body-wind; fart
FLAUNT vaunt; parade; display; (nudity)
mu **FLAUTO** modern traverse flute (It.)
FLAVIN yellow dye
FLAWED defective; wrongly designed
FLAXEN pale yellow; (linen)
FLAYED skinned
FLAYER skinner
ga **FLECHE** arrow; slender spire; running attack (fencing)
FLEDGE grow feathers; become air-worthy (birds)
FLEDGY feathery; downy
FLEECE to strip; plunder; sheepskin
FLEECH flatter; coax (Sc.)
tx **FLEECY** woolly; flocculent
FLENCH FLENSE, to cut up the blubber of a whale
FLESHY carnal; corporeal
FLETCH to feather an arrow (archery)
hd **FLEURY** (fleur-de-lis); dilly-flower; lily
FLEWED deep-mouthed
FLEXED bent; extended (of muscles)
pl **FLEXOR** joint-bending muscle
FLICKS movies
ar **FLIGHT** retreat; exodus; rout; stairs; aerial journey; escape (high-diving) (badminton)
FLIMSY frail; trivial; weak
FLINCH wince; blench; quail
gl **FLINTS** nodules of silica (fossil sponges); flocculation
FLINTY obdurate; hard; miserly
bd **FLITCH** a side of bacon; stack of veneer panels
FLITTY flighty; unstable
nt **FLOATS** (paddle-wheels); mobile platforms (processions); rafts
FLOATY buoyant; light
FLOCCI woolly filaments
tx **FLOCKS** waste wool
FLOCKY downy
FLOPPY flaccid; drooping
FLORAL flowery
mn **FLORAN** tin ore
bt, pr, ar **FLORET** flowerlet; decoration for spacing
FLORID ornate; meretricious
nm **FLORIN** once coined at Florence
FLOSSY silky
FLOURY like flour
to **FLOUSE FLOUSH**, to turn the edge of a tool; to splash (Sc.); (flush)
bt **FLOWER** bloom; blossom
ch **FLUATE** fluoride
mn **FLUCAN** clay
FLUENT flowing; voluble; fluid
FLUFFY downy; fluey
bd **FLUING** of splayed window jambs
FLUKED was fortunate
FLUNKY a lackey; snob
FLURRY agitation; bustle; perturb
FLUSHY reddish
mu, ar **FLUTED** channelled; grooved
mu **FLUTER** flutist; flautist
FLUXED melted; purged
FLUXES fusible substances for soldering
bd **FLY-BOX** receptacle for bait (angling)
FLYING aviation; fleeing; soaring
FLYMAN cabman
FLY-NET morquito curtain
FLY-NUT winged nut
FLY-ROD fishing rod for flies (angling)
FOAMED spurned; frothed
FOBBED imposed on; tricked
pl **FOCILE** a bone (arm or leg)
mu **FOCOSO** spiritedly
nt **FO'C'SLE** forecastle; bows
me **FODDER** a weight; animal food
FOEMAN foe; antagonist; enemy
bl **FOETAL FETAL**, of the unborn (embryonic)
FOETOR a stench; offensive odour
md **FOETUS** life in embryo
FOG-BOW white rainbow
FOGGED blurred; overcast
FOGRAM antiquated; a fogey
FOIBLE faible; weak point; defect
ga **FOIBLE** sharp half of sword (fencing)
FOILED baffled; thwarted; balked
FOILER a frustrator
FOISON plenty; autumn
FOLDED doubled; wrapped; furled

FOLDER leaflet; brochure
FOLIAR (leaves); laminar
FOLIER goldsmith's foil
FOLIOT goblin
gl, pl **FOLIUM** striatum; thin stratum; brain cover
FOLKSY imitation rustic
mu **FOLLIA** (composition)
FOLLOW succeed; chase; pursue; heed
FOMENT fan; excite; stimulate
FONDER tenderer; (preference) (love)
FONDLE pet; caress; dandle
FONDLY affectionately; lovingly
ck **FONDUE** melted cheese/wine dish (Swiss)
FONDUS calico-printing
FONTAL primary; baptismal
FOOLED duped; hoodwinked; hoaxed
FOOLEN (embankment)
FOOTED walked; paid; kicked
ga **FOOTER** football (sl.)
FOOTLE twaddle; bunkum
FOOZLE bungle; mis-hit
FORAGE fodder; search; pillage
FORBID ban; inhibit; taboo; veto
FORBYE besides; hard by
FORCED unnatural; compulsory
FORCER compeller
FORDED crossed by wading
FORE-BY besides (Sc.)
FOREGO yield; resign; relinquish
FOREST woodland; grove; boscage
to **FORFEX** scissors
FORGAT forgot
FORGED fabricated; spurious; welded
FORGER falsifier; hammerman
FORGET overlook; slight
FORGOT neglected; (oversight)
nm **FORINT** Hungarian currency
FORKED bifurcated
FORLAY to ambush; lie in wait for
FORMAL precise; exact; stiff; set
cp, pr **FORMAT** style; layout; size; (printing); data
FORMED arranged; moulded; shaped
FORMER prior; previous; bygone
ch **FORMIC** (acid)
ch **FORMYL** organic radical
md **FORNIX** (shell); (brain)
FORPET **FORPIT**, a fourth part; a quarter (Sc.)
FORREL forel; parchment
FORRIT forward (Sc.)
zo **FORROW** not with calf (Sc.)
FORSAY forbid; renounce
FORTED guarded; castellated
mn **FOSSIL** petrified
FOSTER cherish; nourish; encourage; (-parent)
nt **FOTHER** leak-stopping
me **FOTMAL** 70 lb (31.7 kg) of lead
FOUDRE large storage/transport wine cask
FOUGHT strove; contended; warred
FOULED polluted; sullied
FOULLY scurvily; unfairly; basely
FOURBE a cheat; trickster
mu **FOURTH** ordinal number; 4th; interval (harmonic)
FOWLER bird-shooter
zo **FOX-BAT** flying fox
FOXING deceiving; duping; deluding
FOXISH cunning; sly; shrewd
FOYBLE part of sword-table
FRACAS an uproar; brawl; riot
FRACID overripe; rotten
FRAGOR a crash
FRAISE defence of pointed stakes
FRAMED constructed; devised
FRAMER contriver; frame-maker
nt **FRANCO** free of expense; in bond (storage); duty-free
FRANZY crotchety (dial.)
FRAPPE chilled with ice (Fr.)
FRATCH a quarrel; a brawl (dial.)
rl **FRATER** refectory; brother; friar
FRAYED worn; chafed; fretted
FRAZIL anchor-ice; spicular ice
FREELY unimpeded; willingly; readily
FREEZE chill; numb; congeal; (statues); (golf); (basketball)
FRENCH Gallic
pl **FRENUM** a ligament
FRENZY delirium; madness; fury
FRESCO drink; paint; refreshment
FRESCO coolness; wall painting; (al fresco: out of doors)
mu **FRETTA** increase the pace (It.)
ar **FRETTE** a strengthening band
FRETTY ornate
FRIARY monastery
FRIDAY (Robinson Crusoe); assistant
FRIDGE ice-box; refrigerator
FRIEND ally; chum; intimate
ar **FRIEZE** rough stuff; decorative border
rl **FRIGGA** wife of Odin
FRIGHT alarm; dismay; panic; dread
FRIGID icy; cold; formal
pg **FRILLY** fluted; overdressed
FRINGE border; edge
FRINGY adorned with fringes
FRISKY gay; lively; sportive

FRIVOL to trifle
FRIZEL (flint-lock)
FROGGY abounding in frogs
ck **FROISE** pancake; fraise (Fr.)
FROLIC romp; gambol; play; lark
FRONDE political party (Fr.) 17th cent
FROSTY chilling; wintry
FROTHY empty; unsubstantial; foamy
FROUZY rank; musty; rancid
to **FROWER** a cleaver
FROWST stuffy and hot
FROWSY frowzy; unkempt; disorderly
FROZEN froren; frosty; iced
FRUGAL thrifty; saving; parsimonious
FRUITY fruitful; luscious
FRUMPY dowdy
bt **FRUTEX** a shrub
FRYING cooking with fat
ar **FUCATE** painted; a sham
mn **FUCOID** a fossil seaweed
FUDDLE muddle; inebriate
FUDGED cheated; faked; bungled
FUFFED puffed
mu **FUGATO** like a fugue
md **FUGILE** ear trouble
pc **FUGUES** memoryless wandering
FUHRER Hitler-type dictator; leader; guide; (Ger.)
FULANI tribe (South Sahara)
FULFIL meet; effect; satisfy
FULGID fulgent; flashing; steaming
FULGOR splendour
FULHAM FULLAM, FULLAN, a die loaded at one corner, to throw high
zo **FULICA** coot genus
FULLED scoured and thickened
to **FULLER** hammer
zo **FULMAR** sea-fowl; the petrel
FULVID tawny; yellow
FUMAGE chimney tax; hearth money
FUMBLE grope; bungle; stammer
FUMILY sulkily; smokily
pg **FUMING** ammonia process
zo **FUMMEL** funnel; mule
FUMOUS (fumes); vaporous
FUNDED endowed; financially secure
FUNDIE fundamentalist
ar **FUNDUQ** caravanserai fort (Arab.)
FUNDUS back part
FUNEST doleful; lamentable
bt **FUNGAL FUNGIN,** (fungi) mushrooms
zo **FUNGIA** genus of corals
bt **FUNGUS** plant
FUNKED played the coward
bt **FUNKIA** a lily genus
FUNNEL fummel; smoke-stack
md **FURFUR** dandruff
FURIES avenging deities
FURLED closely rolled
FURORE outburst of excitement anger
FURRED animals bearing winter coat
ag **FURROW** rut; groove; seam; corrugate; track of the plough
bt **FURZEN** furzy; whinny
mn **FUSAIN** friable coal
bt **FUSEAU** macroconidium of dermatophytes
el **FUSING** liquid metals merging; (short circuit)
FUSION melting; amalgamation
bt **FUSOID** wide-middled and end-tapered
FUSSED worried; fretted; fidgeted
FUSTED mouldy; rancid; malodorous
bt **FUSTET** shrub; the sumac
bt **FUSTIC** tropical American tree
FUSURE smelting; fusion
FUTILE bootless; vain; useless
FUTTAH FUTTER, rat-proof raised store-house (NZ)
FUTURE hereafter; prospective
FUZZED ground to powder
FUZZLE intoxicate; fuddle

G

GABBED talked; prattled
GABBLE jabber; prate; chatter
mn **GABBRO** (felspar)
ce **GABION** net frame holder for rocks as wall
bt **GABLED** having gables
GABLET small gable
fr **GABOON** African mahogany-like wood
GADDED wandered about
GADDER a gadabout; a rover
zo **GADFLY** horse-fly
GADGET a cunning device; contraption
zo **GADINE** gadean; cod-type
zo **GADOID** codfish type
GADUIN part of cod liver oil
GAELIC Scottish-Highland dialect; Celtic
GAFFED (fishing)
GAFFER rustic; foreman
GAFFLE spur (cock-fight)
mu **GAGAKU** Japanese court orchestral music

GAGGED silenced; joked
to **GAGGER** an interpolator
zo **GAGGLE** a flock of geese
GAGMAN joke-writer; comic
GAIETY gayety; merriment; vivacity
GAINED acquired; reached; won
GAINER winner; beneficiary
GAINLY comely; conveniently
GAINST against
GAITED having a distinctive walk
GAITER garnash
cf **GALACT-** of milking
zo **GALAGO** lemur (Madagascar)
mu **GALANT** courtly dance
GALAXY Milky Way; brilliant assembly
bt **GALBAN** a gum used in medicine
nt **GALEAS** galley
bt **GALEGA** goat's rue
ch **GALENA** lead sulphide
nt **GALIOT** brigantine
bt **GALIUM** bed-straw genus
GALLED chagrined; fretted; vexed
GALLET stone splinter
nt **GALLEY** ship; boat; cook-house
ch **GALLIC** French; an acid
GALLIO insouciance personified
me **GALLON** 4 quarts (4.5 litres)
GALLOP a dance; full speed of a horse; fast canter
GALLOW to terrify
GALLUP poll (public opinion); voting system
tx **GALOON** galloon; silk fabric
GALOOT lout
GALORE galore; in abundance
GALOSH GALOSH, waterproof overshoe
GAMASH gaiters
zo **GAMBET** a bird; red-shank
ga **GAMBIT** opening move (chess)
GAMBLE stake; hazard; risk; wager
GAMBOL frolic; romp; caper; jump about (lambs)
GAMELY pluckily
pl, zo **GAMETE** mature reproductive cell
tx **GAMGEE** absorbent wool/gauze
GAMING gambling
GAMMER old woman
GAMMON (bacon); hoax; cozen
zo **GAMONT** gamete-bearing individual
cf **-GAMOUS** marital, sexual, union
zo **GANDER** a glance (USA); male goose
rl **GANESA** Hindu elephant god
GANGER foreman; overman
mn **GANGUE** veinstone
zo **GANNET** solan goose
zo **GANOID** sturgeon type of fish
GANOIN fish dermis secretion
rw **GANTRY** travelling crane; signal frame
GAOLED imprisoned; incarcerated
GAOLER jailer; prison warder
GAPING yawning; staring; gazing
mu **GAPPED** pentatonic scale
GARAGE motor shed; repair shop
GARBED clothed
GARBLE misquote; distorted; confused speech
GARCON waiter (Fr.)
GARDEN a pleasance; park; (horticult.); (flowering)
zo **GARDON** roach; ide (Fr.)
GARGET throat inflammation
vt **GARGIL** goose disease
GARGLE a mouth wash
vt **GARGOL** swine disease
zo **GARIAL** gavial; crocodile
GARISH gaudy; ornate; florid
bt **GARLIC** genus of plants
GARNER to store; collect; hoard
mn **GARNET** carbuncle; precious stone
ck **GAROUS** garum; a fish sauce
zo **GARRAN** horse; galloway (Sc.)
GARRET loft; attic
GARRON (see garran)
GARROT a tourniquet; execution; (-cord)
zo **GARROT** ocean duck
bt **GARRYA** flowering evergreen
GARTER stocking supporter
rl **GARUDA** Asian (Hindu) birdgod
nt **GARVEY** small sailing boat (N. Am.)
zo **GARVIE** the sprat
GAS-BAG a blimp; airship; chatterbox
GASCON of Gascony
GASHED severely stabbed
GASHLY ghastly; frightful
GASIFY convert into gas
GAS-JET a burner; flame
bd **GASKET** leafproof joint (materials)
GASKIN cord for lashing sails to yards; hemp fibre
GAS-MAN gas company employee
GASPED panted; blew; puffed
GASPER cigarette; fag (sl.)
GASSED poisoned by gas
GAS-TAR coal-tar
zo **GASTER** hymenoptera abdomen
ck **GATEAU** cake (Fr.); layer cake
GATHER assemble; muster; fold
GATING a university restriction
el **GATING** circuit switching; sensory intake
bt **GATTEN** dogwood

GAUCHE boorish; bad mannered (Fr.)
GAUCHO cowboy rider (S. Am.)
ck **GAUFRE** honey-cake; wafer (Fr.)
GAUGED measured; estimated
to **GAUGER** excise officer; width, size checker
GAUPUS a silly person
vt **GAVAGE** forced bird-feeding
zo **GAVIAL** garial; crocodile (Asia)
GAWPUS a silly person
GAYEST liveliest; merriest; blithest
GAY-YOU fishing boat (Annam.)
GAZEBO garden summer house
GAZING reviewing; gaping; regarding
GAZUMP organize house deal price rises
GEARED harnessed
GEBBIE the stomach (Sc.)
GEEZER man in charge; elder
nt **GEHAZI** dhow; Arab sailboat
GEIGER radioactivity counter
GEISHA mousmee; dancing girl (Jap.)
GELDED castrated; enfeebled
zo **GELERT** Llewellyn's faithful hound
ch **GELTER** one chemical to remove another
rl **GEMARA** (Talmud) (Heb.)
GEMINI Castor and Pollux; (Zodiac)
bt **GEMMAE** leaf-buds
GEMMAN gentleman
GEMMED jewelled; budded
me **GEMMHO** inverse meg-ohm
GEMOTE **GEMOT**, witenagemot, Saxon Council
GENDER sex; (grammar)
GENERA plural of genus; (kinds)
GENIAL hearty; kindly; cordial
GENIUS adept; gift; talent; djinn
zo **GENNET** jennet; small Spanish horse
gn **GENOME** gamete nucleus chromosome
cf **-GENOUS** producing
GENTLE mild; tender; courteous
zo **GENTLE** maggot; larva of fly (angling)
GENTLY tenderly; gradually
zo **GENTOO** a Hindu; a penguin
GENTRY 'the nobs'; 'the upper ten'; (class)
GENUAL of the knee; (curtsey) (-flect)
mn **GEODIC** (crystalline cavity)
GEOGEN environmental factor
zo **GEOMYS** rodents (USA)
nm **GEORGE** a jewel
GERANT gerent; manager
zo **GERBIL** a rodent
GERMAN Teutonic; of Germany
bt **GERMEN** **GERMIN**, an ovary; a germ
GERUND verbal noun
bt **GERVAO** West Indian shrub
bt **GERVAS** plant (W. Indies)
GESTIC legendary
GETTER a sire; obtainer; achiever; collector
ck **GEUSIS** tasting
GEW-GAW **GEE-GAW**, bauble, trinket, gaud
gl **GEYSER** hot spring; steam fountain; water heater (gas)
GHARRY gharri; Indian cart
zo **GHAZAL** **GHAZEL**, a form of Persian verse; gazelle
rl **GHEBER** **GHEBRE**, **GUEBRE**, Zoroastrian
GHETTO exclusively Jewish quarter; area of a minority
nt **GHOBUN** outrigger sail dugout (Papua)
GHURKA Ghurka; native of Nepal
GHURRY clock; time interval (Ind.)
GIAOUR unbeliever (Turk.)
GIBBER jabber; gabble; babble
GIBBET hanging post
zo **GIBBON** an ape
GIB-CAT wornout cat
nt **GIBING** scoffing; jibing
GIBLET internal part of a fowl
GIFTED intellectual; able; talented
GIGGIT to move rapidly (USA)
GIGGLE snigger; titter; cackle
GIGLET **GIGLOT**, a giddy girl; a wanton
nt **GIGLIO** trawler (sail) (Mediterranean)
GIGMAN would-be gent
GIGOLO dancing partner; kept man
GILDED covered in gold; gilt
nm **GILDER** **GUILDER**, Dutch coin
GILLIE attendant; game-keeper (Sc.)
GILPEY boisterous boy or girl (Sc.)
zo **GILPIN** the coal-fish
nt **GIMBAL** compass steadier
to **GIMLET** a boring tool
GIMMAL (machinery)
zo **GIMMER** 2-year-old ewe
bt **GIMPED** crenated
GINETE Spanish trooper
GINGAL Indian musket; swivel gun
bt, ck **GINGER** sandy; reddish; spice
bt **GINGKO** **GINKGO**, Chinese yew; maiden-hair tree
GINGLE jingle; Irish car
tx **GINNED** snared; processed cotton

zo **GINNET** a nag; a jennet
GIRDED reproached; braced; surrounded
ar **GIRDER** a cross-beam (construction)
GIRDLE belt; zone; enclosure
bt **GIRKIN** gherkin (cucumber)
GIRNEL granary; meal-chest
GITANA Spanish; gipsy woman
GITANO Spanish gipsy man
mu **GIUSTO** in time; regular (It.)
GIVING yielding; allowing
GIZZEN to wither; leaky
ar **GLACIS** slope in front of fortress
GLADLY with pleasure; joyously
GLAGOL Slavonic alphabet
GLAIRY viscous; semi-fluid; anti-flow; glue-like
GLAIVE broadsword or falchion
GLANCE glimpse; look; ricochet
GLARED stared; glowered; frowned
GLASSY GLAZED, vitrified; smooth, shiny or mirrorlike surface
GLAZER polisher; calico-smoother
GLEAMY casting rays of light
GLEDGE cunning look; to squint
GLEETY limpid; ichorous
GLIBLY volubly; oily tongued
GLIDED skimmed; skated
GLIDER powerless aeroplane; (towed)
md **GLIOMA** nervous-tissue disease
GLITZY glistery; showiness; sham
GLOBAL globular; world-wide
md **GLOBIN** (haemoglobin)
GLOCAL global and local trade etc.
zo **GLOMUS** capillary-mass glomeruli
GLOOMY dim; dismal; obscure
rl **GLORIA** a hymn; halo
cf **GLOSSO-** of tongue; words
GLOSSY smooth; sheeny; bright; (surface)
GLOVED wearing gloves
GLOVER glove-maker
GLOWED showed warmth; shone; gleamed
GLOWER scowl; frown; glare
GLOZED palliated; wheedled
GLOZER flatterer; sycophant
ch **GLUCIC** (glucose)
GLUING cementing; uniting
GLUISH (glue); sticky; viscous
bt **GLUMAL** of the husk
GLUMLY sulkily; suddenly
GLUMPS the sulks
ck **GLUTEN GLUTIN**, starch free; wheat gum
ch **GLYCIN** gelatin-sugar
ch **GLYCOL** a liquid

GNARLY GNARRY, knotted; crabbed; gnarled
GNAWED fretted; tormented
zo **GNAWER** a rodent; masticator
mn **GNEISS** laminated; metamorphic rocks
bt **GNETUM** plant (E. Indies)
GNOMIC didactic
GNOMON sundial; shadow-caster
cf **-GNOSIA** (of knowledge)
GNOSIS esoteric knowledge
GOADED impelled; spurred; stung
ga **GOALIE GOALER**, goalkeeper (ice hockey) (polo) (football)
zo **GOANNA** iguana (Aust.)
GOATEE a beard
ga **GO-BANG** a game
GOBBET lump; swallow; mouthful
GOBBIN coal refuse
GOBBLE to swallow; bolt; (turkey)
GOBLET tumbler; glass cup; rummer
GOBLIN sprite; gnome; spectre
ga **GO-CART** two-wheeled cart; (racing)
GO-DOWN warehouse; kneel
GODSON protégé
zo **GODWIT** bird of passage
GOETIC (black magic)
GOFFER to plait; to crimp
GOGGLE to roll the eyes; eye piece (tv.)
GOGLET porous vase
GOIDEL Celtic; Gael
md **GOITER GOITRE**, a tumour; bronchocele
GOLDEN gilt; auric; (-handshake etc.)
GOLFER golf player
GOLIAS medieval nom de plume
GOLLAR to scold; speak loudly
GOLORE abundance; galore
GOLOSH GALOSH, waterproof overshoe
ck **GOMMER** soup ingredient
bt **GOMUTI GOMUTO**, sago palm; black fibre
GONGED signalled to stop by police (USA)
md **GONION** angle (of lower jaw)
GOODLY fair; comely; seemly
ga **GOOGLY** a strange delivery (bowling) (cricket)
el **GOOGOL** 10 to the 100th power
zo **GOORAL** Asiatic goat
rl **GOOROO GURU**, Hindu teacher
GOPACK HOPAK, Russian folkdance
zo **GOPHER** American rodent; a short drink
bt, nt **GOPHER** 'timber' of the Ark, reeds and bitumen coracle (Tigris)

GOPURA Hindu temple tower
ar, zo **GORAMY** gourami; fish
hd **GORGED** glutted; stuffed
GORGET throat armour; lady's ruff
md **GORGET** instrument
GORGIO gipsy term for a non-gipsy
GORGON ugly monster (Gr. myth.)
zo **GORHEN** hen grouse
GORIER more blood-stained
GORING a pricking; puncture
rl **GOSHEN** land of plenty (for Israelites)
GOSPEL glad tidings; (New Testament)
mn **GOSSAN GOZZAN**, ferruginous rock
GOSSIP chatter; boon companion
ar, pt **GOTHIC** language (story); style
GOTTEN got; acquired
GOUDIE GOWDIE, goldfinch; jewel; gold lace
GOUGED scooped out
nm **GOURDE** coin (Haiti)
vt **GOURDY** swelling (horse)
GOVERN rule; sway; control; restrain
bt **GOWANS** dandelion
GOWNED robed; arrayed
GOWPEN a handful (Sc.)
gl **GRABEN** land-subsidence structure
GRACED virtuous; chaste
rl **GRACES** 3 goddesses of charm & fertility
GRADED classified; arranged
ce **GRADER** road-making implement; blade; sorter
GRADIN raised step or seat
GRADUS dictionary of prosody
GRÄFIN German countess
GRAINS malt husks; prongs; harpoons
GRAINY granulated
GRAITH accoutrements; equipment (Sc.)
zo **GRAKLE** starling
me **GRAMME** weight (Fr.); (1 cu.cc. water)
GRANGE manor house with farm
nt **GRANNY** grandmother; knot
rl **GRANTH** Sikh Scriptures
bt **GRANUM** pigment globule
cf **GRAPHO-** of drawing; recording
GRAPPA strong spirit from grape refuse
GRASSY green lawn
to **GRATER** kitchen implement; shredder
mn **GRATHE** to repair coal-mine plant
ck **GRATIN** oven-browned (cheese topping)
GRATIS without payment
nt **GRAVED** cleaned; chiselled; cut
md **GRAVEL** disease; embarrass; puzzle
ce **GRAVEL** granular material (stones); fragmented rock
GRAVEN engraved; carved
to **GRAVER** (entraver); more sedate
GRAVES wine
GRAVID pregnant
GRAZED scratched; brushed
zo **GRAZER** browser; herbivore
mu **GRAZIA GRAZIOSO**, elegantly; gracefully
GREASE to oil; lubricate; bribe
GREASY unctuous; sebaceous; slippery
GREATS final exam, in classics, Ox. B.A.
GREAVE GREEVE, leg armour
GREECE GREESE, GRIECE, flight of steps; staircase; a degree
GREEDY eager; voracious; grasping
ck, bt **GREENS** leafy vegetables
GREENY GREENISH (colour)
GREEVE GREAVE, steward; a reeve
GREGAL gregarious
rw **GRICER** train-locomotive-spotter, fan
GRIDED grated; pierced
GRIEVE GREEVE, sadden; lament
wv **GRIFFE** horizontal frame knives
bd, ar **GRILLE** iron grating (tennis); gate
zo **GRILSE** young salmon
GRIMED begrimed; dirtied; foul
GRIMLY fiercely; dourly
GRINGO Yankee in S. America
GRIPED furrowed; trenched
GRIPER extortioner; oppressor
GRIPPED influenza (Fr.)
GRISLY grim; ferocious; fierce; dire
zo **GRISON** weasel (S. Am.)
to **GRITER** teasel spade
GRITTY coarse sand; the intimate
zo **GRIVET** Abyssinian monkey
GRIZEL meek patient wife
GROATS hulled oats
GROCER provisioner; (-shop)
GROGGY tipsy; staggering; unwell
pl **GROINS** loins; between the thighs
bt **GROMEL** gromil; gromwell; a plant
nt **GROMET** a rope ring
cr **GROOVE** furrow; rut; cutting
GROPED searched; picked; sought
bt **GROSER** gooseberry
nm **CROSZY** Polish coin
GROTTO cavern; cave
GROUND earth; clod; domain; cause
zo **GROUSE** complaint; game bird

ck **GROUTS** coarse meal; groats
GROUTY thick; muddy; sulky
GROVEL crawl; cringe; fawn
GROWER husbandman; gardener (commercial)
GROWTH increase; progress
ar, bl **GROYNE GROIN**, arches; breakwater; sea wall
GRUBBY grimy; dirty; dishonest
GRUDGE envy; covet; enmity; dislike
zo **GRU-GRU** edible insect
GRUMLY morosely; surlily
GRUMPH grunt (Sc.)
GRUMPY surly; sullen; churlish
GUACHE style of painting
GUANIN GUANO, bird excrement; fertilizer
GUDDLE to tickle trout (Sc.) (angling)
GUEBRE Gueber; Parsee fire-worshipper
GUELPH Royal (Hanoverian) House
zo **GUENON** African monkey
GUFFAW boisterous laugh
GUGGLE to gurgle
GUIDED regulated; instructed; steered
GUIDER a director; leader; pilot
GUIDON flag; signal (Fr.)
GUILED beguiled; treacherous
bt **GUILLS** corn marigold
GUILTY criminal; culpable; sinful
nm, zo **GUINEA** gold coin; game fowl; (-pig); stable groom; worm
GUISER mummer; strolling actor
mu **GUITAR** type of lute
nm **GULDEN GILDER**, florin (Dutch)
GULLED duped; tricked; hoaxed
GULLER a cheat; imposter
md **GULLET** throat (of bird); trench
GULLEY large knife (Sc.); earth cleft
ch **GULOSE** aldohexose monosaccharide
GULPED swallowed; bolted
GUMLAC resinous matter
GUMMED stuck; cemented
eg **GUNITE** fine cement concrete
GUNMAN armed bandit
GUNMEN gangsters; assassins
zo **GUNNEL** a blenny; butterfish
nt **GUNNEL** ship's side; gunwale
GUNNER artillery-man
GUN-SHY fearful of firearms
nt **GUNTER** emergency sail; instrument
GUNYAH Australian native hut
GUPPIE green or gay yuppie
GURGLE purl; ripple; murmur
GURKHA a native of Nepal
bt **GURJUN** Indian balsam
bd **GURLET** type of pickaxe
el, me **GURLEY** cylinder fall speed
zo **GURNET** fish; gurnard
GURRAH Indian earthen jar
GUSHED rushed; spurted; spouted
GUSHER spurting oil well; voluble person
tx **GUSSET** an insertion (clothing)
GUTNIK swallowable transistor radio
ar **GUTTAE** Doric ornamentation
GUTTED plundered; eviscerated; fed up
hd **GUTTEE** bedewed
ar, bd **GUTTER** trough; drainage; run off
pr **GUTTER** inner margins of book
GUTTLE to guzzle
GUZZLE swill; swallow greedily
nt **GYBING** jibing
ch **GYPSUM** lime sulphate
GYRATE spiral; revolve; spin
bt **GYROSE** like a crook

H

mt **HABOOB** Sudan line-squall
HACKED mangled; hired; kicked
zo **HACKEE** chipmunk; American squirrel
HACKER pirate within computer data storage
zo **HACKET** kittiwake
HACKLE cock's neck feathers
HACKLE fly (angling); comb
HACKLY rough
zo, ck **HADDIE** haddock (Sc.)
HADDIN a holding; residence (Sc.)
gl **HADING** geological fault
rl **HADITH** Moslem oral tradition
nc **HADRON** elementary particle class
pl **HAEMAD** on same side as heart
md **HAEMAL HAEMIC**, relating to blood
ch **HAEMIN** hydrochloride of haematin
HAFFET the temples (Sc.)
HAFFLE to lie; prevaricate
HAFTED handled
HAGBUT arquebuse; hackbut (ancient gun)
zo **HAGDEN** shearwater gull
zo **HAGEEN** dromedary; camel
HAGGED ugly; lean; haggish
ck **HAGGIS** Scottish dish
HAGGLE to mangle; higgle; bargain
zo **HAGLET** shearwater gull
HAIDUK Hungarian yeoman
mt **HAILED** acclaimed; greeted; originated from; iced snow fall
HAIQUE Arab wrap

HAIRDO hairstyle; coiffure
HAIRED hairy; hirsute; comate
HAIRST harvest (Sc.)
HAKEEM physician (Arabic)
zo **HALFER** fallow deer
HALIDE compound of halogen and other radical
HALING hauling
zo **HALION** skipper fish
HALLAN a partition (Sc.)
rl **HALLEL** Passover feast
HALLOA hallo!
HALLOO a hunting cry
HALLOW to reverence
zo **HALLUX** hind toe of bird
HALOED sainted
ch **HALOID** (salt)
HALSED embraced by the neck
nt **HALSER** hawser
HALTED limped; hesitated; stopped
HALTER cord head harness (horses); hesitant; faltering; uncertain
HALVED bisected; fifty-fifty
HALVES moieties
HAMATE set with hooks
HAMBLE mutilate the foot
HAMITE fossil; native (E. Africa)
HAMLET cluster of cottages
HAMMAL HAMAL, Turkish porter
HAMMAM HAMAM, Turkish bath
to **HAMMER** forge; a gavel
ga, pl **HAMMER** throwing (athletics); a shot (squash); bones in ear
bt **HAMOSE HAMOUS**, hooked
HAMPER basket; impede; embarrass
bd **HANDED** served; conducted; led on; right– or left–; tool
HANDLE touch; feel; manipulate
HANGAR aircraft shed
HANGED dangled; depended
HANGER broadsword; wood on hill-side
HANGER (clothes); steel bar; stirrup strap; baseball
HANG-UP unexpected hiatus; breakdown
HANJAR Persian dagger
nt **HANKED** skeined; jibbed
HANKER desire; crave; yearn; want
HANSEL earnest penny; handsel
HANSOM a horse-cab
HANTLE considerable number (Sc.)
HAPPEN occur; betide; chance; befall
HAPTIC pert. to sense of touch
HARASS annoy; tire; vex; worry
HARDEN nerve; steel; brace; injure
HARDER stiffer; firmer
HARDLY barely; scarcely; narrowly
HARD-UP impecunious; indigent
zo **HARELD** sea-duck
HARING speeding; rashly
HARISH like a hare
HARKED listened; hurried; -back (recalled)
HARKEN hearken; listen; attend
HARLED covered with rough-cast
HARLOT strumpet; moll; trollop
HARMAN policeman; a copper
HARMED damaged; injured
bt **HARMEL** Syrian rue
mu **HARPED** iterated; dwelt
mu **HARPER** lyrist; harpist
HARRIS a tweed
ag **HARROW** lacerate; tear; furrow (plough)
HARTAL Indian boycott
ck **HASHED** chopped; mixed; recooked
HASLET roasting meat; pig's fry
HASTED hastened; hurried
HASTEN hurry; speed; despatch; urge
HAT-BOX for hat transport
HATFUL maximum score in an end (bowls)
HATHOR goddess of love (Egypt)
HATING detesting; loathing; abhorring
HAT-PEG place to hang hat
HAT-PIN woman's hat fixer
HATRED odium; enmity; rancour
HATTED wearing a hat
HATTER hatmaker; (mad-); (hats); independent miner (Aus.)
HAULED dragged; tugged; towed
HAULER haulier; carter
ar, pl **HAUNCH** part of an arch; hip to thigh
HAUSSA West African race
zo **HAUTIN** sea-fish in fresh water
mn **HAUYNE** a silicate
HAVERS twaddle; empty talk
HAVING holding; possessing
ar **HAWHAW HAHA** (sunk fence); guffaw
HAWKED peddled; streaked
HAWKER pedlar; retailer; falconer
zo **HAWKEY HAWKIE**, dark cow with white streaked face (Sc.)
nt **HAWSER** halser; cable
ck **HAY-BOX** cooking method
HAYMOW hay in barn
HAYSEL hay-makers' festival
ga **HAZARD** obstacle; risk; chance; peril; jeopardy; old dicing game
HAZILY obscurely; foggily; mistily
HAZING bullying; brutal horse-play
HEADED titled; (direction)

ga **HEADED** (cask); (football)
cp **HEADER** (brick); (diving); headline; identity label
HEAD-ON directly; straight; (collision)
HEALED cured; remedied
HEALER doctor; restorer
HEALTH soundness; hygiene; haleness
HEAPED massed; accumulated; piled
HEARER one of an audience
HEARSE funeral car
HEARTH fireplace; fireside; home
HEARTY robust; sincere; cordial
HEATED agitated; excited; hectic
HEATER warmer
bt **HEATHY** heavy helmet
HEAUME heavy helmet
HEAVED hoisted; dilated; panted
HEAVEN Elysium; Paradise; bliss
HEAVER a lever; strong man
vt **HEAVES** disease (horse); broken wind
HEBREW a Jew; Semitic language
rl **HECATE** goddess of witchcraft
HECKLE to question; to barrack
HECTIC feverish; heated; hot
HECTOR intimidate; bully; a swaggering
wv **HEDDLE** heald shaft in handloom
bt **HEDERA** ivy
HEDGED skulked; avoided; (betting)
HEDGER a trimmer of fences
HEEDED attended; noticed
HEE-HAW to bray (donkey)
HEELED armed; equipped; leant; (well-)
HEELER hanger-on (USA)
rl **HEGIRA HEJIRA**, Mohammed's flight from Mecca to Medina, A.D. 622
zo **HEIFER** young cow
HEIGHT altitude; acme; zenith
as **HELIAC** heliacal; (sun)
HELION virago; shrew; hell-cat
ch **HELITE** an amalgam
ch **HELIUM** a gaseous element
HELLAS ancient Greece
nm **HELLER** German copper coin
HELMED with a helmet; directed
HELMET part of retort; head armour
md **HELOMA** corn on foot
HELPED prevented; aided; succoured
HELPER assistant; abettor; ally
HELVED having a handle; hafted
mn **HELVIN** mineral
me **HEMINA** about 10 oz (283 g)
HEMMED bordered; enclosed
HEMMER a stitcher; a sewer
bt **HEMPEN** made of hemp
bt **HENBIT** dead nettle
HENISM philosophical belief
HEPTAD series of seven
HERALD harbinger; crier; proclaim
HERBAL book describing plants
HERDED tended; massed
HEREAT at this point
HEREBY by this (means) (document) (moment)
HEREIN in this (document) (situation)
HEREOF of this (before-mentioned)
HEREON on this (occasion)
HERESY schism; heterodoxy; recusancy
HERETO in addition
bt **HERIFF** butweed
lw **HERIOT** a fine
HERMAE sculptured busts
rl **HERMES** Mercury (Gr.) the messenger
HERMIT anchorite; recluse
md **HERNIA** rupture
HEROES demi-gods
HEROIC bold; intrepid; valiant
md **HEROIN** a drug
md **HERPES** skin disease; shingles
hd **HERSED** in harrow form
rl **HESPER** evening star; vesper; prayer
HESVAN HESHVAN, Jewish month
cf **HETERO-** of unlike, different (sex) (Gr.)
HETMAN Cossack chief
HEWING hacking; shaping; (digging); (coal)
HEXADE series of six
ch **HEXANE** paraffin
HEXODE a thermionic valve
ch **HEXOSE** monosaccharide subgroup, a sugar
HEYDAY frolic; period of vigour; zenith
md **HIATUS** a chasm; gap; lacuna
md **HICCUP HICCOUGH**, temporary breakdown of breathing
go, ce **HICKEY** pipe-bending tool (USA)
lw **HIDAGE** a tax
HIDDEN latent; covert; recondite
HIDING a beating; screening; masking
HIEING going along; hiking
HIEMAL wintry; hyemal
HIGGLE to bargain; haggle
HIGHER superior; nobler (above)
HIGHLY eminently; loftily
HI-JACK kidnap; rob; armed take-over of transport

HIJRAH Hegira; flight from Mecca
HIKING walking; foot-slogging
lw **HILARY** Law Court session; Oxford term
HILLED earthed up
zo **HILSAH** fish (Ganges)
HILTED hafted; helved
HINDEE North Indian tongue
HINDER delay; interference with flat of ball (handball) (paddle ball)
HINGED depended on; swing on (door)
HINTED implied
HINTER suggester
ar **HIPPED** melancholic; roof
HIPPIC horsy; equine
HIPPIE unkempt wanderer
md **HIPPUS** clonic spasm of iris
HIRAME gold, silver leaf on lacquer (Jap.)
HIRCIN mutton suet
zo **HIRCUS** the goat
HIRING bribing; engaging
rl **HIRMOI HIRMOS**, hymns; ode (Gr. church)
zo **HIRSEL HIRSLE**, flock of sheep (Sc.); a throng; to slide
HISPID bristly
HISSED hizzed; booed; (snake)
HISSER disapprover
HITCHY catchy
HITHER to this place
ga **HIT-OUT** aim blows; verbal attack; aggressive action by players or fans (boxing); starting shot in hockey
ga **HITTER** smiter; slogger; striker
HIVING storing; clustering (bees)
HOARSE guttural; husky; raucous
HOAXED tricked; gulled; gammoned
HOAXEE the victim
HOAXER practical joker
zo **HOAZIN** (S. Am.) pheasant
ga **HOBBER** touching the kob (quoits)
HOBBIT denizen of Middle Earth; (Tolkien)
HOBBLE halt; limp; shackle; clog; leg harness (farm)
HOBJOB an odd job
HOBNOB to be familiar; associate; chat
mu **HOCKET** hiccup (Fr.); extra rests in vocal parts
ga **HOCKEY** 11-a-side stick and ball game
HOCKLE to mow; hamstring
tx **HODDEN** grey cloth
HODMAN mason's labourer
HOEING weeding
HOGGED clipped; bent
HOGGER miser; selfish monopolist; (road-)
zo **HOGGET** young sheep; colt or boar
HOGGIE fishing craft (Brighton)
HOGGIN sand and gravel mixture
HOGPEN hogsty (USA); pigsty
pp **HOG-PIT** waste paper stock pit
HOGSTY pig pen; pigsty
HOIDEN hoyden; a romp; rude; rustic
ga **HOLANI** early form of hockey (Turk.)
bt **HOLARD** whole of soil water
la **HOLDER** a tenant; possessor (-stand) (-case)
HOLD-UP robbery under arms
HOLIER more sacred
HOLILY piously
HOLISM treatment of the body and mind as one entity
HOLLER HOLLOA, shout (distress)
bd **HOLLOW** empty; void; cavity-wall; vacuum; dell
ch **HOLMIA** oxide of holmium
ch **HOLMIC** (holmium)
HOMAGE fealty; devotion; loyalty
HOMELY plain; simple; domestic
HOMILY sermon; address; discourse
ae **HOMING** (pigeons); aerial navigation; returning to base
ck **HOMINY** boiled maize
HONEST fair; just; trusty; sincere
HONING whetting
HONKED tooted (motoring)
HONOUR exalt; dignify; fame; renown
HOODED cowled; cloaked
zo **HOODIE** carrion-crow (Sc.)
rl **HOODOO VOODOO**, witchcraft (W. Indies); column of boulders & earth
HOOFED ungulate (twin-toed)
HOOKAH water smoking pipe; narghile
HOOKED (golf); hamate; addicted (drugs)
nt, ga **HOOKER** fishing boat; prostitute; scrum player (Rugby football)
HOOKUM command; instructions (Ind.)
cp, ro, tc, tv **HOOK-UP** radio connections; (-link)
HOOPED encircled; with handle; whooped
HOOPER (tubs); a cooper
ga **HOOP-LA** game at fairs

zo **HOOPOE HOOPOO**, crested birds, horn-bill type
HOOTED honked
HOOTER a siren
zo **HOOVED** ungulate
vt, zo **HOOVEN** (cattle-disease)
HOOVER dust-removing appliance
zo **HOOVES** pl. of hoof; cleft feet
zo **HOPDOG** pale tussock moth
zo **HOP-FLY** plant louse
HOPING wishing; desiring; trusting
HOPPED jumped; danced; bounced
nt **HOPPER** wooden trough; hop-picker; lighter (dredging)
zo, cp **HOPPER** locust; truck; punched card feeder
rw **HOPPET** hand-basket
ce **HOPPIT** kibble; sinking bucket; skip
rl **HORARY** book of hours (prayers)
HORNED with horns; butted
zo **HORNER** dealer in horns; sand-eel
zo **HORNET** stinging insect
HORNIE the devil; old Nick
HORRID horrific; terrible; dreadful
HORROR terror; panic; alarm; dismay
HORSED mounted (rider)
HOSIER dealer in stockings
HOSTEL an inn; lodging house
bt **HOT-BED** earth-bed; breeding place
ck **HOT-DOG** sausage sandwich
ck **HOT-POT** meat-stew
HOT-ROD supercharged car
HOTTER more ardent; warmer
HOUDAH howdah; seat on an elephant
zo **HOUDAN** breed of fowls
nt **HOUNDS** (mast head)
HOURLY at every hour (trains)
HOUSED resided; sheltered; stored
rl **HOUSEL** the Eucharist
HOUSTY a sore throat (dial.)
HOWDAH houdah; seat on an elephant
HOWDIE midwife (Sc.)
nt **HOWKER** hooker; vessel (Dutch)
HOWLED yowled; cried; lamented
zo **HOWLER** (monkey); grievous error
zo **HOWLET** (owlet); fledgling owl (dial.)
HOYDEN hoiden; tomboy; romp
ck **HRAMSA** garlic-flavoured cheese (Sc.)
HUBBLE an uproar; hubbub
HUBBLY rowdy
HUBBUB disorder; noise; uproar; din
HUCKLE the hip; a haunch
ga **HUDDLE** crowd; confuse; jumble; counsel before line-up (Am. football)
ag **HUDDUP** get up!; fertile; irrigated, 2 crops land
ga **HUFFED** blustered; (draughts) forfeited
HUFFER a bully; blusterer
HUGELY enormously; immensely
nt **HULLED** pierced; husked; (ship's side)
HULLER hulling machine
HUMANE kind; benign; merciful
HUMBLE degrade; abash; meek; lowly
HUMBLY unobtrusively
HUMBUG quackery; charlatan; untruth; peppermint
HUMECT HUMIFY, HUMEFY, to moisten; dampen
md **HUMERI** bones of the upper arm
hd **HUMETE** abbreviated fesse
tx **HUMHUM** coarse cloth (Ind.)
HUMIAN philosophy of David Hume
HUMINE black ground powder; humus
mn **HUMITE** limestone
HUMMED buzzed; droned
HUMMEL hornless; awnless
HUMMER a sledge-runner
HUMMIE small bulge
ck **HUMMUS HUMMUZ, HUMOUS**, chick-pea purée
md **HUMOUR** indulge; pamper; wit
zo **HUMPED** shouldered; hunchback; (camel)
HUMPEN drinking glass (Ger.)
HUMPER meat-porter; carrier
HUNGER hanker; desire; crave
HUNGRY ravenous; famishing
HUNKER to squat down; old fogey
HUNTED searched; sought; hounded
zo **HUNTER** chaser; stalker
bt **HURBUR** burdock
HURDLE wattle fence
HURLED flung; heaved; slung; cast
HURLER a thrower; pitcher
HURLEY shinty; the stick used in hurling (-burley)
HURRAH HURRAY, shout of triumph
HURTER a buffer plank
HURTLE to whirl; to crash
HUSHED quietened; calmed; stilled
HUSKED hulled
HUSKER a remover of husks
HUSSAR light cavalryman
HUSSIF (housewife); a holdall for needles, thread etc.
HUSTLE bustle; jostle; elbow; rush
HUTTED in huts
HUZOOR Indian title of respect

as **HYADES** 5 stars in Taurus
zo **HYAENA** hyena
cp **HYBRID** cross-bred; mongrel; analog; digital mix
HYDRIA Grecian water-vase
ch **HYDRIC** (hydrogen)
ch **HYDRID** hydrogen compound
md **HYDROA** itching skin disease
HYDRON dry/rigid, wet/soft plastic
as, zo **HYDRUS** constellation; water-snake
HYEMAL hiemal; wintry
HYETAL (rainfall)
HYGEEN dromedary
HYGEIA Goddess of Health
HYKSOS Egyptian dynasty
HYLISM materialism
HYMNAL collection of hymns
HYMNED celebrated in song
HYMNIC of hymns
bt **HYPHAE** fungoid filaments
HYPHEN word-join stroke
bt **HYPNUM** a moss genus
bt **HYSSOP** aromatic herb

I

IAMBIC rhythmic
IAMBUS Greek satiric metre
cf, md **-IATRIC** of healing, medical (Gr.)
bt **IBERIS** candytuft
zo **IBEXES** mountain goats (Alps)
IBIDEM in the same place
ICARUS an early aeronaut
ICE-AGE period of icing over
to **ICE-AXE** ice-breaking, -cutting device
ICE-CAP earth ice layer
ICE-MAN ice deliverer
to **ICE-SAW** ice-cutting device
ICICLE frozen water stalactite
ICIEST frostiest; most frozen
ICONIC illustrative
pc, rl **ICONIC** brief visual experience; of sacred portrayal
pc **IDEATE** to fancy; project fantasy
IDIASM a peculiarity
IDIOCY lunacy; dementia; craziness
IDLING nothing doing
IDOLUM IDOLON, mental picture
I'FAITH indeed; truly; verily
cp **IF-THEN** conditional indication operation
IGNAVY laziness; idleness
IGNITE kindle; inflame; fire
cp **IGNORE** disregard; overlook; skip (agent)
zo **IGUANA** lizard; a saurian
bt **ILEXES** holm-oaks
ILL-GOT ill-gotten; (stolen)
ILLISH somewhat unwell
mn **ILLITE** monoclinic clay material
ILLUDE to deceive; conceal; (conjuring)
ILL-USE mistreat
IMAGED imagined; fancied; sculpted
IMBIBE drink; assimilate; absorb
IMBREX pantile; curved roof-tile
IMBRUE to moisten; to drench
IMBUED dyed; inspired; steeped
IMMASK to cover; disguise
md **IMMUNE** secure against attack; (virus)
IMMURE enclose; incarcerate; confine
IMPACT shock; stroke; collision
bd **IMPAGE** horizontal part of door-frame
IMPAIR mar; injure; harm; vitiate
zo **IMPALA** South African antelope
IMPALE cause death on a spear
IMPARK enclose
IMPARL to hold mutual discourse
IMPARL parley
IMPART bestow; confer; divulge
IMPAVE to pave
IMPAWN to pledge
IMPEDE obstruct; hinder; thwart
IMPEND threaten; hover; approach
IMPEST infect with plague
IMPING ekeing; extending; grafting
IMPISH puckish; mischievous
IMPLEX complicated
IMPONE to stake; to wager
IMPORT imply; purport; gist; drift
IMPOSE lay; inflict; charge; dictate
ar **IMPOST** a tax; a duty; a cess; bracket-like base for arches
IMPUGN attack; contradict; question
IMPURE unclean; sullied; tarnished
IMPUTE charge; ascribe; imply
INARCH to graft
bd **INBAND** header stone
bd **INBOND** brick-laying
INBORN innate; inherent; congenital
INBRED in-tribe parentage
INCAGE encage; confine
INCARN to incarnate
INCASE encase; enclose; enshrine
INCASK to put in a cask
INCAST a bonus; thrown in
INCAVO incised stone (cameo)
INCEPT to begin; to commence
INCEST prohibited co-habitation among close kin
INCHED advanced by inches

INCISE engrave; scribe
INCITE stir; goad; foment; rouse
INCLIP to grasp; enclose; surround
INCOME revenue; annual receipts
INCULT uncultivated
INCUSE **INCUSS**, to stamp; forge
INDABA native council (S. Afr.)
INDEED really; truly; verily; actually
ch **INDENE** liquid coal-tar hydrocarbon
ar, lw **INDENT** to notch; order; make a deed; stonework design
INDIAN of India; native American
lw **INDICT** to charge in writing
INDIGN unworthy
INDIGO a blue dye
INDITE endite; write; pen; dictate
ch **INDIUM** metallic element
ch **INDOLE** benzpyrrole
INDOOR within the house
INDUCE urge; actuate; incite
INDUCT introduce; install; initiate
INDUED endued; invested with
INDUNA Zulu chief
INEUNT cusp; fold; tooth; point joint; all enter the stage (theatre)
INFALL an inroad
INFAME defame
INFAMY shame; obloquy; disgrace
INFANT babe; suckling; minor
INFECT taint; spread disease
cp **INFECT** (computer virus)
lw **INFEIF** **INFEFT**, (land transfer)
INFELT heart-felt
INFEST enfest; overrun; throng; beset
INFIMA end species in classification list
INFIRM frail; weak; decrepit
INFLOW that which flows in
INFLUX importation in abundance
INFOLD enfold; embrace
INFORM tell; notify; apprise
rl **INFULA** Roman priestly badge
INFUSE instil; inculcate; steep
INGATE aperture in a mould
INGEST absorb; swallow
ga **IN-GOAL** Rugby football
INGULF engulf; overwhelm
INHALE breathe in; (smoking)
nt **INHAUL** drag in (ropes)
INHERE to be innate
INHIVE to hive (bees)
INHOOP to confine
nc **INHOUR** reactivity unit
INHUME to inter; to bury; entomb
md **INJECT** pump in; interpolate; insert
INJURE harm; hurt; mar; impair
lw **INJURY** ill; detriment; wrong; damage
zo **INK-BAG** (cuttle-fish)
INKING marking with ink
INKNIT to knit in
INKNOT to knot
INKOSI Zulu chief, king
INK-POT ink container
zo **INK-SAC** (cuttle-fish)
INLACE to lace
INLAID fitted flush to surface
INLAND remote from the sea
gl **INLIER** geological formation
pr **INLINE** white-relieved black-letter print
cp **IN-LINE** (traffic) programme instructions
INLOCK enlock
INMATE resident; guest; denizen
INMOST innermost; deepest
INNATE inherent; congenital; inborn
INNING harvest grain
nt **INRAIL** enclose with rails; fencing
INROAD raid; foray; incursion
INRUSH invasion; irruption
INSANE mad; crazy; deranged
INSEAM mark with a seam
INSECT mean; contemptible
zo **INSECT** six-legged invertebrate
INSERT inject; introduce; infix
INSHIP embark; to ship
INSIDE inner; internal; interior
INSIST maintain; demand; urge
INSOLE inner sole
INSPAN to yoke
INSTAL install; induct; invest
INSTAR adorn with stars
pl **INSTEP** part of the foot
INSTIL infuse; ingraft; implant
INSTOP make fast; to stop
pl **INSULA** part of cortex (brain); island
ar **INSULA** middle-class house (Roman)
INSULT abuse; affront; ridicule
INSURE ensure; assure; guarantee
INTACT inviolate; integral; scatheless
INTAKE inlet of a pipe; consume
INTEND mean; purpose; contemplate
INTENT set; bent; eager; attentive
INTERN confine; segregate
zo **INTIMA** innermost organ layer
INTIME private; home-like
bt **INTINE** inner coat of pollen grain
INTOED with toes turned in
INTOMB entomb; bury; inter
mu **INTONE** to chant
INTORT to twist; to wreathe; to wind
ga **IN-TURN** curved sliding shot (curling)
md **INTUSE** a bruise (Spens.)
bt, ck **INULIN** vegetable base (elecampane)

INUNCT anoint
lw **INURED** hardened; accustomed
INVADE raid; infringe; assault; violate
INVENT devise; contrive; create; make
INVERT reverse; upset; overturn; gay
INVEST apply money to purpose
INVITE ask; bid; call; request; solicit
INVOKE adjure; conjure; implicate
INWARD direction inside
INWICK curling cannon
INWORK penetrative work
INWORN inwrought
INWRAP to perplex; enwrap
zo **INYALA** nyala; bushbuck
ch **IODATE** (iodic acid)
ch **IODIDE** salt of hydriodic acid
ch **IODINE** medicinal element
IODISM morbid state
IODIZE treat with iodine
mn **IOLITE** a translucent silicate
ar **IONIAN** scrollshaped pillar capital (Gr.)
IONISM relating to ions, atoms without electrons
ch **IONIUM** (radium)
ps **IONIZE** convert into ions
ch **IONONE** terpene compound
IRANIC Iranian, from Iran
IREFUL angry; wroth; incensed
IRENIC pacific; peaceful
IRIDAL prismatic; iridian
pl, zo **IRIDIN** active principle of iris; (the eye)
IRISED like a rainbow
md **IRITIC** (iritis); inflamed
md **IRITIS** (eye disease)
IRKING irksome; tedious; wearying
IRONED in irons; smoothed
IRONER a laundry operative
IRONIC satirical; sarcastic
IRRUPT rush in; break in
ISABEL brownish yellow
ISAGON equi-angular figure
bt **ISATIC** woad-like
ch **ISATIN** an indigo product
bt **ISATIS** plant providing woad dye
ISLAND isle; isolate; (traffic-)
ISOBAR line of equal barometric prssure
rl **ISODIA** Jewish sacred feast
ps, el **ISOGAM** line of constant acceleration of free fall
ISOGON an isagon
mt **ISOHEL** sunshine comparison map
lt **ISOLUX** same-light-intensity line
ch **ISOMER** (similar substance)
ISONYM paronym
gl **ISOPIC** contemporaneously formed
zo **ISOPOD** (crustaceans)
ISRAEL Jacob and his offspring
ISSUED distributed; emitted; emerged
ISSUER publisher (source)
pr **ITALIC** Italian; semi-cursive script
ITCHED wanted to; craved; hankered
ITSELF reflexive pronoun
zo **IVIGAR** sea-urchin
IZZARD zeta, zee, zed, Z

J

JABBED poked; prodded
JABBER much talk; effusive prattle
JABBLE rough sea; splash (Sc.)
zo **JABIRI** Brazilian stork
zo **JACANA** wading bird
JACENT lying at length
zo **JACKAL** doglike carnivore
JACKED lifted with a jack (motor car)
JACKET cover; jerkin; coat
JADERY tricks of prankster
JADISH worn-out; unchaste
zo **JAEGER** gull; huntsman (Ger.)
JAGGED rough (rocky); uncouth; uneven
JAGGER brass wheel; pastry
JAGHIR a reward (Hindu)
zo **JAGUAR** S. American leopard
JAILED gaoled; incarcerated
JAILER **JAILOR**, gaoler; warder (prison)
ck **JALEBI** saffron batter sweetmeat (Ind.)
JAMBEE a cane; walking-stick
JAMBOK sjambok; hide whip
bt **JAMBUL** Indian evergreen
JAMMED crushed; squeezed
JAMMER radio interferer; competitor blocking Roller Derby race
JAMPAN sedan chair (Ind.)
JANGLE wrangle; clash; bicker
JANKER log-transporter (Sc.)
JARGON routine instruction code; (shop)
bt **JAROOL** Indian blood-wood
bt **JARRAH** tree (W. Australia)
JARRED wrangled; grated; disturbed
JARVEY Irish coach driver (jaunty)
rl **JASHER** lost Hebrew book
bt, ck **JASMIN** shrub; flower; scented tea
mn **JASPER** quartz

rl **JATAKA** nativity (Buddha)
JAUNTY open horse-drawn cart for lovers
JAW-BOX a sink (Sc.)
JAWING scolding
JEAMES a flunkey
JEERED mocked; derided; taunted
JEERER scoffer; sneerer
zo **JENNET** gennet; small Spanish horse
zo **JERBOA** a jumping rodent
JEREED jerid; blunt javelin
JERKED twitched; flipped; jolted
JERKER underhand thrower
le **JERKIN** a leather jacket
zo **JERKIN** a hawk; gyrfalcon
JERQUE examine ship's papers
zo **JERSEY** cow; knitted garment
ch **JERVIN** alkaloid (hellebore)
hd **JESSED** heraldic ornamentation
JESTED joked; made merry; quizzed
JESTER joker; buffoon; wag; fool
JET-LAG disturbance of body time change
lw, nt **JETSAM JETSOM**, goods thrown overboard; jetson; jettisoned
ar **JETTEE** projection
JEWESS female Jew
JEWISH Hebrew
JEZAIL Afghan trifle
tx **JIBBAH** jubbah; Eastern garment
JIBBED refused to go; baulked
zo **JIBBER** restive horse
JIBING sneering; quizzing; taunting
zo **JIBOYA** boa-constrictor; snake
JIFFEY an instant
mu **JIGGED** danced
me **JIGGER** liquid measure; mechanical device
ga, zo **JIGGER** golf club; insect; chigger
JIGGLE wriggle; joggle; jolt
JIGJOG jolting; trotting
ga **JIG-SAW** fret-saw; a puzzle (pictorial)
JILLET a flirt; a wanton
JILTED discarded
bt **JIMSON** thorn-apple
JINGAL Eastern cannon
JINGLE Irish covered car; tinkle; rhyme
JINKER dodged; eluded; turned sharply
JINKER timber-cart (Aust.)
el **JITTER** instability; fear
cp, el **JITTER** cathode ray tube signals
JOBBER stockbroker; book stocker/dealer
bd **JOBBER** builder's handyman
JOB-LOT odds and ends (auction) (sale)
JOCKEY horse race rider; disc–; coax to more favourable position
JOCOSE facetious; humorous; waggish
JOCUND sportive; merry; cheerful
JOGGED travelled slowly; shook
JOGGER slow runner; exerciser
JOGGLE a notch; to jar; to shake
cp **JOGGLE** agitate; punched cards
JOHNNY life and soul of a party
JOINED united; coupled; connected
JOINER a carpenter
ar **JOISTS** floor-board supports
JOKING jesting; bantering; rallying
gl, go **JOKULL** glacial ice-cap
JOLTED jogged; shook; jounced
JOLTER hustler
JORDAN a river; chamber pot (Shak.)
pr **JOSEPH** riding habit; unsized paper
JOSKIN yokel; clown
JOSSER a fellow; a chap; a palooka
JOSTLE push; approach closely; barge
JOTTED noted; recorded
JOTTER memorandum book
JOUNCE to jolt; shake
JOVIAL genial; convivial; blithe
JOVIAN (Jupiter) of Jove
JOWDER JOWTER, fish hawker
zo **JOWLER** hunting dog
JOYFUL happy; pleased; glad; blithe
JOYOUS merry; jocund; happy
JUBATE maned; having a fringe
tx **JUBBAH** Eastern garment
JUDAIC Jewish; Hebrew; Israelitish
cp **JUDDER** shudder; jar; screen scan blurs
JUDEAN native of Judea
JUDGED considered; sentenced
JUDGER a judge; umpire; arbitrator
rl **JUDICA** Passion Sunday
bt **JUGATE** coupled; yoked
me **JUGFUL** filling a jug
JUGGED (hare); imprisoned
JUGGLE conjure; shuffle; swindle
JUG-JUG meat in aspic; nightingale's song
JUICER machine for extracting fruit juice
bt, ck **JUJUBE** shrub; lozenge
JULIAN calendar; system
zo **JUMART** hybrid animal (Fr.)
ck **JUMBAL** crisp sweet cake
JUMBLE confuse; mix; muddle
zo **JUMBUK** a sheep (Aust.)

zo **JUMENT** a mare
JUMPED leapt; bounded; (grabbed)
to **JUMPER** chisel
rl **JUMPER** religious sect; over-blouse
bt **JUNCUS** plants (rush)
go **JUNGLE** tropical wild forest; (concrete-)
JUNGLY jungli; unsophisticated
JUNIOR younger; a son
JUNIUS anonymous writer
JUNKER Prussian landowner, aristocrat
ck **JUNKET** a sweetmeat; to feast; regale
bt **JUPATI** palm yielding raffia fibre
lw **JURANT** swearing
lw **JURIST** a lawyer
JUSTER more equitable
JUSTLE jostle; nudge; elbow
JUSTLY fairly; impartially; rightly
JUTTED projected; protruded
JUZAIL Afghan heavy rifle
JYMOLD gimmal; gimbal

K

KABAKA former ruler of Buganda (Uganda)
rl **KABALA** Moslem Holy of Holies
mn **KABOOK** iron-stone (Sri Lanka)
KABOON backward somersault (trampoline)
KABUKI realistic dramatic art (Jap.)
KABYLE Algerian Berber
KACHIN Burmese borderer
KAFFIR African native
KAFILA caravan; train of camels
tx **KAFTAN** robe (Turk.)
pc **KAIROS** critical moment of decision for changes
KAISER German emperor
zo **KAKAPO** New Zealand parrot
ch **KALIUM** potassium
bt **KALMIA** American laurel
zo **KALONG** Malay fox-bat
tx **KALPIS** Grecian water-vase
KAMEES KAMIS, Eastern garment
bt **KAMELA KAMILA**, orange dye (E. India)
KAMERA CAMERA, private room; secret
KAMMER salon; drawing room (Ger.)
mu **KAMMER** chamber (orchestra)
mt **KAMSIN** a hot wind of the Sahara
KANAKA South Sea islander
wv **KANARA** Persian runner carpet in pairs
bt **KANTEN** a seaweed
KANUCK a Canadian
KAOLIN China day
bt **KARAKA** NZ food tree
ga **KARATE** open-handed fighting (Jap.)
KARMIC relating to Karma
tx **KAROSS** skin blanket (S. Africa)
gl **KARREN** grooved limestone (karst)
go **KARROO** tableland (S. Africa)
bl **KARYON** cell-nucleus
KASBAH Arab town, fort (N. Africa)
KATION cation
zo **KATIPO** Austr. venomous spider
ga **KAYLES** early form of skittles (English)
KAYMAK clotted cream (Turk.)
ps **KAYSER** wave-number unit
KEBBIE a cudgel (Sc.)
rl **KEBLAH KIBLAH**, towards Mecca
KECKLE CACKLE, (rope protection)
bt **KECKSY** dried stalks
KEDDAH kheda; elephant trap
nt **KEDGED** warped; towed into dock
nt **KEDGER** a kedge; small anchor
KEEKER mine inspector (Sc.)
nt, nv **KEELED** carinated; navigated; (-over, capsized)
nt **KEELER** tub; bargee
zo **KEELIE** kestrel; street Arab (Sc.)
KEENER professional mourner
KEENLY sharply; acutely; astutely
KEEPER warden; (zoo-); (time-)
el **KEEPER** guard-ring; magnet; armature
KEEVED tubbed
ck **KELKEL** dried sole
md **KELOID** of scar tissue
KELPIE water spirit; seaweed gatherer
nt **KELSON KEELSON**, inner keel
KELTIC Celtic
zo **KELTIE** kittiwake gull
me **KELVIN** thermo-dynamic temperature
to **KENCHI** ivory carving tool
KENNED recognized; knew; surmised
KENNEL channel; gutter; a haunt; (dog-)
me **KENTLE** 100 lb (45 kg); quintal
gl **KENYTE** fine-grained igneous rock
md **KERION** hair disease
KERITE insulating material
zo **KERMES** crimson dye; cochineal
KERMIS kermess; Dutch fair
pr **KERNED** letter with projecting face
bt, cp **KERNEL** inner nut; heart; set of procedures
bt **KERRIA** Japanese rose

KERRIE knob-kerrie
tx **KERSEY** woollen cloth
ch **KETENE** acetone-based compound
ch **KETONE KETOSE**, acetone; –monosaccheride
KETTLE water-boiling pot
mn **KEUPER** sandstone
KEYAGE quayage
el **KEYING** signals by modulation
KEY-MEN the indispensables
cp **KEYPAD** symbols and digit entry to computer
KEY-PIN key-pivot
eg **KEY-WAY** longitudinal key-slot cut
KHALIF Calif; Caliph; chief of Islam
ar **KHAṆAT** ancient hill tunnels for water supply
wv **KHILIM KILIM**, woven rug (Turk.)
KIBBLE cudgel; hand-mill; hound
me **KIBBLE** iron-ore bucket; coal measure
KICHEL cake
KICKED hacked; objected; punted
ga, ar, ce **KICKER** footballer; thrill-giver; (horse); rebel; base of wall; column
ga **KICKUP** football practice; small dance
tx **KIDDER** a corn cornerer; a carpet
KIDDER forestaller; huckster; con-man
KIDDLE weir
zo **KIDDOW** guillemot
zo **KID-FOX** young fox
KIDNAP abduct; capture; steal
md **KIDNEY** kind; humour
bt **KIEKIE** New Zealand shrub
KIKUYU tribe (Kenya)
me **KILERG** 1000 ergs
fr **KILHIG** tree-pushing pole
mn **KILLAS** slate
KILLED slaughtered; neutralized
zo **KILLER** shark; murderer
mn **KILLOW** a black earth
tx **KILLUT** Indian robe of honour
tx **KILTED** wearing Scots kilt
KILTIE kilted soldier (Sc.)
KIMMER woman neighbour
tx **KIMONO** Japanese robe
bc **KINASE** activator of the true enzymes
ch **KINATE** salt
tx **KINCOB** Indian thread work
KINDER more benevolent
KINDLE provoke; animate; ignite
KINDLY congenial; benevolent
KINEMA cinema; body movement linguistics
zo **KINETY** structure unit in protozoa
KINGLY regal; imperial; august
KINKED snarled; twisted
wv **KINKLE** a kink; twist; ruck
zo **KIPPER** a salmon after spawning
ck **KIPPER** smoked herring
KIRBEH Arab water-skin
rl **KIRKIN** church attendance (Sc.)
KIRPAN Sikh 3 ft (0.9 m) knife
ck **KIRSCH** wild-cherry spirit
tx, me **KIRTLE** a gown; a mantle; (unit of –); weight of flax
ck **KISHKA** Yiddish/Polish sausage
KISMET fate; destiny
ga **KISSED** bussed; (billiards)
ga **KISSER** mouth (sl.); bow-string knot (archery)
KIT-BAG army bag (uniforms etc.)
ga **KIT-KAT** rounders for boys
zo **KITTEN** baby cat
KITTLE ticklish; intractable (Sc.)
KITTLY ticklish; sensitive
KLAXON a motor horn
KLEPHT Greek bandit
ps **K-MESON KILO-MESON**, elementary particles
KLOOCH Indian squaw
KNACKY cunning; (know the knack)
KNAGGY knotty; rough in temper
KNARRY knotty; rugged
bt **KNAWEL** a plant
KNICKS knickers; undergarment; (female)
KNIFED stabbed
KNIGHT a chess-man; a paladin; hereditary title
KNITCH faggot (dial.)
KNOBBY knotty; stubborn
KNOTTY intricate; difficult
KNOWER an erudite man
ch **KOBALT** cobalt
nm **KOBANG** old Japanese gold coin
KOBOLD goblin; gnome
ga **KOLVEN** club and ball game (Holland)
zo **KOODOO** antelope (S. Africa); kudu
nm **KOPECK KOPEK**, Russian farthing
KOREAN COREAN, of Korea
bt **KORKIR** corkir; purple dye
nm **KORUNA** crown (Czech)
ck **KOSHER** of food; ritually prepared (Jew.)
as **KOSMOS COSMOS**, universe
KOTWAL Indian police officer
bt **KOUSSO** plant (Abys.)
bt **KOWHAI** Maori trees
KOW-TOW salutation; obeissance (China)
KOZUKA knife beside a sword (Jap.)

KRAKEN sea monster (Danish)
go **KRANTZ** rocky summit (S. Africa); crown
rl **KRASIS** Eucharistic wine with water
KREESE creese; Malay dagger; kris
rl **K-THIBH** (Hebrew Scriptures)
zo **KUKANG** lemur or loris (Malay); monkey
ck **KULICH** Orthodox Easter cake (Rus.)
KULTUR education; German culture
bt **KUMBAR** Indian coarse wood
bt **KUMBUK** E. Indian tree
ck **KUMISS** koumiss; drink (Tatar)
ck **KÜMMEL** a liqueur
gl **KUNKUR** Indian limestone
KURKEE coarse blanket
nm **KURUSH** (Turkey) small coin
ga **KUSHTI** national wrestling (Iran)
bt, ck **KUSKUS COUSCOUS**, millet dish (Arab); fibre pasta (Indian)
KUTTAR short Indian dagger
K-VALUE thermal conductivity of material
KWAART clear lead glaze (Holland)
KYBOSH insurmountable obstruction
zo **KYLOES** Highland cattle

L

LAAGER Boer wagon encampment
LABEFY impair; weaken
pl **LABIAL** lip (sounds); labia (vagina)
LABILE unstable; liable to err
bt, pl **LABIUM** a lip; fold; (vagina)
LABOUR toil; drudge; industry
md **LABOUR** in birth throes
LABRET lip ornament
pl **LABRUM** upper lip
ch **LACCIC** (a resinous dye)
LAC-DYE (dye); shellac; (plastic)
lw **LACHES** negligence
tx **LACING** twining; beating; intermixing
LACKED short of; needed; wanted
LACKER one in want
LACKEY flunkey; footman; attendant
ch **LACMUS** litmus; lichen-dye
ch, ck **LACTIC** acid, milk, products
LACUNA a void; gap; blank; hiatus
LADDER rent in stockings; climbing aid
ce **LADDER** mud bucket; (snakes and-)
LADDIE youngster; lad; boy (Sc.)
LA-DI-DA (of speech and manners); (superior)
LADIES gentlewoman
LADING freight; cargo; burden; (bill of-)
LADINO Spanish dialect of exiled Jews
to, bd **LADKIN LATTERKIN**, wooden tool to open leaded panes
LADLED spooned; dispensed
LAGENA amphora; vase
LAG-END the bitter end; (the last)
LAGGED loitered; apprehended; (insulated)
LAGGER laggard; loafer; idler
go **LAGOON LAGUNE**, lake; nearly enclosed sea inlet (bayou) (atoll); pool
LAICAL (laity)
pr **LAID-IN** note of inclusion of extra item
LAIDLY loathly; clumsy (dial.)
LAID-ON available; made ready for use
LAID-UP ill; out of action; (mothballs)
zo **LAITHE** pollack fish
LAKIST (Lake school of poetry)
LALLAN lowland (Sc.)
LAMBDA Gr. letter; warmth and energy; gay symbol
LAMBED yeaned
zo **LAMBIE** small lamb (Sc.)
LAMELY haltingly
mu **LAMENT** deplore; wail; a jeremiad; dirge; piece for bagpipes
LAMINA thin plate; ply (laminated)
LAMING crippling; disabling
LAMISH somewhat lame
LAMMAS 1 August
LAMMED thrashed; drubbed
LAMMER amber (Sc.)
tx **LAMMIE** quilted jumper; lammy
vt **LAMPAS** swelling in horse's palate
tx **LAMPAS** damask figured cloth
ch **LAMPIC** (alcohol)
LANARY wool store
tx **LANATE** woolly
LANCED cut open; pierced
LANCER a cavalry-man
md **LANCET** a cutting instrument
ar **LANCET** window
LANDAU a carriage
LANDED disembarked; owning estates
LANDER a miner
tx **LANGET** coarse Dutch lace
LANGUE tongue (linguistics)
zo **LANGUR** Indian monkey
LANKLY ungracefully; clumsily
zo **LANNER** hawk; falcon

zo **LANUGO** prenatal hair in mammals
zo **LAPDOG** small pet dog
LAPFUL load in one's lap
gl **LAPIES** grooved limestone rock (karst)
LAPPED gem cutting; racing; covered
LAPPER folder
LAPPET loose flap; a lobe
LAPSED slipped; become void; (below par)
LAPSUS slip; memory failure; (of pen, tongue) (Lat.); mistake; error
ck **LARDED** smeared with lard; made enticing
LARDER storehouse; cold pantry
ck **LARDON** slice of bacon
LARGER bigger; wider; greater; bulkier
LARIAT lasso; rope with noose
zo **LAROID** pertaining to gulls
LARRUP to beat; to flog
zo **LARVAE** caterpillars; grubs; maggots
zo **LARVAL** (larva)
pl **LARYNX** throat; vocal cord
LASCAR East Indian sailor
LASHED secured; scourged; buffetted
LASHER rope; pool below a weir; whipper
LASHES thongs; eye-lashes; whip strokes
nt **LASKET** loop line in a sail
mn **LASQUE** flat diamond
zo **LASSIE** damsel; maid; lass; collie dog
LASTED endured; remained; continued
LASTER bootmaker; cobbler
LASTLY ultimately; finally; endwise
nt **LATEEN** triangular sail (dhow)
LATELY recently; latterly
LATENT dormant; concealed; potential
cf **LATERO-** lateral, to the side, sideways on (Gr.)
LATEST most up-to-date
LATHEN made of laths
LATHER soapy froth; foam
LATISH somewhat late
rl **LATRIA** highest kind of worship
LATTEN sheet brass
LATTER modern; recent; previous
LAUDED praised; extolled; magnified
LAUDER eulogist; encomiast; panegyrist
zo **LAUNCE** a balance; an eel
LAUNCH hurl; inaugurate; start; float
nt **LAUNCH** craft; lifeboat
bt **LAUREL** the bay-tree
ck **LAURIN** an extract from laurel
rl **LAVABO** ritualistic washing
md **LAVAGE** washing
LAVING bathing
LAVISH squander; dissipate; luxurious
LAVOLT medieval dance; lavolta
lw **LAW-DAY** day of open court
LAWFUL legal; legitimate; rightful
lw **LAWING** litigation; tavern-bill
LAWYER solicitor; counsel; advocate
LAXIST amoral philanderer
LAXITY slackness; latitude; neglect
LAXMAN lacrosse player
nt **LAY-DAY** final loading
LAYING placing; betting; imputing
LAYMAN not a cleric; unprofessional
LAY-OFF dismissal (industrial)
LAY-OUT set out; plan; format
LAZILY slothfully; drowsily; supinely
LAZING idling
mn **LAZULI** blue spar
LEADED set in lead
LEADEN heavy; dully
LEADER head; chief; guide; director
cp **LEADER** (editorial); preceding signal
cp **LEAD-IN** wire connecting an aerial; (TV); computer
bt, pr **LEAFED** having leaves; book binding
LEAGUE combine; union; cabal; distance
LEAKED oozed; percolated; (published)
LEALTY loyalty; fidelity
zo **LEAMER** dog on lead
LEANED relied; leant; inclined
LEANER thinner; skimpier
LEANLY lankly; slenderly; scantily
ar **LEAN-TO** a shed beside a wall
LEAPED sprang; skipped; gambolled
zo **LEAPER** jumper; vaulter; chaser
cp **LEASED** let out; reserved for user
ag **LEASER** gleaner; post-harvester
bt, pr **LEAVED** interleaved; bookbinding
LEAVEN yeast; balm; ferment; imbue
LEAVER a forsaker; quitter; deserter
bc **LECTIN** antibody-like substance
LECTOR reader (university title)
ar **LEDGER** account book
LEERED ogled; gloated
nt **LEEWAY** arrears of work; sideways movement of boat
lw **LEGACY** bequest; gift; (amount devised)
LEGATE ambassador; envoy; delegate
mu **LEGATO** smoothly
LEG-BYE (cricket); penalty

LEGEND myth; fable; fiction; caption
LEGGED dashed off; ran quickly; (four-)
LEGION host; multitude; horde; army
lw **LEGIST** skilled in law; jurist
bt **LEGUME** seed vessel; pod; vegetable
zo **LEIPOA** Australian game-bird
LENDER loaner; creditor
LENGTH extent; duration; reach
LENIFY assuage; mollify
LENITY clemency; leniency
rl **LENTEN** (Lent); sparing; during fast
ec **LENTIC** of standing water
bt **LENTIL** a bean; pulse
LENTOR slowness; tenacity; viscosity
LENVOY postscript
as **LEONID** a meteor from Leo
LEPCHA native of Sikkim
zo, ga **LEPPER LEAPER**, steeplechase horse
LEPPEY soft, kind work
cf, md **-LEPSIA** of seizure, epilepsy (Gr.)
nm **LEPTON** hundredth of a drachma
nc **LEPTON** nuclear particle
zo **LEPTUS** larval form of acarina
ar **LESENE** pilaster-strip moulding (Saxon)
md **LESION** injury; wound
lw **LESSEE** (lease); tenant
LESSEN reduce; mitigate; decrease
LESSER lower; minor; inferior; temporary owner
mu, rl **LESSON** task; precept; warning; Bible reading; short keyboard piece
lw **LESSOR** lease holder
LETHAL fatal; deadly; mortal
LET-OFF a reprieve
LET-OUT release
LETTER note; epistle; missive; initial
LETTIC LETTISH, Latvian language group
LEUCOL coal-tar product
ag **LEVADA** descending irrigation channel (Madeira)
LEVADE horse dressage movement
LEVANT to decamp; the East
LEVIED mustered; taxed
rl **LEVITE** Jewish tribe; priest
LEVITY frivolity; flippancy; giddiness
ck **LEVURE** flour water paste for sealing pot-lids
mn **LEVYNE** zeolite
LEWDLY lustfully; indecently
el **LEYDEN** electrical jar
LIABLE accountable; likely; obnoxious
LIAISE to form a liaison; link-up
LIBANT sipping
LIBATE to make a libation; taste (drink)
LIBIDO life force; sexual urge
go **LIBYAN** of Libya; desert
bt **LICHEN** reindeer moss
md **LICHEN** skin disease
LICKED lapped; lammed; defeated
LICTOR Roman officer
LIDDED having lids; (eyes)
mu **LIEDER** German ballads
pl **LIENAL** of the spleen
ar **LIERNE** cross-rib
LIFTED elevated; stole; upraised
LIFTER raiser; thief; (weight-) (shop-)
ch **LIGAND** outlying ion
ch **LIGASE** catalysing enzyme
md **LIGATE** to tie up
LIGGER thatch ridge stick; bedspread; night-line
LIGHTS (ancient); (Northern); offal; lamps
LIGNIN wood-fibre
bt **LIGNUM** hardwood
bt **LIGULA LIGULE**, grass; petal
mn **LIGURE** precious stone
LIKELY probable; credible
LIKING fondness; regard
LILIED adorned with lilies
LILITH Adam's first wife
mu **LILTED** verse sung rhythmically
LIMBEC a still; a distilling vessel
zo **LIMBED** with limbs; (animal); (furniture)
LIMBER flexible; pliant; supple
pr **LIMBIC** bordering; marginal
LIMBUS limbo; paradise of fools
LIMING snaring; treating with lime
zo **LIMMER** mongrel; idler; jade
LIMNED painted; illuminated
LIMNER artist; delineator
LIMOUS muddy; slimy; sticky
LIMPED walked with disability
LIMPER a lame man
zo, ce **LIMPET** univalve mollusc; leech caisson (for docks); hanger on
LIMPID clear; pellucid; pure
pr **LINAGE** (cost per line) advert rate
bt **LINDEN** lime tree
LINEAL in a direct line (graph) (diagram)
cp **LINEAR** slender; graph; key to combinations
ga **LINE-UP** show of unity; order of batting (cricket); horses at start of race; wave break point (surfing)

rl **LINGAM** sacred symbol (Hindu); penis
LINGEL waxed thread (Sc.)
LINGER lag; loiter; dawdle; tarry
ml **LINGET LINGOT**, an ingot; metal block
LINHAY farm shed
bd **LINING** aligning; inner cover; first coating; ease; painting defect
LINKED connected; united; coupled
cp **LINKED** subroutine, outside program path
zo **LINNET** bird; lintie
tx **LINSEY** mixed wool and linen cloth
bd **LINTEL LINTOL**, joist beam over a doorway, window
tx **LINTER** cotton fibre
zo **LINTIE** linnet; a song-bird (Sc.)
el **LINVAR** linear variometer resolver
zo **LIONEL LIONET**, young lion
ch **LIPASE** enzyme
LIPLET little lip
ch **LIPOIC** an acid regulating oxidation
md **LIPOID** fatty; sebaceous
md **LIPOMA** a fatty tumour
ga **LIPPED** labiate; (gentle golf shot)
LIPPED (tight-)
LIPPEN to reply; to trust (Sc.)
LIPPER a rippling; surface roughness
me **LIPPIE** quarter of a peck (Sc.)
LIQUID fluid; fluent; melting; dulcet
LIQUID (cash); flowing speech sounds 'r' and 'l'
LIQUOR (alcohol); (cooking liquid)
LISPED couldn't pronounce 's' sounds
LISPER person who lisps
LISSOM lithe; agile; pliant; supple
LISTED enlisted; canted over; registered
ar **LISTEL** fillet
LISTEN hark; attend; eavesdrop
LISTER arranger; recorder
rl **LITANY** solemn supplication (repentance)
bt **LITCHI LYCHEE**, fruit (China)
LITHER lazy; worthless; smooth
md **LITHIA** oxide of lithium
ar, md **LITHIC** (stone)
ch **LITMUS** acid-test dye
zo **LITTER** scatter; the newborn; bedding
LITTLE tiny; pygmy; brief; trivial
LITUUS augur's staff
LIVEDO blueness of skin from congestion
LIVELY joyful; active; vigorous; quick
tx **LIVERY** uniform; costume
lw **LIVERY** writ of possession
rl **LIVING** livelihood; animate; alive
zo **LIZARD** saurian reptile
go **LLANOS** plains of South America
LOADED laden; filled; cumbered
LOADER one of the gun's crew; stacker
cp **LOADER** input memory routine
LOAFED lounged
LOAFER idler; vagrant; flâneur; drone
LOANED lent; advanced; borrowed
LOATHE hate; detest; abhor
ck **LOAVES** of bread
pl **LOBATE** (lobes); (of the ear)
LOBBED pitched; gently threw
LOBING gadrooning
LOBOLA wife-purchase (S. Africa)
bt **LOBOSE** lobate
LOBULE small lobe
LOCALE meeting place (hall) (Fr.)
LOCATE fix; place; settle; find
LOCHAN a pond; a loch (Sc.)
LOCKED grappled; embraced; clasped
LOCKER a cupboard; a drawer
LOCKET an ornament; a fastening
LOCK-UP jail-cell, garage with lock
bt **LOCULI** cells
bt, zo **LOCUST** acacia tree; insect
LODGED deposited; dwelt; harboured
LODGER temporary resident
LODORE a cataract
LOFTED skied
LOFTER (golf)
LOGGAN rocking stone; logan
ga **LOGGAT LOGGET**, medieval ninepin; heavy wooden pole
nt **LOGGED** recorded
cp **LOGGER** jumberman; recorder of events
ar **LOGGIA** semi-exposed gallery, arcade
bd **LOG-HUT** log-cabin
ma **LOG-LOG** logarithm of a logarithm
LOGMAN woodman; logger
cp **LOG-OFF** check-out; (register departure)
ce **LOGWAY** chute route beside dam
md **LOHOCK** syrup
md **LOIMIC** (plague)
LOITER linger; dawdle; delay; tarry
zo **LOLIGO** cuttle-fish; squid
bt **LOLIUM** genus of grass
LOLLED hung out; reclined
LOLLER lounger; flâneur
LOLLOP to lounge
bt **LOMENT** a type of legume

LONELY solitary; remote; forlorn
bt **LONGAN** Chinese fruit tree
LONGED craved; desired
LONGER more extensive; taller
bt **LOOFAH** sponge; skeleton; gourd
LOOKED examined; observed; glanced
LOOKER onlooker; spectator
LOOK-IN hasty visit; glance; short participation (Am. football)
cp **LOOK-UP** seek information; select data
nt **LOOMED** came into view
LOOPED encircled; knotted
zo **LOOPER** a caterpillar; wave over surfer; short pass (Am. football)
LOOSED set free
LOOSEN slacken; release; untie; relax
LOOTED ransacked
LOOTER plunderer; pillager; despoiler
zo **LOP-EAR** a lop-eared rabbit
LOPING running easily
LOPPED trimmed; truncated
LOPPER to curdle; trimmer; a cutting
bt **LOQUAT** Chinese fruit
LORATE thong-shaped
nt **LORCHA** junk-rigged Portuguese ship
LORDED domineered
LORDLY noble; magnificent; arrogant
LORICA a cuirass
zo **LORIOT** golden oriole
LOSING mislaying; squandering; failing
LOSSES casualties; damages; privations
LOTION a wash
LOUDER noisier; more stentorian
LOUDLY uproariously; clamorously
LOUNGE open sitting room; (reception-)
LOURED frowned; scowled
LOUSED infested with lice
LOUVER louvre; ventilator
ar **LOUVRE** open turret (Fr.)
bt **LOVAGE** genus of herb; angelica type
LOVELY beauteous; delectable
LOVING adoring; esteeming
LOWBOY low chest of drawers (N. Am.)
LOWERY gloomy; overcast; murky
LOWEST most debased; deepest
LOWING bellowing; mooing
LUBBER heavy; clumsy fellow; (land-)
LUBRIC slippery; lewd
bt **LUCAMA** fruit (Chile)
LUCENT bright; shining; clear
LUCINA Diana or Juno
LUCKIE elderly woman (Sc.)
LUCUMO Etruscan title
md **LUETIC** pestilential
ar **LUFFER** (see Louvre); open turret
LUGGED tugged; hauled; dragged
nt **LUGGER** small sailing ship
LUGGIE vase with ears
LULLED soothed; assuaged; calmed
LUMBAL LUMBAR, of lower backbone
LUMBER walk awkwardly
LUMBER accumulated property (bulk)
lt, me **LUMERG** unit of luminous energy
LUMPED heaped up
LUMPER stevedore
ck **LUMPIA** oriental egg roll
LUNACY mania; dementia; craziness
bt **LUNARY** lunar; moonwort fern
LUNATE like a crescent-moon; (shape)
LUNGED thrust
LUNKAH Indian cheroot
LUNULA LUNULE, crescent-like
LUPINE wolf-likel; wolfish
bt **LUPINE** lupin; a fodder plant
LURING enticing; inveigling; decoying
LURKED hid; lay in wait
LURKER skulker
LUSIAD Portuguese epic poem
LUSTED eagerly desired (sexually)
LUSTIC lusty; vigorous
LUSTRA periods of five years
LUSTRE Roman purification ceremony
LUSTRE gloss; splendour; glory
zo **LUTEAL** of the corpus luteum
ck **LUTEIN** egg yellow
LUTINE (Lloyd's bell) (marine disaster)
LUTING a composition; clay; joining clay pieces using slip
mu **LUTIST** lute player
LUTOSE miry; unsafe; swampy
LUXATE dislocate
LUXURY epicurism; super-comfort
bt **LUZULA** a rush genus
LYCEUM lecture hall; (college)
ck **LYCHEE** Chinese dessert fruit
LYDIAN effeminate
mn **LYDITE** black slate; touchstone
md **LYMPHY** (lymph)
LYRATE lyre-shaped
mu **LYRISM** playing the lyre

LYRIST lyrical writer
ch **LYSINE** diamino-caproic acid

M

bt **MABOLA** Philippine tree
bt **MACACO** a tropical tree
MACHAN platform for tiger-shooting
md **MACIES** emaciation; wasting away
pr **MACKLE** macule; a blur in printing
MACKLE spot, blotch, stain
MACLED spotted
MACRON a mark showing long vowel
pl **MACULA** retinal vision area (eye)
md **MACULE** spot symptom; (small-) (chicken-) pox
MADCAP hair-brained; frolicsome
MADDEN enrage; infuriate
bt **MADDER** a plant; a red dye
MADMAN maniac; bedlamite
tx **MADRAS** bright kerchief; cotton fabric
MAENAD a frenzied woman
MAFFIA MAFIA, Sicilian secret gangsters
zo **MAGGOT** worm; grub; larva; a whim
MAGIAN Wise Men of the East
pt **MAGILP** megilp; painters' varnish
MAGISM Persian philosophy
MAGNET lodestone; attraction; lure
nc **MAGNON** spin-wave energy quantum
ch **MAGNOX** magnesium alloy
me **MAGNUM** 2 quart (2.2 litre) bottle
zo **MAGPIE** (target shooting) (nil); bird
bt **MAGUEY** Mexican aloe
MAGYAR Hungarian
MAHOUN mahound; evil spirit (Arabic)
MAHOUT elephant driver
zo **MAHSIR** mahseer; an Indian fish
MAIDAN Indian parade ground; a plain
MAIDEN lass; damsel; virgin
MAIDEN untaken; non-winner (horse-racing); non-scoring (cricket)
MAILED posted; (clad in chain-mail)
MAILED (fan-); (black-)
MAIMED crippled; disabled; mutilated
MAINLY chiefly; principally; largely
lw **MAINOR** stolen goods; theft
MAJLIS parliament of Iran or Egypt
MAJOON narcotic drug mixture (Hindu)
MAKE-UP fiction; facial embellishment
MAKING forcing; compelling; reaching
bt **MAKORE** African mahogany wood
MALADY ailment; disorder; complaint
MALAGA a Spanish wine
ch **MALATE** a salt of malic acid
MALAWI central African country
MALAXE to rub, knead plaster
ch **MALEIC** obtained from malic acid
MALGRE maugre; in spite of
MALICE spite; rancour; malevolence
MALIGN defame; slander; traduce
MALISM pessimistic belief
MALKIN scarecrow; mawkin
bt **MALLEE** Australian tree
to, ga **MALLET** wooden hammer (croquet) (polo)
rw, zo **MALLET** maul; beetle
bt **MALLOW** plant (marsh); herb
bt **MALTED** malt added (in process)
MALTHA petroleum
zo **MAMMAL** genus of breast-feeders
bt **MAMMEE** West Indian fruit
MAMMER stammer; hesitate; hover
MAMMET puppet; scarecrow
MAMMON god of riches; wealth
MANAGE contrive; control; regulate
MANANA tomorrow or perhaps later (Sp.)
hd **MANCHE** sleeve; the channel (Fr.)
MANCHU former ruling class in China
MANDOM humanity
MANEGE riding school; equitation
MANFUL virile; courageous; bold
MANGAL charcoal brazier (Turk.)
MANGER a trough
MANGLE pre-ironing (laundry)
MANIAC madman; lunatic; fiend
bt **MANILA** Manila cheroot
bt **MANIOC** tapioca; cassava
MANISM belief in nature cult
rl **MANITO** Great Spirit (American Ind.)
MANJAK Barbados asphalt
ch **MANNAN** anhydride of mannose
nt **MANNED** provided a crew
MANNER behaviour; style; deportment
MANQUE 1 to 18 in roulette; missed career
MANTEL a beam; mantel-shelf
MANTIC inspired; prophetic; vatic
zo **MANTID** pertaining to mantis
zo **MANTIS** a praying insect
gl **MANTLE** cloak; hood; covering; suffuse; rock layer between crust

and core of earth; (-piece) (gas-)
MANTON Spanish shawl
rl, pc **MANTRA** a Vedic hymn; meditational prayer, sound ritual
MANTUA lady's cloak or gown
mu **MANUAL** handbook; organ key-board
MANURE compost; fertilizer; dressing
mn **MANWAY** underground ladderway
MAOISM ideas of Mao Zedong
MAOIST follower of Mao Zedong
MAPPED charted; drew; delineated
MAQUIS (resistance movement)
bt **MAQUIS** rough shrub
MARACA Latin-American percussion
MARAUD raid; plunder; pillage
gl, bd, mn **MARBLE** decorative metamorphic rock; balls; famous friezes
MARBLY like marble
MARCEL a hair wave; style of coiffure
mu **MARCIA** (often marcial); (women's name)
MARCID wasting
md **MARCOR** marasmus; weight loss
zo **MARGAY** American tiger-cat
MARGED bordered; edged
MARGIN verge; brim; brink; reserve
zo **MARGOT** fish (perch)
MARIAN concerning the Virgin Mary
rl **MARIAN** Virgin Mary (year)
bt **MARIET** violet campanula
nt **MARINA** yacht-mooring basin
nt **MARINE** nautical; naval; maritime
MARISH a marsh; swamp
MARIST sect, follower of Virgin Mary
nt **MARKAB** dhow, Egypt
MARKED unmistakable; notable
nt **MARKER** examiner; buoy; signpost
tc **MARKER** device determining call paths
MARKET mart; emporium; sale; vend
zo **MARMOT** ground squirrel
MAROON claret-colour; firework (alarm signal)
MAROON runaway slave
MARQUE accredited; boundary; model
bt **MARRAM** sand dune; bent grass
MARRED disfigured; impaired
MARRER spoiler; bungler; botcher
bt, ck **MARRON** chestnut (Fr.); hue, shade
zo **MARROT** guillemot
bt, pl, ck **MARROW** medulla; essence; pith; (veg) (bone)
MARSHY boggy; fenny; paludal
zo **MARTEN** (weasel)
zo **MARTIN** swallow
MARTYR victim; sacrifice; persecute
MARVEL wonder; prodigy; miracle
MARVER iron or stone block
gs **MARVER** glass blower's table
hd **MASCLE** heraldic lozenge
as **MASCON** moon high-gravity region
MASCOT charm; talisman; halidom
MASHAQ Persian goatskin water-bag
MASHED bruised; pulped; kneaded
MASHER fop; dandy; lady-killer
MASHIE a golf-club
nt **MASHVA MUCHVA**, mini-dhow (E. Africa)
rl **MASJID** masjed; a mosque (Arabic)
MASKED disguised; cloaked; screened
MASKER masquerader; mummer
ck **MASLIN** rye-bread
MASORA Hebrew traditions
MASQUE mask; a play; revel
MASSED collected; heaped; lumped
MASSES the proletariat
go **MASSIF** central mountain-mass (Fr.)
zo **MASTAX** gizzard in rotifera
nt **MASTED** having masts
bt **MASTEL** maple tree
MASTER maestro; tutor; teacher; expert
bt, bd **MASTIC** resin; coating with proofing; (pitch); (bitumastic)
ck **MASTIC** liquorice-like flavour
bt **MATHES** may-weed
bt **MATICO** Peruvian astringent plant
zo **MATIES MATJES**, (Dutch); herring; wrasse
zo **MATING** pairing; check-mating (chess)
rl **MATINS** morning service
pr, cp **MATRIX** original die; mould; cavity; array of items; numbers (discs)
MATRON head nurse; dame
MATTED entangled; interlaced
MATTER signify; import; stuff; affair
MATURE ripen; mellow; full grown
MAUDIT one pursued by bad luck
MAUGRE in spite of
MAULED hammered; mangled; bruised
MAUMAU Kenyan nationalists
MAUNDY Thursday before Good Friday
MAUSER rifle
MAWMET maumet; mammet; puppet
MAXIMA highest or top limits
mu **MAXIXE** dance (Brazil)
zo **MAY-BUG** cockchafer

tc **MAYDAY** verbal distress call
MAY-DEW spring
zo **MAY-FLY** a species of ephemera; (angling)
MAYHAP perhaps
lw **MAYHEM** criminal mutilation; maiming
MAYING spring festival (blossom)
bt **MAZARD** skull; cherry
rl **MAZDAH** supreme deity (Zend Avesta)
MAZILY confusedly; distractedly
ch **MAZOUT** petroleum extract
MEABLE easily penetrable
MEADOW mead; lea; sward; field
MEAGRE thin; skinny; lean; gaunt; lank; mean; emaciated
zo **MEAKER** a minnow
MEALER (out-boarder)
ck, bt **MEALIE** maize dish (Africa)
MEANLY ignobly; basely; sordidly
MEASLY stingy; miserly; meagre
ck **MEATHE** mead; a liquor
pl **MEATUS** passage in the body
MEDDLE muddle; intrude; interfere
MEDIAD MESIAD, toward median axis
MEDIAL average; mean; mediocre
as **MEDIAN** traversal; a Mede
bt **MEDICK** lucerne or clover
md **MEDICO** doctor or student
MEDISM Grecian treachery
MEDIUM moderate; means; psychic
pl **MEDIUS** the middle finger
bt **MEDLAR** fruit
mu **MEDLEY** farrago; jumble; olio
MEDLEY mixed selection
zo **MEDUSA** jellyfish; a gorgon
MEEKEN to humble; to abase
MEEKLY lowly; submissively
MEETLY fitly; suitably; correctly
cf **MEGALO-** of great size, power (Gr.)
MEGASS bagasse; cane refuse
me **MEGERG** million ergs
ps **MEGGER** insulation recorder
MEGILP magilp; linseed-oil and varnish
me **MEGOHM** a million ohms
md **MEGRIM** neuralgic pain; migraine
zo **MEGRIM** flat fish; witch/lemon sole
zo **MEHARI** racing dromedary; camel
MEHTAR Ind. house-servant, groom
mu **MEHTER** battle band (Turk.)
MELINE canary-yellow
MELLAY mêlée; affray; broil; brawl
MELLEY scuffle; contest; conflict
vt, zo **MELLIT** a horse-scab
MELLOW mature; ripe; genial; soften
mu **MELODY** air; tune; descant; theme
MELTED molten; dissolved; relaxed
MELTER liquefier
tx **MELTON** woollen cloth
MEMBER part; limb; component
MEMNON desert crier
MEMOIR life; biography; journal
cp **MEMORY** remembrance; recollection; access store
MENACE threat; alarm; intimidate
MENAGE housekeeping; household (group)
MENALD speckled
MENDED restored; rectified; improved
MENDER repairer; restorer
MENHIR obelisk; long grave stone
MENIAL slave; flunky; degrading (chore)
pl **MENINX** a brain-membrane
zo **MENNAD** the minnow
MENSAL monthly
pl **MENSES** menstruation
MENTAL intellectual; psychical
MENTOR guide; monitor; counsellor
zo **MENURA** lyre-bird
MERCER a dealer in silks and cloths
MERELY simply; solely; only; purely
MERESE wine-glass stem flange
MERGED sunk; absorbed; immersed
MERGER an amalgamation
tx, zo **MERINO** sheep; wool
bt **MERISM** development of like members
MERKIN false hair; a mop
zo **MERLIN** falcon; small hawk
ar **MERLON** projecting part of battlement
MERMAN cf. mermaid
zo **MERONT** phase in neosporidia
zo **MEROPS** bird; bee-eater
cf **-MEROUS** of number of parts (Gr.)
zo **MERULA** thrush; blackbird
MESAIL vizor of helmet
MESCAL Mexican drink
go **MESETA** tableland (Spain)
MESHED reticulated; engaged
MESIAL MESIAN, middle; median
bt **MESLIN** maslin; mixed grain
MESODE part of an ode
MESPOT Mesopotamia
MESSED mussed; confused; ate together
zo **MESSIN** a mongrel (Sc.)
MESTEE mixed race; octoroon
me **METAGE** measurement
METEOR aerolite; shooting star
METHAM chemical insecticide; weedkiller

METHER vessel for mead
METHOD order; system; process
ch **METHYL** spirit
METIER role (Fr.); profession (vocational)
METING measuring
ar **METOPE** forehead; sculptural frieze
METRIC decimal system of weights and measures
cf **-METRIC** (isometric) of measure
METTLE courage; ardour; pluck
MEWING caterwauling; confining
MEWLED yowled; squalled
MEWLER a crying child
MIASMA bad air; exhalation
MICHED concealed; played truant
MICHER skulker; beggar; pilferer
MICKLE muckle; great; much
MICMAC an American Indian
me **MICRON** millionth part of metre
MID-AGE middle time of life
MID-AIR up in the air
MIDDAY noon; meridian
MIDDEN dunghill
MIDDLE centre; intermediate; medial
zo **MIDGET** sand-fly; dwarf
ga **MID-LEG MID-OFF**, cricket, fielding position
bt **MIDRIB** largest leaf vein
nt **MID-SEA** at sea
MIDWAY halfway
MIFFED ruffled; annoyed
MIGHTY puissant; potent; dynamic
MIGNON dainty; pretty
rl **MIHRAB** mosque niche facing Mecca
MIKADO Emperor of Japan
MILADY my lady
MILDEN to mollify; make mild
MILDER calmer; softer; gentler
bt **MILDEW** mould; blight; rust; must
MILDLY leniently; placidly; suavely
MILIEU environment
bt **MILIUM** millet grass
MILKED emptied; taken advantage of
MILKEN milk-like
MILKER cow-man
MILLED ground; struggled; levigated
MILLER one who grinds corn
MILLET grain
MILORD my lord
MILSEY milk strainer
zo **MILTER** male fish
ar, rl **MIMBAR MIMBER**, pulpit in mosque
MIMING mimicking; aping; acting (theatre)
bt **MIMOSA** plant genus
ck **MINCED** affected; abbreviated; shredded
MINCER mincing machine; (meat)
MINDED heeded; noted; objected
MINDER care-taker; attendant (nurse)
MINGLE blend; mix; join; jumble
MINIFY diminish; depreciate
MINIMA the lowest
MINING burrowing; sapping
MINION a favourite; sycophant
MINISH diminish; reduce; minify
pt **MINIUM** vermilion (colour)
zo **MINNOW** meaker; mennad, fish
MINOAN Cretan
MINTED coined; stamped; invented
MINTER inventor; creator
MINTON china ware
mu **MINUET** courtly dance
MINUTE small; tiny; minikin; record
fr **MIOMBO** woodland (Tanzania)
MIOSIS rhetorical understatement
pl **MIOTIC** eye-pupil contractor
MIRAGE optical illusion (oasis)
MIRING muddying; besmirching
MIRROR exemplar; reflector
ga **MISCUE** (billiards)
ga **MISERE** (solo whist, no tricks) (cards)
MISERY distress; woe; grief; anguish
MISFIT square peg in round hole
MISGET obtain unjustly
MISHAP accident; ill chance
md **MISHMI** vegetable drug
rl **MISHNA** the text of the Talmud
MISKEN to ignore; be unaware (Sc.)
mu **MISKIN** a little bagpipe
MISLAY misplace; lose
MISLED (mislead); deluded; deceived
rl **MISSAL** Mass-book
MISSAY say wrongly; slander
MISSED failed; wanted; needed
MISSEE view erroneously
zo **MISSEL** thrush; storm cock
MIS-SET to arrange unfitly
MISSIS missus; mistress (Mrs)
MISTER ordinary title for man (Mr)
zo **MISTLE** missel-thrush
MISUSE abuse; profane; misapply
zo **MITHAN** Indian ox; gayal
rl **MITHRA** sun-god (Pers.) (later, Roman)
MITRAL like a mitre; somewhat conical
rl **MITRED** wearing mitre (Bishop)
MITTEN a fingerless glove
MIURUS dactylic hexameter
MIXING mingling; jumbling
nt **MIZZEN** aft mast and sail
MIZZLE fine rain; to drizzle; decamp

MIZZLY misty
pc **-MNESIC** pertaining to memory
MOANED lamented; bewailed; deplored
MOATED surrounded by water (castles)
MOBBED surrounded by hostile crowd
MOBCAP a frilly cap
MOBILE volatile; mercurial; motile
lw **MOB-LAW** lynch-law
MOCKED derided; jeered; aped
MOCKER scorner; scoffer; taunter
MOCK-UP a non-working model
pt **MODENA** crimson
MODERN present; current; up-to-date
MODEST chaste; unassuming; diffident
MODIFY alter; change; vary; moderate
MODISH stylish; fashionable; chic
MODIST a follower of fashion
me **MODIUS** 2 gallons (Roman)
MODOCS Oregon Indian tribe
ar, bd, me **MODULE** model; proportion length; spacecraft
ae, cp **MODULE** hardware; self-contained unit, faculty behaviour; sputnik
ma **MODULO** remaindering formula
MOFFLE bungle
gl, mn **MOGOTE** conical hill (karst) (Sp.)
tx **MOHAIR** hair of the Angora goat
MOHAWK ruffian; N. Am. Indian; (ice-skating)
MOHOLE penetration of earth's crust
MOIDER to toil; confuse; spend (Sc.)
MOIETY a half; a share
MOILED drudged; toiled; soiled
MOIRAE the Fates
pl **MOLARS** grinder teeth of mammals
rl, zo **MOLECH MOLOCH**, Semitic deity; Australian lizard
MOLEST vex; harry; worry; pester
MOLINE mill-stone rynd
ce **MOLING** laying drains with mole plough
rl **MOLLAH MULLAH**, judge; Moslem teacher
MOLTEN melted; liquefied; fused
MOMENT instant; trice; import
MONDAY Solomon Grundy's birthday
zo **MONERA** simple protozoans
MONGER deal; to deal in
MONGOL native of Mongolia
rl **MONIAL** nun
MONIED rich; opulent
MONIES coins; means; specie
MONISM a doctrine of single reality
MONIST believer in monism
zo **MONKEY** tailed tree animal (Rhesus)
MONKEY £500; pile-driver; meddle
mu **MONODY** a dirge
MONOID (versification)
bt **MONOSY** abnormal condition
MONTEM Eton custom of money-raising
mn **MONTON** ore (Sp.)
mu **MONTRE** organ stop; ceramic
zo **MOO-COW** pet word for cow
MOOING lowing; cowtalk
MOONED wandered aimlessly
MOONER listless lounger
MOONET little moon
zo **MOORUK** Bennett's cassowary
tx **MOORVA** fibre; bowstring-hemp
MOOTED debated; discussed
MOOTER disputer
MOPING languishing
MOPISH gloomy; spiritless; despondent
zo **MOPOKE** Australian owl
MOPPED swabbed
MOPPET MOPSEY, a kept person; popsy
MORALE courageous endurance
MORASS bog; fen; swamp; quagmire
MORBID diseased; vitiated; sickly
tx **MOREEN** watered woollen fabric
zo **MORGAY** shark; dog-fish
me **MORGEN** about 2 acres (0.8 hectare)
MORGUE mortuary (Fr.)
MORIAN a Moor; Moroccan
MORION open helmet
MORKIN dead beast
mn **MORLOP** jasper
rl **MORMON** member of sect (Utah)
hd **MORNED** blunted; dawned
MOROSE sullen; surly; churlish
MORRIS folk dance style
MORROW the next day
MORSAL pert. to cutting edge
MORSED signalled by Morse
MORSEL titbit; piece; fragment
MORTAL human; deadly; fatal
MORTAR trench weapon; cement
md **MORULA** button-scurvy
rl **MOSAIC** law; inlaid ornamentation
lw, bt **MOSAIC** green; symptoms of virus in plants
rl **MOSLEM** Muslim; Mohammedan
rl **MOSQUE** temple; mesjid
pt **MOSTIC** maulstick
MOSTLY chiefly; mainly
MOTHER (liquors); dam; generatrix

MOTILE mobile; capable of movement
MOTION proposal; action; impulse
MOTIVE spur; incentive; reason
MOTLEY mixed; clown's costume
zo **MOT-MOT** American bird
MOTORY giving motion
MOTTLE to stain
MOUJIK muzhik; Russian peasant
MOULDY fusty; musty; rusty; fungusy
gl **MOULIN** glacial crevasse
ck **MOULIN** mill (Fr.); grinder
MOUNTY Canadian Mounted Police
zo **MOUNTY** the rise of a hawk
nt **MOUSED** bound with spun-yarn
zo **MOUSER** capable cat
ck **MOUSSE** culinary confection
bt **MOUTAN** tree-peony
MOUTHY ranting; bombastic
nm, zo **MOUTON** sheep; ancient French coin
MOVIES moving pictures (cinema)
MOVING stirring; budging; touching
MOWING grass cutting
tx **MOZING** raising nap (cloth)
MUCAGO mucilage; mucus
ch **MUCATE MUCITE**, mucic acid
MUCHLY rather much
nt **MUCHVA MASHVA**, mini-dhow (E. Africa)
MUCKED muddled; dirtied; spread dung
MUCKER a failure; a fall
MUCKLE much (Sc.)
md **MUCOID** resembling mucus
MUCOSA mucous membrane
md, ps **MUCOUS** mucoid; slimy; viscous
MUDDER muddy course; race-track (racing)
MUDDLE confuse; chaos; derange
MUD-PIE child's inedible confection
MUFFED fumbled and failed
ck **MUFFIN** a winter's delicacy
MUFFLE (furnace); deaden; shroud
MUGGED crammed up; beaten up
zo **MUGGER** Indian crocodile; assailant
bt **MUGUET** lily of the valley
lw **MULIER** wife
MULISH obstinate
rl **MULLAH** (see Mollah); teacher (Moslem)
ck **MULLED** hot; spiced (wine); pondered
bt **MULLEN** mullein plant
MULLER a miller (Sc.)
MULLER heating vessel; pestle
zo **MULLET** genus of fish
hd **MULLET** a star; a rowel
zo **MULLEY** mooly; a cow; hornless
br **MULTUM** adulterant used in brewing
MUMBLE mutter; chew
MUMMER masquerader; actor; histrion
MUMPED nibbled; grinned; chewed
MUMPER a beggar
mn **MUNDIC** iron pyrites
MUNDIL a turban
MUNSHI Eastern teacher
ar **MUNTIN** part of window; glass frame; mullion
MURAGE money for town repairs (Fr.)
MURDER kill; assassinate; slaughter
zo **MURINE** (mice)
MURING immuring; walling up
MURMUR whisper; complain; repine
bt **MURPHY** potato (Irish)
gl **MURREN** a murrain (obs.)
MURREY dark red
zo **MUSANG** East Indian coffee-rat
bt **MUSCAL** (mosses)
bt **MUSCAT** a grape; a wine
pl **MUSCLE** thew; sinew
MUSEUM collection/treasure repository
MUSHED commanded (sled dogs) (forward)
MUSHER snow traveller (Canada)
MUSING ruminating; reflecting
MUSIVE mosaic
go **MUSKEG** swamp; marsh (Canada)
zo **MUSKET** hawk; smooth-bore gun
zo **MUSK-OX** N. American arctic ox
MUSLIM Moslem; Mohammedan
tx **MUSLIN** soft cotton fabric
zo **MUSMON** moufflon; European sheep
MUSNUD Persian throne of state
MUSSAL Indian torch
MUSSED messed; disarranged
zo **MUSSEL** a shellfish
zo **MUSTAC** small tufted monkey
MUSTEE mestee; an octoroon
MUSTER parade; assemble; rally
MUTAGE (checking fermentation)
MUTATE to change
MUTELY dumbly; silently
MUTING guano; silencing; bribing
nt **MUTINY** hijack by crew; riot; revolt
MUTISM dumbness; speechlessness
MUTIVE tending to alter
MUTTER murmur; grumble; maunder
MUTTON proverbially dead
MUTUAL reciprocal; correlative
ar **MUTULE** projection
lw **MUTUUM** loan contract

MUZHIK moujik; Russian peasant
MUZZLE jaw cover (dog)
MUZZLE gun mouth; censor
MYCOID fungus-like
MYELIC pertaining to spinal cord
zo **MYELIN** fatty material round nerve
pl **MYELON** spinal cord
zo **MYGALE** shrew mouse
ch **MYOGEN** water-soluble muscle albumin
md **MYOPIA** near-sightedness
md **MYOPIC** short-sighted; purblind
md **MYOSIN MYOSIS**, disease of the eye
MYRIAD countless; innumerable (stars)
bt **MYRTLE** genus of shrub
bt **MYRTUS** wax-myrtle
MYSELF reflexive pronoun
MYSTIC occult; recondite; enigmatic
MYTHIC legendary; fictitious; fanciful
MYTHUS a myth; a fable
zo **MYXINE** hag-fish
pl **MYXOID** mucoid
md **MYXOMA** a tumour

N

NABBED grabbed; arrested
ck **NABKET** snuff; small cake (Sc.)
md **NAEVUS** birth-mark
md **NAGANA** tsetse fly disease
NAGARI Sanskrit script
nt **NAGGAR** cargo felucca boat
NAGGED scolded; upbraided; pestered
NAGGER a fault-finder
zo **NAHOOR** sheep (Nepal)
hd, zo **NAIANT** (swimming)
NAILED caught; secured; exposed
NAILER nail-maker
zo **NAKONG** water-koodoo (S. Africa)
NAMELY viz, specifically
NAMING christening; nominating
zo **NANDOO** S. American ostrich; Rhea
NANISM dwarfishness
tx **NANKIN** nankeen; cotton cloth
rl **NANNAR** Chaldean moon-god
NANOID dwarf; pigmy
ch **NAPALM** flammable oil/soap gel (warfare)
tx **NAPERY** household linen
NAPKIN serviette; nappy; diaper (ring)
mn **NAPPAL** soaprock
NAPPED dozed; slumbered
bt **NARDOO** Australian plant
bt **NARDUS** mat-grass
bt **NARGIL** coconut tree; hubble-bubble
md **NARIAL NARINE**, nasal
NARROW strait; close; contracted (bowels); -minded; truncate
zo **NARWAL** sea-unicorn; whale
mu **NASARD** organ stop
md **NASION** part of nose
NASUTE captious; critical
hd **NATANT** swimming; naiant
NATION people; race; country
NATIVE aboriginal; intrinsic; congenial
zo **NATRIX** genus of snakes
ch **NATRON** carbonate of soda
NATTER to nag (dial.); to chat, complain
ar **NATTES** surface decoration
bl, bt **NATURE** the biological world
NATURE character traits
me **NAUGHT** O; zero; nought; nothing
NAUSEA sea-sickness; disgust; qualm
NAUTCH dancing girl; a dance
nt **NAUTIC** nautical; naval; maritime
mu **NAZARD** 3-f organ pitch
zo **NEANIC** of adolescent period
nv, nt **NEAPED** aground at low tide
NEARBY adjacent; nigh; at hand
NEARED approached; drew closer
NEARER more adjacent
NEARLY closely; all but; almost
NEATLY smartly; featly; dexterously
bt **NEBBUK** (crown of thorns)
bt **NEB-NEB** acacia pods
NEBRIS fawn-skin worn by Bacchus
as **NEBULA** heavy cloud; whirl (stars)
NEBULE nebula; mist; fog
NEBULY wavy
NECKED embraced; hugged; beheaded
bt **NECRON** dead plant material
ck **NECTAR** ambrosia; honey-sap (juice)
NEED-BE a necessity
NEEDED wanted; lacked; necessitated
NEEDER requirer
to **NEEDLE** critical
NEEDLY thorny
NEESED NEEZED, sneezed
NEGATE deny; mollify
bt, zo **NEKTON** swimming water organisms
NEMEAN (lion killed by Hercules)
go **NEOGEA** neotropical region
NEPALI language (Nepal)
NEPHEW sibling's male child
NERIED sea-nymph
rl **NEREUS** sea-god
bt **NERINE** Guernsey lily
zo **NERITE** mollusc

bt **NERIUM** oleander
bt, ck **NEROLI** oil from orange flowers
NERVAL nervous; sinewy
NERVED fortified; plucky; courageous
NESHEN to soften
NESHKI Arabic script
NESSUS a Centaur
NESTED built a nest
NESTLE snuggle; rest; cherish
NESTOR genus of parrots (NZ)
NETHER lower; under
cy **NETRUM** minute spindle
NETTED reticulated; gained; trapped
bt **NETTLE** to irritate; fret
zo **NEURAD** dorsal
md **NEURAL** (nerves)
NEURIC nervous
NEURIN protein coating; membrane
md **NEURON** nerve cell
pc **NEUROT-** of the nerves (neurotic)
NEUTER neutral; non-partisan; sexless
NEWING yeast; barm
NEWISH somewhat novel
NEW-SAD recently bereaved (Shak.)
me **NEWTON** gravity force
ch **NIACIN** nicotinic acid; B Vitamin
NIBBED complete with nib (pen)
NIBBLE bite; gnaw
NICELY exactly; accurately; adroitly
rl **NICENE** (Nicaea) prayer-book creed (A.D. 325)
NICEST daintiest; choicest
NICETY precision; delicacy
NICHED in a niche or recess
NICHER neigh; snigger
NICKED notched; stolen
nm, mn **NICKEL** 5 cent piece; metal; acoustic delay time
zo **NICKER** a cheat; woodpecker; thief
nt **NICKEY** Manx fishing boat
NIDDER shiver; molest
NIDGED nudged (stone-cutting)
NIDGET a fool
NID-NOD nod repeatedly; (half-asleep)
NIDOSE olfactory
NIELLO engraving; ornamentation
NIFFER exchange (Sc.)
NIFFLE pilfer; steal
NIGGER negro; black
NIGGLE trifle; to be finicky
NIGHLY nearly; adjacent
NIGRIC black
zo **NILGAI** Indian antelope
NIMBLE agile; lively; swift
NIMBLY alertly; briskly; quickly
mt **NIMBUS** a halo; rain cloud
NIMROD a mighty hunter
NINETY cardinal number
NINGAL Nannar's wife
NIPPED pinched; compressed; gripped
zo **NIPPER** tooth (horse); boy (slang); bed-bug
NIPPLE teat; dug; pap; mamilla
NIPPON Japan
rl **NIPTER** feet-washing ceremony
md **NIRLES** herpes; shingles
ch **NITRIC** (nitre); acid
ch **NITRON** reagent for nitric acid
zo **NITTER** bot-fly; body-louse
NITWIT numskull; idiot
NIVOSE 4th French month (Revol.)
nt **NNGGAR NUGGAR**, cargo dhow (Nile)
ga **NO-BALL** (cricket) (penalty)
vt **NOBBLE** dope; lame; cheat
NOBLER more illustrious
NOBODY a nonentity; negative pronoun
ck **NOCAKE** parched corn
NOCENT hurtful; mischievous
zo **NOCTUA** large moth genus
NODDED agreed; auction offer
NODDER a drowsy person
NODDLE the head
NODOSE knotted
NODULE small knot
NOESIS pure knowledge
NOETIC intellectual
me **NOGGIN** small cup; ¼ pint (0.14 litres)
NO-GOOD useless
NOISED reported; rumoured
el **NO-LOAD** normal voltage; speed, but no output
NOMIAL a single term in algebra
NOMISM moral law as basis of conduct
NONAGE immature; minority
ch **NONANE** paraffin hydrocarbon
NONARY group of nine
NON-COM an NCO; under-officer
NON-CON not content
NON-EGO (metaphysics)
NONIUS a graduating instrument
ch **NONOSE** monosaccharide group
ck **NOODLE** simpleton; form of pasta
NOOSED snared; caught; lassooed
NORDIC Scandinavian
gl **NORITE** coarse-grained igneous rock
NORMAL regular; conforming; without deviation; standard
NORMAN of Normandy
hd **NORROY** King at Arms

mn **NOSEAN** a silicate
ga **NO-SIDE** end of a game of Rugby
ar, bd **NOSING** snooping; blunt overhang of stair, sill, roof
NOSISM speaking of self as regal 'we'
bt **NOSTOC** genus of seaweed
lw **NOTARY** official witness of documents
NOTICE see; remark; heed; intimation
NOTIFY warn; advise; apprise
NOTING recording; registering
NOTION idea; belief; theory; concept
NOTOUR notorious (Sc.)
ck **NOUGAT** a sweetmeat
cp **NOUGHT** 0; nought; cypher; zero condition
NOUNAL (noun); of substantive
NOUSLE to nurse; nuzzle
rl **NOVENA** nine days' devotion
NOVENE by nines
NOVICE tyro; neophyte; probationer
NOWAYS in no way
NOWISE nohow
hd **NOWYED** heraldic branches
NOYADE execution by drowning (Fr.)
NOZZLE snout; projecting mouthpiece
NUANCE a subtle distinction
bt **NUBBIN** stunted maize
NUBBLE punch; small lump
NUBBLY bumpy; knotty
NUBIAN of Nubia; Sudanese
NUBILE marriageable
md **NUCHAL** (nape of neck)
NUCLEI cell-centres; cores; kernels
cf **NUCLEO-** of the nucleus (Gr.)
NUCULE a little nut
NUDELY barely; nakedly
NUDGED jogged; poked; pushed
NUDISM NUDIST, naked sun-worshipping
NUDITY nakedness
zo, nt **NUGGAR** mugger; alligator; dhow (Nile)
mn **NUGGET** a lump of gold
go **NULLAH** watercourse; ravine (Ind.)
NUMBED torpid; paralysed; dazed
NUMBER count; compute; figure; identity; amount
tc **NUMBER** code address in network
NUMBLY in a frozen manner
tx **NUMNAH** saddle cloth
NUNCIO Papal representative
NUNCLE mine uncle (Shak.)
tx **NUNOME** mesh fabric
bt **NUPHAR** water-lily
NUPPEN surface droplets glass technique
nm **NURLED** milled like a coin
NURSED fostered; encouraged
NURSER tender; cherisher
NUTANT nodding
bt, ck **NUTMEG** an aromatic kernel
bt **NUT-OIL** paint ingredient
zo **NUTRIA** the fur of the coypu
NUTTER a nut-gatherer
NUZZER a presentation (India)
NUZZLE nousle; fondle
zo **NYLGAU** nilgai; an Indian antelope
zo **NYMPHA** pupa; chrysalis

O

OAFISH idiotic; dull; doltish
ga **OARAGE** rowing
ga **OARING** sculling
bt **OARIUM** an ovary; ovarium
zo **OARLAP** a distinctive rabbit
OBDUCE draw over
bt, fr **OBECHE** African satin/whitewood
OBELUS mark (†); obelisk
OBERON king of the fairies
OBEYED complied; yielded
OBEYER heeder; minder
rl **OBIISM** West Indian witchcraft
OBITER incidentally
OBJECT protest; demur; goal; intent
cp **OBJECT** purpose; thing; (language)
OBJURE to swear
rl **OBLATE** communion wafer-bread
OBLIGE compel; bind; favour; serve
OBLONG longer than broad
mu **OBOIST** oboe-player
nm **OBOLUS** Charon's ferry fee
OBSESS besiege; beset; haunt
OBTAIN get; win; acquire; attain
zo **OBTECT** of pupae unable to move
OBTEST to beseech; supplicate
OBTUND deaden; blunt
OBTUSE dull; stolid; stupid
ma **OBTUSE** open geometrical angle
OBVERT turn toward; to face
OCCAMY silvery alloy
OCCULT mystic; hidden; obscure
OCCUPY fill; possess; inhabit
zo **OCELLI** peacock's 'eyes'
zo **OCELOT** American leopard
bt **OCHREA** cup-shaped plant structure
O'CLOCK on the hour
OCRACY government
ch **OCTANE** petrol purification figure
as **OCTANS** constellation (South Pole)

me, nv **OCTANT** measuring instrument
mu **OCTAVE** ottava; consisting of eight
pr **OCTAVO** (eight leaves to the sheet)
OCTILE octant; eighth of a circle
ps **OCTODE** a thermionic valve
ch **OCTOSE** monosaccharide group
OCTROI monopoly; trade privilege (Fr.)
OCULAR visible
ar **OCULUS** circular office
ODDITY singularity; strangeness
ODIOUS hateful; detested; obnoxious
ODYLIC mesmeric
OECIST founder of Greek colony
md **OEDEMA** localized dropsy; water-retaining cells; obesity; swollen
OEUVRE complete works; artist, writer
OFF-DAY unlucky occasion; free day
OFFEND affront; insult; trespass
rl, tc **OFFICE** post; function; bureau; (holy); (telephone)
nt **OFFING** outer sea; future
OFFISH haughty; snobbish
gl **OFF-LAP** strata conformation
bd **OFFSET** counter-balance; wall ledge; swan neck pipe; accounts; tax
pr **OFFSET** rubber-to-paper process
OGAMIC ancient Irish script
OGDOAD group of 8
OGHAMS ancient Irish alphabet
ar **OGIVAL** arched
OGLING an amorous advance (eyeing)
OGRESS a monstrous lady; giantess
OGRISH orgreish
ga **OH-HELL** card game like whist
bt **OIDIUM** fungus; vine-mildew
pl **OIL-BAG** oil gland
OIL-CAN oil applier
OILERY oilman's stock
ch **OIL-GAS** inflammable gas
OILING lubricating
OIL-MAN oil-dealer
bt **OIL-NUT** butternut
OIL-RIG boring apparatus for oil
OJIBWA puckered moccasins
OLDEST most senile; eldest
OLDISH somewhat ancient
ch **OLEATE** (oleic acid)
ch **OLEFIN** ethylene hydrocarbon
OLEINE liquid fat
ps **OLEOSE** oily; oleic
lw, nt **OLERON** ancient code of sea laws
to **OLIVER** small tilt-hammer; (Roland)
OLIVET mock pearl
OLIVIL gum from the olive tree
md **OLLAMH** ancient Irish doctor
zo **OMASAL** (cow's stomach)
OMASUM ruminant's third stomach
OMBROS madder
OMEDED predicted; augured; presaged
ck **OMELET** omelette; beaten eggs
OMNIFY to render universal
pg **OMNIUM** multi-projector cinema
zo **ONAGER** wild ass; ghorkhar
ONCOME deluge; approach
mn **ONCOST** extraneous mining charges
ONDINE undine; water-spirit
mt **ONDING** fall of rain or snow
ONE-MAN soloist
ONE-TWO successive punches (boxing)
ONE-WAY (traffic); single route
ONEYER (of uncertain origin)
ONFALL storm; attack; assault
ONFLOW gush; on stream
cp **ON-LINE** computer operation
ON-LINE on course; direct hit
mu **ONRUSH** onset; charge
ON-SIDE correct placing (football) (netball)
ONWARD forward; advancing
zo **ONYMAL** (technical group name)
zo **OOCYST** cyst round gametes in protozoa
zo **OOCYTE** cell in meiosis; forming ovum
OODLES quantities; heaps
bl **OOGAMY** union of un-like-sized gametes
OOGENY embryonic development
OOIDAL egg-shaped
mn **OOLITE** a limestone (ovulites)
gl **OOLITH** spherical concretion
OOLOGY the study of birds' eggs
bt, ck **OOLONG** **OULONG**, tea
nt **OOMIAK** kayak, Eskimo boat
zo **OORIAL** wild sheep (India)
zo **OOTYPE** oviduct section
OOZING exuding; seeping; percolating
OPAQUE impermeable to light
OPENED undid; disclosed; revealed
OPENER beginner; cutter
OPENLY publicly; above-board
gn **OPERON** genes in chromosome
mn **OPHITE** porphyry
rl **OPHITE** gnostic serpent-worshipper
ch **OPIANE** narcotine
md **OPIATE** a sedative medicine
OPINED supposed; thought; fancied
OPPOSE prevent; hinder; combat
OPPUGN oppose; obstruct; resist

OPTANT volunteer
OPTICS science of light and vision
OPTIME almost a wrangler
OPTING choosing; co-opting
OPTION choice; wish; selection; right to buy (Am. football)
bt **ORACHE** genus of plants; spinach
ORACLE wiseacre; ambiguous response
ORALLY by word of mouth
bt **ORANGE** Citrus aurantium
ORATED harangued; prated; spouted
ORATOR declaimer; spell-binder
ORBATE bereaved; fatherless
pl **ORBITA** eye-sockets
zo **ORCHIC** of the testis
bt **ORCHID** orchis
bt **ORCHIL** archil; purple dye; a lichen
cf **ORCHIO-** of the testicle (Gr.)
ORCINE lichen dye
ORDAIN prescribe; enjoin; appoint
ORDEAL test; trial; assay; scrutiny
ar **ORDERS** decorated columns
ORDURE excrement
OREIDE imitation gold
md **OREXIS** appetite
md **ORGASM** sexual climax
el **OR-GATE** pulse circuit
br **ORGEAT** liquor (barley)
ORGIES revels; carousals (sexual bouts)
ORIENT eastern; the east
bt, ck **ORIGAN** marjoram (herb)
ORIGIN fount; spring; source; root
pr **ORIHON** continued folded uncut sheet
zo **ORIOLE** a bird species
rl **ORISON** prayer; supplication
ORMULU **ORMOLU**, gilt brass
ORMUZD (Magian system)
ORNATE florid; embellished
ORNERY ordinary; mean; low
mn **OROIDE** alloy; oreide
ch **OROTIC** vitamin B-13; growth acid
ORPHAN child who has lost both parents
ORPHIC (Orpheus)
bt **ORPINE** a yellow plant
ORRERY model of solar system
bt **ORRICE** dried iris root
ORTIVE rising; eastern
zo **OSCINE** of a sub-order of birds
OSCULE small mouth
OSELLA Doge's medal (Venice)
bt **OSIERY** osier-bed
rl **OSIRIS** greatest Egyptian god
mn **OSMIUM** metallic element
me **OSMOLE** unit of osmolic pressure
OSMOSE (diffusion of fluids)
cf **–OSOPHY** belief or doctrine
zo **OSPREY** sea-hawk; an egret plume
pl **OSSEIN** bone-cartilage
OSSIFY to become bone-like; harden to inflexible
OSTEAL pertaining to bone
OSTENT portent; show; appearance
go **OSTIUM** an opening; mouth of river
OSTLER stableman; groom
OSTMEN Danish settlers in Ireland
zo **OSTREA** oyster
md **OTALGY** earache
zo **OTARIA** genus of seals
OTIANT idle; resting
OTIOSE at ease; lazy; idle
md **OTITIS** ear-trouble
mu **OTTAVA** an octave (It.)
OUSTED deposed; ejected; thrown out
OUSTER ejection; dispossession
OUTAGE electrical failure
OUTASK ask for the last time
OUTBAR to shut out
OUTBID offer more; auction; sale
OUTCRY hue; clamour; tumult; bruit
OUTDID excelled; surpassed; exceeded
OUTFIT equipment; clothing
OUTING expedition; trip; holiday
ae **OUTJET** exhaust vent
OUTLAW brigand; bandit; proscribe
OUTLAY expense; disbursement
OUTLET exit; vent; loophole
OUTLIE excel in lying
OUTMAN outnumber
ro **OUTPUT** production; resulting sound; signal
cp **OUTPUT** information from processor
OUTRUN outstrip; beat; surpass; flat, halting terrain; after ski-jump
OUTSET start; beginning; opening
OUTSIT sit longer than
OUTSUM outnumber
OUTTOP over-reach
OUTVIE surpass; out-rival; eclipse
OUTWIT dupe; overreach; circumvent
OVALLY elliptically
OVERBY adjacent
OVERDO carry too far
OVERGO exceed
zo **OVIBOS** musk-ox; buffalo-cow
zo **OVISAC** (ovary)
bt **OVULAR** embryonic
zo **OWLERY** haunt of owls
OWLING smuggling; especially wool
OWLISH as wise an an owl!

OWNING possessing; conceding
ch **OXALIC** an acid; (spinach)
bt **OXALIS** wood sorrel
ch **OXALYL** bivalent acid radical
zo **OXBIRD** the dunlin
zo **OXEOTE** rod-shaped
OX-EYED having large eyes
OXFORD (blue); (shoe); (movement)
OXGALL cleaning/painting agent
OXGANG OXGATE, OXLAND, a bovate; *c.*15 ac./6 ha of land (size cultivable with one ox)
OXHEAD block-head; dolt (Shak.)
bt **OX-HEEL** the setter-wort
OX-HIDE leather
ck **OXTAIL** (soup)
ch **OXYGEN** principal gas in atmosphere
OXYGON a triangle with 2 acute angles
OXYMEL honey and vinegar
zo, ck **OYSTER** shell; pearl; (prairie)
OZALID copy of engineering drawing
md **OZOENA** chronic atrophic rhinitis
OZONIC of ozone

P

PACIFY calm; appease; reconcile
nt **PACING** setting the pace; walking; measuring yards; giring against wind cycle
PACKED crowded; compressed; prearranged fraudulent voting
ce **PACKER** stower; inflatable rubber ring; washer
nt **PACKET** parcel; bale; a mail vessel
go **PADANG** scrub heath (Malaya)
PADDED travelled slowly; (cell); (protective)
PADDER foot-pad; highwayman
nt **PADDLE** canoe oar; wade; to propel (-steamer); semaphore
zo **PADNAG** ambling horse
to **PADSAW** saw blade in toolholder kit
mu **PADUAN** (Padua); the pavan
cf **PAEDIO-** of the feet (Gr.)
ck **PAELLA** rice-seafood dish (Sp.)
cp, pr **PAGING** marking pages; calling (persons); adding data; layout
nm, rl **PAGODA** pagode; temple; (Ind. coin)
lw **PAID-UP** shares; capital; membership
bt **PAIGLE** cowslip
PAINED hurt; distressed; grieved
PAINIM (see Paynim); pagan
PAIRED coupled; yoked; mated; (voting)
PAKEHA white man (Maori)
PALACE ruler's residence; court circles
cf, gl, zo **PALAEO-** of ancient, prehistoric life (Gr.)
zo **PALAMA** toe-webbing
pl **PALATE** roof of mouth; taste-buds
PALELY wanly; ashy; pallidly
PALING a fence; blanching
pt **PALISH** wan; weak colour
PALKEE palanquin (Ind.)
zo **PALLAH** African antelope
rl **PALLAS** Athene, goddess of wisdom
PALLED cloaked; covered (coffin); lost interest
PALLET straw mattress; makeshift bed
PALLID colourless; lifeless
PALLOR paleness
pl **PALMAR** (hand) palm, sole (hand/foot), volar
PALMED concealed; conjured away; stolen
rl **PALMER** pilgrim (with palm leaf)
md **PALMUS** palpitation; twitching
zo **PALOLO** edible worm
zo **PALPAL PALPED**, (antennae-like feelers)
zo **PALPUS** feeler of an insect
PALTER dodge; shuffle; prevaricate
PALTRY mean; petty; despicable
bt, go **PAMPAS** treeless plains; grasses (S.America)
bt, go **PAMPER** indulge; coddle; humour
ck **PANADA** bread pulp
PANAMA sun-hat
PANARY store-house for bread; pantry
PANDER a procurer; cater to (tastes)
PANDIT pundit; a learned man
PANDUR robber; Austrian soldier
ck **PANFRY** method of cooking
ck **PANFUL** filling a pan
PANGED emotionally upset
PANISC Pan as a satyr
PANMUG crockery; butter-pan
mn **PANNED** yielded
PANNEL rustic saddle
PANNER a nagger; faultfinder (gold)
md **PANNUS** birthmark; a dressing
nt **PANSHI** sailing dugout (Bengal)
PANTED gasped; blew; palpitated
zo **PANTER** a snare; panther
PANTON a special kind of horseshoe
PANTRY food storage closet
PANZER armoured corps (Ger.); panser
rl **PAPACY** (pope); popery

md **PAPAIN** disgestive enzyme
bt **PAPAYA** large sub-tropical fruit; pawpaw
PAPERY resembling paper
PAPISH characteristic of Popes
rl **PAPISM** papal doctrine; authority
PAPIST pro-Pope; Roman Catholic
bt **PAPPUS** hairy tuft
PAPUAN from New Guinea
md **PAPULA** pimple
PAPYRI scrolls of papyrus (Egypt)
PARADE show; display; flaunt
go **PARAMO** wind-swept desert in Andes
PARANG heavy Malay knife
PARAPH a flourish to a signature
PARASE movements (fencing)
PARCAE the Fates
lw **PARCEL** packet; bundle; piece; share; (land)
PARDON remit; condone; forgive
PARDON mercy
PAREIL an equal
PARENT author; producer; cause
ck **PAREVE** made without animal products
PARFAY! by, or in, faith!
PARGET plaster decoration
zo **PARIAH** social outcast
PARIAN (marble); (porcelain)
zo **PARINE** pertaining to titmouse (bird)
PARING rind; shaving; reducing
rl **PARISH** church district
cp **PARITY** equality; parage; check on transfer of data
el **PARITY** space; reflection; symmetry
au **PARKED** (left); (cars)
PARKER park-keeper; (nosey-)
ck **PARKIN** perkin; Lancashire cake
PARLAY expand; exploit
PARLEY confer, discuss; talk
PARODY travesty; burlesque; caricature
PAROLE word of honour
zo **PAROUS** offspring liveborn (mammals)
ar **PARPEN** **PARPEND, PARPENT,** transverse 2-faced stone in wall
nt **PARRAL** **PARREL,** collar to prevent spars from slipping from the mast
zo **PARROT** repeat by rote; talking bird
me **PARSEC** interstellar distance unit
PARSED analysed grammatically
PARSEE Persian living in India
rl **PARSON** vicar; clergyman
zo **PARTAN** crab (Sc.)
PARTED left; broke; separated
PARTER distributor; sharer
PARTIM in part
PARTLY not altogether
PARURE set of jewels
rl, ar **PARVIS** court; portico
ga **PASAKA** form of play (pelota)
PASCAL unit of pressure of newton unit
PASSED ignored; spent; elapsed
PASSEE faded (Fr.)
PASSER a passer-by
PASSIM here and there
PASTED basted; gummed
PASTEL crayon; chalk drawing
md **PASTIL** medicated lozenge
rl, zo **PASTOR** shepherd; starling
ck **PASTRY** confiserie
PATCHY unequal standard; mottled
lw **PATENT** proprietary; copyright
PATENT an open fact; truth; (letters-)
PATERA shallow circular dish; ornament
PATHAN tribe of Afghanistan, Pakistan
md **-PATHIC** of diseases
PATHOS deep emotion
nt **PATILE** Ganges barge, India
ar **PATINA** glow given by age; oxidized, lead, bronze effect
rl **PATINE** paten; eucharistic plate
ga **PATLID** stone at start (curling)
PATOIS dialect (Fr.)
PATROL mobile armed guard; police unit
rl **PATRON** customer; supporter; saint
PATTED congratulated; tapped
PATTEN clog (Dutch wooden shoe)
PATTER high speed talk; rain sound
pl **PAUNCH** the belly (obese)
PAUPER indigent person
PAUSAL ceasing; pausing
PAUSED hesitated; halted; tarried
PAUSER a deliberator; a demurer
PAVAGE paving cost
mu **PAVANE** **PAVAN,** court dance
PAVIER **PAVIOR, PAVER,** pavement layer
PAVING surfacing (crazy) (street)
PAVISE great shield
PAWING clawing; touching (rudely)
PAWNED pledged; risked; hazarded
PAWNEE N. American Indian tribe
PAWNEE pawnbroker
PAWNER a borrower on security (possessions)
bt **PAWPAW** papaw; a tropical fruit
zo **PAXWAX** tendon; faxwax
nt **PAYANG** fishing boat (Malaya)

PAY-BOX public coin call box; telephone
PAY-DAY day when wages paid
PAYING gainful; punishing; tarring
PAYNIM painim; infidel; heathen
nt, pc **PAY-OFF** payment; denouement; side-benefits; spin-off
PAYOLA bribe to mention on media
PEACHY like a peach
bt **PEACOD** pea-pod
zo **PEAHEN** a peafowl
PEAKED reached highest form
PEALED resounded; reverberated
bt **PEANUT** the ground-nut
mn **PEA-ORE** oxide of iron
bt **PEA-POD** pea seed envelope
PEARLY transparent; translucent
mn **PEBBLE** a stone; an agate
PEBBLY shingly
PECKED struck (birds); nagged (hen-)
zo **PECKER** woodpecker; courage; mouth; beak; penis
cp **PECKER** tape reader sensing voice
zo **PECTEN** bivalve genus; scallop
zo **PECTEN** eye membrane of a bird
PECTIC congealing; gelatinizing
PECTIN (apple jelly)
zo **PECTUS** insect sclerite; vertebrate breast
rl **PEDALE** altar foot-cloth
PEDANT schoolmaster; precise person
bt **PEDATE** divided like a foot
PEDDLE to sell retail; to trifle; to hawk (drugs)
PEDION single-plane crystal
PEDLAR PEDLER, hawker; vendor; bagman
PEELED stripped; skinned; pillaged
ck **PEELER** policeman (Sir Robert Peel); perfect wave (surfing); rind, skin remover
PEEPED chirped; glimpsed; snooped
zo **PEEPER** (chicken); the eye
bt **PEEPUL** sacred tree; Indian bo-tree
PEERER a peeping Tom
PEERIE peg-top (Sc.)
PEEVED annoyed; fretful
zo **PEEWIT** green plover; lapwing
PEGGED fixed; toiled
PEG-LEG wooden leg
PEG-TOP a spinning top
zo **PELAGE** animal fur
PELIKE double-handled Greek vase
PELION and Ossa, mountains
jn **PELLET** small ball or shot; wood cover over screw
PELMET curtain housing
ga **PELOTA PELOTE**, a Basque ball game
PELTER rainstorm; shower of missiles
PELTRY skins with fur on them
pl **PELVIC** (pelvis)
pl **PELVIS** skeletal cavity (hips)
PENCIL light rays; small brush (graphite pen)
PENDED held up; balanced
PENFUL contents of a pen
pl **PENIAL** pertaining to penis; phallic
PENMAN scribe; author; clerk
PENNAL freshman (Ger.); student
PENNED wrote; indited; enclosed
PENNER writer; scribe
nt **PENNON** pennant; flag; streamer
PENSEE thought (Fr.) (literature)
PENSUM an imposition; examination
PENTAD set of five
PENT-UP confined; mewed
PENULT last but one
PENURY need; want; indigence
PEOPLE mob; rabble; populace; nation
PEPITA nugget of gold (Sp.)
bt **PEPLIS** water-purslane
PEPLUM PEPLUS, robe worn by Greek women
bt, ck **PEPPER** pelt with shot; capsicum, (cayenne) condiment
md **PEPSIN** (gastric juice)
PEPTIC digestive
PERDIE! pardieu!
PERDUE perdu; hidden; concealed
PERIOD age; era; term; epoch; stage
PERISH die; wither; expire; pass
PERKED smartened up; received extra benefits; encouraged
ck **PERKIN** perry; see parkin
PERMIT let; grant; sanction; tolerate
zo **PERNIS** honey-buzzard
PERONE fibula
PERRON external stairway
PERSIC Persian
PERSON individual; party; someone
PERTLY impudently; saucily
PERUKE a periwig; a vallancy
PERUSE read; scrutinize; observe
PESADE an equine evolution
nm **PESETA** Spanish money
PESHWA Mahratta chief (India)
PESTER vex; worry; harass; nettle
PESTLE for grinding with mortar
PETARD explosive machine; bomb
PETARY a peat-bog
PETITE small (Fr.); short and trim figure

zo **PETREL** sea-bird
ch **PETROL** gasoline
PETTED fondled; caressed; indulged
PETTLE indulge (Sc.)
PEWTER an alloy of tin and lead
bt **PEYOTE** cactus; source of mescalin
bt **PEZIZA** cup-shaped fungi
PHANIC visible; obvious
PHAROS lighthouse; world wonder (Gr.)
bt, ck **PHASEL** French bean
PHASIS **PHASE**, a stage of development
zo **PHASMA** leaf insects, etc.
PHATIC of speech as mood implement
ch **PHENIC** carbolic
PHENOL carbolic acid
ch **PHENYL** an organic radical
zo **PHINOC** sea trout
PHLEGM calmness; indifference
md **PHLEME** lancet
bt **PHLEUM** cat's-tail grass, etc.
bt **PHLOEM** bast tissue
md, cf **PHOBIA** morbid fear or aversion (Gr.)
PHOBOS a satellite of Mars
zo **PHOCAL** (seal)
rl **PHOEBE** the moon-goddess
zo **PHOLAS** stone-boring molluscs
PHONED telephoned
PHONEY specious; sham; bogus
cf **-PHONIA** of vocal disorder (Gr.)
PHONIC phonetic
me, ps **PHONON** quantum of thermal energy
md **PHORIA** lack of eye coordination
PHOSSY caused by phosphorus
cf **-PHOTIC** concerning light (Gr.)
me **PHOTON** unit of light energy
mu **PHRASE** idiom; diction; style; theme; motif; melody
bl **PHYLON** **PHYLUM**, biological group
bt, md **PHYSIC** dose; drug; medicine
cf **PHYSIO-** of the physical, body (Gr.)
ch **PHYTIC** of a cereal acid
PHYTON bud
PIACLE sin, crime
PIAFFE a horse gait (Sp.)
PIAZZA square; market place (It.)
PICARD high shoe (Fr.)
ch **PICENE** coal-tar hydrocarbon
PICKED selected; (pickpockets); taken
ag **PICKER** selector; collector; gatherer (fruit-)
PICKET sharp stake; guard; range-pole; striker at gate; railing (Am. football)
ck **PICKLE** to preserve in spices; jumbled
ro **PICK-UP** person of easy virtue; (motoring)
PICNIC alfresco meal
ch **PICRIC** trinitro-phenol; lyddite
PIDGIN merged version made of two (or more) languages
PIECED mended; joined; augmented
PIECER patcher
PIEDOG **PYEDOG**, a pariah; outcast
PIEMAN (Simple Simon); meatpies vendor
PIERCE drill; bore; perforate
zo **PIERID** of certain butterfly group
PIFFLE nonsense; worthless task
zo **PIGEON** a town dove; tell tale; sneak
PIGGIN small bowl
zo **PIGLET** **PIGLING**, a young porker
bt **PIGNON** pine seed
bt, ck **PIGNUT** carrot
PIG-STY pig enclosure
ck **PILAFF** **PILAV**, rice dish; savoury
pl **PILARY** hairy; comate
zo **PILEUM** top of head in birds
PILE-UP crash (motoring)
bt **PILEUS** mushroom cap
PILFER purloin; filch; steal; rob
PILING amassing; stacking; heaping
ar, mo **PILLAR** post; column; support; rock pinnacle
PILLED black-balled; vetoed; rejected
PILLOW a block; bearing; bed cushion
PILOSE **PILOUS**, hairy; comate
md **PILULA** **PILULE**, a small pill
PI-MODE multicavity magnetron operation
md **PIMPLE** a pustule; acne
PIMPLY having pimples
bt **PINANG** betel nut
wv **PINCOP** weft in power loom
PINDAR Greek poet
PINDER pinner; impounder
bt **PINEAL** like a pine-cone
ch **PINENE** terpene
bt **PINERY** hothouse
ro **PINGED** whistled by; bleeped (signalled)
PINGLE dawdle
PINING languishing; losing vigour
PINION feather; cogwheel; disable; bind fast
mn **PINITE** (iolite)
PINKED motoring (petrol effect)
PINNED fastened
PINNER pinmaker; pinder

PINNET pinnacle (Sc.)
PINOLE meal of sorts (USA)
nt **PINTLE** iron bolt
PINXIT he painted it (artist's name)
PIPAGE pipe-distribution
PIPING boiling; shrill; feeble
PIPKIN boiler; small pot
ck **PIPPED** pilled; just defeated; de-stoned
bt **PIPPIN** apple
PIQUED offended; irritated
ga **PIQUET** card game; picket
PIRACY buccaneering; (copyright)
PIRATE freebooter; corsai; picaroon
nt **PIRAUA PIROGUE**, canoe, Atlantic coast
PIRNIE night cap (Sc.)
bt **PISANG** plantain; banana
PISCES the fishes (Zodiac sign)
bt **PISTIL** part of flower
PISTOL a fire-arm
au, mu **PISTON** part of engine; valve (horn)
rl **PITAKA** Buddhist scriptures
PITCHY black; dark; tarry
PITHED central nervous system destroyed
PITHOS round Greek vase
PITIED commiserated
PITIER a compassionate party
PITMAN a miner
to **PITSAW** large saw
ck **PITTED** pock-marked; challenged; de-stoned
PLACED invested; ascribed; put
PLACER auriferous gravel
PLACET Latin affirmation; 'so be it'
PLACID serene; calm; even; tranquil
mu **PLAGAL** (Gregorian music)
PLAGUE pest; contagion; pester
PLAGUY vexatious; harassing
zo **PLAICE** flat fish
lw **PLAINT** lamentation; dirge; wail
zo **PLAISE** plaice
PLANCH to cover with planks
el, me **PLANCK** unit of action, one joule second
PLANED smoothed; (aeroplane)
to **PLANER** planing machine
as **PLANET** a celestial body (solar system)
zo **PLANTA** vertebrate foot sole
PLAQUE commemorative mark; an ornament
md **PLAQUE** destructive coating on teeth
PLASHY sloppy
PLASMA ionised substance at solar gas state temperature for nuclear fusion purposes
md **PLASMA** quartz; blood liquids in cells
bt **PLATAN** plane tree
PLATED overlaid; armoured
ce **PLATEN** the roller of a typewriter; molten steel plates
zo **PLATER** race-horse
PLATEY flat
PLAYED sported; trifled; acted
mu **PLAYER** professional crickets
PLEACH interweave
PLEASE like; prefer; delight; oblige
PLEDGE promise; security for such; pawn; toast
as **PLEIAD** a star
zo **PLEION** flat platelike structure
PLENTY abundance; profusion
PLENUM space; a full assembly
md **PLEURA** (lungs)
lw **PLEVIN** assurance
PLEXOR hammer used with pleximeter
md **PLEXUS** nerve centre
PLIANT flexible; limber; lithe; facile
to **PLIERS PLYERS**, pincers for wire work
PLIGHT promise; dilemma; predicament
ar **PLINTH** pedestal
tx **PLISSE** pleated/woven cloth with shirred effect
PLONGE superior slope of parapet
PLOUGH plow; furrow; to pluck
zo **PLOVER** bird
ag **PLOWED** ploughed; failed (examination)
PLUCKY courageous; brave; bold
PLUFFY puffy (Sc.)
el, ro, cp **PLUG-IN** connect; detachable unit
PLUMAE stiff feathers
PLUMED took pride in
PLUMPY plump; fat; burly
PLUNGE dip; dive; sink; souse; (Am. football)
PLURAL more than one
tx **PLUSHY** like plush (material)
PLUTUS the god of wealth
to **PLYERS** pliers
PLYING practising (trade); supplying
PLYING action of ferry boat
PLYING for hire (taxis); thread twisting
mu **PNEUMA** breath; spirit; florid passage
cf **PNEUMA-** of air, respiration (lung) (Gr.)
POACHY set and soft
md **POCKED** pitted; scarred

POCKET pouch; cavity; (pick-); (thief)
PODERE country estate, farm (It.)
to **PODGER** tightening wrench for tubular coupling
bt **PODIAL** stalk-like
zo **PODITE** lobster's limb
bt **PODIUM** pedestal; rostrum; stylobate
gl **PODZOL PODSOL**, leached subpolar strata (Russian)
POETIC lyrical; metrical
POETRY poesy; verse
rl **POGROM** plunder and massacre (Rus.); persecution (of minorities)
POINTE tip of toes (ballet)
nt, rw **POINTS** switch-point, features of horse; score; angles; of compass, 32
POISED suspended in equilibrium
POISER a balancer
POISON venom; evil; kill (-gas) (-pen)
POKING thrusting
POLACK a Pole
ag, go **POLDER** reclaimed; drained land (Holland)
POLICE constabulary
POLICY statesmanship; strategy; plan
POLING scaffolding; punting
POLISH furbish; burnish; lustre
POLISH pertaining to Poland
POLITE courtly; urbane; civil
POLITY the constitution
lw **POLLAM** jurisdiction of Ind. chief
zo **POLLAN** a salmon-type of Irish fish
POLLED cropped; lopped; voted
bt **POLLEN** flower seed; fine bran
POLLER voter; tree-trimmer
md **POLLEX** thumb
POLLUX twin brother of Castor
ck **POLONY** sausage
ch **POLYAD** polygamous element
md, zo **POLYPE** polyp; aquatic animal; growth
POMACE crushed fruit
POMADE perfumed hair unguent
bt **POMELO** a citrus fruit; shaddock
POMMEL part of saddle; belabour
to, bd **POMMEL** flattener mallet (punner); knob; globular boss or knob; drum (American Indians)
mu **POMMER** ancient bassoon (shawn)
POMONA goddess of fruit
POM-POM quick-firing gun battery
POMPON ornament; a tuft
PONCHO cloak (S. America)
PONDER weigh; meditate; ruminate
PONENT western
tx **PONGEE** soft woven silk
rl **PONGYI** Buddhist priest (Burma)
gs, to **PONTEE** pontil; punty
PONTIC (Black Sea)
to **PONTIL** glass-maker's iron rod
PONTON lighter; pontoon
zo **POODLE** curly-haired dog
mu **POOGYE** nose-flute (Ind.)
POOLED shared; amalgamated
le **POOLER** leather worker
POONAC pulp refuse
POOPED overtaken by a wave (from aft)
POORER more impecunious; inferior (quality)
POORLY indisposed; unwell
POPERY Roman Catholicism
POPGUN an air gun of sorts
POPISH of Catholics; denigratory
bt **POPLAR** genus of trees; abele
tx **POPLIN** silk-cotton mix; shiny cotton
POPPED pawned; proposed; exploded
POPPER a pistol; popcorn; amyl nitrate, drug; plug; (angling)
POPPET puppet; head of a lathe
POPPLE to bob about
zo **PORGIE** bream fish
PORING sweating; brooding; studying
PORISM corollary
mn **PORITE** a species of coral
zo **PORKER** young pig
bt **POROID** having obvious pores
bt **POROSE** of pore-pierced cell walls
gl **POROUS** porose; interstitial limestone
bt **PORRET** small onion; leek
PORRON wine bottle with descending spout
PORTAL gate; entry; entrance
nt **PORTED** conveyed
PORTER door-keeper; carrier
PORTLY burly; stout; imposing
POSADA a Spanish inn (hotel)
POSEUR poser; an affected person (Fr.)
POSING feigning; puzzling; posturing
POSNET small bowl
ck **POSSET** a bedtime drink; potion
zo **POSSUM** opossum
POSTAL (order); (Union); (mail)
POSTEA record of subsequent events
POSTED set; stationed; hastened
POSTER bill; placard; advertisement; ball against goal-post (Am. football)

POSTIL marginal note; a homily
br **POT-ALE** distillery refuse
br **POTALE** grain refuse
ch **POTASH** alkali; potassium
bt **POTATO** murphy; a tuber
POTBOY a junior tapster; barman; bottle-washer
ck **POTEEN** home-made spirits (Irish)
POTENT efficacious; powerful; cogent
POTHER bother; bristle; fuss; ado
POTION dose; draught; philter
ck **POT-LID** a cover; stone on tee (curling)
POTMAN barman; general factotum
POTTAH lease (Ind.)
POTTED preserved; abbreviated
POTTER clay craftsman
me **POTTLE** 4 pints (2.2 litres); a tankard
POTTLE a small basket for fruit
POUDRE powdered (Fr.)
POUFFE a cushion (Fr.)
zo **POULPE** octopus; poulp
POUNCE jump suddenly; snatch; seize; prey
zo **POUNCE** claw of a bird of prey
POUNCE fine blotting powder
POURED uttered; flowed; gushed
POURER the lady of the tea-pot
POUSSE bitters added to a drink
POUTED registered displeasure facially
zo **POUTER POWTER**, pigeon having an inflated breast
POWDER crush; pulverize; sprinkle; ideal light snow surface (skiing)
POW-WOW incantation; conference (American Indian)
PRAISE laud; extol; eulogize; encomium
PRANCE to bound; to spring
ck **PRANZO** meal (It.)
PRATED orated; gabbled; talked
PRATER a chatter-box
PRAXIS use; practice; an example
PRAYED supplicated; craved; besought
PRAYER petition; entreaty; orison
PREACH teach; exhort; declare
rl **PRECIS** prayers
PRECIS summary; abstract
PRECUT ready-sliced; -shaped (portions)
PREDAL rapacious; voracious; ravenous
ar **PREFAB** a prefabricated house
PREFER pick; select; choose; promote
PREFIX appoint beforehand; word; code qualifier
PREPAY pay in advance
cf **PRESBY-** of old, aged (Gr.)
PRESEE foresee; anticipate; foretell
PRESES chairman (Sc.)
mu **PRESTO** quickly; (conjuror) (It.)
cf **PRETER-** beyond
lw **PRETOR PRAETOR**, Roman judge
PRETTY neat; comely; pleasing
PRETTY the fairway of a golf course
PRE-WAR from before a war
PREYED ravened; ravaged; despoiled
PREYER a plunderer; freebooter
PRICED appraised; valued
PRICEY expensive
PRIDED plumed; arrogated
rl **PRIEST** pastor; divine; minister
PRIMAL primary; main; first; original
pt **PRIMER** detonator; pre-paint; text-book
pr **PRIMER** prayer-book; type of type
bt **PRIMET PRIVET**, shrub
PRIMLY precisely; formally; demurely
rl **PRIMUS** bishop (Sc.); first
PRINCE heir to sovereign; ruler; lord
rl **PRIORY** monastery
PRISED prized; levered; (opened)
PRISMY prismatic
PRISON jail; gaol; quod; restrain
bt **PRIVET** genus of shrub; primet
PRIZED valued; esteemed
PRIZER an appraiser
ch, tx **PROBAN** flameproof fabric finish
PROBUD reproductive bodies in cyclo-myaria
PROFIT gain; benefit; advantage
PROKER a poker (dial.)
pl **PROLAN** mammal pregnancy hormone
zo **PROLEG** a caterpillar's leg
PROLIX long-winded; verbose
PROMPT urge; incite; quick; apt
cp **PROMPT** message from system to operator; (theatre) (cues)
PRONTO precipitately; at once!
zo **PROPED** pseudo-leg
PROPEL hurl; cast; throw; impel
PROPER correct; accurate; seemly
PROSED conversed in lengthy periods
PROSER tedious speaker
PROSIT! here's luck! a toast! (Germ.)
bt **PROTEA** S. African flowering shrubs
PROTON electrical nucleus
PROVED tested; verified; established

PROVEN proved; justified
PROVER demonstrator; assayer
PRUINA powdery bloom on plant surfaces
PRUNED trimmed; clipped; lopped
bt **PRUNUS** genus of trees and shrubs
nm **PRUTAH** Israeli coin
PRYING peeping; curious; inquisitive
cp **PSEUDO** false; spurious; imitation; a pre-machine code
md **PSORIC** (psora); itchy
PSYCHE maiden beloved by Cupid; soul; mind
cf, pc **PSYCHO-** of mind; psyche (Gr.)
zo **PTERIC** of wing or shoulder
bt **PTERIS** fern genus
zo **PTERNA** heel-pad in birds
PTERON Greek portico
PTOSIS (fallen eyelid)
bt **PTYXIS** leaf-folding in bud
PUBLIC open; common; general
PUCKER wrinkle; crease; furrow
PUDDLE muddy pool; (iron)
PUDDLY dirty; foul; bespattered
PUDEUR sexual modesty (Fr.)
PUEBLO S. American town or village (Sp.)
PUENTE carved trestle table (Spain)
PUFFED fuffed; blown
zo, nt, rw **PUFFER** globe-fish; coastal steam cargo vessel (Sc.) (loco)
zo **PUFFIN** bird; an auk
zo **PUG-DOG** a lap-dog
PUGREE Indian hat scarf
PUISNE inferior in rank
PUKKHA pucka; real (Ind.)
PULING whimpering; whining
PULLED drawn; hauled; extracted
PULLER hauler; an attraction
zo **PULLET** young hen
to **PULLEY** grooved wheel; tackle (crane)
PULL-IN **PULL-UP**, roadside halt
PULL-ON boxing gloves
PULPED **PULPER**, mashed; machine-shredded
rl **PULPIT** rostrum; ambo
ck **PULQUE** a Mexican beverage
as **PULSAR** space radio-energy source
PULSED throbbed; vibrated
PULTUN native infantry regiment (Ind.)
PULVIL scented powder
ar **PULVIN** dosseret, supercapital (Byzant.)
nt **PULWAR** sailing dugout, cargo boat Ind.
PUMELO pomelo; shaddock; fruit
bd, mn, gl **PUMICE** spongy lava; powder (pounce) for stencils; -stone
PUMPED forced transfer of liquids, gas; interrogated (tyres) (-dry); exhausted
PUMPER cross-examiner; pump man
PUNCHI Kashmiri people
PUNCHY fat; stocky
ga **PUNCTO** point (fencing); punctual
PUNDIT savant; wiseacre; guru; authority
bt **PUNICA** pomegranate
PUNIER weaker; feebler; smaller
PUNISH correct; chasten; scourge
PUNKAH fan (Ind.)
to **PUNNER** a ram; maul; word-joker
PUNNET basket for fruit
PUNTED betted; kicked
PUNTER gambler
zo **PUPATE** from caterpillar to pupa
zo **PUPOID** like a chrysalis
PUPPED whelped; littered
PUPPET doll; marionette; pawn
rl **PURANA** sacred Sanskrit books
PURDAH curtain; seclusion
PURELY simply; clearly; really
PUREST without blemish
tx **PURFLE** embroider
PURFLY wrinkled
PURGED cleaned; purified; shriven
PURGER an aperient; laxative
PURIFY cleanse; clean
ch **PURINE** uric acid compound, toxin
PURISM precision; nicety; exactness
PURIST stickler for style
PURITY chastity; fineness; simplicity
PURLED curled; swirled; knitted
PURLER a fall; a cropper
PURLIN a roof timber
rl **PURPLE** colour; dye; mollusc; imperial; cardinalate
PURPLE ornate (prose); rhetorical
PURRED curred, (cats or pigeons)
PURSED contracted; wrinkled
nt **PURSER** paymaster; supply chief
PURSUE follow; track; chase; practise
PURVEY sell; cater; retail; procure
PUSHED urged; impelled; jostled
nt, rw **PUSHER** type of plane; thruster; tugboat; locomotive
PUSHER thruster; salesman; street hawker
PUSH-IN gatecrash; struggle; (hockey)
PUSHTU Afghan tongue
bt **PUSULE** small plant vacuole
PUTEAL well-curb
nt **PUTELI** Ganges boat

PUTLOG short board; putlock
ga **PUT-OUT** irritated; thwarted; laid; displayed; dismissed (cricket, baseball)
PUTRID corrupt; rotten; decaying
PUTSCH revolt attempt (Ger.)
ga **PUTTED** took short green shot (golf)
PUTTEE cloth legging
PUTTER a golf club
tx **PUTTOO** goat's-wool cloth
PUZZLE bewilder; enigma; problem
PUZZLE a solver's delight (jigsaw) (crossword-)
bt **PYCNID** (fungus' spores)
mu **PYCNON** a semi-tone
zo **PYEDOG** piedog; a pariah
md **PYEMIA** blood-poisoning
md **PYEMIC** septicaemic
zo **PYGARG** antelope (Herodotus)
zo **PYGARG** osprey or sea-eagle
md **PYKNIC** fat (of persons)
zo **PYLOME** opening in sarcodina
md **PYOSIS** formation of pus
bt **PYRENE** fruit stone
ch **PYRENE** tar product
mn **PYRITE** a shining mineral; (poor man's gold)
md **PYROLA** wintergreen
ch **PYRONE** heterocyclic compound
mn **PYROPE** garnet
PYTHIA Delphic oracle priestess
zo **PYTHON** serpent (slain by Apollo)
md **PYURIA** pus in urine

Q

QIVIUT underneath hair of musk-ox (Inuit)
QUADRA square frame or border
zo **QUAGGA** extinct zebra (S. Africa)
QUAGGY boggy; marshy
zo **QUAHOG** clam (N. America)
QUAICH QUAIGH, drinking cup; tassie (Sc.)
QUAINT droll; fantastic; curious; odd
QUAKED shook; quivered; rocked
QUAKER member of Society of Friends
QUALLY wine that has gone off
QUANTA (plural of quantum) a quantity of anything
QUARRY pit; prey; victim; an arrow
QUARTE guard (fencing)
pr **QUARTO** a size of book
mn **QUARTZ** silica (double refracting)
ps, ch **QUARTZ** crystal with varying polarization
as **QUASAR** far-space radio-energy source
mu **QUAVER** quiver; tremble; vibrate; ⅛ note
bd, nt **QUAYED** having a wharf; jettied
QUBBAH domed tomb (Arabic)
QUEASY squeamish; fastidious
zo **QUEEST** ring-dove
zo **QUELEA** weaver-bird
QUENCH extinguish (fire); slake (thirst)
QUERRY equerry; groom; courtier
zo **QUESAL QUEZAL**, resplendent trogon; brilliant green bird
QUEUED lined up (waited turn)
ck **QUICHE** egg flan with savoury filling
QUIDAM somebody (Lat.)
QUIHYE Anglo-Indian (Bengal)
bt **QUILCH** couch grass
zo **QUILLS** feather pens, porcupine spikes
bt, ck **QUINCE** fruit (jelly)
md **QUINIC** (quinine)
bt **QUINOA** Mexican oats
pg **QUINOL** reducing agent
md **QUINSY** tonsilitis
QUINTA manor, large farm (wine grower's) (Portugal)
ga **QUINZE** card game (of 15)
pr, mu **QUIRED** in quires; sang in harmony
QUIRKY evasive; artful; illusive
bt **QUITCH** couch grass
QUIVER case for arrows; vibrate
nt **QUODDY** open fishing boat (Maine, N. America)
ar, bd **QUOINS** dressed corner stones
ga **QUOITS** ring-throwing game (deck)
lw **QUORUM** sufficiency of attendance
QUOTED referred; repeated; mentioned
QUOTER a citer
QUOTHA forsooth
QUOTUM share; proportion
Q-VALUE the amount of energy produced in nuclear reaction

R

RABATE beat down; abatement
RABATO turned-down collar; rebato (It.)
rl **RABBAN** super-rabbi
cr **RABBET** a groove in a plank
RABBIN Jewish lawyer or rabbi
zo **RABBIT** timid breeder and burrower; weak player; lesser person
me **RABBLE** the mob; iron puddling bar

md, vt **RABIES** canine (human) hydrophobia
bt **RACEME** a cluster
bt, zo **RACHIS** backbone; spine
RACIAL ethnic; colour judgement
RACILY piquantly; spicily; pungently
ga **RACING** speed contest (men, horses, cars, etc.)
RACISM ethnic or colour superiority attitude
RACKED strained; wrestled; stretched; (storage)
RACKER a torturer; storer
RACKET snow-shoe; clamour; (tennis) broad bat; fraud
RACKLE rattle; crackle
cp **RACK-UP** video information; lines ascending
RADDLE twist; red ochre
nt **RADEAU** scow defence ship (N. Amer.)
RADIAL extending outward from a centre
RADIAN an angle of 57.3 degrees
bt **RADISH** plant
mn **RADIUM** metal
bt, md **RADIUS** bone of forearm; half a diameter
RADIUS crane load formula based distance
nt **RADOUB** recaulking of ship's hull
zo **RADULA** mollusc's tongue
RAFALE burst of fire; squall
RAFFED swept; huddled together
nt **RAFFEE** schooner sail
bt **RAFFIA** palm fibre
RAFFLE sweeptstake; draw; lottery
bd, nt **RAFTER** roof-timber; lumberman (river)
RAG DAY students' carnival
tx **RAGBAG** odd scraps of fabric
RAGGED jagged; uneven; torn
RAGGED bullied; persecuted
bt **RAGGEE** Indian millet
RAGGLE notch irregularly; raglet
RAGING wroth; rabid; furious; storm
RAGLAN loose overcoat style
ar, bd **RAGLET** narrow masonry groove
RAGMAN rag-picker
ck **RAGOUT** stew; a spicy mixture
RAG-TAG riff-raff
hd **RAGULY** jagged
RAIBLE rabble (Sc.)
RAIDER invader; plunderer (sudden) (night) (cops)
RAILER scoffer; sneerer
RAISER producer
bt, ck **RAISIN** a dried grape
RAJPUT Royal Hindu
RAKERY debauchery
RAKING inclining; enfilading
RAKISH dissolute; licentious
zo **RALLUS** water-rails; etc.; birds
bt **RAMAGE** boughs of tree
nv **RAMARK** non-directional radio beacon
RAMBLE excursion; stroll; roam (on foot)
zo **RAM-CAT** tom-cat (male)
bt **RAMEAL** branching
bt **RAMENT** bristle-shaped leaflet
RAMIFY branch; divide; sub-divide
RAMISM system of logic
ae **RAMJET** open duct combustion
RAMMED butted; crammed
RAMMEL refuse wood
to **RAMMER** sand-packing hand tool
bt **RAMOON** mulberry (W. Indies)
RAMOUS branched
RAMPED bounded; sprang; sloped
RAMPER race-course rough
RAMROD gun-bore stuffer
bt **RAMSON** hedgerow garlic
bt **RAMULE** small branch
RANCHO ranch; stock farm
RANCID sour; musty; fetid
nt **RANDAN** a row boat
RANDLE plate rack
RANDOM casual; haphazard; fortuitous
cp **RANDOM** numbers production
RANGED extended; disposed
fr **RANGER** forest guard (parks); commando; (free-) rover
zo **RANGIA** a bivalve genus
zo **RANINE** frog-like
RANKER fouler; officer from the ranks
RANKLE resent; remain bitter
RANKLY rampantly; excessively
RANSOM money to free a hostage
RANTAN clatter of pots and pans
RANTER spouter; boisterous preacher
md **RANULA** frog-tongue
bt **RAPHIA** raffia; palm fibre
bt **RAPHIS** crystal in plant cell
mu, rw **RAPIDO** with rapidity; express
RAPIER a thrusting sword
RAPINE pillage; spoliation; plunder; rape
RAPING ravishing; violating
RAPPED tapped; struck
RAPPEE snuff
RAPPEL call to arms
nm **RAPPEN** Swiss centime (coin)

RAPPER knocker; arouser (disasters)
zo **RAPTOR** a bird of prey
RAPTUS trance; seizure
RAREFY attenuate
RARELY seldom; infrequently
RAREST sparsest; thinnest; scarcest
RARITY scarcity; fewness; tenuity
RASANT flanking; raking
RASCAL rogue; scamp; knave; caitiff
ck **RASHER** to thin slice (bacon); more reckless
RASHLY audaciously; recklessly
bd **RASING** razing; levelling; demolishing
RASPED filed; abraded; grated
RASPER scraper; stiff fence
tv **RASTER** beam picture on screen; video signal
bt **RATANY** Peruvian shrub
tx **RATEEN** ratteen; woollen fabric
RATHER sooner; preferably; slightly
RATIFY confirm; endorse; approve
tx **RATINE** rough-surface dress fabric
nt **RATING** tonnage; class; seaman; popularity scale; (rowing)
RATION share; quota; portion
zo **RATITE** flat-breasted
nt, tx **RATLIN** (shrouds)
bt **RATOON** sugarcane sprout
RATRAC snow compressor vehicle for clearing pistes (skiing)
bt **RATTAN** drum-beat; basketry
RAT-TAT postman's knock
RATTED deserted; informed upon
RATTEN stealing non-unionists' tools
RATTER rat-catcher
mu **RATTLE** chatter; vibrate; a herb; baby's toy; (snake); (rarely) percussion
RAUCID raucous; hoarse
RAUCLE rough; fearless (Sc.)
RAVAGE spoil; lay waste; ransack
go **RAVINE** gulch; gulley; gorge; defile
RAVING delirious; ranging; frenzied
RAVISH rape; violate; delight
RAWISH somewhat raw
RAYING radiating; shining
zo **RAY-OIL** ray-fish oil
RAZING overthrowing; rasing
pr **RAZURE** rasure; an erasure
RAZZIA a foray (Algerian); police raid
READER proof corrector; reading book
READER (TV news-); University title
REALIA 3-dimensional exhibits
REALLY truly; verily; actually
lw **REALTY** real estate
REAMED frothed; enlarged; edged
to **REAMER** belling tool (drilled holes)
REAPED acquired; cropped; obtained
ag **REAPER** harvester; a machine; death
REARED erected; educated
REARER up-bringer; guardian (foster-)
REASON logic; rational approach; motive; discuss; intelligence; excuse
REASTY rancid; rotting
REAVED bereaved; robbed
REAVER reiver; freebooter
REAVOW avow again; re-pledge
pr **RE-BACK** to repair spine of book
mn **REBATE** discount; abatement; blunt; freestone
REBATO a ruff; rabato
mu **REBECK** Moorish violin
REBIND refasten
pr **REBITE** engraving; acid process
ck **REBOIL** seethe again; re-heat
au **REBORE** worn-cylinder treatment
REBORN re-incarnated ('born again')
ga **REBOTE** (pelota)
REBUFF snub; repel; repulse
REBUKE upbraid; reprove; chide
REBURY inter again
RECALL revoke; rescind; retract
RECANT adjure; renounce; deny
RECAST compute again
RECEDE ebb; decrease; withdraw
RECENT modern; late; new; novel
RECEPT **RECEIPT**, having received; obtained
RECESS niche; alcove; nook; interval; adjournment
ck **RECIPE** prescription; formula; cooking
RECITE tell; relate; repeat; recount
RECKED regarded; heeded
RECKON deem; calculate; estimate
rl **RECOAL** refuel (locomotives)
ck **RECOCT** reconcoct; vamp up
RECOIL kick; rebound (gun); shrink
nm **RECOIN** remint
RECORD enter; note; achievement
mu **RECORD** achievement; (disc) evidence
cp **RECORD** archives; memory; filed data
RECOUP indemnify; make good
rl **RECTOR** academic leader; vicar
RECTUM section of intestine above anus
zo **RECTUS** equal-width muscle
md **RECURE** cure again

lw **RECUSE** reject; withdraw statement
pr **REDACT** to reduce; to edit
bt **REDBUD** Judas tree
zo **REDCAP** goldfinch; military policeman
REDDED tidied; arranged (Sc.)
pt **REDDEN** blush; red colour (rouge)
REDDLE raddle; red chalk
ck **RED-DOG** low-grade flour; (Am. football)
lw **REDEEM** ransom; free; retrieve; repay
zo **RED-EYE** rudd; carp
bt **RED-GUM** eucalyptus
RED-HOT extreme
bt **RED-LAC** Japanese wax-tree
bt **RED-OAK** N. American oak
REDOUT fort
mu **REDOWA** Bohemian dance
REDRAW redraft; copy
bt **RED-TOP** kind of grass
REDUCE degrade; curtail; abridge; decrease
REDUCT a diminution in size
REDUIT redoubt; redout; bastion; fort
RED-WUD stark mad (Sc.)
zo **REEBOK** rhebok; S. African antelope
RE-ECHO repeat; reverberate
REECHY **REEKIE**, smokey (city) (Sc.)
REEDED covered with reeds
bt **REEDEN** (reeds)
RE-EDIT compile new edition
nt **REEFER** wind-jacket; drugged cigarette
nt **REEFER** refrigerated ship
REEKED exhaled; fumed; stank of
REEKIE smoky (city) (Sc.)
REELED staggered; spun; swayed
zo **REELER** the grasshopper warbler
bd, pt **RE-FACE** redecoration (wall); reoppose (ice hockey)
ga **REFAIT** a draw game (Fr.)
pg **REFILL** replenish; film cassette
RE-FIND retrieve
REFINE clarify; purify; cleanse
REFLET iridescent glaze
ae **REFLEX** reactive; introspective; automatic reaction; wing structure
ma **REFLEX** angle greater than ½ circle
REFLOW re-issue
REFLUX ebb; return; redound
REFOLD replicate
lw **REFORM** make; remodel; betterment
REFUEL take in more fuel
REFUGE security; sanctuary; asylum; traffic 'island'
REFUND repay; return; restore
REFUSE veto; decline; deny; trash
REFUTE disprove; confute
REGAIN retrieve; recover; recapture
REGALE feast; entertain; honour
REGALO a gift; a sumptuous repast (Sp.)
REGARD note; watch; repute
REGENT ruling; a ruler during minority
REGIME system; administration; government; diet regimen, rules
REGINA title of queen
REGION province; tract; vicinity
REGIUS **REGIUM**, appointed by the Crown
lw **REGIVE** restore (title, rights)
pr **REGLET** flat moulding
pr **REGLET** spacing block
REGLOW to recalesce; rekindle
REGNAL during the reign of
REGNUM badge of royalty
REGRET rue; deplore; remorse
lw, rl **REGULA** book of rules
REHASH discuss again; rearrange
pr **REHEAD** apply new heading
md **RE-HEAL** to heal again
RE-HEEL shoe repair
REIGLE a channel or guide
REINED harnessed; restrained; steered
REIVER reaver; robber; freebooter
REJECT jilt; spurn; discard; repudiate
REJOIN respond critically
RE-JOIN link up again
REJOLT a new shock
RELAID (carpets)
RELAIS a rampart walk (Fr.)
ae **RELAND** land again
RELATE tell; recite; narrate; report
RELENT become less severe, harsh
RELIED depended on; confided
RELIEF aid; redress; alleviation
RELIER a trusting person
RELISH appreciate; zest; gusto; taste
RELIVE revive
cp **RELOAD** recharge; refill; system recovery time
RELUME to rekindle
REMADE remanufacture; refashioned
REMAIN persist; tarry; stop; survive
REMAKE make anew; revamp
REMAND send back to custody
REMARK state; comment; observation
REMEDY cure; panacea
zo **REMIGE** large wing contour feather
REMIND rearouse memory

lw **REMISE** release; give back; renewed attack (fencing)
REMISS slack; dilatory; negligent
zo **REMORA** a sucking fish
REMOTE distant; (-control); (space, time, relation)
REMOVE transfer (chattels); relationship
REMOVE dislodge; transport; eject
hd **REMPLI** heraldic colouring
lw **RENAME** change name; re-christen
zo **RENARD** Reynard, a fox
RENATE renewed; born again
RENDER return; assign; supply; restore
RENEGE to revoke (cards); break oath or promise
ck **RENNET** enzyme for cheesemaking
md **RENNIN** gastric juice ferment
RENOWN fame; eminence; repute
RENTAL money paid for house, car, tv
lw **RENTED** hired (tenancy) (contract)
RENTER hires out flats, films, cars, tv
RENTES French Government securities
md **RENULE** small kidney
lw **RE-OPEN** restart (file) (case)
REPACE retrace one's steps; re-measure
REPAID compensated; requited (loans)
REPAIR patch; mend; restore; wend
REPAND bent back
RE-PART share; divide again
ck **REPAST** a meal; victuals; food
lw **REPEAL** annul; rescind; nullify
REPEAT iterate; renew; echo
REPENT beg forgiveness; apologize; rue; regret
REPINE fret; complain; murmur
RE-PLAN re-design; re-arrange
lw **REPONE** re-appoint
REPORT rumour; relate; bang
REPOSE lie; recline; rest
REPOUR re-issue
REPPED ribbed
REPUGN oppose (Shak.)
REPUTE reputation; renown; regard
RESAIL put to sea again
RESALE a second sale
RESCUE release from danger; save
RESEAT repair; change-seating
RESEAU a network (Fr.)
md, sv **RESECT** cut off
bt **RESEDA** mignonette genus
RESELL re-market
RESENT dislike; repel; resist; hate
RESIDE live; dwell; lodge; sojourn
RESIGN relinquish a post; submit
RESILE ability to recover; readjust
RESINY resinous; rosiny
RESIST oppose; thwart; withstand
RESORB swallow up
RESORT recourse; (holiday)
RESTED reposed; quieted; paused
RESTEM force back; recheck
bt **RESTIO** plant genus
RESULT ensue; outcome; sequel; end
RESUME renew; summarize; synopsis
RETAIL sell in a shop; explain
RETAIN hold; keep; reserve; detain
RETAKE recapture
RETARD clog; hinder; impede; check
ch **RETENE** coal-tar constituent
lw **RETENT** assets held back
RE-TEST try again; re-adjust; reset
pl **RETINA** a network of optic nerves; screen of sight
md **RETINE** cancer cell growth inhibitor
RETIRE recede; withdraw; shrink
RETOLD already narrated
RETOOK regained; recaptured
RETORT rejoinder; distilling vessel
bt **RETOSE** reticulated
RETOSS throw again
RETOUR return (Sc.)
RETRAD backward
RETRAL posterior; retrorse
pr **RETREE** paper refuse; wastage
RETRIM embellish; smarten up
RETUND to dull; to blunt
RETURN also re-turn; restore; recur
RETUSE blunt
ar, bd **REVALE** of cornices completed in position
REVAMP renovate; remake
ar **REVEAL** disclose; divulge; unveil; part of jamb
REVERE adore; venerate; honour
REVERS revere; lapel (jacket)
lw **REVERT** return of assets (trusts)
REVERT to previous circumstances
REVERY reverie; dream; trance
REVIEW survey; inspect; journal
REVILE asperse; traduce; defame
REVISE reconsider; improve; correct
REVIVE rouse; invigorate; quicken
REVOKE annul; cancel; quash
REVOLT rebel; nauseate; mutiny
REVVED rotated at speed (motor)
REWARD guerdon; repay; premium
REWOOD afforest
REWORD change the phraseology

REXISM REXIST, Royalist party, Belgium
RHAGON form of sponge
bt RHAPIS genus of Chinese palms
zo RHESUS bandar; Indian monkey
md RHEUMY watery; rheumatic
bt RHEXIA genus of flowering plants
md RHEXIS rupture of bodily structure
zo RHINAE shark genus
md RHINAL nasal
bt RHIZIC radicle; root-like
ch RHUSMA a depilatory
RHYMED versified
RHYMER versifier
RHYMIC almost poetic
zo RHYSSA ichneumon flies
RHYTHM cadence; metre; symmetry
RHYTON Assyrian drinking vessel ceramic or metal
ar RIALTO a bridge in Venice
RIANCY gaiety; laughter
RIBALD coarse; rude; gross; lewd
nt, cr RIBAND ribbon (blue-); palisade rail
RIBBED ridged; furrowed
cr RIBBON riband; strip; saw; hand apparatus (gymn)
mu RIBIBE REBEC, old woman (obs.)
RIBLET rudimentary rib
ch RIBOSE pentose sugar in vitamin B-2
bt RICCIA a plant genus
RICHEN enrich; enhance
RICHER wealthier
RICHES abundance; affluence
RICHLY opulently; sumptuously
RICKED piled; sprained
fr RICKER thin round timber
RICKLE small pile or rick (Sc.)
RICTAL gaping
RICTUS open mouth
rl RIDDEL altar-curtain
RIDDEN went riding; (bed-); infested (lice-)
RIDDLE sieve; enigma; rebus (grate)
RIDEAU curtain (theatre) (Fr.)
RIDGED ribbed; furrowed
RIDING county sub-division (Yorks); (horse-)
RIEVER reaver; robber; pirate
RIFELY abundantly
pr, to RIFFLE engraving tool; small shallow rapid (canoeing)
RIFLED pillaged; grooved (gun barrel)
RIFLER robber; freebooter; plunderer; soldier
RIFTED cleft; split
nt RIGGED the setout of sailships; (tackle) (machinery)
RIGGED uniformed; manipulated (finance); (elections) (markets)
to, pt RIGGER mechanic; fitter; long-haired brush; (rowing)
nt RIGGER out-rigger (sailing); equipment (parachuting)
zo RIGGLE sand-eel
cr RIGLET (see reglet); flat piece of wood
RIGOUR rigidity; austerity; harshness
RIG-OUT complete outfit; uniform
RILING annoying; irritating
RILLED trilled; flowed
go RILLET rivulet; stream
RIMIST writer of doggerel
RIMLET thin rim
RIMMED bordered; edged
ck, to RIMMER pastry cutter
rl RIMMON Syrian god
RIMOSE RIMOUS, gnarled
RIMPLE wrinkle; rumple
to RIMSAW edging saw
mn RIMULA fossil limpets
RINDED peeled
RINDLE gutter; runnel; rine
RINGED encircled
RINGER expert shearer (Australia)
RINKED roller-skated
RINSED laved; cleansed; cleared
RINSER (washing machine)
RIOTED brawled; luxuriated
RIOTER disturber of the peace
nt RIPECK REPECK, RYPECK, punt pole for mooring
RIPELY maturely
RIPEST mellowest
RIP-OFF overcharging; defrauding; robbery
RIPPED torn; split; stripped; vandalized
nt, to RIPPER murderer; saw; cutter; speedster
pt RIPPLE flax-comb; small wave; fiddleback (sycamore); finish
RIPPLY rippling
RIPRAP broken stone used for walls
to RIPSAW a ripper
RISALA troop of native cavalry
RISBAN defended ground
ae RISERS parachutists' webbing straps
RISING insurrection; towering
RISKED chanced; ventured (capital)
RISKER gambler; venturer
RISLEY an acrobat
RISQUE indelicate; audacious (Fr.)
RITELY with due rites

RITTER a knight (Ger.)
RITUAL rite; ceremony
go **RIVAGE** the coast; shore; bank (Fr.)
RIVERY riparian; of the shores
bt **RIVINA** the pokeweed genus
RIVING splitting; rending
RIVOSE tabby; furrowed
RIZZER dry in the sun (Sc.)
bt **RIZZER** a red currant (Sc.)
ROAMED ranged; rambled
ROAMER nomad; vagrant; stroller
ROARED bawled; guffawed
zo **ROARER** broken-winded horse
zo **ROBALO** a fish (USA)
ROBBED stole; despoiled; purloined
ROBBER brigand; bandit; burglar
ROBBIN spun-yarn
zo **ROBERD** chaffinch
ROBING attiring; dressing
ROBUST sturdy; vigorous; hale; hearty
zo **ROCCUS** striped bass fish
bt **ROCHEA** a plant genus
zo **ROCHET** fish; the roach
rl **ROCHET** bishop's surplice
ROCKED reeled; tottered
ROCKEL a woman's cloak
ROCKER mining cradle; (swivel chair); compulsory figure (ice skating)
rw **ROCKET** Stephenson's locomotive 1829
ae, sp **ROCKET** firework; jet transport; alarm; salad herb
zo **ROCKIE** rock-linnet
ar **ROCOCO** florid style
bt **RODDIN** rowan-tree (Sc.)
zo **RODENT** gnawing; small mammal
RODING evening flight
gl **ROGGAN** logan; rocking stone
ROILED riled; vexed
ROINEK Boer name for British soldier
ROLAND legendary hero
ROLLED trundled; rotated; turned
ROLLER road-levelling vehicle
zo **ROLLER** wave; blue crow; a sect
cp **ROLL-IN** hockey; to garage; activating process
cp **ROLL-ON** (ferry); copying file
bd **ROLOCK** brick on edge bond
ROMAIC modern Greek
ROMANT exaggerate; romance
ROMANY gipsy; gipsy language
zo **ROMERO** pilot-fish
rl **ROMIST** papist
ROMPED frolicked; gambolled; sported
ROMPER garment; overall costume
mu **RONDEL** **RONDEAU**, poem, music cycle
RONDLE bastion trust
ROOFED covered
ROOFER tiler
ROOKED cheated
ROOKER swindler
ROOKIE recruit
ROOKLE rootle
ROOMED lodged; housed; accommodated
ROOMER lodger (in bedsit or dormitory)
ROOPIT hoarse; roopy; roupy
ROOTED firmly based (plant) (family)
ROOTER grubber; towed scarifier
ROOTLE rookle; poke about like a pig
ROPERY rope walk (factory)
ROPING lassoing
ga **ROQUET** (croquet)
rl **ROSARY** Catholic string of prayer beads
ROSCID dewy; roric
ROSEAL rose-like
ROSERY a rose garden
ROSIED adorned with roses
ROSING sprinkling
ROSINY resiny
ROSSER policeman (slang)
bt **ROSTEL** embryo root; radicle
ROSTER duty list; roll of names
bt **ROSULA** small rose
ROTARY rotatory
ROTATE spin; revolve; take turns; (wheel on axis)
ROTCHE little auk
ROT-GUT bad liquor
ROTTED disintegrated; decayed
ROTTEN corrupt; rank; moribund
ROTTER a pestilent person
md **ROTULA** knee-cap
ROTUND round; spherical
ROTURE plebeian rank (Fr.)
nm **ROUBLE** 100 kopecks (Russian)
ROUCOU a dye (annatto)
ROUGED powdered (rosy cosmetic)
ROUGET swine-fever
ga **ROUNCE** a pulley; card game
zo **ROUNCY** a nag; a hack
ROUSED ruffled; agitated; provoked
ROUSER a stimulator; inciter
ROUTED fled in disorder; defeated
ROUTED planned itinerary; direction
cp, to **ROUTER** sash-plane; message switching selector; plough
ROUTLE grub up; rootle

ROVERY roving; nomadism
ROVING rambling; ranging
ROWING sculling
bt **ROYALS** (family); of Western Red Cedar
bt **ROYENA** ebony
nt **RUA-PET** coastal vessel (Siam)
mn **RUBACE** rock crystal
mu **RUBATO** change of rhythm
RUBBED wiped; scoured; chafed; galled
ga **RUBBER** coagulated latex; set of 3 games (cards, sports)
RUBBLE undressed stone
RUBBLY broken
RUBIAN madder colour
RUBIED red as a ruby
RUBIFY to redden
bt **RUBIGO** mildew; rust (fungi) (rot)
RUBINE crimson dye; rubin
RUB-OFF incidental harm, side-effect of an action
pr, rl **RUBRIC** a heading in red (prayerbook)
RUCKLE wrinkle; pucker
nt, ae **RUDDER** boat guiding device; trailing fin on aircraft
RUDDLE red chalk or ochre
zo **RUDDOC** **RUDDOCK**, robin redbreast
bt, nm **RUDDOC** kind of apple; gold coin
RUDELY boorishly; insolently; impolitely
RUDEST most savage; crudest
RUEFUL mournful; sad; melancholy
RUELLE a coterie
ga **RUFFED** trumped; finessed (bridge)
RUFFER comb for flax
zo **RUFFIN** freshwater perch
RUFFLE a pleated border; disorder
RUFOUS ruddy; florid
RUGATE wrinkled; furrowed
RUGGED ragged; harsh; austere
ga **RUGGER** Rugby football
to **RUGINE** surgeon's rasp
mn **RUGOSA** corals
RUGOSE **RUGOUS**, **RUGATE**, wrinkled
RUINED wrecked; destroyed; beggared
RUINER demolisher
RULING governing; ascendant
RULLEY a dray
RUMBLE carriage-seat; reverberate
RUM-BUD grog-blossom
zo **RUMKIN** tailless fowl
bd **RUMMEL** soakway; dry well; pit
RUMMER drinking glass
RUMOUR report; bruit; hearsay
RUMPLE rimple; crumple; pucker
RUMPUS uproar; disturbance
nt **RUM-TUM** Thames sculling boat
RUNDLE a ladder-rung; a spoke
RUNKLE wrinkle
go **RUNLET** **RUNNEL**, rivulet
nt **RUN-MAN** naval deserter (obs.)
bt, ck **RUNNER** rotating part of water wheel turbine; (coward); (plant gone to seed); (bean)
RUNNER plough guide; timber joists; withies; (ski-) (sledge-)
RUNNER racer; messenger
ck **RUNNET** rennet for cheesing making
RUN-OFF experimental, production-line method
RUN-OFF printing batch; drain; cattle stealing; abduct; compose rapidly; deviate from fixed route (horse racing); rainfall course
RUNOFF final contest; election; river floodwater
RUN-OUT rope length between mountaineers
RUN-OUT cricket; experiment
RUNRIG land tenure (Sc.)
ae, pb **RUNWAY** track; airfield take-off path
nm **RUPIAH** (Indonesia)
bt **RUPPIA** a grass genus
bt **RUSCUS** butcher's broom
RUSHED dashed; flew; ran; plunged
bt **RUSHEN** of rushes
RUSHER impetuous person; thruster
zo **RUSINE** of E. Ind. maned deer
tx, zo **RUSSEL** woollen fabric, fox
tx, bt **RUSSET** homespun; apple
le **RUSSIA** leather
RUSTED oxidized
RUSTIC rural; bucolic; pastoral
RUSTLE quiver; whisper (wind); steal
hd **RUSTRE** heraldic lozenge
gl **RUSURE** earth-slide
zo **RUTELA** beetle genus
ch **RUTILE** an oxide of titanium
RUTTED grooved; furrowed; mated (of stags)
RUTTER a chart; trooper
RUTTLE gurgle; rattle (dial.)
bd **RYBATE** **REBATE** or jamb store
nt **RYPECK** **RIPECK**, **REPECK**, punt pole

S

zo **SABALO** the tarpon; Atlantic fish
SABIAN star worshipper
bt **SABINE** plant; the savin; (raped women)

SABLED darkened; furred
mu **SACBUT** sackbut; stringed instrument
rl, tx **SACCOS** Oriental vestment
zo **SACCUS** pouchlike structure
SACHEM American Indian chief
SACHET scent bag; tea bag
SACKED plundered; dismissed; (packaged)
SACKER sack-filling machine
pl **SACRAL** (pelvic arch)
SACRED holy; divine; consecrated
pl **SACRUM** a pelvis bone
SADDEN to grieve; depress
SADDLE seat on horseback; -bag; burden; encumber
go, ck **SADDLE** contour formation; butcher's cut
SADISM lustful cruelty
SADIST torturer; tormentor
ag **SAETER SETER**, Norwegian hill farm
SAFARI caravan; expedition
SAFELY securely; surely; reliably
SAFEST surest
SAFETY security; protection; safeguard; (measure); score; snooker (Am. football)
SAGELY wisely; sagaciously
SAGENE fishing net; a network
me **SAGENE** 7 ft (2.1 m) (Russian)
SAGEST wisest
SAGGAR sagger; fire-clay pot
SAGGED drooped; bent
SAGGER clay retort for stoneware
bt **SAGINA** pink genus
zo **SAGOIN** S. American monkey
zo **SAGUIN** capuchin monkey
go **SAHARA** a desert (Africa)
nt **SAILED** departed; cruised
nt **SAILOR** A.B.; tar; seaman
nt **SAIQUE SAIC**, small trading ketch
SAIRLY sorely (Sc.)
zo, ck **SAITHE** ling (fish)
SAKIEH Persian water-wheel
SALAAM salutation (India)
ck **SALAMI** spiced sausage (It.)
SALARY pay; wages; stipend
lw **SALIAN** (Mars); salic; male heirs only
ch, ck **SALIFY** to salten; add salt
go **SALINA** sea-salt lagoon; process
SALINE salty; briny
ck **SALITE** to season with salt
mn **SALITE** monoclinic pyroxene
md **SALIVA** spittle
bt **SALLAL** a fruit
SALLET light helmet
bt **SALLOW** yellow; a willow
ck **SALMIS** game-bird; ragout; salmi; a hash
zo **SALMON** highly prized fish
SALOON meeting room (pub) (dance) (carriage)
bt, ck **SALOOP** a decoction of sassafras
SALTED preserved
SALTEN to preserve; made of salt
SALTER salt-seller
zo **SALTIE** dab (fish)
SALTUS a mental jump
zo **SALUKI** hunting dog (Iran)
SALUTE hail; greet; accost
SALVED soothed; rescued
SALVER a tray
bt **SALVIA** sage
SALVOR a salvage expert
bt **SAMARA** winged fruit
SAMARE old-fashioned jacket
ck **SAMBAL** hot spice (Indonesia)
nt **SAMBAR** dhow
zo **SAMBUR** Indian elk
SAMELY in identical manner; (repeatedly)
SAMIAN of Samos
mt **SAMIEL** Arabian/Saharan hot poison wind
SAMIOT native of Samos
tx **SAMITE** silk
zo **SAMLET** a parr; salmon
SAMOAN native of Samoa
nt **SAMPAN** sanpan; Chinese boat
SAMPLE try; taste; specimen
ck **SAMSHU** rice spirit (China)
bt **SAMYDA** West Indian birch
mu **SANCHO** African guitar
nt **SANDAL** a Barbary vessel; footwear
mn **SANDIX SANDYX**, red lead, vermilion
go, gl **SANDUR** glacial outwash alluvial plain (Iceland)
SANELY rationally
SANEST most intelligent; soundest
bd **SANGAR** stone breastwork; masonry
rl **SANGHA** Buddhist church
md **SANIES** discharge from ulcer
SANIFY to restore to health
SANITY wisdom; normality; lucidity
SANJAK division of a vilayet (Turk.)
SANNOP SANNUP, American Indian; brave
mu **SANTIR SANTUR**, Eastern dulcimer
rl **SANTON** Dervish priest
fr **SAPELE** silky-grained Afr. hardwood
bt **SAPFUL** juicy
bt **SAPIUM** gum-tree
bt **SAPOTA** sapodilla
SAPOUR flavour (savour)

SAPPED undermined (tunnels; explosives); weakened
SAPPER Royal Engineer
rl **SAPPHO** Greek poetess
bd **SAP-ROT** dry rot; fungal
zo **SAPYGA** digger-wasps
zo **SARCEL** pinion of a hawk's wing
gl **SARCEN SARSEN**, Stonehenge sandstone; tin worker
zo **SARDEL** herring type of fish
zo **SARGUS** fish of mullet type
zo **SARLAK** sarlac; the yak
SARONG Eastern skirt
zo **SARSIA** jellyfish
SARTOR a well-dressed person
bd **SASHES** window-framings; scarves
lw **SASINE** seizin (Sc.)
rl **SASTRA** sacred book (Hindu)
nm **SATANG** Thailand coin
tx **SATARA** lustred woollen cloth
tx **SATEEN** fabric
bt **SATINE SATIN**, wood (hard-)
SATING satisfying; cloying
SATINY glossy
SATIRE irony; ridicule; sarcasm
SATIVE sown
SATRAP Persian provincial governor
SATURN planet; god of agriculture
nt **SAUCER** a piece of china-ware; flat canoe
zo **SAUGER** American pike
SAUMUR white wine
zo **SAUREL** the horse-mackerel
zo **SAURIA** reptile genus
zo **SAURUS** lizard-fish genus
SAVAGE barbaric; ferocious; brutal
SAVANT a scientist; professor
ga **SAVATE** French boxing
bt **SAVINE** medicinal shrub; red cedar
SAVING preserving; reserves; excepting
bt **SAVORY** aromatic pot-herb
SAVOUR taste; flavour; odour
SAVVEY nous; commonsense
pr **SAW-CUT** groove; binder's sewing mark
SAWDER flattery
zo **SAW-FLY** plant-harmful insect
zo **SAW-NEB** sawbill
tx **SAWNEY** complete yarn breakage
SAW-PIT sawing location
to **SAW-SET** tool for wrenching
SAWYER plank-cutter
tx **SAXONY** type of flannel
SAYING saw; dictum; adage; proverb
zo **SAYNAY** a lamprey
SBIRRO Italian policeman
S'BLOOD an imprecation, exclamation (God's blood)
SCABBY rough; itchy; leprous
SCAITH harm; damage (Sc.)
SCALAR magnitude without direction
SCALER climber
to **SCALER** instrument to register a count
mu **SCALES** a balance; octaves
vt **SCALMA** a horse disease
zo **SCAMEL** bar-tailed godwit
ck, zo **SCAMPI** prawns (It.)
SCANTY meagre; niggardly; chary; see-through (clothing)
md **SCAPHA** (helix of ear)
nt **SCAPHO** sailing cargo ship (Greek)
SCAPUS shaft of column
rl **SCARAB** sacred sunbeetle; gem (Egypt)
SCARCE rare; infrequent; uncommon
SCARED affrightened; panic-stricken
cr **SCARPH** to scarf
SCARRY scarred; disfigured
zo **SCARUS** parrot fish
vt **SCATCH** a horse-bit
SCATHE injury; damage
SCATTY showery; feather-brained; crazy
zo **SCAURY** gull (Shetlands)
SCAZON imperfect rhythm
zo **SCELIO** parasite insects
SCENIC dramatic; theatrical; route
SCHANS fortification (Dutch, Afrikaans)
SCHELM rascal (Boer)
cp **SCHEMA** diagrammatic representation; data base
SCHEME plan; plot; intrigue; devise
SCHEMY cunningly; devised
me **SCHENE** 7½ miles (12 km) (Egyptian)
SCHISM a split; discord; dissent
mn **SCHIST** slaty rock
cf, pc **SCHIZO-** of split, separate, cleavage (Gr.)
SCHOOL train; educate; academy
mn **SCHORL** tourmaline
ga **SCHUSS** unimpeded downhill ski run
nt **SCHUYT** ketch; sloop; (Dutch)
zo **SCIARA** gnats and midges
SCIATH Irish wicker shield
SCIENT knowing; aware
bt **SCILLA** hyacinth
SCLATE slate (obs.)
md **SCLERA** hard coating

zo **SCLERE** skeletal structure
zo **SCOBBY** chaffinch
SCOGIE a drudge (Sc.)
zo **SCOLEX** a worm
zo **SCOLIA** burrowing insects
zo **SCOLUS** thornlike process in larvae
SCONCE skull; bulwark
SCONCE to fine; wall candle with metal reflector
cf, md **-SCOPIA -SCOPIC, SCOPY**, visual; viewing (suffix)
zo **SCOPUS** genus of wading birds
SCORCH singe; char; parch; scar
mu **SCORED** registered; marked out; (-for orchestra)
SCORER recorder
mn **SCORIA** dross; coarse pumice stone
mn **SCORZA** variety of epidote
ck **SCOTCH** to thwart; cut; wedge; (-tape) (-egg)
zo **SCOTER** a sea-duck
ar **SCOTIA** Scotland; a concave moulding
ck **SCOUSE** meat and vegetable broth (Liverpool); Liverpudlian
SCOUTH scope (Sc.)
SCOUTS boys' brigade; guides; talent spotters
SCOVAN tin lode (Cornish)
SCOVED smeared (dial.)
SCOVEL oven-mop
SCRAMB SCRAMP, snatch; scrape together
SCRAPE grate; abrade; rasp; difficulty
SCRAWL hasty writing (illegible)
SCREAK SCREAM, SCREECH, cry; yell; shriek
SCREED tiresome harangue; a shred; wall-edging; jointless
tc **SCREEN** shroud; cloak; hide; sieve; scan; filter; (print); cinema; tv picture
SCREES stony debris
nt, md **SCREWS** divers' bends, caisson disease; fastening bolts, prison warders (sl.); propellors
SCREWY nefarious; underhand; exacting
SCRIBE writer; notary; scrivener
ga **SCRIME** to fence
SCRIMP to stint
pc **SCRIPT** handwriting; typescript; life-scenario; document; drama
SCRIVE scribe; engrave
zo **SCROBE** groove in mandible
SCROLL roll; list; register; flourish
SCROOP to grate; to crack
pl, zo **SCRUFF** back of neck
SCRUNT miser (Sc.)
SCRUTO theatrical trap
SCUFFY SCRUFFY, unkempt; shabby; seedy
SCULPT to sculpture; carve
SCUMMY covered with scum
zo **SCURFF** bull-trout
md **SCURFY SCURVY**, wasting disease; (sores); lack of Vitamin C
ga **SCURRY SKURRY**, haste; skamper; show jumping
SCUTCH to beat; to comb
hd **SCUTUM** Roman shield
SCUTUM middle noturn sclerite in insects
SCYLLA six-headed monster; (Charybdis)
ag, to **SCYTHE** a reaping implement (death)
S'DEATH an imprecation
zo **SEA-APE** sea-otter
zo **SEA-BAR** tern
zo **SEA-BAT** flying fish
nt **SEA-BOY** sailor lad
zo **SEA-BUN** sea-urchin
SEA-CAP a sponge
zo **SEA-CAT** cat-fish
zo **SEA-COB** a gull
zo **SEA-COW** manatee
zo **SEA-DOG** common seal
zo **SEA-EAR** a mollusc; ormer shell
zo **SEA-EEL** conger
zo **SEA-EGG** sea-urchin
zo **SEA-FAN** a polyp
zo **SEA-FIR** another polyp
zo **SEA-FOX** thrasher shark
rl **SEA-GOD** Neptune
zo **SEA-HEN** guillemot
zo **SEA-HOG** porpoise
SEALED ratified; confirmed; shut; closed
nt **SEALER** seal hunter; vessel
nt **SEAMAN** tar; sailor
zo **SEA-MAT** polyzoa
zo **SEA-MAW** sea-mew
tx **SEAMED** united by sewing; lined
SEAMER seamster
zo **SEA-MEW** a gull
SEA-MUD ooze
SEANCE spiritualism session
zo **SEA-ORB** globe fish
zo **SEA-OWL** lump fish
zo **SEA-PAD** star-fish
bt **SEA-PEA** beach-pea
zo **SEA-PEN** quill zoophyte
zo **SEA-PIE** a seafowl
zo **SEA-PIG** the dugong
zo **SEA-RAT** herring-king; a fish

SEARCH scrutiny; seek; inquire; quest
cp, lw **SEARCH** examine for specified conditions
SEARED cauterized; burnt; scorched
zo **SEA-ROD** a polyp
SEASON time; period; flavour
SEATED sited; established; accommodated
nv **SEA-WAY** steerage way
ch **SEBATE** a fatty compound
bt **SECALE SEA-KALE**, plant
nv **SECANT** (geometrical); cutting
SECEDE withdraw; segregate
SECERN secrete; discriminate
bt **SECKEL** variety of pear
me **SECOHM** electrical unit
me **SECOND** support; assist; inferior
mu **SECOND** melodic interval; lower pitched part
SECRET covert; occult; privy; cryptic
SECTOR an area; a cutting; a zone
cp **SECTOR** part of recorded data block
SECUND unilateral
SECURE get; obtain; safe; firm
SEDATE to calm; tranquillize; staid; placid
SEDENT inactive; still; torpid; sediment
bt **SEDGED** flagged; grassed
rl **SEDILE** seat in chancel
SEDUCE entice; tempt; inveigle
SEEDED planted; placed in tournament
to **SEEDER** seed-drill
SEEING observing; viewing; watching
SEEKER inquirer; searcher
SEELOS series of three gates (slalom skiing)
SEEMED befitted; appeared
SEEMER pretentious person; pretender
SEEMLY proper; becoming; decorous
SEEPED oozed; percolated
SEE-SAW teeter-totter; unbalance; pastime
cp **SEE-SAW** sign reversing amplifier
SEETHE to boil; (-with anger)
bt **SEGGAN** sedge (Sc.)
SEGGAR SAGGER, fireclay pot
SEGHOL Hebrew vowel point
nt **SEINER** net-fisherman
lw **SEISED** possessed of
zo **SEISON** a parasite genus
lw **SEIZED** confiscated; held prisoner; possessed (-by devil)
SEIZER thief; snatcher; grasper
lw **SEIZIN SEISIN**, held in possession
SEIZOR bailiff
hd **SEJANT** sitting upright
SELDOM rarely; hardly ever
SELECT pick; choose; prefer
cp **SELECT** courses of action after test
rl **SELENE** Greek Moon-goddess
SELION a ridge of land
SELJUK dynasty; art; empire (Turk.)
SELLER vendor; hawker; retailer
SELVES individualities
zo **SEMELE** genus of bivalves
SEMESE half-eaten
zo **SEMITA** (sea-urchins)
SEMITE descendant of Shem
SEMMIT undershirt (Sc.)
SEMPLE simple (Sc.)
mu **SEMPRE** in the same style
SENARY six of; half a dozen
SENATE assembly; council
SENDAL thin linen
cp **SENDER** transmitter; despatcher; exchange control
tc **SENDER** signal transmission line
SEND-UP compliment; ridiculing
bt **SENEGA** snake-root; an antidote
SENHOR SENOR, gentleman (Port., Sp.)
SENILE aged; doting; tottering; infirm
SENIOR elder; older; higher; superior
mu **SENNET** trumpet call
SENNIT braided cord; plaited straw
SENORA SENHORA, married lady (Sp., Port.)
SENSED perceived, felt
ga **SENSEI** instructor (judo, karate)
SEN-SEN breath-sweetener
SENSOR small-variation detection device
pc **SENSUM** sense datum
SENTRY sentinel; watchman; guardian
ck **SEPAWN** maize-meal
zo **SEPHEN** sting-ray
zo **SEPIUM** cuttle-bone
cn **SEPMAG** 1-magnetic-soundtrack film
cn **SEPOPT** 1-optical-soundtrack film
md **SEPSIN** a ptomaine
md **SEPSIS** (blood poison); putrefication
SEPTAL partitional (Irish)
SEPTAN weekly
mu **SEPTET** seven part ensemble
md **SEPTIC** rotting; putrid
SEPTON (putrefaction)
bt **SEPTUM** a partition
SEQUEL consequence; upshot; result

nm **SEQUIN** a spangle; Venetian
go **SERACS** postglacial ice pillars (Fr.)
SERAIL SERAGLIO, SARAY, oriental palace; (harem)
nt **SERANG** Lascar boatswain
tx **SERAPE** zarafe; Mexican blanket
rl **SERAPH** six-winged angel
SERDAB secret chamber (Egypt)
mt **SEREIN** rain from a cloudless sky
mt **SERENA** damp evening air
SERENE calm; placid; tranquil; clear
cp **SERIAL** a periodical (instalments); identity number; in sequence
pr **SERIAN** Chinese; Seric
SERICA beetle genus
SERIES sequence; succession; order
ch **SERINE** acid from protein hydrolysis
pr **SERIPH SERIF,** typesetting (sans-)
SERMON address; homily; discourse
md **SEROON** package of drugs
pl **SEROSA** chorium; connective-tissue membrane
md **SEROUS** watery; thin
go **SERTAO** jungle wilderness (N.E. Brazil)
zo **SERULA** red-breasted merganser
zo **SERVAL** small African leopard
SERVED ministered; acted; obeyed
rl **SERVER** salver; waiter; mass R.C.; beginner of volley (tennis) (squash) etc
bt **SESAME** plant having oily seeds
bt **SESBAN** a marsh plant
bt **SESELI** saxifrage
mu **SESTET SEXTET,** six part ensemble
oc, zo **SESTON** tiny plankton organisms
pr **SET-OFF** compensation; insulation
SETOSE SETOUS, bristly
SET-OUT display; layout; basic concept
nt **SETTEE** sofa; Mediterranean ship
ga **SETTER** pioneer; placer; (trend-) (tennis)
SETTLE colonize; (pay claims) (disputes); mediate
bt **SETULE** small bristle
SEVERE harsh; cruel; rigorous; plain
ar **SEVERY** part of vaulted ceiling
SEVRES porcelain (Fr.)
SEWAGE drainage; effluent; wastes
SEWING needlework
bt **SEXFID** six-cleft
pc **SEXISM** prejudice; sex discrimination
SEXTAN recurring every sixth day
mu, ga **SEXTET** six part ensemble; team of 6 ice hockey players
SEXTIC of the 6th degree
rl **SEXTON** gravedigger
SEXUAL of sex; sensual
SHABBY threadbare; paltry; beggarly
SHADED screened; obscured
as **SHADOW** umbrage; dark; silhouette; eclipse; follow secretly
SHADUF Nile water-raising device
SHAGGY rugged; rough; uneven; unkempt dog (-story)
zo **SHAHPU** Tibetan wild sheep
tx **SHAIRL** Cashmere cloth
SHAKEN jarred; agitated; moved
rl **SHAKER** religious sect (USA)
md **SHAKES** involuntary trembling; (deep sea divers) hand-split shingles
tx **SHALLI** Indian cotton stuff
bt **SHALOT SHALLOT,** (onion)
zo **SHAMAH** shama; Indian song-bird
mt **SHAMAL** Mesopotamian summer wind
SHAMAN animist; wizard (Siberia)
SHAMED abashed; disgraced
le **SHAMMY** shamoy; chamois-leather
zo **SHANNY** blenny fish
mu, nt **SHANTY** hut; hovel; shack; sea chant
SHAPED moulded; formed; regulated
to **SHAPER** metal-planing machine
SHARED partook; divided; held in common; with joint access
SHARER participator
nt **SHARPY** oysterman's boat
SHAVED swindled; smooth-faced
SHAVEN without hair; shorn; bald
SHAVER a sharp dealer; a barber
SHAVIE a trick; a prank (Sc.)
tx **SHAYAK** coarse cloth (Tripoli)
ag **SHEAFY** of sheaves (cereal harvests)
SHEARS cutters; scissors (sheepwool-)
md **SHEATH** scabbard; condom; (sanitary-)
SHEAVE pulley-wheel (on block & tackle)
SHEENY bright; showy; a Jew
nt **SHEERS SHEERLEGS,** a hoisting appliance; dipod portable crane
nt, pp, ml **SHEETS** sails; broad cloth; bedding (swaddling) (paper) (metal)
me, mn **SHEKEL** Jewish half-crown
SHELFY shelvy; shallow
SHELLY abounding with shells
fr **SHELLY** of shell-shake timber
SHELTA beggars' cant
zo **SHELTY** Shetland pony
SHELVE put aside; to incline
SHELVY sloping shallow
bt **SHE-OAK** Australian shrub

SHEPPY sheep-cote (-pen) (Aust.)
SHERIF shereef; Arab title
ck **SHERRY** a wine from Jerez (Sp.)
SHEUCH SHEUGH, ditch; drain; trench; furrow (Sc.)
SHEWEL scarecrow
SHICER welsher (Australia)
SHIELD shelter; cover; screen; guard
SHIFTY tricky; resourceful; untrustworthy (eyes)
rl **SHI-ISM** faith of a Moslem sect (Iran)
SHI-ITE believer in Shi-ism
SHIKAR big game hunting (Ind.)
SHIMMY chemise; a dance
SHINDY trouble; quarrel; spree; brawl
nm **SHINER** £1; a boot-black
ga **SHINNY SHINTY, SHANDY** bandy ball; West Highland hockey; turmoil; kicking sport
SHINTO Japanese ancestor worship
zo **SHIPOV** small sturgeon
SHIPPO Japanese enamel
nt **SHIPPY** ship-shape; in order; tidy
SHIRES the Shires; midland counties
SHIRTY indignant; wroth; angry
mn **SHIVER** tremble; quiver; slate
nv **SHOALY** shallow; shelfy; seabottom
tx **SHODDY** coarse cloth
SHODER goldbeater's packet
mu **SHOFAR** ram's horn trumpet (Heb.)
SHOGUN Japanese C. in C.
SHONKY shocking; twisting; dishonest
SHOOED drove away
SHOPPY commercial
bd **SHORED** propped; buttressed; braced
nt **SHORER** a support (in dry dock or ashore)
SHORTS bran; pants
zo **SHOUGH** shaggy dog
SHOULD advised to; ought to; duty to
SHOVED obtruded; pushed; jostled
to **SHOVEL** clergyman's hat; spade; upturned tip of ski
SHOVER pusher
mt **SHOWER** distribute liberally; rain; douche
SHRANK contracted; recoiled
SHRAUM mucus deposit in the eye
SHREWD astute; cunning; wise; canny
SHRIEK cry; scream; yell; screech
rl **SHRIFT** confession; absolution
zo **SHRIKE** butcher-bird
mu **SHRILL** high; sharp; piping (note)
zo **SHRIMP** small prawnlike crustacean; young thin child
rl **SHRINE** tomb; reliquary
SHRINK shrivel; contract; decrease in size; withdraw in fear
zo **SHRITE** missel thrush; bird
rl **SHRIVE** to absolve; pardon
SHROFF Indian banker
nt **SHROUD** winding sheet for the dead
rl **SHROVE** pardoned; (Tuesday)
tx **SHRUFF** dross
SHRUNK contracted
SHUCKS! nonsense!
SHUFTI look! (Arab)
bt **SHUNIS** herb; Scotch lovage
SHYING throwing; withdrawing in fear (horses)
bc, ch **SIALIC** derivative of neuraminic acid
SICCAN such (Sc.)
SICCAR sicker; sure (Sc.); certain
SICKEN (disgust); languish; become ill
ag, to **SICKLE** reaping hook
SICKLY faint; unhealthy; morbid
zo **SICSAC** crocodile bird
bt **SICYOS** gourds
rl **SIDDHA SIDDHI**, Buddhist who has attained perfection
rw **SIDING** train parking track
SIDLED moved furtively; sideways
me **SIEMEN** unit of electrical conductance
pt **SIENNA** yellow paint; (burnt)
go **SIERRA** mountain range (Sp.)
SIESTA midday nap (Med., Mexico)
zo **SIFAKA** a lemur
SIFFLE to whistle (Fr.)
ag **SIFTED** sieved; separated; sorted; (winnowed)
SIFTER scrutinizer; analyst
SIGHED breathed heavily, sadly
SIGHER repiner
lw **SIGLUM** seal; mark; initials
ae, nt, rw **SIGNAL** eminent; a sign; lamp; flag; semaphore; traffic
tc **SIGNAL** call (start or end) code
SIGNED signified; endoresed; agreed; autographed
SIGNER one who subscribes
lw **SIGNET** a seal; ring with crest (Sc.)
SIGNOR Mr in Italian
SILAGE ensilage; stored fodder
ch **SILANE** silicon hydride
bt **SILENE** bladder-campion
SILENT mute; dumb; taciturn
mn **SILICA** flint; quartz; etc.
SILKED repaired with silk backings (bks.)

tx **SILKEN** delicate; tender
SILLER silver; money (Sc.)
SILLON a mound in a moat
zo **SILPHA** carrion beetles
nv **SILTED** (waterway) choked with debris
zo **SILURE** cat-fish
fr **SILVAN** **SYLVAN**, wooded; rustic
ml, nm **SILVER** shining metal; coins; cutlery
SIMBIL African stork
zo **SIMIAL** **SIMIAN**, ape-like characteristics
SIMILE parable; comparison
ck **SIMMER** a gentle boil; stew
ck **SIMNEL** sweet fruit cake
rl **SIMONY** buying preferment
mt **SIMOON** summer whirlwind Sahara (Arab.)
zo **SIMORG** **SUMURG**, fabulous Persian bird
SIMOUS snub-nosed; concave
zo **SIMPAI** Sumatra monkey
SIMPER silly affected smile
SIMPLE naive; artless; frank; ingenuous
SIMPLY merely; only; barely; solely
bt **SIMSON** groundsel
SINAIC (Mount Sinai)
ga **SIN-BIN** bench for ice hockey offenders
SINDON a wrapper; winding sheet
SINEWY strong; vigorous; muscular
SINFUL wrong; iniquitous; depraved
SINGED scorched; slightly burnt
mu **SINGER** warbler; songster
cp **SINGLE** choose; select; alone; celibate; unit; score
SINGLY uniquely; individually
mn **SINIAN** Chinese rock formation
SINISM Chinese custom
SINKER a plummet; weight for pets (fishing)
SINNED erred; transgressed
SINNER wrong-doer; transgressor
nt **SINNET** **SENNET**, braided cordage
mn **SINTER** a siliceous deposit
bt **SINTOC** cinnamon bark
SIOUAN Sioux; American Indian tribe
SIPAHI sepoy; colonial soldier
ck, ce **SIPHON** syphon; atmospheric pressure pump (soda)
SIPING perculating; oozing; leaking
SIPPED (tasted); **SIPPET** (small sop)
SIPPER can **SIPPLE** (sup small drops)
SIRCAR sirkar; Hindu clerk
SIRDAR Egyptian commander
mu **SIRENE** a pitchpipe
SIRING begetting; fathering
as **SIRIUS** the Dog Star
SIRRAH sir, sirree
ck **SIRUPY** like syrup; syrupy
zo **SISKIN** bird; a finch
bt **SISSOO** Indian timber-tree
lw **SISTED** summoned (Sc.)
SISTER nun; nurse; sibling
SITTER painter's patient model
rl **SITULA** bucket-shaped vessel liturgical
zo **SIWASH** N. American Indian; Alaskan dog
SIZING size; weak glue; grading
ck **SIZZLE** fry (frypan)
SKATER one who skates (ice) (rollers)
SKATHE scathe; injury; harm; damage
SKEARY scary; scared
SKEELY skilful (Sc.)
pl **SKELIC** pertaining to skeleton
SKELLY to squint (Sc.)
go **SKERRY** rocky island
SKETCH limn; portray; outline; draught
ct **SKEWER** to impale; kitchen implement
SKIING moving; (jumping) on skis
ck **SKILLY** thin gruel; (porridge)
SKILTS trews; Sc. trousers
SKIMPY scanty; meagre
SKINNY lean; lank; (-dipping) (bathing naked)
zo **SKITTY** water-rail
SKIVED sliced; split
SKIVER split sheep-skin
SKIVIE askew (Sc.)
SKLENT to slant; to split (Sc.)
SKRYER a diviner
mt **SKURRY** scurry (Sc.); breeze; puff
SKYISH ethereal
SLABBY viscous; thick; sloppy
SLACKS women's trousers
SLAGGY (slag); scoriaceous
nt **SLAKED** quenched; water-heated (lime)
SLALOM timed ski-race through 'gates'
SLANGY colloquial
SLAP-UP posh; lavish
SLASHY muddy (Sc.)
nt **SLATCH** fair weather
SLATED abused; upbraided; chided
zo **SLATER** a wood louse
SLAVED drudged
nt **SLAVER** dribble; slave ship

SLAVEY serving wench; skivvy; kitchen maid
SLAVIC Slavonic
SLAYER murderer; killer
tx **SLEAVE** unwrought silk; floss
SLEAZE bribery of MPs
SLEAZY sordid; shabby; disreputable
SLEDGE **SLED**, snowcart; (-hammer)
SLEEKY of smooth appearance
SLEEPY soporous; drowsy; somnolent
mt **SLEETY** wet and cold; wet snowfall
ae **SLEEVE** arm cover; (wind indicator)
SLEIGH horse- or reindeer-drawn open snow vehicle
zo **SLEUTH** detective; bloodhound
SLEWED swung askew; tipsy
ga **SLICED** chopped; cut; (golf-shot)
ck **SLICER** ham cutter (in shops)
SLICKS (oil spill at sea); treadless tyres (motor-racing)
SLIDER a moveable part
SLIDER hard curving throw (baseball)
SLIEST slyest; most artful; most crafty
SLIGHT scorn; disdain; minimal
SLINKY lean; furtive
md **SLIP-ON** easily put on (clothing); condom
SLIPPY nimble; unstable
SLIP-UP error; mistake
SLITHY lithe and slimy
SLIVER a cut (splinter-thin)
tx **SLIVER** continuous fibre strand
SLOGAN war-cry (Sc.); curt phrase
SLOKEN **SLOCKEN**, quench with water
SLOPED tilting (ground); walked slowly
SLOPPY maudlin; slipshod
SLOSHY **SLUSHY**, muddy; boggy; watery; miry
SLOUCH depressed gait (clown); hat on head
go **SLOUGH** deep mud; morass; swamp
SLOUGH a cast skin (snake's)
SLOVAK Slav of Slovakia
SLOVEN slattern; slut
fr **SLOVEN** splintered timber stump
SLOWER not so fast
SLOWLY gradually; tardily; sluggishly
SLUDGE mire; wet refuse
SLUDGY muddy
gl **SLUGGA** subterranean cavity
SLUICE floodgate; wash
SLUICY streaming
SLUING turning round
SLUMPY marshy
ce **SLURRY** to smear; to dirty; cement water mix; (trench)
ga **SLURVE** fast, curved throw (baseball)
SLUSHY swampy; muddy; miry
gl **SLUTCH** sediment; muck; mire
SLYEST sliest; most artful
SMALLS exams; underwear
SMALTO glass; enamel; mosaic fragment
SMARMY oily; ingratiating
SMARTY over-bright youth
SMEARY bedaubed; adhesive; glutinous
zo **SMEATH** aquatic bird; smew
SMEIGH being clever
SMELLY odoriferous
SMILED grinned; simpered
SMILET a little smile
SMIRCH depreciate; foul
SMIRKY smart; smiling
ga **SMITER** slogger; hitter
SMITHY blacksmith's forge
SMOKED ridiculed; fumed; reeked
SMOKER a tobacoo addict
mt **SMOKES** dry season mists, coast of Guinea
SMOOTH level; flatten; suave; bland
SMOUCH smack; to kiss
SMOUSE pedlar (S. Africa)
SMUDGE stain; blot; margin decoration (signwriting)
SMUDGY stained; smeary
SMUGLY primly; neatly; complacently
SMURRY misty (Sc.)
SMUTCH to blacken
SMUTTY sooty; lewd; dirty
zo **SNABBY** chaffinch (Sc.)
zo **SNACOT** pipe-fish
SNAGGY full of troublesome difficulties
SNAKED moved like a snake
SNAPED bevelled
SNAPPY abrupt; noticeable style
SNARED netted; caught
SNARER trapper; hunter; poacher
ga **SNATCH** grab; seize; steal; (weight-lifting)
mu **SNATCH** fragment of song
to **SNATHE** scythe-handle
SNEEZE exhale explosively
SNIFFY disdainful; proud
SNIFTY having a luscious smell
SNIPER concealed marksman; gunman
SNIPPY fragmentary; stingy

SNITCH nose
SNIVEL snuffle; blubber; whine
SNOBBY snobbish; bogus superiority
SNOOTY conceited snob
SNOOZE a nap; doze; siesta; drowse
nt **SNOTTY** midshipman
SNOUTY protuberant
SNUBBY somewhat snub; rather blunt
SNUDGE sneak; miser
SNUFFY irritable; peevish
SNUGLY cosily; comfortably
SOAKED sodden; drenched; steeped
SOAKER confirmed toper; alcoholic
pb **SOAKER** watertightness plug in roof
SOAPED lathered; shampooed
SOARED aspired; towered; ascended
SOBBED wept; cried
lw **SOBEIT** if it be so
bt **SOBOLE** budding/rooting stem
lw **SOCAGE** tenure of land by service
ga **SOCCER** association football
SOCIAL genial; civic; civil; festive
SOCKED biffed; whanged; coshed
cp, el, pb **SOCKET** a cavity; (for a plug); pipe joint
lw **SOCMAN** tenant by socage
SODAIC containing soda
ag **SODDED** turfed; grassed; gardening
SODDEN soaked; wet; drenched
ch **SODION** sodium ion
ch **SODIUM** metallic element
md **SODOKU** rat-bite fever
SODOMY anal intercourse
SO-EVER indefinite suffix
SOFFET small sofa
ar **SOFFIT** ceiling; underside of architectural element
SOFTEN to weaken resistance; to impair strength; make malleable
SOFTER tenderer; milder
SOFTLY pliably; quietly; dulcetly
SOGGED saturated; sopped
SOIGNE well-decorated; carefully dressed
SOILED tarnished; smirched
SOIREE evening party (Fr.) (recital)
SOLACE consolation; cheer; relief
zo **SOLAND** the gannet
mt **SOLANO LEVANTER**, rainwind (Spain)
SOLDER fusible metallic cement
SOLEIL worsted dress fabric; the sun (Fr.)
SOLELY singly; alone; solitarily
SOLEMN august; grave; sad; serious
SOLERA cask; blending of sherry vintages
pl **SOLEUS** a leg muscle
ce **SOLING** large stones for road bed; (-and heeling) (pitching)
el **SOLION** audio signal detector
mu **SOLITO** in the usual manner
ar **SOLIVE** joist; cross-timber
ar **SOLLAR SOLLER**, upper gallery; garret
SO-LONG good-bye
SOLUTE readily soluble substance
SOLVED removed; resolved
SOLVER elucidator; interpreter; decoder
SOMALI native (Somalia)
nm **SOMALO** Somali currency
SOMBRE dismal; gloomy; lugubrious
zo **SOMITE** body segment
SOMNUS sleep personified
SONANT sounding; resonant
mu **SONATA** instrumental piece
SONCIE buxom; lucky
tx **SONERI** cloth of gold (Ind.)
eg **SONICS** study of mechanical vibrations
SONNET a poem of 14 lines
mu **SONORE** loudly (It.)
SONSIE good natured (Sc.)
SONTAG knitted cap
SOODRA Hindu castle
ck **SOOJEE SOUJEE, SUJEE**, specially fine flour (Ind.)
SOONER earlier; more readily
SOORMA an antimony cosmetic
zo **SOOSOO** river dolphin
SOOTHE calm; pacific; lull; palliate
SOPHIC teaching wisdom; wise
SOPITE to quash
SOPPED very wet; sogged
SOPPER wet feeder
zo **SORAGE** phase of hawk's life
ck **SORBET** water-ice; sherbet (Turk.)
bt, ck **SORBIC SORBIN**, vitamin C, acid
bt **SORBIN** mountain ash
SORDES sordor; dregs; filth
mu **SORDET** a mute for an instrument
SORDID base; vile; ignoble; foul
SORELY grievously; deeply; sadly
SOREST most grievous
SORNER gate-crasher; uninvited guest
bt **SOROSE** clustered
bt, zo **SORREL** colour; buck
SORROW woe; distress; affliction
SORTED grouped; suited
cp **SORTER** classifier; arranger; punched card machine
SORTIE sally; raid
SOSSLE dabble
as **SOTHIC** dog-star

SOTNIA Cossack troop
SOTTED drunk; infatuated; out of mind; be-
bt **SOUARI** butter-nut tree of Guyana
SOUCAR Hindu banker/usurer
SOUGHT searched; quested; looked for
SOULED full of feeling
SOUPER (a convert) (drinker)
SOUPLE flail arm
tx **SOUPLE** sericin-content yarn/fabric
SOURCE fount; cause; spring; origin
cp **SOURCE** compiled object program language
SOURER more acid
SOURLY tartly; bitterly
SOUSED **SOWSED**, soaked; drenched
SOUTAR **SOUTER, SOWTER**, cobbler; shoemaker
SOVIET Communist Russian council committee
ag **SOWANS** **SOWENS**, oat husk flummery
zo **SOW-BUG** a millipede
ag **SOWING** planting; disseminating; propagating
SOZZLE sossle; muddle
SOZZLY sloppy
SPACED extended
SPACER distance piece; (typewriter)
SPADED dug
SPADER **SPADIX**, clay spade; spike
SPAHEE Algerian cavalryman
zo **SPALAX** mole-rats
SPANDY wholly; completely
SPARED saved; refrained; withheld
SPARER economizer
SPARES spare parts; duplicates
SPARGE to sprinkle
SPARKE battle-axe (Spens.)
SPARKS radio operator
mn **SPARRY** (spar); (crystalline)
SPARSE scanty; meagre; thin
SPARTH halberd; mace
zo **SPARVE** hedge-sparrow
bt **SPATHE** flower sheath
vt, md **SPAVIN** a swollen joint
nm **SPECIE** bullion; coin; cash
SPECKY speckled
SPEECH harangue; oration; palaver
SPEEDY prompt; fast; rapid; hasty
mt **SPEISE** cobalt/lead smelting product
mn **SPEISS** metallic dross
SPELIN form of Esperanto
SPENCE buttery; pantry
le **SPETCH** strip of hide
SPEWED spat; vomited
mn **SPHENE** titanite
SPHERE globe; orb; ball; domain
SPHERY spherical; round
rl **SPHINX** man-lion statue
bt **SPICAL** spiky
ck **SPICED** seasoned
SPICER spice-merchant
zo **SPIDER** a weaver of webs; Ariadne; cue support (billiards, snooker)
SPIFFY spruce; smart (slang)
SPIGOT spile; peg for a cask
SPIKED pointed; put out of action
bt **SPIKES** outside nails; shoe grips for track events; grain
SPILTH anything spilt
md **SPILUS** birth-mark; a naevus
md **SPINAL** (back-bone)
SPINED thorny
mn **SPINEL** (corundum)
mu **SPINET** form of harpsichord
SPINNY a small copse
SPIRAL cork-screw; winding (Am. football) (skating) (parachuting)
ar **SPIRED** having a spire; sprouted
nt **SPIRIC** like an anchor-ring
SPIRIT zeal; soul; essence; spook
SPITAL hospital (obs.)
SPITED thwarted; vexed
SPLASH spatter; splurge; a sensation
md **SPLEEN** anger; melancholy
SPLICE to marry; a junction
SPLINE flexible ruler
md **SPLINT** **SPLENT**, support for broken bone
SPLITS with legs at angle of 180° (gymn.)
SPOFFY officious
SPOKEN told; articulated
zo, ck **SPONGE** porous fibre; cadge; (-cake) (wiper)
SPONGY absorbent
SPOOKY eerie; ghostly
SPOONY weak-minded; amorous
SPOSHY slushy
SPOT-ON accurately placed
SPOTTY speckled
SPOUSE husband or wife
SPRACK sprightly; alert
SPRAID chapped with cold
md **SPRAIN** strain; wrench; injury
SPRANG jumped; leapt; bounded; tea
SPRAWL lounge; spread; straggle
ck, ga, ro **SPREAD** open; broadcast; scatter; savoury paste; banquet; extend; (show-jumping)
SPRENT sprinkled

SPRING well; fount; leap; emanate; coiled energy
SPRING vernal season of new growth
SPRINT running extra spurt
SPRITE elf; fay; pixy; fairy; hobgoblin
SPROUT bud; germinate; shoot; spire
bt **SPRUCE** fir-tree; neat; trim; finical; furniture from the Baltic (Old English)
SPRUIT water-course (S. Africa)
SPRUNG has leapt; tipsy
SPRUNT sprouted
SPRYER more vigorous
SPUDDY potato-like; chubby; podgy
SPUNGE sponge
SPUNKY mettlesome; spirited
bt **SPURGE** a plant
bt **SPURRY** pink weed
SPYING watching secretly; spyism; coding; espionage; (agent)
SQUAIL a disc or counter
SQUALL blast; gust; yell; squeal
bt, zo **SQUAMA** squame bract; scale
SQUARE fair; just; bribe; adjust; straight; equal oblong; (rowing)
bt, ck **SQUASH** a gourd; a game; juice; crush
SQUAWK harsh utterance of protest
SQUEAK small creaking sound
SQUEAL cry out in pain; to inform
bt, zo **SQUILL** hyacinth; shrimp
md **SQUINT** a strabismus; glance
md **SQUIRE** landowner; escort; gallant
SQUIRM writhe; twist; wriggle
SQUIRT syringe; spout; eject
STABLE durable; fixed; constant; horse-house
STABLY firmly; steadfastly; securely
bt **STACTE** myth
to **STADDA** comb-cutting saw
STADIA a range-finder
STAGED performed (dramatics); deceived
STAGER old hand (theatre)
STAGEY melodramatic
STAITH coaling stage; staithe
STAKED (a claim); wagered
STALAG prisoners-of-war camp (Ger.)
STALER less fresh; older
bt **STAMEN** stamina; pollen container of flower
tx **STAMIN** harsh woollen stuff
STANCE position; attitude; station; (sport) (body)
STANCH STAUNCH, firm; stop liquid flow
STANZA verse of poem
md **STAPES** ear-bones
STAPLE essentials; basic materials; needs; requirements; industries; a clip
tx **STARCH** for stiffening clothes, etc.
STARCH feature of green plants; (stored sugar)
STARED gazed; glared; gaped
STAREE one who is stared at
STARER beholder
STARRY stellated (eyed)
STARVE famish; lack; deprive
md **STASIS** static; stable; unchanging state
STATED settled; regular; asserted
nm **STATHER** ancient Greek gold coin
STATHE landing stage
STATIC motionless; in equilibrium; immobile
cp **STATIC** dump; rewriting at end of run
STATOR cf. rotor; circuit holder
STATUE image; figurine
STATUS rank; standing; position
cp **STATUS** situation warning of paper shortage
STAVED burst; delayed
STAVES (staff); rods; sticks
md **STAXIS** haemorrhage; bleeding
STAYER one with endurance; pacing rider
STAY-IN sit-in demonstration
STAYNE deface; stain (Spens.)
STEADY equable; regular; uniform
STEAMY vaporous; humid; overshoot (golf)
zo **STEARE** a steer; an ox (Spens.)
STEBOY! go seek (dog talk)
STEELY hard; firm; obdurate
br **STEELY** of glassy barley grains
STEEPY precipitous
STEEVE to stow; pack closely; (-door)
bt **STEGMA** small silica-filled cell
STEMMA pedigree; family tree
STENCH fetid; odour; effluent
STEP-IN take control; seize power
go **STEPPE** Russian plain
STEREO stereotype
cf **STEREO-** of three dimensions (Gr.)
ch **STERIC** (atomic arrangement)
ch **STEROL** solid alcohol
mu **STESSA** (It.) the same
ck **STEWED** simmered; seethed
STHENE unit of force
ch **STIBIC** (antimony)

ga **STICKS** to raise above shoulders; foul (hockey) (lacrosse)
STICKY gummy; adhesive; viscid
STIDDY a forge; smiddy; smithy
STIFLE suffocate; smother; end (project)
STIGMA brand; mark; disgrace
bt, zo **STIGMA** algae 'eye'; spiracle of insect
STILAR (sundial stile)
STILLY calm; tranquil; silent
STILTY stilted; high-hat
ga **STIMIE** stimy (golf) (balls in line)
STINGO strong ale
STINGY near; close; mean; parsimonious
STINTY stinted; limited
bt **STIPEL** stipule
bt **STIPES** stalk; stipe; stem
STIRPS progenitor; ancestor
STITCH sew; twinge (pain, laughter); manipulate
nm **STIVER** Dutch halfpenny coin
STOCKY sturdy; thick-set; robust
STODGE to cram
ck **STODGY** heavy; indigestible; starchy
STOKED fuelled
nt, rw **STOKER** furnace operator (steamship, locomotive etc)
ps, me **STOKES** kinematic viscosity symbol
STOLEN filched; purloined; taken
STOLID obtuse; phlegmatic
bt **STOLON** a runner
STONED lapidated (killed); drugged; drunk
STONER wall builder
ro, tv **STOOGE** a butt; foil; foolish helper
STOORY dusty
bt **STORAX** resinous balsam
STORED garnered; treasured; deposited
STORER hoarder; stocker
STORES emporium; (department-)
STOREY one of many floors
STORGE natural affection (Greek)
STORMY wild; rough; tempestuous
ck **STOVED** dried; baked
STOVER fodder for cattle
STOWED packed; placed
STOWER stevedore; packer
STRAFE punish (Ger.); attack fiercely
mu **STRAIN** exert; race; filter
rw **S-TRAIN** suburban train (Dan., Ger., etc.)
go **STRAIT** narrows; distress; dilemma
nt **STRAKE** (wheel); flanging
STRAND shore; beach; thread; fibre
STRASS flint glass
STRATA layers; beds
go **STRATH** broad river valley (Sc.)
STRAWY straw-like
STREAK stripe; line; run naked
STREAM flow; pour; brook; burn
cp **STREAM** data from resource to controller
STREET town roadway; avenue
STRESS accent; force; urgency; tension
STREWN scattered here and there
STRIAE stripes; streaks
zo, bt **STRICK** screech-owl; flax
STRIDE long step forward; gait; brisk walk
STRIFE discord; conflict; quarrel
bt **STRIGA** bristle; stripe
ga **STRIKE** to hammer; hit (golf, cricket etc.)
STRIKE work stoppage; break camp; drum (gold)
STRING cord; twine; series
STRIPE band; line (military rank)
ck, tx **STRIPY** streaky (bacon); (pyjamas)
STRIVE vie; compete; attempt
el **STROBE** waveform enlargement
STRODE straddled; bestrode
STROKE blow; knock; caress; seizure; apoplexy; oarsman (stern seat); action of strike (golf); clock chime
STROLL ramble; rove; stray
md **STROMA** tissue
zo **STROMB** a gasteropod
STRONG puissant; bold; lusty
STROUT strunt; to strut (obs.)
STROVE vied; toiled; tried; attempted
STRUCK smote; hit; collided
md **STRUMA** goitre; scrofula
STRUNG threaded; filed
STUBBY stocky; blunt; truncated
ar **STUCCO** plaster facing
STUDIO atelier; broadcasting chamber
STUFFY close; fusty; musty; angry
STUMER bouncer; worthless cheque
ga **STUMPS** tree-boles; legs; wickets (cricket)
STUMPY stubby; short and thick
STUPID witless; dull; idiotic; asinine
STUPOR torpor; coma; lethargy
STURDY robust; stalwart; vigorous
STYING penning
STYLAR pillar-like; pointed
STYLED designed; fashioned; (character)
md **STYLET** **STILETTO**, pointed bristle; dagger; knife

cp, tv **STYLUS** pen; disc needle; torch; stile
ga **STYMIE** (golf); stimy; balls in line
bt **STYRAX** gum plants; storax
STYTHE after-damp
lw **SUABLE** liable to be sued
SUBDUE quell; overpower; tame
lw **SUBFEU** (subinfuedation) (Sc.) tenancy
mu **SUBITO** quickly
lw **SUBLET** make secondary lease
SUBMIT yield; capitulate; acquiesce
SUBORN to bribe; commit perjury
tc **SUBSET** subscriber's phone; part of relay system
ma **SUBSET** subsidiary of mathematics
SUBTLE SUBTLY, sly; crafty; clever manner
SUBULA sharp-pointed organ prolongation
SUBURB city outskirts; (satellite village)
SUBWAY underground passage; metro
mn **SUCCIN** amber (stone)
SUCKED suckled; imbibed via tube; straw
zo, bt **SUCKER** a fish; a shoot; suction pad
SUCKER gullible person
ck **SUCKET** sweetmeat
SUCKLE to wet-nurse
SUDARY a sweat-cloth
SUDDEN abrupt; (unexpected, rapid, happening)
SUDDER chief; supreme (Ind.)
SUEING prosecuting; entreating
SUFFER undergo (pain); endure; tolerate; permit
SUFFIX an affix
rl **SUFISM** Moslem doctrine
SUGARY sweet; honeyed; dulcet
zo **SUIDAE** pigs, hogs; etc.
SUITED contented; dressed
SUITOR wooer; admirer; litigant
mu **SUIVEZ** conductor to follow soloist
SUKAMA native of Tanzania
SULCUS furrow; groove
SULLEN morose; sulky
zo **SULTAN** a fowl; a Moslem ruler, emperor
SULTRY stuffy; oppressive; stifling; (air)
bt **SUMACH** sumak; plant used in tanning
SUMMED counted; added; reckoned
SUMMER season of year
SUMMIT top meeting; peak; zenith; vertex
SUMMON bid; cite; invoke; prosecute
SUMPIT poisoned dart (Borneo)
SUNBOW rainbow
ck **SUNDAE** ice-cream with fruit and syrup
SUNDAY Christian holy day
SUNDER brake; sever; disrupt
bt **SUN-DEW** a bog plant
as **SUN-DOG** a parhelion; mock sun
SUNDRY miscellaneous; various
rl **SUN-GOD** Phoebus; Apollo; Re or Ra
SUN-HAT solar topee (panama)
SUNKEN submerged; engulfed
SUNLIT illuminated by sun
SUNNED exposed to sun; sunbathed
SUNSET sundown
SUN-TAN sun-browned skin; (sun bathing)
SUPERB magnificent; splendid
SUPINE indolent; torpid; inert
ck **SUPPER** evening meal
SUPPLE lithe; pliant; flexible
SUPPLY provide; furnish; grant
bd **SURBED** (stone-laying)
bt **SURCLE** little shoot; sucker
SURELY certainly; positively
SUREST safest; most certain
SURETE crim. investigation service (Fr.)
SURETY bond; guarantee; pledge
SURGED billowed; advanced in mass
zo **SURREY** a fowl; carriage (Amer.)
SURTAX an impost
SURVEY see; review; look; observe
zo **SUSLIK** marmot; ground squirrel
lw **SUSSED** arrested on suspicion
md **SUTILE** wound stitching
SUTLER camp follower; caterer
SUTTEE self-immolation
SUTTLE neat; (tare and tret)
bt, md **SUTURE** stitching thread
SVELTE lissom; slender
SWAGGY bending
SWALED wasted; consumed
SWAMPY marshy; spongy
SWANKY superior; boastful
SWANNY swan-like
SWARAJ home-rule (India)
SWARDY grassy
SWARMY oleaginous; unctuous
SWARTH tawny; apparition
SWASHY squashy; over-ripe
tx **SWATCH** cloth sample; Swiss watch
SWATHE to bind; a bandage
SWATHE harvester's trail
SWATHY like a scythe-cut
SWAYED tottered; unsteady (in wind); persuaded

SWEATY causing sweat; (perspiration)
md **SWEENY** emaciation; atrophy
SWEEPS jeweller's dust/debris
SWEEPY strutting; wavy
SWERVE deviate; turn aside
SWIM-UP regroup in water for polo etc.
SWINGE to belabour; chastise
SWINGY ice conditions (curling)
SWIPED lashed out; slogged
SWIPER a smiter
ck **SWIPES** sweeping blows; small beer
SWIPEY mind-blown; fuddled; (shell-shocked)
SWIRLY curly
SWITCH twig; whip; bypass; shunt; control
el **SWITCH** tap device for electrical circuit
SWIVEL to turn; revolve; rowlock with pivot of oars (rowing)
mn **SYCITE** fig-stone
md **SYCOMA** tumour
fr **SYLVAN** rustic; rural; woodland
cp **SYMBOL** token; badge; emblem; logo
SYNDAW a plant
bt **SYNEMA** column of filaments
SYNEPY interjunction
SYNTAX grammatical sequence, structure
cp **SYNTAX** correct statements in source language
SYNTOL syntagmatic organization lang.
SYPHER to join flush
SYPHON siphon; atmospheric pressure pump (soda)
SYRIAC **SYRIAN**, of Syria; language
zo **SYRINX** vocal organ in birds; fistula
mu **SYRINX** Pan's pipes
SYRTIC like a quicksand
SYRTIS quicksand
ck **SYRUPY** sirupy; sugary
cp **SYSTEM** unit formed by connections
SYSTEM rule; method; order; plan (organized)
as **SYZGY** astronomical conjunction

T

hd **TABARD** heraldic coat; tunic
TABBED labelled; registered; listed
TABEFY to emaciate
TABLED parliamentary motions; catalogued
TABLER boarder
ma **TABLES** data; (conversions); (indoor games)
md **TABLET** flat monument
mu **TABRET** small tabor
ga **TABULA** Roman board game; backgammon; corals
nt **TACKED** attached; stitched; nailed; change of course (sailing)
TACKER he who tacks (nails)
ce, to, nt, ga **TACKLE** grapple; challenge; pulley (football)
TACTIC cunning move; finesse
TACTUS sense of touch
zo **TAENIA** tape-worm; a fillet
TAG-END end of queue; list (last)
TAGGED tabbed; touched; fastened
TAGGER thin metal sheet
TAGGER an appendage (electronic)
ce **TAGLIA** a hoisting device; tackle (crane)
TAG-RAG and bobtail
zo **TAGUAN** Malayan flying squirrel
TAIGLE entangle; delay; tarry
TAILED docked; followed
TAILOR clothes maker
zo **TAJACU** Mexican wild pig; peccary
TAKE-IN a hoax; trick by con-man
TAKE-UP tailor's alterations to clothes
TAKING alluring; attractive; winning
ga **TAKRAW** 7-a-side field game (S.E. Asia)
lt, me **TALBOT** luminous energy unit
zo **TALBOT** hunting dog
nm, me **TALENT** genius; aptitude
mu **TALIAN** Bohemian dance
lw **TALION** retaliation
TALKED discoursed; prated; spoke
TALKER chatterbox; gossip
TALKIE sound film
TALLER higher; sturdier; bolder
TALLOW hard candle fat
rl **TALMUD** Hebrew Bible
go **TALWEG** deep valley (Ger.)
ck **TAMALE** Mexican cornmeal roll
bt **TAMANU** gamboge tree (E. Ind.)
ck **TAMARA** mixed spice
mn, bt **TAMBAC** alloy; also aloes-wood
TAMBOO **TABOO**, **TAMBU**, taboo
zo **TAMBOR** globe-fish
TAMELY meekly; submissively
TAMEST flattest; dullest
tx, wv **TAMINE** **TAMINY**, **TAMISE**, **TAMROY**, worsted cloth
TAMING domesticating; training
TAMKIN tampion
rl **TAMMUZ** Syrian sun-god
zo **TAMPAN** South Afr. venomous tick

TAMPED packed with earth
TAMPER meddle; interfere; screed board
pb **TAMPIN** turning pins; boxwood pipe plug
bt **TAMPOE** an E. Indian fruit
md **TAMPON** medical plug (feminine)
TAMTAM gong of indefinite pitch
TAN-BED bark bed; sunray bed
cp **TANDEM** bicycle for two; two-horse couch; master/slave
TANGED sharply flavoured (smelling); taint suggestion
TANGLE jumble; twisted
rl **TANGLE** Orcadian water-spirit
TANGLY complicated; intricate
zo **TANGUM** Tibetan piebald horse
TANIST land owner (Irish)
TANITE a cement
tx **TANJIB** **TANZIB**, figured muslin (India)
TANKED stored; fuddled
nt **TANKER** oil-carrying ship (truck)
TANKIA boat population, (Canton)
TANNED browned off; leathered
nm **TANNER** sixpence; leather worker
ch **TANNIC** **TANNIN**, acid astringent
TANNOY commerical sound systems
zo **TANREC** hedgehog (Madagascar)
rl **TANTRA** Sanskrit holy book
le **TAN-VAT** tub used in tanning
rl **TAOISM** **TAOIST**, Chinese religion(ist)
TAO-TAI Chinese official
zo **TAPETI** Brazilian hare
to, tv **TAPING** binding; measuring; recording
TAPPED screw-threaded; rapped
rw **TAPPER** rapper (wheels)
au **TAPPET** (motor vehicle); small lever
TAPPIT crested
TARGET shooting butt; production aim
rl **TARGUM** Bible in Chaldee
TARIFF duties on trade; schedule of prices etc.
TARING recording tare allowance
TARMAC road material
TARNAL eternal or infernal
zo **TARPAN** wild horse (Asia)
zo **TARPON** **TARPUM**, Jew-fish
TARRED macadamized; asphalted
TARSAL (tarsus); (the ankle)
zo **TARSEL** hawk; tiercel
TARSIA marquetry
pl **TARSUS** instep; ankle
nt, tx **TARTAN** chequered fabric (Sc.); ship
md, ck **TARTAR** Turkic people; plaque on teeth; wine cask sauce

TARTLY sharply; pungently; acidly
TASCAL informer's reward
TASKED employed; burdened
TASKER taskmaster; overseer
TASLET **TASSET**, thigh armour
tx **TASSEL** pendant (often cloth)
TASSET thigh armour
TASTED **TASTER**, food savoured/sampler
zo **TATLER** a gossip; sandpiper
tx **TATTED** lace making
tx **TATTER** a rag
TATTIE Indian trellis; tatta
TATTLE prattle; gossip; babble
TATTOO army pageantry; skin decoration
TAUGHT imparted; tutored; coached
as **TAURUS** a sign of the Zodiac; the Bull
TAUTEN stretch; strain
TAUTER tighter
zo **TAUTOG** **TAWTOG**, blackfish (N. Am.)
TAVERN inn; hostel
TAWDRY gaudy; garish
le **TAWERY** white leather factory
le **TAWING** leather dressing
zo **TAWTOG** tautog
TAXEME linguistic selection
TAXIED ground movement made by aircraft
ch **TAXINE** alkaloid mixture
TAXING accusing; straining; costing
TCHEKA **CHEKA**, first Soviet Secret Police
TCHICK a click
TEA-BAG tea sachet; tisane
TEA-CUP tea-drinking vessel
TEAGLE a tackle; a hoist
TEAGUE an Irishman
TEAMED associated conjointly
TEA-POT vessel holding tea; (roller skating)
TEA-POY small table for teapot
TEARER render; ripper
TEASED combed; tantalized
bt, tx **TEASEL** **TEAZLE**, burr plant for nap cloth
TEASER a puzzle; aggravator
TEA-SET dishes for tea service
TEATHE (manure)
TEA-URN a samovar
mt **TEBBAD** Centr. Asian simoon wind
TEBETH Jewish month
ar, bd **TECTUM** covering/roofing structure
TEDDED spread (new-mown hay)
TEDDER a tether; hay-maker
ag **TEDDER** machine to loosen windrows

mu, rl **TE DEUM** thanksgiving; choral
TEDIUM boredom; ennui; monotony
ga **TEEING** golf ball mounting for first drive
TEEMED full of life; in myriads
TEEMER a producer
TEEPEE wigwam (N. Amer.)
zo **TEE-TEE** S. Amer. squirrel monkey
TEETER see-saw (USA)
TEETHE to grow teeth
bt **TEGMEN** inner seed coat
pr **TEGULA** subtitle (Italian)
TELARY web-like
zo **TELEDU** stinkard; Malayan badger
TELEGA Russian springless cart
TELESM amulet; charm
rw, ce **TELFER** Telpher monorail; electric hoist
TELLER cashier (bank); narrator; scorer
rl **TELLUS** Goddess of Earth (Roman)
zo **TELSON** tail segment
TELUGA dialect (S. India)
ce **TEMOIN** column of earth
me **TEMPER** mood; tantrum; anneal (steel); mitigate
rl **TEMPLE** Inns of Court; place of worship; fane; upper head
ga **TENACE** (bridge)
lw **TENANT** lease-holder
TENDED cared for; contributed
nt, rw **TENDER** mild; offer; (loco); (boat); (bar-)
md **TENDON** a ligament
TENNER £10 note
ga **TENNIS** net/ball game
mu **TENORA** Catalan instrument
ga **TENPIN** of bowling alley
zo **TENREC** hedgehog (Madagascar)
TENSED keyed up; taut; stretched
TENSER under greater strain
mu **TENSON** **TENZON**, song tournament
md **TENSOR** muscle
TENTED probed
TENTER machine attendant
TENTER machine operative; females' cardroom
TENUIS voiceless stop consonant
lw **TENURE** possession; holding
mu **TENUTO** sustained
bt **TEPARY** hardy Amer. bean
TEPEFY to warm
gl **TEPHRA** erupted material; solids
TERAPH Hebrew household god
ch **TERBIC** containing terbium
zo **TERCEL** male falcon
mu **TERCET** triplet
zo **TEREDO** boring worm; ship-worm

TERETE clyindrical
TERGAL dorsal
TERGUM the back
TERMED terminated; designated
lw **TERMER** **TERMOR**, long-term estate holder
zo **TERMES** white ant genus
TERMLY term by term
mt **TERRAL** land breeze (coast) (Chile, Peru)
TERREL a spherical magnet
TERRET **TERRIT**, harness pad ring
TERROR awe; dismay; dread; panic
TESTED proved; assayed; tried out
ga, nm **TESTER** canopy; time trials (cycling); Henry VIII shilling
pl **TESTIS** male gonad; gland in scrotum
md **TETANY** muscle spasm; lock-jaw
TETCHY testy; peevish
TETHER tie; fasten; stake
TETRAD group of four
zo **TETRAO** capercaillie
ch **TETRYL** yellow detonating compound
md **TETTER** a rash
zo **TETTIX** cicada; tree-cricket
TEUTON ancient German
zo **TEWHIT** peewit; lapwing
TEXTUS authoritative version
nm **THALER** German dollar
THALIA comic Muse
THANKS an expression of gratitude
THATCH roof with straw
THAWED melted (ice and snow)
zo **THEAVE** ewe of the 1st year
THEBAN of Thebes
bt **THECAL** sac-like
zo **THECLA** hair-streak butterflies
ch **THEINE** tea alkaloid
THEIRS of them
rl **THEISM** **THEIST**, one God faith; ditto believer
rl **THEMIS** goddess of law
md **THENAL** **THENAR**, of palm or sole
THENCE for that reason
rl **THEODY** hymn in praise of God
THEORY speculation; hypothesis; (idea)
cf **THERMO-** of heat (Gr.)
THESIS a theme; a dissertation; essay
THETIC dogmatic (thesis)
THETIS sea-nymph; the sea
THEWED trained; muscular
tx **THIBET** heavy woollen fabric
THIBLE to make holes
THIEVE filch; pilfer; purloin; rob
jn **T-HINGE** like a cross-garnet

THINLY scantily; sparsely; (spread-)
lw **THIRDS** widows' rights
THIRST crave; yearn; hanker; desire
THIRTY cardinal number
ar **THOLOS** **THOLUS**, domed chamber; cupola (Gr.)
rl **THORAH** the Pentateuch
THORAL nuptial
md, pl **THORAX** (chest)
THORNY spiny; prickly; sharp
nc **THORON** thorium emanation
THORPE a homestead
THOUGH notwithstanding
nt **THOWEL** thole-pin
THRALL a slave; slavery
THRASH drub; castigate; beat (punish)
THRAVE two stooks (Iceland)
THREAD cord; filament; drift; gist
THREAT menace; intimidation
THRENE a lament (Gr.)
THRESH **THRASH**, (harvest); drub; trounce
THRICE three times
bt **THRIFT** frugality; economy; sea-pink
THRILL excite; rouse; electrify
zo **THRIPS** corn-bugs
THRIVE prosper; flourish
pl, bt, nt **THROAT** constricted passage (neck); (plants); (sail)
lw, rl **THRONE** seat of sovereign (power); (bishop's cathedra)
THRONG crowd; flock; congregate
THROVE thrived; prospered
THROWN cast; propelled; flung
zo, vt **THRUSH** songbird; disease of horses
md **THRUSH** disease of women
THRUST lunge; stab; attack
THUSLY as follows
THWACK belabour; whack; thump
THWART balk; frustrate; obstruct
mn **THYITE** pale green clay
md **THYMOL** oil of thyme
md **THYMUS** a gland
bt **THYRSE** panicle
pl, mu **TIBIAL** leg-bone; flute
TICING enticing; decoying; luring
TICKED clicked; marked; speckled
tx **TICKEN** thick pillow; mattress linen
pl, el **TICKER** rhythmic beat (watch) (heart); (telegraph tape)
TICKET voucher; coupon; pass
mn **TICKEY** coin (S. Africa)
TICKLE gratify; amuse; pleasurable touch
TICKLY ticklish; risky; difficult
TIC-TAC bookie's signalling system
ck **TIDBIT** TITBIT, beakful (birds); small snack (cocktails)
TIDDER to fondle
TIDDLE to potter; to trifle
TIDIED set in order; shipshape
TIDIER neater
TIDILY methodically; neatly
nt, pr **TIED-UP** busy; moored; docked (ship); books heading for cover binding
TIEING binding; confining
TIE-PIN ornament for a cravat
me **TIERCE** 42-gallon (190-litre) cask
mu **TIERCE** 5-f organ pitch
rw **TIE-ROD** connecting rod (steam locomotive)
TIE-WIG court-wig
ck **TIFFIN** Indian lunch; superior snacks
TIGHTS combined stockings and pantie
TILERY tilework; tile factory
bd **TILING** roofing
ag **TILLED** cultivated; ploughed
ag, nt **TILLER** helm; drawer; cultivator; side shoot (grass)
md **TILMUS** floccillation
TILTED covered with awning; aslant
TILTER tent-pegger; jouster (lancer)
mu **TIMBAL** tymbal; kettledrum
TIMBER wood; lumber
mu **TIMBRE** resonance; tone; quality
TIMELY opportune; punctual; apropos
TIME-ON extra time (sports matches etc.)
cp, me **TIMING** clocking; punctuality measuring device
mu **TIMIST** timekeeper (metronome)
mn **TINCAL** **TINGAL**, **TINKAL**, crude borax
TIN-CAN food container
TINDAL Lascar bo'sun's mate
bt **TINDER** touchwood (fire lighting)
zo **TINEID** (small moths)
TINGED coloured; imbued; flavoured
zo **TINGIS** an insect genus
TINGLE thrill; small nail
bt **TINGUY** Brazilian soap-tree
TINIER much smaller
TINKED tinged; tinkled
TINKER bungler; a fish; rubbish man
mu **TINKLE** make bell-like sound
TINMAN expert in tin production; canning
TINNED preserved
TINNER tin miner
TIN-POT inferior
TINSEL finery; glittering; gaudy
TINTED tinged; imbued (coloured)

TINTER colourist
ga **TIP-CAT** a children's game
TIP-OFF secret information; betrayal; (basket-ball)
TIPPED overturned; (racing); gratuity given
tx **TIPPET** garment; small cape
TIPPLE secret (regular) drink
TIP-TOE walk on the toes
TIP-TOP first class
zo **TIPULA** insect genus; daddy-longlegs
TIRADE diatribe; invective; harangue
TIRING dressing; wearying
TIRLED vibrated; twisted
TIRRET handcuff; manacle; fetter
zo **TIRWIT** lapwing
ck **TISANE** herbal drink
md **TISSUE** web; fabric; series
ck **TIT-BIT** tidbit; morsel for birds or cocktails
TITHED taxed (church)
TITHER tithe collector
TITLED yclept; inscribed; named
zo **TITLER** stickle-back
cn **TITLER** lettering screen
bt **TI-TREE** the manuka
TITTER giggle; snigger; laugh
TITTLE an iota; small particle
TITTUP canter (horse-riding)
TMESIS rhetorical intersection
tx **TOBINE** twilled silk
zo **TOCSIN** an alarm; poisonous serum
TODDLE saunter
TOE-CAP boot-tip
ck **TOFFEE** 'butter scotch' sweet
lw **TOFORE** before; heretofore
TOGGED arrayed; dressed up
nt, ae **TOGGLE** wooden pin; ski lift grip; safety rope device
cp **TOGGLE** circut based on stable state
TOILED moiled; strove
TOILER labourer; worker; striver
TOILET dress; attire; washroom (W.C.)
tx **TOISON** a fleece; sheepwool
mu **TOLLED** rang church bells
TOLLER toll-gatherer (highway taxes) (tollgates)
TOLLER bell-ringer
TOL-LOL goodish
TOLSEY toll-booth; mart
TOLTEC early Mexican
ch **TOLUIC TOLVOL**, (methyl) benzine
me **TOMAND** Arabian grain
bt **TOMATO** red fruit-vegetable
nm **TOMAUN** Persion gold coin
mn **TOMBAC TOMBAK**, copper zinc alloy; (bells, gongs)
TOMBED buried and exalted
TOMBIC like a tomb
TOMBOC Javanese weapon
TOMBOY a romping girl; hoyden
zo **TOM-CAT** male feline
zo **TOMCOD** a fish
zo **TOMIAL TOMIUM**, cutting edge of bird's bill
TOMPON inking pad
zo **TOMPOT** blenny fish
zo **TOM-TIT** blue tit
mu **TOMTOM** drum; (N. Amer. Indians)
mu **TONADA** tune, air (Sp.)
TONAME nickname; byname
TONGAN native of Tonga
TONGUE mouth organ; language; lick; scold
rl **TONING** intoning (recitative prayers)
TONING tinting; to suit (colours)
TONISH stylish; having 'tone'
ch **TONITE** an explosive
pl **TONSIL** throat appendage
bt **TOOART** Australian eucalyptus
cr **TOOLED** kitted for production; ornamental style
TOOTED hooted
TOOTER a piper
TOOTHY with teeth too apparent
mu **TOOTLE** play on the flute
TOO-TOO quite so; super
zo **TOPAZA** humming birds
TOP-DOG leader; victor
TOPFUL brimming
TOP-HAT topper
TOPHET place of torment (Hebrew)
md **TOPHUS** (gout)
zo **TOPMAE** insect labrum surface
nt **TOPMAN** top sawyer; dominant partner; demolisher
TOPPED surpassed; filled up; (golf)
TOPPER high hat
TOPPLE fall; tumble; collapse; totter
TORERO bull-fighter on foot
TOROID a symmetrical geometrical fig.
TOROSE TOROUS, swelling; protuberant
TORPID inert; numb; lethargic
TORPOR apathy; dullness; dormancy
TORQUE twisting force (motors)
TORQUE collar; necklace
TORRID sultry; scorching; fiery
TORSEL twisted scroll
bt **TORULA** yeast plant
TOSSED thrown; pitched
TOSSER pitcher; thrower; handy man
TOSS-UP an even chance; spin a coin

T'OTHER the other
TOTING carrying; humping
TOTTED added up
TOTTER topple; reel; rock; stagger
TOTTIE a small tot (rum)
zo **TOUCAN** S. American bird
TOUCHE a palpable hit (fencing)
TOUCHY testy; irascible; petulant
TOUPEE TOUPET, wig; false hair
TOURED journeyed
TOUSED hauled; torn; rumpled
TOUSER a teaser; a worrit
TOUSLE to rumple; ruffle; derange
TOUTED canvassed
TOUTER a tout
nt **TOWAGE** haulage (also by tugs)
TOWARD direction; docile; tractable; apt
TOWERY lofty
zo **TOWHEE** American marsh robin
TOWING dragging; drawing
oc **TOW-NET** water-fauna sample net
zo **TOWSER** a dog
md **TOXOID** detoxified toxin
zo **TOY-DOG** miniature dog
TOYFUL trifling
TOYING dallying; trifling
TOYISH playful; wanton
TOY-MAN a dealer in playthings
ar **TRABAL** beamy
TRABEA Roman consular robe
TRACED trailed; drawn; limned
TRACER investigator; (bullet); artificial isotop; monitor (drawings)
TRADED bartered; vended; sold
TRADER merchant; trafficker
TRAGIC shocking; calamitous
md **TRAGUS** (ear portal)
pc, md **TRANCE** dream state; hypnosis
TRANKA juggler's box
TRAPAN to ensnare; stratagem
TRAPES a slut; a tramp
TRAPPY treacherous
TRASHY rubbishy; worthless
pc, md **TRAUMA** a shock; harsh experience
TRAVEL tour; trip; journey; move; deviation from spin (ice skating)
TRAVIS stable partition
TREATY pact; covenant; alliance
mu **TREBLE** triple; threefold; high voice
TREBLY triply
bt **TREFLE** trefoil; clover
zo **TREMEX** an insect genus
ce **TREMIE** underwater concrete funnel
TREMOR shudder; earth shock (earthquake)
TRENCH deep furrow; groove; -warfare
md **TREPAN** (skull cutting)
TREPAN a cheat; ensnare; trapan
TREPID quaking; trembling; afraid
TRESSY curly
TRIACT having three rays
TRIAGE sorting; classifying state of wounded, injured
lw **TRIALS** performance tests; test cases
TRIBAL clannish
TRICAR motor-cycle
cf **TRICHO-** of the hair (Gr.)
TRICKY intricate; difficult; troublesome
nv **TRICON** on-course signal system
tx **TRICOT** machine-made fabric
bt **TRIFID** three-cleft
ck **TRIFLE** a sweet; gewgaw; daily
zo **TRIGLA** gurnards
TRIGLY dandified
mu **TRIGON** ancient harp; triangle
TRILBY a hat
ch **TRIMER** 3-molecule substance
TRIMLY neatly; compactly; evenly balanced
TRINAL three-fold
zo **TRINGA** sandpiper genus
ro **TRIODE** thermionic valve
ck **TRIOSE** simplest monosaccharide
ga **TRIPLE TRIPLY**, threefold scores (darts) (baseball hit)
TRIPOD three-legged stool or stand
TRIPOS Cambridge examination
zo **TRIPUS** 1 of Weberian vesicles
mu **TRISTE** sad; sorrowful; gloomy
TRITON Neptune's three-pronged fish-spear
zo **TRITON** genus of molluscs
el, ps **TRITON** nucleus of tritium atom
zo **TRITOR** tooth masticatory surface
ch **TRITYL** triphenylmethyl group
rl **TRIUNE** Trinity
TRIVET trevet; small hob; fireside
TRIVIA trivial matters (unimportant)
md **TROCAR** surgical instrument
TROCHE a lozenge; tabloid
zo **TROGON** Central American bird
TROIKA Russian 3-horsed sleigh
TROJAN a champion; a plucky fellow
TROLLY small truck
mu **TROMBA** trumpet (It.)
zo **TROPHI** (insect's mouth)
cf **TROPHO-** of food nourishment (Gr.)
ar **TROPHY** prize; laurels; sculptured arms or armour
TROPIC (Cancer and Capricorn)

md **-TROPIN** benefit of substance on organ
mu **TROPPO** excessively; too much (It.)
ch **TROTYL** explosive
TROUGH groove; trench; furrow; (feeding-)
TROUPE ensemble (circus) (actors)
lw **TROVER** finder (of treasure)
TROWED trusted; believed
to **TROWEL** garden implement
TRUANT shirker; absentee (school)
TRUDGE tramp; plod; march
TRUEST exactest; most veracious
TRUISM axiom; platitude
TRUITE crackled (porcelain)
TRUSTY reliable; staunch; faithful
zo **TRYGON** sting-ray
TRYING irksome; difficult; arduous
TRY-OUT preliminary trial
bt **TSAMBA** black barley (Tibet)
zo **TSETSE** deadly fly (S. Africa)
TSONGA language (Mozambique)
TSWANA language (Africa)
T-TOTUM teetotum; teetotaller (sl.); abstainer
TUAREG tribe (Sahara)
TUBAGE inserting a tube
TUBBED bathed
TUBFUL the contents of a barrel; (bath)
TUB-GIG Welsh open carriage
TUBING piping
TUBULE small tube
TUCHUN Chinese military governor
TUCKED stuffed; folded; pleated
TUCKER bib; frilling
mu **TUCKET** trumpet-call
TUCK-IN large meal; picnic
TUFFET Miss Muffet's seat; grass
TUFTED tufty; crested
zo **TUFTER** a stag-hound
TUGGED TUGGER, heaved/-er; pulled/-er
TUILLE thigh armour
TULWAR Eastern sabre
bt **TUMBAK** coarse Persian tobacco
TUMBLE trip; stumble; somersault
TUMBLY uneven; unstable
TUMEFY to swell; distend; inflate
md **TUMOUR** morbid swelling
TUMPED hilled (gardening)
ck **TUM-TUM** W. Indian food
TUMULI ancient burial mounds
TUMULT uproar; hubbub; turmoil
gl, go **TUNDRA** subarctic plain (permafrost)
TUNDUN a toy; a bull-roarer
ro, tv **TUNE-IN** find station on waveband
TUNGUS Turanian tribe
ro **TUNING** syntonizing
TUNKER dunker; baptist; the great Dipper
TUNNED casked
TUNNEL underground passage (chunnel)
zo **TUPAIA** tree-shrew (Malay)
bt **TUPELO** gum-tree
zo **TUPPED** butted; rammed; served (ewes)
zo **TUPPER** ram; bricklayer's labourer
zo **TURACO** Afr. plantain-eating bird
TURBAN oriental head-dress (Sikh)
TURBID muddy; cloudy; confused
zo **TURBOT** a flatfish
zo **TURDUS** the thrush
TUREEN a receptacle for soup
TURFED sodded; kicked out
TURFEN (turf); covered with sward
TURGID bloated; tumid; bombastic
md **TURGOR** fullness
bt **TURION** runner; underground shoot
zo, ck **TURKEY** straight talk; poultry
mn **TURKIS** turquoise
cr **TURNED** revolved (-hinged); (lathe)
zo **TURNER** lathe-worker; pigeon
TURN-IN part-exchange deal; bed-time
bt **TURNIP** old-fashioned watch; root
TURN-UP attendance; (trousers); (trumps)
zo **TURNUS** swallow-tail butterfly
to **TURREL** tool used by coopers
ar **TURRET** minaret; small tower (castle)
zo **TURTLE** marine tortoise
TURVES plural of turf; sods (peat) (fuel)
ar **TUSCAN** people; art; architecture (It.)
TUSKAR peat cutter
zo **TUSKED TUSKER**, with ivory tusks; elephant
bt **TUSSAC** a tussock; cushion (grass)
tx **TUSSAH TUSSER**, wild silkworm's silk
md **TUSSIS** a cough
TUSSLE scuffle; wrestle; contend
bt **TUTSAN** a plant
TU-WHIT TU-WHOO, owlish night calls
TUXEDO dinner jacket (USA)
TUYERE a pipe; twyer
zo **TWAITE** species of shad
TWAITE THWAITE, arable acreage
TWEENY very small; maid
TWELVE a dozen
TWENTY a score
TWICER compositor and pressman

bt **TWIGGY** abounding in shoots (skeletal)
tx **TWILLY** cotton-cleaning machine
tx **TWINED** twisted; meandered
bt **TWINER** climbing plant; cord maker
TWINGE pang; twitch; spasm
TWITCH twinge; jerk
tx **TWITTY** yarns with twisted portions
tx **TWO-PLY** of 2 layers (wood, wool, etc.)
T'WOULD it would
TWO-WAY (a switch)
TYCOON Japanese prince; oil magnate (Am.)
zo **TYLOTE** sponge-spicule
mu **TYMBAL** kettledrum; timbal
pr **TYMPAN** printing frame
TYPHON evil genius (Egypt)
md **TYPHUS** gaol fever
TYPIFY categorize; symbolize; exemplify
pc **TYPIFY** categorizing of persons; objects; (typewriter)
TYPIST typewriter user
TYRANT autocrat; despot
TYRIAN purple
mn **TYRITE** a mineral
zo **TYSTIE** the black guillemot
mu, zo **TZETZE** Abyssinian guitar

U

zo **UAKARI** S. American monkeys
UBERTY fruitfulness
UBIETY local relation
UBIQUE everywhere
UDMURT native of Central Asia
U-GAUGE laboratory test tube of glass
UGLIFY to make hideous
UGLILY in an ungainly manner
UGRIAN UGRO Hungaric-Finnic-Turkic
UGSOME hideous; gruesome
mn **UIGITE** a silicate of aluminium
md **ULITIS** gum inflammation
ULLAGE ULLING, lack of fullness in a cask
bt **ULMOUS** (elm exudation)
md **ULNARE** cuneiform bone
md **ULOSIS** cicatrization
ULSTER overcoat
ULTIMO last; in last month
ULTION revenge
UMBERY UMBRAL, dark mustard colour; shade
zo **UMBLES** entrails of deer
UMBRAL shady; darksome
UMBRIL umbrel; helmet vizor
UMLAUT vowel inflection (Ger.)
UMPIRE arbiter; referee; judge
UMWELT one's relationship with the environment (Ger.)
UNABLE powerless; impotent; unskilled
UNAWED undismayed; undaunted; unimpressed
UNBANK (stoking)
UNBEAR to release from burden; unharness; ungear
UNBELT remove or undo belt, garment
nt **UNBEND** stand straight; unfasten sails; cast loose (rope)
UNBEND UNBIND, release from bondage
UNBENT relaxed; untied
UNBIAS to free from prejudice
nt **UNBIND** release from tether; knots; set free
nt **UNBITT** (release cable)
UNBOLT unlatch; unlock (doors etc.)
UNBONE remove the bones
UNBOOT to take off shoes, boots
UNBORN non-existent; uncreated
UNBRED of ignoble birth
UNBURY disinter; exhume
UNCAGE release from captivity; (ideas)
UNCALM to disturb; agitate
UNCAMP dislodge; evict; remove
UNCAPE unhood; disrobe; defrock; reveal
UNCART unload (at destination)
UNCASE unpack; display; unsheath
UNCATE hooked
UNCIAL a script used in ancient MSS.
UNCLAD naked; nude
nt **UNCLEW** release guy ropes; (moorings)
UNCLOG clear drains; unhamper
ag **UNCOCK** make gun safe; remove stooks (harvesting)
UNCOIF remove cap
nt **UNCOIL** unwind; straighten out; (snakes); (ropes)
UNCOIN withdraw from currency
mu **UNCOOL** unrelaxed; unpleasant; jazz
UNCORD set free; release knots
UNCORK remove cork from bottle
UNCOWL remove cloak; defrock; expose
lw **UNCURB** remove restrictions; (legal obstacle)

UNCURL straighten out (hair); untwist
rl **UNDEAN** deprive of that office; unfrock
UNDECK divest of ornaments
UNDERN 9 a.m.; the third hour
UNDIES underclothes
UNDINE water-nymph
nt **UNDOCK** to separate space ships; leave dock
UNDOER subversionary agent
UNDONE unfastened (clothes); yet to be done
UNDUKE deprive of duke's rank
UNDULL sharpen; whet
UNDULY excessively; improperly
UNEASE mental unrest; anxiety
UNEASY restive; disturbed
UNEVEN rugged; rough; odd
UNFACE expose the character within
UNFAIR inequitable; unjust; partial
nt **UNFAST** insecurely tied
lw **UNFEED** without fees (salary)
UNFELT callous; insensitive (action)
UNFILE remove from a file
UNFINE shabby
lw **UNFIRM** weak legally; unsound
UNFIST to release; unhand
UNFOLD spread out; reveal (thoughts)
UNFOOL restore from folly; unhoax
lw **UNFREE** tied; restricted
nt **UNFURL** spread out sail; flag; unroll
UNGEAR to unharness; unbear
UNGILD **UNGILT**, remove the gold
UNGILL release from a gill-net
UNGIRD **UNGIRT**, release girdle or girth (harness)
UNGLUE unstick; release
UNGOWN disrobe; expel from university
zo **UNGUAL** **UNGUIS**, having claws; sharp nails
md **UNGULA** instrument; cylinder section
UNGYVE unfetter; free (from chains)
UNHAND **UNHOLD**, cry for release
UNHANG remove from drying line
UNHASP unfasten; (free from a catch)
UNHEAD behead; decapitate
nt **UNHELM** remove helmet or rudder
UNHEWN rough
UNHIVE deprive of habitation (bees)
UNHOLD **UNHAND**, cry for release
UNHOLY impious; profane; ungodly
UNHOOK disconnect; release from fastenings
ck **UNHUNG** (unhanged game meat); (rejected pictures)
UNHURT without injury (personal)
UNHUSK to shell
rl **UNIATE** Greek Catholic sect
UNIBLE **UNIFIC**, unifiable
bt **UNIOLA** American grass genus
UNIPED single-footed
pg **UNIPOD** single support camera mount
UNIQUE peculiar; sole; unexampled
UNISEX for either; or both sexes together
mu **UNISON** harmony; concord; accord
UNITAL unique; singular
UNITED combined; coalesced
UNITER joiner; merger
UNJUST biased; partial
UNKENT unknown
UNKEPT independent; discarded; rejected
UNKIND cruel; harsh; unfriendly
UNKING dethrone
UNKINK straighten out; (loosen knots)
UNKNIT unravel interlocked matter
nt **UNKNOT** untie; unfasten
UNLACE loosen, undo (shoes)
UNLADE discharge cargo; (burdens); unload
UNLAID virginal; untwisted; not allayed
UNLASH let loose; unbind; untie
pr **UNLEAD** remove lead
UNLEAL unloyal
UNLENT not loaned
UNLESS if not; except if; when if
UNLIKE dissimilar; different from
UNLIME extract the lime
tx **UNLINE** remove the lining (clothes)
UNLINK unfasten; undo a chain
el **UNLIVE** not electrified; safe
UNLOAD unburden; remove from; give vent (feeling)
UNLOCK unfasten; open case
UNLORD deprive of that dignity
UNMADE not manufactured
UNMAKE destroy; dismantle
UNMASK expose; denounce; reveal
UNMEET unworthy; unbecoming
nt **UNMOOR** release a ship from moorings
UNMOWN uncut grass (lawn)
UNNAIL open by extracting nails
UNOWED not in debt
UNPACK disburden; open; uncover possessions
cp **UNPACK** recover data from storage

UNPAID still owing; outstanding
UNPICK take apart (clothes)
UNPROP remove a support
UNQUIT not discharged (from profession)
UNREAD not perused; ignorant
UNREAL fantastic; visionary; illusory
UNREEL show; tell a story; (film)
UNREIN slacken the rein
UNREST disquiet; unease; fidgetiness
UNRIPE immature; crude; green
UNROBE deprive of robes of honour
UNROLL open out; uncoil; evolve
UNROOF remove a roof (hurricanes)
UNROOT **UPROOT**, extirpate; eradicate
mo **UNROPE** release from rope (climbing)
UNROVE **UNREEVED**, rope freed from pulley, block
UNRULY riotous; turbulent
UNSAFE risky; hazardous; insecure
UNSAID unspoken (hint)
UNSEAM unpick sewing (clothes); rip; tear
UNSEAT to throw a rider; remove an official
UNSEEL to open the eyes
UNSEEN invisible
UNSELF absence of personality
UNSENT not despatched
UNSEWN unstitched
UNSHED retained; kept
nt **UNSHIP** remove part of a machine, mast of ship
UNSHOD barefoot; without shoes
UNSHUT open
UNSOLD not purchased
UNSOWN not propagated
UNSPAR remove spars
UNSPIN unravel
nt **UNSTEP** remove (a mast)
UNSTOP remove stoppage; make workable
UNSUNG forgotten; neglected
UNSURE uncertain
UNTACK disjoin
UNTAME wild; undomesticated
UNTELL never to narrate
UNTIDY slovenly; disorderly
UNTIED undone; unloosed
UNTILE remove tiles from roof
UNTOLD not narrated; numberless; innumerable
UNTOMB exhume
UNTORN unrent
UNTRIM disarray
UNTROD little frequented
UNTRUE false; fallacious; spurious
UNTUCK open bedclothes
UNTUNE disorder settings of a machine
UNTURN untwist; unscrew
UNUSED new; unaccustomed to; left idle
UNVEIL official opening; uncover a statue; reveal
UNWARM chillsome
UNWARY rash; incautious; indiscreet
UNWELL ailing; sick; indisposed
UNWEPT not lamented
UNWILY lacking in craft
UNWIND uncoil; disentangle; relax
UNWIND to show all instructions used
UNWISE indiscreet; imprudent
UNWOOF unweave
UNWORN new; unimpaired
UNWRAP open parcel; uncloak; disclose
UNYOKE release from harness; set free
UPBEAR sustain; elevate
mu **UPBEAT** unaccentuated rhythm
UPBIND confine
UPCAST uptoss; ventilation shaft
gl **UPCAST** upward strata displacement
UPCOIL to coil
cp **UPDATE** bring into line; modernize
UPFLOW upgush (oil)
UPGROW develop; evolve
UPGUSH upflow
UPHILL gradient; sloping; (effort)
UPHOLD advocate; maintain; champion
nt **UPHROE** awning support
UPKEEP maintenance
UPLAND highland
UPLEAN to incline upwards (Austral.)
UPLIFT improvement; moral encouragement
UP-LINE line to London (railway)
UPMOST topmost
UPPERS of shoes (leather); stimulating drugs
UP-PILE accumulate; upheap
UPPING departing suddenly; price raising; (swan-)
UPPISH **UPPITY**, being over-important; bumptious
UPREAR to raise the backside (horses)
UPRISE to revolt; ascend
UPROAR riot; hubbub; turmoil
UPROOT remove & destroy; (-self from home)

UPRUSH sudden upward surge (air, oil, water)
UPSHOT outcome; issue; result
UPSIDE topside
UPTAKE chimney; speed of learning
UPTILT bend upwards
cp **UPTIME** serviceable time, normal
UPTOWN city centre (if north)
UPTURN create disorder; upheaval
UPWARD ascending; uphill
UPWAYS upward
UPWELL upspring; gush
nt **UNWIND** into the wind; windward
UPWISE top side up
ch **URACIL** pyrimidine; nucleic acid
zo **URAEUM** tail-end of bird
URAEUS serpent emblem (Egypt)
ga **URAKEN** back fist blow (karate)
URANIA Muse of astronomy
URANIC (uranium); celestial
ch **URANIN** yellow dye
URANUS a planet; father of Saturn
ch **URANYL** chemical radical
md **URATES** urine salts
URBANE courteous; polite; affable
URCEUS single-handed jug; urn
zo **URCHIN** hedgehog; brat; gamin
ch **UREASE** enzyme
ch **UREIDE** acid derivative of urea
URESIS passing urine
md **URETER** duct that carries urine
md **URETIC** a medicine
URGENT pressing; imperative
URGING impelling; inciting
URNING consigning to an urn
ch **URONIC** of sugar oxidation compound
zo **UROPOD** abdominal limb
zo **URSINE** bear-like
bt **URTICA** nettle genus
hd **URVANT** turned up
USABLE employable; applicable
rl **USAGER** a religionist
USANCE usury
USEFUL helpful; beneficial
USTION combustion
USURER money-lender; a Shylock
USWARD towards us
UTERUS womb
UTGARD abode of Loki (Scand.)
UTMOST extreme; farthest
UTOPIA a political romance; an ideal society
md **UVEOUS** grape-like
md **UVULAR** (uvula)

V

VACANT void; empty; inane; free
VACATE quit; leave; annul; rescind
VACHER cow-keeper
VACUNA Roman goddess of horticulture
VACUUM void; vacuity; emptiness
VAGARY whim; crotchet; fancy
zo **VAGINA** sexual passage in female
VAGOUS wandering; erratic
VAGUER more indefinite; dimmer
VAIDIC Vedic; (philosophical)
VAILED submitted; tipped
VAILER a yielder
VAINER more conceited; falser
VAINLY ineffectually; proudly
VAISYA (Hindu caste)
rl **VAKASS** Armenian clerical vestment
lw **VAKEEL** Indian attorney
VALETE farewell
VALGUS knock-kneed man; club-foot
ch **VALINE** amino acid
VALING receding; lowering
VALISE portmanteau; holdall
ch, md **VALIUM** tranquillizer
rl, mu **VALKYR VALKYRIES** Odin's Amazons (Wagner)
VALLAR (rampart)
bd **VALLEY** dale; vale; dell; glen; dingle; (roof-edge) tile
VALLUM Roman rampart
VALOUR heroism; courage; prowess
VALUED esteemed; prized; treasured
VALUER appraiser
VALVED having valves
VAMOSE vamoose; to clear out
VAMPED improvised; patched; repaired
mu **VAMPER** a pianist; siren
VANDAL barbarian; destroyer
VANISH fade; disappear; depart
VANITY conceit; egotism; futility
VAN-MAN pantechnicon worker
zo **VANNER** light cart horse
md **VAPORS** vapours; nervous dejection
VAPOUR steam; reek; fume; to boast
VARIED diverse; motley; altered
VARIER an inconsistent person
VARLET scoundrel; rascal; knave
zo **VARMIN VERMIN, VARMINT**, noxious pests (rats)
VARSAL universal
rl **VARUNA** The Creator (Hindu Myth)
go **VARZEA** Amazonian flood plain (Brazil)
VASSAL retainer; dependant; bondman

VASTER on a grander scale
VASTLY spaciously; widely; immensely
md **VASTUS** a thigh muscle
tx **VAT-DYE** oxidation of textiles
br **VATTED** mellowing; maturing
VAULTY arched
VAWARD vanward; in the van
bd **V-BRICK** perforated instead of cavitied
VEADER Jewish intercalary month
VECTOR data display organism transmitting parasites
ma **VECTOR** force with thrust, direction, and magnitude
VEDDAH native Cingalese
VEDUTA painting of recognizable scene
nt **VEERED** changed course; shifted
VEILED concealed; shrouded; glozed
VEINED streaked; variegated; venose
VELARY a sail or awning
bt **VELATE** enveloped; veiled
mu **VELETA** waltz
VELITE lightly armed Roman soldier
VELLED removed turf
VELLON Spanish money of account
VELLUM parchment from calf-skin
zo **VELLUS** downy foetal hair
mu **VELOCE** very quick
VELOUR velvet
VELURE velvet; smoothing pad
tx **VELVET** soft silky stuff
VENDED sold; peddled; hawked
VENDEE the buyer; purchaser
lw **VENDER** **VENDOR**, one who sells
vt **VENDUE** auction; poultry disease
VENEER thin surface layer (fine wood); superficial
ga **VENERY** sport; hunting
ga **VENEUR** head game-keeper
VENGER **AVENGER**, wrathful punisher of wrong doer
VENIAL excusable; pardonable
VENITE 95th Psalm
VENNEL an alley-way (Sc.)
pl **VENOSE** **VENOUS**, veined
VENTED poured forth; uttered; emitted
md **VENTER** the abdomen
mu **VENTIL** (cornet valve)
cf **VENTRO-** ventral from the anterior; stomach, abdomen
zo **VENULE** blood vessel in chordata
VERANO dry season C. Amer. summer (Sp.)
VERBAL oral; by word of mouth
hd **VERDOY** charged with heraldic flowers
VERDUN antique rapier (Fr.)
VERGED sloped; inclined; bordered on
me **VERGEE** about half acre
rl **VERGER** church caretaker
VERIFY confirm; authenticate; identify
VERILY truly; really; certainly
cn **VERITE** realism; film documentary technique
VERITY actuality; fact; reality
zo **VERMES** worms
VERMIL vermilion colour
zo **VERMIN** noxious animal; rabble
zo **VERMIS** main part of cerebellum
VERNAL springlike
VERREL ferrule; see virole
hd **VERREY** vaire; furry
VERSAL universal (Shak.)
VERSED skilled; familiar; accomplished
VERSER versifier; poetaster
mu **VERSET** prelude
VERSUS against; opposing
VERTEX top; apex; acme; zenith
zo **VERVET** S. African monkey
md **VESICA** a bladder; a sac
as **VESPER** evening star; Venus
nt **VESSEL** receptacle; utensil
VESTAL chaste (virgins)
VESTED fixed; legalized; established
rl **VESTRY** sacristy
bt **VETCHY** (vetch)
VETOED prohibited; banned; forbidden
VETTED carefully examined
VETUST ancient
VEXING annoying; tormenting; trying
VIABLE capable of existence
VIANDS food; provisions
VIATIC (journey)
VIATOR wayfarer
zo **VIBRIO** spiral bacillus
VICTIM a dupe; martyr; sacrifice
VICTOR conqueror; winner; champion
zo **VICUNA** cousin of wild llama
VIDAME French noble
VIDEOT media addict (TV)
VIDUAL widowed
mu **VIELLE** antique viol (Fr.)
VIEWED beheld; surveyed; scanned
VIEWER examiner; inspector
VIEWLY striking
VIGOUR force; energy; manliness

rl **VIHARA** Buddhist temple
nt **VIKING** Norse sea-rover; longshipman
VILELY basely; ignobly; malignantly
VILEST lowest; abject
VILIFY defame; traduce; disparage
md **VILLUS** hair; wool
hd **VILNED** wounded beast
rl **VIMANA** Indian temple
VINAGE wine doctoring
VINERY grape house
VINNEY a blue Dorset cheese
VINOSE VINOUS, concerning wine
VINTED made into wine
VINTRY wine shop; bodega; bistro
mn **VIOLAN** violet blue
bt **VIOLET** a colour; flower
VIOLIN fiddle; instrument with bow
VIRAGO nagging; overbearing woman (shrew)
VIRENT verdant; green; fresh
VIRGIN maiden; damsel; spinster; untouched; (city) fresh
VIRILE manly; robust; masculine
zo **VIRION** mature virus
hd **VIROLE** ferrule; hoop
VIROSE VIROUS, venomous; poisonous
VIRTUE integrity; probity; goodness
VISAED endorsed (passport)
VISAGE face; aspect; countenance
VISCID sticky; glutinous; tenacious
bt **VISCIN** mistletoe fruit substance
bt **VISCUM** mistletoe
md **VISCUS** an entrail; singular form of viscera, innards
rl **VISHNU** The Preserver (Hindu God)
VISIER VIZIER, leading Ottoman minister
VISILE with visual preference
VISION view; foresight; dream; eye sight (tele-)
VISIVE visual
cp **VISUAL** visible; perceptible; data display unit
VITALS essential organs (heart, genitals)
VITRIC glassy
mu **VIVACE** lively
VIVARY VIVARIUM, limited zoo
VIVIFY animate; enliven; quicken
VIZARD mask; visor
VOCULE a feeble cry
VOICED said; declared; uttered
VOICER spokesman
VOIDED evacuated; cancelled
VOIDER shallow basket
hd **VOLANT** flying; nimble; active
mu **VOLATA** rapid phrase (It.)
VOLENT exercising will power (gunfire)
VOLERY flight of birds
ga **VOLLEY** salvo (gunfire); strike with racquet (tennis) (ball game)
cp **VOLUME** book; tome; bulk; mass; magnetic storage; sound
VOLUTE spiral scroll
bt **VOLVOX** freshwater algae
md **VOMICA** an abscess in the lungs
md **VOMITO** yellow fever
rl **VOODOO VOUDOU**, Haitian witchcraft beliefs
VORAGO whirlpool; vortex; gull
hd **VORANT** devouring
VORTEX whirlpool; whirlwind
VOTARY a fan; devotee; zealot
VOTING electing; polling
VOTIVE vowed; devoted
VOULGE ancient pike (weapon) (Fr.)
VOWING pledging; promising
VOYAGE trip; cruise; passage
VOYANT seer with psychic vision
VULCAN god of fire
VULGAR coarse; ordinary; vernacular

W

WABBLE WOBBLE, stand unsteadily
ar **WABBLY** insecure; unstable (construction)
WADDED stuffed; filled
WADDIE Australian war club
WADDLE walk like a duck
WADING walking through water (sea)
tx **WADMAL** thick woollen cloth
lw **WADSET** a mortgage
WAFERY wafer-like
ck **WAFFLE** a grilled pancake
WAFTED floated; waved; beckoned
WAFTER a fan
WAGGED WAGGLE, shook about; (dog's tail); (-a finger)
zo **WAGGEL** great gull
WAGGLE vibrate; oscillate (golf)
rw **WAGGON WAGON**, cart; caravan; railway-
WAGING betting; venturing; conducting
WAG-WIT a would-be wit
rl **WAHABI** Puritan Moslem
WAHINE Maori woman; female surfer (Am.)
WAILED bemoaned; lamented
WAILER howler; weeper
WAITED attended; tarried; lingered

WAITER attendant; servitor; garçon
WAIVED **WAIVER**, relax the rules; release penalty
WAKING arousing from sleep; (-to new ideas)
WALING chastising
ce **WALING** trench-timbering plank
WALKED strolled; hiked
WALKER pedestrian; (street-); (sleep-); (jay-); frame
WALLAH Government official (Indian Raj)
WALLED enclosed
WALLER a wall-builder
WALLET purse; scrip; pouch
WALLEY skating jump
br **WALLOP** to hit; to beat; beer
WALLOW lounge in heat; flounder around; grovel
bt **WALNUT** commonest European nut
zo **WALRUS** tusked seal; (morse)
WAMBLE to be queasy
tx **WAMMUS** knitted jacket (USA)
WAMPEE a Chinese fruit
WAMPUM beads used as cash (N.Am. Ind.)
WANDER stroll at random; roam; (mind-)
bt **WANDOO** Australian white gum
WANGLE to obtain by craft, by persuasion
as **WANING** shrinking; ebbing (moon phase)
WANKER winder; handyman
WANKLE weak; unstable
WANNED made pale
WANTED needed; lacked; desired
WANTER a requirer; craver
WANTON frisky; uncontrolled; frolicsome
zo **WAPITI** stag; American reindeer
zo **WAPPER** gudgeon; ball-on-string weapon
zo **WAPPET** yelping cur
mu, vt **WARBLE** cattle tumour; quaver; sing
WAR-CRY slogan
ga **WARDED** guarded; parried (fencing)
WARDEN custodian; protector; curator
WARDER turnkey; keeper; jailer
WARIER more cautious
WARILY cautiously; carefully; cannily
WARMAN warrior; man-at-arms
WARMER hotter; nearer; (a bribe)
WARMLY earnestly; ardently; zealously
WARMTH heat; enthusiasm; fervency
WARM-UP loosening exercises; pre-match
WARNED cautioned; notified; apprised
WARNER an admonisher
WARPED distorted; perverted; biased
tx, wv **WARPER** a weaver; a twister
WARREN labyrinthine; rabbit burrows
WAR-TAX tax to help war
md **WARTED** verrucose
ck **WASABI** Jap. horseradish
WASHED bathed; cleaned (clothes)
pb **WASHER** metal ring; tap root
WASH-IN increase in angle of incidence
WASH-UP cleaning dishes
WASTED frittered; squandered
WASTEL a fine sort of bread
WASTER a cudgel; spendthrift; chisel; defective brick
WATERY aqueous; dilute; thin; insipid
zo **WATTLE** fowl's gills
bt **WATTLE** a acacia; a hurdle
WAULED **WAWLED, HOWLED**, (caterwauled); (street calling)
WAVERY unsteady; tremulous
WAVING undulating; swaying
WAVURE procrastination
WAX-END cobbler's thread
WAXIER more irate
WAXING increasing; growing; (shoe polish); (skiing)
WAYLAY to ambush; kidnap; mug; rob
WAYOUT advanced; unusual
WEAKEN impair; enfeeble; enervate
WEAKER more dilute; thinner; feebler
WEAKLY delicately; infirmly; fraily
WEALTH riches; opulence; abundance
WEANED newly independent (baby); free; withdrawn
WEAPON instrument of combat; (economic)
WEARER bearer; (-of clothing) (-of flag)
zo **WEASEL** explosive carnivore
wv, zo **WEAVER** intertwined cloth maker; bird
WEAZEN wizened; sharp; shrivelled (Sc.)
wv **WEBBED** arachnoid; woven (duck-foot)
md **WEB-EYE** a disease of the cornea
pr **WEB-FED** of printing paper by reel

WEDDED married; espoused; spliced
WEDELN S-course downhill ski technique
WEDGED joined; jammed; crowded
WEEDED hoed; (eradicated) (gardening)
to **WEEDER** garden tool; gardener
WEEKLY hebdomadary; a periodical
WEENED imagined; thought
zo **WEEPER** Niobe; a monkey
zo **WEEVER** sting-fish
zo **WEEVIL** a beetle
ps **WEIGHT** moving force needed to overcome inertia
me **WEIGHT** measure of heaviness; load; burden
WELDED joined; metal parts fused in heat (process)
WELKIN sky, clouds; universe (ring)
WELLED poured forth; spouted; gushed
WELTED edged; bordered
WELTER wallow; flounder; heavy
WENDED journeyed; wandered
WENDIC a Sorabian
WESTER to turn westward
WET-BOB Eton aquatic sportsman
zo **WETHER** a castrated ram
WETTER damper; more showery
nt **WHALER** whale-boat
WHALLY having greenish-white eyes
WHATSO of whatever kind
WHEELY circular
WHEEZE puff; blow; ancient joke
WHEEZY asthmatic; whistling mechanical sound
WHELKY rounded; protuberant
WHENCE wherefrom
nt **WHERRY** a liquor; sailing boat
WHEUGH! exclamation of surprise
zo **WHEWER** the widgeon; duck
ck **WHEYEY** of curdfree, watery milk
zo **WHIDAH** **WHYDAH**, African weaver bird
WHILED of time passing away; beguiled
WHILES meanwhile
WHILLY to cajole; to wheedle
WHILOM formerly
WHILST while
WHIMSY fad; caprice; fancy; crotchet
WHINED **WHINER**, whimper in complaining tone
bt **WHINNY** horsey greeting; gorse
WHIPPY flexible; springy
WHISHT! hush!
WHISKY colour of Napoleon's white horse
WHITEN blanch; bleach; turn pale
WHITER purer; brighter
WHITES flannel trousers (cricket); (eyes); (eggs)
WHOLLY entirely; fully; utterly
WHOMSO every one whom
WICKED evil; sinful; ungodly; nefarious
bt **WICKEN** mountain ash
bt **WICKER** pliant twig; osier
WICKET small gate; (cricket)
bt **WICOPY** American basswood
WIDELY spaciously; extensively; rifely
WIDEST broadest; remotest
WIELDY manageable
WIFELY of the missus
zo **WIGEON** **WIDGEON**, duck
WIGGED scolded; reproved; chid
WIGGLE **WAGGLE**, **WRIGGLE**, snake-like movement
WIGWAG flag-wag; twist
WIGWAM Indian tent (tepee) (Amer.)
WILDER more impulsive; bewildered
WILDLY fiercely; recklessly; savagely
WILFUL wanton; perverse; obdurate
WILIER craftier; slyer
WILILY artfully; cunningly; insidiously
WILING beguiling; deceiving
lw **WILLED** intended; resolved; bequeathed
WILLER one who decides forcefully
zo **WILLET** North American snipe
bt **WILLOW** a cricket bat tree
WILTED drooped; withered
to **WIMBLE** to drill; gimlet
WIMBLE nimble; active
WIMPLE medieval female headdress; ripple
WINCED flinched; quailed
WINCER a shrinker
tx **WINCEY** winsey; a fabric
WINDED blown; lost breath; caught scent
WINDER to fan; to winnow; a key
WINDLE a spindle; reel
WINDOW lattice; casement
WIND-UP crank a machine for starting; (clock); twist
WINERY where wine is bottled/stored
WINGED alate; rapid; wounded
ga **WINGER** enclosed chair; 'outside' forward (football)
WINKED twinkled; flickered; acquiesced

WINKER horse's blinker
zo, bt **WINKLE** sea-snail; (periwinkle)
WINNER victor; conqueror; champion
ag **WINNOW** open-air threshing; separate grain from chaff
tx **WINSEY** wincey; twilled cotton
WINTER hyemal, viernal; cold season
WINTRY icy; frosty; cheerless
WIPING deterging; rubbing
WIRIER capable of greater strain
WIRILY vigorously; tenaciously
WIRING circuits; telegraphing
WISARD WIZARD, sorcerer; necromancer
WISDOM sagacity; knowledge
WISELY sagely; sensibly; sapiently
WISEST most learned and judicious
WISHED listed; wanted; longed for
WISHER desirer; yearner
WISKET a basket
WISTLY earnestly; attentively
WITHAL together with; likewise
WITHED bound with a withe
WITHER fade; pine; languish
WITHIN not exceeding; indoors
WITH-IT up to date; aware of trends
WITTED alert; wise
zo **WITWAL** popinjay; woodpecker
WIVELY WIFELY, of a spouse
hd **WIVERN WYVERN**, winged dragon
WOBBLE wabble; oscillate; vibrate
WOBBLY unstable; unsteady
WOEFUL waeful; tragic; grievous
WOLFER voracious feeder
zo **WOLVES** predacious animals
zo **WOMBAT** burrowing marsupial
WONDER marvel; miracle; prodigy; awe
WONING a dwelling
WONTED accustomed; usual
ck **WONTON** 'Chinese ravioli', cooked in soup
fr **WOODED** afforested; timbered
WOODEN made of timber; impassive
ac **WOOFER** bass loudspeaker
WOOING courting; courtship
tx **WOOLLY** lanate; of wool
WORDED expressed; phrased
WORKED moiled; strove; slaved
WORKER hand; toiler; operative
WORK-UP rehearsal; exercise; obtaining data, become heated
WORMED crept; insinuated; crawled
zo **WORMUL WORNIL**, cow maggot
zo **WORREL** lizard (Eygpt)
WORRIT an annoyance
WORSEN to defeat; to deteriorate
WORSER far worse
WORTHY exemplary; noble; meritorious
WOUNDY excessive; injurious
zo **WOU-WOU** silver gibbon; wow-wow (Java)
WOWSER kill-joy; fanatical Puritan
WRAITH apparition; ghost; spectre
zo **WRASSE** prickly fish
WRATHY apt to wrath; choleric
WREATH festoon; garland; chaplet
to **WRENCH** strain; sprain; twist; spanner
WRETCH villain; vagabond; miscreant
WRIEST most distorted
WRIGHT an artificer; mechanic
WRITER scribe; author; scribbler
WRITHE squirm; wriggle; contort
WUZZLE to jumble (USA)
hd **WYVERN WIVERN**, heraldic dragon

X

XANADU Kubla Khan's country estate
XANGTI Zeus (Chinese)
cf **XANTHO-** of yellowness
XENIAL genial; friendly
XENIUM gift; picture of still life
zo **XENOPS** tree-creeper birds (S. Amer.)
XERXES Persian King; Ahasuerus
X-GUIDE transmission line
XOANON primitive Greek statue
md **X-RAYED** (Rontgen rays)
ch **XYLENE** a benzene derivative
mn **XYLITE** asbestos
XYLOID like wood
bt **XYLOMA** internally spore-forming body
ch **XYLOSE** wood sugar
md **XYSTER** a bone scraper
ar **XYSTOS XYSTUS**, covered portico (Gr.)

Y

YABBER JABBER, speech (Australian)
zo **YAFFLE** the green woodpecker
YAGGER pedlar; hawker (Sc.)
rl **YAHVEH JAHVEH, JEHOVAH**, God of the Hebrews
YAKSKA Hindu gnome
YAMMER whine; blather; grumble
YANKED heaved; pulled up; hauled

YANKEE Northern American
nt **YANKEE** a specially large jib
YANKER a big lie (Sc.)
ck **YAOURT** **YOGHURT**, fermented milk
zo **YAPOCK** S. Amer. water-opossum
YAPPED yelped
zo **YAPPER** a yapping dog
YARDED confined
YARNED related; narrated
YARPHA peaty soil (Shetland)
bt **YARRAH** Australian red gum tree
bt **YARROW** the milfoil
pp **YARYAN** soda-recovery method
YAUPON holly (used as tea)
nt **YAWING** side-to-side movement in rough sea
YAWLED howled; cried
YAWNED gaped; oscitated
YCLEPT by name of; called
YEANED **YEENED**, brought forth
YEARLY annual
YEASTY turbid; frothy; foamy
YELLED bawled; howled; screamed
YELLOW cowardly
YELPED yauped; yapped; barked
YELPER yapper
YEMENI native of Yemen
mn **YENITE** a silicate of iron
nt **YEOMAN** a beefeater; farmer; tower
YERKED jerked
bt **YER-NUT** pig-nut
YES-MAN sycophant; ministerial
YESTER previous; last
YEXING hiccuping
YOGISM a Hindu philosophy
YOICKS! a hunting cry
me **YOJANA** about 5 miles (8 km) (Indian)
YOKING coupling; linking; harnessing; binding
ck **YOLKED** having a yolk; an eggy jolke
YONDER over there
YONKER a stripling
YONNIE pebble (Aus.)
YORKER (cricket)
YORUBA tribe (South Sahara)
YOUTHY young; callow
YOU-UNS you, you ones
YOWLED howled; yelled
zo **YOWLEY** yellow bunting
rw **Y-TRACK** reversing lines for trains
ch **YTTRIA** oxide of yttrium
ch **YTTRIC** containing yttrium
zo **YUCKER** American woodpecker
YURROP US word for Europe

Z

ZABIAN Sabian; non-Christian gnostic
ZABISM Sabianism
zo **ZABRUS** beetle genus
ZACCAB Yucatan wall plaster
ZACCHO the base of a pedestal
mn **ZAFFER** **ZAFFRE**, cobalt ore
bt **ZAMITE** fossil-plant
zo **ZANDER** sander; pike-perch
ZANIES clowns; buffoons
tx **ZANTHA** knitted fabric
bt **ZAPOTE** plums (Mexico)
tx **ZARAPE** **SERAPE**, Mexican blanket
ZAREBA **ZERABA**, **ZARIBA**, fortified camp
mn **ZARNEC** orpiment
ZEALOT fanatic; bigot; partisan
bc **ZEATIN** adenine derivative
nt **ZEBECK** Algerian pirate-ship
ZEDONK offspring of zebra (m.) and donkey (f.)
zo **ZEEKOE** **SEACOW** manatee (S. Africa)
ZEETAK red-coral (S. Africa)
ZEMZEM sacred fountain at Mecca
ZENANA women's quarter (Ind.)
ZENDIK Eastern heretic; magician
ZENITH acme; apex; climax; summit
ZENZIK maths term
mt **ZEPHYR** the west wind; soft breeze
nm **ZEQUIN** **SEQUIN**, gold coin decoration
ZEREBA **ZAREBA**, thorn bush stockade
gl, go **ZEUGEN** table-like masses of rock in deserts
ZEUGMA grammatical conjunction
zo **ZICSAC** sicsac; crocodile bird
ZIG-ZAG alternating turns; hairpin bends; horse show
ZILLAH Indian district
ZIMONE (gluten)
ZINCKY like zinc
zo **ZINGEL** perch; Danube fish
bt **ZINNIA** a flower
ZIPPED whizzed; encoded
ZIPPER zip-fastener
mn **ZIRCON** a silicate
mu **ZITHER** the cithern
zo **ZIVOLA** yellow-hammer
ZODIAC a heavenly-girdle; the ecliptic
ZOETIC vital
ZOMBIE moron; drugged person
ZONARY **ZONOID**, resembling planetary girdle
ZONATE belted
ZONING area allocation; planning

ZONNAR girdle worn in the Levant
ZONULE zonula; small zone
zo **ZONURE** lizard covered with spikes
zo **ZOONAL** embryonic
zo **ZOONIC** zoological
ZOOSIS animal-parasite-caused disease
zo **ZOO-ZOO** wood-pigeon
md **ZOSTER** shingles
ZOUAVE Algerian soldier
ZOUNDS 'God's wounds' (slang)
Z-SCORE standard; sigma score (statistics)
mu **ZUFOLO** zuffolo; flageolet
ch **ZUMATE** **ZYMATE**, a salt of zymic acid
ZUNIAN Pueblo-Indian
ZYGITE an oarsman in a trireme
md **ZYGOMA** the cheek-bone
bl **ZYGOSE** **ZYGOTE**, fertilization; spore; germ cell
ZYMASE a ferment; an enzyme
rl **ZYMITE** priest using leavened bread
ch, ck **ZYMOID** like a ferment; yeasty
ZYMONE insoluble gluten
br **ZYTHUM** ancient type of beer

SEVEN-LETTER WORDS

A

rl **AARONIC** (Jewish priesthood)
ABACIST an accountant
ABACTOR cattle thief, rustler
ABADDON Apollyon; bottomless pit
zo **ABALONE** mother-of-pearl; oyster shell
ABANDON joie-de-vivre; forsake; quit
ABASHED shamed; embarrassed
ABASING degrading; humbling
ABATING mitigating; stopping
ABATTIS military obstacles
ABATURE beast tracks
pg, bt **ABAXIAL** outward rays from stem
ABBOZZO preliminary sketch
tx **ABB-WOOL** warp-yarn
ABDOMEN lower belly
ABDUCED abducted; separated
ABETTED incited; aided; assisted
lw **ABETTER** an abettor; instigator
ABEYANT in abeyance
ABIDING residence; lasting; durable
bt **ABIETIC ABIETIN**, conifers; resin
ABIGAIL serving-girl; Hebe; waitress
lw **ABIGEAT** cattle theft
ABILITY legal power; wealth; talent
ABIOSIS absence of life
ABIOTIC incompatible with life
lw **ABJUDGE** deprive by law
ABJURED recanted; repudiated
ABJURER forswearer
md **ABLATOR** heat-protection material; instrument
ABLEISM pro able-bodied discrimination
md **ABLEPSY** blindness
ABLINGS aiblins; perhaps
ABLUENT detergent
ABOLISH destroy; extirpate; annul
pc, md **ABOULIA** atrophy of reasoning
ABRADED scraped; worn away
ABRAXAS Gnostic god; amulet
ABREAST side by side
ABRIDGE curtail; epitomize; summarize
md **ABSCESS** inflamed body tissue
ABSCIND cut off
ABSCISS a geometric line
ABSCOND quit secretly
ABSENCE lack; deficiency; non-presence
ar, rl **ABSIDAL** apse-like
ck **ABSINTH** liqueur; wormwood
ABSOLVE release; exonerate; shrive
ABSTAIN refrain; desist; avoid
ABUSING perverting, violating
ABUSION deception; disparagement
ABUSIVE ribald; reviling; calumnious
ABUTTAL the boundary of lands
ABUTTED contiguous; bordered on
lw **ABUTTER** neighbour
ABYSMAL fathomless; profound
ABYSSAL bottomless
ACADEMY also academe; institution
ACADIAN Nova Scotian
ACALEPH jelly fish
bt **ACANTHA** prickly plant
md **ACAPNIA** loss of CO_2 in blood
ACARDIA heart-less
zo **ACARIDA ACARINA**, mites; ticks
ACCEDED assented; succeeded
ACCEDER one who concurs
ACCLAIM applaud; applause; proclaim
lw **ACCOMPT ACCOUNT**, reckon; bill; statement
ACCRUED resulted; accumulated
ACCURSE curse; condemn; execrate
ACCURST accursed; damned; diabolical
ACCUSAL an accusation; indictment
lw **ACCUSED** defendant; arraigned
lw **ACCUSER** plaintiff
ch **ACERATE** (aceric acid)
ACERBIC sour; caustic; astringent
bt **ACEROLA** Amer. cherry-like fruit
bt **ACEROSE** acerous; prickly
ACETARY acid pulp
ch **ACETATE** (vinegar)
ch **ACETIFY** acidify
ch **ACETONE** liquid ketone; solvent
ACETOUS also acetose; sour
ACHAEAN of Achaia (Greek)
bt **ACHAENE** seeded fruit
ACHATES a true friend
ACHERON river of woe
ACHIEVE perform; perfect; attain
ck **ACHIOTE** red colouring matter from seeds
md **ACHOLIA** lack of bile

ACHTUNG beware!; look out! (Ger.)
ACICULA spiked crystals
ACIDITY sourness; tartness
ACIDIZE to add acid
ACIDOID potentially acid (soil)
ACIFORM needle-shaped
ACINOSE ACINOUS, granular consistency
ACLINIC no magnetic dip
md **ACOLOGY** the healing art
rl **ACOLYTE** also acolyth; assistant
bt **ACONITE** plant genus; monkshood
zo **ACONTIA** free threads of anthozea
zo **ACOUCHY** guinea pig; agouti
lw **ACQUEST** acquisition
ACQUIRE get; gain; procure; win
pc **ACRASIA** inability of self-restraint
ACRATIA impotence
ACREAGE area in acres
md **ACRISIA** therapeutic uncertainty
ACROBAT a tumbler; funambulist
bt **ACROGEN** (club-moss); (tree-fern)
as **ACRONIC** non-cosmical (astronomy)
ACRONYM word composed of initials
ACRONYX ingrowing nail
ar **ACROTER** pinnacle
md **ACROTIC** superficial
ch **ACRYLIC** acid, resins for plastics
ACTABLE performable
ACTAMER substance stopping bacteria growth
zo **ACTINIA** (sea-anemones)
ACTINIC chemical ray action (solar)
ACTRESS a lady of parts
ACTUARY statistical expert; registrar
ACTUATE impel; urge; instigate; incite
zo, bt **ACULEUS** sting; prickle
ACUTELY keenly; intensely; poignantly
ACYESIS sterility of female
ADACTYL fingerless
ADAGIAL proverbial
mn **ADAMANT** the diamond; unshakable; unyielding
ADAMITE a nudist
ADAPTED conformed; attuned; adjusted
ADAPTOR ADAPTER, fitment; joining device
bt **ADAXIAL** axis-face of leaf
ma **ADDABLE ADDIBLE**, easily joined for increase
ADDENDA appendix; augmented matter
ADDIBLE addable
ADDLING going rotten; confusing
ADDRESS skill; accost; speech
ADDRESS stance over ball (golf); domicile; archery
ADDUCED cited; brought forward; alleged
ADDUCER a deducer
ADDULCE to sweeten
ch **ADENINE** purine derivative
md **ADENOID** growth in nasal pharynx
md **ADENOMA** glandular tumour
md **ADENOUS ADENOSE**, glandular
ADHERED stuck; clung; held; cleaved
ADHERER partisan; ally; parasite
ADHIBIT attach; administer
md **ADIPOMA** morbid obesity
ADIPOSE fatty; adipous; sebaceous
md **ADIPSIA** never thirsty
ADJOINT united; connected
ADJOURN suspend; postpone; defer
ADJUDGE condemn; decree; ordain
ADJUNCT a concomitant
ADJURED charged on oath
ADJURER adjuror
ADJUTOR a helper; colleague; ally
nt **ADMIRAL** highest naval officer
ADMIRED wondered; appreciated
ADMIRER a lover; adorer
ADMIXED adulterated; infused
ADOLODE distillation tester
ADONAÏS Shelley's elegy on Keats
ADONIZE beautify; worship youth
ADOPTED (foster-child); appropriated
ADORING worshipping; idolizing
ADORNED embellished; decked
hd **ADORSED** back to back
md **ADRENAL** (kidneys); gland
ADULATE flatter; cajole; belaud
ADVANCE to extoll; loan; promote; move forward
ADVENED acceded
ADVENER an assentor
ADVERSE contrary; hostile; inimical
ADVISED notified; informed; apprised
ADVISER informer; cautioner
ADVISOR advice giver; counsellor
rl **ADVOWEE** a patron of a benefice
md **ADYNAMY** weakness
mu, gl, go **AEOLIAN** aerial; deposits, sanddunes, caused by wind
AEOLIST wind-bag
AEONIAN eternal
AERATED gassy
AERATOR soda-water machine
AEROBAT an aerial stunter
md **AEROBIA** bacteria
md **AEROBIC** microbial; gymnastic dance
AEROBUS passenger plane

AEROGEL gel containing gas
ch **AEROSOL** sprayed mist
AERO-TOW record heights achieved (gliding)
AETATIS at the age of
AFFABLE benign; gracious, sociable
AFFABLY cordially, courteously
AFFICHE notice; placard
AFFINAL akin; related
AFFINED united; allied; related
AFFIXED attached; appended; annexed
AFFLICT distress; torment; chasten
AFFORCE reinforce
AFFRONT insult; outrage; abuse
AFFUSED sprinkled
AFFYING betrothing
nm **AFGHANI** native (Afghanistan)
AFRICAN of Africa
AGAINST opposite; counter; despite
md **AGALAXY** lack of milk
AGAMIST matrimonial objector
AGAMOUS crytpogamic
mn **AGATINE AGATIZE**, like agate; become agate
AGELESS timeless
AGELONG ancient; antiquated
AGENDUM a business item
md **AGEUSIA** loss of taste
AGILELY, AGILITY gracefully and mentally quick
AGISTER, AGISTOR grazing controller
AGITATE arouse public feeling; shake
mu **AGITATO** spasmodic; restless
zo **AGNATHA** lampreys; hagfish
AGNATIC akin
AGNOMEN added surname
md **AGNOSIA** perceptionlessness
AGONISE AGONIZE, to suffer anguish amid effort
ga **AGONISM, AGONIST** competing; contestant (prot-)
AGRAFFE clasp or hook (armour)
nt **AGROUND** stranded (also figuratively)
bt **AGYNOUS** non-reproductive
AHRIMAN evil spirit (Persian)
AIBLINS ablings; perhaps
AIDANCE help; succour; bounty
AIDLESS unsupported; unbacked; solo
AIGULET aglet; pendant
bt **AILANTO** tree of Heaven
ae **AILERON** wing lateral-control
AILETTE armoured epaulet
AILMENT malady; complaint; disorder
AIMLESS pointless; random; haphazard
AIR BASE strategic air supply point
AIR GLOW atmospheric luminosity
AIR MAIL post carried by air
AIR MARK par avion
AIR RAID attack by aeroplanes
AIR-BATH nudity for health
AIR-BONE hollow bone
ae **AIR-BUMP** sudden jolt during flight
AIRCAST sow seed from the air
tc **AIR-CORE** cable
AIR-FLUE hot air distributor
AIRFOIL aileron
eg **AIR-FUEL** gas-liquid ratio
AIRHEAD unintelligent; vapid; forward supply (airport)
AIRHOLE ventilator; (cavern)
AIRLESS stuffy
AIRLIFT aerial transportation
AIRLINE flight transport company
AIR-LOCK pump flow stoppage
AIRPARK fleet of aeroplanes
AIRPORT aeroplane landing area
AIR-PUMP vacuum maker
zo **AIR-SACS** quill vesicles
ae **AIR-SHED** a hangar
ae **AIRSHIP** dirigible; zeppelin
AIRSIDE post control embarkation areas (airports)
ae **AIRWAYS** airlines
ch **AJACINE** cycactonine acid ester
AJUTAGE vent pipe
bt **AKINETE** oil/food storage cell
ar **ALAMEDA** shaded promenade (Moorish)
A-LA-MODE stylish
A-LA-MORT till death
md **ALANINE** amino acid
bt **ALANTIN** starch
ALARMED shocked; appalled; daunted
ALASKAN (Alaska)
ALASTOR Nemesis
hd **ALBERIA** shield without arms
ch **ALBITIC** (felspar)
ALBORAK Mahomet's mount to heaven
ALBUMEN white of egg
md **ALBUMIN** (endosperm)
ALCAICS Alcaic verse
ALCALDE judge; Spanish mayor
bt **ALCANNA, ALHENNA** henna, dye for hands
ALCAZAR Moorish palace
ALCHEMY alchymy; medieval chemistry
ch **ALCOHOL** pure wine spirit

as **ALCYONE** star in Pleiades
bt **ALECOST** costmary; ale flavouring
ALE-GILL medicated liquor
bt **ALEHOOF** ground ivy
ALEMBIC distilling retort
ALENGTH full length
ALERTER brisker; more wakeful
ALERTLY vigilantly; actively; warily
pc **ALETHIA** inability to forget
ALETUDE fatness; bulkiness
bt **ALEURON** albuminoid
zo **ALE-WIFE** kind of skad; mackerel
bt **ALFALFA** lucerne grass
md **ALGAROT** antimony emetic
ALGATES by all means; always
as **ALGEBAR** the constellation Orion
ALGEBRA number-properties' investigation
ALGESIA sensitiveness to pain
ALGIFIC producing cold
ALHENNA henna; alkenna; orange dye
sv **ALIDADE** surveyor's sight rule
ALIFORM wing-like
ALIGNED adjusted; regulated; aimed
ALIMENT nutriment; sustenance; food
lw **ALIMONY** maintenance
ALIQUOT integral factor
bt **ALKANET** henna dye
rl **ALKORAN** alcoran; the Koran
md **ALLALIA** loss of speech
ALLAYED quieted; alleviated; pacified
ALLEGED averred; asserted; declared
mu **ALLEGRO** gaily; cheerful pace
ALLERGY distaste; repugnance
ar **ALLETTE** building wing; buttress
bt **ALL-GOOD** a plant
ALL-HAIL a greeting
ALL-HEAL a panacea; valerian, etc.
nc **ALLOBAR** non-natural-isotope form of element
ALLONGE added leaf; lunge
ALLONYM assumed name; pseudonym
ALLOWED abated; authorized
ch **ALLOXAN** cyclic ureide
ALLOYED debased; tempered
ALL-PASS phase-shift for any frequency
bt **ALLSEED** flax
ALL-TIME unprecedented occurrence
ALLUDED suggested; insinuated; hinted
ALLURED enticed; inveigled; decoyed
ALLUVIA waterborne desposit
el **ALL-WATT** induction motor
ro **ALL-WAVE** multi-wave
ALL-WISE of infinite wisdom
ALLYING betrothing; leaguing
nt **ALMADIE** bark canoe
ALMANAC calendar
ALMOIGN charitable endowment
ALMONER giver of alms
ALMONRY almsgiving place; cupboard
ALMS-BOX charity receptacle
ALMS-FEE Peter's pence
ALMSMAN receiver of alms
ALNAGER wool inspector
lw **ALODIUM** freehold
md **ALOETIC** purgative
ALOGISM illogical statement
ALONGST along with
mu **ALP-HORN** Swiss cow-horn
ALREADY before; previously
ALSIRAT bridge to paradise
ALTERED modified; transmuted
bt **ALTERNE** sudden plant-life change
bt **ALTHAEA** hollyhock genus
ALTHING Iceland Parliament
mu **ALT-HORN** saxhorn
ALTRICE bird hatching immature young
ch **ALTROSE** glucose stereoisomer
mn **ALUMINA** aluminium clay
ALUMINE oxide of aluminium
ALUMING impregnating with alum
ALUMISH resembling alum
ALUMNUS college student
mn **ALUNITE** alum-stone
pl **ALVEARY** hive; ear cavity
ALVEATE to hollow out
bt **ALVEOLA** small cavity
pl **ALVEOLE** tooth socket
bt **ALYSSUM** a rock plant
ch **AMALGAM** mercury alloy
bt **AMANDIN** (almonds)
AMANOUS lacking hands
bt **AMARANT** **AMARANTH**, a fadeless flower
AMASSED heaped; collected
AMATEUR not a professional
AMATIVE loving; lovesome
AMATORY ardent; erotic; passionate
AMAZING astounding; bewildering
AMAZONE riding habit
AMBAGES circumlocution; subterfuge
AMBARIE covered howdah
AMBETTI speck-containing glass
AMBIENT encompassing; enfolding
AMBITAL pertaining to skeletal parts
AMBITUS outer edge
AMBLING at an easy gait; sauntering

bt **AMBOYNA** a decorative wood
AMBREIN **AMBERGRIS**, sea wax used in perfumes
AMBROID moulded amber
ga **AMBSACE** **AMESACE**, double-ace dice
AMBULET small ambulance
bt **AMELLUS** purple star-wort
AMENAGE domesticate; manage
AMENDED emended; ameliorated
AMENING ratifying; sanctioning
AMENITY pleasantness; agreeableness
bt **AMENTAL** bearing catkins
md **AMENTIA** mental deficiency
bt **AMENTUM** a catkin
AMERCED fined
AMHARIC language (Ethiopia)
AMIABLE lovable; benign; winsome
AMIABLY kindly; charmingly
el **AMMETER** ampere meter
ch **AMMONAL** an explosive
ch **AMMONIA** pungent gas
md,pc **AMNESIA** loss of memory
md,pc **AMNESIC** loss of language ability
AMNESTY pardon; absolution; oblivion
zo **AMNIOTE** embryo sac classification
AMOEBAN pertaining to amoeba
AMONGST amid; between
AMORIST philanderer
AMOROSA, AMOROSI sweetheart; gallants
mu **AMOROSO** **AMOROUS**, tenderly, passionate
bt **AMORPHA** indigo
lw **AMOTION** deprivation
AMPASSY **AMPERSAND**, the &
AMPHORA two-handled wine jar
AMPLEST most lavish; most copious
AMPLIFY expand; enlarge; augment
md **AMPOULE** container for hypodermic dose
AMPULLA glass vial for oil, perfume
AMUSING **AMUSIVE**, entertaining; droll
AMUTTER muttering
ch **AMYLASE** starch-hydrolysing enzyme
ch **AMYLENE** amyl
bt,ch **AMYLINE** **AMYLOID**, starchy cellulose
ch **AMYLOSE** starch constituent
ANABION anabolism-dominated organism
bt **ANACARD** cashew-nut
md **ANAEMIA** general debility
md **ANAEMIC** bloodless
ANAGOGUE **ANAGOGY**, mindless interpretation
ANAGRAM word puzzle
ANALECT anthology
ANALGIA analgesia
md **ANALITY** anal libidinous energy
ANALOGY similarity; likeness
ANALYSE examine critically
ANALYST a resolver
ANANICE absolute necessity
ANAPEST poetic metre
ANAPHIA loss of sense of touch
zo **ANAPSID** having roofed skull
ANARCHY chaos; disorder; violence
ch **ANATASE** titanium oxide
md **ANATOMY** a skeleton; dissection
ANATRON glass scum
ANAUDIA loss of voice
zo **ANAXIAL** asymmetrical
zo **ANCHOVY** a small fish
bt **ANCHUSA** alkanet, red dye
ANCIENT antique; pristine ensign
ANCONES ornamental brackets
ANCORAL like an achor; hooked
ANCRESS **ANKRESS**, female anchorite
mu **ANDANTE** slow; walking pace
ANDARAC a red pigment
ANDRASE male-producing enzyme/hormone
ANDROID automaton; robot; imitation man
ANDVARI a dwarf (Norse myth.)
ANELACE anlace; a broad dagger
rl **ANELING** annointing with oil
bt,zo **ANEMONE** anemony; windflower
md **ANERGIA** lack of energy
ANEROID a kind of barometer
ANESONE white anise liqueur
bt **ANETHOL** oil of anise
ANEURIA lack of nervous energy
ANEURIN B-group vitamin
ANGARIA war rights
ANGELIC seraphic; cherubic; heavenly
ck,mu,nm **ANGELOT** cheese; lute; coin
rl **ANGELUS** a prayer; (bell-ringing)
ANGERED exasperated; enraged; roused
ANGERLY angrily; wrathfully
ANGEVIN dynasty of Anjou
ANGIOID like blood/lymph vessel
md **ANGIOMA** dilated-blood-vessel tumour
ANGLIFY anglicize, make English
ANGLING hopefully fishing
ANGLIST expert in English
ANGRILY wrathfully, irately
ANGUINE snake-like
ANGUISH agony; distress; rack; pang
ANGULAR sharp cornered
ANIDIAN shapeless

ch **ANILINE** indigo derivative
ANILITY dotage; senility; imbecility
mu **ANIMATE ANIMATO**, actuate; lively
rl **ANIMISM ANIMIST**, soul as vital principle
bt **ANISEED** the seed of the anise
rl, lw **ANNATES** first fruits
bt **ANNATTO** annotto; a reddish dye
zo **ANNELID** worm
ANNEXED affixed; subjoined; attached
ANNOYED harassed; pestered; molested
ANNOYER an irritator; teaser
ANNUENT nodding
ANNUITY a yearly payment
bt **ANNULAR** ring-like growth markings
ANNULET small fillet round a column
pl, md **ANNULUS** ring; ring-shaped; sphincter
bt **ANODERM** skinless
ANODISE dyeing aluminium
zo **ANODONT** a freshwater mussel
ANODYNE pain-killer; opiate; sedative
pc **ANOESIA** comprehension failure
ANOESIS state of non-cognitive mind
ANOETIC responds only to emotion
ck **ANOLINI** ravioli
el **ANOLYTE** portion of electrolyte
ANOMALY irregularity; eccentricity
md **ANOPSIA** blindness; (cataract); squint
md **ANOREXY** appetite failure illness
ANORMAL ABNORMAL, exceptional
md **ANOSMIA** loss of smell power
ANOTHER one more
ANSATED with a handle
ch, md **ANTACID** a corrective; neutralizer
as **ANTAPEX** point opposite to apex
zo **ANT-BEAR** American ant-eater
ANTE-ACT an act preceding
ANTEFIX ornamental tiling
zo **ANT-EGGS** the pupae of ants
ro, zo **ANTENNA** a feeler
zo **ANT-HILL** a formicary
bt **ANTHOID** flower-like
rl **ANTHONY** saint; piglet
md **ANTHRAX** wool-sorter's disease
bt **ANTICAL** stem/leaf upper surface
ae **ANTICER** anti-icing means
ANTICOR animal disease
ANTICUM a front porch
ANTI-GAS for combating gas
md **ANTIGEN** cause of antibodies
ma **ANTILOG** anti-logarithm
ch **ANTIPYR** formalin
pr **ANTIQUA** printing type
ANTIQUE archaic; old; ancient
ANTI-RED anti-communist
ar **ANTISAG** preventing sagging
ANT-LIKE industrious
zo **ANT-LION** a neuropterous insect
ANTONYM the opposite of a synonym
ANXIETY ANXIOUS, concern, apprehensive
ANYBODY person unspecified
ANYWAYS anyhow
ANYWHEN any old time
ANYWISE somehow
APAGOGE APAGOGY, progressively absurd
APANAGE natural attribute; perquisite
APANDRY male impotence
mn **APATITE** lime phosphate
hd **APAUMEE** open hand
APE-HOOD APELIKE, apishness; simian
md **APEPSIA** poor digestion
md **APERTOR** eye-opener; muscle
bt **APETALY** absence of petals
APHACIA APHAKIA, lensless eye
md, zo **APHAGIA** inability to swallow, feed
md **APHASIA** temporary dumbness
as **APHELIA** maximum distances (earth from sun)
md **APHEMIA** loss of speech
APHETIC APHESIS, vowel curtailment
zo **APHIDES** plant-lice; ants' milchcows
md **APHONIA** loss of voice
APHONIC speechless
APHORIA sterility
bt **APHOTIC** able to grow without light
mn **APHRITE** carbonate of lime
md **APHTHAE** ulceration of the mouth
bt **APHYLLY** absence of leaves
APICIAN epicurean; gastronomic
md **APINOID** clean
APISHLY monkey-like
A-PITPAT palpitating
APLANAT lens lacking spherical aberration
md **APLASIA** defective structural growth
APOCOPE elision; verbal curtailment
bt **APOCYTE** cell-less protoplasm
APODAL APODOUS, footless
bt **APOGAMY** sex-function loss
APOGEAN culminating; climactic
bt **APOGYNY, APOGENY** sterility
APOLOGY excuse; explanation; plea
as **APOLUNE** point in moon satellite orbit
APOSTIL marginal note; postscript

rl **APOSTLE** closest to Jesus; messenger
ma **APOTOME** mathematic difference
mu **APOTOMY** major semitone
APPAREL equipment; attire; vesture
APPEASE pacify; assuage; placate
APPLAUD praise; commend; extol
APPLIED referred; exercised; used
APPOINT nominate; prescribe; enjoin
APPOSED placed side by side
APPOSER an examiner; questioner
APPRISE inform; acquaint; warn
APPRIZE appreciate; appraise
APPROVE ratify; assent; encourage
APPULSE rapprochement
pc **APRAXIA** loss of movement ability
bt, ck **APRICOT ABRICOCK**, fruit (-brandy)
APRONED wearing an apron
APROPOS pertinent; opportune; timely
ch **APROTIC** high-dielectric solvent
ar, rl **APSIDAL ABSIDAL**, apse (church)
APSIDES perigee and apogee
zo, ar **APTERAL** wingless; end columns
zo **APTERYX** kiwi-bird (New Zealand)
md **APTHOUS** (thrush); ulcerous
APTNESS suitability; felicity
APTOTIC indeclinable
md **APYREXY** absence of fever
APYROUS unchanged by heat
gl **AQUAFER AQUIFER**, permeable strata
zo **AQUARIA** (aquariums)
ch **AQUASOL** sulphonated castor oil
AQUATIC in/of water
AQUEOUS water; humid; damp
AQUILON the north wind
ARABIAN of Arabia
bt **ARABINE** gum arabic
ARABISM Arab idiom
ARABIST Arabic expert
bt **ARACHIS** peanut genus
ARAMAIC Syriac; Aramite
ARAMEAN Chaldaic; Chaldean
ARATION ploughing
ARBITER umpire; judge; referee
ARBLAST crossbow
ARBORED arboured
bt **ARBORET** shrub
bt **ARBUTUS** mountain strawberry
ar **ARCADED** having arched galleries
ARCADIA pastoral country
ARCANUM a mystery; a secret
ARCHAIC Noachian; antiquated
ga **ARCHERY** bowmanship
ARCH-FOE Satan
ARCHING curved; vaulting
ARCHIVE home for public documents; file
ARCHLET small arch
ARCHWAY gateway; gatehouse
ARC-LAMP carbon-pole-bridge lamp
ARCTOID like a bear
ARCUATE bow-shaped
ARDENCY passion; warmth; fire
ARDUOUS laborious; toilsome
AREFIED withered; arid; parched
ARENOSE sandy; arenaceous
bt **AREOLAR** areolic; cell nucleus
mu **ARGHOOL** Arab reed pipe
ARGOTIC slangy
ARGUING discussing; debating
md **ARGYRIA** silver poisoning
ARGYROL silver antiseptic
ARIDITY dryness; aridness; sterility
mu **ARIETTA ARIETTE**, operatic air
bt **ARILLED ARILLUS**, husk; seed coating
ARISING emerging; originating
tx **ARMHOLE** clothing aperture for arm
hd **ARMIGER** bearer of coat of arms (crest)
ARMILLA antique bracelet
ARMLESS lacking arms
hd **ARMOIRE** cupboard for coats of arms
ARMORIC Breton dialect
ARMOURY arsenal; magazine
bt **ARNOTTO** annatto; orange dye
AROUSAL awakening; uprising
AROUSED excited; provoked
lw **ARRAIGN** accuse; summon
ARRANGE group; classify; dispose
ARRAYED marshalled; equipped
ARREARS payments overdue
ARRIVAL advent; coming; newcomer
ARRYISH festive; jovial
ARSENAL armoury; depository
ch **ARSENIC** a metallic element
nt **ARTEMON** bowsail on Rome vessel
cf, md **ARTERIO- ARTERIAL**, concerning arteries
ARTICLE essay; paper; indenture
ARTISAN artizan; workman; operative
ARTISTE a fine performer
ARTLESS simple; ingenuous; naive
ARTSMAN a craftsman
ARTWORK creative design
ARUSPEX soothsayer; seer; diviner
ASARONE form of camphor
ASBOLIN oil from soot
zo **ASCARID** parasite worm
rl **ASCESIS** self-discipline
ASCETIC austere; rigid; abstemious
ASCIANS equator dwellers
zo **ASCIDIA** molluscs
md **ASCITES** peritoneal fluid collection
md **ASCITIC** dropsical
ASCRIBE attribute; assign; impute

md **ASEPSIS** sterilization
ASEPTIC sterilized
ASEXUAL algamic; sexless
ASHAMED abashed; confused
ck **ASH-CAKE** pastry cooked in ashes
ASH-FIRE chemical operations fire
ASH-HEAP tip for ashes
ASH-TRAY cigarette-butt tray
bt **ASH-WORT** a weed
ASIARCH Asiatic Proconsul
ASIATIC of Asia
ASINEGO ASINICO, a dolt; dunce; dulled
ASININE ass-like; idiotic; obstinate
ASKANCE obliquely; aslant; awry
pc **ASOCIAL** drop-out from society
mn **ASPHALT** bitumen
md **ASPHYXY** suffocation
ASPIRED soared; aimed high; yearned
ASPIRER aspirant; competitor
ASSAGAI ASSEGAY, Zulu spear
zo **ASSAPAN** flying squirrel (N. Amer.)
ASSAULT onset; attack; storm; assail (fencing)
ASSAYED tested; tried; endeavoured
ASSAYER metallurgist; analyst
ASS-HEAD blockhead; Bottom
ASSIZER inspector of weights
lw **ASSIZES** Courts of jurisdiction
lw **ASSIZOR** juror
ASSUAGE allay; pacify; mollify; quell
ASSUMED usurped; feigned; supposed
ASSUMER pretender, arrogant person
ASSURED pledged; guaranteed
ASSUROR ASSURER, underwriter (insurance)
ro **ASTABLE** free-running; self-sustaining
md **ASTASIA** inability to keep erect
ASTATIC unstable; lacking polarity
ASTEISM refined irony
mn **ASTERIA** (sapphire)
zo **ASTERID** star-fish
ASTOUND amaze; daze; stupefy
ASTRAEA Goddess of Justice
ASTRICT restrict; bind
ASTRIDE astraddle
mn **ASTRITE** star-stone
ASTROID star-shaped
ar **ASTYLAR** without columns
ASUNDER apart; divided; divergent
ch, tx **ATACTIC** of random polymer constituents
ATARAXY impassiveness; coolness
ATAVISM ATAVIST, reversion to ancestral type
nt **ATCHEEN** banting, sail dugout (Malaya)
ATEKNIA childlessness
ATELENE amorphous; imperfect
ATELIER studio; sculptor's workshop
ATHALIA saw-fly
ATHANOR alchemist's furnace
ATHEISE ATHEIZE, proselytize unbelief
ATHEISM disbelief
ATHEIST a nullifidian
ATHLETE athleta; a contestant
ATHWART across; askew; aslant
md **ATHYMIA** lack of feeling
md **ATHYMIA** thymus gland deficiency
md **ATHYRIA** absence of thyroid gland
ATOBOMB atomic bomb
ATOKOUS lacking offspring
bt **ATOMATE** covered by small particles
ATOMISM atomic theory
ATOMIST atomic theorist
ATOMIZE vaporize
ATONING expiating; reconciling
ATRESIA failure of opening development
bt **ATROPAL** not inverted; upturned
md **ATROPHY** wasting away
md **ATROPIA** bella-donna
bt **ATROPIN** deadly nightshade
ATTABOY a panegyric (USA)
mu **ATTACCA** continue without break (It.)
ATTACHE important embassy man (-case)
zo **ATTAGAS** a pheasant
ATTAINT corrupt; convicted
ck **ATTELET** ornamental meat skewer
ATTEMPT try; aim; endeavour; effort
ATTICAL classical
ATTINGE touch
ATTIRED garbed; dressed; arrayed
ATTRACT draw; allure; charm; decoy
ATTRIST to sadden
ATTRITE worn by friction; penitent
ATTUNED in harmony
AUBERGE an inn (Fr.)
AUCTION roup; vendue
AUDIBLE able to be heard
AUDIBLY spoken clearly
AUDIENT listening; attentive
AUDILES preference for heard images, stimuli
ma **AUDITED AUDITOR**, books examined; accountant
mn **AUGITIC** (augite); (pyroxene)
AUGMENT amplify; increase; enhance

AUGURAL, AUGURED ominous; foretold; portended
pl **AURALLY** concerning the ears; sound
AURATED AUREATE, AUREITY, golden; gilded
zo **AURELIA** a chrysalis
rl **AUREOLA AUREOLE,** golden halo
md, bt **AURICLE** ear; heart; leaf base
AURIFIC gold bearing
AURITED having ears
zo **AUROCHS** urus; wild ox; (prehistoric)
as **AURORAL** dawn (-Borealis) Northern Lights
AUSLAUT final syllable/word sound (Ger.)
AUSONIA Italy
AUSPICE augory; omen; portent
AUSTERE severely simple; ascetic
AUSTRAL southern
AUTARCH autocrat; tyrant
AUTARKY national self-sufficiency
AUTOBUS omnibus
AUTOCAR motor car
AUTONYM true name
md **AUTOPSY** post-mortem exam.
AUTOSET quick-levelling in surveying
au **AUTO-VAC** vacuum
AUXESIS hyperbole
AUXETIC amplifying
AVAILED answered the purpose; helped
AVARICE greed; rapacity; cupidity
lw **AVENAGE** barley-corn rent
AVENGED retaliated; revenged
AVENGER vindicator
md **AVENOUS** lacking veins
AVERAGE mean; moderate; ordinary
AVERNUS infernal regions
AVERRED affirmed; alleged; stated
AVERTED warded off; prevented
AVERTER preventer; diverter
AVIATED AVIATOR, flew; pilot (air navigation)
AVICIDE killing of birds
AVICULA kind of pearl oyster
AVIDITY greed; voracity; eagerness
AVIETTE a glider
AVIFORM bird-shaped
bt, ck **AVOCADO** alligator-pear
bt **AVODIRE** African hard-wood
AVOIDED eschewed; annulled; eluded
AVOIDER dodger; shunner
lw **AVOWANT** defendant in replevin
AVOWING owning; admitting; averring
AWAITED eagerly expected; tarried
AWAKING emerging from sleep; arousing
AWELESS without fear
AWESOME full of awe; fearsome
AWFULLY dreadfully; portentously
AWKWARD clumsy; ungainly; inapt
zo **AWL-BIRD** woodpecker
bt **AWL-WORT** an aquatic plant
bt **AWNLESS** beardless
AXIALLY from pole to pole
AXIFORM like a spindle or aborr
zo, bt **AXILLAR** a feather
au **AXLE-BOX** automobile part
AXLE-PIN linch-pin
zo **AXOLOTL** larval salamander
md **AXOTOMY** severing of axon nerve
AZALINE emulsion-sensitizing dye mixture
bt **AZAROLE** medlar
ch **AZELAIC** rancid-fat acid
AZILIAN pre-Neolithic
me, nv, as **AZIMUTH** angle over horizon (distance)
ch **AZOTITE** nitrous acid
AZOTIZE to nitrogenize
AZOTOUS nitrous
AZTECAN concerning the Aztecs (Mexico)
AZULEJO bright-coloured Iberian tile
AZUREAN sky-blue
AZURINE azure
mn **AZURITE** copper carbonate
AZYGOUS not in pairs
rl **AZYMITE** Armenian churchman
AZYMOUS unleavened; unfermented

B

rl **BAALISM BAALITE,** of Baal, idolatry
BABASSU oil in shampoo
BABBARI hare
BABBING catching eels (angling)
BABBLED chattered; jabbered
zo **BABBLER** betrayer; talker; thrush
rl **BABIISM** Persian religion
zo **BABUINA** female baboon
BABYISH BABYISM, infantile expression
ga **BACCARA BACCARAT,** gambling cardgame
BACCARE stand back!
bt **BACCATE** berry-shaped; pulpy
BACCHUS BACCHIC, carousing wine god
md **BACILLI** bacteria; microbes

BACK OUT withdraw
fr **BACK-CUT** tree-felling
BACKERS supporters; target background
nt **BACKING** aiding; abetting; retiring; strengthening; (finance); anticlockwise (wind)
BACK-LOG delayed work
BACK-OFF back-out; retire; leave; withdraw
BACK-OUT reversal of missile drill
cr **BACK-SAW** thick-backed saw
BACKSET an eddy
bt **BACTRIS** peach-palm
BADDISH rather bad
BADIAGA small sponge
bt **BADIANE BANDIAN**, aniseed (flavour)
BADNESS depravity; evil; wickedness
BAFFLED foiled; checked; bewildered
BAFFLER thwarter; confounder
BAGASSE refuse sugar stalks
BAGGAGE luggage; belongings
nt **BAGGALA** 2-masted Arab vessel
BAGGING bag-cloth; pouching (theft)
mu **BAGPIPE** windbag instrument, Gr./Sc.
ce **BAGWORK** bagged concrete, gravel for sea wall
BAHADUR Indian title
lw **BAILAGE** ancient export duty
lw **BAILIFF** land steward; overseer
ag **BAILING** packing (hay bundles)
nt **BAILING** of water (emptying a boat)
ae **BAILING** -out; parachuting (pilots)
lw **BAILING** court release (money pledged)
BAILLIE councillor of Scottish burgh
BAITING taunting; (bear-); angling
el **BAKE-OUT** electrode/valve pre-heating
BALANCE poise; weigh; surplus
zo **BALANUS** crustacean; acorn-shell
ar, bd **BALCONY** hanging porch
BALDEST barest; plainest
BALDING BALDISH, losing head hair
BALDRIC baudric; shoulder-belt
BALEFUL evil; noxious; pernicious
BALKING BAULKING, horse's refusing jump
mu **BALLADE BALLATA**, poetic aria
nt **BALLAST** non-cargo weight (gravel, sand)
ga **BALL-BOY** ball returner (tennis, football)
mu **BALLETT** dance-like vocal composition
BALLING becoming clogged; partying
md **BALLISM** motor nerve disorder
BALLIUM bulwark
ae **BALLOON** hot-air (gas) skycraft
ga **BALLOON** idea tryout; up-hit (cricket)
BALLS-UP muddled (confusion)
BALMIER sweeter; milder; gentler
BALMILY soothingly; tranquilly
md **BALNEAL** spa treatment (mineral)
md **BALNEUM** curative public bath
BALONEY unbelievable nonsense
BALSAMY fragrant; aromatic
BAMBINO a child (It.)
BAMMING hoaxing; cheating
BANABAN Micronesian language
ck **BANBURY** a cake
tx **BANDAGE** wound dressing fabric
tx **BANDANA** colourful silk hankie, tie
BANDBOX hat box, new-clothes box
BANDEAU brow-band
bt **BANDIAN** badiane; aniseed
BANDIED discussed; tossed; agitated
BANDING uniting together; decorative multiwood inlay; border
BANDLET bandelet; a flat moulding
mu **BANDORA PANDORA**, ancient cittern, zither
mu **BANDORE** lute-like plucked continuo
BANDROL banderole; small flag
to **BAND-SAW** saw over wheels
BANEFUL baleful; deadly; venomous
BANGING overwhelming; clattering
BANGLED with bangles
mn **BANK-BAR** mine-shaft lining
ae **BANKING** relying; (financial); earthworks; tilting of aircraft
bt **BANKSIA** dwarf yellow climbing rose
BANNING cursing; proscribing; barring
ck **BANNOCK** oaten-cake (Sc.)
ck **BANQUET** feast; regalement
BANSHEE ghost (Irish)
BANTENG Malayan wild ox
BANTERY mild repartee
BANTING reducing the diet; slimming
nt, zo **BANTING** wild ox (Ind.); atcheen, sail-dugout craft (Malaya)
BANYULS Pyrenean wine
rl **BAPTISM** immersion at christening
BAPTIST member of Protestant sect
BAPTIZE christen
tx **BARACAN** camel-hair cloth
BARBARY a Saracen country (N. Africa)
bt **BARBATE** bearded; awned

BAR-BELL dumb-bell; weight-lifting bar
BARBING shaving; trimming; piercing
BARBOLA modern gesso
bt **BARBULE** small beard on plant
gl **BARCHAN BARCHANE**, windblown deposit
BARCODE lined stockcode label
BARDISH BARDISM, Celtic poetry & its lore
BARDLET BARDLING, young bard (poet)
BAREBOW without sighting or aiming (archery)
BARGAIN chaffer; haggle; compact
BARGING shoving; elbowing; jostling; intrusion of line (yachting)
BARILLA raw seaweed alkali
BAR-IRON malleable iron in bars
le **BARK-BED** tanner's hot-bed
le **BARKERY** tan-house
gl **BARKHAN** lone crescentic sandhill
BARKING peeling; (shins); dog noise
le **BARK-PIT** tan-vat
BARMAID Hebe; tavern server; sleeper
BARMIER flightier; more crazy
BARMKIN outer castle ward
BARNABY the apostle Barnabas
zo **BARNAGH** large whelk
BARNING storing; garnering
zo **BARN-OWL** screech owl; night-bird
BARONET bart; hereditary title; Sir
mu **BAROQUE** 17th cent. style architecture, music
BARRACK army lodgement house; to boo
BARRAGE embankment; barrier; dam
mu **BARRAGE** (artillery fire); guitar chords
BARRENS elevated plateaux (arctic)
BARRICO small keg (Sp.)
BARRIER hindrance; embargo; obstacle
BARRING excluding; banning
hd **BARRULY** heraldic division
BAR-SHOE special horseshoe
BAR-SHOT double connected shot
bt **BARTRAM** the plant pellitory
bt **BARWOOD** red dye-wood
ch **BARYTES** barium sulphate
BARYTIC (baryta)
mu **BARYTON** tenor-bass viol
BASBLEU blue stocking
BASCULE balanced drawbridge; perfect arc of horse jumping
ml **BASE-BOX** metal-plate measurement unit
BASENET bascinet; basnet; a helmet
zo **BASENJI** Congo barkless dog
BASHFUL strikingly modest; shy
BASHING coshing; slugging
BASHLYK Russian hood
BASILAR serving as a basis
BASILIC basilican style
BASINED in a basin
BASINET BASNET, round helmet
zo **BASKING** luxuriating; revelling (-shark)
BASLARD a small dagger
BASSOCK fibre mat
mu **BASSOON** bass oboe
BASTARD illegitimate offspring; spurious
BASTILE castle on wheels
tx, ck **BASTING** coarse stitching; (roasting)
ar **BASTION** outer fortification; stronghold
bt, ck **BATATAS** sweet potatoes; yams
ae, nt **BAT-BOAT** sea-plane
nt **BATEELE, BATELO** small dhow
BATEFUL contentious; disputable
ck **BATH BUN** a comestible
BATHING giving/having a bath
BATHMAN attendant
BATH-MAT thick towel-like mat
BATHYAL pert. to deep-sea zone
BATISTE cambric
BATSMAN a cricketer
BATTELS provisions (Oxford)
el, zo **BATTERY** stored electricity; hens
lw **BATTERY** (assault); test group; (baseball)
BATTERY (artillery) gun group unit; site
BATTING quilting; cricket; angling
BATTISH bat-like
BATTLED fought
BATTLER resident at Oxford
go **BATTURE** raised sea/river bed
mu **BATTUTA** 3 bar rhythm beat (It.)
BAUDRIC shoulder sash
BAULKED shield; balked; jibbed
zo **BAUSOND** badger-like
mn **BAUXITE** (aluminium)
BAWCOCK fine fellow
BAWDILY lewdly; obscenely
rl **BAWDKIN BALDACHIN**, canopy
BAWLING shouting; clamouring
BAYONET rifle-dagger
BAY-SALT evaporated sea-water
bt **BAY-TREE** the laurel
bt **BAYWOOD** mahogany
BAY-YARN woollen yarn

BAZIGAR nomadic Ind. gypsy
BAZOOKA anti-tank gun
nt **BEACHED** aground; on the beach
BEADING narrow moulding
BEADMAN an almsman
BEAKING (cock-fighting)
BEAMILY broad on the beam
BEAMING radiant; gleaming; bright
zo **BEAN-FLY** a garden pest
BEARDED awned; defied; opposed
zo **BEARDIE** the whitethroat bird
BEARING (magnetic); (rein); (ball); wheel bearing
BEARISH uncouth; boorish; rude
BEAR-PIT enclosure for bears
BEASTLY brutal; sensual; bestial
BEATIFY (sainthood); canonize
BEATING chastisement; battering
BEATNIK latter-day Bohemian
BEAUISH foppish
bt **BEBEERU** greenheart tree
BECAUSE owing to
BECKING servile bowing
bt, tx, bd **BEDDING** planting out; bedclothes; foundation; gun mounting
BEDEAUX piece-work system
BEDELRY BEADLERY, street orderlies
BEDEMAN the bead-maker
BEDEVIL bewitch
BEDEWED covered with dew; affused
BEDFAST bed-ridden
BED-GOWN night gown
BED-MATE bed-fellow
BEDOUIN nomadic Arab
BED-POST bedstead support
BED-REST recuperation
gl **BEDROCK** basic stratum
BEDROOM sleeping apartment
BEDSIDE (table); (lamp); (manner)
md **BED-SORE** sore from bed-lying
zo **BED-TICK** bed bug
BEDTIME time to sleep
BEDWARF to belittle; to dwarf
BEDWORK easy toil; copulation
zo **BEE-BIRD** bee catcher
bt **BEECHEN** of the beech tree, wood
BEEF-TEA meat-extract drink
BEE-GLUE beeswax
BEE-HIVE home for bees
BEE-LINE straight line
zo **BEE-MOTH** wax-moth
BEESWAX product of hives
zo **BEET-BUG** agricultural pest
zo **BEET-FLY** a dipterous insect
BEETLED speeded along
bt **BEE-TREE** American linden
BEFFANA befana; Epiphany fairy
BEGGARY mendicancy; indigence
BEGGING soliciting; craving; imploring
rl **BEGHARD BEGUINE**, religious order
bt **BEGONIA** elephant's ear plant
BEGUILE pass pleasantly; amuse
BEGUILE deceive; delude; trick
rl **BEGUINE BEGHARD**, religious almshouse
BEHAVED acted correctly
BEHOVED was necessary; befitted
BELATED overdue; retarded
nt **BELAYED** fastened; held
BELCHED eructated
BELCHER coloured kerchief
BELDAME old hag
BELGIAN of Belgium
BELIEVE credit; opine; accept
BELL-HOP page boy
BELLIED dilated
zo **BELLING** full and ripe; bellowing; of deer in rut
BELL-JAR vacuum enclosure
BELL-MAN town crier
BELLONA goddess of War
BELLOWS draught producer (organ) (forge)
BELOVED dear; darling
BELTANE May Day fire festival
BELTING beating; a belt
BEMUSED confused, bewildered
BENCHED furnished with seating
lw **BENCHER** senior (Inns of Court)
BENDING curving; flexing; inclining
hd **BENDLET** small heraldic bend
BENEATH inferior; subordinate; under
BENEFIC favourable (astrol.)
BENEFIT boon; profit; gain; enrich
BENELUX Belgium, Netherlands and Luxemburg
BENGALI of Bengal
BENISON benediction
bt **BENTEAK** Nana-wood
zo **BENTHOS** ocean-bed organisms
ch **BENZENE BENZINE**, cleaning solvent; paint remover
bt **BENZOIN** resinous incense
ch **BENZOLE** tar product
ch **BENZOYL BENZOIC** acid
lw **BEQUEST** legacy; inheritance
BERATED scolded; nagged; chided
BEREAVE deprive; divest; despoil
zo **BERGYLT** red sea-fish
BERHYME to lampoon in verse
BERLINE berlin; a vehicle
BERSERK Norse warrior; in a fury
nt **BERTHED** moored; situated
nt **BERTHON** collapsible lifeboat

bt **BERTRAM** bastard pellitory
BESEECH implore; entreat; crave
BESHMET grape pulp
BESIDES except; save; moreover
BESIEGE beset; invest; beleaguer
BESPOKE ordered
BEST MAN groomsman (weddings)
BESTIAL brutal; uncivilized
BESTING winning
BETROTH affiance; plight
BETTING wagering; staking
zo **BETTONG** kangaroo rat
BETULIN birch camphor
BETWEEN amid
BETWIXT amidst
BEVATON proton synchrotron
BEWITCH fascinate; enchant; charm
ga **BEZIQUE** card game
BHANDAR store; library (Hindu)
BHISTEE water-carrier (India)
BIALATE with 2 wings
BIARCHY rule by 2 persons
BIASING prejudicing; influencing
BIAXIAL with 2 axes
eg **BIB-COCK** down-curving draw-off tap
BIBELOT personal trinket, snuffbox, etui
rl **BIBLIST** zealous Bible quoter
ce **BI-CABLE** multi-line aerial ropeway
mu **BICHORD** doubly strung
to **BICKERN** pointed anvil
BICOLOUR having 2 colours
bt **BICONIC** double-cone-shaped
BICYCLE bike; 2-wheeler
BIDDERY metal alloy
BIDDING enjoining; directing
ck **BIFFINS** dried apples
BIFIDLY cleft
BIFILAR double-threaded
BIFOCAL type of spectacles (twin lenses)
BIFROST Rainbow Bridge (Norse)
BIG-BORE larger rifles (8 mm) shooting
nv **BIGELOW** flexible sailing boom
BIGENER cross-breed
BIGGEST largest; greatest
BIGGISH somewhat massive
zo **BIG-HORN** wild sheep
BIGNESS of a size; bulkiness
BIGOTED dogmatic; intolerant
BIGOTRY zealotry; fanaticism
BILBOES bars and shackles
BILGING rubbishing others' remarks
md **BILIARY** **BILIOUS**, of bile glands
BILKING defrauding; eluding; cheating
BILLING invoicing (charging); petting
BILLION a large number
BILL-MAN hedger; pruning hook
BILLOWY roughish
BILOBED double-lobed
cp **BILSTED** mahogany substitute
ck **BILTONG** dried meat (S. Africa)
BIMANAL two handed
el **BIMETAL** of 2 different metals
ma **BIMODAL** 2 similar frequencies
BINDERY bookbinding
BINDING obligatory; a fillet; fastening; (boot to ski); books
md **BINDWEB** (nervous system)
BINNING wine storage; (rubbish bin)
BINOCLE double-telescope
BINOTIC binaural
BIOCIDE plant-life-destroying substance
BIOGENY life origin science
gl **BIOLITH** rock from living organisms
bl **BIOLOGY** science of life
ec **BIOMASS** population living weight
cp **BIONICS** study of functions of brains and computers
BIORGAN physiological organ
zo **BIOTAXY** grouping of organisms
zo **BIOTICS** living organisms (viruses, bacteria)
mn **BIOTINE** (alumina)
mn **BIOTITE** magnesia mica
BIOTOMY vivisection
BIOTOPE uniform habitat
BIOTYPE uniform genetic make-up
BIPEDAL having two feet
BIPLANE 2-winged aeroplane
BIPOLAR with 2 poles
pg **BIPRISM** obtuse-angle prism
BIRCHED beaten with stick or cane
BIRCHEN made of birchwood
BIRDEYE bird's eye
BIRDING snaring
BIRDMAN fowler; single flyer (hang-glider)
BIRETTA clerical cap
BIRLING whirling; spinning
BIRLINN Gaelic barge
BIRYANI type of pilaw (India)
ck **BISCUIT** thin, hard cookie; ceramic process
mn, ch **BISMUTH** metal ochre
BISSEXT (leap year)
bt **BISTORT** snakeweed
BITLESS no bit
zo **BITTERN** also bittour
BITTERN brine

BITTERS wormwood-impregnated liquor
BITTILY disjointedly
BITTING harnessing a horse
BITTOCK small bit
zo **BITTOUR** the bittern
mn **BITUMED BITUMEN**, bituminous asphalt; pitch
zo **BIVALVE** a mollusc
BIVIOUS two ways
mo **BIVOUAC** make-do camp (army)
BIZARRE fantastic; whimsical; strange
BIZONAL double zone ticket
BLABBED babbled; told; revealed
BLABBER sneak; tell-tale; prattler
BLACKED inked; obscured
BLACKEN darken; defame; decry
BLACKER darker; more sullen
BLACKLY sombrely
md **BLADDER** urine collection organ
BLADING fitting a blade to
BLAMING censuring; reproaching
BLANDLY mildly; benign; affably
bt **BLANKET** the mullein
nc **BLANKET** cover (bed, snow); group usage; yacht; surrounder of nuclear reactor core
BLANKLY vacantly
BLARING strident; obvious
BLARNEY whimsical flattery (Irish)
ck **BLARNEY** yellow Irish cheese
BLASTED withered; blighted; ruined
BLASTER froth-blower; golf
BLATANT obtrusively vulgar
BLATHER BLATTER-BLETHER, to babble
bt **BLAWORT** harebell
BLAZING flaming; proclaiming
BLEAKER more exposed; barer
BLEAKLY cheerlessly; drearily
md **BLEEDER** haemophiliac; (baseball)
BLEMISH defect
BLENDED mingled; blent; mixed
ck, to **BLENDER** mixing device; paint brush of badger hair; (tea)
BLESBOK S. African antelope
BLESSED extolled; glorified; adored
BLETTED decayed
bt **BLEWART** the germander speedwell
bt **BLEWITS** mushrooms
BLIGHTY England (soldiers' slang)
BLINDED shuttered; deceived
BLINDER more obtuse; a blinker
BLINDLY ignorantly; heedlessly
BLINKED twinkled; flickered; connived
md, nt **BLISTER** abraised skin spot; extra hull for stability
BLOATED swollen; distended
zo **BLOATER** smoked herring
zo **BLOBBER BLUBBER**, whale or seal fat
BLOCKED obstructed; jammed
ar **BLOCKER** headstone of column; offensive player (Am. football)
BLOMARY a forge
BLONDIN tight-rope walker
BLOODED foxhunting rite; wounded
bt **BLOOMED BLOSSOMED**, flowered, throve
tx **BLOOMER** error; woman's undergarment
bt **BLOSSOM** bloom; bud; flower
BLOTCHY patchy; smeary
BLOTING drying by smoke
BLOTTED stained; sullied
BLOTTER a blotting pad
zo **BLOWFLY** blue-bottle
BLOW-GUN blow-pipe
gl, pb **BLOWING** puffing; disclosing; (glass); surface pits; hollows in sand, soil
BLOW-OUT a spread; banquet; short work-out of horse (racing)
BLOWZED frowsy; slovenly
zo **BLUBBER** wail; whale fat (blobber)
zo **BLUE-CAP** a titmouse (bird)
zo **BLUE-CAT** Siberian cat
zo **BLUE-EYE** honey-eater bird
bt **BLUE-GUM** eucalyptus
BLUEING a metal finish; expanding
zo **BLUE-JAY** North American jay
BLUFFED concealed; spoofed
BLUFFER a deceiver; con-man
BLUFFLY bluntly; frankly; openly
BLUNDER gross mistake; howler
BLUNGER clay-mixer
BLUNTED took the edge off; dulled
BLUNTER more outspoken
BLUNTLY stolidly; obtusely
BLURRED dimmed; obscured
BLURTED uttered abruptly
BLUSHED flushed; coloured
BLUSHET a damsel
BLUSTER turbulence; swagger; storm
nt **BOARDED** lodged; embarked
BOARDER paying guest
BOARISH swinish; brutal
BOASTED vaunted; bragged; blustered
to **BOASTER** a broad chisel; a vain proud fellow
BOAT-CAR canal trolley
zo **BOAT-FLY** water-boatman
nt **BOATFUL** ship-load
BOATING an aquatic pastime

BOATMAN a rower; an oarsman
BOBBING cheating; curtseying
BOBBING (winter sports); angling
BOBBISH hearty; energetic; uppish
BOB-SLED bob-sleigh
nt **BOBSTAY** bowsprit stay
BOBTAIL rabble; caudal abbreviation
lw **BOCLAND** feudal freehold
BODEFUL ominous
bt **BOG-BEAN** marsh plant
BOGGARD bugbear; scarecrow
BOGGART hobgoblin; spectre
BOGGLED hesitated; vacillated
BOGGLER a waverer; demurrer; doubter
BOG-LAND fen; marsh; swamp
bt **BOG-MOSS** sphagnum
bt **BOG-RUSH** a sedge
mt **BOHOROK** Föhn-like winds in Sumatra
BOILING enraged; seething; pasteurizing
BOLDEST bravest; most valiant
bt **BOLETIC** fungoid extract
bt **BOLETUS** fungus genus
BOLIVAR Venezuelan currency unit
nt **BOLLARD** mooring post; kerb-post
bt **BOLLING** a pollard; a lopped tree
pl **BOLLOCK** testicle; nonsense; rubbish
BOLONEY phoney palaver
BOLSTER to support; prop; pillow
BOLTING sifting; swallowing
BOMBARD to pump with projectiles, (artillery); drop bombs
mu **BOMBARD** large leather water bottle; jug; larger shawm (bassoon)
BOMBAST fustian; rodomontade
BOMBING blitzing
BOMBOUS rounded, convex
BONANZA stroke of luck
zo **BONASUS** bison or wild ox
BONDAGE captivity; thraldom; helotry
BONDING (Customs); (bricklaying); pairing; linking
BONDMAN villein; peon
ga **BONE-ACE** card game
BONE-ASH burnt bones
gl **BONE-BED** strata with fossils
zo **BONETTA BONITA,** tunny fish
BONFIRE a beacon; (Guy Fawkes)
BONNILY handsomely
BOOKFUL theoretical
BOOKING reserving; buying; on record; (office)
BOOKISH studious
BOOKLET brochure; pamphlet
BOOKMAN scholar
cp **BOOLEAN** truth, algebra, and calculus system
BOOMING in demand; resounding
nt **BOOMKIN** short boom overhanging the stern
zo **BOONDER** Rhesus monkey
BOORISH mannerless; clumsy; lubberly
BOOSING tippling; bousing
BOOSTED advertised; eulogized
bd **BOOSTER** output or energy raising device; pump; compressor
BOOTING foot-wear; sacking
ga **BOOTLEG** sell prohibited goods; Am. football
BOOZING boosing; toping; getting drunk
ch **BORACIC** a boron derivative
ch **BORAZON** boron/nitrogen compound
BORDAGE feudal tenure
BORDMAN feudal tenant
hd **BORDURE** heraldic border
BOREDOM ennui; tedium; dullness
ch **BORNEOL** camphor-yielding chemical
mn **BORNITE** erubiscite; copper ore
BOROUGH electoral division; municipality
BORSTAL a reformatory for youth
ck **BORTSCH** beetroot soup (Rus.)
bt **BOSCAGE** undergrowth; macchia (It.); scrubs; shrubbery
zo **BOSHBOK** bush-buck
BOSOMED embraced
BOSQUET an arbour
BOSSAGE (projecting stones)
BOSSING controlling; dominating; bullying
BOSSISM political dictatorship
BOTANIC botanical; floral
ck **BOTARGO** special sausage
ck **BOTARGO** grey-mullet roe
BOTCHED bungled; patched
BOTCHER incompetent worker
BOTTINE small boot
BOTTLED inebriated
BOTTLER person or machine that fills bottles
hd **BOTTONY** heraldic cross
bt **BOUCHET** a pear
hr **BOUCHON** hollow watch plug
BOUDOIR a lady's private room
ck **BOUILLI BOUILLON,** boiled meat (broth)
gl **BOULDER** a large rock
md **BOULIMY, BULIMY** morbid appetite
BOULTER fishing line

BOULTIN convex moulding
BOUNCED rebounded, bluffed
BOUNCER chucker-out; bad cheque; (baseball); (cricket)
BOUNDED sprang; limited; bordered
BOUNDER inconsiderate ass
bt **BOUQUET** nosegay
BOURBON Kentucky corn whisky
mu **BOURDON** bass stop
BOURDON mule; pilgrim's staff
BOURLAW local jurisprudence
BOURREE lively dance (Fr., Sp.)
BOW-BACK crooked; hog-back
BOW-BENT bent as a bow
BOW-HAND left hand (archery)
BOWLESS no bow
nt **BOWLINE** a rope; a non-slip knot
BOWLING (bowls); (cricket); trundling
BOW-SHOT about 80 yards (73 m) (archery)
BOWSOCK bow cover (archery)
BOX-CALF tanned calfskin
BOX-COAT heavy coat
nt **BOXHAUL** luffing; sailing to windward
BOX-IRON heater receptacle
BOX-KITE scientific kite
tx **BOX-LOOM** multiple-shuttle-box loom
cr **BOX-SLIP** boxwood planing face
eg **BOX-TOOL** single-point lathe cutter
bt **BOXWOOD** odoriferous shrub; its wood
BOYCOTT ostracize; refuse to do business with
BOYHOOD puerility
BRABBLE squabble; a quarrel; broil
bl, nt **BRACING** strengthening; invigorating
bt **BRACKEN** brake-fern
BRACKET brace; corbel; a support; (figure-skating); small ornamental shelf
bt **BRACTED** (irregular leaf)
to **BRADAWL** boring tool
BRAGGED boasted; blustered
rl **BRAHMAN** **BRAHMIN**, Hindu priest
BRAIDED plaited; embroidered
nt **BRAILED** trussed
BRAILLE raised letters
BRAINED brainy; bashed
ck **BRAISED** stewed
BRAKING retarding
bt **BRAMBLE** brier-brush
BRAMBLY thorny; prickly
BRANCHY spreading; ramifying
BRANDED marked; disgraced
BRANDLE waver; shake
BRANGLE wrangle; a brawl
zo **BRANLIN** striped worm
BRANTLE a dance
BRASIER **BRAZIER**, brass-workers' charcoal pan; for hot chestnuts
BRASSET casque or helmet
BRATINA loving cup (Russia)
BRATTLE clatter
BRAVADO arrogant bluster; showing off; dare-devil
BRAVELY gallantly; daringly
BRAVERY valour; heroism
BRAVEST most courageous
BRAVING defying; daring
BRAVOES hired assassins
mu **BRAVURA** florid virtuoso performance needed
BRAWLED wrangled; quarrelled
BRAWLER rowdy ruffian
zo **BRAWNER** boar-meat
BRAYING clamour; pounding
BRAZIER brasier
ce **BRAZING** soldering; capillary jointing (metals)
BREACHY unruly
BREADTH broadness; beaminess
BREAKER small water cask
el **BREAKER** wave; circuit stop; gyratory or jaw (rocks, cask) (ice)
BREAK-IN interruption; burglary
BREAK-UP disrupt; disillusion
nt **BREAMED** cleaned of barnacles
BREATHE respire; exhale; express
mn **BRECCIA** conglomerate
BREEDER (animal husbandry) (sire)
pr **BREVIER** a size of type
BREVITY terseness; conciseness
ch **BREVIUM** uranium
br **BREWAGE** a brew
br **BREWERY** brewhouse
BREWING plotting; beer-making
zo **BRIABOT** angler-fish
BRIBERY palm-oil; graft
BRIBING illicit payments for illegal acts
BRIBRIS Costa Rican Indian
BRICKED blocked completely
BRIDGED spanned; linked; covered; (loan)
BRIDLED **BRIDLER**, curbed; checked; controller
BRIDOON snaffle bit
lw **BRIEFED** informed; instructed; courtcase
BRIEFER shorter; more concise
BRIEFLY curtly; pithily; in short
BRIERED set with briars
BRIGADE subdivision of army

BRIGAND bandit; outlaw; freebooter
BRIMFUL almost overflowing
BRIMMED edged
BRIMMER a hat; a full glass
BRINDLE streaky-brown
ck **BRINING BRINISH,** salting (brackish)
bt, ck **BRINJAL** egg-plant (Indian)
ck **BRIOCHE** light pastry (Fr.)
BRISKER sharper; quicker; sprier
ck **BRISKET** breast of meat
BRISKLY quickly; vivaciously
BRISTLE BRISTLY, (beard); rough and prickly
BRISTOL (glass); (china)
BRISURE rampart deviation
BRITISH of Britain
BRITTLE easily broken; fragile
BROADEN BROADER, widen; extend; amplified
BROADLY tolerantly, more liberally
tx **BROCADE** woven silk
BROCAGE brokerage; brokery
BROCARD maxim or canon; wise words
tx **BROCART** gold, silver thread cloth patterns
BROCKED black and white
zo **BROCKET** young red deer
BRODKIN a buskin; brodekin
ck **BROILED BROILER,** flame-cooked; gridiron
BROKAGE, BROKERY, BROKERAGE shares sales
BROKING bargaining; negotiating
ch **BROMATE** a salt of bromic acid
ch **BROMIDE** a sedative
ch **BROMINE** a liquid element
md **BROMISM** state after overdose
pt **BROMOIL** oil pigment prints
zo **BRONCHO** unbroken horse
BRONZED tanned
BROODED cherished; meditated
BROOKED allowed; enjoyed; endured
BROOMED swept and dusted
BROTHEL sex-workers' den; bawdy house
BROTHER sibling; kinsman; friar
BROUGHT conducted; led; fetched
ck **BROWNED BROWNER,** bronzed; tanned; gratinated
BROWNIE young girl guide; elfin
BROWSED pastured; grazed; (bookshop)
zo **BRUCHUS** pea-beetle
bt **BRUCINE** nux vomica
ch **BRUCITE** hydrate of magnesia
BRUISED injured; contused; pounded
BRUISER a boxer
BRUITED rumoured; noised abroad
zo **BRUMMER** large fly (S. Africa)
BRUMOUS foggy; wintry
bt **BRUNION** nectarine
BRUSHED swept; grazed; (hair)
BRUTIFY brutalize; bestialize
BRUTISH BRUTISM, gross; cruel; savage
md **BRUXISM** teeth-grinding
zo **BRYOZOA** incrustations
zo **BUBALIS** antelope genus
zo **BUBALUS** buffalo
ck **BUBBLED** gurgled; burbled; (boiling); aerated
BUBBLER a cheat
md **BUBONIC** plague
ch **BUBULUM** neat's-foot
md **BUCCATE** with protruding cheeks
BUCCULA double chin
zo **BUCEROS** rhinoceros horn-bill
gl **BUCHITE** clay/shale fusion rock
BUCKEEN Irish squireen
bt **BUCKEYE** horse-chestnut
BUCKING BUCKISH, (horse); boasting; foppish
BUCKLED BUCKLER, bent in; fastener; shield; belt
BUCKRAM stiffened cloth
to **BUCKSAW** frame-saw
BUCOLIC Arcadian; pastoral; rural
ar **BUCRANE** garlanded ox-skull frieze; Doric
bt **BUDDING** germinating; blossoming
nt **BUDGERO** Bengal boat
BUDGING shifting; stirring
bt **BUDLESS** barren; sterile
zo **BUFFALO** cattle-like animal
BUFFING polishing
BUFFOON a rough fool; clown
nt **BUGALET** square-rigger ship, Brittany
BUGBEAR bugaboo; hobgoblin; bogey
bt **BUGLOSS** borage
bt **BUGWORT** a plant
to **BUHL-SAW** spaced-back frame-saw
BUILDED built; erected; raised
BUILDER constructor
BUILD-UP favourable publicity
BUILT-UP urban area; compounded (timber) (interest)
BULBING BULBOUS, BULGING, swelling; expanding
bt **BULBLET BULBULE,** small bulb
zo **BULCHIN** bull-calf
BULGING protuberant; distended
md **BULIMIA** rapid over-eating disorder

BULKIER BULKING, more massive; becoming huge
bt **BULLACE** wild-plum
rl **BULLARY** (papal bulls)
BULLATE blistered
zo **BULL-BAT** night-hawk
zo **BULL-BEE** stag-beetle
zo **BULLDOG** college police
zo **BULL-FLY** gadfly
BULLIED blustered; hazed; (hockey)
BULLIES browbeaters; hectors
BULLING boosting
BULLION uncoined metal
BULLISH obstinate; mulish
zo **BULLOCK** steer
BULLPEN pitcher's enclosure (baseball)
zo **BULL-PUP** young bulldog
bt **BULRUSH** the reed-mace
BULWARK ship's side
BUMBAZE bamboozle
BUMBOAT refuse and slops removal boat
bd **BUMICKY** masonry repair cement
ck **BUMMALO** Bombay duck (dried fish)
BUMMILY preposterously; protuberously
BUMMING sodomizing; begging; loafing
BUMMOCK ale
BUMPERS shock absorbers (cars); extra portions
BUMPING thumping; jarring; knocking
BUMPKIN short boom; rustic; swain
BUNCHED clustered; concentrated
BUNDLED packed together closely
BUNGLED BUNGLER, mismanaged; botcher
nt **BUNKAGE** coaling charge
BUNKING decamping; sharing dormitory
zo, tx **BUNTING** bird; celebration flaglets
nt **BUOYAGE** placing buoys
BUOYANT light; floating
BUOYING sustaining
zo **BUPHAGA** beef-eater bird
BURDASH fringed sash
bt **BURDOCK** dock with prickly head
BURETTE graduated glass tube; phial
BURGAGE tenure in socage
BURGEON to bud; expand rapidly (status)
BURGESS freeman of a borough
BURGHAL of a borough
BURGHER inhabitant
BURGLAR house-breaker; cracksman
BURGLED stole; robbed
ck **BURIDDA** Ital. fish stew
BURKING smothering; concealing
bt **BURLACE** a variety of grape
BURLIER more robust; sturdier
BURLING removing knots
BURMESE (Burma)
BURNING vehement; ardent; fervent
BURNISH polish; furbish; brighten
BURNOUS Arab attire
pc, el **BURNOUT** excess emotional reaction; voltage change
bt **BUR-REED** a plant
bt **BURRELL** pear; russet cloth
zo **BURRHEL** wild sheep of Tibet
BURRING raising a ridge
BURROCK small weir
BURSARY educational grant for students
BURSTER eruptor; exploder; terrorist
cp **BURSTER** offline separation of output
BURTHEN burden
bt **BUR-WEED** a plant
BURYING burial; concealing; sepulture
zo **BUSH-CAT** the serval
BUSHIDO Japanese code of chivalry
BUSHING detachable lining
BUSHMAN aborigine
zo **BUSH-TIT** long tailed titmouse
BUSKING street entertainment; (begging)
BUSSING conveying; (anti-racialism); kissing (Am.)
BUS-STOP here by request sign!
zo **BUSTARD** large bird
BUSTLED BUSTLER, hastened; (noisily); (ostentatiously); hurrier
BUSY-BEE a finger in every pie
BUSYING meddling; interfering
ch **BUTANOL** an alcohol
BUTCHER murder; slay; slaughter
ck **BUTLERY BOTTLERY**, pantry (of kitchen area)
bl **BUTMENT** houses' end to end contact
BUTT-END ditto; fag end (cigarette)
ck **BUTTERY** larder; cold area in kitchen
BUTTING clash of goats (rutting); ramming
pl **BUTTOCK** thigh as sit-upon; backside
BUTTONS BUTTONY, fastening knobs; (decorative)
ch **BUTYRIC** rancid
BUVETTE refreshment bar
bt **BUXEOUS** (box-tree)
BUXOMLY generously breasted
BUYABLE for purchase; available

zo **BUZZARD** rapacious bird
to **BUZZ-SAW** circular saw
BY-AND-BY presently
BYE-ROAD secondary road
BY-GOING passing by
BYRONIC cynical
BYSSINE of flax
BYSSOID fringed
BY-THING a minor detail
BYWONER squatter (S. Africa)

C

CABARET entertainment show (night club)
bt, ck **CABBAGE** green vegetable
CABBALA rabbinic mysticism
CABBLED fragmented
CABEIRI deities of Semitic origin
tx **CABESSE** Indian silk
CAB-FARE money for taxi ride
CABINED confined; cribbed
CABINET governing ministers; chamber; WC
CABINET show case; (furniture)
CABIRIC (nature worship)
CABLING telegraphing
rw, bd **CABOOSE** guard's van; shanty
CAB-RANK row of cars for hire
CA'CANNY work in slow time
md **CACHEXY** morbid state
mt **CACIMBO** heavy mists, low cloud, Angola
CACIQUE cazique; Mexican chieftain
CACKLED CACKLER, a noisy hen
ch **CACODYL** oily compound
CACOEPY false pronunciation
CACOLET mule-chair
CACONYM wrongly derived name
CADAVER corpse; dead body
CADDISH impolite; trickster; impostoring
CADENAS condiment casket
mu **CADENCE** falling tones; flow sequence
CADENCE rhythmical movements
CADENCY regularity of movement
CADENUS Dean Swift
mu **CADENZA** a flourish
CADGING hawking; sponging; soming
CADMEAN (Cadmus); moral victory
ch **CADMIUM** a metal
to **CADRANS** (jewel cutting)
ch **CAESIUM** a metal
CAESURA poetic pause
CAFENET Turkish inn
CAFFEIC CAFFEIN, coffee alkaloid
mo **CAGOULE** waterproof hooded garment
CAINITE (Cain); a Gnostic
nt **CAISSON** floatable, sinkable dock port
CAITIFF knave; miscreant; churl
bt **CAJEPUT CAJUPUT**, pungent oil (tree)
CAJOLED CAJOLER, inveigled; beguiler
bt **CAJUPUT** pungent oil
CALABER squirrel-fur
zo **CALAMAR** cuttle-fish
bt **CALAMUS** dragon's blood palm
pr **CALAMUS** antique Islamic reed pen
mu **CALANDO** diminuendo
CALCIFY turn to lime
CALCINE pulverize by heat
mn **CALCITE** calc-spar
ch **CALCIUM** a metallic element
md **CALCULI** gall-stones
gl **CALDERA** lava collapse crater; steep cliffs
CALDRON cauldron; boiler; kettle
CALECHE a vehicle; calash (Fr.)
CALENDS first of month
CALIBAN a tempestuous monster
CALIBER CALIBRE, diameter of bore gauge; capacity; faculty; talent
ch **CALICHE** sodium nitrate
bt **CALICLE** small cup
CALINDA W. Indian dance
CALIPEE calipash; turtle fat
to **CALIPER** measuring instrument
CALIVER a musket
nt **CALKING CAULKING**, water-proofing hulls
CALL-BOY prompter's attendant; (rent-boy)
pg **CALLIER** photographic ratio
CALLING vocation; profession; trade; game-, dance instructions
CALLOUS insensitive; hard; obdurate
bt **CALLUNA** heather
md **CALMANT** a sedative
CALMING tranquillizing
CALMUCK Kalmuck; Mongolian
md **CALOMEL** mercuric chloride
CALORIC heating
me **CALORIE** unit of heat
ar, rl **CALOTTE** skull-cap; dome
rl **CALOYER** Greek monk
CALTRAP CALTROP, 4-pin spike against cavalry
bt **CALUMBA** climbing plant
CALUMET Indian peace-pipe
CALUMNY slander; aspersion; obloquy

rl **CALVARY** Golgotha (skulls) crucifixion place
CALVING bringing forth (of cattle)
CALVING icebergs from polar ice
zo **CALYCLE** coral-polyp
bt **CALYPSO** sea nymph; (Odysseus)
CAMAIEU cameo; a monochrome
ar, rl **CAMARIN** chapel behind high altar (Sp.)
CAMARON freshwater prawn; Sp. shrimp
CAMBIAL pertaining to cambium
CAMBISM art of exchange; (cambio It.)
CAMBIST banker; financier
CAMBIUM cellular tissue
tx **CAMBLET** camel-hair cloth
bt **CAMBOGE** gamboge
CAMBREL meat-hook
tx **CAMBRIC** white linen
rl **CAMBUCA** pastoral staff
CAMELOT King Arthur's Court
CAMELRY camel corps
CAMORRA secret society (It.)
bt, mu **CAMPANA** an anemone; bell (It.)
bt **CAMPHOR** aromatic laurel
CAMPING encamping; struggling
bt **CAMPION** plant
nt **CAMSHIP** merchant ship with fighter aircraft
bt **CAMWOOD** a red wood
mu **CANARIE** triple time dance
ga **CANASTA** two-pack card game
CAN-BANK collection container for recycling
nv **CAN-BUOY** conical buoy
me **CANDELA** luminous intensity
CANDENT incandescent; glowing
CANDIED CANDIFY, sweetmeat preserve in sugar
bt **CANDOCK** yellow water-lily
CANDOUR frankness; openness
bt, ck **CANELLA** cinnamon tree (W. Indies)
CANHOOK cask-hook
CANIKEN CANAKIN, small container
CANKERY cankered
tx **CANNELE** horizontally ribbed silk fabric
CANNERY CANNING, food processing (factory)
CANNIER more artful, cunning
CANNING preserving; tinning
md **CANNULA** surgical tube
rl **CANONIC** canonical
rl **CANONRY** residence of cathedral canon
CANOPIC (Canopic case)
as **CANOPUS** star in Argo
CANTARO drinking glass (Spain)
rl, mu **CANTATA** sung mass; choral work
ck **CANTEEN** factory restaurant; cutlery box; tin
pl **CANTHAL CANTHUS**, corner of the eye
CANTING hypocritical; sanctimonious
rw **CANTING** curve adjustment slope
CANTLET CANTLE, fragment; cutting
tx **CANTOON** cotton material
CANTRED hundred; county division
CANTRIP a witch's spell
pt **CANVASS** seek votes (lobby); (painting)
nt, ga **CANVASS** (sails) (tentcloth) (flooring)
mu **CANZONE** song or melody
CAPABLE CAPABLY, efficient; able; competent
CAP-A-PIE from head to foot
CAP-CASE travelling case
zo **CAPELIN** small smelt fish
CAPERED CAPERER, frolicked; bounded; dancer
cr **CAP-IRON** cutting-iron stiffener
CAPITAL money; main; excellent
nt **CAPITAN** naval officer
CAPITOL Roman temple
CAPORAL shag tobacco
CAPOTED won all tricks at piquet
rl **CAPOUCH** monk's cowl
CAPPING topping; limiting (finance)
ch **CAPRATE** a salt
mu **CAPRICE** whim; light fugue; (humour)
zo **CAPRINE CAPROIC**, like a goat
ck **CAPRINO** goat-milk cheese (Argentina)
CAPRONE flavouring oil
CAPSIZE upset; overturn
nt, cp **CAPSTAN** windlass; tape-winder
bt **CAPSULA** seed-vessel; a cap
md **CAPSULE** soluble envelope
ae **CAPSULE** detachable compartment
nt **CAPTAIN** leader; chief; master
CAPTION certificate; title; arrest
CAPTIVE prisoner
CAPTURE take; apprehend; catch
rl **CAPUCHE** a Capuchin's hood
CAPULET father of Romeo's Juliet
bt **CAPULIN** Mexican cherry
CAR PARK parking area
zo **CARACAL** Persian lynx
ar **CARACOL** snail; spiral shell; staircase
zo **CARACUL** Bukhara sheep
ck **CARAMEL** a sweetmeat; caromel
bt **CARANNA** aromatic resin (Amazon)

CARAVAN house on wheels
nt **CARAVEL** four-masted ship
bt **CARAWAY** seed; plant; spice
ch **CARBIDE** (lamp)
CARBINE short rifle
CARCAKE pancake
CARCASE body; bomb; framework
CARCASS a fire-work; shell arch
nm **CARDECU** French quarter-crown
md **CARDIAC** (heart); cardial
CARDING combing flax
bt **CARDOON** artichoke
bt **CARDUUS** thistle genus
CAREFUL meticulous; heedful; wary
CARGOES argosies
zo **CARIAMA** bird of prey
zo **CARIBOU** Arctic reindeer (N. Amer.)
CARIOLE light cart
CARIOUS decayed
rl **CARITAS** love of God and neighbour
CARKING anxious
bt **CARLINE** a witch; thistle genus
CARLISM CARLIST, royal faction (Sp.)
CARLOCK motor door; isinglass
CARMINE red pigment
CARNAGE slaughter; butchery
CARNIFY turn to flesh
CARNOSE CARNOUS, fleshy; meatlike
nm **CAROLUS** sovereign of Charles I
CAROSSE sheepskin or fur rug (S. Africa)
md **CAROTID** arterial
md **CAROTIN** carrot pigment, vitamin
CAROUSE revel; feast; tipple
CARPING captious; cavilling; objecting
CARPORT open garage
nt **CARRACK** armed trading ship; argosy
CARRIED borne; upheld; transported
CARRIER transporter; conveyor
CARRION putrid meat
CARROTY rufous (rufus); colour of carrots
rw **CAR-SHED** carriage depot for buses, trains
CARTAGE conveyance
CARTING transporting
CARTOON topical sketch
CARVING slicing; cutting; engraving
zo **CARVIST** hawk on hand
ch **CARVONE** caraway oil ketone
mu **CARYOKE** video-led pub singing
bt **CARYOTA** fish-tail palms
CASCADE waterfall; collar
md **CASCARA** herbal laxative
CASEASE casein-decomposing enzyme
ck **CASEATE CASEOUS**, cheese-like
lw **CASE-LAW** based on judgements
CASEMAN compositor
CASHIER cash desk teller; discharge
CASHING (cheques)
bt, ck **CASSADA CASSAVA**, tapioca
ga **CASSINO CASINO**, card game
CASSIUS (purple)
rl **CASSOCK** a vestment
CASSONE bridal chest (It.)
CASTING rejecting; pitching; (mould); (spell); (roles); angling
CASTLED (chess)
CASTLET small castle
CAST-OFF laid aside
CASTRAL (camp)
CASUIST a quibbler; sophist
CATALAN Catalonian
zo **CATALLO** hybrid; buffalo and cow
CATALOG university calendar (USA)
bt **CATALPA** Shawnee-wood
CATAPAN Byzantine governor
CATARRH (inflammation)
CATASTA slave-block
bt **CATAWBA** Ohio grape
zo **CAT-BIRD** American thrush
nt **CAT-BOAT** boat with mast in bow
CAT-CALL derisive yell
CATCHER (base-ball)
CATCHES songs; (fish)
ck **CATCHUP CATSUP, KETCHUP**, tomato and spices sauce
CATCH-UP draw level; chance-taking
md **CATECHU** an astringent
CATERED provided for; food obtained
CATERER restaurant meals purveyor
CAT-EYED (night vision)
nt **CAT-FALL** anchor rope
zo **CAT-FISH** wolf-fish; nurse-hound
CATHEAD anchor rest
CATHECT to direct feelings
el, pc **CATHODE** negative electrode; (TV)
nt **CAT-HOLE** hawser hole
CATHOOD cf. spinsterhood
CATLIKE feline character
zo **CATLING** small cat; cat-gut
bt **CAT-MINT** a species of Nepeta
CAT-SALT rough salt
mn **CAT'S-EYE** a quartz
CAT'S-PAW a dupe; a ripple
zo **CATTALO** hybrid; buffalo and cow
CATTISH spiteful
nt **CATWALK** narrow plank bridge
bt **CATWHIN** needle-gorse

CAUDATE with a tail
bt **CAULINE** stalky
CAULKED rendered watertight
CAULKER a dram; a whopper
bt **CAULOME** all organs of a shoot
CAUSING resulting in; occasioning
CAUSTIC corrosive; mordant
md **CAUTERY CAUTERIZATION**, searing treatment
CAUTION care; heed; warning
CAVALRY horse-soldiers
CAVEMAN a troglodyte; grotto-dweller
CAVETTO hollow moulding
zo **CAVIARE** sturgeon's roe
bt **CAYENNE** red pepper
CAZIQUE cacique; West Ind. chief
CEASING desisting; ending; stopping
zo **CEBIDAE** class of monkeys
fr **CEDARED** cedar forest
CEDILLA c like s sign
bt **CEDRELA CEDRINE**, types of cedar
bd, ae **CEILING** upper limit; (room, prices, flights)
CELADON stoneware (ceramics) (Ch.)
mu **CELESTA** keyboard; bell effects
ch **CELLASE** apricot-kernel enzyme
mu **CELLIST** violoncellist
cy **CELL-SAP** cell fluid constituents
CELLULE small cell
ps **CELSIUS** centigrade heat scale
mu **CEMBALO** It. clavichord, harpsichord
CENACLE supper-room
CENSING burning incense
CENSION assessment
CENSUAL (census)
CENSURE blame; rebuke; chide
CENTAGE percentage
CENTAUR mythological horse-man
nm **CENTAVO** Portuguese halfpenny
bd, ar **CENTERS** temporary supports (arch, dome)
ma **CENTILE** scores system below 100
nm **CENTIME** hundredth part of a franc
me **CENTNER** foreign cwt
nc, me **CENTRAD** one hundredth of a radian
CENTRAL mediate; middlemost
CENTRED concentrated; based; located
CENTRIC central
zo **CENTRON** neuron
pl **CENTRUM** part of spinal vertebra
ga **CENTURY** hundred (years, runs – cricket)
CERAMIC (pottery)
bt **CERASIN** plum-gum
CERATED waxed
CEREALS edible grass crops; breakfast food
CEREOUS CERESIN, wax
CEROTIC beeswax extract
CERTAIN assured; infallible; undeniable
CERTIFY avouch; attest; witness
CERULIN indigo
md **CERUMEN** ear-wax
CERUSED white-leaded
CERVINE (stags)
CESIOUS bluish-grey
CESSING taxing
CESSION relinquishment; surrender
bd **CESS-PIT** midden; sewage tank
zo, md **CESTODA CESTOID**, tapeworm
zo **CETACEA** whales, etc.
CHABLIS white wine
CHABOUK Eastern whip
mu **CHACONY CHACONNE**, slow dance; repeated theme
CHAFERY welding furnace
CHAFFED bantered; scoffed; derided
CHAFFER haggle; bargain
CHAFING fretting; fuming; rubbing
CHAGRIN vexation; irritation
CHAINED fettered; measured
CHAIRED presided over; carried in triumph
bt **CHALAZA** the base of an ovule
CHALDEE Chaldean
me **CHALDER** 96 bushels
rl **CHALICE** communion cup; goblet
CHALKED scored; recorded (blackboard)
tx **CHALLIS** fine silk
md **CHALONE** an internal secretion
CHAMADE invitation to a parley
CHAMBER room; closet; hall; cavity
CHAMFER groove; polish
CHAMLET camlet; camel-hair
zo **CHAMOIS** leather
bt **CHAMPAC** Indian tree; champak
CHAMPED crunched; chewed; bit
CHANCED happened; befell; risked
rl, bd **CHANCEL** clergy's area of church
CHANDOO prepared opium
CHANGED altered; varied; shifted
CHANGER exchanger; shifter
cp, nt, tc **CHANNEL** canal; strait; gutter
mu **CHANSON** song (Fr.)
CHANTED (horse-coping); intoned
rl **CHANTER** a precentor
mu **CHANTER** (bagpipes)
rl **CHANTRY** chapel for mass
CHAOTIC confused; disordered
gl **CHAPADA** tableland in Bahia, Brazil
ck **CHAPATI** unleavened bread (India)

CHAPEAU a hat (Fr.)
CHAPLET garland; wreath; coronal
CHAPMAN pedlar; hawker
CHAPNET **CHAPNUT**, pewter salt-cellar
CHAPPED seamed; cleft; cracked
CHAPPIE ghost (Sc.)
rl **CHAPTER** cathedral council; (freemasonry)
CHAPTER a division within history, novel, etc.
CHARACT a character (Shak.)
CHARADE dramatic enigma
CHARGED rushed forward; accused; billed; loaded
zo **CHARGER** platter; war horse
CHARILY stingily; warily; reluctantly
CHARING drudgery
CHARIOT Roman vehicle
CHARISM sense of power
CHARITY benevolence; alms
CHARLEY night-watchman
CHARLIE pointed beard
CHARMED enchanted; fascinated
CHARMER a siren; beguiler
CHARNEL mortuary; house of the dead
CHARPOY Indian bedstead
CHARQUI dried beef (Peru)
CHARRED scorched; seared; burnt
nt **CHARTED** tabulated; recorded
CHARTER right; privilege; hire
CHASING engraving; pursuing; hunting
CHASSIS frame-work; base structure of vehicle
CHASTEN correct; punish; humble
CHATEAU country seat
CHATTAH Indian umbrella
CHATTED gossiped; prattled
lw **CHATTEL** movable property
CHATTER talk; prate; tattle
CHAUVIN French patriot; chauvinism (excessive group loyalty)
CHAWING chewing; munching
ck **CHAYOTE** custard marrow
CHEAPEN belittle; depreciate; reduce price, quality
CHEAPER not so dear
CHEAPLY inexpensively
CHEATED bobbed; duped; gulled
CHEATER trickster; swindler
CHECHIA Arab skull-cap
CHECKED restrained; hindered; verified
ce **CHECKER** chess board; to variegate; section leader
CHECK-IN arrival formality (airport, hotel)
ck **CHEDDAR** a cheese
CHEEKED sauced; was impertinent
CHEEPED chirped
zo **CHEEPER** young game bird
CHEERED applauded; enlivened
CHEERER vociferous supporter
CHEERIO convivial salutation
zo **CHEETAH** hunting leopard
zo **CHELATE** (claw)
zo, bt **CHELONE** tortoise; shell flower
ck **CHELSEA** china porcelain; spiralled buns
CHEMISE shift; smock; slip
ch **CHEMISM** chemical action
CHEMIST chymist; pharmacist; druggist
CHEMOSH a Moabite god
CHENILE fluffy cord
CHEQUER checker; diversify
mt **CHERGUI** Saharan wind, Morocco
CHERISH to foster; harbour; treasure
CHERMES **KERMES**, a crimson dye
CHEROOT Burmese or Manila cigar
bt **CHERVIL** culinary herb
CHESSEL a cheese mould or vat
CHESTED boxed; (flat-)
bt **CHESTON** a species of plum
CHETNIK guerilla (Croat)
zo **CHEVIOT** sheep bred on the Cheviots
CHEVRON zigzag badge
CHEWING chawing; munching
CHIANTI Italian red wine
md **CHIASMA** nerve intersection
CHICANE trick; artifice; (cards); evasion; diversion of circuit turns (motor cycling)
CHICKED sprouted; hatched
CHICKEN young fowl; young person
bt **CHICORY** salad plant, root (coffee)
CHIDING rating; scolding; blaming
CHIEFLY principally; mainly; mostly
CHIEFRY rent; chief's lands
tx **CHIFFON** gauzy material
mu, zo **CHIKARA** Indian guitar; antelope
CHILEAN Chilian; native of Chile
CHILIAD a thousand years
CHILLED discouraged; depressed
CHILLER an iceberg or wet blanket
CHILLUM hookah
zo **CHILOMA** camel's lip
zo **CHIMERA** mythical monster; illusion
zo **CHIMERA** graft; hybrid; fish
rl **CHIMERE** bishop's robe
mo, gl **CHIMNEY** funnel; smoke-stack; narrow rock cleft
zo **CHINCHA** S. American rodent

CHINDIT Burmese guerilla
CHINESE Sinesian
CHINING cutting the backbone
CHINKED jingled; clinked
mt **CHINOOK** N. American Indian tribe; föhn wind by East Rocky mountains, Canada
CHINSED caulked
CHINWAG chatty conversation
to **CHIPAXE** light axe
CHIP-HAT hat made of palm leaves
nv **CHIP-LOG** log-line attachment
CHIPPED chaffed; chopped; cut
CHIPPER lively; twitter; cutter; sculptor
CHIPPIE holed shot (golf); (basket ball)
CHIRPED bird song
zo **CHIRPER** grasshopper
CHIRRUP bird noise
CHISLEU a Jewish month
CHISLEY gravelly
CHITTER shiver with cold
zo **CHITWAH** panda; red bear-cat
md **CHLORAL** a narcotic
ch **CHLORIC** chlorine derivative
bd, mu, rl **CHOIRED** in chorus (church)
CHOKING stifling; strangling; coughing
md **CHOLEIC** of bile
md **CHOLERA** deadly infectious disease
md **CHOLINE** B vitamin; organic base
CHOLTRY caravanserai; Eastern inn
CHOOSER a picker; a selector
CHOPINE clog or patten
CHOPPED cut; minced; changed
to, ae, cp **CHOPPER** cleaver; axe; helicopter; pulsator
CHOPPER high-bouncing ball (baseball)
mu **CHORALE** choral composition
eg **CHORDAL** of chords
mu **CHORDED** strung
CHOREUS a trochee
bt **CHORION** a membrane
rl **CHORIST** chorister
md **CHOROID** eye-membrane
CHORTLE chuckle noisily; exult
ck **CHOWDER** dish of clams
CHOWTER grumble; croak
rl **CHRISOM** baptismal cloth
ml **CHROMAX** iron-based alloys
ch **CHROMIC** of chromium
ch **CHROMYL** chrome radical
CHRONIC long continuing; inveterate
nc, ps **CHRONON** hypothetical particle of time
CHUCKED pitched; tossed; thrown
zo **CHUCKIE** a chicken
CHUCKLE exult; crow
tx **CHUDDAH** chudder; cloak or cloth (Ind.)
rw **CHUFFED** proud; satisfied; steamed
ga **CHUKKUR** **CHUKKA**, period of play (polo)
CHUMMED roomed together
ck **CHUPATI** unleavened bread (Ind.)
rl **CHURCHY** pious; ritualistic
CHURNED agitated; jostled; upset
CHURRED made deep whirring sound
ck **CHUTNEY** fruit pickle (Ind.)
ch **CHYAZIC** (hydro-cyanic)
ch **CHYMIFY** to digest
CHYMIST **CHEMIST**, pharmacist
rl **CIBORIA** canopies
zo **CICHLID** Tanganyika fish
zo **CICONIA** storks genus
zo **CIDARIS** sea-urchins
md **CILIARY** (eyelashes)
CILIATE with hairs
CIMARRE ceremonial wine vessel (2 handles) (Fr.)
CIMBRIC a language of Jutland-Germanic invaders of Imperial Rome
CIMELIA stored treasures
CIMETER scimitar
CINDERY full of cinders; ashy
ch **CINEOLE** eucalyptole
md **CINEREA** nerve tissue
mn **CIPOLIN** green marble
CIRCEAN of a witch; enchantress; (Circe)
CIRCLED went right round; circumnavigated
CIRCLER **CIRCLET**, small ring (finger)
cp, el, lw, tc, ga **CIRCUIT** judicial itinerary; round tour; racing track; electrical layout; water course; (cars, greyhounds), channel (radio, TV, telex); rotational route; golf; revolution (planetary); turn
mt **CIRRATE** curly (of clouds)
bt **CIRROSE** **CIRROUS**, with tendrils; curls
pt **CISSING** retreat of paint from surface
CISSOID geometric curve
CISTERN **CYSTERN**, waterholder; wine cooler (table)
md **CISTRON** gene (function)
CITABLE quotable
bd **CITADEL** inner stronghold of city fort
CITADIN alpine races for part-time skiers

lw **CITATOR** a summoner; quoter; speaker
mu **CITHARA** Greek lyre
mu **CITHERN** guitar
CITIZEN burgher; burgess; resident
ch **CITRATE** lemon salts
CITRENE oil of lemons
CITRINE a yellow
mu **CITTERN** cithern; zither
CIVILLY courteously; politely
CIVVIES mufti; civilian clothes
CLABBER thicken
CLACHAN small village (Sc.)
CLACKED clucked; clicked; jabbered
CLACKER clack-valve; football fan's rattle; turnstyle rachet
CLADISM evolutionary classification by common factor
bt **CLADODE** leaflike branch
CLAIMED demanded; insisted; usurped
ga, lw **CLAIMER CLAIMANT**, horse when racing; appellant (court) challenger
CLAMANT insistent crying (demonstration)
CLAMBER climb; scramble
CLAMMED clogged; smeared
CLAMOUR din; uproar; hubbub
CLAMPED clumped; held down
CLAMPER iron patch
CLANGED clashed; pranged
CLANKED clinked; clanged
CLAP-NET bird fowler's net
CLAPPED applauded; shut
CLAPPER tongue of a bell
CLAQUER claqueur; hired applauder
CLARAIN fine coal
CLARIFY make clear; strain; purify
mu **CLARINO** It. trumpet, horn parts; clarionet
mu **CLARION** a shrill trumpet
CLARITY cleanness; distinctness
bt **CLARKIA** a flowering annual
mu **CLASHED** suddenly opposed; cymbals
CLASPED grasped; gripped; fastened
bt **CLASPER** tendril; embracer
CLASSED ranked; grouped; ranged
CLASSER classificationist
CLASSIC first rate; standard; masterly
rl **CLASSIS** assembly or convention
mt **CLASTIC** fragmental; brittle
CLATTER clash; rattle; crash; (breakage)
CLAVATE club-shaped
mu **CLAVIER** keyboard
CLAWING scratching; fawning
CLAYING puddling; purifying
CLAYISH clay-like
CLAY-PIT marl pit
CLEANED purified; washed; scoured
CLEANER dirt remover
CLEANLY spotlessly; adroitly
rl **CLEANSE** wash; purify; (ritual)
CLEAN-UP to tidy; make respectable; purge; cartoon technique; (baseball)
CLEARED acquitted; absolved
CLEARER more obvious; less opaque
CLEARLY distinctly; patently
CLEAVED split; parted; adhered
CLEAVER butcher's chopper
CLEDDYO Celtic sword
CLEMENT merciful; lenient; mild
CLEMMED held fast (crowd, rocks); starving
CLERKLY learnedly; scholarly
nt **CLEWING** coiling; securing
CLICKED found favour; ticked
CLICKER cobbler; compositor
CLICKET knocker; door-latch
mt **CLIMATE** clime; weather
CLIMBED scaled; ascended
bt **CLIMBER** a creeper; mountaineer
CLINKED clanked; jingled (of chains); jailed
CLINKER slag; (ship design)
CLINOID like a bed
CLIPPED shorn; pared; snipped; docked
nt **CLIPPER** schooner; cutter; trimmer
CLIPPIE bus-conductress
ec, mt **CLISERE** climate changes and climaxes
CLITTER clatter
bt **CLIVERS** goose-grass
CLIVITY slope; incline
CLOAKED disguised; concealed; hidden
CLOBBER clothing; cobbler's paste; assault
ar, rl **CLOCHER** belltower (Fr.)
CLOCKED timed; (-in)
CLOCKER time-keeper; clock-watcher
CLODDED clotted; mired
CLOGGED congested; coalesced
CLOGGER clog-maker
CLOSELY intimately; accurately
CLOSEST nearest
CLOSE-UP (to action) (movies); frank
CLOSING conclusion; sealing; clogging; deadline date; (horse-racing)

CLOSURE also cloture; enclosure
bt **CLOT-BUR** the burdock
CLOTHED attired; arrayed; draped
CLOTHES apparel
CLOTTED curdled
CLOTTER to coagulate
CLOTURE closure; conclusion
CLOUDED obscured; blended; dimmed
CLOUTED patched; buffeted
CLOVATE inverse taper
CLOWNED played the fool
CLUBBED coshed; bludgeoned
CLUBBER clubbist; club member
CLUB-LAW might is right
CLUB-MAN member of clubs
CLUCKED clocked; cackled
zo **CLUMBER** a spaniel
CLUMPED in clusters; mustered
CLUMPER to form clumps
rl **CLUNIAC** Benedictine monk
mu **CLUSTER** group; clump; assemble; adjacent notes played together
CLUTTER confused mass
CLYPEAL like a shield; scutate
zo **CLYPEUS** insect's forehead
CLYSMIC cleansing
md **CLYSTER** an injection
COACHED tutored; trained
COACTED compelled; concentrated
COAGENT an associate; colleague
COAKING dowelling
COAL-BED stratum of coal
COAL-GAS extraction from coal
nt **COALING** taking on coal fuel
COALISE **COALESCE**, come together
COALITE a form of fuel
COAL-PIT mine
ch **COAL-TAR** extraction from bituminous coal
zo **COAL-TIT** a passerine bird
nt **COAMING** raised border surrounding cockpit of kayaks
CO-ANNEX join jointly
COARSEN roughen
COARSER rougher; ruder; cruder
COASTAL **COASTER**, shorewise, inshore vessel
COASTED free-wheeled (cycles and cars)
COASTER plate for glasses; decanters; bottles
pt, tx **COATING** layer; covering
eg **CO-AXIAL** having common axis
COAXING cajoling; wheedling; (manipulating)
COBBING rounding up swans; picking cherries
bd **COBBING** mixing clay, chalk and straw for walls
COBBLED mended; tinkered; patched
COBBLER shoe repairer; botcher
ce **COBBLES** stones for paving
COBIRON andiron; firedog (open fire place)
COBLOAF crusty loaf
zo **COB-SWAN** male swan
COB-WALL mud-wall
ar **COBWORK** log-house construction
md **COCAINE** drug
zo **COCALON** large cocoon
md **COCHLEA** ear-cavity
ch **COCINIC** cocoa extract
COCKADE badge on 3-cornered hat
pl **COCKEYE** imperfect vision; a squint
ag **COCKING** making hay cocks; stooks; strutting
COCKLED puckered; wrinkled; (like a cockleshell)
COCKLER purveyor of seafood; shell-fish
COCKNEY true Londoner
ae, nt **COCKPIT** cock-fighting arena; enclosure for pilot, kayak canoeist; deck for wounded (Navy)
gl **COCKPIT** sinkhole in karst areas
COCK-SHY coconut shy; target (Aunt Sally)
bt, ck **COCONUT** tropical tree fruit
COCOTTE light of love (Fr.); faithless
ck **COCTILE** baked
COCTION cooking, (con-) result
CODDING fishing; codswallop; nonsense
ck **CODDLED** simmered (eggs); pampered
bt **CODEINE** an alkaloid from opium
mu **CODETTA** rounding off passage (It.)
zo **CODFISH** esteemed food fish
CODICES manuscript books
lw **CODICIL** addition to a will
bt **CODILLA** coarse hemp
CODILLE card-term at ombre
zo **CODLING** young cod
CODLING codlin apple
COELEBS bachelor
md **COELIAC** abdominal
zo **COENURE** young tape-worm
COEQUAL a peer; a compeer
COERCED **COGENCE**, **COGENCY**, compelled to; forced to
bl **COEXIST** be coeval; live together
ga **COGGERY** **COGGING**, cheating at dice
COGNATE related; allied; akin to
bt **COG-WOOD** a Jamaican tree
lw **COHABIT** live together as married

COHERED adhered; cleaved; coalesced
ro **COHERER** early form of detector
COIFFED (hairdressing)
COIGNED billeted (Irish)
COILING entangling; winding up
COINAGE money; specie
COINING minting; counterfeiting
COITION sexual intercourse
lw **COJUROR** witness to credibility
bt **COLA-NUT KOLA-NUT**,
COLD-CUT buffet items; cold lacquer solvent
COLDEST iciest; frostiest
COLDISH chillsome
COLD-PIG cold douche
zo **COLIBRI** species of humming-bird
COLICKY with pains
md **COLITIS** colic; colonic infection
bt **COLLAGE** real objects on art forms
COLLARD cole-wort
COLLATE collect and compare
COLLAUD unite in praising
COLLECT a prayer; assemble; amass
COLLEEN Irish girl
COLLEGE academy; seminary; guild
COLLIDE crash; encounter; clash
nt **COLLIER** miner; vessel
COLLING embracing; necking
COLLOID gelatinous
COLLUDE connive fraud in collaboration
zo **COLOBUS** a monkey genus
COLONEL highest regimental rank
COLOSSI gigantic statues
COLOURS tints; (army flags; sports awards)
COLOURY coloured
COLTISH frisky (of young horses)
zo **COLUBER** a snake genus
COLUMBA holy vessel; (Iona)
COLUMEL a small column
COMBINE unite; blend; coalesce
COMBING breaking into foam; smoothing; (hair); removing wet paint
as **COMBUST** astrological term
COMETIC (comets)
COMFORT console; solace; ease; cheer
COMFORT luxury (furniture; financial)
bt **COMFREY** a plant
COMICAL droll; diverting; farcical
COMITIA assemblies
COMMAND govern; rule; enjoin; decree
COMMARK marches; frontier land
COMMEND laud; praise; eulogize
COMMENT remark; note; criticize
COMMERE a gossip
COMMODE chest of drawers; (portable toilet)
ck **COMMONS** food; fare; non-nobility
COMMOVE agitate
COMMUNE converse; discourse
COMMUNE a self-sufficient group sharing family tasks
COMMUTE exchange; replace; travel
mu **COMPACT** mini-pack; cosmetics; (-disc)
COMPANY society; group; business firm
COMPARE examine for likeness or difference
go, ma **COMPASS** to encircle; scope; magnetic pointer N
COMPERE introducer; leader of an entertainment
COMPETE strive as rival
COMPILE amass; combine; arrange
COMPLEX intricate; complicated
pc **COMPLEX** mental inhibition
COMPLOT conspiracy
nv, ps **COMPOLE** auxiliary magnetic pole
COMPORT behave fittingly; glass stand for syllabub glasses
ar, mu, pt, ck **COMPOSE** create; assemble; formulate
ag **COMPOST** convert decayed debris to fertility
ck **COMPOTE** dessert of cooked fruit
cp **COMPUTE** reckon; analyse; solve
COMRADE pal; mate; associate
COMTISM COMTIST, (Comte's Positivism)
CONATUS volition; effort; impulse
CONCAVE hollow; scooped; turning inwards; converging
CONCEAL cloak; hide; cover; disguise
CONCEDE yield; allow; grant
CONCEIT vanity; egotism; pride
CONCEPT basic idea expanded
CONCERN trouble; regard; firm
mu **CONCERT** devise; concoct
CONCISE terse; pithy; laconic
CONCOCT plot; hatch; brew
mu **CONCORD** harmony; amity; union
md **CONCUSS** stuns by fall or blow
CONDEMN declare doom; convict; punish
CONDIGN deserved; merited; appropriate
CONDITE to pickle; to preserve
CONDOLE console; share sorrow with sympathy

CONDONE to overlook wrong-doing with apathy; pardon
CONDUCE to lead to desirable result; promote
CONDUCT guide; escort; deportment
mu **CONDUCT** direct a musical performance
CONDUIT passage; pipe; channel; canal
md **CONDYLE** knuckle
bt **CONEINE** coniine; hemlock
ck **CONFECT** a sweetmeat; to prepare
CONFERVA freshwater algae
CONFESS admit; own; disclose; avow
CONFIDE close trust (secrets); depend; rely
CONFINE imprison; limit (of freedom); in bounds
CONFIRM ratify; endorse; re-establish
CONFLUX crowd; confluence of people
CONFORM comply with obedience; similarity
CONFUSE confound; mislead; muddle
CONFUTE disprove; refute; find wrong
CONGEAL make solid (freeze, coagulate)
CONGEST clog; overfill; overpack
CONGIES vitamin-rich rice-cookery water
CONICAL cone-shaped; tapering
bt **CONIFER** evergreen (bearing spores)
CONJOIN unite for link-up; common aim
CONJURE spirit-raising; creating illusions
CONJURY sleight of hand tricks; entertainment
CONKERS chestnuts (challenging game)
CONNATE congenital; innate; inherent
CONNECT couple; conjoin; hyphenate
CONNING studying situation; confidence deception
CONNIVE overlook; permit wrong; abet
CONNOTE imply a logical connection
CONQUER overpower; vanquish
CONSENT concur; agree; assent
CONSIGN despatch; send; trasmit
CONSIST comprised of; made up of
mu **CONSOLE** sympathize (sadness); organ (control point)
CONSOLS government Consolidated Funds
mu **CONSORT** associate with; chamber orchestra; spouse
CONSULT deliberate together; confer
CONSUME devour (eat) (fire); expend
el **CONTACT** get in touch; (communication) (-lens)
CONTAIN include; embody; comprise
CONTEND strive; vie; assert; cope
CONTENT volume; satisfy; mollify; (contained)
ga **CONTEST** struggle; compete (arena)
CONTEXT applicable background situation
CONTORT bend; twist (body) (facts)
CONTOUR outline; height line; profile
el **CONTROL** check; steer; master; (switches)
CONTUSE bruise; crush (physical)
CONVENE assemble; muster; summon
rl **CONVENT** a nunnery
rl **CONVERT** change; alter; transform; win over; after-try (goal) rugby; Canadian football
CONVICT prove guilty; (judge); criminal
CONVOKE summon to a meeting; convene
ck **COOKERY** **COOKING**, concocting; cuisine
COOLANT liquid or gas preventing overheating
COOLEST most impudent; exciting; least warm
COOLING moderating
COOLISH somewhat cool
COONCAN card game
bt **COONTIE** arrowroot
COOPERY barrel production
COOPING confining; penning
CO-OPTED invited to elected body
bt **COPAIBA** **COPAIVA**, balsam
zo **COPEPOD** minute water organism
mu **COPERTO** muffled covered drums
ae, nt **CO-PILOT** assistant aviator; partner
COPIOUS abundant; plenteous; ample
COPLAND angular piece of land
ml, pt **COPPERY** copper-coloured
COPPICE spinney; clump of trees; thicket
COPPING catching; arresting; (policeman)
zo **COPULAR** linking; of mating; coupling

md **COPULIN** vaginal secretion
COPYCAT apeing others' ideas
COPYING aping; transcribing
COPYISM copyist's work
COPYIST plagiarist; imitator
bt **COQUITO** palm with edible sap/seeds
nt **CORACLE CURRAGH**, river craft (Wales)
mu **CORANTO** a running dance
CORBEAU raven-black
CORBEIL sculptured basket
nt **CORBITA** cargo vessel of Imperial Rome
CORCASS Irish salt marsh
bt **CORCULE** an embryo
CORDAGE rope
bt **CORDATE** heart-shaped
CORDIAL cocktail; hearty; ardent
CORDING cordage; binding
CORDITE a propellant
fd **CORE-BOX** sand-moulding container
zo **CORINNE** gazelle; small deer
bt **CORINTH** a currant
CO-RIVAL competitor
CORKAGE charge for guests' own wine
CORKING stopping; sealing wine bottles
CORK-LEG artificial limb
ag, lw **CORNAGE** agricultural land tenure
bt **CORN-COB** spike of maize
md **CORNEAL** (eye-membrane)
mu **CORNETT CORNET**, woodwind 17th c.
zo **CORN-FLY** destructive insect
mo, ar **CORNICE** ledge of snow; a top moulding
bt **CORNINE** quinine type
CORNING preserving; granulating
CORNISH (Cornwall)
mu **CORNIST** hornist; cornet blower
lw **CORN-LAW** regulating corn trade
ck **CORN-OIL** maize oil
CORN-RIG strip of growing corn
CORNUAL CORNUTE, horny
CORN-VAN winnowing machine
bt **COROLLA** floral whorl
CORONAL circlet; wreath
CORONER official of causes of death
zo **CORONET** a moth; tiara
CORONIS elision; word contraction
CORRECT amend; exact; precise; true
CORRODE destroy slowly (rust)
CORRUPT degraded; depraved; putrid
tx **CORSAGE** flowery female dress
CORSAIR pirate (Barbary coast)
mn **CORSITE** diorite
CORSLET sleeveless armour
CORSNED an ordeal
ga **CORTADA** shortened; low shot (pelota)
CORTEGE solemn procession
md **CORTICO-** of outer layer tissue
ar **CORTILE** courtyard
ch **CORUBIN** aluminium oxide
CORVINE like a cow
CORYDON a rustic lover
bt **CORYLUS** hazel
bt **CORYPHA** fan-palm
COSAQUE cracker; bon-bon (Fr.)
COSHERY billeting (Irish)
COSHING bashing; slugging
COSIEST snuggest; warmest (intimate)
COSMISM COSMIST, of secular philosophy
COSSACK KHAZAK, cavalryman (Russian)
bt, ck **COSTARD** apples (and custard)
ar **COSTATE** ribbed construction
COSTING calculation of right sales price
COSTIVE obstructive; constipated
COSTREL pilgrim's bottle
COSTUME dress; uniform; livery
COTERIE social circle (similar interests)
COTIDAL contemporaneous tides
zo **COTINGA** chattering birds
COTLAND cottage land
COTTAGE cot; lodge; hut
hd **COTTICE** heraldic barulet
COTTIER Irish tenant
zo **COTTOID** fish genus; miller's thumb
COTTONY downy; nappy
COUCHED expressed; reclined; (bedded)
COUCHEE soirée; evening reception (Fr.)
COUGHER splutterer
rl **COULDST** thou could; (prayer form)
gl **COULOIR** cleft; canyon; eroded gully
el **COULOMB** unit of electrical charge
COULTER fore-end of plough
COUNCIL ministry; assembly; diet
lw **COUNSEL** advice; barrister
COUNTED reckoned; relied; numbered
COUNTER contrary; adverse; opposed; small chest (Am. football) (curling)
me, mu **COUNTER** token, meter; table; (-point) (-foil)
ga **COUNTER-** being against trend; (ice-hockey)
COUNTRY region; nation; state

COUPLED paired; bracketed; joined
mu **COUPLER** connector; duplicated organ controls
mu **COUPLET** two lines (rhyming) (musical)
COURAGE pluck; valour; heroism
mu **COURANT** disseminator; dance form
COURIER messenger; runner
zo **COURLAN** S. American crane
COURSED hunted; pursued; chased
zo **COURSER** war-horse; plover
nt **COURSES** some sails
COURTED wooed; invited; solicited
COURTER a wooer; swain
COURTLY elegant; urbane; debonair
COUTEAU long knife
COUTURE (haute); clothes for the jet-set
COUVADE a curious custom
COVELET small bay
COVERED enveloped; veiled; spread
zo **COVERTS** certain feathers
COVER-UP boxing; concealment
COVETED longed for; desired
bt **COW-BANE** water-hemlock
zo **COW-BIRD** American cuckoo
zo **COW-CALF** female calf
COWERED cringed; shrank; crouched
COWHAGE a bean (Hindu)
ck **COW-HEEL** ox-foot stewed to a jelly
COWHERD a cow tender
COWHIDE leather
mu **COW-HORN** alphorn; drinking-
bt **COW-ITCH** cowhage
COW-LICK salt lick, in fields
COWLIKE ruminant; placid
ae **COWLING** hood
bt **COWSLIP** paigle
bt **COW-TREE** moraceous tree
bt **COW-WEED** herb
COXCOMB conceited fellow; dandy
COYNESS shyness; bashfulness
COZENED deceived; gulled
COZENER white collar bandit
me, ps **C-PARITY** charge parity (quantum)
CRABBED morose; surly; disparaged
nt **CRABBER** small open boat
CRABITE fossil crab
bt **CRAB-OIL** carap-oil
CRACKED crazy; snapped; split; broke
CRACKER cosaque; biscuit; firework
CRACKLE glazed fissures in china
pc **CRACK-UP** nervous breakdown; crash
CRACOWE KRAKOW, pointed shoe (Poland)
CRADLED nurtured
CRAGGED rugged; jagged
CRAKING cawing
zo **CRAMBUS** grass moth
CRAMESY crimson
CRAMMED stuffed; studied
CRAMMER intensive teacher; packer-in
CRAMPED confined; cabined
CRAMPIT curlers' stand
CRAMPON spiked shoe cover (Alpine)
CRANAGE dockyard crane dues
zo **CRANIAL** skull
CRANING stretching the neck
md **CRANIUM** a skull
CRANKED bent; turned; wound
CRANKLE crinkle; wrinkle; a turn
CRANNOG lake dwelling
CRAPING curling
CRAPNEL grapnel; hook
zo **CRAPPIE** N. Amer. sunfish
CRASHED smashed; shattered; fell
CRASHER (gate-), uninvited guest; clumsy
CRATING encasing; packaging
CRAVING longing; yearning; desiring
CRAWLED crept; (swimming)
CRAWLER a reptile; a baby's overall
CRAZIER madder
CRAZILY daftly; distractedly
ar **CRAZING** weak, broken (crazy pavement)
bd **CREAKED** grated, squeaked (floor noise)
ck **CREAMED** take the best of milk; foamed
CREANCE hawk-leash line
ga **CREASED** folded; wrinkled; lined (cricket)
CREATED originated; formed; produced
md **CREATIN** muscular constituent
CREATOR maker; originator; inventor
CREDENT credulous; trusting
CREEING softening grain
zo, bt, ga **CREEPER** crawler; ski-aid; plant; bird; larva of stonefly; bait (angling); low ball (cricket)
CREMATE reduce to ashes; incinerate
mu **CREMONA** a violin
bt **CRENATE** notched
CRENAUX loop-holes
ch **CREOSOL** (phenol)
CREPANE wound due to brushing
CRESSET beacon; torch
hd **CRESTED** capped; surmounted; (badge)

CRETIFY impregnate with lime
CRETISM a falsehood
CRETOSE chalky
mo **CREVICE** fissure; rift; breach
CREWELS embroidery
CRIBBED cradled; plagiarized; cheated
CRIBBLE coarse sieve; a temse
CRICKED sprained
CRICKET a low stool; an insect; 11 a side bat and ball game
CRICOID ring-shaped
lw **CRIMING** making criminal accusations
tx, ck **CRIMPED CRIMPER, CRIMPLE,** corrugated edging (pies); shrunk
CRIMSON blood red colour
CRINGED cowered; fawned
CRINGER a yes-man; sycophant
nt **CRINGLE** eyelet in sail
CRINITE hairy; a fossil
CRINKLE crankle; wrinkle; crimp
mn **CRINOID** fossilized sea-lily
CRINOSE crinite; pilose; hairy
bd **CRIPPLE** disable; impair; hobble
ck **CRISPED** frizzled; toasted; made brittle
CRISPER curler; more friable
CRISPIN the cobblers' saint
CRISPLY briskly
CRIZZEL CRIZZLE, cloudy roughness on glass
zo **CROAKED** uttered; grumbled; decried (frog)
zo **CROAKER** a fish; a pessimist
CROCHET fancy-work
CROCKED blackened; broken down
ar **CROCKET** pinnacle adornment
CROESUS a wealthy man
ag **CROFTER** hill farmer
CROOKED tortuous; awry; bent
CROONED sung (chromatic); lamented
CROONER sentimental singer
CROPFUL full stomach; satiated
CROPPED mowed; reaped; cut
pr, ce **CROPPER** printing machine; heavy fall; steel bar cutter
ga **CROQUET** up to date pall-mall
rl **CROSIER CROZIER,** bishop's crook
hd **CROSLET** crossed cross
CROSSED thwarted; interbred
CROSSLY peevishly; testily; petulantly
mu **CROTALO** Turkish cymbal
CROTTLE lichen-dye
ck **CROUTON** chopped fried bread
to **CROWBAR** lever; jemmy
CROWDED huddled; thronged
mu **CROWDER** Welsh fiddler
zo **CROWGER** striped wrasse; fish
CROWING rejoicing; boasting; cocks
CROWNED honoured; completed; (king)
bt **CROW-TOE** the buttercup
rl **CROZIER CROSIER,** pastoral crook
CRUBEEN cooked pig's trotter (Irish)
CRUCIAL cross-like; critical; decisive
zo **CRUCIAN** goldfish; crusian
CRUCIFY hang to death on cross
mn **CRUCITE** red iron ore
CRUDELY unpolished; roughly
CRUDEST rawest; coarsest
ck **CRUDITY** rawness; immaturity; salad
CRUELER more brutal; harsher
CRUELTY savagery; barbarity
nt **CRUISED** moved watchfully; voyaged
nt **CRUISER** patrol warship; powered yacht
CRUISIE primitive lamp
ck **CRULLER** a cake
ck **CRUMBED CRUMBLY,** friable; fragmented
ck **CRUMBLE** disintegrate; (fruit dish)
CRUMPED artillery; bomb noise; exploded
ck **CRUMPET** hot griddled tea-bun; (love)
ck **CRUMPLE CRUNKLE,** collapse; crimp
md **CRUORIN** haemoglobin
CRUPPER severe fall; saddle-strap
rl **CRUSADE** idealists' campaign
nm **CRUSADO** Portuguese coin
CRUSHED overwhelmed; compressed
CRUSHER pulverizer; chucker-out
zo **CRUSIAN CRUCIAN,** carp; goldfish
CRUSTED hard surface; en- with debris
CRY-BABY a weakling
CRYOGEN a freezing mixture
CRYPTIC hidden; occult; secret
ch **CRYPTON** krypton; a gas
mn **CRYSTAL** cut-glass; quartz; (-gazing)
CRYSTIC pertaining to ice
CSARISM TSARISM, CZARISM, despotic
CTENOID comb-shaped
CUADROS division lines (pelota Sp.)
CUBBING whelping; hunting fox cubs; scouting
CUBBISH ill-mannered
md **CUBEBIN** cubeb extract
CUBICAL cubic
CUBICLE little bedroom
me **CUBITAL CUBITED, CUBITUS,** (cubit *c.*50 cm)

CUCKOLD husband of loose wife
zo **CUCULUS** cuckoo
bt **CUDBEAR** a lichen; a purple dye
CUDDLED hugged; fondled; caressed
bt **CUDWEED** a plant
CUE-BALL (billiards)
CUFFING scuffling; buffeting
CUINAGE tin stamping
CUIRASS breastplate (armour)
ck **CUISINE** style of cookery
mu **CUIVRES** brass band instruments (Fr.)
CULETTE hip-armour
CULLIED duped; gulled; hoaxed
CULLING gathering; reducing animal population
bt **CULLION** bulbous root
CULPRIT delinquent; offender
rl **CULTISM CULTIST**, ritual supporter
CULTURE arts; enlightenment; customary beliefs
md **CULTURE** clinical lab. cultivation
CULVERT small bridge; (waterway)
bt **CUMQUAT** kumquat; Chinese fruit
mt **CUMULUS** large cloud formation
CUNEATE wedge-shaped
CUNNING crafty; sly; wily; astute
ag **CUP-FEED** seed drill system
bt **CUP-GALL** an oak-gall
ce **CUPHEAD** rivet shape
bt **CUP-MOSS** a lichen
CUPPING blood-letting
mn **CUPRITE** oxide of copper
bt **CUP-ROSE** poppy
ch **CUPROUS** copper compound
CURABLE remedial
CURACAO orange liqueur
CURATOR custodian; keeper; warden
CURBING repressing; restraining
bt **CURCUMA** (arrowroot, etc.)
CURDING coagulating
CURDLED congealed; thrilled
CURE-ALL universal remedy; panacea
md **CURETTE** surgical scraper
CURIOSA collection of exotic objects
CURIOSO unconventional object collector
CURIOUS inquisitive; strange; novel; odd
ga **CURLING** bowls played on ice
nt **CURRAGH CORACLE**, Celtic water craft
bt **CURRANT** ribes; a dried raisin
nt, el, pr **CURRENT** up-to-date; flow (tide); (-account)
ck **CURRIED** spiced Indian food; flattered; groomed
le **CURRIER** leather-dresser
CURRISH doglike snarling; spiteful
CURSING evil invocation of harm; swearing
pr **CURSIVE** running; ongoing; script
CURSORY hasty; superficial; transient
CURTAIL abridge; contract; shorten
CURTAIN window, theatre drapery; (-call)
CURTANA sword of mercy (Coronation)
cp **CURTATE** cut short; reduced; punched
CURT-AXE short broad-sword
CURTEST bluntest; briefest; shortest
CURVATE CURVITY, bending (surface of globe)
CURVING turning; change of direction
ga **CUSHION** pad; pouffe; lining (billiards)
CUSSING cursing; swearing
ck **CUSTARD** milk, egg and vanilla sauce
CUSTODE a watchman; custodian
CUSTODY care; imprisonment; duress
CUSTOMS duties on merchandise
CUSTREL buckler-bearer; a costrel
tx **CUT-AWAY** tailored coat, dress
CUT-BACK decrease of work; retreat
CUT-DOWN reduce; cheapen (prices etc.)
pl **CUTICLE** fingernail skin area
nt **CUTLASS** short broad sword
CUTLERY edged steel tools (knives etc.)
CUTLINE across front wall (pelota)
CUT-OVER attack (fencing)
CUT-RUSH technique (croquet)
CUTTING satirical; sardonic; sarcastic
bt, rw **CUTTING** trough; gap; sproutling
CUTTING tailoring; escaping; ignoring
CUT-WORK type of embroidery
zo **CUT-WORM** caterpillar pest
CUVETTE crucible; trench; cunette
ch **CYANATE CYANIDE, CYANINE**, poison
mn **CYANITE KYANITE**, aluminium silicate
CYCLING CYCLIST, two wheeling, biker
CYCLOID geometric curve
mt, zo **CYCLONE** tornado; hurricane; typhoon; genus, waterfleas
CYCLOPS one-eyed Sicilian giant
CYCLORN a cycle horn

mu **CYMBALO** the dulcimer
CYNICAL disparaging; ironical
bt **CYPERUS** a sedge
bt **CYPRESS CYPRINE**, funereal tree
CYPRIAN CYPRIOT, of Cyprus
md **CYSTINE** calculus growth
md **CYSTOID CYSTOSE**, cystlike
md **CYSTOMA** tumour
ch **CYTIDIN** nucleic acid
bt **CYTISUS** the broom genus
md **CYTITIS** dermatitis
mu **CZARDAS** Hungarian dance
CZARINA TSARINA, empress (Russia)

D

pt **DABBING** daubing; adding oil or paint
DABBLED sprinkled; meddled; trifled
DABBLER dilettante; trifler
DABSTER an expert; adept
DACOITY DAKOITY, brigandage
DADAISM art movement
DADDLED tottered
DADDOCK the heart of a rotten tree
DAFTEST silliest; maddest; craziest
DAGGING wool clotted with dung, earth
DAGGING cutting into strips
DAGGLED befouled; smirched
DAG-LOCK hanging lock of wool
DAGONET King Arthur's fool
bt **DAGWOOD** dog-wood; sandwich
nt **DAHABIA** dhow for cargo, Nile
bt **DAHLINE** dahlia starch
DAKOITY DACOITY, brigandage
DALLIED DALLIER, dawdled; trifler; flâneur
DALRIAD an Ulster Scot
DAMAGED marred; injured; hurt
DAMMING embanking
DAMNIFY DAMNING (injure) (condemning)
DAMOSEL DAMSEL, maiden; lady
mu **DAMPFER** dampered; mute (Ger.)
DAMPING discouraging; moistening; lulling
ro, el **DAMPING** decreasing wave motion
DAMPISH moist; dank; humid
DANAKIL nomad fisher tribe
DANCING social rhythmic movement to music
DANDIFY overdone dress; dandy's movement
DANDLED fondled
DANELAW DANELAG, Danish East England
DANGLED DANGLER, suspended, cause to swing
DANKISH damp and dark
DANTEAN sombre; infernal
DANTIST specialist of Dante's works
bt **DAPHNAL DAPHNIN**, laurels (bay leaf)
zo **DAPHNIA** water-fleas
DAPIFER meat-bearer; royal steward
bd **DAPPING** fly-fishing; cement patterns
DAPPLED variegated grey; (horses)
DARBIES handcuffs
zo **DARCALL** long-tailed duck
zo **DARCOCK** water-rail
DARIOLE rich cake
DARKEST most secret; blackest
DARKISH sombre; gloomy; blackish
DARLING beloved; dear; pet; idol
DARNING mending clothes
ga **DARTING** swift movements; sprinting
DASHING rushing; impetuous; spirited
el **DASHPOT** snubber
DASTARD poltroon; coward; craven
DATABLE traceable to epoch; of friendships
rl **DATARIA** (papal chancery)
bt **DATISCA** hemp
DATIVAL of dative case (grammar)
DAUBERY DAUBING, poor painting; smearing; graffiti
DAUNTED discouraged; cowed
DAUPHIN king's eldest son (Fr.)
DAWDLED lagged; dallied; tarried
DAWDLER time-waster; laggard
DAWNING day-break; day-spring
DAY-BOOK daily register
mn **DAY-COAL** (upper stratum)
DAY-GIRL non-resident schoolgirl
bt **DAY-LILY** the hemerocallis
DAY-MAID dairy-maid; daily girl
DAY-PEEP dawn
DAY'S-MAN umpire
DAY-STAR the morning star
zo **DAYSURE** a wolf genus
DAY-TIME not night
DAYWORK (paid daily)
DAZZLED dazed by lights; confused
DEAD-END blind street; cul-de-sac; without future
nt **DEAD-EYE** 3-eyed naval tackle (pulley)
DEADISH rather moribund; decaying
DEAD-MEN empty bottles
DEADPAN expressionless (facial)

DEAD-PAY (pay drawn; death concealed)
DEAD-SET determined effort
bt **DEAD-TOP** arboreal disease
DEAF-AID hearing device
bt **DEAF-NUT** without kernel
DEALATE divest of wings
ga **DEALING** handling; trading; (card games)
rl **DEANERY DECANAL**, office of dean (university)
DEAREST costliest; closest loved one
DEARNLY secretly; grievously
DEASIUL DEASOIL, opposite of widdershins
DEATHLY mortal; deadly; destructive
DEBACLE fiasco; theatrical ending; rout; stampede
DEBASED DEBASER, degraded; shady dealer
DEBATED DEBATER, deliberated; disputed; arguer
DEBAUCH intemperate sensual action; deprave
DEBITED DEBITOR, DEBTOR, owing; charged with
DEBOUCH emerge into open area
DECADAL DECADIC, units of ten; decimal system
DECAGON ten-sided figure
rl **DECANAL DEANERY**, office of deans
zo **DECAPOD** having ten limbs; (lobster)
DECARCH commander over 10
DECAYED rotted; degenerated; wasted
DECAYER source of decay
DECEASE perish; die; expire; demise
DECEIVE beguile; mislead; overreach
DECENCY propriety; decorum
me **DECIARE** tenth of an are (Fr.)
me **DECIBEL** unit of noise
DECIDED resolute; firm; unwavering
ga **DECIDER** umpire; referee; final contest
ma **DECIMAL** system based on tens, tenths
DECKING ornament; embellishment
DECKLED with edges uncut
cp **DECKLET** record, set of IBM cards
DECLAIM orate; harangue; rant; spout
DECLARE avouch; assert; proclaim
DECLINE refuse; decay; wane; languish
DECODED deciphered
DECODER info. locater/fetcher/solver
DECORUM seemliness; decency
DECOYED allured; snared; inveigled
DECREED ordered; resolved; enacted
DECREET announce court judgement
DECRIAL DECRIER, clamorous censure; vilifier
DECRIED disparaged; traduced
DECROWN discrown; dethrone
DECUMAN main gate; tenth; principal
DECUPLE tenfold
DECURVE straighten
lw **DEDIMUS** judicial commission
DEDUCED inferred; concluded; reasoned
bd **DEDUCTS** calculation (excluding doors, windows etc)
DEEDFUL DEEDILY, manly; valiantly
lw **DEEDING** conveying by deed
DEEMING opining; considering
DEEPEST most profound; lowest
ck **DEEP-FRY** cooking method
DEEP-SEA in deep ocean
DEERITE iron/manganese hydrous silicate
DEFACED DEFACER, disfigured; mutilator
DEFAMED DEFAMER, libelled; slandered; detractor
DEFAULT lapse; financial failure
DEFENCE plea; excuse; protection
DEFIANT provocative; contumacious
DEFICIT shortage
DEFILED DEFILER, polluted; taken; seducer
DEFINED DEFINER, accurately described; clarifier
DEFLATE release air; reduce credit; erode
DEFLECT divert; turn aside
DEFRAUD trick; cheat; deceive
DEFUNCT deceased
DEFYING challenging; flouting
DEGAUSS antimagnetic device
DEGLAZE to clear thick gravy
DEGRADE lower; humble; debase
DEICIDE a god-destroyer
DE-ICING removing ice
rl **DEIFIED DEIFORM**, idolized; godlike
DEIGNED condescended; vouchsafed
rl **DEISTIC** theory of non-active God
DELAYED procrastinated; deferred
DELAYER a cunctator; procrastinator
DELETED expunged; effaced
DELIGHT charm; ravish; joy; ecstasy
DELIMIT fix limits
DELIVER cede; consign; rescue; save
DELOUSE to remove lice
DELPHIC oracular

go **DELTAIC** delta-like
md **DELTOID** a muscle
DELUDED misled; beguiled; gulled
DELUDER deceiver; trickster; hoaxer
DELUGED flooded; inundated; swamped
DELVING digging; excavating
DEMENTI official denial (Fr.)
DEMESNE DOMAIN, lord's land (feudal)
DEMIGOD almost worshipped person
DEMIREP a lady of doubtful virtue
DEMISED bequeathed; willed
DEMODED old fashioned
DEMONIC fiendish; satanic; diabolical
DEMONRY devilry
DEMONYM pseudonym using pop. style
DEMOTIC popular; common
DENDRAL living in trees; arboreal
DENDRON dendrite of nerve-cell
DENIZEN inhabitant; naturalized plant, animal
DENOTED indicated; signified
DENSELY closely; thickly
DENSEST thickest; closest
DENSITY compactness; stolidness
pl **DENTARY** (teeth); dermal bone
DENTATE toothed
DENTELS toothed ornaments
pl **DENTINE** ivory tissue of teeth
DENTING dinting; notching
md **DENTIST** tooth doctor
DENTOID tooth-like
DENTURE false teeth
DENUDED stripped; bared; divested
DENYING controverting; refuting
DEPLANE cf. detrain
DEPLETE to empty; exhaust; drain
DEPLORE lament; grieve; bewail
DEPLUME to pluck
lw **DEPONED** testified
DEPOSAL dismissal; sacking
DEPOSED bore witness; ousted
cp **DEPOSIT** store; lodge; intrust; part payment
DEPRAVE corrupt; debase; vitiate
DEPRESS damp; dishearten; sadden
DEPRIVE strip; rob; divest
DEPUTED delegated; authorized
DERANGE disturb; upset; ruffle
DERATED freed from local taxation
DERIVED deduced; traced; obtained
DERMOID like skin
DERNFUL solitary; mournful
DERNIER final; last (Fr.)
DERRING daring
DERVISH Moslem monk
rl **DESCANT** counterpoint superimposed on melody
DESCEND dismount; alight; drop; sink
DESCENT slope; decline; origin; raid
DESERVE earn; win; merit; justify
DESIRED wanted; solicited; coveted
DESIRER craver; yearner; fancier
DESKILL simplify industrial work
mn **DESMINE** stilbite; zeolitic mineral
DESPAIR hopelessness; despondency
DESPISE disdain; contemn; scorn; scout
DESPITE in spite of; malice
DESPOIL rob; bereave; strip; rifle
DESPOND despair; dejectedness
ck **DESSERT** fruit course; pudding; afters
DESTINY fate; fortune; doom; Kismet
DESTROY devour; demolish; raze
mu **DETACHE** violin bowing technique (Fr.)
DETENTE relaxing political strain
fr **DETERMA** a useful wood from Guyana
lw **DETINUE** writ of distraint
DETRACT defame; disparage; traduce
DETRAIN alight from train
DETUNER jet-engine noise-reduction
bt **DEUTZIA** a white flower
DEVALUE depreciate
DEVELOP grow; unfold; expand
DEVIATE swerve; turn; tack; digress
DEVILED stuffed; seasoned before frying
DEVILET small demon; imp
DEVILRY cruel mischief; diabolism
DEVIOUS wandering; erratic; tortuous
DEVISED contrived; willed; concocted
DEVISEE legatee; inheritor
DEVISER inventor; schemer; planner
DEVISOR testator
DEVOLVE deliver; depute; impose
DEVOTED loving; ardent; attached
DEVOTEE an addict; a fan; zealot
DEW-DROP drop of earth condensation
DEW-FALL aqueous precipitation
DEWLAPT with a dewlap
DEW-POND pond fed by condensation
zo **DEW-WORM** earthworm
md **DEXTRAD** to the right side (body)
DEXTRAL (not left)
DEXTRAN synthetic blood plasma

DEXTRIN starch gum
mn **DIABASE** variously defined rock type
ga **DIABOLO** game (devil on two sticks)
DIAGRAM graph; sketch; drawing
DIALECT local parlance; idioms
DIALIST dial-maker
ch **DIALIZE** separate
DIALLED rang up (telephone call)
ch **DIAMINE** 2-amino-group compound
mn, hd, ga **DIAMOND** hard valuable stone; (cards); lozenge; baseball
bt **DIANDER** (two stamens)
zo **DIAPSID** condition of skulls
DIARCHY dual monarchy
DIARIAL DIARIES, daily memoranda
DIARISE DIARIST, to record; chronicler
cy **DIASTER** stage in cell-division
bt **DIATOMS** seaweed
bd **DIATONI** face-dressed quoins
zo **DIAXONE** bipolar nerve cell
ch **DIBASIC** giving two salts
zo **DIBATAG** N. African gazelle
DIBBING dipping
DIBBLED made hole in the ground
DIBBLER planter
DICE-BOX dice holder
ga **DICEING** throwing dice; (gambling) (game)
zo **DICERAS** clams
mu **DICHORD** lyre
mn **DICKITE** hydrated aluminium silicate
bt **DICLINY** state of sex separation
DICTATE record; command; state
DICTION style; speech; clear enunciation
DIDACHE apostolic teaching
DIDDLED out-witted; cajoled; cozened
DIDDLER a cheat; swindler; cajoler
DIE-AWAY languishing; losing sound
DIE-CAST (condenser construction)
DIEDRAL dihedral
DIE-HARD last ditcher; anti-reformist
ck **DIETARY DIETING**, system of diet
ck **DIETIST DIETITIAN**, diet advisor
DIE-WORK die-cutting
DIFFUSE spread; copious; prolix
DIGAMMA obsolete Greek letter
DIGGING delving; excavating
ma **DIGITAL** integral; decimal; binary
el, cp **DIGITAL** numeric system data
DIGLYPH grooved face
DIGNIFY ennoble; exalt; grace
DIGNITY majesty; decorum; rank
DIGRAPH (two letters)
DIGRESS deviate; wander; swerve
bt **DIGYNIA** curious plant; (two pistils)
ch **DIKETEN** ketene dimer
DILATED enlarged; expatiated
DILATER an expander; amplifier
md **DILATOR** a muscle
DILEMMA quandary; plight; strait
md **DILL-OIL** a carminative
DILUENT a diluter; reducer
DILUTED watered; attenuated
DILUTEE unskilled worker (industrial)
DILUTER thinner
DIMETER (poetry)
DIM-EYED with weak vision; weepy
DIMMING blurring; clouding; dulling
DIMMISH somewhat obscure
DIMNESS vagueness; dinginess
DIMPLED showing dimples
DINETTE a dining compartment
bd **DINGING** ringing; urging; single coat stucco walls
zo **DINGOES** wild dogs of Australia
DINNING advocating clamorously
DINTING denting; striking
rl **DIOCESE** a bishopric
zo **DIOCOEL** diencephalon lumen
DIODONE iodine x-ray preparation
bt **DIOECIA** genus of plants
bt **DIONAEA** Venus's fly-trap
zo **DIOPSIS** fly genus
me **DIOPTER** optical measurement
DIOPTER speculum; theodolite
pg **DIOPTRE** unit of lens power
DIORAMA panorama
DIORISM definition
mn **DIORITE** igneous rock
ch **DIOXIDE** oxygen-based oxide
DIPHONE a shorthand sign
md **DIPLOID** twin chromosomes
DIPLOMA a certificate
DIPLONT diploid-nuclei-bearing plant body
DIPOLAR with two poles
DIPPING dibbing; plunging; immersing
DIPTERA two-winged insect
DIPTOTE noun with 2 cases only
DIP-TRAP bend in a pipe
rl **DIPTYCH** pictorial altar-piece
DIREFUL calamitous; baleful; awful
DIRKING stabbing
DIRT-BED (quarrying)
DIRTIED soiled; sullied; begrimed
DIRTIER DIRTILY, grubbier; more soiled; filthily
DIRT-PIE mud-pie
DISABLE unfit; incapacitate; maim
cp **DISABLE** suppress an interrupt

DISAGIO money-exchange charge
DISALLY separate; sunder
DISAVOW repudiate; disown; deny
DISBAND disperse; disembody
DISCARD cast; reject; abandon
DISCERN espy; perceive; discriminate
DISCOID flat like a disc
mu **DISCORD** strife; brawl; animosity; dissonance
DISCUSS debate; argue; consume
DISDAIN spurn; contemn; ignore
md **DISEASE** malady; complaint
DISEUSE woman reciter (Fr.)
DISGOWN unfrock (clergy)
DISGUST nausea; aversion; loathing
DISHFUL filling a dish
ck **DISHING** thwarting; preparing food
DISJOIN part; detach; sunder; sever
DISLIKE hate; detest; antipathy
DISMALS unhappy pessimists (anti-social)
nt **DISMAST** remove masts (sea battle)
DISMISS cashier; discharge; sack
DISOBEY transgress; disregard; infringe
DISPLAY parade; flaunt; show; evince
cp, lw **DISPLAY** reveal; put on screen
lw **DISPONE** hand over
DISPORT sport; gambol; frolic; wanton
DISPOSE sell; transfer; arrange
DISPUTE argue; wrangle; bicker
DISROBE unrobe; strip; divest; bare
DISRUPT break up; disintegrate
DISSECT anatomize; analyse; cut
DISSENT disagree; differ
DISTAFF staff for holding unspun flax
DISTAFF the opposite of spear-side
DISTANT remote; far; aloof; reserved
DISTEND dilate; swell; expand; bloat
DISTENT distended (Spens.)
DISTICH rhyming couplet
zo **DISTOMA** genus of worms
DISTORT pervert; misrepresent
DISTURB molest; confuse; vex; annoy
DISUSED obsolete; neglected; abandoned
DITCHED fallen into the sea (RAF); discarded; failed examination
DITCHER ditch clearer
nt **DITHERY** nervous; agitated; tremulous
bt **DITTANY** candle plant
DITTIED **DITTIES**, sung sea shanties
DIURNAL daily; quotidian; journal
DIVERGE fork; radiate; part
DIVERSE unlike; different; varied
DIVIDED severed; sundered; separated
cp, tc **DIVIDER** distributor; apportioner
DIVINER predictor; seer; magician
DIVISOR (arithmetic)
DIVORCE dissever; part; alienate
DIVULGE tell; reveal; disclose; impact
DIVVY-UP provide dividend (on profit); divide
DIZENED **DIZZIED, DIZZIER**, dazed; confused
DIZZARD blockhead; idiot
DIZZILY confusedly
rl **DOCETAE** **DOCETIC**, ungodly heretic sect
DOCKAGE dock dues
nt **DOCKING** taking ships into dock; curtailing (dog)
DOCQUET **DOCKET**, list sheet (cargo) loads
DODDING lopping tails; polling horns (cows, deer)
DODGERY trickery; prevarication
DODGING evading; quibbling
le **DOESKIN** soft leather
DOFFING divesting; putting off
bt **DOG-BANE** plant with a bitter root
DOG-BELT part of dog harness
DOG-BOLT arrow; dog-meal
DOG-CART two-wheeled vehicle
nt **DOG-DAYS** (occur in July and August)
DOGEATE office of Doge (Venice)
zo **DOG-FISH** tope; small shark
DOGGING following closely; tailing
DOGGISH rather posh; doglike
DOGHEAD gunlock hammer
nt **DOG-HOLE** **BOGHOLE**, ship's WC
DOGHOOD cf. manhood
DOGLIKE having canine attributes
DOG-NAIL large nail
bt **DOG-ROSE** wild rose
DOG'S-EAR a fold in a page in a book
DOGSHIP of dogs; dogginess
DOG-SICK sick as a dog
le **DOGSKIN** glove leather
bt **DOG'S-RUE** a plant; Scrophularia
as **DOG-STAR** Sirius
zo **DOG-TICK** a parasite
DOGTROT jog
nt **DOG-VANE** wind-vane
bt **DOGWOOD** flowering bush
DOLABRA Roman hatchet
DOLEFUL woe-begone; dismal; rueful

DOLLIED hammered; laundered
DOLLIER an ore-crusher
zo, nt **DOLPHIN** cetacean; (pilot); a spar buoy
DOLTISH stupid; stolid; witless
DOMABLE tamable; tractable
DOMICAL dome-shaped
DOMINIE schoolmaster (Sc.)
DOMINUS Master; Lord
DONATOR donor; presenter; giver
DONNING putting on; assuming
DONNISH like a don
DONNISM self-importance
DONSHIP estate of being a don
DOOMING condemning; judging
DOORING door-case
DOORMAT boot-scraping mat
DOORWAY portico
ps **DOPPLER** change of frequency (colour, sound) (distance)
ar, rl **DOPSKAL** font for baptism
zo **DORHAWK** nightjar
DORMANT quiescent; latent
zo **DORMICE** sleepy rodents
tx **DORNICK DORNOCK**, figured linen
rl **DORTOUR** dorter; dormitory
DOSSIER file of papers; a brief (Fr.)
DOTTARD decayed tree
DOTTIER barmier; more foolish
DOTTING spotting; stippling
zo **DOTTREL** plover
DOUBLED turned; ran; repeated
DOUBLER duplicator; increaser
DOUBLES two teams of two against each other (golf, tennis, sculls)
DOUBLET jerkin; one of a pair
DOUBTED distrusted; suspected
DOUBTER an unbelieving Thomas
DOUCELY sweetly
zo **DOUCETS DOWCETS**, stones of deer
DOUCEUR tip; vail; gratuity
DOUCHED sprayed
DOUCINE ornamental moulding
DOUGHTY valiant, intrepid; dauntless
zo **DOUPION** double cocoon
DOUREST grimmest; staunchest
vt **DOURINE** breeding-horse infection
DOUSING dipping; extinguishing;
DOWSING water-divining
DOUTING extinguishing; quenching
zo **DOVECOT** dove-cote
zo **DOVELET** young dove
DOVERED slumbered
DOWABLE endowable
DOWAGER widow with a jointure
DOWDILY untidily; slovenly
DOWERED gifted
DOWN-BED feather bed
mu **DOWN-BOW** playing motion (violin)
DOWNING felling; overcoming
DOWSING water-divining
DOYENNE senior lady
DOZENTH 12th
DRABBER more dingy
DRABBET smocking
DRABBLE befoul; draggle
nt **DRABLER** additional sail
nm **DRACHMA** Greek silver coin
bt **DRACINA** dragon's blood palm
bt **DRACINE** dracina; a dye
DRACONE nylon/rubber liquids container
DRACULA Transylvanian vampire
DRAFTED outlined; detached
zo **DRAFT-OX** draught-ox
DRAG-BAR draw-bar
DRAGGED tugged; hauled; lingered
DRAGGLE bemire; drabble
DRAG-MAN a fisherman
DRAG-NET his net
DRAGOON compel; coerce; cavalryman
DRAINED filtered; exhausted; emptied
DRAINER a colander
DRAPERY haberdashery
DRAPIER a Swift 'nom de plume'
DRAPING covering; dressing
DRASTIC severe; forcible; efficacious
DRATTED confounded
DRAUGHT dose; breeze; outline
rw, me **DRAWBAR** connecting rod; train couplings; tractive force
DRAWBOY a weaving assistant
DRAWING pulling; sketch; plan
DRAWLED dawdled; droned
DRAWLER monotonous speaker
DRAW-NET bird net
DRAWN-ON printing technique
DRAYAGE charge for a dray
DRAYMAN dray-driver; brewer's driver
DREADED apprehended; feared
DREADER an alarmist
DREAMED dreamt; imagined
DREAMER visionary; idealist
DREDGED sprinkled
nt **DREDGER** tea cup with strainer lid; salt pot; vessel for deepening waterways
DREEING enduring; bearing (Sc.)
DRESDEN Meissen porcelain
DRESSED cooked; decked; arrayed in
DRESSER kitchen sideboard; (window-); (attendant)
to **DRESSER** lead beater

DREULED slavered; dribbled
DRIBBED inveigled; filched
DRIBBLE (football); trickle; drip; ooze
DRIBLET driplet; a small quantity
DRIFTED floated
nt **DRIFTER** wanderer; fishing boat with drift net; amateur aimless wanderer; dilettante
DRILLED trained; perforated; pierced
DRINKER reveller; carouser; toper
DRIP-DRY non-iron fabric
DRIPPED dropped; oozed; trickled
bt **DRIP-TIP** a leaf-point
DRIVE-IN service for motorists
DRIVING dragooning; urging; forcing
mt **DRIZZLE DRIZZLY**, (fine rain)
DROILED toiled tediously
DROLLED jested; clowned
DROLLER farceur; funnier; odder
nt **DROMOND** fast sailing ship
DRONING prosing; humming
DRONISH lazy
DROOLED slavered; dribbled
DROOPED withered; declined
DROPLET a drip; bead of moisture
DROP-NET a fishing-net
cp **DROP-OUT** computer error; failure
ga **DROP-OUT** social non-participant; (dropkick) (Rugby football)
DROPPED dripped; let fall (clanger); quitted
DROPPER end fly of a cast (medicine)
bt **DROSERA** sun-dew
DROSHKY Russian vehicle
DROUGHT aridity; dryness
DROWNED submerged; blotted out; drenched
DROWSED dozed; napped; slept
DRUBBED DRUBBER, thrashed; mauled; beater
DRUDGED DRUDGER, toiled; labourer
md **DRUGGED** stupefied (medicated); lulled
nt **DRUGGER** drogher; small ship
DRUGGET floor covering (over carpet)
rl **DRUIDIC** of Druids (ancient bards)
DRUMBLE to drone
gl **DRUMLIN** long glacially-formed hill
DRUMMED expelled; tapped; played
DRUMMER salesman (USA); drum player
DRUNKEN inebriated; crapulous; tipsy
DRUSIAN Levantine sectarian (Moslem)
DRY-BEAT thrash without bleeding
mn **DRY-BONE** silicate of zinc
el **DRY-CELL** type of battery
nt **DRY-DOCK** (graving-) exposing whole ship
DRY-EYED tearless
DRYNESS aridity; drought; thirst
DRY-PILE voltaic battery
lw **DRY-RENT** (no distress)
DRY-SALT preserve; cure
DRYSHOD with shoes not wet
DUALISE DUARCHY, split in two; dual control
rl **DUALISM** doctrine; Manichaeism
DUALIST DUALITY, twofoldness in universe
DUBBING ennobling; sound translation (films)
DUBIATE DUBIETY, DUBIOUS, doubtful; uncertainty
DUCALLY like a duke in style
DUCHESS consort of a duke
zo **DUCK-ANT** Jamaican termite
DUCKING evading; thrusting under water
DUCTILE tractile; malleable
zo **DUCTULE** narrow-lumen duct
DUDDERY rags; old clo' shop
DUDGEON dagger; sullenness
DUE-BILL accepted debt
DUELIST DUELLED, antagonist; fought for; combated
DUELLER combatant in single fight
DUENESS fitness; propriety; seemliness
DUFFING sham; furbishing up
DUKEDOM duke's realm
DULCIFY sweeten
DULCINE DULCITE, DULCOSE, manna; saccharine
DULLARD stupid fellow; blockhead
DULLEST bluntest; most obtuse
DULLING allaying; benumbing
DULLISH rather dull; somewhat inert
DULNESS dullness; stupidity; apathy
zo **DULOSIS** ant slavery
DUMPING heaping (exporting)
DUMPISH in the dumps
zo **DUN-BIRD** pochard duck
DUNCERY dulness; stupidity
DUNCISH not clever
DUNEDIN Edinburgh (Celtic form); also N.Z.
ck **DUNFISH** cured cod-fish
DUNGEON dark prison; cell
DUNKERS Tunkers; triple baptists
DUNKING jumping to score (basketball)

DUNNAGE packing; baggage; timber
DUNNING debt collecting; fish curing
DUNNISH dirty brown
zo **DUNNOCK** hedge-sparrow
lw **DUODENA** ancient jury
DUOTONE two-colour half-tone printing
pr **DUO-TYPE** 2 like plates for different colours
DUPABLE credulous; gullible
DUPPING opening as a door
DURABLE DURABLY, long lasting; stable
bt **DURAMEN** heart-wood
lw **DURANCE DURANTE**, permanent restraint
ml **DURIRON** acid-resistant iron alloy
bt **DURMAST** an oak
lw **DURSLEY** bloodless blows; assault
DUSKIER more sable or swarthy
DUSKILY DUSKISH, dimly; darkly (twilight)
DUSTBIN garbage receptacle
DUSTIER unswept; flocculent state
DUSTING a beating
DUSTMAN garbage collector
DUSTPAN house-cleaning implement
DUTEOUS DUTIFUL, deferential; respectful
DUUMVIR Roman magistrates
DVORNIK Russian concierge
DWARFED stunted; eclipsed
DWELLED sojourned; abode; inhabited
DWELLER resident; inmate; indigene
DWINDLE diminish; decrease; shrink
DYARCHY duarchy; dual control
pr **DYELINE** document-copying process
bt **DYE-WOOD** (various woods)
DYE-WORK dyeing establishment
DYINGLY in the process of death
DYNAMIC forceful; energetic; mobile
cp **DYNAMIC** influx message handling
DYNASTY family; succession; house
DYSLOGY disapproval; disapprobation
DYSNOMY bad laws
md **DYSOPSY** poor sight
md **DYSURIA** impaired urination
zo **DYTICUS** water-beetles
lw **DYVOURY** bankruptcy

E

EAGERLY avidly; ardently; fervently
zo **EANLING** young lamb
md **EARACHE** a pain in the ear
EARDROP a pendant; earring
md **EAR-DRUM** tympanum
EAR-HOLE aural portal
EARLDOM the seignory of an earl
EARLESS reluctant to hear
EARLIER sooner
EARLOCK love-lock
EARMARK identity cut (sheep, reindeer)
EARNEST serious; steady; persevering
EARNING bread-winning; meriting
EAR-PICK tool for cleaning ears
EARRING pendant; eardrop
EARSHOT hearing distance
el **EARTHED** driven to den (hunting); circuit
EARTHEN (-ware); clay pottery
EARTHLY carnal; mundane; terrestrial
EASEFUL restful; tranquil; contented
EASIEST least difficult; simplest
EAST-END east part of city
EASTERN oriental; auroral
nt **EASTING** east of any meridian
EATABLE edible; succulent; esculent
nt **EBB-TIDE** recede from flood (sea movement)
EBONIST ebony-wood artisan
ch **EBONITE EBONIZE**, artificial ebony; vulcanite
EBRIETY intoxication; intemperance
EBRIOSE EBRIOUS, fond of drink; fuddled
ECBASIS ECBATIC, rhetorical treatment
md **ECCRINE** cell-excretory; glandular
md **ECDEMIC** foreign; not inbuilt
ECDYSIS moulting (feathers); sloughing
ECHAPPE (horse-breeding)
ECHELLE ECHELON, ladder formation; cycling to minimize crosswind
zo **ECHIDNA** ant-eater (Australia)
zo **ECHIMYD** S. American dormouse
ar, zo **ECHINUS** egg and dart moulding; sea urchin
ECHOING resounding; repeating
ECHOISM onomatopoeia
ECHOIST a yes-man
as **ECLIPSE** hide; blot out; surpass; obscuration of sun or moon
ECLOGUE pastoral poem
ec **ECOLOGY** wide environmental studies; (-ist)
ECONOMY thrift; (national) household keeping

bt, ec **ECOTONE** plant-community limit
bt, ec **ECOTYPE** habitat-adapted plants
ECOUTES listening posts (Fr.)
ECSTASY rapture; fervour; delight
ECTASIS mispronunciation
md **ECTHYMA** a rash
md **ECTOPIA ECTOPIC**, dislocation, displaced
zo **ECTOZOA** parasites
ECTYPAL actual copy
ck **ECUELLE** two handled dish with cover
EDACITY greed; voracity; rapacity
EDAPHIC pertaining to soil
EDAPHON soil community of living organisms
bt **EDDERED** a top-pruned hedge
EDDYING swirling; whirling; vortical
mn **EDELITE** a silicate
EDENTAL toothless
EDICTAL laid down; ordered
EDIFICE a stylish building
EDIFIED EDIFIER, spiritually benefited; uplifter
EDITING EDITION, preparing a publication
EDUCATE teach; tutor; school; train
EDUCING extracting; eliciting
EDUCTOR corkscrew
EELBUCK basket-net
zo **EEL-FARE** a young eel
zo **EEL-POUT** blenny
EFFABLE explicable; utterable
EFFACED erased; became inconspicuous
EFFECTS personal estate; theatrical illusions
EFFENDI master; sir; gentleman (Turk.)
EFFULGE gleam; glisten; coruscate
EFFUSED emanated; diffused
EGALITY parity; equality
zo **EGG-BIRD** tern
bl **EGG-CELL** within an ovum or zygote
EGG-COSY cap for a boiled egg
ck **EGG-FLIP** (-nog); thick alcoholic drink
EGGHEAD intellectual; highbrow
EGOTISM EGOTIST, of hyper self-importance
EGOTIZE (excess of 'I')
EGRETTE (egret); spray of gems; aigrette
pc **EIDETIC** having vivid mental pictures
EIDOLON apparition; phantom
EIRENIC irenic; peaceful
EJECTED threw out; dispossessed
ae **EJECTOR** chucker-out; pilot's safety seat
ch **ELAIDIC ELAIDIN**, of oil products
ELAPSED slid away; passed, of time
ELASTIC ELASTIN, resilient; stretchable; (rubber)
ELATERY elastic force; elasticity
bt **ELATINE** water-wort
ELATING stretching to joy; high spirits
ELATION gratification; exhilaration
hy **ELAULIC** with oil in pipes
mn **ELBAITE** tourmaline variety
ELBOWED thrust aside; nudged
ELDERLY getting on in years
ELEATIC philosophic
ELECTED chosen; picked; preferred
ELECTOR voter; German title
cf **ELECTRO-** (plate); (magnetic); electric
ELEGANT refined; graceful; tasteful
ELEGIAC a lament; dirge
ELEGIST plaintive writer
ELEGIZE lament in writing
zo **ELEIDIN** skin cells substance
ELEMENT part; component; ingredient
ELEVATE elate; raise; hoist; promote
ga **ELEVENS** teams (cricket, football etc.)
ELF-BOLT ELF-SHOT, small arrow; flint head
ELF-LAND fairy-land
ELF-LOCK tangled hair
bt **ELF-WORT** elecampane
ELIDING ELLIPSIS, shortening words
ELIMATE to file; to polish
ELISION suppression of metre (poetry)
bt **ELK-WOOD** umbrella-tree
bt **ELLAGIC** of gall-nuts
ma, as **ELLIPSE** oval; orbit of a comet
me **ELL-WAND** (a yard and a quarter)
ELOGIST ELOGIUM, funeral orator; panegyric speech
rl **ELOHIST** Pentateuch author (O.T.)
ELOINED removed; separated; banished
ELOPING sloping; bolting; decamping
ELUDING dodging; evading; baffling
ELUSION evasion; avoidance
ELUSIVE illusory; deceptive; fugitive
ELUSORY hard to solve; intangible
ELUVIUM detritus from rock weathering
ELYSIAN ELYSIUM, heavenly paradise (Gr.)

zo **ELYTRAL** shield-like
zo **ELYTRON ELYTRUM**, (wing sheath beetles)
EMANANT EMANATE, proceeding from origin
EMARCID wilted
EMBALED packed; bundled
EMBARGO a prohibition; veto
EMBASSY ambassadorial residence
EMBATHE to soak (industrial process)
hd **EMBLAZE** embellish
EMBLEMA inlaid ornament
bt **EMBLICA** Indian tree
md **EMBOLUS** wedge; a clot
EMBOSOM caress
EMBOWED arched
EMBOWER give shelter
EMBRACE hug; welcome; include
EMBROIL involve in dispute, confusion
hd **EMBRUED** ensanguined heraldically
pl, zo **EMBRYON** of an embryo, zygote
EMENDED text corrected
EMERALD smaragdus; brilliant green
EMERGED resulted; appeared from; arose
EMERITI honourably retired
EMINENT exalted; prominent
EMIRATE the domain of emir
EMITRON early UK TV tube
EMITTED circulated; exhaled; gushed
cp **EMITTER** electrode; punched card signal
md **EMMENIA** menstrual flow
pc **EMOTION** moody excitement; strong feelings
pc **EMOTIVE** arousal of reactions
EMPANEL coopt; enrol to a committee
EMPATHY sympathetic reaction of agreement
EMPERIL endanger
EMPEROR head of an empire
EMPIRIC based on practical experience
lw **EMPLEAD** prosecute
EMPLUME to put on feather, apparel, dress
EMPOWER authorize; warrant; allow
EMPRESS female ruler of empire
EMPTIED drained; discharged
EMPTIER remover; less complete
EMULATE to vie; compete; rival
EMULOUS striving to equal
md **EMULSIC** emulsive
ch **EMULSIN** almond ferment
zo **EMU-WREN** an Australian bird
ENABLED authorized; allowed
ENACTED decreed; ordained
lw **ENACTOR** law-maker
ENAMOUR charm; fascinate; enslave
ENCAGED cooped up; in captivity
ENCASED stored in; stowed in
ENCAVED trapped in cave
ENCHANT enamour; bewitch; captivate
ENCHASE set with jewels; engrave
md **ENCHYMA** injection; infusion
ENCLASP embrace; hug; enfold
rl **ENCLAVE** secret meeting (election, Vatican)
ENCLAVE separated zone (land)
lw **ENCLOSE** fence in, claim land
ENCLOSE cover; pack in box (letter)
mt **ENCLOUD** mystify; make obscure
cp, tc **ENCODER** data; official converter (into code)
ENCORED repeated after applause
ENCRUST achieve overlay of sediment; (jewels)
bt **ENDARCH** xylem strand characteristic
ENDEMIC local; indigenous
md **ENDERON** true skin
END-GAME chess; final stage
ENDIRON andiron; firedog
ENDLESS eternal; interminable
ENDLONG not sideways
cp **END-MARK** code conclusion signal
ENDMOST furthest in
END-NOTE footnote; (postscript)
bt **ENDOGEN** botanical growth
ENDORSE assign; ratify
ENDOWED supplied; bequeathed
ENDOWER benefactor; donor
ENDUING imbuing; endowing; providing (finances)
ENDURED ENDURER, stayer; bore suffering
cp **ENDWAYS ENDWISE**, upright; card feed in
ENDYSIS development of new hair/skin
pr **ENFACED** paper headings
lw **ENFEOFF** assignment
hd **ENFILED** heraldic sword thrust
ENFLESH turn into flesh
ENFORCE compel; oblige; coerce
ENGAGED fiancé; occupied; betrothed; committed
ENGAGER employment agent; fixer
ENGINED powered
ENGLISH of England; language
ENGORGE stuff with food; engulf
ENGRACE bring into favour

ENGRAFT insert; graft
hd **ENGRAIL** spot with dots
ENGRAIN dye; permeate
ENGRASP clutch; seize
ENGRAVE cut; chisel; carve
ENGROSS monopolize; absorb; copy
ENHANCE to intensify; heighten
ENJOYED ENJOYER, liked; appreciator; (gourmet)
ENLACED entwined; spliced
ENLARGE amplify; extend; expand
ENLIVEN wake; arouse; quicken
ENMEWED cooped up in a mews; encaged
ENNICHE to enshrine
ENNOBLE exalt; raise; aggrandize
ENNUIED bored stiff
ENODING unknotting
ENOMOTY Spartan band
ENOUNCE to pronounce words clearly
ENQUIRE ENQUIRY, ask searching questions
cp, tc **ENQUIRY** search address control for terminal
ENRAGED exasperated; incensed
ENRIPEN to mellow; mature
ENROBED attired; invested
ENROUGH to roughen
ag **ENSILED** stored in a pit; silage
ENSLAVE enthral; captivate; subjugate
ENSNARE entrap; allure; inveigle
ENSUING resulting; issuing; accruing
ENSURED made certain; guaranteed
md **ENTASIA** spasm
ENTASIS architectural swell
ENTENTE understanding; alliance
ENTERED joined; penetrated; registered
md **ENTERIC** typhoid fever
zo **ENTERON** collenterata body cavity
ENTHEAL divinely inspired
ENTHUSE to spread enthusiasm
ENTICED ENTICER, cajoled, drawn into; seducer
ENTITLE permit; qualify; grant
zo **ENTOMIC** of insects
ENTONIC of high tension
md **ENTOTIC** (interior of ear)
zo **ENTOZOA** internal parasites
ENTRAIL interweave; plait
ENTRAIN to board a train
ga **ENTRANT** who enters profession; competitor
ENTREAT beg; implore; importune
pl **ENTROPY** lost energy and body functions
ENTRUST confide; commit to others
ENTWINE weave; interlace; twist; (rope)
ENVELOP enwrap; enfold; encase
ENVENOM to poison
ENVIOUS jealous; invidious; grudging
ENVYING grudging; coveting
ag, gl **EOAPHIC** soil-related
EOBIONT stage in creation (nature)
bt **EPACRID** of heathlike shrubs
EPAGOGE figure of speech
EPARCHY prefecture
EPAULET shoulder-piece
EPAXIAL above the axis
EPEEIST duelling by sword (fencing)
EPERGNE ornamental stand
zo **EPHEBIC** adult; of optimum period
EPHEBUS young Greek citizen
md **EPHELIS** freckle
zo **EPIBOLY** overgrowth
bt, ag **EPICARP** of the rind, skin of fruit
EPICEDE funeral ode
EPICENE common to both sexes
bt **EPICHIL** orchid labellum end
EPICISM sagas; heroic poems; etc.
EPICIST epic writer
ec **EPICOLE** harmless parasite animal
EPICURE gourmet; voluptuary
zo **EPICYTE** ectoplasm cuticular layer
zo **EPIDEME** wing articulation sclerite
mn **EPIDOTE** a silicate
EPIGEAL low growing
bt **EPIGEAN** found on ground
bt **EPIGEIC** with stolons on soil surface
EPIGENE mineral change
bt **EPIGONE** a descendant; seed container
zo **EPIGONE** spore-bag
EPIGRAM barbed wisdom
zo **EPIHYAL** hyoid arch element
EPILATE remove (hair)
md **EPILOIA** development defect affliction
EPIMERE mesothelial-wall zone in vertebrates
EPIMYTH moral of story
zo **EPIOTIC** a bone in vertebrate skull
EPISODE separate event within a narrative
ba **EPISOME** of genetically active bacteria
rl **EPISTLE** lengthy letter (N.T.)
EPITAPH monumental inscription
EPITAXY crystal growth or deposition
EPITHEM lotion; poultice

EPITHET a disparaging, abusive description
EPITOME brief summary; abstract
zo **EPIZOAN EPIZOIC, EPIZOON**, parasitic
EPOCHAL of outstanding memorable period
EPOXIDE plastic resin
EPULARY festive
EQUABLE fair; severe; uniform; calm
EQUABLY uniformly; justly
EQUALLY evenly
EQUATED made equal; balanced
go **EQUATOR** Great Circle; tropical centre
EQUERRY court gentleman; adjutant
EQUINAL pertaining to horses
vt **EQUINIA** glanders disease
as **EQUINOX** equality of day and night
md **EQUINUS** hoof-like; foot deformity
EQUITES Roman cavalry, knights (Lat.)
pr **ERASING ERASURE**, obliterating; cancellation
ar, bd **ERECTED ERECTER**, raised; constructed; builder
ERECTOR penis; enlarger
ERELONG before long; later on
ERGODIC probability theory
bt **ERGOTED** afflicted with fungus
ERGUSIA vitamin A
bt **ERICOID** with heather-like leaves
bt **ERINEUM** leafy excrescence
mn **ERINITE** arseniate of copper
ERINOID a plastic material (milk)
ERINYES the Furies
ERISTIC controversial
cf **ERITHRO-** of redness
zo **ERMELIN ERMINED**, fur garment; stoat
hd **ERMINES** white marked spots
ERODENT EROSIVE, gnawing; acid
gl **ERODING EROSION**, denudation; weathering
EROTEME interrogation mark
EROTICA of sex (pornographic)
ERRATIC of no fixed course; inconsistencies
pr **ERRATUM** misprint; mistake; text error
ERUDITE scholarly; learned
ERUGATE smoothed
ERUPTED exploded; ejected
ESCAPED eluded; avoided; leaked
ESCAPER danger dodger
zo **ESCHARA** net-like coral
lw **ESCHEAT** forfeiture; confiscate
ESCRIME fencing; swordsmanship (Fr.)
hd **ESCROLL** heraldic scroll
ESCUAGE feudal tenure
ch **ESCULIN** alkaloid (horse chestnut)
ch **ESERINE** alkaloid (Calabar bean)
ESKIMOS inhabitants of Arctic America
ESOTERY mysticism; necromancy
ESPADON Spanish sword
bt **ESPARTO** exportable grass
mn **ESPINEL** kind of ruby
ESPOUSE to marry; support a cause
ESQUIRE gentleman (bodyguard); shield bearer
ESSAYED wrote serious article
ESSENCE extract; kernel of matter
rl **ESSENES** Jewish sect, fraternity
ESTIVAL of summer
hd **ESTOILE** heraldic star
ESTRADE a dais (Fr.)
lw **ESTREAT** true extract
md **ESTRIOL ESTRONE**, female hormone
ESTUARY river mouth; firth; frith
ETATISM central control (government)
ch **ETCHANT** copper-removing chemical
ETCHING engraving; an impression
ETERNAL endless; perennial; immortal
ETESIAN Levant wind
zo **ETHERIA** river-oyster
ETHICAL conduct conforming to morality
ETONIAN of Eton (College)
mn **EUCLASE** beryl
gl **EUCRITE** coarse-grained igneous rock
EUDOXID monogastric stage in siphonofora
zo **EUGAMIC** of maturity-period
bt **EUGENIA** a large genus of spices
md **EUGENIC** (-s), control of hereditary genes
EUGENIN clove camphor
ck **EUGENOL** item of clove/cinnamon oil
bt **EULALIA** ornamental grass
EULOGIA EULOGIC, praises; laudatory
EUPATHY contentment with moderation
md **EUPEPSY** hearty digestion
EUPHONY melodious sound
EUPHROE ridge-pole
bl **EUPLOID** cell chromosome valve
md **EUPNOEA** free respiration
EURIPUS strait having violent tides
mn **EURITIC** like granite
bt **EURYALE** water-lilies
EUSTYLE columnar building style

EUTERPE muse of music
md **EUTONIA** firmness of tone
EUTROPY variation in chemical compounds
EVACUEE a displaced (rescued) person
EVADING EVASION, EVASIVE, avoiding; dodging
EVENING eventide; night-fall; twilight
lw **EVICTED** dispossessed of house (property)
EVICTOR tenant remover; chucker-out
EVIDENT obvious; patent; manifest
EVIL-EYE a bewitching look
EVINCED manifested; proved
EVIRATE castrate; geld
EVOCATE EVOCATION, to summon spirits
EVOKING rousing; exciting (of memory)
EVOLUTE geometric curve
EVOLVED unfolded; emitted; educed
EWE-LAMB poor man's only possession
EXACTED demanded; levied
EXACTER extortioner
EXACTLY just so; precisely; literally
EXACTOR a tax collector
EXALTED lofty; ennobled; elevated
EXALTER magnifier; extoller
EXAMINE inquire; scrutinize
EXAMPLE model; pattern; sample
md **EXANGIA** blood-vessel
zo **EXARATE** of pupae with free members
EXARCHY a vice-royalty
EXCERPT an extract; cutting; citation
lw **EXCHEAT** escheat; confiscate
EXCISED cut out; removed
EXCITED EXCITER, provoked; stimulant; agitator
el **EXCITON** electron pair in semiconductor
zo **EXCITOR** stimulating to activity
EXCLAIM cry out; utter sharply; vociferate
lw **EXCLUDE** to shut out; bar from; omit
md **EXCRETA** human or animal waste
EXCUSED released; pardoned; condoned
lw **EXECUTE** accomplish; put to death
EXEDRAE halls; recesses
EXEGETE theological exponent
EXERGUE date space on coin
EXERTED strove; applied; used
EXHALED emitted; evaporated; breathed
EXHAUST drain; empty; expend; tire
EXHIBIT display; manifest; evince
EXHUMED disinterred; unearthed
EXIGENT urgent; critical; importunate
EXILIAN exiled Jew
EXILING banishing; proscribing
EXILITY EXILE, period of enforced absence
EXISTED was; lasted; endured; subsisted
EXITIAL destructive to life
zo **EXOCONE** of insect compound eyes
zo **EXODERM** outer cell layer in porifera
EXODIST an emigrant
EXOGAMY outbreeding; beyond tribal group
EXOMION Greek sleeveless vest
EXOTISM EXOTIC, not native; strikingly different
zo **EXOTYPE** a non-heritable creature
EXPANSE wide area (to spread out)
lw **EX-PARTE** prejudiced; biased
EXPENSE cost; outlay; charge; price
EXPIATE atone; sin no more
EXPIRED exhaled; ended; dead
EXPLAIN elucidate; interpret; expound
EXPLODE burst; detonate; discharge
EXPLOIT feat; deed; achievement
EXPLORE search; prospect; examine
EXPORTS outward trade goods (foreign)
EXPOSED EXPOSER, unmasked; open; revealer (nark)
EXPOUND explain; unfold; interpret
EXPRESS explicit; exude; speedy
EXPUNGE erase; abrogate; cancel
EXSCIND cut out; exsect
EXTINCT defunct; obsolete; quenched
EXTRACT decoction; essences; juice
lw **EXTRACT** extort; derive; select; (copy) (spy)
EXTREME utmost; ultimate; excessive
EXTRUDE swelling; push out (unsightly)
EXUDING sweating; oozing; dripping
EXULTED crowed; triumphed; boasted
zo **EXUVIAE EXUVIAL,** of cast-off animal skins
pl **EYE-BALL** the eye itself (orb)
EYE-BATH basin for lotions
EYE-BEAM EYELIAD, a strong glance

nt **EYE-BOLT** (for hooks)
ar **EYE-BROW** a hairy arch; dormer window
EYE-DROP a falling tear; ciliary
EYE-FLAP blinker (horses)
ar **EYE-HOLE** (peep-hole)
EYELASH cilary hair
EYELESS blind; unobservant
EYESHOT range of vision observed
EYESORE a hideosity
bl **EYESPOT** (peacock's feather); 'stigma' in algae
EYEWASH spoken rubbish; humbug
lw **EZEMENT** **EAZEMENT**, gymnastics; legal benefit

F

pg **F NUMBER** relative aperture, stop
zo **FABELLA** sesamoid bone (in mammals)
FABLING **FABULAR**, inventing stories
FABRILE (handicraft)
FACE-OFF ball into play (ice hockey etc.)
mn, pc **FACETED** having differing faces (gems)
FACETIA facetiousness; witty jokes
wv **FACONNE** woven figurative design
FACTION dissenting clique within an association
FACTORY works; mill; workshop
FACTUAL real; actual; authentic
FACTURE manufacture; workmanship
FACULAE large bright areas of sun photosphere
FACULTY skill; ability; section of university
FADAISE trivial remark (Fr.)
FADDING shellac lacquering
FADDISH **FADDIST**, idiosyncratic craze; follower (diet)
FADDLED trifled (of dilettantes)
cn **FADE-OUT** end of film sequence; disappear
FADGING suiting; prospering
FAGGERY drudgery
FAGGING domestic slavery in schools
mu **FAGOTTO** musical bundle of wind; bassoon (It.)
FAIENCE **FAYENCE**, glazed pottery, ceramics
FAILING a foible; defect; no pass (exams)
FAILURE fiasco; non-success; ruin
cp **FAILURE** disruption by defect
FAINING willingly; desiring; wishing
md **FAINTED** swooned; lost consciousness
FAINTER **FAINTLY**, weaker; paler; dimmer
FAIREST most beautiful, attractive
FAIRIES benevolent enchantresses; pixies; gays
FAIRILY of elf-like, ethereal qualities
FAIRING a present; streamlining
pl **FAIRISH** moderately fair; blondish (hair)
ga, nt **FAIRWAY** (golf); navigable channel
FALANGE Spanish fascist party
tx **FALBALA** furbelow; pleated lining; seam
FALCADE (equitation); curvetting
zo **FALCATE** **FALCULA**, beaked; hooked; claw
lw **FALDAGE** privilege; right of farming
FALLACY a sophism; mistaken idea; not so
FALLALS showy trifles (ornament)
FALLING dropping; tumbling; (error) (loss)
FALLOUT spread of nuclear radioactivity
FALLOUT secondary result; pollution
nt **FALLUCA** Nile dhow
FALSELY wrongly; untruthfully
FALSEST most disloyal
FALSIES artificial bust; dentures
FALSIFY counterfeit; belie; fake
FALSISH somewhat erroneous
FALSISM obvious falsity
FALSITY fallacy; fabrication
FANATIC bigot; zealot; visionary
FANCIED favoured; imagined; thought
FANCIER expert; breeder
FANFARE flourish of trumpets
FANGLED newly contrived
FAN-MAIL letters of adulation
FANNING extending; winnowing; (flames); cowboy's balance tactics
bt **FAN-PALM** the talipot palm
zo **FANTAIL** pigeon; a gas burner
FANTASM spook; phantasm
FANTAST visionary; enthusiast
mu **FANTASY** imaginative idea (arts)
el, me, ps **FARADAY** **FARADIC**, inductive electrolysis unit
FARAWAY distant; remote
FARCEUR satirical jester
FARCIFY to burlesque
ck **FARCING** edible stuffing; force-meat
nt **FARDAGE** dunnage; packing (Fr.)
ag **FARMERY** rural homestead

FARMING agriculture; leasing out
FARMOST uttermost; furthest
FARNESS remoteness
FARRAGO a medley; hodge-podge
FARRIER shoeing-smith; a vet
mu **FARRUCA** Andalusian dance
FARTHEL farl; oatcake
FARTHER besides; further; beyond
to **FASCETS** glass-making tools
FASCIAE fillets; name boards
FASCIAL of fasces (Roman emblems)
FASCINE bound brushwood
FASCISM FASCIST, party, dictatorship (It.)
FASHERY FASHING, annoyance; bothering
FASHION mode; vogue; style; mould
rl **FAST-DAY** non-eating day
FASTEST swiftest; fleetest; closest
FASTING abstaining from food
FASTISH rather quickly; reckless
FATALLY mortally; calamitously
zo **FAT-BODY** fatty tissue in amphibians
FATEFUL ominous; portentous
FAT-HEAD blockhead; moron; dunce
FATIDIC prophetic; oracular
FATIGUE tire; jade; lassitude
zo **FATLING** young fatted animal
mu **FATLUTE** a broad guitar
pl **FATNESS FATTEST**, of corpulence; obesity
ck **FAT-RICH** greasy; high calorie (food)
FATTISH rather plump; adipose
FATUITY self-complacency; folly
FATUOUS illusory; imbecile; witless
FAUCIAL pertaining to fauces
ga **FAULTED FAULTY**, mistaken; displaced
FAVOURS free services; party badges
FAWNING sycophantic; cringing
FAYENCE faience; pottery
FEARFUL dismayed; dire
FEARING dreading; revering; timid
FEASTED caroused; gratified
FEASTER a Lucullus
zo **FEATHER** adorn; quill; (oar)
FEATURE aspect; trait; (film) (press)
FEAZING unravelling
FEBRILE feverish
FECULUM starchy extract
FEDERAL confederated; (state)
FEEDING eating; grazing; providing food (machine)
lw **FEE-FARM** tenure without fealty
FEELING touching; sensibility; perception
lw **FEE-TAIL** entailed estate
FEEZING twisting; unscrewing
FEIGNED FEINTED, simulated; shammed
zo **FELIDAE FELINAE**, the cat genus
FELLING hewing; cutting down
mn **FELSITE** igneous rock
mn **FELSPAR** metamorphic rock
FELTING felt cloth
nt **FELUCCA** Nile, Red Sea lateen sailboat
bt **FELWORT** mullein
FEMINAL womanly
md **FEMORAL** (thigh)
ga **FENCING** enclosing; evading; sword duelling
FENDING warding off; averting
zo **FEN-DUCK** shoveller-duck
FEN-FIRE will o' the wisp
mn **FENGITE** alabaster
FENNISH marshy; boggy; swampy
lw **FEODARY** feudal tenure
lw **FEOFFEE FEOFFOR**, receiver; granter of a fief
FERDWIT a quittance; penalty
FERINGI foreigner (European team) in India
mu **FERMATA** a pause
ck **FERMENT** inflame; commotion; yeast
ps **FERMION** particle (statistical theory)
ch **FERMIUM** man-made element
bt **FERNERY** fern garden
zo **FERN-OWL** night-jar
FERRARA a sword-blade (It.)
ch **FERRATE** an iron salt
FERRIED transported
FERRIES ferry-boats; air-lift transport
ch, cp **FERRITE** ferro-magnetic (ceramics)
ch **FERROUS** (iron)
bt **FERRUGO** plant-rust; fungus
mu **FERRULE** protecting cap; shaft of hunting horn
FERTILE inventive; prolific; fruitful
FERULED caned; punished
FERVENT zealous; ardent; glowing
FERVOUR eagerness; intensity; ardour
FESTIVE joyous; convivial; gay
FESTOON wreath; garland
bt **FESTUCA** grass genus
FETCHED brought; conveyed; reached
FETCHER collector; heaver
zo **FETLOCK** a tuft of hair
lw **FEUDARY FEODARY**, rights; medieval fee
FEUDING quarrelling (ice hockey)
lw **FEUDIST** writer on feudal law
lw **FEU-DUTY** annual payment, fee (Sc.)

FEVERED agitated; febrile
FEWMAND fouling (on a carpet)
FEWNESS paucity; scarcity; sparsity
FEYNESS otherworldliness
FIANCEE betrothed woman
FIBBERY FIBBING, telling lies; prevaricating
bc **FIBROID FIBROIN**, of fibre; cobweb; elastic protein
md **FIBROMA** fibrous tumour
FIBROSE FIBROUS, filamental; stringy
FIBSTER petty liar
md **FIBULAR** (leg bone)
bt **FICARIA** celandine
FICTILE plastic; mouldable
FICTION romance; fantasy; invention
FICTIVE imaginative; feigned
FIDALGO Portuguese hidalgo
FIDDLED trifled; meddled
zo **FIDDLER** a crab; violinist
nt **FIDDLEY** small finger's work; hatchway railing
FIDGETY restless; uneasy; impatient
FIDIBUS taper to light a pipe
FIELDED (cricket); (baseball)
ga **FIELDER** defender; not batting side
FIERCER more violent
FIERILY vehemently; ardently
ga **FIFTEEN** a Rugby team
ck **FIG-CAKE** a sweetmeat
FIGGING dressing up
FIGHTER combatant; warrior
bt **FIG-LEAF** early dress material
FIGMENT a fabrication
bt **FIG-TREE** Mediterranean plant
FIGURAL pictorial; figurate
FIGURED computed; depicted
bt **FIGWORT** a plant
lw **FILACER FILAZER**, writs and pleas officer
zo **FILARIA** parasitic worms
bt **FILBERT** hazel-nut
FILCHED FILCHER, stole; pickpocket; pilferer
FILEMOT dead-leaf colour
cp **FILESET** magnetic data; (manicure)
FILIBEG the kilt (Scots' national dress)
FILICAL FILICES, the ferns
FILINGS fragments (sawdust, metal)
ck **FILLING** replenishing; stuffing; ballast; putting in
mt **FILLING** atmospheric pressure in depression
FILM-FAN a devotee; star-worshipper
FILMING recording in celluloid
pl **FIMBRIA** brain neural fibre; bundle
FIMETIC foul in thought
FINABLE liable to a fine; amerceable
FINALLY ultimately; lastly; eventually
FINANCE money affairs; revenue
zo **FINBACK** rorqual whale
FINCHED striped; spotted
FINDING verdict; discovering
FINECUT chopped into small pieces
FINESSE subtletly; craft; artifice
zo **FIN-FISH** finback whale
zo **FIN-FOOT** tropical bird
FINGENT moulding
FINICAL fastidious; dainty; faddy
FINICKY niggling; meticulous
zo **FINLESS** without steering propulsion
FINNACK FINNOCK, white sea trout
FINNISH language; of the Finns
zo **FIN-RAYS** bony fin supports (fish)
FIN-TOED web-footed
mn **FIORITE** volcanic residue
FIRE-ARM weapon
FIRE-BAR furnace bar
FIRE-BOX boiler fuel chamber
FIRE-BUG an incendiary
FIREDOG an andiron
zo **FIREFLY** a luminous beetle
ga **FIREMAN** fire fighter; pitcher (baseball)
FIRE-NEW brand-new (ceramic)
FIRE-PAN brazier; priming pan
FIRE-POT incendiary device
lw **FIRMARY** tenant's rights
FIRMING confirming; establishing
bd **FIRRING** wood strips for roof boarding
pb **FIRRING FURRING** encrusting; lathing
rl **FISH-DAY** Friday
FISHERY fish-breeding station
FISH-FAG wife of gay male
zo **FISH-FLY** a bait
FISH-GIG fishing appliance
FISH-GOD Dagon (coastal Palestine)
FISHIFY become a fish
FISHILY in a fishy manner
FISHING angling; piscatorial pursuit
FISH-MAW swimming bladder
FISH-OIL nutrient-rich oil
FISHWAY fish-ladder
FISKERY friskiness
ps **FISSILE FISSIVE**, of spontaneous cleavage (nuclear)
gl,ps **FISSION FISSURE**, rift; fracture; cleft; crevice
FISTING pommelling; boxing; fisticuffs
FIST-LAW might is right
bd **FISTUCA** pile-driving machine

bt, md **FISTULA** reed; ulcer
hd **FITCHED FITCHEE**, pointed
zo **FITCHET FITCHEW**, polecat; foumart
FITMENT a fitting (small part of whole)
FITNESS aptness; decency; seemliness
lw **FITTAGE** brokerage
FITTING try on (clothes); appropriate
bt **FITWEED** anti-hysteric plant
FIXABLE securable
FIXEDLY firmly; steadfastly
jn **FIXINGS** fasteners holding joinery
FIXTURE appointment; engagement; (match); building; fitment
FIZZING spluttering; hissing
FIZZLED failed; flopped
FLACCID flabby; loose; limp
FLACKER flutter like a bird
FLAG-DAY charity or national funds day
FLAGGED FLAG-MAN, signalled by flag (motor circuits)
bd **FLAKING** crumbling; peeling
FLAMING blazing fire; glowing
FLAMMED shammed; hoaxed
to **FLAMMER** splitting knife
FLANEUR an idling gossip
rw **FLANGED** having a raised edge; wheel
ga **FLANKED FLANKER**, side by side (wingers)
tx **FLANNEL** woollen garment; persuasion
ae **FLAPPER** emancipated girl; wing adjunct
FLARING funnel-shaped; trousers
FLASHED glistened; sparkled; gleamed
FLASHER would-be wit; male exposed
bd **FLATLET** small flat; dwelling
bd **FLATTED FLATTEN**, of levelling; laid low
FLATTER compliment falsely; cajole
FLAUNTY showy; gaudy
bt **FLAVEDO** yellowness
FLAVIAN (T. Flavius Vespasianus)
bt **FLAVINE** a yellow dye
ch **FLAVONE** yellow plant pigment
FLAVOUR zest; savour; taste; relish; quality
FLAWING cracking; marring
FLAYING skinning; excoriating
FLEABAG sleeping bag
bd **FLEAPIT** dosshouse; shabby theatre
FLECKED FLECKER, dappled; to add spots
FLEDGED chicks ready for flight (birds)
FLEECED FLEECER, sheepshearer; overcharged
FLEEING absconding; retreating
FLEERED mocked; scoffed
FLEERER a derider; flouter
FLEETED flitted; flew; sped
FLEETLY swiftly; nimbly; rapidly
FLEMING native of Flanders (Belgium)
FLEMISH variant of Dutch language
FLENSED skinned (of whale blubber)
FLESHED well-fed; satiated (carnally)
zo **FLESHER** butcher; red-backed shrike
FLESHLY carnal; sensual; fat; obese
bd **FLETTON** pink/yellow indented brick
FLEURET floral decoration; fencing-foil
FLEURON type flower in printing
FLEXILE pliable; pliant; supple
ga **FLEXING FLEXION**, bending (muscles); (archery)
FLEXURE curvature
FLICKED flipped
FLICKER FLICKS, failing light; (movies)
FLIFFIS double somersault; trampoline
FLIGHTY volatile; mercurial; fickle
FLINDER splinter; fragment
ga **FLINGER** hurler; thrower; caster
FLIP-DOG 'feet' of marine divers
FLIPPED boosted; flicked (pages); be enthused
zo **FLIPPER** feet of marine denizen, diver
FLIRTED showed amorous interest
FLITTER change frequently (jobs etc.)
FLOATED drifted (aimlessly); launched; (loan)
pb **FLOATER** indifferent voter; ballcock
FLOCCUS tuft of hair; down
FLOCKED crowded; swarmed; thronged
FLOGGED scourged; lashed; sold (illegally)
pt **FLOGGER** graining brush; whipper; overdoer
FLOODED inundated; swamped (market)
FLOOKAN slimy clay
bd **FLOORED** overthrown; baffled; storeyed
ga **FLOORER** knockdown blow (boxing)

FLOPPED fell; failed (business) (show)
FLOPPER faller; failure; splasher
FLOREAL 8th month (Fr. Revolution)
FLORIST a nurseryman
FLOROON flower border
FLORUIT a life-time
FLOTAGE buoyancy
FLOTSAM recovered wreckage
FLOUNCE a jerky movement
FLOURED powdered
FLOUTED jeered; insulted
FLOUTER mocker; derider
FLOWAGE flow; current; discharge
FLOWERY florid; ornate; figurative
FLOWING of river; fluent; smooth
ps **FLUENCE** energy (f); particle (f-)
FLUENCY lingual mastery; exuberance
FLUEWAY smoke and gas duct
FLUFFED bungled; foozled
FLUIDAL flowing; liquid
FLUIDIC FLUIDLY, of liquids
FLUKILY by a fluke
FLUKING scoring by chance
FLUMMOX perplex; defeat
FLUMPED slumped
FLUNKEY footman; snob; toady
ch **FLUORIC** (fluorine)
FLUSHED blushed; roused; disturbed
zo **FLUSHER** toilet device; emptier; butcher bird
FLUSTER agitation; disconcert; bustle
zo **FLUSTRA** sea-mat; polyzoa
mu **FLUTINA** accordion
ar **FLUTING** decorative grooving
mu **FLUTIST FLAUTIST**, flute-player
md **FLUTTER** speculation; palpitation (heart); wave
el, ps **FLUTTER** undue modulation; scare; excitement
go **FLUVIAL FLUVIATILE**, of rivers; soil deposits
fd **FLUXIDE FLUXING, FLUXION**, melting; welding; fusion
FLYAWAY flighty; impracticability; gymnastic move
el, tc **FLYBACK** restart of scanner beam cycle
FLY-BILL handbill; poster (advert)
FLY-BOAT canal boat
FLY-BOMB pilotless aerial torpedo
FLY-BOOK (fishing)
FLY-FLAP fly-whisk
FLY-HALF (football)
FLY-LEAF blank page
FLY-LINE fishing line
FLY-OVER road or rail crossing
FLY-PAST flight by aircraft
FLY-RAIL table leaf support
bt **FLY-TRAP** an insectivorous plant
FOALING colt-birth
FOAMING raging; bubbling; creaming
FOBBING cheating; tricking
FOCUSED clarity of aim (optics, lens)
FODIENT pertaining to digging
FOE-LIKE hostile; inimical; adverse
FOG-BANK accumulation of fog
FOG-BELL sea warning device
FOG-DUST cloud of groundbait (angling)
bt **FOGGAGE** coarse grass
go **FOGGARA** underground water channel (Arab.)
FOGGIER FOGGILY, FOGGING, murkier; obscurance
nt **FOGHORN** sea warning device
FOGLAMP penetrating headlight
FOGLESS clear
FOG-RING bank of fog
FOGYISH FOGYISM, senile; dull notions
FOILING tracery; deer track
ga **FOILIST** fencer
FOINING thrusting; tilting
FOISTED FOISTER, thrust on one; imposer; cheat
lw **FOLDAGE** sheep folding rights
FOLDING sheep penning; (clothes); bankruptcy
FOLIAGE leafage; boscage
FOLIATE a curve; laminate
FOLINIC acid constituent of folic acid
pr **FOLIOED FOLIOLE**, in pages; leaflet
FOLIOSE FOLIOUS, leafy; thin; insubstantial
FOLLIES imbecilities; revue show
ch **FOMITES** porous substances
ck **FONDANT** sugar icing (cakes) (sweets)
FONDEST dearest; most affectionate
FONDING doting
FONDLED caressed; dandled
FONDLER sugar daddy
FONTEIN spring (Afrikaans)
rl **FONTLET** small font
FOOLERY FOOLING, clowning; playing
FOOLISH doltish; stupid; irrational
ae **FOOT-BAR** aeroplane rudder control
FOOTBOY page; bell-hop
ar **FOOTING** walking; basis; foundation

FOOTLED bungled; wasted time ineptly
FOOTMAN servant; lackey; flunkey; (coach)
FOOTPAD highwayman; pickpocket; robber
vt **FOOT-ROT** disease of sheep
FOOTSIE linked feet; (flirting)
me **FOOT-TON** a measure of work
FOOTWAY footpath
FOOZLED footled; mishit
FOOZLED deceived; bungled
FOPPERY FOPPISH, affectation; dressy
FORAGED FORAGER, pillaged; plunderer
md **FORAMEN** a pore
FORAYED raided
FORBADE FORBIDDEN, permission refused
FORBEAR ancestor; refrain; abstain
FORBORE desisted; withheld; shunned
to, md **FORCEPS** pliers; graspers (surgery)
FORCING plant culture; coercing
FORDING riding, wading across a stream
FORDONE tired out; exhausted
pl **FOREARM** lower part of arm
hy **FOREBAY** pipeline head reservoir
FORE-BOW front of saddle
FOREDAY forenoon
nt **FORE-END** front end; bow
pl **FORE-GUT** beginning of alimentary canal
FOREIGN alien; exotic; strange
FORELAY ambush
FORELEG front leg
lw **FOREMAN** boss; overseer; ganger
FORERAN preceded; ushered
FORERUN herald
FORESAW foretold; forecast
FORESAY predict; presage; augur
FORESEE anticipate; forecast
nt **FORETOP FOREMAST** (part of ship)
FOREVER everlasting; always
lw **FORFANG** an ancient felony
FORFEIT confiscation; lose rights
FORFEND to avert; ward off
FORGAVE pardoned; absolved
FORGERY counterfeiting
FORGING shaping an imitation; falsifying
FORGIVE pardon; excuse
FORGONE abstained from; past
ck **FORKFUL** fork load (mouthful)
el **FORKING** branching; dividing (routes) (circuits)
mu **FORLANA FORLANE**, old dance (It.)
FORLORN desolate; lost; hapless; scruffy
FORMANT vowel pitch (phonetics)
ch **FORMATE** a salt from formic acid
FORMICA rigid laminated plastic material
FORMING shaping; moulding
ch **FORMOXY** organic radical
FORMULA order; ritual; ingredients
FORSAKE abandon; quit; desert
FORSOOK renounced; relinquished
FORTIFY strengthen; brace
FORTLET small redoubt
FORTUNE luck; Kismet; felicity; wealth
FORWARD bold; brazen; despatch
ga **FORWARD** -gear; front ranker (football)
FORWENT FOREGONE, past; a missed chance
FOUGADE fougasse; mine
tx **FOULARD** silk
ga **FOULING** soiling; blocking; agin rules
zo **FOUMART** the polecat; fitchew
FOUNDED started; established
nt **FOUNDER** originator; to sink
FOUNDRY (metal casting)
FOURGON baggage wagon
md **FOVEATE FOVEOLA**, dented; notched
bt **FOVILLA** pollen; plant seed
FOWLING bird catching; (shooting)
FOWLRUN chicken run; poultry yard
FOX-CASE foxskin
md **FOX-EVIL** baldness
FOXHOLE safety pit; bivouac (army)
FOXHUNT with horses and hounds
FOXLIKE FOXSHIP, cunning; craftiness
bt **FOXTAIL** a grass
FOX-TRAP a snare to catch foxes
FOX-TROT ballroom dance step
FRABBIT peevish
FRACHES glass annealing trays
hd **FRACTED** broken
FRAGILE delicate; infirm; brittle
FRAILTY foible; weakness; infirmity
FRAISED defended by pointed stakes
FRAKTUR German black-letter type
FRAME-UP plot; conspiracy for entrapment
FRAMING putting together; devising
FRANCIC FRANKISH, French culture etc.
FRANION boon companion; paramour
FRANKED exempt; post paid

FRANKLY candidly; openly; unreserved
FRANTIC frenzied; raving; distracted
nt **FRAPPED** bound
FRATCHY quarrelsome
rl **FRATERY** refectory in monastery
FRAUGHT laden; pregnant; surcharged
FRAYING peeling; tattering of clothes
FRAZZLE to make extremely upset; exhausted
FREAKED STREAKED, ran naked; took drugs
pl **FRECKLE** small facial spot (macula)
pl, pt **FRECKLY FRECKLED**, spotted design (skin)
FREEBIE complimentary ticket, meal etc.
FREEDOM liberty; informality; scope
FREEING loosing; liberating
FREEMAN privileged citizen
bt **FREESIA** bulbous plant
FREEWAY bypass; motorway
FREEZER refrigerator
ps **F-REGION F-LAYER**, ionosphere
FREIGHT cargo; burden; burthen
ae **FREMLIN** beery; female gremlin
zo **FRENATE** bristly
FRESHEN refresh; invigorate; revive
FRESHER freshman; less faded
FRESHES a flood; a spate
FRESHET flooding of a river; clear stream
FRESHLY recently; briskly; newly
me **FRESNEL** unit of optical frequency
FRETFUL petulant; testy; fractious
to **FRETSAW** for jigsaw puzzle making
ml, pc **FRETTED** frayed; abraded; sorrowed
pc **FRETTER** one with extreme anxiety
ck, gl **FRIABLE** crumbly; powdery
FRIAGEM wintry spell in Brazil
FRIARLY monkish; unsophisticated
FRIBBLE frivolous; to trifle; totter
ar **FRIEZED** with ornamental border; unshaven
nt **FRIGATE** a patrol warship
bt **FRIJOLE** Mexican bean
FRILLED with decorative collar (ham); (pastor)
FRINGED decorative border (hairstyle)
FRINGES light and dark lines on bordering
FRIPPER second-hand clothes merchant
FRISEUR hairdresser
zo **FRISIAN** Frieslander cattle race
FRISKED gambolled; made personal search
FRISKER a gad-about; a searcher
FRISKET a printing frame
FRISLET small ruffle
FRISURE a crisping of the hair
FRITTED fused; baked
ck **FRITTER** food fried in batter
FRIZING inducing curls; (hairstyle)
pl **FRIZZED FRIZZLY**, curled (hair)
FRIZZLE to fry; to crisp; to splutter
FROCKED wearing a frock; of clergy
bt **FROGBIT** acquatic plant
zo **FROGERY** a frog pool
FROGGED braided
nt **FROG-MAN** special type of diver
bt **FRONDED** leafy
FRONTAL a pediment; head on
FRONTED faced; encountered
FRONTIS front wall of court (pelota)
FRONTON a pelota ground (Sp.)
FROSTED roughened; decorative glass effect
FROTHED foamed; (at the mouth) (beer)
FROUNCE wrinkle; frown
FROWNED scowled; glowered
FROWSTY foul and stuffy
FRUCTED bearing fruit
FRUGGIN oven stirring pole
FRUIBLY do something with enjoyment
FRUITED bore fruit
FRUITER fruit grower
FRUMPED jeered
FRUMPER scoffer; mocker
FRUSTUM a conic section
FRUTIFY fructify; team; produce
FUBBERY deception
FUCATED painted deceptively
bt **FUCHSIA** a flowering shrub
FUCHSIN red fuchsia dye
FUDDLED bemused; fuzzled
FUDDLER drunkard; toper
FUDGING faking; of poor workmanship
FUEHRER German (Nazi) leader
FUELLER stoker; petrol salesman
FUFFING puffing (with exhaustion)
mu **FUGUIST** fugue composer
FULCRUM of leverage; rowing oars
FULGENT dazzling; radiant; brilliant
zo **FULGORA** lantern fly
FULGOUR splendour
tx **FULLAGE** fee for cleansing woollen cloth
tx **FULLERY** a fuller's cloth factory
FULLEST amplest; most exhaustive

FULL-HOT vehement; blazing
FULLING (cloth process)
FULL-PAY salary without deductions
FULMINE FULMINATE, to denounce with thunder
FULNESS FULSOME, plenitude; repletion
FULVOUS FULVID, tawny yellow colour
bt **FUMARIA FUMARIC**, tobacco plant genus
FUMBLED FUMBLER, bungled; groper
ck **FUMETTE** smell of high game
bt **FUMITER** plant genus
FUN FAIR amusement park
bt **FUNARIA** genus of mosses
FUNCTOR performer (of process)
FUNDING obtaining financial resources
mu **FUNEBRE** funeral; march
rl **FUNERAL** interment occasion (burial)
ch **FUNGATE** (fungic acid)
mn **FUNGITE** fossil coral
bt **FUNGOID FUNGOUS**, of fungi
FUNGOUS of fungi; behaving like fungus
pl, bt **FUNICLE** ligature; ovule stalk
FUNKING afraid to take any action
FUNNILY comically; humorously
FURBISH burnish; rub; polish
FURCATE forked
zo, ck **FURCULA** merrythought; wishbone (of chicken)
mu **FURIANT FURIOSO**, quick Czech dance
FURIOUS frantic; raging; frenzied
FURLANA forlana; Venetian dance
tx **FURLING** wrapping; rolling
me **FURLONG** running; horse racing; (201m)
FURMETY FRUMENTY, Elizabethan porridge
FURNACE coal firebox (in steam locomotive); (iron- and steelworks)
FURNISH equip; supply; produce
FURRIER a dealer in furs
pb **FURRING FIRRING**, encrusting pipes and leads
ag **FURROWY** in furrows
FURTHER FARTHER, increase in distance
FURTHER promote; support (cause) (fund)
FURTIVE stealthy; sly; clandestine
FUSCINE FUSCOUS, oil extract; swarthiness
FUSIBLE able to be melted
FUSSIER FUSSILY, more bothered; fidgety
FUSSING bothering; making trouble
FUSS-POT anxious busy-body
FUSTIAN coarse cloth; bombastic
FUSTIER mouldier; mustier
FUTCHEL supporting bar
FUTHORC Runic alphabet
nt **FUTTOCK** ship's timber
FUZZIER curlier; more crinkled
FUZZLED fuddled; inebriated
FYRDUNG whole country military array (Saxons)

G

nt **GABBARD GABBART**, a barge
GABBING gossiping
GABBLED GABBLER, chattered; babbler
GADDING GADDISH, restless roving
ck, bt **GADELLE** currant (Fr.)
GADLING gauntlet spike
GADROON ornamented edge
GADSMAN ploughman
zo **GADWALL** migratory duck
GAFFING fish spearing; gambling
GAGGING preventing speech; silencing
GAGGLED sound of noisy geese
mn **GAHNITE** spinel-group mineral
nt **GAIASSA** cargo felucca, Nile
GAINFUL lucrative; beneficial
GAINING profiting; winning; acquiring
GAINSAY (against); contradict; dispute
GAIRISH garish; gaudy colours
tx **GAITERS GAMBADOES**, mudguards for legs
as **GALACTO-** of constellations; galaxies
GALANTY (shadow pantomime)
GALATEA Pygmalion's statue
tx **GALATEA** cotton fabric
zo **GALEATE** crested
zo **GALEENY** guinea-fowl
GALENIC (lead)
GALERIA ancient Mexican water system
ck **GALETTE** a small gateau; (cream cake)
rl **GALILEE** West porch of cathedral
bt **GALIPOT** pine-resin
GALLANT courtly; valiant; a beau
zo **GALLA-OX** Abyssinian ox
ch **GALLATE** (gallic acid)
nt **GALLEON** carrack; trader (Sp.)

ar **GALLERY** grand corridor; mining passage
ga **GALLERY** balcony; (play to-) (tennis)
zo **GALL-FLY** a pest
GALLICE in French
GALLING irritating; exasperating
nt **GALLIOT** galiot; brigantine; later, barge
ch **GALLIUM** a metallic element
GALLIZE (wine-making)
bt **GALL-NUT** a pestiferous growth
tx **GALLOON** woven fabric; lace
GALLOWS for hanging criminals (noose)
GALOCHE GALOSH, rubber over-shoe
GALUMPH wild price rise (property)
GAMBADO mud gaiter
GAMBIAN native of Gambia (W. Africa)
bt **GAMBIER** catechu; a dye
mu **GAMBIST** cello player; (viol da gamba)
GAMBLED GAMBLER, hazarded; speculator
pt **GAMBOGE CAMBOGE**, yellow gum
ar **GAMBREL** butcher's crook; roof
GAME-BAG hunter's bag
zo **GAME-EGG** a bad egg
GAMEFUL sportive; playful
mu **GAMELAN** Indonesian ensemble
GAME-LEG lameness
GAMETAL gametic; reproductive
zo **GAMETID** sporont-body bud cell
GAMMOCK sky-larking; gammon
GAMPISH bulging; slatternly (Mrs G-)
GANGING grouping; teaming
md **GANGLIA** nerve-centre
GANGREL vagrant; vagabond
to **GANG-SAW** multiple saw
nt, bd **GANGWAY** ship's ladder; passage; scaffolding
GANOIDS fish of sturgeon type
GANOSIS reducing shine on marble
wv **GANTREE** loom jacquard frame
GAPPING opening; cleaving
cp **GARBAGE** litter; unwanted data
ga **GARBAGE** easy goal (basketball); soft shot (tennis)
GARBLED GARBLER, distorted sound, meanings
ck **GARBURE** Pyrenean ragout
hd **GARDANT** full-faced
zo **GARFISH** sea-fish; belone
GARGLED warbled
bt, ga **GARLAND** festoon; sideslip (skiing)
tx **GARMENT** clothing; apparel; vestment
ck **GARNISH** adornment (food) (ceramics)
GAROTTE GARROTTE, strangling collar
zo **GARPIKE** the garfish
nt **GARUKHA CARUCA**, dhow; Arab vessel
nv **GAS-BUOY** lightbuoy; marine warning
mn **GAS-COAL GAS-COKE**, anthracite for gas
GASEITY GASEOUS, containing gas
GAS-FIRE domestic heating unit
GASHFUL GASHING, mutilated; slitting
tx **GASKINS** leggings for warmth
GAS-LAMP Victorian lighting
GAS-LIME (gas filtration)
GAS-MAIN chief gas conduit
GAS-MASK protection against poison gas
GAS-OVEN gas-fired (kitchen) oven
md **GASPING** spasmodic breathing
GAS-PIPE gas conduit
GAS-RING cooking grid
GASSING loquacity; chattering
GAS-TANK portable gas cylinder
cf, pl, md **GASTERO- GASTRIC**, of stomach (acid)
ar **GATEMAN GATEWAY**, door keeper; portal
GATLING a gun
tx **GAUDERY GAUDIED**, loud coloured finery
GAUDILY ostentatiously; embellished
ck **GAUFFER GAUFFRE**, crimped; wafer (Fr.)
rw **GAUGING** measuring widths (rail gauge) etc.
bd, to **GAUGING GAULTER**, estimating mortar mix; marking timber
GAULISH of France (Caesar's Gallia)
GAUMING daubing; smearing
GAUNTLY lankily; leanly
rw **GAUNTRY GANTRY**, overhead signals
lw **GAVELET** land forfeiture
zo **GAVILAN** species of hawk
mu **GAVOTTE** a country dance
GAYNESS of homosexuals; cheerfulness
GAYSOME blithe; vivacious; jolly
GAZEFUL regardant; contemplative
zo **GAZELLE** graceful animal
GAZETTE journal; newspaper; record
GEAR-BOX GEARING, varying motor wheels
GEHENNA place of abomination; (Hell)

ck **GELABLE GELATIN**, glutinate; jelly
zo **GELDING** castrated stallion
ck, pt **GELIDLY GELLING**, liquid to set jelly
to **GELLOCK** crowbar; gavelock
GEMMATE budding
GEMMERY GEMMARY, collection of mounted gems and precious stones
bt **GEMMING GEMMULE**, budding; small bud
zo **GEMSBOK** S. African antelope
GENAPPE worsted yarn
GENERAL high officer; over all; (in-)
GENERIC of general features classified
rl **GENESIS** starting point; birth of; (Bible)
bl **GENETIC** of heredity; chromosomes; DNA
zo **GENETTE GENET**, civet
rl **GENEVAN** of Geneva; Calvinist
ck **GENEVER** 'Holland's gin'
bt **GENIPAP** orange-like fruit
bt **GENISTA** broom (bush) (Plantagenet)
bl, pc **GENITAL** of reproductive organs
GENIZAH store-room for ancient relics
GENOESE of Genoa
GENTEEL elegant; polite; mincing
bt **GENTIAN** plant genus
GENTILE not a Jew
GENTLER milder; more kindly
GENUINE sincere; authentic; veritable
bl **GEOCOLE** soil-dwelling organism
gl **GEODESY** (earth measurements)
go **GEOGONY** (earth formations)
gl **GEOIDAL** globe, earth-shaped
gl **GEOLOGY** history of globe through rocks
go **GEONOMY** physical geography
go **GEORAMA** globular map
nm **GEORDIE** miner's lamp; guinea coin
GEORGIC poetic metre (verse form)
bt, gl **GEOTOME** soil-sample taker
bl **GEOXENE** soil-dwelling organism
GERMANE relevant; apposite; pertinent
md **GERMULE** a small germ
ck **GERVAIS** cream cheese (Fr.)
pc **GESTALT** total perception; art as unity
GESTAPO Nazi secret police
bl, pl **GESTATE** of pregnancy; (womb time)
pc **GESTURE** an act expressing feeling
GETABLE obtainable; procurable
GET-AWAY escape
GETTING acquisition; gaining; reaching
ps **G-FACTOR** magnetic energy level changes
GHASTLY fearsome; spectral; awful
bt **GHERKIN** small cucumber
GHILGAI Australian dewpond
GHILLIE game-keeper (Sc.)
GHOSTLY weird; spiritual; spectral
GIANTRY large human monsters
as, pl **GIBBOSE GIBBOUS**, convex; of moon; humpbacked
ck **GIBLETS** edible internal organs (fowls)
GIDDILY whirling around; unsteady
GIFTING endowing; bestowing; donating
GIG-MILL nap-raising device
GILBERT magnetic potential
pt **GILDING** enhancing with gold
GILLIAN sweetheart
ma, me **GILLION** 10 to the 9th power
zo **GILL-LID** 'lung cover' of fish
bt, pt **GILVOUS** brownish gold
nt **GIMBALS** compass holder; magnet balancer
to, nt **GIMBLET GIMLET**, hand borer
GIMMICK publicity trick
GIN-FIZZ a long drink based on gin
GINGALL swivel gun
ck **GINGERY** hot-flavoured; spicey
tx **GINGHAM** umbrella; gamp; (material)
bt, ck **GINGILI** sesame-oil
mn **GINGING** mine-shaft lining
GIN-MILL off-licence (Amer.)
GINNING cotton making
bt, ck, md **GINSENG** Chinese elixir root
GIN-SHOP gin-palace
GIN-TRAP snare; leg-trap (poachers)
mu **GIOCOSO** jocund; playful (smiling) (It.)
GIPPING gutting; cleaning out meat
GIPSIES Romanies; caravanners; Zingari
zo **GIRAFFE** long-necked camelopard
mn **GIRASOL** fire-opal
GIRDING dressing for war (action)
GIRDLED belted (of surround); zoned
GIRDLER belt or girth-surround maker
GIRLISH childish; young ladyish
zo **GIRROCK** garfish
GIRTHED girdled; bound
GISARME battle-axe; bill; halberd
mu **GITTERN** cither; guitar
zo **GIZZARD** birds' food-grinding organ
GJETOST Norwegian goat's-milk cheese
gl, go **GLACIAL** of Ice Age, glaciers

mo, gl, go **GLACIER** slowly moving icefield
GLADDEN delight; gratify; rejoice
GLADDER brighter; more cheerful
GLAD-EYE an invitation
zo **GLADIUS** swordfish
bt **GLADWYN** purple iris
GLAIDIN glutin; (wheat)
GLAIRED varnished
pc **GLAMOUR** illusory fascination
GLANCED glimpsed; bounced away
GLARING obvious; staring fiercely
md **GLASSES** eye-; sun-; (spectacles)
zo **GLAUCUS** genus of molluscs
GLAZIER instals window-glass
ck **GLAZING** glassy; glossy; surfacey
GLEAMED shone; flashed; glinted; smiled
GLEANED GLEANER, post reaping (remnants) harvesting
GLEBOUS cloddy, turfy ground
GLEDGED squinted
GLEEFUL gay; lively; hilarious
mu **GLEEMAN** minstrel; chorister
md **GLENOID** of being bled; cupped
GLEYING squinting
ae **GLIDING** non-powered flight
GLIDING skimming; sliding; skiing
GLIMMER soft gleam (light); inkling (idea)
GLIMPSE glance; hasty look or impression
GLINTED gleamed; sparkled; reflected
GLIRINE rodent-like
GLISTEN give sparkling radiance
GLISTER glitter; lustre; sparkle
GLITTER deceptive; ornamental; sparkle
GLOAMED grew dark
GLOATED exulted; revelled
zo **GLOBARD** a glow-worm
GLOBATE spheroidal
GLOBING encircling
GLOBOID spherical
GLOBOSE round
GLOBOUS globular
GLOBULE corpuscule
GLOOMED made dark, sombre
GLORIED exalted; took pride in
GLORIFY honour; magnify; extol; bless
GLOSSAL vocabulary; tongue
GLOSSED explained; palliated
GLOSSER polisher; commentator
GLOSSIC phonetic alphabet
md **GLOTTAL GLOTTIC**, phonetical stop
pl **GLOTTIS** larynx; vocal cord
GLOWING vehement; ardent; fervid
GLOZING specious representation
ch **GLUCIDE** saccharin; gluside
ch **GLUCINA** an oxide
GLUCOSE sugar
GLUE-POT gum receptacle
GLUMMER more dismal and dejected
bt **GLUMOUS** husky
GLUTEUS hind-limb muscle in vertebrates
GLUTTED gorged; surfeited; crammed
zo **GLUTTON** the wolverine
ch **GLYCINE** amino-acetic acid
pr **GLYPHIC** coded; ideogram; cartouche
GLYPTIC engraved; figured
bt **GMELINA** (verbena)
GNARING snarling; growling
bt **GNARLED GNARRED**, knotty timber
pc **GNASHED** teeth ground in anger
pl **GNATHAL GNATHIC**, of the jaws
GNAT-NET mosquito-net
GNAWING champing; eroding
ck **GNOCCHI** maize/potato dumplings (It.)
GNOSTIC speculative believer
GOADING inciting; annoying
GO-AHEAD enterprising
GOATISH lustful; satyr-like
GOBBING coal refuse
zo **GOBBLER** turkey-cock
GOBBLER gourmandizer
GOBELIN French tapestry
GODDARD pewter cup
GODDESS female deity
bt **GODETIA** a garden annual
ce **GO-DEVIL** concrete pipeline cleaner
GODHEAD divine nature
GODHOOD state of being god
GODILLE wavy ski-descent technique
GODLESS atheistic; irreligious; profane
GODLIER more righteous
GODLIKE deific
GODLILY devoutly
GODLING an inferior deity
GODROON gadroon; beading
GODSEND windfall; a crowning mercy
GODSHIP deification
GODWARD heavenward
GOGGLED lobster-eyed
GOGGLES eye-protectors
GOITRED afflicted with bronchocele
bt **GOLD-CUP** buttercup
zo **GOLDNEY** a bream
ga **GOLFING** playing golf (social pastime)
GOLIARD wandering jester

zo **GOLIATH** Biblical giant; beetle
GOMBEEN money-lending; usury (Irish)
GOMELIN cotton starch
md **GONAGRA** gout (of uric acid)
nt **GONDOLA** canal boat (Venice); galley
ae, mo **GONDOLA** passenger car of airship, cable funicular
GONGING prelude to speeding fine (USA)
bt **GONIDIA** lichen-moss spores
vt **GONITIS** stifle joint inflammation
zo **GONOPOD** insect reproduction organ
GOOD-BYE adieu
GOOD-DAY conventional greeting
GOOD-EGG cordial approval
GOODISH not so bad
GOODMAN a husband
GOOD-NOW exclamation of wonder
GOONDIE Australian native hut
zo **GOOSERY** cf. swannery
ar **GOPURAN** Hindu gate tower
zo **GORCOCK** red grouse
zo **GOR-CROW** carrion crow
GORDIAN intricate; (knot)
zo **GORDIUS** hair-worm
GORGING cramming; stuffing
zo **GORILLA** largest anthropoid ape
GORMAND gourmand; glutton
GORSEDD Welsh bardic assembly
zo **GOSHAWK** short-winged hawk
zo **GOSLING** a young goose
zo **GOSNICK** small sea-fish; skipper
GOSSIPY chatty; loquacious
GOSSOON a boy (Irish)
pt **GOUACHE** (water-colour painting)
GOUGING scooping out (eyes)
ch **GOULARD** lead acetate
ck **GOULASH** a ragout; (cards)
zo **GOURAMI** tropical fish
GOURMET a dainty feeder; epicure
zo **GOURNET** **GURNARD, GURNET**, a fish
rl **GOWN-MAN** of university or church
nc, ps **G-PARITY** particle quantum number
GRAB-BAG lucky-dip bag
GRABBED clutched; snatched
GRABBER gripper; pincher
GRABBLE sprawl; grope; paw
GRACILE slender
GRACING honorary adorning
to **GRADINE** sculptor's chisel
GRADING classifying; (quality) (results)
GRADUAL step by step progress
lw **GRAFFER** notary; scrivener
bt **GRAFTED** one plant on to another
GRAFTER financial swindler
bt **GRAINED** pattern of cross-section of wood, marble
GRAINER painter of above (imitator)
zo **GRALLAE** genus of wading birds
GRALLIC stilted
GRAMARY magic; wizardry
GRAMMAR linguistic treatise
zo **GRAMPUS** blunt-headed delphinoid cetacean
GRANARY grain-store
GRANDAD grandpa
GRANDAM a grannie
GRANDEE Spanish nobleman
GRANDER finer; superior; sublime
GRANDLY splendidly; superbly
GRANDMA grandam
GRANGER farm bailiff
gl **GRANITE** coarse, igneous, plutonic rock
GRANNOM grandam
GRANTED ceded; allotted; vouchsafed
lw **GRANTEE** the receiver
GRANTER the bestower
lw **GRANTOR** conveyor
GRANULE small particle
bt **GRAPERY** vinery
cp, pt, pr **GRAPHIC** pictorial, vivid comic strip
nt **GRAPNEL** **GRAPPLING**-iron (boarding ships)
GRAPPLE close-up fighting grip
GRASPED **GRASPER**, gripped; understood; clasp
GRASSED informer told police
pr **GRASSER** extra printing hand
GRASSUM a premium
GRATIFY to satisfy; gladden; please
GRATING scratching, rasping sound
pc **GRATING** harsh; offensive; annoying
cp **GRAUNCH** unplanned fault of machine
GRAVEDO cold in the head
GRAVELY seriously; staidly; sober
GRAVEST most serious; very cogent
GRAVIED served with gravy
nt **GRAVING** engraving; scraping
GRAVITA of seriousness
ps **GRAVITY** law of falling weight
GRAVITY seriousness; dignity; importance
pr **GRAVURE** photo printing technique
GRAZIER shepherd
GRAZING animals browsing; glancing blow
GREASED lubricated; oiled (machinery)
GREASER lubricator; machine-minder

GREATER larger; more important
GREATLY notably; immensely
GREAVES leg-armour; old tallow
GREAVES tallow refuse; cracklings
GRECIAN Greek or man of Greece (poet)
GRECISM a Greek expression
GRECIZE to Hellenize
GRECQUE in Greek style; coffee-machine
GREENED hoaxed; duped; cheated
GREENER verdant; easily fooled
GREETED accosted; welcomed
mt **GREGALE GREGAL**, NE Med. winter wind
rl **GREMIAL** bishops' pinafore
GREMLIN aerial imp; pilot's illusion
ga **GREMLIN** unskilled skateboardist
GRENADE hand-bomb
GREY-HEN stone bottle
zo **GREY-HEN** female grouse
GREYISH grayish
zo **GREYLAG** wild goose; grey goose
zo **GREY-OWL** tawny owl
zo **GRIBBLE** marine borer (crustacean)
GRIDDED marked in squares
ck **GRIDDLE** circular iron baking plate
GRIDING grating; jarring
GRIEVED lamented; mourned
hd **GRIFFIN GRIFFON**, mythical dragon-eagle
GRIFFIN greenhorn; a duenna
GRILLED broiled; cross-examined
GRIMACE a moue; facial distortion
GRIMING fouling; soiling
GRIMMER dourer; fiercer; more grisly
pl **GRINDER** molar tooth; quern; peppermill
GRINNED smiled broadly
md **GRIPING** causing intestinal pains
GRIPPED seized; held; clutched
GRIPPER a bailiff
GRIPPLE usurious; tenacious
GRIQUAS Dutch half-castes
GRISKIN lean bacon
GRISLED grizzled; grey
ck **GRISTLE GRISTLY**, cartilage; indigestible (meat)
GRITTED grated; ground
GRITTER road, salt-spreading device
GRIZZLE whimper; gray
zo **GRIZZLY** grey; a bear
GROANED moaned; bewailed
GROBIAN clumsy lout
GROCERY provision shop
tx **GROGRAM** fabric of silk and mohair
GROINED thigh cleft; breakwater
GROLIER of book-binding technique
nt **GROMMET GRUMMET**, rope-ring for mooring
GROOMED made smart, tidy (horses)
GROOVED furrowed channel; rut
GROPING seeking by touch
GROSSER GROSSLY, coarser; rougher; outrageously
lw **GROTIAN** (legal philosophy)
ga, ck **GROUNDS** arenas; reasons; dregs
GROUPED GROUPER, graded; arranger
GROUSED GROUSER complained; grumbler
GROUTED filled with cement
GROWING raising; waxing
GROWLED snarled
nt, zo **GROWLER** a wandering iceberg; dog
GROWN-UP an adult
to **GRUB-AXE** a hoe
GRUBBED GRUBBER, dug up; investigator
GRUBBLE grope; grabble
GRUDGED envied; resented
GRUFFER surlier; rougher; (voice)
GRUFFLY churlishly; roughly; bluntly
GRUMBLE grouse; complain; repine
nt **GRUMMET GROMMET**, rope-ring for mooring
GRUMOSE GRUMOUS, clustered; clotted
zo **GRUNDEL** loach or rock-goby
zo **GRUNTER** a pig; a gurnet
ck **GRUYERE** a Swiss cheese
GRYLLID pertaining to crickets
hd **GRYPHON GRIFFIN**, dragon-eagle
zo **GRYSBOK** S. African antelope
GUAJIRA peasant dance (Cuba)
zo **GUANACO HUANACO**, llama genus
bc **GUANINE** purine base in living tissues
bt **GUARANA** Brazil cocoa
nm **GUARANI** (Paraguay)
GUARAPO sweet drink (Peru)
GUARDED wary; watchful; defended
zo **GUDGEON** an axle; a fish
bt **GUELDER** rose; snowball tree
zo **GUENONS** a monkey genus
GUERDON a reward; recompense
zo **GUEREZA** the Abyssinian monkey
GUERITE watch-tower
GUESSED divined; solved; supposed
GUESSER a conjecturer
bt **GUIACUM** lignum vitae
GUICHET small ticket window (Fr.)
GUIDING leading; directing; piloting
nm **GUILDER** Dutch golden coin
GUINEAN (W. African)

tx **GUIPURE** a heavy lace
rl **GUISARD GUIZER**, Christmas mummer (actor)
zo **GULLERY** bird sanctuary; easy deception
go **GULLIED** of water-eroded ravines
go, to **GULLIES** small narrow canyons; knives
GULLING greening; duping
md **GUM-BOIL** inflamed swelling
GUM-BOOT rubber shoe
GUMDROP a confection
bt **GUMMING** fruit-tree disease; cementing
GUMMOUS gummy; mucilaginous
md **GUM-RASH** red gum; strophulus
bt **GUM-THUS** resin from Amer. pine
bt **GUM-TREE** (quandary); (rubber)
bt **GUMWOOD** similar grain to rosewood
nt **GUNBOAT** small warship
nt **GUN-DECK** ships' artillery deck
nt **GUNDELO GUNDELOW**, cargo (felucca) vessel
GUN-FIRE war-sound; ceremonial salute
GUNLOCK firing mechanism
nt **GUNNAGE** (number of guns)
GUNNERY the craft of the artillery
GUNNING shooting
nt **GUN-PORT** port-hole
nt **GUN-ROOM** a mess-room
GUNSHOT distance of effective range
GUN-SITE location of gun
nt **GUNWALE** topmost plank (ship's side)
GURGLED GARGLED, rippling sound; water-warbled
zo **GURNARD** gurnet fish
GUSHING spouting; flowing; effusive
GUSTATE to taste, consume
GUSTILY in gusts; fitfully; breezily
GUTTATE spotted
GUTTING gipping; eviscerating
GUTTLED gulped; swallowed
GUTTULE small drop
GUZZLED ate greedily; swilled; caroused
GUZZLER gourmand
zo **GWINIAD** freshwater salmon
zo **GWYNIAD** small white fish
GYMNAST athlete
zo **GYPLURE** moth sex attractant
GYRATED twirled; span; spun; rotated
el **GYRATOR** component used at microwave frequencies
zo **GYRINID** whirligig beetle
hd **GYRONNY** heraldic triangulation
ae **GYROSYN** flux-gate gyro compass
GYTRASH a ghost

H

bt, zo **HABITAT** natural life-environment
HABITED dressed; attired
HABITUE a frequenter; regular
pr **HACHURE** engraved line; groove
HACKBUT arquebus; musket
HACKING cutting; notching; kicking
cp **HACKING** penetrating computer secrets
HACKLED combed
HACKLER flax-comber
HACKLES feathers; imitation flies (angling)
zo **HACKLET** sea-bird; shearwater gull
HACKLOG chopping block
zo **HACKNEY** horse; cab; trite
to **HACK-SAW** a saw for metal
zo **HADDOCK HADDIE**, (Sc.)
HAFFLED prevaricated
ch **HAFNIUM** metallic element
HAFTING fitting a handle
HAGANAH Jewish militia
nt **HAGBOAT** hull design of sailing vessels
zo **HAGDOWN** shearwater gull
zo **HAGFISH** parasite fish
HAGGADA Jewish commentary
zo **HAGGARD** stackyard; wild falcon
HAGGING HAGGISH, ugly; nagging female
HAGGLED HAGGLER, bargainer
HAGSEED offspring of a witch
HAGSHIP haggishness
bt **HAGWEED** witches' broom (transport)
mt **HAILING** greeting; raining ice
HAIRCUT barber's service
HAIRNET coiffure cover
HAIR-OIL hair dressing
HAIRPIN coiffure; (sharp bend)
HAITIAN native of Haiti
HALACHA HALAKAH, Jewis oral laws
HALBERD HALBARD, pike-axe
HALBERT guard's weapon; pike-axe
zo **HALCYON** kingfisher; calm
bd **HALF-BED** stone laying term
HALF-ONE a golf handicap
HALF-PAY semi-retirement
HALFWAY intermediate position
HALF-WIT nitwit; moron
zo **HALIBUT** the largest flounder
HALIDOM mascot; sanctuary
md **HALITUS** foul exhaled breath

HALLAGE market-hall dues
HALLIER bird net
HALLING national folk dance (Norway)
HALLION hallyon; hallian; rascal
ch **HALOGAN** salt producer group
HALOGEN one of the 7th-group elements
HALTING faltering; hesitating
mn **HALVANS** ore-mining refuse
HALVING tieing; bisecting
nt **HALYARD** halliard; running rope
HAMBLED mutilated the foot
zo **HAMBURG** domestic fowl
HAMITIC sons of Ham (of Noah)
tc **HAMMING** overacting; radio hobby
cp **HAMMING** code signal distance error
nt **HAMMOCK** a slung bed
zo **HAMSTER** rodents; (pets)
HAMULAR **HAMULUS**, small crooked hook
HANAPER **HAMPER**, basket-box (picnic)
HANDBAG women's closed everyday bag
HANDFUL small amount; difficult person
HANDIER more manageable (size)
HANDILY conveniently; adjacently
HANDING presenting; delivering
HANDJAR Persian dagger
HANDLED dealt with; manipulated
HANDLER dealer
HAND-OFF self-defence; fending off a tackle (rugby football)
HANDOUT prepared statement; sample; advertising material
to **HANDSAW** carpenter's tool
HANDSEL earnest money; a present
tc **HANDSET** telephone receiver and microphone (mouthpiece)
HANDS-ON direct participation
HANGDOG sullen; morose; abject
HANGING dangling; depending
HANGMAN topsman; public executioner
HANG-NET vertical net
tx **HANKIES** handkerchiefs
nt **HANKING** coiling ropes; skeining wool
HANKLED entangled (in coils); involved
HANSARD Parliamentary Debate Reports
HANSTER a freeman of a guild
rl **HANUKAH** Jewish feast day
HANUMAN Hindu monkey-god
HAPLESS luckless
HAPLOID single chromosomes
HAPLONT special-nucleus-type plant
nm **HAP'ORTH** halfpenny-worth
HAPPIER pleased; luckier
HAPPILY joyously; blissfully; gaily
HAPPING happening
HARBOUR shelter; haven; asylum
HARDEST densest; firmest; harshest
HARDIER pluckier; braver; tougher
HARDILY stoutly; intrepidly; resolutely
HARDISH somewhat hard
bt **HARDOCK** harlock; burdock; coarse weed
gl **HARDPAN** bedrock; level of soil horizon
HARD-RUN greatly pressed
HARDSET beset by difficulty; hungry
HARDTOP fixed roof on a car
HARD-WON barely victorious
HAREING speeding
md **HARELIP** fissured lip
bt **HARICOT** French bean
HARKING listening; hurrying
bd **HARLING** of steel-clad houses
bt **HARMALA** wild rue
HARMFUL noxious; baneful; baleful
ch **HARMINE** wild rue extract
HARMING molesting; scathing
mu **HARMONY** chord structure
HARMONY amity; agreement; literary notes
eg, ae **HARNESS** safety gear; (pilots)
ag **HARNESS** fastenings; yoke (horses) (carts)
HARNESS control and utilize
pc **HARPING** repeating endlessly
mu **HARPIST** minstrel; musician
to **HARPOON** barbed spear on rope (whaling)
HARRIED harassed; raided; ravaged
zo **HARRIER** hound; hawk; hare courser
HARRIER cross-country runner
HARSHEN stiffen; embitter
HARSHER rougher; severer; sterner
HARSHLY raucously; stridently
mn **HARTALL** orpiment (stone)
cp **HARTLEY** unit of information; bits
me, nc **HARTREE** atomic unit of energy
HARVEST crop; yield; produce
HAS-BEEN diminished fame
ck **HASHING** muddling; mangling; cooking a medley
pr **HASHIRA** narrow print (Jap.)
ch, md **HASHISH** bhang; the assassin's drug
HASLOCK wool on sheep's throat
rl, tx, bt **HASSOCK** prayer cushion; tuft grass
bt **HASTATE** arrowhead-shaped leaf

HASTIER quicker; rasher; brisker
HASTILY rapidly; hurriedly; abruptly
HASTING ripening early; expediting
HASTLER (turn-spit); cook's help
HATABLE odious; obnoxious
HATBAND ribbon on hat
HATCASE bonnet-box
vt **HATCHED** new chicken; graduated
cp **HATCHEL** to heckle; to tease; public speaker
HATCHER plotter; conspirator; information thief
nt **HATCHES** deck trapdoor
to **HATCHET** an axe
HATEFUL detestable; execrable; odious
HATLESS bareheaded
HAT-RACK place to hang hat
HAUBERK coat of mail
HAUGHTY arrogant; proud
HAULAGE a charge for conveyance
HAULIER carter
HAULING tugging; drawing; dragging
HAUNCHY with full hips
HAUNTED frequented; followed; (ghost)
HAUNTER frequent visitor; (ghost)
HAURLED dragged; rought-cast
HAUSTUS adult medicine dose
mu **HAUTBOY** **HAUTBOIS**, oboe (woodwind)
HAUTEUR disdain; arrogance; loftiness
HAUTPAS a dais
HAVENOT under-privileged
HAW-BUCK a clown
bt **HAWKBIT** a plant
HAWKING falconry; peddlary; touting
HAWKISM war-minded advice
zo **HAWK-OWL** snowy owl
HAYBAND hay-rope
HAYCOCK gathered hay in stack
HAYDITE expanded clay (USA)
to **HAYFORK** farm implement
HAYLOFT part of barn
HAYRICK regular hay pile
bt **HAYSEED** hick, bumpkin
HAY-TIER hay bundler
HAYWARD a warden
HAYWIRE in confusion
HAZELLY light brown
HAZIEST foggiest; vaguest
HEADILY impetuously; precipitately
HEADING adit; headline; intercepting
HEADMAN chief; boss
HEAD-PIN no. 1 pin (bowling)
HEADWAY progress
bt **HEAL-ALL** valerian; a panacea
HEALING mollifying; remedying
HEALTHY hygienic; bracing; hale
HEAPING collecting; amassing
lw **HEARING** audition; trying
HEARKEN listen; attend; heed
HEARSAY rumour; report; gossip
HEARSED put in a hearse
HEARTED emboldened; cheered
HEARTEN encourage; rally; inspire
HEATHEN pagan; paynim; infidel
bt **HEATHER** ling; erica
HEATING warming; exciting
HEAVERS stevedores; dockyard unloaders
nt **HEAVE-TO** command: stop!; storm tactic
HEAVIER weightier; denser
HEAVILY ponderously; onerously
HEAVING a rising; hoisting; throwing
HEBAMIC pert. to Socratic method
bt **HEBENON** hen-bane; poison
HEBETIC occurring at puberty
HEBRAIC Hebrew
HECKLED combed; questioned
HECKLER political enquirer; demonstrator
me **HECTARE** 100 ares
HECTOID flushed; feverish; hectic
bt **HEDEOMA** penny-royal
HEDERAL of ivy
bt **HEDGING** natural garden fence
HEDGING guarding against losses
HEDONIC pleasure-seeking
HEEDFUL mindful; wary; cautious
HEEDING paying attention; regarding
HEELING (cock fighting); (football)
HEFTIER stronger; more vigorous
HEFTILY vigorously; powerfully
rl **HEGUMEN** Greek abbot
HEIGH-HO exclamation of complaisance
HEINOUS infamous; flagrant; atrocious
HEIRDOM succession
HEIRESS female inheritor
md **HELCOID** ulcerous
HELIBUS **HELICAB**, helicopter bus/taxi
HELICAL spiral
HELICES circumvolutions; spirals
HELICON mount of Muses
mu **HELICON** tuba; sousaphone (brass; wind)
HELIOID like the Sun
ch **HELIXIN** an ivy extract
pr **HELL-BOX** receptacle for broken type
HELL-CAT malignant hag

HELLENE Greek
HELL-HAG witch
HELLISH diabolical; infernal; fiendish
nt **HELMAGE** guidance; steering
md **HELOSIS** corns in feet
HELOTRY serfdom; bondage; (Sparta)
HELPFUL assistant; useful; beneficial
HELPING share; aiding; abetting
HELVING hafting; fitting a handle
mn **HELVITE** beryllium silicate
mu **HEMIOLA HEMIOLIA**, rhythmic change (Gr.)
zo **HEMIONE** half-ass; dziggetal
bt, md **HEMLOCK** poison plant; conine
HEMMING edging; besetting; sewing
bt **HENBANE** narcotic plant
HENCOOP a fowl abode
HENNAED dyed with henna
HENNERY poultry farm
HENOTIC conciliatory
HENPECK nag; dominate
HENTING final furrow
HENWIFE chicken-girl
HEPARIN anticoagulant
md **HEPATIC** of liver ailments
HEPTADE seven
ch **HEPTANE** petrol constituent
HEPTODE type of electric valve
ch **HEPTOSE** monosaccharide subgroup
HERBAGE pasture
HERBARY herb garden
HERBIST herbalist; collector of natural remedies
HERBLET small herb
HERBOUS herbaceous; herbose
HERDING tending; crowding; group instinct; driving groups about
HERDMAN herdsman; ranchero
HEREOUT out of this
HERETIC unorthodox; schismatic
HERISSE bristled
HERITOR inheritor
zo **HERLING** young sea-trout
md **HERNIAL** (rupture)
HEROINE intrepid damsel
HEROISM valour; bravery; fortitude
HEROIZE lionize
zo **HERONRY** bird sanctuary
zo **HERRING** tasty fish
HERSELF reflexive pronoun
HERSHIP cattle-theft (Sc.)
HESSIAN jute fabric; burlage (USA)
mn **HESSITE** telluride of silver
HETAIRA Greek dancing girl
HEXAGON a six-sided figure
HEXAPLA a Bible edition
HEXAPOD with 6 feet
bt **HEXARCH** with 6 protoxylem strands
HEXERIS galley with 6 oar banks
HEXONIC chemical base
HEYDUCK Haiduk; Hungarian
HEY-PASS conjuror's command
HIBACHI charcoal brazier (Jap.)
zo **HICATEE** Central American tortoise
bt **HICKORY** American nut-bearing tree
zo **HICKWAY** small woodpecker
as **HIDALGO** Spanish Don; asteroid
HIDEOUS unshapely; monstrous; grisly
HIDE-OUT a cache
HIEMATE hibernate; to winter
HIGGLED negotiated; peddled; chaffered
HIGGLER haggler; bargainer; hawker
HIGHBOY TALLBOY, pillar chest of drawers
HIGHDAY holiday
HIGHEST tallest; loftiest
HIGHFED pampered
HIGH-HAT high-brow
HIGHLOW sort of shoe
HIGHWAY main road; (-code) (-signals)
cp **HIGHWAY** digital transmission canals
HILDING paltry; base; a deceiver
HILLIER steeper
HILLING earthing
HILLMAN a mountaineer
HILLOCK small hill
HILLTOP summit
HIMSELF reflexive pronoun of 'he'
HINDBOW saddle cantle; equestrian
zo **HIND-GUT** posterior of alimentary canal
zo **HINNIED WHINNIED**, greeting of a horse
HINTING implying; suggesting
HIP-BATH portable sitting bath
HIP-BELT swordbelt
md **HIP-GOUT** sciatica
HIP-KNOT gable ornament
HIP-LOCK wrestling trick
HIPPING grieving; glooming
HIPPOID like a horse
HIP-ROOF a type of roof
HIPSHOT dislocated hip
HIPSTER clothes held by a belt
HIRABLE for hire; leasable
zo **HIRCINE** goatish
HIRSUTE hairy; rude
HIRUDIN anticoagulant chemical from leeches
HISKING breathing heavily
HISSING audible disapproval
ch **HISTONE** simple-protein group

HISTORY chronicle; annals; account
HISTRIO histrion; an actor
HITCHED caught; fastened; attached
HITTING smiting; striking; succeeding
HITTITE ancient Near-Eastern people
zo **HIVE-BEE** honey-bee
HOARDED garnered; amassed; secreted
HOARDER miser; husbandman
zo **HOATZIN** S. American bird
HOAXING duping; gammoning
HOBBISH clownish
HOBBISM a moral philosophy
HOBBIST follower of Hobbes
HOBBLED hoppled; tethered
HOBBLER horse-soldier
HOBLIKE boorish; clownish
HOBNAIL boot-nail
HOBOISM vagrancy (USA)
HOCK-DAY old English festival
HOCKLED houghed; hamstrung
HODADDY incompetent surf boarder
ck **HOE-CAKE** Indian meal cake
HOE-DOWN American folkdance
HOGBACK ridge; eskar
ag **HOGCOTE** pig-sty (America)
HOGGERS miner's leg-wear
HOGGING bending
HOGGISH swinish; sordid; greedy
HOG-HERD swineherd
HOG-MANE clipped mane
bt **HOG-PLUM** tropical tree
tx **HOGSKIN** pigskin; leather
HOGWASH swill; pig food
bt **HOGWEED** cow parsnip
HOISTED raised; heaved
HOISTER an elevator; lift
HOITING capering
HOLDALL a pack; luggage
lw **HOLDING** tenure; company finance
HOLDING climb-grip; horse-race conditions
HOLIDAY festival; vacation; free day
HOLIEST most sacred
tx **HOLLAND** coarse linen
ch **HOLMIUM** metallic element
bt **HOLM-OAK** evergreen oak
HOLSTER leather pistol case
rl **HOLY-DAY** feast day; sacred day
HOMAGER a vassal
HOMBURG gentleman's hat
HOME-BOY of home town; (-street kid)
HOMELOT home-plot
zo **HOMELYN** spotted ray
HOMERIC of Homer; grandiose
HOMINID man (ancient and modern)
HOMONYM equivocation
HONESTY best political creed
HONEYED flattering; sweet
HONITON centre for lace
HONKING (motoring); (geese)
HONOURS of university degree; court cards
HOODING covering; blinding
HOODLUM hooligan; rowdy; mobster
HOOFING walking
HOOGAAR cutter rigger pleasure boat (Dutch)
HOOKING ensnaring; bending; (polo)
HOOKPIN floor nail
bt **HOOP-ASH** nettle-tree
HOOPING binding; encircling
HOOTING decrying; booing
HOP-BACK brewer's vessel
bt **HOPBIND HOPBINE**, hop stem
HOPEFUL eager; expectant; confident
mn **HOPEITE** hydrated zinc phosphate
zo **HOP-FLEA** a parasite
HOPKILN an oast
HOPLITE Greek heavy-armed soldier
HOP-OAST hop-kiln
ga, rw **HOPPERS** a game; gravel spreaders
HOPPING leaping; (netball fault)
HOPPLED hobbled; tethered
HOPPLES hobbles; rope shackles
HOP-POLE husbandry implement
bt **HOP-TREE** American shrub
bt **HOP-VINE** hopbind
HOP-YARD hop-garden
bt **HORDEIN HORDEUM**, barley genus
HORDING crowding; herding; amassing
HORIZON where sea meets sky
md **HORMONE** gland secretion
HORNBAR crossbar
zo **HORN-BUG** stag beetle
lw **HORNING** debtor's summons
HORNISH ungual
HORNITO volcanic smoke-hole
bt **HORN-NUT** a water-plant
zo **HORN-OWL** tufted owl
HORRENT bristling
HORRIFY appal; terrify; alarm; shock
rl **HOSANNA** beatific invocation
HOSEMAN fireman
HOSIERY stock of stockings
HOSPICE home for terminally ill patients
HOSTAGE personal pledge (prisoner)
HOSTESS woman giving hospitality
HOSTILE inimical; opposed; (-bid)
HOSTLER ostler
HOTFLUE drying room

HOT-FOOT in haste
HOT-HEAD impetuous; rash
HOTNESS fieriness; ardency; fervency
HOT-SPOT internal combustion
HOTSPUR impetuous
HOTTEST most vehement
HOT-TROD Border pursuit
HOT-WALL (fruit culture)
nt **HOUARIO** pleasure sail boat (Mediterranean)
zo **HOUBARA** ruffed bustard
HOUGHED hockled; hamstrung
HOUNDED pursued; harassed; dogged
HOUSAGE storage fee
ce **HOUSING** saddle-cloth; sheltering; protective cover (machinery)
HOVERED vacillated; lingered
HOVERER waverer; flutterer
HOWBEIT nevertheless
HOWDY-DO ado; fuss; commotion
HOWEVER notwithstanding
HOWLING dreary; lamenting; wailing
zo **HUANACO** **GUANACO**, llama (Andes)
HUDDLED heaped; piled; mixed
HUDDLER bungler; confused cogitator
HUELESS colourless
HUFFILY petulantly; angrily; irritably
HUFFING puffing; swelling; (draughts)
HUFFISH hectoring; furious
ck **HUFFKIN** hot larded bread bun (Eng.)
HUGGING clasping; embracing; necking
HUKILAU Polynesian party
HULKING big and clumsy
HULLING husking; shelling
HUMANLY ethically; rationally
HUMBLED abashed; humiliated
HUMBLER an abaser; mortifier
HUMBUZZ a bull-roarer
HUMDRUM commonplace; prosaic
rl **HUMERAL** Jewish shoulder-veil
pl **HUMERUS** shoulder bone
hd **HUMETTE** heraldic fesse
HUMIDLY damply; dankly
HUMMING bumming; droning
HUMMOCK hommock; hillock
HUMORAL vapourish
bt, br **HUMULIN** **HUMULUS**, hop extract
HUNCHED bunched; crooked
HUNDRED cantred; county division
HUNGRED hungry; famished
HUNKERS the hams; haunches
HUNTING blood sport; searching; chase
el **HUNTING** of thermostat temperature
HURDLED enclosed with a wattle fence
HURDLER racing jumper
HURDLES 10 obstacles to overcome per event
HURLING casting; flinging; pitching
HURLING ancient form of hockey
HURRIED scurried; accelerated; ran
HURRIED cursory; superficial
HURRIER hastener; quickener; urger
HURTFUL noxious; baleful; detrimental
HURTLED whizzed; crashed
HURTOIR a bumper
HUSBAND male spouse; breadwinner
HUSHABY lullaby
HUSHING repressing; calming
zo **HUSKIES** Eskimo dogs; toughs
HUSKING removing husks
HUSSIES worthless women
HUSSITE (John Huss); Moravian
HUSTING an assembly; a council
HUSTLED bustled; elbowed
HUSTLER rent boy
HUSWIFE hussif; housewife
HUTCHED cooped; boxed; confined
HUTMENT a hut
HUTTING temporary building
HYALINE glassy
mn **HYALITE** clear opal
HYALITH dense black Bohemian glass; dark sealing wax
HYALOID vitreous
HYDRANT fire-plug
ch **HYDRATE** hydride; hydrous
HYDRIAD water-nymph
HYDROID hydra-like
HYDROUS containing water
HYGEIAN hygienic
HYGIENE sanitary science
vt **HYGROMA** fluid-filled swelling
HYLOIST materialist
HYMNARY hymn-book
HYMNING lauding
HYMNIST hymn-writer
HYMNODY hymn-singing
HYODONT pig-toothed
nc **HYPERON** cosmic-ray particle
zo **HYPNODY** larval resting period
HYPNOID resembling sleep
HYPOGEA cellars; basement
zo **HYPOPUS** cheesemites
HYPPISH hippish; depressing
zo **HYPURAL** below the tail
zo **HYSTRIX** the porcupine

I

IAMBICS classic verse metre
IAMBIZE satirize; versify
IBERIAN Spanish and Portuguese
ICARIAN of Icarus; rash; adventurous
go **ICEBELT** region of ice
ICEBERG floating ice mass
zo **ICEBIRD** little auk
nt **ICEBOAT ICE-FOOT**, with sled hull
go **ICE-FALL ICE-FLOE**, calving of a glacier
ICE-FERN with frosty encrustations
ICE-HILL slalom; tobogganing slope
ICEPACK polar glácial barrier
ICEPAIL for chilling wine
ICE-RINK skating rink (natural ice)
mn **ICE-SPAR** ryacolite
ICHABOD calamity (Heb.)
ICHNITE fossil footprint
ICHTHYS (fish); Christian symbol
ICINESS chilled drinks
pl, pc **ICINESS** frigidity; personality
md **ICTERIC ICTERUS**, of jaundice
ICTINUS designer of the Parthenon
IDALIAN sacred to Venus
IDEALLY perfectly; for best result
IDIOTCY IDIOTIC, imbecility; witless; fatuous
IDOLISM IDOLIST, of fan club
IDOLIZE venerate; adore (as fan)
IDYLLIC pastoral; poetic
IGNEOUS volcanic in origin
IGNITED lit; kindled; inflamed
IGNITER primer; detonator
IGNITOR electrode of ignition
IGNOBLE dishonourable; low; base
IGNOBLY infamously; unworthily
IGNORED disregarded; neglected
IGOROTE Filipino
gl **IJOLITE** coarse-grained igneous rock
md **ILEITIS** ileum inflammation
ILL-BRED poorly brought up
ILLEGAL unlawful; illegitimate; illicit
ILLEISM too much 'he'
ILL-FAME of bad repute
ILLICIT forbidden; banned; prohibited
ILLNESS malady; disease; ailment
ILL-TIME mistime
ILL-TURN unkindly act
ILL-USED badly treated
ILL-WILL enmity; odium; spite; malice
mn **ILVAITE** hydrous iron silicate
IMAGERY fanciful concept
IMAGINE dream; think; suppose
IMAGING imagining
rl **IMAMATE** the parish of a Moslem Imam (priest)
IMBIBED IMBIBER, swallowed; toper
IMBOUND impound
bt **IMBREKE** houseleek
IMBROWN embrown; tan
IMBRUED drenched; soaked; stained
IMBRUTE to brutalize
IMBUING pervading; drenching
IMBURSE financing services in advance
IMITATE copy; ape; mimic; counterfeit
IMMENSE titanic; colossal; boundless
IMMERSE plunge into; souse; engross
IMMORAL against code of conduct; vicious
IMMURED shut up; imprisoned
IMPALED fenced in; speared through (executed)
IMPASSE deadlock; no escape from
IMPEACH charge with official misconduct
IMPEDED hindered; obstructed
IMPERIL endanger; hazard; jeopardize
IMPETUS momentum
zo **IMPEYAN** Indian pheasant
IMPFING crystallization technique
IMPIETY iniquity; profanity
IMPINGE to touch upon; infringe
IMPIOUS irreverent; ungodly
IMPLANT to graft; infuse; instil
IMPLATE to cover with metal; sheathe
IMPLIED understood; insinuated
IMPLORE entreat; crave; adjure
IMPORTS inward-bound trade goods
IMPOSED forced; misled
IMPOSER impostor; charlatan
IMPOUND confine; confiscate
IMPRESS stamp; mark; imprint respect
IMPREST cash from pressgang enrolment
IMPRINT impress; fix on the mind
IMPROVE armed; ameliorate; raise
cp **IMPULSE** stimulus; urge to action; short signal
IMPUTED attributed; implied
IMPUTER ascriber
IN-AND-IN overly inbred
INANELY vapidly; stupidly
INANITY fatuity; emptiness
INAPTLY untimely; unsuitably
INBEING inherence

INBOARD within the ship (including motor); oar handle
INBOUND inward bound; ball thrown into play (basketball)
INBREAK inburst
INBREED mate with relative
INBURST break in; irruption
INCENSE holy smoke; to enrage; anger
INCHEST embox; encase; (jewels)
INCHING moving gradually
INCHPIN deer's sweetbread
mu **INCIPIT** here begins (Lat.); identifying reference with first bars
INCISED cut; engraved
INCISOR cutting tooth
INCITED roused; fomented; egged
INCITER agitator; agent provocateur
INCIVIL uncivil; impolite
hd **INCLAVE INCLEAVE**, dovetail joint design
INCLINE gradient slope; prefer (opinion)
INCLUDE embody; comprise; contain
INCOMER new arrival; invader; infiltrator
pc, rl **INCUBUS** incumbrance; dead weight; intercourse with devil
rw **INCURVE** circumference of decreasing circle
ml **INCUSED** stamped, hammered; code
ch **INDICAN** a glucoside or acid
ma **INDICES** maths terms; plural of index
INDICIA indications
lw **INDITED INDICTED**, formal accusation
lw **INDITER** legal accuser; prosecuting party
pc **INDOLES INDOLENT**, disposition (anti-effort)
INDOORS within house
INDRAFT INDRAUGHT, inflow of manpower, wind power
ae, zo **INDRAWN** retracted (aircraft wheels during flight); (claws)
INDUCED impelled; prompted; effected
INDUCER persuader; instigator
INDUING ENDUING giving moral strength
INDULGE gratify; humour; pamper
INDWELL of aboriginal inhabitants
el **INEARTH** inter; bury; return contact
INEPTLY not professionally; pointlessly
ps **INERTIA** stationary state (overcome by movement)
INERTLY sluggishly; torpidly
INEXACT unexact; incorrect; faulty
INEYING inoculating; grafting; immunity
lw **INFANCY** stage of the child (birth–18)
INFANTA princess (Spain)
INFANTE prince (Spain – second son)
md **INFARCT** coronary thrombosis; blood stoppage
INFAUST cursed as was Dr Faustus
INFERNO INFERNAL, of hell, heating, destruction
rl **INFIDEL** non-adherent to majority faith
ga **INFIELD** land nearest mansion; (cricket)
INFIXED positioned; fastened; (radar)
md **INFLAME** excite; kindled; body infection sign
INFLATE expand; distend (balloon) (economy)
INFLECT vary pitch (linguistics) (curves)
INFLICT power causing others to suffer
rl **INFULAE** priestly badges
INFUSED inspired; instilled; inculcated
INFUSER a coffee machine; tea-maker
INGENUE naive girl
md **INGESTA** food
INGLOBE ENGLOBE, encircle; ensphere
INGOING direction entering; joining; enrolling
bd **INGOING** visible frame of door, window
INGRAIN root deeply; instil
bd, ar **INGRESS** entrance; portal
IN-GROUP influential, dominant elite
INHABIT dwell; occupy
INHALED breathed in
INHALER respirator
INHERIT acquire by bequest
cp **INHIBIT** ban; prohibit; restrain; warn
INHUMAN merciless; cruel
INHUMED interred; buried
cp **INITIAL** first steps; pre-sign; acronym
INJURED offended; marred; maltreated
INJURER abuser; impairer
INKATHA Zulu loyalist movement
INKHORN portable inkpot
INKLING hint; suggestion; innuendo

INKNEED knock-kneed
INKWELL ink-cup
INLACED enlaced; entwined
INLAWED cf. outlawed
INLAYER cabinet-maker; mosaic decorator
ck **INMEATS** offal; innards
ga **INNINGS** batting turn (baseball; cricket)
INNUENT of significance; allusion; slight of character
IN-PHASE (electrical)
cp **IN-PLANT** automatic data handling
lw **INQUEST** judicial inquiry
INQUIRE enquire; ask; interrogate
INQUIRY ENQUIRY, (information); investigation
cp **INQUIRY** access to programs
INSHOOT pitch to batter (baseball)
INSHORE close to the beach
INSIDER in the know; (-trading, dealing)
INSIGHT vision; perception
INSINEW innerve; invigorate
INSIPID tasteless; vapid; flat; tedious
INSOOTH in truth
INSPECT supervise; investigate
INSPIRE animate; inflame; imbue
INSTALL instal; instate; induct; invest
INSTANT current; urgent; prompt
INSTATE install; inaugurate; introduce
INSTEAD in place of; in lieu
INSULAR of islander; narrow-minded
md **INSULIN** (diabetes treatment)
INSURED risks covered against loss
INSURER insurance underwriter
INSWEPT narrowed
INTEGER whole; a whole number
INTENSE acute; vehement; extreme
INTERIM pause; provisional
md **INTERNE** inmate; boarder; (doctor)
mu **INTONED INTONER**, chanted; pitched
mu **INTRADA** entry; preliminary piece (It.)
mu, rl **INTROIT** opening anthem (mass)
INTRUDE trespass; butt in
md **INULASE** an enzyme
INURING enuring; habituating
INUTILE useless (Fr.)
INVADED violated; entered; occupied
INVADER aggressor; raider; attacker
INVALID null and void; infirm; weak
INVEIGH revile; reproach; upbraid
INVERSE reciprocal; inverted
hd **INVEXED** arched
INVIOUS impassable; untrodden
INVITED offered; requested; bid
INVITER welcomer; enticer; allurer
INVOICE sales note (commercial); bill
INVOKED adjured; implored; besought
INVOKER summoner; conjuror
INVOLVE implicate; entangle; embrace
INWARDS internally; to inside (direction)
tx **INWEAVE** of woven pattern (cloth)
INWHEEL circling tactics (military)
tx **INWOVEN** patterns intertwined (cloth)
md **IODIZED** treated with iodine
ch, ps **IONIZED** converted into ions
pc **IPSEITY** essence of the self
IRACUND irascible; petulant; angry
IRANIAN Persian
IRENICS pacifist theology
IRICISM Irish (Celtic) phrasing
ch **IRIDIUM** metallic element
IRIDIZE make iridescent
IRISHRY Irish people
IRKSOME tiresome; tedious
IRONIES unexpected contradictions
IRONING flattening; (-out faults)
IRONIST writes dramatic incongruity
ISAGOGE introduction; handbook
ch **ISATINE ISATIN**, indigo; woad colour
zo **ISCHIUM** pelvic bone in tetrapods
ISERINE titanic steel
bt **ISIDIUM** excrescence on lichen
ISLAMIC Mohammedan; Moslem
ISLEMAN islander
ISMATIC faddish; fond of isms
gl **ISOBASE** land-depression line
ISOBATH under-sea contour
ISODOMA form of masonry
ISODONT uniform teeth
bt **ISOETES** quill-worts
bt, zo **ISOGAMY** union of equal gametes
ISOGENY similar origin
ISOGRAM map line linking like places
ISOHYET (seasonal) rainfall map
ISOLATE insulate; segregate; dissociate
nc, ps **ISOMERS** of same weight molecules
mt **ISONEPH** equal-cloudiness line
mt **ISONETH** cloud map
ISONOMY equal rights
lw **ISONYMY** paronymy; equal
zo **ISOPODA** crustaceans
mn **ISOPYRE** impure opal
nc **ISOSPIN** quantum isotopic spin
mt **ISOTACH** equal wind-speed line

ISOTAXY polymerization characteristic
ISOTONE stable nucleus (atom)
ch **ISOTOPE** allied element
nc **ISOTRON** isotope-separating device
pr **ISOTYPE** picture writing
bc **ISOZYME** like/unlike enzyme form
ISRAELI Jew (Israel)
hd **ISSUANT** issuing
ISSUING emanating; proceeding
go **ISTHMUS** narrow land joining masses
ITACISM Greek egotism
ITALIAN of Italy
pr **ITALICS** sloping letters
ITCHING skin irritation; restless desires
ITEMIZE note particulars in detail
ITERACY ITERANT, repetition; repeating
ITERATE recapitulate an argument
pl, zo **IVORIED** with teeth or tusks
bt **IVY-BUSY** Bacchus's bush
md, vt **IXIODIC** infested with ticks
mn **IXOLITE** fossil resin

J

JABBING prodding; stabbing; injecting
zo **JACAMAR** tropical kingfisher
zo **JACCHUS** marmoset
bt, mn **JACINTH** hyacinth; a gem
zo, nt **JACKASS** donkey; bird; schooner
mn **JACKBIT** blast-hole drill end
zo **JACKDAW** a daw
JACKING lifting; abandoning; pulling off
ga **JACKPOT** poker; total prize; gambling
to, zo **JACKSAW** metal saw; goosander
nt **JACK-TAR** a sailor
JACOBIN French revolutionary
nm **JACOBUS** James (Latin form) coin
tx **JACONET** muslin
JADEDLY of tiredness; worn out
mn **JADEITE** a silicate
JADOUBE adjust chesspiece on square
JAGGERY palm sap sugar
JAGGING notching; carousing
JAGHIRE land revenues (Hindu)
JAHVIST scriptural writer
ga **JAI-ALAI** pelota court, festival
JAILING gaoling; imprisoning
JAINISM an Indian religion
md **JALAPIN** a purge
ga **JAMBONE** (cards on table, euchre)
tx **JAMDANI JAMDARI**, flowery figured muslin
tx **JAMEWAR** goat hair cloth
JAMMING rock climbing; becoming wedged
JAMMING interference in radio reception
JAMRACH animal mart
JAMSHID King of the genii
JANEITE fan of Jane Austen (writer)
JANGADA timber raft
JANGLED jingled; discordant sound
JANGLER wrangler; petty disputant
JANITOR doorkeeper; (caretaker)
JANIZAR JANISSARY, Turkish palace-guard
ck **JANNOCK BANNOCK**, scone-like cake
JANNOCK straightforward
JANTILY jauntily; airily; finically
JANTING jaunting; rambling
JANUARY 1st month
tx **JAP-SILK** a thin kind of silk
mn **JARGOON** a gem; zircon
JARKMAN begging letter writer
JARRING discordant; grating; clashing
bt, ck **JASMINE** fragrant flower; (tea)
mn **JASPERY JASPOID**, like jasper
JAUNTED took a pleasure trip
ga **JAVELIN** hurling-, spear field event
md **JAWBONE** Samson's lethal weapon
zo **JAW-FOOT** maxilliped
JAW-HOLE a sink
nt **JAW-ROPE** sailing tackle
JAY-WALK careless road-walking, crossing
JAZZING making garish imitations
JEALOUS envious; covetous; resentful
pl **JECORAL** pertaining to the liver
zo **JEDCOCK JUDCOCK**, jack snipe
JEERING derision; taunting; scoffing
md **JEJUNUM** digestive organ
JELLIED congealed
JELLIFY to become gelatinous
JEMIMAS elastic-sided boots; galoshes
lw **JEOFAIL** an oversight
JEOPARD to hazard; to endanger
JERKING JERK-OFF, spasmodic motion
ch **JERVINE** white hellebore alkaloid
bt **JESSAMY** jasmine; a dandy
hd **JESSANT** heraldic uprising
JESTFUL humorous; witty; sportive
JESTING joking; quipping
nt **JETTIED** with landing pier (harbour)

nt **JETTIED JUTTED** (-out); breakwater
JETTING spouting (fountains); emitting
mn **JEWELRY JEWELLERY**, gems, trinkets
bt **JEW'S-EAR** edible fungus
JEZEBEL a flagrant courtesan
JIBBING balking; shying
nt **JIB-BOOM** triangular bowsprit sail
JIB-DOOR flush (fire-proof) door
JIGAJOG JIGJOG, feet movement (horse)
md **JIGGERS** tropical foot complaint
JIGGING shaking (drinks); dancing
ma **JIGGING** (machines)
JIGGISH frivolous; frolicsome
JIGGLED joggled; wriggled
JILTING discarding; rejecting lovers
JIMCROW of black segregation (Amer.)
JIM-JAMS nervous apprehension
JINGLED jangled; tingled
JINGLET sleigh-bell clapper
JINKING dodging; twisting
el **JITTERS** fear; distortion
JITTERY nervy; agitated; dithery
JOBBERY financial cheating conspiracy
JOBBING doing small jobs
JOBLESS unemployed
JOCULAR jokey; jolly; cheerful
JOGGING shaking movement; stimulation
JOGGING slow running exercise
JOGGLED jostled; shook
bd **JOGGLES** stone jointing
JOG-TROT easy running pace
lw **JOINDER** united action
JOINERY carpentry
JOINING uniting; linking; connecting
JOINTED articulated
to **JOINTER** smoothing plane
JOINTLY in concert; unitedly
bd **JOISTED** floor laying; roof making
JOLLIER merrier; more genial
JOLLIFY celebrate; carouse
JOLLILY heartily; mirthfully
JOLLITY joviality; hilarity; frolic
JOLTING jerking; shaking
JONGLER a wandering minstrel
bt **JONQUIL** narcissus
JOOKERY jokery; trickery
JOTTING memorandum; reference note
JOUNCED shook; jolted
JOURNAL diary; newspaper; log
JOURNAL spindle bearing; gazette
JOURNEY jaunt; excursion; travel
JOUSTED tilted
JOYANCE gaiety; festivity
JOY-RIDE a trip for pleasure
J-STROKE to correct trim (kayaking)
JUBILEE (fiftieth) anniversary
rl **JUDAISE JUDAIST**, practises Judaism
rl **JUDAISM** Jewish doctrine and rites
rl **JUDAIZE** enforce Jewish religious rules
zo **JUDCOCK JEDCOCK**, jack snipe
JUDGING trying; deeming; estimating
JUFFERS square timber
JUGATED coupled; yoked; (con-) verbs
JUGGING imprisoning; stewing
JUGGINS a simpleton
JUGGLED manipulated; balanced; swindled
JUGGLER thrower and catcher; (performer)
pl **JUGULAR** main veins in the neck
zo **JUGULUM** breast/neck region in birds
ga **JUJITSU JUJUTSA**, Japanese defence art
mu **JUKE-BOX** a pay-record player
ga **JUKSKEI** horse-shoe throwing (S. Africa)
JUMBLED disordered; confused
JUMBLER a muddler
JUMPING leaping; bounding (equestrians)
JUMPING sudden change; (conclusions)
JUMP-OFF beginning point
JUNCATE JUNKET, picnic; spree (party)
JUNCOUS rush-like
bt **JUNIPER** coniferous tree; gin-berry
mn **JUNKING** coal-cutting process
JUNKING discarding as worthless
JUNKMAN second-hand dealer
JUPETTE short petticoat
JUPITER a planet
lw **JURALLY** lawfully; legally
JURY-BOX where jury sits
lw **JURY-MAN** juror
JUSSIVE imperative
JUSTICE equity; fairness; impartiality
JUSTIFY vindicate; exonerate; excuse
pr **JUSTIFY** adjust text
JUTTING projecting; beetling
JUVENAL JUVENILE, a youth
bt **JUWANZA** camel-thorn
zo **JYNGINE** a wryneck bird family

K

KABADDI 12-a-side field game (Far East)
rl KABBALA CABBALA, Jewish oral tradition
KACHINA doll (Amer. Indian)
ck KADAYIF baklava-type pastry (Turk.)
rl KADDISH Jewish funeral prayer
ck KAKAVIA fish soup; cooking pot (Gr.)
KAKODYL cacodyl; noisome liquid
KALENDS 1st day of Roman month
KALMUCH Calmuck; Mongolian
KAMERAD COMRADE! surrender call (German)
zo KAMICHI Brazilian tropical bird
KAMPONG (Malay) court-yard
KANAGAI lacquer work (Japan)
mn KANDITE kaolin minerals group
ml KANTHAL high-resistivity alloy
KANTIAN (Kant); Kantist
KANTISM a philosophy
KAPITIA lacquer (Sri Lanka)
zo KARAGAN Russian fox
rl KARAITE strict Jewish sect
bt KARATAS W. Indian pineapple
KARTING GOKART, primitive motor racing
mu KARYOKE CARYOKE, video-led pub singing
tx KASHGAR white silky Asian wool
KATHODE negative electrode
mn KEATITE synthetic silica form
KECKLED CACKLED, noise of hens (laying)
nt KEDGING warping; moving ships by rope
bt KEDLACK wild mustard
KEEKING PEEPING, prying; spying
KEELAGE harbour tax
nt, zo KEELING codling (codfish); heeling over
nt KEELMAN bargee (skipper or crew)
nt KEELSON keel-plate; (foundation plate)
KEENING wailing; mourning
KEEPING holding; maintaining; conforming
KEEP-NET live fish storage (angling)
KEEVING (fermentation)
zo KEITLOA S. African rhinoceros
KELKING beating; thrashing
KENNING range of vision; knowing
KENOSIS KENOTIC, denial of godhood
KENTISH of West Kent
ch KERASIN brain-substance cerebroside
md KERATIN (horn and hair)
ar KERFING curving bullnose stairs
rl KERMESS Dutch fair
KERNING granulating
KERNISH clownish
mn KERNITE sodium borate
zo KESTREL a falcon
ck KETCHUP a sauce (tomato)
md KETOSIS fat-metabolism toxaemia
KEYBOLT part of lock
KEYCOLD cold as a key
KEYED-UP tense with suspense
KEYHOLE orifice for key
mu KEYNOTE which sets tone
KEY-RING key holder
KEY-SEAT a groove
KEYWORD word showing topic discussed
cp KEYWORD retrieval; significant entry
rl KHALIFA KHALIF, CALIF, Mohammed's representative on earth
mt KHAMSIN hot wind of the Sahara
KHANATE khan's jurisdiction
KHEDDAH enclosure; (elephant hunting)
KHEDIVA wife of a khedive
KHEDIVE chancellor-viceroy of Egypt, 19th C.
rl KHOTBAH KHUTBAH, Moslem prayer and service
KIBBLED fine-ground in a hand mill
KIBBUTZ communal farm (Israel)
KIBITKA Russian vehicle
KICKING spurning; punting
ga KICK-OFF start of play (football)
KIDDIES kids; small youngsters
KIDDING bluffing; joking; jesting
bt KIDDING replanting riverbanks
zo KIDLING young kid-goat; infant
KIDSKIN goat leather
KIKUMON imperial crest of Japan
zo KILLDEE N. Amer. ring plover
nt KILLICK KILLOCK, small stone anchor
KILLING slaying; butchering; tiring
KILL-JOY a sourpuss; puritan
KILN-DRY desiccate; dry in kiln
el KILOVAR volt-ampères unit
tx KILTING wearing national costume (Sc.)
KINDEST most benevolent; helpful
KINDLED set ablaze; incited
KINDLER lighter; an igniter; pyromaniac
KINDRED related; kin; of groups
md KINESIA motion sickness

KINETIC force in motion
bt **KINETIN** plant growth substance
bt **KINGCUP** marsh marigold
KINGDOM monarchy; realm; dominion
zo **KINGLET** golden-crested wren
KING-PIN head of organization
KINKING twisting; looping
KINLESS without kindred
KINSHIP relationship
KINSMAN of same family; clan
KIP-SHOP bawdy house; brothel
KIPSKIN sleeping bag
KIRGHIZ of Central Asia (Turkic)
bt **KIRIMON KIKUMON**, a chrysanthemum
KIRTLED wearing a petticoat
KIRUNDI language of Burundi (Africa)
KISSING lips touching lovingly
KISSING bowl by jack; bussing
ck, nt **KITCHEN** cook-house; galley
ga **KITCHEN** shuffleboard (court area)
mu **KITHARA** ancient lyre (Gr.)
KLICKED CLICKED, fell in love; (doors)
gl **KLIPPEN** hill-top outliers
KLISMOS revived ancient chair (Gr.)
ck **KLODNIK** iced beetroot soup (Pol.)
KNABBED gnawed; bitten
KNACKER cat's meat purveyor; slaughterer of horses
KNAPPED snapped; nibbled
KNAPPER flint worker
KNAPPLE snap; nibble
KNARRED knotted
KNAVERY roguery; trickery; fraud
KNAVISH rascally; fraudulent
KNEADED massaged; mixed
KNEADER dough-mixer
md **KNEECAP** knee-pan
KNEELER prayer cushion; hassock
bd **KNEELER** pad-stone; kneestone; skew table, panel
mu **KNELLED** tolled (church bells)
KNESSET Israeli Parliament
KNIFING stabbing
tx **KNITTED** (garments) of wool stitch
KNITTED joined; contracted; contrived
KNITTLE a draw-thread
KNOBBED with protruberance
KNOBBLE small boss; handle
KNOBBLY irregular; with knobs on
KNOCKED buffeted; rapped; hit
KNOCKER door rapper; (waker up)
ga **KNOCK-ON** ball falling forward (football)
KNOCK-UP practice game (tennis)
mu **KNOLLED** pealed (church bells)
bt **KNOPPER** gall-nut
KNOTTED tied; kinked; entangled
KNOW-ALL a wiseacre
KNOW-HOW technical expertise
KNOWING canny; shrewd; astute
pl **KNUCKLE** clenched fist; (-duster)
KNUCKLE threaten; (-under); submit
bd **KNUCKLE** pinholes in a hinge
KOFTGAR metal inlayer (Hindu)
bt **KOLA-NUT** cola-nut
KOLKHOZ Soviet collective farm
pc **KOLYTIC** inhibitory processes, hindering (Gr.)
KOMATIC long Eskimo sledge
KORANIC (Koran)
KOUMISS fermented mare's milk
KOWTOWED made obeisance
KREATIN creatin; muscle constituent
KREMLIN citadel (Moscow)
KRIMMER grey lambskin fur
KRISHNA an incarnation of Vishnu
KRUPSIS a theological doctrine
KRYPTOL electrical resistant
ch **KRYPTON** gaseous element
mu **KUH-HORN** Alpine horn
bt **KUMQUAT** Chinese citron
KURBASH Arab hippo-hide whip
KURDISH (Kurd)
KURHAUS spa pavilion (Ger.)
KURSAAL the pump-room of a spa
KUWAITI native of Kuwait
KYANISE rot-proofing of timber
mn **KYANITE** aluminium silicate

L

LABARUM symbolical banner
LABIATE lip-like
LABROSE thick-lipped
bt **LACCATE** as if varnished
LACCINE (shellac)
LACEMAN lace-dealer
zo **LACERTA** lizard genus
bt, zo **LACINIA** leaf incision; maxilla lobe
LACK-ALL destitute
LACKING needing; wanting
LAC-LAKE lac dye
LACONIC concise; pithy; curt; terse
LACQUER varnish
LACTASE lactose-dissolving enzyme
ch **LACTATE** (lactine); to suckle; milk salt
ck **LACTEAL LACTEAN**, of milk
ch **LACTONE** hydroxy acid anhydride
LACTOSE LACTINE, a sugar in milk

bt **LACTUCA** lettuce genus
LACUNAE gaps; blanks; chasms
LACUNAL discontinuously
LACUNAR (panelled ceiling)
md **LADANUM** resinous extract
LADINOS Judeo-Spanish Sephardim
ck **LADLING** serving with deep-bowled spoon
zo **LADY-BUG** **LADY-FLY**, insect
zo **LADY-COW** **LADYBIRD**, red-cased beetle
LADY-DAY 25 March
LADYISH **LADYISM**, of affected gentility
LAETARE 4th Sunday in Lent
LAGGARD sluggard; lazy-bones
bd **LAGGING** dawdling; insulation cover
ga **LAGGING** order of play in billiards
LAGOTIC rabbit-eared
rl **LAICIZE** commit to laymen
LAIRAGE cattle depot yard
nt **LAKATOI** large sailing raft (Papua)
LAKELET pool; mere; pond
rl **LAKSHMI** wife of Vishnu
LALIQUE artistic glassware
LALLANS Lowland Scottish dialect
LALLING repetition of a sound
rl **LAMAISM** **LAMAIST**, of Tibetan Buddhism
LAMBADA fast erotic dance (Brazil)
LAMB-ALE shearing feast
LAMBENT softy radiant
me **LAMBERT** unit of brightness
LAMBING giving birth
zo **LAMBKIN** baby lamb
LAMBOYS armoured kilts
zo **LAMELLA** thin plate or scale
pl **LAMETER** **LAMIGER**, a cripple
LAMETTA metal foil
LAMINAL **LAMINAR**, in plate form
LAMMING thrashing
ch **LAMPATE** a salt
zo **LAMPERN** **LAMPREY**, eel-fish
zo **LAMP-FLY** **FIRE-FLY**, illuminated flies
LAMPING ultraviolet detection
LAMPION fairy lamp
LAMP-LIT artificially illuminated
LAMPOON a satirical article
zo **LAMPREY** eel-fish
LANATED woolly
mu **LANCERS** cavalry; a dance
LANCING piercing; cutting
go **LAND-ICE** fresh water; inland, ice
LANDING disembarking; floor; (fish)
mu **LANDLER** Tyrolean waltz; folk song (Ger., Austrian)
LANDMAN country dweller
LANDTAG Federal parliament (Ger.)
LAND-TAX type of impost
zo **LANGAHA** snake (Madagascar)
mn **LANGITE** copper sulphate
me **LANGLEY** unit of radiation
LANGREL chain-shot
hd **LANGUED** heraldic tongue
LANGUET tongue-shaped
LANGUID **LANGUOR**, listless; lassitude
LANIARY slaughter-house
LANIARY canine tooth
LANIATE tear in pieces
LANKIER taller and thinner
md **LANOLIN** wool grease; ointment
bt **LANTANA** verbena; herb
LANTERN hand lamp
LANYARD **LANIARD**, sailor's uniform rope
LAO-THAI language of Laos
LAOTIAN native of Laos
gl **LAPILLI** volcanic stones; cinders
LAPPING covering exposed copper (over-)
LAPPING how cats and dogs drink
LAPPISH of Lapland; Saami
ck **LAPSANG** for afternoon tea (China)
LAPSING slipping; failing
LAPUTAN visionary
zo **LAPWING** peewit
LAPWORK overlapping work
lw **LARCENY** theft, pilfering
bt **LARCHES** conifers
LARDING smearing with lard
LARD-OIL a lubricant
ck **LARDOON** **LARDON**, strip of bacon
LARGELY greatly; abundantly
LARGESSE bounty; alms; gift
LARGEST most capacious; biggest
LARGISH somewhat extensive
mu **LARIGOT** 6-f organ pitch
LARIKIN **LARRIKIN**, hooligan (Australia)
LARKING having fun; pranking
LARMIER drip-stone; corona
mn **LARNITE** orthosilicate of calcium
zo **LARVATE** larval; masked
ck **LASAGNE** flat pasta dish (It.)
LASHING whipping; scourging; upbraiding
LASHKAR **LASCAR**, N. W. Indian tribe
eg **LASKETS** **GASKETS**, anti-leak sealing
LASSOED **LASSOES**, steer-catching noose rope
LASTAGE ballast; fishing dues
LASTING abiding; enduring; durable
tx **LASTING** strong twill cloth
bt **LATAKIA** Syrian tobacco
LATCHED fastened; locked; secured

LATCHES door bolts; lock systems
LATCHET shoe-fastening
zo **LATCHET** sapphirine gurnet
zo **LATEBRA** an egg cavity
LATENCE suspended activity
LATENCY force in suspense
LATERAL side by side
cp **-LATERAL** beside; parallel; (bi-) joint
rl **LATERAN** papal palace; church (-councils)
cr **LATHING** lathe workmanship; carving
LATRANT barking
LATRINE camp privy; toilet
LATROBE a form of stove
cp **LATTICE** grid form; network
LATVIAN Lettish; of Latvia
LAUDING extolling; praising
LAUGHED expressed amusement (-at)
LAUGHER game won by a wide margin
LAUNDER wash; ore trough
LAUNDRY the wash
bt **LAURELS** bay leaf crowns of victory
mn **LAURITE** a sulphide
LAUWINE **LAVINE**, avalanche
LAVOLTA an old dance
zo **LAVROCK** **LARK**, a song bird
lw **LAW-BOOK** case book (common law)
LAW CALF ditto bound in calf leather
LAWLESS wild; rebellious; disorderly
lw **LAW-LORD** House of Lords' judge
LAW-LORE in a lawyer's library
lw **LAW-SUIT** case in court
md **LAXATOR** a muscle
LAXNESS slackness; negligence
mo **LAYBACK** rock-climbing technique
nt **LAY-DAYS** harbour days; cargo lading
LAYERED stratified
LAYETTE infant's outfit
LAYLAND pasture land
bt **LAYLOCK** lilac
nt **LAY-LORD** civil lord
LAYOUTS aerial somersaults (skiing)
LAZARET hospital
md **LAZARLY** of Lazarus the leper; leprous
LAZIEST most sluggish; idlest
LAZY-BED potato-bed
L-DRIVER learner driver
ch, ps **LEACHED** elements filtered from a mix
LEADING metal roof or cover
LEADING high-ranking; famous; guiding
mu **LEAD-OFF** opening; overture; departure
ga **LEAD-OUT** well-positioned player
LEAFAGE foliage; boscage
bt **LEAF-BED** gemma
LEAF-FAT fat in layers
LEAFING leaf-growth; (gold-)
pt **LEAFING** floating of metal particles
pr **LEAFLET** **PAMPHLET**, hand-out; advert
ga **LEAGUED** **LEAGUER**, placed in groups
LEAKAGE divulgence (secrets); liquid loss
LEAKING liquid oozing out, escaping
LEANDER Hellespont swimmer (Gr.)
LEANEST thinnest; lankiest
LEANING penchant; bias; relying
LEAPING jumping; springing
LEARNED erudite; scholarly
LEARNER pupil; tyro; student
LEASHED bound; under control
LEASING falsehood; letting
LEASOWE a pasture
LEATHER tanned animal skin; to thrash
lw **LEAVING** resigning; departing; donating
LECTERN **LETTERN**, reading desk
LECTION a reading
LECTUAL necessitating bed-rest
LECTURE reproof; rebuke; discourse
md **LEECHED** healed
bt, ck **LEECHEE** **LYCHEE**, Chinese fruit
nt **LEEFANG** jib sheet
nv **LEEMOST** most leeward
LEERILY wideawake; sly; fly
LEERING ogling
nt **LEE-SIDE** **LEE-GAGE**, sheltered side
nv **LEE-TIDE** tide with the wind
nv **LEEWARD** down wind
LEFT-ARM cricket
LEGALLY legitimately; licitly
lw **LEGATEE** inheritor of legacy; bequest
LEG-BAIL (absconding)
LEGGATT thatcher's wooden mallet
mu **LEGGERO** light and easy (It.)
LEGGERS barge-pushers
LEGGING a gaiter
LEGGISM black-leggism
zo **LEGHORN** straw hat; fowl
LEGIBLE readable
LEGIBLY clearly written
LEG-IRON ankle to wall fetter
lw **LEGITIM** Bairn's Part
LEGLESS apodal
LEG-PULL a draw; a joke; a hoax
ga **LEG-SIDE** right-handed cricketer's bat side

ga **LEG-SLIP** fielding position (cricket)
LEGTRAP (cricket)
bt **LEGUMEN** vegetable casein; pulse
LEISTER fishing spear (Ice.)
LEISURE restful ease
LEMMATA logical premises
zo **LEMMING** Arctic rodent
LEMNIAN (Lemnos)
nm **LEMPIRA** coin, Honduras
LEMURES spirits in the Roman household
LENDING loaning; advancing
LENGTHY extended; protracted
LENIENT mild; clement; merciful
md **LENTIGO** a rash; freckle
bt **LENTISK** mastic tree
LENTOID lens-shaped
LENTOUS viscous; tenacious
zo **LEONERO** puma-hunting dogs
as **LEONIDS** meteor shower
LEONINE like a lion
zo **LEOPARD LIBBARD**, the spotted tree cat
LEOTARD one-piece, stretch costume
md **LEPROMA** leprous swelling
md **LEPROSE** scurfy
md **LEPROSY LEPROUS**, a disease
bt **LEPTOME** phloem elements
LESBIAN female homosexual
LETCHED percolated; filtered
LET-DOWN an avoidable failure
LETHEAN oblivious
LETTERN LECTERN, reading desk
LETTING preventing; hindering
LETTISH Latvian; Lettic
bt **LETTUCE** salad plant
md **LEUCINE** (decomposition)
mn **LEUCITE** volcanic rock
md **LEUCOMA** wall-eye
LEUCOUS albino
md **LEVATOR** a muscle
mt **LEVECHE** dry S. W. wind in Spain
LEVELER leveller
LEVELLY evenly; horizontally
LEVERED raised; lifted
zo **LEVERET** young hare
rl **LEVITIC** of Levites (Hebrew priests)
LEVYING collecting; exacting
LEXICAL alphabetically arranged
LEXICON dictionary
LIAISON co-ordination; intrigue
bt **LIANOID** ground-rooted climbing plant
gl **LIASSIC** geological formation
LIBERAL bounteous; generous
LIBERTY freedom; emancipation
LIBRARY collection of books (Public-)
cp **LIBRARY** software; routes
LIBRATE to balance; poise; oscillate
LICENCE permission; excess; warrant
LICENSE to permit; allow; authorize
zo **LICH-OWL SCREECH OWL**, night bird of prey
rl **LICH-WAY LYCH-WAY**, funeral path to church
LICITLY lawfully; legally; legitimately
LICKING a thrashing; a beating
LICKING sucking from the tongue; tasting
LIE-ABED a sluggard
LIFT-BOY LIFTMAN, elevator operator
LIFTING raising; elevating; stealing (shop-)
md **LIGATED** bandaged
LIGHTED lit; ignited; illumined
LIGHTEN enlighten; alleviate; ease
LIGHTER barge; brighter; igniter
LIGHTLY buoyantly; airily; joyfully
LIGNIFY become woody
bt **LIGNINE** woody fibre
mn **LIGNITE** brown coal
LIGNOSE cellulose
LIGROIN paraffin
bt **LIGULAR** strap-shaped
LIKABLE attractive; lovable; amiable
LIKENED resembled; compared
bt **LILY-PAD** water-lily leaf
ma **LIMAÇON** heart-shaped curve
LIMBATE bordered; edged
LIMBING dismembering
zo **LIMBOUS** overlapping
tx **LIMBRIC** plain-weave cotton cloth
LIME-LIT illuminated
LIME-PIT limestone quarry
LIMINAL almost conscious
LIMITED restricted; circumscribed
LIMITED liability company, Ltd
LIMITER restraining factor; agent; signal
LIMNING water-colour painting
mn **LIMNITE** iron ore
md **LIMOSIS** abnormal hunger
LIMPING halting; walking lamely
zo **LIMPKIN** tropical crane
md **LINCTUS** soothing syrup
LINEAGE ancestry; extraction; race
LINEATE lined; (paper) (graphs)
ga **LINEMAN** railwayman; marker (football)
ga **LINE-OUT** for throw-in (football)
LINGUAL of the tongue, language
LINKAGE cross-cultural mergings
ma **LINKAGE** in mechanics, and mathematics

pl **LINKAGE** genetics (genes and chromosomes)
ps **LINKAGE** analog; magnetic flux in coils
LINKBOY relay torchbearer (Olympic)
LINKING connecting; joining; merging
ga **LINKMAN** go-between; midfield (football)
bt **LINNEAN** floral classification
pt **LINOXYN** dried film of linseed oil
zo **LINSANG** Indian civet cat; fox
bt **LINSEED** flax-seed
hd **LIONCEL** small lion
zo **LION-CUB** baby lion
zo **LIONESS** lady lion
LIONISM LIONIZE, to build up a person's importance
LIP-BORN hearsay; not genuine
ch, pl **LIPIDIC** of fats, waxes in cells
LIPPING uttering impudent remarks
LIQUEFY melt to liquid state
LIQUEUR a distilled cordial
bt **LIRELLA** ridged apothecium
LISPING speaking with a lisp
LISSOME svelte; lissom; agile
LISTFUL attentive; heedful
LISTING tabulation; choosing
LITERAL verbatim; prosaic exactness
ch **LITHATE** (lithium)
LITHELY actively; pliantly
LITHIUM metallic element; salts
ch, pc **LITHIUM** anti-psychotic drugs
LITHOID stone-like
LITOTES (figure of speech)
LITTERY covered with litter
LITUATE forked
rl **LITURGE** leader in public worship
rl **LITURGY** ritual
LIVABLE habitable
LIVENED cheered up; enlivened
bt **LIVE-OAK** American oak
LIVERED lily-livered; cowardly
LLANERO S. American plain dweller
LOADING cargo; lading; charging
tc **LOADING** distance versus power loss
LOAFING loitering; idling
LOAMING earthing
LOANING lending; advancing
LOATHED hated; detested
LOATHER an abhorrer
LOATHLY reluctant; unwilling; hateful
LOBBIED sought votes
LOBBIES vestibules (in Parliament)
ga **LOBBING** pitching; throwing a ball
LOBCOCK lubber; clumsy fellow
pl, zo **LOBELET** small protrusion; leg
bt **LOBELIA** a flower genus
zo **LOBIPED** having extended feet
zo **LOBSTER** a decapod (10 feet) crustacean
LOBULAR LOBULUS, lobed (ears) etc.
zo **LOBWORM LUGWORM**, sea-bait
LOCALLY in the vicinity
LOCANDA rough Italian doss-house
LOCATED placed; fixed; found
LOCATOR finder
LOCKAGE canal dues; water losses
LOCKIAN (Locke's philosophy)
LOCKING grappling; securing
LOCKIST philosopher
md **LOCK-JAW** tetanus
LOCK-MAN in charge of lockgates (canals)
lw **LOCK-MAN** Under-Sheriff (Isle of Man)
LOCK-OUT exclusion of employees
cp, el **LOCK-OUT** activation of hardware unit
tx. **LOCKRAM** coarse linen
LOCULAR cell-like
LOCULUS small cell
bt **LOCUSTA** carob-tree
LODGING abode; accommodation
LOFTIER of greater eminence
LOFTILY arrogantly
LOFTING raising; lifting
ac **LOGATOM** artificial testing word
LOG-BOOK motorcar documentation
nt **LOG-BOOK** official daily record
nt **LOG-CHIP LOG-SHIP**, speed recorder
ga **LOGGATS** (ninepins)
nt **LOGGING** recording
LOG-HEAD a blockhead
LOG-HEAP log-pile; wood-pile
LOGICAL reasonable; deductive; sensible
cp **LOGICAL** entities as appearing to user
nt **LOG-LINE** speed-measuring line
LOGOGEN exact words for clear speech
nt **LOG-REEL** for winding in log-line
LOG-ROLL pulling strings (influence)
bt, pt **LOGWOOD** red dye; openfire wood
rl **LOLLARD** religious sect
LOLLING lounging; (tongue)
bt **LOMARIA** ferns
LOMBARD a banker; a money lender
LONG-AGO remote in time
LONGBOW for medieval archery
LONGEST most protracted
ga **LONG-HOP** (cricket)
LONGING eager desire; yearning

LONGISH somewhat long
ga **LONG-LEG** (cricket)
pt **LONG-OIL** high-oil-content varnish
LONG-RUN record amount (theatre shows)
LOOBILY lubberly; clumsily
LOOKING watching; scanning; searching for
LOOKING with threatening eyes
LOOKOUT duty seaman; watcher; sentinel
LOOKOUT panorama point; gazebo
LOOK-SAY word recognition
LOOK-SEE glance; hasty visit
LOOMING coming into sight, approaching
zo **LOONING** cry of the loon bird
zo **LOOPERS** (moth caterpillars)
LOOPING circling; knotting; bypassing
LOOPING coloured thread in glass
LOOSELY vaguely; diffusely; slackly
LOOSING relaxing; releasing
LOOTING pillaging; stealing; (war)
LOPPING amputating; curtailing; (trees)
LORDING bossing others
LORELEI a Rhine maiden; rock
LORGNON an eye-glass (magnifying)
LORIMER LORINER, bridle; harness maker
LOTTERY draw (chance); (lots)
LOTTING allocating; cataloguing
LOUDEST showiest; noisiest
ck **LOUKOUM LOKUM**, Turkish delight
LOUNGED reclined; lolled
LOUNGER flâneur; loafer; idler
LOURING threatening; menacing
LOUSILY despicably; uselessly; badly
LOUTISH clumsy; uncouth; oaflike
LOVABLE amiable; charming; winsome
LOVE-ALL no score (tennis)
bt **LOVEMAN** a plant
LOVERED having a lover
LOW-BORN of humble birth
LOW-BRED poorly reared
LOWBROW unintellectual
LOWDOWN rascally
LOWERED threatened; frowned
au **LOW-GEAR** low speed machine
LOWLAND netherland
LOW-LIFE in poverty; degradation; crude
LOWLILY humbly; meekly
LOWNESS dejection; depression
LOW-TECH absence of technology
LOW-TIDE when tide is out
LOXOTIC oblique; distorted
LOYALLY faithfully; devotedly
LOYALTY fealty; fidelity
hd **LOZENGE** a rhomb; diamond-shaped
LOZENGE a throat pastille
LOZENGY pertaining to above
LUBBARD LUBBER, clumsy fellow
zo **LUCANUS** stag beetle (insect)
ar **LUCARNE LUTHERN**, dormer window
LUCENCE LUCENCY brightness; radiance
ag **LUCERNE** clover for fodder
LUCIDLY clearly; simply; exactly (style)
LUCIFER Satan; a match
LUCIGEN powerful oil lamp
LUCKIER more fortunate
LUCKILY happily; fortunately
nt **LUFFING** turning toward wind
LUGGAGE baggage; impedimenta
LUGGING tugging; dragging; hauling
LUGMARK earmark
nt **LUGSAIL** 4-cornered sail
zo **LUGWORM** lob-worm
LUK-CHIN hybrid Chinese
LULLABY soporific song
LULLING soothing; waning; subsiding
md **LUMBAGO** muscular rheumatism
md **LUMINAL** narcotic drug
LUMPIER bumpier; more awkward
LUMPING accepting without satisfaction
LUMPING mixing together for sales; lots
LUMPING laying ready-made rail track
LUMPISH dull; heavy
LUMP-SUM cash down payment
LUNATIC maniac; crazy; insane
ar **LUNETTE** half-moon; small window
LUNETTE bastion; watch glass; ornament
LUNULAR crescent (moon) shaped
bt, br **LUPULIN LUPULUS**, extract of hop plant
LURCHED pitched; lurked; shifted
zo **LURCHER** a lurker; dog
LURKING skulking; awaiting
LUSHING swilling; toping
LUSTFUL lascivious
LUSTIER stronger; sturdier
LUSTILY vigorously
LUSTING desirous
LUSTRAL (purification)
LUSTRUM period of 5 years
LUTEOUS fulvous; tawny
LUTETIA old name for Paris

LUTHERN lucarne; dormer-window
mu **LUTHIER** lutemaker (and viols) (Fr.)
zo **LUTRINE** (otter)
LUXATED dislocated
LYCHNIC (vespers, Greek church)
bt **LYCHNIS** campion plants
bt **LYCOPOD** a moss
zo **LYCOSID** wolf spider
LYDDITE a high explosive
md **LYING-IN** maternity confinement
LYINGLY falsely; mendaciously
pt **LYMNATO** spray-gun decorating technique
zo **LYNCEAN** lynx-eyed; cat's night-sight
LYNCHED victim of mob-law
LYNCHET unploughed strip
LYRATED lyre-shaped
mu **LYRICAL** musically poetic

M

MACABRE gruesome; grisly
zo **MACACUS** baboon
MACADAM road material (asphalt)
zo **MACAQUE** monkey
bt **MACCHIA MAQUIS**, scrub; Resistance (Fr.)
pt **MACCHIA** first sketch of painting (It.)
MACE-ALE spiced ale
mn **MACERAL** elementary coal constituent
MACHAIR low-lying ground (Gael.)
MACHETE West Indian knife
MACHINE complicated device
MACKITE asbestos plaster
tx **MACRAME** corded fringe; lace (Arab)
md, pc **MACRONT** post-schizogony stage
nt **MACSHIP** merchant ship (helicopter carrier)
MACULAE dark sun-spots
MACULAR of body tissue spots
MAD-BRED passionately conceived
MADDEST craziest
MADDING raging; distracted
MADEIRA a wine; a cake
MADLING a lunatic
MADNESS mania; delirium; frenzy
MADONNA Our Lady
zo **MADOQUA** Abyssinian antelope
mn **MADRIER** mine-plank
bt **MADRONA MADRONO**, evergreen tree (USA)
bt **MADWEED** black horehound
MADWORT mugwort; cure for rabies
mu **MAESTRO** eminent conductor (orchestra)
MAESTRO N.W. wind (Mediterranean)
MAFFICK rejoice riotously
MAFFLED muddle-headed
MAGALOG magazine-mail-catalogue
MAGENTA purple aniline dye
MAGGOTY grub-ridden (inedible meat)
MAGICAL talismanic; supernatural
MAGINOT French defensive line
MAGNATE wealthy, influential businessman
MAGNETO a generator in a car
el **MAGNETO-** recording disc; tape (-phone)
MAGNIFY praise; enlarge; augment
bt **MAHALEB** cherry (Arab.)
MAHATMA adept in esoteric Buddhism
rl **MAHDISM** restoration of faith (Islam)
rl **MAHDIST** of Mahdism; Mahdi supporter
ga **MAHJONG** Chinese game
MAHOUND Moslem evil spirit
zo **MAHSEER** Indian river fish
MAIL-BAG post sack
MAIL-CAR postal van
MAILING posting
MAIL-VAN post vehicle
MAIMING mutilating; crippling
lw **MAINOUR** stolen property
nt **MAINTOP** part of rigging
MAISTER maestro; master
bt **MAIZENA** maize-meal
MAJESTY grandeur; magnificence
MAJORAT primogeniture (Fr.)
bt **MALACCA** cane
md **MALACIA** pathological tissue softening
mn **MALACON** variety of zircon
MALAISE unease; disquiet
md **MALARIA** fever
MALAYAN of Malaysia; citizen; language
MALEFIC maleficent; baneful; noxious
MALICHO villainy
MALISON a curse; malediction
zo **MALLARD** wild duck
vt **MALLEIN** glanders inoculum
md **MALLEUS** ear bone
MALLING MAULING, biting; injuring
MALMSEY canary wine
ch **MALTASE** an enzyme (glucose-splitting)
MALTESE native or language of Malta

br **MALTING** brewing
br **MALTMAN** maltster
ch **MALTOSE** sugar-extracting enzyme
ck **MALTOSE** barley starch sugar
pl **MAMELON MAMMARY**, rounded; glands
zo **MAMMATE** breasted mammals
MAMMOCK shapeless mass; (mangle flat)
MAMMOSE like a bosom
pl **MAMMOTH** elephantine; colossal
zo **MAMMOTH** hairy, extinct elephants
pl **MAMMULA** small protuberance; nipple
MANACLE handcuff; shackle; fetter
MANAGED contrived; administered
MANAGER controller; director
zo **MANAKIN MANIKIN**, small bird; dwarf
zo **MANATEE** sea-cow; dugong
ck **MANCHET** small French loaf
MANCHOO MANCHU, Chinese dynasty
rl **MANDALA** mystic cosmos symbol
MANDATE trust territory; authorization
bt **MANDIOC MANIHOC**, cassava (tapioca) shrub
mu **MANDOLA** mandora; guitar
MANDREL lathe-head
MANDRIL mandrel; spindle
ae **MANETON** heavy gripping pinch-bolt
zo **MANGABY** monkey (Madagascar)
MANGLED laundered; spoiled by bad work
MANGLER indifferent carver (worker)
bt **MANGOLD** mangel-wurzel
MANHOLE underground-channel exit
MANHOOD man's ideal
me **MAN-HOUR** unit of work
MAN-HUNT search for fugitive
bt **MANIHOC MANIHOT, MANDIOC**, cassava shrub
nm **MANILIO** arm-ring; copper coin
MANILLA cheroot; cigar
ga **MANILLE** a card value
lw **MANIPLE** handful; scarf
MANITOU Great Spirit
MANKIND blot on creation
MANLIKE as a man
mn, nt **MAN-LOCK** air lock for pressure changes
MAN-MADE hand-made
MANNING providing a crew
MANNISH masculine
bt **MANNITE** manna-sugar
ch **MANNOSE** a hexose
nt **MAN-ROPE** handrail
ar **MANSARD** two-slope roof
MANSION residence; house
MANTLED cloaked; disguised
MANTLET cloak; testudo
MAN-TRAP snare for trespassers
MANUALE case for papyrus rolled text
MANUMIT free from slavery
ag **MANURED** land spread with droppings
ag **MANURER** cultivator (machine)
MANX-CAT tailless, from Isle of Man
MAPPERY MAPPING, surveying; delineating
MAPPIST cartographer artist
ar, rl **MAQSURA** VIP's concealment in mosques
zo **MARABOU** adjutant stork
zo **MARACAN** parrot
mu **MARACAS** Cuban instrument
MARATHI Mahratta language
ar, ck **MARBLED** veneer grain (marble, cheese)
MARBLER stone-slab decorator
ga **MARBLES** friezes in stone; balls game
mu **MARCATO** as indicated previously (It.)
MARCHED movement of troops on foot
MARCHEN folk-stories
MARCHER border-defender
go **MARCHES** borderland territories
md **MAREMMA** marsh; malaria
mn **MARGODE** bluish stone
bt **MARGOSA** Indian tree
zo **MARIKIN** marmoset
mu **MARIMBA** kind of xylophone
nt **MARINER** sailor; seafarer
zo **MARIPUT** civet cat
pc **MARITAL** of husband and wife relationship
zo **MARKHOR** wild goat
MARKING branding; labelling
MARLINE rope
nt **MARLING** binding
mn **MARLITE** variety of marl
MARLPIT clay-pit
zo **MARMOSE** opossum
MARPLOT spoil-sport
MARQUEE large tent
MARQUIS French nobleman
MARRANO Jew converted to Christianity
MARRIED spliced; wedded
MARRING spoiling; interrupting
MARROWY full of marrow
MARSALA a light wine
MARSHAL arrange; harbinger; officer

MARTEXT careless preacher
MARTIAL warlike; military
MARTINI rifle; cocktail
mn **MARTITE** variety of haematite
hd, zo **MARTLET** house martin (bird)
MARXIAN according to Marx's theories
MARXISM MARXIST, the idea; communist
MARYBUD marigold
MASCARA eye shading (cosmetics)
MASCLED net-like
hd **MASCULE MASCULY,** lozenge-shaped
ck **MASHING** rendering mushy
MASHLIN MASHLUM, mixed grain
ck **MASH-TUB** where malt processed
MASKING disguising; hiding; revels
cp **MASKING** bit pattern
MASONIC of freemasons; fraternity
bd, ar **MASONRY** stone work (construction)
md **MASSAGE** kneading body and muscles
cp **MASSAGE** manipulate figures, data
md **MASSEUR MASSEUSE,** physiotherapist; osteopath
MASSING assembling; accumulating; heaping
MASSIVE bulky; weighty; ponderous
MASSORA Biblical references
MASTABA Egyptian tomb
MASTERY skill; supremacy
MASTFUL full of beech-nuts
bt **MASTICH** gum; mastic
zo **MASTIFF** large strong dog
nt **MASTING** system of masts
md **MASTOID** nipple-shaped
md **MASTOID** bone behind ear
MATADOR bull-fighter
MATADOR a domino game
MATCHED tallied; harmonized
MATCHES contests; lucifers
to **MATCHET MACHETE,** cutlass
MATELOT a sailor (Fr.)
MATERIA as substance
MATINAL MATINEE, early theatre show
MATRASS chemical retort
bt **MAT-REED** reed-mace
cp **MATRICE MATRIX,** (dieplate); key
nt **MATROSS** assistant gunner
md **MATTERY** purulent; pus discharge
MATTING floor cover; silver technique
to **MATTOCK** pick-adze for roots and stiff ground
MATTOID cogenital idiot
MATURED experienced; ripened; payable

MAUDLIN drunk and silly
ga **MAULING** tearing flesh; attacking (rugby)
MAUNDER move idly; mutter drivel
rl **MAURIST** a Benedictine monk
MAWASHI silk cummerbund belt of sumo wrestler
MAWKISH squeamish
bt **MAW-SEED** poppy-seed
zo **MAW-WORM** tape-worm
pl **MAXILLA** upper jaw bone
MAXIMAL greatest; upper limit
MAXIMED proverbial
MAXIMUM greatest quantity, value etc.
MAXIMUS senior (of a group)
el **MAXWELL** unit of magnetic flux
zo **MAY-BIRD** wood-thrush
MAY-DAY *M'aider* International 'Help' Call
MAY-DAY 1 May, Spring Labour day
bt **MAY-DUKE** cherry
MAY-GAME May-day sport
MAY-LADY May-queen
bt **MAY-LILY** spring flower
MAY-MORN start of May celebrations
MAYORAL of the town mayor; official
MAY-POLE ribboned for folk dancing
MAY-TIME of hawthorn and spring revels
bt **MAY-WEED** camomile flower
bt **MAZAGAN** bean
MAZARIN deep blue
MAZDEAN godlike
MAZEFUL intricate, labyrinthine
mu **MAZURKA** Polish country dance
ga **MAZURKA** ice-skating jump
MAZZARD skull; cherry
MEADOWY pasturable
MEAL-ARK meal-chest
MEALMAN grain merchant
MEANDER aimless wandering river course
MEANING purport; import; signifying
md **MEASLED** spotted
md **MEASLES** spotty diseases; tapeworms
ma, pr **MEASURE** unit of amount or dimension
MEASURE estimate; regulate; mark out
zo **MEAT-FLY** blow-fly or other parasite
MEAT-TEA consommé of meat base
MEAT-TUB for preserved or pickled meat

MECCANO do-it-yourself construction kit
MECHLIN lace
md **MECONIC** (opium)
rl **MEDALET** small medal
MEDDLED interfered; muddled
MEDDLER busybody
MEDIACY dispute-solving process
mu **MEDIANT** a tone
MEDIATE negotiate a settlement (claims)
md **MEDICAL** concerning doctors' treatments
md **MEDINAL** soporific drug
pl **MEDIOLA** bone in cochlea (ear)
md **MEDULLA** marrow; pith; inner core of organ
zo **MEDUSAE** Gorgons; hydrozoans
MEDUSAN (petrifying, of gorgons)
zo **MEERKAT** mongoose (S. Africa)
MEETING encounter; conference; (sport)
cp **MEGABIT** one million binary digits
MEGAERA one of the Furies
me **MEGA-ERG** a million ergs
MEGAFOG multiple foghorn
zo **MEGAPOD** having large feet
MEGARON ancient Gr. house
MEGASSE megass; cane residue
me **MEGATON** measure of explosive force
vt **MEGRIMS** giddiness; staggers
MEIOSIS hyperbole; cell division in gametes
MEISSEN (Dresden china)
MELANGE medley; farrago; jumble
MELANIC black
md **MELANIN** black skin pigment
md **MELASMA** black spots
bt **MELILOT** sweet-scented clover
mu **MELISMA** melodic ornamentation
bt **MELISSA** herb; balm
mn **MELLITE** honey-stone
MELLOWY mellow; soft; unctuous
mu **MELODIC** tuneful; harmonious
MELROSE honey of roses
MELTING from solid to liquid; fusion
pl **MEMBRAL** concerning limbs, body
MEMENTO keepsake; souvenir
MENACED alarmed; frightened
MENACER threatener; intimidator
MENDING repairing; amending
MEN-FOLK in contrast to women
pl **MENINGE** of brain, spinal membranes
MENIVER miniver; white fur
ch **MENTHOL** peppermint camphor
MENTION remark; state; cite; declare
fr **MERANTI** Malayan hardwood
MERCERY haberdashery
MERCIES small fortunate circumstances
as **MERCURY** planet; Hermes (messenger)
ch, cp **MERCURY** quicksilver; acoustic delay
MERGING absorbing; blending; uniting
cy **MERISIS** cell-division size increase
MERITED deserved; earned; incurred
zo, ck **MERLING** the whiting (fish)
MERMAID sea woman with fish tail
MERRIER more cheerful; festive
MERRILY joyously; blithely; happily
MESHING netting
mt **MESOBAR** region of normal atmospheric pressure
MESODIC (intermediate system)
MESOPIC night vision
bt **MESOPOD** central-stipe fungus fruit
zo **MESOTIC** paired cartilage in birds
MESSAGE despatch; missive; errand
tc **MESSAGE** information to be transmitted
rl **MESSIAH** **MESSIAS**, heavenly saviour
MESSING muddling; communal feeding
ck **MESS-TIN** a soldier's canteen food-dish
MESTINO **MESTIZO**, half-caste Sp. Indian
zo **METAGON** cytoplasmic particle; amoeba
zo **METAZOA** multicellular animals
ch, mn **METHANE** marsh-gas; firedamp
pm **METHOIN** anticonvulsant chemical
METOCHE an architectural interval
as **METONIC** lunar cycle of 19 years
METONYM attribute representing a thing
METOPIC superficial
md **METOPON** opium-based drug
zo **METOTIC** behind auditory vesicle
zo **METOVUM** nutrition-surrounded ovum
METRICS versification; mensuration
ma **METRIFY** metricate; decimalize
METRIST a ballad-monger
METTLED high-spirited
MEWLING squalling
MEXICAN citizen of Mexico
MEXICAN wave, ripples in crowds; statistics
bt **MEZQUIT** **MESQUIT**, a Mexican tree
md **MIASMAL** airborne infection
MIAUING mewing
MIAULED caterwauled

MICELLA foundation structure of cell walls
ch **MICELLE** aggregate of molecules
MICHING pilfering
md **MICROBE** germ; bacillus
me **MICROHM** electrical resistance
MIDDEST middlemost
MIDGARD cf. Asgard (Scand.)
MID-HOUR crossword combination
MIDI-BUS medium-sized bus
MID-IRON golf-club
MIDLAND some way from the coast
MID-LIFE halfway to death
MIDMOST middlemost; central
MID-NOON midday
MIDRASH Jewish commentary
md **MIDRIFF** diaphragm; garment
nt **MIDSHIP** middle of ship
bd **MIDSPAN** between beam support
MIDWIFE birth assistant
mn **MIEMITE** limestone
MIGRANT nomad; wandering; roving
MIGRATE annual transit of birds (reindeer)
MILDEST calmest; blandest
MILDEWY mouldy; musty; rusty
MILEAGE distance travelled
bt **MILFOIL** the yarrow
md **MILIARY** a fever
MILITIA citizen army
MILK-BAR snack bar
MILKMAN milk distributor
MILK-RUN routine round
MILKSOP effeminate fellow
MILL-COG water-wheel tooth
MILL-DAM mill reservoir
MILLIAD 1000 years
me **MILLIER** a thousand kilos (2204 lbs)
MILLING struggling; grinding
MILLION 1,000,000
nm **MILLREA MILLREIS**, Port., Brazilian coins
MILTING spawning
MILVINE (kite family)
MIMESIS MIMETIC, MIMICRY, imitative miming
bt **MIMULUS** musk plant
rl **MINARET** prayer tower (mosque)
MINCING grinding; affecting; -words
MINDFUL heedful; wary; attentive
MINDING attending to; objecting to
pc **MINDSET** imprinted, accepted attitudes
mn **MINERAL** planetary substance
rl **MINERVA** Pallas Athene (Gr.)
MINETTE biotite-orthoclase lamprophyre
MINEVER MINIVER, plain white fur
MINGLED joined; associated; jumbled
MINGLER a mixer; blender; compound
MINIATE to paint red
MINIBUS bus for a dozen or so
MINICAB private hired car
MINIKIN small pin; pet; favourite
MINIMAL MINIMUS, smallest (youngest son)
MINIMUM least quantity
MINIOUS vermilion
MINIVER plain white fur
zo **MINORCA** a fowl
rl **MINSTER** cathedral; monastery church
MINTAGE coinage; mint dues
MINTING coining; inventing
MINTMAN coiner
ma **MINUEND** number to be diminished; subtraction
MINUTED briefly recorded
MINUTIA detailed detail (trivial)
MIOCENE geological period
MIOLNIR Thor's hammer
MIRACLE prodigy; supernatural event
MIRADOR balcony; viewpoint (Sp.)
ck **MIRATON** beef/onion stew (Fr.)
MIRBANE (bitter almonds)
MIRIFIC marvellous; wondrous
MISBORN of illegitimate, improper origin
MISCALL revile; with abusive title
MISCAST actor in unsuitable role
MISCITE misquote; mislead
MISCOPY reproduce falsely
ga **MISCUED** wrong aim (snooker; billiards)
MISDATE put wrong date on
MISDEAL faulty card distribution
MISDEED fault; crime; trespass
MISDEEM judge wrongly
MISDOER delinquent; malefactor
MISDONE ill-done
MISDRAW draft badly
MISERLY parsimonious; niggardly
MISFALL mishap; misadventure
cp **MISFEED** hopper fault (punched cards)
MISFIRE fail to go off; (firearm)
MISGAVE filled with doubt
MISGIVE mistrust; doubt
rl **MISHNAH MISHNIC**, Jewish oral law
MISKICK (football) misdirections
MISLAID temporarily lost
MISLEAD dupe; delude; hoodwink
MISNAME misterm; miscall
MISPLAY foozle

MISRATE rate erroneously
MISREAD read incorrectly
MISRULE anarchy; chaos; riot
MISSAID incorrectly stated
MISS-HIT cricket
MISSILE bullet; projectile
MISSING lost; lacking; absent
MISSION trust; errand; embassy
MISSISH girlish; affected
MISSIVE missile; letter; message
MISSUIT not harmonize
MISTAKE err; error; fault; oversight
MISTELL misstate; misrepresent
MISTILY hazily; obscurely
MISTIME judge occasion poorly
mt **MISTRAL** a cold N. or N.W. wind (Fr.)
MISUSED abused; squandered
rl **MITHRAS** **MITHRA**, Persian/Roman god
MITOGEN **MITOSIS**, somatic cell division
MITRATE mitre-shaped
cr **MITRING** carpenters' wood joint
MIXABLE can be blended or united
MIXEDLY with mixed feelings
MIXED-UP confused; disordered; hotch-potch
MIXTION gold-leaf fixative
MIXTURE combination formula; rigid blend
mt **MIZZLED** mist-and-drizzled
rl **MJOLNIR** **MIOLNIR**, Thor's hammer (Norse)
MOABITE a tribe (in modern Jordan)
MOANFUL mournful; grievous
MOANING deploring; repining
MOBBING crowding around
MOBBISH tumultuous; disorderly
MOBILES free-hanging ornaments
MOB-RULE lynch law (Mafia dominance)
MOBSMAN well-dressed swindler
MOBSTER gangster; hoodlum; ruffian
MOCKADO ancient woollen fabric; tawdry
MOCKERY scorn; derision; ridicule
MOCKING taunting; jeering
mn **MOCK-ORE** a zinc ore
MOCK-SUN a parhelion
MODALLY conditionally
MODESTY chastity; propriety
MODICUM small quantity
mu **MODINHAR** Portuguese popular song
MODISTE dressmaker
MODULAR **MODULUS**, factor of a function
bd, el **MODULOR** proportional units (buildings)
zo **MODWALL** bee-eater (bird)
ga **MOEBIUS** aerial somersault (skiing)
MOELLON masonry-filling
MOFETTE (earth-fissures)
MOHICAN Algonquin Indian
mn **MOHSITE** titanite of iron
nm **MOIDORE** Portuguese gold coin
MOILING toiling; drudging
MOINEAU bastion (Fr.)
MOISTEN damp; add water
mn **MOLASSE** sandstone
zo **MOLE-RAT** a rodent
nt **MOLETTA** **MULETTA**, fishing boat (Port.)
MOLIMEN strenuous effort
MOLLIFY pacify; alleviate; soothe
MOLLINE emollient base
zo **MOLLUSC** (snail; cuttlefish; octopus)
MOLOSSI (3 long syllables)
MOMENTA masses having velocity
ch **MONACID** with one hydroxyl group
ch, cp **MONADIC** single operand process
MONARCH ruler of Kingdom, Empire
zo **MONAXON** of one axis only
MONEPIC comprising one word
zo **MONERAL** **MONERON**, protozoans
MONERGY saving money and energy
MONEYED rich; wealthy; opulent
MONEYER coiner
MONGREL mixed breed
MONIKER nickname
MONITOR overseer; mentor; adviser
nt **MONITOR** big-gun naval craft
cp **MONITOR** radio deviation censor; nozzle
rl **MONKERY** **MONKISH**, monastic; monk-like
zo **MONKEYS** non-human primates; scamps
MONKISH monastic
MONOCLE eye-glass
MONODIC monotonous and mournful
zo **MONODON** narwhal
bt **MONOGYN** type of plant
ch **MONOMER** single-molecule substance
MONONYM **MONOMIAL**, single-term name
MONOPOD single-foot chair; table (Roman)
md **MONOTIC** affecting 1 ear only
MONSOON **MAVSIM**, Indian rainy season
MONSTER abnormal; horrifying; huge (ogre)

MONTAGE film editing
MONTANT fencing term
MONTERO horseman-cap (Sp.)
MONTHLY menses
MONTOIR mounting-stone (Fr.)
zo **MONTURE** saddle-horse (Fr.); mount
MOOCHED loitered; mouched
MOOCHER thief; aimless wanderer
MOODILY morosely; capriciously
lw **MOOKTAR** Indian lawyer
MOOLVEE doctor of Moslem law
zo **MOONEYE** lake fish
MOONING day-dreaming
MOONISH fickle; variable
MOONLIT visible in moonlight
MOON-MAD moonstruck
MOON-SET the setting of the moon
MOORAGE anchorage
zo **MOORHEN** water-hen
MOORING boat tie-up
ar, rl **MOORISH MORESQUE**, Arab décor (Morocco)
MOOTING suggesting; debating
lw **MOOTMEN** debating law students
MOPPING dabbing; wiping
gl **MORAINE** glacial debris; pile-up
pc **MORALLY** of right, ethic conduct
MORASSY marshy; swampy; boggy
mu **MORBIDO** of gloom; disease; dire situation (It.)
MORDANT biting; caustic; (style)
mu **MORDENT** a trill
bt, ck **MORELLO** sour red cherry
mu **MORENDO** dying; slowing down (It.)
ar **MORESCO MORESQUE**, Moorish art design
bt **MORICHE** American palm
bt **MORINGA** Malay tree
MORISCO Moorish; moresco
MORLING dead sheep or its wool
zo **MORMOPS** repulsive-looking bats
MORNING dayspring; daybreak
MOROCCO goatskin leather
MOROSIS feeble-mindedness
md **MORPHEW** scurf
MORPHIA opium extract
bl **MORPHIC** form and structure; shapes
MORRION open helmet
MORSURE the act of biting
pc **MORTIDO** death wish; energy (Thanatos)
MORTIFY putrefy; fester; corrupt
MORTIFY bodily self-denial; humiliate
cr **MORTISE** and tenon joint; door lock
lw, rl **MOSAISM MOSAIC**, of Moses
ck **MOSELLE MOSEL**, light wine (Germany)
MOTHERY MOTHERLY, maternally; protective
MOTTLED variegated; spotted
pt **MOTTLER** brush for graining, marbling
MOTTOES pithy maxims
MOUCHER skulker
zo **MOUFLON** wild sheep
MOUILLE liquid tone
MOULAGE casting footprints
MOULDED kneaded; shaped
MOULDER metal-caster; crumble
MOUNDED banked; fortified
MOUNTED on horseback; ascended; framed
MOUNTER climber
MOURNED grieved; keened; wailed
MOURNER bewailer
ck **MOUSAKA** moussaká; Gr. dish
MOUSING cat-work
MOUTHED orated; chewed
MOUTHER stump-orator; ranter
MOVABLE portable; mobile
ag **MOW-BURN** slash-burn (field clearance)
ar **MOZARAB** Christianized Arab (Sp.) art
rl **MOZETTA** cardinal's cape
MUCKING dung-raking; seeking scandal
md **MUD-BATH** skin, health treatment
nt **MUD-BOAT** dredger
MUD-CART night-soil pick-up service
MUD-CONE mud volcano
MUDDIED fouled; dirtied; soiled
MUDDING smearing with mud
MUDDLED misused; confused; fuddled
MUDDLER mixer; fuddler
zo **MUD-FISH** the bow-fin
MUD-FLAT low-tide bank
MUD-HOLE waterside residence
MUD-LARK to play in/with mud
mn **MUDLINE** water/slurry division line
MUD-SCOW (dredging)
cr **MUD-SILL** tide mud level; soleplate
MUD-WALL soil embankment
bt **MUD-WORT** aquatic plant
rl **MUEDDIN MUEZZIN**, Moslem prayer-caller
MUFFING botching; fluffing; bungling
MUFFLED wrapped; deadened; dulled
tx **MUFFLER** silencer; scarf
MUFFLON MOUFLON, wild sheep

MUGGARD sullen; displeased
zo **MUGGENT** wild freshwater duck
MUGGING ruffianly street assault
MUGGINS simpleton; a juggins
MUGGISH damp and warm
MUGIENT bellowing like cattle
bt **MUGWORT** wormwood plant
MUGWUMP independent politician; idiot
MULATTO with black and white parentage
ag **MULCHED** applied compost dressing on soil
MULCTED fined; swindled
nt **MULETTA MULETTO**, fishing boat (Port.)
MULETTE Portuguese sailing vessel
bt **MULLEIN** yellow plant
MULLING warming and spicing
MULLION munnion; uprt. window bar
mn **MULLITE** aluminium silicate
MULLOCK rubbish; dirt
MULTURE grain grinding
MUMBLED muttered
MUMBLER indistinct articulator
nc **MU-MESON** elementary particle
MUMMERY MUMMING, pantomiming; merrymaking
MUMMIED embalmed; caused to shrivel
MUMMIFY make a mummy
MUMMOCK ragged coat
MUMPING mockery; begging tricks
MUMPISH dull; sullen
MUNCHED crunched; chewed
MUNCHER a masticator
MUNDANE worldly; secular; temporal
MUNDIFY cleanse; purify
bt **MUNJEET** Siberian madder
MUNNION a mullion
MUNTING a door upright
zo **MUNTJAK** barking deer
ar **MUQARNA** stalactite decoration; arabesque
zo **MUREXAN MURICES**, Tyrian purple (shellfish) dye
ch **MURIATE** hydrochloric
MURKIER more overcast
MURKILY duskily; luridly; darkly
vt **MURRAIN** cattle disease
mn **MURRINE** fluorspar
MURRION morion; helmet
bt **MUSCARI** grape hyacinth
mn **MUSCITE** fossil moss
MUSCLED muscular
bt **MUSCOID** moss-like
MUSEFUL pensive; meditative
MUSETTE refreshments haversack (cyclists)
MUSHING dog-sleighing
MUSICAL tuneful; harmonious
zo **MUSIMON** moufflon
MUSK-BAG perfume sachet
zo **MUSK-CAT** civet cat
MUSKILY like musk
zo **MUSK-RAT** the musquash
MUSROLE nose-band of a bridle
zo **MUSTANG** wild horse
bt **MUSTARD** sinapis
zo **MUSTELA** weasel
MUSTILY sourly; acridly; frowsily
MUSTING growing mouldy and rank
MUTABLE changeful; fickle; unstable
MUTABLY variably; inconstantly
md **MUTAGEN** mutation producer
MUTANDA things to be altered
MUTTONY resembling mutton
MUZZILY confusedly; dizzily
MUZZLED forcibly restrained
md **MYALGIA** cramp
md **MYALGIC** tense; stiff
MYALISM W. Ind. magic cult
zo **MYARIAN** (mussels)
bt **MYCELIA** mushroom spawn
zo **MYCETES** howler monkeys
md **MYCOSIS MYCOTIC**, fungoid growth (infection)
MYELOID marrow-like
md **MYELOMA** bone-marrow malignancy
vt **MYIASIS** parasitism by fly lavae
zo **MYLODON** extinct sloth
md **MYOCELE** muscle hernia
zo **MYOCOEL** coelomic space in myotome
zo **MYOCYTE** ectoplasm layer of protozoa
zo **MYODOME** eye-muscle chamber
MYOGRAM (muscular movement)
md **MYOLOGY** (muscles)
zo **MYOMERE** somite muscles
zo **MYONEME** ectoplasm fibril in protozoa
zo **MYOTOME** muscle merome
md **MYOTOMY** dissection
MYOXINE pertaining to doormice
MYRINGA ear-drum
bt **MYRRHIC MYRRH**, labdanum and resin scent
MYRRHIN MYRRHOL, extract and oil
MYSTERY a craft; enigma
MYSTICS a sect
MYSTIFY nonplus; perplex; bewilder
MYTHIST a recorder of legends
zo **MYTILUS** mollusc genus; mussels
zo **MYXOPOD** a protozoan

N

NABBING grabbing; seizing
NACARAT bright orange-red colour
NACELLE body of aeroplane
NACODAH Arab sea-captain
mn **NACRITE** pearl-like
mn **NACRITE** clay mineral
NACROUS pearly
md **NAEVOID** (birthmark)
NAEVOUS freckled
NAFFING make oneself a fool
NAGGING incessant scolding
NAIADES water nymphs
NAILERY nail factory
NAILING spiking; fastening
NAIL-ROD nail material
NAIVELY artlessly; candidly
NAIVETE ingenuousness
NAIVETY unaffected simplicity
NAKEDLY uncovered; starkly
zo **NAMAQUA** African dove
zo **NANDINE** civet cat (W. Africa)
tx **NANKEEN** buff-coloured cloth (Nankin)
NAOLOGY study of church buildings
mn **NAPHTHA** rock-oil
NAPLESS threadbare
NAPPING dozing; snoozing; unalert
ga **NAPPING** horse's refusal to perform
pc **NARCISM** **NARCISSISM**, self-love (Gr.)
md **NARCOMA** narcotics coma
md **NARCOUS** **NARCOSE**, stupor-inducing
bt **NARDINE** spikenard
NARGILE Eastern pipe; hubble-bubble
NARRATE chronicle; describe; report
rl **NARTHEX** church porch with lean-to roof
zo **NARWHAL** sea-unicorn; whale
zo **NASALIS** proboscis monkey
NASALLY through the nose
mu **NASARDE** organ stop
NASCENT natal; originating; incipient
md **NASITIS** nasal inflammation
NASTIER more disagreeable
NASTILY offensively; nauseously
NATTERY peevish; captious
NATTIER French blue; smarter
NATTILY neatly; sprucely
NATURAL an idiot; normal; inherent
NATURED temperamentally disposed
NATUREL unadulterated
NAUGHTY forward; perverse
NAUPEGY ship-building
zo **NAUPLII** crustaceans
nt **NAUTICS** art of navigation
zo **NAUTILI** cephalopods with chambered shells
NAVARCH an admiral (Greek)
NAVARHO aircraft navigation system
ck **NAVARIN** mutton/vegetable stew
bt **NAVETTE** rape plant
NAVVIES labourers; canal diggers
NAVY-CUT rope-bound tobacco sliced
NAYWORD by-word; watch-word
NAZIISM German national socialism
NEAD-END show end
md **NEALOGY** embryology
NEAREST closest; stingiest
NEARING approaching; drawing nigh
NEATERY place to buy meat (17th c.)
NEATEST sprucest; tidiest; trimmest
NEATNIK anti-beatnik
NEBULAE gaseous matter
NEBULAR cloudy; vague; hazy
ar **NECKING** embracing; an annulet
NECKLET small necklace
NECKTIE cravat
bt **NECTARY** honey-gland
NEEDFUL essential; vital; requisite
NEEDIER rather worse off
NEEDILY necessitously
NEEDING wanting; lacking
NEEDLED pierced; sown; embroidered
NEEDLED persuaded against will
NEEZING **NEESING**, sneezing
NEGATED denied; mollified
NEGATER computer inverter
el **NEGATON** negative electron
cp **NEGATOR** NOT element; reverse binary
lw **NEGATUR** it is denied
NEGLECT disregard; omission
NEGLIGE loose attire; negligee
NEGRESS **NEGROID**, woman
NEGRITO pygmy (Polynesia)
NEGROID negro-type
bt **NEGUNDO** box-elder
zo **NEIGHED** whinnied call (of horse)
NEITHER not either; not the one
bt **NELUMBO** water-lily; lotus
ps **NEMATIC** with parallel orientation
NEMESIC retributive; final judgement
NEMESIS goddess of vengeance
NEMORAL arboreal
gl **NEOCENE** geological epoch
gl **NEOCENE** rock formation
mn **NEOLITE** silicate of aluminium
NEOLITH 'stone-ager' slang epithet
NEOLOGY (new terms); rationalism

NEONATE reborn; immaturity; new ideas
NEORAMA interior view of building
zo **NEOTENY** larval-character retention
zo **NEOTYPE** evolution within species
NEOZOIC geological system
md **NEPHRIA** Bright's disease
pl **NEPHRIC** of the kidney
pl **NEPHRON** excretory unit in kidney
NEPOTIC favouring the family
as **NEPTUNE** sea-god; planet
mn **NEREITE** fossil centipede
nt **NERITIC** of shallow coastal waters
bt **NERVATE** veined
md **NERVINE** nerve tonic
NERVING summoning resolution
NERVOSE having nerves
NERVOUS sensitive; timid; fearful; tense
pl **NERVOUS** neural system; neuronal
bt **NERVULE** vein in leaf
zo **NERVURE** vein in insect wing
NESIOTE living on an island
NEST-EGG cash savings
NESTING nidification (birds); home-making
cp **NESTING** instructional loops
NESTLED cherished; lay close
NESTLER a snuggler; cuddler
ga **NETBALL** 7-a-side; like basketball
ga **NET-CORD** divides the tennis court
NETSUKE Japanese fastening
NETTING wall or curtain of net; trap
NETTLED stung; fretted; irritated
NETTLER a provoker
tx **NETWORK** mesh; cord; fabric; curtain
NETWORK social, influential contacts
cp, tc **NETWORK** chain series; data transmission
md **NEURINE** nerve-matter
NEUROID nerve-like
md **NEUROMA** tumour
NEURONE nerve cell
NEUROSE veined
zo **NEURULA** stage of embryo development
ec **NEUSTON** water-surface animals
NEUTRAL unbiased; indifferent
nc **NEUTRON** uncharged particle
mt **NEVADOS** mountain wind, Andes, S. America
NEW-BORN just hatched
NEWCOME recently arrived
NEW-LAID fresh eggs
NEW-MADE novel; fresh; neoteric
NEWNESS novelty
NEWSBOY paper seller
NEWSMAN reporter
gl **NIAGARA** waterfall; torrent (N. America)
NIBBLED lightly chewed
NIBBLER dainty feeder
NIBLICK a golf club
NICKING stealing; notching
NICTATE wink
NIDGING stone dressing
bt **NIGELLA** love-in-a-mist
NIGGARD a miser; covetous; sparing
NIGGLED trifled
NIGGLER fuss-pot
NIGHTED benighted
NIGHTIE nightdress; robe de nuit
NIGHTLY every evening
mn **NIGRINE** an ore of titanium
NIGRITE insulating material
NILLING unwilling
NILOTIC of the river Nile
NIMBLER more agile; quicker; swifter
NIMIETY excessiveness
ml **NIMONIC** high-temperature-work alloy
ga **NINE-PIN** skittle
NIOBEAN (Niobe); lachrymose; tearful
ch **NIOBIUM** metallic element
bt **NIPBONE** herb comfrey
to, zo, pl **NIPPERS** pincers; crabs' claws; youth
NIPPIER quicker; more agile
NIPPING biting; pinching; fleeing
NIRVANA peace in unity with creation
rl **NIRVANA** liberation from desires
NITENCY effort; brightness
NITHING poltroon; idiot
ch **NITRATE NITRIDE**, nitrogen salts
ch **NITRIFY** convert to nitre
ch **NITRILE** alkyl cyanide
ch **NITROUS NITROSE**, of nitrogen
rl **NJORTHR** a Vanir (Norse god)
NOACHIC of Noah's time
NOBBLED stole; tampered with a horse
NOBBLER confederate; doper
pc **NOBLESS** noblesse oblige; nobility attitudes
NOBLEST most illustrious
NO-CLAIM (insurance)
zo **NOCTUID** nocturnal moth
zo **NOCTULE** bat (night-flyer)
mu, rl **NOCTURN** psalm service; (-al) of night
NOCUOUS harmful; noxious; baleful
NODATED knotted

NODDING (auction); unwary; nutation
as **NODICAL** (ecliptic point)
NODULAR (intersections)
NODULED knotted
NODULUS small knop
NOEMICS intellectual science
NOETIAN a dogmatic theologian
NOGGING brick and wood-work
NOISILY rowdily; loudly; uproariously
NOISING bruiting; rumouring
NOISOME noysome; disgusting
NOMADIC wandering; migratory
NOMANCY divining; (chiro-) healing
NOMARCH frontier province governor, Gr.
NOMBLES entrails of deer
NOMBRIL escutcheon centre
NOMINAL titular; ostensible
NOMINEE prospective candidate
NON-ACID alkali
NON-AGED under 18; minor (USA)
NONAGON nine-sided figure
NONPLUS perplex; astound; bewilder
NON-SKID steady grip tyres
NONSTOP uninterrupted (cinema); (chatter)
bt **NONSUCH** fodder plant
lw **NON-SUIT** no case
NON-TERM vacation
NONUPLE 9-fold
pc **NOOLOGY** psychology
NOONDAY 12 o'clock midday
NOONING siesta
NOOSING lassoing; snaring
NORFOLK loose jacket; turkey
cp **NOR-GATE** logic with binary digits
NORIMON Japanese palanquin
NOR-LAND north country
mt **NORTHER** north wind (USA)
NORWICH school of painting
NOSE-BAG horse's lunchbox
NOSEGAY bouquet
NOSE-LED befooled
pl **NOSTRIL** nose passage
NOSTRUM panacea; medicine; (Mare-) sea
NOTABLE remarkable; memorable
NOTABLY conspicuously; notoriously
zo **NOTAEUM** bird's back
NOTAGEA Australian region
NOTANDA memoranda
NOTCHED inscribed; scored; nicked
NOTCHEL to repudiate
NOTCHER marker; scorer
ce **NOTCHER** steel flange stripper (machine)
NOTEDLY markedly; particularly
NOTELET small note
mu **NOTE-ROW TONE-ROW**, 12-note octave
NOTHING nihil; zero; naught
NOTHOUS spurious; bastard
tx **NO-THROW** barely twisted silk thread
ga **NO-THROW** foul (football, cricket)
NOTICED observed; heeded; marked
NOTITIA a catalogue
NOUMENA opp. to phenomena
NOURISH cherish; foster; encourage
NOVALIA reclaimed land
NOVELLA NOVELETTE, short novel, story
NOVELTY new; unusual; knick-knack
NOWHERE address unknown
NOXIOUS hurtful; nocuous; baneful
bl, nc **NUCLEAL NUCLEAR**, of nucleus
bl, nc **NUCLEIC NUCLEIN**, central cell; (-protein)
nc **NUCLEON** proton; neutron; isospin
nc **NUCLEOR** core; kernel; centre
bl, nc **NUCLEUS** essence of being; comet-head
ch, nc **NUCLIDE** atom isotope of nucleus
NUDGING elbowing; jostling
NULLIFY annul; rescind; revoke; repeal
NULLITY invalidity; noughtiness
ma, rl **NUMBERS** amounts; biblical book
NUMBING deadening; paralysing
NUMBLES entrails of deer
ma **NUMERAL NUMERIC**, digit; figure; character
NUMMARY numismatics
NUNATAK projecting rock (Eskimo)
NUN-BUOY conical buoy
NUNDINE market day (Roman)
NUNHOOD nunation
rl **NUNNERY** convent
NUNNISH sisterly; conventual
NUPTIAL conjugal; bridal; hymeneal
NURAGHE Sardinian fort
NURLING milling an edge
NURSERY infants' room; care centre
bt, fr **NURSERY** plants; tree-propagation area
ga **NURSERY** handicap; 2-year old; horserace
NURSING fostering; developing
NURTURE upbringing; sustenance
bt **NUT-BUSH** hazel
bt **NUT-GALL** dyestuff source
NUT-HOOK crooked stick
ck **NUT-LOAF NUT-MEAT**, vegetarian rissole/meal
ck **NUT-MEAL** nut-flour rissole

bt **NUT-PINE** food-producing tree
NUTTING gathering nuts
bt **NUT-TREE** hazel
bt **NUT-WOOD** panel wood
NUZZLED nestled; cuddled
zo **NYCTALA** genus of owls
NYMPHAL NYMPHLY, NYMPHIC, maiden-like

O

OAFLIKE doltish; stupid; idiotic
bt **OAK-BARK** could be cork
bt **OAK-FERN** 3-branched polypody
bt **OAK-GALL** tree excrescence
bt **OAK-LEAF** colonel's decoration
bt **OAKLING** young oak
OARFISH ribbon-fish
nt **OARLOCK** rowlock
nt, ga **OARSMAN** sculler; (rowing) (racing)
ck **OAT-CAKE** Scottish delicacy
ck **OAT-MALT** malt from oats
ck **OATMEAL** meal from oats (porridge) (Sc.)
OBCONIC funnel-shaped
OBDUCED drawn over; covered
OBDURED hardened; inured
OBELION part of skull
OBELISK monolith; memorial pillar
pr **OBELISK** printer's dagger (†)
OBELIZE mark as spurious
OBESITY corpulence; fatness
OBEYING submitting; complying
OBITUAL funereal
OBLIGED favoured; forced to; constrained
OBLIGEE under bond to recompense
OBLIGER favourer; lender; helper
lw **OBLIGOR** bond giver
OBLIQUE askew; crooked; aslant
OBLOQUY calumny; censure; odium
OBOLARY poverty-stricken
OBOVATE OBOVOID, egg-shaped
OBSCENE repulsive; lewd; indecent
OBSCURE abstruse; indistinct; hidden
OBSEQUY funeral ceremony etc.
OBSERVE mark; notice; espy; remark
OBTRUDE thrust; disturb; interfere
nm **OBVERSE** head side (coin); truth
OBVIATE get round; preclude
OBVIOUS evident; patent; palpable
mu **OCARINA** Sicilian keyless oval flute
md **OCCIPUT** back of head
OCCLUDE absorb; include
OCEANIC of oceans
OCEANID ocean nymph
OCEANUS ocean god
zo **OCELLAR** ocellate; with 'eyes'
OCELLUS single eye; a spot
zo **OCELOID** spotted leopard; jaguar (cat)
OCHROID pale yellow
OCREATE wearing boots/leggings
OCTAGON 8-sided figure
OCTAPLA eight-fold text
OCTAVUS eighth (Latin)
mu **OCTETTE OCTET,** 8 instrumentalists
OCTOBER 10th month
bt **OCTOFID** eight segments
zo **OCTOPOD** eight-footed
zo **OCTOPUS** cephalopod with 8 suckered arms
OCTUPLE eightfold
ch **OCTYLIC** (organic radicle)
OCULATE eyed
md **OCULIST** eye doctor
OCYPETE one of the Harpies
ODALISK concubine of Sultan; whore
ODD-BALL eccentric; peculiar person
cp **ODD-EVEN** street numbers; parity
ODDMENT remnant; something left over
ODDNESS oddity; eccentricity
ODFORCE mesmeric force
zo **ODONATA** dragonflies
ODONTIC pertaining to teeth
ODORANT odorous; fragrant
ODORINE a bone distillate
ODOROUS fragrant; also smelly
ODYSSEY wandering; quest; saga (Odysseus/Ulysses)
md **OEDEMIA** overweight; palsy; liquescent
pc **OEDIPUS** a child's parental complex
ck **OENOMEL** wine and honey
me **OERSTED** magnetic field intensity
OESTRUM frenzy; on heat; rut
OESTRUS ESTRUS, gadfly; ovarian cycle
mu **OFF-BEAT** unconventional; advanced
lw **OFFENCE** insult; outrage; crime
OFFERED proffered; tendered; essayed
OFFERER a bookie; volunteer
OFFHAND casual; impolite; (volleyball)
OFFICER commissioned office holder (army)
nt, cp **OFF-LINE** off-course; off-centre
OFF-LINE impromptu; off-cue
OFF-LOAD unload; discharge; cargo
OFF-PEAK at time of least demand
ga **OFF-ROAD** dirt-track motor racing

OFF-SCUM offscouring; cleansing
ga **OFF-SIDE** fault (football)
OFFWARD leaning overboard; departing
OGHAMIC Irish (Celtic) style script
OGREISH like an ogre
OGYGIAN prehistoric; primeval
OIL-BATH bicycle accessory
zo **OIL-BIRD** the guacharo
OIL-CAKE cattle food
OIL-GOLD (gold leaf)
OIL-MEAL ground linseed cake
OIL-MILL oil factory
bt **OIL-PALM** oil source
OIL-SHOP lubricatorium
tx **OILSILK** oil-impregnated fabric
OILSKIN waterproof garment
OIL-SUMP drainage cavity in motor
OIL-WELL petroleum well
OJIBWAY Algonquin Indian
OLDNESS senility
OLDSTER middle-aged
OLD-TIME old fashioned; quondam
ch **OLEFINE** hydrocarbons
OLIGIST haematite
OLITORY (kitchen-garden)
OLIVARY olive shaped; oval
mn **OLIVINE** chrysolite
OLYMPIC of Olympus; Games
OLYMPUS abode of the gods
OMENING auguring; presaging
pl **OMENTAL** **OMENTUM**, of peritoneum
OMICRON Greek short 'o'
OMINOUS portentous, inauspicious
OMITTED left out; neglected; dropped
OMNEITY state of including all things
OMNIBUS public bus; compendium; for all
OMNIFIC all-creating
ONANISM self-pleasuring
ONCOSTS extras; overhead costs
ONCOTIC osmotic pressure of colloids
ONDATRA musk-rat
ONE-EYED round-eyed; a cyclops
ONEFOLD single
pc **ONEIRIC** pertaining to dream
ONENESS unity; concord
ONEROUS burdensome; weighty
ONESELF me, you or anybody
ONE-STEP a dance
ONE-TIME former; previous
ONGOING continuous event (course)
mn **ONICOLO** cameo-onyx
bt **ONOCLEA** fern genus
ONOLOGY prattle
ONSHORE landbased (services)
md **ONYCHIA** a whitlow
ONYMIZE categorize
ONYMOUS identified; not anonymous
bl **OOCYTIN** substance in spermatozoa
zo **OOECIUM** brood pouch
OOGRAPH ovum-drawing device
OOLITIC granular
zo **OOLOGIC** (birds' eggs)
bt **OOLYSIS** conversion to leaf
OOMETRY egg measurement
bt **OOPHYTE** gametophyte
OOPLASM central cytoplasm in oomycetes
zo **OOSPORE** fertilized ovum
zo **OOTHECA** egg-carrying structure
zo **OOZOOID** zooid arising from ovum
OPACITY opaqueness; obscurity
OPACOUS opaque; untransparent
OPALINE opalescent
OPALIZE make opaque
OPEN-AIR outdoor (activity)
ro, lw **OPEN-END** radio contract; of contracts
OPENING vacancy; opportunity; chance
pg, pl **OPENING** aperture; breach; orifice
ga **OPENING** ceremony; first gambit (chess)
OPEN-JAW air ticket (two routes)
cp, ma **OPERAND** sum to be worked on
OPERANT a worker; artisan; employee
md **OPERATE** drive (machine); apply surgery
OPEROSE **OPEROUS**, laborious; tedious
nt **OPETIDE** spring-tide
zo **OPHIDIA** snakes
zo **OPHIURA** starfish
OPIATED drugged
ch, md **OPIATES** **OPIOIDS**, classes of drugs
OPINANT of opinion
OPINING a notion; supposing
OPINION conception; idea; conjecture
OPORICE preserved fruit
zo **OPOSSUM** a marsupial
OPPIDAN town boy (Eton)
OPPOSED combated; competed
OPPOSER rival; resister
OPPRESS persecute; crush; maltreat
md **OPSONIC** **OPSONIN**, germ-resistant blood
OPTICAL of vision
zo **OPTICON** brain zone in insects
OPTIMUM best value
OPULENT wealthy; affluent

bt **OPUNTIA** cactus family
OPUSCLE opusculum; a small work
rl **ORAISON** orison; a prayer
ORALITY oral eroticism; oral disorder
ORARIAN coastal
rl **ORARION ORARIUM**, clerical stole
ORATING speech-giving; declaiming
ORATION speech; harangue; address
rl **ORATORY** eloquence; chapel
ORATRIX lady speaker
ORBIFIC world-creating
as **ORBITAL** encirclement course; elliptic
pl **ORBITAL** of the eye; sphere of influence
pl, ps, ch **ORBITAL** bony cavity; molecular
ORBLIKE globular; spherical; earth shape
ORCHARD garden of fruit-trees
ORDERED regulated; commanded
ORDERLY methodical; soldier-servant
ga **ORDINAL** figure (ice)-skating penalty
ma **ORDINAL** numerical order (rank)
rl **ORDINAL** RC book of forms of services
rl **ORDINEE** newly ordained (deacon, priest)
OREADES mountain nymphs
ORECTIC pert. to desire/satisfaction
ORGANIC vital; radical; fundamental
ORGANIC natural farming (no chemicals)
ORGANON ORGANUM, enquiry; dissertation
mu **ORGANRY** organ music
ORGIAST a Bacchanalian extremist
ORIENCY brightness of sunrise; colour
ORIFICE aperture; vent; pore
ORIFORM mouth-shaped
ORIGAMI paper cut-out, fold designs (Jap.)
bt **ORLEANS** cloth; plum
OROGENY (mountain formation)
OROLOGY mountain lore
OROTUND full voiced
ORPHEAN enchantingly musical
ORPHEUS made music sweet and low
ORPHISM cult of Bacchus
ORPHREY embroidered border
mn **ORTHITE** allanite
ORTHROS morning service (Greek)
zo **ORTOLAN** garden bunting
ck **ORVIETO** a white wine (It.)
OSCHEAL of the scrotum
zo **OSCINES** singing birds
OSCULAR (kissing)
OSCULUM exhalant aperture in porifera
OSIERED made with reeds
OSMANLI of the Turkish Ottoman dynasty
OSMATIC having olfactory organs
ch **OSMIOUS** containing osmium
mn **OSMOSIS** diffusion balance of dissolved minerals
bt **OSMOTIC** diffusible respiration
bt **OSMUNDA** royal fern
OSSELET morbid growth
OSSEOUS bony
OSSICLE small bone
md **OSSIFIC** bony
OSSUARY charnel-house
OSTEOID like bone (material)
OSTERIA hostelry (It.)
rl **OSTIARY** church janitor
bt **OSTIOLE** spore-door
md **OSTIOMA** bone tumour
md **OSTITIS** inflammation
zo **OSTRICH** also estrich
md **OTALGIA** ear-ache
zo **OTARINE** referring to seals
zo **OTIDINE** pertaining to bustards
md **OTOCYST** auditory vesicle
md **OTOLITH** ear-stone
md **OTOLOGY** ear science
OTTOMAN Turk; sofa; divan
OURSELF our kingly self
OUSTING ejecting; evicting; dislodging
OUT-BACK one from the interior (Australia)
OUTBRAG out-boast
OUTBURN burn away
OUTCAST pariah; exile
OUTCOME issue; sequel; upshot
OUTCROP geological fault
OUTDARE outventure
OUTDONE surpassed; eclipsed
OUTDOOR open air
OUTEDGE farthest extremity
OUTFACE to brave criticism
OUTFALL the place of discharge
OUTFLOW outlet
OUTFOOT out-pace; outsail
OUTGATE exit
OUTGAZE look longer than
OUTGIVE surpass in liberality
OUTGOER opposite of incomer
OUTGONE over-reached; went beyond
OUTGROW get too old for
OUTGUSH outpour; outwell
nt **OUTHAUL** a rope

OUTHIRE to let out
OUTJEST write dictionary definitions
OUTLAND foreign
OUTLASH sudden outburst
OUTLAST survive; outlive; outwear
OUTLEAP sally attack from besieged town
gl **OUTLIER** outcrop of rocks
OUTLINE draft; sketch; profile
OUTLINE précis; synopsis; description
OUTLIVE survive
OUTLOOK prospect; future; view
OUTMATE overmatch; checkmate
OUTMOST furthest outward
OUTMOVE out-manoeuvre
OUTNAME surpass in reputation
OUTNESS externality; objectiveness
OUTPACE outrun
OUTPART remote part
ga **OUTPEER** **OUTPLAY**, prove superior to rival
nt **OUTPORT** ship's gun-port (shutters)
OUTPOST detached fort; look-out point
OUTPOUR stream; spout
OUTPRAY surpass in prayer
OUTRAGE wanton mischief; abuse
OUTRANK precede
OUTRASE exterminate; destroy
OUTRIDE win horse race
ga **OUTROAR** competing football-team fans
OUTROOT uproot; eradicate garden weeds
ga **OUTRUSH** besieged; make a foray
OUTSAIL win yacht race
OUTSELL succeed in America
pr **OUTSERT** extra outside binding leaf
OUTSHOT a projection
OUTSIDE external; exterior; superficial
OUTSIZE extra big (clothing)
OUTSOAR fly higher than high
OUTSOLD sold out; no more stock
OUTSOLE outer sole of shoe
OUTSPAN to unyoke
OUTSTAY stay longer than
OUTSTEP overstep
OUTTALK continue talking endlessly
OUTTURN output; production; delivery
ga **OUTTURN** ball throw (rugby football)
OUTVIED surpassed; exceeded
OUTVOTE get majority
OUTWALK outpace
OUTWALL outer wall
OUTWARD ostensible; apparent
OUTWEAR last longer; outlast
OUTWELL gusher (oil)
OUTWENT outstripped; overtook
ga **OUT-WICK** shot on other stone (curling)
OUTWIND unwind; extricate
OUTWING out-flank (battle)
OUTWORE lasted longer than
ar **OUTWORK** redoubt; bastion
OUTWORN worn out
pl **OVARIAN** of the ovary
OVATION enthusiastic applause
zo **OVEN-TIT** willow-warbler
OVERACT act too much
OVERALL protective garment
OVERARM bowling (cricket)
OVER-ATE surfeited
OVERAWE intimidate; daunt; cow
OVERBID succeed at auction
OVERBUY buy too much
OVERDUE in arrears; outstanding; (debt)
OVERDYE dye too deeply
OVEREAT gourmandize
OVEREYE flirt openly
OVERFAR too far
OVERFLY soar beyond; fly over
OVERLAP one extending over another
tc **OVERLAP** dialling; fax-scan faults
tc **OVERLAY** bedcover; spread across
tc **OVERLAY** multiple-store program
OVERLIE to smother
OVERMAN foreman; manager; umpire
OVERMAN to employ too many
OVERPAY pay too much
OVERPLY over-exert
OVERRAN outran; invaded
pr **OVERRUN** swarm; infest; printing
OVERSAW superintended
OVERSEA foreign
OVERSEE superintend
pr **OVERSET** carried over (bookkeeping)
OVERTAX tax too highly
OVERTLY openly; publicly; patently
OVERTOP surpass
zo **OVICELL** brood-pouch in ectoprocta
OVICIDE killing of sheep
OVIDIAN narrative verse form
md **OVIDUCT** ovary passage
OVIFORM oval
OVIFORM **OVOIDAL**, egg-shaped; oval
OVOLOGY all about eggs
bt **OVULARY** (seed)
mn **OVULITE** fossil egg
OWENITE of cooperative ideals (R. Owen)

OWL-EYED global eyes; alert
OWL-LIKE as wise as an owl
ga **OWN-GOAL** scoring for opponents (fault)
ch **OXALATE** of oxalic acid
mn **OXALITE** oxalate of iron
ch **OXAMIDE** oxalic acid amide
bt **OXHEART** kind of large sweet cherry
ch **OXIDANT** combustive agent
ch **OXIDASE** enzyme
ch **OXIDATE OXIDIZE**, to rust (of iron)
ch **OXIMIDE** oxamic acid compound
OXONIAN of Oxford
OX-STALL home for non-bulls
ch **OXYACID** proton-giving hydroxide
ae **OXYDANT** oxygen component in rocket
OXYNTIC secreting acid (of stomach glands)
md **OXYOPIA** acute vision
ch **OXYSALT** containing oxygen
OXYTONE accented syllable
ch **OZONIDE** explosive organic compound
ch **OZONIZE OZONOUS**, charge with ozone

P

PABOUCH oriental slipper
PABULAR yielding food
PABULUM aliment; fodder; nutriment
PACABLE appeasable
PACATED calmed; quieted; pacified
PACEMAN runner; fast bowler (cricket)
ga **PACHISI** pachesi; Indian backgammon
bt **PACHYMA** fungus genus
PACIFIC peaceful; tranquil; irenic
PACKAGE bale; bundle; parcel; (holiday)
cp **PACKAGE** multipurpose programs' set
go **PACK-ICE** icy-sea barrier (Arctic)
PACKING packeting; stowing; crowding
PACKMAN peddler; hawker; tallyman
zo **PACKWAX** tendon in animals' necks
PACKWAY bridle path (for horsemen)
PACTION a pact; covenant; bond
PADDING stuffing
PADDLED dabbled; propelled
zo, nt **PADDLER** canoeist; wader; steamship
zo **PADDOCK** frog or toad
PADDOCK puddock; field
PADELLA small lamp
PADISHA Persian title
PADLOCK durable, portable lock
PADRONE employer (Iberia, It.)
PAD-TREE harness frame
rl **PAENULA** chasuble (church vestment)
PAEONIN red colouring matter
PAGEANT historic spectacle; display show
PAGINAL (pages)
PAHLEVI pehlevi; early Persian dialect
PAILFUL the contents of a bucket
PAILLON metal backing
PAINFUL grievous; vexatious; sore
PAINING afflicting; tormenting; aching
PAINTED limned; bedizened; daubed
PAINTER artist in colour; depictor
nt **PAINTER** R.A.; mooring rope
PAIRING matching; mating; MPs' voting
tx **PAJAMAS PYJAMAS**, slumber wear
PAKFONG PAKTONG, silver (Germany)
PALABRA wordy discussion
PALADIN knight errant, crusader
zo **PALAMAE** toe-webbings
md **PALATAL** of the palate (tasting)
PALAVER parley with chieftains
br **PALE-ALE** type of brew
PALEOUS like chaff
PALETOT loose overcoat
PALETTE artist's board; (pelota)
zo **PALFREY** saddle-horse
md **PALINAL** retrogressive
zo **PALLIAL** (mantle of mollusc)
PALLING covering; surfeiting
zo **PALLIUM** brain-shell of mollusc; mantle of bird
rl **PALLIUM** archbishops' mantle (pall)
ga **PALLONE** ball game (It.)
ar **PALMARY** worthy; capital decoration
zo **PALMATE** web-footed
bt **PALMERY** palm-house
PALMING sleight of hand; (trick)
PALMIST hand-reader; fortune teller
PALM-OIL bribery
cp **PALM-TOP** a hand-held computer
bt **PALMYRA** East Indian palm
PALOOKA incompetent boxer; simpleton
md **PALPATE** touch gently (medical)
PALSHIP comradeship
md **PALSIED** of palsy (paralysis, tremors)

PALUDAL marshy; malarial; fenny
mt **PAMPERO** cold S.W. squall (Argentina)
PANACEA universal remedy
PANACHE plume; self-esteem
rl **PANAGIA** all holy; an ornament
ck, ae **PANCAKE** fried batter; flat landing
rl **PANDEAN** of Pan, god of Nature (Gr.)
PANDECT digest of Roman Law
zo **PANDION** osprey genus
zo **PANDORA** (her fateful box); sea bream
mu **PANDORA BANDORA**, plucked lyre; zither
mu **PANDORE** a lute
PANDOUR Hungarian soldier; robber
mu **PANDURA** Neapolitan guitar
rl **PANEITY** state of being bread
PANFISH small non-commercial food fish
gl, go **PANGAEA** sial; primeval single landmass
PANGANI East African ivory
PANGING paining; causing anguish
PANICKY jumpy; nervous; fearful
bt **PANICLE** a small web
bt **PANICUM** millet-grain
PANIKIN tin mug
nt **PANJANG** sampan, Malaysia
PANNADE curveting
PANNAGE swine food
tx **PANNIER** 2 bread-baskets; hooped skirt
mn, pg **PANNING** gold washing; photo-spanning
PANNOSE like felt
PANOCHA coarse sugar (Mexico)
PANOPLY complete armour
mu **PAN-PIPE** piped wind instrument
PANSIED with pansies
zo **PANTHER** leopard
PANTHOS Divinity made manifest
PANTIES undies
PANTILE S-shaped roof tile
PANTING palpitating; desirous
PANTLER butler
mu **PANTOUM** Malayan quatrain
PANURGE a Rabelaisian rascal
PANURGY skill in work
rl **PAPALLY** popishly (ceremoniously)
PAPBOAT small feeding vessel for infants
PAPERED sand-papered
PAPERER paperhanger
PAPHIAN (worship of Venus)
zo **PAPILIO** butterfly
md **PAPILLA** nerve extremity
PAPMEAT soft food
PAPOOSE North American Indian infant
PAPPING feeding with pap
PAPPOSE pappous; downy
bt **PAPRIKA** red pepper (Hungarian)
PAPULAE dermal gills in echinodermata
md **PAPULAR** pimply
bt **PAPYRUS** sedge; scroll
PARABLE allegorical similitude
PARACME decline; decadence
PARADED displayed; vaunted
PARADOS rampart
PARADOX surprising statement
PARAGON model of perfection
PARAMOS semi-tundra (Andes)
PARAPET rampart
PARASOL sunshade
ck **PARBAKE** bake partially
ck **PARBOIL** boil partially
PARCHED scorched; dried; shrivelled
PARDIEU in truth
PARDINE like a leopard; spotted
bt **PAREIRA** drug (Brazilian plant)
bt **PARELLA PARELLE, PERELLE**, litmus lichen
PARERGY subsidiary work
md **PARESIS** paralysis
md **PARETIC** partially paralysed
ck **PARFAIT** cold egg/whipped cream dessert
PARGING pargeting; external decorative plaster work
gs **PARISON** intermediate glass shape
PARITOR beadle; apparitor
PARKING lodging; collecting
PARLOUR the Mayor's 'front room'
PARLOUS perilous; difficult; precarious
PARODIC (parody); farcical
md **PAROTIC** auricular
md **PAROTID PAROTIS**, salivary gland
PARQUET wooden flooring; stalls of theatre
PARRIED avoided; warded off; fended
PARSING grammatical exercise
bt **PARSLEY** a culinary herb
ck, bt **PARSNIP** root vegetable
PARTAKE to share; participate
PARTIAL biased; restricted; fond
ga **PARTIDO** 15-point limit (pelota)
lw **PARTIES** social; political; legal
PARTING division; separating; breaking
mu **PARTITA** notation scores
bt **PARTITE** partially parted

zo **PARTLET** a ruff; a collar; a hen
PARTNER colleague; associate; buddy
md **PARULIS** gumboil
PARVENU upstart
rl **PARVISE** porch; church garden
PARVULE tiny pill
PASCHAL (Easter)
PASCUAL grazing; pasturing
PASGANG striding technique (skiing)
PASQUIL **PASQUIN**, lampoon, satire
PASSADE sword thrust
PASSADO equestrian exercise
lw **PASSAGE** clause; context; law
mu **PASSAGE** extract (music, literature)
PASSAGE corridor; alley; voyage
hd **PASSANT** walking
PASSING brief; transient; exceeding
PASSION ardour; fervour; wrath
PASSIVE patient; submissive; inert
PASS-KEY a master-key
PASSMAN of examinations (university)
PASSOUT ice-skating movement
pr **PASTE-IN** late correction, insert
PASTERN (fetlock); part of horse's foot
pr **PASTE-UP** extended arrangement of proof sheets
ck **PASTIES** patties; pies
PASTIME recreation; sport; diversion
PASTING cementing; gumming
PASTOSE painted thickly
PASTURE herbage; meadowland
nt **PATACHE** fishing boat from Malaysia
nt **PATAMAR** coasting vessel; dhow; India
ga **PATBALL** tennis of sorts
PATCHED repaired clumsily
PATCHER repairer; botcher
zo, pl **PATELLA** limpet; kneecap
PATELLA saucer; shallow dish
PATHWAY footway; track; trail; (garden)
md **PATIENT** steadfast; calm; (hospital-)
PATNESS quick in the uptake
ga **PATOLLI** Aztecs' board game
hd **PATONCE** heraldic curved cross
PATRIAL racial; national
PATRICO gipsy priest; patercove
PATRIOT staunch non-cosmopolitan
rl **PATRIST** a theologian
PATROON American proprietor
PATTERN design; model; sample
PATTERN exemplary (ideal)
ck **PATTIES** pasties; pies
ck **PATTING** tapping; stroking; (butter-)
PATTRAS wooden wall-plug
PAUCITY fewness; exiguity; lack

rl **PAULINE** (St Paul); sect
PAUNCHY obese; stout
PAUSING halting; wavering; tarrying
PAVIOUR pavement layer
PAWLATA method of righting a kayak
PAWNING pledging; hypothecating
PAYABLE due for payment
PAYBILL cheque; order to pay
PAYBOOK record of wages (military)
PAYCOCK vain husband of Juno
PAYDIRT alluvial deposit
PAYLIST **PAYROLL**, of employees
PAYLOAD amount of cargo permitted
PAYMENT financial transaction
PAYNISE to preserve wood
PAYROLL paylist
PAYSAGE landscape (painting) (Fr.)
PEACHED divulged
PEACHER an informant
PEA-COAT pea-jacket
zo **PEACOCK** pavonine
zo **PEACRAB** small crustacean
zo **PEA-FOWL** a species of Pavo genus
PEAKING reaching full performance
nt **PEAKING** sail raising
PEAKISH off colour; sickly
PEALING bellringing; resounding
PEANISM song of praise or triumph
PEARLED made success as oyster
nt **PEARLER** fishing boat (Japan)
tx **PEARLIN** lace made of silk thread
PEASANT rustic; swain; farm labourer
PEASCOD Tudor genitals' protector; pod
PEA-SOUP London fog
PEAT-BED damp moss
PEAT-BOG Irish fuel source
PEAT-HAG peat-hole
PEAVIES lumbermen's levers
PEBBLED shingled
zo **PEBRINE** silk-worm disease
PECCANT sinning; guilty; criminal
zo **PECCARY** S. American pig
PECCAVI confession of error
PECKING picking up; striking; (-order)
PECKISH hungry
bt **PECTASE** gel-forming plant enzyme
PECTATE **PECTOSE**, gelatinous
ck, bt **PECTINE** jelly from apple acid
PECTOSE carbohydrate plant constituent
PEDDLED retailed; trifled
PEDDLER hawker; huckster
PEDESIS molecular vibration
bt **PEDICEL** **PEDICLE**, small stalk

PEDLARY hawking; (street) selling
gl, ag **PEDOCAL** calcium rich zonal soil
PEDRAIL tracked vehicle
PEELING excoriating; skinning
PEELITE follower of Sir R. Peel
PEENING hammer-blow metal-working
PEEPING snooping; peering
PEERAGE Debrett; rank of peer
PEERESS consort of a peer
PEERING prying; peeping; gazing
PEEVISH querulous; snappish
zo **PEEWEEP** peewit; pewit
PEGASUS winged horse of the Muses
as, zo **PEGASUS** (fish); constellation
PEGGING fastening; (croquet)
PEGWOOD clock-hole cleaning sticks
PEHLEVI PAHLEVI, Persian dialect
PELAGIC (deep sea)
zo **PELAMID** bonito; mackerel type
PELASGI Greek tribe
zo **PELICAN** genus of birds
md **PELIOMA** livid spot
PELISSE fur-coat
PELLAGE duty on skins
PELOPID a son of Pelops
md **PELORIA PELORIC**, abnormalism
nv **PELORUS** pivoted dial
PELOTON bunch of racing cyclists
PELTAST soldier with buckler
PELTATE shield-like
PELTING raining; pouring; throwing
PENALLY by way of punishment
PENALTY handicap; retribution
ga **PENALTY** free kick; throw (-goal)
PENANCE punishment; humiliation
PENATES Roman household gods
PEN-CASE pen-holder
PENDANT an ornament; pennant
PENDENT hanging; dangling
PENDING awaiting decision
PENEIAN (river Peneus in Vale of Tempe)
zo **PEN-FISH** sparoid fish
ag **PENFOLD PINFOLD**, cattle enclosure
zo **PENGUIN** Antarctic sea-bird
PENICIL paint-brush
PEN-NAME pseudonym; nom de plume
nt **PENNANT** a long streamer
zo **PENNATE** Penguin genus of birds
PENNIED having a cash asset
nm **PENNIES** pence
PENNILL stanza (Eisteddfod)
PENNINE magnesium/aluminium silicate
PENNING inditing; cooping

PENSILE pendulous; suspended
PENSION retirement income; (social)
PENSION annuity; boarding house
PENSIVE meditative; thoughtful
PENTACT five-rayed
ch **PENTANE** (paraffin)
bd **PENTICE** pent-house; a sloping roof or weather cover
PENTODE pentone; wireless adjunct
ch **PENTOSE** a form of sugar
bt **PENTZIA** S. African shrub
ck **PENUCHE** type of fudge
PENWORK drawings; calligraphy
PENWORK on japanned lacquer furniture
PEONAGE PEONISM, agricultural slavery
bt **PEONIES PAEONIES**
PEOPLED inhabited; populated
mn **PEPERIN** volcanic tufa
PEPPERY irascible; choleric
PEP-PILL stimulant
md **PEPSINE** an enzyme
PEP-TALK encouragement
md **PEPTICS** digestion
ch **PEPTIDE** protein-breakdown substance
md **PEPTONE** digestive product
PERBEND bonding stone
PERCALE woven cambric
PERCASE perhaps
PER-CENT out of 100
PERCEPT that which is perceived
PERCHED roosted; settled
zo **PERCHER** candle; rooster
zo **PERCINE** like a perch; percoid
PERCOCT well cooked
zo **PERCOID** perch-like
PERCUSS strike; tap
PERDURE endure; persist
PEREGAL fully equal
zo **PEREION** thorax of crustacea
bt **PERELLE PARELLE, PARELLA**, lichen
mu **PERFECT** complete; faultless; pitch
PERFIDY betrayal; treachery
PERFORM fulfil; act; execute; effect
PERFUME scent; aroma; fragrance
PERFUSE sprinkle; bedew; permeate
PERGOLA PERGULA, garden arbour
PERHAPS aiblins; peradventure
PERIAPT amulet; charm; talisman
mn **PERIDOT** green jewel; olivine
PERIGREE point nearest to earth of other orbits
ro **PERIKON** detector
PERIQUE Louisiana tobacco
PERIWIG peruke
PERJURE forswear

lw **PERJURY** false testimony
PERKIER more irrepressible
PERKILY saucily; jauntily; airily
PERKING peering; smartening up
bd, mn **PERLITE** in sandless gypsum plaster
gl **PERLITE** vitreous rock
gl **PERMIAN** geological era
PERMUTE commute; change
zo **PEROPOD** rudimentary leg
zo **PERORAL** surrounding the mouth
vt **PEROSIS** slipped tendon
PERPEND ratiocinate; cogitate
PERPEND bonding stone
PERPLEX puzzle; nonplus; embarrass
PERRIER catapult; a table water
PERSEID a meteor from Perseus
PERSEUS slew Medusa; a constellation
PERSIAN Iranian
PERSIST persevere; continue; last
PERSONA (grata); actor's mask
PERSPEX a glazing material
PERTAIN to relate to; concern
PERTURB disturb; agitate; disquiet
PERTUSE riddled; bored
PERUSAL careful reading
PERUSED read; studied; examined
pr **PERUSER** a scrutineer of pages
PERVADE perfuse; impregnate; imbue
PERVERT deviate; lead astray
rl **PESHITO** Syriac Testament
PESKILY annoyingly
PESTLED pounded in a mortar
PETASUS Mercury's winged cap
PETERED pottered; exhausted; (cards)
bt **PETIOLE** leaf-stalk; pedicle
cr **PETRAIL** heavy framing beam
PETRARY catapult for stones
PETREAN stony
PETRIFY stupefy; dumbfound; stun
rl **PETRINE** according to St Peter
PETROUS rocklike
PETTILY meanly; trivially
PETTING fondling; canoodling
PETTISH peevish; fretful; querulous
bt **PETUNIA** a flower
mn **PETZITE** silver/gold telluride
rl **PEW-RENT** rent paid for use of pew
PEWTERY (pewter)
nm **PFENNIG** German copper coin
md **PHACOID** lenticular
PHAETON sky-hog; four-wheel carriage
zo **PHAETON** boastwain-bird
PHALANX compact body
pl **PHALLIC** **PHALLUS**, penis, symbol
PHANTOM spectral; illusive; ghost
PHARAOH ancient Egyptian ruler
PHARATE of development phase in insects
md **PHARYNX** upper part of gullet
tc, tv **PHASING** correcting screen picture of facsimiles
bt **PHELLEM** tissue external to phellogen
ch **PHENATE** (phenol)
ch **PHENOIC** carbolic
PHIDIAS Greek sculptor
PHILTRE **PHILTER**, love potion
bt **PHLOEUM** **PHLOEM**, bark fibre
zo **PHOCINE** of seals
PHOEBUS Apollo; the sun
zo **PHOENIX** date palm; fabulous bird
PHONATE to utter inarticulately
PHONEME relevant sound (linguistics)
PHONICS harmony; phonetics
PHONING telephoning
PHONISM synesthesia; noises off
zo **PHORESY** transport by clinging to animal
pg **PHOTICS** science of light
pg **PHOTISM** colour sensation
pg **PHOTOMA** hallucinated flash of light
zo **PHRAGMA** septum or partition
PHRASED expressed; styled
PHRASER phrase-monger
PHRATRY tribal subdivision
md **PHRENIC** diaphragmatic
PHYSICS a science
bt **PHYTOID** plant-like
mu **PIACERE** at pleasure
PIAFFER a horse gait
mu **PIANINA** small piano
mu **PIANISM** musical technique
mu **PIANIST** an expert on the ivories
mu **PIANOLA** self-playing piano
nm **PIASTRE** coin (Egypt)
mu **PIBROCH** a tune; bagpipe (Sc.)
PICADOR mounted bull-fighter
PICAMAR tar extract
lw **PICCAGE** pitch-money
mu **PICCOLO** small flute
PICEOUS pitch-black
to **PICKAXE** pointed chopper
PICKING petty larceny; choosing
PICKLED preserved
PICK-OFF automation device
bt **PICOTEE** carnation
PICOTTE little lace loop
PICQUET piquet; card game
ch **PICRATE** an explosive; lyddite
bt **PICRINE** foxglove extract
mn **PICRITE** olivine; peridot

PICTISH Celtic
PICTURE portrait; drawing; imagine
zo **PIDDOCK** mollusc
PIEBALD **PYEBALD**, motley (horses)
PIECING patching; uniting
PIERAGE pier tolls
PIERCED transfixed; impaled
PIERCER borer; gimlet; drill
PIERIAN (Muses); (of Pieria)
PIERROT an entertainer
PIETISM sanctimoniousness
rl **PIETIST** religious sect
zo **PIEWIFE** lapwing
el **PIEZOID** crystal blank
mu **PIFFERO** oboe; organ-stop
PIFFLED chattered; drivelled
zo **PIG-DEER** invented animal
PIGEYED with small eyes
PIGGERY pig-sty
PIGGING living higgledy-piggledy
PIGGISH hoggish; swinish; messy
PIGHTLE small enclosure
PIG-IRON iron ingots
PIG-LEAD cast lead
PIGMEAN of pygmies; Lilliputian
pt **PIGMENT** paint; colour; tincture
PIGMIES **PYGMIES**, diminutive Africans
bt **PIGNONS** fir-cone seeds
le **PIGSKIN** (leather); (saddle)
PIGTAIL plait of hair
PIG-WASH hog-wash
ck **PIKELET** **PIKELIN**, small crumpet, tea cake
PIKEMAN turnpike gatekeeper
mn **PIKRITE** igneous rock
PILCHER a scabbard
PILEATE cap-shaped
lw **PILFERY** petty theft; larceny
PILGRIM palmer; devotee; wayfarer
bt **PILKINS** pill-corn; oats
PILLAGE rifle; sack; ravage; loot
PILLBOX concrete defensive emplacement
PILLBOX medicine box; hat (ladies, pages)
PILLING blackballing (vetoing membership)
PILLION saddle, 2nd rider's seat
PILLORY expose to ridicule
PILLOWY yielding; soft
PILOTED steered; conducted; guided
ar **PILOTIS** building on columns
zo **PILTOCK** coalfish
PILULAR (pills)
bt, ck **PIMENTA** **PIMENTO**, red capsicum
PIMPLED blotched (skin)
zo **PINBONE** hipbone of quadruped
PIN-CASE pin etui
to **PINCERS** pliers
PINCHED gripped; purloined
zo **PINCHER** sea fish
PINCHES wee drams; nips
PINDOWN children in punishment room
PINE-OIL oil from resin
bt **PINETUM** plantation of pine-trees
PIN-FIRE (cartridge)
zo **PIN-FISH** a scaly fish; sailor's choice
PINFOLD cattle pound
PINGING bullet noise (rifle)
pt **PINGUID** greasy; unctuous
PINHEAD top of a pin; minute
PIN-HOLD pin-housing
PINHOLE tiny aperture
vt **PINK-EYE** a horse disease
PINKING scalloping; knocking
PINKISH somewhat pink
nt **PINNACE** a man-of-war's boat
bt **PINNATE** pennate; feathered
PINNING making fast
zo **PINNOCK** tom-tit
bt, zo **PINNULA** **PINNULE**, branchlet; small feather
zo, tx **PINTADO** guinea-fowl; chintz, 18th c.
zo **PINTAIL** a duck
me **PINT-POT** vessel holding pint
PIN-WORK (flexing flax)
PIONEER forerunner; initiator
PIONEER 1st bowler; pilot
PIOUSLY devoutly; religiously
PIP-EMMA p.m. (signalling)
PIPERIC peppery
PIPETTE graduated tube
bt **PIPLESS** seedless
bt, ck **PIPPING** piling; de-seeding
PIQUANT stimulating; caustic; tart
PIQUING irritating; nettling
nt **PIRAGUA** a dug-out canoe
PIRATED plundered; marauded
PIRATIC infringing; piratical
lw **PISCARY** fishing rights
PISCINA **PISCINE**, swimming pool (Sp., Fr.)
zo **PISMIRE** an ant; emmet
nm **PISTOLE** Spanish golden coin
PITAPAT in a flutter; raindrops
PITCHED flung; tossed; planted; cast
ga **PITCHER** eared jug; thrower (baseball)
mn **PITCOAL** from underground
PITEOUS woeful; sorry; compassionate
PITFALL a trap; snare; danger
PIT-HEAD top of coal mine

PITHILY tersely; concisely; briefly
PITHING extracting the marrow
bt **PITH-RAY** root or stem cell sheet
PITIFUL humane; lenient; wretched
PIT-MIRK dark as pitch (Sc.)
PITTING striving; seed removal
bd **PITTING** plaster-blowing technique
PITTING setting one against another
PITTITE playgoer (in the pit)
md **PITUITA** **PITUITE**, phlegm
PITYING commiserating
PIVOTAL axial
PIVOTED hinged; centred on
PIXY-LED bewildered
PLACARD bill; poster; notice
PLACATE conciliate; appease
md, rl **PLACEBO** fake drug; prayer (mass)
PLACING identifying; assigning
PLACKET slit; pocket
zo **PLACODE** platelike structure
PLACOID scaly
PLACULA small plate; plaque
PLAGUED persistently annoyed
PLAGUER a vexatious person
tx **PLAIDED** wearing tartan (Scots)
PLAINER clearer; more obvious
PLAINLY simply; clearly; candidly
tx **PLAITED** folded; woven
tx **PLAITER** an interlacer; interweaver
PLANARY as foundation; flat; level
PLANCHE body position (gymnastics)
fr **PLANCON** octagonally hewn log
PLANING smoothing; aeroplaning
PLANISH to hammer smooth
bd **PLANKED** floorboards laid
PLANNED sketched; schemed
PLANNER a projector; designer
PLANTAR (sole of foot)
PLANTED instilled; inculcated; sown
PLANTER settler; grower
zo **PLANULA** embryo protoplasm
PLANXTY Welsh lament
PLASHED splashed; dabbled
PLASMIC proto-plasmic
bl **PLASMID** of cytoplasmic structure
ch **PLASMIN** fibrin-destructive blood item
PLASMON flour-like food
PLASTER sinapism; daub; stucco
PLASTIC elastic; pliable; yielding
zo **PLASTID** living cell
bt **PLATANE** plane-tree
ma **PLATEAU** flattened graphic curve
go **PLATEAU** high tableland; stand on plinth
ch **PLATINA** platinum
PLATING sheathing
ga **PLATOON** army squad; sports team
PLATTED plaited; weaved
PLATTER wooden plate
PLAUDIT applause; approbation
PLAY-BOX theatre seat
PLAYBOY man of pleasure
ga **PLAYDAY** sports day
PLAYFUL frolicsome; joker
PLAYING acting; competing; romping
ga **PLAY-OFF** repeat match after a tie
ga **PLAY-OUT** finish the game
PLAYPEN children's play enclosure
lw **PLEADED** entreated; argued
lw **PLEADER** barrister; advocate
PLEASED delighted; contented; obliged
PLEASER charmer; gratifier
PLEATED platted; interlaced
mu **PLECTRE** plectrum; plectron
PLEDGED pawned; engaged
PLEDGEE pawnbroker
PLEDGER pawnbroker's customer
md **PLEDGET** lint compress
PLEIADS the Pleiades; 7 stars in Taurus
PLENARY in full; complete; entire
PLENISH provide; equip
PLENIST spacious materialist
zo **PLEOPOD** fin-paws of whale
PLEROMA abundance; fullness
bt **PLEROME** centre of apical meristem
md **PLEURAL** (lungs)
zo **PLEURON** shell extension
PLEXURE weaving; texture
PLIABLE tractable; supple
PLIABLY flexibly; lithely
PLIANCY flexibility
PLICATE folded; plaited
PLIFORM in the form of a fold
PLIMMED swollen
PLODDED toiled; drudged
PLODDER steady worker
PLOPPED plumped
PLOSIVE phonetic sound-group
PLOTFUL full of schemes
PLOTTED planned; schemed
nt **PLOTTER** intriguer; conspirator; radar
PLOW-BOY ploughboy
ag **PLOWING** **PLOUGHING**, furrowing
PLOWMAN ploughman, (lunch)
PLUCKED failed examination; pulled
PLUCKER feather remover
PLUGGED plodded; shot; sealed
PLUGGER stopper
PLUMAGE plumery; feathers
PLUMBED measured; made vertical

PLUMBER lead-worker; water-system worker
ch **PLUMBUM PLUMBIC**, of lead
bt **PLUMCOT** plum-apricot
PLUMERY display of plumes
PLUMING self-congratulation
PLUMIST feather-dresser
PLUMMET lead bob
PLUMMET fall headlong downwards
PLUMOSE plumous; feathery
PLUMPED fell suddenly
PLUMPER chubbier; fatter; stouter
PLUMPLY roundly; fully
bd **PLUMULE** plumula; bud
PLUNDER loot; spoil; pillage; booty
PLUNGED dived; gambled heavily
PLUNGER part of a pump
PLUNKET blue colour
zo **PLUTEUS** pelagic larval form
PLUVIAL rainy; humid
PLUVIUS Jupiter
PLY-WOOD laminated wood
bt **POACEAE** the grasses
POACHED trespassed; stabbed; (eggs)
POACHER thief; setter of snares
zo **POCHARD** a duck
pr **POCHOIR** stencil colour process
md **POCK-PIT** pox-mark
md **PODAGRA** gout
PODALIC pertaining to feet
PODDING producing pods
PODESTA Italian magistrate
zo **PODITIC** (crab's leg)
PODRIDA Spanish stew
zo **POE-BIRD** tui; parson bird; (NZ)
POEISIS creation
POETESS lyrical lady
POETICS criticism of poetry
POETIZE versify
lw **POINDED** pounded; distrained
POINTED acute; sharp; keen; significant
POINTEL pencil; spike; stylo
zo **POINTER** indicator; hunting dog
POISING balancing; loading
POITREL horse-armour
nt **POLACCA FALLUCA**, sailing vessel
nt **POLACRE** Mediterranean dhow
mu **POLACKA** polonaise (Polish dance)
POLAIRE ancient leather book-satchel
POLARIS guided missile
el **POLARON** trapped electron
POLDERS reclaimed land
to **POLE-AXE** poll-axe
zo **POLE-CAT** civet
POLEMIC controversial; contentious
POLENTA Italian maize porridge
POLICED regulated
POLIGAR S. Ind. village chieftain
POLITER more courteous or civil
POLITIC statesmanlike; discreet
zo **POLLACK** sea-fish; pollock; chub
POLLARD stag after casting his antlers
zo **POLLARD** lopped; bran; the chub
POLLCAP capping municipal spending
POLLENT strong; mighty; puissant
POLLING voting; lopping (trees)
tc, bt **POLLING** multidrop network act
POLL-MAN pass-man (Cam.)
POLL-TAX capitation tax
POLLUTE contaminate; defile
POLOIST polo player
POLONYM joint-authorship name, work
bt **POLSTER** lichen moss on glacial rock
zo **POLSTER** glacier mouse (Scand.)
POLYACT rayed
POLYGON angular figure
bt **POLYGYN** plant genus
ch **POLYMER** complex compound
POLYOPY multiple vision
ch **POLYOSE** polysaccharide
zo **POLYPOD** many-footed
zo **POLYPUS** sea-anemone; coral
zo **POLYZOA** barnacles
ch **POMATUM POMADE**, an ointment
bt, ck **POMELOE POMERANCE**, shaddock citron
bt **POMEROY** the king-apple
zo **POMFRET** a fish
POMMAGE crushed apples
POMMARD a Burgundy wine
zo **POMPANO** edible fish (N. Amer.)
bt **POMPION** pumpkin
bt **POMPIRE** an apple
mu **POMPOSO** with due pomp
POMPOUS self-important; grandiose
bt **PONCEAU** poppy; poppy-coloured
PONDAGE water in a pond
PONDING collecting into a pond
mt **PONENTE** W. wind, Mediterranean (It.)
zo **PONGIDS** long-armed gibbons (apes)
PONIARD dagger
PONTAGE bridge toll
rl **PONTIFF** high priest; pope
PONTINE Roman marsh
PONTOON bridge of boats; card game
POOH-BAH a pluralist
POOLING merging; combining
POOPING (following sea)
POOR-BOX alms for the poor
POOREST most necessitous; neediest

POOR-LAW charity provisions
bt **POPCORN** parched maize
rl **POPEDOM** papality
POP-EYED with protruding eyes
ck **POPOVER** Amer. 'Yorkshire pudding'
POPPIED drowsy; slumbrous; narcotic
POPPING exploding; darting eyes; (-in)
POPPING surface pitting; uncorking
POPPLED rippled; bubbled
POP-SHOP soda-fountain bar
POPULAR commonly liked; (prices)
bt **POP-WEED** bladder-wort
PORCATE ridged
zo **PORCINE** piggy; swinish; suiform
PORIFER a sponge
ck **PORK-PIE** type of hat; meat in pastry
md **POROSIS** bone formation
md **POROTIC** (porosis); callous
ch **PORPHIN** pyrrole/methene nucleus
PORRECT erect; extended
md **PORRIGO** dandruff
nt **PORTAGE** conveying boats overland
nt **PORT-BAR** harbour bar; (sand spit)
PORTEND foretell; augur; bode
PORTENT an evil omen; presage
PORTICO porch; stoa; colonnade
PORTIFY aggrandize
PORTING **PORTAGE**, conveying; carrying
PORTION bit; part; share; division
pr **PORTRAY** depict; describe (art) (words)
zo **PORZANA** water-rail; crake
mu **POSAUNE** German trombone
POSITED affirmed; postulated
mu **POSITIF** small choir organ (Fr.)
POSSESS own; hold; keep; control
POSTAGE mail carriage fee
POST-BAG sack for letters
POST-BOX letter-box
POST-BOY mail collector
POST-DAY day for sending/getting mail
POSTEEN Kashmir sheepskin coat
POSTERN back-door; small gate
POSTFIX affix; suffix; append
POSTING mailing; recording
POSTMAN letter carrier
POSTURE pose; attitude; position
POST-WAR since hostilities ended
POTABLE drinkable; liquid
POTAGER porringer; soup-bowl
zo **POTAMIC** pertaining to rivers; (hippo-)
POTANCE part of a watch
POTARGO a pickle
ch **POTASSA** potash
POTATOR an imbiber; toper
pp **POTCHER** paper-pulp machine
hd **POTENCE** heraldic gibbet
hr **POTENCE** inverted clock
ch **POTENCY** effectiveness; strength
POT-HEAD dunderhead
POTHEEN home-distilled spirits (Irish)
ck **POT-HERB** herbal cookery flavouring
gl **POT-HOLE** earth cavity (water-course)
POT-HOOK kettle-holder (fireplace)
POTICHE porcelain vase
ce **POT-LIFE** period in pot etc.
ck **POT-LUCK** makeshift meal; make-do
POTOROO rat kangaroo
POT-SHOP pub; off-licence
POT-SHOT random round; sly remark
ck **POTTAGE** nourishing thick soup; (mess)
POTTERY ceramics (factory)
POTTING preserving; shooting; (plants)
zo **POUCHED** bagged; marsupial
zo **POULARD** plump hen; pullet
zo **POULTRY** fattened fowls
POUNCED with claws; sprang; swooped
me **POUNDAL** unit of force
md **POUNDED** struck; to crush; (heartbeats)
POUNDER weight of projectile (gunnery)
POUNDER grinder; pestle; hand-mill
POURING streaming; gushing; (rain)
POUTING sulking; grimacing; (displeasure)
POVERTY want; penury; indigence
POWDERY pulverous; floury; dusty
POWERED engined
PRAESES academical disputers
PRAETOR Roman magistrate
go **PRAIRIE** treeless grassy lands
PRAISED lauded; glorified
PRAISER laudator; extoller; eulogizer
PRAKARA temple passage (India)
PRAKRIT Sanskrit and allied languages
ck **PRALINE** chocolate sweetmeat
PRANCED strutted; bounded; (horses)
PRANGED bombed heavily; struck
PRANKED played comic tricks
PRANKER practical joker
bt **PRATIES** potatoes (Irish)

PRATING babbling; boasting
PRATTLE idle chatter
rl **PRAYING** addressing God; entreating
PREACHY tediously didactic
rl **PREBEND** canon's stipend
PRECEDE herald; usher; introduce
PRECEPT behest; maxim; rule; canon
lw **PRECIPE** writ
PRECISE exact; accurate; finical
PREDATE ante-date
PREDIAL (farm estate)
PREDICT foretell; calculate future
PREDONE completed in advance
PREDOOM judge in advance of facts
PRE-ECHO prior sound from record defect
cp **PRE-EDIT** run of input data, records
PREEMPT appropriate in advance
PREENED tidied up
PREFACE preamble; prologue
PREFECT French magistrate; monitor
PREFINE limit; delimit
PREFORM form beforehand
PREFORM larger moulding composition
ck **PREHEAT** heat (oven) up for use
rl **PRELACY** episcopal church government
rl **PRELATE** church dignitary
PRELECT discourse; lecture; address
PRELIMS introductory features of book
PRELIMS examinations
mu **PRELUDE** preface; exordium
PREMIAL at a premium
PREMIER first; principal; P.M.
PREMISE antecedent proposition
PREMISS logical premise
PREMIUM bounty; fee; reward; bonus
lw **PRENDER** right of seizure
md **PREORAL** in front of the jaw
PREPAID paid in advance
PREPARE make ready (for process, action)
md **PREPUCE** foreskin; penile cover
zo **PREPUPA** insect larval stage
PRESAGE foretell; predict; prophesy
PRESEEN foreseen
PRESELL promote products in advance
PRESENT here; now; existing; current
PRESENT exhibit; proffer; gift
PRESIDE officiate; direct; control
PRESSED urged; crushed; encroached
PRESSER squeezer (clothes-)
mu **PRESSEZ** increase speed (Fr.)
md **PRESSOR** causing arterial pressure rise
PRESTER medieval king; (priest-king)
PRESUME assume; suppose; reckon
PRETEND feign; simulate; claim (title)
PRETEST pre-examine; check; control
PRETEXT excuse; plea; cloak
PRETONE (accented syllable)
PRETZEL crisp biscuit
PREVAIL dominate; win; succeed
PREVENE precede
PREVENT hinder; hamper; thwart
PREVIEW foresee
PREVISE forewarn; foresee
PREWARN give notice of
PREYFUL predatory
PREYING plundering; wasting; robbing
rl, pl **PRIAPUS** god of procreation; (erection)
PRICING costing; valuing; rating
PRICKED spurred; punctured; bored
PRICKER prickle; light horseman
PRICKET early candlestick
zo **PRICKET** a young buck
bt **PRICKET** stone-crop
bt **PRICKLE** to prick; a thorn
PRICKLY spinate; spicate
PRIDIAN of yesterday
PRIDING valuing; esteeming highly
PRIDWIN King Arthur's shield
PRIGGED filched; purloined; nabbed
PRIGGER thief; pincher
rl **PRIMACY** leading archbishopric
PRIMAGE a lading charge
PRIMARY main; first; pristine; initial
zo, rl **PRIMATE** genus of apes; archbishop
PRIMELY originally; excellently
PRIMERO card game
ck **PRIMEUR** early wine (Beaujolais) (Fr.)
bt **PRIMINE** outer husk
pt **PRIMING** (powder); first coat
PRIMMED formed precisely
bt **PRIMULA** primrose genus
PRINKED pranked; all dressed up
PRINKER (dressed showily)
PRINTED published; pressed; issued
PRINTER typographer
PRISAGE a levy on wines
bt **PRISERE** primary succession
PRISING forcing open; levering
zo **PRISTIS** saw-fish

PRITHEE I pray thee
PRIVACY seclusion; solitude; retreat
PRIVATE soldier; personal; unofficial
PRIVILY privately; confidentially
PRIVITY secrecy; cognizance
PRIZING appreciating; valuing
md **PROBANG** whalebone swab
lw **PROBATE** proof of a will
PROBING scrutinizing; testing; sifting
PROBITY proved integrity; sincerity
PROBLEM enigma; query; conundrum
bt **PROCARP** female organ in rhodophyta
PROCEED advance; continue; act
PROCESS operation; course; progress
cp **PROCESS** method; patterning of data
lw **PROCTOR** university official
PROCURE get; obtain; induce
PROCYON lesser Dog-star
PRODDED goaded; shoved; poked
PRODDER inciter; stimulator
PRODIFY modify production car (motor racing)
mu **PRODIGY** marvel; wonder; (infant)
PRODUCE engender; show; bring forth
cp, ck **PRODUCT** arithmetic; concoction
PRODUCT staple; yield; commodity
PROFACE May it profit you!
PROFANE desecrate; secular
PROFESS own; aver; proclaim
PROFFER offer; tender; volunteer
bd **PROFILE** outline view; biography
PROFUSE lavish; prodigal; copious
PROGENY offspring; issue; young
PROGGED begged; prodded; (proctored)
PROGRAM programme; syllabus
PROJECT propel; contrive; jut
PROLATE extended
zo **PROLEGS** legs of caterpillars
ch **PROLINE** protein cleavage product
PROLONG protract; lengthen; sustain
md **PROMINE** cancer-cell growth stimulant
PROMISE pledge; engage; stipulate
PROMOTE further; sponsor; organize
PRONAOS temple porch
PRONATE face or palms downwards
PRONELY lying down
PRONGED fork-like; bifurcated
zo **PRONOTA** beetles' backs
PRONOUN word for known person, thing
PROOFED **PROVEN**, tried, tested
md **PROOTIC** an ear-bone
PROPALE to disclose
PROPANE paraffin gas
PROPEND to favour; lean forward
ch **PROPENE** propyl alcohol
PROPHET seer; augur; preacher
PROPINE pledge; guarantee
ch **PROPINE** methyl acetylene
ae **PROPJET** a turboprop aircraft
PROPOSE suggest; intend; purpose
PROPPED shored; strutted; supported
PROPUGN vindicate; defend
PRORATE assess pro rata
md **PRORSAD** prorsal; anterior
PROSAIC unexciting; dull; humdrum
PROSIFY turn into prose
PROSILY unimaginatively
PROSING talking tediously
PROSODY (harmonious writing)
PROSPER thrive; flourish; succeed
PROTEAN in many guises
PROTECT shield; defend; ward
PROTEGE trusted nominee
ch **PROTEID** complex essential food
ch **PROTEIN** dietetic energy component
PROTEND hold out; extend
PROTEST expostulate; exclaim; object
PROTEUS sea-god of Carpathian Sea
ch **PROTIUM** hydrogen isotope
PROTYLE hypothetical nucleus
PROUDER more arrogant and haughty
PROUDLY majestically; imperiously
PROVANT of inferior quality
PROVERB saw; adage; epigram; maxim
PROVIDE supply; produce; survey
PROVINE (vine culture)
cp **PROVING** truth; fault-testing program
lw **PROVING** establishing; trying; trial
PROVISO a condition
PROVOKE infuriate; enrage; rouse
rl **PROVOST** magistrate
PROWESS valour; skill; dexterity
PROWLED slunk; roved; roamed
PROWLER stealthy stalker
PROXIME nearest
PROXIMO next month
PRUDENT wise; cautious; frugal
PRUDERY mock modesty
PRUDISH very formal; puritanical
bt **PRUNING** lopping; clipping; trimming
md **PRURIGO** an itch
ch **PRUSSIC** acid; a cyanide

PRY-OVER Canadian canoe sideways movement
PRYTANY Athenian Council division
PRYTHEE I pray thee
PSALTER psalm book; rosary
PSCHENT royal crown of ancient Egypt
md **PSOATIC** (tenderloin)
PSYCHAL spiritualistic
PSYCHIC not based on materialism
cl **PSYCHRO-** of coldness (Gr.)
md **PTARMIC** sneezing mixture
md **PTERION** (craniology)
PTEROMA Greek peridrome; side-wall
zo **PTEROPE** flying fox; fruit-bat
md **PTOMAIN PTOMAINE** toxic poison
md **PTYALIN** (saliva)
PUBERAL of age
PUBERTY the generative age
PUBLISH announce; disclose; blazon
gs **PUCELLA** wine-glass top opener
PUCELLE Joan of Arc
zo **PUCERON** plant louse
PUCKERY wrinkled
PUCKISH impish; mischievous
PUCK-OUT free hit by defenders (hurling)
PUDDING fruity farinaceous food
PUDDLED stirred up the mud
PUDDLER iron-worker
PUDENCY modesty; bashfulness
PUEBLAN Mexican aborigine
pc **PUERILE** child-like, irresponsible acts
le **PUERING** skin-steeping/softening
PUFF-BOX powder compact
PUFFERY PUFFING, overdone advertisement
PUFFIER more swollen (skin)
PUFFILY bombastic; conceited
PUFF-OUT breather pause; exhale (smoke)
PUGMILL clay mill
pl **PUG-NOSE** boxer's flattened nose
bt **PULIALL** pennyroyal herb
nt **PULLIES** pulley-wheels (block/tackle)
PULLING towing; drawing back; extract
PULLING (weapon) (votes) (punches) (oars)
rw **PULLMAN** luxury railway carriage
PULL-OUT extensible; withdrawal; quit
ck **PULPIFY** make mash; purée
PULPOUS like pulp
PULSATE throb (rhythm); vitality
pl **PULSING** heart beats; vibration
el **PULSION** electric waves; surges
ck **PUMMAGE** crushed apples (cider)
PUMPAGE the amount pumped
PUMPING extracting information
PUMPING syphoning liquids
ga **PUMPING** to vary weight (skateboards)
bt **PUMPKIN** pumpion; quashey; a gourd
au **PUMP-ROD** part of engine
PUNCHED perforated; struck
PUNCHER a bruiser; cattle drover
PUNCH-UP fist-fight (boxing)
zo **PUNCTUM** marking dot; tiny aperture
PUNGENT acrid; caustic; tart
PUNJABI an Indo-Aryan language
PUNNING play on word similarities
PUNSTER a maker of puns
PUNTING gambling against banker
PUNTING poling a punt forward
ga **PUNTING** football pool chancing
zo **PUPATED** formed a chrysalis
rl **PURANIC** (Brahmin scriptures)
mn **PURBECK** Dorset stone
ar **PURFLED** decorated
PURFLEW wrought border
PURGING cleaning up; pruning
PURITAN religious bigot
PURLIEU slum; environs
PURLINE timber-work
PURLING rippling
PURLOIN steal; pilfer; filch
PURPLED dyed purple; imperial
md **PURPLES** livid spots
PURPORT significate; state intent
PURPOSE aim; reason for action
zo, hd **PURPURA** Tyrian heraldic purple
PURRING curring; (feline felicitude)
PURROCK PADDOCK, witch's cat
PURSING wrinkling
PURSUED continued; hunted; practised
lw **PURSUER** plaintiff (Sc.)
PURSUIT chase; search; hobby
ga **PURSUIT** track-cycling start-points
PURVIEW extent; scope; range
PUSHFUL enterprising; self-assertive
PUSH-OFF leave hastily; forced departure
ga **PUSHPIN** a child's game
au **PUSH-ROD** auto engine part
PUSTAKA Indonesian magic book (on bark)
md **PUSTULE** a pus-pimple
go **PUSZTAS** Hungarian open plain
bt **PUTAMEN** fruit-stone; husk

md **PUTAMEN** lenticular nucleus
bd **PUTLOGS** horizontal bearers (scaffolding)
PUTRIFY rot; decay; decompose
PUTTIED fixed with putty
PUTTIER glazier
PUTTIES leg-wear; puttees
PUTTING (golf); (the weight)
zo **PUTTOCK** kite; buzzard
PUTWITH acknowledgement, addenda for book
PUZZLED perplexed; mystified
PUZZLER poser; riddler
md **PYAEMIA** blood-poisoning
md **PYAEMIC** suffering from pyaemia
mn **PYCNITE** topaz
bt **PYCNIUM** spermogonium in uredinales
zo **PYEBALD PIEBALD**, 2 colours (horses)
PYE-BOOK rules to determine Easter date
PYGMEAN PIGMEAN, dwarfish
PYGMIES negrillos; negritas; 1.5 m. tall
tx **PYJAMAS PAJAMAS**, nightwear
zo **PYLORIC** of stomach-intestine entry
md **PYLORUS** an outlet
rl **PYRAMID** triangular on a square; tomb
cy **PYRENIN** paranuclein
md **PYRETIC** fever-reducer
PYREXIA PYREXIC, of fever
mn **PYRITES PYRITIC**, flints
md **PYROGEN** fever inducer
md **PYROSIS** indigestion; heartburn
md **PYROTIC** caustic; burning
PYRRHIC victory at great cost
ch **PYRROLE** coal-tar constituent
bc **PYRUVIC** of an α-keto acid
PYTHIAD a period
PYTHIAN oracular
bt **PYXIDIA** capsules

Q

el **Q-FACTOR** efficiency, reactive circuit
me, nc **Q-FACTOR** ditto electrical components
zo **QUABIRD** night heron
QUACKED boasted; practised quackery
QUACKLE CAKKLE, croak; quack (ducks)
pr **QUADRAT** filling piece in printing
QUADREL square tile
QUADRIC four-sided, oblong shape
QUAFFED tippled; swilled; caroused
QUAFFER deep drinker; soaker; toper
zo **QUAHAUG** American clam
QUAILED flinched; cowered; blenched
rl **QUAKERS QUAKERY, QUAKERISM**, a sect
QUAKING shaking; quivering
QUALIFY entitle; regulate; dilute
QUALITY trait; attribute; grade
bt **QUAMASH** camass lily
zo **QUANACO** S. American llama
to **QUANNET** flat file
cf **QUANTAL** small changes, amounts
QUANTIC algebraic function
QUANTUM a sufficiency; elemental unit
el, nc **QUANTUM** radiant energy; theory
QUARREL wrangle; brawl; bicker
QUARREL cross-bow bolt; diamond pane
QUARTEN every fourth day
ma **QUARTER** one fourth; district; mercy
mu **QUARTET** 4-part music
mn **QUARTZY** of quartz silicon
as **QUASARS** quasi-stellar radio sources
QUASHED rendered void; nullified
bt **QUASHEY** pumpkin; a gourd
bt **QUASSIA QUASSIN**, bitter, tonic
QUATERN a quarter; 4-pound loaf
QUAVERY tremulous; quivery; tottery
QUAYAGE quay dues
QUEACHY bog-like; unsteady; yielding
QUEENED played the queen
QUEENLY regal
QUEERED put at a disadvantage
QUEERER odder; rummier; stranger
QUEERLY quaintly; whimsically
QUELLED crushed; allayed; quenched
QUELLER subduer; represser
bt **QUERCUS** oak
QUERELA complaint
lw **QUERENT** inquirer; plaintiff
QUERIED doubted; challenged
QUERIST questioner; interrogator
QUERLED twirled
QUERNEL oaken
QUESTED sought; requested
QUESTER a seeker; searcher; candidate
QUESTOR Roman treasury official
nm, zo **QUETZAL** resplendent trogon
QUIBBED quipped; sneered
QUIBBLE prevaricate; cavil; trifle
QUICKEN revive; rouse; expedite
QUICKER faster; more swiftly
QUICKIE a fatuous film

QUICKLY rapidly; speedily; pronto
QUIDDIT a quibble
QUIDDLE to potter
QUIETED calmed; assuaged; mollified
QUIETEN lull; allay; pacify; soothe
QUIETER more placid or secluded
QUIETLY peacefully; serenely
QUIETUS discharge; death
QUILLED pleated; crimped
QUILLER adept at paper-filigree art
QUILLET a quibble; a furrow
QUILLON part of a sword-guard
QUILTED padded; tufted
QUILTER coverlet maker
ma **QUINARY** in fives (biquinary= 2×binary)
bt **QUINATE** five-leafed
bt, md **QUININE** bitter (tonic water)
zo **QUINNAT** king salmon
ch **QUINONE** (benzene)
QUINTAD pentad
me **QUINTAL** a hundredweight
me **QUINTAL** 100 kilograms weight
md **QUINTAN** recurring ague
nm **QUINTAR** (Albania)
mu **QUINTET** 5-part music
ma **QUINTIC QUINTUS**, of the fifth degree
QUIPPED quibbled; taunted
QUIRING singing in unison
QUISCHE be still; calm; be silent
QUITTAL repayment; requital
QUITTED abandoned; forsook; left
vt **QUITTER** shirker; horse ulcer; deserter
vt **QUITTOR** foot cartilage suppuration
QUI-VIVE alert; on the look-out
QUIXOTE a chivalrous Don
QUIZZED queried; bantered; chaffed
QUIZZER questioner; a joker
bt, ck **QUODLIN CODLING**, cooking apple; boy
QUONDAM former
QUOTING citing; pricing
QUOTITY quantity

R

RABBANA raffia matting (Madagascar)
RABBITY petty; rabbit-like
RABBLER puddler; iron-worker
RABBONI Jewish title
RABIDLY frantically; maniacally
md **RABIFIC** causing hydrophobia
RABINET ancient gun
RABIOUS raging mad
zo **RACCOON** N. American racoon
RACE-CUP a trophy
bt **RACEMED** clustered
ch **RACEMIC** acid from grapes
RACEWAY sluice
RACKETS raquet and ball game in court; (squash)
mu **RACKETT** woodwind, 'sausage bassoon'
RACKETY bobbery; clamorous
RACKING decanting; straining
ga **RACQUET RACKET**, (tennis, badminton)
RADDLED interwoven; infested
zo **RADDOCK RUDDOCK**, robin red-breast
md **RADIALE** radiocarpal bone
RADIANT beaming; effulgent; shining
RADIATE sparkle; glitter; emit
RADICAL essential; root; basic change
RADICAL Liberal; molecular atoms
ga **RADICAL** exacting skateboarding
bt **RADICEL** small root of seedling
RADICLE root; corm; rootlet
RADIOED transmitted by wireless
RADULAR rasping; rough
RAFFING sweeping; snatching
RAFFISH rakish; dissipated
RAFFLED notched; (lottery)
RAFFLER lottery organizer
RAFT-DOG iron clamp
RAFTING raft-work
RAG-BOLT iron holdfast
bt **RAG-BUSH** heathen shrine
RAG-DUST rag refuse
RAGEFUL angered; wroth; ireful
RAG-FAIR old clothes sale
RAGGERY rags collectively
RAGGING boisterous pranks; rampaging
RAGGING teasing; students' stunts
tx **RAGSHOP** used clothes junk shop
mu **RAGTIME** syncopation with rhythm (jazz)
hd **RAGULED** jagged
bt **RAG-WEED RAGWORT**
tx **RAG-WOOL** shoddy
bd **RAGWORK** mason's work with stones
RAIDING foraying; pillaging
rw **RAILBUS** bus-engine railway coach
rw **RAILCAR** self-propelled rail coach
RAILING fencing; nagging; rating
to, rw **RAILSAW** portable saw
rw **RAILWAY RAILROAD**, iron road (trains)
RAIMENT garb; vesture; apparel
RAINBOW water-refracted sunlight

RAINING pouring; showering
mt **RAINMAP** weather chart
RAISING growing; erecting; lifting
RAISING levying; (old) pipe-making
RAKE-OFF share of crooked profits
RALLIED recovered; reformed
RALLIES bouts; jamborees
zo **RALLINE** waterbirds
rl **RAMADAN RAMAZAN**, month of fasting
RAMBADE boarding platform
RAMBLED sauntered; maundered
RAMBLER footpath, pleasure walker
bt **RAMBLER** climbing rose; long-winded
bt, ck **RAMEKIN RAMSKIN**, cheese savoury
bt **RAMENTA** scales on ferns
bt **RAMEOUS RAMULOUS**, branching out
RAM-HEAD iron lever; a cuckold
RAMLINE guide line in ship-building
RAMMING thrusting; forcing
zo **RAMMISH** of ram; strong-scented
RAMPAGE wild uncontrolled behaviour
hd **RAMPANT** exuberant; rearing stance
bd **RAMPART** fortified wall; bastion
bt **RAMPICK RAMPIKE**, tree-stump; log
RAMPING creeping; climbing; bounding
bt **RAMPION** campanula
bt, ck **RAMSKIN RAMEKIN**, cheese savoury
RAMSONS garlic, broad-leaved
bt **RAMULUS** small branch
RANCHED (stock farming)
RANCHER stock-breeder
RANCOUR deep-seated enmity
RANGERS National Parks' patrol men
hd **RANGIER** scythe
RANGING ranking; roving; extending
zo **RANIDAE** the frogs
RANKEST coarsest; most rancid
RANKING grading; ranging
RANKLED festered; smouldered
RANSACK rummage; pillage; plunder
RANTING orating; declaiming; raving
zo **RANTOCK** goosander
bt **RAPE-OIL** cole-seed oil
nt **RAPFULL** full of wind
RAPHAEL an archangel; a painter
bt **RAPHIDE** plant-cell crystal
RAPIDLY speedily; swiftly; despatch
RAPPING knocking; hitting; beating
fd **RAPPING** mould pattern loosening
pc **RAPPORT** harmony; understanding
RAPTURE ecstasy; beatitude; bliss
ck **RAREBIT** Welsh cheese savoury
nt **RASCONA** sail cargo boat, Venice
mn **RASHING** thin layer of shale/poor coal
zo **RASORES** gallinaceous birds
RASPING grating; abrading
mu **RASTRUM** a music-pen
RATABLE taxable; assessable
RATABLY by rate
RATAFIA almond-flavoured biscuit
mu **RATATAT** drumming
RATCHED stretched; racked
RATCHEL ratchil; loose stones
RATCHET pawl; toothed bar
RAT-HOLE retreat for rat
zo **RATITAE** (ostriches, emus, kiwis)
nt **RATLINE RATLING**, rigging ladder step
RAT-RACE career competition
RAT-TAIL tapering
tx **RATTEEN** twilled wool
RATTERY apostasy
RATTING quitting; abandoning
RATTLED clattered; shaken
RATTLER snake
bt **RATTOON** young sugar-cane
RAT-TRAP bicycle pedal
RAUCITY hoarseness
RAUCOUS harsh; noisy
RAUNCHY male ruggedness; strength
RAVAGED laid waste; devastated
RAVAGER despoiler; plunderer
RAVELIN part of a fort
RAVENED preyed; plundered
RAVENER ravager; devourer
RAVINED gullied
ck **RAVIOLI** small filled pasta cases (It.)
RAWBONE gaunt, lean person
RAWCOLD damp and cold
RAWHEAD bughead; devil; scarecrow
RAWHIDE untanned skin
RAWNESS immaturity; callowness
nt **RAWPORT** porthole for an oar
RAYLESS dark
REACHED attained; arrived; stretched
REACHER stretcher
REACTED took violent action
nc **REACTOR** atomic power generator
READIED prepared
READIER prompter; more glib
READILY willingly; cheerfully
READING recital; version; studying
READMIT glove used when reading
cp **READ-OUT** transfer of data
READ-OUT data display on screen
ch **REAGENT** active agent
REAGREE reconcile
mn **REALGAR** red arsenic

REALIEN objects for study; teaching aids
REALISM natural limits accepted
REALISM naturalism in art
REALIST a facer of facts
REALITY actuality; truth; verity
REALIZE convert into cash
REALLOT re-assign
REALTOR estate agent (USA)
REAMING enlarging a hole
REANNEX claim back; reunite
REAPING harvesting
RE-APPLY repeat a process
RE-ARGUE rediscuss a matter
REARING breeding; lifting; raising
REARISE reascend
REARMED re-equipped
RE-AROSE got up again
ps **REAUMUR** scale of temperature
REAVING bereaving; ravaging
REAWAKE rouse again
REBATED blunted; diminished
REBIRTH renascence
REBLOOM impossible action
REBOANT resounding; reverberating
REBORED facelift for gun-barrel
REBOUND bounce back; recoil
ga **REBOUND** regain the ball (basketball)
REBUILD REBUILT, re-erected
REBUKED chided; upbraided
REBUKER reproacher; gainsayer
RECEDED retreated; withdrew
RECEIPT a recipe; formula; quittance
RECEIVE welcome; acquire; get
RECENCY newness
RECITAL concert; narration
RECITED RECITER, narrated; narrator
RECLAIM rescue; salve; regain
RECLASP refasten
RECLINE lean; lie; rest; repose
RECLOSE fail to keep open
RECLUSE sequestered; a hermit
RECOAST coast back
RECOUNT tell; relate; enumerate
hd **RECOUPE** heraldic division
RE-COVER cover anew
RECOVER rally; revive; retrieve
RECROSS go back over
RECRUIT enlist; novice
RECTIFY amend; correct; redress
RECTION grammatic influence
rl **RECTORY** rector's benefice
zo **RECTRIX** steering feather
RECURVE concave; backwards
zo **RED-BIRD** bull-finch
RED-BOOK a register
nm **RED-CENT** copper cent
RED-CLAY raddle; reddle
REDCOAT a soldier
REDCOCK incendiary fire
mn **RED-CRAG** Pliocene rock
zo **RED-DEER** the common stag
REDDEST ultra-radical
REDDISH colour; rubicund; Titian
zo **RED-DRUM RED-BASS**, fish
REDEYED needing sleep
zo **RED-FISH** Pacific salmon
RED-HAND (Ulster)
zo **REDHEAD** red-haired; a duck
REDLEAD oxide as orange pigment
zo **REDLEGS** purple sandpiper
REDNESS ruddiness
REDORSE reverse of dorsal
REDOUBT fort
REDOUND conduce; lead; tend
zo **REDPOLL** linnet
REDRAFT revised copy
REDRAWN drawn again
REDRESS remedy; reparation
REDRIVE drive back
bt **RED-ROOT** buckthorn
RED-SEAR to break when too hot
zo **RED-SEED** small crustaceans
REDSKIN N. American Indian
zo **RED-TAIL** N. American buzzard
RED-TAPE bumbling officialdom delays
REDUCED curtailed; abridged; (prices)
REDUCER contractor; diminisher
RED-WEED the poppy
zo **REDWING** fieldfare
bt **REDWOOD** sequoia tree
tx, ar **REEDING** combing (yarns); moulding
nt **REEFING** shortening sail
REEKING fuming; smoking
REELING staggering; vacillating
nt **REEMING** caulking
RE-ENTRY regress; return
RE-EQUIP rearm
RE-ERECT rebuild
nt **REEVING** (passing a rope)
REFEOFF reinvest in a fief
REFEREE umpire; arbitrator; judge
REFINED highly cultivated
REFINER purifier; clarifier
REFLAME flare up again
REFLECT mirror; muse; meditate
REFORGE fashion anew
REFRACT to bend at an angle
REFRAIN chorus; forgo; abstain
REFRESH invigorate; revive; brace
REFUGED took sanctuary
REFUGEE a displaced person
REFUSAL declination; denial

REFUSED declined; denied; vetoed
REFUSER repudiator
REFUTED disproved; confuted
REFUTER rebutter
REGALED entertaining sumptuously
REGALIA insignia of royalty
REGALLY royally
nt **REGATTA** waterborne competitions
REGENCY rule of a stand-in (heir)
ar **REGENCY** fashions and of arts
REGIBLE governable
REGIMEN regulation; diet
REGNANT ruling
REGORGE vomit
REGRADE re-assess
REGRANT grant again
bd **REGRATE** retail; treating hewn stone
REGREET welcome again
pc **REGRESS** return; revert to (hypnosis)
REGULAR steady; systematic; normal
gn **REGULON** enzyme-production gene
as **REGULUS** star in Leo
ma **REGULUS** line set in ruled surface
REIGNED ruled; administered
REINING curbing; restraining
REINTER to bury again
zo **REIT-BOK** S. African buck
REJOICE revel; exult; gladden
cr **REJOINT** make a new joint
RELAPSE revert; backsliding
RELATED akin; connected; recited
RELATER gives an honest account
cp, lw **RELATOR** linkup factor; informant
RELAXED loosened; slackened; abated
ro **RELAYED** transmitted
RELEASE set free; emancipate; liberate
RE-LEASE lease again
RELIANT confident; self-assured
RELIEVE release; allay; assuage
RELIEVO rilievo; in relief
RELIGHT rekindle; reignite
rl **RELIQUE** a holy relic (Fr.)
RELIVED lived again
RELUMED rekindled
RELYING depending; trusting
REMAINS (literary productions)
REMAINS evidence of past history
lw **REMANET** delayed lawsuit
REMERGE merge again
zo **REMIGES** flight feathers
zo **REMIPED** oar-shaped feet
lw **REMISED** released; surrendered
REMNANT residue; odd lot; fragment
REMODEL refashion; remake; redesign
REMORSE anguish; compunction
REMOTER farther off
REMOULD shape anew
zo **REMOUNT** a fresh horse
REMOVAL euphemism for murder
REMOVED dislodged; abstracted
REMOVER homestead shifter
REMPHAN Israelitish idol
RENAMED rechristened
RENDING ripping; tearing; severing
RENEGED denied; revoked
RENEWAL refreshment; extension
RENEWED repeated; rejuvenated
RENEWER renovator
RENT-DAY time to pay or flit
RENTIER estate or fund holder
RENTING letting; leasing
RENUENT nodding
ga **RENVERS** half-pass in horse-dressage
REORDER bid again; repeat request
REPAINT (a golf ball); a fresh coating
REPAPER (a palindrome); redecorate
mu **REPIANO** **REPIENO**, all performers (It.)
REPINED fretted; murmured; envied
REPINER plaintive person
REPIQUE (piquet)
REPLACE reinstate; refund
REPLAIT refold
REPLETE crammed; fraught
lw **REPLEVY** to bail
REPLICA a copy; duplicate; model
REPLIED answered; folded back
REPLIER respondent
REPLUME to preen
REPOINT sharpen; accentuate
bd **RE-POINT** restore brickwork joins
REPONED replaced; relied
REPOSAL rest; sleep; ease
REPOSED settled; reclined
REPOSER slumberer
REPOSIT replace item in right place
REPRESS crush; check; restrain
REPRINT a subsequent edition
lw **REPRISE** repeat of music, song; estate charge; (fencing)
REPRIVE deprive (obs.)
REPROOF censure
REPROVE chide; upbraid
zo **REPTANT** creeping; reptilian
zo **REPTILE** crocodile; snake
REPULSE rebuff; deter; reject
REPUTED alleged; deemed; reckoned
REQUEST demand; entreat; solicit
rl **REQUIEM** a mass
REQUIRE want; lack; desire; need
REQUITE repay; reward; avenge
rl **REREDOS** altar screen

RESCIND revoke; quash; cancel
mu **RE-SCORE** try again
RESCUED freed; liberated
RESCUER deliverer; saviour
lw **RESEIZE** (legal confiscation)
RESERVE withhold; restraint
RESERVE set aside (for future) (land)
RESHAPE remould; remodel
lw **RESIANT** resident
RESIDED abode; inhered
RESIDER sojourner; dweller
RESIDUE remainder; dregs
RESILED showed ability to recover
RESOLVE determine; resolution
RESOUND reverberate; extol; echo
RE-SOUND reconsult; second opinion
RESPEAK repeat; reply
RESPECT revere; honour; esteem
RESPIRE breathe; inhale
RESPITE reprieve; pause; rest
RE-SPOKE reiterated; maintenance (bicycle)
RESPOND answer; accord; tally; react
ar **RESPOND** pillar set under arch
ar **RESSAUT** a projection
RESTANT persistent; remaining
RESTART return to paid work
cp **RESTART** recommence re-run
RESTATE re-assert; recite
lw **RESTAUR** claim for indemnity
REST-DAY the Sabbath
RESTFUL tranquil; quiescent; irenic
RESTING reposing; relaxing; leaning
RESTIVE refractory; obstinate
RESTOCK replenish
RESTORE reinstate; repair; heal
RE-STORE return to store
mn **RESUING** pre-mining technique
RESUMED renewed; continued
rl **RESURGE** rise again
RETABLE altar shelf for candles
RETAKEN recaptured
RETAKER recaptor
RETENUE self-control
RETIARY net-like, (gladiator)
RETICLE small net; reticule
md **RETINAL RETINA**, of eyes and sight
RETINOL resin oil; vitamin A
RETINUE suite; escort; bodyguard
zo **RETIPED** having veined feet
RETIRAL withdrawal; departure
RETIRED left; retreated; secluded
RETOUCH re-engrave; revise
RETRACE return by the same road
RETRACT adjure; recant; withdraw
RETREAD repair of a tyre
RETREAT recede; asylum; refuge
lw **RETRIAL** repeating court case
RETRUDE to thrust back
RETRUSE abstruse; hidden; occult
RETTERY flax mill
RETTING prepared flax
RETYRED renewed motor tyre surfaces
REUNIFY rejoin
REUNION social gathering
REUNITE reconcile; recombine
REURGED entreated again
REUTTER repeat; reiterate
REVALUE re-assess
REVELRY carousal; debauch; orgy
REVENGE requite; retaliate; vindicate
REVENUE income; return; reward
nt **REVENUE** (-man) (-cutter) ship
REVERED honoured; worshipped
REVERER venerator
REVERIE dreaminess; trance; vision
REVERSE backwards; setback; backspin
REVERSE misfortune; opposite; turnround
ga **REVERSI** a counter-game
REVERSO left-hand page of a book
hd **REVESTU** heraldic squaring
REVILED aspersed; vilified; abused
REVILER a despiser; contempt spreader
REVISAL revision; reviewal
REVISED amended; altered
REVISIT return to the same place
REVISOR editor; checkman
REVIVAL comeback; repeat; recall
rl **REVIVAL** religious reawakening
REVIVED quickened; resuscitated
REVIVER invigorator; rouser
lw **REVIVOR** renewed action
REVOKED reneged; repealed; quashed
REVOLVE rotate; spin; whirl; circle
REVVING spinning at speed
REWAKEN re-arouse
REWRITE recall; transcribe; revise
cp **REWRITE** return data to former location
zo **REYNARD** the fox
RHAETIC Ladino; Latin-Swiss
pl **RHAGADE RHAGOSE**, spongy wet skin crack
bt **RHAMNUS** buckthorn, etc.
bt **RHATANY** Peruvian shrub
RHEMISH (Rheims)
RHENISH (Rhine) (wine)
ch **RHENIUM** metallic element
zo **RHESIAN RHESUS**, sacred monkey (India)
zo **RHIZOTA** small aquatic animals

bt **RHIZOTE** rooted
RHODIAN RHODESIAN, (Cecil Rhodes)
ch **RHODIUM** hard white metal
bt **RHODORA** rhododendron
RHOMBIS RHOMBUS, oblique parallelogram
md **RHONCUS** harsh bronchial-tube sound
zo **RHOPODE** a marine invertebrate
bt, ck, cp **RHUBARB** pudding plant; statists' talk; rubbishy argument
RHYMING versifying
RHYMIST ballad-monger
RHYNCHO snouted; (rhinoceros)
nt **RIB-BAND** shipbuilding technique
RIBBING lampooning; ridiculing
nt, bd **RIBBING** corrugation frame
tx **RIBBONS** decorative bands (medals etc.)
mu **RIBIBLE REBEC** (forerunner of violin)
RIBLIKE lying like slats
bt **RIBSTON** pippin; an apple
RICASSO part of rapier-blade
zo **RICE-HEN** American fowl
bt **RICINUS** castor-oil plant
RICKERS tree stems for spars
md **RICKETS** softness of the bones
RICKETY shaky; unstable; feeble
RICKING wrenching; spraining
RICKSHA jinricksha; carriage
ck **RICOTTA** bland creamy It. cheese
RIDABLE rideable
RIDDING freeing; banishing; clearing
RIDDLED full of holes
RIDDLER propounder of riddles
RIDE-OFF bumping and pushing (polo)
RIDERED stakes laid across bars
mu **RIDOTTO** musical entertainment (It.)
zo **RIETBOK** rietboc; reedbuck (S. Africa)
to **RIFFLER** curved file
RIFLING spiral grooving; ransacking
nt **RIFTING** riving; cleaving; splitting
gs **RIGAREE** broken design band; collar
nt **RIGGING** ropes, lines (masts, sails)
RIGGING fraudulent accounting, deals
RIGHTED redressed; rectified; adjusted
RIGHTEN set right; adjusted
RIGHTER redresser of wrongs
RIGHTLY properly; correctly
RIGIDLY inflexibly; staunchly
RIG-VEDA Vedic doctrine (India)
RIKSDAG Swedish Parliament
RILIEVO bas-relief
RILLING flowing; purling; rippling
RIMFIRE a cartridge
RIMLESS unframed
RIMMING making a border or edge
RIMPLED wrinkled; rumpled
ar **RINCEAU** vine-foliage moulding motif
RINDING peeling; excoriating
fr **RING-DOG** used for hauling timber
RINGENT irregular and gaping
zo **RINGHAL** spitting cobra
RINGING resounding
RINGLET circlet
RINGMAN Zulu chief
RING-NET butterfly-net
to **RING-SAW** scroll-saw
ga **RINKING** roller-skating; ice-skating
RINSING cleansing
mn **RIOLITE** silver selenide
RIOTING disorder; lawlessness
RIOTOUS turbulent; tumultuous
RIPCORD parachute release cord
mu **RIPIENO** supplementary
RIPOSTE lightning repartee; (fencing)
RIPPING splendid; tearing
RIPPLED purled; rilled
to **RIPPLER** comb for flax
RIPPLET tiny ripple
zo **RIPSACK** Californian whale
RIPTIDE fast flowing current
RISIBLE laughable; droll; absurd
RISIBLY amusingly; farcically
RISKIER more hazardous
RISKING venturing; chancing; hazarding
ck **RISOTTO** Italian rice dish
ck **RISSOLE** an entrée
RISTORI woman's jacket
zo **RITTOCK** tern
RIVALRY emulation; competition
RIVERET small river; stream; rivulet
RIVETED fastened
RIVETER clincher
RIVIERA fashionable resort
RIVIERE a necklace of jewels
RIVULET stream; brook; riveret
hd **RIZOMED** heraldic grains
ROADBED road foundation
ROADCAR rural streetcar
ROAD-HOG a motor pest
ROADING team racing
ROADMAN road repairer
ROAD-MAP plan of road network
ROADWAY highway; turnpike; autobahn
ROAMING roving; wandering

ROARING bellowing; shouting; bawling
ck **ROASTED** cooked in oven or embers
ROASTED cross-questioned; parched
ck **ROASTER** micro-oven; (pig, fowl etc.)
ROBBERY piracy; spoliation; pillage
ROBBING stealing; depriving; theft
zo **ROBINET** chaffinch
bt **ROBINIA** acacia
ROCK-CAM cam on rocking shaft
zo **ROCK-DOE** chamois
zo **ROCK-EEL** slippery customer
ROCKERY rock garden
ROCKIER more unstable
ROCKILY reeling; tottery
ROCKING lulling; staggering
mn **ROCK-OIL** petroleum; naphtha
sp **ROCKOON** balloon/rocket technique
mn **ROCK-TAR** petroleum
pb **RODDING** piping; drain-cleaning
RODLIKE cylindrical
ROD-LINE fishing line
RODOMEL roses and honey
ROD-RING (fishing-rod)
RODSTER an angler
zo **ROE-BUCK** male roe-deer
zo **ROE-DEER** small deer species
ROGALLO delta-shaped hang-glider
ROGUERY knavery; fraudulence
ROGUISH arch; wanton; puckish
ROILING rilling; angering
vt **ROINISH ROINOUS**, mangy; spotty
ROISTER to bluster; swagger; bully
ROKEAGE parched Indian corn
ROKELAY short cloak; roguelaure
ROLLICK frolic
ROLLING trundling; wallowing; lurching
ck **ROLLMOP** cured spiced herring
nt **ROLL-OFF** car ferry; primitive file
ae **ROLL-OUT** launching a new aircraft
ROLLTOP desk with sliding slats cover
ga **ROLLWAY** an incline, indoor bowls
ROMAIKA modern Greek dance
ROMAINE cos; firm-leafed lettuce
ROMANCE love story; (love affair)
ROMANCE ROMANIC, Latin-based tongue
ROMAUNT romance (exaggeration)
mn **ROMEINE** (antimony and lime)
mn **ROMEITE** antimonite of calcium
ROMMANY ROMANY, gipsy; (-language)
ROMPERS children's overalls
ROMPING frolicking; capering
ROMPISH frisky; sportive; frolicsome
zo **RONCHIL** ronquil; a N. Pacific fish
mu **RONDEAU** verse with a refrain
mu **RONDENA** Andalusian serenade
RONDEUR rounded contour; shape
md **RONGEUR** surgical forceps
zo **RONQUIL** ronchil, sea-fish
RÖNTGEN (X-rays)
ROOFING materials for roof
ROOFLET small roof
ROOF-TAX community tax
ROOINEK a Englishman (S. Africa)
zo **ROOKERY** (rooks); (seals)
ROOKING defrauding; fleecing
ROOK-PIE unsavoury dish
ROOMAGE stowage
ROOMFUL quantity of roses
ROOMIER more extensive
ROOMILY spaciously
ROOMING shared lodging
ROOSTED perched; slept
zo **ROOSTER** chanticleer; cock
ROOTAGE manner of rooting
bt **ROOTCAP** tip at end of root
ROOTERY pile of stumps
ROOTING eradicating; implanting
ROOTLED rummaged; dug
bt **ROOTLET** radicle; a root fibre
ROPALIC club-shaped
ROPEWAY aerial transport
zo **RORQUAL** a whale
mu **ROSALIA** progressive melody
ROSATED crowned with roses
ROSEATE rosy; blushing
bt **ROSEBAY** willow-herb
to **ROSE-BIT** (for countersinking)
bt **ROSE-BOX** a plant
bt **ROSE-BUD** what Citizen Kane said
zo **ROSE-BUG** rose-chafer
ROSE-CUT (diamond-cutting)
bt, ck **ROSE-HAW ROSE-HIP** wild rose fruit
ROSELET ermine's summer fur
zo **ROSELLA** a parakeet
bt **ROSELLE** rose-mallow
md **ROSEOLA** a rash
bt **ROSE-RED** deep-red (of roses)
ROSETTA inscribed (-lingual) stone
tx **ROSETTE** coloured cloth; a favour
ROSETTE party election badge
ROSIEST most blushing; reddest
ROSINED resined; gingered up
ROSLAND moorland
ck **ROSOLIO** raisin brandy
ROSSING bark removal
nt **ROSTRAL** Roman bow-beak (rammer)
ROSTRUM platform; pulpit; a beak
ROSULAR (leaves in clusters)
zo **ROTALIA** foraminifers

ROTATED revolved; spun; twirled
ROTATOR a rotor
zo **ROTCHET** red gurnard
zo **ROTCHIE** little auk; sea-dove
ROTELLA round shield
zo **ROTIFER** an animalcule
ROTODIP car-painting technique
ROTONDE ruff; cope (Fr.)
ROTTING decaying; fooling
me **ROTTOLO** Levantine weight
md **ROTULAR** (patella)
ROTUNDA circular building
ROUCHED puckered
ROUELLE wheel-like amulet
ROUERIE debauchery
ROUGHED rasped; (horse-shoes)
ROUGHEN scarify; coarsen
ROUGHER ruder; harsher; coarser
ROUGHIE hoodlum; hooligan
ROUGHLY boisterously; crudely
ROUGH-UP violent fight
ROUGING painting with rouge
ck **ROULADE** rolled meat
ROUNDED curved; turned
ROUNDEL a Norman shield; a ballad
ROUNDER more like a circle
ROUNDLY boldly; openly; plainly
ROUND-UP cowboys' work; rodeo show
hd **ROUSANT** starting up
ROUSING stimulating; brisk; lively
ROUSTER vagrant; vagabond
ROUTIER long-distance delivery-man
ROUTIER armed brigand (Fr.)
cp **ROUTINE** workstyle; regularity system
ROUTING utterly defeating; furrows
cp **ROUTING** itinerary; transmissions
ROUTISH clamorous; disorderly
ROWABLE a truly oarful state
nt **ROWBOAT** oars-boat
ROWDIER more uproarious or rampant
ROWDILY turbulently; noisily
nt **ROWLOCK** oarlock (rowing)
bd **ROWLOCK** bricklaying pattern
ROWPORT oar-hole
ROYALLY regally; imperially
ROYALTY author's perquisite
ROYNISH roinish; mangy
zo **ROYSTON** hooded crow
bt **ROZELLE** hibiscus
RUB-A-DUB beat of drum
mn **RUBASSE** Ancona ruby
RUBBING brass/stone tracing (brasses, tombstones)
RUBBING abrasion; chafing; erosion
RUBBING friction; massage (-down)
RUBBISH litter; trash; worthless
RUB-DOWN aphrodisiac
md **RUBELLA** German measles
RUBIATE madder
RUBICAN roan
mn **RUBICEL** variety of ruby
RUBICON boundary; fateful river
RUBIFIC making red
RUBIOUS ruby-red
RUBYING reddening
RUCHING a plaited frilling
RUCKING creasing; ruffling
RUCKLED wrinkled; rucked
RUCTION uproar; turmoil; disturbance
RUDDIED reddened
RUDDIER rosier; more rubicund
RUDDILY glowingly
tx **RUDDLED** interwoven; ochred
zo, bt **RUDDOCK** robin; apple
RUDERAL waste growth
bt **RUE-WORT** herb of grace
RUFFIAN desperado; apache; rascal
RUFFING trumping; ruffling
RUFFLED disordered; agitated
RUFFLER a bully
tx **RUGGING** heavy napped cloth
RUINING wrecking; demolishing
RUINOUS pernicious; calamitous
RULABLE allowable; governable
RULLION veldt-shoe; virago
RUMBLED reverberated
RUMBLER tum; (record-deck chafing)
RUMINAL of cud chewer; ruminant
RUMMAGE search; ransack
RUMMIER stranger; droller; quainter
RUMMILY oddly; whimsically
RUMNESS queerness; oddity
RUMPLED rimpled; crushed
RUM-SHOP a tavern
RUNAWAY fugitive; deserter; renegade
RUNDLED rounded like a rung
RUNDLET small barrel; runlet
RUN-DOWN exhausted; weak; anaemic
RUN-DOWN tracked to lair
RUN-LINE factory production; (stadium)
ce **RUNNERS** timber sheet piles (excavation)
RUNNING managerial; organizing
nt **RUNNING** sailing downwind; in order
RUN-OVER continuation over (body)
RUPTION eruption
RUPTIVE ruptile; liable to snap
RUPTURE fracture; breach; rift

RURALLY rustically
RUSALKA water-nymph (Rus.)
RUSHING dashing; careering; flying
RUSH-MAT reed pad
bt **RUSH-NUT** edible tuber
RUSSETY reddish-brown
RUSSIAN of Russia
RUSSIFY to enforce Russian style
bt **RUSSULA** red fungus
RUSTFUL rusty
RUSTICA ancient Rom. manuscript style
RUSTIER less practised
RUSTILY fustily; mustily
RUSTING oxidizing
RUSTLED stirred
RUSTLER cattle-thief
hd **RUSTRED** lozenge-shaped
RUTHFUL compassionate
nv **RUTTIER** routier; bearings chart
RUTTING grooving; furrowing; pairing
RUTTISH lustful; of mating season (deer)
me, nc **RYDBERG** atomic ionizing energy unit
zo **RYE-MOTH** a harvest pest
zo **RYE-WOLF** (German folk lore)
zo **RYE-WORM** larva of rye-moth

S

rl **SABAISM SABEISM**, Chaldean star worship
SABAOTH armies (Heb.)
SABBATH day of rest
zo **SABELLA** sea-worms
SABREUR user of sabre (fencing)
SABRING cutting with a sabre
SABURRA grittiness of the tongue
pl **SACCADE** rapid eye movement (dreams)
mu **SACCADE** sudden check
zo **SACCATA** molluscs
SACCATE sack-like
SACCULE small pouch
SACELLA altars; sanctuaries
SACKAGE pillage
mu **SACKBUT** dulcimer trombone
SACKFUL bagful
SACKING looting; plundering
rl **SACRIST** sacristan; a sexton
SADDEST most dismal and depressing
SADDLED loaded; hampered
SADDLER a saddle maker (horses)
SAD-EYED mournful
SADIRON box-iron; flat-iron
SADNESS sorrowfulness; melancholy
bt **SADTREE** night jasmine
mn **SADWARE** pewter dishes; plates etc.
SAFFIAN (tanned skins)
bt, ck **SAFFRON** plant; a colour; flavour
SAGAMAN a bard; narrator of sagas
tx **SAGATHY** woollen stuff
SAGESSE wisdom (Fr.)
ck **SAGGARD** box for baking porcelain
SAGGING drooping; sinking; failing
as **SAGITTA** arrow; star in Great Bear
zo **SAGOUIN** capuchin monkey
bt **SAGUARO** giant cactus
mn **SAHLITE** augite
SAIL-ARM (windmill)
nt **SAILING** voyage with wind
zo **SAIMIRI** squirrel monkey
SAINTED canonized
SAINTLY holy; devout; religious
rl **SAIVISM** worship of Siva
SALABLE saleable; vendible
SALADIN a Sultan (Crusades)
SALAMBA fishing device (Manila)
zo **SALAMIS** insect genus
SALCHOW skating jump
mu **SALICET** soft tone organ stop
bt, md **SALICIN** willow extract (aspirin)
SALIENT projecting front-line sector
SALIERE salt-cellar (Fr.)
bt **SALIGOT** water caltrops
lw **SALIQUE SALIC**, male succession law
pl, ch **SALIVAL SALIVARY**, of mouth enzymes
SALLIED when besieged attacked
pt, md **SALLOWY** yellowish (jaundice)
SALMIAC sal-ammoniac
ch **SALMINE** fish-testicle protamine
zo **SALPIAN** ascidian
md **SALPINX** Eustachian tube
bt **SALSAFY** oyster plant saxifrage root
bt **SALSIFY** purple goat's beard root
bt **SALSOLA** glass-wort
SALTANT dancing; leaping
bl **SALTANT** suddenly developed variant
SALTATE to dance; leap; jump; skip
SALT-BOX salt cellar
SALT-CAT pigeon medicine
SALTERN salt factory
SALTIER saltire
SALTING sea-marsh; pickling; curing
SALTIRE St Andrew's cross
SALTISH brackish; briny
SALT-PAN evaporating pan
SALT-PIT open salt mine
SALUTED honoured; kissed; greeted
SALUTER that which salutes

SALVAGE rescue; compensation
SALVETE greetings to new members
SALVING healing; restoration
SAMADHI broken; mind/body link in yoga
zo **SAMBHUR** Indian stag
SAMBUCA SAMBUKE, ancient harp
SAMIOTE native of Samos (Gr.)
mu **SAMISEN SHAMISEN**, Japanese lute
SAMNITE Sabine tribe (It.)
ck **SAMOGON** illicit vodka (Russia)
bt **SAMOLUS** primrose genus
SAMOVAR Russian tea-urn
zo **SAMOYED** arctic people; sledge dog
SAMPLED tried; tasted
SAMPLER needlework; pattern picture
ce **SAMPLER** soil, sand crusher for testing
SAMSARA transmigration; reincarnation
SAMSHOO rice spirit (China)
SAMURAI Japanese military class
rl **SANCTUM** a refuge; a shrine
rl **SANCTUS** a hymn
SANDBAG ballast; defence; weapon
SAND-BAR estuarine barrier
SANDBED a mould
rw **SANDBOX** on loco for slippery rails
bt **SANDBOX** for wet ink; tree (W. Indies)
SAND-BOY a happy lad
zo **SANDBUG** digger wasp
bt **SANDBUR** a weed
zo **SAND-DAB** plaice
zo **SAND-EEL** small fish
bt **SANDERS** red sandal-wood
zo **SAND-FLY** a biting midge
SANDING burying oysters (in moisture)
jn, pt **SANDING** smoothing; flattening down
SANDISH gritty; friable
SANDJET sand-blast
zo **SAND-LOB** lug-worm
SANDMAN children's sleep-giver
SAND-PIT source of sand
zo **SAND-RAT** the camass rat
SANHITA Vedic hymns
bt **SANICLE** healing plant
SANKHYA Hindu philosophy
zo **SAPAJOU** S. Amer. spider-monkey
zo **SAPERDA** boring beetles
SAP-HEAD (fortification)
md **SAPHENA** prominent vein
SAPIENT wise; sage; clever; astute
SAPLESS dry; not juicy
bt **SAPLING** young tree
zo **SAPLING** young greyhound
SAPONIN soapwort extract
SAPPHIC SAPPHO, stanzas; lifestyle
bt **SAPPING** draining juices; undermining
SAPROBE plant growing in foul water
ck **SAPSAGO** a green Swiss cheese
bt **SAPWOOD** the alburnum
SARACEN Arab; Selçuk Turk
SARAFAN Russian gala-dress
SARAWAK glossy yellow cane
SARCASM irony; satire; ridicule
SARCELE partly cut through
bt **SARCINA** fungoid plant
md **SARCINE** (muscular tissue)
SARCODE protoplasm
SARCODY conversion to fleshlike state
SARCOID flesh-like
md **SARCOMA** tumour; skin cancer
SARCOUS fleshy
mu **SARDANA** folk dance (Catalan)
zo **SARDINE** fish; (pilchard)
nt **SARDINE** sea-boat (Portugal)
mn **SARDIUS** sard; a quartz
zo **SARGINA** mullet (fish)
zo **SARIGUE** opossum (Brazil)
SARKING roof sheathing
bt **SARMENT** a runner; filiform stem
tx **SARPLAR** sarpler; packing cloth
tx **SARSNET** fine woven silk
SARTAGE forest clearing
SASHERY dress bands; court orders
SASHING framework for windows
zo **SASSABY** tsessebe; hartebeest
SASSING (-out); ascertaining
SATANIC infernal; diabolical; abuse
SATCHEL small sack or container
SATIATE glutted; to cloy; to gorge
SATIETY surfeit; over-gratification
tx **SATINET** thin satin
SATIRIC sarcastic; ironical; mordant
SATISFY gratify; requite; settle
SATRAPY stand-in governorship
bt **SATSUMA** Japanese pottery; citrus fruit
tx **SATTARA** ribbed woollen material
tx **SATTEEN** ratteen; thick woollen fabric
rl **SATYRAL SATYRIC**, satyr; woodland goat-god of lustful revelling
SATYRUS orang-utan (wild-man)
SAUCIER ruder; more impudent
SAUCILY pertly; flippantly; pungently
SAUCING sassing; seasoning
SAUNTER dawdle; stroll; dally

zo **SAURIAN** lizard; reptile; crocodile
zo **SAUROID** reptilian; (dino-)
ck **SAUSAGE** minced meat inside skin
hd **SAUTOIR** diagonal ribbon
SAVABLE SAVEABLE, salvageable
SAVAGED attacked brutally
go **SAVANNA** treeless plain
ck **SAVARIN** syrup-soaked yeast cake
SAVE-ALL an economizer
ck **SAVELOY** red smoked pork sausage
SAVIGNY red Burgundy wine
SAVINGS 'nest-egg'; reserve cash
rl **SAVIOUR** Messiah; Redeemer
ck **SAVOURY** piquant, stimulating dish
zo **SAW-BACK** a caterpillar
zo **SAWBILL** goosander; merganser
SAWBUCK sawhorse
SAWDUST carpentry by-product
to **SAWFILE** triangular file
zo **SAWFISH** serrated-proboscis fish
zo **SAWHORN** an insect
SAWMILL lumber factory
zo **SAWWHET** Acadian owl
bt **SAWWORT** a plant
mu **SAXHORN** brass wind-instrument
SAXONIC of Saxony, Germany
tx **SAY-CAST** coarse part of wool, from tail
tx **SAYETTE** serge; woollen yarn
SCABBED worthless; black-listed
SCABBLE SCAPPLE, (stone-dressing)
md **SCABIES** itch; mange; parasitic mite
md **SCABRID SCABROUS**, skin scabs
SCADDLE skaddle; hurtful; impish
mn **SCAGLIA** Italian calcareous rock
SCALADE scaling ladder (Fr.)
SCALADO escalade assault (It.)
SCALARY stepped like a ladder
SCALDED immersed in boiling water
SCALDIC (Norse eddas, sagas)
SCALENE irregular triangle
mn **SCALING** removal of loosened rock
SCALING evaluation; measurement
bd **SCALING** ladder; (siege-ladder)
SCALING fish scales etc.
SCALING ornament; overlapping circles
SCALLED scurfy; scabby
zo, ck **SCALLOP** shellfish; baking mould
SCALLOP pilgrim badge; (border) (pattern)
zo **SCALOPS** American shrew-moles
SCALPED head-skin removed as trophy
SCALPED speculators' quick profits
md **SCALPEL** surgeon's dissecting knife
SCALPER hair-raising savage
SCAMBLE SHAMBLE, SCRAMBLE, mangle
zo **SCAMMEL** bar-tailed godwit
SCAMMUM geometrical figure
SCAMPED skimped
SCAMPER scurry; run; hasten
SCANDAL disgrace; infamy; discredit
bt **SCANDIX** Venus' comb
SCANNED scrutinized; perused
tv **SCANNER** television or radar beam
md, cp **SCANNER** (medical) sampling device
SCANTED limited; stinted
SCANTLE cut into small pieces
SCANTLY scantily; niggardly
SCAPNET minnow-net
SCAPPLE stone-dressing
md **SCAPULA** shoulder blade
SCARCER rarer; less plentiful
SCARFED (timber joint)
SCARIFY to scratch; to harrow
SCARING affrighting; daunting
SCARLET bright orangish red
SCAROID like parrot fish
SCARPED made precipitous
SCARRED disfigured
SCARVES kerchiefs; cravats
SCATHED injured; damaged; hurt
ag **SCATTER** disperse; strew; sow seed
cp **SCATTER** distributing data within store
to **SCAUPER** engraver's tool
SCENERY prospect; view; landscape
SCENTED perfumed; smelt; suspected
SCEPSIS philosophic doubt
SCEPTIC skeptic; a doubter
SCEPTRE royal staff; power
tx **SCHAPPE** spun silk
zo **SCHELLY** white fish
SCHEMED plotted; planned; contrived
SCHEMER intriguer; plotter
SCHEPEN magistrate (Dutch)
mu **SCHERZO** playfully
SCHESIS habitude; wont
SCHETIC constitutional; habitual
bt **SCHINUS** mastic-tree
to **S-CHISEL** well-boring cutter
mu **SCHISMA** tonal difference
SCHLICH ore slime
SCHLOSS castle; ancient seat (Ger.)
SCHMUCK unsophisticated person; idiot
SCHNAPS SCHNAPPS, akvavit
SCHOLAR student; pupil; disciple
SCHOLIA marginal notes
mn **SCHORLY** tourmaline
md **SCIATIC** affecting the hip

SCIBILE knowable
SCIENCE knowledge; reduced to system
zo **SCINCUS** lizard; skink; a saurian
mu **SCIOLTO** with abandon
bt **SCIRPUS** bulrush genus
SCISSEL **SCISSIL**, metal clippings
SCISSOR to cut
zo **SCIURUS** squirrel genus
md **SCLERAL** hard; ossified
bt **SCLERIA** sedges
bt **SCOBINA** ends of grass
SCOFFED mocked; jeered; derided
SCOFFER a taunter; ridiculer
SCOLDED chided; nagged; rebuked
SCOLDER railer; upbraider
mn **SCOLITE** fossil worm
zo **SCOLLOP** scallop
zo **SCOMBER** mackerel genus
SCOONED skimmed; glided
nt **SCOONER** a schooner
SCOOPED hollowed out; dredged
zo **SCOOPER** a water-fowl; the avocet
SCOOTED bolted; squirted
SCOOTER ice-boat; toy; light motorcycle
SCOPATE brush-like
SCOPTIC bantering; jesting
zo **SCOPULA** small tuft of hairs
SCORIAC ashy
mn **SCORIAE** volcanic ashes
SCORIFY reduce to ashes
SCORING recording points, runs etc.
SCORING scratching; making marks
SCORNED disdained; spurned
SCORNER contemner; flouter
to **SCORPER** a gouge
zo **SCORPIO** (Zodiac); scorpion
rl **SCOTICE** in Scottish
SCOTISM doctrine of Duns Scotus
rl **SCOTIST** a theologian
md **SCOTOMA** blind spot
md **SCOTOMY** dizziness
SCOURED made searching survey
SCOURED vigorously cleansed
SCOURER scrubber; polisher; scraper
SCOURGE lash; chastise; plague
SCOUTED made an intensive search
SCOUTER stone flaker
SCOWLED registered displeasure
SCRAGGY lean and lanky
SCRANCH **SCRUNCH**, grinding noise
SCRANNY lean and spare
SCRAPED erased; rubbed; rasped
to **SCRAPER** plane
SCRAPER miser; fiddler; scourer
vt **SCRAPIE** nervous sheep disease
SCRAPPY fragmentary; incomplete
SCRATCH lacerate; zero handicap
SCRATCH withdraw from contest
cp **SCRATCH** reusable tape; (-an income)
SCRAWLY scribbled; ill-formed script
SCRAWNY raw-boned
SCREECH shrill sound; owl call
SCREEVE to write begging letters
SCREWED twisted; tipsy; bored
SCREWER screw-driver; extortioner
SCRIBAL clerical
SCRIBED wrote; recorded; marked
to **SCRIBER** engraving tool
SCRINGE **CRINGE, FLINCH**, grate
zo **SCRITCH** **SCREECH**, a thrush
SCROGGY having thick undergrowth
SCROOGE scrudge; squeeze
SCROTAL of the scrotum
zo **SCROTUM** testicle sac in mammals
SCROUGE squeeze; to crowd
SCRUBBY stunted; squabby
SCRUFFY unkempt; untidy; uncouth
SCRUNCH **CRUNCH**, crush; (-dry)
SCRUNCH for tousled -look hair-style
me **SCRUPLE** honesty; 20 grains Troy wt
SCRYING crystal gazing
nt **SCUDDED** ran before the wind
SCUDLER scullion; kitchen boy
ag **SCUFFLE** struggle; a hoe
SCULLED rowed gently
nt **SCULLER** rowed water taxi
SCULPIN sea-fish; dragonet; bull-head
zo **SCUMBER** fox-dung
SCUMBLE overlay painting
SCUMMER a skimmer of scum
SCUPPER vent; annihilate
SCUPPET **SCOPPET**, scoop; shovel
SCURRIL **SCURRIT**, foul-mouthed rogue
md **SCURVEY** vitamin-deficiency disease
SCUTAGE feudal tax
SCUTATE like a shield
SCUTTER scurry
nt **SCUTTLE** (coal); hatchway; sink
zo **SCYMNUS** ladybirds; sharks
SCYPHUS a large drinking-cup (Gr.)
bt **SCYPHUS** podetium end widening
SCYTALE secret message (Gr.)
zo **SCYTALE** coral snake
SCYTHED mowed; cut
SCYTHIC Scythian (of Ukraine)
SEA-BANK protective bank
zo **SEA-BASS** marine fish
bt, zo **SEA-BEAN** small univalve shell

zo **SEA-BEAR** seal; polar bear
SEA-BEAT lashed by the waves
bt **SEA-BEET** rare vegetable
bt **SEA-BELT** fucus plant
zo **SEA-BIRD** aquatic bird
nt **SEA-BOAT** manageable at sea, stable
SEA-BORN produced by the sea
zo **SEA-CALF** common seal
nt **SEA-CARD** compass card
zo **SEA-CLAM** a bivalve
mn **SEA-COAL** cash
zo **SEA-COCK** gurnard; a valve
nt **SEA-COOK** marine father
zo **SEA-COOT** exotic ocean bird
zo **SEA-CORN** spawn
zo **SEA-CRAB** ocean crustacean
zo **SEA-CROW** cormorant
zo **SEA-DACE** bass
zo **SEA-DOVE** little auk
zo **SEA-DUCK** eider-duck
SEA-FIRE phosphorescence
zo **SEA-FISH** cod and others
mn **SEA-FOAM** meerschaum
SEA-FOLK sailors
zo **SEA-FOOD** fish as food
SEA-GAGE depth gauge
SEA-GATE harbour bar
SEA-GIRT insular
SEA-GOWN dress worn at sea
zo **SEAGULL** marine bird
SEA-HAIR sea-mist
SEA-HALL hall below the sea
zo **SEA-HARE** mollusc
zo **SEA-HAWK** a skua
bt **SEAHOLM** sea-holly
bt **SEAKALE** a cruciferous plant
SEA-KING a viking
bt **SEA-LACE** (seaweed)
ce **SEALANT** adhesive compound; plastic coating
zo **SEA-LARK** the dunlin
SEA-LEGS ability to balance at sea
nt **SEALIKE** shipshape; spirits up
zo **SEA-LILY** sea-urchin
nt **SEA-LINE** horizon; sky-line
zo **SEALING** culling
zo **SEA-LION** large seal
SEAL-OFF closure
zo **SEA-LUCE** hake
SEA-MAID mermaid
zo **SEA-MALL** sea-gull
nv **SEA-MARK** spar; buoy; light
me **SEA-MILE** 1853m or 2000 yards
SEAMING sewing together; scarring
zo **SEA-MINK** whiting
zo **SEA-MONK** monk-seal
bt **SEA-MOSS** seaweed
to **SEAM-SET** tinman's punch
SEA-OOZE soft mud
SEA-PASS passport
zo **SEA-PEAR** sea-squid
zo **SEA-PECK** the dunlin
zo **SEA-PERT** the opah fish
zo **SEA-PIKE** pike
bt **SEA-PINK** the thrift
zo **SEA-PORK** an ascidian
SEAPORT harbour for large ships
bt **SEA-REED** mat grass
SEARING cauterizing
SEA-RISK marine hazard
zo **SEA-ROLL** sea-cucumber
SEA-ROOM manoeuvre space
zo **SEA-ROSE** sea-anemone
zo **SEA-RUFF** sea-bream
mn **SEA-SALT** cookery condiment
SEASICK mal-de-mer
SEASIDE beach
zo **SEA-SLUG** a nudibranch
SEASONS climate and growth; (-of events)
SEA-TANG sea-tangle-weed
SEATING (bums on seats) (capacity)
zo **SEA-TOAD** angler fish
SEA-TOST common or garden tost
SEA-TURN a gale from the sea
SEAVIEW glimpse of the briny
SEA-WALL retaining wall
SEA-WANE wampum
SEAWARD toward the sea
bt **SEA-WARE** seaweed; sea-wreck
bt **SEAWEED** tangle; algae
zo **SEA-WHIP** a zoophyte
zo **SEA-WIFE** wrasse; mermaid
SEA-WING a sail
SEA-WOLD imaginary tract
zo **SEA-WOLF** wolf fish; pirate
zo **SEA-WORM** marine annelid
ch **SEBACIC** fatty acid
SEBILLA wooden bowl (meals)
SEBUNDY **SEPOY**, Indian soldier
SECANCY intersection
SECEDED withdrew; separated
SECEDER separationist
bt **SECHIUM** gourds
SECLUDE segregate; isolate
mu **SECONDO** bass of duet
SECONDS imperfect items; (stale); rejects
SECONDS deputies; assistants; extras
SECONDS time units; (boxing) (duelling)
SECRECY privacy; stealth; reticence
SECRETE hide; conceal; cache; yield
SECTANT geometric figure
SECTARY sectarian
SECTILE sliceable

SECTION portion; division; segment; (cross-); (-leader); (maps)
cp **SECTION** part of magnetic tape block
SECTIST dissenter
SECTIVE divisible
SECULAR of the world; lay; temporal
SECURED obtained; ensured; fastened
SECURER protector; guardian; safer
rl **SEDILIA** altar seats
SEDUCED enticed; led astray
SEDCUCER a libertine
SEEABLE visible
zo **SEE-CAWK** the American skunk
SEED-BAG germ-pouch
SEED-BED plantation
bt **SEED-BUD** germ of the fruit
SEED-COD seed-basket; husk
SEEDFUL promising; hopeful
SEEDILY shabbily
SEEDING (tournaments); sowing
SEED-LAC dried resin
bt **SEED-LOP** seed container
SEED-OIL linseed oil
SEEKING inquiring; questing
SEELING closing the eyelids
SEEMING specious; guise; apparent
SEEPAGE leakage; oozings
SEETHED boiled; soaked
SEETHER boiling pot
bt **SEGGROM** ragwort
SEGMENT a portion; section of a whole
cp **SEGMENT** redivide into chapters
SEINING netting fish
lw **SEISING** taking possession
SEISMAL seismic; (earthquake)
mt **SEISTAN** Persian summer north wind
zo **SEISURA** Australian fly-catchers
zo **SEIURUS** wagtail genus
SEIZING (ropes); grappling; binding
lw **SEIZURE** grasp; legal confiscation
md **SEIZURE** stroke; attack; theft
hd **SEJEANT** seated
zo **SELACHE** shark
ch **SELENIC** (selenium)
SELFBOW of single yew, archery
SELF-FED automatic feeding
SELFISH egotistical; mean; ungenerous
SELFISM me first and me only
SELFIST egoist
bt **SELINUM** milk-parsley
SELLING vending; hawking; betraying
SELTZER mineral water
SELVAGE selvedge; border
SEMATIC significant
SEMEION metrical mark
zo **SEMI-APE** a lemur
SEMI-GOD demi-god
SEMILOR imitation gold
SEMINAL rudimentary; original
SEMINAR special study occasion
zo **SEMIPED** prosody; a half-foot
SEMIPED verse, metre
SEMI-RAG paper with some rag content
SEMITIC Jewish; Hebrew
SENATOR a counsellor
SENATUS governing body
bt **SENCION** groundsel
SENDING despatching; forwarding
SEND-OFF farewell party
SENECAN style of philosophy of Seneca
bt **SENECIO** ragwort
zo **SENEGAL** African fire-bird
SENIORY council of elders
SENSATE sensible
SENSILE sensitive
SENSING understanding; feeling
SENSING perceptual awareness
SENSION perception
SENSISM sensualism
SENSIST sensationalist
md **SENSORY** nerve system
SENSUAL voluptuous
zo **SEPIARY** relating to cuttlefish
zo **SEPIOID** ink producers
zo **SEPIOST** cuttle-bone
SEPPUKU hara-kiri (Jap.)
SEPTATE partitioned
SEPTIME fencing posture
SEQUELA a consequence
SEQUELA abnormal, chronic condition
SEQUENT following; succeeding
bt **SEQUOIA** Californian red-wood
SERAPIS Apis; goddess of fertility
SERBIAN of Serbia; Yugoslav
SERENED tranquillized
SERENER calmer; more placid
bt **SERENOA** dwarf-palms (Florida)
SERFAGE serfdom; slavery
SERFDOM villenage; thraldom
SERIATE in series; serial
tx **SERICIN** silk
SERICON alchemic red
zo **SERIEMA** cariama; (heron)
SERIFIC silk-producing
bt **SERINGA** flowering shrub
zo **SERINUS** canary genus
zo **SERIOLA** amber fish
SERIOUS grave; sedate; staid

SERMENT oath
zo, mu **SERPENT** snake; old bassoon
md **SERPIGO** ring-worm
zo **SERPULA** sea-worms
SERRATE serrous; notched
SERRIED at close interval
zo **SERRULA** comblike ridge on chelicerae
zo **SERTOLI** of seminiferous tubule cells
bt **SERTULE** collection of plants
SERVAGE servitude; enthralment
SERVANT retainer; henchman; menial
SERVIAN Serbian; Serb
SERVICE duty; performance; utility
rl, mu **SERVICE** Anglican worship and music
ga **SERVICE** start of rally; (squash) (tennis)
SERVICE maintenance; employment
SERVICE military-; public-; social-; tip
SERVILE fawning; sycophantic; slave-like
rl **SERVING** ministering; (tennis)
SERVITE mendicant monk, 13th cent.
bt **SESAMUM** sesame genus
SESOTHO Basuto language (S. Africa)
bt **SESSILE** (no stalk)
lw **SESSION** meeting; assize; sitting
cp, tc **SESSION** open-time transmission
SESTINA sestine; verse (Fr.)
SESTOLE sextuplet
bt **SETARIA** spiky grasses
ar **SET-BACK** check; reverse; recess
SET-DOWN a rebuff
mu **SETLESS** no score; tennis
mu **SETTIMA** interval of a seventh
mu **SETTIMO** a seventh (It.)
SETTING appointing; congealing
SETTLED fixed; paid; sank; serene
SETTLER colonizer; arbitrator
bt **SETWALL** valerian
SETWORK (boat-building); (plaster)
SEVENTH ordinal number
SEVENTY cardinal number
SEVERAL sundry; diverse; various
SEVERED cut; rent; divided
SEVERER stricter; simple
zo **SEVRUGA** caviare-fish
nt **SEWED-UP** stranded
bt **SEXFOIL** six-leafed plant
SEXLESS of inteterminate gender
SEXTAIN (six lines)
nm **SEXTANS** Roman bronze coin
nt **SEXTANT** optical instrument
pp **SEXTERN** quire of 6 sheets
SEXTILE planet aspect
zo **SEXUALE** sexually reproducing being
SHABASH bravo! (Pers.)
SHACKED tramped; hibernated
SHACKLE manacle; gyve; bond; fetter
zo **SHADFLY** May-fly
SHADIER more dubious
SHADILY umbrageously
zo **SHADINE** American sardine
SHADING screening; tinting
SHADOOF water-raising device (Nile)
SHADOWY obscure; dim; gloomy
SHAFTED handled; hafted
SHAGGED shaggy; rough; rugged
zo **SHAHEEN** peregrine falcon
SHAITAN Satan (Arabic)
SHAKE-UP upheaval; reorganization
SHAKILY insecure; precariously
SHAKING quaking; jarring; jolting
bt **SHALLON** an edible fruit
nt **SHALLOP** rowing boat; skiff; gun-boat
nt **SHALLOP** fishing boat; tender
bt **SHALLOT** small type of onion
zo **SHALLOW** superficial; rudd-fish
SHAMBLE shuffle along
SHAMING humiliating; abasing
SHAMMED simulated; feigned
SHAMMER impostor; malingerer
SHAMPOO hair-washing
SHANDRY rickety conveyance (Irish)
SHANGIE shackle (Sc.)
rl **SHANGTI** Chinese for God
SHANKED (golf); shin; legged
zo, bt **SHANKED** shanks's pony; stem
SHAPELY finely formed
SHAPING moulding; fashioning
zo **SHARDED** beetle-winged
SHARING apportioning; dividing
SHARKED cheated; duped; gulled
SHARKER shark-hunter
SHARPED tricked; defrauded; duped
SHARPEN strop; point; whet
SHARPER a trickster; cheat; rogue
nt **SHARPIE** oyster boat, New England
SHARPLY keenly; acutely; tartly
rl **SHASTER** Hindu Bible
rl **SHASTRA** sacred Hindu book
SHATTER splinter; disrupt; smash
SHAVIAN (Bernard Shaw)
SHAVING slicing; pairing; grazing
SHEAFED bundled in sheaves
SHEARED reaped; cut through
SHEARER clipper; reaper; cutter
SHEATHE encase; cover
SHEATHY like a scabbard

SHEAVED collected in sheaves
SHEBANG store; saloon
nt **SHEBECK** **CHEBEK, XEBEC,** mixed rig boat
SHEBEEN Irish whiskey shop
SHEDDER emitter; diffuser
SHEERED moved away
SHEETED covered with sheets
bt **SHELLAC** resin lac
SHELLED bombarded; husked
SHELLER huller; shucker
SHELTER screen; asylum; refuge
zo **SHELTIE** Shetland pony
SHELVED put aside; pigeonholed
SHELVES ledges
SHEPPEY sheep-cote
SHERBET a cooling drink
SHEREEF an amir; emir
lw **SHERIAT** Islamic law
lw **SHERIFF** county officer
SHEWING showing; demonstration
SHIFTED changed; altered; quitted
SHIFTER remover; contriver
SHIITES Persian sectarians
SHIKARI hunter (India)
SHIMMED wedged
SHIMMER gleam; glisten; glimmer
SHINGLE style of hair cutting
gl **SHINGLE** pebbles on sea shore
bd **SHINGLE** wooden roof tiles
SHINGLY pebbly
SHINING resplendent; coruscating
SHINNED climbed
nt **SHIP-BOY** sailor's solace
SHIPFUL boat-load
cr **SHIPLAP** rebate-cut sheathing boards
nt **SHIP-MAN** a sailor
SHIPPED embarked; (oars)
SHIPPEN sheep-pen; stable
SHIPPER exporter
SHIPTON a prophetess
SHIP-WAY (dry dock)
SHIRKED evaded; avoided; scamped
SHIRKER malingerer; dodger
zo **SHIRLEY** bull-finch
bt **SHIRLEY** poppy
SHIRRED puckered
SHIRTED wearing a shirt
bt **SHITTAH** **SHITTIM** acacia; (Tabernacle wood)
SHIVERY brittle; chilly
SHIZOKU Japanese gentry
SHOALED became shallow
nt **SHOALER** coasting-vessel
SHOCKED offended; surprised
SHOCKER sensational novel
SHOE-BOY a shiner
SHOEING farrier's work
SHOE-PEG a nail
SHOE-TIE shoe-lace
SHOGGED jolted; jogged
SHOOING scaring away
SHOOKED packed
SHOOTER marksman; sniper
ga **SHOOTER** goal scorer (netball, football)
SHOPBOY assistant; errand boy
SHOPMAN shop/factory foreman
SHOPPED imprisoned; framed
SHOPPER peripatetic buyer
SHORAGE landing charge
SHORING props; buttressing
el **SHORTED** circuit fault
SHORTEN abbreviate; abridge; curtail
SHORTER briefer; terser; curter
SHOTGUN light sporting gun
ga **SHOT-PUT** putting the weight (sport)
SHOTTED loaded
SHOTTEN dislocated; curdled
pc **SHOULDS** internalized demands
SHOULDS acceptable behaviour
SHOUTED yelled; bawled; roared
SHOUTER crier; vociferator
SHOVING propelling; pushing; jostling
SHOW-BOX presentation carton
SHOW-END (roll of cloth)
SHOWERY pluvial
SHOWILY ostentatiously; flashily
SHOWING representation; displaying
SHOWMAN exhibitor; actor-manager; artiste
SHOW-OFF play for admiration; swank
SHREDDY ragged; fragmentary
SHRILLY piercingly; sharply; high-toned
SHRINAL sacred; hallowed
SHRINED enshrined
SHRIVEL to dry up; parch
rl **SHRIVEN** given absolution
rl **SHRIVER** a confessor; absolver
SHROUDS winding sheets
nt **SHROUDS** mast to ship's sides' rigging
SHROUDY giving shelter
bt **SHRUBBY** full of shrubs
SHUCKER husker; huller; sheller
SHUDDER shake; quiver; shiver
SHUFFLE mix; cavil; quibble; (cards)
SHUNNED avoided; eluded
SHUNNER eschewer; evader
SHUNTED put in siding
SHUNTER a railway-man
SHUT-EYE sleep; a nap

nt **SHUT-OFF** turn off (steam)
SHUT-OFF stoppage; isolated
ga **SHUT-OUT** no score for opponent (sport)
bd, pg **SHUTTER** window aperture cover
SHUTTLE sliding thread-holder
ae, rw **SHUTTLE** service (space, chunnel)
SHYLOCK rapacious usurer
SHYNESS bashfulness; coyness
SHYSTER rascally lawyer
zo **SIAMANG** Malay gibbon
md **SIAMESE** joined, before birth
SIBILUS sibilant rhoncus
SIBILUS (nasal) phonetics
SIBLING one's brother or sister
SIBSHIP brothers and sisters of one family
SICCATE desiccate; dry; parch
SICCITY aridity; dryness
nt **SICKBAY** hospital ward
md **SICKBED** in-patient at home
SICKEST very poorly
SICKISH unwell; out of sorts
SICKLED with sickle
SICK-PAY wages during illness
SIC-LIKE such like
SIDEARM sword or bayonet
SIDEBOX (theatre)
SIDECAR cocktail (motorcycle)
SIDECUT branch canal; not off the grand joint (butchers' meat)
SIDE-OUT loss on a service
ga **SIDEOUT** losing a rally (tennis)
SIDE-ROD coupling rod (steam locomotive)
SIDLING edging away
el, me **SIEMENS** electrical conductance unit
SIENESE of Sienna
mn **SIENITE** syenite; hornblende
SIFFLED whistled
SIFFLET small whistle
SIFTING scrutinizing; sorting; sieving
SIGHFUL grievous
SIGHING lamenting; repining
SIGHTED seen; viewed; glimpsed
SIGHTER a trial shot
SIGHTLY handsome
SIGMATE (sigma)
SIGMOID curve of beauty
nt, tc **SIGNALS** lights; sounds; radio flags
SIGNATE designate
SIGNIFY indicate; betoken; portend
SIGNING subscribing; gesturing
SIGNORA an Italian lady
SIGNORY seigniory; overlordship
rl **SIKHARA** spire of Indian temple
SIKHISM monotheistic sect
SILENCE quiescence; dumbness
SILENUS foster-father of Bacchus
tx **SILESIA** cotton fabric
ch **SILICIC** (silica)
bt **SILICLE** broad pod
ch **SILICON** an element
bt **SILIQUA** seed vessel
me **SILIQUE** carat
SILKIER more lustrous
SILKING silk chiffon
pt **SILKING** books on paint lining
SILKMAN silk-mercer
zo **SILLAGO** a fish genus
SILLERY a white wine
SILLIER more witless
SILLILY inanely; foolishly; ineptly
ch **SILOXEN** polymerized silicon analogue
go **SILTING** depositing mud
zo **SILURUS** cat-fish
SILVERN of silver
SILVERY bright; clear; sweet
SIMARRE a cymar; a costume
SIMILAR alike; analogous; twin
SIMILIA similes; metaphors
SIMILOR semilor; imitation gold
zo **SIMIOUS** ape-like; simian
SIMPLER herbalist; plainer; easier
tc **SIMPLEX** one-way circuit flow
SIMPLEX centre shafted putter (golf)
bt **SIMPSON** groundsel
SIMULAR counterfeit; feigned
SIMURGH fabulous bird (Pers.)
bt **SINAPIS** sinapin; mustard
SINBORN illegitimate
SINBRED raised to vice
SINCERE true; genuine; honest
SINEWED powerful; vigorous
SINGING the vocal art
el **SINGING** oscillation transmission
SINGLED selected; separated
SINGLES tennis; reeled silk
SINGLET undervest
SINGULT a sob; a sigh
ma **SINICAL** of sine (trigonometry)
SINKAGE excess margins of headings
nt **SINKING** foundering; declining
jn **SINKING** greater screw cavity
SINLESS innocent; blameless
SINNING transgressing
SINOPIA red pigment
SINOPIS sinople; sinoper
SINSICK repentant
SINSYNE since (Sc.)
SINUATE insinuate; curved
SINUOUS sinuose; winding

SINWORN fabulous monster
SIPPING supping
zo **SIREDON** larval salamander
zo **SIRENIA** sea-cows
zo **SIRGANG** green jackdaw
SIRLOIN surloin
mt **SIROCCO** **SCIROCCO**, hot African desert wind
SISTINE **SIXTINE**, (Vatican chapel)
lw **SISTING** summoning (Sc.)
mu **SISTRUM** holy rattle (Egypt)
md **SITFAST** ulcer
SITHENS since; after that
zo **SITTINE** (nut-hatches)
SITTING session; incubating; bent-knee stance (fencing)
SITUATE permanently fixed
rl **SIVAITE** follower of Siva
SIXFOLD 6 times as much
SIXTEEN age of sweetness
SIZABLE of a size; bulky
SIZZLED frizzled
SJAMBOK S. Afr. rawhide whip
zo **SKEETER** mosquito
SKELDER swindle
SKELLUM a rascal; scamp; scoundrel
SKELTER skedaddle
SKEPFUL basketful
SKEPTIC sceptic; doubting
SKETCHY vague; incomplete
SKEWGEE crooked; skewed
SKIDDED scotched; slipped
SKIDLID crash helmet
SKID-PAN motorists' training ground
mu **SKIFFLE** folk-song and jazz
SKI-JUMP skiing slide
SKILFUL dexterous; adept; expert
SKI-LIFT cable or funicular lift
SKILLED expert; artful; adroit
SKILLET iron cooking pot
SKIMMED glided; grazed
zo **SKIMMER** scoop; bird
SKIMPED stinted
SKINFUL amount of drunkenness
SKINKER tapster; barman
SKINNED peeled; fleeced
SKINNER a furrier
SKIPPED omitted; jumped
nt **SKIPPER** a captain on board
nt **SKIPPET** seal-box; boat
SKIRLED shrieked shrilly
bt **SKIRRET** water-parsnip
SKIRTED bordered
SKIRTER a dodger
SKI-SUIT winter-costume
SKITTER glide; skim
SKITTLE bowl out; knock down
SKIVING leather splitting; work dodging
SKULKED lurked
SKULKER a shirker; malingerer
zo **SKULPIN** sea-fish
SKYBLUE azure
SKYBORN heaven-born
SKYHIGH excessively elevated
nt **SKYHOOK** overhead crane
zo **SKYLARK** the laverock
SKYLINE horizon; sea-line
nt **SKYSAIL** sail above royal
tx **SKYTEEN** satin weave shirting
SKYWARD heading upward
SLABBED cut into thick slices
SLABBER slobber; dribble; slaver
SLACKED eased off
SLACKEN relax; mitigate; abate
SLACKER skulker; sluggard; idler
SLACKLY negligently; laxly
SLAINTE! Good health! (Irish)
SLAKING quenching; allaying
SLAMKIN a slut; loose gown
SLAMMED banged
SLANDER malign; traduce; obloquy
SLANGED abused; vituperated
SLANKET strip of land; slang
SLANTED sloped; tilted
SLANTLY slantwise; atilt; obliquely
SLAPPED smacked; spanked
SLAPPER slap-up affair
SLASHED gashed; cut
to **SLASHER** cutting tool
SLASHER violent attacker (films)
SLATHER lots of
SLATING roofing; reprimand; abusing
SLATTER wasteful; slovenly
bd **SLATTER** slater; tile mason
SLAVDOM Slavs collectively
SLAVERY serfdom; thraldom; bondage
SLAVING drudging; moiling
SLAVISH servile; obsequious
SLAYING destroying; despatching
SLEAVED not spun; raw
SLEAVED separated; divided
SLEDDED travelled across snow
SLEDGED sledded; mushed
SLEEKED glided; smoothed
SLEEKEN to smooth
to **SLEEKER** slicker
SLEEKLY fair spoken; glossily; silky
cr, rw **SLEEPER** track bed; overnight (train)
ga **SLEEPER** slumberer (bowling)
SLEEPER honeycomb wall; valley
bd **SLEEPER** board (roof) earstud
mt **SLEETED** rained and snowed

SLEIDED unwoven; sleaved
SLEIGHT dexterity; skill; adroitness
SLENDER frail; slim; slight
nt **SLEWING** rotatory roll of crane, ship
SLEYING swinging askew
SLICING severing; (golf)
SLICKER smarter; more deft
SLIDDER to slither; slip; slide
SLIDING a lapse; varying
SLIMILY viscously; muddily
SLIMMER more slender; lankier
SLIPPED conveyed secretly
SLIPPER steel cradle; mule
SLIPWAY (shipbuilding)
SLITHER slide about
SLITTED slashed; split
to **SLITTER** a cutter
SLOBBER slabber; dribble; slaver
SLOCKEN slake; quench
SLOE-GIN pleasant drink
SLOGGED hit hard
SLOGGER mighty smiter
SLOPING inclined; declinous; oblique
SLOPPED spilt
SLOTTED grooved
SLOTTER to foul; filth
SLOUCHY slackly
SLOUGHY swampy; miry; queachy
SLOVENE language, people of Slovenia
SLOWEST dullest; tardiest
SLOWING delaying; retarding
SLUBBER to scamp; slabber
nt **SLUDGER** sewage dumping; bum boat
to **SLUDGER** sandpump; hole cleaner
SLUGGED bashed; coshed
SLUGGER big hitter (baseball)
SLUICED drenched; flushed
SLUMBER sleep; repose; doze
SLUMGUM honey and wax polish
SLUMMER slum visitor
SLUMPED fell heavily
SLUNKEN shrivelled
mu **SLURRED** sullied; disparaged
ce, mn **SLUSHER** scraper (USA)
SLUTCHY residual; mucky
SLYNESS sliness; craft; cunning
SMACKED slapped; spanked
SMACKER a resounding kiss
mn **SMARAGD** the emerald
SMARTED endured sharp pain
SMARTEN brighten; quicken
SMARTER brisker; sprucer
SMARTLY promptly; readily; alertly
SMASHED disrupted; broken; drunk
SMASHER blow; fine thing; (argument)
SMASH-UP a crash; raid; gangsters
SMATTER slight superficial knowledge
SMEARED daubed; contaminated
tc **SMEARER** overshoot-cancelling circuit
ps **SMECTIC** with parallel-oriented atoms
SMEDDUM energy; powder
SMELLED had an odour; smelt
pl **SMELLER** nose; proboscis
SMELTER ore worker; iron furnace
zo **SMERLIN** loach fish
SMICKER to smirk; ogle; leer
SMICKET a smock
SMICKLY amorously
SMIDGEN a bittock; a trifle
SMILING smirking
SMIRKED simpered
SMITING striking; buffeting; hitting
SMITTEN afflicted; chastened
SMITTLE to infect
SMOKIER reekier
SMOKILY fumily
SMOKING bloating; quizzing
SMOLDER smoulder
SMOOTHE palliate; flatter; flatten
SMOTHER stifle; suppress
SMOUSER pedlar (S. Africa)
SMUDGED blurred; blotted
SMUDGER plumber
SMUGGLE convey secretly; snuggle
SNABBLE snaffle; plunder; eat
SNAFFLE a bit; appropriate; filch
SNAGGED snaggy
to **SNAGGER** a cutter
nt **SNAKING** rope-winding
SNAKISH reptilian; serpentine
SNAPING bevelling
SNAPPED caught; broke; photographed
zo **SNAPPER** a turtle
SNARING entrapping; catching
SNARLED entangled; complicated
zo **SNARLER** growler; grumbler; dog
SNATCHY irregular
SNEAKER soft-soled shoe
SNEAKER short drink
SNECK-UP go hang!
zo **SNEDDEN** sand-eel
SNEERER derider; taunter
SNEEZED snorted violently
SNICKER snigger; giggle
SNIFFED snuffed; inhaled
SNIFFLE snuffle
SNIFTER dram; radio-detector

SNIGGER snicker; giggle
SNIGGLE ensnare
SNIPING shooting from ambush
SNIPPER a tailor
SNIPPET a cutting
SNIRTLE snigger
SNOODED wearing a fillet
ga **SNOOKER** potting game; pool
SNOOPER a nosy Parker
SNOOZER a daydreamer
nt **SNORKEL** breathing pipe (U-boat)
SNORTER a fast one (cricket)
nt **SNOTTER** bowsprit housing
SNOUTED with snout
SNOW-BOX (stage snowstorm)
SNOW-FED (streams)
zo **SNOW-FLY** a stone-fly
SNOW-ICE frozen slush
SNOW-MAN snowball in human form
zo **SNOW-OWL** the great white owl
SNUBBED deliberately slighted
SNUBBER shock absorber
SNUFFED sniffed
SNUFFER a snuff taker
md **SNUFFLE** nasal catarrh
SNUGGLE smuggle; cuddle; fondle
SNUGIFY to make cosy
SNUZZLE nuzzle
SOAKAGE absorption
SOAKING drenching; steeping; imbruing
SO-AND-SO a vague definition; (derogatory)
SOAP-BOX orator's platform
SOAPING flattering; lathering
SOAP-PAN soap boiler
hd **SOARANT** heraldic flying
ae **SOARING** airborne on upward currents
SOARING (gliding) (eagle) (at zenith)
SOARING mental uplift; aspiring
SOBBING lamentation; ululation
SOBERED enjoyed morning after
SOBERLY staidly
bt **SOBOLES** botanical suckers
SOCAGER socage tenant
lw **SOCCAGE** land tenure
SOCIETY company; sodality; élite
zo **SOCKEYE** Pacific salmon
SOCKING beating; throwing
mn **SODA-ASH** impure sodium carbonate
SODDING turfing
SOFA-BED day-bed; divan; ottoman
SOFTEST gentlest; easiest
SOFTISH yielding; compliant
SOGGING saturating
SOIGNEE admirably turned out (Fr.)
bt **SOILING** replacing topsoil; (re-)
SOILING dirtying; staining; tarnishing
SOILURE pollution
SOJOURN visit; tarry; remain; abide
lw **SOKEMAN** tenant by socage
SOLACED consoled; comforted
bt **SOLANUM** night-shade genus
ar **SOLDIER** warrior; man-at-arms
bd **SOLDIER** brick as vertical support
SOLICIT importune; canvass; crave
SOLIDLY compactly; firmly; densely
SOLIDUM complete sum
nm **SOLIDUS** 's' for shilling
zo **SOLIPED** not cloven-hoofed
mu **SOLOIST** lone musician
bt **SOLOMON** wisdom personified; (seal)
SOLONIC wise like Solon
zo **SOLPUGA** a spider genus
SOLUBLE capable of solution
SOLVEND a substance to be dissolved
SOLVENT able to pay all debts
SOLVING elucidating; unravelling
SOMATIC corporeal; bodily
SOMEHOW in one way or another
SOMEONE unspecified person
SOMNIAL dreamy
bt **SONCHUS** sow-thistle genus
zo **SONDELI** Indian musk-rat
SONGFUL full of glee
SONGMAN balladmonger
SONLESS defiliated
rl **SONNITE SUNNITE**, orthodox Moslem
SONSHIP cf. daughterdom
SOOPING sweeping ice away (curling)
SOOTHED assuaged; pacified; cajoled
SOOTHER diplomatist; mollifier
SOOTHLY truly
SOOTING (sparking plugs)
SOOTISH like soot
SOPHISM a fallacy; specious argument
SOPHIST captious reasoner
bt **SOPHORA** pagoda tree
SOPIENT a soporific
SOPPING soaking; steeping
mu **SOPRANO** female treble
SORBENT an absorbent
SORBIAN SORBISH, Slavonics in Saxony
SORBILE that can be sipped/drunk
bt **SORBINE** sorbate extract
bt **SORBITE** sweet berry
ch **SORBOSE** keto hexose
SORCERY witchcraft; enchantment
mu **SORDINA** damper pedal on piano
mu **SORDINO** bowed/wind instrument mute

mu **SORDONO** (oboe)
SOREHON Irish tenure
bt **SORGHUM** sugar-cane
SORICID like a shrew
SORITES syllogistic argument
SORNING obtruding; sponging on
md **SOROCHE** altitude sickness (Andes)
SORORAL sisterly
bt **SOROSIS** mulberry type of fruit
SOROSIS woman's club
SORRILY meanly; pitiably
cp **SORTING** disposing; classifying
SORTING sequence; order
mu **SOSPIRO** a breathing rest
SOSTRUM life-saving reward (Gr.)
SOTTING tippling; toping; boozing
SOTTISE blundering act (Fr.)
SOTTISH besotted; foolish
ck **SOUBISE** onion sauce
ck **SOUCHET** boiled fish
ck **SOUFFLE** frothy egg-dish
md **SOUFFLE** blowing sound over heart
SOULFUL spiritually emotional
nt **SOUNDED** vibrated; tested
SOUNDER (Morse)
zo **SOUNDER** boar; herd of swine
SOUNDEX consonant-based coding system
SOUNDLY thoroughly; validly
SOUPCON a suspicion; a taste (Fr.)
SOUREST most acid; rankest
SOURING acidulating
SOURISH tart; acetous; acrid
bt **SOUROCK** sorrel
bt **SOURSOP** American custard apple
SOUSING pickling; drenching
rl **SOUTANE** cassock
mu **SOUTENU** sustained; smooth flow (Fr.)
SOUTHER south wind
SOUTHLY southerly
SOU'WEST S.W.
SOVKHOZ state-owned farm (U.S.S.R.)
SOWBACK gravel ridge
bt, ck **SOYBEAN** protein-rich Asiatic legume
SOZZLED sossled; tipsy; fuddled
SPACIAL extensive; commodious
SPACING arranging intervals
to **SPADDLE** spittle; small spade
SPADING digging
SPADONE double-handed sword
SPAEMAN diviner (Sc.)
SPAIRGE sparge; sprinkle
SPALING a bracing; cross-band
SPALLED chipped; splintered
SPANCEL cow-hobble
SPANDAU German light machine gun
SPANGLE glittering disc
SPANGLY sparkling
zo **SPANIEL** fawning; mean
SPANISH Iberian
SPANKED slapped; speeded
nt **SPANKER** a sail
SPANNED measured; embraced
SPANNER monkey-wrench
SPARELY sparingly; charily
SPARGED sprinkled; sprayed
SPARGER sprinkler; diffuser
SPARING frugal; parsimonious
SPARKED played the gallant
SPARKLE coruscate; twinkle
SPAROID like sea bream
SPARRED disputed; wrangled; boxed
SPARRER boxing partner
zo **SPARROW** a small finch
SPARSIM here and there (Lat.)
SPARTAN austere; hardy; undaunted
tx **SPARVER** type of bed curtain
SPASTIC spasmodic
SPATHED ensheathed
SPATHIC laminated; foliated
SPATIAL spacial; wide; spacious
SPATTER asperse; besprinkle; splash
ch **SPATTLE SPADDLE**, mouth enzymes
SPITTLE saliva
md **SPATULA** a blade; a small spade
zo **SPATULE** (tail feather)
SPAWLED slavered
SPAWNED deposited eggs
zo **SPAWNER** female fish
SPAYING gelding
SPEAKER (House of Commons)
SPEARED lanced; pierced; impaled
SPEARER spearman
SPECIAL distinctive; particular
SPECIES group; genus; class; kind
SPECIFY definite; indicate; detail
SPECKED spotted; speckled
SPECKLE small speck or stain
SPECTRA (spectrum); images
SPECTRE apparition; spook; hobgoblin
SPECULA mirrors; reflectors
SPEEDED ran; hastened; executed
SPEEDER pace-maker
SPEED-UP accelerate
SPELDER a splinter; chip
SPELEAN troglodytic
SPELLED charmed; entranced; spelt
SPELLER spelling book
ml **SPELTER** solder alloy; zinc compound
SPENCER butler; jacket

nt **SPENCER** gaff-sail
SPENDER prodigal; wastrel; waster
SPERKET spirket; harness hook
SPEWING vomiting
md **SPHACEL** gangrene
SPHENIC wedge-like
SPHERAL ball-like; globular
SPHERED englobed
SPHERIC spherical
SPHYRNA hammer-headed sharks
SPICATE SPICOSE, prickly
ck **SPICERY** of various spices
SPICILY pungently; piquantly
SPICING seasoning; varying
SPICOUS SPINATE, thorny
SPICULA spike ear
bt **SPICULE** small pine
zo **SPIDERY** thin of legs and web
SPIEGEL steel alloy
bt **SPIGNEL** baldmoney; a plant
SPIKING impaling; transfixing
bd **SPILING** building-piles
gl **SPILITE** fine-grained igneous rock
SPILLED spilt; wasted; slopped
nt **SPILLER** reefing rope; surfing
ga **SPILLER** slow, even wave; (bowling)
SPILLER lucky strike; oil gusher
md **SPILOMA** birthmark; a naevus
bt, ct **SPINACH** vegetable
bt **SPINATE** spiky; spicate
SPINDLE axis; arbor
SPINDLY fusiform; slender
SPINNER a bait; textile operator
SPINNEY spinny; copse
SPINODE cusp in a curve
SPIN-OFF chance; side effect; product
bt **SPINOSE** spinous; thorny
bt **SPINULA** spicule
bt **SPINULE** small spine
bt **SPIRAEA** a plant genus
SPIRANT fricative consonant; a sibilant
SPIRING tapering; sprouting
mu **SPIRITO SPIRITOSO**, spirited
SPIRITY mettlesome; alcoholic
SPIRKET sperket; harness hook
SPIRTLE to spin; to spurt
zo **SPIRULA** cephalopods; cuttlefish
SPITBOX a cuspidor
SPITING grudging; thwarting
ck **SPITTED** transfixed
zo **SPITTER** young deer
SPITTLE small spade; saliva
zo **SPIZINE** (buntings; finches)
SPLASHY wet and muddy
SPLAYED sloped; slanted
SPLEENY ill-humoured; fretful
md **SPLEGET** a swab
SPLENIC spleeny; fretful; melancholy
nt **SPLICED** main brace; hit
tx **SPLICED** married, interwoven
nt, cp **SPLICER** joiner (ropes) (tapes)
md **SPLINTS** surgical appliances
SPLODGE daub; patch
SPLODGY stained; blotched
SPLOTCH smear; stain
SPLURGE rowdiness
SPLURGY boisterous; spend freely
SPODIUM ivory-black
SPOFFLE to bustle; to fuss
SPOILED pillaged; ruined; marred
SPOILER plunderer; bungler
rl **SPOLIUM** church property
SPONDEE poetic foot (2 long syllables)
md **SPONDYL** a vertebra; a joint
SPONGED deleted; purged; moistened
SPONGER a parasite; sorner
SPONSAL (marriage)
nt **SPONSON** protecting bracket
SPONSOR guarantor; a surety
SPOOFED hoodwinked; hoaxed
SPOOLED wound on spools (films)
SPOOMED scudded before the wind
SPOONED hit into the air; courted
SPOONEY love-sick
SPOORER tracker; detective
bt **SPOROID** sporous; sporelike
SPORONT stage in protozoa life history
SPORRAN kilt-pouch
SPORTED wore; trifled; romped
SPORTER jester; player
bt **SPORULE** small spore
SPOTTED spied; detected; pied
nt **SPOTTER** sharp-sighted look-out
rw **SPOTTER** (train-); (talent-)
ga **SPOTTER** assistant to gymnast
SPOUSAL nuptial; matrimonial
SPOUTED orated; spirted; pawned
zo **SPOUTER** declaimer; whale
SPRAYED sprinkled; spurned; affused
SPRAYER water cart; town cleansing
bt **SPRAYER** fountain; flow aimer (garden)
bt **SPRAYER** (crops-) (fruit-)
SPRAYEY branching
SPREAGH plunder (Sc.)
SPRIGGY full of sprigs
SPRIGHT sprite; a spirit; a ghost
SPRINGE spring trap; a gin
SPRINGY vernal; elastic

SPRINTS bicycle wheels
SPRUCED smartened up; prinked
SPRUNNY spruce; a sweetheart
SPRYEST spriest; gayest; pertest
SPUMING spumous; frothy; foamy
ck **SPUMONE** ice-cream in varied layers (It.)
SPUN-HAY twisted hay
SPUN-OUT long drawn
zo **SPUR-DOG** a shark
zo **SPURIAE** bastard quills
SPURNED rejected; scouted; contemned
SPURNER a disdainer
SPURRED goaded; impelled; galloped
SPURRER inciter; instigator
bt **SPURREY** a plant
SPURTED gushed; sprinted
SPURTLE spurt; spirtle
SPURWAY bridle-path
SPUTNIK earth satellite (Rus.)
SPUTTER splutter
nt **SPY-BOAT** vessel for secret agents
SPY-HOLE peep-hole; Judas' hole
SPYNDLE unit of length of jute/flax yarn
SQUABBY squaddy; squat; tubby
zo **SQUACCO** crested heron
SQUAILS form of table bowls (19th cent.)
SQUALID sordid; unclean; filthy
SQUALLY gusty; blustering
SQUALOR dirtiness; foulness
zo **SQUALUS** shark
SQUARED adjusted; tallied; bribed
SQUARED oar-blades (rowing) (circle)
SQUASHY pulpy; soft
SQUATTY squabby; clumsy
SQUEAKY clean; more than true
SQUEASY scrupulous; squeamish
SQUEEZE compress; crush; pinch; nip
ga **SQUEEZE** (money); block players
SQUEEZY congested; squashy
SQUELCH crush; suppress; (wet noise)
SQUIFFY tipsy; inebriated; sozzled
SQUINCH small stone arch; tight squeeze
SQUINNY to look asquint; meagre
SQUIRED escorted
bt **SQUITCH** quitch-grass
rl **SRADDHA** Hindu devotional offerings
STABBED wounded; pierced
to **STABBER** awl; marlinspike
STABLED stalled; horses
STABLER stable-keeper
mu **STABLES** a trumpet call (cavalry)
bt **STACHYS** hedge-nettle genus
STACKED piled; (cards)
STACKER washer-up (kitchen)
STACKER haymaker; storeman
cp **STACKER** punched-cards receptacle
STADDLE crutch; support
STADIUM arena; running track
STAFFED manned by
STAGERY scenic exhibition
STAGGER astound; lurch; reel; sway
STAGGER (time-); (hours)
STAGING a structure; producing
STAIDLY steadily; sedately; soberly
STAINED foxed; tarnished; sullied
STAINER a dyer
STAITHE coaling stage
STAKING hazarding; wagering
STALDER cask rack; horizontal bar (gymnastics)
STALELY mustily; effetely; insipidly
STALEST most trite
bt **STALKED** with peduncle
STALKER stealthy sportsman
STALLED fatted; lost speed
ml **STALLOY** silicon-content steel
STAMINA endurance; vitality; vigour
tx **STAMMEL** rough red cloth
STAMMER stutter
STAMNOS Greek urn
STAMPED impressed; crushed; branded
STAMPER ore crusher
STAND-BY a reserve
STANDER provider; candidate (elections)
STAND-IN deputy; substitute
STAND-TO military readiness
STAND-UP well fought
zo **STANIEL STANNEL**, kestrel bird
STANINE statistical unit
STANNIC (of tin)
ch **STANNUM** tin, metallic element
zo **STANYEL** windhover
STAPLED connected together
STAPLER a dealer; clipping machine
STARCHY stiff; formal; precise
STARDOM film eminence
STARING glaring; gaping; prominent
STARKEN stiffen; make obstinate
STARKLY completely; absolutely
STARLET junior actress
STAR-LIT almost invisible
STARRED shone; bespangled
STARTED winced; roused; began
ck **STARTER** first course; foretaste
STARTER (self-); also ran (horses)

STARTLE alarm; frighten; surprise
START-UP of a business, refinery
STARVED famished; emaciated
STASIMA choral odes (Gr.)
hd **STATANT** standing
STATELY lofty; magnificent; imposing
bt **STATICE** sea-lavender
STATICS conditions for equilibrium
STATING narrating; affirming
rw, ag **STATION** train-; bus-; stockfarm
STATION petrol-; office; status
cp **STATION** network computer terminal
STATISM policy; art of government
STATIST statistical expert
STATIVE fixed; standing still
el, me **STATOHM** obsolete electrostatic unit
STATUED with statues
STATURE natural height
lw **STATUTE** an enactment; decree
STAUNCH stanch; trusty; steadfast
STAVING delaying; broaching
STAYING enduring; detaining; abiding
STAY-PUT semi-permanent
STEALER purloiner; peculator
STEALTH furtiveness; secrecy
ck **STEAMED** cooked in vapour
nt **STEAMER** cooking vessel; ship
ch **STEARIC** of candle grease
STEARIN fat; wax; stearic acid
STEELED hardened; nerved
STEEPED soaked; drenched
STEEPEN to make steep
STEEPER soaking vat
rl **STEEPLE** a spire
STEEPLY almost sheer; abruptly
STEERED conned; controlled; directed
STEERER pilot; guide; director
STEEVED packed closely
STELENE pillar-like; columnar
STELLAR astral; starry
STEMLET small stalk
STEMMED compressed
jn, bd **STEMPLE** crossbeam
nt **STEMSON** jointing timber
STENCHY odoriferous
STENCIL pattern plate
STENGAH whisky and soda (Malay)
STENODE supersonic heterodyne receiver
tx **STENTER** fabric-sketching machine
STENTOR a loud speaker
STEP-INS elastic-held shoes; underwear
STEPNEY spare-wheel; (born at sea)
STEPPED paced; walked; fixed
STEPPER horse with high action
STEPSON spouse's earlier product
STERILE barren; germ-free; acarpous
zo **STERLET** sturgeon
md **STERNAL** (breast-bone)
STERNER harsher; more austere
STERNLY severely; strictly; dourly
nt **STERN-TO** in reverse; backwards
md **STERNUM** breast-bone
ch **STEROID** sterol compound
STEROLS cholesterols (universal)
md **STERTOR** noisy breathing
STETSON a hat (USA)
nt **STEVING** stowing
STEWARD seneschal; bailiff
nt **STEWARD** airline; purser (ship); agent
STEWARD (horse-racing) (rally); waiter
ck **STEW-CAN STEW-POT**, cooking vessel
STEWING simmering; worrying
md **STHENIA** strength
STIBIAL (antimony)
ch **STIBINE** antimony hydride
ch **STIBIUM** antimony
STICHIC rhythmic
STICHOS a line of verse
STICKER last ditcher; adherent
STICKLE a rapid in a stream
STIFFEN harden
STIFFER more rigid; harder; primmer
STIFFLY rigidly; firmly; starchy
STIFLED suffocated; smothered
STILLED hushed; calmed; distilled
STILLER pacifier
STILTED pompous; bombastic
ck **STILTON** a cheese
STIMIED obstructed; (golf)
STIMULI incentives; spurs
zo **STINGER** insect organ; injects poisons
nt **STINGER** pontoon; lay barge
STINKER despicable person
STINTED restricted; rationed
STINTER pincher; restrainer
bt **STIPATE** crowded
STIPEND salary; emolument
STIPPLE to make dots
md **STIPTIC** astringent
bt **STIPULA STIPULE**, leaf appendage
STIRPES forefathers; races
STIRRED roused; incited; bustled
STIRRER thriller; agitator; disturber
STIRRUP foot-holder for rider; pump; cup
STIVING stewing
nt **STOAKED** choked; stopped

STOCKED stored; saved; hoarded
STOCKLI pommel horse; gymnastics
STOICAL passionless; unfeeling
STOKING adding fuel
ck **STOLLEN** sweet German currant bread
pl **STOMACH** digestive organ
STOMACH to brook; to resent
STOMACH desire for courage
md **STOMATA** breathing pore
bt **STOMIUM** fern-sporangium-wall part
STONIED astonished; amazed
STONILY obdurately; unrelentingly
STONING pelting; (fruit)
STOOGED loitered; filled in time
STOOKED set up in sheaves
STOOKER harvest worker
STOOMED fermented
STOOPED condescended; swooped
STOOPER bender
nm **STOOTER** Dutch silver coin
STOPGAP locum tenens
STOPING series of ledges
STOPPED restrained; repressed; closed
STOPPER STOPPLE, restraint; a centre-back (soccer)
STORAGE space; safe-custody
STORAGE warehouse facilities
el **STORAGE** accumulator cell
cp **STORAGE** memory system (computer)
STORIED legendary; fabled
STORIES floors; tales
STORING garnering; hoarding
STORMED assaulted; raved; raged
STORMER blusterer
STOTTER rebound; a bounce (Sc.)
STOUTEN hearten; cheer
STOUTER more corpulent; braver
STOUTLY sturdily; stalwartly; robust
STOVING a heat treatment
STOWAGE packing; loading
STOWING arranging; packing
STRAIKS wheel-plates; strakes
STRANGE unfamiliar; abnormal; exotic
STRAPPY strong; fit; many straps
gl **STRATUM** rock formation
mt **STRATUS** cloud formation
STRAWED strewed
STRAYED erred; roved; deviated
STRAYER wandered; vagrant
ck **STREAKY** striped; bacon with fat
STREAMY well watered
STRELLI parallel bars (gymnastics)
STRETCH reach; strain; expand; (baseball)
mu **STRETTO** quick and sharp (It.)
STREULI backward roll to handstand
STREWED strewn; scattered
STRIATE streaky; scratched
STRIDOR harsh noise
zo **STRIGES** the owl genus
STRIGIL skin-scraper
STRIKER (industrial action)
STRIKER blacksmith's assistant
ga **STRIKER** firing-pin; batsman (cricket)
mu **STRINGS** viol family instruments
STRINGY filamentous
STRIOLA small/weak stria; scratch
STRIPED streaked
STRIPES tiger; denoting military, naval rank
STRIP-IN recombining photo material
STRIVEN strove; struggled; tussled
STRIVER emulator; trier; competitor
STROBIC rate of turning; spinning
STROCAL glass-maker's shovel
STROKED rubbed gently; (rowing)
STROKER rubber; soother
STROPHE a stanza; verse; (Gr.)
ck **STRUDEL** Austrian thin-dough pastry
STUBBED blunted; obtuse; extirpated
bt **STUBBLE** corn stumps
STUBBLY like stubble; unshaven
STUCKLE clump of sheaves
STUCK-UP arrogant; pompous
STUDDED (shirts); (nails)
STUDDLE a trestle
STUDENT pupil; scholar; philomath
STUDIED conned; pondered; worked
STUDIER student; scrutinizer
STUFFED padded; crowded; rammed
STUFFER packer; crammer
STUMBLE trip; slip; blunder; lurch
STUMBLY apt to stumble
STUMMED fortified; doctored
STUMMEL tobacco pipe (Ger.)
STUMPED at a loss; (cricket)
STUMPER wicket-keeper; difficult problem
STUMPER heavy walker; tree-cutter
STUNNED unconscious after blow, fall
STUNNED dumbfounded; amazed
STUNNER an astonisher; stupefier
STUNTED dwarfed; pygmean; runty
STUPEFY bemuse; dope; benumb
STUPENT struck with stupor
STUPOSE tufted; scaly; matted
zo **STURNUS** starling genus

STUTTER stammer; hesitant utterance
STYGIAN infernal; black; murky
STYLATE styloid; like a style or pen
STYLING naming; designating
STYLISH modish; chic; elegant
STYLIST fine writer
STYLITE pillar-dweller
STYLIZE to make average
STYLOID pen-like
STYMIED stimied; obstructed; (golf)
md **STYPSIS** use of styptics
md **STYPTIC** stiptic; astringent
SUASIVE urbane; agreeable
SUASORY convincing
SUAVELY pleasantly; blandly
SUAVITY affability; sweetness
SUBACID rather acid
SUBADAR Mogul governor
SUBARID slightly arid
nt, ce **SUB-BASE** (submarines); road undersurface
mu **SUBBASS** low organ note
SUBBING acting as substitute; subediting
zo **SUBCOXA** segment of primitive leg in insects
rl **SUBDEAN** under-dean
SUBDUAL conquest; subjugation
SUBDUCE withdraw
SUBDUCT subtract
SUBDUED piano; routed; worsted
SUBDUER queller; vanquisher
SUBEDAR native captain
SUBEDIT (edit)
SUBERIC of cork
bt **SUBERIN** cork-cell fatty mixture
SUBFUSC subfusk; dusky
SUBGENS sub-clan
SUBGOAL intermediary goal or achievement
SUB-HEAD sub-title
lw, mu **SUBJECT** thesis; topic; subservient; conquer; impose; grammar; (fugue)
SUBJOIN append; affix; postfix
SUBLATE carry off; take away
SUBLIME exalted; lofty; superb
bt **SUBNUDE** almost leafless
SUBOVAL almost ovate
lw **SUBPENA** subpoena; writ
SUBRENT sublet
ch **SUBSALT** below the salt
SUBSIDE sink; ebb; wane; abate
SUBSIDY a grant; dole; monetary aid
SUBSIGN undersign
bd **SUB-SILL** steel window-level wall covering
SUBSIST live; exist; endure
SUBSOIL the under-soil
SUBSUME include as comprehended
SUBTACK an under-lease (Sc.)
SUBTEND embrace; enfold
SUBTILE subtle; cunningly devised
SUBTLER wilier; craftier
SUBTYPE subdivision
SUBURBS outlying districts
SUBVENE aid; support
SUBVERT overthrow; ruin; corrupt
SUCCADE candied fruit
SUCCEED follow; prosper; win
SUCCESS prosperity; victory; triumph
bt **SUCCISE** ending below abruptly
SUCCOSE sappy
SUCCOUR aid; help; support; foster
SUCCUBA battering demons; spirits
SUCCULA capstan; winch
SUCCUMB yield; submit; die; capitulate
SUCCUSS to shake suddenly
SUCKING absorbing; imbibing
SUCKLED nursed
SUCKLER an infant; a suckling
SUCROSE cane sugar
SUCTION vacuum-filling
SUDANIC group of languages (Sudan)
SUDORAL sweaty; perspiring
SUFFETE Punic official
SUFFICE to content; be enough; avail
SUFFUSE diffuse; blush; overspread
SUGARED candied; sweetened
SUGGEST hint; insinuate; propose
nt **SUGGING** sea-rocked when stranded
SUICIDE taking one's own life; felo-de-se; self-destruction
SUIFORM pig-like; swinish
tx **SUITING** pleasing; according
SULCATE grooved; furrowed
SULKIER more sullen
SULKILY morosely; sullenly; surlily
SULKING glowering
SULLAGE dross; scum
SULLENS morose; temper; the sulks
SULLIED tainted; tarnished; defamed
ch **SULPHUR** brimstone
bt, zo **SULTANA** raisin; marsh bird
mt **SUMATRA** Malaccan summer squall
SUMLESS beyond count
SUMMARY epitome; abstract; digest
cp **SUMMARY** report
lw **SUMMARY** to be done without delay
SUMMERY summerlike; hot weather
SUMMING summary; adding; counting

SUMMIST writer of a compendium
lw **SUMMONS** writ; citation
mn **SUMPERS** cut holes (shaft sinking)
zo **SUMPTER** pack-horse
SUN-BATH outdoor near-nudity
SUNBEAM ray from the sun
SUNBEAT struck by the sun's rays
zo **SUNBIRD** humming bird
SUNBURN tan; browned skin
SUNCLAD radiant
bt **SUNDARI** hardwood tree (Borneo)
SUNDAWN dawn-light
SUNDIAL stylish timepiece
SUNDOWN sunset
bt **SUNDROP** primrose (Amer.)
zo **SUNFISH** shark
SUN-KIST kissed by the sun
SUN-LAMP ultra-violet ray
SUNLESS cloudy; overcast
SUNLIKE solar
SUNMYTH a solar myth
SUNNING sun-bathing
SUNNITE orthodox Muslim
SUNRISE dawn; cock-crow
bt **SUNROSE** sunflower
as **SUNSPOT** solar phenomenon
SUNWARD towards the sun
SUNWISE clock-wise
SUPPING eat evening meal
SUPPLED made pliant
SUPPORT prop; uphold; assist; position on arms (gymnastics)
SUPPOSE surmise; fancy; deem
SUPREME dominant; paramount
zo **SURANAL** above the anus
SURBASE cornice; base moulding
SURCOAT coat worn over chain mail
SURDITY lack of resonance; deafness
SURFACE exterior; superficies
SURFARI safari in search of good surfing
SURFEIT excess; plethora; cloy; gorge
SURFING to plane on forward portion of wave on a surfboard
SURFMAN skilled swimmer
SURGENT swelling; heaving
SURGEON who treats people by operation
md **SURGERY** cutting into bodies
SURGING billowing regularly
SURGING regular increase of power
SURGING Faradayism; (running)
SURLIER more churlish and crusty
SURLILY gruffly; sullenly; morosely
ck **SURLOIN** sirloin beef
SURMISE conjecture; suppose; imagine
SURNAME cognomen
SURPASS excel; exceed; outdo
SURPLUS residuum; balance; excess
lw **SURSIZE** feudal penalty
SURTOUT overcoat
SURVIVE outlive; endure; outlast
SUSCEPT parasite's host
SUSPECT doubtful; mistrust; distrust
SUSPEND hang; postpone; relieve
SUSPIRE sign; yearn; breathe
SUSTAIN uphold; bear; endure
SUTLERY sutler's occupation
SUTLING commissariat (Turk.)
SUTURAL sewn; seamy; stitched
SUTURED sewn together
SWABBED washed; mopped
SWABBER scrubber; mopper-up
SWABIAN (South German)
SWADDLE swathe; wrap; bind
SWAGGED sagged; leant
SWAGGER strut; ruffle; boast
SWAGING assuaging; mitigating
mt **SWAGING** metal-rod tapering
SWAGMAN burglar
SWAHILI East African language
SWALING wasting; consuming; burning
go **SWALLET** underground stream
zo **SWALLOW** voracity; engulf; absorb
SWAMPED overwhelmed; inundated
SWANKED boasted; bragged
SWANKIE swipes; thin beer
SWANPAN Chinese abacus
SWAPPED bartered; exchanged
SWARAJI home rule (India)
SWARDED grassy; turfy
SWARFED fainted; swooned; dwalmed
SWARMED thronged; teemed; clustered
SWARTHY tawny; swart; dark
SWASHED blustered; swanked
SWASHER swash-buckler
SWATTED hit with a fly swat
SWATTER fly-killer
SWAYING governing; oscillating
SWEALED guttered like a candle
SWEARER blasphemer
SWEATED drudged; perspired; reeked
SWEATER a pullover; jersey
SWEDISH (Sweden)
SWEEPER road cleaner; artist brush
SWEEPER defensive (soccer, hockey)
SWEETEN to palliate; dulcify
SWEETER more fragrant
SWEETIE sweetmeat; confectionery
SWEETLY dulcetly; fragrantly

zo **SWELLED** inflated; heaved; bulged
zo **SWELLEL** American squirrel
SWELLET rush of water in a mine
SWELTER perspire; sweat
SWELTRY sultry; oppressive
SWERVED deviated; turned aside
SWERVER curve-swinger
SWIFTER faster; nimbler; quicker
SWIFTLY rapidly; promptly; suddenly
SWIGGED drank deep; quaffed
SWILLED rinsed; washed; boozed
SWILLER copious absorber
zo **SWIMMER** water-spider
SWINDLE fraud; dupe; cheat
SWINERY piggery
SWINGED beaten up; punished
SWINGEL SWINGLE, flail
SWINGER disco dancer; pendulum
SWINGER wife-swapper; trench bar
SWINGER a wielder
SWINISH hoggish; suiform
SWINKED drudged; moiled; toiled
SWIPING slogging; lashing out
SWIPPLE at a loose end
SWIRLED whirled; eddied
SWISHED flogged
SWISHER a wielder of the birch
SWISHER shot for goal (basketball)
SWITHER hesitate; doubt; fright
SWITZER Swiss bodyguard; a Swiss
SWIZZLE a mixed drink
SWOLLEN distended; enlarged; bloated
SWOONED fainted; swarfed; dwalmed
SWOOPED caught on the wing
SWOPPED swapped; bartered
SWOTTED studied hard
SYBOTIC pertaining to swineherd
md **SYCOSIS** barber's itch
mn **SYENITE** Egyptian granite
SYLPHID small sylph; fairy
ch **SYLVINE** potassium chloride
ch **SYLVITE** potassium chloride
zo **SYMBION** symbiotic organism
SYMPTOM indication (of illness)
bt **SYNACMY** floral maturity
md **SYNAPSE** nerve junction
rl **SYNAPTE** Greek litany
SYNAXIS an assembly for worship
bt **SYNCARP** multiple fleshy fruit
SYNCHRO transformer for transmitting
SYNCHRO right-angular
SYNCOPE contraction; collapse
SYNERGY co-operation
SYNESIS harmonious construction
bt **SYNNEMA** erect bunch of hyphae
md **SYNOCHA** fever
SYNOCIL a growth on sponges
rl **SYNODAL** bishop's benefit
SYNODIC (synod); conventional
SYNONYM a word of similar significance, meaning
zo **SYNOTUS** long-eared bat
md **SYNOVIA** lubrication
SYNTONY wireless tuning
bt **SYRINGA** mock-orange
SYRINGE a squirt; to spray
md **SYSTOLE** contraction of the heart
ar **SYSTYLE** a stylish portico
ar **SYSTYLE** type of colonnade

T

TABANAC French white wine
zo **TABANUS** horse-fly or gad-fly
tx **TABARET** satin striped silk
md **TABELLA** lozenge
md **TABETIC** consumptive
TABIDLY tabific; tabetic
TABINET curtain material
TABLEAU vivid picture (Fr.)
TABLIER apron; chess-board
TABLING setting down in order
md **TABLOID** multum in parvo
TABOOED banned; barred; accursed
mu **TABORER** drummer
mu **TABORET** small drum
TABULAR listed; tabulated; catalogued
cp **TABULAR** program language
nc **TACHYON** fast-moving particle
TACITLY noiselessly implied
TACKILY stickily; adhesively
TACKING stitching; fastening
nv **TACKING** zigzag course against wind
TACKLED seized; grappled with
pt **TACK-RAG** dust/grit remover
TACTFUL diplomatic and sensitive
TACTICS cunning moves
TACTILE tangible; perceptible
TACTION sense of touch; contact
ch, ps **TACTOID** double-reflecting droplet
TACTUAL tactile; palpable
zo **TADORNA** duck genus
zo **TADPOLE** embryonic frog
TADZHIK Central Asian people
mn **TAENITE** iron-nickel solution
tx **TAFFETA** wavy fabric
tx **TAFFETY** taffeta; lustrous silk
TAGALOG language (Philippines)
bt **TAGETES** French marigolds
TAGGERS thin sheet iron

TAGGING following; tailing; tacking
TAGMEME smallest meaningful speech unit
vt **TAGSORE** sheep disease
vt **TAGTAIL** worm; parasite
lw **TAILAGE** entail
TAILCAP leather fold on book spine
TAILEND fag-end
TAILING following; a winter sport
lw **TAILZIE** deed of entail
TAINTED infected; stained; sullied
TAIPING Chinese rebel
ae **TAKE-OFF** a burlesque; ascent from earth
ga **TAKE-OFF** a stroke (golf) (croquet)
TAKE-OUT withdraw; (insurance)
lw **TAKE-OUT** courtship; (patents) (export)
TAKINGS cash receipts
TAKOURA golf-like game (Morocco)
ar **TAKSPAN** pine-roof shingles
TALARIA Mercury's winged sandals
mn **TALCITE** nacrite
TALCOSE a talc
TALEFUL newsy
TALIPED club footed
md **TALIPES** slub-foot
bt **TALIPOT** **TALIPAT**
bt **TALIPUT** fan-palm
TALKIES talking films
TALKING prating; discoursing
TALLAGE ancient tax
TALLBOY chest of drawers
TALLEST loftiest; highest
TALLIED agreed; correspond; fitted
TALLIER tally-keeper
TALLISH rather tall; of good height
TALLITH praying mantle (Heb.)
TALLOWY fatty
TALLY-HO hunting call
TALONED with claws
TAMABLE docile; tractable
zo **TAMANOA** ant-eater
zo **TAMARIN** S. American monkey
TAMASHA entertainment (India)
mu, tx, ar **TAMBOUR** drum; embroidery; vestibule; dome-(holding walls)
mu **TAMBURA** **TANPURA**, long Indian lute
mu **TAMBURO** It. small snare drum
TAMILIC **TAMULIC**, Tamil language (Sri Lanka)
TAMMANY corrupt political organization, USA
TAMPING (blasting)
TAMPION also tompion; a stopper
TANADAR Hindu police officer
zo **TANAGER** American finch
zo **TANAGRA** finches
TANAGRA terracotta ware
TANGENT meeting but not intersecting
mu **TANGENT** a clavichord; tongue
TANGENT squaring the circle
bt **TANGHIN** poison tree (Madagascar)
TANGING twanging; flavouring
TANGLED jumbled; matted; twisted
ga **TANGRAM** Chinese jigsaw
TANKAGE storage
TANKARD drinking vessel
TANKCAR tanker; oil-tank
TANKING waterproofing a basement
TANLING sun-bather
TANNAGE tanning materials
ch **TANNATE** a salt of tannic acid
le **TANNERY** leather factory
le **TANNING** leathering
ch **TANNINS** organic compounds for ink and leather – T for two
TANRIDE riding school
to **TANSPUD** bark-peeling tool
mu **TANTARA** fanfare
TANTITY tantamount
TANTIVY coach horn call; (hunt)
zo **TANTONY** smallest pig in litter
TANTRUM temper; petulance
TANYARD tanning place
TAPBOLT screw bolt
TAPERED conical; pointed
md **TAPETUM** (retina)
bt **TAPIOCA** cassava
TAPLASH stale swipes
TAPPJNG broaching; screwcutting
TAPROOM bar
bt **TAPROOT** main sustenance root
TAPSTER bartender
TARACEA inlaid wood (Spanish style)
mu **TARAGOT** Transylvanian clarinet
TARBUSH tarboosh; fez; Muslim cap
TARDIER slower; later; slacker
TARDILY slowly; reluctantly
TARDIVE tardiness; lateness
TARNISH sully; soil; stain
TARRACE volcanic earth
TARRIED loitered; lingered; sojourned
lw **TARRIER** dawdler; estate register
TARRING covering with bitumen
zo **TARROCK** arctic tern
zo **TARSIER** lemur; the malmag
nt **TARTANE** coastal trader, Mediterranean
TARTARY Tartarus; nethermost hell
TARTISH somewhat sharp
ck **TARTLET** small tart; (sweetmeat)
TASHRIF respect; compliment (Ind.)

TASKING taskwork; drudgery; toiling
TASTIER choicer; more succulent
TASTILY artistically; with gusto
TASTING relishing; enjoying; gustation
TATARIC Mongolian, Turkish, etc.
zo **TATOUAY** armadillo; peba; tatou
TATTERY in rags; not riches
TATTING lace work
TATTLED gossiped; chatted; prated
TATTLER tale-bearer; a wag
TAUNTED derided; flouted; scorned
TAUNTER mocker; upbraider; reviler
TAURIAN (bulls)
TAURIDS meteoric shower
ch, md **TAURINE** ox extract; amino acid
TAUTEST tightest; tensest
TAXABLE rateable; inescapable
TAXCART small farm cart
TAXFREE scot-free
TAXICAB hire car for lower price
ae **TAXI-ING** runway movements
TAXI-MAN cab driver
ck **TEA-CAKE** scone or bun for tea
TEACHER master; tutor; pedagogue
TEACH-IN active seminar discussion
TEACHTA member of parliament (Irish)
TEA-COSY pot warmer
TEA-GOWN long afternoon dress
TEA-LEAD (tea-chest linings)
bt **TEA-LEAF** blade of tea
TEAMING grouping; selecting
md **TEARBAG** lachrymal gland
TEARFUL maudlin; weeping; Niobean
ch **TEAR-GAS** riot repellant; eye irritant
TEARING rending; raving; raging
bt **TEA-ROSE** tea-scented rose
TEARPIT a lachrymal depression
TEA-SHOP shop serving tea
TEASING tantalizing; plaguing
TEATHED manured by livestock
TEA-TIME 4/5 o'clock
TEA-TRAY on which tea carried
bt **TEA-TREE** Asian camellia; shrub
TECHILY fretfully; peevishly
TECHNIC technique; technical
zo **TECTRIX** a wing or tail feather
TEDDING spreading; bedding
TEDESCO German (It.)
TEDIOUS wearisome; hum-drum
TEEBEAM rolled steel; concrete flow
TEEIRON golf club (driver)
TEEMFUL prolific; swarming
TEEMING fruitful; abundant
TEENAGE thirteen to nineteen
TEENING troubling; provoking
TEGULAR of tiles
mn **TEKTITE** non-volcanic natural glass
TELAMON statue supporting masonry
TELECAR mobile telegraph office
TELEOST osseous
TELERGY telepathy
mn **TELESIA** sapphire
TELLING effective; informing
el **TELPHER** **TELFER**, electric traction
TEL-QUEL exchange rate
TELSTAR television satellite
TEMENOS temple precinct (Gr.)
TEMPEAN delightful; (Vale of Tempe)
TEMPERA oilless paint; distemper
TEMPEST hurricane; typhoon; gale
lw **TEMPLAR** student of law
TEMPLED in a temple
to **TEMPLET** template; jig
TEMPTED allured; tried; solicited
TEMPTER a decoy; an enticer
TENABLE maintainable; rational
TENANCY tenure
TENDING tendentious; trending
bt **TENDRIL** twining shoot
zo **TENERAL** immature
TENFOLD decuple
zo **TENIOID** like tapeworms
TENONED mortised
to **TENONER** tenon cutter
TEN-PINS cf. nine-pins
TENSELY tautly; tightly
TENSEST stiffest; most emotional
TENSILE ductile
TENSION strain; stress; exigency
TENSITY tenseness; urgency
TENSIVE intensive
TENTBED canopied bed
TENT-FLY part of tent
TENTFUL tent fully occupied
TENTGUY tent-rope; not its occupant
TENTING camping
TENTORY the awning of a tent
TENTPEG **TENTPIN**, used to secure a tent
TENTURE wall hangings
TENUATE thin; attenuate
TENUITY rarity; thinness
TENUOUS diffused; slender
nt **TEPUKEI** Polynesian sail canoe
TEQUILA fermented sap drink (Mex.)
ch **TERBIUM** a metallic element
bt **TERCINE** seed-coat
bt **TEREBIC** (turpentine)
zo **TEREBRA** Roman ram; ovipositor
zo **TEREKIA** sandpiper genus

hd **TERGANT** recursant
zo **TERGITE** back of an anthropod
lw **TERM-FEE** periodic payment
TERMING naming; denominating
rw **TERMINI** boundaries; stations
zo **TERMITE** white ant
TERNARY in threes
bt **TERNATE** three-leafed
TERNERY tern breeding ground
TERNION (twelve pages)
ch **TERPENE** terebene
ar **TERRACE** raised level (vines)
TERRACE continuous house row
go **TERRAIN** geological features
gl **TERRANE** area covered by certain rock
TERRENE terrestrial; earthy
zo **TERRIER** fine fighter
lw **TERRIER** tarrier; register
TERRIFY alarm; appal; dismay
TERRINE earthenware cooking dish
TERSELY concisely; briefly; laconically
TERSION wiping
zo **TERTIAL** wing feather
TERTIAN on alternate days
TESSERA mosaic block
lw **TESTACY** testate
lw **TESTATE** leaving a will
TEST-BAN nuclear weapons agreement
bt **TESTBED** for horticultural experiments
cp **TESTBED** software for program testing
nm **TESTERN** testril; a sixpence
TESTIER more irritable or irascible
TESTIFY affirm; avow; depose; depone
TESTILY peevishly; petulantly
TESTING proving; trying
nm **TESTOON** Henry VIII shilling
nm **TESTRIL** a tester; a sixpence
zo **TESTUDO** tortoise; early tank
md **TETANUS** lock-jaw disease
TETRACT having four rays
TETRODE a thermionic valve
ch **TETROSE** monosaccharide
TEXTILE woven fabric
TEXT-MAN a quoter
rl **TEXTUAL** valid; literal; written source
TEXTURA medieval handwriting
pr **TEXTURA** Gothic dark type
TEXTURE a web; structure; fabric
THALIAN comic; theatrical
THALLUS a stem formation
gl **THALWEG** longitudinal river profile
THANAGE thanedom (Scottish rank)
THANATO- of death (instinct) (Gr.)
THANKED gratefully acknowledged
THAWING melting; dissolving
THAYYAM board game with sticks (Ind.)
md **THEATRE** operations; drama
md **THEBAIA** **THEBAIN**, opium
THEBAIC Theban
bt **THECATE** sheathed; encased
bt **THECIUM** spore-case
mu **THEORBO** lute with 11 strings
THEOREM logical proposition
md **THERAPY** curative art
THEREAT on that account
THEREBY in consequence
THEREIN inside that
THEREOF about that
THEREON upon that
THERETO in addition
md **THERIAC** alleged antidote
THERMAE public steam baths (Roman)
THERMAL thermic; warm
THERMIE heat-calory unit (Fr.)
THERMIT incendiary mixture
THERMOS flask
zo **THEROID** animal-like
THESEUS slew Minotaur in Labyrinth
THESPIS founder of Greek drama
THEURGY miracle making
ch **THIAMIN** B vitamin
THICKEN condense; coagulate; curdle
THICKER closer; duller; muddier
THICKET underwood
THICKLY solidly; densely; closely
nm **THICKUN** £1; a sovereign
THIEVED stole; peculated; purloined
THIGGED cadged; begged
THIGGER threatening beggar; sorner
zo **THILLER** wheel-horse; shaft-horse
nt **THIMBLE** iron rope ring; sleeve piece
tx **THIMBLE** fingertip sewing shield
THINKER cogitator; (Rodin)
THINNED attenuated; reduced
THINNER slimmer; slighter; (paint)
pt **THINNER** solvents; (turpentine)
THIRSTY dry; parched; craving
bt **THISTLE** emblem of Scotland; weed
THISTLY overgrown with thistles
THITHER to there; yonder
THOLING enduring; yielding
rl **THOMISM** doctrine of Thomas Aquinas
nc **THORIDE** radioactive isotope
mn **THORITE** thorium silicate
ch **THORIUM** a metallic element

THOUGHT solicitude; concern; care
THOUGHT concept consideration
THOUING treating with familiarity
THRATCH gasp for breath (Sc.)
THREADY filamentous
THREAVE 24 sheaves
THRIFTY frugal; economical; thriving
THRIVED waxed; luxuriated
THRIVER prosperer
THROATY guttural (sounds)
THRONAL like a throne
THRONED exalted
THROUGH clear; unobstructed
THROWER caster; hurler; heaver
ga **THROW-IN** football
THRUMMY shaggy cloth; fringed
THUGGEE practice of thugs, assassins
mn **THULITE** Norwegian rock
ch **THULIUM** a metallic element
THUMBED beckoned for a lift
THUMPED struck heavily; drubbed
THUMPER whacker; wammer
THUNDER denounce; rumble
THURIFY to cense frankincense
THWAITE reclaimed land
bc **THYMINE** of animal nucleoprotein
md **THYMOMA** tumour in thymus
el **THYRITE** voltage-rise limiting device
md **THYROID** shield-like gland
bt **THYRSUS** branched inflorescence
THYSELF reflexive pronoun of deity
TIARAED wearing a tiara, mini-coronet
TIBETAN of Tibet
mu **TIBICEN** flute player
TICKING bedding material; marking
TICKLED titillated; amused
TICKLER enlivener
zo **TIDDLER** small fry
TIDERIP rough water
TIDEWAY a channel
TIDIEST neatest; sprucest
TIDINGS news; intelligence; message
TIE-BACK window drape fastener
TIE-BEAM rafter retainer
nt **TIE-LINE** ship's mooring rope
cp **TIE-LINE** channel link
zo **TIERCEL** male hawk
TIERCET triple rhyme
tx **TIFFANY** gauze; thin silk
bt **TIGELLA** short stem
TIGHTEN increase the strain
TIGHTER more compact; closer
TIGHTLY tautly; tensely
bt **TIGLINE** croton oil
zo **TIGRESS** fierce female tiger
TIGRINE marked like a tiger
TIGRISH fierce
cy **TIGROID** of nerve-cell granules
TILBURY dog-cart
mn **TILE-ORE** copper ore
TILE-RED brownish-red
TILLAGE cultivation
TILLING husbandry
TILLITE till; boulder clay
bt **TILSEED** seed of sesamum indicum
TILTING jousting; forging
ga **TILTING** slanting; twist throw (bowls)
ck, mu **TIMBALE** a fowl dish; kettle-drum
mu **TIMBREL** tambourine
TIMEFUL seasonable; timely
TIME-GUN parting shot
TIME-LAG an interim; delay
TIME-OFF leisure break; free period
ga **TIME-OUT** entertainment; sports news
TIMIDLY fearfully; diffidently
bt **TIMOTHY** cat's tail grass
mu **TIMPANI** kettle drums; percussion
zo **TINAMOU** S. American quail
zo **TINCHEL** **TINCHIL**, deer culled
TINDERY inflammable
nt **TIN-FISH** torpedo
TINFOIL leaf aluminium
TINGING ringing; tinking
TINGLED thrilled; smarted
TINIEST smallest; puniest; microscopic
TINKLED rang; clinked
TINKLER small bell
TIN-MINE Cornish hole
TINNING covering with tin
zo **TINNOCK** blue tit
TINSICA cartwheel and half-twist
TINSICA somersault (gymnastics)
TIN-TACK tack of/for tin
TINTAGE colouring; shading
pt **TINTERS** stainers; dyers
TINTIES coloured films
TINTING tingeing
TINTYPE ferro-type
TINWARE tin pots
ml **TIN-ZINC** metal finish
TIPCART rubbish barrow
TIPPING hinting; donating
TIPPLED drank deep
TIPPLER steady drinker
TIPSIFY inebriate
TIPSILY drunkenly
TIPSTER racing tout
TIPTOED walked warily
md **TIQUEUR** person suffering from tic
mu **TIRASSE** pedal coupling
TIRLING quivering; vibrating; twisting

TISSUED woven; variegated
TITANIA fairy queen
TITANIC gigantic; colossal
TITHING township
zo **TITLARK** meadow pipit
pr **TITLING** title pages
zo **TITLING** hedge sparrow
zo **TITMICE TITS**, birds
TITOISM political practice
ch **TITRATE** (volumetric analysis)
TITTUPY frisky
TITULAR nominal
TIVERED marked with ochre
TOADIED cringed; truckled; fawned
TOADIES sycophants
TOASTED lightly grilled
TOASTER toast maker
TOBACCO insidious narcotic
TOBASCO red pepper
TOBYMAN highwayman
mu **TOCCATA** a touchy composition
TODDLED strolled; meandered
TODDLER a tiny tot
TOE-HOLD foot grip for climber
TOENAIL horn on foot digits
TOFTMAN a cottager
TOGGERY raiment
TOILFUL wearisome
TOILING moiling; labouring; snaring
TOKENED spotted; marked
TOLLAGE dues
TOLLBAR toll-gate
lw **TOLLING** knelling; annulling
TOLLMAN toll-gatherer
ch **TOLUENE** methyl benzene
zo **TOMALLY** lobster liver
ch **TOMATIN** tomato antibiotic
TOMBOLA a form of lottery
go **TOMBOLO** sand, shingle bar (beach)
TOMFOOL buffoon
bt **TOMOSIS** disease of cotton plant
TOMPION inking pad; clockmaker
TONGUED possessing a tongue
TO-NIGHT night of this day
TONNAGE amount of tons
au **TONNEAU** back-seat part of motor-car
TONSILE clippable
TONSURE shaving; (shorn)
TONTINE co-operative loan
bd, cr, jn **TOOLBOX** container for toolkit
TOOLING (bookbinding); driving
TOOTHED dentate; serrated edge
ar **TOOTHED** (saw-); (dog-)
bd **TOOTHER** projecting horizontal brick
TOOTING prying; hornblowing
mu **TOOTLED** played the flute
TOPARCH a Greek governor
TOPBOOT boot with high top
TOPCOAT overcoat
TOP-EDGE smooth gilded upper book edge
TOPFULL brimming over
TOPHOLE first-rate; best quality
bd **TOP-HUNG** of top-hinged window-sash
TOPIARY ornamental clipping
TOPICAL local; particular; allusive
zo **TOPKNOT** plume or crest of feathers
TOPLESS without a lid; bare-bosomed
nt **TOPMAST** elevated mast
TOPMOST highest
TOPONYM topographical name
cr **TOPPING** upper layer (decor); splendid
ga **TOPPING** beheading; hitting top of ball
TOPPLED tumbled down
nt **TOPSAIL** part of rigging
TOPSIDE the upper part
TOPSMAN bailiff; public hangman
TOPSOIL planting earth
ga **TOPSPIN** rotary motion of ball in play
TORBITE peat fuel
TORCHER torch-bearer; linkman
TORCHON geometric lace
zo **TORGOCH** a species of char
TORMENT rag; rack; plague; harry
md **TORMINA** griping pains
TORNADO cyclone; hurricane; typhoon
TORNOTE with blunt extremities
zo, nt **TORPEDO** ray fish; the tin fish
TORPENT torpid; inert
TORPIFY benumb
hd **TORQUED** wreathed
TORREFY parch; roast; scorch
TORRENT stream; flood; current
TORSADE twisted scroll
TORSION twisting force
TORSIVE spiral
mn **TORSTEN** an iron ore
hd **TORTEAU** red circlet
TORTILE coiled; wreathed
TORTIVE twisted; tortile; tortuous
zo **TORTRIX** a moth genus
TORTURE torment; agony; pang
zo **TORULUS** antenna socket
TORVOUS grim; stern in aspect
TORYISM Conservatism
TOSSILY perty
TOSSING flipping; heaving
TOSSING throw a coin; a caber; one's head

TOSSING twisting and turning; shaking
TOSS-POT toper; quaffer; drinker
TOTALLY wholly; entirely; completely
TOTEMIC (totems); emblematic
TOTTERY shaky; unsteady
TOTTING adding up
TOUCHED sympathetic; impinged
TOUCHED made body contact; handled
TOUCHED emotionally moved; aroused
TOUCHER confidence trickster
ga **TOUCHER** bowls; snooker; billiards
TOUGHEN indurate; harden
TOUGHLY stubbornly; tenaciously
zo **TOURACO** African bird
TOURING journeying
TOURISM co-ordinated travel
TOURIST tripper; excursionist
TOURNEY tournament
TOUSING teasing; worrying
TOUSLED unkempt; in disarray
TOUTING seeking custom
TOWARDS in direction of
nt **TOWBOAT** tug
TOWERED with towers
TOWIRON whaling toggle-iron
nt **TOWLINE** tow rope
TOWNISH urban
TOWPATH boat-haulage path
nt **TOWROPE** boat-haulage rope
md **TOXEMIA** blood poisoning
md **TOXEMIC** septicaemic
TOXICAL poisonous
zo **TOXODON** extinct rhinoceros
TOYSHOP plaything emporium
TOYSOME playful
bt **TOYWORT** shepherd's purse
TRACERY ornamental stonework
md **TRACHEA** wind-pipe
TRACING a copy; traversing
TRACKED trailed; traversed
TRACKER a sleuth
TRACTOR agricultural field vehicle
TRADE-IN part exchange
TRADING commerce; barter
TRADUCE misrepresent; libel; slander
TRAFFIC communications; movement
TRAFFIC flow of social intercourse
TRAFFIC transport; trade; exchange
TRAGEDY drama; calamity
TRAIKET worn out (Sc.)
TRAILED followed; dragged; dogged
TRAILER towed vehicle; follower
TRAILER tracker; preview (play, film)
cp **TRAILER** signal of filed data
TRAINED proficient; skilled
TRAINEE man under instruction
TRAINER a coach
TRAIPSE to tramp
TRAITOR quisling; betrayer
TRAJECT ferry; project
TRAMCAR passenger carriage on lines
TRAMMEL bird-net; compass; hamper
TRAMPED walked; trudged
TRAMPER vagrant; stroller; hiker
TRAMPLE crush; spurn; squelch
TRAMPOT socket for a spindle
rw **TRAMWAY** street railway; (factory)
TRANCED in a dream; enraptured
TRANCHE slice; book-edge; life aspect
hd **TRANGLE** small band
TRANKUM a gew-gaw
TRANNEL wooden rail
TRANSIT conveyance; passage
bd,nt **TRANSOM** window beam; stem of yacht
TRANTER pedlar
TRAPEZE swinging cross-bar aloft
TRAPEZE daring circus gymnastics
TRAPPED adorned; caught
TRAPPER setter of snares
TRASHED lopped; crushed; hindered
TRAVAIL toil; labour; affliction
TRAVERS equestrian dressage act
nt **TRAWLED** fished
nt **TRAWLER** fishing boat
TREACLE molasses; dark syrup
TREACLY viscous and sweet
TREADER trampler
TREADLE pedal
TREASON treachery; disloyalty
TREATED entertained; doctored
TREATER negotiator
TREBLED tripled; threefold
TREEING cornering
ar **TREFOIL** (clover)
el **TREGOHM** million megohms
bt **TREHALA** Turkish manna
TREKKED migrated
TREKKER (ox-wagons, S. Africa)
TRELLIS lattice work
TREMBLE quiver; shake; oscillate
TREMBLY tottery; unsteady
mu **TREMOLO** trembling; shaking; vibrato
TRENDED tended; inclined; gravitated

TRENDLE a roller
rl **TRENTAL** 30 masses
zo **TREPANG** sea-slug
TRESSED curled
TRESSEL trestle; a movable framework
TRESTLE wooden construction support for tables, bridges, scaffold
ce **TRESTLE** ropeway bridges
TREVISS cross-beam
lw **TRIABLE** (jurisdiction)
ch **TRIADIC** trivalent
zo **TRIAENE** spicule in porifera
bt **TRIARCH** with 3 xylem strands in stele
nt **TRIATIC** jumper stay
TRIAXON with three axes
TRIBADE lesbian
TRIBBLE paper drying frame
to **TRIBLET** a goldsmith's mandril
TRIBUNE Roman magistrate; platform
TRIBUTE tax; impost; toil; offering
md **TRICEPS** extensor muscle
zo **TRICHAS** American warblers
nt **TRICING** hauling; clewing
TRICKED defrauded; hoaxed
TRICKER trickster
TRICKLE drip; ooze; percolate
TRICKLY trickling
TRICKSY artful; deft
TRICORN three-cornered
TRIDARN having three tiers
TRIDARN Welsh drying cupboard
TRIDENT Neptune's sceptre
TRIDUAN every third day
TRIDUUM period of three days
TRIFLED dallied; toyed; played
TRIFLER philanderer; idler; fribbler
bt **TRIFOLY** **TREFOIL**, leaf grouping
TRIFORM triple form
TRIGAMY cf. bigamy
TRIGGED skidded; obstructed
TRIGGER firing catch (gun); (-happy)
TRIGGER activate; detonate
TRIGGER switching device; bistable circuit
TRIGLOT in three languages
TRIGONE triangular area
TRIGRAM a triphthong; a trigraph; 3 letter sequence
md **TRILABE** surgical fork
ar **TRILITH** stone doorway
TRILLED warbled; quavered
TRILOGY a series of three linked books
zo **TRIMERA** type of beetle
TRIMMED clipped; balanced; rebuked
cr **TRIMMER** fishing float; beam joists
TRIMMER shearer; timeserver
el **TRIMMER** trimming capacitator
TRINARY ternary; threefold
TRINDLE trundle; trickle
TRINGLE curtain rod (Fr.)
rl **TRINITY** unit of 3
TRINKET small ornament
TRINKLE trickle or tinkle
TRIOLET poetic stanza
md **TRIONAL** hypnotic drug
as **TRIONES** 7 stars in Ursa Major
pg **TRIPACK** 3-emulsion-base process
TRIPARA woman giving birth 3 times
TRIPERY tripe-booth
TRIPLED trebled
TRIPLES series of midair jumps (skating)
mu **TRIPLET** three of a kind; (birth)
TRIPODY verse measure of 3 feet
TRIPOLI polishing powder; diatomite
bt **TRIPOLY** Michaelmas daisy
TRIPPED erred; slipped; stumbled
TRIPPER excursionist; dancer
TRIPSIS shampooing; pulverizing
nt **TRIREME** a galley
TRISECT cut into three
TRISEME (tribrach)
md **TRISMUS** lock-jaw; tetanus
md **TRISOMY** genetic basis of syndrome
TRISULA Siva's trident
TRITELY jejunely; hackneyed
TRITIUM very rare isotope of hydrogen
bt **TRITOMA** red-hot poker
mu **TRITONE** dissonant interval
TRIUMPH exultation; success; ovation
TRIVIAL trifling; slight; paltry
TRIVIUM grammar, logic and rhetoric
zo **TROCHAL** wheel-shaped
TROCHEE long and short foot metre
zo **TROCHUS** gastropod genus
TRODDEN trampled
TROGGIN pedlary
TROLAND unit of illuminance (optics)
TROLLED sang; fished
TROLLER fishing style
TROLLEY truck; metal pulley
TROLLOL sing; troll; trill
TROLLOP a slattern; a slut
TROMLET side pommel horse (gymnastics)

TROMMEL coal sieve with rotary screen
TROMPIL blast regulating device
TRONAGE wool-tax
TROOPED thronged; (the colours)
nt **TROOPER** mounted man; ship
TROPHIC (nutrition)
TROPICS (Cancer and Capricorn)
md **TROPINE** constituent of atropine
TROPISM enforced turning movement
TROPIST figurative speaker
TROTTER pig's foot; (globe-); horse
TROUBLE disturb; worry; trial; dolour
TROUNCE to larrup; castigate
TROUPER strolling player
md **TROUSSE** set of instruments
TROWING trusting; believing
TRUANCY vagrancy
TRUCAGE counterfeiting a picture
TRUCKED bartered; trafficked
TRUCKER exchange agent; driver
TRUCKLE roller; yield; submit
TRUDGED walked wearily; tramped
TRUDGEN a swimming stroke
bt **TRUFFLE** an edible fungus
TRUMEAU part of a wall
TRUMPED deceived; ruffed
mu **TRUMPET** proclaim; blazon; instrument
TRUNCAL main; principal
zo **TRUNCUS** main blood vessel
TRUNDLE wheel; truck; to roll
TRUNDLE spool of golden thread
TRUSSED bound; tied up
TRUSTED credited; confided
TRUSTEE guardian; fiduciary
TRUSTER an optimist; creditor
lw **TRYABLE** triable (law courts)
zo **TRYPETA** boring flies
md **TRYPSIN** pepsin
md **TRYPTIC** peptic; digestive
nt **TRY-SAIL** part of rigging
TRYSTED rendezvoused; appointed
TRYSTER tryst convener; go-between
TSANTSA head-shrinking technique
TSARINA Empress of Russia
TSARISM of the tsar (czar)
TSARIST Russian royalist
T-SQUARE draughtsman's tool
TSUKPIN Proa canoe, Micronesia
TSUNAMI seismic sea wave tremor, Japan
zo **TUATERA** tuatara; NZ lizard
mn **TUBBING** mine shaft lining; bathing
zo **TUBBISH** rotund; tub-like
zo **TUB-FISH** sapphirine gurnard
mu **TUBICEN** trumpeter
TUB-SIZE strengthening dip for handmade paper
TUBULAR hollow; fistular; capillary
TUCK-BOX for schoolboys' treats, delicacies
TUCKING cramming; folding; gathering
TUCK-OUT gorge of eating; blow-out
TUESDAY a weekday
mn **TUESITE** slate-pencil material
TUFTING knotting (carpets); adorning
nt **TUGBOAT** ship-towing craft
TUGGING lugging; pulling; hauling
nm **TUGHRIK** (Mongolia)
TUITION instruction; education
TULCHAN spoof calf
TULLIAN Latin style of M. Tullius Cicero
TUMBLED rumpled; fallen; twigged
zo **TUMBLER** pigeon; glass; acrobat; lock system
TUMBREL tumbril; two-wheeled cart
TUMIDLY pompously; turgidly; puffily
bt **TUMPING** stamping (after planting)
TUMULAR heaped
TUMULUS burial mound
TUNABLE melodious; musical
TUNABLY harmoniously
bd **TUNDISH** wine funnel; flue; condensation collector
TUNEFUL musical; dulcet
bt **TUNG-OIL** wood-oil
zo **TUNICIN** animal cellulose
TUNICLE small tunic
TUNMOOT village council
TUNNAGE (and poundage) wine tax
TUNNERY tunny-netting area
TUPPING hammering; butting
TURACIN carmine
zo **TURAKOO** gaudy bird; plantain-eater
TURBARY turf digging rights
TURBINE rotary engine
TURDINE thrush-like
TURFING laying turf; swarding
TURFITE racing fan
TURGENT swelling; distended; tumid
mn **TURGITE** a form of haematite
TURKISH of Turkey; language
TURKMEN Turkic people
TURMOIL tumult; ado; hubbub
TURNCAP chimney cowl
TURNERY lathe work
TURNING flexure; spinning; fermenting

TURNKEY prison warder
TURN-OUT parade; clearout; tidying
TURNPIN **TAMPIN**, boxwood roller (USA)
TURN-UPS trouser leg folds
bt **TURPETH** purgative plant
TURTLER turtle-hunter
ar **TUSKING** projecting stones (toothing)
TUSSIVE afflicted with a cough
TUSSLED struggled; fought; battled
TUSSOCK tuffet; tuft
tx **TUSSORE** coarse silk
TUTAMEN a protection; a defence
TUTANIA Britannia metal; alloy of copper, calamine, antimony, tin (1770)
TUTELAR protective
TUTENAG a Chinese alloy; zinc
TUTORED taught; educated; instructed
TUTULUS Etruscan head-dress
mn **TUT-WORK** excavation piece-work
TWADDLE verbiage; balderdash; prattle (sl.)
mu **TWANGED** played the banjo
TWANKAY green tea
TWANKED twanged; twangled
TWEAKED twitched; pinched
TWEEDLE (fiddle); wheedle
TWEENIE maid; diminutive
ac **TWEETER** loudspeaker
mu **TWELFTH** ordinal number; mutation stop organ
to **TWIBILL** mattock; axe
TWIDDLE twist; tweedle
TWIGGED understood; observed (sl.)
TWIGGEN of wicker
TWINGED twitched; pained
TWINING twisting; meandering; coiling
TWINKLE wink; glimmer; scintillate
TWINNED two at a time
TWINSET matching sweater and cardigan
TWINTER beast, two winters old
au **TWIN-TOP** (motoring)
TWIRLED span; rotated; whirled
TWIRLER spinner; twister
TWISTED spun; contorted; tangled
TWISTER a puzzle; cheat; tornado
TWISTLE twist; a wrench (Sc.)
TWISTOR computer memory device
TWITTED reproached; rallied; taunted
TWITTEN by-lane
TWITTER an upbraider; chirp; palpitate
TWIZZLE turn and twist; a step-dance on one spot; jig
TWO-FOLD double
pr **TWO-LINE** size of printing type; whip (parliamentary)
TWONESS doubleness
TWOSOME a couple
mu **TWOSTEP** a dance
TWO-TIME double-cross
tc **TWO-WIRE** (AC or DC) transmit and receive channel
TYCHISM theory based on chance
pt **TYING-IN** tubular scaffolding, interior grip
nt **TYING-UP** mooring a vessel; securing
pr **TYING-UP** binding; setting book bands
zo **TYLARUS** padded hoof
TYLOPOD camel-footed
md **TYLOSIS** eye-trouble
md **TYLOTIC** eye-inflammation
md **TYMPANA** ear-drums
md **TYMPANY** turgidity; flatulence
TYNWALD parliament (Isle of Man)
pr **TYPE-BAR** a line of type
md **TYPHOID** a fever
mt **TYPHOON** cyclone; hurricane
TYPICAL emblematic; characteristic
TYPONYM type-name
TYRANNY despotism; iron rule
TZARINA Tsarina (Russia)
TZIGANE gipsy (Hungary)

U

UBEROUS fruitful
lw **UDALLER** **ODALLER**, freehold
UDARNIK 'shock' worker (Rus.)
mu **UKULELE** Hawaiian guitar
mn **ULEXITE** sodium calcium borate
ULLALOO Irish lament
pl **ULNARIA** arm-bones
md **ULONCUS** swollen gums
ULULANT wailing; sobbing
ULULATE howl; hoot
ULYSSES Odysseus; a wanderer
UMBERED tinged with brown colour
UMBONAL protuberant
UMBONES bosses on shields
UMBONIC humpy
UMBRAGE shade; resentment
UMBRERE helmet visor
UMBRIAN of Umbria province (It.)
zo, pt **UMBRINE** fish; darkish brown
UMBROSE shady; umbrageous
ga **UMPIRED** refereed; arbitrated
UMPTEEN more than ten

UNACTED never staged
UNAGING remaining youthful; immortal
UNAIDED single-handed
UNAIRED stuffy; unventilated; hidden
rl **UNALIST** holding one benefice
UNAPTLY not à propos
UNARMED defenceless
UNASKED gratuitously; unrequested
UNAWARE ignorant; uninformed
ga **UNBATED** unblunted point (fencing)
UNBAYED opened up
UNBEGUN not started
UNBLIND restore vision
UNBLOCK to clear; (cards)
UNBLOWN not sounded; in the bud
UNBORNE not carried
UNBOSOM freely disclose
UNBOUND loose; limitless
UNBOWED unsubdued
UNBRACE relax; free from tension
UNBRAID disentangle
UNBRUTE domesticate; tame
UNBUILD destroy (a house)
UNBUILT not yet constructed
UNBURNT unconsumed
UNCAGED released; freed
UNCANNY eerie; weird; mysterious
UNCARED untended; unheeded
UNCASED taken out; displayed
UNCEDED not transferred or granted
UNCHAIN free; let loose; unfetter
UNCHARM unspell; exorcise
UNCHARY heedless; not frugal
UNCINAL hook-shaped
md **UNCINUS** small hook
UNCIVIL incivil; impolite
UNCLASP unfasten; disconnect
UNCLEAN foul; dirty; leprous
UNCLEAR confused; unintelligible
UNCLING unclasp; disengage
UNCLOAK disrobe; unveil; unmask
UNCLOSE open; babbling
UNCLOUD free from obscurity
UNCOUTH boorish; rustic; rough
UNCOVER lay open; disclose
UNCROSS straighten (the legs)
UNCROWN dethrone
rl **UNCTION** an anointing
UNCULAR avuncular
md, ck **UNCURED** unremedied; unpreserved
UNDATED unrecorded; timeless
UNDEIFY remove a god
ck **UNDERDO** cook insufficiently
UNDERGO experience; bear; suffer
UNDIGHT to undress
UNDOING opening; unravelling; ruining
UNDRAPE strip; uncover
UNDRAWN not delineated
UNDREAM abandon a scheme, fantasy
UNDRESS disrobe; casual wear
UNDRIED wet; green
UNDYING immortal; continuing
UNEARTH disclose; reveal; discover
UNEATEN not consumed
UNEQUAL varying; not uniform
UNEXACT **INEXACT**, inaccurate
UNFADED remaining fresh; unwithered
UNFENCE remove a hedge
UNFILED unsorted reports; unrasped
UNFITLY unsuitably; improperly
UNFIXED unsettled; unsecured
UNFLESH reduce to a skeleton
UNFLUSH lose colour
UNFOUND still lost; not met with
rl **UNFROCK** deprive of office
UNFUMED not fumigated
el, mn **UNFUSED** unmerged; (unsafe)
UNFUZED shells unset for gunnery
UNGIVEN not conceded
UNGLAZE remove the glass
UNGLOVE bare the hand
UNGLUED unstuck
UNGODLY sinful; impious; profane
UNGUARD leave defenceless
md **UNGUENT** an ointment
zo **UNGULAR** (hoof; nails; etc.)
UNGYVED unfettered
UNHANDY awkward; clumsy
UNHAPPY sad; grievous; sorrowful
bt **UNHARDY** irresolute; delicate
UNHASTY slow; deliberate
UNHEARD inaudible; obscure
UNHEEDY careless; rash
UNHINGE to unsettle; derange
UNHIRED not engaged
UNHITCH loosen; unfasten
UNHIVED driven from shelter
UNHOARD dissipate; spend
UNHOPED unexpected
UNHORSE force to dismount
UNHOUSE evict
UNHUMAN not of mankind
UNIAXAL on one plane; uniaxial
UNICATE to make as one
UNICITY uniqueness; city sprawl
zo **UNICORN** a fabulous animal; oryx
UNIDEAL realistic; prosaic
UNIFIED united; merged
UNIFIER amalgamator; merger
bt **UNIFOIL** bearing only one leaf

UNIFORM consistent; steady; standard
ma **UNITAGE** of measurement
UNITARY (method); integral
UNITATE remainder after division
UNITERM key-word graphic index system
cp **UNITERM** information retrieval
UNITING combining; concerting
UNITION conjunction
UNITIVE harmonizing
UNITIZE to treat as one unit
UNJOINT separate; individualized
UNKEMPT uncombed; rough
UNKNOWN nameless; anonymous
UNLACED not done up; untied
nt, rw **UNLADED UNLADEN**, unloaded (of cargoes)
UNLATCH unlock; open
UNLEARN to forget
UNLEASH remove all constraint
UNLEAVE strip of leaves
UNLEVEL uneven; rough
UNLIMED freed from lime
UNLINED (paper); unruled
UNLIVED bereft of life (Shak.)
UNLOOSE unleash from restraints
UNLOVED disliked; unrequited
UNLUCKY ill-starred; hapless
UNLUSTY weak; infirm; sickly
UNLUTED unglued; uncemented
UNMANLY effeminate; cowardly
UNMARRY divorce
UNMATED single; unconsummated
UNMEANT not intended
UNMETED not measured
UNMEWED set free; released
UNMIXED pure; unadulterated
UNMORAL immoral; licentious
UNMOULD change the form of
UNMOVED impassive; serene; quiet
UNNAMED anonymous
UNNERVE frighten; intimidate
UNNOBLE ignoble; unworthy
UNNOTED unremarked
UNOFTEN infrequently
UNOILED free from lubrication
UNORDER countermand
UNOWNED unacknowledged
UNPAGED unnumbered (of prelim. pages)
UNPAINT remove paint
UNPANEL remove from committee
UNPAVED uncobbled (streets)
UNPENAL without penalty
UNPERCH dislodge; unroost
UNPLAIT unbraid; unravel
UNPLUMB not vertical
UNPLUME pluck
UNQUEEN dethrone; expose
UNQUIET unease; restless; noisy
UNQUOTE end quotation
UNRAKED untilled
UNRATED unvalued; unregarded
UNRAVEL disentangle; solve
UNREADY irresolute; slow
nt **UNREEVE** withdraw a rope
ck, pl **UNRISEN** unbaked; flaccid
UNRIVET undo; loose; detach
UNROYAL unkingly; not in lineage
UNRULED uncontrolled; unlined
UNSATED rapacious; not satisfied
rl **UNSAVED** lost; condemned
zo **UNSCALY** without fish scales
UNSCREW untwist; unfasten
UNSEXED undetermined or castrated
UNSHORN unshaven; unclipped
UNSHOWN not exhibited; hidden
UNSIGHT lose sight of; (cricket)
UNSIZED not stiffened; ungraded
UNSLING release from slings
UNSLUNG not projected
UNSOLID fluid; unsubstantial
UNSOUND erroneous; defective
UNSPENT unexhausted; still moving
UNSPIED unobserved; undetected
UNSPIKE pull put prickles
UNSPILT not shed; not slopped
UNSPLIT undivided
UNSTACK disperse; dishevel
UNSTAID unsteady; unstable
UNSTATE deprive of dignity
UNSTEEL soften; disarm
UNSTICK ungum; tear free
UNSTRAP loosen
UNSTUCK loosened; dished
UNSWEAR recall an oath
UNSWEET inharmonious; acid
UNSWEPT unbrushed
UNSWORN not on oath
UNTAKEN left; relinquished
UNTAMED savage; barbaric
UNTAXED not charged
UNTHINK dismiss from the mind
UNTILED detesselated
UNTIRED unwearied
UNTOOTH extract
UNTRIED inexperienced; new
UNTRULY falsely; erroneously
UNTRUSS take apart; dissect
UNTRUTH lie; imposture; error
ro, mu **UNTUNED** not set to play
UNTWINE untwist; unravel
UNTWIST disentangle
UNTYING unknotting
UNURGED unsolicited

UNUSUAL bizarre; queer; odd; rum
UNVEXED unharassed; untroubled
UNVOWED not bound by oath
UNWAGED unsalaried
UNWAYED trackless
UNWEARY unspent; unflagging
UNWEAVE unplait
UNWHIPT unbirched
UNWIRED unstrung
UNWITCH uncharm; unspell
UNWITTY lacking humour; prosaic
UNWOOED uncourted; unsolicited
UNWOUND untwined; uncoiled
UNWOVEN not made into cloth
UNWRUNG untwisted; undrained
UNYOKED freed (of oxen)
UNZONED unpartitioned (area)
UPBRAID rebuke; chide; taunt
UPENDED stood on end
UPFIELD cricket
UPGRADE promote
UPHEAVE lift up; raise
UPHOARD secrete; amass; garner
go **UPLYING** elevated ground
UPRIGHT vertical; honest; just
UPRISEN ascended
UPSHIFT change gear
bt **UPSHOOT** a sprout; result
UPSIDES horses exercising together
UPSTAGE theatrical; steal attention
bt **UPSTART** parvenu; meadow saffron
UPSURGE upswell
ga **UPSWEEP** woman's coiffure
UPSWELL upsurge; crowds; tide
UPTIGHT unduly inhibited
UP-TRAIN train to London
UPWARDS upward; upwardly
md **URAEMIA** kidney disease
mn **URALITE** fireproof material
URA-NAGE rear throw (judo)
URANIAN astronomical
ch **URANIDE** element beyond protactinium
mn **URANITE** a green uranium ore
ch **URANIUM** metallic element
ch **URANOUS** containing uranium
zo **URETHRA** urinary duct
URGENCY importunity; stress
URICASE uric acid salt
ch **URIDINE** crystalline nucleoside
hd **URINANT** bent fish
md **URINARY** of the bladder/urine
md **URINATE** to pass body water
zo **UROCYCON** American grey fox
pl **UROCYST** the bladder
zo **URODELA** newts and salamanders
md **UROLOGY** study of urinary tract
md **UROSOME** caudal segment
zo **URSINAL** ursine; bearish
bt **URTICAL** (nettles)
USELESS vain; bootless; abortive
USHERED introduced; foreran; heralded
USITATE usually; customary
USUALLY normally; generally
USURPED arrogated; seized; assumed
USURPER a dictator
UTENSIL implement; vessel
md **UTERINE** of the uterus
UTILISE utilize; employ; apply
UTILITY usefulness
UTOPIAN imaginary; chimerical; ideal
UTOPISM unpractical hopefulness
UTOPIST optimist; visionary
md **UTRICLE** small cell or bladder
UTTERED issued; pronounced; said
UTTERER promulgator; (counterfeit)
UTTERLY absolutely; completely
md **UVEITIS** eye congestion
UXORIAL dotingly fond of a wife

V

VACANCY job, place available
VACATED left; abandoned
VACATOR a quitter
lw **VACATUR** annulment
md **VACCINE** anti-disease extract
VACHERY cow-house; dairy
VACUATE make a vacuum
VACUIST vacant believer
VACUITY emptiness; a void
VACUOLE minute cavity
VACUOUS void; unfilled
VAGITUS cry of a newborn child
VAGRANT vagabond; nomad; tramp
VAGUELY dimly; indefinitely
VAGUEST most uncertain
VAILING veiling; tipping
VAINEST most conceited
VALANCE draped border
ch **VALENCE VALENCY**, combining power; compatibility of elements
bt **VALERIC** derived from valerian
VALIANT intrepid; gallant; doughty
VALIDLY with legal force
VALINCH cask tap
VALLARY (rampart)
VALLATE cup-shaped
bt **VALONIA** acorn-cup (Levant)
bt **VALSOID** with perithecia in circle
VALUING esteeming; appraising
VALVATE valvular
VALVLET valvula; small valve

VALVULA cerebellum process in fish
zo **VALVULE** valvula; small valve
VAMOOSE to retire
VAMOSED decamped
mu **VAMPING** patching; bewitching
mu **VAMPING** simplified reissuing
zo **VAMPIRE** blood-sucker; a bat
VAMPLET spear buckler
ch **VANADIC** of vanadium
ch **VANADYL** electrolyte cation
VANDYKE lace collar
zo **VANESSA** butterfly genus (Swift)
VAN-FOSS a moat
bt **VANILLA** orchid; a flavour
VANNING mining; transporting
zo **VANSIRE** mongoose (Madagascar)
ga **VANTAGE** (tennis); advantage
VANTAGE sighting point
VANWARD vanguard; ahead
VAPIDLY inertly; insipidly; languidly
md **VAPOURS** nervous malady
VAPOURY hypochondriac
VAQUERO S. Amerian cow-puncher
zo **VARANUS** monitor lizard
VAREUSE seaman's jersey, jacket
VARIANT different; diverse
VARIANT differing version
VARIATE to vary; altered form
md **VARICES** knotted veins
VARIETY diversity; assortment
VARIETY music hall; revue
md **VARIOLA** smallpox
bl **VARIOLE** pitted (of skin, stem)
VARIOUS sundry; several; numerous
zo **VARMINT** vermin
VARNISH to gloss over; palliate
VARSITY university
VARVELS vervels; rings on a hawk
VARYING differing; deviating; altering
VASTATE make immune
VASTEST bulkiest; greatest
rl **VATICAN** papal capital
VATTING mixing wines; customs
VAUDOIS Waldensian of Swiss canton
ar **VAULTED** arched; sprang; (of ceiling, roof)
ga **VAULTER** bounder (athletics)
VAUNTED boasted; bragged
VAUNTER braggart; boaster
VAVASOR titled landowner
VECTION porterage; convection
VEDANGA Veda commentary
VEDANTA Veda philosophy
VEDETTE vidette; mounted scout
nt **VEERING** shifting; changing; varying; wind moving clockwise
bt, ck **VEGETAL** of vegetable, plant
VEHICLE car; conveyance; art form
rl, tx **VEILING** covering; concealing; cloth
md **VEINAGE VEINOUS**, of the vein system
md **VEINING** pattern of veins
pl **VEINLET VEINULE**, smaller vein
pl **VELAMEN** membrane; of palate
VELARIA Roman amphitheatre awnings
zo **VELIGER** larval stage of mollusca
VELLING cutting turf
VELLUMY like vellum
tx **VELOURS** plush fabric
ck **VELOUTE** creamy meat sauce
VELVETY smooth
VENALLY mercenary
VENATIC sporting
zo **VENDACE** a lake fish
VENDING selling; bartering
ck **VENISON** deer meat
VENOMED poisoned
VENTAGE escape hole
VENTAIL helmet visor
VENTING releasing; uttering; emitting
VENTOSE windy; breezy
VENTOSE Republican month (Fr.)
VENT-PEG a plug for a cask (wine)
pl **VENTRAD VENTRAL, VENTRIC**, abdominal
VENTURE to undertake (risks); dare
ae **VENTURI** convergent/divergent duct
ar **VERANDA VERANDAH**, roofed open gallery
bt, ck **VERBENA VERVAIN**, herbal tea
VERBIFY VERBALIZE, express thoughts
VERBILE VERBOSE, loquacious; wordy
bt **VERDANT VERDURE**, green growth
lw **VERDICT** decision; finding; judgement
mn **VERDITE** green S. Afr. rock
VERGENT VERGING, bordering; adjacent
VERGLAS thin ice or frost layer
VERIEST absolute; truest
VERISMO expressionist objectivity (art)
VERITAS French shipping register
VERMEIL a glaze; ormolu
zo **VERMIAN** wormlike
pt **VERMILY VERMILION**, red pigment
VERNANT VERNATE, of spring; to flourish
VERNIER measuring device

md **VERONAL** an opiate
bt, md **VERRUCA** a wart; foot ailment
VERSANT conversant; familiar
ch **VERSENE** sodium versenate
VERSIFY VERSING, relate in rhyme
ma **VERSINE** function of an angle
VERSION an account; interpretation
VERSUAL paragraphic
VERSUTE crafty; wily
md **VERTIGO** dizziness; giddiness
hd **VERULED** ringed
hd **VERULES** concentric rings
bt, ck **VERVAIN VERBENA**, herbal tea
VERVELS varvels; rings on a hawk
md **VESANIA VERSANIC**, insanity; psychoses
pl **VESICAL VESICLE**, bladder-like cavity
zo **VESPINE VESPOID**, wasplike
VESTIGE footprint; trace; remains
VESTING fabric for vests; investing
zo **VESTLET** a sea-anemone
VESTRAL (vestry)
VESTURE clothing; garment; dress
VETERAN experienced; seasoned (war-)
VETERAN pre-1918 used cars (crocks)
bt **VETIVER** a fragrant grass
VETOING prohibiting; barring; banning
VETTING examining; checking
VETTURA Italian cab
VEXILLA processional banners
VIADUCT raised road
VIARIAN wayfarer
md **VIBICES** feverish spots
VIBRANT resonant; undulous
VIBRATE oscillate; quiver; sway
mu **VIBRATO** tremolo
md **VIBRION** mobile bacterium
VICEROY king's deputy
VICIOUS depraved; sinful; defective
VICTORY success; mastery; triumph
VICTRIX a lady winner
VICTUAL provide provisions
VIDENDA things to be seen
VIDEOCY media addiction (TV)
VIDETTE vedette; mounted scout
VIDIMUS an inspection; summary
VIDUOUS widowed
VIEWING surveying; scanning; eyeing
tx **VIGONIA** llama wool fabric
VILAYET Turkish province
VILLAGE hamlet; thorpe
VILLAIN miscreant; rascal; rogue
VILLEIN serf; villager
VILLINO small villa in a park
VILLOSE VILLOUS, shaggy; hairy
mu **VILUELA** ancient Spanish lute
VIMINAL of twigs
VINALIA Roman wine festival
VINASSE wine dregs
VINCULA chains; (prisoners); brackets
ma **VINCULA** similarly treated terms
VINEGAR fermentation acid; sour wine
VINGT-UN card game
VINTAGE season's yield of wine (harvest)
VINTAGE year of an extra fine wine
VINTAGE cars of 1919–30
VINTNER wine-seller
mn **VIOLANE** violet-blue diopside
VIOLATE outrage; break; profane
VIOLENT fierce; vehement; furious
bt **VIOLINE** poisonous extract
mu **VIOLINO** ancient high-pitched viol (It.)
mu **VIOLIST** viola player
mu **VIOLONE** ancient double-bass (It.)
mt **VIRAZON** sea breeze, Chile, Peru
mu **VIRELAY VIRELAI**, medieval roundelay (Fr.)
VIRGATE wand-like; slender and straight
me **VIRGATE** a quarter of a hide
VIRGULE small rod; a comma
md **VIROSIS** viral infection
VIRTUAL almost entirely; de facto
pg **VIRTUAL** image by light-convergences
cp **VIRTUAL** environment for code data
VISAGED of face; aspect; appearance
VIS-A-VIS face to face
md **VISCERA** internal organs
VISCOUS sticky; glutinous; tenacious
mn **VISEITE** zeolite
VISIBLE patent; evident; apparent
VISIBLY obviously; manifestly
VISITED stayed; chastised; afflicted
VISITOR visiter; a caller
VISORED masked; helmeted
VITALLY essentially; (-necessary)
ck **VITAMIN** vital organic compound (diet)
VITIATE to spoil; impair; debase
VITRAIL stained-glass window
mn **VITRAIN** a type of coal
md **VITREUM** eye-fluid
VITRICS VITRIFY, glassmaking; glazing
VITRINE glass show case
ch **VITRIOL** sulphuric acid
VITRIOL virulent speech; feeling

VITRITE black glass
bt **VITTATE** with longitudinal stripes
VITULAR (calf); (veal)
VIVENCY existence
zo **VIVERRA** civet genus
VIVIDLY animatedly; brilliantly
VIVIFIC enlivening
VOCABLE call-able
VOCALIC concerning, containing vowels
VOCALLY by voice, speech, song
VOCODER synthetic speech device
VOCULAR vocal
mn **VOGLITE** uranium ore
VOICING expressing
VOIDING ejecting; emptying
VOIVODE VAIVODE, Hungarian, Polish, Romanian governor
VOLABLE nimble-witted; volatile
mu **VOLANTE** Sp. vehicle; fast and light (It.)
VOLCANO eruptive mountain
VOLSUNG Odin's grandson
el, me **VOLTAGE** amount of volts
VOLTAIC galvanic
VOLUBLE having the gift of the gab
VOLUBLY glibly; fluently
VOLUMED bulky
VOLUMEN rolled papyrus text
VOLUSPA song of the sybil (Scand.)
VOLUTED with spiral scroll
md **VOMITUS** vomited matter
VORLAGE forward leaning position (skiing)
VOTABLE enfranchised
VOUCHED warranted; attested
lw **VOUCHEE** warrantee
VOUCHER a witness; a pass
VOWELLY full of vowels
VOYAGED cruised; traversed
VOYAGER ocean traveller
rl **VULGATE** authentic Latin Bible
VULPINE foxy; cunning
zo **VULTURE** carrion-eating bird
zo **VULTURN** Australian turkey

W

WADABLE fordable
WADDING stuffing; non-edible filling
WADDLED walked like a duck
WADDLER wobbly walker
to **WAD-HOOK** an extractor
tx **WADMOLL** woollen cloth
lw **WADSETT** a mortgage
lw **WAFERED** sealed; secured
WAFTAGE transportation
WAFTING floating; airing; beckoning
WAGERED hazarded; risked; staked
WAGERER a better
WAGGERY sportive merriment
WAGGING swaying (flags) (dogs)
WAGGISH droll; facetious; jocular
WAGGLED wiggled
WAGONED carted; transported
WAGONER cart-driver
WAGSOME whimsical; witty
zo **WAGTAIL** bird; joinery
bt **WAGWANT** totter-grass
rl **WAHABEE** primitive Moslem
WAILFUL mournful; sorrowful; grievous
WAILING bemoaning; lamenting
WAINAGE transport
WAISTED narrowed
WAISTER whaling greenhorn
WAITING attendance; biding; tarrying
WAIVING relinquishing; remitting
WAKEFUL alert; wary; vigilant
WAKEMAN a watchman
WAKENED stimulated; excited
WAKENER a rouser; knocker-up
WALKING pedestrianism; hiking; rambling
WALK-OUT industrial strike; protest
bt **WALLABA** timber tree (Guyana)
zo **WALLABY** kangaroo-like animal
WALLACH Wallack; a Wallachian
md **WALL-EYE** eye condition
WALLING wall material
WALLOON Belgian (French-speaking)
bt **WALL-RUE** a fern
WALTZED danced (Viennese style)
WALTZER ballroom athlete
WAMBLED rumbled
WAN-EYED languid; sad
WANGHEE a cane; a stick
WANGLED acquired by craft
WANHOPE despair
bt **WANHORN** a plant
WANNABE aspiring to be liked
WANNESS pallor; paleness
WANNISH sickly
WANTAGE deficiency; lack
WANTING absent; desiring; needing
WANTWIT a numbskull; nitwit
zo **WAPACUT** American snowy owl
bt **WARATAH** Australian shrub
WARBLED trilled (bird-song)
zo **WARBLER** crooner, bird
WARBLES saddle-sores; tumours

WARDAGE watch-tax
WARDING repelling; fending; guarding
WARD-WIT warder's quittance
WAREFUL wary; cautious; vigilant
WARFARE strife; hostilities
WARHEAD explosive part of missile
WARHOOP war-cry; slogan
WARIEST most circumspect
WARISON a reward; a gift
WARLIKE belligerent; martial
WARLOCK wizard (devil's own)
WARLORD Junker militarist
WARMEST keenest; most ardent
WARMING heating
WARNING caution; notification; omen
WARPATH hostile expedition
WARPING twisting; distorting (the mind)
WARPING expansion of wood
nt **WARPING** docking by ropes (ships)
WARRANT authorize; justify
WARRANT police permission; guarantee
WARRING contending; striving
WARRIOR veteran fighter
WAR-RISK (insurance)
WAR-SCOT war-tax; a levy
nt **WARSHIP** battleship, etc.
WARSONG song on martial theme
zo **WART-HOG** an African ungulate
WARTIME during hostilities
WARWORN battle-weary
WASH-DAY laundry day
WASHING ablution; rinsing
ga, rw **WASHOUT** sports; track; unusable (rain)
ga **WASHOUT** failure; fiasco (bowling)
WASHTUB (mobile) bath; (clothes)
zo **WASP-FLY** fly resembling wasp
WASPISH resentful; irritable
WASSAIL carolling outside houses
WASSAIL festival; punch (drink)
WASTAGE dissipation; debris
WASTING emaciation
WASTREL waif; a dud
WATCHED guarded; tended; noted
WATCHER observer; (bird-); overseer
WATCHET light blue
WATERED wavy; moistened; sprinkled
WATERER irrigator
WATTLED (hurdles); (cocks-comb)
WAULING howling; caterwauling
WAVELET a ripple
WAVERED faltered; swayed
WAVERER hesitator
nt **WAVESON** flotsam; floating wreckage
ps **WAVICLE** quantum mechanical entity
bt **WAX-BEAN** butter-bean
zo **WAXBILL** (weaver-bird)
WAX-DOLL poupée (Fr.)
WAX-JACK sealing wax taper stand
zo **WAX-MOTH** (a bee scourge)
bt **WAX-PALM** wax-producing tree
bt **WAX-TREE** American gamboge tree
zo **WAXWING** a crested bird
WAXWORK wax statue counterfeiting life
WAYBILL a list (transport)
WAYGONE exhausted; wayworn
WAYLAND a legendary smith
WAYLESS pathless; trackless
WAY-MARK direction pointer; sign
WAY-POST guide-post
WAYSIDE of the roadside
WAYWARD froward; wilful; unruly
WAYWISE directional capacity
WAYWORN exhausted; spent
WEAKEST puniest
WEALDEN WEALD, old woodland (Kent, E. Sussex)
WEALTHY opulent; affluent; rich
WEANING ending milk-child stage
WEARIED fatigued; jaded; careworn
WEARIER more jaded and tired
WEARILY tediously
WEARING exhausting
WEARISH withered; washy
WEAR-OFF effect decreasing gradually
WEAR-OUT to become worn and torn
md **WEASAND** windpipe; throat
WEATHER climate; endure; overcome
tx **WEAVING** interlacing threads (cloth)
nt **WEAVING** zigzag course; (pattern)
WEBBING hempen fabric
md **WEB-EYED** filmy-eyed
WEB-FOOT characteristic of aquatic birds
WEBSTER a weaver
WEB-TOED frog-footed
WEDDING nuptials; espousal; marriage
WEDGING timber joint; doorstop jamb
WEEDING eliminating; purging
WEDLOCK BEDLOCK, matrimony; marriage
rl **WEE-FREE** church group (Sc.)
WEEKDAY WORKDAY, (not Sunday)
WEEKEND Saturday and Sunday
WEENING thinking; imagining
WEEPING sobbing; crying; bewailing

zo, ck **WEEVILY** maggoty; meat infestation
WEFTAGE texture
pc **WE-GROUP** in-group; elitism
WEIGHED pondered; pressed; (anchor)
WEIGHER weighing machine
WEIGH-IN pre-contest weight check
WEIGHTY ponderous; onerous; grave
WEIRDER more fantastic
WEIRDLY eerily; uncannily
WELADAY **LACKADAY**, alas!
WELCHER welsher; absconding bookie
WELCOME salutation; greeting
WELDING welded joint
WELFARE comfort; prosperity; weal
WELLING springing; gushing
WELL-MET all hail! welcome!
WELL-OFF well-to-do; prosperous
WELL-SET firmly set
WELL-WON honestly gained
WELSHED betrayed
WELSHER absconding bookie
WELTING shoe-edging
WENDING wandering; strolling
WENDISH **WEND** (Baltic) dialect
mn **WENLOCK** limestone
WENNISH cyst-like
WERGILD **WERGOLD**, blood money (Scand.)
rl **WERWOLF** **WEREWOLF**, wolfman (Scand.)
WEST-END stylish city district
WESTERN occidental; democratic
WESTING westerly; wind
nt **WET-DOCK** dock where ship can float
WETNESS dampness; humidity
WET-SHOD with wet feet
WETTEST supersaturated
WET-TIME wages for rainy days
WETTING moistening; drenching
WETTISH rather rainy
fr **WETWOOD** high-water-content wood
WHACKED beaten; defeated; smitten
WHACKED exhausted
WHACKER of large size; formidable
WHALERY port and factory base for whaling
WHALING whale-fishing; thrashing
bt **WHANGEE** bamboo cane
WHAPPED struck; fluttered
nt **WHARFED** brought to jetty
WHARVES quays; docks
WHATNOT small, 3-shelf stand
WHATSIT unspecified; forgotten item
bt **WHEATEN** of wheat
WHEEDLE to coax; to cajole
WHEELED with wheels
zo **WHEELER** shaft-horse; cyclist
WHEELER wheelwright
WHEEZED breathed asthmatically
WHEEZLE whaizle; whaisle; obtain
WHELKED ridged; shell-like ornamentation
zo **WHELPED** littered; gave birth to brood
WHEREAS in view of fact that
WHEREAT thereupon
WHEREBY through which
WHEREIN within which
WHEREOF whence
WHEREON upon which
WHERETO to which
WHETHER if; in the case of
zo **WHETILE** woodpecker
WHETTED stimulated; urged
WHETTER a sharpener
WHEWING whistling with surprise
WHEYISH like whey
WHEY-TUB cream-tub
WHIFFED puffed
WHIFFER a puffer
WHIFFET whipper-snapper
mu **WHIFFLE** whistle; flute; prevaricate
WHILERE while here; recently
WHILING loitering; passing the time
WHIMPER whine; cry; moan
WHIMPLE **WIMPLE**, pointed headdress
WHIMSEY **WHIMSY**, a caprice; crotchet
WHINING complaining; snivelling
WHIPCAT a tailor
WHIPPED lashed; beaten; thrashed
WHIPPER a flagellant
zo **WHIPPET** greyhound; small tank
zo **WHIP-RAY** a sea-fish
to **WHIPSAW** frame-held narrow saw
WHIP-TOP whipping top
WHIRLED span; spun; revved
WHIRLER a whirligig
WHIRRED **WHURRED**, rotated rapidly
WHIRRET **WHERRIT**, vex; a blow
WHISHED **WHIZZED**, hurtled
WHISKER facial hair (man, cat etc.)
WHISKET a basket
WHISKEY (Irish), **WHISKY** (Scotch)
WHISKEY light dog-cart
WHISPER murmur; disclose
nt, mu **WHISTLE** bosun's pipe; tin; police
WHISTLY silently
WHITELY palely; pallidly
WHITEST purest; lightest
WHITHER to which place
zo **WHITING** whitewash; a fish
WHITISH near white

md **WHITLOW** an abscess on finger or toe
WHITSUL curds and whey
rl **WHITSUN** Whitsuntide; Pentecost
WHITTAW a saddler
WHITTLE shawl; to cut; pare
WHIZZED tore through the air
WHIZZER a fast one; motorist
ga **WHIZZER** form of arm-lock wrestling
WHOEVER anyone at all
WHOLISM in entirety; holistic
WHOMMLE confusion; overwhelm
WHOOBUB hubbub
WHOOPED hooted; yelled; shouted
WHOOPEE a joyous cry; a revel
zo **WHOOPER** the hooper swan
WHOPPED beat; defeated
ga **WHOPPER** whacker; very large
WHORLED spiral; convoluted
ga **WICKING** cannoning when curling (bowls)
WICKIUP shelter (Amer. Indian)
WIDENED extended; broadened
WIDENER an enlarger; a reamer
zo **WIDGEON** migratory duck
WIDOWED bereaved; viduous
WIDOWER bereaved husband
WIELDED handled; plied; governed
WIELDER a controller; user
bt **WIGGERS** dandelion
WIGGERY creations with false hair
WIGGING a scolding; reprimand
WIGGLED waggled
WIGGLER a wriggler
WIGLESS deperuked
zo **WILD-ASS** the onager
zo **WILDCAT** speculative; strike (indust.)
WILDEST most turbulent and rash
bt **WILDING** growing wild; crab-apple
WILDING city youth rampaging
WILDISH rather wild
bt **WILD-OAT** youthful crop
WILIEST craftiest; pawkiest
WILLING devising; agreeing; consenting
zo **WILLOCK** young guillemot
WILLOWY slender; pliant
WILSOME wilful; stubborn; wayward
WILTING drooping; fading
bt **WIMBERY** whortleberry
WIMBLED drilled; bored
zo **WIMBREL** whimbrel; small curlew
WIMPLED puckered; wrinkled
WINCHED hoisted; hauled up
WINDAGE clearance
WINDBAG a would-be orator
zo **WIND-EGG** an addled egg
WIND-GUN air-gun
WINDIER breezier; more alarmed
pc **WINDIGO** Red Indian hunter syndrome
WINDILY breezily; panic-struck
WINDING tortuous; changing; scenting
WINDROW hay or peat in rows
WINDSOR Royal House; dynasty
WINEBAG wine-skin; a tippler
WINEFAT a vat
bt **WINESAP** American winter apple
WING-ICE (ice on aircraft)
WINGING flying; wounding
zo **WINGLET** bastard wing
au **WINKERS** flashing lights
WINKING nictitating; conniving at
WINNING first; successful; acquiring
WINSOME childish; engaging; seductive
WINTERY WINTRY, hibernal; cold
WIPE-OUT exterminate; slaughter
tc **WIPE-OUT** intense interference
ga **WIPE-OUT** fall into wave (surfing)
ml **WIREBAR** copper in tapered ingots
WIREMAN linesman
WIREWAY telpherage; aerial transport
WIRIEST leanest; toughest
WISE-GUY clever trickster; smart Alec
WISHFUL desirous; eager and anxious
WISTFUL pensive; meditative; yearning
zo **WISTITI** marmoset
WITCHED bewitched; charmed
bt **WITCHEN** mountain ash; rowan
WITHERS (horse's neck)
bt **WITHIES** willow twigs
WITHOUT outside; except; lacking
WITLESS indiscreet; thoughtless
WITNESS attest; testimony; see
WITTIER droller; more facetious
WITTILY jocularly; humorously
WITTING wotting; knowing
zo **WITWALL** golden oriole
WIZENED shrivelled; wimpled
WOBBLED swerved; staggered; quavered
mu **WOBBLER** unsteady singer; rocker
ga **WOBBLER** erratic fast glide (curling)
WOESOME WOEFUL, sorrowful; grievous
zo **WOLF-DOG** fierce guard-dog
WOLFISH rapacious; ravenous
WOLFKIN young wolf
WOLF-MAN werewolf
WOLF-NET large fishing net
ch **WOLFRAM** tungsten

WOLSUNG grandson of Odin
WOMANLY feminine
WONGSHY yellow dye (Chinese)
zo **WOOD-ANT** the red ant
WOODCUT a print from a wooden block
rl **WOOD-GOD** sylvan deity; Pan
WOODMAN a forester
bt **WOODNUT** hazel-nut
bt **WOOD-OIL** balsam
zo **WOOD-OWL** brown owl
ch **WOOD-TAR** a distillate
mn **WOOD-TIN** tin-stone
WOOLDED roped; lashed
WOOLDER lashing stick
zo **WOOLFAT** lanolin
WOOLLEN of wool
WOOLMAN wool dealer
WOOLSAW evil spirit (C. American)
tx **WOOLSEY** a dress material
WOOMERA spear, throwing stick (Aust.)
bt, ch **WOORALI WORRARA**, curare (arrow) poison
WORDILY verbose; prolix; garrulously
WORDING phrasing; expressing
WORDISH wordy; loquacious
WORKBAG lady's sewing bag
WORKBOX box of work materials
WORKDAY M., T., W., Th., Fr.
WORKING fermenting; drudging
WORKMAN a toiler; operative
WORK-OUT gymnastic exercise
WORKSHY allergic to labour
WORLDLY earthy; secular; mundane
WORMING (rope); squirming
WORN-OUT exhausted
WORRIED harassed; bothered; troubled
WORRIER a worrit; a hector
WORSHIP adoration; idolize; venerate
WORSTED wool yarn
WOULD-BE aspiring
WOULDST (thou) would
WOUNDED injured; hurt; damaged
WOUNDER a pain-giver
WRANGLE bicker; brawl
WRAPPED covered; swathed; wound
WRAPPER envelope; scarf
WREAKED inflicted; (vengeance)
WREAKER an avenger
WREATHE entwine; to garland
WREATHY twisty; interlaced
WRECKED shattered; ruined; destroyed
WRECKER saboteur; blighter
zo **WREN-TIT** Californian bird
WRESTED wrenched; forced; pulled
WRESTER a twister
WRESTLE grapple; strive; contend
WRIGGLE worm; squirm; writhe
WRIGGLY tortuous; sinuous
WRINGER a mangle
WRINKLE crinkle; pucker
bd, cr **WRINKLE** unglued fault in veneer
WRINKLY creased; ruffled
WRITE-UP flattering notice
WRITHED squirmed; wriggled
WRITING calligraphy; penmanship
WRITING literature; (desk); (paper)
cp **WRITING** electronic, fax, computer
WRITTEN inscribed; indited, forever
WRONGED maltreated; oppressed
WRONGER a wrong-un; evil-doer
WRONGLY falsely; unjustly
WROUGHT worked; effected
zo **WRYBILL** a New Zealand plover
zo **WRYNECK** (woodpecker)
WRYNESS irony; twisted humour; crooked
mn **WUSTITE** cubic iron oxide
zo **WYANDOT** Iraquoian Indian; fowl
bt **WYCH-ELM** witch-elm

X

ch **XANTHIC XANTHIN**, acid; yellow extract
XANTHOS colour of Greek chariot horses
zo **XENURUS** genus of armadillos
md **XERASIA XEROSIS**, hair disease; dry scalp
md **XERODES XEROTIC**, body dryness
zo **XIPHIAS** sword-fish genus
as **XIPHIAS** a Southern constellation
XIPHOID ensiform
ch **XYLENOL** monohydric phenol
XYLOLIN wood pulp fabric
bt **XYLOPIA** bitter plants

Y

YACHTED cruised
YACHTER yachtsman
rl **YAHWISM** worship of Jehovah
rl **YAHWIST** Jehovist
YAKAMIK S. Amer. bird
bt **YAMADOU** nutmeg oil
YANKING jerking; heaving; hauling
YAPPING yelping; yauping
YAPSTER a barking dog

nt, me **YARDAGE** sail dues (yachting); distance
nt **YARD-ARM** end of sail-support spar
YARDING enclosing
ag, rw **YARD-MAN** (farm-); (railway-)
YARNING tale-spinning; narrating
YARRING snarling
YASHMAK Moslem woman's double veil
YATAGAN Turkish curved knife
YAUPING yelping
YAWLING howling; screaming
YAWNING gaping; gasping; yawing
YEANING lambing; bring forth young
YEARNED desirous; grieved
YEGGMAN criminal tramp (USA)
zo **YELDRIN** yellow bunting
YELLING howling
vt **YELLOWS** an animal disease
YELLOWY yellowish; sallowy
YELPING yauping; yapping
YERKISH lingo for chimpanzees
YEW-TREE (bow-wood; archery)
YEZIDIS devil worshippers
YIDDISH Jewish dialect
YIELDED rendered; resigned; conceded
YIELDER capitulator; abdicator
YODELER Tyrolese singer
YOGHURT fermented milk
YOICKED chanted Lappish motifs
zo **YOLDING YOLDRIN**, yellow-hammer
zo, ck **YOLK-SAC** within the white of an egg
YORKIST (War of Roses)
YOUGHAL needle-point lace
YOUNGER not so old
YOUTHLY YOUTHFULLY, immature
YOWLING howling; bawling
ch **YPERITE** poison gas
ch **YTTRIUM** a metallic element
YULE-LOG midwinter feast of light (Scand.)
mn **YU-STONE** high-quality jade

Z

bt **ZALACCA** dragon's blood palm
ZAMARRA sheepskin jacket (Sp.)
zo **ZAMOUSE** W. African ox
ZANELLA umbrella fabric
bt, ck **ZANONIA** cucumber
rl **ZANSHIN** awareness; alertness (Jap.)
ZANYING fooling
ZANYISM buffoonery
mu **ZAPATEO** shoe dance (S. Amer.)
ZAPHARA sky blue dye used in pottery
mn **ZARNICH** realgar; orpiment
ZEALFUL eager; keen; enthusiastic
ZEALOUS fervent; ardent; extreme
zo **ZEBRASS** a cross-breed; zebra and ass
zo **ZEBRINE ZEBROID**, of zebra type
zo **ZEBRULA** (zebra and horse)
bt **ZEDOARY** aromatic root
ZEMSTVO Russian local assembly
mn **ZEOLITE** aluminium silicate
ZEROING concentrating firepower
cp **ZEROIZE** to reset a meter to zero
ZESTFUL piquant; eager; keen
ZESTING flavouring; relishing
ZETETIC a seeker; a Pyrrhonist
nc **ZEUGITE** nuclear-fission cell
mn **ZEUXITE** a silicate of aluminium
ZIMOCCA bath-sponge
ZINCALI ZINGARI, gipsies
ch **ZINCATE** zinc oxide
ZINCIFY coat with zinc
mn **ZINCITE** red zinc ore
ZINCODE positive pole electrode
mn **ZINCOID ZINCOUS**, of zinc (metal)
ZINGARI (cricket); gipsies (lt).
ZIONISM Jewish Nationalism
ZIONIST who supports free Israel
ZIPCORD parachute release cord
zo **ZIPHIUS** swordfish genus
ZIPPING pinging; whizzing; fastening
mu **ZITHERN ZITHER**, plucked strings (board)
mu **ZITHERN CITHARA**, hand-held lyre
bt **ZIZANIA** aquatic grasses; (rice)
zo **ZOARIUM** polyzoan
ar **ZOCCOLO** square base
ZOILEAN supercritical
ZOILISM carping criticism
ZOILIST a caviller
mn **ZOISITE** a silicate; an epidote
ZOLAISM Zola's excessive naturalism
go **ZONALLY** of divisions, sectors, areas
go **ZONULAR** belted; girdled; divisions
ZONULET a small girdle
zo **ZONURUS** saurian (reptile) genus
zo **ZOOECIA** polyp cells
zo **ZOOGAMY** of reproduction; sex
zo **ZOOGENY ZOOGONY**, zoological origins
zo **ZOOIDAL** animal-like
mn, zo **ZOOLITE ZOOLITH**, fossil animal
zo **ZOOLOGY** study of animals
pg **ZOOMING** flying low; closing in (films)
ZOONITE articulated segment

ZOONOMY natural laws
ZOOPERY experimenting on lower animals
ZOOTAXY systematic zoology
ZOOTOMY animal anatomy
md **ZOPISSA** pitch used medicinally
mn **ZORGITE** a metallic ore
zo **ZORILLA ZORRINO**, American skunk
ZOTHECA alcove (Gr.)
mu **ZUFFOLO** Italian flute
mn **ZUNYITE** orthosilicate of aluminium
mn **ZURLITE** a Veruvian mineral
zo **ZYGAENA** a shark genus
bt, zo **ZYGOSIS ZYGOTIC**, uniting as zygote
ch **ZYMOGEN** a fermentor
md **ZYMOSIS** inflammation
md **ZYMOTIC** bacteriological
ch **ZYMURGY** fermentation

EIGHT-LETTER WORDS

A

zo **AARDVARK** antbear (S. Afr.)
rl **AARONITE** Hebrew priest
ABACTION cattle-theft; rustling
ABACULUS counting-frame; tavola
ABAMPERE absolute electromagnetic unit
bd **ABAMURUS** buttress; wall support
ABAPICAL distant from opposite pole
ABASHING humiliating; shaming
ABATABLE reducible; alleviable
ABAT-JOUR skylight; reflector
ABATTOIR slaughter-house
rl **ABAT-VOIX** canopy over pulpit
rl **ABBATESS** abbess; Lady Superior
rl **ABBATIAL** under abbey control
bt **ABDALAVI** Egyptian musk melon
ABDERIAN given to laughter
ABDERITE a Thracian; Democrites
ABDICANT renouncing; an abdicator
ABDICATE resign; cede; renounce
rl **ABDITORY** secret repository
ar, rl **ABDOCULE** shrine between 2 columns
md, pc **ABDUCENS** outward movement
ABDUCENT retracting; separating
lw **ABDUCTED** removed; taken by fraud
md **ABDUCTOR** kidnapper; a muscle
rl **ABELIANS ABELITES**, sect practising marriage chastity (Abel)
bt **ABELMOSK** Syrian mallow
zo **ABERDEEN** a terrier; (-Angus) beef breed
ABERRANT abnormal; rambling
ABERRATE deviate; diverge; wander
ABERRING straying; digressing
lw **ABETMENT** aiding and abetting
ABETTING conniving; encouraging
ABEYANCE suspension; dormancy
ABEYANCE cessation; contemplation
ABHORRED hated; loathed; detested
ABHORRER Tory nickname, A.D. 1680
ABIDANCE abode; dwelling; habitation
ABIOGENY spontaneous generation
ABJECTLY servilely; despicably
ABJURING apostasy; forswearing
md **ABLATION** removal; attrition
ABLATIVE the sixth case in Latin
rl **ABLEGATE** a Papal envoy
ABLENESS ability; skill; vigour
md **ABLEPSIA** ablepsy; blindness
ABLOCATE hire; lease; let
rl **ABLUTION** purification; baptism
ABLUVION water-deposited detritus
ABNEGATE deny; adjure; renounce
ABNODATE untie; remove the knots
ABNORMAL odd; irregular; monstrous
ABOCOCKE peaked cap of 15th century
zo **ABOMASUS** abomasum; cow's stomach
ABORTING miscarrying; frustrating
md **ABORTION** a premature expulsion of a foetus; hideosity
ABORTIVE premature; broken off
ABRADANT disintegrator; scraper
ABRADING grinding; abrasing; fraying
ABRASION surface wound; attrition
ABRASIVE scratchy; gritty; rough
ABRIDGED epitomized; curtailed
ABROGATE cancel; repeal; quash
ABRUPTED rent; torn asunder
ABSCISSA an axial line in geometry
ABSENTED played truant
ABSENTEE deliberate duty dodger
ABSENTLY dreamily; inattentively
bt **ABSINTHE** wormwood; French liqueur
ABSOLUTE pure; despotic; supreme
ABSOLVED acquitted; excused
ABSOLVER a pardoner; forgiver
ABSONANT irrational; discordant
ABSONOUS incongruous; out of tune
ABSORBED imbibed; preoccupied
ABSTERGE purge; wipe away
ABSTRACT summarized gist; theoretical
ABSTRUSE recondite; occult; obscure
ABSURDLY irrationally; foolishly
ABUNDANT profuse; plentiful; copious
ABUSABLE improper usage; violable
bt **ABUTILON** plant genus; the jute
ar **ABUTMENT** an arch support; adjacency
lw **ABUTTALS** estate boundaries
ABUTTING bordering; alongside

ACADEMIC scholastic; literary
zo **ACALEPHA** hydrozoa (jellyfish)
bt **ACANTHUS** a 'capital' plant
ACARDIAC heartless
zo **ACARIDAE** mites; ticks; etc
bt **ACARPOUS** sterile; barren
zo **ACAUDATE** tailless; acaudal
bt **ACAULOUS** acauline; stalkless
ACCEDING complying; consenting
rl **ACCENSOR** R. C. candle-trimmer
ACCENTED stressed; emphasized
zo **ACCENTOR** the hedge-sparrow
mu **ACCENTOR** leading singer
ACCEPTED received; acknowledged
ACCEPTED admitted; entered for race
lw **ACCEPTER ACCEPTOR**, recipient; official
ACCIDENT mischance; mishap; fortuity
ACCLINAL sloping; atilt
ACCOLADE act of knighting; award
ACCOLENT neighbour; borderer
hd **ACCOLLED** collared
ACCORDED harmonized; granted
ACCOSTED hailed; solicited boldly
ACCOUNTS recorded transactions
ACCOUNTS newspaper reports; hearsay
ACCOUTRE dress in military array
ACCREDIT authorize; empower; entrust
ACCRUING accumulating; resulting
ACCURACY precision; exactness; truth
ACCURATE correct; unerring
ACCURSED execrable; doomed
lw **ACCUSANT** informer; accuser
ACCUSING charging; impeaching
ACCUSTOM habituate; familiarize
ACELDEMA the field of blood (Hebrew)
ACENTRIC out of centre
zo **ACEPHALA** oyster genus
ACERBATE exasperate; embitter
ACERBENT caustic; astringent
ACERBITY bitterness; sour taste
ACERVATE clustered
ACESCENT turning sour
ch **ACETATED** (acetic acid)
bt **ACHENIUM** single-seeded fruit
me **ACHERSET** 8-bushel measure
bt **ACHEWEED** gout-weed
ACHIEVED won; attained; perfected
ACHIEVER a performer; an executant
bt **ACHILOUS** lipless
mn **ACHIRITE** dioptase
mn **ACHROITE** tourmaline
ACHROMAT colour-blind individual; lens
bt, zo **ACICULAE** spikes and prickles
ACICULAR needle-shaped
ch **ACIDIFIC** producing acid
ACIDNESS bitterness; tartness
md **ACIDOSIS** acidity
ACIERAGE steel electro-plating
ACIERATE turn into steel
zo **ACNESTIS** part of spine
ACOEMETI religious community
bt **ACONITIC** (wolf's-bane, monk's-hood)
bt **ACORN-CUP** acorn top, case
md **ACOUSTIC** relating to sound
ACQUAINT notify; apprise; teach
ACQUIRED scrounged; won; procured
zo **ACRIDIAN** locust
ACRIDITY pungency; harshness
ACRIMONY sharpness of temper
ACRITUDE corrosive quality
ACROATIC esoteric; (oral instruction)
ch **ACROLEIN** acryl aldehyde, propenal
ACROLITH statue with wooden body
ACROMIUM ventral process
zo **ACROSOME** head of sperm
ACROSTIC word puzzle in verse
md **ACROTISM** lack of pulsation
ACTINISM effect of light rays
ch **ACTINIUM** radio-active element
zo **ACTINOID** star-shaped
ACTIVATE to move to activity
ACTIVELY energetically; sedulously
ACTIVISM practical idealism
ACTIVIST production promoter (indust.)
ACTIVITY pastime; happening
ACTIVITY quick movement
ACTUALLY really; as a fact
ACTUATED influenced; set in motion
ACUITION mental, physical keenness
bt **ACULEATE** spiky; pointed
pt **ACUTANCE** clarity of enlargement
ADAMITIC Adamic; nudistic
ADAPTING adjusting; suiting
ADAPTIVE adaptable; conformable
ADDEEMED adjudged; considered
ADDENDUM adjunct; appendix
zo **ADDER-FLY** dragonfly
ADDICTED wont; prone; inclined
cp **ADDITION** accession; summation
ck, ch, ps **ADDITIVE** an added substance
hd **ADDORSED** back to back
md **ADDUCENT** retracting (muscles)
ADDUCING citing; alleging
pl **ADDUCTOR** a muscle

md **ADENOIDS ADENITIS**, inflammation of nasal glands
ADEPTION attainment; perfection
ADEQUACY sufficiency; fitness
ADEQUATE suitable; condign
ADHERENT adhesive; partisan
ADHERING sticking to; supporting
ADHESION coalescence; attachment
rw **ADHESION** railways on easy inclines
ADHESIVE tenacious; gummy
bt **ADIANTUM** maidenhair fern
md **ADIPOSIS** fat-deposit illness
ADJACENT contiguous; close by
ADJOINED connected; neighbouring
ADJUDGED awarded; deemed
lw **ADJURING** charging on oath
ADJUSTER arranger; fitter
ADJUTAGE tubular connection
ADJUTANT assistant; regimental officer
zo **ADJUTANT** Indian scavenging stork
ADJUTRIX lady help
md **ADJUVANT** helping; intensifier
pc **ADLERIAN** of human inferiority
ADMIRING respecting; marvelling
ADMITTED included; conceded
ADMIXING mingling with
ADMONISH warn; reprove; exhort
bt **ADNATION** length attachment of organs
ADOPTING choosing; embracing
ADOPTION formal acceptance; (child)
ADOPTIVE selective
ADORABLE reverential; venerable
ADORABLY worshipfully; devotedly
ADORNING embellishing; decking
md **ADRECTAL** adjacent to the rectum
ADROITLY dexterously; adeptly
ADSCRIPT conscript; postscript
ADSORBED condensed
mn **ADULARIA** moonstone
ADULATED lauded; flattered
ADULATOR scyophant; yes-man
ADULTERY extra-marital cohabitation
bt **ADUNCATE** hooked
md **ADUSTION** cauterization
ADVANCED in the van; lent; progressed
ADVANCER promoter
ADVENING acceding
ADVERTED drew attention to
ADVISING counselling; notifying
ADVISORY advice service offer
ck **ADVOCAAT** egg-yolk liqueur (Dutch)
ADVOCACY defence; support
lw **ADVOCATE** barrister; recommend
rl **ADVOWSON** patronage of benefice

md **ADYNAMIA** loss of vitality
ADYNAMIC slack; lifeless; listless
md **AEGROTAT** academic certificate
AERARIAN voteless Roman freeman
AERATING charging with gas
AERATION gasification
AERIALLY ethereally
AERIFIED inflated
AERIFORM unsubstantial
AEROBICS gymnastics with music
bt **AEROCYST** seaweed air cell
AERODART dart dropped by airman
ae **AERODYNE** aircraft
AEROFOIL lifting surface (gliding)
AEROGRAM wireless message; letter
mn **AEROLITE AEROLITH**, meteoric stone; meteorite
AEROLOGY meteorology
AERONAUT airman; balloonist
AEROSTAT barrage balloon
bt **AESCULIN** horse-chestnut extract
AESTHETE professes beauty lover
AESTIVAL estival (summer)
md **AFEBRILE** unaccompanied by fever
AFFECTED moved; unnatural; insincere
md **AFFERENT** conducting inwards
AFFIANCE confidence; betroth
AFFINAGE metal refining
AFFINING refining; purifying
AFFINITY relationship; attraction
AFFIRMED confirmed; ratified
rl **AFFIRMER** testifier; a Quaker
AFFIXING attaching; connecting
AFFLATUS inspiration; ecstasy
AFFLUENT flowing with wealth
AFFORDED bore the cost easily; gave
fr **AFFOREST** convert into forest
AFFRIGHT sudden tremor; frighten
hd **AFFRONTE** confronting
rl **AFFUSING** spraying; bedewing
rl **AFFUSION** baptismal sprinkling
AFTER-ALL in conclusion
AFTER-WIT wisdom after the event
bt **AGAL-WOOD** aloes-wood
bt, ck **AGAR-AGAR** seaweed; edible gel
zo **AGASTRIC** stomachless
mn **AGATIZED** turned into agate
AGEDNESS antiquity; senility
AGENBITE remorse
AGENESIS imperfect development
AGENTIAL acting through an agent
AGERASIA healthy-looking elder
AGGRIEVE give sorrow; injure
AGIOTAGE (stock jobbing)
lw **AGISTAGE** tax on pasturage
AGITABLE excitable; tremulous
AGITATED roused; instigated

AGITATOR agent provocateur
AGLIMMER shimmering
zo **AGLOSSAL** tongueless
md **AGLOSSIA** tongueless; inarticulate
lw **AGNATION** male descent
AGNOSTIC humanist; positivist
AGONIZED tormented
md **AGRAPHIA** inability to write
AGRARIAN of farming, land, rural
AGREEING matching; tallying
mu **AGREMENT** adornment (Fr.)
bt **AGRESTAL** weedlike
bt **AGRIMONY** liverwort
AGRONOMY scientific farming
md **AGRYPNIA** insomnia
md **AGUE-CAKE** a tumour
bt **AGUE-TREE** sassafras tree
md **AHEDONIA** depressive listlessness
ce, ag **A-HORIZON** podsol; uppermost of soil layers
zo **AIGRETTE** egret's plume
AIGUILLE spire; peak; rock-drill
ae **AILERONS** wing brake flaps (gliding)
AILLETTE ailette; epaulet
AIR-BORNE no earthly connection
AIR-BRAKE brake operated by air
AIR-BRICK ventilating brick
AIRBRUSH fixative spray
AIR-BUILT chimerical; baseless
AIRCRAFT flying machines
ar **AIR-DRAIN** an airspace
AIR-DRAWN imaginary; visionary
zo **AIREDALE** terrier
AIRFIELD landing ground
AIR-FLEET unified collection of aeroplanes
mn **AIR-FLOAT** sand-shaking process
zo **AIRFRAME** fuselage
AIRGRAPH air mail letter; microfilm
AIRINESS lightness; gaiety
AIR-LINER commercial passenger plane
AIR-PILOT a flyer; a navigator
AIRPLANE aeroplane
AIRPOISE aneroid barometer
AIR-POWER air war potential
AIRSCREW propeller
AIRSHAFT ventilation shaft
AIRSPACE supra-construction; of territory
AIRSPEED rate relative to airflow (gliding)
AIR-STOVE heating apparatus
AIRSTRIP landing ground
mn **AIR-SWEPT** dry grinding process
AIRTIGHT impermeable to air
AIRTRUNK ventilating shaft
md **AKINESIA** muscular weakness/ paralysis
ALACRITY briskness; agility; readiness
ALARM-GUN signal of distress
ALARMING calling to arms; ominous
ALARMIST Jeremiah; panic-monger
zo **ALBACORE ALBICORE**, tunny-fish; species of thynnus
ALBANIAN of Albania
ALBINESS female albino
ALBINISM deficiency of pigment
mu **ALBORADA** folk music (Sp.)
bt **ALBURNUM** sap-wood
ALCAHEST alkahest; alchemists' solvent
zo **ALCATRAS** ocean birds; pelican
ALCHEMIC relating to alchemy
ch **ALDEHYDE** a volatile liquid
ALDERMAN a civic dignitary
ch **ALDOLASE** an enzyme
ALEATORY depending on dice
ALEBENCH alehouse bench
ALEBERRY hot ale with sops
ALEHOUSE (no spirit licence)
ALEMBDAR Sultan's standard-bearer
ALE-STAKE an alehouse sign
bt **ALEURONE** a protein in seeds
ALFRESCO in the open air
ALGERINE Algerian; pirate
ALGIDITY chilliness
bt **ALGOLOGY** the study of seaweeds
ALGONKIN Canadian Indian
ALGORISM the decimal system
ALGRAPHY aluminium printing
ALHAMBRA Moorish palace
ALICANTE Spanish red wine
ALIENAGE estrangement
ALIENATE transfer; estrange
pc **ALIENISM** study of insanity
pc **ALIENIST** mental specialist
ALIGHTED stepped off; descended
ALIGNING adjusting; dressing
ar **ALIGNING** straight lines; common cause
ALIQUANT a remainder
zo **ALITRUNK** winged segment
ALIZARIN madder; synthetic dye
ch **ALKAHEST ALCAHEST**, solvent
ALKALIES caustic bases
ch **ALKALIFY ALKALIZE**, neutralize an acid
ch **ALKALINE** salty
md **ALKALOID** active part of a drug
ALKERMES a crimson cordial
ch **ALLANITE** cerium silicate
ALLAYING stilling; mitigating

ch **ALL-BURNT** rocket-fuel exhaustion point
ALL-CLEAR end of danger
ALLEGING asserting as a fact
ALLEGORY parable; metaphor
ALLELULA alleluyah; halleluiah
ALLERGIC antipathetic
hd **ALLERION** heraldic beakless eagle
ga **ALLEY-WAY** board-game
ALL-FIRED infernal; hell-fired
ALL-FOURS (cards); mode of progress; crawling
ALLIANCE union by treaty; coalition
ALLIGATE to bind together
ALLOCATE allot; assign; share
ALLODIAL freehold; not feudal
lw **ALLODIUM** freehold estate
bt **ALLOGAMY** cross-fertilization
md **ALLOPATH** user of healing drugs
cy **ALLOSOME** non-typical chromosome
ALLOTTED meted; assigned; dispensed
ALLOTTEE shares received
ALLOTYPE varying type specimen
ALL-OUTER extremist; zealot
ALLOWING conceding; admitting
ml **ALLOYAGE** the alloying of metals
ALLOYING blending; debasing
bt **ALLSPICE** Jamaica pepper
ALLUDING hinting; insinuating
ALLURING enticing; tempting
ALLUSION hint; reference
ALLUSIVE relative; innuent
ALLUSORY symbolical; figurative
ALLUVIAL sedimentary
ALLUVION alluvial land
ALLUVIUM water-borne silt
as **ALMAGEST** astronomical problems
ALMIGHTY all-powerful; omnipotent
ALMSDEED act of charity
ALMSGATE (where alms were given)
ALOMANCY divination by salt
md **ALOPECIA** baldness; fox-evil
ALPHABET order or list of letters
ALPHA-RAY a radio-active ray
ck **ALPHENIC** white barley-sugar
ALPINIST mountaineer
mn **ALQUIFOU** Cornish lead ore
zo **ALSATIAN** sheep-dog
rl **ALTARAGE** altar offerings
ALTERANT production of change
ALTER-EGO second self
ALTERING varying; changing
ALTERITY being otherwise
ALTERNAT precedence by rotation
bt **ALTHEINE** asparagine
ALTHOUGH notwithstanding
ch **ALTINCAR** unrefined borax
ae **ALTITUDE** height; eminence; (aircraft, gliders) data
mu **ALTO-CLEF** C on 3rd line of staff
ALTRUISM devoted to others' welfare
ALTRUIST philanthropist
mn **ALUMINIC** containing aluminium
ch **ALUMINUM** aluminium
ch **ALUNOGEN** aluminium sulphite
ALVEATED hollowed out; saucer-shape
ALVEOLAR speech sound; honeycomb-like
ALVEOLUS alveole; tooth socket
zo **AMADAVAT** a weaver-bird
AMANDINE sweet almond ointment
mn **AMANDOLA** green marble
ch **AMANITIN** poison in fungi
bt **AMARACUS** marjoram
bt **AMARANTH** love-lies-bleeding
AMASSING piling up; accumulating
AMAZEDLY confusedly; dazedly
ch **AMBERITE** smokeless explosive
AMBITION desire; aspiration
pc **AMBIVERT** one turned both ways
AMBLYGON obtuse-angled
AMBREADA spurious amber
ch **AMBREATE** salt of ambreic acid
AMBROSIA food of the gods; bee-bread
nm **AMBROSIN** Milanese coin
AMBULANT peripatetic; hiking
AMBULATE saunter; walk; stroll; hike
AMBUSHED attacked in surprise trap
AMENABLE liable; pliant; subject
AMENABLY docilely; responsively
AMENDING rectifying; correcting
AMERCING fining; mulcting
AMERICAN Yankee
mn **AMETHYST** anti-inebriation jewel
mn **AMIANTUS** fibrous asbestos
AMICABLE friendly; neighbourly
AMICABLY benignly; peacefully
nt **AMIDMOST** in the very centre
AMITOSIS constriction-division of nucleus
cy **AMITOTIC** characterized by amitosis
zo **AMMODYTE** sand-eel
ch **AMMONIAC** of nature of ammonia
AMMONITE explosive
zo **AMMONITE** spiral fossil
ch **AMMONIUM** base of ammonia
md **AMNIOTIC** a membrane
AMOEBEAN alternately answering
AMOEBEUM poetic dialogue
zo **AMOEBOID** **AMOEBOUS**, of protozoan structure
AMORETTO cupid; a lover

lw **AMORTIZE** transfer property
AMOUNTED reached; rose; resulted
mn **AMPELITE** anti-pest earth
zo **AMPHIBIA** amphibians
bt **AMPHIGEN** a lichen-like plant
zo **AMPHIONT** a zygote; an egg-shell
AMPHORAL like a two-handled vase
md **AMPHORIC** hollow sounding
AMPULLAR like a two-handled flask
AMPUTATE lop; prune; sever
AMULETIC like an amulet; charming
AMURCOUS foul with dregs
AMUSABLE capable of enjoyment
AMUSETTE light field gun (salutes)
pl **AMYGDALA** limbic system
ch **AMYLASES** diastase enzymes
ANABASIS epic of 10,000 mercenary Greeks (Xenophon)
mt **ANABATIC** hot-air convection winds
md **ANABOLIC** body-building
zo **ANACONDA** python (S. America)
md **ANACUSIA** total deafness
mt **ANAFRONT** frontal-zone warm-air rise
ANAGLYPH a cameo; stereoscopic
ANAGOGIC mystical; allegorical
ANAGRAPH catalogue; inventory
ANALECTS collection of literary fragments
ANALEMMA pedestal of sundial
md **ANALEPSY** recurring epilepsy
ANALOGIC analogous; alike; akin
ANALOGON similarity; synonym
ANALOGUE corresponding part
ANALYSED examined
ANALYSER scrutator; analyst
ANALYSIS opposite of synthesis
ANALYTIC inductive
md **ANANDRIA** lack of maleness
pl **ANANGIAN** lacking vascular system
ANAPAEST a reversed dactyl
ANAPHASE nuclear division stage
rl **ANAPHORA** rhetorical repetition
ANARCHIC lawless and turbulent
md **ANASARCA** dropsy
rl **ANATHEMA** excommunication
md **ANATOMIC** internal
ANCESTOR forefather; forebear
ANCESTRY lineage; descent
ANCHORED fixed securely
rl **ANCHORET** anchorite; hermit
md **ANCONEAL** relating to the elbow
ANDERSON steel air-raid shelter 1940
mn **ANDESINE** felspar; andes
mn **ANDESITE** igneous rock, Andes
ANDIRONS fire-dogs
ANDORRAN (Andorra)
bc **ANDROGEN** male hormone
ANECDOTE a chatty relation
ac **ANECHOIC** echoless
md **ANEURISM** dilated artery
md **ANEURYSM** abnormal enlargement
ANGEL-BED open bed without posts
bt **ANGELICA** plant; Californian wine
ANGERING inflaming; infuriating
rl **ANGLICAN** Church of England
ANGLOMAN anglo-maniac
ANGRIEST exceedingly irate
lt, me **ANGSTROM** light wave-length unit
ANGULATE angular
gl **ANHEDRAL** allotriomorphic
md **ANHYPNIA** insomnia
pc **ANICONIA** lack of mental energy
ANIENTED annulled
ANIMALLY beastly
ANIMATED enlivened
ANIMATOR a rouser
rl **ANIMETTA** cloth for chalice
md **ANIRIDIA** absence of iris
ANISETTE liqueur from aniseed
md **ANISOPIA** unequal vision
ANNALISE record historical events
ANNALIST writer of annals
ml **ANNEALED** tempered steel
zo **ANNELIDA** worms
ANNEXING attaching; taking over
ANNOTATE add notes to; commentate
ANNOUNCE pronounce; proclaim
ANNOYING irritating; vexatious
ANNUALLY yearly; every year
ANNULARY ring bearing (fourth finger)
ANNULATE dividing into rings
ANNULLED rendered void; abolished
ANNULLER a voider
zo **ANNULOSE** annular; ringed
ANODISED treated electrically
rl **ANOINTED** consecrated; Messiah
zo **ANOPLURA** parasitic lice
md **ANOREXIA** loss of appetite
ANORTHIC oblique angled (crystals)
pl **ANOVULAR** eggless
ANSERINE gooselike; stupid; silly
ANSWERED solved; responded; refuted
md **ANTALGIC** anodyne; pain-killer
zo **ANT-EATER** ant-bear, etc.
ANTECEDE precede
ANTEDATE anticipate
ANTEFIXA ornamental tiling
zo **ANTELOPE** deer
ANTENATI born before a given date
zo **ANTENNAE** feelers; aerials
ANTENNAL relating to the above

el **ANTENODE** (maximum displacement)
ANTEPORT outer gate or harbour
ANTERIOR prior; before
ANTEROOM antechamber
ANTHELIA luminous rings around sun
pl **ANTHELIX** antihelix; part of the ear
bt **ANTHEMIS** plant genus; camomile
bt **ANTHERAL** (pollen bearing anthers)
bt **ANTHESIS** full bloom
zo **ANTHOZOA** sea-anemones; corals
cf **ANTHROPO-** related to man
md **ANTIACID** antacid medicine
ANTI-ARMY pacifist
md **ANTIBODY** a counteractive
ANTICIZE to play antics
bt **ANTICOUS** centripetal
ANTIDOTE counter-measure
gl **ANTIDUNE** sandhill, dune
zo **ANTIGENY** sexual dimorphism
ANTI-ICER anti-freeze
ANTILOGY contradiction; antinomy
ANTIMASK grotesque interlude
ch **ANTIMIST** preventing misting up
mn, ch **ANTIMONY** stibium; a white metal
ANTINAZI anti-Hitlerite
ro **ANTINODE** radio term
lw **ANTINOMY** legal contradiction
ANTINOUS ideal of youthful beauty
ANTIPHON anthem; alternate chanting
ANTIPODE Australia (down under)
ANTIPOLE South Pole (down under)
ANTIPOPE opposition pope; (Avignon)
ANTIQUED simulated parchment
md **ANTISERA** antibiotics
ANTISPIN assisting recovery from spin
rl **ANTISTES** chief priest or prelate
ANTI-TANK (guns, mines, etc.)
ANTITYPE typical example
ANTLERED furnished with antlers
ANTRORSE up-turning
ANYTHING an unspecified object
ANYWHERE an undefined locality
AORISTIC indefinite as to time
md **AORTITIS** inflammation of artery
APAGOGIC reducing to an absurdity
md **APELLOUS** without a skin
md **APERIENT** a laxative; an opening
APERITIF a cocktail
pg **APERTURE** gap; hole; lens
md **APEX-BEAT** heartbeat visibility point
APHANITE hornblende, quartz, etc.
as **APHELION** max. earth–sun distance
zo **APHIDIAN** (green-fly)
bt **APHLEBIA** lateral fern outgrowth
md **APHONOUS** voiceless; dumb
APHORISM a maxim; a saw
APHORIST a writer of adages
APHORIZE define briefly
pc **APHRENIA** without mind
md **APHTHOUS** ulcerous
zo **APIARIAN** concerning bees
APIARIST a bee expert
APICALLY topmost; at the apex
APLASTIC not easily moulded
nt **APLUSTRE** ornament on stern
APNEUSIS state of maintained inspiration
APOCONYM foreshortened word-name
md **APOCRINE** of gland-cell breakdown
APODOSIS consequent clause
APOGAEIC (apogees and aphelions)
APOGRAPH a copy; transcript
APOLLYON the destroying angel
APOLOGIA vindication; formal defence
APOLOGIA excuses
APOLOGUE moral fibre; allegory
ar **APOPHYGE** base of column
md **APOPLEXY** loss of mental control
md **APOSITIA** aversion to food
rl **APOSTASY** renunciation of faith
APOSTATE a renegade
md **APOSTEME** apostume; an abscess
APOTHEGM sententious maxim
APPALLED terrified; dismayed
APPANAGE territorial dependency
APPARENT obvious; evident; palpable
APPEALED implored; entreated
APPEALER a suppliant; invoker
APPEARED emerged; dawned; arrived
APPEASED soothed; allayed; mollified
APPEASER pacifier; tranquillizer
lw **APPELLEE** defendant in an appeal
APPELLOR prosecutor
APPENDED subjoined; attached
md **APPENDIX** supplement; addendum
APPESTAT appetite controller
APPETENT desirous; solicitous
APPETITE craving; longing; hunger
APPETIZE to create a desire
APPLAUSE praise; laudation
APPLE-PIE dessert; orderly; (bed!)
bt **APPLE-PIP** apple-seed
APPLIQUE applied work
APPLYING employing; requesting
APPOSITE fit; suitable; pertinent
APPRAISE set a value to; rate; survey
APPRISED informed; notified; told

APPRIZED appreciated; valued
APPROACH advance; resemble; avenue
APPROVAL approbation; sanction
APPROVED commended; ratified
APPROVER ratifier; king's evidence
tx **APRES-SKI** Alpine late party; (dress)
APRON-MAN a mechanic
zo **APTEROUS** wingless
APTITUDE natural ability; talent; faculty
md **APYRETIC** feverless
md **APYREXIA** intermittent fever
AQUACADE musical water show
AQUALUNG diver's oxygen pack
AQUARIUM tanks of aquatic animals
AQUARIUS water-carrier (zodiac)
AQUASTAT boiler temperature regulator
AQUATINT a print; (engraving on copper)
pg **AQUATONE** photo printing process
AQUEDUCT artificial water channel
AQUIFUGE (clay strata) low permeability
AQUILINE like an eagle; hooked
gl **AQUITARD** slow permeability strata
AQUOSITY sloppiness
zo **ARACHNID** spider; mite or scorpion
ARAINGEE gallery of a mine
ARAMAISM an Aramaic idiom
zo **ARANEOUS** araneose; cobwebby
zo **ARAPUNGA** the bell-bird; campanero
ARBALIST arbalest; cross-bow
ARBITRAL arbitrational
bt **ARBOREAL** tree-like
ARBORETA shrubberies
ARBORIST tree expert; herbalist
ARBOROUS woody; arboreal
ARBOURED with shady bowers
bt **ARBUSCLE** dwarf tree
bt **ARBUSTUM** copse; shrubbery
bt **ARBUTEAN** (strawberry tree)
ARCADIAN pastoral; rustic
ARCATURE a small arcade
ARCHAEAN geologically remote
ARCHAISM an archaic expression
ARCHAIZE employ archaisms in speech
ARCHDUKE a princely title
ARCHICAL chief; primary
ARCHIVAL documentary
ARCHIVES record office; records
ARCHLIKE arcuate; iridian
mu **ARCHLUTE** double-stringed lute
ARCHNESS roguishness
ARCHPOET Poet Laureate
ARCHWISE bowed
as **ARCTURUS** Bear-guard; star in Boötes
ar, bd **ARCUATED** built on arches
ARDENTLY fiercely; zealously
AREFYING withering; desiccating
bt **ARENARIA** sandwort; chickweed
AREOLATE divided into small areas
bt **ARESCENT** drying
bt **ARGEMONE** silver-weed
ARGENTAN German silver
ARGENTIC argental; silvery
ch **ARGENTUM** silver; Ag
pl **ARGINASE** enzyme
ARGONAUT (golden fleece)
ARGOSIES richly laden vessels
ARGUABLE debatable
ARGUFIED wrangled
ARGUMENT discussion; an abstract
ARGUTELY keenly; shrewdly; piercing
rl **ARIANISE** convert to Arianism
rl **ARIANISM** doctrine of Arius
ARIDNESS dryness; sterility
bt **ARILLARY** (exterior coating of a seed)
nt **ARISINGS** irregularities after refit
bt **ARISTATE** awned; bearded
ARMAMENT munitions; arms; guns
ARMARIAN monastic librarian
ARMARIUM scroll; book cupboard
ARMATURE armour; rotor of dynamo
ARMCHAIR chair with arm rests
rl **ARMENIAN** of Armenia; Christian sect
ARMIGERO esquire; armour-bearer
ARMILLET small bracelet; armlet
rl **ARMINIAN** (opposed to Calvinism)
hd **ARMORIAL** relating to coats-of-arms
hd **ARMORIST** expert in heraldry
ARMOURED plated
ARMOURER artificer; manufacturer
tx, rl **ARMOZEEN ARMOZINE**, taffeta or silk, used for clerical gowns
AROMATIC fragrant; pungent
AROUSING stirring
mu **ARPEGGIO** harplike chord
ARQUEBUS heavy musket
ARRANGED settled; grouped
ARRANGER planner; orchestrator
ARRANTLY infamously; notoriously
ARRASENE Arras embroidery
ARRAUGHT taken by force
ARRAYING disposing; adorning
ARRESTED halted; seized; captured
lw **ARRESTER** an apprehender
ga **ARRIMADA** front wall shot (pelota)
ARRIVING reaching; attaining; landing

ARROGANT haughty; overbearing
ARROGATE usurp; assume
hd **ARRONDEE** segmented heraldic cross
pl **ARSEHOLE** the anal orifice
ch **ARSENATE ARSENITE**, arsenical salts
ARSONIST ARSONITE, felon who deliberately sets fire to property
ARTEFACT man made, modified object
md **ARTERIAL** (arteries); (roads)
gl **ARTESIAN** well water-table pressure
ARTFULLY craftily
lw **ARTICLED** bound by agreement
ARTIFACT product of primitive art
ARTIFICE stratagem; trick; device
ARTISTIC tasteful; aesthetic
ARTISTRY vocation; workmanship
ARUSPICE haruspex; soothsayer
ARUSPICY divination by augury
zo **ARVICOLA** vole genus
mn **ASBESTIC** made of asbestos
ASBESTOS incombustible material
ASCENDED rose; mounted
pr **ASCENDER** part of letters in printing
bt **ASCIDIUM** bottle-like appendage
ch **ASCORBIC** acid; vitamin C
ASCRIBED attributed; assigned
md **ASEMASIA** symbol-blindness
ga **ASHIKUBI** ankle kick (karate)
ga **ASHIWAZA** leg throwing (judo)
ASH-LEACH tub for washing wood-ash
ASH-PLANT ash sapling; walking stick
ASH-STAND ash-tray
ASHY-GRAY ashy in colour
bt **ASPARTIC** obtained from asparagus
ASPERATE to roughen
rl **ASPERGES** ceremonial sprinkling
ASPERITY harshness; sourness; acerbity
ASPERSED sprinkled; slandered; abused
bt **ASPHODEL** a lily; a daffodil
md **ASPHYXIA** suffocation; pulse failure
ASPIRANT suitor; candidate
ASPIRATE to emphasize the 'h' sound
ASPIRING longing; hoping; soaring
bt **ASPOROUS** without spores
ASPORTED stolen away
ASSAILED assaulted; attacked; vilified
ASSAILER aggressor; invader; traducer
ASSAMESE native of Assam; (language)
ASSARTED grubbed up trees and bushes
ASSASSIN a thug primed with hashish
ASSAYING testing; analysing
ASSEMBLE convene; muster; congregate
ASSEMBLY parliament; synod; meeting
ASSENTED agreed; concurred
ASSENTER assentor; approver
ASSERTED maintained; averred
ASSESSED taxed; rated; appraised
lw **ASSESSOR** tax-master; valuer
ASSIETTE oblong dish; dinner plate (Fr.)
nm **ASSIGNAT** paper currency, Fr. Rev.
ASSIGNED allotted; specified
ASSIGNEE a recipient
ASSIGNOR transferer of an interest
zo **ASSINEGO** small donkey; fool; dolt
ASSISTED aided; abetted; sustained
ASSIZING assessing; regulating
ASSONANT harmonious; rhythmical
mu **ASSONATE** correspond in sound
ASSORTED mixed; varied; classified
ASSUAGED allayed; abated; appeased
ASSUAGER mitigator; alleviator
ASSUMING arrogant; presumptuous
ASSURANT holder of insurance policy
ASSURING affirming; pledging
ASSYRIAN a descendant of Shem
zo **ASTACIAN** shellfish; lobster type
zo **ASTERIAS** starfish genus
pr **ASTERISK** printers' mark (*)
as **ASTERISM** small cluster of stars
ASTERNAL not joined to breastbone
as **ASTEROID** minor planet; star-shaped
ASTHENIA lack of vitality; debility
md **ASTHENIC** feeble; weak
zo **ASTOMATA** an order of infusoria
ASTOMOUS astomatous; mouthless
ASTONIED astounded; stunned; dazed
ASTONISH amaze; startle; surprise
ASTRINGE constrict; constrain
ASTUNNED astonished; mazed; dazed
ASTUTELY cunningly; craftily
md **ASYSTOLE** heart failure
md **ATABRINE** quinine type
ATARAXIA stoical indifference
ATHEIZED converted to disbelief
ATHELING Anglo-Saxon noble
ATHENIAN a Greek (Athens)
zo **ATHERINE** fish genus; mullets; smelts
md **ATHEROMA** disease of arteries

ATHLETIC strong; vigorous; sinewy
ATLANTES male supporting figures
go **ATLANTIC** western ocean
ATLANTIS lost continent
ATMOLOGY science of vaporization
ATOMICAL atomic; minute
ATOMIZED vaporized
ATOMIZER a spray
ATONABLE expiable; amendable
ATREMBLE dithering
ATROCITY a cruel barbarous act
ATROPHIC emaciated; withered
md **ATROPINE** bella-donna
md **ATROPISM** illness due to atropine
bt **ATROPOUS** upturned; erect
lw **ATTACHED** fond; bound; arrested
ATTACKED assaulted; set about
ATTACKER assailant; invader; violater
ATTAINED achieved; secured; won
ATTENDED served; escorted; hearkened
ATTENDER attendant; close listener
ATTENTAT attempted assassination
ATTESTED invoked; endorsed
ATTESTOR attester; a witness
ATTICISM witty remark; Attic salt
ATTICIZE to use Athenian idioms
ATTINGED touched lightly; affected
ATTIRING arraying; adorning; robing
ATTITUDE pose; posture; opinion
ATTORNED transferred loyalty
lw **ATTORNEY** lawyer; solicitor
ATTRITED worn away; abraded; erased
mn **ATTRITUS** a grade of coal
mu **ATTUNING** harmonizing
ATYPICAL not conforming
AUBUSSON style of carpet
AUCUPATE to go bird-catching
AUDACITY boldness; effrontery; daring
AUDIENCE formal interview; listeners
AUDITING examining accounts
AUDITION vocal test; also sound tests
AUDITIVE audible
md **AUDITORY** sense of hearing
AUGURATE foretell by divination
AUGURIAL ominous
AUGURIES prognostications; portents
AUGURING presaging; prophesying
AUGUSTAN (Emperor Augustus)
AUGUSTLY majestically; imposingly
AULARIAN member of an Oxford Hall
AURELIAN (Emperor Aurelius); philosophy
rl **AUREOLED** in a halo
bt **AURICLED** eared
bt **AURICULA** the primula
AURIFORM ear-shaped
md **AURILAVE** ear-washing instrument
AUROREAN rosy; dawning; (aurora borealis)
AURULENT golden
AUSONIAN Italian
AUSTRIAN of Austria
md **AUTACOID** a hormone; a chalone
AUTARCHY autocracy; absolutism
AUTARKIC self-sufficient
pc **AUTISTIC** withdrawn
AUTOBAHN fast motorway
AUTOCADE motor cavalcade
bt **AUTOCARP** self-fertilized fruit
AUTOCODE computer operation procedure
rl **AUTOCRAT** absolute ruler
zo **AUTOCYST** parasite-formed membrane
AUTO-DA-FE Inquisition burnings
AUTO-DYNE frequency stabilizer
bt **AUTOGAMY** self-fertilization
AUTOGENY spontaneous generation
ae **AUTOGYRO** a type of aircraft
AUTOLOGY the study of self
AUTOMATA automatons; robots
AUTOMATH a self-taught man
AUTONOMY self-government
md **AUTOPSIA** autopsy; post-mortem
AUTOPTIC seen with one's own eyes
AUTOSLED snow vehicle
cy **AUTOSOME** non-sexual chromosome
AUTOTOMY amputation; cell division
AUTOTYPE carbon copy process
AUTUMNAL peculiar to the autumn
ch **AUTUNITE** phosphate of uranium
AUXILIAR subsidiary; assisting
cy **AUXOCYTE** cell with meiosis
AVAILING profiting; sufficing; using
hd **AVELLANE** heraldic cross of filberts
AVENGING vindicating; retaliating
AVENTAIL visor; opening in a helmet
lw **AVENTURE** fatal accident
AVERAGED equated; proportional
ck **AVERCAKE** oatcake
AVERMENT affirmation
AVERNIAN Plutonic; infernal
AVERRING declaring; alleging
hd **AVERSANT** heraldic reversal
AVERSELY unwillingly; reluctantly
AVERSION dislike; hatred; allergy
AVIARIST keeper of caged birds
AVIATING flying
AVIATION travel by air
zo **AVIFAUNA** local birdlife
AVOIDING eschewing; shunning

AVOIDISM trouble evasion
AVOUCHED guaranteed
AVOWABLE affirmable; declarable
AVOWABLY deposably; admittedly
AVOWANCE avowel; confession
AVOWEDLY openly; frankly
AWAITING abiding; expecting
AWAKABLE not dead-asleep
AWAKENED spurred; stimulated
AWAKENER a rouser
AWANTING wanting; lacking; absent
AWARDING decreeing; bestowing
AWEARIED jaded; spent; worn
nt **AWEATHER** the weather-side
AXE-HELVE handle of an ax
mn **AXE-STONE** jade
bt **AXILLARY** (armpit); branch angle
AXIOLOGY theory of value
AXIOTRON value with controlled stream
AXLETREE spindle
AXOIDEAN axial
AXOPLASM material around axon
AZOTIZED nitrogenized
AZULEJOS glazed blue-white tiles (Port.)

B

zo **BABAKOTO** a large lemur
BABBLING prattling; gossiping
BABELDOM state of confusion
zo **BABIRUSA** pig deer of Sri Lanka
BABISHLY childishly
BABOODOM realm of red tape
BABOOISM plethora of verbiage
BABOUCHE oriental slipper
BABY-FACE term of endearment
BABY-FARM baby-boarding house
BABYHOOD state of infancy
ga **BACCARAT** a card game
BACCHANT bacchanalian
BACHELOR a degree-man; unmarried man
md **BACILLAR** like bacilli
md **BACILLUS** rod-like organism
md **BACHACHE** persistent vertebral pain
BACKAWAY retreat; withdraw
BACK-BAND cart-saddle band
lw **BACKBEAR** poacher stealing venison
BACK-BITE to speak evil; asperse
BACK-BOND conditional deed
pl **BACKBONE** reliability; spine
BACK-CAST anglers' thrust (fishing)
BACK-CHAT impertinent rejoinder
hr **BACK-COCK** pendulum bracket
BACKCOMB reverse combing (coiffeur)
BACKDATE retrospective (cheques)
BACK-DOOR clandestine; furtive
BACKDOWN retire; resign; withdraw
BACK-DROP drop scene
lw **BACK-DUTY** unpaid tax
BACK-FALL a wrestling throw
BACKFIRE create reverse effect
BACKFIRE a blow back (motoring)
BACKFIST a punch (karate)
BACK-FLAP folding shutter
hy **BACK-FLOW** reverse liquid flow
jn **BACK-FOLD** foldable part of shutter
eg **BACK-GEAR** lathe speed-reducer
ga **BACKHAND** negative compliment; (tennis)
ga **BACK-HEEL** wrestling throw; football
bd **BACKINGS** furring strips on joints
BACKINGS financial support; data
BACKINGS picture mounts (framing)
bd **BACK-IRON** fireplace heat reflector
BACK-KICK violent engine reversal
BACK-KICK gun recoil; horse bucking
BACKLASH political counter-reaction
BACKLASH whipping; gear wear
BACKMOST hindermost
BACKPACK rucksack; snail's burden
eg **BACK-RAKE** surface/base relation
BACK-RENT dues
tx **BACK-REST** loom bar
BACK-ROOM behind the scenes
BACKSEAT rear in bus, car, theatre
BACKSIDE posterior; buttocks; behind
ga **BACKSPIN** rotary motion of ball
nt **BACKSTAY** mast-, stern-, sides-support
BACK-STEP cycle mounting step
BACKSTOP armature-travel-limit relay
ga **BACKSTOP** manor fence; screen; (baseball)
eg **BACK-WALL** conductor; photovoltaic
BACKWARD retarded; reluctant
BACKWARD unadvanced; in reverse
nt **BACKWASH** backward current; wake
BACKWASH after suction (air current)
BACKWASH aftermath of event (results)
tc **BACK-WAVE** spacing wave
BACKWORK non-mining colliery activity
zo **BACKWORM** filanders; hawk-disease
BACONIAN (Bacon); inductive
md **BACTERIA** fungoid growths

zo **BACTRIAN** two-humped camel
BACULINE rod-like
mn **BACULITE** fossil cuttlefish
BADGERED pestered; worried
BADGERLY grey like a badger
BADIGEON sculptor's cement
BADINAGE persiflage; chaff
BADLANDS arid, gullied, highland (Nevada)
tx **BAFFETAS** Indian muslin
BAFFLING defeating; hoodwinking
zo **BAGHEERA** the black panther (India)
mu **BAGPIPER** a bagpipe player
BAGUETTE baton-like crustbread (Fr.)
lw **BAILABLE** able to be bailed
BAIL-BALL cricket ball bail high
BAIL-BOND security for appearance
lw **BAIL-DOCK** room at Old Bailey
lw **BAILMENT** delivery of goods in trust
lw **BAILSMAN** guarantor of bond
BAKELITE a plastic material
ck **BAKEMEAT** pastry; pies
BAKSHISH discount; commission; tip
BALANCED in equilibrium
BALANCER acrobat; tumbler
mn **BALANITE** fossil barnacle
BALCONET miniature balcony
zo **BALDCOOT** baldicoot; coot; monk
BALDHEAD no hair apparent
bt **BALDMONY** gentian
md **BALDNESS** alopecia
zo **BALD-PATE** species of wild duck
BALDRICK shoulder belt
BALE-FIRE signal-fire; funeral pyre
BALESTRA lunge (fencing)
tx **BALK-BACK** fibrous-back cloth
BALK-LINE baulk-line (billiards)
BALLADER ballad-monger
BALLADRY patriotic or epic verse
gl **BALL-CLAY** fine-textured detrital clay
BALL-COCK stopcock in a cistern
BALLIAGE an export duty
BALLISTA ancient catapult
BALLONET small balloon; gas bag
BALLOTED drew lots for; voted
to **BALL-PANE** part flat, part globular
BALLROOM location for stately measures
BALLYHOO bunkum; false fame
BALLYRAG bullyrag; torment
BALMORAL bonnet; boot; petticoat
md **BALNEARY** of spa treatments
BALOTADE an equine feat
BALSAMIC soothing; demulcent
ar **BALUSTER** supporting column
BANALITY triviality; triteness
BANDAGED surgically bound
BANDANNA Indian silk kerchief
BANDEAUX hair-bands or fillets
el **BAND-EDGE** between 2 defined limits
ar **BANDELET** bandlet
BANDEROL bannerol; small banner
zo **BANDFISH** long lean fish
BANDITTI bandits; robbers; outlaws
el **BAND-PASS** free for specific currents
mu **BANDSMAN** musician in a band
BANDSTER sheaf-binder
BAND-STOP attenuating specific currents
BANDYING tossing about
bt **BANEWORT** deadly nightshade
am **BANG-BANG** serco control mechanism
BANGSTER bully; victor
BANGTAIL square-cut tail
BANISHED expelled; outlawed
BANISTER baluster; stair railings
mu **BANJOIST** fretful player
BANKABLE receivable at a bank
BANK-BILL note of exchange
BANK-BOOK depositor's account book
BANK-NOTE promissory note
BANK-RATE Bank of England rate
BANKRUPT insolvent; broke
BANKSMAN overseer at pit-mouth (coal)
ce **BANKSMAN** driver's help
BANLIEUE environs of a town (Fr.)
BANNERED beflagged
BANNERET knighthood
BANNEROL banderol; small banner
BANTERED railed; chaffed
BANTERER joker; jester
BANTLING young child; bratling
zo **BANXRING** insect-eating squirrel
BAPHOMET Templar's idol
rl **BAPTIZED** immersed
tx **BARATHEA** woven fabric
BARBACAN barbican; outer defence
BARBARED shaved; shorn
BARBARIC foreign; savage; Hunnish
bt **BARBATED** bearded; awned
ck **BARBECUE** out-door grill
bt **BARBERRY** thorny shrub; berberry
BARBETTE armoured defence
ar **BARBICAN** **BARBACAN**, gun-port in wall; outer defence of castle
mu **BARBITON** antique form of lyre
to **BAR-CRAMP** plank-gluing bar
BARDLING bardlet; poetaster; rhymster
BAREBACK unsaddled

lw **BAREBOAT** chartering contract
BAREBONE (Parliament); lean; thin
BAREFOOT bootless
BARESARK without shirt of mail
BARGEMAN barge owner; bargee
BARGHEST a dog-like goblin
BARILLET watch-spring case
mu **BARITONE** (between tenor and bass)
BARKMILL bark-crusher
bt **BARNABAS** cornflour
zo **BARNACLE** a twitch; cirriped; goose
BARN-DOOR a farm portal
BARNEKIN outermost castle ward
BARNYARD the rooster's realm
mt **BAROGRAM** record of atmospheric pressure from barograph
BAROLOGY the science of weight
bt **BAROMETZ** a fern
BARONAGE cf. peerage
BARONESS wife or widow of baron
BARONIAL noble and spacious
ps **BAROSTAT** pressure device
BAROUCHE four-wheeled carriage
BAR-POSTS supports of field-gate
tx **BARRACAN** material of camel-hair
BARRACKS the soldier's home
BARRANCO barranca; deep gorge
lw **BARRATOR** encourager of litigation
rl **BARRATRY** traffic in church offices
BARRENLY sterilely; unfruitfully
hd **BARRULET** horizontal heraldic bar
to **BAR-SHEAR** bar-cutter
BARTERED exchanged commodities
BARTERER a dealer
BARTIZAN small overhanging turret
mn **BASALTIC** allied to basalt
mn **BASANITE** touchstone; flinty slate
BASCINET helmet of 15th century
ga **BASEBALL** national game (USA)
BASEBAND frequency modulation
BASE-BORN of low parentage
BASE-BRED of low breeding
BASELESS lacking any foundation
me **BASE-LINE** a surveyor's base
BASEMENT floor below ground level
BASENESS vileness; meanness
BASE-PAIR complementary acid bases
BASE-RICH iron-rich soil
mu **BASE-VIOL** bass-viol; violoncello
BASHLESS unashamed; undaunted
ch **BASICITY** ratio of acid to base
ch **BASIFIER** an alkali
rl **BASILIAN** monk of St Basil
rl **BASILICA** church
BASILICA public hall (Roman)
BASILING grinding to an angle
zo **BASILISK** dragon; lizard; cannon
BASINFUL bowlful
zo **BASIPHIL** attracted to basic dyes
BASKETED hampered
BASKETRY wickerwork
BASOPHIL attracted to basic dyes
BASQUINE Basque outer petticoat
mu **BASS-DRUM** deep-noted drum
mu **BASSETTE** tenor or small bass viol
mu **BASS-HORN** deep-toned bassoon
BASSINET wickerwork perambulator
mu **BASS-TUBA** euphonium
mu **BASS-VIOL** base-viol; violoncello
bt **BASSWOOD** (N. Amer.)
BASTAARD Dutch half-breed (S. Afr.)
BASTARDY illegitimacy
BASTERNA mule-borne litter
BASTILLE old castle; state prison
BATAVIAN native of Batavia; (Indonesian)
BATELESS irrepressible
BATHABLE washable
BATHETIC anticlimatic; bombastic
BATHMISM inherent divergence
zo **BATHORSE** pack-horse
BATH-RAIL side-grip
BATHROOM tub- and wash-room
BATSWING flat gas flame; flittermouse
nt **BATTENED** dependent; doors secured
BATTERED pounded; shattered
BATTLING striving; warring
mu **BATUCADA** batuque; dance (Brazil)
rl **BAUDEKIN** silk brocade; canopy
BAUDRONS Scottish name for the cat
BAULKING **BALKING**, checking; refusal (horse-jumping); jibbing
BAVARIAN of Bavaria
BAWDRICK baldrick; shoulder belt
BAYADERE Indian nautch girl
BAYARDLY blindly
bt **BAYBERRY** war-myrtle
bt **BDELLIUM** aromatic gum-resin
nt, ce **BEACHING** running ashore; loose-graded stones
ae, nt **BEACONED** aircraft guided; seamarks lit
BEADLERY beadle's jurisdiction
rl **BEAD-ROLL** names for masses
BEADSMAN almsman
bt **BEAD-TREE** the azedarac
tx **BEADWORK** ornamental, with coloured glass beads on cloth
BEAGLING hare-coursing on foot with dogs
nt **BEAK-HEAD** head; (ship's WCs)
nt **BEAK-HEAD** ramming projection (Roman)

BEAKIRON bickern; anvil point
zo **BEAM-BIRD** spotted flycatcher
lt **BEAM-EDGE** searchlight angle
lt **BEAM-FLUX** total light flux
el **BEAM-TRAP** beam-catching electrode
bt **BEAM-TREE** a hardwood tree
BEAN-KING king of the revels
BEARABLE tolerable; supportable
BEARABLY endurably; moderately
bt **BEARBIND** bearbine; bindweed
BEARDING meeting face to face
BEAR-HERD bear-keeper
BEARINGS sense of direction
BEARLIKE rude and rough; ursine
bt **BEAR'S-EAR** primula auricula
BEARSKIN headgear of the Guards
BEARWARD bear-leader; Arcturus
zo **BEASTIES** small animals
BEASTISH brutal; animal
BEATIFIC ecstatic; rapturous
BEAT-NOTE rhythmic accentuation
BEAUFREY beam or joist
BEAUPERE father-in-law (Fr.)
BEAUTIES lovelies
BEAUTIFY adorn; array; garnish
BEAVERED covered with beaver fur
BECALMED motionless; tranquillized
ck **BECHAMEL** savoury sauce (white)
BECHANCE befall; accidentally
BECKONED nodded; called; invited
BECOMING befitting; graceful
nt **BECUEING** anchor dragging on rocks
BECURLED with ringlets
BEDABBLE dabble; sprinkle
BEDAGGLE drag through the mire
BEDARKEN obscure; eclipse
BEDASHED bespattered
BEDAUBED smeared; plastered
BED-CHAIR bed back-rest
BEDECKED robed; embellished
bt, zo **BEDEGUAR** a rose scourge
rl **BEDESMAN** see beadsman
bt **BEDEWEEN** the birch tree
BEDEWING sprinkling
BED-GOING retiring
pt **BEDIMMED** tarnished; lights lowered
BED-LINEN sheets, etc.
BEDMAKER college servant
BEDPLATE foundation plate
eg **BEDPLATE** engine-frame base
BED-QUILT an overlay
BEDRENCH saturate; immerse; soak
BEDSTAFF cudgel; truncheon
BEDSTEAD a framework for a bed
BEDSTOCK part of bed (gardening)
bt **BEDSTRAW** a plant
BED-TABLE table for use in bed

BEDUCKED soused
BEDUSTED smothered with dust
BEDWARDS on the way to bed
bt **BEE-BREAD** pollen collected by bees
ck **BEECH-OIL** beechnut oil
zo **BEE-EATER** a bird
BEEFIEST heftiest; lustiest
bt **BEEFWOOD** an Australian wood
BEER-PUMP beer-pull, spout
BEERSHOP inn; alehouse; tavern
BEESWING dregs of port
BEETLING overhanging; projecting
bt **BEETRAVE** beetroot
bt **BEETROOT** beetrave
BEFITTED suitable; becoming; worthy
BEFLOWER cover with flowers
BEFOGGED dimmed; confused
BEFOOLED deluded; hoaxed; gulled
BEFOULED polluted; begrimed
BEFRIEND favour; patronize; aid
BEFRINGE adorn with fringes
BEFURRED covered with fur
BEGETTER a sire; father
BEGGABLE borrowable
BEGGARED rendered penniless
BEGGARLY paltry; mean; abject
BEGINNER tyro; novice; neophyte
BEGIRDED belted
BEGIRDLE encompass; encircle
BEGOTTEN born; produced
BEGREASE lubricate
BEGRIMED soiled; grubby
BEGRUDGE envy
BEGUILED deluded; diverted
BEGUILER cheat; deceiver
BEHAVING comme il faut
BEHEADAL an execution
BEHEADED decapitated
zo **BEHEMOTH** Job's hippopotamus
BEHOLDEN grateful; indebted
BEHOLDER observer; surveyor
BEHOVING being necessary
pc **BEINNESS** acceptedness socially
BEKISSED smothered in kisses
BELABOUR to thrash and whack
BELACING adorning with lace
BELAMOUR a gallant; a fair lady
BELATING being late
BELAUDED eulogized
nt **BELAYING** fastening
BEL-CANTO refined singing technique
BELCHING eructating
BELFRIED having belfries
rl **BELFRIES** steeples; watch-towers
BELIEVED credited; fancied
BELIEVER theist; devotee; pietist

BELITTLE disparage; deprecate
bt **BELLBIND** **BELL-BINE**, bindweed
zo **BELL-BIRD** New Zealand bird
nt **BELL-BUOY** the sailor's warning
BELLCOTE small belfry
BELLOWED roared; bawled
BELL-PULL bell-rope
el **BELL-PUSH** push-button bell switch
BELL-ROPE a ringer of clangers
BELL-TENT conical canvas tent
bt **BELLWORT** a campanula
BELLYFUL a bun in the oven
BELLY-GOD greedy; epicure; gourmand
BELLYING swelling; billowing
BELONGED owned by; pertained
BELOVING loving; fond; doting
eg **BELT-FORK** belt-transfer prongs
eg **BELT-SLIP** pulley-face belt slippage
BELZEBUB Beelzebub; satan; the devil
BEMASKED wearing a mask
BEMIRING soiling
BEMOANED bewailed; lamented
BEMUDDLE mess up
BEMUFFLE take a wrap for warmth
bd **BENCHING** extended seating; berm-ledge
ce **BENCHING** over ditch; manhole of iron
BENDABLE not rigid; over-bearing
nt **BENEAPED** aground at low tide
BENEDICK newly married man
rl **BENEDICT** an orderly saint
BENEFICE church living
BENIGNLY kindly; benevolently
BENITIER holy water vessel
BENJAMIN gum; overcoat
BENOTING noting fully
eg **BENT-TAIL** having a bent shank
BENUMBED torpid
ch **BENZOATE** a salt
BEPEPPER shoot repeatedly
BEPESTER annoy persistently
BEPITIED commiserated
BEPLUMED with plumes
BEPOMMEL belabour
BEPOWDER pulverize
BEPRAISE laud
BEPUFFED flattered with hot air
mu **BEQUADRO** natural (It.)
lw **BEQUEATH** of bequest, legacy (will)
BERATING scolding
ch **BERBERIN** barberry extract
bt **BERBERRY** the barberry
BERCEUSE cradle lullaby; song (Fr.)
BERDACHE Indian transvestite
BEREAVED bereft; widow; widower
bt, ck **BERGAMOT** herbal perfume; (tea)
mn **BERGMEHL** crystalline earth
BERGMOTE a miner's court
BERHYMED celebrated in verse
md **BERI-BERI** a tropical disease
BERNOUSE burnouse; Arab mantle
BERRYING producing berries
BERTHAGE dock fees
nt **BERTHING** docking
BESCRAWL scribble
BESCREAM yell the house down
BESCREEN shelter
BESEEMED befitted
BESEEMLY becoming; fit; suitable
BESETTER an assailant
BESHADOW overshadow
bt **BESIDERY** variety of pear
BESIEGED beleaguered; encircled
BESIEGER an investor
BESILVER electro-plate
BESLAVED enslaved
BESLAVER slobber
BESLIMED bemired
BESMIRCH besmutch; beslime
BESNOWED snowed up
BESOILED defiled; dirtied
BESORTED suited; fitted
BESOTTED drunk; crapulous; inebriated
BESOUGHT entreated; implored
BESOULED endowed with a soul
BESPICED highly seasoned
BESPOKEN made to order
BESPREAD broadcast; disseminate
BESSEMER a steel process
BESTIARY book about beasts
BESTOWAL gift; grant; distribution
BESTOWED gave; presented; awarded
BESTOWER donor; feoffer
BESTREAK mark with streaks
BESTREWN scattered; dispersed
BESTRIDE astride
BESTRODE traversed; mounted
mn **BETAFITE** hydrous uranium
BETAKING removing to; applying to
BETA-RAYS radium-rays
BETATRON electron speeding machine
BETEARED tearful; bedimmed
bt **BETEL-NUT** areca nut palm
BETIDING happening; befalling
BETONGUE scold; rail; nag
BETOSSED thrown about
BETRAYAL breach of trust; treachery
BETRAYED ensnared; beguiled; deceived
BETRAYER seducer; a Judas; traitor
BETTERED ameliorated; improved

bt **BETULINE** birch camphor
BEVELLED basiled; on the slant; smoothed, rounded
BEVERAGE drink; potion; potation
hd **BEVILLED** sloping lines
BEWAILED lamented
BEWARING minding; avoiding
lw **BEWIGGED** wearing a wig (law courts)
BEWILDER perplex; confuse
BHEESTIE Hindu water-carrier
ag **B-HORIZON** lower level of soil
BIANCONI Irish car
BIATHLON skiing and shooting; running and swimming trophies
ck **BIBATION** tippling; a drink
BIBLE-BOX container for Bible
rl **BIBLICAL** scriptured
BIBULOUS over-indulgence in alcohol
eg **BIB-VALVE** disc-closed draw-off tap
BICAUDAL with two tails
BICKERED squabbled
BICOLOUR of two colours
ps **BICONVEX** lens
BICRURAL two-legged
bt **BICUSPID** having two cusps
BICYCLED cycled
BIDDABLE worth bidding for (auction)
BIDENTAL with two teeth
BIENNIAL once in two years
BIER-BALK right of way for funerals
BIFACIAL doublefaced
bt **BIFEROUS** two crops each year
bt **BIFIDATE** cleft in twain
BIFORATE having two pores
lw **BIGAMIST** husband of two or more wives
lw **BIGAMOUS** situation of plural marriage
bt **BIGAROON** white-heart cherry
BIG-BONED bony; osseous
BIGGONET cap; deerstalker
bt **BIGNONIA** plant genus
BIJOUTRY bijouterie; trinkets
bt **BIJUGATE** twin
BIJUGOUS paired
BIJWONER squatter (S. Africa)
BILABIAL with both lips (phonetic)
nt **BILANDER** Dutch barge
bt **BILBERRY** blueberry
md **BILEDUCT** a canal
BILL-BOOK account book
BILLETED quartered
BILLETEE person billeted
zo **BILLFISH** lake fish (N. Amer.)
pr **BILLHEAD** letterhead; printing
to **BILLHOOK** hedge-cutting tool
BILLIARD- for a special green smooth cloth-covered table
BILLOWED surged; swelled (waves)
nt **BILLY-BOY** bluff-bowed ketch
BILLY-CAN bush teapot (Aust.)
BILOBATE with two lobes
BIMANOUS two-handed
md **BIMANUAL** done with both hands
BIMARINE between two seas
BIMENSAL every other month
BIMESTER two-month term
BIMIRROR slightly inclined mirror pair
nt **BINABINA** canoe (S. Pacific)
BINAURAL adapted for two ears
BINBASHI Turkish army officer
bt **BINDWEED** bearbine; convolvulus
nt **BINNACLE** mounting for ship's compass
ma **BINOMIAL** two-term system
ch **BINOXIDE** a peroxide
pm **BIO-ASSAY** drug-power test on animals
BIOBLAST parturient protoplasm
BIOCYTIN vitamin in yeast
BIOGENIC produced by living organisms
cn **BIOGRAPH** bioscope; cinema; zoetrope
BIOLYTIC destructive to life
bl **BIOMETER** life-measuring instrument
BIOMETRY life mensuration
bl **BIONOMIC** ecological
BIOPHORE minute growth-capable particle
zo **BIOPLASM** protoplasm
BIOSCOPE early cinematograph
BIOSOPHY made of life
BIPAROUS twin-producing
BIPENNIS two-edged battle-axe
BIQUARTZ saccharimeter analyser
zo **BIRADIAL** part radial, part bilateral
BIRAMOUS double-branched
BIRCHING corporal punishment
BIRD-BATH garden ornament
BIRD-BOLT blunt arrow
BIRDCAGE prison for birds; mini-aviary
BIRD-CALL bird song
BIRD-EYED quick-sighted; eagle-eyed
zo **BIRD-LICE** avian irritants
BIRDLIKE aviform
BIRDLIME sticky stuff for catching birds
BIRDSEED aviary food

BIRD'S-EYE of avian view
BIRD-SONG warbling of birds
lw **BIRRETUM** judge's black cap
BIRTHDAY an anniversary
BIRTHDOM privilege of birth
BISCAYAN Basque
BISCOTIN sweet biscuit
mu **BISCROMA** demisemiquaver
ma **BISECTED** halved angles (geometry)
BISECTOR an equal divisor
BISERIAL in two series
bt, zo **BISETOSE** double-bristled
BISEXUAL hetero- and homosexual
vt, zo **BISHOPED** horse ailment
ga **BISHOPED** bishop's conquest (chess)
pl, zo **BISMATIC** with two nipples
nt **BISQUINE** fishing lugger (Fr.)
tc **BISTABLE** with 2 stable states
rd **BISTATIC** transmitter/receiver apart
md **BISTOURY** surgical knife
pr **BITING-IN** acid process (etching)
BITINGLY acidly; mordantly
BITMAKER lorimer; loriner
BITMOUTH bit of a bridle
to **BITSTOCK** carpenter's brace
nt **BITTACLE** compass housing
BITTERED of acid flavour; distressed
BITTERLY acrimoniously
ch **BIVALENT** diatomic valency
BI-WEEKLY periodically
zo **BIZCACHA** chinchilla, rodent
BLABBING telling; tatling; weeping
BLACK-ART necromancy
ae **BLACK-BOX** computer control unit; flight recorder
zo **BLACKCAP** a warbler
zo **BLACK-FLY** turnip-flea
bt **BLACK-GUM** N. American tree
BLACKING boot-polish; black-listing
BLACKISH somewhat dark
BLACKLEG non-participant in works' strike
BLACKLET speck of dust
BLACK-NEB beak of crow, crane etc.
BLACKOUT loss of consciousness
BLACKOUT darkened city (war)
BLACKPOT coarse ceramic
BLACK-ROD Usher to House of Lords
mn **BLACK-WAD** ore of manganese
md **BLADDERY** of the gall, urine bladder
BLAMABLE censurable
BLAMABLY reprehensibly
BLAMEFUL culpable
BLANCARD bleached woven cloth
BLANCHED deprived of colour
BLANCHER white-washer
BLANDEST smoothest; mildest
BLANDISH flatter; coax; cajole
BLANKEST most vacant
BLANKING off-putting; frustrating
bt **BLASTEMA** an off-shoot
BLASTING detonating; cursing
BLAST-OFF launching of rocket
bl **BLASTULA** embryonic cell
BLATANCY obtrusive vulgarity
zo **BLAUWBOK** antelope (S. Africa)
hd **BLAZONED** decorated with
BLAZONER a broadcaster
BLAZONRY heraldic painting
BLEACHED blanched
BLEACHER colour extractor
BLEAKEST coldest; barest; chilliest
BLEAKISH cold and cheerless
BLEATING sheep calls (blethering)
BLEEDING blood-letting; gluing; separation of liquids
BLENCHED flinched; paled
BLENDING intermingling; harmonizing
zo, bt **BLENHEIM** spaniel; apple; plane
rl **BLESSING** divine favour; boon; gain
BLETTING decaying
BLIGHTED mildewed
BLIGHTER pestilent fellow
BLIMPERY blatant reactionary; obstinacy
BLINDAGE art of camouflage
BLINDERS **BLINKERS**, eye directors (horses)
BLINDEST most ignorant and heedless
ce **BLINDING** hoodwinking; (light); mat; mathers; sight-losing
BLINKARD a blinker or winker
BLINKERS vision restrictors (horses)
BLINKING ignoring; winking; gleaming
BLISSFUL rapturous; ecstatic
md **BLISTERY** swollen; vesicated; painful
BLITHELY joyously
BLITHEST merriest
BLITZING terror bombing (Blitzkrieg – Ger.)
BLIZZARD violent (arctic) snowstorm
ck **BLOATING** smoking (curing) fish
BLOATING inflating; swelling
nt **BLOCKADE** hostile closure of ports as act of war
BLOCKING obstructing; shaping; angling tool
BLOCKISH like a blockhead
BLOCK-OUT defensive trick (baseball)
pb **BLOCK-TIN** pure tin
BLODWYTE penalty for bloodshedding

BLONCKET gray
md **BLOOD-HOT** body temperature (37°C/98.6°F)
BLOODIED stained with gore
BLOODILY sanguinely
BLOODING fox-hunting rite
BLOOD-RED a gory hue
BLOOD-TAX conscription
BLOOD-WON dearly bought
BLOOMERS garments; blunders
BLOOMERY forge for smelted iron
BLOOMING flourishing
BLOSSOMY full of blossom
BLOTCHED pimpled; maculose
BLOTTING drying-up; leaving smudges
bt **BLOWBALL** dandelion head
zo, gl **BLOWHOLE** a whale's nostril; vent in cavern roof with fountain
BLOWLAMP intense local-heat apparatus
BLOWMILK skim-milk
BLOWPIPE a tube; blow-gun
BLUDGEON truncheon; heavy stick
BLUDGEON to assault with violence
BLUE-BACK the field-fare
zo **BLUEBIRD** dreambird; warbler (Am.)
BLUE-BOOK Parliamentary report
BLUECOAT Christ's Hospital schoolboy
BLUE-EYED innocent; promising
zo **BLUE-FISH** mackerel
BLUE-FUNK alarm and despondency
BLUEGILL common Amer. sunfish
lw **BLUEGOWN** King's bedesman, almsman
BLUEJOHN decorative fluorspar
BLUENESS of colour; of despondency
zo **BLUENOSE** Nova Scotian whale
md **BLUE-PILL** mercurial pill
zo **BLUE-POLL** salmon type
zo **BLUE-WING** a duck
BLUFFEST most outspoken
BLUFFING acting deceptively
BLUISHLY rather blue
BLUNGING puddling clay
BLUNTING dulling; benumbing
BLUNTISH not sharp
BLURRING indistinct; confusion
BLURTING uttering hastily
BLUSHFUL modest
BLUSHING flushing; reddening, milky effect; lacquer
BLUSTERY stormy
nt **BOARDING** embarking; lodging
zo **BOARFISH** red and silver fish
BOASTFUL vaunting
BOASTING bragging; bucking; crowing; stone surfacing
BOATABLE navigable
zo **BOATBILL** a heron
to, nt **BOATHOOK** grasping pole
ga, nt **BOATRACE** oars, sailing contest
BOATROPE a painter
BOBBINET netted lace
zo **BOBOLINK** the rice-bird
BOBOLYNE fool (16th c.)
zo **BOB-WHITE** American partridge
br **BOCK-BEER** dark beer
zo **BOCKELET** a hawk
lw **BOCKLAND** freehold land
BODEMENT a presentiment
BODILESS incorporeal
BODLEIAN (Oxford Library)
BODY-LINE bowling at batsman; (penalty); (cricket)
zo **BODY-WALL** perivisceral cavity wall
bt, ck **BOGBERRY** cranberry
mn **BOG-EARTH** peat
BOGEYISM frightfulness
BOGEYMAN hobgoblin
BOGGLING wavering; havering
bt **BOG-WHORT** whortleberry
BOHEMIAN unconventional
BOISERIE wood panelling (Fr.)
BOLD-FACE brazen
BOLDNESS courage; audacity
BOLIVIAN (Bolivia)
zo **BOLL-WORM** cotton-worm; weevil
nt **BOLT-BOAT** cobble
BOLT-HEAD a matrass
BOLT-HOLE escape hole
nt **BOLT-ROPE** rope round sail
nt **BOMBARDA** a polacre brigantine (It.)
mu **BOMBARDA** euphonium (brass band)
mu **BOMBARDE** organ stop (16 ft)
BOMB-FREE no raiders
ch **BOMBIATE** a bombic salt
pr **BOM-PROOF** book-club advance copy
BONA-FIDE in good faith
BONDAGER helpful event
lw **BOND-DEBT** bond-held debt
BONDMAID slave
lw **BONDSMAN** surety; bondman
md **BONEACHE** a pain
BONECAVE (prehistoric bones)
ag **BONEDUST** fertiliser
BONE-IDLE a good-for-nothing; shirker
BONE-LACE bobbin-lace
BONELESS spineless
BONHOMIE geniality
BONIFACE an innkeeper
BONING-IN peg-lining
BONNETED with hat or hood

BONSENSE opposite of nonsense
BONSPIEL curling match
zo **BONTEBOK** S. African antelope
BOOBYHUT covered sleigh
BOOBYISH idiotic
BOOBYISM stupidity
BOOHOOED lamented loudly
BOOKCASE shelved case
BOOK-CLUB literary association
BOOK-DEBT outstanding account
BOOKLESS unlearned
BOOKMARK book-marker
BOOKMATE schoolfellow
BOOKNAME nonce name
BOOK-OATH Bible oath
BOOK-REST bed or table lectern
BOOKSHOP voluminous emporium
BOOKWORM avid reader
BOOSTING advertising, pushing
BOOTHOSE spats
BOOTIKIN leggings
BOOTJACK a boot remover
BOOTLACE shoestrings
BOOTLAST boot/shoe makers' model
BOOTLESS unavailing; barefoot
BOOTLICK a lickspittle
BOOT-TREE (for a shapely boot)
BORACHIO leather wine bag
ch **BORACITE** magnesium borate
BORDEAUX claret
BORDERED edged
BORDERER border dweller
lw **BORDLAND** reserved domain land
BORD-LODE timber carrying
bt **BORECOLE** winter cabbage
BOREHOLE geological research site; (well); (irrigation); (oil)
zo **BOREWORM** teredo
BORROWED assumed; hypothesized
BORROWER cadger
go **BORSTALL** hill road
bt **BOTANIST** plant studier
BOTANIZE pick flowers
BOTCHERY patchwork
BOTCHING clumsy repair work
BOTHERED plagued
ck **BOTTLING** preserving; storing in a bottle
nt **BOTTOMED** constructed (keels); butted; fathomed
BOTTOMRY loan secured by ship
md **BOTULISM** form of poisoning
BOUDERIE pouting; petulance
BOUDEUSE sofa with adjustable back-rest
BOUFFANT puffed out
ck **BOUILLON** broth; soup
BOUNCING resilient; fraud (of cheques); playing ball down (netball)
BOUNDARY limit; (cricket)
BOUNDING leaping; bordering
bt **BOUNTREE** **BOURTREE**, the elder
tx **BOURETTE** tufted waste-silk yarn
bt **BOURTREE** the elder
BOUTIQUE trendy fashionable shop
mu **BOUZOUKI** Greek mandolin
BOVIFORM ox-like
BOW-BRACE archer's string-guard
BOW-DRILL rotary drill
nt **BOW-GRACE** a fender
BOWINGLY subserviently; courteously
nt **BOW-PIECE** bow-chaser; (gun)
BOWSIGHT adjustable aimer (archery)
nt **BOWSPRIT** a spar forward beyond the bows
BOX-DRAIN enclosed drain
bt **BOX-ELDER** ash-leaved maple
el **BOX-FRAME** 1-piece traction-motor frame
BOX-LOBBY passage in theatre
bd **BOX-PLATE** web-plate steel
BOX-PLEAT a double fold
bt **BOX-THORN** a shrub
BOYISHLY puerilely
BOY'S-PLAY a prank; trifling
zo **BRACCATE** with feathered feet
BRACELET a handcuff; ornament
BRACHIAL belonging to the arm
BRACKISH somewhat salt (of water)
bt **BRACTEAL** leaf formation
BRADBURY £1 note (obs.)
BRADSHAW railway guide
BRADYPOD a sloth
nt **BRAGAGNA** felucca, Adriatic
BRAGGART boaster
BRAGGING vaunting
nt **BRAGOZZI** luggers, Venice
BRAIDING plaiting; (ribbon); (sword)
BRAIDISM hypnotism
nt **BRAILING** hauling in; trussing
BRAIN-FAG nervous exhaustion
BRAINING dashing out the brains
BRAINISH brain-sick; furious
md **BRAINPAN** part of the skull
ck **BRAISING** a form of cookery
rw **BRAKE-MAN** a controller; (bobsledding)
rw **BRAKE-VAN** the guard's domain
BRAMBLED overgrown
BRANCARD horse-borne litter; float; platform vehicle
BRANCHED forked; ramified
zo **BRANCHER** young bird

BRANDIED laced with brandy
BRANDING stigmatizing; marking
BRANDISE a trivet
BRANDISH flourish; wave; shake
BRAND-NEW unused; branded
BRANGLED wrangled
zo **BRANTAIL** the redstart; a warbler
zo **BRANT-FOX** a kind of small fox
BRASSAGE cost of mintage
BRASSARD an armlet
BRASSART arm armour
BRASS-HAT big-wig; officer
bt **BRASSICA** the cabbage genus
bt **BRASSOCK** field mustard
BRATLING small brat; youngster
bd **BRATTICE** **BRETTICE**, (partition)
ch **BRAUNITE** manganese oxide
BRAWLING drunken disorder
BRAZENED shameless
BRAZENLY impudently; boldly
BRAZENRY effrontery
bt **BRAZILIN** a red dye
BREACHED violated; (pact); tore open
BREACHES gaps; pact-violations
bt **BREAD-NUT** a fruit
BREAKAGE rupture; fracture
BREAKING smashing; infringing
BREAK-OUT escape; epidemic; war; molten metal
nt **BREAK-OUT** canoeing off course
BREAKVOW a perjurer
BREAMING cleaning ship's bottom
BREASTED confronted
BREATHED exhaled; respired
BREATHER a respite
BREECHED put into trousers
BREECHES pantaloons
ps **BREEDING** lineage; begetting; nuclear transformation
cn **BREEZING** of unclear photo image
BRELOGUE watch-chain ornament
BRENNAGE an ancient tribute
zo **BREPHNIC** neanic; of adolescent period
BRETHREN brotherly group; kindred
bd **BRETTICE** **BRATTICE**, partition
BREVETCY nominal rank
rl **BREVIARY** prayer-book, R.C.
lw **BREVIATE** epitome; a brief
zo **BREVIPED** short-legged
zo **BREVIPEN** short-winged
BREWSTER brewer; maltster
BRIAREAN many handed
BRIBABLE venal; corrupt
BRICK-AXE 2-bladed brick-dressing axe
BRICKBAT half-a-brick (thrown)
BRICKING building; wrecking
BRICK-RED dark orange-red
BRICK-TEA tea in blocks
BRIDE-ALE ale at a marriage
BRIDE-BED marriage-bed
mo **BRIDGING** joining up; loan; rock chimney climbing technique
BRIDLING controlling; scorning; ruffling
BRIEFING giving final instructions
BRIEFMAN brief compiler
BRIGADED combined
BRIGHTEN clarify; illumine
BRIGHTLY brilliantly
BRIGUING canvassing
BRIMLESS rimless
BRIMMING full; verging
mu **BRINDISI** It. toast; drinking song
BRINDLED streaky brown
BRINEPAN **BRINEPIT**, salt extraction by evaporation
BRINGING conveying; fetching
BRISANCE shattering effect
BRISKING quickening
BRISKISH rather spry
zo **BRISLING** small sardine or sprat
BRISTLED ruffled
ck **BRITTLED** (cooking venison)
BROACHED pierced
BROACHER first proposer
to **BROAD-AXE** heavy axe
BROADEST vastest; amplest
BROADISH rather broad
BROCADED embroidered
BROCATEL coarse brocade
bt, ck **BROCCOLI** green cauliflower
BROCHURE pamphlet; leaflet
BRODEKIN buskin; half-boot
ck **BROILING** grilling
BROKENLY disconnectedly
BROKERLY mean (of brokers)
bt **BROMELIA** the pineapple
ch **BROMELIN** proteolytic enzyme
md **BROMIDIC** dull; calming
ch **BROMIZED** made to smell
pl **BRONCHIC** (windpipe)
BRONZIFY make into bronze
pt **BRONZING** metallic-lustre-giving
mn **BRONZITE** lustrous diallage
BROODING pondering; incubating
zo **BROOD-SAC** cockroach egg chamber
BROOKING bearing; enduring
mn **BROOKITE** crystalline titanium oxide
BROOKLET streamlet
BROOMING sweeping; breaming
ce **BROTHERS** male siblings; rope or chain sling
BROUGHAM one-horsed carriage

BROUHAHA fuss and bother
BROWBEAT bully; overbear; haze
BROWLESS shameless
BROWNING tanning; rifle
mu **BROWNING** song variations
BROWNISH somewhat sunburnt
rl **BROWNIST** Congregationalist (now URC)
BROW-POST a main beam
BROWSICK dejected; melancholy
BROWSING grazing; casual reading
BRUISING inflicting tissue injury
BRUMAIRE November (Fr. Rev. cal.)
BRUNETTE dark hair and eyes
el **BRUSH-BOX** brush-holding container
BRUSHING sweeping, skirmishing; brisk
BRUSH-OFF curt rebuff; (lacrosse)
BRUSSELS (carpets); (sprouts)
BRUSTLED crackled; bullied
BRUTALLY ferociously; ruthlessly
BRYOLOGY study of mosses
ch **BRYONINE** extract of bryony
BUBBLING boiling; frothing; cheating
bd **BUBBLING** surface film effect (defect)
ck **BUCCANED** (smoked meat)
BUCCINAL like a trumpet
zo **BUCCINUM** a whelk
fr **BUCHERON** Canadian forest worker
bt **BUCKBEAN** a water-plant
mt **BUCKETED** rode or rained furiously
zo **BUCKHORN** deer horn
BUCK-JUMP quick plunging leap
BUCKLING curling; fastening
ck **BUCKLING** pickled fish
bt **BUCKMAST** beech-mast
ag **BUCKRAKE** tractor transport attachment
BUCKSHEE gratuity; commission; free
BUCKSHOT large shot
BUCKSKIN soft yellow leather
BUCRANIA ornamental ox-skulls
rl **BUDDHISM BUDDHIST**, religion founded by Sakyamuni *c*.500 BC
BUDDLING ore washing
BUDGEREE good (Australian)
BUDGETED made provision
BUFFCOAT a jacket (former regiment)
BUFFERED cushioned; shielded
BUFFETED struck; clouted
mn **BUFONITE** toadstone
BUHL-WORK inlaid tortoiseshell
BUILDING erecting; pile; structure
BULGARIC Bulgarian
BULKHEAD water-tight wall in ships; water tank cover
nc **BULK-TEST** radiation test sample
BULL-BEEF coarse beef
zo **BULL-CALF** male calf
BULLDOZE to raze; intimidate; coerce
BULLETIN official report
zo **BULL-FROG** North American frog
rw **BULLHEAD** rail-type
ar **BULLNOSE** rounded edge
BULLRING Spanish arena
BULL'S-EYE glass window; sweet
bt **BULLWEED** knap-weed
bt **BULLWORT** bishop's-weed
BULLYING BULLYISM, browbeating; tormenting
BULLYRAG BALLYRAG, to badger; intimidate
bt **BULRUSHY** full of rushes
zo **BUMMALOE** Bombay duck (fish)
BUMMAREE fish vendor; money-lender
nc **BUNCHING** clustering; grouping; velocity modulation
BUNDLING hurrying; packaging
BUNDLING offering intimate hospitality
BUN-FIGHT tea party
BUNGALOW one-storeyed house
BUNGHOLE hole in a cask
BUNGLING awkward; clumsy
BUNGVENT spile-hole in bung
BUNKERED coaled; in difficulties
md **BUNODONT** a dental malady
nt **BUNTLINE** a sheet
nt **BUOYANCY** specific lightness; floatability
BURBERRY a waterproof
BURDENED laden; overloaded
BURGANET BURGONET, Burgundian helmet
BURGLARY felony at night
BURGLING stealing; robbing
BURGRAVE German governor
BURGUNDY French wine
BURINIST engraver
mu **BURLETTA** burlesque; comic operetta
BURNOOSE Arab cloak
bt **BURNT-EAR** corn-disease
BURROWED excavated; tunnelled
BURROWER a rabbit
nt **BURR-PUMP** large pump
md **BURSALIS** a muscle
md **BURSITIS** bursa inflammation
BURSTING exploding; rending
zo **BUSH-BABY** night-ape (S. Africa)
BUSH-BRED reared in back country
zo **BUSHBUCK** antelope (S. Africa)

BUSHELER a clothes-repairer (USA)
bt **BUSH-ROPE** a liana; a creeper
BUSH-VELD bush country (S. Africa)
BUSINESS stage-craft; occupation; commerce
BUSKINED booted
BUSYBODY officious person
BUSYLESS being idle
BUSYNESS state of being busy
BUTCHERY slaughter; massacre
BUTCHING being tough; lesbian
ck, ga **BUTTERED** of teacake; missed a catch
to **BUTTERIS BUTTRICE**, farrier's (horse-shoeing) knife
BUTTONED fastened
ar, bd **BUTTRESS** extra wall, roof support
ch **BUTYRATE** salt of butyric acid
ck **BUTYROUS** buttery; oleaginous; greasy
BUZKASHI equestrian team game (Japan)
BY-BIDDER auction-bid encourager
BYCOCKET peaked cap (15th cent.)
BY-CORNER odd corner
BY-DESIGN spin off
nt **BY-LANDER BILANDER**, coastal hoy (ship)
BY-MATTER something incidental
BY-MOTIVE unavowed motive
BY-PASSED avoided
BYRONISM Lord Byron's phrase
BY-SPEECH casual speech
BY-STREET side street
BY-STROKE sly stroke
BY-THE-BYE by the way

C

bt, fr **CAATINGA** thorn forest of N.E. Brazil
CABALISM CABALIST, of cliques in politics
CABALLED CABALLER, intrigue of schemers
CABBAGED filched; purloined; stole
CABBLING smashing into small pieces
CABIN-BOY waits on ship's passengers
nt **CABINING** allotting cabins; sorting in groups
CABIRIAN fire-worshipper (Lemnos)
rw **CABLE-WAY** funicular railway; rope-linked
hd **CABOCHED CABOSHED**, neck-less head
CABOCHON gem without facets
CABOODLE the whole lot
CABOTAGE coasting trade
CABRIOLE leap; furniture
CAB-STAND taxi rank
zo **CACHALOT** the sperm whale
md **CACHEMIC** unhealthy
CACHEPOT ornamental flower-pot cover
CACHESEX miniwear for beach
md **CACHEXIA** severe emaciation
mu **CACHUCHA** Spanish dance
md **CACHUNDE** aromatic medicine
zo **CACKEREL** a species of fish
CACKLING gossiping; chattering; (hens)
CACODOXY erroneous opinion
CACOLOGY bad pronunciation
pc **CACOSMIA** aversion to smells
CADASTRE a survey of land
mu **CADENCED** modulated; rhythmical
bt **CADILLAC** a pear; motor car
CADUCEUS Mercury's wand
CADUCITY frailty; transitoriness
bt **CADUCOUS** early falling (leaves)
CAERLEON King Arthur's residence
CAESIOUS blue-grey
CAESURAL (metric pause)
ch **CAFFEINE** coffee alkaloid
CAGELING a bird in a cage
CAJOLERY persuading; coaxing
CAKESHOP (confectionery)
mu **CAKE-WALK** pre-ragtime plantation dance (USA)
bt **CALABASH** gourd
bt **CALADIUM** plant genus
zo **CALAMARY** cuttlefish, squid
bt **CALAMBAC** aloes-wood
mn **CALAMINE** zinc ore
bt **CALAMINT** aromatic plant
mn **CALAMITE** tremolite
CALAMITY disaster; affliction
zo **CALANDER** a lark
zo **CALANDRA** grain-weevil
zo **CALANGAY** white cockatoo
CALATHUS work-basket
CALCEATE shod; to shoe
mn **CALCEDON** opaline quartz
CALCINED reduced to quick-lime
CALCINER high-temperature heat device
mn **CALC-SPAR** calcite
mn **CALC-TUFF** a limestone
bd, me **CALCULON** size of brick
ma **CALCULUS** mathematical system
CALENDAR almanac; roster list
CALENDER hot-rolling machine
CALFLESS spindle-shanked
CALF-LOVE an early attachment

CALF-SKIN binding leather
CALIBRED bored; gauged
CALIDITY warmth; fervency; ardency
CALIDUCT a heating pipe
rl **CALIFATE CALIPHATE**, Islamic rulership
CALIPASH calipee; green turtle fat
me **CALIPPIC** (Metonic cycles)
bt **CALISAYA** Peruvian bark
rl **CALIXTIN** Hussite
mn **CALLAITE** turquoise
zo **CALL-BIRD** a decoy
CALL-GIRL prostitute
mu **CALLIOPE** muse of epic poetry; organ
to **CALLIPER** a measuring device
CALL-LOAN cash on demand
CALL-NOTE bird-call
pl **CALLOSUM** left-right brain link
md **CALLOUSE** wart; hardening of skin
CALL-OVER a roll-call; betting odds on horses
CALMNESS placidity; tranquillity
CALORIST a heat theorist
ml **CALORIZE** aluminium-spray steel surfaces
CALOTYPE talbot-type
bt **CALTROPS** a plant
ps **CALUTRON** electromagnetic separator of images
CALVERED crimped; pickled
bt **CALVILLE** an apple
bt **CALYCINE** cuplike
zo **CALYCOID** cup-like animal structure
zo **CALYMENE** trilobite genus
bt **CALYPTRA** a covering
bt **CAMASSIA** kind of hyacinth
CAMATINA acorns for tanning
CAMBERED slightly arched
mu **CAMBIATA** changed, device in counterpoint (It.)
ch **CAMBOGIA** gamboge gum
gl **CAMBRIAN** Welsh; era
CAMELEER camel driver
zo **CAMELEON** chameleon
CAMELINE camlet; camel hair
CAMELISH obstinate
bt **CAMELLIA** an evergreen
ar **CAMERATE** to build arch shape
tx **CAMISADE CAMISADO**, night attack with white shirts over armour
tx **CAMISOLE** short bodice (fem. underwear)
rl **CAMISTER** a clergyman
bt, ck **CAMOMILE** soothing herbal flowers
CAMPAIGN military operation; the countryside
CAMP-FIRE for outdoor warmth
ch **CAMPHENE** camphine; camphor
CAMP-SHOT a pile revetment
au **CAM-SHAFT** pan of machinery
CAMSTONE whitening for doorsteps
CAM-WHEEL off-centric oval mechanism
CANADIAN Canuck
bt **CANAIGRE** Texan dock (plant)
ce, cp **CANALIZE** make into a canal; direct flow
CANARESE natives of Canara
mu **CANARIES** triple tune, old dance
bt **CANASTER** a kind of tobacco
rl **CANCELLI CANCELLO**, lattice-work in choir, chancel, of church
zo **CANCRINE** crab-like
md **CANCROID** like cancer
CANDIDLY frankly; sincerely; naively
CANDYING preserving in sugar
CANE-HOLE trench for sugar canes
CANE-MILL sugar crushing mill
CANEPHOR basket-bearing figure
CANEWARE yellowish stoneware dishes
CANICULA the dog-star; Sirius
CANISTER a tin; tea chest; case-shot
md **CANITIES** whiteness of the hair
CANKERED corroded; infected
ch **CANNABIN** cannabic extract
bt **CANNABIS** hemp; bhang
CANNIBAL anthropophagite
CANNIKIN pannikin; a billy
CANNONED (billiards); collided
CANNULAR tubular
CANOEIST canoe paddler
CANON-BIT cannon-bit; (horse-bit)
rl **CANONESS** lady canon; a beneficiary
rl **CANONIST** ecclesiastical expert
rl **CANONIZE** besaint
lw, rl **CANON-LAW** ecclesiastical law
CANOODLE caress; fondle
CANOPIED with an awning
CANOROUS tuneful; musical; melodious
CANTERED galloped easily
to **CANTHOOK** lumberman's lever
rl **CANTICLE CANTICUM**, chant or song
bd **CANTLING** brick-firing course
CANTONAL referring to a district
CANTONED divided into cantons
rl **CANTORIS** of the precentor
CANZONET air or song
CAPACITY volume; capability; faculty; motor power in terms of cylinder size
CAPE-CART two-wheeled vehicle (SA)
md **CAPELINE** bandage; lady's wrap

CAPELLET enlarged hock
CAPERING frolicsome frisking
bt **CAPER-TEA** black tea
zo **CAPIBARA CAPYBARA**, Brazilian rodent
CAPITANO a head-man
bt **CAPITATE** growing to a head
CAPONIER gallery in a fort
CAPONISE castrate; geld; emasculate
CAPOTING winning all tricks at piquet
CAP-PAPER wrapping or writing paper
CAPRIOLE equestrian jump
CAPRIPED goat-footed
ch **CAPROATE** a butyric salt
ch **CAPRYLIC** normal; acidic
eg **CAP-SCREW** nutless screw-bolt
bt **CAPSICUM** red pepper; chilli
mn, bd **CAPSTONE** fossil sea-urchin; a coping, wall ridge
CAPSULAR in capsule form
CAPTIOUS hypercritical; censorious
CAPTURED caught; arrested
CAPUCCIO a hood or cowl
rl **CAPUCHIN CAPUCINE**, hooded cloak
zo **CAPUCINE** hooden monkey; pigeon
CARABINI CARBINES, short rifle
zo **CARACARA** Brazilian carrion-hawk
ar **CARACOLE** spiral staircase
zo **CARACOLE** equestrian turn; shell
CARACOLY alloy of gold and silver
nt **CARACORE** patrol sail boat, Indonesia
zo **CARAPACE** tortoise shell; etc.
bt **CARAP-OIL** crab-wood oil
nt **CARAVELA CARAVELLE, CARAVEL, CARVEL**, lateen; atlantic rig (Sp., Port.)
ch **CARBOLIC** phenol
CARBOLOY carbide alloy for cutting tools
ch **CARBONIC** of carbon
ch **CARBONYL** metal/carbon-monoxide product
CARBURET impregnant with carbon
CARCAJOU wolverine or glutton
CARCANET collar of jewels
bt **CARDAMOM** aromatic spice (India)
CARD-CASE a receptacle
CARDIACE heart-shaped jewel
CARDIGAN knitted woollen jacket
rl **CARDINAL** member of Vatican Council
rl **CARDINAL** principal; short cloak
CARDIOID heart-shaped curve
md **CARDITIS** inflammation of heart
nt **CAREENED** laid on one side
CAREENED caressed; fondled
CAREERED raced; rushed; dashed
CAREFREE joyous
CARELESS heedless; remiss; incautious
CARESSED fondled; embraced; petted
CAREWORN grief-stricken
zo **CARGOOSE** crested grebe
zo **CARIACOU** Virginian deer
CARIBBEE a Caribbean
bt **CARICOUS** like a fig
mu **CARILLON** a unit (ringing) of church bells
bt **CARINATE** keel-shaped
bt **CARL-HEMP** female hemp plant
CARNAGED slaughtered; butchered
CARNALLY of the flesh; sensuously
bt **CARNAUBA** Brazilian palm
CARNEOUS fleshly
CARNIFEX public executioner
CARNIVAL revelry; masquerade
CAROLINE time of King Charles
mu **CAROLLED** sung (as choral group)
me **CAROTEEL** East Indian weight
CAROTENE vitamin A
CAROUSAL CAROUSED, feasted, drunkenly; held orgies, noisily
CAROUSEL tournament; tourney
CAROUSER a reveller
CARPETED a covered floor; rebuked
CARRIAGE passenger coach; deportment
CARRIERS hauliers; containers
CARRIOLE open carriage; sledge
CARRYING transporting; conveying
CART-LOAD a measure of capacity
rl **CARTOUCH CARTOUCHE**, hieroglyph (Eg.)
CARUCAGE tax on ploughs
CARUCATE (plough-land)
md, bt **CARUNCLE CARBUNCLE**, fleshy excrescence; wart; outgrowth on seeds
CARYATIC (Caryatides)
ar, rl **CARYATID** a lady supporter (ancient Gr.)
bt **CARYOKAR** butter-nut tree
ck **CASANOVA** loves all; type of salad
CASCABEL swell on cannon's mouth
CASCADED fell in torrents
CASCALHO diamond-bearing earth
CASEMATE armoured chamber
CASEMENT hinged window
CASE-SHOT short range ammunition
zo **CASE-WORM** caddis-worm
CASHMERE silky goat's hair
CASKETED enshrined; coffined

mu **CASSETTE** container; reel of taped music
bt **CASS-WEED** shepherd's purse
bt **CASTANEA** chestnut-tree
CASTANET a chestnut-like dance clapper
CASTAWAY wrecked; rejected (Crusoe)
CAST-IRON rigid; inflexible
CASTLERY feudal castle control
CASTLING (chess)
CASTRATE geld; emasculate
mu **CASTRATO** high voiced singer
CASTWORK moulded parts of a silver object
CASUALLY by chance; fortuitously
CASUALTY of accident; death; wounded
CATACOMB cave sepulchre
ch **CATALASE** hydrogen-peroxide-decomposing enzyme
CATALYST CATALYSE, (unchanged substance assisting chemical action)
CATAPULT a pellet projector
md **CATARACT** waterfall; eye trouble
nt **CAT-BLOCK** anchor-tackle
CATCH-ALL general jumble container
bt **CATCHFLY** certain plants
CATCHING infectious; charming
CATCH-PIT sump; matter-retaining catchment
CATEGORY order; class; division
CATENARY like a chain
bt **CATENATE** chain-like
ma **CATENOID** catenary revolution surface
CATERESS lady provider
ck **CATERING** of food and entertainment
rl **CATHEDRA** bishop's throne
CATHETUS perpendicular line
CATHEXIS concentration of psychic energy
CATHISMA part of the psalter
el **CATHODAL** negative electrode
el **CATHODIC** produced by cathode reaction
rl **CATHOLIC** universal; liberal; Roman church
CATILINE daring conspirator
CATODONT teeth on lower jaw only
el **CATOLYTE** electrolyte next to cathode
CATONIAN resembling Cato; severe
CATOPSIS morbid keen-sightedness
bt **CAT'S-FOOT** ground ivy
bt **CAT'S-TAIL** the reed mace
CAT-STICK tip-cat's stick
CAUDATED having a tail; tailed
bt **CAUDICES** stems of trees
bt **CAUDICLE** an orchid stalk
CAUDILLO leader (Sp.)
ar, ck **CAULCOLE** Corinthian cabbage
ck **CAULDRON** bowl-shaped cooking pot
bt **CAULICLE CAUDICLE,** small stalk
nt **CAULKING** filling in cracks
CAUSALLY resultantly; productively
CAUSERIE gossip; small talk
CAUSEUSE settee for two
CAUSEWAY roadway over wet ground
CAUTIOUS wary; discreet; watchful
CAVALIER romantic; daring; royalist; beau; earth platform
mu **CAVATINA** short simple air
CAVATION excavation
lw **CAVEATED** warned by writ
lw **CAVEATOR** deliverer of writs
zo **CAVE-BEAR** extinct animal
CAVERNED hollowed out
CAVESSON horse-breaking appliance
zo **CAVICORN** hollow-horned
CAVILLED objected; carped; criticized
CAVILLER captious critic
CAVORTED pranced
bt **CELERIAC** turnip-rooted celery
CELERITY rapidity; swiftness; speed
CELIBACY the unmarried state
CELIBATE unwed
CELLARER wine steward; Simon
CELLARET small wine container; ornamented wooden chest
CELLULAR honeycombed; alveolated
CEMENTED glued; united; stuck
CEMETERY burial ground; necropolis
CENATION supping
rl **CENOBITE** religious order
CENOTAPH a monument; memorial
gl **CENOZOIC** era of mammals
CENSORED blue-pencilled
CENSURED reprimanded; rebuked
bt **CENTAURY** rose-pink flower
CENTERED centred; localized
md **CENTESIS** puncturing a cavity
me **CENTIARE** a square metre
me **CENTIBAR** measurement of pressure
CENTOISM literary patchwork
CENTOIST platitudinarian
ce **CENTRING** football kick; temp. dome or arch support
CENTROID centre of gravity
CENTUPLE a hundredfold
CENTURIA division of 100 horsemen (Roman)
md **CEPHALGY** headache

md **CEPHALIC** remedy for head-pains
CEPHALIN phosphatide substance in brain
CERAMICS pottery
bt **CERASINE** plum gum
zo **CERASTES** a horned snake
mn **CERATITE** species of ammonite
CERATODE horny structure
CERATOID ceratose; horny
rl **CERBERUS** watch-dog of Hell
bt, ag **CEREALIA** of corn types and grasses
ch **CEREALIN** a bran extract
pc **CEREBRAL CEREBRIC**, of the brain; ingenious
CEREBRIN something in the brain
md **CEREBRUM** part of the brain
CEREMENT shroud dipped in wax
CEREMONY prescribed formality
el **CERESINE** refined ozocerite
bt **CERNUOUS** drooping
pg **CERTINAL** a phenol developer
CERULEAN sky-blue
CERULEIN olive-green
mn **CERUSITE** white lead
CERVELAT saveloy; pork-brain sausage
pl **CERVICAL** of the neck of womb
md **CESAREAN** childbirth by operation
CESSPOOL drainage pit; midden
md **CESTODES** tapeworm
zo **CETACEAN** whale or dolphin
bt **CETERACH** fern; cryptogam
zo **CETOLOGY** natural history of cetaceans
bt **CETRARIA** lichen; Iceland moss
mu **CHACONNE** slow courtly dance
CHADBAND a canting hypocrite
CHAFEWAX sealing-wax officer
CHAFFERY haggling; bargaining
CHAFFING bantering; scoffing
CHAFFRON horse armour
CHAINAGE measure of length or steel tape
CHAINING restraining; fettering
CHAINLET small chain
ag **CHAINMAN** survey team member; axeman (USA)
CHAIR-BED convertible contraption
CHAIRING carrying in triumph; (meeting)
CHAIRMAN president of meeting
CHALDAIC Babylonian
me, mn **CHALDRON CAULDRON**, 25 cwt (1270 kg) of coal; portable cauldron; truck-load in mines
CHALICED cup-like
bd **CHALKING** writing in chalk; break up of pigmented films
CHALKPIT a quarry
zo **CHALONIC** inhibitory, depressive
CHAMBREL horse's hind leg joint
CHAMFRON horse's head armour
CHAMORRO native; language (Guam, Marianas)
CHAMPFER bevelled angle on a surface
CHAMPING chewing; gnawing; biting
CHAMPION defender; hero; victor
lw **CHANCERY** court of justice (civil)
CHANCING risking; happening
CHANDLER candle-maker; supplies dealer
CHANFRIN fore-part of horse's head
CHANGE-UP let-up; slow pitch throw (baseball)
CHANGING altering; varying
rl **CHANTING** intoning; reciting; (choral)
ck **CHAPATTY CHUPATTY**, unleavened bread (Ind.)
CHAPBOOK book hawked by chapmen
CHAPELET stirrups and leathers
rl **CHAPELRY** chapel district
CHAPERON to escort (for single ladies)
ar **CHAPITER** capital of a column
rl **CHAPLAIN** a sky-pilot; padre; priest to service groups
fr **CHAPLASH** yellow-brown durable wood
CHAPLESS without a lower jaw
CHAPPING cleaving
ar **CHAPTREL** arch-supporting capital
CHARCOAL charred wood
CHARGING rushing; costing; enjoining
CHARISMA magnetic personality; grace
CHARLIES night watchmen
bt **CHARLOCK** wild mustard
CHARMING fascinating; captivating
CHARRING scorching; toasting
CHARTING mapping; recording; planning
CHARTISM CHARTIST, of suffrage reform
CHASSEUR light-armed soldier; (hunter)
CHASTELY virtuously; modestly
CHASTISE flog; castigate; discipline
CHASTITY sexual abstinence
rl **CHASUBLE** vestment over alb
CHATELET small castle
CHATONES ornamental nailhead
CHATTELS miscellaneous property

CHATTING friendly conversation
CHATWOOD fuel; ducal mansion
mu **CHAUNTER** note-piece (bagpipes)
CHAUSSES trunk-hose; leg-armour
bt **CHAY-ROOT** Indian red dye
CHEATERY fraud; deception
CHEATING knavery; duping; (card-sharper)
nt **CHEBACCO** fishing boat (N. America)
CHECHAKO tenderfoot (Alaska)
cp **CHECKBIT** binary check digit
CHECKERS a draughts game
CHECKING reproving; impeding
CHECKOUT departure formality
CHEEKING saucy behaviour
CHEEPING piping; chirping
CHEERFUL merry and bright
CHEERILY joyfully; gaily; blithely
CHEERING applause; comforting
zo **CHELIFER** book-scorpion
CHELLEAN early Palaeolithic
zo **CHELONIA** tortoises and turtles
ch **CHEMICAL** substance of chemistry
md **CHEMOSIS** eye-disease symptom
CHEMURGY applied organic chemistry
CHENILLE cord with short threads of silk, wool
CHERUBIC angelic
CHERUBIM a celestial spirit
zo **CHESHIRE** cheese; fading cat
CHESSMAN a piece in chess
CHESTING encasing; boxing
bt **CHESTNUT** old joke; conker
CHEVEREL **CHEVERIL**, kid-skin; flexible
CHEVERET small table (English)
mu **CHEVILLE** bridge of a violin
CHEVYING chasing, pursuing
CHIASMUS inverse parallelism
CHIASTIC crossed
CHICANED cheated; tricked
CHICANER a swindler; artful dodger
CHICKING hatching; sprouting (plants)
bt **CHICK-PEA** edible pealike seed
CHIEFAGE capitation; poll tax
lw **CHIEFRIE** small feudal rent
CHILD-BED in labour; confinement
CHILDISH puerile; infantile
CHILDREN family juniors; kids
CHILIASM doctrine of millennium
CHILIAST believer in that doctrine
CHILLIER cooler; colder
CHILLING discouraging; depressful; freezing; (damage); (wine)
CHILTERN (stewardship by the hundred)
CHIMAERA fabulous monster; illusion
zo **CHIMAERA** graft; hybrid; fish
CHIMERIC fanciful; delusive
CHINAMAN Chinese; left hander's googly (cricket)
CHINAMPA floating garden
CHIN-CHIN a toast
CHINKING jingling; tinkling sound
CHINOITE green mineral
CHINREST violin
vt **CHINSCAB** a sheep-disease
CHINSING caulking
zo **CHIPMUCK** **CHIPMUNK**, ground-squirrel
CHIPPING chaffing; chopping; fracturing
CHIPSHOT golf
md **CHIRAGRA** gout in the hands
CHIRPING cheeping
CHIRRING cooing; curring; purring
CHIT-CHAT small talk
CHIVALRY gallantry
md **CHLOASMA** a skin disease
ch **CHLORATE** salt of chloric acid
ch **CHLORIDE** compound of chlorine
ch **CHLORINE** a yellow gas
mn **CHLORITE** olive-green mineral
ch **CHLOROID** **CHLOROUS**, of chlorine
zo **CHOANATA** vertebrates; (nasal-oral)
mn **CHOANITE** fossil sponge
CHOICELY discriminately; exquisitely
rl **CHOIR-BOY** in church choir
CHOIRING singing in unison
CHOLERIC irascible; testy; petulant
CHOLIAMB iambic metre
md **CHONDRAL** cartilaginous
md **CHONDRIN** gelatinous liquid
CHOOSING selecting; picking
CHOP-CHOP hurry; (army)
CHOPNESS kind of spade
CHOPPING and changing; veering; cutting with axe; shortening stride (running)
ck **CHOP-SUEY** a succulent Chinese dish
mu **CHORAGIC** **CHORAGUS**, musical production
mu **CHORALLY** sung by choir or chorus
zo **CHORDATA** vertebrates, etc.
mu **CHORDING** stringing; time-spaced tonal effect
CHORIAMB iambic metre
bt **CHORISIS** separation
ag **C-HORIZON** soil level
CHORTLED chuckled loudly

CHORUSED concerted; in unison
CHOUSING swindling
ck, zo **CHOW-CHOW** ginger chutney; Chinese dog
ck **CHOW-MEIN** Chinese dish
CHRESARD plant water supply in earth
rl **CHRISMAL** (consecrated oil)
rl **CHRISTEN** baptize
ga **CHRISTIE CHRISTIANIA**, ski turn
CHRISTIE position for skateboard riding
ch **CHROMATE** salt of chromic acid
ch **CHROMIUM** a metallic element
bt **CHROMULE** colouring matter
ch **CHRYSENE** coal-tar component
CHTHONIC subterranean
CHUCKIES a game with pebbles
CHUCKING throwing; hurling; pat on chin
CHUCKLED laughed privately
CHUFFILY clownishly; churlishly
CHUMMAGE chamber-fellowship
CHUMMERY friendship; intimacy
CHUMMING sharing accommodation
CHUMMING ground bait for angling
CHUMP-END the buttocks; thick-end
CHURINGA Australian amulet
CHURLISH surly and sullen
CHURNING agitating; rotating; foaming
CHUTZPAH bold, impudent (Jew.)
md **CHYLIFIC** producing chyle
CHYMICAL chemical
ch **CHYMOSIN** gastric enzyme, rennin
CIBATION feeding
rl **CIBORIUM** eucharistic vessel
md **CICATRIX** a scar
CICERONE guide (tourism)
CICISBEI sword-knots
CICISBEO philanderer
CICURATE to tame
CIDER-CUP a beverage
CIDERIST cider-maker
CIDERKIN inferior cider
CILIATED with eyelashes
bt **CILIFORM** (fine filaments)
mu **CIMBALOM** Hung. concert dulcimer
CIMBRIAN a German tribe
mn **CIMOLITE** fuller's earth
cn **CINCHING** tightening roll of film
md **CINCHONA** Peruvian bark (quinine)
CINCTURE girdle; belt
CINDROUS ashy
cn **CINEFILM** moving-picture film
cn **CINERAMA** wide-screen film
CINERARY cindery
CINEREAL like ashes
CINGULUM band; zone; belt
mn **CINNABAR** dragon's blood
bt **CINNAMIC** cinnamon type
bt **CINNAMON** a spicy bark
CIPHERED written in code
CIRCAEAN infatuating (Circe)
as **CIRCINUS** the Compasses (constellation)
ae **CIRCLING** moving around in circles
CIRCUITY circuitous indirect approach
CIRCULAR round; printed leaflet
bt **CIRRHOSE CIRRHOUS**, terminating in a tendril or curl
zo **CIRRIPED** a barnacle
CISELEUR engraver; chaser
CISELURE chased metal-work
bt **CISTELLA** capsular shield
CISTVAEN stone tomb
CITATION mention in despatches
CITATORY citing; summoning
CITREOUS citric; lemon-flavoured
CITRININ bacteriostat
CITY-BRED raised in town
zo **CIVET-CAT** muskily perfumed carnivore
CIVETING scenting with civet
CIVILIAN non-military
CIVILIST civil law expert
CIVILITY politeness; courtesy
CIVILIZE reclaim from barbarism
CLACK-BOX valve container
CLACKING clicking; jabbering
ar **CLADDING** metal-surfacing coins; extra wall or roof surfaces; siding (USA)
bt **CLADONIA** reindeer moss
ml **CLAGGING** adhesion of blacking
CLAIMANT assertor of claims
CLAIMING demanding; arrogating
CLAMANCY urgency; exigency
ck **CLAM-BAKE** clam dish (Am.)
CLAMMING daubing; clogging; stickiness
CLAMPING fastening
mu **CLANGING** resounding; arousing
CLANGOUR din and noise; clamour (crowd)
CLANGOUS resonant
CLANKING metallic clashing noise
CLANNISH tribal; cliquish
CLANSHIP loyalty; sodality
CLANSMAN one of a clan
CLAP-DISH wooden platter
CLAPOTIS increasing pressure of larger waves breaking on sea wall
CLAPPING applauding; (–in jail)
CLAP-SILL frame of lock-gates

CLAP-TRAP speciosity; theatrical
CLAQUEUR hired applauder
CLARENCE four-wheeled cab
mu **CLARINET** reed instrument
mu **CLARSACH** Gaelic small Celtic harp
CLASHING colliding; jarring; differing
CLASHING unmatching colours
CLASPING fastening; grasping; hugging
eg **CLASP-NUT** split/lathe nut
CLASSIER superior; loftier; finer
CLASSIFY arrange; tabulate
CLASSING grading; grouping; ranging
CLASSMAN a graduate
CLASS-WAR social enmity (Marxism)
CLAUDIAN (Roman Emperors)
CLAUSURE closure; stoppage
CLAVATED with knobs on
mu **CLAVECIN** harpsichord
CLAVIARY index of keys
md **CLAVICLE** collar-bone
CLAVIGER clubman; key-man
CLAWBACK a sycophant
md **CLAW-FOOT** foot deformity
md **CLAW-HAND** hand deformity
CLAWLESS no claws
CLAWSICK foot-rot
CLAY-COLD lifeless
mn **CLAY-MARL** chalky clay
CLAY-MILL clay mixing mill
CLAYMORE Scottish broad-sword
bt **CLAYWEED** coltsfoot
eg **CLEADING** coffer dam; lock-gate boarding
CLEANING washing; purifying; clearing
CLEANISH rather clean
CLEANSED purged; purified
CLEANSER a detergent; purifier
CLEARAGE removal
CLEAR-CUT sharply outlined
CLEAREST plainest; purest
CLEARING meadow in forest; banking
CLEARING emptying; tidying up
CLEAVAGE fracture; bosom; separation
bt **CLEAVERS** goose-grass
CLEAVING splitting; riving
CLEAVING clinging; uniting; adhering
zo **CLECKING** a brood; a clutch
bt **CLEMATIS** traveller's joy, etc.
CLEMENCY clemence; leniency; mercy
CLENCHED clinched; gripped
CLERICAL priestly; secretarial
CLERKAGE clerical work
CLERKDOM babooism
CLERKERY accountancy
CLERKISH somewhat learned
mn **CLEVEITE** Norwegian pitchblende
CLEVERER more astute; abler
CLEVERLY dexterously; adroitly
CLICKING progressing satisfactorily
CLIENTAL dependent
CLIENTED supplied with clients
CLIMATIC due to climate
mo **CLIMBERS** undersurfaces for skis for uphill; ascenders (social-)
CLIMBING scrambling; scaling heights
CLINCHED **CLENCHED**, held fast; agreed on
CLINCHER decisive reply
bt **CLINGING** embracing tenaciously
md **CLINICAL** casework; analytic
CLINKING jingling (coins, keys etc.)
CLIPPERS **CLIPPING**, trimming (shearing) (toenails) (haircutting)
CLIQUISH **CLIQUISM**, clannish; exclusiveness (interests)
ec, mt **CLISSERE** climate changes and climaxes
zo **CLITELLA** bands of worms
bt **CLITHERS** burweed
CLITHRAL completely roofed
pl **CLITORIS** female erectile tissue
CLOAKAGE disguise; pretext
CLOAK-BAG portmanteau
CLOAKING hiding; veiling; screening
CLOCHARD tramp (Fr.)
CLOCKING checking in; timing
CLODDING clotting
CLODDISH boorish; rustic
CLODPATE dolt; blockhead
CLODPOOL dullard; clotpoll
CLOGGING coalescing; impeding
rl **CLOISTER** an ambulatory; veranda
CLOSE-CUT close-bodied; cropped
CLOSEOUT collapse of surfing wave
CLOSETED secluded
CLOTHIER cloth merchant; tailor
CLOTHING garments; dress; draping
CLOTPOLL **CLODPATE**, fathead; idiot
CLOTTING coagulating; curdling
CLOUDAGE cloudiness
CLOUDERY cloudage
CLOUDILY mistily
CLOUDING obscuring; dimming
CLOUDLET a little cloud
ar **CLOURING** chisel indentations on walls

CLOUTING patching; buffeting; clothing
CLOVERED in clover
CLOWNERY buffoonery; burlesque
CLOWNING playing the fool; jesting
CLOWNISH ungainly; rude; boorish
CLOYLESS insatiable
CLOYMENT a surfeit; a glut
CLOYSOME palling
CLUBBING combining; bludgeoning
CLUBBISH rustic; congenial
CLUBBISM the club system
CLUBBIST frequenter of clubs
CLUB-FIST large heavy fist
md **CLUBFOOT** taliped
nt **CLUBHAUL** tacking
CLUB-LAND (Pall Mall, etc.)
bt **CLUB-MOSS** lycopodium
CLUB-ROOM a meeting room
bt **CLUB-ROOT** a plant disease
bt **CLUB-RUSH** bulrush
CLUCKING fowl hen-talk
CLUELESS without a trace
CLUMPING (bootmaking); bunching
CLUMSIER more awkward
CLUMSILY maladroitly
zo **CLUPEOID** like a herring
bt **CLUSTERY** in clusters or bunches
CLUTCHED caught; gripped; clasped
CLYFAKER a pickpocket
CLYPEATE like a shield; oscutate
COACHBOX driver's seat
zo **COACH-DOG** Dalmatian; (spotted)
COACHFUL full inside
COACHING tutoring; driving; training; racing
COACHMAN a coachee
COACTING alliance; working together
COACTION compulsion; coercion
COACTIVE working in unison
COAGENCY joint action
md **COAGULUM** a blood clot
cp, tc **COALESCE** merge; unite; amalgamate
zo **COALFISH** black-backed cod
COAL-HOLE small coal-cellar
COAL-MINE coal-pit
nt **COAL-SHIP** a collier
COALWORK a colliery
nt **COAMINGS** raised work
COARSELY crudely; churlishly
COARSEST roughest; grossest
COARSISH rather coarse
CO-ASSUME agree
nt **COASTING** of navigation; free wheeling
COAT-LINK two buttons and a link
COBALTIC rather blue
COBBLING shoe-repairing
mn **COBCOALS** cobbles
rl **CO-BISHOP** joint bishop
mn **COBSTONE** large rounded stone
COBWEBBY araneous
bt **COCCAGEE** cider apple
md **COCCIDIA** parasites
bt **COCCULUS** narcotic plant
COCHLEAN COCHLEAR, spiral (of seashell); twisted pattern
COCKADED with rosette (on hat) (vanity)
zo **COCKATOO** crested parrot
COCKAYNE cocaigne; land of plenty
COCK-BEAD hanging decorative bead; moulding on edges of drawer fronts
nt **COCK-BILL** (anchor-dropping)
nt **COCK-BOAT** cog; lifeboat; tender
COCK-CROW dawn
COCKERED pampered
zo **COCKEREL** young cock
md **COCK-EYED** asquint; crooked
COCKLING puckering; wrinkling
COCKLOFT top loft; (highest perch)
COCKSHOT COCK-SHY, random shot fired
COCK-SHUT eventide; twilight; curfew
COCKSPUR Virginian hawthorn
COCKSURE determinedly certain
zo **COCKTAIL** mixed (coloured) drink; beetle
bt **COCOA-NUT** seed of cacao (chocolate) tree
COCOBOLO hard wood used for knife handles
bt, ck **COCOYAMS** product of Ghana
COCTIBLE able to be cooked
CODDCELL single electric cell
ck **CODDLING** pampering; indulging; (egg)
CODIFIED CODIFIER, systematized; sorted; a compiler; collator
tx **CODPIECE** Tudor genitals protector
nt **CODSHEAD** type of yacht
CO-EDITOR joint editor
COENZYME a fellow enzyme
COERCING compelling; curbing
COERCION force; constraint
COERCIVE repressive; compulsive
COESTATE union of estates
COEXPAND dilate simultaneously
COEXTEND march together
COFFERED COFFERER, packed in a box; sluice treasurer (safe-keeper)
COFFINED sealed; enclosed in box (funeral)
COGENTLY forcibly; potently

COGITATE ponder; meditate; ruminate
lw **COGNIZEE** fine receiver
lw **COGNIZOR** exacter of a fine
COGNOMEN the surname
lw **COGNOSCE** give judgment
lw **COGNOVIT** acceptance of claim
COGWHEEL spur-wheel
COHERENT connected; consistent; logical; comprehensible
COHERING adhering; uniting
COHESION congruity; adhesion
COHESIVE sticky; gummy
ch **COHOBATE** distil
COIFFEUR hairdresser
COIFFURE hairstyle; (wig)
COINCIDE happen simultaneously
CO-INHERE exist together
COINLESS impecunious; broke
COISTRIL a groom; see coystrel
COKE-OVEN coal carbonization process
COKERNUT coconut
COLANDER perforated bowl
COLATION filtration
COLATURE straining
COLDNESS frigidity
COLD-SETT Smith's chisel
COLDSHUT casting imperfection
pr **COLD-TYPE** printing
bt, ck **COLE-RAPE** kohlrabi; cabbage-turnip
bt **COLESEED** cabbage seed
COLESLAW cabbage salad
bt **COLEWORT** young cabbage
COLISEUM Roman ruin
ch **COLLAGEN** gelatine
ga **COLLAPSE** breakdown; subside; faint; fall; tactic
COLLARED pressed; caught
rl **COLLARED** necked shirt; band (dog-)
COLLARET small neck of garment; neck band
COLLATED collected; assembled
cp **COLLATOR** codifier; interpolator; verifier; assembler
COLLEGER Eton scholar
COLLETIC sticky; mucilaginous
COLLIDED crashed; encountered
COLLIERY coal-mine
COLLOGUE plot; confer
COLLOIDS the gummy sector of life (gelatin starch, paste); clay particles; smallest matter
COLLOQUY dialogue; conversation
COLLUDED acted in collusion
COLLUDER conspirator; plotter
COLLYING fouling
COLONIAL colonist
COLONIST a settler in the colonies
COLONIZE establish a colony
md **COLOPEXY** abdominal operation
COLOPHON publisher's tally mark
COLORATE coloured; dyed
bt **COLORINE** madder extract
COLOSSAL gigantic; titanic
COLOSSUS Apollo's statue
md **COLOTOMY** removal of colon
COLOURED specious; painted; tinged
COLSTAFF carrying pole
mn **COLUMBIC** containing niobium
COLUMNAR in columns
COLUMNED having pillars
COMATOSE lethargic; drowsy
COMATOUS sleepy; torpid
COMBINED united; coalesced
COMBINER a merger; blender
COMBLESS lacking comb or crest
COME-BACK repartee; return to fame
COMEDIAN actor; player; performer
COMEDIST writer of comedy
COME-DOWN humiliation; anti-climax
COMELILY attractively; gracefully
COMETARY planetarium; orrery
COMING-IN entrance; income
COMITIAL relating to assemblies
COMMANDO special raiding force
mu **COMMATIC** staccato; concise
COMMENCE initiate; begin; originate
COMMERCE barter; trade; traffic
COMMIXED blended; combined
COMMONED held in common
COMMONER not a nobleman
COMMONEY a playing-marble
COMMONLY usually; frequently
lw **COMMONTY** common land
COMMUNAL public
COMMUNED held private converse
COMMUTED exchanged; altered; bussed
COMMUTER season ticker holder
COMPAGES a complex structure
COMPARED likened
COMPETED strove; emulated
COMPILED amassed; composed; set in order
cp **COMPILER** literary hack; editor; computer program
COMPLAIN grumble; grouse; repine
COMPLETE ended; perfect; fulfil
COMPLICE to aid a crime
COMPLIED met; yielded; fulfilled
COMPLIER an active agent
rl **COMPLINE** evening service (Catholic)
hd **COMPONED** heraldic squares

COMPOSED calm; invented; produced
mu **COMPOSER** a creator; writer
mu **COMPOSTO** compounded; medley
COMPOUND combine; agree; mingle
COMPRESS abridge; condense; bandage
lw **COMPRINT** pirate
COMPRISE include; embrace; contain
COMPTOIR cash-desk
COMPUTED calculated; rated
COMPUTER actuary; reckoner
lw **CONACRED** sub-let
md **CONARIAL** **CONARIUM**, of the pineal gland
CONATION volition
CONATIVE endeavouring
CONCAUSE secondary cause
CONCAVED hollowed
CONCEDED granted; allowed; yielded
CONCEDER a donor; relinquisher
CONCEIVE imagine; think; fancy; plan
CONCEIVE become pregnant
mu **CONCERTO** orchestral work
CONCETTO a right merry conceit
mn **CONCHITE** fossil shell
CONCHOID shell-like curve
CONCLAVE synod; assembly; council
CONCLUDE close; terminate; infer
CONCOURS celebratory occasion; (fair)
CONCRETE not abstract; solid; cement
CONDENSE compress; solidify; shorten
CONDENSE steam change
ck **CONDITED** pickled; preserved
CONDOLED sympathized; commiserated
CONDONED pardoned; forgave
CONDUCED aided; led; promoted
CONE-GEAR variable-speed belt drive
CONFALON gonfalon; banneret
bt **CONFERVA** a seaweed
CONFETTI rice, petals thrown (wedding)
CONFIDED entrusted; hoped; relied
CONFIDER entruster of secrets
CONFINED limited; shut-up; restrained
CONFINED secluded for childbirth
CONFINER imprisoner
CONFLATE collect; assemble
CONFLICT combat; clash; discord
CONFOUND put to shame; refute; confuse
CONFRERE colleague; companion
CONFRONT to face a challenge
CONFUSED muddled disorder
CONFUTED overwhelmed by facts
CONGENER an affinity
CONGIARY Roman gift of wine
CONGRESS meeting for legislation etc.
CONGRESS representative assembly (Am.)
md **CONICINE** hemlock
CONICITY conicalness
bt **CONIFERS** (fir or pine) evergreens
CONIFORM conical
CONJOINT associated; connected
CONJUGAL matrimonial
CONJUNCT concurrent; united
lw **CONJURED** bound by oath; juggled
CONJURER **CONJUROR**, magician; juggler; wizard; marabout
mu **CONJUSTO** with gusto
CONNIVED overlooked; permitted
CONNIVER confidence man; accessory
CONNOTED included; implied
CONOIDAL almost conical
CONOIDIC conoidal
CONQUEST victory; subjugation
ck **CONSERVE** preserve; maintain
CONSIDER contemplate; regard; ponder
CONSOLED solaced; assuaged; cheered
CONSOLER a comforter; soother
CONSOMME clear soup
bt **CONSOUND** herb comfrey
CONSPIRE plot; intrigue; machinate
CONSTANT unchangeable; perpetual
CONSTRUE translate; interpret
CONSULAR Foreign Office service
CONSUMED eaten; used up; destroyed
CONSUMER customer; eater
lw **CONTEMPT** disdain; scorn; (–of court)
CONTENTS materials contained (written)
CONTINUE endure; extend; persist
mu **CONTINUO** harmonized keyboard accompaniment
pr **CONTLINE** intervening space
CONTRACT agreement; abridge
mt **CONTRAIL** condensation trail
CONTRARY otherwise; opposite
cp, el, pg **CONTRAST** difference; clash; comparison
CONTRITE penitent; repentant; humble

CONTRIVE bring about; scheme
CONTUSED bruised; crushed; knocked
CONUSANT knowing; cognizable
CONVENED called together; gathered
CONVENER summoner
CONVERGE approach; incline
CONVERSE talk; parley; reciprocal
CONVEXED vaulted
CONVEXLY in convex form
CONVEYED delivered; imparted
CONVEYER mechanical moving belt
CONVEYOR carrier (haulage)
CONVINCE persuade; satisfy; prove
CONVOKED convened; mustered
CONVOLVE roll together
CONVOYED escorted; guarded
CONVULSE writhe; agitate; perturb
CONY-SKIN rabbit-skin
CONY-WOOL rabbit's fur
mt **COOEEING** hailing in Australia
ck **COOK-ROOM** cook-house
ck **COOK-SHOP** eating-house
COOLNESS indifference; frigidity
COOPERED barrels constructed, repaired
CO-OPTING adding to a committee
CO-OPTION without election
zo **COPEPODA** water-boatmen; crustacea
md **COPHOSIS** deafness
COPHOUSE tool-house
md **COPOPSIA** eye-strain
ch **COPPERAS** sulphate of iron
COPPERED covered with copper
COPULATE unite; couple; mate
COPYBOOK exercise book; example
lw **COPYHOLD** land held under manorial records
COQUETRY flirtation; philandery
COQUETTE courtesan; jilt
COQUILLE conch-shaped guard of epée (fencing)
mn **CORACITE** uraninite
CORACOID like a crow's beak
CORANACH a dirge
bt **CORDATED** heart-shaped
le **CORDINER** **CORDWAINER**, leather worker (Sp.)
el, tc, cp **CORDLESS** without plug-in connection
le **CORDOVAN** **CORDWAIN**, goatskin leather of Cordoba (Spain)
tx **CORDUROY** ribbed cloth
CORD-WOOD firewood; tinder wood
CO-REGENT joint ruler
CORE-SAND linseed moulding mixture
CORK-SOLE inner shoe-sole
bt **CORK-TREE** cork-oak (quercus suber)
zo **CORKWING** a sea-fish
bt **CORKWOOD** balsawood (USA)
ck **CORN-BALL** pop-corn; maize
bt **CORN-BIND** convolvulus
ck **CORNCAKE** Indian meal cake
CORNEOUS horny
CORNERED brought to bay; controlled
CORNETCY rank of a cornet (army)
bt **CORNFLAG** gladiolus
CORNICLE a little horn
zo **CORNICLE** honeydew tube in aphids
CORNIFIC horn-producing
CORNLAND grain-land
CORNLOFT granary
ck **CORNMEAL** coarse maize flour
CORN-MILL a grinder; quern
bt **CORN-MINT** calamint
zo **CORN-MOTH** a pest
CORN-PIPE straw-pipe
ck **CORN-PONE** bread (Indian corn)
CORN-RENT rent paid in corn
CORNUTED with horns
CORN-WAIN farm-cart; (haywain)
nt **COROCORE** Malay boat
bt **COROLLET** a floret
CORONACH coranach; a lament
md **CORONARY** crown-shaped, heart artery
CORONATE crowned
ch **CORONIUM** gaseous element
zo **CORONOID** **CORACOID**, of a crow's beak
bt **CORONULE** downy tuft on seeds
CORPORAL bodily; material; an N.C.O.
rl **CORPORAS** fine linen
CORRIDOR passage-way; gallery
CORRODED eaten away; rusted; eroded
CORSELET corslet; leather cuirass
CORSICAN of Corsica; (Napoleon)
md, bt **CORTICAL** outer tissue (brain), bark (tree)
pm **CORTISOL** adrenal hormone extract
CORUNDUM emerald; ruby; sapphire
nt **CORVETTE** sloop; convoy escort; naval
CORYBANT priest of Cybele
CORYMBUS top-knot
mu **CORYPHEE** ballet-dancer
zo **CORYSTES** masked crab
COSECANT an inverse sine
lw **COSENAGE** **COSINAGE**, cousinhood; a writ
COSHERED pampered; coddled

COSHERER (free board and lodgings)
COSINESS snugness
COSMETIC a beautifier
COSMICAL relating to the universe
COSSETED petted; fondled; caressed
COSTATED ribbed
COST-BOOK account book
COST-FREE free of charge
COSTLESS without price; free
COSTLIER more expensive; dearer
bt **COSTMARY** aromatic plant
COST-PLUS of contracts
COSTUMED garbed; dressed; robed
COSTUMER costumier; dressmaker
CO-SURETY joint security
COTCHELL privately sold timber
tx **COTELINE** ribbed muslin
lw **CO-TENANT** joint tenant
COTHOUSE a cottar's house
mu **COTILLON** cotillion; round dance
COTQUEAN a womanly man
zo **COTSWOLD** sheep
COTTABUS wine-throwing contest
COTTAGED covered with cottages
COTTAGER small holder
COTTONED attracted to; understood
COTYLOID cup-shaped
hd **COUCHANT** reclining
md **COUCHING** removing cataract
COUGHING a raucous noise
COULISSE theatrical side-scene
bt **COUMARIC** from Tonka beans
bt **COUMARIN** a scent
COUNTESS wife of earl or count
COUNTING reckoning; enumerating
COUNT-OUT adjournment; boxing
COUPELET cabriolet
mu, rw **COUPLING** linking; a link; mating
COURANTE French dance; a paper
mu **COURANTO** musical piece
COURSING racing; chasing; pursuing
lw **COURT-DAY** sessions-day
COURTESY polished manners
COURTIER courtesy personified
COURTING wooing; soliciting; inviting
ck **COUSCOUS** a millet dish (N. Africa)
COUSINLY friendly
COUSINRY kin; relations
COUTILLE material for corsets
ch **COVALENT** bond: 1 electron to 2 atoms
lw, rl **COVENANT** contract; bond; pact
COVENTRY ostracism (sent to–)
COVERAGE protection; insurance
COVER-ALL an overlay; genital protection
COVERCLE a lid
COVERING protecting; including; roof
COVERLET bed cover; counterpane
COVERLID coverlet
COVERTLY surreptitiously; insidiously
COVETING acquisitiveness
COVETOUS avaricious; rapacious
COVINOUS collusive; fraudulent
COWARDLY timidly; cravenly
mu **COWBELLS** alpine percussion
bt **COWBERRY** whortleberry
COWERING crouching; cringing
bt **COWGRASS** meadow trefoil
COWHIDED whipped
COWHOUSE a byre; milking-shed
COW-LEECH cow doctor (veterinerary)
CO-WORKER fellow toiler
zo **COWPILOT** West Indian fish
bt **COWPLANT** plant (Sri Lanka)
COW-THIEF a rustler
bt **COW-WHEAT** annual plant
md **COXALGIA** hip disease
COXINESS conceit; bumptiousness
nt **COXSWAIN** steersman; cox
COYSTREL **COYSTRIL**, **COISTRAL**, a groom; a knave
COZENAGE deception; deceit; fraud
COZENING cheating; swindling
CRABBING peevish criticism; grousing
bt **CRABTREE** crab-apple
bt **CRABWOOD** S. American tree
md **CRAB-YAWS** foot disease
CRACKING distilling; splitting
CRACK-JAW difficult to pronounce
CRACKLED crepitated
CRACKNEL a biscuit
CRACK-POT a maniac; crazy
CRACOWES pointed shoes
CRADLING timber framework; goal pass (lacrosse)
CRAFTIER slyer; more cunning
CRAFTILY shrewdly; pawkily
CRAGSMAN rock-climber
CRAM-FULL no more room
CRAMMING stuffing; tutoring
CRAMOISY **CRIMSON**, **CREMOSIN**, blood red
CRAMPING restraining; impeding
CRAMPONS mountaineering spiked boots
zo **CRANE-FLY** daddy-longlegs
zo **CRANIATE** vertebrates with skull
CRANKING winding; turning; twisting
eg **CRANK-PIN** link; crank/connecting rod
CRANNIED full of chinks

CRANNIES nooks; fissures
CRASHING blundering; clashing; colliding
CRATCHES mangers; swollen pastern
CRAVENLY cowardly
md **CRAW-CRAW** tropical skin disease
zo **CRAWFISH** **CRAYFISH**, langouste
CRAWLING on all fours; creeping; paint cracking, cissing
CRAWLWAY high duct, man-size
CRAYONED drawn with chalk
CRAZIEST maddest; most idiotic
CREAKING grating
CREAMERY milk-bar; dairy
CREAMING foaming; mantling
CREAM-NUT Brazil nut
CREAM-POT cosmetic container
CREASING folding
ck, md **CREATINE** gristle on meat; chemical in muscle
CREATING begetting; fashioning
CREATION the universe; cosmos; product
CREATIVE inventive; productive
CREATRIX a designing lady
CREATURE term of contempt
rl **CREDENCE** belief; credit; reliance; sacrament table
rl **CREDENDA** articles of faith
CREDENZA low cupboard on floor
CREDIBLE trustworthy; believable
CREDIBLY conceivably
CREDITED trusted; accepted
CREDITOR a lender; mortgagee
CREEPING crawling; cringing; stealing
CREMATED reduced to ashes
CREMATOR incinerator
CREMORNE French-window bolt
CREMOSIN crimson; cramoisy
CRENATED notched
CRENELET small loophole
CRENELLE arrow hole; loophole
CREOLIAN of **CREOLES**
ch, md **CREOSOTE** tar product; wood seasoning
CREPANCE brushing, grooming of horses
md **CREPITUS** lung-rattle
CRESCENT Turkish emblem; moon
CRESCIVE growing; increasing
CRESTING topping; surfing; decorating; coloured identity of arrow (archery)
CRETATED chalked
CRETONNE patterned cloth
nm **CREUTZER** Austrian copper coin
CREVASSE fissure in glacier
CREVICED rent; cracked; flawed
CRIBBAGE card game
CRIBBING shift lining; copying
CRIBBLED sifted; riddled
CRIBRATE perforated
CRIBROSE full of holes
ce **CRIB-WORK** a form of structure; bridge foundation
zo **CRICETUS** genus of rodents
CRIMEFUL criminal; wicked; culpable
lw **CRIMINAL** felon; convict; illegal
CRIMPAGE press-gang work
ck **CRIMPING** plaiting; pattern on pastry
CRIMPLED curled
CRINATED hairy
CRINGING fawning; crouching; servile
CRINKLED wrinkled; corrugated
CRIPPLED disabled; impaired; maimed
CRISPATE curly
CRISPING crimping; twisting; waving
CRISTATE crested; tufted
CRITERIA standards of judgement
bt **CRITHMUM** the samphire
CRITICAL crucial; fault-finding; serious
nc **CRITICAL** nuclear transformation; chain reaction
CRITIQUE literary notice
CROAKING woeful; sound (frogs)
CROCEOUS yellow; like saffron
CROCKERY earthenware
CROCKING blackening with soot
mn **CROCOITE** chromate of lead
ag **CROFTING** farming; hill-farming
CROMLECH ancient stone circle
mu **CROMORNA** organ-stop
CROODLED cowered
CROOKING bending; inflecting
mu **CROONING** warbling; chromatic singing
CROPPING harvesting; lopping; cutting
CROP-SICK sick of a surfeit
CROSS-BAR transverse bar
CROSSBIT cheated
CROSS-BOW a weapon
ck **CROSS-BUN** hot cross-bun
to **CROSS-CUT** short cut; large saw
CROSSING a ford; traversing
hd **CROSSLET** small heraldic cross
au **CROSS-PLY** standard flexible-tread
pr **CROSS-ROW** the alphabet
CROSS-SEA choppy tide versus wind
CROSS-TIE railway sleeper

CROSSWAY by-way
mu **CROTALUM** castanet; small bell
mu **CROTCHED** forked
CROTCHET whimsey; fancy; conceit
bt **CROTONIC** (croton-oil)
bt **CROTTLES** lichens used for dyeing
CROUCHED cringed; fawned; truckled
CROUPADE equestrian feat
CROUPIER a raker of shekels; (casino)
md **CROUPOUS** croupy; hoarse coughing
md **CROW-BILL** forceps
CROWDING urging; pressing; swarming
bt **CROWFOOT** buttercups (ranunculus)
CROWMILL crow-trap
CROWNING a coronation
CROWNING (-mercy) completing
CROWNLET small crown
to **CROWN-SAW** circular saw
bt **CROW-SILK** aquatic plant
CRUCIATE cruciform
CRUCIBLE melting pot
CRUCIFER cross-bearer
rl **CRUCIFIX** religious emblem
ck **CRUDITES** raw-vegetable salad
CRUELEST most ruthless; harshest
nt **CRUISING** voyaging; sailing
nt **CRUISING** zigzag patrolling
CRUMBING covering with crumbs
CRUMBLED disintegrated; crushed
CRUMENAL a purse
CRUMPLED ruffled; rumpled; wrinkled
CRUNCHED munched
CRUSADED campaigned for Holy Land
CRUSADED undertook reforming activities
CRUSADER valiant reformist
CRUSHING subduing; overpowering
CRUSTILY morosely; sullenly
bt **CRUSTOSE** uninterrupted crust
CRUTCHED on crutches
zo **CRUTCHET** the perch, fish
nm **CRUZEIRO** Brazil currency unit
mn **CRYOLITE** a transparent stone
ps **CRYOSTAT** low-temperature thermostat
el **CRYOTRON** small electronic switch
ma **CUBATION CUBATURE**, determination of cubic contents
md **CUBEBINE** a carminative
CUBIFORM cubical
CUBOIDAL cube-like
CUCHILLA uplands (S. Amer.)
bt **CUCUMBER** a creeping plant
ch **CUCURBIT** distilling vessel
CUDDLING fondling; petting; hugging
CUFFLINK wrist adornment (shirt)
CUL-DE-SAC dead-end; blind alley
CULINARY au cordon bleu
CULLYING imposing on
CULLYISM being a simpleton
CULPABLE censurable; blameworthy
CULPABLY guiltily; sinfully
CULTRATE knife-like
CULTURAL of group norms; of the arts
CULTURED intellectual; refined
CULVERIN a cannon
CUMBERED hampered; clogged
gl **CUMBRIAN** of Cumbria (Cumberland)
CUMBROUS unhandy; clumsy
CUMULATE a mass; collect
CUMULOSE heaped
CUNABULA a cradle; incunabula
CUNABULA books prior to A.D. 1500
CUNARDER a Cunard steamship
CUNEATED wedge-shaped; cuneiform
CUNIFORM Assyrian writing, etc.
CUPBOARD a repository
eg **CUP-CHUCK** bell-chuck on lathe
CUPIDITY covetousness; avarice; desire
CUP-JOINT male/female pipe joint
CUPREOUS like copper
ch **CURARINE** curari extract
CURARISE to poison with curari
zo **CURASSOW** S. American turkey
CURATIVE healing; restorative
CURATORY remedial; antidotal
CURBLESS without restraint
CURB-ROOF bent roof
zo **CURCULIO** corn-worm; weevil
CURDLING congealing; thickening
CURLICUE a fantastic curl; pig's tail
CURLIWIG a curved piece
CURRENCY coin; flow; circulation
CURRICLE two-wheeled chaise
ck **CURRYING** Indian cooking; seasoning
CURRYING combing, brushing horses; (–favour)
CURSEDLY as deserving a curse
lw **CURSITOR** Chancery writ writer
zo **CURSORES** running birds
CURTNESS abruptness; terseness
CURTSIED made obeisance (women)
CURVATED curved; bent
CURVITAL not straight
CUSPIDAL pointed
CUSPIDOR a spittoon

CUSTOMED specially made to order
CUSTOMER purchaser; client; patron
lw **CUTCHERY** Indian court
CUT-GLASS art glassware
rl **CUTHBERT** Northumbrian apostle
CUT-PRICE bargain offer; cheap
CUTPURSE pickpocket
CUT-UNDER (fencing)
nt, ce **CUTWATER** prow; wedge shape of stone piers; breakwater
ch **CYANOGEN** poisonous gas
md **CYANOSIS** skin disease
md **CYANOTIC** (blue jaundice)
bt **CYCLAMEN** primrose family
CYCLE-CAR side-car (motorbike)
ch, ps **CYCLICAL** of circle; ring of atoms
mt **CYCLONIC** like a hurricane
zo **CYCLOPIA** one median eye (cyclops)
CYCLOPIC gigantic; monstrous
CYCLOSIS circulation; cell movement
cp **CYLINDER** closed tube (combustion) (expansion) (gas) (steam); data store
ce **CYLINDER** solid roller; monolith, bored piles
ar **CYMATIUM** cyme; a moulding
md **CYNANCHE** sore throat
CYNICISM misanthropy
CYNOSURE centre of attraction
CYRENAIC of Cyrene
CYRILLIC (Slavic alphabet)
md **CYSTICLE** small cyst
md **CYSTITIS** inflammation of bladder
CYTISINE laburnum alkaloid
CYTOLOGY study of cells
ch **CYTOSINE** nucleic acid hydrolysis
zo **CYTOSOME** cell cytoplasm
CYTOZOIC intra-cellular; living in a cell
CZECHISH characteristic of Czechs

D

DABBLING meddling; trifling; ducks feeding
zo **DAB-CHICK** grebe; diving bird
md **DACRYOMA** defective tear duct
md **DACRYOPS** eyelid cyst
DACTYLAR (finger); (toe)
DACTYLIC (verse)
DADDLING tottering locomotion
ga **DADDLUMS** form of skittles
ar **DADO-RAIL** edge of border panelling
DAEDALUS human glider
DAEMONIC diabolical; satanic
bt **DAFFODIL** Lent lily
DAFTNESS lunacy; stupidity
DAGGERED stabbed
DAGGLING trapesing
tx **DAG-SWAIN** coarse woollen fabric
nt **DAHABIAH DAHABIEH**, state barge of Nile
DAINTILY delicately; elegantly
ag **DAIRYING** supplying milk
DAIRYMAN dairy keeper; milkman
DALESMAN northern English dale dweller
DALLYING trifling; delaying; fondling
DALMAHOY bushy bob-wig
rl **DALMATIC** long white vestment
DAMAGING injuring; impairing
DAMASKED variegated
DAMASKIN Damascus sword
tx **DAMASSIN** damask cloth
DAMBOARD draughtboard
bt **DAME-WORT** dame's violet
DAMNABLE pernicious; execrable
DAMOCLES his sword was a hanger
DAMPENED moistened; discouraged
DAMPNESS humidity
mn **DANALITE** iron/beryllium silicate
ar **DANCETTE** Norman zigzag moulding
DANDIEST neatest; eye-catching
DANDLING fondling; caressing
md **DANDRUFF** scurf
DANDYISH foppish
DANDYISM elegance in attire
DANDYIZE dress ostentatiously
DANE-GELD tribute paid to Danes by Anglo-Saxons
DANELAGH Danish England (A.D. 878)
bt **DANE-WEED** a plant
bt **DANE-WORT** dwarf elder
DANGLING hanging by a thread
DANSEUSE ballerina
DANUBIAN (Danube)
zo **DAPEDIUS** ganoid fish
mn **DAPHNITE** iron-rich chlorite
DAPPERLY in neat, spruce style
DAPPLING with patches of shade
DARING-DO derring-do; act of high daring, mischief
DARINGLY intrepidly; bravely
DARKENED obscured; clouded
DARKNESS night; ignorance
DARK-ROOM a developing locality
DARKSOME mysterious; dismal
DASTARDY cowardice; base timidity
zo **DASYURES** Australian marsupials
DATELESS immemorial; timeless
DATE-LINE where East meets West
bt, rl **DATE-PALM** Biblical palm
bt **DATE-PLUM** persimmon

bt **DATE-TREE** (many varieties)
mn **DATOLITE** a silicate
ch **DATURINE** thorn-apple alkaloid
DAUBSTER poor painter
DAUGHTER person's female child
DAUNTING intimidating; dismaying
DAUPHINE dauphin's wife
mn **DAVY-LAMP** miner's safety lamp
DAWDLING dallying; lagging; trifling
DAYBREAK dawn; dawning; day-spring
DAY-DREAM reverie; visionary scheme
pc **DAYDREAM** mental meandering
DAYLIGHT illumination
DAYSHIFT working period (industrial)
DAY-SIGHT night-blindness
DAY-TO-DAY of successive days; programme
DAY-WOMAN daily cleaner; charlady
DAZZLING bewildering; confusing (light)
DEAD-BEAT exhausted
DEAD-BORN still-born
DEADENED retarded; benumbed
DEAD-FALL animal trap
DEAD-FIRE death omen
DEAD-HEAT equal winners
DEADLIER more malignant
DEAD-LIFT (no leverage or help)
DEADLINE a boundary; time-limit
DEADLOCK no compromise; impasse
DEAD-LOSS complete loss
DEAD-MEAT meat for market
DEADNESS inertness; inertia
DEAD-PULL dead-lift
nt **DEADRISE** design of rise from ship's bottom
DEAD-ROPE fixed rope in dead-eye
DEAD-SHOT unerring marksman
DEAD-WALL windowless wall
mt **DEAD-WIND** calm
DEAD-WOOD decayed or useless wood
DEAD-WORK unprofitable work
bt **DEAD-WORT** species of elder
DEAFENED stunned
DEAF-MUTE deaf and dumb
md **DEAFNESS** hard of hearing
zo **DEAL-FISH** a thin fish
rl **DEANSHIP** offfice of dean
DEARNESS costliness; tenderness
DEARNFUL solitary; mournful
DEATH-BED place of dying
DEATHFUL fateful; moribund
bt **DEBARKED** tree with bark removed
DEBARRED excluded; prohibited
DEBASING degrading; vitiating
DEBATING discussing; disputing
DEBILITY functional weakness
DEBITING charging
DEBONAIR genial; cheerful; merry
DEBOUCHE emerge from narrow to wider place
DEBTLESS owing naught
DEBUNKED shown up
DEBUTANT a starter
DECADENT degenerate
me **DECAGRAM** 10 grams
ae **DECALAGE** wing chords angle
DECAMPED sloped off; fled; bolted
DECANTED poured out
DECANTER glass wine bottle
zo **DECAPODA** prawns, lobsters, crabs
DECAYING rotting; declining; ebbing
DECEASED dead; departed; defunct
DECEIVED beguiled; duped; gulled
DECEIVER impostor; trickster
DECEMBER 10th Roman month
bt **DECEMFID** ten-cleft
DECEMVIR Roman magistrate
DECENTLY in fitting good taste
lw **DECERNED** judged; decreed
pm **DECICAIN** local anaesthetic
DECIDING settling; resolving
bt **DECIDUAL** able to be cast off (leaves)
me **DECIGRAM** one-tenth of gram
DECIMATE kill one in ten
DECIPHER decode
cp **DECISION** verdict; firmness; chosen action
DECISIVE final; conclusive
ga **DECKGAME** shipboard game
nt **DECK-HAND** seaman
DECK-LOAD deck-cargo
DECLARED said; announced; averred
DECLINED pined; sank; shunned
DECLINER a refuser
DECLUTCH gear-changing (motoring)
DECOCTED boiled down; concentrated
DECODING deciphering
DECORATE deck; embellish; garnish
DECOROUS proper; befitting; seemly
DECOYING luring; enticing; inveigling
DECREASE minimize; reduce; curtail
DECREPIT broken down
rl **DECRETAL** a Papal decree
DECRYING disparaging; vilifying
DECUPLED tenfold
DECURION controller of ten
DECURVED straightened; (unbent)
DEDENDUM wheel/cylinder radial distance

DEDICATE devote; consecrate; assign
DEDUCING inferring; drawing; deriving
DEDUCTED subtracted; withdrawn
lw **DEEDLESS** without document of legality
lw **DEED-POLL** a legal instrument
lw **DEEMSTER** **DEMPSTER**, Manx judge
DEEP-DYED extreme; rascally
DEEPENED became more mysterious
DEEP-LAID cunning; intricate
DEEP-MOST uttermost
DEEPNESS profundity
DEEP-READ scholarly
to **DEERFOOT** leathercraft
bt **DEER-HAIR** heath club-rush
DEER-HERD a herd of deer
DEER-LICK salt lick
DEER-NECK scraggy
DEER-PARK paddock enclosure, zoo
DEERSKIN leather
DEFACING disfiguring; marring; spoiling
DEFAMING slandering; traducing
DEFEATED frustrated; overthrown
DEFECATE purge; empty bowels
DEFECTOR deserter; traitor
DEFENCED fortified; walled; covered
DEFENDED warded off; shielded
DEFENDER protector; advocate
DEFERRED postponed; adjourned
DEFERRER a procrastinator
DEFIANCE a challenge; provocation
DEFILING polluting; corrupting
DEFINING explaining; specifying
DEFINITE precise; exact; certain
DEFLATED punctured; of economics
DEFLEXED relaxed of muscles
DEFLEXOR metal outrigger (hang gliding)
DEFLOWER deprive of virginity; rape
DEFOREST clear of trees
DEFORMED disfigured; misshapen
DEFORMER destroyer of symmetry
DEFRAYAL payment
DEFRAYED met the cost; paid
DEFRAYER liquidator; settler
DEFTNESS adroitness; dexterity
pc **DEFUSION** breakup of balance
DEGRADED reduced in rank
DEGREASE remove the grease
DEHORNED dodded (cattle)
DEIFICAL making divine
DEIFYING exalting to Godship
DEIGNING condescending; vouchsafing
DEISHEAL clockwise
DEJECTED downcast; chapfallen
DEJECTLY gloomily; dolefully
DEJEUNER breakfast; lunch (Fr.)
ps **DEKATRON** cold cathode sealing tube
DELAYING retarding; hindering
DELECTUS classical anthology
DELEGACY spreading responsibility
DELEGATE appoint in one's stead
DELEGATE official conference attendee
DELETING obliterating; effacing
DELETION erasure; expunction
DELETIVE delible
DELETORY erasive; blotting
DELIBATE cleanse mouth between tastings
DELICACY consideration; tact; relish
DELICACY a (luxury) edible
DELICATE dainty; frail; slight
DELIMING hide lime-salt removal
DELIRIUM mental aberration; mania
DELIVERY rescue; distribution; (childbirth)
DELOUSED cleared of vermin
DELPHIAN oracular
zo **DELPHINE** dolphin
DELUBRUM shrine; sanctuary
DELUDING duping; gulling; misleading
DELUGING pouring; inundating
DELUSION fallacy; imposture
DELUSIVE deceptive; fallacious
DELUSORY illusory; deceitful
DEMAGOGY popular oration technique
DEMANDED queried; exacted; claimed
DEMARCHE ultimatum; counter-stroke
DEMEANED degraded; behaved
DEMENTED daft; crazy; deranged
md **DEMENTIA** insanity; lunacy
bt **DEMERARA** brown sugar
DEMIBAIN sit-bath
DEMI-FOND motor-paced cycle race
DEMIJOHN super flask in basket
DEMILUNE ravelin; fortification
DEMISING bequeathing; devising
DEMISSLY humbly
au **DEMISTER** windscreen condensation preventive
DEMI-TINT a shade
mu **DEMI-TONE** semitone
DEMITTED dismissed; resigned
DEMIURGE Plato's world-maker
DEMI-VOLT an equestrian trick
zo **DEMI-WOLF** progeny of dog and wolf
DEMOBBED demobilized; discharged
DEMOCRAT upholder of democracy

DEMOLISH destroy; raze; dismantle
DEMOLOGY social statistics
DEMONESS a diabolical lady
DEMONIAC possessed; infernal
DEMONISM Satanic cult
DEMONIST devil worshipper
DEMONIZE turn into a devil
DEMONOMY dominion of devils
DEMPSTER see deemster
DEMURELY gravely; sedately; modestly
DEMURRED hesitated; wavered; paused
lw **DEMURRER** a plea; objector
DEMYSHIP an Oxford scholarship
nm **DENARIUS** former English penny; d
DENATURE denaturalize
bl **DENDRITE** receptor; neuron
mn **DENDROIT** tree-like fossil
DENEGATE deny; contradict; refute
DENEHOLE shaft cut in chalk
DENIABLE controvertible; refutable
DENOTATE denote; signify
DENOTING indicating; designating
DENOUNCE impeach; censure; threaten
md **DENTAGRA** toothache
DENTATED with teeth; notched
ar **DENTELLE** tooth-like decoration or edging
zo **DENTICLE** small projection; teeth in fish
DENTIZED toothed
gl **DENUDATE** strip bare; divest; erosion
DENUDING the soil (by erosion, chemicals)
DEPARTED left; gone away; withdrew
DEPARTER metal refiner
DEPENDED relied on; trusted factor
DEPICTED described; limned; portrayed
DEPICTOR painter; artist
DEPILATE remove hair
DEPLETED emptied; drained
DEPLORED lamented; bewailed; grieved
DEPLOYED extended; unfolded
DEPLUMED plucked
lw **DEPONENT** a witness
lw **DEPONING** testifying under oath
DEPORTED expelled; banished
DEPORTEE person forcibly removed
DEPOSING ousting former ruler
DEPRAVED corrupt; vicious; profligate
DEPRAVER vilifier; reprobate
DEPRIVED robbed; dispossessed
DEPRIVER a despoiler; brigand
DEPUTING authorizing; charging
DEPUTIZE delegate; act for another
rw **DERAILED** off the lines
rw **DERAILER** train-wrecker
DERANGED disordered; insane; mad
DERATING reducing liability
DERATION to end limits of purchase
DERBY-DAY in June (horse race)
DERBY-DOG also ran
DERELICT abandoned; deserted; ruin
DERIDING mocking; lampooning
DERISION laughing stock; mockery
DERISIVE scoffing; ridiculous
DERISORY scornful; contemptuous
DERIVATE a derivative
DERIVING deducing; tracing; obtaining
md **DERMATIC** relating to the skin
DEROGATE disparage; detract
DESCRIBE portray; narrate; tell
DESCRIED observed; espied; discerned
DESERTED forlorn; left; abandoned
DESERTER quitter; renegade; turncoat
DESERVED justified; merited; earned
DESERVER meritorious person
DESIGNED projected; invented; drew
DESIGNER schemer; contriver
DESILVER extract silver from
DESIRING craving; wanting
DESIROUS covetous; eager; longing
DESISTED stopped; ceased; forbore
DESK-WORK clerical work
DESOLATE solitary; deserted
DESPATCH **DISPATCH**, expedite; send
DESPISAL contempt; scorn
DESPISED disdained; ignored; scouted
DESPISER scorner; contemner
DESPITED vexed; offended; teased
DESPOTAT territory under despot
DESPOTIC tyrannical; arbitrary
DESTINED ordained; fated
zo **DESTRIER** second charger
pc **DESTRUDO** desire for death, destruction
DETACHED isolated; disengaged
DETAILED particularized; recounted
DETAILER enumerator; narrator
DETAINED delayed; restrained; held
lw **DETAINER** withholder of goods
DETECTED found out; unmasked
DETECTOR detecter; discoverer
DETERGED cleansed; wiped
DETERRED prevented; hindered

DETESTED odious; abominated; loathed
DETESTER abhorrer
DETHRONE depose; discrown
DETONATE explode violently
DETONIZE fulminate
DETRITAL (detritus); residual
gl **DETRITUS** disintegrated material; eroded
DEUCE-ACE a throw at dice
DEUCEDLY confoundedly
ch **DEUTERON** charged particle
zo **DEUTOVUM** development stage in acarina
DEVALUED depreciated
pc **DEVIANCE** differing from norms
DEVIATED swerved; strayed; veered
DEVIATOR a wanderer
DEVILDOM kingdom of hell
DEVILESS demoness
DEVILISH fiendish; malignant; diabolic
DEVILISM devil worship
DEVILKIN imp
ck **DEVILLED** highly seasoned; curried
DEVISING scheming; bequeathing
DEVISING producing (entertainment)
lw **DEVOLVED** transferred; handed over
gl **DEVONIAN** of county; era
DEVOTING dedicating; consecrating
DEVOTION zeal; piety; attachment
DEVOURED bolted; consumed; gobbled
DEVOURER absorber; destroyer
DEVOUTLY earnestly; piously; holily
bt **DEWBERRY** the bramble
DEWINESS precipitation
DEW-POINT a critical temperature
mn **DEWSTONE** a limestone
ch **DEXTRINE** starch gum
DEXTRONE synthetic blood
ch **DEXTROSE** glucose sugar
DEXTROUS dexterous; skilful
DEZINKED freed from zinc
mn **DIABASIC** greenstone type
md **DIABETES** sugar sickness
md **DIABETIC** of diabetes
DIABLERY diablerie; impishness
DIABOLIC satanic; demoniac; fiendish
DIACETYL colour/flavour constituent in butter
bt **DIACHYMA** cellular tissue
zo **DIACOELE** 3rd brain ventricle in craniata
rl **DIACONAL** concerning deacons
DIACTINE having two rays
bt **DIADELPH** twin
DIADEMED crowned
md **DIADEXIS** disease mutation
DIADOCHI ancient governors (Gr.)
DIAGLYTH an intaglio; carved gem
md **DIAGNOSE** identify
DIAGONAL cross-tie
DIAGRAPH drawing instrument
mn **DIALLAGE** monoclinic pyroxene
DIALLAGE rhetorical argument
tc **DIALLING** selecting telephone numbers
DIALOGIC in dialogue form
cp, tc **DIALOGUE** two talking; two-way exchange
md **DIALYSED DIALYSER**, of kidney-cleaning process
ch, md **DIALYSIS DIALYTIC**, filtration of body salts; unbracing
DIAMANTE artificial glitter stones
ma **DIAMETER** line halving a circle
bt **DIANDRIA** two-stemmed plants
DIANODAL traversing a node
bt **DIANTHUS** carnations, pinks, etc.
mu **DIAPASON** concord of sounds
zo **DIAPAUSE** life-cycle stage in insects
mu **DIAPENTE** interval of a fifth
tx **DIAPERED** clothed with nappy
tx **DIAPHANE** transparent-woven silk
DIAPHONE electrical fog-signal
mu **DIAPHONY** part-writing based on plainsong
DIARIZED recorded in a diary
DIASPORA Jew dispersion
mn **DIASPORE** aluminium hydrate
DIASTASE malt sugar
DIASTEMA tooth-gap in jaw; stage of protoplasm
md **DIASTOLE** heart dilatation
ar **DIASTYLE** proportion in colonnades
ch **DIATOMIC** (two atoms)
mu **DIATONIC** natural scale
DIATRIBE stream of invective; tirade
DIBBLING planting
DIBSTONE stone used in a game
cy **DICARYON** simultaneously dividing nuclei
mn **DICE-COAL** small coal
bt **DICENTRA** bleeding-heart
DICE-PLAY dicing
ch **DICHLONE** chemical fungicide
md **DICHOTIC** contrasting ear stimulation
DICHOTIC doubled; twinned
DICHROIC double refraction
DICKERED bargained
DICLINIC crystalline shape
ch **DICLORAN** chemical fungicide
md **DICROTIC** double pulsation
DICTATED bid; prescribed; ordained

DICTATOR autocrat; despot; tyrant
bt **DICYCLIC** with 2-whorled perianth
DIDACTIC instructive; moral; directive
DIDACTYL with all hind-foot toes separate
zo **DIDAPPER** dabchick; grebe
DIDDERED couldn't decide; dithered
DIDDLING cheating; trifling; dawdling
bt, zo **DIDYMATE** in pairs; twins
ch **DIDYMIUM** a rare metal
bt **DIDYMOUS** growing in pairs
DIEGESIS explanation; narrative
bt **DIELYTRA** the bleeding-heart
DIE-STOCK die-holder
DIETETIC (food regime)
DIFFERED disagreed; diverged; varied
DIFFRACT break; refract
DIFFUSED disseminated; spread
bd **DIFUSER** a spray; a damper for chimney or ducts
mn **DIGENITE** cubic copper sulphide
DIGESTED classified; codified; arranged
ch **DIGESTER** an industrial 'cooker' (chemical)
DIGGABLE suitable for spade work
DIGGINGS (gold); archaeological
bt **DIGITATE** having five leaflets
el **DIGITRON** numerical read-out glow tube
zo **DIGITULE** fingerlike process
bt **DIGONOUS** with two angles
bt **DIGYNIAN** **DIGYNOUS**, flowers having cleft styles
DIHEDRAL angle between planes
DIHEDRON geometric figures
el **DIHEPTAL** of 14 in number
gn **DIHYBRID** from parents different in 2 aspects
ch **DIKETONE** CO-group-containing compound
DILATANT swelling; elastic
DILATING expanding; stretching
md **DILATION** distention; amplification; by stimulation
DILATIVE expansive
DILATORY tardy; dallying; lagging
DILIGENT busy; industrious; assiduous
DILLY-BAG for billycan (Australian)
DILUTING attenuating; weakening
DILUTION watering; reducing
DILUVIAL alluvial
DILUVIUM glacial or flood deposit
ch **DIMEDONE** alcohol-detecting reagent
zo **DIMEGALY** with different-sized spermatozoa
DIMERISM duplex arrangement
DIMEROUS in two parts
DIMETRIC tetragonal
DIMINISH cut; abate; lessen; curtail
DIMPLING smiling
zo **DIMYARIA** molluscs
DINAMODE unit of work, metre-ton
DINARCHY dual control
DINER-OUT a table companion
DING-DONG hammer and tongs; church bells
nt **DINGHIES** small boats
DINGIEST dullest; dirtiest
zo **DINORNIS** moa-bird, N. Zealand
DINOSAUR of extinct reptile community
rl **DIOCESAN** a bishop's council
DIOGENIC (Diogenes); cynical outlook on life
mn **DIOPSIDE** augite
DIOPTASE copper silicate
DIOPTRIC (refraction of light)
DIORAMIC of small tableaux exhibition
mn **DIORITIC** (igneous rock, diorite)
DIOSCURI Castor and Pollux
zo **DIPCHICK** **DABCHICK**, grebe
DIPHASIC in two phases
DIPHENYL coal-tar chemical
md **DIPLEGIA** paralysis
el **DIPLEXER** two-way transmitter
DIPLOGEN deuterium; heavy hydrogen
DIPLOMAT ambassador; envoy
md **DIPLOPIA** double vision
cy **DIPLOSIS** chromosome doubling
zo **DIPNOOUS** having lungs and gills
DIPROTON two-proton system
bt **DIPSACUS** the teasel
md **DIPSOSIS** morbid thirst
zo **DIPTERAL** with two wings
zo **DIPTERAN** a fly
ar **DIPTEROS** (double peristyle)
DIPTYCHA writing tablets
DIRECTED addressed; enjoined
DIRECTLY expressly; soon; forthwith
DIRECTOR manager; controller
DIRENESS horror; calamity
pl, md **DIRHINIA** of both nostrils
DIRIGENT directing
DIRTIEST filthiest; most sordid
DIRTYING fouling; soiling
DISABLED incapacitated; crippled
DISABUSE enlighten; undeceive
ch **DISACRYL** acrolin polymer
DISADORN deprive of ornament

DISAGREE differ; vary; deviate
DISALLOW reject; forbid; disclaim
DISANNEX surrender former gains
DISARMED subdued; stripped
DISARRAY disorder; undress
DISASTER calamity; catastrophe
lw **DISBENCH** of judges (unseat)
DISBOSOM reveal
DISBURSE expend; spend
DISCIPLE learner; follower; pupil
DISCLAIM disown; reject; renounce
DISCLOSE reveal; tell; betray
DISCOUNT allowance; forestall; deduct
DISCOVER detect; espy; divulge
ch **DISCRASE** a silver salt
DISCREET circumspect; prudent
DISCSEAL form of valve
DISEASED indisposed; unhealthy; sickly
DISENDOW deprive of endowments
rl **DISFROCK** expel from clergy
lw **DISGAVEL** a change in tenure
DISGORGE surrender; eject; vent
DISGRACE ignominy; dishonour
DISGUISE conceal; mask; cloak
DISHEVEL disarray
DISHORSE unhorse
DISINTER exhume; unbury
DISINURE render unfamiliar
zo **DISIPPUS** an American butterfly
DISJOINT dislocate
DISLEAVE deprive of leaves
DISLIKED detested; hated; loathed
DISLODGE evict; eject; oust
DISLOYAL false; perfidious
DISMALLY drearily; dolefully
DISMAYED terror-struck; appalled
DISMOUNT alight; descend; unhorse
DISORDER confusion; turbulence
DISOWNED repudiated; denied
DISPATCH despatch; expedite; send
DISPATHY antipathy; allergy
DISPENSE administer; dispence
DISPERSE scatter; diffuse; dispel
cp **DISPERSE** redistribute data
DISPIRIT discourage; dishearten
DISPLACE remove; discharge; oust
DISPLAIT untwist; unravel
DISPLANT uproot; eradicate
DISPONED disposed
lw **DISPONEE DISPONER**, (conveyance of property in legal form)
lw **DISPONGE DISPUNGE**, expunge
rl **DISPOPED** deprived of popedom
lw **DISPOSAL** right of bestowing
DISPOSED inclined; arranged; biased
DISPOSER administrator
DISPROOF refutation; rebuttal
DISPROVE confute; refute
DISPUNGE disponge; expunge
DISPUTED contested; wrangled
DISPUTER arguer; debater
DISQUIET to vex; unease; anxiety
DISRATED reduced in rank; degraded
DISROBED divested; denuded
DISROBER raiment remover
DISSEVER cut in two; rend
DISSOLVE loosen; liquefy; end
DISSUADE deter; disincline
zo **DISTALIA** 5 bones in tetrapod limb
DISTANCE interval; space; outstrip
DISTASTE aversion; antipathy
mn **DISTHENE** cyanite; kyanite
DISTINCT definite; clear
DISTITLE deprive of right
zo **DISTOMUM** liver-fluke parasite
DISTRACT divert; harass; bewilder
lw **DISTRAIN** seize for debt
DISTRAIT absent-minded
DISTRESS anguish; suffering; worry
DISTRICT territory; region; quarter
DISTRUST discredit; doubt; suspect
DISTUNED put out of tune
DISUNION breach of concord
DISUNITE separate; disrupt
DISUNITY isolation; dissension
DISUSAGE disuse; desuetude
DISUSING abandoning
DISVALUE underrate; disprize
DISYOKED untrammelled
zo **DITCH-DOG** dead dog
DITCHING excavating; clearing
bt **DITHECAL** with two spore-cases
rl **DITHEISM DITHEIST**, co-existence of a good and an evil god
DITHERED hesitated
DITOKOUS having twins
mn **DITROITE** coarse-grained alkali/syenite rock
DITTY-BAG sailor's kit-bag
DITTY-BOX sailor's treasure-box
md **DIURESIS** increased urination
md **DIURETIC** urination stimulant
DIVAGATE digress; wander
ch **DIVALENT** bivalent
DIVE-BOMB aerial attack
DIVERGED deviated; digressed; veered
DIVERTED distracted; amused
DIVERTER an entertainer
DIVESTED stripped; deprived; bared
DIVIDEND interest; share; profit
ce, nv **DIVIDERS** drawing, measuring instrument

DIVIDING cleaving; parting
bt **DIVI-DIVI** pods used in tanning
DIVINELY heavenly; exquisitely
DIVINIFY treat as divine
rl **DIVINITY** deity; theology
DIVINIZE deify
DIVISION category; army unit
DIVISIVE dissentient; discordant
DIVORCED forced assunder
DIVORCEE person divorced
DIVORCER divorcing person
DIVULGED communicated; revealed
DIVULGER betrayer of secrets
DIZZYING confusing
rl **DOCETISM** doctrine of a sect
rl **DOCETIST** a 2nd-century heretic
DOCHMIAC Greek metrical foot
DOCILITY pliance; tameness
DOCIMACY metallurgy
nt **DOCKYARD** naval establishment
DOCTORAL (doctor)
md **DOCTORED** treated; doped
DOCTORLY scholarly
DOCTRINE dogma; creed; tenet
lw **DOCUMENT** writing; record; writ; account
DODDERED quaked; tottered
DODDERER senile senior
ch **DODECANE** paraffin
DODIPOLL dolt; numbskull
DODONIAN oracular
DOGBERRY ignorant parish official
bt **DOG-BRIER** dog-rose
DOG-CHEAP bargain price
DOG-EARED crinkled corner
DOGESHIP chief Venetian office
DOG-FACED unprepossessing
DOGGEDLY obstinately; stolidly
DOGGEREL bad verse
DOGGONED confounded
bt **DOG-GRASS** couch grass
DOG-HOUSE kennel
DOG-LATIN barbarous Latin
DOG-LEECH a vet
DOGMATIC dictatorial; arbitrary
bt **DOG'S-BANE** a poisonous plant
DOG'S-BODY utility man
DOG-SLEEP cat-nap
DOG'S-MEAT offal
DOG'S-NOSE beer and gin
DOG-TIRED spent
ar **DOG-TOOTH** a Norman moulding
DOG-TRICK a currish wile
nt **DOG-WATCH** short ½ watch
DOG-WEARY exhausted
bt **DOG-WHEAT** dog-grass
zo **DOG-WHELK** kind of mollusc
DOLDRUMS calm zone; depression
gl **DOLERITE** medium-grain-size igneous rock
DOLESOME dismal; rueful
bt **DOLICHOS** hyacinth bean
DO-LITTLE lazy-bones
DOLLARED flush; wealthy
DOLLED-UP dressed showily
DOLLHOOD dollship
DOLLY-MOP handled mop
DOLLY-TUB washing tub
mn **DOLOMITE** magnesian limestone
mu **DOLOROSO** pathetically
DOLOROUS sorrowful; dolesome
DOMAINAL DOMANIAL, (landed estate); (scope)
DOMELIKE dome shaped
lw **DOMESMAN** judge; umpire
DOMESTIC household; maid
DOMICILE habitation; residence
mu **DOMINANT** prevailing; ruling; 5th note of scale
DOMINATE control; override
DOMINEER to hector; to sway
DOMINION sovereignty
DOMINIUM ownership
DOMINOES hooded capes; a game
DONATING giving; bestowing
DONATION presentation; offering; alms
rl **DONATISM** a Christian cult
DONATIVE gratuity; benefice; largesse
lw **DONATORY** recipient of land
DOOLTREE duletree; the gallows
bt **DOOM-PALM** Egyptian palm
DOOMSDAY domesday (Book)
DOOMSDAY end of the world
DOOMSMAN domesman; judge
DOOR-BELL a ringer
DOOR-CASE door framework
DOOR-KNOB a handle
DOORLESS without portal
DOORNAIL considered as dead
DOOR-POST regarded as deaf
DOOR-SILL lower framework
DOOR-STEP slice of bread (slang)
DOOR-YARD an enclosure
DORICISM Doric in expression
DORMANCY abeyance; latency
zo **DORMOUSE** somnolent rodent
zo **DORR-HAWK** night jar
zo **DORSALIS** dorsal organ artery
md **DOSOLOGY** science of doses
DOTATION donation; dowry
DOTINGLY stupidly; fondly
zo **DOTTEREL** a plover
DOUANIER custom-house officer (Fr.)

DOUBLETS Tudor dress; (dice)
DOUBLING folding; running
nm **DOUBLOON** Spanish guinea
DOUBLURE book-binding
DOUBTFUL uncertain; ambiguous
DOUBTING distrusting; querying
DOUBTIVE questionable; dubious
DOUCHING spraying
DOUGHBOY American infantryman
DOUGHNUT a confection
bt **DOUM-PALM** doom-palm
DOURNESS obstinacy; grimness
DOVECOTE pigeon house
DOVE-EYED meek-eyed
DOVELIKE gentle; innocent
DOVESHIP qualities of a dove; (man of peace)
DOVETAIL a joint; synchronize
DOWDYISH rather slovenly
DOWDYISM shabbiness
DOWELLED pinned together
DOWEL-PIN a fastening
DOWERING endowing; bequeathing
DOWFNESS lethargy; dullness
DOWNBEAR depress
mu **DOWN-BEAT** descending stroke (conductor); gloomy; relaxed; informal
DOWNBORE discouraged
DOWNCAST dejected
DOWNCOME sudden fall
DOWNFALL debacle; ruin
nt **DOWNHAUL** a sheet
DOWNHILL a declivity
DOWNLAND hilly pasture land
rw **DOWN-LINE** (railways)
DOWNPIPE rainwater runaway
DOWNPOUR continuous heavy rain
DOWNRUSH downward draught
pc, cp, tc **DOWN-TIME** depression; machine inoperable
DOWNTOWN business centre
DOWNTROD trampled; tyrannized
DOWNWARD descending
bt **DOWNWEED** cotton weed
rl **DOXOLOGY** hymn of praise
DOZINESS drowsiness
tx **DRABBETT** DRABETTE, twilled linen used for smocks
DRABBISH slatternly; dowdy
DRABBLED fouled with mire
nt **DRABBLER** a sail extension
bt **DRACANTH** gum; tragacanth
DRACONIC (Draco); severe
DRAFTING sketching; drawing up; conscripting; formulating
DRAFTING technique of cycling, driving
DRAG-BOLT draw-bar
DRAGGING tugging; tedious; pulling; forbidden footwork (netball); (motor racing)
DRAGGLED wet and dirty
DRAG-HOOK a connection
DRAG-HUNT foxing the hounds with a scented trail
DRAGOMAN guide; interpreter
zo **DRAGONET** small dragon; a fish
hd **DRAGONNE** heraldic lion-dragon
DRAG-SHOE a brake
DRAINAGE sewage system
DRAINING emptying; exhausting
DRAMATIC theatrical; powerful voice
DRAMMOCK drummock; skilly; gruel (Sc.)
DRAM-SHOP shebeen; illicit bar
DRAUGHTS a game
DRAUGHTY inconveniently airy
DRAWABLE representable
DRAWBACK detriment; defect
DRAWBOLT coupling pin
DRAWBORE carpentry
DRAWGATE sluice gate
DRAW-GEAR harness; railway coupling
DRAWLING droning
DRAW-LINK a couple
DRAW-WELL deep well
DREADFUL frightful; dire; horrific
DREADING fearing; awing
DREAMERY reverie
DREAMFUL fanciful; dreamy
DREAMILY vaguely
DREAMING imagining
DREARILY gloomily; dismally
ce **DREDGING** deepening; sprinkling; underwater excavation
DREGGISH foul with lees
DRENCHED saturated; inundated
DRENCHER a soaker
DRESSAGE training of horses competition
md, bd **DRESSING** alignment; draping; binding; finishing stonework
ck **DRESSING** putting on apparel (–room); (salad–)
DRIBBLED slobbered; footwork with ball
ga **DRIBBLER** (baby); footballer
DRIBBLET a small drop
nt **DRIFTAGE** leeway
DRIFT-ICE polar ice; iceberg
DRIFTING passively awaiting events
DRIFT-NET drifting herring net
DRIFT-WAY cattle-road; leeway
to **DRILL-BOW** a boring device

DRILL-BOX seed-box
DRILLING training; perforating
DRINKING imbibing; carousing
ae **DRIP-FLAP** part of balloon
ck **DRIPPING** pork or suet fat spread; running tap
DRIVABLE condition of road for traffic
DRIVEWAY **DRIVE**, private access road
DRIZZLED rained softly
DROGHING coastal trade, W. Indies
DROILING drudging; loitering
DROLLERY buffoonery; waggery
DROLLING jesting; clowning
DROLLISH fairly facetious
DROMICAL (race-course)
zo **DRONE-FLY** drone-bee
DROOLING slavering; slobbering
DROOPING withering; languishing
DROP-DOWN short first title in book
DROP-GOAL two points
au **DROPHEAD** convertible automobile
DROPKICK football
zo **DROPPING** spoor of animals; sheldrakes (flock)
DROPPING letting fall; releasing; abandoning
DROP-RIPE fruits ready to fall
DROPSHOT tennis
DROP-SLIP book stockist's order
DROPWISE in drops
bt **DROPWORT** meadow-sweet
DROTCHEL idle wench; slut
DROUGHTY thirsty; arid
DROWNING submerging; overwhelming
DROWSILY sleepily
DROWSING dozing
DRUBBING beating; mauling
DRUDGERY slavery; ignoble toil
DRUDGING moiling; plodding
DRUDGISM menial occupation
md **DRUGFAST** drugproof; immune
DRUGGING inducing stupor
DRUGGIST chemist; chymist
DRUIDESS lady soothsayer
DRUIDISM Celtic cult
DRUMFIRE continuous fire
zo **DRUMFISH** North American fish
DRUMHEAD (service; court-martial)
DRUMMING vibrating
DRUNKARD toper; dipsomaniac
zo **DRY-BIBLE** cattle-disease
DRY-CLEAN without using water
DRY-FLIES artificial gnats as bait (angling)
DRY-GOODS drapery
DRY-PLATE photographic plate
DRY-POINT engraving needle
DRY-STEAM (no unevaporated water)
DRY-STONE (no mortar used)
DRY-STOVE hot-house
DUALIZED halved; split in twain
DUBITATE to doubt; to vacillate
nm **DUCATOON** scudo; silver coin
ck **DUCHESSE** a table-cover; potato dish
zo **DUCKBILL** platypus; duck-mole
DUCK-DIVE swimming-dive
pr **DUCK-FOOT** lowered inverted commas
zo **DUCK-HAWK** marsh-harrier
DUCK-HOOK very low stroke to left (golf)
zo **DUCKLING** young duck
zo **DUCK-MOLE** duckbill
DUCKPINS variation of ten-pin alley
DUCK'S-EGG a zero (cricket)
DUCK-SHOT pellets for wild fowl
bt **DUCK-WEED** a water weed
md **DUCTLESS** endocrine gland
DUELLING **DUELLIST**, fighting in single combat
DUELSOME prone to duelling
mu **DUETTINO** short duet
mu **DUETTIST** a performer
DUKELING a petty duke
DUKERIES ducal country seats
DUKESHIP ducal rank
mu **DULCIANA** (It.) soft organ stop
mu **DULCIMER** stringed cimbalom (Hung.)
DULCITOR saccharine; sweetener
DULE-TREE **DOOL-TREE**, the gallows
DULL-EYED lacking expression
DULL-HEAD a dolt
DULLNESS dulness; apathy
DUMB-BELL no ringing tone
DUMB-CAKE (baked on St Mark's Eve)
bt **DUMB-CANE** (causing dumbness)
DUMBNESS muteness
DUMB-SHOW pantomime
DUMMERER bogus mute
DUMOSITY prickliness
ck **DUMPLING** pudding
DUNCEDOM the class of dunces
zo **DUN-DIVER** goosander
DUNGAREE Indian cloth; overalls
DUNG-FORK a gardening implement
DUNG-HILL cock's castle
DUNG-MERE **DUNG-YARD**, manure pit
pl **DUODENAL** **DUODENUM**, first of the small intestines
DUOLOGUE two in conversation; a debate
el **DUOPHASE** choke-use in valve circuit

ps **DUPLEXER** two channel multiplexer (radar)
DURATION indefinite length of time
DUSKNESS twilight
DUST-BALL horse disease
DUST-CART rubbish conveyor
DUST-COAT light house-coat
DUST-HOLE ash-bin
gl **DUSTWELL** dust in glacial hollow
DUTCHMAN Hollander
DUTIABLE subject to customs
DUTY-FREE off-shore transit purchases
DWARFING stunting; overshadowing
DWARFISH pygmy; undersized; tiny
md **DWARFISM** growth-hindering condition
DWELLING domicile; habitat
DWINDLED declined; shrank
DYE-HOUSE where dyeing is done
DYE-STUFF dye material
DYEWORKS coloration factory
ps, mu **DYNAMICS** masses in motion; gradations (loud, soft) in music
DYNAMISM DYNAMIST, theory of imminent energy
DYNAMITE powerful explosive
nt **DYNASHIP** modern automaton sailing ship
DYNASTIC in succession
DYNATRON electrical oscillation
md **DYSBASIA** walking difficulty
md **DYSCHROA** skin disease
DYSGENIC detrimental to the race
DYSLALIA over-age baby talk
DYSLEXIA reading learning difficulty
mn **DYSLUITE** manganese ore
mn **DYSODILE** lignite
md **DYSOPSIA** dimness of sight
md **DYSOREXY** depraved appetite
DYSPATHY antipathy
md **DYSPEPSY** indigestion
DYSPHONY difficulty of speaking
md **DYSPNOEA** difficulty in breathing
md **DYSTOCIA** difficult birth-labour
mn **DYSTOMIC** (imperfect fracture)
md **DYSTONIA** impaired muscle tone

E

zo **EAGLE-OWL** great horned owl
zo **EAGLE-RAY** devil-fish
EAR-BORED (for ear-rings)
EARPHONE a receiver
zo **EAR-SHELL** a sea-shell
EARTH-BAG sandbag
EARTH-FED earthly contented
zo **EARTH-HOG** aardvark
EARTHING burrowing; burying
bt **EARTH-NUT** pig-nut, peanut
bt **EARTH-PEA** hog peanut
EAR-TO-EAR a definite distance
lw **EASEMENT** relief; privilege; right of passage
EASINESS facility; comfort; quiet
EASTERLY oriental
EASTLAND the Orient
EASTMOST farthest east
EASTWARD toward the rising sun
tx **EASY-CARE** minimal-creasing fabrics
EAU-DE-NIL dull green colour (Nile)
EAU-DE-VIE brandy; akvavit; (vodka)
EBENEZER memorial stone; chapel
rl **EBIONIZE EBIONISM, EBIONITE,** Jewish-Christian sect that upheld the Mosaic laws
ch **EBLANINE** volatile crystal
EBONIZED blackened
EBURNEAN EBURNINE, like ivory
zo **ECAUDATE** tailless; Manx
rl **ECCLESIA** an assembly; a church
ECCYESIS external foetus development
ch **ECGONINE** coca-base alkaloid
ECHINATE prickly; bristled
mn **ECHINITE** fossil sea-urchin
zo **ECHINOID** like a sea-urchin
bt **ECHINOPS** globe thistle, etc.
zo **ECHIODON** sand-eel type
ECHOLESS no repetition
md **ECLAMPSY** epilepsy
ECLECTIC derived from selected sources
as **ECLIPSED** obscured; disgraced
ECLIPTIC a great circle
mn **ECLOGITE** crystalline rock
zo **ECLOSION** emergence from egg case
pc **ECMNESIA** loss of short items of memory
ec **ECOCLINE** variations based on unalike habitats
ECONOMIC frugal; thrifty; careful
ECOPHENE physiologically habitat-affected type
bt **ECOSTATE** ribless
ECPHASIS explicit declaration
pc **ECPHORIA** establishing memory trace
md **ECRASEUR** surgical instrument
ECSTATIC rapturous; beatific
zo **ECTOCYST** outer cyst layer; exoskeleton
md **ECTODERM** outer skin, also of embryo
bt **ECTOGENY** pollen effect on female plant organs

zo **ECTOLOPH** mammalian tooth edge
zo **ECTOZOAN** an external parasite
rl **ECUMENIC** promoting universal Christian unity
EDACIOUS greedy; voracious
EDDERING making up fences
EDDY-WIND back draught
zo **EDENTATA EDENTATE**, animal lacking front teeth
EDGE-BONE aitch bone; rump bone
EDGELESS blunt
EDGE-RAIL an iron rail
to **EDGE-TOOL** cutting tool
EDGEWAYS EDGEWISE, sideways
EDGINESS angularity
EDIFYING enlightening; instructive
EDITRESS woman editor
EDUCABLE teachable
EDUCATED instructed; taught; literate
EDUCATOR tutor
EDUCIBLE show from various evidence
EDUCTION extraction; deduction
bt **EEL-GRASS** grass-wrack
EEL-SPEAR fisherman's fork
zo **EELWORMS** plant-parasites; nematodes
EERINESS weirdness; creepiness
EFFACING expunging; deleting; erasing
EFFECTED accomplished; executed
EFFECTOR effecter; creator; doer; realizer
pl **EFFECTOR** active organ cells
EFFERATE irritating person
EFFERENT conveying outward
EFFICACY production power
EFFIGIAL relating to images
EFFIGIES images; likenesses; guys
EFFLUENT a stream; outflow; with sewage
EFFLUVIA noxious exhalations
EFFULGED shone in radiant splendour
EFFUSING emanating; pouring
EFFUSION unrestrained expression of words, feelings
EFFUSIVE emotionally demonstrative; gushing
EFTSOONS soon after; again
EGESTING discharging
EGESTION excretion
bt **EGG-APPLE** brinjal; aubergine
EGG-DANCE ancient blindfold hop
pt **EGG-GLAIR** pre-gilding eggwhite surface
EGG-GLASS sand-glass
bt **EGG-PLANT** brinjal; aubergine
EGG-SHELL thin porcelain; paint
ck **EGG-SLICE** frying spatula
EGG-SPOON small pointed spoon
EGG-TOOTH knob on chick's beak
EGG-WHISK wire brush
bt **EGLATERE** eglantine; sweetbriar
pc **EGO-ALIEN** refusal to accept self
EGOISTIC self-assertive; self-contained
pc **EGOMANIA** self-preoccupation
pc **EGOPATHY** aggressive; boasting
md **EGOPHONY** a pleurisy symptom
EGOTIZED self-conceited
EGRESSED departed; left
EGYPTIAN (Egypt); gipsy; tiny peg
EIGHTEEN 1½ dozen
EIGHTHLY an ordinal number
EJECTING rejecting; cashiering
EJECTION discharge; dismissal
EJECTIVE expulsive; emissive
ch **ELAIDATE ELAIODIC**, castor-oil derivative
ELANCING darting; casting; launching
zo **ELAPHINE** like a stag
ELAPHURE a deer
ELAPSING slipping away
ELAPSION lapse; interval
ELASTICS pack-opening bands (parachuting)
ELATEDLY in high spirits
ch **ELATERIN** cucumber extract
ELBOWING jostling; nudging
ELDER-GUN pop-gun
ELDORADO land of fabulous wealth
ELECTING choosing; preferring
ELECTION freewill; choice; acceptance
ELECTION voting for candidates, parties
ELECTIVE selective; preferential
el **ELECTRET** permanently polarized material
ELECTRIC stimulating
ELECTRON (negative electricity)
ELECTRUM silver and gold alloy
ELEGANCE refinement; taste; grace
ELEGANCY beauty of propriety
ELEGANTE lady of fashion
ELEGIAST sorrowful bard
ELEGIZED lamented in verse
ELENCHIC elenctic; refutatory
ELENCHUS a sophism
pr, zo **ELEPHANT** size of paper; mammoth
bt **ELEUSINE** tropical grass
ELEVATED high; exalted; dignified
ELEVATOR a lift; animator; tail plane flap; (wrestling)

ELEVENTH ordinal number; (last hour)
ELF-ARROW flint arrow-head
ELF-CHILD a changeling
ELICITED deduced; extracted; evoked
ELIDABLE suppressible
ELIGIBLE fit; fully qualified
ELIGIBLY desirably; worthily
ELIMATED polished; smoothed
ELINGUID tongue-tied
ELLIPSIS gap; omission; hiatus
ELLIPTIC oval
ELOCULAR without partitions
ELOINING banishing
ELONGATE stretch; extend; lengthen
ELOQUENT fluent and impressive
ELSEWISE otherwise; differently
ELUDIBLE avoidable; escapable
mn **ELVANITE** crystalline rock
ELVE-LOCK elf-lock
ELVISHLY mischievously; impishly
ELYDORIC oil and water-colour
zo **ELYTRINE** (beetle wing material)
EMACIATE waste away; decline; pine
EMANATED derived from; originated
EMBALING bundling; packing
EMBALMED cleansed body (Egypt)
EMBALMER preserver; mortician
EMBANKED mounded
EMBARKED ventured; undertook
nt **EMBARKED** entered a ship
EMBARRED encaged; shut in
EMBATTLE draw up for battle
nt **EMBAYING** enclosing in a bay
EMBEDDED firmly established
EMBEZZLE appropriate; peculate
EMBITTER exacerbate; exasperate
EMBLAZED displayed; bedecked
EMBLAZON blaze; adorn; embellish
EMBODIED incorporated; integrated
EMBODIER codifier; merger
EMBOGGED mired; bogged
EMBOGUED emptied; discharged; fell
EMBOLDEN encourage; reassure; impel
md **EMBOLISM** intercalation; obstruction
mn **EMBOLITE** a silver ore
EMBOLIUM narrow corium strip in hemiptera
EMBORDER adorn with a border
EMBOSSED ornamented in relief
EMBOSSER a craftsman
EMBOTTLE to bottle
EMBOWING arching; vaulting
EMBRACED embodied; clasped; hugged
lw **EMBRACER** corrupter of a jury
EMBRONZE fashion in bronze
EMBRUTED brutalized
EMBRYOUS inaugural
EMBUSSED loaded on a bus
EMENDALS repair-work
EMENDATE to correct; to rectify
EMENDING amending; reforming
EMERGENT pressing; urgent
EMERGING issuing; arising
EMERITED put on retired list
EMERITUS retired with honour
EMERSION reappearance; emergence
md **EMETICAL** ejective
EMIGRANT distant home seeker
EMIGRATE migrate; remove
EMINENCE distinction; celebrity
EMINENCY a title
EMISSARY envoy; spy; agent
EMISSILE capable of being emitted
EMISSION discharge; ejection
EMISSIVE emanative; expulsive
md **EMISSORY** a duct; channel
EMITTING issuing; delivering
rl **EMMANUEL** Immanuel; Messiah
EMMARBLE enmarble; petrify
EMMEWING confining; penning
EMPACKET to pack up
EMPALING IMPALING, transfixing
EMPARKED enclosed
EMPATRON patronize
EMPAWNED pledged
EMPHASIS stress; force; accent
EMPHATIC definite; positive; earnest
EMPLANED boarded an aeroplane
EMPLOYED at work; occupied
EMPLOYEE a wage earner; hand
EMPLOYER the boss
EMPLUMED plumed
EMPOISON embitter; envenom
EMPORIUM large store; mart
EMPTYING exhausting; discharging
md **EMPTYSIS** haemorrhage
EMPURPLE to dye
EMPUZZLE mystify; bewilder; nonplus
EMPYREAL ethereal; aerial; sublime
EMPYREAN highest; heaven
EMULATED vied; strove; competed
pc **EMULATOR** rival; copyist; bridging device
EMULGENT flowing; oozing
EMULSIFY liquate; blend
EMULSINE a fermented mixture
EMULSION milky liquid
EMULSIVE milk-like
ENABLING empowering; allowing
ENACTING decreeing; ordaining
ENALLAGE change of tense, etc.
hd **ENALURON** heraldic bordure

ENARCHED like a rainbow
ENCAGING confining; immewing
bd **ENCALLOW** brick claypit surface mould
ENCAMPED pitched; settled
ar **ENCARPUS** festoon of fruit
ENCASHED realized; cashed
ENCASING boxing; packing
bd **ENCASTRE** end-fixed, of a beam
ENCAVING hiding in a cave
ENCHARGE to trust
ENCHASED decorated
ENCHISEL to chisel
ENCHORIC demotic
ENCIRCLE encompass; hem; environ
ENCLISIS ENCLITIC, (grammatical accentuation)
ENCLOSED wrapped; enveloped
ENCLOSER fencer of land
ENCLOTHE to clothe
ENCOFFIN prepare for burial
ENCOLLAR encircle
ENCOLOUR tinge
ENCOLURE horse's mane
ENCOMIUM panegyric; eulogy
ENCORING calling for a repeat
ENCRADLE lay in a cradle
mn **ENCRINAL ENCRINIC**, (fossilized sea-lilies)
ENCROACH trench; intrude; infringe
ENCUMBER burden; clog; obstruct
ENCURLED interlaced
ENCYCLIC Catholic circular
md **ENCYSTED** enclosed in a wart or shell
ENDAMAGE cause loss; spoil
ENDANGER hazard; imperil; jeopardize
ENDEARED beloved; made fond
ENDEMIAL locally prevalent
ENDENIZE naturalize
md **ENDERMIC** (through the skin)
bt **ENDOCARP** inner coat of fruit
zo **ENDOCYST** inner membrane
zo **ENDODERM** inner skin
ENDOGAMY tribal intermarriage
pl **END-ORGAN** receptor, motor nerve
ENDORSED ratified; approved
ENDORSEE the assignee
bt **ENDOSARC** endoplasm
zo **ENDOSOME** protozoa nuclei central mass
ENDOWING presenting; bequeathing
bt **ENDOZOIC** living inside animal
pr **ENDPAPER** link between cover and book
zo **END-PLATE** muscle motor-nerve ending
el **END-PLATE** type of electrode
ENDURING lasting; persisting
mu **ENERGICO** with vitality
ENERGIZE animate; excite; force
ENERVATE weaken; sap; relax
ENFEEBLE debilitate; paralyse
ENFETTER manacle; shackle
ar **ENFILADE** to rake; gunfire volley in battle; doors in sequence
ENFOLDED clasped; enclosed
ENFORCED compelled; obliged
ENFORCER active agent; rules referee; cop; pressurizer
ENGAGING winning; charming
ENGENDER produce; beget
ENGILDED gilt
ENGINEER scheme; a sapper; (civil); mechanic; fitter; contriver
ENGINERY implement of war
ENGINING contriving; racking
ENGIRDED encircled
ENGIRDLE encompass; encircle
hd **ENGLANTE** heraldic acorns, etc.
ENGORGED glutted
hd **ENGOULED** heraldic absorption
ENGRAVED scribed; chiselled; cut
ENGRAVER carver; sculptor
ENGROOVE cut a furrow
ENGULFED devoured; overwhelmed
ENHANCED heightened; raised
ENHANCER augmenter
ENJOINED commanded; directed
ENJOINER prohibiter
ENJOYING appreciating; delighting in
ENLACING encircling; entwining
ck **ENLARDED** basted with fat
ENLARGED dilated; expanded
ENLARGER an amplifier
ENLISTED enrolled; engaged
ENMESHED entrapped; caught
ENNEADIC nine of
ENNEAGON nine-sided polygon
ENNEATIC ninth
ENNOBLED made illustrious
ENORMITY atrocity; depravity
ENORMOUS vast; monstrous; gigantic
ENQUIRED inquired; investigated
ENQUIRER a snooper; questioner
ENRAGING maddening; exasperating
ENRAVISH enrapture; entrance
ENRICHED endowed; adorned
ENRICHER a fertilizer
ENRIDGED furrowed; corrugated
ENRINGED encircled
ENROBING dressing
ENROLLED registered; recorded
ENROLLER inscriber

ENROOTED firmly fixed; established
ck **ENSALADA** onion/tomato salad (Sp.)
ENSCONCE protect; hide; harbour
mu **ENSEMBLE** all together
ENSHIELD guard; screen
ENSHRINE treasure; cherish
ENSHROUD veil; mask; conceal
ENSIFORM like a sword
ENSIGNCY rank of ensign
ENSLAVED in bondage; enthralled
ENSLAVER captor; subjugator
ENSNARED trapped; inveigled
ENSOULED animated
ENSURING guaranteeing; safe-guarding
ENTAILED settled on heirs
ENTAILER a deviser
ENTANGLE mat; ravel; implicate
zo **ENTELLUS** sacred monkey
ENTERING penetrating; noting
ps **ENTHALPY** thermodynamic property
ENTHRONE install; exalt; elevate
ENTHUSED became ardent
ENTICING alluring; coaxing
ENTIRELY fully; perfectly
ENTIRETY aggregate; completeness
ENTITLED styled; dubbed; empowered
ENTOMBED buried; interred
zo **ENTOMOID** like an insect
ENTOPTIC inner vision
zo **ENTOZOIC** **ENTOZOON**, of internal parasites
mu **ENTR'ACTE** an interval
md **ENTRAILS** internal parts; offal
ENTRANCE entry; to ravish
ENTREATY urgent request; petition
ck **ENTREMET** sweet dish
ENTRENCH fortify; encroach
ENTREPAS an amble (Fr.)
ENTREPOT emporium; transit depot
ENTRESOL mezzanine storey
ENTWINED woven; plaited; twisted
md, pc **ENURESIS** incontinence
ENVEIGLE inveigle; lure; seduce
ENVELOPE a cover; surround; dirigible gasbag (airship)
cp, tc **ENVELOPE** pre- and suffix data code signals
ENVIABLE most desirable
ENVIABLY covetously; grudgingly
ENVIRONS suburbs; vicinity
ENVISAGE to face; to consider
zo **ENZOOTIC** (localized disease)
EOLIENNE dress material; silk and wool
EOLIPILE experimental flask
gl **EOLITHIC** pre-paleolithic
EPAGOGIC inductive
zo **EPALPATE** no feelers
EPANODOS rhetorical recapitulation
EPENDYMA spinal cord epithelium in vertebrates
EPENETIC laudatory
zo **EPHEMERA** may-flies; etc.
EPHESIAN debauchee; (Ephesus)
md **EPIBLAST** outer skin
bt **EPICALEX** outer calyx
EPICERIE grocery; spices (Fr.)
zo **EPICOELE** cerebellum ventricle in craniata
md **EPICOLIC** (abdomen over colon)
bt, zo **EPICOTYL** axis of feather or seedling
cy **EPICRINE** type of secretion gland
EPICYCLE circulating circle
md **EPIDEMIC** locally prevalent
mn **EPIDOTIC** (vitreous ore)
zo **EPIGAMIC** appealing to opposite sex
bt **EPIGEOUS** low growing
EPIGRAPH motto; inscription
md **EPILEPSY** fits
EPILOGIC concluding
EPILOGUE farewell speech
hd **EPIMACUS** heraldic griffin
zo **EPIMERAL** (segment above joint)
EPIMERON posterior of sclerites in insects
mn **EPIMORPH** crystal natural cast
bt **EPINASTY** curvature
pc **EPINOSIC** advantage by illness
zo **EPIORNIS** extinct bird (Madagascar)
rl **EPIPHANY** 6 January
md **EPIPHORA** streams of tears
bt **EPIPHYTE** (mistletoe, orchids), non-parasitic cohabiting plant
bt **EPIPLASM** residual cytoplasm in ascus
EPIPLOCE rhetorical climax
zo **EPIPODIA** lateral foot lobes in gastropoda
EPIPOLIC fluorescent
zo **EPIPROCT** plate over insect anus
zo **EPIPUBIC** before or above pubis
lt **EPISCOPE** projection lantern
rl **EPISCOPY** superintendence; search
EPISEMON city badge (Gr.)
EPISODAL digressive; accidental
EPISODIC incidental; subordinate
bt **EPISPERM** outer seed cover
bt **EPISPORE** outside spore-wall layer
EPISTLER letter-writer; scribe; Paul
EPISTOME face/mouth region in various creatures
ar **EPISTYLE** the architrave
EPITASIS climax; culmination
bt **EPITHECA** diatom cell valve

EPITONIC overstrained
EPITRITE metrical foot
EPITROPE rhetorical concession
zo **EPIZOITE** sedentary attached animals
zo **EPIZOOTY** animal epidemic
EPLICATE unplaited
EPONYMIC yclept; named after
EPOPOEIA epic poetry
mn **EPSOMITE** Epsom salts
md **EPULOTIC** cicatrizing
EQUALISE equalize; even
EQUALITY uniformity; sameness
EQUALLED rivalled
EQUATING balancing
EQUATION allowance for inaccuracy
EQUIFORM of equal shape; similar
EQUIPAGE outfit; effects; train
EQUIPPED accoutred; armed
EQUITANT riding astraddle
ERASABLE effaceable
ERASTIAN follower of Erasmus
ERECTILE capable of elevation
ERECTING raising; building
bd **ERECTION** structure; edifice; building; (penile)
EREMETIC hermit-like; solitary
md **ERETHISM** acute irritation
EREWHILE formerly
zo **ERGATOID** like a worker insect
ERGONOMY physiological distinction of functions
bl **ERGOSOME** unit of cell-protein synthesis
bt **ERGOTINE** **ERGOTIZE**, **ERGOTISM**, parasitical, poisonous fungus
bt **ERIGERON** flea-bane genus
mn **ERIONITE** uncommon zeolite
hd **ERMINOIS** heraldic fur
EROTICAL amatory; amorous; (Eros)
ERRANTLY like knights of old
ERRANTRY rambling; roving
ERRORIST fallacious fellow
ERUCTATE belch
ERUGATED wrinkled; corrugated
bt **ERUMPENT** breaking out
ERUPTING casting out
gl, md **ERUPTION** outburst; volcanic; suppuration; boil
ERUPTIVE explosive
zo **ERYCINIA** insect genus
bt **ERYSIMUM** hare's ear, etc.
md **ERYTHEMA** a skin disease
ERYTHRON red blood cell
ESCALADE **ESCALADO**, attack by means of scaling ladders
ESCALATE increase in scope
zo **ESCALLOP** scallop; a bi-valve
ck **ESCALOPE** boneless meat slice
ESCAPADE prank; adventure; frolic
ESCAPADO desperado; on the loose
ESCAPING evading; eluding
ESCAPISM **ESCAPIST**, the quest of a mental anodyne
ck **ESCARGOT** edible snail
ck **ESCAROLE** dark green salad plant
ESCARPED steeply sloped
ESCHEWED shunned; avoided
ESCHEWER non-joiner; loner
ESCORTED attended; conducted
lw **ESCOTTED** taxed; maintained
ESOTERIC secret; mysterious
ESPALIER trellised trees
bt **ESPARCET** sainfoin
ESPECIAL particular; special
bt **ESPIBAWN** ox-eye daisy
bt **ESPIOTTE** species of rye
ESPOUSAL betrothal
ESPOUSED married
ESPOUSER wooer
md **ESPUNDIA** S. Amer. skin infection
ESQUIRED promoted to esquire (adjutant)
ESSAYING attempting; endeavouring
ESSAYISH experimental
ESSAYIST a scribe; writer
ESSAYKIN short essay
ESSENCED perfumed
ESSENISM Essene doctrine
gl **ESSEXITE** alkali-gabbro igneous rock
ESSOINED excused for absence
lw **ESSOINER** attendance excuser
mn **ESSONITE** yellow garnet
hd **ESSORANT** heraldic wings
mu **ESTAMPIE** Fr. instrumental dance form
ESTANCIA cattle ranch, S. America
ESTEEMED held in high regard
ESTEEMER valuer; admirer
ch **ESTERASE** ester-hydrolysing enzyme
ESTHESIA **ESTHESIS**, sensitivity
cf **-ESTHESIC** of sensibility
ESTHETIC aesthetic; perceptive
ESTIMATE appraise; calculate
nt **ESTIVAGE** method of ship loading
ESTIVATE pass the summer
ESTONIAN of Estonia (Baltic republic)
lw **ESTOPPED** impeded; barred
lw **ESTOPPEL** a plea
lw **ESTOVERS** timber supplies
ESTRANGE alienate; disaffect
zo **ESTRIDGE** ostrich down
ESTROGEN female genital hormone
ESTUANCE heat, warmth
ESURIENT greedy; hungry
ps **ETA-MESON** zero spin elementary particle

ETA-PATCH balloon patch
ETCETERA etc; etc.
ETEOSTIC a chronogram
ETERNITY perpetuity
ETERNIZE immortalize
ETHEREAL airy; heavenly; celestial
ch **ETHERENE** etherine; a gas
ETHERISM effects of ether
md **ETHERIZE** to gas
ch **ETHEROLE** a light oil
ETHICIST moralist
ETHIOPIC Abyssinian; Ethiopian
ETHNARCH Greek governor
ETHNICAL of mankind (cultural, linguistic groupings)
pc **ETHOGRAM** behaviour pattern
pc **ETHOLOGY** cultural customs; animal behaviour in wild
ch **ETHYLENE** carburetted hydrogen
ETIOLATE to blanch
ETIOLOGY study of causes
mu **ETOUFFEZ** (Fr.) stuff it down; dampen
ETRURIAN **ETRUSCAN**, of Etruria
ETYPICAL exceptional; aberrant
bt **EUCALYPT** eucalyptus
EUCARPIC with vegetative and reproductive organs
bt **EUCHARIS** Amazon lilies, etc.
EUCTICAL supplicatory
EUCYCLIC made up of matching successive whorls
EUGENICS eugenism
EUGENIST (race culture)
EUGUBINE (bronze tablets)
bl **EUKARYON** higher-organism nucleus
EULACHAN candle-fish oil
EULOGIST panegyrist
EULOGIUM laudatory speech; encomium
EULOGIZE extol; applaud; flatter
zo **EUMERISM** aggregation of like parts
md **EUMYDRIN** atropine-like medicament
zo **EUNICEAE** a worm genus
bt **EUONYMIN** **EUONYMOUS**, spindle-tree extract
bt **EUPATORY** hemp agrimony
EUPATRID Athenian aristocrat
md **EUPEPSIA** good digestion
EUPEPTIC highly digestible
EUPHONIA smooth enunciation
EUPHONIC harmonious; felicitous
mu **EUPHONON** **EUPHONIUM**, brass instrument
EUPHORIA satisfaction of the artist
md **EUPHRASY** the eye-bright plant
EUPHUISM bombastic diction
EUPHUIST affected speaker; pedant
EUPHUIZE over-emphasize
cy **EUPLOIDY** polyploidy involving exact haploid multiples
EUPYRENE typical, of spermatozoa
EUPYRION a quick match, etc.
EURASIAN European-Asiatic
ch **EUROPIUM** metallic element
EURYTHMY symmetry; regularity
rl **EUSEBIAN** (Eusebius)
zo **EUSOCIAL** division of labour (insects)
EUTECTIC easily melted
zo **EUTHERIA** genus of mammals
EUTHROPY good digestion
pc **EUTHYMIA** tranquillity; relaxed state
mn **EUXENITE** uncommon rare-element mineral
pm **EVACUANT** purgative; laxative
EVACUATE quit; abandon; forsake; empty
EVADIBLE escapable; evasible
EVANESCE disappear; vanish
EVASIBLE avoidable; elusory
EVECTION convection
EVEN-DOWN downright
EVENFALL twilight
EVENNESS levelness; regularity
rl **EVENSONG** end of day service
EVENTFUL full of incident; stirring
EVENTIDE evenfall; evening
EVENTUAL last; ultimate; final
EVERMORE always; eternally
EVERYDAY usual; common; routine
EVERYONE everybody
EVERYWAY in all ways
EVICTING expelling; ousting
EVICTION dispossession
EVIDENCE testimony; witness
EVILDOER malefactor; criminal
EVILNESS malignity; depravity
EVINCING demonstrating; exhibiting
EVINCIVE indicative
EVITABLE avoidable; escapable
lw **EVOCATOR** a summoner
EVOLVING on-going evolution
EXACTING enforcing; critical; rigid
EXACTION extortion; tribute
EXALTING extolling; honouring
EXAMINED inquired; studied
EXAMINEE candidate
EXAMINER scrutinizer; inspector
EXAMPLAR model; exemplar; pattern
md **EXANTHEM** surface rash
EXCAVATE delve; dig; scoop
EXCEEDED surpassed; capped; excelled
EXCEEDER outdoer; surpasser
EXCEPTED excluded; omitted

EXCEPTOR objector; abstainer
EXCERNED excreted; exuded
EXCESSED exceeded
EXCESSES surpluses; over the limits; orgies
cp **EXCHANGE** barter; commute; transaction
EXCISING cutting out
EXCISION extirpation; amputation
EXCITANT a stimulant
EXCITING rousing; inciting; inflaming
EXCITIVE provocative
EXCITRON mercury-arc rectifier
EXCLUDED banned; barred; vetoed
EXCURSED digressed; wandered
EXCURSUS supplemented treatise
EXCUSING remitting; condoning
EXECRATE curse; detest; abhor
EXECUTED beheaded; achieved
lw **EXECUTER EXECUTOR**, testamentary agent; deed drafter
EXEGESIS explanatory discourse
EXEGETIC elucidative
EXEMPLAR pattern; examplar; model
EXEMPTED excused; released
EXEQUIAL funereal
EXEQUIES obsequies; funeral rites
EXERCISE use; task; drill; exert
EXERGUAL date space on coin
EXERTING striving; wielding
EXERTION effort; strain; attempt
EXERTIVE labouring; toilsome
EXHALANT exhalent; evaporative
EXHALING breathing; emitting
EXHORTED encouraged; warned
EXHORTER incitor; adviser
EXHUMATE disinter; exhume
EXHUMING digging up
EXIGEANT exacting; importunate
EXIGENCY exigence; urgency
EXIGIBLE able to be levied
EXIGUITY scantiness; fineness
EXIGUOUS tiny; diminutive; minute
bt **EXINTINE** floral membrane
EXISTENT extant; living
EXISTING being; continuing
ps **EXITANCE** (luminous); (radiant)
EX-LIBRIS (book-plate)
EXOCHITE outer layer of fucales macrosporangium
zo **EXOCOELE** portion of coelenteron
zo **EXOCRINE** of gland secretion; duct-carried
pc **EXOGAMIC** of marriage outside social group
EXOPHAGY selective cannibalism
EXORABLE not relentless; lenient
rl **EXORCISM EXORCIST, EXORCIZE**, deliverance from evil spirits
EXORDIAL introductory
EXORDIUM the beginning; preamble
EXOSMOSE diffusion
bt **EXOSPORE** outer layer of spore wall
bt **EXOSTOME** part of ovule
EXOTERIC openly professed; superficial
EXOTHERM heat liberator
ba **EXOTOXIN** bacterium-released toxin
EXPANDED stretched; dilated
el, cp **EXPANDER COMPANDOR**, with built-in volume compressor
EXPECTED awaited; forecast
EXPEDITE hasten; accelerate
EXPELLEE expelled; dismissed; sacked
EXPENDED consumed; money used
EXPERTLY dexterously; adroitly
EXPIABLE atonable
EXPIATED made reparation
EXPIATOR indemnifier
EXPIRANT a dying person
EXPIRING at death's door
EXPLICIT clearly stated; categorical
EXPLODED burst; repudiated
EXPLODER a machine
EXPLORED scrutinized; plumbed
EXPLORER investigator
ma **EXPONENT** an executant; idea supporter; power
EXPORTED shipped; sent abroad
EXPORTER foreign trader
EXPOSING exhibiting; revealing
EXPOSURE disclosure; revelation
EXPUGNED overcome; conquered
EXPUNGED erased; deleted
EXTENDED stretched; protracted
EXTENDER dilator; expander
pl **EXTENSOR** joint muscle
EXTERIOR outer; outward
EXTERNAL outer; foreign; exotic
EXTOLLER eulogizer
EXTORTED wrested; extracted
EXTRADOS convex surface of vault
EXTRUDED pointed outwards; visible
EXULTANT triumphant; jubilant
EXULTING crowing; rejoicing
EXUVIATE moult; shed a skin
EYEGLASS monocle
EYEPIECE telescope lens
EYESALVE eyewash; ointment
EYESIGHT vision
zo **EYE-STALK** eye-bearing stalk in crustacea
md **EYESTONE** optical adjunct
EYE-TO-EYE vis-à-vis; face to face

EYETOOTH a canine tooth
EYEWATER tear; lotion

F

FABLIAUX French metrical tale
FABULIST an Aesop
FABULIZE narrate a romance
FABULOUS super; better than real
mu **FABURDEN** plainsong with simple harmony
md **FACE-ACHE** neuralgia
FACE-CARD court card
cp **FACE-DOWN** submissive; of punch cards
FACELESS lacking a physiognomy
FACE-PACK cosmetic
FACETIAE witticisms; pleasantries
FACETING cutting facets
FACIALLY superficially; externally
FACILITY dexterity; readiness; address
FACINGLY oppositely
FACTIOUS turbulent; riotous
FACTOTUM general assistant; dog's body
FACULOUS spotted
FADDLING trifling; playing
FADEAWAY old soldier; screwball (baseball)
FADELESS imperishable; enduring
FADINGLY decreasingly; vapidly
bt **FAE-BERRY** fea-berry; gooseberry
mu **FAGGOTED** bundled (firewood); of bassoon
FAGOTING a kind of embroidery
cp **FAIL-SAFE** automatic close-down device
cp **FAIL-SOFT** slowdown device
FAINTEST barely perceptible; dimmest
FAINTING swooning
FAINTISH giddy; languid
FAIR-COPY correct copy
FAIR-HAND freehand
FAIRINGS small porcelain ornament (Ger.)
FAIRINGS first milk after calf-birth
nt **FAIR-LEAD** a rope-guide
FAIRNESS honest dealing; equity
FAIR-PLAY justice; impartiality
FAIRYDOM fairyland
FAIRYISM enchantment
FAITHFUL leal; loyal; steadfast
FAKEMENT makeshift; swindle
FAKIRISM mysticism; poverty
FALCATED like a sickle
FALCHION short curved sword
FALCONER a hawker
zo **FALCONET** small hawk; cannon
FALCONRY hawking
FALDERAL meaningless refrain
FALDETTA hood and cape (Malta)
ga **FALL-AWAY** rocket launching pad; to pass (ball games)
FALL-BACK reserve; retreat; (wrestling)
FALL-DOWN inadequacy; failure
FALLIBLE capable of errors
FALLIBLY erroneously
FALLOWED (field) ploughed but not sown
FALL-TRAP a snare
mu **FALSETTE FALSETTO**, shrill and unnatural tone of voice
pr **FALSTAFF** fat face
FALTERED wavered; hesitated
FAMELESS undistinguished
FAMILIAL common to a family
FAMILIAR unceremonious; intimate
rl **FAMILIST** (16th-century sect)
FAMISHED anhungered; starved
FAMOUSLY remarkably; eminently
FAMULIST magician's attendant
FAN-BLAST forced delight
FANCIFUL whimsical; capricious
FANCYING preferring; (love); imagining
mu **FANDANGO** Spanish national dance
FANFARON swaggering bully; braggart
FANGLESS toothless; (without venom)
FANLIGHT lunette; window over doorway
mu **FANTASIA** musical medley
FAN-WHEEL ventilating device
me **FARADAIC FARADIZE, FARADISM**, of a farad
FARCICAL ludicrous; absurd; droll
vt **FARCY-BUD** glanders
FARDELED in bundles
FAREWELL adieu; good-bye; parting
FAR-FLUNG widely disseminated
FARINOSE mealy; floury
FARMABLE cultivatable
FARMYARD rooster's realm
FARRIERY veterinary work
FARROWED littered
FAR-SPENT well advanced
FARTHEST ultimate; yondmost
nm **FARTHING** four a penny (d)
FASCHING winter masquerade season (Ger.)
FASCICLE a cluster

zo **FASCIOLA** narrow band of colour
FASCIOLE ciliated spines in spatangoidea
FASCISTI Italian fascists
FASCISTS opponents of socialism
FASHIOUS vexatious; provocative
mn **FASSAITE** monoclinic pyroxene
FASTBALL pitch at full speed (baseball)
FASTENED secured; bound; tied
FASTNESS a stronghold; security
FATALISM FATALIST, (belief in the inevitable)
FATALITY a calamity; disaster
FATHERED adopted; begat; sired
FATHERLY paternal; benign
FATHOMED comprehended; plumbed
FATIGUED weary; jaded; tired
FATTENED overfed
FATTENER a fat producer
FAULTFUL defective
FAULTILY imperfectly
FAULTING accusing
FAUTEUIL arm-chair; stall
zo **FAUVETTE** garden warbler
FAVONIAN (west wind)
FAVOURED encouraged; approved
FAVOURER patron; supporter
mn **FAYALITE** an iron ore
bt **FEABERRY** faeberry; gooseberry
FEARLESS intrepid; undaunted; heroic
FEARSOME dread; awe inspiring
FEASIBLE FEASIBLY, workable; achievable; possibly
rl **FEAST-DAY** a festival
FEASTFUL sumptuous; luxurious
FEASTING banqueting; carousing
FEAST-WON (elections) bribed by feasting
FEATEOUS dexterous; deft
FEATHERY with plumes; golf-shot (raising soil); oar-stroke (spray)
FEATNESS adroitness; neatness
FEATURED details, items, actors shown
FEBRIFIC causing fever
FEBRUARY month of expiation
FECKLESS inefficient; spiritless
FECULENT muddy; turbid; fetid
FEDERACY confederacy; alliance
FEDERARY a confederate
FEDERATE league together
FEEBLISH weakish
el **FEEDBACK** sound; energy phenomenon
cp **FEED-BACK** reaction report
FEED-HEAD cistern of a boiler
FEED-PIPE water-pipe
FEED-PUMP a force-pump
pg **FEER-TYPE** positive process
FEETLESS footless; apodal
FEIGNING counterfeiting; shamming
FEINTING pretending; misleading
mn **FELDSPAR** felspar
FELICIDE cat-killing
FELICITY happiness; bliss; blessedness
FELINITY cattishness
FELLABLE capable of being felled
FELLAHIN Egyptian peasants
FELLATIO oral penis stimulation
FELLNESS ruthlessness; ferocity
FELLOWED matched
FELLOWLY companionable
FELLSIDE mountain side
lw **FELO-DE-SE** suicide
mn **FELSITIC** like porphyry
mn **FELSTONE** (quartz and felspar)
FELTERED matted together
FELTMARK imprint left in papermaking
FELTSIDE smooth side of roll of paper
bt **FELTWORT** the mullein
FEMALITY feminality
FEMERELL louvre or ventilator
FEMICIDE lady-killing
FEMININE female; effeminate; tender
FEMINISM (women's rights)
FEMINIST advocate of feminism
FEMINITY womanliness
FEMINIZE to make effeminate
bt **FENBERRY** cranberry
FENCEFUL affording defence
FENCE-OFF exclude; preliminary bout (fencing)
ch **FENCHONE** dicyclic ketone
FENCIBLE a home guard
FENESTER FENESTRA, a window
zo **FEN-GOOSE** greylag goose
FENTHION chemical insecticide
bt **FENUGREC** sort of clover
lw **FEOFFING** granting fief, feudal rights
FERACITY fecundity; fruitfulness
rl **FERETORY** shrine for relics
FERINELY wildly; savagery
bt **FERN-SEED** spores
bt **FERNSHAW** a thicket of ferns
FEROCITY cruelty; savagery
FERREOUS of iron
FERRETED unearthed
FERRETER ferret-like investigator
FERRETTO for colouring glass
nt **FERRIAGE** ferry charge

FERRITES ferro magnetic materials (ceramics)
FERRITIN liver protein
FERRULED tipped
FERRYING transporting
FERRY-MAN Charon (river Styx)
FERULING caning (as punishment)
FERVENCY ardour; devotion; eagerness
FERVIDLY hotly; zealously; with heat
FESTALLY joyously; jovially; merrily
md **FESTERED** rankled; turned septic
FESTIVAL mirthful; an occasion
FETCHING attractive; bringing
bt **FETERITA** dwarf sorghum
FETISHES charms; talismans; amulets
FETTERED shackled; manacled
FETTLING conditioning
bt **FEVERFEW** a febrifuge
FEVERING agitating; heating
FEVERISH inconstant; sultry
FEVEROUS restless; excited
FEWTRILS trifles (dial.)
FIBERKIE fluff on a blanket
bt **FIBRILLA** a filament
FIBROGEN protein
FIBROSIS fibrous growth
md **FIBROTIC** of fibrosis
FIBULATE tell fibs, untruths
pl **FIBULATE FIBULOUS**, of real leg-bones
mu **FIDDLING** playing the violin (folk occasions)
FIDELITY faithful honesty; reliability
FIDGETED worried; fretted; chafed
mu **FIDICULA** small lute
FIDUCIAL honesty in money transactions
FIELD-BED camp-bed
FIELD-DAY tactical exercise
FIELD-GUN mobile gun
FIELDING cricket
FIENDISH malicious; devilish
FIERCELY zealously; vehemently
FIERCEST most ferocious
FIERY-HOT blazing; impetuous
FIERY-NEW brand-new
nt **FIFE-RAIL** belaying pin rack
FIFTIETH ordinal of fifty
bt **FIG-APPLE** a coreless apple
zo **FIG-EATER** garden warbler
FIGHTING contention; strife; faction
zo **FIG-SHELL** a univalve shell
FIGULATE moulded
mn **FIGULINE** potter's clay
FIGURANT male ballet dancer
FIGURATE of determinate form
FIGURIAL represented by a figure
FIGURINE small statuette (Fr.); Oscar (prize)
FIGURING calculating; symbolizing
FIGURIST one skilled in figures
FILAMENT slender thread
FILATORY spinning machine
FILATURE the reeling of silk
FILCHING pilfering; purloining
zo **FILE-FISH** a sea-fish
FILIALLY like a son or daughter
FILIATED adopted; amalgamated
bt **FILICORD** fern-like plant
FILIFORM thread-like
FILIGREE metal lacework designs
rl **FILIOQUE** (clause in Nicene creed) concerning status of God's son
FILIPINO (Philippines)
ck **FILLETED** meat, fish less the bones
FILLIBEG a kilt (Sc.)
FILMGOER a frequenter of cinemas
FILM-STAR popular actor/actress
ga **FILOPINA PHILOPINA**, a nut-game
FILTERED percolated; strained
FILTHIER grubbier
FILTHILY dirtily
FILTRATE filtered solution
FINALISM conclusiveness; purposeful; teleology (ends)
FINALIST in the last round
FINALITY kismet; eventuality
FINANCED capitalized
FINDABLE discoverable
FINE-DRAW invisible mending
FINELESS endless; unlimited
FINENESS purity
FINE-SPUN elaborated
FINESSED acted artfully
FINESSER crafty person
FINGERED handled
FINGROMS woollen cloth
FINISHED ended
FINISHER final blow
FINITELY within limits
FINITUDE limitation
FINNESKO shoe made from reindeer skin
zo **FINNIKIN** crested pigeon
bt **FINOCHIO** sweet fennel
zo **FINSCALE** rudd, fish
zo **FIN-WHALE** rorqual
FIREARMS offensive weapons
ar **FIREBACK** ornamental heat refraction plate
FIRE-BALL explosive-like outbreak
FIRE-BARS furnace bars
FIRE-BOAT fire-fighting steamboat

FIREBOMB incendiary missile; grenade
mn **FIRECLAY** used for fire-bricks
FIRECOCK hydrant connexion
FIREDAMP explosive gas in mines
FIRE-EYED with fiery eyes
FIREFLAG flash of lightning
FIRE-GIRL woman fire fighter
FIRE-HOOK demolition hook
FIRE-HOSE portable piping
FIRE-KILN an oven
FIRELESS showing no flames
FIRELOCK antique musket
FIRE-PLUG valve in a water-main
nt **FIRESHIP** incendiary ship
FIRESIDE the hearth
FIRE-STEP firing-step (warfare) trench
zo **FIRETAIL** the redstart
FIRETRAP (no means of escape)
FIREWARD towards the fire! (as seaward)
bt **FIREWEED** a plant
FIREWOOD chopped sticks
FIRMLESS wavering; unstable
FIRMNESS solidity; resolution
FIRST-AID emergency help
FISHABLE capable of being fished
FISH-BALL fish-cake
FISHBEAM beam of special form
FISH-CAKE fish-ball
FISH-COOP box used for ice-fishing
FISh-GLUE an adhesive; isinglass
zo **FISH-HAWK** the osprey
FISH-HOOK barbed hook
FISH-MEAL fodder; fertilizer
FISH-POND fish storage tank
FISh-ROOM part of ship
FISH-SKIN fish epidermis
FISHTAIL a gas jet; jewellery
FISH-WEIR a fishgarth
FISH-WIFE fish vendor
FISSIPED cloven hoof
FISSURED cleft; cracked
FISTIANA boxing annals
bt **FISTINUT** pistachio nut
FISTULAR tubular
FITFULLY spasmodically; inconstantly
FIVEFOLD 500%
FIVELEAF cinquefoil
FIXATION cast-iron attitudes, opinions
pc **FIXATION** obsessive attachment
pg **FIXATIVE** a stabilizer; adhesive; gum
FIXATURE hair cream
FIXIDITY permanence; constancy
FIZZLING sizzling
FLABBILY limply; weakly
FLAGGING naval fore to aft celebration
FLAGGING becoming exhausted; weakening
FLAGGING denoting winner of horse races, Olympics
FLAGRANT notorious wrongdoing
nt **FLAG-SHIP** leading ship; with flag officer
zo **FLAG-WORM** green gentle
FLAMBEAU a lighted torch
FLAMELET small flame
mu **FLAMENCO** folk dance, music (Sp.)
zo **FLAMINGO** long-legged waterbird
FLAMMING deluding
FLAMMULE pictorial Japanese flame
hd **FLANCHED** heraldic term; flanged
FLANERIE lounging (Fr.)
FLANKING bordering; touching
ck **FLAP-JACK** cookie; compact
FLAPPING flopping; waving; shaking
FLASHILY transiently; gaudily
FLASHING bursts of light; signals; lightning
nt **FLAT-BOAT** invasion landing-craft
zo **FLAT-FISH** flounder, sole, dab, plaice etc.
FLAT-FOOT fallen arches; (of policemen)
FLAT-IRON smoothing iron
FLATNESS monotony; depression
FLAT-RACE not a steeplechase
FLATTERY insincere compliment
FLATTEST dullest; lowest; very level
FLATTING a process
FLATTISH comparatively level
FLATWISE not edgewise
zo **FLAT-WORM** tape worm
FLAUNTED vaunted; paraded
FLAUNTER ostentatious person
mu **FLAUTATO FLAUTANDO**, flute-like effect from violins (It.)
mu **FLAUTIST FLUTER**, flute player
FLAWLESS perfect; without blemish
FLAX-COMB a heckle
bt **FLAX-LILY** New Zealand flax
FLAX-MILL a factory
bt **FLAX-SEED** linseed
bt **FLAX-TAIL** the reed-mace
bt **FLAX-WEED FLAX-WORT**, plants of doubtful provenance
bt **FLEA-BANE** flea-discouraging plant
FLEA-BITE an inconvenient trifle
FLEAKING reed covering under thatch
bt **FLEA-WORT** a plant
FLECKING dappling

FLECTION flexion; bending
FLEECING shearing; swindling
FLEERING mocking; taunting
FLEETEST fastest; swiftest
FLEETING transient; passing; brief
FLENCHED fists as for punching
FLENSING removing skin (whaling)
zo **FLESH-FLY** blow-fly; bluebottle
FLESHING tights; scraping leather
FLESHING add colour to portraits; filling
FLESHPOT stock-pot; good living; night life
FLETCHED feathered (arrows)
ga **FLETCHER** and bow-man (archery)
FLEXIBLE FLEXIBLY, pliant; tractable; not rigid
FLEXUOSE FLEXUOUS, winding; wavering; curving; elastic
FLIC-FLAC back handspring (gymnastics)
FLICKING flipping
mu **FLICORNO** brass band instruments including sax-like instrument (military) (It.)
FLIGHTED took wing
FLIMFLAM humbug; nonsense
FLIMSIES carbon copies
FLIMSILY unsubstantially
FLINCHED winced; shrank back
FLINCHER shrinker; coward
FLINDERS fragments; flitters
FLINGING hurling; casting; pitching
FLINTIFY turn into flint
FLIPFLAP an entertaining device; scenery; theatre
cp, el **FLIPFLOP** walking noise; two state circuit
FLIPPANT pert; saucy; glib
FLIPPERS swim fins of seal and surfer
FLIPPING flicking
FLIRTING philandering; (fan)
FLIRTISH somewhat coquettish
FLITTERS vagrant non-rent payers
FLITTING hastening; leaving hurriedly
bt **FLIXWEED** a hedge plant
lw **FLOATAGE FLOATSAM, FLOTSAM**, shipwrecked goods
md **FLOATERS** 'flying flies' in the eye
FLOATERS markers; inconstants, voters
FLOATING circulating; wafting
FLOATING sideways movement (basketball)
FLOCCOSE tufted
FLOCCULE small tuft of wool
FLOCK-BED bed stuffed with flock
FLOCK-GUN dry spray for textile finishes
FLOCKING congregating; crowding
FLOGGING a chastisement
FLOODING inundating; swamping
FLOOD-LIT illuminated
FLOOKING cross vein or fissure
FLOORAGE floor space
FLOORING material for floors
FLOORMAN bookies' runner at races
mn **FLOPGATE** diverting materials moving gate
FLOPPILY limply; flaccidly
FLOPPING falling; collapsing (exhaustion)
FLORALLY with flowers
tx **FLORENCE** wine; cloth
FLORIAGE blossom
zo **FLORICAN** Indian bustard
FLORIDLY ornately; exuberantly
bt **FLORIGEN** hypothetical hormone
bt **FLOSCULE** a floret; a bloom
nt **FLOTILLA** small fleet
FLOUNCED threw oneself about
zo **FLOUNDER** struggle; a fish
FLOURING reducing to powder
mu **FLOURISH** prosper; wave; fanfare
FLOUTING showing off; exhibiting oneself
FLOUTING mocking conventional behaviour
FLOWERED blossomed
FLOWERED peak of artistic endeavour
FLOWERER plant flowering periodically
cp **FLOW-LINE** production, transport diagram
FLUENTLY volubly; easily
mu **FLUE-PIPE** organ pipe (without reed)
FLUFFING muffing
ps **FLUIDICS** science of liquid tube flow
FLUIDIFY fluidize
FLUIDITY fluidism; liquidity
FLUMMERY a drink; humbug
ch **FLUORIDE** tooth protector
ch **FLUORINE** a gas
mn **FLUORITE** fluorspar
FLUOROUS derived from fluor
FLURRIED agitated; disconcerted
FLUSHING blushing; colouring
FLUSTERY confused; agitated
md **FLUTTERY** flapping; oscillating; (pulse)
FLUXIBLE fusible
FLY-BLOWN shopworn; stale; dated; mouldy

FLY-BOARD container for artificial flies (angling)
FLY-MAKER (fishing)
FLYPAPER a fly-trap
FLY-SHEET handbill; broadside
FLY-WATER an arsenical solution
FLY-WHEEL a conserver of momentum
bt **FOAL-FOOT** colt's foot
FOCALIZE conveying/focus
pg **FOCUSING** correcting perspectives
FODDERER cattle-feeder
FOG-BOUND wrapped in mist
FOGEYDOM senility
FOGGIEST most obscure; murkiest
FOG-SMOKE thick fog
FOILABLE able to be frustrated
FOILPLAY fencing
FOILSMAN fencer
FOLDEROL refrain of old song
FOLDLESS uncreased
FOLD-YARD cattle enclosure
FOLIATED leafy
FOLIATED laminated; process
bt **FOLICOLE** feeding on leaf material
lw **FOLKLAND** common land
FOLK-LORE legendary traditions
FOLKMOTE assembly of freemen
mu **FOLK-SONG** traditional song
FOLK-TALE fairy story
FOLKWAYS group tradition
pl, bt **FOLLICE** small secreting cavity; pod
FOLLOWED imitated instructions given
FOLLOWED tracked; pursued
FOLLOWER partisan; adherent; copier
FOLLOW-ON giving second innings to opponents with lower score (cricket); strongly delivered bowl
FOLLOW-UP second stage support
FOMENTED growth promoted; treated by heat
FOMENTER agitator; agent provocateur
FONDLING a beloved one
FONDNESS affection; predilection
md **FONTANEL** a cavity
FONTANGE wire cap-frame
FOOD-CARD a rational requirement
FOODLESS lacking sustenance
FOOLSCAP paper, 17 × 13½ inches
FOOL-TRAP snare for simpletons
FOOSLING bungling
ga **FOOTBALL** national sport
FOOT-BATH bath to ease feet
FOOT-FALL footstep; tread
FOOTGEAR shoes and stockings
vt **FOOT-HALT** a sheep disease
go **FOOT-HILL** mini relative of mountain
FOOTHOLD support niche
FOOT-IRON carriage step; fetter
FOOTLESS with nothing to stand on
FOOTLING trifling; trivial; trumpery
FOOT-MARK foot-print
FOOT-MUFF foot-warmer
FOOT-NOTE an addendum
FOOT-PACE slow rate of progression
FOOTPATH pedestrian way
FOOT-POST pedestrian messenger
FOOT-RACE running match
nt **FOOT-ROPE** rope along a yard
me **FOOT-RULE** a 12-inch measure
FOOT-SLOG march; walk; tramp; hike
FOOTSORE with aching feet
FOOTSTEP footfall
FOOTWEAR foot-gear
FOOTWORK movement (sport)
FOOTWORN feet feeling over-used
FORAGING ravaging; searching
pl **FORAMINA** openings; orifices
FORAYING plundering; raiding
FORBORNE refrained; spared
FORCEDLY compulsorily; unnaturally
FORCEFUL coercive
FORCIBLE cogent
FORCIBLY violently
FORDABLE crossable wetshod
FORDOING ruining; exhausting
FOREBEAR ancestor; forefather
FOREBODE prognosticate; portended
nt **FORE-BODY** forward part of ship
FORECAST prediction; prognosis
FOREDATE antedate
nt **FOREDECK** in the bows
FOREDONE overpowered
FOREDOOM predestinate
FOREDOOR front door
FORE-EDGE front edge of book
FOREFEEL sense in anticipation
FOREFELT anticipated
nt **FOREFOOT** foremost end of keel
FOREGIFT lease premium
FOREGOER vor-trekker; precursor
FOREGONE already decided
FOREHAND cf. backhand
FOREHEAD brow; audacity; metope
nt **FORE-HOOK** strengthening piece
FOREKNEW foresaw
FOREKNOW know already
FORELAID previously arranged
go **FORELAND** headland; bluff; cape
FORELAND lend in anticipation
FORELENT previously loaned
FORELOCK sometimes a quiff

nt **FOREMAST** forward lower mast
FOREMEAN intend
FOREMOST in the van; leading
FORENAME home name, not surname
FORENOON from sunrise to noon
lw **FORENSAL FORENSIC**, of law-court procedure
FOREPART the beginning
nt **FOREPEAK** (in the bows)
FOREPLAY precopulation frolic
FOREPLAN to scheme
ce **FOREPOLE** tunnel cutter
FORE-RANK front rank
FORE-READ prognosticate
FORE-RENT rent due before reaping
FORESAID previously mentioned
nt **FORESAIL** one of various sails
FORESEEN expected; anticipated
FORESEER prophet
nt **FORESHIP** fore-part of ship
FORESHOW introductory frolic; portend
FORESIDE front side
FORESTAL concerning forests
nt **FORESTAY** part of rigging
FORESTER woodsman
FORESTRY arboriculture
FORETELL predict; augur
FORETIME the past; days of yore
FORETOLD presaged; warned
FOREWARD the van; the front
FOREWARN caution; admonish; advise
FOREWENT foregone; by-gone
FOREWIND favouring breeze
FOREWISH look foward to
FOREWORD preface; prologue
nt **FOREYARD** (yard on foremast)
FORGEMAN at blacksmith's workshop
FORGIVEN condoned; absolved
FORGIVER pardoner; remitter
FORGOING preceding
FORKEDLY furcated
FORKHEAD (knuckle-joint)
FORKLESS not branching
zo **FORKTAIL** salmon; kite; crow
ch **FORMALIN** an antiseptic
FORMALLY precisely; ceremoniously
ar **FORMERET** wall rib in medieval vault
FORMERLY ci-devant; whilom
FORMLESS shapeless; chaotic
FORMULAE sets of symbols
FORMULAR prescribed; formal
ar **FORMWORK** shuttering (concrete mould)
FORRADER further forward (slang)
FORSAKEN left; abandoned; renounced
FORSOOTH in truth; indeed
FORSPEAK forbid; bewitch
FORSPEND exhaust; squander
FORSWEAR deny upon oath; abjure
FORSWINK exhaust; wear out
FORSWORE FORSWORN, pledged falsely; recanted
ar **FORTRESS** castle; citadel
FORTUIST believer in chance
FORTUITY luck; accident
FORTUNED presaged
ga **FORWARDS** onward; football players
mu **FORZANDO** emphatically (It.)
FOSSDYKE Roman earthwork (Lincs.)
FOSSETTE dimple
zo **FOSSORES** burrowers
FOSTERED brought up; cherished
FOSTERER a nurse
FOSTRESS foster-mother
nt **FOTHERED** stopped a leak
FOUGASSE land-mine
zo **FOUL-FISH** fish when spawning
FOUL-HOOK not hooked in gills
FOULNESS dirt; grossness; scurrility
FOUL-PLAY unfair action
ml **FOUNDERY** foundry
FOUNDING establishing; endowing
FOUNTAIN jet of water
FOUNTFUL full of springs
FOURBALL four singles match (golf)
hd **FOURCHEE** cross
FOURFOLD quadruple
FOURLING one of a quadruplet
FOURNEAU explosion chamber (Fr.)
ga **FOURSOME** four together (golf, bridge)
FOURTEEN twice seven
FOX-BRUSH a trophy of the chase
FOX-CHASE hunting
FOX-EARTH reynard's home
bt **FOXGLOVE** digitalis
bt **FOXGRAPE** variety of grape
zo **FOXHOUND** hunt dog
FOXINESS craftiness; slyness
zo **FOX-SHARK** thresher shark
FOX-SLEEP pretended sleep
FRACTION part; particle; fragment
FRACTURE break; rift; fissure
bt **FRAGARIA** the strawberry
FRAGMENT shard; scrap; remnant
FRAGRANT odoriferous; redolent
FRAILISH somewhat weak; delicate
FRAMABLE can be framed
to **FRAME-SAW** Italian saw
bt **FRANCATU** russetin apple

ch **FRANCIUM** heaviest alkali metal
lw **FRANK-FEE** tenure in fee-simple
FRANKING remitting postage
FRANKISH (Frank); proto-French
FRANKLIN old English freeholder
FRAPPAGE sharp slapping
nt **FRAPPING** binding; lashing
zo **FRASLING** the perch
FRAUDFUL dishonest; knavish
FRAULEIN German spinster
ch **FRAXININ** extract from ash bark
bt **FRAXINUS** ash-tree genus
FREAKFUL FREAKISH, capricious; abnormal; erratic
pl **FRECKLED** with natural speckled skin
FREEBORN neither vassal nor slave
FREE-CITY independent town
FREE-COST cost free
FREED-MAN emancipated slave
FREEHAND without instrumental aid
lw **FREEHOLD** held in fee-simple
FREE-LOVE promiscuity
FREENESS freedom; liberty
FREE-PORT (duties not levied)
mu **FREE-REED** vibrating reed
FREE-SHOT legendary hunter
FREE-SOIL (no slavery)
FREE-TRIP complimentary tour
FREE-TRIP trip-close mechanisms
FREE-WILL voluntary; spontaneous
FREEZE-UP immobility; infrozen
FREEZING congealing; chilling
md **FREMITUS** palpable vibration
FRENETIC frenzied; distracted
zo **FRENULUM** a butterfly's bristle
FRENZIED maddened; furious
FREQUENT oft repeated; recurrent
FRESCADE a cool walk
FRESCOED painted on plaster
FRESCOER a washy painter
FRESHISH almost fresh
FRESHMAN first year student
FRESH-NEW unpractised
FRETTING worrying; fuming; abrading
FRETWORK interlaced ornament
FREUDIAN psycho-analytic
FRIATION crumbling
FRIBBLED frivolled; tottered
FRIBBLER trifler
FRICTION attrition; abrasion; sliding; rolling
ps **FRICTION** kinetic; coefficient (dynamic, static)
FRIENDED befriended; well-disposed
FRIENDLY kind; favourable; amicable (society); (match)
FRIESIAN FRISIAN, of Friesland, Netherlands
FRIGHTED affrighted; dismayed
FRIGHTEN alarm; scare; intimidate
FRIGIDLY coldly; icily
FRILLING edging material
FRINGENT FRINGING, encircling; bordering; tasselating
FRIPPERY fallals; old clothes
FRISETTE artificial curl
FRISKFUL lively; sportive
FRISKILY briskly; wantonly
FRISKING capering; skipping; romping
FRISKING rapid search for arms on person
gs, ml **FRITTING** pasty condition of powdered ore
FRIZETTE see frisette
FRIZZLED curled; fried
tx **FRIZZLER** hairdresser; cloth-worker
FROCKING coarse jean
zo **FROG-FISH** angler-fish
FROGGERY an abode of frogs
zo **FROGLING** tadpole
zo **FROG-SPIT** froth-fly
FROMWARD away from
FRONDAGE leafage
bt **FRONDENT FRONDOSE, FRONDOUS**, leafy
FRONTAGE building line
FRONTATE widening like a leaf
FRONTIER boundary; border; march
FRONTING facing; opposing
FRONTLET fillet or browband
ar **FRONTOON** a pediment
FROSTILY frigidly; icily; freezingly
FROSTING icing
FROTHERY mere froth; foam
zo **FROTH-FLY** numerous parasites
FROTHILY verbosely
FROTHING bubbling
FROTTAGE coin-rubbing; erotic stimulation
FROTTEUR performer of frottage
FROU-FROU flounced petticoat
FROUNCED plaited hair
FROWNING glowering; scowling
FRUCTIFY to make fruitful; teem
FRUCTOSE fruit sugar
FRUGALLY economically; thriftily
FRUITAGE crop; harvest; produce
bt **FRUIT-BUD** flower to be fruit
FRUITERY fruit-loft
zo **FRUIT-FLY** a pest
FRUITFUL productive; fecund; prolific
FRUITING bearing fruit

FRUITION fulfilment; realization
FRUITIVE enjoying; gratifying
bt **FRUITLET** a small fruit
FRUMENTY porridge of sorts
FRUMPING insulting; flouting
FRUMPISH old-fashioned; ill-natured
bt **FRUSTULE** shell of a diatom
ch **FUCHSINE** magenta; rosaniline hydrochloride; dye
mn **FUCHSITE** green muscovite
FUDDLING making drunk or confused
FUELLING taking in fuel
FUGACITY instability; uncertainty
mu **FUGHETTA** (It.) a little fugue
FUGITIVE volatile; vagabond; refugee
FUGLEMAN exemplary soldier
bt **FULCRATE** with supports
FULGENCY effulgence; brilliance
FULGURAL (lightning); flashy
FULL-AGED of mature age
FULL-BACK (football)
FULL-BUTT head-on crash
FULL-EYED with prominent eyes
FULL-FACE cf. profile
FULLNESS fulness; repletion; profusion
nt **FULL-ROLL** swell and yawing; croquet shot
pr **FULL-STOP** end of a period
FULL-TIME normal working hours
FULL-WAGE wireless rectifier
FULMINED fulminated; thundered
FULMINIC explosive; detonative
FUMARASE catalysing enzyme
FUMAROLE volcanic smoke hole
FUMATORY fumigating chamber
FUMBLING clumsy; groping
FUMELESS smokeless
bt **FUMEWORT** the fumitory plant
FUMIGANT fume-producing; incense
FUMIGATE disinfect by smoke
FUMITORY fumewort
FUMOSITY smokiness; flatulence
FUNCTION duty; power; office
cp **FUNCTION** purpose; meeting; instruction
FUNDABLE able to be financed
FUNDLESS broke
FUNEBRAL **FUNEREAL**, sombre; woeful
FUNERARY mournful; dismal
FUNGIBLE interchangeable
FUNK-HOLE coward's corner
FURBELOW puckered flounce
FURCATED forked; branching
FURCULAR fork-shaped
ch **FURFURAL** fural solvent
ch **FURFUROL** organic liquid
FURIBUND raging; furious; frenzied
FURLOUGH leave of absence
FURMENTY see frumenty
FURRIERY the fur trade
FURROWED corrugated; ploughed
FURTHEST most distant; remotest
md **FURUNCLE** a boil
FURY-LIKE furious; violent; frantic
ar **FUSAROLE** a classic moulding
FUSELAGE body of aircraft
FUSEL-OIL malodorous spirit
FUSIFORM spindle-shaped
FUSILIER armed with flint-lock muskets
bt **FUSTERIC** a yellow dye
FUSTILUG fat unwieldy person
FUTILELY unavailingly; ineffectually
FUTILITY uselessness; vanity
FUTURELY in time to come
FUTURISE anticipate; antedate
FUTURISM art movement
FUTURIST (Biblical prophecies)
FUTURITY future time; the hereafter; gamble on future commodities
bt **FUZZ-BALL** puff-ball fungus
FUZZLING confusing; intoxicating

G

GABARAGE packing cloth
GABBATHA Pilate's judgement seat
GABBLING chattering; jabbering
GABIONED with gabions
ar **GABLE-END** part of house silhouette
GADABOUT roving busybody
GADHELIC Gaelic Celt language
GADLINGS steel spikes
GADZOOKS a mild expletive
GAGGLING noise of geese; cackling
GAG-TOOTH projecting tooth
mu **GAIEMENT** in lively style
GAIETIES vivacities; jollities
GAIGEOUR a wager, bet
GAINABLE procurable; attainable
GAINLESS unprofitable; bootless
GAINSAID contradicted; denied
zo **GAIR-FOWL** **GARE-FOWL**, great auk
ch **GALACTAN** anhydride of galactose
md **GALACTIA** excess of milk
as **GALACTIC** of galaxies (Milky Way)
bt **GALACTIN** sap of cow tree
GALALITH material made from milk
bt **GALANGAL** spicy tropical plant
GALATIAN inhabitant of Galatia
mn **GALAXITE** rare form of spinel
bt **GALBANUM** a gum

bt **GALBULUS** fleshy-scaled strobilus
GALEATED floral helmet
GALENISM Dr Galen's principles
GALENIST one of his followers
mn **GALENITE** sulphide of lead
GALENOID (galenite)
mn **GALERITE** fossil sea-urchin
GALILEAN of Galileo; of Galilee
md **GALL-DUCT** body channel
nt **GALLEASS GALLIASS,** galley-galleon trader (W. Europe)
GALLIARD gay fellow; brisk; a dance
GALLICAN of Gaul; later of France
GALLIPOT a glazed pot; artist's pot; apothecary's pot
nt **GALLIVAT** Malay pirate ship
GALLIZED (wine production)
GALLOPED rode at a gallop
GALLOPER mounted orderly
zo **GALLOWAY** a hardy horse
el **GALVANIC** variable pulsating current (Galvani)
GAMBESON GAMBISON, doublet worn under armour
GAMBLING playing recklessly
bt **GAMBOGIC** of gamboge, yellow; gum
tx **GAMBROON** twilled linen cloth
GAMEBIRD bird to be shot at
zo **GAMECOCK** fighting cock
lw **GAME-LAWS** hunting regulations
GAMENESS courage; endurance
GAMESOME sportive; playful
GAMESTER a gambler
zo **GAMMARUS** genus of crustaceans
ck **GAMMONED** pickled ham; bamboozled
GAMMONER cook; practical joker
GAMOBIUM sexual generation in metagenesis
GAMODEME permitted close marriage
zo **GAMOGONY** sporogony; gamete formation
rl **GANG-DAYS** (Rogation week)
GANGETIC (River Ganges)
GANGLAND criminal resort
GANGLING slender, awkward in movement
pl **GANGLION** cyst on tendon; nerve centre
GANGLION a focus of strength; energy
pc **GANGRENE** fatal blood poisoning
GANGSMAN foreman of a team
GANGSTER desperado; ruffian
rl **GANGWEEK** (Rogation week)
mn **GANISTER** sandstone; fire-brick
zo **GANNETRY** haunt of solan geese
nt **GANTLINE** rope for sails/clothes
GANYMEDE cupbearer to Zeus
GAOLBIRD habitual criminal; old lag
GAPINGLY widely open
GARBAGED worthless writing; household waste
GARBLING distorting the facts
nt **GARBOARD** plank next to keel
bt **GARCINIA** plant genus; mangosteen
GARDENER a cultivator
bt **GARDENIA** sub-tropical shrub; flower
zo **GARE-FOWL** gair-fowl; great auk
zo **GARGANEY** sea-duck
GARGLING warbling; throat cleansing
GARGOYLE grotesque gutter-spout
GARISHLY gaudily; showily; tawdrily
bt **GARLICKY** like garlic
GARNERED harvested; stored
GARRETED with watch-towers
GARRISON an armed force
GARROTTE strangle; throttle
zo **GARRULUS** crow genus; jay
GARTERED with socks well up
GASALIER hanging pendant for gas
pt **GAS-BLACK** carbon-black pigment
GAS-GAUGE (for testing pressure)
GASIFORM gaseous
GAS-LIGHT 19th-cent. lighting
GAS-METER (for measuring volume)
GAS-MOTOR a gas engine
GASOGENE aerating; apparatus
GASOLINE rectified petrol; fuel
GAS-STOVE cooking stove
GASTIGHT air-tight
zo **GASTRAEA** primordial organism
zo **GASTRULA** embryonic cup
GAS-WATER (coal-gas purification)
GAS-WORKS a source of illumination
GATE-BILL GATE-FINE, university penalty for lateness
GATEFOLD folded insert in a book
GATELESS without a gate
GATE-POST gate supporter
md **GATE-VEIN** portal vein
GATHERED collected; acquired
GATHERER gleaner; collector; fruit picker
GAUDY-DAY colourful festival (-ing)
GAUDYING making merry
GAUNTLET iron glove; (run the-)
lw **GAVELMAN** tenant in gavelkind
GAVELOCK crowbar; javelin
GAWNTREE barrel stand; gantry
GAZETTED published; recorded
ck **GAZPACHO** Andalusian cold soup
GAZUMPED thwarted by gazumper
GAZUMPER raiser of agreed selling price

au **GEAR-CASE** part of auto works
ch **GEGENION** simple ion
GELASTIC risible
GELATINE an animal jelly
GELATION solidification by cold
GELIDITY extreme cold
GEMATRIA a cabbalistic method
bt **GEMINATE** in pairs
as **GEMINIDS** meteoric shower
GEMINOUS double
bt **GEMMATED** budded
GEMMEOUS gemlike
mu **GEMSHORN** an organ stop
GENDARME armed policeman (Fr.)
GENDERED begat; sired; bred
GENE-FLOW gene-mix within populations
GENERALE general principle
GENERANT a cause of production
GENERATE originate; beget; produce
GENEROUS munificent; liberal
GENESIAC (Genesis)
GENETICS study of heredity
GENETRIX **GENITRIX**, a mother, female parent
GENEVESE of Geneva, Genevan
GENIALLY heartily; cordially; jovially
zo **GENITALS** reproductive organs
GENITIVE possessive case
GENITURE birth; procreation
GENOCIDE racial extermination
gn **GENOMERE** hypothetical gene constituent
cy **GENOSOME** chromosome part
GENOTYPE individual's genetic constitution
GENTILIC tribal; non-Jewish
ec **GEOBIONT** soil organism
bt **GEOCARPY** underground fruit ripening
GEOCLINE cline across organism's range features
GEODESIC **GEODETIC**, of earth measurements
GEOGNOST student of geognosy
gl **GEOGNOSY** petrography
GEOGONIC (formation of the earth)
GEOLATRY earth-worship
GEOMANCY a form of divination
GEOMETER a mathematician
GEOMETRY mensuration
bt **GEONASTY** groundward curvature
GEONOMIC (physical laws)
GEOPHAGY earth-eating
gp **GEOPHONE** portable shock-wave recorder
bt **GEOPHYTE** subterranean-budding plant
GEOPONIC agricultural; husbandry
GEORDIES Tynesiders
GEORGIAN period; Caucasian; (Georgia)
GEOSCOPY observational knowledge
GEOTAXIS gravity-stimulated movement response
ch **GERANIOL** perfumery ester constituent
bt **GERANIUM** showy pink flower
GERMANIC Teutonic
GERMCELL gamete
GERMINAL sprouting; French month
md **GEROCOMY** regime for the aged
GERONTIC of individual's senescent period
ch **GESTAGEN** hormone promoting pregnancy
GESTURAL gesticulating
GESTURED acted; posed; signalled
GHANAIAN native of Ghana
GHETTOES Jewish quarters
zo **GHORKHAR** Asiatic wild ass; onager
GHOSTING pattern staining; stand-in authorship
GHOULISH gruesome; fiendish
GIANTESS colossal lady
GIANTISM hugeness
GIANTIZE play the giant
mn **GIBBSITE** aluminium-hydroxide constituent of bauxite
GIBINGLY scornfully; mockingly
GIB-STAFF water-gauge; pole
GIDDIEST most thoughtless
GIDDYING making dizzy
GIFTLING a small present
GIGANTIC enormous; elephantine
GIGGLING tittering; sniggering
GIG-LAMPS carriage lamps; spectacles
zo **GILLAROO** species of trout
bt **GILLENIA** rose genus
zo **GILL-FLAP** a membrane
GILT-EDGE aureate; (securities)
zo **GILT-HEAD** sea-bream
zo **GILT-TAIL** species of worm
GIMCRACK a gewgaw; jimcrack
GIMLETED holed; bored
GINGERLY cautiously; warily
md **GINGIVAL** relating to the gums
zo **GIN-HORSE** mill-horse
GIN-HOUSE cotton factory
ck **GIN-SLING** a short drink (Singapore cocktail)
GIPSYDOM gipsy life
GIPSYISM cheating; flattery
bt **GIRASOLE** sunflower

GIRDLING encompassing; surrounding
GIRLHOOD juvenile femininity
GIRONDIN moderate republican
GIRTHING saddling; girdling
nt **GIRT-LINE** rigging line
GIVEABLE bestowable; presentable
GIVE-AWAY unintended disclosure
GLABRATE **GLABROUS**, smooth; without hair or down
GLACIATE freeze; polish by ice
GLADDEST very cheerful; merriest
GLADDING rejoicing; delighting; elating
GLADIATE sword-shaped
bt **GLADIOLE** sword-lily
bt **GLADIOLI** plural of gladiolus
GLADNESS joy; joyfulness; cheer
GLAD-RAGS party frocks
GLADSOME pleasurable; pleasant
GLAIRING varnishing
GLAIROUS viscous
GLANCING glimpsing; ricocheting
GLANDAGE feeding on acorns
vt **GLANDERS** a horse disease
md **GLANDULE** small gland
GLAREOUS glairous; viscous
GLASSEYE a horse disease
GLASSFUL a measure of content
GLASSILY in a vitreous manner
GLASSING glazing
GLASSITE one of a Scottish sect
gs **GLASS-POT** (used for melting glass)
bt **GLAUCIUM** the yellow poppy
md **GLAUCOMA** an eye-disease
GLAUCOUS a sea-green colour
GLEAMING resplendent; radiating
GLEANING harvesting; culling; picking
GLEDGING squinting
GLEESOME frolicsome; hilarious; lively
gl **GLEISOIL** poor-drainage-influenced soil type
bt **GLIADINE** yellow extract
GLIBNESS gift of the gab
GLIMPSED viewed hurriedly; glanced
GLINTING gleaming
cy **GLIOSOME** cytoplasmic granule
GLISSADE a glide on a glacier
zo **GLISSAUN** the coal-fish
GLOAMING dusk; twilight
GLOATING revelling; crowing; exulting
GLOBATED spherical
GLOBULAR spheric; round
GLOBULET round particle
md **GLOBULIN** (a blood constituent)
GLOOMILY despondently
GLOOMING obscuring; depressing
GLORIANA Queen Elizabeth I
rl **GLORIOLE** a halo; saintly aura
bt **GLORIOSA** a lily
GLORIOUS illustrious; noble; eminent
GLORYING exulting; boasting
bt **GLORY-PEA** an Australian pea
GLOSSARY explanatory vocabulary
GLOSSILY smoothly; sleekly
zo **GLOSSINA** the tsetse fly
GLOSSING commenting; polishing
GLOSSIST annotator; glossarist
GLOWERED scowled; frowned
GLOW-LAMP incandescent lamp
zo **GLOW-WORM** a beetle
bt **GLOXINIA** flowering plant
md **GLUCAGON** hormone increasing blood sugar
GLUCINUM white metal; beryllium
ch **GLUCONIC** acid derived from glucose
ch **GLUCOSID** sugar compound
GLUE-LINE dielectric heating
GLUMMEST gloomiest; very morose
GLUMNESS sulkiness; depression
GLUMPISH sullen; splenetic; moody
md **GLUTAEUS** posterior muscle
ch **GLUTELIN** water-insoluble protein
ch **GLUTENIN** wheat glutelin protein
GLUTTING sating; saturating; cloying
GLUTTONY voracity; greed
ch **GLYCEROL** glycerine
ch **GLYCOGEN** animal starch
GLYCONIC kind of verse
GLYPTICS gem engraving
GNARLING gnawing
GNARRING snarling; growling
GNASHING grinding the teeth
GNATHISM (jaw measurement)
zo **GNATHITE** insect mouth-part
zo **GNATLING** small gnat
zo **GNAT-WORM** larva of gnat
GNOMICAL of dialling
nt **GNOMONIC** of shadow casting; (sundial) (suncompass)
bt **GOA-CEDAR** a cypress
GOAL-LINE back-line (football)
GOAL-POST (football)
GOATHERD goat-minder
zo **GOATLING** small goat
zo **GOAT-MOTH** fabulous insect
GOATSKIN skin of goat
bt **GOAT'S-RUE** a plant
GOBBLING guzzling; turkey-noise
GODCHILD protégé
GOD'S-ACRE a graveyard
GODSMITH idol maker

GOD-SPEED a benediction
mn **GOETHITE** a hydrated iron oxide
GOFFERED crimped
GO-GETTER pushing person
GOGGLING rolling the eyes
GOINGS-ON unexpected, strange happenings
md **GOITERED GOITROUS**, afflicted with the goitre
bt **GOLD-DUST** a plant
GOLDENLY splendidly; aureately
zo **GOLDFISH** a carp
GOLD-FOIL GOLDLEAF, thin gold
GOLD-LACE sumptuary decoration
GOLDLESS destitute of gold
bt **GOLD-LILY** the yellow lily
GOLD-MINE source of wealth
GOLD-RUSH prospector's scramble
GOLD-SIZE a varnish
GOLD-WIRE thread gold
GOLD-WORK replacement teeth; dental bridges
GOLF-CLUB striker rod; association
rl **GOLGOTHA** place of a skull (crucifixion)
GOLLYWOG doll (black native)
GOLOSHES GALOSHES, rainproof overshoes
GOMARIST opponent of Armenians
GOMBROON Persian pottery
md **GONALGIA** pain in the knee
GONENESS that sinking feeling
GONFALON a banner
bt **GONGYLUS** (seaweed)
bt **GONIMIUM** lichen thallus cell
zo **GONOCOEL** gonad cavity
zo **GONOCYTE** sexual cell in porifera
zo **GONODUCT** genital products duct
GONOPORE reproductive elements opening
zo **GONOSOME** repro. individuals in animal colony
zo **GONOTOME** embryo somite
GOOD-DOER benefactor; patron
GOOD-FOLK the fairies
GOOD-LACK expression of pity
GOODLIER more excellent; fairer
GOODNESS kindness; beneficence
GOODWIFE a term of respect
GOODWILL benevolence; an asset
ga **GOOGLIES** bouncing cricket bowling
GOOSE-CAP a silly person
ga **GOOSE-EGG** a 'duck'; zero; no score (cricket)
GORGEOUS splendid and showy
zo **GORGONIA** corals
GOSPODAR Slav governor
GOSSAMER filmy cobweb
GOSSIPED chatted; tattled
GOSSIPRY small talk; intimacy
GOURMAND glutton; epicurean
bt **GOUTWEED** goutwort
GOVERNED controlled; ruled; swayed
GOVERNOR regulator; guardian
GOWNSMAN cf. townsman (university)
GRABBING snatching; clutching
nt **GRABLINE** lifeline on a lifeboat
GRACE-CUP loving cup
GRACEFUL elegant and easy
zo **GRACILIS** land-vertebrate thigh muscle
mu **GRACIOSO** Spanish clown; graciously
GRACIOUS dignified; polite; benign; charming
GRADATED stages of change
GRADATIM step by step
me, rw **GRADIENT** slope; incline; variable quantity ratio
el **GRADIENT** rate of change of potential in volts per metre
GRADUAND about to be a graduate
GRADUATE pass; proportion; divide
GRAECISM a Greek idiom
GRAECIZE to turn into Greek
GRAFFITI (ancient) wall scribblings
GRAFFITO two-colour plaster layers
GRAFTING implanting one stem into another plant
GRAINAGE duties on grain
bd, zo **GRAINING** imitating wood or marble using paints etc.; a fish
GRAIN-TIN melted tin
zo **GRALLINE** (wading birds)
zo **GRALLOCK** entrails of deer
GRAMARYE necromancy; magic
GRANDDAD grandfather
GRANDEST most magnificent; noblest
GRANDEUR pomp; splendour; majesty
GRANDSON son's son
mn **GRANITIC** of granite
GRANTING conceding; conferring
GRANULAR in grains
GRAPHICS art of drawing
mn **GRAPHITE** blacklead
GRAPHIUM a style (for writing)
GRAPPLED seized; grasped; clutched
GRASPING gripping; avaricious
GRASSING turfing; laying low
bt **GRASS-OIL** an essential oil
GRATEFUL thankful; beholden
bt **GRATIOLA** hedge hyssop
GRATUITY tip; bonus; pourboire

lw **GRAVAMEN** principal charge
GRAVELLY full of gravel
GRAVITAS weight of dignity
ps **GRAVITON** quantum of gravitation (hypothetical)
GRAY-EYED grey-eyed
zo **GRAYLING** freshwater fish
mu **GRAZIOSO** gracefully (It.)
GREASILY unctuously
GREASING lubricating; corrupting
GREATEST largest; biggest; bulkiest
GRECIZED Hellenized
GREEDILY voraciously; eagerly
GREENERY verdure; foliage
zo **GREEN-FLY** a pest
GREENING hoaxing
GREENISH somewhat green
ck **GREEN-TEA** for Chinese meals
GREETING cheerful welcoming message
lw **GREFFIER** notary (Channel Isles)
GREMLINS malignant aerial imps
ga **GREYCING** greyhound racing
GREYNESS grayness
ro **GRIB-BIAS** adjustment
GRIDIRON a grill; squared plan; map; traffic system
GRIEVOUS burdensome; heinous
ck **GRILLADE** grilled meat (Fr.)
GRILLAGE a cross-beam construction
GRILLING broiling; interrogating
GRIMACED smirked
GRIMALDI prince of clowns (It.)
GRIMMEST sternest; dourest
GRIMNESS fierceness; dourness
GRIMOIRE ancient handbook of black magic
GRINAGOG someone who is always smiling
GRINDERY shoemakers' materials
GRINDING pulverizing; crushing
GRINNING smiling broadly
GRIPEFUL distressing; colicky
GRIPPING holding tight; clutching
GRISELDA a very patient lady
GRISEOUS grey; grizzled
GRITTING grating; grinding; abrading
GRIZZLED grey; grumbled
GROANFUL mournful; lugubrious
GROANING moaning; complaining
GROGGERY a dram-shop; liquor-shop
nt **GROGGING** adding water to rum
GROG-SHOP pub; bar
pl, ar **GROINING** where thighs meet; intersecting vaults
bt **GROMWELL** a plant
GROOMING making neat and tidy; appearance
GROOMING (of horses); fur picking (animals)
GROOVING furrowing; scoring
zo **GROSBEAK** a finch
nm **GROSCHEN** Austrian coin
GROTTOES caves
GROUNDED on the ground
GROUNDER low ball at baseball
GROUPING arranging; disposing
GROUSING grumbling
GROUTING filling in with concrete
GROWABLE cultivatable
GROWLERY a private den
GROWLING grumbling; snarling
GRUBBIER dirtier
GRUBBING digging up
GRUBBLED groped
GRUDGING envying; coveting
GRUESOME horrible; grisly; grim
GRUMBLED complained; repined
GRUMBLER grouser
GRUMNESS surliness; dourness
zo **GRUMPHIE** a sow
bt **GRUNDSEL** groundsel
zo **GRYSBOCK** steinbock (S. Africa)
zo **GUACHERO** oil-bird (S. Amer.)
ch **GUAIACOL** an odorous liquid
bt **GUAIACUM** resinous lignum vitae
GUANCHOS natives of Canary Islands
mu **GUARACHA** a Cuban dance
GUARANTY basis of security
hd **GUARDANT** facing
GUARDFUL wary; cautious
GUARDIAN warden; protector
GUARDING watching; defending
GUBBINGS wild Devonians
GUELPHIC of Hanoverian royal family; (the Georges)
GUERILLA **GUERRILLA**, irregular warrior
zo **GUERNSEY** a garment; a cow
GUESSING imagining
GUGGLING gurgling
GUIDABLE readily conducted, led
GUIDANCE direction; government
GUILEFUL crafty; insidious
GUILTILY criminally; culpably
bt **GUIMAUVE** marsh-mallow
GUJARATI language (Bombay)
mn **GULCHING** pre-rock-fall sound
bt **GULF-WEED** tropical seaweed
GULLIBLE easily deceived
GULLIVER Swift traveller
GULLYING making a watercourse
GULOSITY voracity
GUMPTION shrewd sense; nous

bt **GUM-RESIN** gamboge
nt **GUNDALOW** weighted felucca sail barge, New England
GUN-LAYER who prepares guns for firing
GUNMETAL alloy; copper and tin
GUN-REACH gunshot; range; (target distance)
GUNSMITH gun-maker
GUNSTICK ramrod
GUNSTOCK part of gun
GUNSTONE stone projectile
GURGLING purling; rippling
GURKHALI language (Nepal)
GUSTABLE tasty; savoury
GUTTATED sprinkled; bedewed
GUTTERED of roof drainage run-off
GUTTLING gorging; swallowing
GUTTURAL throaty
GUYANESE (Guyana; S. Amer.)
GUZZLING swilling; tippling; quaffing
GYMNASIC of Gymnasium College levels
GYMKHANA equestrian competitions meeting
GYMNICAL athletic
zo **GYMNOTUS** electric eel
bt **GYNANDER** a plant
GYNANDRY male characteristics of the female
GYNARCHY female government
GYNECIUM women's quarters
bt **GYNERIUM** pampas grass
mn **GYPSEOUS** (gypsum)
GYPSYISM Romany, gypsy lore, language
GYRATING spinning; rotating; whirling
GYRATION rotation; revolution
GYRATORY circling; revolutionary
ae **GYRODYNE** speedy helicopter
GYROIDAL spiral; winding
mn **GYROLITE** hydrated calcium silicate
ae **GYROPTER** helicopter
nt **GYROSTAT** gyroscope compass housing

H

mu **HABANERA** Cuban dance with singing
lw **HABENDUM** descriptive clause
HABITANT inhabitant; native
HABITING dressing; arraying
HABITUAL customary; usual; wonted
HABITUDE customary manner
pr **HACHURES** shaded height; indications by pen hatchings
HACIENDA estate or ranch (S. Amer.)
zo **HACKBOLT** great shearwater gull
ga **HACK-LINE** of curling (bowls on ice)
tx **HACKLING** strands separating flax
HAEMATIC acting on the blood
md **HAEMATIN** (haemoglobin)
bt **HAGBERRY** bird-cherry
rl **HAGGADAH HAGGADIC**, Rabbinical commentary on O.T.
HAGGLING chaffering; bargaining
bt **HAGTAPER** the mullein
HAILSHOT small shrapnel shot
HAILSHOT coastal patrol warning: stop!
tx **HAIRCORD** kind of carpet
HAIR-LACE hair ribbon
HAIRLESS bald
HAIRLINE a fine line
mu **HAIRPINS** colloquial; diminuendo and crescendo signs
mn **HAIR-SALT** epsomite
HAIRWORK work done with hair
zo **HAIRWORM** freshwater worm
pg **HALATION** photographic defect
HALENESS robustness; health
HALF-BACK (football)
HALF-BOOT (halway to the knee)
HALF-BRED mongrel
el **HALF-CELL** electrode with electrolyte contact
HALF-COCK gun, using safety lever setting
HALF-DEAD almost dead
nt **HALF-DECK** half length deck
HALF-DONE incomplete; under-done
HALF-FACE the profile
HALF-HALT equestrian exercise
HALF-INCH map scale
ps **HALF-LIFE** radio-activity period
pr **HALF-LINE** light-shading technique
HALFLING a youth
nm **HALF-MARK** old coin, value 33p
HALFMAST a sign of mourning (flag salute)
HALF-MILE athletics
HALF-MOON a semicircle; demilune
HALF-NOTE a semitone
HALF-PASS two-step for horses
HALF-PAST HALF-HOUR, clock time
HALF-PIKE short pike
nt **HALF-ROLL** light swell; croquet shot
nt **HALF-SEAS** half-drunk; half-storm
ar **HALF-SPAN** lean-to; half-arch
HALF-SUIT body armour
HALF-TIDE neither in nor out
HALF-TIME an interval

HALF-TINT intermediate tint
pr **HALF-TONE** a printing process
zo **HALICORE** dugong; sea-cow
zo **HALIOTIS** mother-of-pearl shell
HALL-DOOR front door
nt **HALLIARD HALYARD**, rigging ropes; lines for sails
HALL-MARK a guarantee
HALLOOED shouted
HALLOWED reverenced; sanctified
HALTERED roped; tethered
zo **HALTERES** balancing wings
HAMBLING mutilating the foot
HAMIFORM hook-shaped
ck, rl **HAMINDAS** egg/peppers/onion casserole (Jew.)
HAMMERED expelled from Stock Exchange
HAMMERER hammer-man; smith
HAMPERED impeded; packed; clogged
HANDBALL an old pastime; 11 a side field game
mu **HANDBELL** one rung by hand
HANDBILL anouncement; broadcast
HANDBOOK a manual
HANDCART transport to hell
HANDCUFF manacle; fetter; restrict in baseball
HANDFAST hold; custody; betroth
HANDGEAR (manual control)
mo **HANDGRIP HANDHOLD**, climbing
mu **HAND-HORN** with only harmonic series (valveless)
HANDICAP penalty; allowance
HANDLESS awkward
HANDLINE line without a rod
HANDLING manipulation
HANDLIST convenient list
wv **HANDLOOM** for home weaving
HAND-MADE product of home industry
HANDMAID Abigail (maid-servant)
HANDMILL home corn-grinder
HANDPICK select carefully
HANDPOST finger-post; guide
HANDRAIL support
HAND-SALE handshake deal
HANDSOME generous; good-looking
HAND-WORK sloyd; handicrafts
HANDYMAN jack-of-all-trades
HANGABLE dependable; suspensible
HANGER-ON parasite; retainer
mn **HANGFIRE** explosive-detonation delay
md **HANGNAIL** agnail
zo **HANGNEST** a bird
HANGOVER after-alcohol reaction
HANKERED coveted; longed; yearned
zo **HAPLODON** mountain beaver
cy **HAPLOSIS** chromosome halving
HAPPENED chanced; occurred; befell
bt **HAPTERON** of plant attachment organs
HAQUETON padded jacket
HARA-KIRI ritual shame suicide (Jap.)
HARANGUE tirade; declaim
HARASSED wearied; persecuted
HARASSER a guerilla; annoyer; molester
HARDBACK book published in stiff covers
HARDBAKE cookery and baking techniques
bt **HARDBEAM** horn beam
HARD-CASH ready money
bd **HARD-CORE** unwavering resistance; stone fillers, essence of construction
HARDENED inured; obdurate
ch **HARDENER** toughener
bt **HARD-FERN** the northern fern
bt **HARD-HACK** steeple-bush
HARDIEST most robust; boldest
HARDNESS most solid firmness
HARDSHIP injustice; tribulation
nt **HARDTACK** ship's biscuit
cp **HARDWARE** ironmongery; computers and equipment etc.
bt **HARDWOOD** close-grained timber
bt **HAREBELL** hairbell; campanula
HAREFOOT swift of foot
bt **HAREHUNE** horehound
HAREPIPE a snare
bt **HARE'S-EAR** a yellow flower
HARLEIAN a literary society
HARLOTRY prostitution
HARMLESS innocuous; inoffensive
mu **HARMONIC** concordant; consonant; tone
HARMONIE windband (Ger.)
nt **HARPINGS** battens
HARRIDAN gaunt old woman; vixen
HARROWED lacerated; tortured; torn
HARROWER sensationalist
HARRYING harassing; raiding; vexing
bt **HARTWORT** plant; seseli type
bt **HASTATED** spear-shaped
HASTENED expedited; urged
HASTENER urgent reminder
bt **HASTINGS** early peas
HATBRUSH brush for hats
HATCHERY incubator
HATCHETY sharp featured
HATCHING plotting; shading; breeding

nt **HATCHWAY** deck opening
HATEABLE odious; detestable
HATSTAND like a hatrack; but different
zo **HATTERIA** tuatara; lizard (NZ)
HAT-TRICK 3 times (a winner); successful
HAUNCHED in squatting position
HAUNTING frequenting; obsessing
hd **HAURIANT** (fish on end)
HAURLING dragging; trailing
HAUSFRAU housewife (Ger.)
mu **HAUTBOIS** Fr. 'high (tone) wood', Italianized as oboe
HAVANNAH HABANA, (Cuban) cigar
HAVELOCK white cover for cap
HAVOCKED devastated; ruined
HAWAIIAN of Hawaii island group
zo **HAWFINCH** grosbeak
HAWK-BELL small bell on hawk's foot
HAWK-EYED lynx-eyed
zo **HAWK-MOTH** genus of moth
bt **HAWK-WEED** genus of weed
bt **HAWTHORN** the may
md **HAY-FEVER** pollen allergy
HAY-FIELD meadow
HAY-KNIFE stack-cutter
HAY-MAKER a swipe
ag **HAY-STACK** (thatched) hay storage pile
HAZARDED imperilled; ventured
HAZARDER a gambler; speculator
zo **HAZEL-HEN** ruffled grouse
bt **HAZEL-NUT** filbert
HAZINESS uncertainty; vagueness
md **HEADACHE** occipital disorder
HEADACHY off colour
HEAD-BAND book top; fillet
nt **HEAD-BOOM** jib-boom
nt **HEADFAST** mooring rope
HEADGEAR head-dress
HEAD-HOLD HEAD-LOCK, (wrestling)
HEADIEST most exhilarating
HEADLAMP (motor-car)
HEADLAND cape; promontory; ness
HEADLESS decapitated
HEADLINE newspaper superscripture
HEADLONG precipitately; steep; hasty
HEAD-MAIN main water supply
HEAD-MARK outstanding feature
md **HEAD-MOLD** skull; a moulding
HEADMOST most advanced
HEAD-NOTE introductory note
nt **HEAD-PUMP** latrines pump in bow of ship
HEAD-RACE lead to water-wheel; power
HEAD-RENT payment for use of a head
HEAD-REST a support
HEAD-RING Kaffir coiffure
bd, me **HEADROOM** ceiling clearance height
nt **HEADSAIL** set forward of mast (sailing)
HEADSHIP supreme authority
HEAD-TIRE head-dress
HEAD-WIND a contrary wind
HEAD-WORD title word
HEAD-WORK intellectual labour; sport
HEALABLE remediable; curable
HEARABLE audible
HEARTILY cordially; sincerely; warmly
HEARTLET small heart
bt **HEART-ROT** central decay
bt **HEATHERY** heathy; heath-clad
zo **HEATH-HEN** black grouse
bt **HEATH-PEA** legendary plant
HEAT-SPOT a freckle
me **HEAT-UNIT** lot of hot air
HEAT-WAVE calorific undulation
HEAVENLY celestial; seraphic
HEAVIEST most ponderous
HEBDOMAD a group of seven
HEBETANT making blunt; dulling
HEBETATE to dull; stupefy
HEBETUDE dullness; stupidity
HEBRAIST HEBRAISM, HEBRAIZE, of Hebrew customs and literature
HECATOMB sacrifice of 100
HECKLING interrupting, arguing against speaker
zo **HECKYMAL** blue tit
HECTORED boasted; swaggered
HECTORER brawler; bully; braggart
HECTORLY insolent; domineering
zo **HEDGEHOG** 'Mr Prickles'
HEDGEHOP a low flight
zo **HEDGEPIG** young hedgehog
bt **HEDGEROW** bushy boundary
HEDONICS HEDONISM, HEDONIST, 'pleasure is the highest good' doctrine
HEEDLESS regardless; rash
HEELBALL black wax
pr **HEEL-NICK** cut-out portion of movable type
HEFTIEST sturdiest; beefiest
HEGELIAN (process of the spirit)
HEGEMONY leadership
rl **HEGUMENE** prior
HEIGHTEN enhance; raise
lw **HEIRLESS** lacking heirship; no heir
HEIRLOOM family jewel

lw **HEIRSHIP** inherent right
md **HELCOSIS** ulceration
md **HELCOTIC** ulcerous
HELIACAL (sunlight)
HELICOID spiral
mn **HELIODOR** S. Afr. yellow beryl
md **HELIOSIS** sunstroke
zo **HELIOZIA** protozoa
ae **HELIPORT** helicopter airfield
HELLBENT reckless
HELLBORN HELLBRED, of satanic origin
HELLENIC Grecian
HELL-FIRE Satan's illumination
HELL-GATE approach to inferno
zo **HELL-KITE** bird of ill-omen
HELLWARD devilish progress
HELMETED double-domed
zo **HELMINTH** a worm
HELMLESS rudderless
HELMSMAN steersman
HELOTAGE HELOTISM, slavery; bondage; servitude; serfdom
HELPLESS impotent; weak; powerless
HELPMATE wife; partner
HELPMEET helpmate; helper
HELVETIA Switzerland
HELVETIC Swiss
mn **HEMATITE** haematite
zo **HEMIGALE** Malayan civet
mu **HEMIOLIA HEMIOLA, HEMIOLIC**, change of rhythm in ratio 2 to 3
zo **HEMIONUS** dziggetai
md **HEMIOPIA** faulty vision
zo **HEMIPODE** sort of quail
zo **HEMIPTER** cicada or bug
zo **HEMISOME** symmetrical half of animal
bt **HEMP-PALM** a pretend plant
bt **HEMP-SEED** flaxseed
HENCHMAN servant; page; valet
bt **HENEQUEN HENEQUIN**, sisal hemp
HEN-HOUSE coop
HEN-HUSSY a cotquean
HEN-MOULD black spongy soil
HEN-PARTY ladies' gossip group
HEN-ROOST poultry park
HEN-WOMAN hen-wife
mn **HEPATITE** barium sulphate
HEPATIZE of the liver function
md **HEPATOMA** liver tumour
HEPTAGON 7 sided figure
HEPTARCH ruler of a heptarchy
HERALDED proclaimed; blazoned
hd **HERALDIC HERALDRY**, armorial bearings and ceremonial orders
HERBAGED grass-covered
bt **HERBARIA** hortus siccus
bt **HERBELET** small herb
HERBLESS lacking vegetation
rl **HERCULES** strong man of labours
HERD-BOOK cattle stud-book
HERDSMAN cow-puncher
HEREAWAY hereabouts
HEREDITY inherent propensity
HEREINTO into this
HERESIES schisms
HEREUNTO unto this
HEREUPON upon this; then
HEREWITH by saying this
HERISSON spiked obstruction
HERITAGE patrimony; legacy
HERMETIC air-tight; mystic; occult
md **HERNIOID** ruptured; hernial
zo **HERNSHAW** heronshaw; handsaw
HEROICAL intrepid; valiant; epic
HEROICLY dauntlessly; daringly
HEROIZED lionized; idealized
HEROSHIP heroism (the Argonaut)
md **HERPETIC** of shingles (herpes)
HERTZIAN (low frequency waves)
mn **HERTZITE** galena
HESITANT vacillating; doubtful
HESITATE pause; waver; demur
as, nt **HESPERUS** the evening star; a wreck
HEXAGRAM Solomon's seal
HEXAPLAR sextuple
HEY-GO-MAD joyous interjection
HIBERNAL wintry
bt **HIBISCUS** tropical mallow
zo **HICCATEE** Cen. Amer. tortoise
HICCOUGH hiccup
HICCUPED belched politely
zo **HICKWALL** small woodpecker
HIDDENLY privily; furtively; covertly
HIDE-ROPE a reim (S. Afr.)
md **HIDROSIS** sweat
HIELAMAN native shield (Aust.)
rl **HIERARCH** chief priest
rl **HIERATIC** priestly
HIERONYM sacred name used as surname
HIGGLING haggling; chaffering
HIGH-BALL whisky and soda
HIGHBORN of noble birth
HIGHBRED not a hybrid
HIGHBROW so-called intellectual
HIGH-HUNG elevated
HIGH-JUMP athletics; dismissal
HIGHLAND where the heart is; (cattle)
HIGH-LIFE the jet set
rl **HIGH-MASS** special service
HIGHMOST topmost
mo **HIGHNESS** royal rank; altitude

HIGHROAD thoroughfare; main street
HIGH-SPOT climax
HIGH-TIDE floodtide
HIGH-TIME almost overdue
bt **HIGTAPER** the mullein
HI-JACKED transport passengers forcibly seized
HI-JACKER aerial super-pirate
HILARITY gaiety; jollity; merriment
HILL-FOLK hillmen; Covenanters
HILL-FORT stronghold; fastness
HILLOCKY hummocky
HILLSIDE a declivity
HINDERED delayed; thwarted; impeded
HINDERER obstructionist; opposer
HINDMOST last; posterior
HINDUISM doctrine and rites
HINGEING depending on
HINNIBLE ability to neigh or whinny
HIP-JOINT with-it nightclub
HIREABLE on hire
HIRELESS wageless
HIRELING mercenary
HIRPLING running lamely
HIRRIENT trilling sound
HIRUDINE like a leech
HISPANIC Spanish
md **HISTIOID** resembling tissue
HISTORIC authentic; genuine; famous
HISTRION play-actor
HITCHING fastening; attaching
HITHERTO till now
HIVELESS not a single skep
zo **HIVE-NEST** multiple bird's nest
zo **HOACTZIN** hoatzin; S. Amer. bird
HOARDING storing; treasuring; fence
HOARSELY discordantly; raucously
HOASTMAN member of a guild
HOBBLING walking lamely; limping
HOBBYISM **HOBBYIST**, cult of favourite pursuit
HOCKCART (last harvest load)
bt **HOCKHERB** a mallow
HOCKLING mowing
HOCK-TIDE harvest festival
HOCUSSED pocussed; dopey; drugged
nt **HOG-FRAME** (shipbuilding)
zo **HOGGEREL** sheep of second year
HOGMANAY New Year's Eve party (Sc.)
HOG-REEVE medieval parish officer
bt **HOG'SBEAN** henbane
ga **HOG-SCORE** block line on a curling rink
HOGSHEAD large cask of beer, wine
zo **HOGSTEER** wild boar
ac **HOHLRAUM** black-body radiator cavity
HOISTING raising; lifting; elevating
HOISTWAY trap-door
HOLDBACK check; retainer
bd **HOLDFAST** catch; grip; anchor spike with eye for joinery
HOLDINGS stock possessed by library
bt **HOLEWORT** moschatel
rl **HOLINESS** sanctity; devoutness
HOLLANDS genever gin
HOLLOAED shouted
HOLLOWED excavated; scooped
HOLLOWLY insincerely; vacantly
bt **HOLOGAMY** mature-cell fusion
ps **HOLOGRAM** laser optical imaging
zo **HOLOPTIC** side eyes meeting
zo **HOLOZOIC** eating other organisms
rl **HOLYROOD** holy cross; Palace (Edinburgh)
HOLY-WEEK the week before Easter
rl **HOLY-WRIT** the Scriptures
HOMAGING paying respects
HOMEBIRD stay-at-home
HOMEBORN native; domestic
HOMEBRED natural; unpolished
HOME-FARM nearest fields to farmhouse
HOMEFELT inward; private
HOMEGOER anti-social recluse
HOMELAND native land
HOMELESS on the streets
HOMELIKE not ornate
HOME-MADE better-tasting
HOME-RULE autonomy
HOMESICK nostalgia
HOMESPUN rough worsted
HOMEWARD return journey
HOMEWORK out of school task
lw **HOMICIDE** man-slaughter
HOMILIST sermonizer
bt **HOMOBIUM** alga/fungus association
zo **HOMODONT** teeth all alike
tc **HOMODYNE** (wireless telephony)
bt **HOMOGAMY** hermaphroditism
HOMOGENY similarity of nature
HOMOLOGY affinity of structure
HOMONYMY (similar-sounding words)
HOMOSOTE material for walls of huts
HOMOTYPE **HOMOTYPY**, structural affinity
HONDURAN (Honduras)
HONESTLY uprightly; sincerely
bt **HONE-WORT** herb parsley-piert
zo **HONEY-BAG** nectar sac of bee
zo **HONEY-BEE** nectar-sucker

bt **HONEYDEW** tobacco; melon
bt **HONEYPOT** a grape (S. Afr.)
HONORARY gratuitous; unpaid
HONOURED respected; revered
HONOURER venerator
HOODWINK befool; cheat; delude
HOOFMARK imprint of animal
zo **HOOK-WORM** a parasite
HOOLIGAN ruffian; rascal; bully
HOOP-IRON iron band on cask
cp **HOOT-STOP** audible stop signal
HOOT-TOOT toot-toot!; motor horn signal
HOPELESS despairing; despondent
HOPINGLY thinking wishfully
HOPPLING hobbling
HORATIAN (Horace)
bt **HORMESIS** non-toxic organism stimulus
zo **HORNBEAK** garfish
bt **HORNBEAM** a tree
zo **HORNBILL** picarian bird
zo **HORNFISH** garfish
HORNFOOT hoofed
HORNGATE gate of dreams
mn **HORN-LEAD** chloride of lead
HORNLESS dodded
mu, nt **HORNPIPE** air; dance; sailors'
ar **HORNWORK** outer ramparts; bastions
bt **HORNWORT** water-plant
HOROLOGY works on clocks
HOROPTER normal combined vision
HORRIBLE revolting; fearful; dire
HORRIBLY hideously; appallingly
HORRIDLY foully; alarmingly
HORRIFIC terrific; awful; frightful
HORSE-BOX van for horses
HORSE-BOY stable-boy
HORSE-CAR a carriage
zo **HORSE-FLY** large blood-sucking fly
HORSE-HOE a harrow
HORSEMAN rider; equestrian
HORSE-WAY road or track
HOSE-PIPE a duct
HOSE-REEL firefighting equipment
HOSPITAL an almshouse
HOSPODOR GOSPODAR, Slav governor
HOSTELRY inn; tavern
HOT-BLAST pre-heated air
ck **HOTCHPOT** farrago; mixture; medley
HOTELIER hotel-keeper
HOTHOUSE greenhouse
HOT-PLATE a heating appliance
HOT-PRESS a machine
HOT-SHORT brittle
bt **HOTTONIA** water-violet
HOT-WATER trouble
HOUGHING ham stringing
HOUNDING pursuing; tracking; trailing
HOUR-HAND time indicator
HOUSE-BOY serving lad
zo **HOUSE-DOG** watch dog
zo **HOUSE-FLY** musca domestica
lw **HOUSE-TAX** a levy
HOVELLED meanly housed
HOVELLER longshoreman
HOVERING in suspense; maintaining a fixed observation level above earth
mn **HOWIEITE** triclinic hydrous silicate
HOWITZER short cannon
HUCKSTER underhand dealer, rogue, advertiser
HUDDLING cowering in mass
HUDIBRAS political satire by S. Butler
HUGENESS bulk; immensity; vastness
rl **HUGUENOT** French Protestant
zo **HUIA-BIRD** New Zealand bird
HUMANELY mercifully; benignly
HUMANISM HUMANIST, HUMANITY, pragmatism; human interests; rhetoric
HUMANIZE enlighten; civilize
HUMATION burial
HUMBLING abasing; shaming
HUMEFIED moistened
HUMIDIFY to dampen
HUMIDITY moisture content in air
HUMILITY humbleness; meekness
HUMMOCKY hillocky
HUMORISM facetiousness; jocularity
HUMORIST jester; merryman
HUMOROUS witty; droll; comical
HUMOURED indulged; pampered
zo **HUMPBACK** a whale; road-bridge
HUMPLESS no depression here
HUMSTRUM humdrum; monotonous
HUNG-BEEF dried beef
HUNGERED famished; hankered
HUNGRILY cravingly; with appetite
HUNKERED squatted
HUNTRESS female hunter; lioness
HUNTSMAN chasseur
HURDLING (athletics)
zo **HURLBONE** a horse bone
HURRYING urging; speeding
HURTLESS uninjured; innoxious
HURTLING whizzing
HUSHED-UP undisclosed
HUSH-HUSH very secret
HUSH-MUSH highly confidential
HUSKIEST very hoarse

HUSTINGS electioneering platform
HUSTLING bustling; jostling; elbowing
HUTCHING cooping
HUZZAING shouting with joy
mn, bt **HYACINTH** a gem; flower
md **HYALITIS** optic inflammation
md **HYBODONT** irregular teeth
md **HYDATISM** a watery sound
HYDATOID aqueous
zo **HYDRANTH** nutrition polyp
HYDRATED combined with water
HYDROFIN high speed motor-boat
ch **HYDROGEL** water soluble colloid
ch **HYDROGEN** gaseous element
zo **HYDROIDS** animal growths on seaweed
HYDROMEL watered honey
zo **HYDROMYS** water-rats, etc.
HYDROPIC thirsty
md **HYDROPSY** dropsy
HYDROSOL colloidal solution
zo **HYDROZOA** **HYDROIDS**, jelly fish
ch **HYDRURET** hybrid
HYGIENIC salubrious; healthy
HYLICISM materialism
HYLICIST a philosopher
zo **HYLOBATE** a gibbon
HYLOZOIC materialistic
HYMENEAL conjugal; matrimonial
HYMENEAN nuptial; bridal
bt **HYMENIUM** part of fungus
rl **HYMN-BOOK** for singing praises
zo **HYOIDEUS** nerve branch in vertebrates
md **HYOSCINE** poisonous alkaloid
HYPALGIA insusceptibility
zo **HYPAXIAL** below the axis
sp **HYPERGOL** rocket fuel
HYPERION a Titan
md **HYPHAEMA** interior eye bleeding
pr **HYPHENED** **HYPHENIC**, linked; jointed
md **HYPNOSIS** hypnotism
HYPNOTIC mesmeric; sleep-inducing
zo **HYPOARIA** brain lobe in fish
HYPOBOLE form of argument
zo **HYPOCONE** molar cusp
bt **HYPODERM** cell layer under epidermis
HYPOGEAL underground
HYPOGEAN subterranean
mn **HYPOGENE** rock formation
ar, mn **HYPOGEUM** underground gallery, vault, or mine
zo **HYPOHYAL** hyoid arch element
zo **HYPOMERE** mesothelial wall zone
zo **HYPONOME** water escape funnel
HYPOSMIA dimished smell sensitivity
HYPOTHEC mortgage house; debt security
gl **HYPOZOAN** **HYPOZOIC**, below the limit of life
md **HYSTERIA** nervous disorder
HYSTERIC hysterical; in a fit

I

zo **IANTHINA** purple sea-snails
md **IATRICAL** medical
IBSENISM of Henrik Ibsen's works
ICE-BLINK a reflection; mirage
ICE-BOUND immobilized by ice
ICE-BROOK frozen brook
ICE-CREAM the content of a cornet
ICE-FIELD glacier terrain
ICE-FLOAT sea ice-floe
ICE-HOUSE ice storage building
ICE-LEDGE en route for Everest
ICE-PLANT crystalline snow as flower
ICE-SHEET glacial arctic regions
ICE-WATER Amer. national drink
ICE-YACHT for sailing on sea ice
md **ICHOROUS** like ichor
zo **ICHTHINE** (fishes' eggs)
ICHTHYIC fishlike
ICTERINE yellow
IDEALISM transcendency
IDEALIST visionary
IDEALIZE attribute perfection to ideals
IDEATING fancying
IDEATION conception
IDEATIVE imaginative
IDENTIFY recognize; integrate
IDENTITY individuality; sameness
IDEOGRAM ideograph; logo; picture word (cp. Chinese)
IDEOLOGY metaphysics
IDIOTISH doltish; fatuous; inane
IDIOTISM imbecility; inanity
IDIOTIZE ridicule; befool
IDLEHOOD idleness
IDLENESS dolce far niente
mn **IDOCRASE** silicate of lime
IDOLATER a heretic
IDOLATRY image worship
IDOLIZED idolised
IDOLIZER a fan
rl **IGNATIAN** (St Ignatius)
IGNITING kindling; inflaming
IGNITION firing; lighting
el **IGNITRON** mercury arc rectifier
IGNOMINY public disgrace; obloquy

IGNORANT uninstructed; unaware
IGNORING disregarding; overlooking
ILLATIVE deducive; grammatical case (direction to)
ILL-BLOOD enmity; discord; rancour
ILL-FATED calamitous; unlucky
ch **ILLINIUM** metallic element
ILL-TIMED ill-judged
ILL-TREAT maltreat
ILLUDING creating illusions; deceiving
ILLUMINE enlighten; irradiate
ILLUMING elucidating
ILL-USAGE harsh treatment
ILLUSION delusion; dream; fantasy
ILLUSIVE ILLUSORY, deceptive; fugitive; hallucinatory
ILLYRIAN of Illyricum; of Dalmatian coast (Croatia)
mn **ILMENITE** titanate of iron
zo **IMAGINAL** relating to an image
IMAGINED fancied; thought
IMAGINER dreamer
IMBECILE idiot; moron
IMBEDDED firmly fixed
IMBELLIC pacific; unwarlike
IMBIBING absorbing; swallowing
pg **IMBITION** dye transfer
IMBOWING arching
IMBRUING drenching
IMBRUTED degenerated
IMBUMENT deep tincture
IMBURSED supplied with cash
IMITABLE easy to forge
IMITANCY mimicry
IMITATED parodied; aped
IMITATOR copy-cat; impersonator
IMMANENT inherent; innate
IMMATURE unripe; crude; untimely; undeveloped
IMMERGED IMMERSED, submerged; soused; plunged; inundated
IMMERSED held under water (baptism)
IMMINENT impending; perilous
IMMOBILE still; motionless; static
IMMODEST bold; indelicate; coarse
IMMOLATE sacrifice; surrender
IMMORTAL imperishable; deathless
IMMUNITY privilege; freedom
IMMUNIZE exempt
IMPACTED collided; struck
IMPAIRED enfeebled; blemished
IMPAIRER saboteur; marrer
IMPALING transfixing
IMPALMED grasped; handled
IMPANATE to sandwich
IMPARITY inequality; disproportion
IMPARKED enclosed
IMPARLED conversed; discussed
IMPARTED communicated; divulged
IMPARTER bestower; donator
IMPASTED kneaded
IMPAWNED pledged; mortgaged
IMPEDING obstructing; thwarting; personal foul in water polo
IMPELLED urged; induced; drove
IMPELLER instigator; inciter; centrifugal pump
IMPENDED threatened; hovered
IMPENNED enclosed; encompassed
IMPERIAL shorn beard; a goatee
IMPERIUM sovereignty
md **IMPETIGO** an eruption
IMPIERCE bore; drill; penetrate
mn **IMPINGER** dust-measuring device
IMPISHLY mischievously; wantonly
IMPLATED sheathed
IMPLEACH interweave
IMPLEDGE pawn; hypothecate
IMPLICIT tacit; implied; inferred
IMPLORED entreated; craved
IMPLORER supplicant; petitioner
IMPLUMED plucked
IMPLUNGE immerse; dive
IMPLYING indicating; connoting
IMPOCKET filch; steal
IMPOISON envenom; infect
IMPOLDER reclaim from sea (Holland)
IMPOLICY inexpedience
IMPOLITE positively rude; insolent
lw **IMPONENT** a backer; imposer; con-man
lw **IMPONING** wagering; betting
IMPORTED conveyed; denoted
IMPORTER foreign dealer
IMPOSING impressive; stately
IMPOSTOR IMPOSTER, trickster
IMPOTENT non-erectile; unable
IMPRIMIS in the first place
IMPRISON incarcerate; immure
IMPROPER unseemly; indelicate
IMPROVED bettered; amended
IMPROVER developer; rectifier
IMPUDENT saucy; shameless
IMPUGNED gainsaid; contradicted
IMPUGNER attacker; assailant
IMPUNITY exemption; immunity
IMPURELY unchastely; licentiously
IMPURITY an adulterant
IMPUTING charging; insinuating
INACTION inertia; sloth; indolence
INACTIVE idle; torpid; supine
INAQUATE turn into water
INARABLE unfit for tillage

INASMUCH because
INAURATE gild
INBONDED brick-laying technique
INCAGING confining; mewing
INCANTON merge into a canton
INCARNED incarnated
hd **INCENSED** inflamed; enraged
INCENSOR incense burner
INCEPTOR beginner; inaugurator
bd **INCERTUM** early rubble-filled masonry
INCHMEAL gradually
INCHOATE begun; immature; incipient
cp **INCIDENT** episode; event; fracas; breakdown
INCIRCLE encircle; encompass
INCISELY clear cut; acutely
INCISING scribing; engraving
INCISION cut; gash; slit
INCISIVE trenchant; sarcastic
INCISORY sharpness
INCISURA body notch; scar
pl **INCISURE** a cut; wound
INCITANT stimulant; provocative
INCITING goading; arousing; spurring
INCIVISM lack of communal spirit
INCLINED disposed; biased; tilted
INCLINER sloping dial
INCLUDED contained; embodied
INCOMING entrance; arrival
INCOMITY incivility; rudeness
INCREASE aggravate; augment
INCREATE create within
INCUBATE hatch
bt **INCUBOUS** (leaf formation)
zo **INCUDATE** characteristic of rotifera
INCURRED contracted; ran into
INCURVED bent
INCUSING stamping
INCUSSED forged; struck
INDAGATE investigate
ch **INDAMINE** used in dye-making
INDEBTED under obligation
INDECENT unbecoming; coarse
INDENTED notched; toothed
INDEVOTE disloyal; unloving
INDEVOUT irreverent; impious
INDEXING compiling an index
nt **INDIAMAN** trading ship
INDICANT symptomatic
INDICATE show; suggest; denote
INDICTED impeached; charged
INDICTEE a defendant
INDICTER an accuser
INDIGENE a native; aboriginal
INDIGENT poor; needy; necessitous
INDIRECT devious; tortuous; oblique grammar (speech)
INDITING dictating; writing; penning
INDOCILE intractible; stubborn
INDOLENT lazy; sluggish; inert
INDUCING actuating; urging; causing
rl **INDUCTED** invested; installed
INDUCTOR officiating minister
INDULGED gratified; humoured
INDULGER favourer
ch **INDULINE** a dye
INDURATE harden; inure
zo **INDUSIAL** (caterpillar skins)
bt **INDUSIUM** skin or cover
INDUSTRY trade; assiduity; diligence
bt **INDUVIAE** withered leaves
INEDIBLE uneatable
INEDITED unpublished
INEQUITY injustice; unfairness
bt **INERMOUS** no prickles
INERTION sluggishness; indolence
INEXPERT unskilled; unversed
INFAMING defaming; discrediting
INFAMIZE publicly brand with infamy
INFAMOUS vile; notorious; heinous
INFANTLY childishly; infantile
INFANTRY foot-soldiers
INFECTED tainted; corrupted; disease-ridden
INFECTER carrier of disease
INFECUND sterile; barren; unprolific
INFERIAE Roman sacrifices
INFERIOR poor; subordinate; mediocre
INFERNAL diabolical; fiendish; satanic
INFERRED deduced; argued; surmised
INFESTED overrun; thronged; beset
INFILTER permeate; seep
INFINITE boundless; unlimited
mu **INFINITO** perpetual
INFINITY immensely
INFIRMLY irresolutely; feebly
INFLAMED exasperated; infuriated
INFLAMER agent provocateur
INFLATED distended; bloated; swollen
INFLATOR air-pump
INFLATUS inspiration
INFLEXED bent inwards
INFLOWED ran in
INFLUENT a tributary
INFOLDED embraced
INFORMAL unconventional; simple
INFORMED told; apprised; notified
INFORMER a sneak

INFRA-DIG beneath one's social standing
INFRA-RED beyond red in spectrum
INFRINGE violate; transgress
INFRUGAL prodigal; extravagant
INFUMATE to smoke
INFUSING inculcating; inspiring
INFUSION instillation; introduction
INFUSIVE penetrative
zo **INFUSORY** protozoic
INGENIUM bent of mind
INGROOVE engroove; furrow
INGROWTH opposite of outgrowth
INGUINAL (between thighs)
md **INHALANT** a vapourizer
INHALING breathing
INHERENT innate; congenial
INHUMING burying; interring
INIMICAL allergic; hostile; contrary
INIQUITY vice; sinfulness; offence
INITIATE a novice; start; inaugurate
INJECTED forced in; introduced
md **INJECTOR** kind of pump, syringe
INJURING damaging; maltreating
INKINESS state of being inky
INKMAKER squid
INKSTAND ink-holder
mn **INK-STONE** sulphate of iron
INLANDER not an islander
lw **INLAWING** clearing of attainder
INLAYING ornamenting
INNATELY instinctively; naturally
INNOCENT guileless; blameless; sinless
INNOVATE make changes; alter; new
INNUENDO an insinuation
INORNATE plain
ch **INOSITOL** yeast growth agent
INQUIRED asked; investigated
INQUIRER questioner; scrutineer
nt **INRIGGED** with rowlocks on gunwhale
INSANELY crazily; deliriously
INSANITY dementia; mania; lunacy
INSCIENT ignorant; illiterate; unread
cp **INSCRIBE** dedicate; engrave; imprint; rewrite data
INSCROLL write on a scroll
INSEAMED marked by a seam
INSECTED segmented
INSECURE uncertain; hazardous
INSERTED introduced; injected
INSETTED implanted
INSHADED tinted
INSHRINE enshrine; dedicate
INSIGNIA badges; emblems; tokens
INSISTED persisted; maintained; urged

INSITION ingraftment
INSNARED entangled; caught; ginned
INSNARER trapper
INSOLATE dry in the sun
INSOLENT contumacious; hubristic
md **INSOMNIA** sleeplessness
INSOMUCH so that
INSPIRED inhaled; animated
INSPIRER spiritual leader
INSPIRIT enhearten; infuse
INSTABLE unstable; transient
INSTANCE specify; occurrence; incident
INSTANCY urgency; solicitation
INSTATED established
INSTINCT natural propensity
INSTREAM to flow
INSTRUCT edify; direct; enjoin; order
INSTYLED entitled; named; yclept
lw **INSUCKEN** milling restriction
INSULATE isolate; enisle
INSULTED affronted; outraged
INSULTER taunter; abuser; offender
INSURANT policy holder
INSURING assuring; underwriting
INTAGLIO opposite to cameo
INTARSIA pictorial inlay
INTEGRAL whole; entire; complete
INTENDED betrothed; meant; purposed
INTENDER activator; planner
INTENTLY with fixed attention
INTERACT interplay of various similar factors
tc **INTERCOM** two-way communication system
INTEREST concern; attention
INTERIOR indoors; within
INTERLAY insert
INTERMIT suspend
INTERMIX blend; commingle
INTERNAL domestic; within; inside
INTERNED confined; imprisoned
INTERNEE arrested alien
INTERPOL international criminal police
INTERRED buried; inhumed; entombed
INTERREX a regent; protector
INTERTIE connecting piece
cp, mu, tc **INTERVAL** gap; pause; (music); interim, specific time period
INTER-WAR of period between wars
bt **INTEXINE** pollen cover
INTIMACY **INTIMITY**, extreme closeness; familiarity
INTIMATE declare intentions in advance

INTONATE intone
INTONING chanting
INTRADOS lower surface of arch
INTREPID dauntless; doughty; daring
INTRIGUE cabal; interest; conspiracy
INTROMIT insert; admit
INTRORSE facing inwards
INTRUDED butted in; thrusted
INTRUDER trespasser; interloper
INTUBATE insert a tube
INUNDANT overflowing; overwhelming
INUNDATE flood; swamp; deluge
INURBANE rude; uncouth; discourteous
INURNING putting in an urn
INUSTION a branding
INVADING violating; raiding; entering
INVARIED set; constant; uniform
INVASION foray; attack; assault
md **INVASIVE** aggressive; intrusive (tumours); (epidemic)
INVECKED **INVECTED**, scalloped
hd **INVECTED** engrailed
INVEIGLE entice; wheedle; decoy; lure
INVEILED veiled
INVENTED devised; created; fabricated
INVENTOR innovator; contriver
el **INVERTER** conversion device
cp **INVERTER** sign reverser; negative binary signal
INVESTED arrayed; indued; beset
INVESTOR buyer; purchaser
INVITING attractive; alluring
INVOCATE adjure; invoke; beseech
INVOICED billed; charged
INVOKING conjuring; summoning
INVOLUTE spiral
INVOLVED complicated; complex
INWALLED enclosed
INWARDLY privily; secretly
INWORKED inset
ch **IODAZIDE** iodine azide
md **IODIZING** with iodine effect
ch **IODYRITE** iodide of silver
mu **IOLANTHE** a fairy; an opera
IONICIZE Grecianize
IONIZING electrolysing
IOTACISM excessive use of 'I'
pc **IPSATIVE** reflected, measured against self
IREFULLY angrily; furiously
IRENICAL tranquil; pacific
IRENICON peace propaganda
md **IRIDITIS** eye inflammation
IRISATED like a rainbow
IRISCOPE spectroscope
IRISHISM Celtic expression, humorous
IRISHMAN (Ireland)
bt **IRONBARK** eucalyptus
nt **IRONCLAD** metal-hulled warships
mn **IRON-CLAY** yellow iron ore
IRONGREY a colour
IRONICAL satirical; sarcastic; derisive
ch **IRON-SAND** firework mixture
IRONSICK rusty and leaky
IRONSIDE a Cromwellian
IRONWARE ironmongery
bt **IRONWOOD** tough timber
IRONWORK smithery
IRRIGATE supply with water; moisten
IRRISION derision; banter
IRRITANT annoying; exasperating
IRRITATE gall; nettle; provoke
bt **IRRORATE** as if dew-covered
IRRUPTED burst in; invaded; raided
ISABELLE yellowish grey
ISAGOGIC introductory
zo **ISENGRIM** a fabulous wolf
rl **ISLAMISM** Mohammedanism
rl **ISLAMITE** worshipper of Allah
rl **ISLAMIZE** proselytize
ISLANDED isolated
ISLANDER not an inlander
ISLESMAN (from the Hebrides)
mt **ISOBARIC** (equal barometric pressure)
ISOCHEIM line indicating equal winter temperatures
zo **ISOCHELA** equal-jointed chela
ISOCHORE gas pressure and temperature
ISOCORIA equal size of eye pupils
ISOCRYME line indicating equal winter temperatures
rl **ISODICON** short anthem
bd **ISODOMON** **ISODOMUM**, masonry composed of uniform blocks
ISOGONAL equi-angular
ISOGONIC (equal magnetic angles)
el **ISOLATED** solitary; (fever epidemic); (sheltered); (prison); (hermit)
el **ISOLATOR** device for 2-way microwave flow
ch **ISOLOGUE** like/unlike compound
ch **ISOMERIC** **ISONYMIC**, different properties of similar compounds
md **ISOPATHY** homeopathy
ISOPLETH map showing weather constituents
ch **ISOPRENE** synthetic rubber

ISOSTASY equal-pressure-caused equilibrium
mt **ISOSTERE** atmospheric volume line
ISOTHERE (equal summer heat)
ISOTHERM line of equal heat
ISOTONIC having equal tension
nc **ISOTOPES** nuclides of similar number but different mass
ISOTOPIC of isotopes
ISSUABLE distributable
ISSUANCE delivery
go **ISTHMIAN** of an isthmus, narrow neck
ITALIOTE a Greek colonist in Italy
zo **ITCH-MITE** burrowing insect
ITERANCE repetition
ITERATED repeated; recapitulated
ITHURIEL cherub; guardian angel
bt **IVORY-NUT** a palm-nut

J

JABBERED gabbled; chattered
JABBERER wind-bag
JACKAROO greenhorn squatter (Aust.)
JACKETED having a paper cover
zo **JACKFISH** pike
nt **JACK-FLAG** smaller than ensign
JACK-FOOL perfect fool
JACK-HIGH raise car level with jack (tool)
bt **JACKWOOD** jaca-tree
nt **JACKYARD** uppermost short extension to main-mast
JACOBEAN (James I)
JACOBITE partisan of James II
wv **JACQUARD** loom mechanism
JACULATE to throw; to dart
JAGGEDLY raggedly; unevenly
JAILBIRD old lag; often convicted
JALOUSIE Venetian blind
JAMAICAN of Jamaica
JAMBEAUS leggings
JAMBOREE Boy Scouts' rally, frolic, carousal
JAMBOREE hand with 5 highest trumps (cards)
JAMPANEE chair carrier
JANGLING wrangling
md **JANICEPS** 2-headed monstrosity
JANUFORM double-faced; of doorways
JAPANESE of Japan
JAPANNED varnished; enamelled
JAPANNER a shoeblack
JAPAN-WAX lacquer from sumac tree berries
JAPHETIC Armenian alphabet
bt **JAPONICA** Japanese quince
zo **JARARAKA** poisonous snake
mn **JAROSITE** iron-potassium sulphate
mn **JASPONYX** an onyx
md **JAUNDICE** bile-obstruction disorder
JAUNTIER more sprightly
JAUNTILY debonairly
JAUNTING an outing
JAVANESE an Indonesian
zo **JAVELINA** wild boar
JAW-LEVER veterinary instrument
pl **JAW-TOOTH** a molar
JEALOUSY anxiety caused by rivals
tx **JEANETTE** coarse cloth
JEBUSITE a Canaanite
rl **JEHOVIST** Hebrew theologian
JELLYBAG a strainer
fr **JELUTONG** pale Malayan hardwood
zo **JENTLING** Danube chub
JEOPARDY danger; peril; hazard; risk
JEREMIAD lamentation
JEROBOAM super wine bottle
nt **JERQUING** customs searching
JERRICAN 5-gallon (22 litres) petrol tin
JEST-BOOK collection of jokes
rl **JESUITIC** **JESUITRY**, of Jesuit Order
JET-BLACK deepest black
JET-CRAFT **JET-PLANE**, jet-propelled aircraft
nt **JETTISON** throw overboard
JETTYING projecting
JEWELLED set with gems
JEWELLER a craftsman with gems
JEWISHLY judaical
mu **JEW'S-HARP** small mouth instrument
JICKAJOG a shake; a push
JIGGERED flabbergasted
JIGGLING wriggling; joggling
JIGMAKER a tool-maker
JINGLING tinkling; rhyming
JINGOISH super-patriotic
JINGOISM ultra-patriotism
JOBATION a tedious scolding
JOCKEYED jostled; outwitted; set aside
JOCKEYED race-horse ridden by –
JOCOSELY facetiously; joyously
JOCOSITY sportiveness; fun
JOCUNDLY mirthfully; waggishly
JODHPURS riding breeches
JOGGLING shaking; jostling; elbowing

nm **JOHANNES** old Portuguese gold coin
pr **JOIN-HAND** connected script
vt **JOINT-ILL** umbilicus disease
bd **JOINTING** finishing joints between timber/bricks
JOINT-OIL synovia
lw **JOINTURE** a settlement (estate)
JOISTING fitting with laths
JOKINGLY in jest; hilariously
JOLLIEST very merry and bright
JOLT-HEAD dunderhead; simpleton
JONGLEUR juggler (Fr.)
mu **JONGLEUR** wandering minstrel
bt **JORDANON** faintly varied breeding race
JOSTLING pushing; hustling; crowding
JOUNCING shaking; jolting (slang)
JOUSTING a tourney; simulation of middle-aged knights
JOVIALLY festively; blithely
JOVIALTY merriment; conviviality
JOYFULLY rapturously; gladly
JOYOUSLY blissfully; happily
ae **JOYSTICK** aeroplane control lever
JUBILANT triumphant; exulting
JUBILATE celebrate; rejoice
rl, lw **JUDAICAL** Jewish
rl **JUDAISED** conformed to Mosaic law
rl **JUDAISER** opponent of St Paul
JUDGMENT sentence; decree; award
JUDICIAL legal; legitimate; sagacious
JUGGLERY manual dexterity
JUGGLING conjuring; swindling
JUGO-SLAV Yugoslav
ck **JULIENNE** sliced vegetables (soup)
JUMBLING confusing; mixing
JUMP-SEAT collapsible seat
bd, rw **JUNCTION** union; coalition; coupling; (-pipe); (-box of circuits) (railway)
JUNCTURE exigency; moment of crisis; joined speech sounds
JUNKBALL slow, breaking pitch (baseball)
JUNKETED feasted; caroused
JUNK-RING piston-packing
JUNONIAN queenly
gl **JURASSIC** geological period
lw **JURATORY** comprising an oath
lw **JURISTIC** legal jurisdictive
nt **JURYMAST** temporary mast
JUSTLING jostling; jolting
JUSTNESS equity; impartiality
JUVENILE young; puerile; adolescent

K

KAILWIFE scold; cabbage seller
KAILYARD KALEYARD, kitchen garden
KAKEMONO Japanese picture
KAKIEMON style of pottery (17th c.)
pc **KAKOSMIA** abnormal reaction to smell
md **KALA-AZAR** black fever
KALAMDAN Persian writing case
tx **KALAMKAR** Indian printed cotton
KALENDAR calendar; almanac
bt **KALERUNT** cabbage stalk
KALEVALA Finnish epic
mn **KALINITE** alum
KALIYUGA Hindu mythological era
KALOLOGY science of beauty
KALOTYPE early photograph
KAMADEVA Indian Eros
KAMIKAZE suicide bomber plane (Jap.)
KANARESE language (Mysore, India)
tx **KANDAHAR** East Indian wool
zo **KANGAROO** marsupial (pouched)
rl, mu **KANTIKOY** religious dance
KARELIAN of Karelia (N & E of Ladoga and East Finland)
cy **KARYOTIN** nuclear reticulum substance
KASHMIRI people and language (Kashmir)
bl **KATABION** katabolic-predominant organism
KATAKANA Japanese script
bt **KAURI-GUM** a resin (Aust.)
KAYMAKAM Turkish governor
nt **KECKLING** binding rope
ck **KEDGEREE** a breakfast dish of rice, egg, fish
nt **KEEL-BOAT** type of yacht
nt **KEEL-HAUL** (punishment)
KEENNESS acuity; astuteness
KEEPSAKE memento; relic
el **KENETRON** large vacuum diode
ro **KENOTRON** wireless valve
KERASINE KERATOSE, horn
md **KERATOMA** skin tumour
KERCHIEF a head cover
KERMESSE annual fair in Low Countries; also circuit road racing events
bt **KERN-BABY** harvest image
bt **KERNELLY** full of seeds
mn **KEROSENE** paraffin
ch **KETOXIME** ketone reaction product
pr **KEYBLOCK** printing
mu **KEYBOARD** clavier, piano, organ

cp, tc **KEYBOARD** type, digit, encoder; enigma; typewriter
cp, tc **KEYBOARD** systematic select-
mu **KEY-BUGLE** Kent bugle
bt **KEY-FRUIT** ash, sycamore, etc.
bd **KEYING-IN** bonding a brick wall
KEY-MONEY levy on a tenant
KEYPLATE keyhole escutcheon
cp **KEYPUNCH** punch-card recording system
ar **KEYSTONE** main arch support
mu **KHOROVOD** Russian round dance with singing
KIBITZER critical observer (USA)
KICKABLE suitable for booting; (ball)
KICK-DOWN switch
KICKSHAW a fallal
KID-GLOVE soft delicate glove
mn **KIEFEKIL** meerschaum
KIELBASA smoked Polish sausage
KILL-CROP a changeling
zo **KILLDEER** American plover
KILL-TIME a pastime
KILN-HOLE mouth of kiln
me, cp **KILOBITS** one thousand binary digits
me **KILODYNE** 1000 dynes; units of force
me **KILOGRAM** 1000 grams, weight
KILOMEGA one thousand million (10^9)
me **KILOWATT** 1000 watts
KINDLESS unnatural; merciless
KINDLIER more forbearing
KINDLING animating; tinder
KINDNESS benevolence; generosity
KINEMICS gestural expression
KINESICS gestural body movements
KINETICS dynamics
zo **KINGBIRD** American fly-catcher
zo **KING-CRAB** tropical crab
zol **KINGFISH** the opah
KINGHOOD sovereignty
KINGLESS republican
KINGLIKE truly regal
KINGLING ruler of petty state
KINGPOST principal strut and support for rigging (gliding/hang-)
KINGSHIP kingcraft
KINGWANA language
bt **KINGWOOD** ebony (S. Amer.)
zo **KINKAJOU** raccoon; honey-bear
KINSFOLK kindred; relations
KIPPERED cured
KIRIKANE gold-foil application (Jap.)
rl **KIRKYARD** graveyard (Sc.)
zo **KIROUMBO** tropical bird
ga **KISS-CURL** stymie in ice curling
bt **KITEFOOT** a tobacco plant
KITTENED had a kitty litter
KITTLISH ticklish
KLYSTRON electron converter
KNABBING gnawing
KNACKISH knavish
KNAPPING flint breaking
KNAPSACK haversack; rucksack
bt **KNAPWEED** bachelor's buttons
KNEADING dough work
KNEE-DEEP **KNEE-HIGH**, nearly thigh-high
bt **KNEEHOLM** knee-holly
KNEELING kotowing; worshipping
mu **KNEE-STOP** organ lever
rl **KNELLING** tolling; church bells
KNICKERS knickerbockers (men)
KNICKERS undergarments (women)
KNIFE-BOY kitchen scullery lad
KNIGHTED now Sir
KNIGHTLY courtly
bt **KNIT-BONE** herb comfrey
KNITTING uniting; interlacing
KNITWEAR reticulated fabric
KNOCKING rapping; hitting; motoring
KNOCK-OUT K.O.; defeat of boxer
KNOTLESS free from ties
KNOTTIER more intricate
tx, pt **KNOTTING** securing; entangling; (carpets); (nauti-knots); dissolved shellac
KNOTWORK ornamental work
KNOUTING scourging with knotted rope
KNOWABLE ascertainable; scibile
KNOW-ALLS wiseacres
KNUCKLED yielded; jointed
ar **KNULLING** fluting and reeding
mt **KOEMBANG** fohn wind, Java
KOFTGARI **KOFTWORK**, inlaying steel with gold
rl **KOHELETH** Preacher (Solomon)
mn **KOHINOOR** famous diamond
bt **KOHLRABI** cole-turnip
zo **KOLINSKY** Siberian mink
KOMITAJI Balkan guerilla band
KONISTRA orchestra of a Greek theatre
KOORBASH **KOURBASH**, whip made from rhino hide
KORFBALL 12-a-side field game (handball)
KOTOWING making obeisance
nm **KREUTZER** small Austrian copper coin
KUKUKUKU people (New Guinea)
KURVEYOR transport rider (S. Afr.)
KUTTROLF Waldglas vessel with curved neck (Ger.)

ch **KYANIZED** cyanized
md **KYLOSSIS** club-foot
md **KYPHOSIS** vertebral deformity

L

ch **LABDANUM LADANUM** opium
LABELLED directed
bt **LABELLUM** lower petal
LABIALLY lipwise
LABIATED lipped
pc **LABILITY** quick emotional variations
LABOURED strove
LABOURER a toiler
ck **LABSKAUS** meat/vegetable stew (Scand.)
LABURNIC derived from laburnum
bt **LABURNUM** flowering tree
bt **LACE-BARK** bark of a tree
LACE-BOOT (no buttons)
bt **LACE-LEAF** aquatic plant
LACERATE tear
zo **LACEWING** an insect
LACEWORK decoration
LACE-YOKE needlework
LACHESIS one of the Fates
LACING-IN attaching end-boards to book body
LACK-A-DAY sorrowful exclamation
LACKEYED valeted
LACONISM brevity; pithiness
ga **LACROSSE** a Canadian game
LACRYMAL LACRIMAL, tearful
LACTEOUS milk-like
LACTIFIC milk producing
bt **LACTUCIC** (lettuce)
LACUNOSE pitted; furrowed
LADDERED (stockings)
ck **LADLEFUL** soup measure
LADYBACK tandem cycle
zo **LADYBIRD** a helpful beetle
bt **LADY-FERN** tall slender fern
LADY-HELP distressed gentlewoman
LADYHOOD gentility
LADYLIKE well-bred; delicate
LADYLOVE a sweetheart
LADYSHIP a title for dame, wife of lord, knight
LAGTHING Norwegian Upper House (Parliament)
LAICIZED opened to the laity
bd **LAITANCE** milky mortar scum
LAKE-LIKE merely?
LALLYGAG necking (USA)
zo **LAMANTIN** the manatee
rl **LAMASERY** Tibetan monastery
LAMBDOID lambda-shaped (Gr.)
LAMBENCY play of light
LAMBLIKE gentle; meek
zo **LAMBLING** lambkin
LAMBSKIN soft fleece
LAME-DUCK President without power (USA)
LAMELLAR of thin plates
LAMENESS halting; crippledness
LAMENTED deeply regretted
LAMENTER deplorer; bewailer
LAMINARY in thin plates
LAMINATE in layers
LAMPHOLE sewer lighting shaft
LAMP-POST support for drunk
LANCEGAY a kind of spear
zo **LANCELET** primitive vertebrate
nt **LANCHANG** lugger sailboat (Malaya)
zo **LAND-CRAB** land-dwelling crustacean
nt **LANDFALL** landslip; sighting of land
LAND-FISH fish out of water
LAND-GIRL wartime farm help
zo **LAND-HERD** a herd of animals
LANDLADY boarding-house boss; rentier
LANDLESS without land (tenure)
LANDLINE overhead cable
LANDLOCK protect from wind and sea
LANDLORD mine host; house or estate owner
LANDMARK notable event; conspicuous feature; boundary stone
LANDMINE parachuted bomb
LANDNAMA Domesday Book (Ice.)
zo **LANDRAIL** corncrake
LAND-ROLL clod-crusher
LAND-SHIP a tank
LANDSLIP landslide
LANDSMAN antithesis of seaman; farmer
LAND-TURN land-breeze
nt **LANDWARD** in the direction of land; sea-breeze
LANDWEHR German militia
LAND-WIND off-shore wind
LANGLAUF cross-country skiing (Ger.)
LANGRAGE grape shot
zo **LANGSHAN** black Chinese hen
LANGSYNE time long past
cp **LANGUAGE** diction; vernacular; digital codes
LANGUISH pine; droop; decline
LANIATED torn to pieces
LANKIEST leanest
LANKNESS length without breadth

zo **LANNERET** small falcon
LANOLINE wool fat
LANTHORN hornsided lantern
LAP-BOARD board used by tailors
LAPELLED with lapels; (coat collar)
LAPIDARY stone-cutter
LAPIDATE pelt with stones
LAPIDIFY turn into stone
LAPIDIST stone-worker
mn **LAPILLUS** fragment of lava
LAP-JOINT an overlapping joint
LAPPETED with flaps
LAPSABLE terminal; transient
LAPSTONE (used by a shoemaker)
nt **LARBOARD** port side
LARCENER a thief; pilferer
LARDERER a store keeper
LARGESSE liberality; generosity
bt **LARKSPUR** a delphinium
LARRIKIN Australian hooligan
zo **LARVATED** masked
md **LASER-RAY** searing ray
nt **LASH-DOWN** secure firmly
LASHINGS an abundance; great quantity
LASSLORN jilted
pr **LAST-FOLD** last folded sheet in a book
LATCH-KEY domestic open sesame
LATENESS tardiness
LATENTLY inherently; not obvious
mn **LATERITE** brick-clay
LATHERED soapy; larruped
LATHWORK lath and plaster
LATINISM Latin idiom
LATINIST Latin scholar
LATINITY purity of Latin style
LATINIZE make like Latin
go, nt **LATITUDE** width; scope; laxity
LATITUDE north and south parallels
LATTERLY more recently; lately
LATTICED cross-barred
LAUDABLE praiseworthy; honourable
LAUDABLY commendably
md **LAUDANUM** an opiate
LAUGHING riant
LAUGHTER convulsive merriment
LAUNCHED hurled; began; initiated
gl **LAURASIA** primeval northern landmass
LAUREATE crowned with laurel
LAVA-LIKE hard and full of holes
LAVATION washing; purification
LAVATORY a wash-house; W.C.
bt **LAVENDER** greyish blue
zo **LAVEROCK** skylark
LAVISHED spent; squandered
LAVISHLY prodigally; wastefully
LAWFULLY legally; justly; validly
lw **LAWGIVER** a legislator; a Solon
LAWMAKER an M.P.
LAWYERLY verbose
LAXATION relaxation; slackness
md **LAXATIVE** colonic purgative
LAY-ABOUT lazy; good for nothing
rl **LAY-CLERK** a responder
rl **LAY-ELDER** Presbyterian elder
gl **LAYERING** strata process; horticultural
LAYSTALL refuse heap
LAYSTOOL table for newly printed/clean paper
rl **LAZARIST** R.C. missionary
LAZARONE Neapolitan beggar
LAZINESS inertness; slackness
mn **LAZULITE** a blue stone
mn **LAZURITE** lapis lazuli constituent
gl, mn **LEACHATE** extraction of salt in solution
gl **LEACHING** making an alkali; rain-aided descent of soluble topsoil minerals
LEAD-MILL lapidary's plate
nt **LEADSMAN** a lead-swinger
LEAF-LARD leaf-fat lard
LEAFLESS destitute of leaves
bt **LEAFSCAR** a mark
LEAGUING confederating; coalescing
pr **LEANFACE** narrow-width type
LEANNESS thinness; gauntness
LEAPFROG play; overtake; location
cp **LEAPFROG** of memory programs
LEAP-YEAR a year of 366 days
LEARNING scholarship; erudition
LEASABLE able to be let
LEASHING binding; securing
LEATHERN made of leather
LEATHERS protective paramilitary uniform (baseball); (hockey); (motor/motorcycle racing)
LEATHERY tough
ck **LEAVENED** baked with yeast; modified; tempered
LEAVINGS (left overs); residue; relics; departures
LEBANESE a native of Lebanon
bt **LECANORA** lichen; manna
LECITHIN egg tissue
LECTURED reprimanded; chided
LECTURER an expositor
LED-HORSE spare horse
nt **LEE-BOARD** anti-drift device
md **LEECHING** doctoring
nt **LEEFANGE** sheet guide
nt **LEE-SHORE** windward shore
LEFT-HAND sinister

LEFTWARD to the left
LEFT-WING (politics)
LEGACIES bequests; gifts
lw **LEGALISM** adherence to law
LEGALIST stickler for law
LEGALITY lawfulness
LEGALIZE authorize; sanction
lw **LEGATARY** powers of a legatee
LEGATINE of official deputy
LEGATION later an embassy
LEG-BREAK crooked course bowling (cricket)
LEGERITY lightness
bt **LEGUMINA** pods
bt **LEGUMINE** nitrogenous proteid
LEMONADE a soft drink
zo **LEMUROID LEMURINE**, monkey-like
LENDABLE loanable
LENGTHEN extend; elongate; protract
LENIENCE LENIENCY, mildness; clemency; mercifulness; forbearance
LENINISM LENINIST, follower of Lenin
LENITIVE mitigating; sedative
pg **LENS-HOOD** light-shield
mu **LENTANDO** slowing up
bt **LENTICEL** cell-formation
gl **LENTICLE** lenslike mass; glass door of grandfather clock
bt **LENT-LILY** daffodil
nt **LEPALEPA** dugout outrigger sail canoe (New Guinea)
md **LEPEROUS** leprous
zo **LEPIDOID** ganoid; scaly
bt, zo **LEPIDOTE** with scalelike hairs
zo **LEPORINE** like a hare
LESSENED diminished; decreased
LETHARGY dullness; apathy; oblivion
pr **LETTERED** with degree, diploma; printed
LETTERER sports award winner (USA)
mn **LEUCITIC** containing volcanic ore
md **LEUCOSIS** pallor; albinism
LEVANTED decamped; welshed
LEVANTER N. African wind
LEVELING LEVELLING, smoothing over; reduction to intake capacity
LEVELLED flattened; raged; demolished
LEVELLER ultra-republican, 1649
LEVERAGE mechanical advantage
LEVERING exerting pressure
LEVIABLE taxable; imposable
LEVIGATE to smooth; to polish
LEVIRATE Hebrew marriage custom
LEVITATE cause to float
LEVITIES frivolities; flippancies
LEVOLOSE fruit sugar
LEWDNESS licentiousness
LEWDSTER a profligate
pc **LEWINIAN** field theory; life-space; group dynamics
ch **LEWISITE** poison gas
rl **LIBATION** offering of sacred drink (wine)
LIBATORY oblatory
LIBELLED slandered; defamed
LIBELLER lampooner; calumniator
LIBERATE set free; emancipate
LIBERIAN (Liberia)
LIBRATED balanced
mu **LIBRETTO** words of musical play, opera
LICENSED authorized; allowed
LICENSEE holder of a licence
LICENSER licence issuer
bt **LICHENIC** made from lichen
LICHENIN moss starch
rl **LICHGATE LYCHGATE**, gate for a hearse
LICHWAKE post-funeral party
tx **LICKER-IN** toothed carding roller
bt **LICORICE** liquorice
LIEGEMAN vassal; henchman
nt **LIFEBELT LIFEBOAT**, marine lifesaving equipment
nt **LIFEBUOY** floating navigation marker
lw **LIFEHOLD** lease for life
LIFELESS dull; inanimate; extinct
LIFELIKE as if living
LIFELINE vital cord
LIFELONG till death
LIFE-PEER (not hereditary)
nt **LIFE-RAFT** (for shipwreck)
LIFE-RATE (life insurance)
lw **LIFE-RENT** rent during lifetime
LIFE-SIZE full scale
LIFE-TIME from birth to death, (actuarial); life-time of particle until recombination in a charge
LIFE-WORK reason for a career
LIFTABLE capable of elevation
LIGAMENT binder; tendon
ps **LIGASOID** gaseous/liquid colloidal system
md **LIGATING** binding; bandaging
LIGATION a fastening
mu **LIGATURE** bandage; band
LIGHTFUL cheery; happy; radiant
LIGHTING illuminating; kindling
LIGHTISH not heavy; fickle
tv, cp **LIGHT-PEN** photo electric torch for screens
gl **LIGNEOUS** previously of trees; (coal)

mn **LIGNITIC** (lignite; brown coal)
LIGULATE straplike
mn **LIGURITE** pea-green gem
LIKEABLE pleasant enough
LIKENESS resemblance; similarity
LIKENING comparing
LIKEWAKE LICHWAKE, post-funeral party
LIKEWISE also; moreover; besides
bt **LILACINE** extract of lilac
LILLIPUT miniature
LILY-IRON harpoon for swordfish
bt **LILY-STAR** feather-star
zo **LIMACOID** like a slug
LIMATION filing; polishing
LIMATURE filings
bt **LIMA-WOOD** Peruvian red-wood
LIME-FREE clear of calcium
LIME-KILN a furnace
LIMERICK verse often perverse
LIME-SINK a depression
bt **LIME-TREE** linden tree
LIME-TWIG a snare
LIME-WASH whitewash
bt **LIMEWORT** lychnis viscaria
LIMITARY finite; bounded
LIMITING confining; restricting
mn **LIMONITE** haematite ore
md **LINAMENT** bandage material
mn **LINARITE** a lead compound
LINCHPIN keeps the wheel on
md **LINCTURE** linctus; medicine
LINEALLY in a direct line
LINEARLY directly
pr **LINE-FEED** counting control device
LINE-FISH fish taken on a line
zo **LINELLAE** filament system in sarcodina
ga **LINESMAN** referee's assistant (football)
zo **LING-BIRD** meadow-pipit
LINGERED lagged; delayed; tarried
LINGERER dawdler; loiterer; (ma-)
tx **LINGERIE** ladies' underwear
LINGUIST seldom tongue-tied?
LINIMENT embrocation
LINNAEAN of Linnaeus; (botanical)
LINOLEUM lino; floorcloth
pr **LINOTYPE** type-setting machine
LINSTOCK flame-holder
LIONIZED heroized
md **LIPAEMIA** fatty blood
gl **LIPARITE** rhyolite; granitic lava rock
LIPIODOL X-ray-opaque substance
LIPO-GRAM (letter omission)
bt **LIPOSOME** fatty/oily globule
LIPSTICK a cosmetic
LIQUABLE fusible; fluent
LIQUATED liquefied
LIQUIDLY smoothly; fluidal
ch **LIQUIDUS** solidification temperature line
LIQUORED in drink; tipsy
LIRIPOOP hood; trick; nincompoop
LIROCONE floury; powdery
LISTENED hearkened; attended; heard
LISTENER eavesdropper
LISTLESS languid; apathetic; torpid
LITERACY ability to read and write
LITERARY erudite; scholarly
LITERATE learned; studious
LITERATI writers; critics; intelligentsia
LITEROSE bookish
mn **LITHARGE** lead oxide
LITHERLY mischievous; lazy
lw **LITIGANT** engaged in a lawsuit
lw **LITIGATE** to go to law
LITTERED scattered; strewn; deranged
LITTLE-GO examination (Camb.)
go **LITTORAL** a coastal strip
LITURATE blurred; spotted
rl **LITURGIC** ritualistic
LIVEABLE habitable; of a residence
LIVE-AXLE driving axle
LIVE-BAIT living worms for fishermen
LIVELILY vivaciously; briskly; alertly
bt **LIVELONG** lasting; the orpine
LIVENING cheering up; animating
el, rw **LIVE-RAIL** power track
LIVERIED in uniform
LIVERIES garbs; uniforms
pt **LIVERING** thickening of paints, varnish
md **LIVERISH** bilious; testy
LIVE-WELL kind of aquarium
LIVE-WIRE human dynamo
LIVIDITY discoloration
LIVINGLY lively; energetically; agilely
ch **LIXIVIAL** residual
ch **LIXIVIUM** lye; residuum
nt **LOAD-LINE** Plimsoll's loading mark on ships' sides
LOANABLE available for borrowing
LOAN-WORD borrowed word
LOATHFUL abhorrent; detestable
LOATHING hating; antipathy
LOBBYING endeavouring to influence
LOBBYIST pressurist (parliamentary)
ch **LOBELINE** monoacidic alkaloid
LOBLOLLY gruel; lout; attendant
md **LOBOTOMY** brain surgery

LOCALISM provincialism
LOCALITY situation; district; spot
LOCALIZE assign to a place
LOCATING positioning; fixing
cp **LOCATION** film-setting; place; information storage site
LOCATIVE grammatical case of place (Lat.)
LOCHLANN Irish word for Scandinavian
LOCKFAST firmly fastened
LOCK-GATE (on canal or river)
LOCKLESS without a lock
LOCK-SILL threshold of a lock
LOCKSMAN a turnkey
LOCKSPIT digging mark
LOCK-WEIR weir with lock
bt **LOCULATE LOCULOSE, LOCULOUS,** divided internally into cells
LOCUTION diction; phrase
rl **LOCUTORY** place for conversation
nt **LODESMAN** pilot
as **LODESTAR** pole-star
LODGINGS digs; accommodation
LODGMENT occupation; golf
bt **LODICULE** grass stamen scale
nt **LOG-BOARD** rough log
LOG-CABIN timber hut
nt **LOG-CANOE** dugout
nt **LOG-GLASS** timing device
LOGICIAN one skilled in logic
LOGICIZE deduce from reasoning
LOGISTIC transport problems
LOGOGRAM puzzle in verse
LOGOTYPE twin letters in printing
nt **LOG-SLATE** recording slate
LOITERED lingered; tarried
LOITERER an idler; flaneur
LOKWEAVE carpet-splice
rl **LOLLARDY** Lollard doctrine
LOLLIPOP sweet; (traffic sign)
LOLLOPED lounged; lurched
bt **LOMENTUM** branching fruit
mn **LOMONITE** a zeolite
LONDONER citizen of capital
LONENESS seclusion; solitude
LONESOME solitary
nt **LONGBOAT** naval lifeboat (sail), tender
ae **LONGERON** main spar of aeroplane
LONGEVAL long lived
LONG-FIRM swindling company
LONGHAND handwriting
LONG-HAUL long distance; lengthy time
zo **LONG-LEGS** flying daddy (- -); flying insect
bt **LONG-MOSS** tillandsia
nt **LONG-SHIP** Viking sailing vessel
ga **LONG-SLIP** (cricket fielder)
LONGSOME tiresome; tedious; irksome
LONG-SPUN protracted; extended
LONG-STOP (cricket)
LONG-TAIL not docked
LONG-TERM far seeing
LONGUEUR tedious patch, padding in literature
LONGWAYS lengthways
LONGWISE in extenso
bt **LONICERA** honey-suckle genus
LOOKER-ON spectator; observer
mt **LOOM-GALE** minor gale
LOOP-HOLE gun port in castle; (escape)
lw **LOOP-HOLE** legal evasion clause
LOOP-LINE alternative, passing track
cp **LOOP-STOP** program stopper
LOOSE-BOX a stall for horses
md **LOOSENED** undone; relaxed; slackened
md **LOOSENER** a laxative
LOP-EARED with drooping ears
gl **LOPOLITH** lens-shaped igneous intrusion
LOP-SIDED unbalanced; biased
LORD-LIKE haughty; imperious
LORDLING a would-be lord
md **LORDOSIS** spinal curvature
LORD'S-DAY Sunday
LORDSHIP title; domain of peerage
LORICATE to encrust
zo **LORIKEET** Australian parrot
LOSINGLY wastefully
LOTHARIO a libertine; a filly-buster
LOUDNESS uproar; clamour; resonance
LOUNGING reclining; lolling; idling
zo **LOVEBIRD** a budgerigar
LOVEKNOT a tangle
LOVELACE a libertine
LOVELESS passionless; frigid
LOVELIES beauteous damsels
LOVE-LIFE romance
LOVELILY delectably; enchantingly
LOVELOCK a manly curl
LOVELORN jilted
LOVE-NEST romantic abode
LOVESICK languishing
LOVESOME adorable
LOVESUIT courtship
LOVINGLY affectionately; fondly
LOWERING depressing; threatening
nt **LOW-WATER** at the ebb (tide)
LOYALIST patriot; faithful follower
LUBBERLY clumsily; maladroit

LUCIDITY clearness; luminosity
LUCKIEST most fortunate; happiest
LUCKLESS singularly unfortunate
ga **LUCKYBAG** **LUCKYDIP**, a bran tub with hidden gifts
LUCULENT translucent; lucid; clear
LUCULLUS an epicure
gl **LUGARITE** rare analcite-gabbro form
LUKEWARM tepid
LUMBERED rumbled along
LUMBERER woodman
LUMINANT shining; radiant
LUMINARY a heavenly body
LUMINATE illuminate; brighten
LUMINOUS phosphorescent; lucent
zo **LUMPFISH** a sea fish
LUNARIAN a moon observer
LUNATION a lunar month
LUNCHEON midday repast
LUNCHING eating in early afternoon
LUNGEING fencing; horse training
zo **LUNGFISH** queer fish
LUNGLESS not breathing
bt **LUNGWORT** a lichen
LUNIFORM moon-shaped
LUNULATE like a crescent
LUPERCAL Roman festival
ch **LUPININE** lupinus-seed alkaloid
bt **LUPINITE** a bitter extract
br **LUPULONE** soft hops resin
LURCHING stumbling; rolling
LUSCIOUS rich in flavour
LUSTIEST beefiest; heftiest; sexiest
LUSTRATE polish; cause to shine
tx **LUSTRING** silk cloth
LUSTROUS shining; luminous
bt **LUSTWORT** the sun-dew
LUTATION sealing (fastening) documents
ch **LUTECIUM** a metallic element
mu **LUTENIST** a lute player
bt **LUTEOLIN** yellow dye
LUTETIAN of Paris
rl **LUTHERAN** Protestant
LUTIDINE bone-oil/coal-tar constituent
LUXATING displacing
LUXATION dislocation
LUXMETER illuminance measurement device
LUXURIES unnecessary pleasures
LUXURIST an indulger
LYCHGATE hearse gateway to churchyard
bt **LYCOPODE** yellow powder
md **LYMPHOID** of lymph (from -gland)
LYNCHING mob law
LYNCH-LAW short-shrift
LYNX-EYED can see like a cat
ch **LYOLYSIS** acid/base formation process
zo **LYRE-BIRD** Australian bird
LYRICISM of lyric composition
ch **LYSERGIC** L.S.D. acid; (dream-trances)
bl **LYSOSOME** sac of hydrolytic enzymes
bl **LYSOZYME** bacteriolytic enzyme

M

rl **MACARIAN** blessed
rl **MACARISM** a beatitude
rl **MACARIZE** to bless
ck **MACARONI** fop; food (pasta)
ck **MACAROON** almond biscuit
MACASSAR hair oil
MACERATE harass; to steep; to rot
MACHINAL mechanical
MACHINED turned on a machine
MACHINER factory operative (worker)
zo **MACKEREL** cloud pattern; fish
zo **MACRANER** large male ant
zo **MACROPOD** long-legged
zo **MACROPUS** kangaroo genus
MACULATE to spot; to stain
MADDENED infuriated; incensed
md, pc **MADHOUSE** bedlam; lunatic asylum
mu **MADRIGAL** pastoral glee; part song
MAECENAS rich art patron
MAENADIC bacchanalian
mu **MAESTOSO** majestically
MAFFLING a simpleton
MAGAZINE depot; store; periodical; feeder (gun) (slides)
MAGDALEN home for repentants
mu **MAGGIORE** It. major, greater
MAGICIAN wizard; marabout
MAGIRICS the culinary art
md **MAGISTER** master; doctor
MAGNADUR ceramic magnet/insulator material
md **MAGNESIA** a medicine
ch **MAGNESON** magnesium reagent
el **MAGNETIC** attracted to poles
el, ps **MAGNETON** constant of M, movement of an eletron
MAGNIFIC splendid; majestic
bt **MAGNOLIA** a flowering tree
zo **MAGOT-PIE** magpie
rl **MAHADENA** Hindu god, Siva
MAHARAJA Indian rajah
bt **MAHOGANY** tropical tree
MAIDENLY virginal; demure

MAIDHOOD girlhood; virginity
MAIEUTIC delivering; evolving
MAILABLE postable
nt **MAIL-BOAT** a packet
MAIL-CART post wagon
MAIL-CLAD armour-plated
MAIL-DRAG mail-coach
nt **MAIN-BOOM** part of sailing ships
nt **MAIN-DECK** part of sailing ships
MAINLAND continent
nt **MAINMAST MAINSAIL**, chief rigging units
cp **MAIN-PATH** main course; written routine
nt **MAINSTAY** supporting brace (mainmast)
MAINTAIN support and care; assert; hold
nt **MAINYARD** part of rigging
MAJESTIC imperial; august; regal
MAJOLICA artificial pearls (Majorca)
MAJORATE army rank; attain age of 18
MAJORITY overwhelming proportion
MAKEBATE quarrel-maker
MAKELESS matchless
MAKIMONO Japanese picture
MALACOID soft-bodied
md **MALADIES** disorders; ailments
MALAGASH MALAGASY, of Madagascar
zo **MALAMUTE** Arctic sledge dog
MALAPERT saucy; impertinent; flippant
MALAPROP muddled misuse of words
md **MALARIAL** (malaria)
gl **MALCHITE** malachite; diorite rock
md **MAL-DE-MER** sea-sickness
bt **MALE-FERN** common lowland fern
MALEFICE evil deed; enchantment
MALENESS having male physical characteristics
lw **MALETOLT MALETOTE**, illegal exaction
MALIGNED traduced; slandered
MALIGNER defamer; reviler; abuser
MALINGER feign illness
MALLEATE to soften (using hammer, mallet)
mn **MALMROCK** sandstone
MALODOUR a smell; stench
MALT-DUST malt grains
ch **MALTHENE** asphaltic bitumen constituent
MALT-KILN MALT-MILL, comprise malt factory
MALTREAT abuse; hurt; harm; injure
MALTSTER malt-maker
zo **MALT-WORM** a tippler; weevil
md **MALUNION** improper bone-knitting
ck **MAMALIGA** maize-meal porridge
MAMBRINO source of Don Quixote's helmet
MAMELUKE Turkic military dynasty in Egypt; Caucasian slave
MAMMALIA breast-suckling animals
MAMMARED stammered
zo **MAMMIFER** a mammal
md **MAMMILLA** a nipple
tx **MAMMODIS** Indian muslin
MANACLED shackled; fettered
MANAGING controlling; contriving
MAN-CHILD a boy
MANCIPLE a steward; purveyor
MANDAEAN Babylonian sect
lw **MANDAMUS** a writ
bt **MANDARIN** official; orange; language
MANDATOR responsible entrustor; administrator
bt **MANDELIC** bitter almond extract
zo **MANDIBLE** a jaw of insect
MANDINGO tribe (South Sahara)
bt **MANDIOCA** cassava; manioc
mu **MANDOLIN** a guitar
MANDORLA oval panel
bt **MANDRAKE** white bryony
zo **MANDRILL** a baboon
zo **MAN-EATER** cannibal; tiger
MANELESS without a mane
MANELIKE like a mane; (of lion, horse)
MANFULLY boldly; courageously
zo **MANGABEY** Malagasy monkey
MANGANIN copper-base alloy
MANGCORN (many corn) mixed grain crop
MANGLING calendering; mutilating
MANGLING drying cloth by squeezer rollers
MANGONEL a ballistic machine
bt **MANGROVE** a tree
MAN-HATER allergic to man
MAN-HOURS labour measure
MANIACAL raving; frenzied; lunatic
bt **MANICATE** hairy
rl **MANICHEE** of God and Devil sect
MANICURE hand, finger nails beauty care
nt **MANIFEST** invoice of ship's cargo
MANIFEST evince; clear; obvious
MANIFOLD multiplied; numerous
MANNERLY of good address
MANNIKIN manikin; dwarf
ch **MANNITOL** hexahydric alcohol

bt **MANOCYST** receptive papilla in oomycetes
nt **MAN-OF-WAR** warship
MANORIAL referring to a manor
eg **MANOSTAT** pressure-constancy device
MAN-POWER male potential (labour reserve)
MAN-SIZED of adult dimensions
MANTELET small cloak
hd **MANTIGER** heraldic term
MANTILLA hanging lace and comb hair style (Sp.)
MANTISSA decimal part of logarithm
cp, ma **MANTISSA** number with floating point
MANTLING blushing; flushing; suffusing
MAN-TO-MAN close, confidential; intimate; frank
MANUALLY by hand
zo **MANUCODE** bird of paradise
MANURING fertilizing
MANUTYPE hand-painted
zo **MAORI-HEN** the weka
MAQUETTE mock-up model, sketch (Fr.)
zo **MARABOUT** Indian stork
rl **MARABOUT** Moslem priest or wizard
ml **MARAGING** steel-hardening heat treatment
MARASMUS emaciation
MARATHON long-distance race
MARAUDED roved; plundered; pillaged
MARAUDER raider; bandit; outlaw
nm **MARAVEDI** small Spanish copper
MARBLING form of décor
mu **MARCANDO** with precision
MARCHING bordering; foot slogging
MARGARIC pearly
MARGARON a fatty substance
pr **MARGINAL** in the margin; slight amount
pr **MARGINED** edged; bordered
MARGRAVE German prince
bt **MARIGOLD** orange flower
sv **MARIGRAM** tidal-height record
ck **MARINADE** steeping liquor
ck **MARINATE** steep in liquor; preserve
MARITIME marine; naval; nautical
bt **MARJORAM** aromatic plant
MARKEDLY unmistakably; eminently
MARKETED sold; vended
MARKSMAN crack shot
nt **MARLINED** twined with twine
mn **MARLITIC** (clay)
zo **MARMOSET** American monkey
tx **MAROCAIN** fine-rep dress fabric
MARONITE Jewish sect
MAROONED left on desert island
MAROQUIN morocco leather
MARQUESS a marquis
MARQUISE marchioness
MARRIAGE wedlock; espousal
MARRYING wedding; uniting
ch **MARSH-GAS** methane
zo **MARSH-HEN** moorhen
zo **MARSH-TIT** blackheaded tom-tit
bt **MARTAGON** turk's cap lily
MARTELLO circular tower
mu **MARTENOT** electronic keyboard
MARTINET a disciplinarian
MARTYRED died for their faith
bt **MARYGOLD** **MARIGOLD**, flower
zo **MARY-SOLE** a flat-fish
mu **MARZIALE** martial (It.)
ck **MARZIPAN** a sweetmeat of almonds
MASCARON grotesque head as decoration
MASORITE a theologist
MASSACRE pogrom; carnage
MASSAGED kneaded; rubbed
rl **MASS-BELL** serving bell
rl **MASS-BOOK** R.C. missal
pl **MASSETER** a jaw muscle
md **MASSEUSE** a manipulator
mn **MASSICOT** lead oxide
MASSORAH Hebrew tradition
MASTERED conquered; overcame; learned; competent
MASTERLY expertly; dexterously
MASTHEAD head of (esp.) lower mast
pr **MASTHEAD** newspaper heading
md **MASTITIS** breast inflammation
nt **MASTLESS** dismasted; steam-diesel-powered vessels
zo **MASTODON** early mammoth
nt **MASTSHIP** masts, timber carrier vessel
ch **MASURIUM** a metallic element
MATADORE bull-fighter; domino game
zo **MATAMATA** S. Amer. river tortoise
MATCHBOX chez Lucifer
cp **MATCHING** equalling; suiting; comparing records; matchboard
ck **MATELOTE** fish/wine stew (Fr.)
MATERIAL stuff; essential; relevant
MATERIEL equipment (Fr.)
MATERNAL motherly
MATESHIP comradeship
bt **MAT-GRASS** weavable reeds
MATHESIS mathematics; learning
MATHILDA army tank (obsolete)

MATRONAL motherly; sedate
MATRONLY elderly
MATTERED signified; imported
ce **MATTRESS** stuffed base of bed; concrete base (slabs)
md **MATURANT** a cataplasm
md **MATURATE** to poultice
MATURELY acting on experience and maturity
MATURING ripening; mellowing
MATURITY repayment date (insurance policies)
MATURITY fullness of age; ripeness
to **MAUNDRIL** a pick-axe
ch **MAUVEINE** synthetic dyestuff
MAVERICK unbranded animal
MAXIM-GUN single-barrelled machine gun
MAXIMIST a dealer in old saws
MAXIMIZE raise to maximum (prices, production)
bt **MAY-APPLE** N. American fruit
bt **MAY-BLOBS** marsh marigold
bt **MAY-BLOOM** hawthorn
MAYORESS wife of mayor
MAY-QUEEN spring deity
ck **MAZARINE** deep blue; flat plate within a dish; cake
MAZDAISM Zoroastrianism
MAZINESS perplexity; haziness
zo **MAZOLOGY** a zoological science
mu **MAZOURKA** mazurka; Polish folk dance
MEAGRELY scantily; sparsely; meanly
MEAL-POCK MEAL-POKE, beggar's meal bag
MEALTIME breakfast, lunch or dinner
zo **MEALWORM** one infesting flour
MEAN-BORN of humble origin
MEANNESS sordidness; paltriness
MEANTIME meanwhile
MEASURED meted; ascertained; steady
MEASURER computer; gauger
ck **MEAT-BALL** rissole; mini-hamburger
ck **MEATLESS** of vegetarian foods
MEAT-RACK hooked storage facilities
MEAT-SAFE storage cupboard
MECHANIC artisan; fitter
bt, zo **MECONATE MECONINE, MECONIUM,** opium; poppy-juice; foetal intestine contents
MEDALIST a prize winner
MEDALLIC relating to medals
MEDDLING interfering; intruding
MEDIATED intervened; reconciled
MEDIATOR an intercessor; arbitrator
MEDICATE to doctor; to dose
MEDICEAN (Medici of Florence)
md **MEDICINE** the curative art
MEDIEVAL (Middle Ages)
MEDIOCRE middling; ordinary
rl **MEDITATE** deep reflection; focus; spiritual exercise
bt **MEDULLAR** pithy (heart)
bt **MEDULLIN** lilac cellulose
MEEKENED became gentle
MEEKNESS submissiveness; humility
MEETNESS fitness; propriety
el **MEGALINE** magnetic flux unit
MEGALITH stone monument
zo **MEGALOPS** last larval stage in crabs
zo **MEGAPODE** mound bird
MEGATRON light-house valve
MEGAVOLT million volts
MEGAWATT million watts
mn **MEIONITE** a silicate
bt **MEIOTAXY** whorl development failure
ch **MELAMINE** organic compound
MELANISM black coloration
mn **MELANITE** black garnet
MELANOMA pigmented mole
MELANOUS dark-visaged
zo **MELANURE** sea-bream
MELIBEAN alternately responsive
mn **MELILITE** complex mineral
MELINITE a high explosive
MELLIFIC honeyed
MELLOWED matured; ripened; enriched
MELLOWLY sweetly; melodiously
mu **MELODEON** harmonium
mu **MELODIST** song and tune maker; composer
mu **MELODIZE** render harmonious
MEMBERED having limbs
bt, zo **MEMBRANE** tissue wall; tent roof; film (surface)
MEMORIAL relic; monument; memento
MEMORIZE learn by heart
MEMPHIAN MEMPHITE, of Memphis (Egypt)
MEMSAHIB white lady (India)
MENACING threatening; intimidating
MENDABLE repairable
zo **MENHADEN** American herring
mn **MENILITE** brown opal
md **MENINGES** brain membranes
MENISCAL MENISCUS, crescent-shaped type of lens
MENOLOGY calendar of saints
zo **MENOPOME** mud-devil

MENSURAL measurable
MENTALLY intellectually
MEPHITIC noxious; pestilential
MEPHITIS an exhalation; miasma
MERCABLE saleable; vendible
MERCHAND to traffic; to trade
MERCHANT trader; dealer; monger
MERCIFUL humane; clement; lenient
MERCURIC mercurial; quick witted; changeable
MERCYISM rumination; infantile regurgitation
bt **MERICARP** seed carpel
go **MERIDIAN** great circle; noon
go **MERIDIAN** longitude line through terrestrial poles
ck **MERINGUE** eggwhites and sugar cake
zo **MERIONES** Can. jumping mouse
MERISTEM formative tissue
zo **MERISTIC** segmented
MERITING deserving; earning
bt **MEROGAMY** individualized-gamete union
md **MEROSMIA** smell sense deficiency
zo **MEROSOME** a segment; a somite
mn **MEROXENE** biotite class
zo **MEROZOON** protozoon fragment
MERRYMAN mountebank; jester
md **MESCALIN** alkaloid 'truth drug'
MESDAMES ladies
MESHWORK network; reticulation
mn **MESITITE** a carbonate
MESMEREE one mesmerized
MESMERIC hypnotic
bt **MESOCARP** central carpel
md **MESODERM** inner skin
mn **MESOLITE** needlestone
zo **MESOMERE** muscle-plate zone in vertebrates
zo **MESOSOMA** abdomen division in arachnida
MESOTRON electron-directing device
mn **MESOTYPE** zeolitic mineral
gl **MESOZOIC** Triassic period
bt **MESQUITE** African thorn-bush
MESSIDOR 19 June – 18 July (Fr.)
MESSMATE table companion
MESSROOM forces' dining room
MESSUAGE premises and garden
METACISM excess of 'M'
zo **METACONE** cusp of mammal molar
el, ps **METADYNE** generator, converter
METALLED plated; macadamized roads
ch **METALLIC** compound of metals; lustrous; harsh
METALMAN metal-worker
zo **METAMERE** similar body segment
mn **METAMICT** glassy amorphous state
METAPHOR allegory; image; (comparison)
zo **METASOMA** abdomen part in arachnida
zo **METASOME** mid-body of cyclops
METATOME an architectural space
METAYAGE produce sharing (Fr.)
zo **METAZOAN** **METAZOIC, METAZOON,** multi-cellular construction of an animal
METECORN a corn issue
METEORIC transient; dazzling; flashing
METERAGE measurement
me **METEWAND** **METEYARD**, yard-stick
ch **METHANOL** methyl alcohol
METHINKS I think
METHODIC systematic; orderly
METHYLAL chemical solvent
ch **METHYLIC** (methyl)
md **METHYSIS** drunkenness
METONYMY a trope
ME-TOOISM alsoiology
md **METOPISM** (frontal suture)
ch **METOPRYL** anaesthetic
METRICAL rhythmic
bt **MEZEREON** aromatic shrub
MIASMATA nauseous exhalations
zo **MICRANER** small male ant
ps **MICROBAR** unit of pressure
zo **MICROBIC** microbial
zo **MICROZOA** animalculae
bl **MICRURGY** cell-study technique
pl **MIDBRAIN** sight and hearing
MIDDLING mediocre; medium; average
MIDFIELD players (cricket, lacrosse)
MIDNIGHT 24.00 hours
MIDPOINT central position (place, opinion)
MIDRANGE average distance achieved
nt **MIDSHIPS** on bow-aft line, in the beam
MIGHTILY vigorously; potently
md **MIGRAINE** the vapours
MIGRATED left; moved
MIGRATOR emigrant; nomad; rover
MILANESE (Milan)
MILDEWED mouldy; musty; rusty
MILDNESS gentleness; blandness
MILEPOST milestone
MILESIAN early Irish race
MILITANT eager to fight; warring
MILITARY martial; soldierly; warlike
MILITATE oppose; contend; fight
MILK-MAID dairy-maid

bt **MILK-TREE** the messaranduba
MILK-WALK milk delivery route (locally)
MILK-WARM tepid
bt **MILK-WEED** the sow-thistle
bt **MILK-WORT** flowering plant
as **MILKY-WAY** our galaxy group
MILL-HAND factory operative
MILLIARD a thousand millions
MILLIARE thousandth of an are (Fr.)
me **MILLIBAR** unit of barometric pressure
gp **MILLIGAL** 1000th of a gal
lt **MILLILUX** unit of illumination intensity
MILLINER bonnet-maker
MILLPOND reservoir for working millwheel
MILLRACE actuating stream
MILLTAIL (used) water past mill-wheel
jn **MILLWORK** mill machinery; prefabricated joinery
MILTONIC (of Milton's writings)
mn **MIMETITE** lead compound
MIMICKED aped; took off; imitated
MIMICKER impersonator; mime
MINATORY menacing; threatening
ck **MINCE-PIE** fruit-filled tart (Christmas)
MINDLESS stupid; heedless
MINGLING mixing; blending
MINIATED illuminated
bd **MINIBORE** (central heating); small-bore piping
MINIFIED depreciated
MINIMIZE treat slightingly
MINISTER servant; pastor; succour
MINISTRY agency; cabinet
rl **MINORITE** Franciscan friar
MINORITY the smaller number
MINOTAUR half man, half bull
MINSTREL ballad-monger
nm **MINTMARK** identification mark
mu **MINUETTO MINUET**, triple-time dance (Fr.)
MINUTELY particularly; exactly
MINUTEST smallest; tiniest
MINUTIAE small details
MINUTING recording; noting
zo **MIRE-CROW** black-headed gull
ck **MIREPOIX** vegetable bed for braised meats
MIRINESS muddiness; swampiness
mu **MIRLITON** Fr. kazoo, hum-through toy
MIRRORED reflected
MIRTHFUL festive; jocund; vivacious
MISAIMED ill-directed
MISAPPLY pervert; misuse; abuse
MISARRAY disarray; disorder
MISBEGOT shapeless
pr **MISBOUND** pages in wrong order
MISCARRY expulsion of a foetus
MISCARRY failure to execute a plan
ch **MISCELLA** oil/solvent solution
MISCHIEF injury; harm; hurt; trouble
MISCHOSE made wrong choice
MISCIBLE mixable
MISCLAIM claim in error
MISCOUNT reckon wrongly
MISCUING faulty move (billiards, snooker)
MISDATED wrong date ascribed
MISDEALT uneven dealing of cards
MISDOING wronging; offending
MISDOUBT to be wrong in doubting
MISDRAWN wrong file or information extracted
cp **MISENTER** enter facts wrongly (book-keeping)
MISENTRY erroneous record
mu, rl **MISERERE** Catholic repentance anthem
ar, rl **MISERERE** curiously decorated under-seats (choir-stalls)
MISFAITH distrust; perfidy; wrong reliance
MISFEIGN failure to disguise
MISFIELD failure to stop batsman's score
MISFIRED faulty gun shot
MISGUIDE lead astray
bt **MISGRAFT** fail to graft plant correctly
MISHEARD wrongly heard
mu, ck **MISHMASH** jumble; hotchpotch
rl, lw **MISHNAIC MISHNOTH**, (Jewish Oral Laws)
MISINFER deduce erroneously
MISJUDGE misconstrue; mistake
MISLABEL address incorrectly
MISLAYER untidy person
bt **MISLETOE MISTLETOE**, parasitic plant
MISLIKED disapproved; disliked
MISMATCH out-class
MISNAMED wrong appellation
MISNOMER incorrect appellation
MISOGAMY hatred of marriage
MISOGYNY hatred of women
MISPLACE displace; mislay
lw **MISPLEAD** win case for opponent
pr **MISPOINT** punctuate improperly
pr **MISPRINT** typographical error
MISPRISE to mistake

MISPRIZE slight; undervalue; belittle
MISQUOTE cite erroneously
MISRATED rated erroneously
MISRULED governed badly
MISSABLE not necessary or desirable to attain
MISSERVE serve unfaithfully
MISSHAPE to deform
MISSPEAK utter wrongly
MISSPELL write wrong
MISSPELT an error in orthogaphy
MISSPEND squander; misuse
MISSPENT wasted; dissipated
MISSTATE state falsely
MISTAKEN in error; wrong; incorrect
MISTEACH teach wrongly
MISTHINK think ill of
MISTIMED chronologically erroneous
MISTITLE use wrong title
MISTRAIN to educate amiss
MISTRESS lady of the house
lw **MISTRIAL** (jury fail to agree)
MISTRUST want of confidence
mu **MISTUNED** discordant
MISTUTOR educate wrongly
MISUSAGE abuse; perversion
MISUSING misapplying; profaning
MISVOUCH to bear false witness
MISWRITE write incorrectly
MISYOKED unevenly matched (2 plough-horses)
MITCHELL hewn Purbeck stone
MITHRAIC (Mithras)
MITIGANT alleviating; lenitive
MITIGATE lessen; allay; assuage
MITTENED wearing mitts (fingerless gloves)
lw **MITTIMUS** a writ
mt **MIZZLING** ceasing to rain; drizzling
MNEMONIC sound association (memory aid)
MOBILITY readily mobile; uncertain
MOBILIZE gather armies, manpower, for war
MOBOCRAT demagogic speaker
zo **MOCCASIN MOCASSIN**, leather shoe; venomous snake
MOCKABLE ridiculous; derisive
MODALISM Sabellian doctrine
MODALIST theorist
MODALITY logical custom; sensory-system
MODELLED fashioned; designed
MODELLER copyist; plastic planner
MODERATE so-so; fair; pacify; mollify
mu **MODERATO** at moderate pace
MODESTLY decently; unobtrusively
MODIFIED altered; varied; changed
MODIFIER moderator
mu **MODINHAR** Portuguese popular song
MODIOLAR like a bushel measure
zo **MODIOLUS** central pillar of cochlea
MODISHLY foppishly; fashionable
MODULATE regulate; harmonize
MOFUSSIL rural districts (Hindu)
rl **MOHARRAM** Mohammedan fast
MOIDERED spent; toiled
MOISTFUL damp; humid
MOISTURE humidity
ch **MOLALITY MOLARITY**, mole/solvent solution ratio
MOLASSES treacle
MOLE-CAST a molehill
ch **MOLECULE** group of atoms
MOLE-EYED having small eyes
MOLE-HILL miniature mountain
tx **MOLE-SKIN** strong cotton fustian
MOLESTED troubled; pestered
MOLESTER an annoyer; harasser
rl **MOLINIST** a Jesuit
MOLLIENT assuaging; softening
zo **MOLLUSCA** invertebrates
ch **MOLYBDIC** (molybdenum)
MOMENTLY every moment
MOMENTUM impetus; impulsive weight
rl **MONACHAL** monastic
MONANDRY (one husband only)
MONARCHY royal family in kingdom
rl **MONASTIC** a monk
MONAURAL uni-aural; one ear only
mn **MONAZITE** a phosphate
MONDAINE woman of fashion
MONETARY financial; (money-wise)
MONETIZE manufacture money from gold
MONEYBOX cash-box
MONGERED dealt in
zo **MONGOOSE** cobra-killing ichneumon
MONISTIC single-minded
lw **MONITION** a summons
MONITIVE warning
MONITORY cautionary
MONITRIX woman instructor
MONKEYED played about with
zo **MONKFISH** angler-fish
rl **MONKHOOD** monastic state
zo **MONK-SEAL** kind of sea creature
MONNIKER sobriquet; nickname
pg **MONO-BATH** developing/fixing solution; for single person only
au **MONOBLOC** integral cylinder casting
bt **MONOCARP** an annual plant
MONOCLED wearing an eye-glass
MONOCRAT autocrat

zo **MONOCULE** one-eyed animal
zo **MONOCYTE** uninuclear leucocyte
MONODIST writer of dirges
zo **MONODONT** having a single tooth
MONOGAMY (one wife)
bt **MONOGERM** seed producing single seedling
MONOGONY asexual reproduction
MONOGRAM interwoven initials
MONOGYNY (one wife)
MONOLITH stone monument
MONOLOGY soliloquizing
MONOMIAL expressed by one term
MONOPODE single-footed
MONOPOLY exclusive privilege
MONOPTIC with one eye; monocular
rw **MONORAIL** single-rail system
MONOTINT picture in one colour
MONOTONE unvaried tone
MONOTONY dull uniformity; tedium
pr **MONOTYPE** printing machine
MONSIEUR a Frenchman
MONTANIC mountainous
MONTEITH punch-bowl; kerchief
MONTEURS artificial flower makers
MONTICLE hillock; molehill
MONUMENT a memorial; cenotaph; beacon
MOOCHING loitering
MOONBEAM a lunar ray
MOONCALF monster; dolt
MOON-EYED purblind
MOONFACE a round face
MOONLESS (a dark night)
MOONLING born last day of month and moon
nt **MOON-SAIL** a small sail
bt **MOONSEED** climbing plant
MOONSHEE Moslem linguist
pr **MOONTYPE** embossed lettering
bt **MOONWORT** a fern
MOON-YEAR lunar year
zo **MOORCOCK** red grouse
zo **MOORFOWL** moorcock
zo **MOORGAME** grouse
zo **MOORHAWK** marsh harrier
go **MOORLAND** moreland; peaty soil
bt **MOORWHIN** a genista
bt **MOORWORT** marsh andromeda
MOOTABLE debatable; doubtful
MOOT-CASE a moot-point
MOOT-HALL judgement hall
MOOT-HILL a rendezvous
MOPE-EYED myopic; purblind
MOPISHLY gloomily; dejectedly
MOQUETTE a carpet (Fr.); of coarse wool and linen
MORALIST virtuous man
MORALITY ethics; virtue
MORALIZE philosophize on morality
MORATORY of moratorium agreement to delay
rl **MORAVIAN** of Moravia; Hussite sect
MORBIDLY unhealthily
md **MORBIFIC** causing disease
MORELAND moorland
MOREOVER besides; also; likewise
ar **MORESQUE MOORESQUE**, arabesque decorative style
MORIBUND decaying; dying
bt, zo **MORILLON** grape; duck
zo **MORMYRUS** Egyptian pike
MOROCCAN (Morocco)
MOROLOGY foolish talk
MOROSELY sullenly; sourly
mn **MOROXITE** a phosphate
MORPHEAN sleepy; dreamy
MORPHEMA minimal meaningful linguistic unit
MORPHEUS god of sleep
md **MORPHINE** morphia
MORTALLY fatally; deadly
bd **MORTARED** of gunfire; solid brickwork
lw **MORTGAGE** loan on house security
cr **MORTISED** wood-joint; door lock
gl **MORTLAKE** ox-bow (ex-river, lake)
zo **MORTLING** morling; dead sheep
lw **MORTMAIN** inalienable property
MORTUARY charnel house; morgue
le **MOSLINGS** curried leather
zo **MOSQUITO** an insect
MOSS-BACK a Rip van Winkle character (USA)
MOSS-CLAD mossy
go **MOSSLAND** peat-land
bt **MOSS-PINK** a phlox
bt **MOSS-ROSE** house plant
bt **MOSS-RUSH** bog plant
MOTHBALL naphthalene; anti-moth
MOTHERED adopted
MOTHERLY parental; tender
MOTILITY movement; mobility
MOTIONAL of parliamentary motion (debate)
MOTIONED gestured; proposed
MOTIONER a mover; proposer of motion
MOTIVATE actuate; impel; induce
MOTIVITY power of energizing
MOTOR-BUS coach
MOTOR-CAR automobile
MOTORIAL motory; giving motion
MOTORING travelling by car
MOTORISE equip with motors
MOTORIST car driver

rw **MOTORMAN** chauffeur; one-man-train driver
MOTORWAY fast main road
MOTTLING variegating
MOUCHING slouching; skulking
zo **MOUFFLON** wild sheep
MOULD-BOX box for casting
MOULDING shaping; fashioning
MOULINET drum of capstan
MOULTING shedding feathers, fur
MOUNDING banking
MOUNTAIN a light wine; peak
MOUNTANT photographic paste
MOUNTIES R. Can. Mounted Police
MOUNTING surround for a picture
MOUNTING ascending; copulating
MOUNTING sword movement (army)
MOURNFUL lugubrious; grievous
MOURNING lamenting; sorrow
bt **MOUSE-EAR** a herb
ck **MOUSSAKA** aubergine dish of minced meat, eggs etc. (Gr.)
MOUSSEUX sparkling frothy wine (Fr.)
ck **MOUTHFUL** pithy statement; tasty snack
MOUTHING con molta espressione
MOVABLES personal belongings; chattels, furniture
MOVELESS fixed; stationary
MOVEMENT motion; speed; crusade
mu **MOVEMENT** part of a musical work
MOVINGLY affectingly; eloquently
MOWBURNT (hay)
MUCCHERO rose and violet infusion
bt **MUCEDINE** a fungus
MUCHNESS almost abundance
bt **MUCILAGE** gum
zo **MUCIVORA** insects
MUCKERED made a muck of
MUCK-HEAP midden
MUCK-HILL dung-hill
MUCK-RAKE dig up dirt
bt **MUCK-WEED** white goosefoot
zo **MUCK-WORM** a miser; a grub
md **MUCOCELE** mucus accumulation
MUCOSITY mouldiness
MUCULENT slimy; viscous
bt **MUDARINE** an extract
MUDDLING confusing; deranging
MUDDYING miring
MUDGUARD a screen
gl **MUDSTONE** argillaceous sedimentary rock
MUD-VALVE of drainage
MUFFLING noise deadening; shrouding
MUG-HOUSE ale-house
MUHARRAM a Moslem month
bt **MULBERRY** a fruit-tree
MULCHING fertilizing
MULCTING fining; amercing
zo **MULE-DEER** N. American deer
MULETEER mule-driver
bt **MULEWORT** a fern
MULISHLY obstinately; stubbornly
MULTEITY multiplicity
MULTIFID many cleft
MULTIPED with many feet
cp **MULTIPLE** factor; combined units; paralleling
ma, cp **MULTIPLY** increase; augment; spread
bd **MULTI-PLY** more than 3 ply (-wood)
MUMBLING muttering incoherently
MUMMYING embalming (ancient Egypt)
MUNCHING chewing; masticating
MUNERARY donative
lw, bd **MUNIMENT** title-deed; stronghold
MUNITION military stores; equipment
ga **MUNSHETS MUNSHITS**, stick and hole field game
MURALLED painted on a wall
MURDERED assassinated; slain
MURDERER a Cain
mn **MUREXIDE** a crystal
MURIATED soaked in brine
ch **MURIATIC** hydrochloric
MURICATE prickly; thorny; spiky
MURIFORM like a wall
MURKSOME darksome; obscure
MURMURED complained; repined
MURMURER grumbler; grouser
mn **MURRHINE** (fluor-spar)
bt **MUSCADEL** muscatel
bt **MUSCATEL** grape; wine
MUSCULAR brawny; sturdy; powerful
MUSELESS uncultured
bt, ck **MUSHROOM** upstart; blewit; edible fungus
mu **MUSICALE** private recital
mu **MUSICIAN** instrumentalist
MUSINGLY in contemplative fashion
MUSK-BALL perfumed sachet
zo **MUSK-CAVY** a rodent
zo **MUSK-DEER** Cent. Asian ruminant
zo **MUSK-DUCK** Muscovy duck
MUSKETRY rifle-shooting
bt **MUSK-PEAR MUSK-PLUM**, odoriferous fruits
bt **MUSK-ROSE** rambling rose
bt **MUSK-WOOD** musky tree
tx **MUSLINET** coarse muslin
zo **MUSQUASH** musk-rat

MUSTACHE moustache
bt **MUSTAIBA** Brazilian hardwood
MUSTERED assembled; gathered
MUTACISM mytacism
MUTATION discontinuous variation
MUTENESS dumbness
bt **MUTICATE** without a point
zo **MUTICOUS** lacking defence structures
MUTILATE maim; dismember
MUTINEER insurgent crew member
nt **MUTINIED** rebelled; revolted
MUTINOUS seditious; unruly; turbulent
MUTTERED mumbled; whispered
MUTTERER grumbler; grouser
MUTUALLY reciprocally
MUZZLING restraining (jaws); silencing (opinion)
bt **MYCELIUM** mushroom spawn
md **MYCETOMA** a foot disease
zo **MYCETOME** special insect organ
md **MYCODERM** fungoid pellice
MYCOLOGY study of fungi
md **MYELITIS** spinal disease
zo **MYLODONT** (extinct sloth)
gl **MYLONITE** compact streaky rock
zo **MYOBLAST** embryonic-muscle cell
md **MYOGENIC** of spontaneous muscle contraction
md **MYOGRAPH** recording machine
MYOMANCY divination by mice
md **MYONOSUS MYOPATHY**, muscular disease
zo **MYOPHORE** muscle-connected structure
cy **MYOPLASM** contractile part of muscle cell
md **MYOSITIC MYOSITIS**, muscular inflammation
bt **MYOSOTIS** the forget-me-not
pl **MYOTASIS** muscular tension
pl **MYOTONIA** excessive muscle rigidity
zo **MYRIAPOD** centipede
MYRIARCH a commander
MYRICINE (bee's wax)
MYRMIDON desperate ruffian
bt **MYRRHINE** myrrh (gum and ladanum mix)
ch **MYRTENOL** myrtle oil monoalcohol
MYSTICAL enigmatical; occult
MYSTIQUE reverence for cleverness/skills
MYTACISM excess of 'M' in speaking
MYTHICAL legendary; fabulous
zo **MYTILITE** fossil mussel
MYTILOID mussel-like
md **MYXEDEMA** severe depression of nervous system activity
zo **MYXOPODA** protozoans

N

NACREOUS pearly; iridescent
bd **NAILABLE** material that tolerates nails
NAIL-FILE manicurist's implement
NAILHEAD visible outer portion of nail
ar **NAILHEAD** early English embellishment
NAIL-HOLE surface depression after hammering
bt **NAILWORT** whitlow grass
tx **NAINSOOK** jaconet muslin
hd **NAISSANT** issuing from; parentage
NAMEABLE identifiable
NAMELESS obscure; inglorious
NAMESAKE having identical name
md **NANOSOMA** dwarfism
ch **NAPHTHOL** coal-tar constituent
NAPIFORM turnip-shaped
nm **NAPOLEON** nap; 20 francs
mn **NAPOLITE** volcanic substance
md **NARCEINE** opium extract
bt **NARCISSI** flowers
md **NARCOSIS** stupefaction; stupor
NARCOTIC anodyne; sedative; opiate
NARGHILE hookah-pipe
zo **NARICORN** horny beak
NARIFORM beak-like
NARRATED recited; related; recounted
NARRATOR story-teller; historian
NARROWED contracted; cramped
NARROWER closer; nearer
NARROWLY nearly; barely; scarcely
NASALITY nosiness
NASALIZE enunciate nasally
NASCENCY growth; production
zo **NASICORN** horn-beaked
NASIFORM nose-shaped
ec **NATALITY** population's increase ability
zo **NATANTES** water-spiders
NATANTLY buoyantly
NATATION swimming
NATATORY of aquatic habits
NATHLESS nevertheless
NATHMORE never more
NATIONAL public; general; racial
NATIVELY by birth; naturally
NATIVISM doctrine of genetics versus experience

NATIVITY birth; Christmas; base of horoscope
NATTERED chatted
NATTIEST neatest; smartest
NATURISM nature worship
NATURIST practiser of nudism
nt **NAUMACHY** a sea-fight
zo **NAUPLIUS** larva of crustaceans
nt **NAUSCOPY** ship-sighting
NAUSEANT disgusting; revolting
NAUSEATE to sicken
nt **NAUSEOUS** offensive; repulsive
nt **NAUTICAL** marine; maritime; naval
zo, nt **NAUTILUS** cephalopod with chambered shell; diving bell
nt **NAVALISM** sea power
nt **NAVARCHY** admiralship
nt **NAVICERT** naval permit
NAVICULA incense-boat
nt **NAVIFORM** art; boat-like
nv **NAVIGATE** voyage; cruise; steer; pilot
nt **NAVY-BLUE** dark blue
NAZARENE of Nazareth
rl **NAZARITE NAZIRITE**, early Christian sect
NAZIFIED Hitler-minded
NEALOGIC adolescent
NEARCTIC N. of N. America
NEARHAND nigh; nearly
NEARNESS propinquity; closeness; togetherness
NEAR-SIDE left side looking forward
NEATHERD cow-herd
NEATNESS spick and span; dexterity
as **NEBULIUM** questionable element
NEBULOSE NEBULOUS, nebular; cloudy; hazy; misty; obscure
NECKATEE kerchief; scarf
NECKBAND collar
ck **NECKBEEF** coarse flesh
NECKLACE rivière
rl **NECKWEAR** scarves; ties; dog-collar
NECROPSY post-mortem
md **NECROSIS** mortification; death
NECROTIC moribund
NECTARED honeyed
zo **NECTOPOD** swimming appendage
NEED-FIRE fire by friction (Scouting)
NEEDLESS unnecessary; superfluous
NEEDLING embroidering; sewing
NEGATING denying; disclaiming
NEGATION denial; refusal; confute; absence
cp **NEGATION** mirror-wise; reversal of digits
pg **NEGATIVE** right of veto; not; (photo)
el **NEGATRON** thermionic tube
NEGLIGEE loose apparel
NEGRITOS pygmies (Malay)
NEIGHING whinnying; horse language
NEMALINE fibrous
mn **NEMALITE** hydrate of magnesia
zo **NEMATODA** eel worms
zo, md **NEMATOID** like a thread; internal parasite
zo **NEMERTEA** worms
NEMOROSE growing in groves
NEMOROUS woody
bt **NENUPHAR** water-lily
zo **NEOBLAST** large amoeboid cell
NEOCRACY rule by upstarts
NEO-LATIN modern Latin
NEOLOGIC of adding new words to language (neologisms)
pm **NEOMYCIN** antibiotic
md **NEONATAL** of newborn infants
zo **NEOPHRON** genus of vultures
NEOPHYTE novice; tyro; proselyte
NEOPLASM new tissue
NEPALESE a native of Nepal
md **NEPENTHE** drug causing oblivion
mn **NEPHRITE** jade
NEPHROID kidney-shaped
md **NEPHROMA** kidney tumour
zo **NEPIONIC** of embryonic period
NEPOTISM favouritism of family
NEPOTIST favours relatives
NERONIAN concerning Emperor Nero
NERVE-WAR cold war
NESCIENT NESCIOUS, ignorant; unlettered; unaware; agnostic
NESISTOR bipolar-field-dependent transistor
zo **NESTLING** young bird
NETHINIM temple servants (Heb.)
NETTLING irritating; provoking
md **NEURALGY** neuralgia
NEURAXIS spinal cord-brain axis
md **NEURITIS** nerve inflammation
NEURONAL concerning the neuron
zo **NEUROPIL** brain nerve fibre maze
NEUROSAL neurotic; temperamental
md **NEUROSIS** nervous disease
NEUROTIC highly strung
nc **NEUTRINO** subatomic particle
gl **NEVADITE** rhyolite; acid lava
NEWBLOWN just blossoming
NEWCOMER late arrival
NEW-MODEL Cromwell's army (Civil War)
NEWS-HAWK journalist; reporter
NEWS-REEL cinematic news

NEWS-ROOM incoming news; room where news is prepared
NEXTNESS nearest proximity
NIBBLING consuming tiniest morsels
NIBELUNG a Rhine gnome
NICENESS politeness; precision; choice
NICKELIC of nickel
NICKNACK a trifle; gewgaw
NICKNAME a monniker; sobriquet
el, ps, ml **NICKROME** alloy for electrical heating elements
ch **NICOTINE** tobacco constituent
NIDERING rascal; coward
ck **NIDOROSE NIDOROUS**, smelling of cookery
zo **NIDULANT NIDULATE**, nestling, birdling
NIELLURE metal-work
NIFFNAFF a trifle; nicknack
NIFLHEIM region of mist (Teutonic)
NIGERIAN of Nigeria
NIGGLING finicking; trifling
NIGHNESS nearness; proximity
NIGHTCAP cap or drink; horsehood (baseball)
NIGHT-DOG nocturnal venatic hound
zo **NIGHT-FLY** nocturnal moth
NIGHT-HAG a witch
zo **NIGHT-JAR** night-churr; goat-sucker
NIGHTMAN watchman
NIGHT-OWL who stays out late
NIHILISM extreme negation (doctrine)
NIHILIST Russian revolutionary (Tsarist era)
NIHILITY nothingness
cp **NINE-EDGE** feeding in punch cards
zo **NINE-EYES** lampreys
NINEFOLD 9 times
NINEPINS skittles
NINETEEN cardinal number
NINEVITE of Nineveh
bt **NISBERRY** naseberry; medlar
bt **NITIDOUS** lustrous; shining; reflecting
ch **NITRATED** (nitric acid)
ch **NITROGEN** an inert gas
NITROLIC acid
NITROXYL halogen/metal-attached radical
NIVATION snow-caused erosion
NOACHIAN (Noah); archaic; bygone
NOBBLING doping; injuring; swindling
ch **NOBELIUM** man-made element
NOBILITY distinction; aristocracy
NOBLEMAN a peer
NOBLESSE obliges all; (nobility)
zo **NOCTILIO** bat-genus
NOCTUARY night record
mu **NOCTURNE NOTTURNO**, serenade; lyrical; (It.) night scene
NODECUSP intersection of orbits
bt **NODIFORM** knots on stems
NODOSITY an entanglement
NODULOSE knotty; nodulous
NOEMATIC NOETICAL, intellectual; mental; thoughtful
ck **NOISETTE** small round piece of meat etc.
NOMADISM of regular seasonal migration
NOMADIZE migrate with flocks
NOMARCHY provincial rule
NOMINATE designate; name; appoint
NOMISTIC lawful
NOMOGENY life origin
ce **NOMOGRAM** alignment chart; diagram
NOMOLOGY psychology
lw **NON-CLAIM** failure to claim (insurance)
ch **NON-CREEP** smooth flow additive
NON-ELECT not of the elect
NONESUCH without parallel; paragon
rl **NON-JUROR** (Jacobite clergy)
ch **NONMETAL** negative-ion former
NON-MORAL amoral
NON-NASAL (phonetics)
NON-PARTY independent
NON-RIGID limp
NONSENSE balderdash; inanity; trash
md **NON-TOXIC** not poisonous
NON-UNION not accepting trades unions
NOONTIDE midday
NORMALCY regularity; standard
NORMALLY usually; ordinary
NORSEMAN NORTH-MAN, (Viking) Scand.
NORTHERN of the north
NORTHING distance northward
NORWEYAN Norwegian (Shak.)
NOSEBAND part of bridle
ae **NOSE-DIVE** a sudden plunge
zo **NOSE-LEAF** a bat appendage
NOSELESS non-nasal
NOSE-RING bull's ornament
md **NOSOLOGY NOSONOMY**, classification of diseases
md **NOTALGIA** backache
NOTANDUM a memorandum
NOTARIAL clerical
NOTATION system of figures
NOTCHING nicking; scoring

NOTEBOOK jotting pad
NOTELESS insignificant; petty; trivial
NOTICING observing; remarking
NOTIFIED made known; apprised
NOTIONAL fanciful; imaginative
zo **NOTORNIS** coot, (extinct) NZ
mu **NOTTURNO NOCTURNE**, night serenade; lyrical (It.)
ag **NOTWHEAT** of cereals without beard forms
NOUMENAL not phenomenal
NOUMENON a definite conception
rl **NOVATIAN** puritanical sect
lw **NOVATION** debt transference
NOVELESE inferior-novel language style
NOVELISH resembling a novel
NOVELIST author of romances; fiction
NOVELIZE to spin yarns, tell tales
NOVEMBER eleventh month
NOVENARY nine collectively
NOVERCAL like a step-mother
lw **NOVERINT** a writ
NOWADAYS in these days; at present
mt **NUBECULA** cloudiness
NUBILITY marriage
mt **NUBILOSE NUBILOUS**, cloudy; overcast
bt **NUCAMENT** a catkin
bt **NUCELLUS** nucleus of ovule
NUCIFORM nut-like
ch **NUCLEASE** nucleic-acid-hydrolisis enzyme
NUCLEATE having a nucleus
NUCLEOLE small nucleus
bl **NUCLEOME** protoplast's nuclear substance
bt **NUDATION** stripping area of plants
NUDISTIC scantily attired
NUGATORY ineffectual; futile; bootless
NUISANCE pest; annoyance; bother
NUMBERED reckoned; computed; limited
NUMBERER counter; numerator
NUMBNESS torpor; stupefaction
NUMERARY of numerals
NUMERATE as literate, but in numbers
NUMEROUS plentiful; manifold; frequent
NUMMULAR numismatic
NUMSKULL blockhead; dunce
NUPTIALS a marriage (occasion)
NURIMONO lacquer-ware (Jap.)
NURSLING an infant; child
NURTURED brought up; tended
NUTARIAN nut-eater
ma **NUTATION** nodding; Euler's angles showing position of body around a point
NUT-BROWN colour of ale
zo **NUTHATCH** small bird
NUTHOUSE lunatic asylum
ck **NUTMEGGY** of nutmeg flavour etc. as spice
NUTRIENT nourishing; alimental
NUT-SCREW monkey wrench
NUTSHELL receptacle for small amount
NUZZLING nestling
bt **NYMPHAEA** water-lilies
NYMPHEAN NYMPHISH, maidenly; like a nymph
NYSTATIN antifungal antibiotic

O

bt **OAK-APPLE** wen on oak tree
OAK-PAPER a wall paper
bt **OAT-GRASS** sort of straw
OATHABLE capable of being sworn
OBDUCING enveloping; covering
OBDURACY stubbornness; callousness
OBDURATE harsh; hardened; inflexible
OBEDIENT dutiful; submissive
OBEISANT reverencing; respectful
pr **OBELIZED** marked as spurious (†)
OBERHAUS upper house (Ger.)
OBITUARY list of the dead
OBJECTED protested; interposed
OBJECTOR opposer; heckler
OBLATION an offering; libation
rl **OBLATORY** of divine bread
lw **OBLIGANT** bound by contract
OBLIGATE oblige; pledge; mortgage
mu **OBLIGATO** obbligato; of special import
OBLIGING gratifying; constraining
OBLIQUED slanted
zo **OBLIQUUS** obliquely placed muscle
OBLIVION forgetfulness; (nepenthe)
zo **OBLONGUM** wing-vein cell coleoptera
OBSCURED eclipsed; clouded; dimmed
OBSCURER a concealer; hider
OBSERVED saw; remarked; obeyed
OBSERVER spectator; commentator
OBSESSED besieged; beset; haunted
mn **OBSIDIAN** volcanic rock
OBSOLETE discarded; archaic; effete

OBSTACLE hindrance; barrier; check
OBSTRUCT block; clog; impede; choke
OBTAINED got; won; earned; acquired
OBTAINER procurer; achiever
OBTRUDED thrust out; assertive
OBTRUDER importunate gate-crasher
OBTUNDED blunted; deadened
OBTURATE to close up; seal; shut
OBTUSELY stolidly; stupidly
OBTUSION bluntness
OBVERTED faced; confronted
OBVIATED avoided; prevented
bt **OBVOLUTE** wavy; enfolded
rl **OCCAMISM OCCAMIST**, doctrine of Occam
OCCASION create; event; incident
OCCIDENT the west
as **OCCLUDED** eclipsed; hidden
OCCLUSOR a shutter; valve
OCCULTED one eclipsed by another
OCCULTLY by secret (planetary) forces
OCCUPANT holder; tenant; resident
OCCUPIED engaged; employed
OCCUPIER inhabiter
OCCURRED chanced; happened; befell
OCEANIAN (Oceania)
mn **OCEANITE** basaltic igneous rock
zo **OCELLARY OCELLATE**, with spots like eyes; leopard-like genus
OCHEROUS yellow
zo **OCHIDORE** shore-crab
md **OCHLESIS OCHLETIC**, illness due to overcrowding
bt **OCHREATE** sheathing
OCHREOUS yellowish
mn **OCHROITE** cerite
OCTAPODY verse of 8 feet
OCTARCHY government by 8
mu **OCTOBASS** lower than double bass cello
OCTONARY referring to 8
zo **OCTOPODA** sub-order of molluscs
OCTOROON one-eighth negro blood
mu **OCTUPLET** (eight notes)
OCULARLY visibly; demonstrably
ODIOUSLY hatefully; offensively
ODOGRAPH distance and course meter
ODOMETER mileage recorder
md **ODONTIST** dentist
ODONTOID toothlike
md **ODONTOMA** tooth tumour
bt **OENANTHE** water dropwort
OENOLOGY study of wine
OERLIKON light A.A. gun
OESTROUS female reproductive cycle
ga **OFF-BREAK** of erratic bowling (cricket)
ga **OFF-DRIVE** batsman's stroke (cricket)
OFFENDED violated; affronted
OFFENDER transgressor; delinquent
OFFERING tendering; proposing
OFFICIAL functional; authorized
pr **OFFPRINT** a reprint; copy
OFFSHOOT branch outwards; new direction
OFFSHOOT scion; extension of company; gutter; water run-off
OFFSHORE non-domestic (banking etc.)
OFF-STAGE behind the scenes; unrecorded
OFF-WHITE variation shade
OFT-TIMES frequently; repeatedly
me **OHMMETER** (resistance)
OILCLOTH linoleum
OIL-FIELD oil well area
OIL-FIRED boiler; furnace
md **OIL-GLAND** secreting gland
OILINESS greasiness; lubricity
OILING-IN pre-painting surface preparation
OIL-PAPER transparent paper
OIL-PRESS olive squeezer
OILSKINS weatherproof garments
OILSTONE whetstone; sharpening stone; hone
md **OINTMENT** an unguent
fr **OITICICA** oil from nut tree (Brazil)
OLD-TIMER old-stager
OLD-WORLD antiquated
bt **OLEANDER** an evergreen
bt **OLEASTER** wild olive
OLEFIANT oil producing
pg **OLEOBROM** developing process
zo **OLEOCYST** oil-containing diverticulum
bt **OLEOSOME** cell fat inclusion
me **OLFACTIE** odour intensity unit
bt **OLIBANUM** frankincense
OLIGARCH one of power-sharing few
zo **OLIPHANT** elephant (obs.); cup made of ivory-tusk (medieval)
bt, ck **OLIVE-OIL** food oil of purity
rl **OLIVETAN** a Benedictine
OLYMPIAD period of 4 years
OLYMPIAN godlike
ga **OLYMPICS** competitive games, athletics
OMELETTE beaten-egg dish

OMISSION oversight; failure; disregard
OMISSIVE exclusive; neglectful
OMITTING missing; skipping; dropping
zo **OMMATEUM** compound eye
OMNIFORM of all shapes; protean
md **OMOHYOID** (shoulder-blade)
md **OMOIDEUM** pterygoid bone
md **OMOPLATE** shoulder-blade
md **OMPHALIC** (navel)
OMPHALOS boss on a shield; hub
ONCE-OVER comprehensive glance
bt **ONCIDIUM** orchid genus
md **ONCOLOGY** science of tumours
ONCOMING approaching
md **ONCOTOMY** cutting a tumour
ONE-HORSE poorly equipped
ONE-SIDED partial; biased
ONE-TRACK single interest or file
zo **ONISCOID** like a woodlouse
ONLINESS managing independently, alone
ONLOOKER spectator (match) (occasion)
mn **ONOFRITE** a mercury salt
ONOMANCY divination
ONRUSHES onsets
ONTOGENY development during individual life history
ONTOLOGY metaphysics
zo **ONYCHIUM** pulvillus in insect
zo **ONYMATIC** genetic
bt **OOGONIUM** algae/fungi female sex organ
zo **OOKINETE** vermiform stage in protozoa
OOLOGIST collector of bird's eggs
zo **OOSPHERE** an egg
zo **OOTOCOUS** oviparous
OPALESCE to be iridescent
OPALIZED make like an opal
mn **OPENCAST** excavating surface coal
OPEN-EYED watchful; alert; awake
OPENNESS frankness; sincerity
ar **OPEN-WELL** uncovered well
OPEN-WORK metal/lace pattern
OPERA-HAT a gibus
rw, md **OPERATED** as service (trains etc.); - on (as patient)
OPERATIC in opera style
OPERATOR service organizer; businessman
OPERATOR factory machinist; artisan; hand-
mu **OPERETTA** light, humorous musical
zo **OPHIDIAN** reptilian
zo **OPHIDION** conger eel
zo **OPHIURAN** starfish
OPIFICER artificer
OPINABLE conjecturable
OPIUM-DEN centre for drug addicts
bt **OPOPONAX** a perfume; a gum
OPPILATE block up; obstruct
zo **OPPONENS** muscle related to digits
OPPONENT foe; rival; antagonist
OPPOSING resisting; withstanding
OPPOSITE contrary; adverse; inimical
OPPUGNED contested; fought
OPPUGNER adversary; competitor
OPTATIVE optional; elective; voluntary
OPTICIAN spectacle-maker
OPTIMACY the nobility
OPTIMISM hopefulness
OPTIMIST a sanguine person
OPTIMIZE take a bright view
OPTIONAL left to choice; discretional
OPTOGRAM image of object seen on retina
OPULENCE wealth; affluence; profusion
OPULENCY riches; possessions
OPUSCULE a small work
ORACULAR portentous; ominous
ORANGERY orange garden
ORANGISM of Ulster Protestantist power
mn **ORANGITE** thorium silicate
mu **ORATORIO** sacred musical drama
ORATRESS a woman orator
ORCADIAN (Orkney Islands)
bt **ORCHANET** alkanet
ORCHESIS art of dancing
rl **ORDAINED** invested as priest; enacted
rl **ORDAINER** bishop; assigner; prescriber
ORDERING disposing; directing
rl **ORDINAND** candidate for orders
rl **ORDINANT** a prelate
ORDINARY a dinner; usual; customary
ORDINATE methodical; orderly
ORDINATE vertical axis on two dimensional graph
ORDNANCE war material (national)
ORDNANCE survey; mapping (national)
tx **ORGANDIE** figured muslin
ORGANIFY add organic matter
ORGANISM living structure
mu **ORGANIST** a player
ORGANIZE frame; constitute; construct

ORICHALC imitation gold
ORIENTAL of matters, cultures in the East
ar, bd **ORIENTED** lined up; on course
ORIGINAL authentic; an eccentric; new approaches
ORILLION a bastion
ORINASAL mouth and nose sound
ORNAMENT embellishment; decoration
ORNATELY elaborately; in florid style
zo **ORNITHIC** referring to birds
zo **ORONASAL** of mouth and nose
ORPHANCY orphanhood
ORPHANED parentless
ch **ORPIMENT** sulphurous yellow pigment; (arsenic sulphide)
tv **ORTHICON** type of camera tube
ORTHODOX true; conventional; correct
ORTHOEPY correct pronunciation
mn **ORYCTICS** fossils
ch **ORYZENIN** rice glutelin protein
zo **OSCINIAN** (singing birds)
OSCITANT drowsy; yawning
OSCITATE to gape
OSCULANT kissing
OSCULATE to buss
zo **OSETROVA** sturgeon; caviar
OSMAZOME meat extract
tx **OSNABURG** coarse linen
ac **OSOPHONE** headphone for the deaf
OSSIANIC (Ossian)
OSSIFIED turned into bone
ck **OSSOBUCO** stew of veal with bone, wine (It.)
md **OSTEITIS** bone inflammation
md **OSTEOZOA** the vertebrata
bt **OSTERICK** bistort plant
mu **OSTINATO** recurrent theme
OSTIOLAR cellular
OSTRAKON engraved pottery shard (Gr.)
OTAHEITE Malay apple (Pacific)
zo **OTOCONIA** concretions in mollusca
OTOLITHS tiny calcium crystals (in ear)
md **OTORRHEA** discharge from ear
md **OTOSCOPE** ear examiner
md **OTOSCOPY** ear examination
mu **OTTAVINO** It. small flute, piccolo
zo **OUISTITI** marmoset
OUTBLUSH outflush
nt **OUTBOARD** external, portable, boat motor
OUTBOUND outward bound
OUTBRAVE defy; dare; challenge
OUTBREAK fray; riot; broil; revolt
OUTBURST eruption; ebullition
OUTCASTE rejected; casteless Hindu
OUTCLASS excel; outvie; surpass
OUTCROSS (cross-breeding)
OUTDARED defied; flouted
OUTDATED outmoded; old-fashioned
OUTDOING surpassing; outstripping
OUTDOORS not at home; fresh airing
OUTDWELL outstay
OUTFACED braved
OUTFIELD (cricket); nearer to the boundaries
OUTFLANK asssault from side or rear
OUTFLASH outshine
OUTFLING sharp retort
OUTFROWN show the greater dissatisfaction
OUTGOING expenditure; outlay
pc **OUT-GROUP** the excluded ones; pariahs
OUTGROWN become too constricting
OUTGUARD outpost
OUTGUIDE file marker for removed entries
OUT-HEROD be bigger stinker
OUTHOUSE shed; shack; shanty; barn
OUTLAWED beyond the pale
OUTLAWRY exile; banishment
ga **OUTLEAPT** higher than competitors sprang
OUTLEARN excel in learning
OUTLINED delineated; sketched
OUTLIVED outlasted
OUTLYING far; remote; distant
OUTMARCH walk until drop
OUTMODED out of fashion
OUTPACED over-run; run faster
cp **OUT-PLANT** system with remote data terminals
OUTPOINT win (sport)
OUTPOWER overpower; vanquish
OUTRAGED insulted; maltreated
OUTRANGE extend further
OUTREACH exceed; surpass
OUTREIGN sit on throne longer
OUTRIDER mounted attendant
OUTRIGHT at once; utterly
OUTRIVAL excel; outvie; beat
lw **OUTROPER** kind of bailiff
OUTSCOLD upbraid excessively
OUTSCORN despise; disdain; contemn
OUTSHINE eclipse; overshadow
OUTSHONE outrivalled
OUTSIDER not a favourite; onlooker; as alien
OUTSIDES backs or three quarters (rugby football)

OUTSIGHT outlook
OUTSKIRT border
OUTSLEEP perchance to outdream
OUTSLEPT snored longer than
OUTSLIDE slide better than everyone else
OUTSMART diddle; outwit; overreach
OUTSPEAK speak boldly
OUTSPENT over tired
OUTSPOKE bad English
OUTSPORT outdo in sport
OUTSTAND resist; withstand
OUTSTARE look longer than
OUTSTOOD withstood
OUTSTRIP outrun; undress faster
OUTSWEAR collect cursing prize
OUTSWELL overflow
OUT-TO-OUT overall measurement
OUTVALUE appraise too highly
OUTVOICE talk down
OUTVOTED won election
OUTVOTER imaginary elector
OUTWARDS externally
OUTWATCH peer superiorly
OUTWEARY bore stiff
OUTWEIGH exceed in value; offset; overbalance
zo **OVARIOLE** egg-tube in insects
zo **OVARIOUS** consisting of eggs
zo **OVEN-BIRD** a tree-creeper
OVER-AGED disqualified by age
tx **OVERALLS** garments
OVERARCH overhang
OVERAWED quelled; intimidated
OVERBEAR overwhelm; domineer
OVERBODY head, shoulders and breast
OVERBOIL let kettle blow top
OVERBOLD impudent; presumptuous
OVERBOWL cricket
OVERBRIM overflow
OVERBUSY officious
OVERCAME vanquished; subdued
mt **OVERCAST** lowering; cloudy
OVERCOAT winter topcoat
OVERCOME defeat
OVERCROW to insult; exult; brag
OVERDATE post-date
OVERDONE exaggerated
OVERDOSE too many pills
OVERDRAW take too much from bank
OVERDREW exaggerate in drawing
OVER-FACE requiring horse to jump beyond its limits
OVERFALL tidal effect
OVERFEED glut; cloy; satiate
OVERFILL flood
OVERFISH trawl too many
OVERFLOW overrun; inundate; swamp; annex (space)
tc, cp **OVERFLOW** reserve circuits; excess (location); (audience)
gl **OVERFOLD** inverted strata
OVERFOND doting
OVERFULL too full
OVERGAZE look over
OVERGIVE give lavishly
OVERGROW grow excessively (overgrown)
OVERHAND throwing; hand higher than shoulder
OVERHANG jut; impend
OVERHAUL repair; overtake; examine
OVERHEAD aloft
OVERHEAR eavesdrop
OVERHEAT scorch
OVERJUMP neglect; pass by
OVERKILL excess of casualties (nuclear war)
OVERKIND indulgent
OVERKING control lesser kings
OVERKNEE (above the knee)
OVERLADE overburdened
mn, gl, tx **OVERLAID OVERLAIN**, smothered; with decorative layers, (jewellery; gems)
OVERLAND cross-country
OVERLEAF on the next page
OVERLEAP skip
OVERLIVE outlive; survive
OVERLOAD encumber
OVERLOCK lock up too much
OVERLONG too long
OVERLOOK to slight; connive; condone
OVERLORD feudal superior
OVERMOST highest; topmost
OVERMUCH in excess
OVERNEAT finicky
OVERNICE fastidious
OVERPAID given excessive wages
OVERPASS traffic routing
OVERPLAY gambling
OVERPLUS remainder; surplus
OVERRAKE to sweep over like a wave
OVERRATE esteem too highly
OVERRIDE trample; quash; annul; exhaust a horse
OVERRIPE passé; past the prime
OVERRULE prevail; repudiate; rescind
OVERSEAM a seam
OVERSEAS abroad
OVERSEEN observed; overlooked
OVERSEER superintendent; foreman

OVERSELL make excess profits
OVERSEWN sewn over the edge
OVERSHOE a galosh (waterproof)
OVERSHOT beyond the target; went too far
nt **OVERSIDE** when water floods into a ship
OVERSIZE outsize; exaggerated
OVERSKIP leap-over; overtip
OVERSLIP pass without notice
ga **OVERSMAN** umpire (cricket)
OVERSOLD sales exceeded stocks
OVERSOUL divine being
ga **OVERSPIN** of twisted bowling (cricket)
OVERSTAY remain too long
OVERSTEP exceed; transgress
OVERSWAY overrule
OVERTAKE catch up with and pass
OVERTASK overtax; overtoil
bd **OVERTILE** imbrex; (It.); (Sp.)
OVERTILT upset
OVERTIME extra-pay and -play hours
OVERTOIL overexert
mu **OVERTONE** harmonic; partial tone, vibrating body
OVERTRIP be tripped by tripwire
mu **OVERTURE** offer; proposal; prelude (opera)
OVERTURN cause revolution
OVERVEIL overmantel; covering
OVERVIEW an inspection
OVERWASH glacial formation
OVERWEAR outdoor clothing
OVERWEEN to be conceited
OVERWIND overtax clock-mechanism
OVERWISE too clever by half
OVERWORK excess toil
tx **OVERWORN** exhausted by above; threadbare
zo **OVIPOSIT** lay an insect's eggs
OWL-LIGHT dusk to darkness
OXIDABLE oxidizable
ch **OXIDATOR** source of oxidation
OXIDIZE OXIDIZER, combined with oxygen; oxidizing agent
zo **OX-PECKER** African bird
bt **OX-TONGUE** a plant
OXYGONAL having acute angles
OXYMORON bitter-sweet
zo **OXYTOCIC** causing muscle contraction
md **OXYTOCIN** pituitary hormone strengthening uterus, mammary glands
OZOKERIT waxen material
ch **OZONIZED** converted to ozone
ch **OZONIZER** oxygen-to-ozone converter

P

PABULARY alimentary
PABULOUS nourishing
PACHYOTE thick-eared
PACHYPOD thick-footed
PACIFIED calmed; lulled; assuaged
PACIFIER tranquillizer; conciliator
PACIFISM PACIFIST, refusal to participate in armed warfare
PACKETED made into a parcel
PACK-LOAD load for an animal
PACK-MULE beast of burden
PADDLING walking in shallow water
nt **PADDLING** canoeing; of side wheelers
bt **PADELION** lady's mantle
PADELOUP inlaid leather book decoration
PADISHAH Turkish title; sultan; supreme ruler
PADSTONE kneeler; template
PADUAKAN coasting ketch (Celebes)
tx **PADUASOY** corded silk
ga **PAGANICA** feather filled leather ball
PAGANISH heathen
PAGANISM of polytheistic religions
PAGANIST follower of above
PAGANIZE proselytizing others to this
pr **PAGINATE** to number the pages
mn **PAGODITE** pagoda-stone
zo **PAGURIAN** (hermit-crabs)
gl **PAHOEHOE** ropy or cordel lava (Hawaii)
PAILLONS spangles (Fr.)
PAINLESS pangless
PAINTBOX box of colours
pt **PAINTING** a picture; limning; coating; application of paints
pt **PAINTOUT** test of pigment
PAIR-WISE in pairs
zo **PALAMATE** web-footed
PALATIAL royal; magnificent; stately
PALATINE with royal privileges
zo **PALEBUCK** the oribi
PALE-FACE white man among Red Indians
PALENESS wanness
PALESTRA wrestling school
bt **PALIFORM** stake-shaped
PALILOGY repetition
PALINODE recantation
bd **PALISADE** fortified paling enclosure

ga **PALISADE** horse-jumping obstacle
PALLIATE extenuate; mitigate; gloss
PALLIDLY palely; wanly
ga **PALL-MALL** ancient croquet
PALMETTE palm-leaf decor
bt **PALMETTO** fan-palm; hat
zo **PALMIPED** web-footed
PALMITIN natural oil fat
PALM-WINE fermented palm juice
zo **PALOMINO** cream coloured horse with light-coloured mane and tail (Sp.)
PALPABLE perceptible; evidently
PALPABLY obviously; tangibly
zo **PALPACLE** tentacle in siphonophora
PALPATED handled; felt
pl **PALPEBRA** eyelid
zo **PALPIFER** lobe of maxilla
zo **PALPLESS** absence of palpi
zo **PALPOCIL** sense hairlet in coelenterata
PALSTAFF PALSTAVE, Celtic stone axe
PALSYING paralysing
PALTERED shuffled; quibbled
PALTERER dodger; prevaricator
PALUDINE marshy
md **PALUDISM** malaria
PALUDOSE boggy
pm **PAMAQUIN** synthetic antimalarial drug
PAMPERED coddled; humoured
PAMPERER over-indulgent person
PAMPHLET a broadsheet; brochure
rl **PANAGHIA** bishop's pendant
ae **PANCAKED** landed flat
PANCARTE royal charter
PANCHEON earthenware pan
md **PANCREAS** sweetbread
bt **PANDANUS** (screw-pines)
PANDEMIC epidemic in an area
PANDERED appeased others' desires
ck **PANDOWDY** apple-charlotte dessert
PANEGYRY eulogy; encomium; adulation
PANELESS no glass
PANELLED (walls; a jury)
to **PANEL-SAW** a cutting tool
zo **PANGAMIC** of indiscriminate mating
zo **PANGOLIN** scaly ant-eater
PANICKED terrorized; affrighted
bt **PANICLED** in clusters
PANIONIC (Ionian people)
zo **PANMIXIA** cessation of natural selection
PANNIKEL brain-pan; skull
PANNIKIN small vessel
PANOPTIC all seeing
PANORAMA extensive view
PANOTYPE antique photograph
mu **PANPIPES** a scale of wood pipes
PANSOPHY all wisdom
ar, rl **PANTHEON** complete mythology; burial place of monarchs
mu **PANTONAL** synthesis of keys; atonal
PANURGIC skilled in all craft
PAPABILE suitable for papal/other office
mt **PAPAGAYO** northerly wind (Mexican plateau)
rl **PAPALISM** popery
rl **PAPALIST** an R.C.
rl **PAPALIZE** proselytize (R.C.)
PAPERBOY newsagent's delivery boy
PAPERING wall and house-decorating
zo **PAPILLAE** nipples
PAPILLAR warty
rl **PAPISHER** a papist
rl **PAPISTIC** popish
ck **PAPPADAM PAPPADUM**, Indian bread wafer
PAPULOSE pimply
PAPYRINE like paper
rl **PARABEMA** Byzantine sacristy
PARABLED used a parable
PARABOLA a conic section
PARABOLE similitude
PARACHOR molecular volume
zo **PARACONE** molar cusp in mammals
PARADIGM example; model; grammar pattern
PARADING displaying; flaunting
PARADISE Heaven; Eden; Elysium; oasis; open court; atrium
mn **PARAFFIN** an oil
ch **PARAFORM** fumigant; formaldehyde
PARAGOGE literal addition
PARAGRAM a pun
zo **PARAGULA** region of insect head
zo **PARAKEET** paroquet; small parrot
PARAKITE tailless kite
PARALLAX alternation; displacement
PARALLEL side by side
PARALOGY false reasoning
PARALYSE benumb; deaden; unnerve
zo **PARAMERE** an antimere
PARAMOUR a lover; mistress
bt **PARANEMA** paraphysis
PARANGON matchless jewel
md **PARANOEA PARANOIA**, chronic monomania; hallucination
zo **PARAPSID** reptile skull condition
zo **PARAPSIS** (thorax)

ch **PARAQUAT** weedkiller toxic to humans
me **PARASANG** about 4 miles (Pers.)
rl **PARASEVE** Jewish Saturday night
PARASHOT an anti-parachutist
zo **PARASITE** a sycophant; toady
ac **PARASTAT** gramophone record cleaner
PARATYPE not the type specimen
PARAVAIL inferior; cf. paramount
nt **PARAVANE** minesweeping aid
pg **PARAXIAL** near to axis
lw **PARCENER** co-heir
PARCHING scorching; drying
rl **PARCLOSE** screen
PARDONED excused; absolved
rl **PARDONER** sells papal indulgences
PARENTAL affectionate; fatherly
mu **PARERGON** subsidiary work (Gr.)
PARGETED decorated exterior house-walls
PARGETER plasterer; artist-modeller
PARHELIA mock suns (illusory)
pl **PARIETAL** walls of anatomical cavity
pl **PARIETES** of organ cavities; skull
PARISIAN (Paris)
mn **PARISITE** a marble
PARLANCE mode of speech
mu **PARLANDO** articulation in singing
mu **PARLANTE** crisp (piano playing)
PARLAYED conferred; discussed
PARMESAN a cheese
PARODIED took off; burlesqued
PARODIST burlesqued in literature, on stage
PARONYME similar-sounding word
zo **PAROQUET** small parrot; parakeet
md **PAROSMIA** smell sense abnormality
rl **PAROUSIA** second Advent
md **PAROXYSM** fit; convulsion
PARROTER copyist
PARROTRY servile imitation
PARRYING warding; frustrating
PARSONIC like a parson
PARTAKEN consumed
PARTAKER sharer; partner
PARTERRE (flower beds, etc.) ground floor; stalls; auditorium
PARTHIAN (Parthia)
PARTIBLE divisible
lw **PARTIBUS** marginal note
PARTICLE an atom; scrap; fragment
PARTISAN firm adherent to a faction
PARTNERS couples (dancing) (wedded); associates
mu **PART-SONG** glee; for several parts
PART-TIME works for part of day only
PARTYISM party loyalty
PASCUAGE grazing
PASCUOUS growing in pastures
PASHALIK pasha's jurisdiction
PASILALY universal speech
PASSABLE tolerable, up to standard
PASSABLY acceptably; reasonably
zo **PASSAGER** free tripper (falconry)
PASSBOOK identity documents; pay; bankbook
PASSCODE secret entry requirement
PASSER-BY street pedestrian on his way
zo **PASSERES** perching birds (genus)
PASSLESS trackless; without pass, identity
rl **PASSOVER** Jewish festival
PASSPORT document of nationality, identity; visas
PASSROLL stroke in croquet
PASSWORD secret watchword for entry
PASTICHE comic imitation, entertainment
md **PASTILLE** medicated lozenge
PASTORAL rustic
PASTORLY pastorlike; priestly
ck **PASTRAMI** smoked/sun-dried seasoned meat
ck **PASTRIES** confectionery
PASTURED grazed
zo **PATAGIUM** wing membrane
PATCHBOX for decorative black spots
PATCHERY botchery
PATCHING repairing; cobbling
pl **PATELLAR** of the knee-cap
PATENTED protected by law
PATENTEE to whom a patent is granted
PATENTOR the Patent Office; issuer
PATERERO **PEDERERO**, ancient swivel gun (Sp.)
PATERNAL fatherly; parental
PATHETIC sad; grievous; emotional
PATHLESS no beaten track
zo **PATHOGEN** disease-causing parasite
PATIENCE cards; an opera
ec **PATOCOLE** forest-floor animal
hd **PATONCEE** heraldic cross
ec **PATOXENE** accidental forest-floor animal
PATRONAL condescending
nt **PATTAMAR** large 3-masted dhow (East India)
PATTENED wearing clogs
PATTERED falling rain; children's feet
PATTERER with flowing salestalk

ck **PATTY-PAN** baking dish
PATULOUS spreading
PAULDRON a shoulder plate
PAUNCHED obese
PAVEMENT footway; sidewalk
PAVILION large tent; canopy; sports house
PAVILLON grand opening of horns, bells (Fr.)
PAVISADO galley defence
PAVONINE like a peacock
PAWNSHOP pawnbroker's pledged goods shop
PAYCLERK employee charged with paying
PAYPHONE public coin callbox; telephone
PAYSHEET list of wages owed
PEACEFUL placid; serene; pacific
PEACHERY a hothouse
zo **PEACHICK** young peafowl
PEACHING divulging; informing
PEAGREEN a colour
el **PEAK-LOAD** maximum activity
mn **PEARL-ASH** potash
md **PEARL-EYE** cataract
PEARLIES coster's buttons
PEARLING diving for pearls
ml **PEARLITE** iron/steel microconstituent
mn, bd **PEARLITE** granules of volcanic glass, insulation aggregate
bt **PEARMAIN** an apple
bt **PEASECOD** pea-pod
mn **PEASTONE** limestone
PEAT-MOOR peat-bog
bt **PEAT-MOSS** sphagnum
PEAT-REEK peat smoke
PECCABLE weak; frail; erring
PECCANCY sinfulness; offence
PECTINAL like a comb
PECTORAL breast-plate
PECULATE embezzle; steal; purloin
PECULIAR odd; singular; unusual
PECULIUM prerogative; privilege
PEDAGOGY instruction
ag, gl **PEDALFER** cyclist; iron-clay rich zonal soil
PEDALIAN referring to feet
PEDALIER pedal keyboard
PEDALITY foot measurement
PEDALLED worked by foot
PEDALLER PEDALFER, cyclist
PEDANTIC finical; exact; precise
PEDANTRY priggishness; conceit
PEDDLERY hawking
PEDDLING retailing; trifling
PEDERERO paterero; swivel gun (Sp.)
PEDESTAL plinth; base
md **PEDIATRY** childish diseases
md **PEDICURE** foot treatment
PEDIGREE lineage; stock; genealogy
PEDIMENT portico decoration
zo **PEDIPALP** whip-scorpion
zo **PEDIREME** a crustacean
PEDOLOGY study of soil
bt, pl **PEDUNCLE** stalk; nerve fibre stalks in brain
PEEK-A-BOO punching cards with identity code
PEEK-A-BOO children's frolic
PEEP-HOLE chink for illicit observation
PEEP-O'-DAY dawn
PEEP-SHOW galanty-show
PEERLESS unrivalled; matchless
zo **PEESWEEP** peewit
zo **PEETWEET** spotted sandpiper
PEGAMOID imitation leather
PEGASEAN (Pegasus)
PEIGNOIR loose wrapper
PEINTURE special consistent use of paints
PEJORATE deteriorate
zo **PEKINESE** small pug-nosed dog
PELAGIAN (deep sea)
PELARGIC stork-like
PELASGIC early Grecian
PELERINE a tippet or cape
md **PELLAGRA** acute anaemia
PELLICLE thin skin or crust
PELL-MELL rapidly; in disorder; confusedly
PELLUCID transparent; vitreous; clear
bt **PELORISM** abnormality
PELTATED shield-shaped
PELT-WOOL wool from a hide
ck **PEMMICAN** dried meat/berry food
PENALIZE handicap; punish
PENCHANT inclination; turn; bent
PENCRAFT penmanship
PENDENCE suspense
PENDENCY indecision
PENDULUM swinging weight
zo **PENELOPE** currasow-bird (S. Amer.)
PENITENT contrite; repentant
nt **PENJAJAP** square-lug trade vessel (Malaya)
PENKNIFE pocket-knife
PENNORTH a pennyworth
zo **PENNY-DOG** a kind of shark
PENOLOGY prison management
PENSTOCK duct to waterwheel
PENTACLE five-pointed star
PENTAFID cleft in five

PENTAGON five sided figure
mn **PENTELIC** (marble)
ch **PENTOSAN** polysaccharide
bd **PENT-ROOF** lean-to; sloped roof
as **PENUMBRA** partial shadow; (partial solar eclipse)
PENWIPER rag for pen user
PENWOMAN lady journalist; author
PEOPLING populating
mn **PEPERINO** granular tufa
PEPPERED hit with shot
PEPTOGEN PEPTONIC, digestive principle; digestive
PEPYSIAN (Samuel Pepys) (diary)
PERACUTE very sharp or violent
PERCEIVE apprehend; discern; descry
PERCHING roosting
hd **PERCLOSE** screen; railing
mu **PERDENDO** dying away
PERDURED endured; lasted
PERFORCE of necessity; forcibly
PERFUMED scented; odoriferous
PERFUMER perfume seller
PERFUSED sprinkled; bedewed
nt **PERIAGUA** dug-out canoe, W. Indies (Sp.)
pl **PERIANAL** anal/rectal region
bt **PERIANTH** floral envelope
bt **PERIBLEM** portion of apical meristem
bt **PERICARP** seed-vessel
rl **PERICOPE** scriptural passage
md **PERICYTE** small-blood-vessel cell
bt **PERIDERM** outer bark
bt **PERIDIUM** outer wall of fungus fruitbody
as **PERIGEAL PERIGEAN**, of moon's orbit nearest to the earth
bt **PERIGONE** perianth
PERILLED endangered; risked
PERILOUS hazardous; risky; parlous
as **PERILUNE** point in lunar satellite orbit
PERIODIC at stated intervals
PERIOTIC around inner ear
PERIPETY climax; solution
PERIPLUS circumnavigation
zo **PERISARC** chitinous layer in hydrozoa
PERISCII polar people
PERISHED decayed; died; expired
ch **PERISSAD** (odd atomic valency)
el **PERITRON** special cathode-ray tube
PERJURED perfidious; forsworn
PERJURER false witness
gl **PERKNITE** coarse-grained igneous rock
mn **PERLITIC** vitreous obsidian
ec **PERMEANT** highly mobile animal
PERMEATE penetrate; percolate; seep
PERMUTED changed; transmuted
lw **PERNANCY** rent in kind
PERNETTI kiln support
ch **PEROLENE** heat exchange organic fluid
bt **PERONATE** with thick-sheathed stipe
md **PERONEAL** (fibula)
zo **PERONEUS** fibula or leg muscle
PERORATE declaim; harangue
ch **PEROXIDE** a bleacher
bd **PERPENDS** face joints, corners (brick)
PERRUQUE peruke; a wig
PERSICOT peach cordial
bt **PERSIMON** date-plum
PERSONAL distinctive; individual
PERSPIRE sweat
PERSUADE induce; sway; entice
PERTHITE potassium/sodium-felspar intergrowth
PERTNESS sauciness; flippancy
PERTUSED punched
PERUSING reading; scrutinizing
PERUVIAN (Peru)
bt **PERUVINE** Peruvian balsam
PERVADED permeated; diffused
PERVERSE stubborn; vexatious
PERVIOUS porous; permeable
zo **PESSULUS** osseus trachea band in birds
PESTERED plagued; harassed; worried
PESTERER tormentor; teaser
PESTLING pounding; abrading
bt **PETALINE** (petal)
PETALISM banishment; ostracism
mn **PETALITE** silicate of alumina
bt **PETALODY** stamen-to-petal transformation
bt **PETALOID** petal-shaped
bt **PETALOUS** having petals
ga **PETANQUE** of boule (French bowls)
md **PETECHIA** tiny haemorrhage spot
PETERING calling at cards
PETERING collapsing, drying (of machines)
PETERMAN a fisherman
bt **PETIOLAR** having a leaf-stalk
PETITION supplication; ask; beseeching
PETITION of right demand of Govt.
PETITORY of petitioning; demanding
PETRIFIC turning to stone
PETRONEL horse pistol
zo **PETROSAL** otic-fusion bone

PETTIFOG quibble over details
PETULANT irritable; querulous; testy
mn **PETUNTSE** china clay
mn **PETWORTH** variety of marble
PEWTERER worker in pewter
bt **PEZIZOID** like cup-shape apothecium
md **PHAKITIS** eye inflammation
pl **PHALANGE** finger-bone
PHANTASM spectre; chimera
PHANTASY airy speculation; fancy
PHARISEE formalist
PHARMACY drug-store
zo **PHEASANT** a game bird
bt **PHELLOID** plant-surface cell crust
PHENETIC maximum observable similarity
mn **PHENGITE** species of mica
PHENOLIC plastic mould
bt **PHIALIDE** flask-shaped sterigma
PHIALLED filled small one-dose flask
tx **PHILABEG PHILIBEG**, the kilt
zo, mu **PHILOMEL** the nightingale; unit of melody (Shak.)
md **PHLYCTEN** nodule on conjunctiva
zo **PHOCENIC** (dolphins)
PHONATED gurgled
PHONE-BOX public telephone; call box
PHONEMIC phoneme minimal unit of speech in language
PHONETIC vocal
pl **PHORESIS** ion passage through membrane
bt **PHORMIUM** New Zealand flax
ch **PHOSGENE** poisonous gas
PHOSPHAM ammonia compound
ch **PHOSPHOR** morning star; Venus; fluorescent substance
zo **PHOTOGEN** phosphorescent organ
PHOTOPIC normal daylight vision
md **PHOTOPSY** an eye trouble
PHRASING expressing; uttering
bt **PHRYGANA** scattered thorn scrub (Greece)
PHRYGIAN a Montanist
md **PHTHISIS** consumption
PHYLARCH Greek tribal leader
md **PHYLAXIS** body defence against infection; protection
PHYLETIC tribal
mn **PHYLITTE** clay state
bt **PHYLLARY** bract outside capitulum
zo **PHYLLIUM** leaf insects
PHYLLODE a form of leaf
bt **PHYLLODY PHYLLOID**, leaf-like structure
bt **PHYLLOME** foliage
PHYSALIA Portuguese man-of-war
bt **PHYSALIS** Cape gooseberry
zo **PHYSETER** sperm whale
PHYSICAL material; corporeal; tangible
PHYSIQUE bodily structure
bt **PHYTOMER** phyton; plant unit
bt **PHYTOSIS** vegetable parasites
zo **PHYTOZOA** sea anemones, etc.
PIACULAR atrociously bad
mu **PIANETTE** small piano
bt **PIASSABA PIASSAVA**, Brazilian palm; fibre for ropes and brooms
PIAZZIAN like a piazza
PIBLOKTO culture syndrome (Eskimos)
zo **PICARIAN** (woodpeckers)
fr **PICAROON** small hooked pulling pole
PICAROON pirate; rogue
PICCADIL high collar
zo **PICIFORM** woodpecker type
zo **PICKEREL** pike; dunlin
PICKETED enclosed; guarded
PICKLING preserving
PICKLOCK master (skeleton) key
PICK-ME-UP a cordial; stimulant
PICKWICK a club
mn **PICOTITE** a spinel
PICTURED described; represented
PIECENER a piecer; joiner of threads
PIECRUST tart pastry
gl **PIEDMONT** zonal character at foot of mountain
PIEDNESS spotted diversity
bd **PIEDROIT** pier without cap or base
PIERCING keen; shrill; acute
PIERHEAD jetty
PIERIDES the nine Muses
PIFFLING trifling; peddling
PIGEONED fleeced; swindled
PIGEONRY pigeon loft
PIG-FACED swine-visaged
mn **PIGOTITE** aluminium compound
PIGSTIES pig-pens
PIGSWASH swill; hogwash
PIKEHEAD head of a pike
ar **PILASTER** square column
zo **PILCHARD** sea-fish
PILEATED capped
bd **PILE-WORK** foundation of piles
zo **PILE-WORM** teredo; boring worm
PILE-WORN threadbare
bt **PILE-WORT** celandine
PILFERED filched; peculated
PILFERER thief; purloiner
zo **PILIDIUM** larval form of nemertea
PILIFORM slender as a hair
PILING-UP accumulating to surfeit
PILLAGED ransacked; looted

PILLAGER plunderer; rifler; robber
PILLARED columnar
bt **PILLCORN** oats
PILLOWED cushioned
bt **PILLWORT** a plant
PILOSELY hairily
PILOSITY hairiness
nt **PILOTAGE** harbour pilot's fee
ac, nt **PILOTING** directing; guiding; steering
mn **PIMELITE** aluminium silicate
nc **PIMPLING** fuel can surface swelling
PINACOID crystalline structure
nt **PINAFORE** apron; ship of line (Gilbert-rigged)
bt **PINASTER** the cluster-pine
cp **PINBOARD** bagatelle; plugboard (cordless)
PINCE-NEZ eye-glasses
PINCHERS pincers; pliers
nv **PINCHING** nipping; being frugal; sailing too close to the wind
el, ps **PINCH-OFF** breakdown point in field transmissions
PINDAREE Mogul freebooter
PINDARIC in the style of Pindar
PINE-CLAD crowned with pines
bt **PINE-CONE** fir-cone
PINE-WOOD deal
PINE-WOOL fibrous substance
PING-PONG table tennis
cp **PINGPONG** twin-tape multiple recording
PININGLY longingly; languishingly
PINIONED bound; shackled
PINK-EYED having small eyes
bt **PINK-ROOT** a vermifuge
PINKSTER Whitsuntide; a pink flower
PINMAKER who makes pins
PIN-MONEY an allowance
PINNACLE apex of tower decoration; zenith; crown
PINNATED feathered
bd **PINNINGS** different coloured stones set in rubble wall
zo **PINNIPED** fin-footed; a seal
PINOCHLE card game (USA)
PINOLEUM wood and canvas sunblind
bt **PINPATCH** periwinkle
PINPOINT locate exactly
PINTABLE bagatelle gambling
hr **PIN-WHEEL** firework; clock part
PINWHEEL revolving coloured wheel on stick
bt **PIONNATE** fungal spore layer
PIPE-CASE pipe-holder
mn **PIPE-CLAY** a kaolin-like clay
zo **PIPE-FISH** sea-horse type
w **PIPELINE** cross-country oil-lead
PIPERACK storage for tobacco smoker
ck **PIPERINE** pepper concentrate
PIPE-ROLL Great Roll of Exchequer
bt **PIPE-TREE** the lilac
PIPE-WINE wine from the cask
mn **PIPE-WORK** a pipe-vein of ore
bt **PIPEWORT** pepperwort
PIQUANCY pungency; raciness
PIRATING illegal action at sea; (radio)
PIRATING infringing a copyright
PIRIFORM pearshaped
PISCATOR Izaak Walton; fisherman
PISCINAL (fishpond)
zo **PISIFORM** fishlike
mn **PISOLITE** coarse oolite
bt **PISTACIA** the pistachio-tree
PISTOLET small pistol
PITCHING flinging; casting; lurching
PITCH-OUT (baseball)
mn **PIT-FRAME** framework round mine
zo **PITHECUS** an ape
PITHLESS lacking energy; sapless
PITIABLE arousing pity or contempt
PITIABLY deplorably; movingly
PITILESS merciless; ruthless
PITTACAL a blue dye
PITTANCE dole; small allowance
pl **PITUITAL** (pituitary gland)
PITYROID branlike
PIVOT-GUN swivel-gun
PIVOTING moving around; hingeing
PIVOT-MAN key-man
PIXY-RING fairy-ring
PLACABLE relenting; forgiving
PLACATED pacified; appeased
PLACEMAN office-holder
PLACENTA the afterbirth
PLACIDLY serenely; tranquilly; calmly
PLAGIARY literary theft
PLAGUILY pestiferously
PLAGUING tormenting; pestering
lw **PLAINANT** plaintiff
PLAITING pleating; braiding
PLANCHED planked
PLANCHET disc; a blank
PLANETIC planetary; revolving
PLANGENT resounding; reverberating
PLANKING flooring; putting down
zo **PLANKTON** drifting organic life
PLANLESS unsystematic; aimless

PLANNING scheming; plotting; devising
bt **PLANTAIN** banana-like fruit; a weed
PLANTING inculcating; inserting
bt **PLANTLET** a small shrub
bt **PLANTULE** embryo of a plant
zo **PLANULAR** (embryo of hydrozoa)
PLASHING dabbling; splashing
bd **PLASHING** hurdle-making process
ps **PLASMOID** characteristic plasma section
ar **PLASTERY** plasterwork
ch **PLASTICS** industrial synthetic resins; organic polymer materials
PLASTRON breastplate (fencing)
bd **PLATBAND** impost; lintel; projecting; moulding
PLATEFUL a meal
md **PLATELET** blood corpuscle form
rw **PLATFORM** party policies; raised level
ch **PLATINIC** (platinum)
ch **PLATINUM** metallic element
PLATONIC philosophical; (-friendship)
PLATTING plaiting; weaving
zo **PLATYPUS** duck bill
zo **PLATYSMA** dermal musculature
PLAUSIVE applauding
PLAYABLE stageable drama, music, pageant
PLAYBILL programme
PLAYBOOK book of rules; log (Am. football); script
PLAYBOOK book of dramas
PLAY-DEBT gambling debt
PLAYGOER stage fan
PLAY-MARE hobby-horse
PLAYMATE sportive companion
PLAYSOME frolicsome; wanton
PLAYTIME recreation
PLEACHED interwoven; plaited; matted
PLEADING arguing; disputing
PLEASANT welcome; delectable
PLEASING grateful; charming
PLEASURE indulgence; gladness; joy
PLEATING folding
PLEBEIAN popular; vulgar; ignoble
mu **PLECTRUM** plucking quill for lute, lyre, mandolin, banjo
PLEDGING plighting; pawning
as **PLEIADES** group of 7 stars
rl **PLENARTY** (benefice)
PLEONASM verbosity
PLEONAST a sprouter; demagogue
PLESSITE entectic intergrowth in meteorites
PLETHORA super abundance; surfeit
md **PLEURISY** lung inflammation
md **PLEXITIS** nerve plexus inflammation
PLIANTLY easily bent; flexibly
PLICATED folded; involved; intricate
PLIGHTED betrothed; promised
PLIGHTER one who pledges
PLIMMING becoming plump
PLIMSOLL rubber shoe; ship's load line
gl **PLIOCENE** a geological strata
el **PLIOTRON** hot-cathode vacuum tube
PLODDING slow but sure
PLOPPING dropping into water
PLOTTING conspiring; contriving; planning
nt **PLOTTING** demonstrating movements (radar)
PLOUGHED furrowed; failed exam
PLOUGHER husbandman; persister
PLUCKILY courageously; valorously
gl, mu **PLUCKING** glacial theft and misplacement of rocks; stripping; (examination); (strings)
el **PLUGGING** stopping; blocking; core; inserting a lead
el **PLUGMOLD** duct for laying cables; raceway (Amer.)
PLUG-UGLY thug; street ruffian; fister; slasher
cp **PLUGWIRE** two live sockets (also earth) circuits
mn, bt **PLUMBAGO** graphite; blue or violet flower
pb **PLUMB-BOB** test for vertical alignment
PLUMBEAN leaden; dull; heavy
PLUMBERY lead work
nt **PLUMBING** sounding for depth of ocean
bd **PLUMBING** water piping system
bd **PLUMBING** heating; sanitation
md **PLUMBISM** lead poisoning
ck **PLUMCAKE** fruit cake (Christmas) (wedding)
ck **PLUMDUFF** plain flour pudding with raisins/currants
zo **PLUMELET** downy feather
zo **PLUMIPED** feathered feet
PLUMMING sinking a shaft
PLUMPEST fattest
PLUMPING going all out
zo **PLUNGEON** a sea-bird
PLUNGING immersing; ducking
PLURALLY more than once
PLUTONIC infernal; dark; igneous
PLUVIOUS rainy; pluvial; humid
bd **PLYMETAL** metal-faced plywood

POACHING stabbing; trespassing (It.)
ck **POACHING** hunting unlawfully; (eggs)
POCHETTE POCHETTO, pocket wallet; book; violin; kit (Fr., It.)
POCKETED stolen; concealed; filched
md **POCKMARK** a scar
bt **POCKWOOD** a hard wood
md **PODAGRAL PODAGRIC**, gouty
md **PODALGIA** neuralgia in foot
zo **PODARGUS** genus of nocturnal birds
to **PODAUGER** grooved auger
PODIATRY chiropody; foot care
md **PODISMUS** spasm of foot
bt **PODOCARP** stalk to a carpel
zo **PODOMERE** limb segment in arthropoda
PODOSOMA leg-bearing segments in acarina
POEMATIC poetical; lyric; metrical
POETICAL imaginative; rhyming
POETIZED versified
POIGNANT acutely painful; caustic
POIGNARD small dagger
lw **POINDING** distraining
POINTING directing; aiming; indicating
bd, mu **POINTING** exposed mortar treatment; allocation of syllables to notes
POISONED corrupted; envenomed
POISONER who gives poison
POLARITY united opposites
POLARIZE magnetize
ga **POLE-JUMP** assisted leap
nt **POLEMAST** (without a topmast)
POLEMICS controversies
as, nv **POLE-STAR** Polaris; a lode-star
POLICIES lines of conduct; insurance–
POLICING maintaining public order
POLISHED smooth; burnished
POLISHER shoe or furniture shiner
POLITELY courteously; urbanely
POLITICO opportunist politician
POLITICS art of government
to **POLL-ADZE** blunt-headed adze
POLL-BOOK register of voters
vt **POLL-EVIL** bursa inflammation in horse
pl **POLLICES** thumbs or great toes
bt **POLLINAR** covered with pollen
zo **POLLIWOG POLLYWOG**, tadpole; children's rag doll (Moorish)
POLLSTER opinion taker
POLLUTED contaminated; filth-laden
POLLUTER defiler; contaminator
zo **POLOCYTE** polar body
POLONIUM radio-active element
POLTROON coward; dastard; craven
bt **POLYARCH** of many-stranded stele
zo **POLYAXON** having many axes
zo **POLYCARP** gonad form in urochorda; (philosophy)
POLYFOIL circular ornamentation
POLYGAMY POLYGYNYplurality of wives just then
POLYGLOT in several languages
POLYGRAM many sided figure
POLYMERS POLYMERY, organic, synthetic resins; rubbers
bt **POLYMERY** whorl of many members
md **POLYOPIA** multiple vision
POLYPARY hard covering of polyps
zo **POLYPIDE** compound polyzoan
POLYPODE having many feet
bt **POLYPODY** a fern
zo **POLYPOID POLYPOUS**, resembling polyps; octopus type
pg **POLYPOSE** multi-pose portrait
POLYSEMY multi meanings of word, root
ch **POLYSOME** cluster of ribosomes
cy **POLYSOMY** multiple-chromosome state
POLYTENE identical chromatids (genes)
POLYTERM unit concept heading
POLYTYCH many-leaved ancient book
POLYTYPE cast of an engraving
md **POLYURIA** excessive urine secretion
zo **POLYZOAN** colony of polyzoa
zo **POLYZOIC** zoolatrous; sporozoic
zo **POLYZOON** barnacle type
POMANDER perfumed ball
POMIFORM like an apple
bt **POMOLOGY** apple culture
POMPEIAN of Pompeii
PONDERAL ascertained by weight
PONDERED meditated; thought
PONDERER cogitator; ruminator
bt **POND-LILY** inhabitant of lily-pond
bt **POND-WEED** aquatic plant
bt **POND-WORT** water-soldier plant
PONTIFEX a Roman pontiff
rl **PONTIFIC** of a bishop; papal
PONTINAL bridging
PONY-SKIN soft hide
PONY-TAIL hairstyle for girls and youths
POOH-POOH sneer at; deride
POOL-ROOM billiard-room
bt **POONSPAR** an Indian tree
POOR-JOHN salted hake
lw **POOR-LAWS** former legislation concerning paupers

POORNESS poverty; indigency
POOR-RATE a tax
POPE-JOAN a card game
rl **POPELING** a would-be pope
zo **POPE'S-EYE** fatty gland
rl **POPESHIP** popehood
POPINJAY parrot; coxcomb; fop
rl **POPISHLY** in popish style
md **POPLITIC** (knee joint or ham)
zo **POPODERM** dermal layer of hoof
POPPLING bubbling
POPPY-OIL slow-drying paint ingredient
POPULACE rabble; mob; masses
POPULATE propagate
bt **POPULINE** aspen bark extract
POPULOUS thronged; crowded; dense
zo **PORIFERA** the sponges
PORIFORM like a pore
PORISTIC porismatic; inferential
PORK-CHOP meat of pig
zo **PORKLING** young pig; piglet
zo **POROCYTE** tube-pierced cell in porifera
bt **POROGAMY** pollen-tube entry in micropyle
POROROCA tidal bore wave, Amazon
POROSITY porousness
POROTYPE a reproduction
mn **PORPHYRY** igneous rock
zo **PORPOISE** sea-hog
PORRIDGE Scotch oatmeal dish; prison sentence (sl.)
PORTABLE easily carried
mu **PORTANDO** carrying the voice; singing (It.)
PORTERLY coarse; vulgar
rl **PORTESSE** a breviary
PORTFIRE an igniter
nt **PORTHOLE** gun-port; scuttle; ship's window
PORTIERE doorway curtain
mn **PORTLAND** (stone; cement)
nt **PORTLAST** gunwale
lw **PORTMOTE** court held in port
nt **PORTOISE** gunwale
nv **PORTOLAN** old grid charts
PORTRAIT likeness; representation
PORT-ROPE rope for porthole lid
rl **PORTUARY** portable breviary
POSEIDON sea-god; Neptune
POSHTEEN sheepskin coat
POSINGLY so as to puzzle
POSITING postulating; affirming
POSITION spot; post; locality
mu **POSITIVE** actual; real; true; small organ
nc **POSITRON** radioisotope decay product
md **POSOLOGY** science of quantity
POSSIBLE feasible; likely
POSSIBLY practicably
POSTABLE mailable
nt **POSTBARK** mailboat
POST-BILL placard
POST-CARD card sent by post
POST-DATE future date on a cheque
POST-FACT a later occurrence
POST-FREE postage paid
POSTICHE counterfeit; coil of false hair; wig
POSTIQUE added ornament
POSTLUDE conclusion
POST-NATI born after a certain date
POST-NOTE promissory note
POST-OBIT payable after death
POST-PAID prepaid
POSTPONE defer; adjourn; shelve
POST-TEST final examination
POST-TIME hour of despatch
POST-TOWN district mail office
POSTURAL body position, reflexes, attitudes
POSTURED posed
POSTURER acrobat
cf, ec **-POTAMOUS** living in streams
POTATION drinking bout
bt **POTATOES** edible tubers
POTATORY draughty
POT-BELLY a paunch
POTENTLY forcibly; powerfully
POTHERED bothered; harassed
POT-HOUSE drinking booth
POTLATCH custom of giving presents (N. Amer. Indian)
POT-METAL lead and copper alloy
bt **POT-PLANT** (grown in a pot)
ck **POT-ROAST** braised meat
POTSHARD POTSHARE, broken pieces of earthenware; potsherd
ck **POT-STICK** stirring stick
ck **POT-STILL** for distilling spirits
mn **POTSTONE** soapstone
POTTERED spent time aimlessly
POTTERER desultory worker
zo **POTTOROO** rat kangaroo
POTULENT rather tipsy
POUCHING pocketing
bt **POUCHONG** black tea
POULAINE long pointed shoe
POULTICE a cataplasm
POUNCING sudden onset
POUNDAGE discount; taxation
POUNDING bruising; braying; hammering

POWDERED sprinkled
POWERFUL potent; puissant
POWERGAS coal-gas
pt **POYOK-OIL** W. African drying oil
ce, mn **POZZOLAN** volcanic dust; hydraulic cement; fly-ash (It.)
lw **PRACTICE** profession; normal method, conduct
PRACTICK practical training
PRACTISE work repeatedly for proficiency
PRACTISE perpetuate; pursue activities
PRACTIVE practised; adept; dexterous
lw **PRAECIPE** writ or instruction
lw **PRAEFECT** magistrate
PRAISING lauding; exalting; eulogizing
PRANCING bounding; capering
PRANDIAL concerning dinner
ae **PRANGING** crash-landing; bombing
PRANKING of practical jokes; frolicking
PRANKISH freakish; impish
nt **PRATIQUE** clearance certificate
PRATTLED babbled; chattered
PRATTLER chatterbox
PREACHED proclaimed; exhorted
PREACHER pastor; divine; declarer
PREAMBLE an introduction; preface
PREBOUND (books) in a library binding
PRECEDED anticipated; headed; led
PRECINCT a close; enclosure
PRECIOUS dear; prized; treasured
PRECLUDE shut out; obviate; debar
PRECURSE a prognostication
PREDABLE raptorial; predacious
PREDATED antedated
PREDATOR carnivorous (preying) plunderer
PREDELLA altar decoration; stool
PRE-ELECT choose beforehand
zo **PREENING** smartening (self, dress); trim feathers
PRE-ENTRY prior to joining (formalities)
PRE-EXIST of an earlier life
PREFACED introduced by
PREFACER preface writer
PREFINED limited beforehand
PREFIXED anticipated; put before
PREGNANT mother-to-be; prolific; suggestive
mn **PREHNITE** silicate of alumina
PREJUDGE condemn unheard
PRELUDED prefaced; started
PRELUDER prelude player
PREMIANT incentive
PREMIATE to reward
PREMIERE first performance
PREMISED introduced
lw **PREMISES** a messuage
md **PREMOLAR** bicuspid tooth
PREMORSE ending abruptly
PRENASAL in front of your nose
PRENATAL before birth
PRENOMEN Christian name
PREORDER arrange beforehand
PREPARED provided; planned; made
PREPARER arranger
PREPENSE premeditated
PREPUBIC prepubertal; preadolescence
PRESAGED foreboded; foretold
PRESAGER seer; soothsayer
PRESBYTE a far-sighted person
PRESCIND cut off; distract
PRESENCE mien; demeanour; company
PRESERVE conserve; defend; keep
PRESIDED controlled; officiated
PRESS-BED collapsible bed
PRESS-BOX reporter's box
PRESSING urgent; importunate; vital
PRESSION compression
PRESSMAN journalist
PRESSURE straits; urgency; stress; preparation for attack (fencing)
PRESTIGE reputation; fame; renown
cp **PRESTORE** deposit data temporarily
PRE-STUDY con; cogitate; ponder
PRESUMED surmised; thought
PRESUMER conjecturer
PRETENCE cloak; mask; guise
PRETERIT the past tense
PRE-TRIAL court case dry run
PRETTIFY beautify; adorn
PRETTILY neatly; daintily
PREVIOUS antecedent; prior; former
PREVISED foreseen
md **PRIAPISM** chronically erect penis
PRICKING inciting; spurring; needlepoint decoration; perforating
PRICKLED minor pain sensation (needle)
PRIDEFUL haughty; scornful
rl **PRIEDIEU** folding stool; praying desk
PRIESTLY sacerdotal
PRIGGERY super-respectability
PRIGGING larceny; pinching
PRIGGISH conceited; prim; affected
PRIGGISM coxcombry; pedantry
zo **PRIMATES** monkeys; archbishops

PRIMEVAL antediluvian; pristine
PRIMMING decking; pranking
PRIMNESS formality; demureness
bt **PRIMROSE** flower; a badge
PRINCELY regal; stately; lavish
PRINCEPS of first-rank status
PRINCESS king's daughter
PRINCOCK a prig; coxcomb
PRINKING strutting; pranking
PRINTIES concave circles; ovals cut in glass
PRINTING typography
cp **PRINTOUT** reproduction of stored information
rl **PRIORATE** office of prior
rl **PRIORESS** lady prior
PRIORITY precedence
PRISMOND prismatic
PRISONED incarcerated; gaoled
PRISONER captive
PRISTINE original; ancient
PRIZEMAN a winner
zo **PROATLAS** bone between skull and vertebra
PROBABLE credible; likely
PROBABLY maybe; peradventure
PROBATOR examiner; approver
pm **PROCAINE** crystalline solid
PROCEEDS results; produce
lw **PROCHEIN** next; nearest
PROCINCT complete preparation
PROCLAIM bruit; trumpet; blazon
PROCURED got; obtained; acquired
PROCURER provider of women and other services
PRODDING goading
PRODIGAL wasteful; reckless; lavish
PRODITOR traitor
PRODROME preliminary treatise
PRODUCED created; caused; made
PRODUCER generator; manufacturer
PROEMIAL introductory
PROFANED violated; debased
PROFANER blasphemer; desecrater
PROFILED outlined; drawn; described in brief
PROFITED benefited; gained
PROFITER PROFITEER (speculator) (contriver)
PRO-FORMA advance checking for confirmation
PROFOUND deep; abysmal; occult
PROGERIA stunted; dwarfism; early senility
PROGGING begging food
zo **PROGONAL** of genital ridge portion
PROGRESS advancement; growth
PROHIBIT inderdict; forbid; ban
md **PROLAPSE** anatomical slippage
PROLIFIC productive; fertile; fecund
PROLIXLY at great length
PROLOGUE dramatic preface; poem
PROLONGE rope; rings and toggle
ml **PROMETAL** heat-resistant cast iron
PROMISED guaranteed, engaged
PROMISEE assured person
PROMISER PROMISOR, assuror; warranter; pledger; stipulator
PROMOTED elevated; preferred
PROMOTEE advanced person
PROMOTER active agent
PROMPTED suggested
PROMPTER encourager; souffleur (theatre)
PROMPTLY readily; quickly
PROMULGE announce; publish
PRONATED naturally leaning forwards, downwards
md **PRONATOR** an arm-muscle
PRONG-HOE a gardening tool
zo **PRONOTUM** prothorax notum in insects
zo **PRO-NYMPH** a stage of insect life
PROOFING making waterproof
PROOFING establishing alcohol quantity in spirits
ch **PROPANOL** propyl alcohol
ch **PROPENOL** allyl alcohol
PROPENSE inclined; disposed
PROPERLY correctly; formally; exactly
PROPERTY quality; wealth; chattels
bt **PROPHAGE** inactive bacteriophage
cy **PROPHASE** mitosis/meiosis early stage
PROPHECY forecast; divination
PROPHESY to prognosticate; foretell
bt **PROPHYLL** bracteole
PROPLASM mould; matrix
PROPOLIS beeswax
PROPOSAL suggestion; tender (offer)
PROPOSED suggested; meant marriage; planned
PROPOSER mover; instigator
PROPOUND advocate; enunciate
PROPPAGE support
PROPPING shoring up
PROPRIUM self-hood; egotism
PROPYLON temple gateway
PRORATED assessed
PROROGUE adjourn; defer; postpone
PROSAISM prose writing
PROSAIST prosy person
PROSEMAN writer of prose
zo **PROSODUS** canal in porifera
PROSPECT aspect; outlook; survey

bt **PROSPORY** sporangia formation
pl **PROSTATE** male gland near bladder
PROSTYLE pillared portico
PROTASIS maxim; prologue
PROTATIC introductory
ch **PROTEASE** protein enzyme
PROTEGEE a ward
ch **PROTEIDS PROTEINS**, albuminoids
zo **PROTELES** the aard-wolf
ch **PROTEOSE** protein derivative
zo **PROTHECA** coral calyx rudiment
bt, zo **PROTISTA** organisms
PROTOCOL treaty; draft agreement
tc, tv **PROTOCOL** etiquette; precedence; information flow
PROTOPOD early abdominal phase in insects
mn **PROTOSET** mine rescue equipment
zo **PROTOZOA** early life forms
PROTRACT draw out; prolong; delay
PROTRUDE bulge; jut; project
PROVABLE demonstrable
PROVABLY verifiably
PROVIANT provender; fodder; provisions
PROVIDED if in that case; supplied
PROVIDER donor; furnisher; caterer
PROVINCE department; tract
PROVINED (vine culture)
PROVISOR purveyor; treasurer
PROVOKED exasperated; stung; vexed
PROVOKER inciter; annoyer; offender
PROWLING roving for prey; slinking
PROXIMAL adjoining; adjacent
PRUDENCE discretion; judiciousness
PRUINOSE PRUINOUS, powdery; mealy
bt **PRUNELLA** self-heal plant
bt **PRUNELLO** dried plum
PRURIENT interested in the obscene
md **PRURITIS** persistent severe itching
PRYINGLY inquisitively; curiously
rl **PSALMIST** poet; psalm writer
rl **PSALMODY** psalms collectively
mu **PSALTERY** stringed instrument
mn **PSAMMITE** sandstone
md **PSELLISM** stammering
zo **PSITTACI** the parrot tribe
PSYCHICS mental phenomena
PSYCHISM spiritualism
PSYCHIST psychologist
zo **PTEROMYS** flying squirrel
zo **PTEROPOD** class of molluscs
zo **PTEROTIC** skull ear-wall bone
zo **PTERYLAE** clump of feathers
zo **PTILINUM** cephalic sac in dipters
zo **PTILOSIS** plumage
md **PTOMAINE** organic poison
md **PTYALISM** salivation
PUBCRAWL round all the taverns
PUBLICAN pub manager; collector of tribute
PUBLICLY open to all
PUCELAGE virginity
bt **PUCKBALL** puffball
PUCKERED wrinkled; crinkled
mn **PUDDLING** clay/iron refining process
PUDICITY modesty
bt **PUFF-BALL** lycoperdon (mushroom)
zo **PUFF-BIRD** S. American bird
PUFF-PUFF onomatopoeic locomotive
PUG-FACED monkey-faced
PUGGAREE scarf round helmet
PUGILISM prize-fighting
PUGILIST a pug; a boxer
PUISSANT powerful; forcible
PULINGLY fretfully; whiningly
PULLBACK a restraint
to **PULL-LIFT** chain or rope-operator pulling device
PULLOVER jersey; sweater
md **PULMONIC** consumptive
PULPITER preacher
PULPITUM stone screen in major church
PULSATOR vibrator
PULSIFIC throbbing
pl **PULVINAR** a cushion; brain fibres in visual sector
bt **PULVINUS** swollen leaf base
PUMICATE polish; make smooth
PUMP-DALE water trough
PUMP-ROOM mineral spring at spa
PUMP-WELL water pumped from well
PUNCHEON steel tool; large cask
PUNCHING perforating; striking
PUNCTATE pointed
PUNCTUAL punctilious; timely
PUNCTURE a hole; perforate; prick
PUNGENCE acridness
PUNGENCY keenness; acuteness
PUNINESS feebleness; frailty
PUNISHED chastised; penalized
PUNISHER disciplinarian
PUNITIVE punishing; penal
PUNITORY corrective
PUNTILLA lace-work
PUNTSMAN poleman on a river punt
zo **PUPARIAL PUPIFORM, PUPARIUM**, pupa; a chrysalis
zo **PUPATION** incubation
PUPILAGE wardship; minority
PUPILARY in statu pupillari

PUPILATE having a central spot
zo **PUPIPARA** viviparous inspects
PUPPETRY puppet-show; finery
PUPPYISH of a young wag; conceited
PUPPYISM dog-like loyalty, affection
PURBLIND dim-sighted
PURCHASE buy; procure; leverage
PURENESS purity; chastity
PURFLING embroidering
PURIFIED ceremonially cleansed
PURIFIER refiner
md **PURIFORM** resembling pus
PURISTIC scrupulously stylish
lw **PURPARTY** share of an estate
PURPLING dyeing with purple
PURPLISH somewhat purple
PURPOSED resolved; meant; intended
PURPURIC madder-purple
PURSEFUL enough to fill a purse
PURSE-NET purse with strings
PURSLANE salad herb
PURSUANT conformably
PURSUING prosecuting; chasing
md **PURULENT** suppurating
PURVEYED procured; retailed
PURVEYOR caterer
rl **PUSEYISM** of Pusey; Tractarianism
rl **PUSEYITE** high-church doctrinaire
PUSHBALL a great ball game
PUSHBIKE pedal bicycle
PUSHCART barrow; handcart; (street sales)
PUSHOVER easy success; easily conned victim
cp, rw **PUSHPULL** parallel amplifiers; two-way train
zo **PUSS-MOTH** large hairy moth
bt **PUSS-TAIL** a bristle grass
bt, zo **PUSSY-CAT** willow-catkin
zo **PUSSYCAT** domestic feline pet
md **PUSTULAR** pimpled
PUTATION computation; sum
PUTATIVE reputed; alleged
bt **PUTCHOCK** root used for incense
pr **PUT-TO-BED** stopped press
PUTTYING cementing glass panes with putty
PUZZLING bewildering; perplexing
cy **PYCNOSIS** staining-matter shrinkage
md **PYELITIS** kidney pelvis inflammation
md **PYOGENIC** pus-producing; (inflammation)
pl **PYRAMIDS** elevated medulla nerves (ear)
PYRAMOID of pyramid form
ch **PYRAZOLE** heterocyclic compound
bt **PYRENOID** refractive protein mass
bt **PYRENOUS** globular; nucleiform
md **PYREXIAL** feverish
ch **PYRIDINE** organic compound
PYRIFORM pear-shaped
PYRITIZE turn into pyrites
mn **PYRITOUS** like pyrites
PYROGRAM mechanical firework
PYROLOGY blowpipe analysis
zo **PYROSOMA** luminous animalculae
PYROSTAT a thermostat
nc **PYROTRON** thermonuclear device
mn **PYROXENE** augite
ch **PYROXYLE** gun-cotton
PYRRHOUS reddish
PYTHONIC oracular; of Delphi
bt **PYXIDATE** having a lid
bt **PYXIDIUM** lidlike capsule

Q

QUABLING tropical fish
QUACKERY charlatanism; humbug
QUACKING boasting; duck-talk
QUACKISH somewhat bogus
QUACKISM medical pretence
QUACKLED almost choked
nm **QUADRANS** Roman farthing
nv **QUADRANT** quarter-circle; for sun-sighting
QUADRATE square; to agree
QUADRIGA four-horsed chariot
QUADROON (quarter negro blood)
mn **QUADRUNE** gritstone
QUAESITA to be decided on later
QUAESTOR treasurer
QUAFFING swallowing; imbibing
QUAGMIRE a bog; swamp
QUAGMIRY yielding; boggy
QUAILING flinching; blenching
QUAINTER odder; stranger
QUAINTLY whimsically; fancifully
QUAKERLY soberly
QUALMISH squeamish; queasy
bt **QUANDANG** Australian peach
QUANDARY dilemma; predicament
QUANTIFY determine quantity
QUANTITY measure; amount; bulk
QUARRIED stone hewn from the rocks
QUARRIER quarryman
QUARRIES arrows; panes of glass
QUARRIES animals hunted; targets shot at
me **QUARTERN** a gill (liquid); 4 lb (1.8 kg) loaf
QUARTERS living places

as **QUARTILE** planetary aspect; point of quarter division
bt **QUARTINE** a seed covering
QUASHING annulling; crushing
md **QUASSINE QUASSITE**, extract of quassia, a febrifuge
QUATERON a quadroon
ga **QUATORZE** 14; a count in piquet (cards)
QUATRAIN four line stanza
mu **QUAVERED** of musical notation
QUAVERED QUIVERED; shook; vibrated
QUAVERER a warbler
QUAY-WALL harbour-wall
QUEASILY squeamishly
QUEBRADA a ravine (Sp.)
zo **QUEEN-BEE** ruler of hive
QUEENDOM queenly state
QUEENING playing the queen
QUEENLET a petty queen
QUEEREST quaintest; oddest
QUEERING spoiling; disarranging
QUEERISH rather strange
mn **QUELLERZ** limonite
QUELLING crushing; subduing; curbing
QUENCHED extinguished; (fire); (appetite); (thirst)
QUENCHER a long drink; thirst or fire subduer
QUENELLE forcemeat
bt **QUERCITE** acorn extract
QUERLING twirling
QUERYING challenging; inquiring
QUESTFUL adventurous
QUESTING seeking; searching
QUESTION interrogation; catechize
QUESTMAN authorized inquirer
QUEUEING lining up; taking one's turn
QUIBBLED evaded the question
QUIBBLER prevaricator
QUICKEST speediest; fastest
QUICKIES quickly done films; drinks, etc.
bt **QUICKSET** living plant
QUIDDANY a dish of quinces
vt **QUIDDING** spitting out chewed food
QUIDDITY captious question; quibble
QUIDDLED wasted time; pottered
QUIDDLER a trifler
QUIDNUNC tattler; know-all
QUIESCED silenced; subsided
QUIETAGE tranquillity
QUIETEST calmest
QUIETISE pacify
QUIETISM placidness
QUIETIST a mystic
QUIETIVE sedative
QUIETUDE rest; repose
QUILLING crimping; goffering; decorating surface of glass with coloured glass ribbons (Amer.)
QUILL-NIB penpoint
QUILTING of eiderdown coverings
mu **QUINABLE** interval of a fifth
fr **QUINCUNX** plantation of 5 trees
ga **QUINIEZA** pelota with bets
ga **QUINTAIN** balanced tilting beam
QUINTILE aspect of the planets
mu **QUINTOLE** five-stringed viol
QUIPPING taunting; jesting
QUIPPISH sarcastic
QUIRINAL Italian Court
QUIRINUS defied Romulus
QUIRITES Roman citizens
QUIRKING twisting
QUIRKISH evasive
QUISLING traitor; betrayer
QUIT-RENT rent in lieu of service
QUITTING deserting; ratting; hiatus; (golf)
QUIXOTIC QUIXOTRY, romantic and absurd notions and actions
QUIZZERY ridicule
QUIZZIFY hoax; puzzle
QUIZZING bantering; chaffing
QUIZZING asking questions (of knowledge)
QUOTABLE citable
QUOTIENT how many times
QUOTIETY proportionate frequency

R

RABATINE turned-down collar
RABBETED grooved
RABBINIC Hebrew language, etc.
RABBITER rabbit catcher
RABBITRY enclosure for rabbits
RABIDITY of rabies; raving madness
RABIETIC of rabies; maniacal; demented
ga **RACE-CARD** record of runners, horse races
ga **RACEGOER** watcher of winners
bt **RACEMOSE RACEMOUS**, in clusters
bt **RACEMULE** small bunch
bt **RACHILLA** leaf-rib
md **RACHITIC RACHITIS**, of rickets
RACIALLY pertaining to race (mixed)
RACINAGE acid technique for leather twig effects
RACINESS piquancy

RACKETED made noisy
RACKETER dishonest business man
rw **RACK-RAIL** (cogwheel) mountain track
RACK-RENT highest the market will fetch
RACK-TAIL part of clock
rw **RACK-WORK** rack and pinion locomotive
ck **RACLETTE** Swiss melted cheese
RACOVIAN Polish Socinian
RADARMAN radar petty officer R.N.
el **RADECHON** mesh-grid storage tube
RADIALLY like spokes of a wheel
as, ps, el, me **RADIANCE** effulgence; lustre; energy in watts per steradian per m^2 directional intensity
RADIANCY brilliancy; glitter; sheen
RADIATED shone; sparkled
RADIATOR heating apparatus
RADICANT taking root
RADICATE to plant; emplant
bt **RADICOSE** having a large root
bt **RADICULE** a small root
RADIOING transmitting by wireless
zo **RADIOLUS** part of a feather
zo **RADULATE** (rasping tongue)
RAFFLING lottery for an article or articles
zo **RAFT-DUCK** black-headed duck
RAFTERED timbered
nt **RAFT-PORT** (timber loading)
RAFT-ROPE thickish piece of string
RAFTSMAN castaway
RAGABASH ragamuffin
RAGGEDLY in tatters
RAGINGLY furiously; rabidly
RAGNAROK twilight of the gods (Norse mythology)
RAG-PAPER high-quality paper
mn **RAGSTONE** impure limestone
RAG-WHEEL polishing wheel
rw **RAILHEAD** a terminus
RAILLERY banter; chaff; ridicule
rw **RAILROAD** railway; forceful insistence; overhead serve (tennis); (bowls)
RAINBAND band in solar spectrum
zo **RAINBIRD** Jamaican bird
RAINCOAT waterproof
RAINDROP single drop of rain
RAINFALL shower
RAINLESS state of drought
RAINPOUR downpour
bt **RAINTREE** S. American tree
gl **RAIN-WASH** gravity/rain soil creepage
RAISINEE a confection
RAKEHELL a rip; debauchee
RAKISHLY set at an angle
RAKSHASA Hindu ghoul
RALLYING reuniting; gathering; track and trek events; cycling; motor racing
RAMAYANA Indian epic poem
RAMBLING roaming; wandering
RAMBOOZE a cordial
bt **RAMBUTAN** Malayan fruit tree
bt **RAMENTUM** brown scale on ferns
bt **RAMICOLE** living on twigs
RAMICORN horny sheath
RAMIFIED diverse
RAMIFORM like a branch
RAMPAGED romped; rioted; gambolled
RAMPANCY excessive prevalence
RAMPSMAN highwayman
RAMRODDY stiff
mn **RAMSHORN** an ammonite
RAMULOUS ramulose; branching
zo **RANARIUM** frog aquarium
RANCHERO cow-puncher
RANCHING cattle-raising
RANCHMAN stockbreeder
RANCIDLY fustily; mustily; sourly
RANDOMLY at a venture; fortuitously
zo **RANGIFER** a reindeer
zo **RANIFORM** froglike
RANKLING festering; smouldering
RANKNESS overgrowth; exuberance
RANSOMED redeemed; released; purchased; (release money)
RANSOMER liberator; indemnifier
RAPACITY greed; avarice; voracity
RAPE-CAKE cattle fodder
bt **RAPE-SEED** (hence colza oil)
RAPHANIA ergotism; blight
bt **RAPHANUS** radish
RAPHIDES crystals in plants
RAPIDITY celerity; despatch; speed
RAPPAREE Irish robber; bandit
zo **RAPTORES** birds of prey
RAPTURED ravished; ecstatic
RAQUETTE (pelota); (racket)
RAREFIED tenuous
RARENESS infrequency; scarceness
RARERIPE early ripe; untimely
RASCALLY knavish; roguish; dishonest
RASHLING reckless fellow
RASHNESS foolhardiness; unwariness
RASORIAL scratching
RATAPLAN beat of drum
RATCHETY jerky
wv **RATCHING** yarn-tightening process

RATEABLE assessable
RATE-BOOK book of valuations
zo **RAT-GOOSE** brent goose
RATHRIPE early ripe
RATIFIED confirmed; endorsed
RATIFIER approver; authorizer
RATIONAL reasonable; judicious; sane
RATIONED on an allowance
RAT'S-BANE rat poison
zo **RATSNAKE** rat-killing snake
RAT'S-TAIL tapering
RATTINET a woollen stuff
RATTLING quick; lively; clattering
RAVAGING despoiling; plundering
to **RAVEHOOK** ripping iron
RAVELLED entangled; untwisted
RAVENING plundering; devouring
RAVENOUS starving; voracious
RAVINGLY with fury; frantically
RAVISHED enchanted; charmed
RAVISHER abductor
RAW-BONED gaunt
REABSORB soak up again
REACCESS fresh approach
REACCUSE indict again
nv **REACHING** extending; attaining; sailing, wind abeam
ch **REACTANT** substance involved in chemical reaction
REACTION counter-measure; recoil
REACTIVE capacity to react
READABLE well written; good style
READABLY clearly; legibly
tc **READ-HEAD** of tape recorder, cassette
cp **READ-HEAD** electro-magnetic pickup
READJUST reset; modify
READ-ONLY on loan; unalterable
READ-RATE speed of reading
cp **READ-TIME** access to screen; delay
REAFFIRM swear on oath; state anew
pc **REAGENCY** reflex influence; reaction
REALISED felt; understood; comprehended
REALLEGE assert a 2nd time
REALNESS actuality; verity; fact
REANOINT relubricate
REANSWER reply again
REAPPEAR turn up again
REAR-LINE behind the army
REARMING re-equipping
REARMOST last; ultimate
REAR-RANK back line
REARWARD rearguard
REASCEND climb again
REASCENT a further climb
REASONED argued; disputed
REASONER debater
REASSERT re-affirm
REASSESS re-impose; revalue
REASSIGN give different job to
REASSURE console; comfort
REATTACH refix
REATTAIN get again
REAVOWED said so again
REBATING deducting from
REBELLED revolted; mutinied
REBELLER a rebel; insurgent
REBELLOW re-echo
REBITING re-engraving
ch **REBOILER** vessel at still bottom
REBRACED restrengthened
REBUFFED repulsed; snubbed
REBUKING chiding; carpeting
REBURIED re-interred
REBUTTAL refutation; retort
REBUTTED confuted; refuted
lw **REBUTTER** a legal reply
RECALLED revoked; annulled; denied
RECANTED retracted; abjured
RECAPTOR one who retakes
RE-CASING rebinding of book in original cover
RECEDING retreating; ebbing
RECEIVED got; allowed; welcomed
lw **RECEIVER** a recipient; receptionist; (bankruptcy); (telephone); (stolen goods)
RECENTLY lately
RECEPTOR sensory organ; nerve transmitter
RECESSED dimpled; secluded
RECESSES niches; vacations
RECESSUS a recess; a niche
RECHAMPI gold ornamentation on chair frames
RECHARGE attack anew; reload
RECISION cutting back; pruning
RECITING rehearsing; relating
RECKLESS heedless; rash; headstrong
zo **RECKLING** weakest in a litter
RECKONED considered; judged
RECKONER calculator; computer
RECLINED leant; lay; reposed
RECLINER a reclining dial
RECLOSED shut again
RECLOTHE provide new garments
RECOALED refilled the bunkers
RECOILED retreated; reacted
RECOILER flincher
RECOINED minted afresh
rl **RECOLLET** Franciscan monk
RECOLOUR repaint
RECOMMIT refer again; re-entrust

RECONVEY transfer back
lw **RECORDED** entered; minuted
mu, lw **RECORDER** flageolet; judge
el, mu **RECORDER** permanent sound receptor
RECOUPED regained
RECOURSE reference; resort; refuge
lw **RECOURSE** right to demand compensation
RECOVERY convalescence; revival; body renewal; return (rowing)
lw **RECOVERY** to regain possession
RECOVERY economic upturning
RECREANT craven; apostate
RECREATE reproduce with exact resemblance
el **RECTIGON** thermionic gas diode
rl **RECTORAL** duties of an incumbent rector
RECTORAL ditto of university rector
RECUBANT recumbent
RECUMBED reclined; reposed
RECURRED remembered; repeated
RECURVED bent back
rl **RECUSANT** Elizabethan R.C.
REDACTOR editor
REDARGUE to refute; disprove
zo **RED-BELLY** terrapin; char
bt **RED-CEDAR** pencil-wood
mn **RED-CHALK** reddle
mn **RED-CORAL** living coral
RED-CROSS humanitarian organization
lw **REDDENDA** rent clauses
lw **REDDENDO** (vassal's duties)
REDDENED blushed; flushed
mn **RED-EARTH** reddish loam
REDEEMED ransomed; freed; retrieved
REDEEMER liberator; saviour
REDELESS unwise; ill-advised
REDEMAND request again
lw **REDEMISE** reconveyance
REDENTED indented
REDEPLOY movement of army; industrial
RED-FACED florid; rubicund
REDIGEST reduce to form again
REDIRECT re-address
REDITION return
REDIVIDE re-allot
RED-METAL a copper alloy
REDNOSED nose red with cold
REDOLENT aromatic; fragrant
REDOUBLE a bridge call
REDRIVEN herded back again
zo **REDSHANK** red-legged sandpiper
RED-SHIRT follower of Garibaldi; athlete (USA)
RED-SHORT brittle
RED-STAFF millstone trimmer
REDUBBER old clothes merchant
REDUCENT reducing
REDUCING curtailing; abating
zo **REDUVIUS** predacious bug
RE-DYEING recolouring
RE-ECHOED reverberated; repeated
mu **REED-BAND** clarionets, etc.
zo **REED-BIRD** bobolink
REEDLESS no rush
zo **REEDLING** bearded titmouse
bt **REED-MACE** cat's tail
mu **RED-PIPE** an organ pipe
mu **REED-STOP** an organ stop
zo **REED-WREN** greater reedwarbler
nt **REEF-BAND** strip of canvas
REEF-KNOT secure flat knot
nt **REEF-LINE** a rope
REELABLE able to be wound in
REEL-LINE fishing line
REEL-SEAT reel housing on rod
RE-EMBARK get back in a boat
RE-EMBODY reform into a body
RE-EMERGE come out again
RE-ENLIST sign on again
RE-EXPORT ship out again
REFASTEN refix
REFERRED attributed; assigned
REFERRER enquirer
REFIGURE present anew
REFILLED replenished
REFINERY purification plant
REFINING purifying
REFITTED re-equipped
REFLEXED curved back
REFLEXLY reactively
REFLOWED ebbed
REFLOWER bloom again
REFLUENT flowing back
REFOREST plan anew
REFORGED kept signing false name
REFORMED remodelled; restored
REFORMER innovator
REFRAMED re-modelled; traduced all over again
REFREEZE make icebound again
REFRINGE infringe
REFUGIUM locality remaining unchanged despite climatic alteration
REFUNDED reimbursed; repaid
REFUNDER one who pays back again
REFUSING declining; repudiating
REFUTING gainsaying; rebutting
REGAINED retrieved; recaptured

REGALIAN regal; sovereign
REGALING faring sumptuously
REGALISM sovereignty
REGALITY royalty
REGARDED noticed; heeded; gazed
REGARDER observer; watcher
REGATHER recollect
REGICIDE killer of a king
REGILDED made golden once more
REGIMENT organize; a military unit
REGIONAL topographical
REGIONIC local
cp, mu **REGISTER** record; chronicle; fit; list; filed data storage; range or compass of voice, instruments, organ stops
REGISTRY labour agency
sv **REGLETTE** measuring tape scale
REGNANCY predominance; supremacy
REGOLITH mantle rock; topsoil
zo **REGORGED** of chewing the cud
REGRATED furnace fire area renewed
REGRATER boiler maker
REGROUND knives resharpened
REGROWTH new growth
REGULATE adjust; control; arrange
REGULIZE readjust
REHANDLE start again from beginning
REHASHED restyled
REHEARSE recapitulate
ce **RE-HEATED** warmed up again; superheated
ce **REHEATER** part of steam or compressed air machines
REHOUSED given new homes
REIGNING prevailing; governing
RE-IGNITE rekindle
REIMBODY re-incorporate
REIMPORT bring back
REIMPOSE retax
REINCITE reanimate
REINDEER Father Christmas's sleigh steeds
md **REINFECT** spread disease again
REINFORM renotify
REINFUND pour in again
REINFUSE reanimate
REIN-HOOK bearing-rein hook
REINLESS unchecked
REINSERT put in again
REINSMAN accomplished driver
REINSURE make doubly certain
REINVENT create anew
REINVEST put money in again
REINVITE bid home again
pr **REISSUED** revalidated; reprinted
REJECTED excluded; rebuffed
REJECTOR decliner; rejecter
el **REJECTOR** impedance of circuit (due to overloading)
REJOICED exulted; gloried; delighted
REJOICER reveller; merry-maker
REJOINED knit together; reunited
REJUDGED re-examined; reconsidered
REKINDLE arouse anew; relight
RELANDED came down twice
RELAPSED retrogressed
RELAPSER backslider
RELATING narrating; telling
RELATION connection; kinsman; (harmony)
cp, mu **RELATIVE** comparative; kinsman; parallel common key-signature
lw **RELATRIX** female informant
RELAXANT a loosener
RELAXING slackening; unbending
ro **RELAYING** transmit programmes
RELEASED emancipated; freed
RELEASEE discharged person
RELEASER releasor; liberator
RELEGATE consign; transfer
RELESSEE releasee
lw **RELESSOR** releaser
RELEVANT applicable; apt; pertinent
RELIABLE trustworthy; trusty; safe
RELIABLY dependably
RELIANCE confidence; trust
lw **RELICTED** left bare
RELIEVED palliated; soothed; eased
RELIEVER mitigator; assuager
RELIGION faith
RELISHED appreciated
RELISTEN hear once more
RELIVING experiencing again
RELOADED ready to fire again
RELUCENT transparent; shining
RELUMINE rekindle
REMAINED left over; stopped
REMAKING rebuilding
REMANENT remaining
REMANNED provided with a new crew
REMARKED said; declared; mentioned
REMARKER commentator; observer
REMARQUE marginal etching
REMEDIAL curative; healing
REMEDIED repaired; rectified
REMEMBER recall; recollect
REMIFORM oar-shaped
REMINDED brought to notice
REMINDER keepsake; souvenir
lw **REMISING** releasing

REMISSLY negligently; slackly
REMITTAL surrender; remittance
REMITTED relaxed; forgave
REMITTEE consignee
REMITTER pardoner; remittor
REMODIFY remodel
ck **REMOLADE** salad dressing
REMOLTEN remelted
REMOTELY faintly
REMOVING dislodging; abstracting
REMURMUR complain again
RENAMING rechristening
RENDERED translated; gave
RENDERER supplier; assignor
RENDIBLE able to be torn; note not renderable; degradable
gl **RENDZINA** intrazonal dark soil on chalk (Poland)
RENEGADE RENEGADO, RENEGATE, quisling; apostate; runagate; traitor; recreant; rebel
ga **RENEGING** revoking agreement; (cards)
RENEWING renovating; rejuvenating
RENIDIFY build a new nest
RENIFORM kidney-shaped
RENITENT allergic; resistant
RENOUNCE disclaim; forsake; abjure
RENOVATE renew; repair; refresh
RENOWNED famous; eminent
RENOWNER swaggerer; braggart
RENTABLE leasable
RENTERER invisible mender
RENT-FREE living without paying rent
RENT-ROLL list of tenants
RENUMBER put new numbers on
RENVERSE inverted; reverse
REOBTAIN get again
REOCCUPY move back in
REOPENED no longer shut
REOPPOSE not capitulate
REORDAIN refrock the defrocked
REORIENT arising again
REPACIFY calm down again
zo **REPAGULA** egg-protection bodies
REPAIRED redressed; went
REPAIRER restorer
REPARTEE witty retort; riposte
REPASSED went by twice
REPASTED fed
REPAYING refunding
REPEALED rescinded; annulled
REPEALER abrogator; revoker
REPEATED iterated; echoed
tc **REPEATER** a watch; transmission channel amplifier
REPELLED repulsed; checked; rebuffed
REPELLER deterrer; rejecter
REPENTED truly contrite; rued
rl **REPENTER** penitent person; (sect)
REPEOPLE repopulate
REPERTOR a finder
REPERUSE read again
REPETEND recurring decimal
REPINING fretting; murmuring
REPLACED reinstated; restored
REPLACER a substitute
REPLEDGE swear again
lw **REPLEVIN** a legal action
REPLUNGE dive again
REPLYING answering
REPOLISH shine up again
lw **REPONING** replacing
REPORTED communicated; related
REPORTER announcer; journalist
REPOSING reclining; resting
REPOSURE repose; peace; tranquillity
REPOTTED (gardening)
REPOUSSE embossed
REPRIEVE respite; pardon; acquit
RE-PRIMER recapping machine
REPRISAL retaliation; revenge
REPROACH reprimand; upbraid
REPROVAL admonition; censure
REPROVED blamed; rebuked; chided
REPROVER reprehender
REPRUNED lopped again
zo **REPTILIA** snakes and crocodiles, etc.
REPUBLIC democratic state
REPUGNED resisted; opposed
REPUGNER a rebel
REPULPIT restore a preacher
REPULSED checked; refused; rebuffed
REPULSER repeller
REPURIFY purify again
REPUTING esteeming
REQUIRED wanted; demanded; lacked
REQUIRER exactor; claimant
REQUITAL recompense; punishment
REQUITED reciprocated
REQUITER avenger
rw **RE-RAILED** got back on track
lw **REREFIEF** an under-fief (Sc.)
REREWARD rear-guard
REROOFED given new roof
RESAILED sailed again
RESALUTE put hand to head again
mu **RE-SCORED** rearranged
RESCRIBE rewrite
RESCRIPT edict; decree

RESCUING extricating; liberating
RESEARCH scientific enquiry
RESEATED given chair again
lw **RESEIZED RESEIZER**, legal seizure of disseized property
RESEMBLE liken; compare; collate
RESENTED strongly objected; resisted
RESENTER an injured party
RESERVED shy; distant; unsociable
RESERVER withholder
RESETTER jeweller; repairer
RESETTLE repopulate
mt **RESHABAR** dry wind in Near East
RESIANCE residence
cp **RESIDENT** occupier; dweller; agent; routine
ps **RESIDUAL** left over; difference between observation and true value
RESIDUUM residue; surplus; excess
RESIGNED abdicated; relinquished
RESIGNEE he who becomes resigned
RESIGNER renouncer; quitter
RESILING applying resilience in recoil
RESINATA RESINATE, Greek resinous white wine
RESINIFY RESINIZE, to make resinous
RESINOUS olfactory quality (pine, pitch)
RESISTED withstood; repelled; opposed
RESISTER opposer
el **RESISTOR** non-conductor
RESMOOTH smooth again
RESOLDER solder again
RESOLUTE steadfast; staunch
RESOLVED determined; settled
mu **RESOLVER** solver; mediator; catalyst; chord
RESONANT resounding; sonorous
RESONATE re-echo; vibrate
RESORBED absorbed
ch **RESORCIN** crystalline phenol
RESORTED betook; repaired; flew
RESORTER frequenter
RESOURCE expedient; means; natural wealth; ingenuity
RESOWING broadcasting again
RESPECTS compliments
RESPIRED exhaled
RESPITED postponed; reprieved
RESPOKEN repeated
RESPONSE answer; reply; rejoinder
RESTATED reaffirmed
REST-CURE convalescence
RESTLESS agitated; turbulent; uneasy
RESTORED returned; renewed; cured
RESTORER reviver; healer
RESTRAIN check; curb; suppress
RESTRICT limit; confine; hamper
RESTRIKE lay down work a second time
RESTRING tennis racket; violin
RESULTED caused; followed; ensued
RESUMING renewing; continuing
RESUMMON call again
RESUPINE lying on the back
RESURVEY review
RETAILED gossiped; peddled
RETAILER not a wholesale merchant
hd **RETAILLE** divided twice
RETAINED detained; kept; withheld
RETAINER henchman; lackey; servant
RETAKING recapturing
RETARDED slowed up; delayed
RETARDER hinderer; obstructionist; hardening reducing admixture
md **RETENTOR** retaining muscle
zo **RETEPORE** a coral
RETICENT taciturn; reserved; quiet
RETICULE lady's workbag; graticule; linked webs
hd **RETIERCE** heraldic arrangement
zo **RETIFERA** the true limpet
RETIFORM meshed; reticulated
ch **RETINENE** rhodopsin; pigment of retina (eye)
mn **RETINITE** obsidian; amber
RETINOID resin-like
zo **RETINULA** pigmented cells
RETIRING unobtrusively withdrawing from service
hd **RETORTED** rejoined; replied
RETORTER responder
RETOSSED thrown back
RETRACED returned by same route
lw **RETRAXIT** loss of action
RETRENCH curtail; economize
RETRIEVE recover; regain; rescue
RETROACT oppose
RETRORSE bent back
RETRUDED thrust back
RETRYING attempting again
RETUNDED blunted
RETURNED rendered; reverted
RETURNER remitter; (reappeared)
REUNITED rejoined
RE-UPTAKE reabsorption of a substance
REURGING pressing on again
mn **REUSSITE** magnesium compound
REVALUED re-assessed
REVAMPED repatched

REVANCHE revenge (Fr.)
REVEALED disclosed; published
REVEALER betrayer; divulger
REVEHENT taking away
REVEILLE trumpet-call; dawn
REVELLED wantoned; feasted
REVELLER carouser
REVENANT returned from the dead; ghost
REVENGED requited; repaid
REVENGER vindicator
REVEREND respectful epithet
REVERENT submissive; humble
REVERING venerating; honouring
REVERIST a dreamer
REVERSAL complete change
REVERSED subverted; overthrew
lw **REVERSER** mortgager of land
REVESTED reappointed
REVETTED faced with masonry
REVIEWAL a reconsideration
REVIEWED revised; edited; surveyed
REVIEWER an inspector; critic
REVILING aspersing; maligning
REVISING checking; amending
REVISION re-examination
REVISORY correctional
REVIVIFY reanimate; revive
REVIVING renewing; rousing
REVOKING repealing; quashing
REVOLTED felt disgust
REVOLTED rebelled
REVOLTER guerilla; partisan
REVOLUTE rolled back
REVOLVED rotated; wheeled; circled
REVOLVER a firearm
md **REVULSOR** h. and c. apparatus
REWARDED decorated; requited
REWARDER guerdon giver
REWORDED redrafted
zo **RHABDITE** rod-like structure
zo **RHABDOID** spindle-shaped body
md **RHABDOME** lens supporter
RHAETIAN (Rhaetia) Latin-Swiss linguistic area, population
md **RHAGADES** fissures of the skin
bt **RHAGODIA** grapelike genus
ch **RHAMNOSE** methyl-pentose
RHAPSODE rhapsodist
mu **RHAPSODY** rambling composition
RHEOBASE minimal electrical response stimulus
RHEOCORD resistance wire
ps **RHEOLOGY** formation of matter
RHEOSTAT (variable resistance)
RHEOTOME a switch
RHETORIC florid oratory
zo **RHINIDAE** sharks
md **RHINITIS** nasal inflammation
zo **RHINODON** immense shark
bt **RHIZANTH** flowering root
bt **RHIZOGEN** parasite plant
zo **RHIZOMYS** genus of mole-rats
zo **RHIZOPOD** locomotive protozoa
ch **RHODANIC** rose-red colour
zo **RHODEINA** goldfish
ch **RHODEOSE** isomer of rhamnose
zo **RHODITES** genus of gall-flies
ch **RHOEADIC** (poppy extract)
RHOMBOID quadrilateral figure
ml **RHOMETER** molten-metal impurity measurer
md **RHONCHAL** bronchial
md **RHONCHUS** a raâle
RHOPALIC a hexameter
nv **RHO-THETA** distance/bearing navigation system
bt, md **RHUBARBY** cathartic
mn **RHYOLITE** a quartz
RHYTHMIC harmonious; metric; lilting
RHYTHMUS rhythm; cadence; verse
RIBALDRY **RIBAUDRY**, irreverent jesting; obscenity
RIBBONED striped; streaked
bt **RIB-GRASS** ribwort
RIB-NOSED like a baboon
RIBOSOME nuclear source of protein synthesis
RIB-ROAST beat soundly
zo **RICE-BIRD** the bobolink
nt **RICEBOAT** backward-sailing river craft (Burma)
RICE-DUST rice-meal
RICE-GLUE a cement
RICE-MEAL oriental flour
RICE-MILK milk with rice
RICHNESS wealth; opulence; affluence
zo **RICINIAE** mites; ticks, etc.
RICINIUM Roman mantle
RICK-RACK openwork edging
RICKSHAW Indian or Chinese vehicle
RICOCHET rebound
mn **RICOLITE** ornamental stone
RIDDANCE deliverance; release
RIDDLING perforating; sieving
RIDEABLE broken in
RIDICULE deride; lampoon; mock
RIFENESS prevalence
RIFFRAFF sweepings; refuse; rabble
RIFLEMAN modern musketeer
RIFLE-PIT short trench
RIGHTFUL genuine; true; lawful
RIGHTING doing justice; rectifying

RIGIDITY stiffness; tautness; contraction (muscle); social strictness
RIGORISM austerity
RIGORIST a martinet
RIGOROUS inflexible; severe; harsh
RILL-MARK corrugation
RIMIFORM having a rim
RIMOSITY roughness
RIMULOSE fissured
RIND-CALL defect in timber; (callus)
RING-BARK make a circular cut
zo **RING-BILL** ring-necked duck
RINGBOLT embedded ring
vt **RINGBONE** exostosis on horse foot bones
RINGBONE callus on pastern
RING-DIAL portable sundial
zo **RING-DOVE** cushat; wood-pigeon
tc **RINGDOWN** operator-signalling method
RING-GOAL a ball game
RINGLETY with ringlets
RING-LOCK a puzzle lock
RING-MAIL chain armour
RING-NECK ring-plover
RING-ROAD by-pass
nt **RING-ROPE** a cable rope
RING-SIDE close to the scene
zo **RING-TAIL** hen-harrier
RING-TIME time for marriage
RING-WALL ring fence
RINGWISE experienced; of boxing
vt **RINGWOMB** incomplete cervix dilatation
RING-WORK mail construction
md **RING-WORM** skin disease; fungoid
ps **RIOMETER** ionosphere absorption measurer
RIPARIAN riparial; riverbanks
RIPENESS maturity; mellowness
RIPPLING flax cleaning
RISE-WOOD tinderwood; hedge cuttings
RISKIEST most reckless
RISORIAL ludicrous
mu **RITENUTO** restrained; slower tempo
RITUALLY ceremoniously
RIVALISE compete
RIVALITY equality in rank
RIVALLED emulated; vied; matched
RIVER-BED a channel
RIVER-GOD tutelary deity
zo **RIVER-HOG** the capybara
RIVERINE riparian
RIVER-MAN river-liver
zo **RIVER-PIE** water-ousel
RIVETING clinching
RIVULOSE wavy; rivose
RIXATION brawl; quarrel
RIZZERED salted and sun-dried
ROAD-BOOK guide-book; route; list; itinerary
ROADLESS unwayed
ROAD-POST signpost
ROADSIDE footpath; wayside
ROADSMAN road repairer
ROADSTER coachdriver; cycle
bt **ROAD-WEED** plantago
ROAD-WORK highway repairs
ROAN-TREE rowan tree; mountain ash
ROASTING parching; bantering
ROBURITE an explosive
ROBUSTLY lustily; stoutly; sturdily
ROCAILLE scroll ornament
bt **ROCCELLA** dyers' lichen
mn **ROCK-ALUM** alum stone
ROCKAWAY American carriage
zo **ROCK-BIRD** a pigeon
ck **ROCK-CAKE** small, hard bun
bt **ROCK-CIST** a plant
zo **ROCK-COOK** rock-fish
mn **ROCK-CORK** asbestos
zo **ROCK-CRAB** stony crustacean
ROCK-DOVE pigeon nesting on rocks
ROCKETED shot away
ROCKETER a high flier
ROCKETRY science of rockets
ROCK-FIRE firework mixture
zo **ROCK-FISH** wrasse, bass, etc.
zo **ROCK-GOAT** ibex
zo **ROCK-HAWK** merlin
mn **ROCK-HEAD** bed-rock
ROCK-HEWN cut from rock
zo **ROCK-LARK** rock pipit
bt **ROCK-LILY** (various types)
zo **ROCK-LING** cod; haddock
bt **ROCK-MOSS** lichen
bt **ROCK-ROSE** member of rock garden
mn **ROCK-RUBY** a garnet
mn **ROCK-SALT** native salt
zo **ROCK-SEAL** common seal
mn **ROCK-SOAP** a kind of bole
mn **ROCK-WOOD** ligniform asbestos
ROCK-WORK a rockery
zo **ROCK-WREN** stone-preferring bird
zo **RODENTIA** rats; mice; squirrels
RODOMONT vain boaster; braggart
me **ROENTGEN** unit of radiation
mn **ROE-STONE** oolite
ROGAILLE decorative work with rocks, shells
ROGATION litany; supplication
zo **ROITELET** kinglet; gold-crest
ROLLBACK price legislation

ROLL-CALL a check of all present
ck **ROLY-POLY** rolled suet and jam pudding
ROMANCED economized the truth
ROMANCER tall tale teller
ROMANESE Wallachian language
ROMANIAN RUMANIAN, of Romania
rl **ROMANISH** Catholic
rl **ROMANIST** R.C.
rl **ROMANIZE** Latinize; convert
ROMANSCH Swiss dialect
ROMANTIC quixotic; fanciful
rl **ROME-SCOT** Peter's pence
ROMEWARD verging on Romanism
zo **RONCADOR** Pacific fish
RONDELET form of poem
RONDELLE ladder rung
ROOD-ARCH (over rood-screen)
ROOD-BEAM beam supporting rood
zo **ROODEBOK** bush-buck
ROOD-LOFT gallery over screen
ROOD-TREE Holy-rood; the cross
ROOFLESS open for the rain
ROOF-RACK automobile baggage holder
ROOF-TREE a beam
ROOSTING perching; lodging
ROOT-BEER dandelion ale
ROOT-CROP (esculent roots)
ROOT-FAST firmly rooted
ROOT-FORM shape of a root
bt **ROOT-HAIR** delicate filament
bt **ROOT-KNOT** an abnormality
bt **ROOT-LEAF** a leaf that roots
ROOTLESS footloose
ROPE-PUMP (by an endless rope)
ROPE-WALK shed for spinning ropes
ROPE-YARN manilla; hemp; sisal, etc.
ROPINESS stringiness
ROQUETED (croquet)
bt **RORIDULA** sundew plants
RORULENT dewy
ROSARIAN sect
ROSARIUM rose garden
mn **ROSASITE** copper/zinc carbonate
bt **ROSE-BUSH** where the rose thorns
bt **ROSE-DROP** rose-flavoured orange
ROSEFISH redfish; Atlantic food fish
ROSE-GALL an excrescence
ROSE-HUED rosy
ROSE-KNOT a rosette
mn **ROSELITE** cobalt arseniate
bt **ROSEMARY** aromatic plant
ROSE-PINK sentimental
md **ROSE-RASH** German measles
bt **ROSE-ROOT** herbaceous plant
bt **ROSE-TREE** a standard rose
ROSETTED wearing a rosette (party colours)
bt **ROSEWOOD** Brazilian timber tree
zo **ROSE-WORM** a caterpillar
ROSINESS rubicundity
ROSINING impelling; hustling
ROSIN-OIL a lubricant
zo **ROSMARUS** walruses, etc.
ROSOGLIO red wine of Malta
ROSTRATE beaked
ROSTROID like a rostrum
bt **ROSULATE** having rosetted leaves
ROSY-DROP a grog blossom
zo **ROSY-WAVE** a moth
zo **ROTALIAN ROTALINE**, protozoan
ROTALITE fossil rotalian
ROTARIAN (Rotary Club)
ROTATING spinning; turning
ROTATION revolution; series
ROTATIVE in succession
ROTATORY circulatory
ROT-GRASS butterwort
zo **ROTIFERA** animalculae
ROTIFORM wheel-shaped
ROT-STEEP cotton purification
ROTTENLY putridly
bt **ROTTLERA** dye yielding plant
ROUGHAGE fibre food to keep regular
ROUGH-DRY not ironed
ROUGH-HEW back formation from rough-hewn
ROUGHING (ice-nails)
ROUGHISH rather boisterous
ROULEAUX bundles of fascines
ROULETTE a game of chance
ROUND-ALL acrobatic feat
ROUND-ARM (bowling)
ROUNDERS a game; 9-a-side forerunner of baseball (UK)
ROUNDING encircling
ROUNDISH not quite spherical
ROUNDLET a small circle
nt **ROUND-TOP** masthead platform
ROUTEING selecting a route
ROWDYISH riotous; noisy
ROWDYISM turbulence; brawling
ROWELLED spurred
ROXBURGH a book-binding
ROYALISM ROYALIST, king-supporter
ROYALIZE become a king
RUBBISHY trashy
zo **RUBECULA** robin redbreast
RUBEDITY ruddiness
mn **RUBELIAN** magnesia mica
RUBEZAHL mountain imp (Ger.)
RUBIANIC madder-coloured
RUBICUND ruddy; florid

ch **RUBIDIUM** metallic element
RUBIFORM like a ruby
RUBRICAL marked in red
RUBSTONE whetstone
zo **RUBY-TAIL** cuckoo-fly
bt **RUBY-WOOD** red sandalwood
zo **RUCERVUS** East Indian deer
RUCKLING crumpling; creasing
RUCKSACK knapsack
RUDDLING marking with ochre
RUDENESS unmannerliness
RUDENTED ornamented
RUDIMENT first principle; embryo
RUEFULLY sorrowfully; regretfully
RUFFLING disturbing; agitating
RUGGEDLY jaggedly; unevenly
RUGOSELY wrinkly
RUGOSITY roughness
RUINABLE of delicate virtue
RULE-CASE a printing tray
RULE-WORK tabulation
RULINGLY dominantly
RUMANIAN ROMANIAN, of Romania
RUM-BARGE a warm drink
RUMBLING noise from stomach
zo **RUMINANT** chewing the cud
RUMINATE meditate; muse; ponder
RUMMAGED ransacked; rifled
RUMMAGER searcher
RUMOURED bruited; reported
RUMOURER a gossip; tattler
RUMPLESS having no tail
RUMPLING puckering; rimpling
RUM-SHRUB an odd decoction
nt **RUNABOUT** vagabond; convenient motorcar; motorboat
RUNAGATE renegade; vagabond
RUNMAKER cricket
RUNNER-UP second
RUNOLOGY rune-craft
RUNRIDGE open-field husbandry
RUN-ROUND railway shunting
zo **RUPICOLA** cocks of the rock
RURALISM country life
RURALIST country bumpkin
RURALITY ruralness
RURALIZE rusticate
RUSH-HOUR commuter-time
RUSHLIKE reedy; weak
RUSH-LINE football
zo **RUSH-TOAD** the natterjack
RUSTICAL rustic; sylvan
RUSTLESS stainless
RUSTLING cattle lifting
zo **RUST-MITE** gall-mite
bt **RUTABAGA** Swedish turnip; swede
RUTHLESS pitiless; barbarous
RUTILANT shining
RUTILATE emit rays of light
bt **RYE-GRASS** fodder grass
RYOT-WARI RYOT-WARY, land tenure (Ind.)

S

SABAEISM star worship
bt **SABBATIA** gentian
rl **SABBATIC** holy rest day; or year off
SABBATON armoured boot
zo **SABELINE** sable type of skin
ch **SABINENE** terpene derivative
SABLIERE sand-pit
SABOTAGE wanton destruction
SABOTEUR a wrecker
SABOTIER a wearer of wooden shoes
bt **SABULOSE** growing in sandy places
SABULOUS sandy; gritty
SACCATED pouched
SACCULAR baggy; saclike; vesiculate
zo **SACCULUS** a small sac or cyst
rl **SACELLUM** makeshift altar
SACK-RACE race run in sack
SACREDLY divinely; holily
rl **SACRISTY** the vestry
SADDENED mournful; downcast
SADDLERY horse furniture
SADDLING loading
rl **SADDUCEE** Jewish ritualist
SADFACED gloomy; depressed
SAFENESS security; trustiness
SAFFRONY saffron coloured
ch **SAFRANIN** saffron dye
SAGACITY wisdom; shrewdness
SAGAMORE American Indian chief
zo **SAGE-COCK** American grouse
SAGENESS sapience; sagacity; wisdom
mn **SAGENITE** crystals of rutile
bt **SAGE-ROSE** an evergreen
SAGINATE pamper; fatten
SAGITTAL like an arrow
bt **SAGO-PALM** food-giving tree
bt **SAGUINUS** marmoset
SAHIB-LOG Europeans
zo **SAIBLING** the char
SAILABLE navigable
nt **SAIL-BOAT** yacht
zo **SAIL-FISH** basking shark
nt **SAIL-HOOP** mast-hoop
SAILLESS steam-driven
SAIL-LOFT (where sails are made)
nt **SAIL-PLAN** layout of sails
nt **SAIL-ROOM** storage place for sails
nt **SAIL-YARD** spar for sails
bt **SAINFOIN** a fodder-plant

SAINTISH rather saintlike
SAINTISM sanctimoniousness
SALACITY lustfulness
bt **SALADING** salad vegetables
ck **SALAD-OIL** vegetable oil for dressing
SALARIED receiving wages
SALEABLE marketable
SALEABLY vendibly
SALE-ROOM auction room
SALESMAN persuading to buy
SALE-WORK work carelessly done
SALICINE extract of willow bark
SALIENCE prominence
SALIFIED made into salt
SALINITY saltiness
SALITRAL saltpetre mine
md **SALIVANT SALIVARY, SALIVATE,** of saliva
SALLYING dashing out
zo **SALMONET** young salmon
SALOPIAN from Shropshire
ck **SALPICON** Spanish savoury dish
bt **SALSILLA** edible tuber
bt **SALT-BUSH** Australian plant
mn **SALT-CAKE** sulphate of soda
SALT-COTE salt-pit
SALT-FOOT (below the salt)
ck **SALTJUNK** former ships' supplies
ck **SALTLESS** without the savour
gl **SALT-LICK** animals' balancer source
SALT-MINE mine of rock salt
SALTNESS salinity
SALT-WELL salt spring
SALT-WORK salt factory
bt **SALT-WORT** (several species)
SALUTARY beneficial
SALUTING greeting; hailing
SALVABLE rescuable
SALVAGED saved
bt **SALVINIA** genus of ferns
ch **SAMARIUM** spectroscopic metal
bt **SAMAROID** (winged fruit)
rl **SAMAVEDA** Veda with chants
bt **SAMBUCUS** honeysuckle type
SAMENESS monotony; similarity
bt **SAMPHIRE** a herb
tx **SAMPLARY** test of pictorial sewing
ck **SAMPLING** selection; tasting; matching value
SANATION a cure
SANATIVE healing
SANATORY curative; remedial
el **SANATRON** valve circuit
rl **SANCTIFY** make holy; hallow
SANCTION ratification; approve
SANCTITY holiness; godliness
mn, bt **SANDARAC** realgar; resin
SANDARIC N. Afr. resin for map varnishes
SAND-BALL pumice soap
SAND-BAND protecting band
go, nv **SAND-BANK** a shoal
SAND-BATH household pets' toilet
zo **SAND-BEAR** Indian badger
zo **SAND-BIRD** sandpiper
zo **SAND-COCK** redshank
zo **SAND-CRAB** the lady crab
zo **SAND-DART** a moth
SAND-DUNE a ridge of drifted sand
SANDEVER SANDIVER, glass scum in state of fusion
zo **SAND-FISH** dry land fish
mn **SAND-FLAG** a sandstone
zo **SAND-FLEA** chigoe or jigger
ch **SAND-HEAT** heat of sand-bath
SAND-HILL mound of sand
ga **SAND-IRON** niblick; golf club
zo **SAND-LARK** a wading bird
zo **SAND-MOLE** S. African rodent
zo **SAND-PEEP** American stint
SAND-PUMP (rock drilling)
bt **SAND-REED** a shore grass
SAND-REEL a windlass
SAND-ROLL a casting
SAND-SHOT small shot
zo **SAND-STAR** starfish
SAND-TRAP sand eliminator
zo **SAND-WASP** the digger-wasp
SAND-WELD silica fusing
ck **SANDWICH** a snack between slices
ga **SANDWICH** rubber-layered ping-pong bat
ce **SANDWICK** vertical sand drain construction
zo **SAND-WORM** lob-worm; lug-worm
bt **SAND-WORT** genus Arenia
SANENESS sanity; mental equilibrium
SANGAREE W. Indian drink
SANGLANT bleeding
zo **SANGLIER** wild boar
rl **SANGRAAL** holy grail
SANGREAL sangraal
SANGUIFY to make blood
SANGUINE optimistic; hopeful
mn **SANIDINE** potassium feldspar
SANITARY hygienic; healthful
pr **SANSERIF** serifless type face
SANSKRIT ancient Indian language
bt **SANTALIC** (sandal-wood)
SANTALIN red dye
bt **SANTALUM** sandal-wood genus
ch **SANTONIN** wormwood
SAP-GREEN yellow green
SAPIDITY tastiness

SAPIENCE wisdom; sagacity; intellect
bt **SAPINDUS** the soapberry
zo **SAPI-UTAN** wild ox (Celebes)
SAPONIFY convert into soap
SAPONINE soapwort extract
mn **SAPONITE** hydrous silicate of magnesium
SAPOROUS tasty; piquant (savour)
mn **SAPPHIRE** blue, green or red gem
SAPPHISM lesbianism; (Sappho)
md **SAPREMIA** blood poisoning
gl **SAPROPEL** stagnant water sediment
fr **SAPSTAIN** fungus-caused discoloration
bt **SAPUCAIA** Brazil nut-tree
SARABAND Spanish dance
SARATOGA American travelling trunk
zo **SARCELLE** a teal
tx **SARCENET** sarsenet; woven silk
bt **SARCINIC** fungoid
md **SARCITIS** eye inflammation
bt **SARCOCOL** gum Arabic
zo **SARCODIC** protoplasmic; resembling flesh
md **SARCOSIS** a tumour
md **SARCOTIC** generating flesh
zo **SARDELLE** herring-like fish
SARDONIC ironical; cynical
mn **SARDONYX** variety of onyx
SARGASSO sea of seaweed
SARPLIER packing cloth
SARRASIN a portcullis
bt **SARRIZIN** buckwheat
SARSENET sarcenet; woven silk
SASH-DOOR door having panes of glass
SASSANID a Persian ruler
mn **SASSOLIN** native boracic acid
zo **SASSOROL** rock-pigeon
go **SASTRUGI** hard wind-ridges on winter snow surface (Russia)
SATANISM devil worship
SATANITY devilry; diablery; (witchcraft)
SATELESS insatiable
SATHANAS Satan
SATIABLE appeasable
SATIATED glutted; gratified
SATIRIST lampoonist; ironic writer
SATIRIZE ridicule
SATRAPAL province of a satrap
SATURANT saturating
SATURATE soak; drench
SATURDAY Jewish sabbath
zo **SATURNIA** a moth genus
SATURNIC (lead poisoning)
bt **SATYRIUM** orchid genus
SAUCEBOX impudent fellow
SAUCEPAN cook-pot
SAUCISSE powder bag for use in mines
mu **SAUDADES** Port. 'remembrance of past' pieces
mn **SAURODON** fossil fish
bt **SAURURUS** pepper plants
SAUTERNE white wine (Fr.)
mu **SAUTILLE** rebounding violin technique (Fr.)
hd **SAUTOIRE** heraldic ribbon
SAVAGELY barbarously; inhumanly
SAVAGERY ferocity; brutality
SAVAGING maltreating
SAVANNAH savanna; a treeless plain
SAVEABLE rescuable; salvable
SAVINGLY thriftily; frugally
SAVOURED tasted
SAVOURLY well seasoned
SAVOYARD Gilbert and Sullivan operas enthusiast
md **SAWBONES** a surgeon
zo **SAW-FLIES** boring insects
to **SAW-FRAME** blade holder
bt **SAW-GRASS** a marsh grass
SAW-HORSE cradle for sawing logs
SAW-TABLE boring table
SAW-WREST a saw-set
SAXATILE rock-inhabiting
zo **SAXICAVA** mollusc genus
zo **SAXICOLA** the stone-chats
bt **SAXICOLE** growing on rocks
SAXONDOM Anglo-Saxon world
SAXONISM a Saxon idiom
SAXONIST Saxon scholar
gl **SAXONITE** coarse-grained igneous rock
SCABBARD sheath
ce **SCABBING** worn road surface; fretting; working non-strikers
SCABBLED rough hewn; scappled
bt **SCABIOSA** teasel plants
bt **SCABIOUS** plant; scabby
zo **SCAB-MITE** a parasite
SCABROUS rough; rugged
bd **SCAFFOLD** temporary structure for construction also ski-jumps
SCALABLE climbable; measurable
zo **SCALARIA** ladder-shells
SCALAWAG scallywag; scamp
SCALDING injuring with boiling water
SCALDINO Italian brazier
SCALENUM scalene triangle
pl **SCALENUS** a muscle
SCALIOLA imitation marble
bt **SCALLION** shallot; leek

bd **SCALLOPS** short withies (thatching willows)
SCALPING selling tickets at surcharge
SCALPING removing skin from skull
SCAMBLED mauled; mangled
SCAMBLER gate-crasher
bt **SCAMMONY** convolvulus
SCAMPING shirking; skimping
SCAMPISH knavish; rascally
SCANDENT climbing
ch **SCANDIUM** a metal
md **SCANNING** scrutinizing; viewing (tests)
cp **SCANNING** action of a scanner
SCANSION rhythm
SCANTIES light attire
SCANTILY meagrely; sparingly
SCANTING stinting
SCANTLED in small pieces
SCANTLET a small pattern
zo **SCAPANUS** shrew-moles
SCAPHISM a Persian torture
mn **SCAPHITE** fossil ammonite
zo **SCAPHIUM** beetle genus
SCAPHOID boat-shaped
SCAPPLED rough hewn; scabbled
SCAPULAR (shoulder-blade); scarf
zo **SCARABEE** scarab; beetle
SCARCELY hardly; barely
SCARCITY dearth; rarity; lack
SCARE-BUG a bugbear
SCARFING uniting timber
SCARF-PIN male decoration
zo **SCARIDAE** parrot-fish
SCARIOUS dry; scaly
zo **SCARITID** (carabid beetles)
SCARLESS unwounded; unscathed
zo **SCARN-BEE** dung-beetle
bd **SCARPHED** (a timber joint)
SCARRING wounding; injuring
SCATCHES stilts
SCATHING bitterly severe; caustic
SCATHOLD open pasture ground
SCATLAND peat and pasture land
SCATTERY dispersed
SCAVENGE to collect/eat refuse
mn **SCAWTITE** calcium silicate/carbonate
SCELERAT villain
zo **SCELIDES** the hind-legs
SCENARIO plan of a play
SCENE-MAN scene shifter
SCENICAL scenic; dramatic
zo **SCENT-BAG** animal's pouch
SCENT-BOX perfume pack
SCENTFUL highly odoriferous
SCEPTRAL regal
SCEPTRED kingly (isle)
SCHEDULE catalogue; inventory; list
SCHEDULE programme; timetable; (to-) punctuality
SCHELLUM rascal; rogue
SCHEMING planning; intriguing
SCHEMIST projector; astrologer
md **SCHEROMA** dryness of the eye
SCHILLER bronze lustre
mn **SCHISTIC** laminated; slaty
pc **SCHIZOID** tendency to dementia
zo **SCHIZONT** trophozoite ready to reproduce
SCHLAGER duelling sword (Ger.)
SCHMALTZ grease (Ger.); sentimental
SCHMELZE enamel (Ger.)
SCHNAPPS akvavit; firewater
bt **SCHOENUS** a sedge genus
nt **SCHOKKER** fishing vessel, Holland
SCHOLION **SCHOLIUM**, marginal note in old classics
SCHOOLED disciplined; trained
SCHOONER large drinking glass
nt **SCHOONER** fore-and-aft rigged ship
md **SCIAGRAM** X-ray picture
md **SCIATICA** neuralgia
SCIENTER knowingly; deliberately
SCIENTLY fully aware
SCILICET to wit; namely
SCIMITAR curved sword
zo **SCINCOID** pertaining to the skink
SCIOGRAM radio photograph
SCIOLISM superficiality
SCIOLIST a know-all
SCIOLOUS shallow; skin-deep
SCIOPTIC (camera obscura)
md **SCIRRHUS** cancerous tumour
SCISSILE able to be cut
SCISSION division
to, rw **SCISSORS** acrobatic feat; forfex; cutters; secateurs; crossing
SCISSURA fissure; cleft
SCISSURE rupture division
zo **SCIURINE** **SCIUROID**, rodent mammals
md **SCLERITE** hardened tissue
SCLEROID ossified
md **SCLEROMA** sclerosis
SCLEROUS bony
SCOFFING deriding; taunting; jeering
SCOFF-LAW contemptuous to law
SCOLDING nagging; chiding; rating
zo **SCOLEINA** earth-worms, etc.
zo **SCOLOPAX** woodcock genus
zo **SCOLYTUS** destructive beetle
bd **SCONTION** inside quoin
SCOONING skimming

SCOOPING ladling
SCOOP-NET a hand-net
SCOOTING decamping
bt **SCOPARIA** sweet bromweed
SCOPEFUL with wide prospect
zo **SCOPIDAE** African wading birds
zo **SCOPIPED** having brushy feet
SCORCHED parched; charred
SCORCHER road-hog
mu **SCORDATO** out of tune
SCORIOUS ashy; clinkery
SCORNFUL mocking; insolent
SCORNING spurning; scouting
zo **SCORPION** stingtail
SCOTCHED wounded; blocked
SCOT-FREE untaxed
SCOTOPIC night vision
SCOTSMAN Scot
SCOTTICE in Scottish manner
SCOTTIFY Caledonianize
SCOTTISH Scots
SCOURAGE refuse water
SCOURGED chastised
SCOURING scurrying; scrubbing
SCOUTING rejecting; scorning
SCOUT-LAW Scout Code
SCOWLING glowering; frowning
SCRABBLE scribble; scrawl
SCRAGGED strangled; throttled
SCRAGGLY rough-looking
ck, mo **SCRAMBLE** hurry; strife; clamber; (eggs); (code); (jumble); (Amer. football)
ae **SCRAMJET** spacecraft
nt **SCRAN-BAG** food sack
SCRANNEL squeaking; slender; meagre
SCRAPING abrading; rasping
SCRAPPED discarded; fought
SCRAPPLE to grub about; scrabble
SCRATCHY ragged; sketchy
SCRATTLE to scuttle
SCRAWLED scribbled
SCRAWLER slovenly writer
SCREAMED yelled; cried; squalled
zo **SCREAMER** tropical bird; monkey; human offspring
SCREECHY shrill and harsh
SCREENED veiled; hidden; sieved
SCREEVER begging-letter writer
SCREWING exacting; twisting; racking
to **SCREW-KEY** a spanner
bt **SCREW-POD** screw-bean
SCRIBBET painter's pencil
SCRIBBLE scrawl; write
SCRIBING recording
SCRIBISM Jewish literature
SCRIGGLE wriggle
SCRIMPED stinted
SCRIMPLY miserly
SCRINIUM scroll/relic container
SCRIPTOR ancient book-copier, handwriter
SCRIVANO Italian clerk
SCRODDLE to variegate
md **SCROFULA** the king's evil
SCROGGIE full of brushwood
SCROLLED convoluted
SCROOPED grated; cracked
SCROUGED squeezed
SCROUGER a whopper
SCROUNGE acquire by stealth; cadge
SCRUBBED scoured
ch **SCRUBBER** charlady; removal of gas impurities
bt **SCRUB-OAK** stunted oak
SCRUPLED hesitated; wavered
SCRUPLER demurrer; doubter
SCRUTINY close inquiry; search
SCUDDICK scuttock; a trifle; a shilling
SCUDDING speeding
le **SCUDDING** pre-tanning hide treatment
SCUFFLED tussled
SCUFFLER brawler
SCULLERY room for washing dishes
SCULLING rowing
SCULLION dish-washer
SCULPSIT he engraved it
SCULPTOR image maker
SCUMBLED painted over
SCURRIED scampered; hastened
SCURRIES pony races
SCURRILE scurrilous
SCURVILY basely; shabbily
SCUTCHED separated
SCUTCHER hedger
zo **SCUTELLA** sea-urchin genus
SCUTIFER shield-bearer
zo **SCUTIPED** having scaly shanks
SCUTTLED ran; bolted; scampered; sabotaged
SCUTTLER ship-sinker
SCUTTOCK see scuddick
gl **SCYELITE** coarse-grained igneous rock
SCYTHIAN (Scythia)
zo **SCYTODES** a genus of spiders
zo **SEA-ACORN** a barnacle
zo **SEA-ADDER** stickle-back
bt **SEA-APRON** a seaweed
zo **SEA-ARROW** flying squid
SEA-BEACH seashore
zo **SEA-BEAST** a sea monster

bt **SEA-BELLS** bindweed
nv **SEA-BOARD** the coast
nt **SEA-BORNE** shipped
zo **SEA-BRANT** brent goose
zo **SEA-BREAM** mackerel type
nv **SEA-CHART** marine map
nt **SEA-COAST** seashore
nt **SEA-CRAFT** seamanship
bt **SEA-DAISY** the lady's cushion
zo **SEA-DEVIL** ray; angel-fish
zo **SEA-DRAKE** sea-crow
zo **SEA-EAGLE** the osprey
nt **SEA-FARER** voyager; sailor
nt **SEA-FIGHT** marine engagement
SEA-FRONT shore promenade
SEA-FROTH foam
nv **SEA-GATES** (tidal basin)
nt **SEA-GAUGE** ship's draught
nt **SEA-GOING** deep water line ship
zo **SEA-GOOSE** a dolphin
bt **SEA-GRAPE** glasswort
bt **SEA-GRASS** the thrift
SEA-GREEN marine colour
bt **SEA-GROVE** under-water grove
bt **SEA-HEATH** beach plant
bt **SEA-HOLLY** the eryngo
zo **SEA-HORSE** the walrus
zo **SEA-HOUND** dog-fish
zo **SEA-JELLY** sea-blubber
zo **SEA-LEECH** an annelid
zo **SEA-LEMON** a doridoid mollusc
SEA-LEVEL mean tide level
zo **SEA-LOACH** a gadoid fish
zo **SEA-LOUSE** a parasite
SEAL-PIPE a dip pipe
SEAL-RING signet ring
SEAL-SKIN pelt; fur
zo **SEA-LUNGS** a comb-jelly
bt **SEAL-WORT** Solomon's seal
SEAMANLY seamanlike
nv **SEA-MARGE** seashore; tide-line
zo **SEA-MELON** sea-cucumber
SEAMIEST most sordid
SEAMLESS in one piece
zo **SEA-MOUSE** the dunlin; a worm
SEAM-RENT a tear at the seam
SEAMSTER one who sews
SEA-NYMPH an Oceanid
bt **SEA-ONION** a squill
zo **SEA-OTTER** marine otter
bt **SEA-OXEYE** seashore plant
zo **SEA-PEACH** sea-squirt
zo **SEA-PERCH** bass
mu **SEA-PIECE** seascape; poem; song; music
SEA-PLANE hydroplane; floatplane
bt **SEA-PLANT** a seaweed
SEA-POWER strategic
zo **SEA-PURSE** eggcase of skate
zo **SEA-QUAIL** the turnstone
SEA-QUAKE marine earthquake
zo **SEA-RAVEN** cormorant
SEARCHED quested; probed; sought
SEARCHER inquirer; examiner
SEA-REEVE customs officer
SEARNESS dryness; sereness
zo **SEA-ROBIN** gurnard fish
nt **SEA-ROVER** pirate; pirate ship
SEARWOOD dry wood
SEASCAPE marine view, painting
zo **SEA-SHARK** man-eater shark
zo **SEASHELL** marine shell
SEASHORE the beach
zo **SEA-SHRUB** a sea-fan
zo **SEA-SNAIL** the periwinkle
zo **SEA-SNAKE** sea-serpent
zo **SEA-SNIPE** sandpiper
SEASONAL not always available
SEASONED matured; inured
ck **SEASONER** a relish; strong flavouring
zo **SEA-SQUID** cuttlefish
SEA-STICK herring cured at sea
zo **SEA-SWINE** porpoise
SEAT-BACK loose cover
zo **SEA-TENCH** black sea-bream
bt **SEA-THONG** cord-like seaweed
SEAT-LOCK a catch
SEAT-MILE transport statistic
SEAT-RAIL a crosspiece
zo **SEA-TROUT** saltwater trout
zo **SEAT-WORM** pin-worm
SEA-WATER brine
zo **SEA-WOMAN** mermaid; dugong
SEA-WRACK coarse seaweed
bt **SEBESTAN SEBESTEN**, tree with plumlike fruit
SEBUNDEE Indian militia-man
bt **SECAMONE** shrubby climber
to **SECATEUR** pruning shears
SECEDING withdrawing; retiring
SECERNED secreted
SECESHER a secessionist
SECLUDED aside; shut off
zo **SECODONT** with cutting teeth
SECONDED aided; transferred
SECONDER supporter; abettor
SECRETED cloaked; concealed
bc **SECRETIN** secretion-stimulating hormone
SECRETLY privily; covertly
SECTATOR an adherent
SECTORAL in a sector
bd **SECTROID** space between groins
SECUNDUM according to (Latin)
SECURELY fast; safely

SECURING acquiring; getting
SECURITE an explosive
SECURITY safety; surety; pledge; secrecy
cp **SECURITY** protection from risks of data losses
SEDATELY calmly; seriously; soberly
md **SEDATIVE** tranquillizing; soothing
lw **SEDERUNT** court session (Sc.)
zo **SEDGE-HEN** marsh-hen
rl **SEDILIUM** chancel seat
SEDIMENT lees; dregs; grounds
SEDITION treason; mutiny; rebellion
SEDUCING enticing; inveigling
SEDUCTOR tempter; corrupter
SEDULITY assiduity; diligence
SEDULOUS industrious; busy
SEECATCH Alaskan male seal
zo **SEED-BIRD** water-wagtail
SEED-CAKE caraway cake
bt **SEED-COAT** husk
bt **SEED-CORN** corn for sowing
bt **SEED-DOWN** down on cotton, etc.
zo **SEED-FISH** spawn; roe
zo **SEED-FOWL** grain-fed bird
SEED-GALL plant disease
bt **SEED-LEAF** a cotyledon
SEED-LEAP seed-basket
SEEDLESS pipless
SEEDLING young plant
bt **SEED-LOBE** seed-leaf
SEED-PLOT a hot-bed
SEEDSMAN dealer; sower
zo **SEED-TICK** a parasite
SEEDTIME sowing season
SEED-WOOL cotton-wool and seeds
vt **SEEDY-TOE** a horse disease
zo **SEER-FISH SEIR-FISH**
SEERSHIP talent of foretelling
SEESAWED oscillated
SEETHING boiling
hd **SEGREANT** rampant and salient
SEIGNEUR lord of the manor
SEIGNIOR seigneur; feudal lord
oc **SEINE-NET** long shallow net
zo **SEIR-FISH** seer-fish
SEIZABLE apprehendable
zo **SEIZLING** the carp
bt **SEJUGOUS** (six pairs of leaflets)
SEKITORI sumo wrestler
zo **SELADANG** Malayan tapir; bison
ar **SELAMLIK** men's quarters (Turk.)
nt **SELANDER** post-Roman trireme, Mediterranean
SELECTED chosen; culled; preferred
cp **SELECTOR** picker and chooser; specified conditions finder
tc **SELECTOR** electromagnetic switching device
ch **SELENATE** a selenic salt
ch **SELENIDE** a compound
mn **SELENITE** gypsum
ch **SELENIUM** a chemical element
SELF-BORN self-begotten
SELF-ENDS endpaper leaves in books
bt **SELF-HEAL** burnet saxifrage
SELF-HELP unaided effort
SELFHOOD conscious personality
SELFLESS unselfish
SELF-LIKE indulgence
SELF-LIKE twin
SELF-LOVE wrapped up in self
SELF-MADE independent
SELFMADE hermaphrodite solves chess problem
SELFNESS egotism
SELF-PITY sorriness for self
SELFSAME identical; equivalent
SELF-SOWN plant from windblown seed
SELF-WILL obstinacy
SELF-WISE self-conceit
SELLABLE saleable; marketable
SELVAGEE untwisted rope
SELVEDGE woven border
cp **SEMANTIC** significant; expressive; symbol-meaning link
SEMBLANT resembling; like
SEMESTER period of six months
SEMI-ACID half-acid
go **SEMI-ARID** between desert and savannah
rl **SEMI-BULL** a papal bull
SEMI-COPE outer monastic garment
SEMI-DOME half-dome
SEMI-FLEX to half bend
SEMI-MUTE half deaf
SEMINARY academy; college; school
SEMINATE propagate; sow
SEMINOLE American Indian tribe
SEMI-NUDE barely clothed
mn **SEMI-OPAL** half-opal
SEMI-OPEN sport
SEMIOTIC sign language
SEMI-OVAL half-oval
SEMI-PULP ground-wood impurities in paper
SEMI-RING half-circle
SEMITAUR half-bull, half-man
SEMITISM Hebrew idiom
SEMITIST Hebrew scholar
mu **SEMITONE** musical interval
ck **SEMOLINA SEMILINO**, granules of flour; manna; grits
mu **SEMPLICE** simply

SEMPSTER seamstress
nm SEMUNCIA Roman coin
SENARIUS verse of six feet
SEND-DOWN expel; rusticate
zo SENG-GUNG Java badger
bt SENGREEN the houseleek
SENILITY dotage; old age
SENNIGHT a week
gl SENONIAN geological formation
SENORITA Spanish young lady
SENSEFUL judicious; rational
SENSIBLE intelligent; wise; discreet
SENSIBLY sagaciously; sanely
SENSIFIC exciting
SENSUISM sensuality
SENSUIST amorist; materialist
SENSUOUS carnal; voluptuous
SENTENCE doom; maxim; clause
SENTIENT perceptive; aware of; alert
SENTINEL sentry; watchman; warder
cp SENTINEL signal ending tape recording
SENTRIES watchers; guards
SENTRY-GO sentry duty
bt SEPALINE (leaf of calyx)
bt SEPALODY SEPALOID, reversion of petals to sepals
SEPALOUS sepaline
SEPARATE sort; divorce; sever
cn SEPDUMAG 2-magnetic-sound-track film
cn SEPDUOPT 2-optical-sound-track film
zo SEPIACEA cuttlefish
zo SEPIIDAE cephalopods
SEPIMENT hedge; boundary
mn SEPTARIA turtle-stones
bt SEPTATED divided into cells
mu SEPTETTE (seven performers)
bt SEPTFOIL the tormentil
SEPTUARY group of seven
bt SEPTULUM small cell
SEPTUPLE sevenfold
SEQUENCE continuity; series
mu SEQUENZA repetition in higher key; hymn for mass; solo pieces (It.)
SERAFILE serrefile
SERAGLIO Ottoman sultan's palace
SERAPHIC angelic; sublime
rl SERAPHIM celestial being
bt SERAPIAS genus of orchids
mu SERENADE SERENATA, Nachtmusik (Ger.); piece for woodwind in several movements
SERENELY tranquilly; calmly; placidly
SERENEST calmest; most tranquil
SERENISE glorify
SERENITY peacefulness; quiet
SERGEANT serjeant
tx SERGETTE thin serge
SERIALLY consecutively
SERIATIM in regular order
SERICATE silky; downy
mn SERICITE potash mica
SERIFORM Chinese writing
mu SERINGHI Indian viol
SERJEANT sergeant
rl SERMONER preacher
SERMONET short address
rl SERMONIC admonitive
md SEROLOGY study of blood, serum
md SEROSITY (exuding serum)
zo SEROTINE species of bat
to SERPETTE pruning knife (Fr.)
me SERPLATH 80 stone (Sc.)
bt SERPOLET wild thyme
zo SERRANUS perch; bass
SERRATED notched; like a saw
zo SERRATUS a thorax muscle
zo SERRIPED with serrated feet
SERVIENT subordinate; slavish; abject
SERVIOUS obsequious; sycophantic
SERVITOR waiter; henchman
md SESAMOID (toe bones)
nm SESTERCE Roman 2d. coin
mu SESTETTE sextet
mu SESTOLET sextuplet
SET-ASIDE reserve(d)
SETIFORM bristly
SET-PIECE stage scene; battle
SETTLING colonizing; deciding; fixing
SETULOSE prickly; spinate; spicate
SEVERELY rigorously; strictly
SEVERING disrupting; sundering
SEVERITY harshness; austerity
zo SEWELLEL mountain beaver
SEWERAGE drainage
SEWER-GAS bad smell
SEXAGENE angle of 60 degrees
SEXANGLE a hexagon
SEXOLOGY study of sex and sexuality
mu SEXTETTE sextet
mu SEXTOLET sextuplet; group of 6 notes
SEXTUPLE sixfold
SEXUALLY in a sexual way
mu SFORZATO emphatically
SGABELLO stool or bench (It.)
SHABBIER more ragged
SHABBILY despicably; meanly
SHABRACK saddle-cloth
SHACKING sharing digs, lodgings

SHACKLED fettered; manacled
zo **SHAD-BIRD** American snipe
bt **SHAD-BUSH** the June-berry
bt **SHADDOCK** grapefruit
SHADEFUL umbrageous
zo **SHAD-FROG** jumping frog
SHADIEST most obscure
SHADOWED followed; obscured
SHAFTING of propeller drive; copulation
SHAGGING of intercourse; exhausting
SHAGREEN sharkskin and rayfish tea caddies; untanned leather (Persia)
SHAKE-OUT return to normal; economics
tx **SHALLOON** woollen fabric
SHAMANIC magical
SHAMBLES slaughter-house; ruin
SHAMEFUL humiliating; heinous; base
SHAMMING feigning; counterfeiting
bt **SHAMROCK** Irish emblem
SHANGHAI kidnap
SHANKING mishitting at golf
SHANTIES sea songs; huts
tx **SHANTUNG** coarse silk
SHAPABLE fashionable
SHARKING of commercial scoundrel
SHARP-CUT clearly defined
SHARPING tricking
SHARP-SET keen
ck **SHASHLIK** grilled lamb on skewer
SHATRANJ board game for two, like chess
SHATTERY brittle; rickety
zo **SHAW-FOWL** a wappenshaw fowl
SHEADING district, Isle of Man
SHEALING **SHEILING**, shepherds' shelter
zo **SHEARHOG** shorn sheep
SHEARING clipping; shaving; fleecing
SHEARMAN cloth-cutter
SHEATHED encased; sheeted
bt **SHEA-TREE** butter tree
SHEAVING collecting; harvesting
SHEDDING discarding; diffusing
SHEEP-DIP cleansing pool
zo **SHEEPDOG** shepherd's flock-director
zo **SHEEPFLY** a parasite
SHEEPISH shy; timid
SHEEP-PEN an enclosure
SHEEP-RUN tract of pasture
SHEERING moving aside
nt **SHEER-LEG** a crane spar
ce **SHEETERS** steel poling boards for trenches
pr **SHEET-FED** separate-sheet printing
SHEETING cloth for sheets
bd **SHEETING** **SHEATHING**, vertical boards with struts for trenches
SHEKINAH Divine Aura
zo **SHELDUCK** female sheldrake
SHELL-GUN a cannon
SHELL-ICE (no water below it)
SHELLING bombarding; husking
SHELL-OUT spend cash; pay for (sl.)
SHELTERY affording shelter
SHELVING sloping; shelves
SHEMITIC Semitic; (Shem)
SHEPHERD a swain; shove; impede, shoulder (Australian football)
SHERATON furniture designer
SHIELDED sheltered; screened
SHIELDER projector
SHIFTILY deceitfully; evasively
SHIFTING moving; varying; changing
SHILLALY Irish blackthorn cudgel
nm **SHILLING** a bob
SHIMMING wedging
md **SHIN-BONE** the tibia
SHINGLED bobbed
md **SHINGLES** herpes
SHINNING climbing
SHIPLESS without boats
nt **SHIPLOAD** a full cargo
SHIPMATE fellow seaman
SHIPMENT embarkation
nt **SHIPPING** freighting; seaborne craft
SHIP-TIRE head-dress
zo **SHIP-WORM** the teredo
nt **SHIPYARD** building yard
SHIREMAN sheriff
SHIRKING evading; scamping
tx **SHIRTING** material for shirts
SHIVAREE mock serenade; charivari
SHIVERED shattered; quaked; trembled
SHOALING thronging
zo **SHOCK-DOG** a poodle
SHOCKING offensive; outrageous
zo **SHOEBILL** whale-headed heron
SHOEHORN footwear aid
SHOELACE a latchet
SHOELESS barefoot
SHOGGING shaking; jogging
SHOGUNAL (of Japanese C. in C.)
SHOOTING a game-preserve; slaughter-sporter
SHOOTOUT police versus gangsters
SHOP-BELL bell at shop door
SHOPGIRL shop assistant
SHOPLIFT pilfer; rob a store
SHOPPING purchases
SHOPWORN faded
zo **SHORLING** newly shorn sheep
SHORTAGE deficiency; lack

pr **SHORT-AND** the ampersand; &
SHORT-CUT (tobacco); a quick way
SHORT-LEG (cricket)
md **SHORT-RIB** a false rib
SHOT-BELT bandolier
SHOT-FREE Scot free; untaxed
SHOT-HOLE hole for explosives
SHOT-SILK iridescent silk
SHOTTING loading with shot
SHOULDER carry; hump; a prominence
SHOUTING cheering; crying; calling
SHOW-BILL a show-card
SHOW-CARD card of patterns
SHOW-CASE display case
SHOW-DOWN cards on the table
SHOWERED bestowed liberally
SHOW-ROOM display salon
SHOW-YARD (horses and cattle)
SHRAPNEL a projectile
SHREDDED cut into strips
SHREDDER machine for shredding
SHREWDLY sagaciously; astutely
SHREWISH vixenish
SHRIEKED yelled; squealed; cried
SHRIEKER screamer
SHRIEVAL (sheriff)
SHRILLED squeaked; piped
SHRIMPED went fishing for shrimps
SHRIMPER boat or catcher
SHRINKER (head-); psychiatrist
SHRIVING absolving; pardoning
SHROUDED veiled; hidden; screened
SHROVING Shrove-tide festivity
SHRUGGED uplifted
SHUCKING husking; stripping
SHUCKING SHACKING, sharing a shelter
SHUFFLED (cards); evaded
SHUFFLER palterer; quibbler
SHUNNING avoiding; evading
SHUNPIKE a byroad
SHUNTING switching railway cars
SHUTDOWN closure
SHUTTING fastening; barring
SHWANPAN Chinese abacus
SIBERIAN of Siberia
mn **SIBERITE** red tourmaline
SIBILANT hissing; buzzing
SIBILATE to hiss
SIBILOUS sibilant
SIBYLLIC oracular; prophetic
SICANIAN Sicilian
SICELIOT a Greek in Sicily
SICILIAN (Sicily)
SICK-CALL doctor's visit
SICKENED languished; ailed; wearied
SICKENER a cause of disgust
nt **SICK-FLAG** quarantine-flag
SICKLIED pallid; wan
SICKLILY languidly
SICK-LIST register of patients
SICKNESS malady; disease; illness
md **SICK-ROOM** patients' room
SICULIAN early Sicilian
SIDE-ACHE side stitch or pain
SIDE-ARMS sword or bayonet
ro **SIDEBAND** close frequencies
tc **SIDEBAND** signal for close transmission
au **SIDE-BEAM** (above crank-shaft)
SIDE-COMB ornamental comb
SIDE-DISH subsidiary, extra dish
mu **SIDE-DRUM** snare-drum; small drum
SIDELINE subsidiary activity
SIDELING sideways; sloping
SIDE-LOCK a curl
SIDELONG obliquely
SIDE-NOTE marginal note
as **SIDEREAL** of interval between 2 transits
mn **SIDERITE** ironstone
SIDE-SEAT seat not in front
SIDE-SHOW raree show at fair, circus, amusement park
SIDE-SLIP a skid; descending technique (skiing)
rl **SIDESMAN** deputy churchwarden
SIDE-STEP evade
SIDE-SWAY wind-caused side movement of frame
SIDETONE telephony
SIDE-VIEW profile
SIDEWALK pavement; footway
SIDEWAYS crabwise
SIDE-WIND undue influence
pr **SIDE-WIRE** wire-staple stitching
SIEGE-GUN heavy gun
SIFFLEUR whistler
SIFFLING whistling
bt **SIGATOKA** fungal banana disease
SIGHTERS first six arrows on target (archery)
SIGHTING spotting; aiming; viewing
SIGMATIC (sigma)
SIGNABLE able to have a name written on
SIGNALLY eminently; notably
SIGNIEUR seignior; feudal lord
SIGNLESS making no sign
SIGN-POST modern milestone
bt **SIKYOTIC** plasma-fusing parasitic
SILENCED stilled; hushed
SILENCER (cars, guns, etc.)
SILENTLY mutely; dumbly; taciturnly

ch **SILICATE** silicon compound
ch **SILICIDE** silicon-content compound
SILICIFY make into silica
mn **SILICITE** labradorite
ch **SILICIUM** silicon
bt **SILICOLE** plant on silica-rich soil
ch **SILICONE** organo-silicon compound
bt **SILICULA SILICULE**, seed vessel
tx **SILKENED** made glossy
SILK-MILL cloth factory
zo **SILK-REEL** spool for silk
zo **SILKWORM** source of silk
ck **SILLABUB** syllabub; a drink; jelly sweetmeat
SILLADAR Indian cavalryman
pl **SILLY-HOW** a caul; foetal membrane
bt **SILPHIUM** rosin-weed
mn,gl **SILURIAN** rock formation; geological era
SILURIST a Silurian
SILVANUS a forest-god
SILVERLY like silver
bt **SIMARUBA** quassia; bitterwood
SIMILIZE find similarities; compare
SIMMERED boiled gently
rl **SIMONIAC** one guilty of simony
SIMPERED smiled fatuously
SIMPERER smirker
SIMPLIFY make plain and easy
SIMPLING gathering herbs
SIMPLIST herbalist
SIMULANT like unto
SIMULATE pretend; imitate; sham
rl **SINAITIC** (Mount Sinai)
md **SINAPISM** mustard plaster
pl **SINCIPUT** the skull
SIN-EATER (a Welsh custom)
SINECURE salary for no work
SINEWING strengthening
SINEWOUS strong; vigorous
mu **SINFONIA** a symphony
SINFULLY unrighteously; naughtily
SINGABLE vocable
SINGEING scorching; searing
SINGERIE monkeys represented as human
SINGLING selecting; picking
mu **SING-SONG** community singing
SINGULAR peculiar; unique; quaint
SINICISM a Chinese custom
ch **SINIGRIN** black-mustard-seed glucoside
SINISTER evil; unlucky; baneful
gl **SINK-HOLE** a vent; swallow hole; pot hole in depression
SINN-FEIN Irish home-ruler
SINOLOGY Chinese lore
SINOPHIL lover of China
SINUATED insinuated; wound
SINUSOID geometric curve
SIPHONAL working on the siphon principle
SIPHONED extracted to a lower level
SIPHONET aphid cornicle
SIPHONIC working on the siphon principle
ch **SIPYLITE** niobite of erbium
zo **SIRENIAN** mermaid-like sea mammal
SIRENIZE entice; allure
md **SIRIASIS** sunstroke
SIRVENTE troubadour's song
zo **SISCOWET SISKIWET, SISKOWET**, variety of trout from Lake Superior
SISTERLY affectionate; sororal
SISYPHUS stone-roller
md **SITOLOGY** dietetics
SITTYBUS papyrus-roll title label
SITUATED placed; located; sited
SITZ-BATH hip-bath
nm **SIXPENCE** a tanner
SIXPENNY worth sixpence
SIXTIETH ordinal number
SIZEABLE of some bulk
SIZINESS adhesiveness
SIZING-UP estimation; rapid evaluation
SIZZLING hissing; seething; frying
SKEAN-DHU Highland dirk
SKELETAL like a skeleton
SKELETON outline; nucleus; cadre
SKETCHED drafted; depicted; drew
SKETCHER delineator
SKEWBACK an abutment
SKEWBALD piebald
SKEWERED impaled
SKEWNESS deviation of curve of frequency distribution
md **SKIAGRAM** X-ray photograph
el **SKIATRON** type of cathode-ray tube
SKIDDING side-slipping
SKILLESS maladroit; artless
SKILLING outhouse; bay of a barn
SKIM-MILK weightwatcher's drink
SKIMMING scan superficially
SKIMMITY a burlesque
SKIMPING scamping; stinting
SKIN-DEEP superficial
SKINLESS flayed
SKINNING flaying
bd **SKINTLED** of irregularly laid brickwork
SKIN-WOOL wool from dead sheep
SKIPETAR an Albanian
zo **SKIP-JACK** upstart; click-beetle

nt **SKIPJACK** sail cargo boat, Chesapeake, N. America
SKIPPING leaping; bounding; hopping
mu **SKIRLING** bagpipe music
SKIRMISH contest; brush; fray
SKIRTING bordering
SKITTISH mettlesome; fickle
ga **SKITTLES** ninepins
zo **SKUA-GULL** the great skua
SKULKING lurking; slinking
SKULL-CAP the sinciput
zo **SKUNKISH** like a skunk
SKURFING **SKURFER**, skateboarding
SKYLIGHT glazed hole in roof
rl **SKY-PILOT** aviator; padre
SKYSCAPE cloud painting
pg **SKY-SHADE** lens; hood
SLABBING cutting into slabs
nt **SLABLINE** a running rope
SLACKING relaxing; loosening
SLAMMING banging
SLANGILY colloquially
SLANGING vituperating
SLANTING sloping; tilting; oblique
SLAP-BANG violently
SLAP-DASH carelessly; rashly
ck **SLAPJACK** flapjack; pancake
SLAPPING large; strong; spanking
SLASHING showy; severe; gashing; swing of ice hockey stick
to **SLATE-AXE** a seax
SLATTERN slovenly person
SLAVERED dribbled
SLAVERER driveller; idiot
SLAVONIC (Czechs; Poles; etc.)
SLEAVING separating
SLEDDING sled-transport
SLEDGING sleighing
SLEEKING gliding; smoothing
SLEEPFUL somnolent
SLEEPILY drowsily
SLEEPING dormant; slumbering
mt **SLEETING** rain, snow and hail
SLIDABLE capable of sliding
SLIGHTED insulted; peeved
SLIGHTLY slenderly; faintly; scantily
SLIGHTLY superficial
SLIME-PIT pit of viscous mire
SLIMMING banting; reducing; dieting
SLIMNESS craftiness; artfulness
SLINGING throwing; flinging; tossing
SLINKING skulking; lurking; sneaking
nt **SLIP-DOCK** slipway
nt **SLIP-KNOT** sailor's device
SLIPOVER sleeveless sweater
SLIPPERY evasive; shifty; elusive
SLIPPING tripping; erring; sliding
SLIP-RAIL form of gate (Australian)
rw **SLIP-ROAD** minor by-pass; siding
SLIPSHOD down at heel
SLIPSLOP jejune; trash; slovenly
SLIPWARE lead-glazed earthenware with relief slip pattern
SLITHERY slimy; deceitful
SLITTING splitting
SLIVERED cut into strips
SLOBBERY moist
SLOGGING smiting
SLOP-BOWL slop-basin
SLOP-DASH weak cold tea
SLOP-PAIL household bucket
SLOPPING spilling
SLOPSHOP (ready-made clothes) R.N.
SLOPWORK slovenly work
SLOTBACK (Am. football)
SLOTHFUL idle; dronish; dilatory
SLOTTERY squalid; dirty
SLOTTING grooving
SLOUCHED bent; depressed
SLOUGHED cast off
SLOVENLY negligently; unkempt
SLOVENRY slovenliness; disorder
SLOWBACK lazy lubber
SLOW-DOWN ca' canny; reduce capacity
SLOWNESS tardiness; sluggishness
zo **SLOW-WORM** limbless lizard
SLUBBING twisting
SLUGFEST high scoring (baseball)
SLUGGARD laggard; lounger; slacker
SLUGGING slogging
SLUGGISH slothful; inert
mu **SLUG-HORN** a trumpet
SLUICING flushing
SLUMBERY somnolent; soporous
SLUMMING visiting slums
SLUMPING falling heavily
tx **SLURGALL** knitted-fabric fault
SLURRIED smeared
SLURRING disparaging
SLUTTERY of prostitutes
SLUTTISH dirty; slovenly
SLY-BOOTS a wag
zo **SLY-GOOSE** the sheld-duck
SMACKING tasting of; slapping
bt **SMALLAGE** wild celery
SMALL-ALE (no hops)
SMALLEST minutest; tiniest
SMALLISH on the small side
md **SMALLPOX** variola
mn **SMALTINE** **SMALTITE**, cobalt-arsenic compound

SMARTING stinging; rankling
SMASH-HIT popular song; musical
SMASHING shattering (blow); excellent
SMATCHET person of no importance
SMEARING daubing; begriming
mn **SMECTITE** fuller's earth
SMELLING redolent; scenting
SMELTERY foundry
SMELTING producing metal
SMIRCHED soiled; clouded
SMIRKING simpering
SMITCHEL a particle
SMITHERY a smiddy; a smithy
SMITHING iron-working
SMOCKING pleating
SMOKABLE fumable
rw **SMOKE-BOX** of steam locomotive
ck **SMOKE-DRY** cure; bloat (of fish)
SMOOTHED palliated; levelled
SMOOTHEN to allay; mollify
SMOOTHLY suavely; blandly
mu **SMORZATO** diminuendo
SMOTHERY stifling; stuffy
SMOULDER hangfire
SMOULDRY slow burning
SMUDGING blotting
nt **SMUG-BOAT** smuggling boat
SMUGGLED brought in illegally
SMUGGLER a night-owler
SMUGNESS self-satisfaction
bt **SMUTBALL** a fungus
SMUTCHED blacken with soot
ck **SNACK-BAR** buffet
SNAFFLED purloined; filched
nt **SNAGBOAT** (removing snags)
SNAGGING lopping trees
SNAILERY small farm
zo **SNAKE-EEL** sinous fish
pt **SNAP-LINE** chalked-string design marker
SNAPPING biting; breaking; cracking
SNAPPISH short-tempered
cp **SNAPSHOT** amateur photograph; store data for correcting errors
SNAP-VOTE sudden vote
bt **SNAP-WEED** balsams, etc.
SNARLING entangling (traffic hold-ups)
SNATCHED plucked; clutched; wrested
SNATCHER grasper; grabber
SNATTOCK fragment
SNEAK-CUP insidious scoundrel
SNEAKING telling; secret; slinking
SNEERING taunting; jeering; mocking
SNEEZING sudden, involuntary, explosive expiration
SNICKING cutting; nicking
SNIFFING inhaling drugs; dogs detecting same
SNIGGLED snared
SNIPPETY fragmentary
SNIPPING shearing; clipping
SNIP-SNAP smart sharp dialogue
SNITCHER handcuff; informer
SNIVELLY whining
SNOBBERY tuft-hunting
SNOBBISH feeling superior
SNOBBISM aping gentility
SNOBLING a little snob
SNOGGING illicit intercourse
SNOOPING furtive enquiry; prying
SNOOZING dozing; drowsing
SNORTING puffing
bt **SNOWBALL** guelder-rose
zo **SNOWBIRD** American finch
SNOWBOOT long boot; galosh
SNOWCAPT crowned with snow
SNOWCOLD cold as snow
bt **SNOWDROP** first sign of spring
SNOW-EYES snow goggles
SNOWFALL frozen precipitation
SNOWLIKE cold, white and soft
SNOWLINE line of perpetual snow
rw **SNOWSHED** railway protection
SNOWSHOE wide-framed shoe for walking on snow
SNOWSLIP avalanche
SNOWSUIT winter garments
SNUBBING checking a rope
SNUBBISH petulant
SNUB-NOSE short nose
SNUFFBOX collector's item
SNUFFERS candle trimmers
SNUFFLED obstructed nasal air intake
SNUFFLER one who snuffles
md **SNUFFLES** infantile breathing noise
SNUGGERY cosy quarters
SNUGGLED cuddled
SNUGNESS warmth and comfort
SOAKAWAY dry well; rummel; pit
SOAPSUDS froth on soapy water
SOAP-TEST (for hardness of water)
bt **SOAP-TREE** a Chilean tree
SOAPWORK soap factory
bt **SOAPWORT** a genus of plants
SOBERIZE to calm down
SOBRANJE Bulgarian tobacco
SOBRIETY dispassion; temperance
SOB-STORY false, pathetic tale
SOB-STUFF synthetic emotion
SO-CALLED incorrectly known as

SOCIABLE companionable
SOCIABLY friendlily
SOCIALLY gregariously
SOCIETAL of society; social in nature
SOCINIAN a polemic theologian
SOCKETED shanked
lw **SOCMANRY** feudal tenure
SOCRATIC (Socrates)
SODA-LIME soda and quicklime
mn **SODALITE** a soda compound
SODALITY comradeship; association
ch **SODAMIDE** ammonia-sodium compound
SODA-SALT baking ingredient
SODDENED saturated; drenched
SOFTBALL rounders; derivative of baseball
SOFTENED mollified; melted; assuaged
SOFTENER mitigator; mollifier
SOFT-EYED compassionate
SOFTLING weakling
SOFTNESS tenderness
SOFT-SHOE light tap-dancing
SOFT-SOAP flattery
cp **SOFTWARE** computer programs, subroutines
bt **SOFT-WOOD** sap-wood
SOILLESS untarnished
SOIL-PIPE drain-pipe
SOLACING consoling; comforting
SOLANDER case for prints
bt **SOLANINE** an alkaloid
md **SOLANOID** potato-shaped
SOLARISM solar myths
SOLARIST mythologist
SOLARIUM suntan parlour
SOLARIZE injure by sun's rays
zo **SOLASTER** starfish
SOLATIUM compensation
bt **SOLDANEL** blue moonwort
SOLDERED cemented
SOLDERER a joiner of metals
SOLDIERY the military
SOLECISM incongruity; impropriety
SOLECIST SOLECIZE, breaches of manners or syntax
SOLEMNLY gravely; formally; staidly
SOLENESS singleness
mn **SOLENITE** fossil razor-shell
tc **SOLENOID** switch based on copper coil
mu **SOLFAISM SOLFAIST**, use of sol-fa for sight-reading songs
SOLIDIFY harden; congeal; petrify
md **SOLIDISM SOLIDIST**, medical theory of diseases
SOLIDITY compactness
SOLITARY lonely; single; remote
SOLITUDE isolation; seclusion
SOLLERET foot armour
lw **SOLONIAN** (Solon, a lawgiver)
SOLSTICE an ecliptic point
SOLUTION release; elucidation
SOLUTIVE loosening
SOLVABLE explainable; resolvable
SOLVENCY all debts payable
zo **SOMACTID** bony fin rod in fish
SOMATISM a doctrine
SOMATIST materialist
SOMATOME homologous segment
SOMBRELY gloomily; darkly; gravely
SOMBRERO broad-brimmed hat (S. Amer.)
SOMBROUS gloomy; sombre; doleful
SOMEBODY more than a nobody
SOMEDEAL in some degree
SOMESUCH similar
SOMETIME formerly; once
SOMEWHAT more or less
SOMEWHEN some time or other
SOMNIFIC inducing sleep; soporific
mu **SONATINA** short sonata
zo **SONG-BIRD** warbler
mu **SONG-BOOK** collection of songs
mu **SONGFORM** ternary; (3 sections)
mu **SONGLESS** not in good voice
mu **SONGSTER** vocalist
SON-IN-LAW daughter's husband
SONOBUOY underwater noise-fixing equipment
mu **SONORITY** resonance
mu **SONOROUS** melodious; audible
SOOTHING pleasing; calming; lulling
SOOTHSAY foretell; augur; predict
SOPHERIM Hebrew scribes
SOPITION lethargy
SOPOROUS drowsy; somnolent
bt **SORALIUM** group of soredia in lichen
ch **SORBITOL** hexahydric alcohol
SORCERER wizard; magician
SORDIDLY ignobly; basely; meanly
bt **SOREDIUM** a brood-bud
SOREHEAD disgruntled person
SORENESS regret; rancour
zo **SORICINE** (shrew-mice)
SORORATE marriage of widower to dead wife's sister
SORORISE be a sister to
SORORITY women's club (Amer. university)
ch **SORPTION** absorption, adsorption, etc.
SORROWED grieved; lamented; wept
SORROWER mourner; repiner
SORTABLE befitting; suitable

SORTMENT assortment; distribution
SOTADEAN satirical and malicious
SOTERIAL about salvation
SOUCHONG black China tea
SOUGHING moaning; sighing
rl **SOUL-BELL** dying funeral bell
SOULLESS dull; spiritless
rl **SOUL-SCOT SOUL-SHOT**, requiem fee
SOUL-SICK morally diseased
SOUND-BOW part of a bell
nt, me **SOUNDING** swinging the lead; determination of sea depths and speed in knots of vessel
SOUR-BALL tart hard spherical sweet
mu **SOURDINE** a muffler; sordet
bt **SOUR-DOCK** sorrel
SOUR-EYED morose
SOURNESS tartness; asperity
SOUR-PUSS a kill-joy
SOUTHERN of the south
as **SOUTHING** of star crossing meridian
SOUTHING maintaining direction towards the south
SOUTHPAW boxer's stance in ring
SOUVENIR memento; relic; keepsake
bt **SOW-BREAD** a tuber
SOW-DRUNK beastly drunk
bt **SOYA-BEAN** protein/oil plant (Manchuria)
SOZZLING getting fuddled
SPACE-AGE era of astronautics
SPACE-BAR typewriter gadget
SPACEMAN astronaut
SPACIOUS vast; roomy; ample; wide
ga **SPADILLE SPADILIO**, ace of spades in ombre and quadrille
SPADROON double-handed sword
SPAGIRIC chemical
SPALLING stonework fragmentation
SPALPEEN scamp; rascal (Ir.)
ar **SPANDREL SPANDRIL**, triangular space beside an arch
md **SPANEMIA** anaemia
SPANGLED glittering
SPANGLER sparkler
SPANIARD an Iberian
SPANKING dashing; open-hand striking
SPANLESS immeasurable
me **SPAN-LONG** 9 inches (22 cm)
SPANNING bridging; extending
SPAN-ROOF roof with eaves
SPARABLE shoe nail
nt **SPAR-DECK** the upper deck
SPARE RIB a piece of pork
SPARGING sprinkling
zo **SPAR-HAWK** sparrow-hawk
SPAR-HUNG (with fluorspar)
SPARKFUL lively; gay
SPARKING playing the gallant
SPARKISH well-dressed; airy
mn **SPARKLER** a diamond
SPARKLET charge of gas
zo **SPARLING** a smelt
SPARRING boxing
SPARSELY thinly; meagrely
SPARSILE scanty; infrequent
bt **SPATHOSE SPATHOUS**, foliated or lamular
zo **SPATHURA** humming-birds
SPAVINED (leg swelling)
SPAWLING slobbering
SPAWNING putting forth eggs
SPEAKING hailing; addressing
SPEARING lancing
SPEARMAN he who spears
cp **SPECIFIC** distinctive; peculiar; particular; absolute address
SPECIFIC qualifier per unit mass for physical property
SPECIMEN sample; type; exemplar
SPECIOUS plausible; ostensible
SPECKING staining
SPECKLED variegated
SPECTRAL ghostly; spooky
SPECTRAL of spectrum or of monochromatic radiation; of separation of wavelengths
SPECTRUM (colour bands); of refracted light waves
SPECULAR reflective
SPECULUM a mirror
SPEEDFUL speedy; hasty; impetuous
SPEEDIER faster; quicker
SPEEDILY with rapidity
SPEEDWAY racing track; specially built light racing vehicles
bt **SPEKBOOM** S. African shrub
SPELDING SPELDRIN, SPELDRON, dried haddock; fish split and dried in the sun
SPELLING charming
SPEND-ALL spendthrift
SPENDING exhausting; squandering
SPERABLE hopeful
bt **SPERGULA** spurry; sandweed
SPERM-OIL whale by-product
bt **SPHAGNUM** bog-moss
zo **SPHECIUS** digger-wasps
SPHENOID wedge-shaped
SPHERICS spherical geometry
SPHEROID almost a sphere
SPHEROME cell-inclusion causing oil globule
SPHERULE small globe
mn **SPHRAGID** ochreous clay

md **SPHYGMIC** pulsative
mu **SPIANATO** smoothed out evenness (It.)
SPICATUM herring-bone work
mu **SPICCATO** rapid detached notes (violin)
SPICE-BOX condiment-holder
SPICEFUL aromatic
bt **SPICKNEL** baldmoney plant
SPICULAR spiky; pointed
bt **SPICULUM** small spike
SPIFFING delightful
bt **SPIGELIA** worm-grass; pink-root
bt **SPIKELET** unit of grass inflorescence
ga **SPILIKIN** spillikin; splinter of wood
SPILLING upsetting; shedding
SPILLWAY overflow
zo **SPILOTES** a snake genus
SPINDLED tapering
mu **SPINETTO** It. spinet (harpsichord type)
bt **SPINIFEX** porcupine grass
md **SPINITIS** spinal fever
SPINNERY spinning mill
SPINNING whirling; twirling
SPINSTER unmarried woman
SPINSTRY spinning industry
zo **SPIRACLE SPIRICLE**, breathing-hole; pore
SPIRALLY whorled
mn **SPIRIFER** fossil brachiopod
SPIRITED sprightly; alert
SPIRITUS aspiration; breathing
SPIRTING spurting; sprinting
SPITBALL illegal pitch in baseball
SPIT-CURL soap-lock
SPITEFUL vindictive; malicious
SPITFIRE fighting aircraft; irascible
SPITTING piercing
SPITTOON a cuspidor; receptacle
SPLASHED spattered
SPLASHER ornamental nameplates
nt **SPLASHER** protecting paddle-box; mudguard
rw **SPLASHER** locomotive driving wheels
SPLATTER to splash
SPLAYING sloping
SPLEENED angered
SPLENDID lustrous; refulgent
md **SPLENIAL** splint-like bone
zo **SPLENIUM** posterior bend of commissure
pl **SPLENIUS** a neck muscle
SPLICING joining; binding
SPLINTER fragment; cleave
SPLITTER separator
SPLOTCHY unevenly daubed
SPLUTTER a bustle; a stir
SPOFFISH fussy; officious
SPOILFUL wasteful; rapacious
SPOILING marring; vitiating
SPOLIARY Roman mortuary
SPOLIATE plunder; pillage
SPOLVERO perforation cartoon technique
SPONDIAC metre of drinking songs (spondees)
bt **SPONDIAS** hog-plums, etc.
pl **SPONDYLE** a vertebra
SPONGING cadging; sorning
SPONSION sponsorship
SPONTOON kind of halberd
SPOOFING bluffing
SPOOKISH ghostly
cp **SPOOLING** winding on reels (cinema), (fishing), (recording)
SPOONFUL a bite
SPOONILY amorously
SPOONING courting
SPORADIC scattered; irregular
zo **SPOROSAC** a gonophore
SPORTFUL frolicsome; jocose
SPORTING generous
SPORTING romping; displaying
SPORTIVE wanton; hilarious
SPOT-BALL billiards
SPOTLESS pure; untainted
pt **SPOTTING** observing; raining; appearance of defect, disease; choosing correct moment to jump (parachuting)
SPOUTING orating; gushing
SPRACHLE SPRACKLE, to clamber up with difficulty
SPRAGGED scotched up
SPRAINED overstrained
SPRAINTS dung of an otter
SPRAWLED straggled; spread
SPRAWLER lounger
SPRAYING atomizing
ag, ce, rw **SPREADER** extender; distributor; disperser; trench strut
SPRIGGED adorned with sprigs
SPRINGAL catapult; youth
SPRINGAR Norw. folkdance
mu, zo **SPRINGER** arch support; ornamental short note; spaniel dog
SPRINKLE bedew; perfuse
SPRINTED speeded; spurted
SPRINTER racer
cp **SPROCKET** a cog; (film); (tape)
SPRUCELY neatly; tidily
SPRUCIFY to smarten
SPRUCING refurbishing
SPRUNTED sprang; sprouted

ce **SPUDDING** lifting potatoes; enlarging hole with piles
SPUNYARN loosely twisted rope
SPUR-GALL wound with a spur
SPUR-GEAR gear wheels
SPURIOUS bastard; faked
SPURLESS without incentive
zo **SPURLING** the smelt
SPURNING disdaining; scouting
SPURRIER spur-maker
SPURRING inciting
SPURRITE carbonate/silicate of calcium
SPURTING gushing
SPURTLED showered
SPY-CRAFT secret service
SPY-GLASS a telescope
SPY-MONEY pay to secret agent
SQUABBED stuffed; crashed
SQUABBLE wrangle; brawl; printing
SQUAB-PIE pigeon-pie
SQUADDED grouped
SQUADRON military grouping
ch **SQUALENE** symmetrical triterpine
SQUALLED yelled; cried
SQUALLER screamer; informer
zo **SQUALOID** like a shark
zo **SQUAMATA** reptile genus
SQUAMATE **SQUAMOID**, scale-like
zo **SQUAMOSE** **SQUAMOUS**, scaly
SQUAMULA **SQUAMULE**, a small scale
SQUANDER dissipate; lavish; fritter
SQUARELY evenly; quadrilaterally
SQUARING adjusting; regulating; resetting; blade turning (rowing)
SQUARISH not quite square
rl **SQUARSON** squire-parson
SQUASHED compressed; squeezed
SQUASHER suppresser
SQUATTED cowered; crouched; sat
SQUATTER settler without title
SQUAWKED squalled
SQUAWMAN transvestite wife (N. Am. Indian)
SQUEAKED shrilled
SQUEAKER informer
SQUEALED squalled
SQUEEGEE rubber mop
SQUEEZED crushed; constricted
SQUEEZER playing card
SQUEGGER self-quenching circuit
SQUIBBED wrangled
SQUIGGLE squirm; wriggle
SQUILGEE squeegee
SQUINTED peered with narrowed/crossed eyes
SQUIREEN a petty squire
SQUIRELY gallantly
SQUIRING escorting
SQUIRMED wriggled
zo **SQUIRREL** plume-tailed rodent
SQUIRTED ejected; gushed
SQUIRTER a syringe
STABBING piercing; thrusting
STABLING accommodation for horses
STABLISH establish
mu **STACCATO** abruptly
STACKING piling
STADDLED supported
STAFFING providing personnel
STAFFMAN right-hand man; assistant
vt **STAG-EVIL** horse disease
zo **STAGGARD** 4-year-old stag
STAGGERS giddiness
bt **STAGHORN** large fern
STAGNANT motionless; inert
STAGNATE become dull
md **STAHLIAN** **STAHLISM**, medical theory
STAINING sullying; discolouring
STAIR-ROD carpet retainer
STAIRWAY a staircase
STAKE-NET fishing net
STALKING approaching prey warily
STALLAGE street traders' stall rent
STALL-FED luxuriously nurtured
STALLING losing speed when flying; to remain motionless (basketball)
zo **STALLION** male horse
STALLMAN stall-holder
STALWART resolute; sturdy; valiant
bt **STAMENED** having stamens
STAMINAL constitutional; vigorous
STAMPEDE panic; rush; flight
STAMPING pounding; impressing
STANCHED staunched; stopped
STANCHER a tourniquet
STANCHLY steadily; staunchly
ce **STANDARD** banner; colours; size; quantity; U-shaped metal casting
STANDARD normal; plant with treelike stem
STANDARD (street or house lamp)
STANDING rank; duration; status; (-order)
STAND-OFF (Rugby football)
STAND-PAT decline to budge
STANHOPE dog-cart
zo **STANK-HEN** moorhen
ch **STANNANE** tin hydride
STANNARY tin mine
ch **STANNATE** a salt
STANNINE a tin alloy
STANNITE sulphostannate of copper/iron
STANNOUS containing tin

STANZAIC (stanzas)
bt **STAPELIA** milkweed plants
STAPLING sorting; binding
STARCHED formal; stiff
STARCHER stiffener
STARCHLY rigidly; punctiliously
STAR-DUST cosmic dust
STARE-CAT over-inquisitive neighbour
zo **STAR-FISH** an echinoderm
STAR-FORT angular redoubt
STAR-GAZE astronomize
STARLESS lacking stars
STAR-LIKE stellate
as **STARLING** small heavenly body
zo **STARLING** ring of piles; bird
zo **STAR-NOSE** N. American mole
STAROSTA Polish noble
STAROSTY life-estate
bt **STAR-REED** Peruvian plant
STARRING taking the lead
ck **STARTERS** introductory meal course
STARTFUL skittish; jumpy
STARTING beginning; (post); (price)
STARTISH nervous; fearful; scared
STARTLED affrighted; dumbfounded
STARTLER a shock; a rouser
STAR-TURN revue or circus act
STARVING famished; hungry
bt **STARWEED** star-shaped plant
bt **STARWORT** aster genus
rl, mu **STASIMON** choral ode
STATABLE declarable; affirmable
STATEDLY regularly
STATICAL in equilibrium; restful
STATUARY sculpture
STATURED full grown
nt **STAYBAND** mast hoop to take stay wires
STAY-BOLT a holdfast
STAY-LACE corset cord
nt **STAYSAIL** triangular upper mainsail (schooner)
STEADIED supported; upheld
STEADILY constantly; firmly
STEADING farm out-houses
STEALING filching; purloining
STEALTHY clandestine; furtive; sly
STEAM-GUN steam-propelled firearm
ck **STEAMING** evaporatng; reeking; cooking
nt **STEAM-TUG** steam-driven boat
STEANING well-shaft lining
zo **STEAPSIN** fat-digesting enzyme
STEARATE a fatty acid
STEARINE tallow; suet; etc.
mn **STEATITE** soapstone
md **STEATOMA** wen or tumour
STEELING hardening; bracing; nerving
STEEL-PEN a nib
STEENING well-shaft lining
STEEPING soaking; macerating
STEEPLED having a thick spire
nt **STEERAGE** third class at sea
STEERING directing; piloting; guiding
STEEVING stowing
zo **STEINBOK** African antelope
STEINGUT lead glazed earthenware (Germ.)
ce **STEINING** process of well-lining
STELLARY starry
STELLATE radiated
zo **STELLION** a lizard
mn **STELLITE** zeolitic mineral
nt **STEM-HEAD** bow-post (forward end)
bt **STEM-LEAF** part of plant
STEMLESS no stalk
STEMMING techniques of stopping and turning (skiing)
zo **STENLOCH** overgrown coalfish
STENOSED contracted
STENOSIS constriction
STEP-DAME step-mother
STEP-GIRL doorstep cleaner
STEPOVER wrestling manoeuvre
STEPPING pacing; working; chorus dancing; (stones); (netball)
STEPWISE photocopying method
zo **STERCOME** faecal matter in sarcodina
bt **STEREOME** mechanical plant tissue
bt **STERIGMA** fungal-spore-bearing hypha
STERLING genuine; pure; pound
nt **STERNAGE** steerage
zo **STERNITE** part of an insect
STERNWAY backward movement
md **STEROIDS** bile acids; vitamin D hormones; saturated hydrocarbons
rl **STIBBLER** clerical locum tenens
STIBNITE antimony compound
mu **STICCADO** xylophone
STICKBOY oddjobs boy (ice hockey)
STICKING adhering; fixing; piercing
STICKJAW toffee
STICKLED interposed; obstructed
STICKLER purist over trifles
STIFF-BIT horse's bit
STIFFISH rather tight
STIFLING suffocating; muffling
rl **STIGMATA** bearing crucifixion marks
ch **STILBENE** S-diphenylethylene
mn **STILBITE** zeolitic mineral
bt **STILBOID** having stalked spore-head

STILETTO small dagger; high heel
br **STILLAGE** cask-storing platform
STILLING calming; distilling; ceramics
STILLION stand for a cask
STIMMUNG tone; atmosphere, mood (Ger.)
STIMULUS spur; incitement; goad
STINGILY parsimoniously; miserly
STINGING pricking; wounding
zo **STING-RAY** a fish
zo **STINKARD** teledu; badger
STINKPOT night-soil pot
STINKPOT grenade; hand-bomb; insult
STINTING limiting; pinching
STIPPLED dotted
STIPPLER engraver
zo, bt **STIPULAR STIPULED**, having pin-feathers; (leaf lobe)
STIRLESS quiescent; still; dull
STIRRING rousing; exciting; lively
STITCHED united; sewn
STITCHEL a hairy wool
STITCHER seamstress
ga **STOCCADE STOCCADO**, thrust in fencing
STOCKADE palisaded defence
STOCKIER stouter built
STOCKILY thickset
STOCKING footwear; storing
STOCKISH stupid; blockish
STOCKIST a tradesman
STOCKMAN herdsman
ck **STOCKPOT** soup, stew of the day
STOICISM imperturbation
STOLIDLY impassively; obtusely
mn **STOLZITE** lead tungstate
md **STOMATIC** mouth medicine
zo **STOMIDIA** disc apertures in actinaria
STONE-BOW (for shooting stones)
zo **STONE-FLY** a lure for trout
mn **STONE-OIL** petroleum
STONEPIT quarry
STOOGERY clownish fraudulence
STOOKING corn gathering
STOOLING ramifying
STOOMING fermenting
STOOPING condescending; bending
STOP-BATH developing accessory
STOP-BUTT safety bank behind targets
pb **STOP-COCK** regulating valve; cistern system
STOP-CODE colours of traffic lights
cp **STOP-CODE** emergency stop signal
STOP-OVER intermediate landing
STOPPAGE a deduction of pay
STOPPING a filling; checking
STOPPLED corked
ga **STOP-SHOT** stroke in croquet, snooker
rw **STOP-TIME** deceleration time (trains)
STORABLE tolerates being stored
STORMILY angrily; tempestuously
STORMING assaulting; ranting
STORYING narrating
md **STOVAINE** an anaesthetic
nt **STOWAWAY** secret passenger
STOWDOWN arrange cargo
STRADDLE bracket; striddle
STRAGGLE stray; digress; wander
STRAIGHT direct; honest; upright
STRAINED stressed; exerted; taxed
STRAINER a filter; percolator
STRAITEN confine; perplex; constrict
STRAITLY narrowly; closely
bt **STRAMMEL** straw
STRANDED driven ashore; aground
STRANGER odder; quainter; alien
STRANGLE choke; suppress; smother
STRAP-OIL a thrashing
STRAPPED secured; stropped
STRAPPER harness-maker
STRATEGY military art
STRATIFY laminate (plywood)
bt **STRATOSE** of well-defined layers
STRATULA thin rock layer
STRAW-HAT Panama headgear
STRAYING roving; deviating; erring
STREAKED variegated; striped
STREAKER dare-naked runner
STREAMED flowed; poured; gushed
STREAMER a pennant; wind-drift indicator (parachuting)
STREAMER ecliptic corona; wet fly (angling)
STRELITZ Muscovite militia-man
STRENGTH power; vigour; might
STREPENT noisy; strident
zo **STREPERA** crow-shrikes
STREPHON love-sick swain
STRESSED emphasized; accented
STRESSOR factor of stress
STRETCHY elastic
STREWING scattering; broadcasting
STRIATED furrowed; streaked
md **STRIATUM** brain ganglion
STRICKEN afflicted; smitten; struck
STRICKLE a template
STRICTLY exactly; literally; severely
STRIDDEN strode
STRIDDLE straddle; bracket
STRIDENT harsh; grating; creaking
STRIDING bestriding; stalking
STRIGATE striped; variegated

STRIGGED with fruit stalks removed
zo **STRIGINE** owl-like
zo **STRIGOPS** owl-parrots
bt **STRIGOSE STRIGOUS**, bristly; setous; aciform; setiform
bd **STRIKING** impressive; forcible; breaking camp; removal of support structure
mu **STRINGED** (rackets; billiards)
STRINGER horizontal tie rod; binder; surfboard slat
STRINKLE sprinkle sparingly
STRIPING making stripes
STRIP-OFF dismantling; undressing
STRIPPED deprived; naked; fleeced
STRIPPER pillager; peeler; husker
zo **STROBILA** tape-worm
bt **STROBILE** hardened catkin
STROKING (rowing); caressing
STROLLED sauntered; wandered
STROLLER actor; vagrant
zo **STROMBUS** wing-shells, etc.
STRONGLY forcibly; mightily
ch **STRONTIA** strontium oxide
mu **STROPHIC** choral ode for turning chorus (Gr.)
STROPPED (razors) sharpened
tc **STROWGER** relay selectors in telephone exchanges
STRUGGLE wrestle; strive; contend
mu **STRUMMED** vamped
bt **STRUMOSE** with cushion-like swellings
md **STRUMOUS** scrofulous
STRUMPET trollop; fly-by-night
zo **STRUTHIO** ostrich genus
STRUTTED braced
STRUTTER proud walker
STUBBING uprooting
STUBBLED bristly
STUBBORN refactory; wilful; perverse
STUB-IRON (used for gun-barrels)
STUB-NAIL short thick nail (boots)
STUCCOED plastered
STUDBOLT headless bolt
STUD-BOOK pedigree book
STUDDING putting in studs
STUD-FARM (horse breeding)
STUDIOUS diligent; scholarly
zo **STUD-MARE** breeding mare
STUDWORK form of brickwork
STUDYING conning; learning
STUFFING cramming; taxidermy
STULTIFY deaden; dull the mind
STUMBLED tripped; lurched
STUMBLER blunderer
STUMMING fermenting
STUMPING (cricket); nonplussing
STUNDISM STUNDIST, (Russian dissenters)
STUNNING dazing; marvellous
nt **STUNSAIL** studding-sail
STUNTING dwarfing; performing
zo, bt **STUPEOUS** with matted hair
STUPIDLY doltishly; senselessly
STUPRATE to ravish
STURDILY stoutly; stalwartly
zo **STURGEON** caviare fish
zo **STURNOID** (starlings)
SUASIBLE persuasible
SUBACRID pungent
SUBACUTE slightly blunt; dull
SUB-AGENT an underling
SUBAHDAR Indian captain
sv **SUBCHORD** way-measuring chord length
SUB-CLASS subdivision
zo **SUBCOSTA** primary wing vein in insects
SUBCRUST layer between pavement and foundation
SUBDUING overpowering; mastering
SUBDUPLE ratio of one to two
zo **SUBDURAL** under dura mater
SUB-ENTRY subdivision
SUB-EQUAL nearly equal
SUBERATE compound derived from cork
SUBERECT half upright, half nodding
SUBERINE compound derived from cork
bt **SUBEROSE** somewhat gnawed
SUPEROUS corky texture
bd **SUB-FLOOR** basic underfloor; blind or rough floor base
bt **SUB-FLORA** floral division
bd **SUBFRAME** fixing for cladding
zo **SUBGALEA** parastipes in insects
SUB-GENUS subdivision
as **SUB-GIANT** bright star
ce **SUB-GRADE** lower division; original natural road surface; strata
SUB-GROUP subsidiary part
SUB-HUMAN almost human
md **SUBHYOID** under the tongue
zo **SUB-IMAGO** a state of change
zo **SUBIMAGO** stage in mayfly life history
SUB-INDEX index within an index
pr **SUBITISE** not counting dots
SUBLATED taken away
SUB-LEASE an underlet
SUBLIMED exalted
SUBLUNAR under the moon

SUBMERGE plunge; drown; flood
SUBMERSE duck; douse; dive
SUBNASAL under your nose
bt **SUBNODAL** below a node
SUBORDER subdivision; sub-genus
SUBORNED bribed; led astray
SUBORNER perjurer; false witness
SUBOVATE almost egg-shaped
lw **SUBPOENA** writ of attendance
SUBPOLAR adjacent to polar sea
eg **SUBPRESS** die set; punch and die unit
SUBPRIOR prior's deputy
SUBRIGID fairly stiff
SUBSERVE help forward; promote
SUBSIDED sank; abated; waned
SUBSOLAR under the sun
SUBSONIC slower than sound
SUBSTAGE microscopic device
SUBSTYLE line on sundial
SUBSUMED logically included
SUBTENSE chord of an arc
SUBTEPID lukewarm
SUBTITLE secondary title
SUBTLETY cunning; artfulness
mu **SUBTONIC** leading note of scale
SUBTOPIA suburban ideal
SUBTRACT withdraw; deduct; take
SUBTRIBE section of a tribe
SUBTRIST somewhat sad
SUBTUTOR under-master
SUBULATE awl-shaped
SUBURBAN built-up area surrounding a city
SUBURBIA the suburbs
SUBVENED relieved; subsidized
SUBZONAL below the belt
SUCCINCT concise; compact; terse
SUCCINIC derived from amber
rl **SUCCUBUS** night demon; intercourse with the devil
SUCHLIKE in such manner; similar
SUCHWISE in like manner
zo **SUCKERED** arms of an octopus
SUCKLING unweaned child
md **SUDAMINA** sweating fever
SUDANESE (Sudan)
SUDARIUM sweat room of Roman bath
SUDATION perspiration
SUDATORY connected with sweating
SUDDENLY hastily; abruptly; quickly
SUFFERED underwent; allowed; bore
SUFFERER victim; martyr
SUFFICED satisfied; was adequate
SUFFIONI volcanic fumes
SUFFIXED added; subjoined; appended
SUFFLATE inflate; blow up
SUFFRAGE vote; prayers; intercession
SUFFRAGO hock joint
SUFFUSED permeated; overspread
rl **SUFISTIC** (Moslem pantheism)
SUGARING sweetening
SUICIDAL self-destructive
zo **SUILLINE** of the pig family
SUITABLE appropriate; convenient
SUITABLY fittingly; aptly
SUITCASE portable oblong bag
ck **SUKIYAKI** Jap. meat/vegetable dish
SULCATED grooved; furrowed
zo **SULCULUS** siphonoglyph of anthozoa
SULLENLY morosely; gloomily
SULLYING smirching
ch **SULPHATE SULPHITE**, sulphur compounds
ch **SULPHONE** hexavalent sulphur compound
SULPHURY containing sulphur
SULTANIC despotic
SULTANRY Sultan's dominion
cp **SUM-CHECK** digit produced by summation check
SUMERIAN pre-Babylonian
SUMMERED passed the summer
SUMMONED bid; cited; arraigned
SUMMONER invoker; prosecutor
SUMPITAN Malay blow-pipe gun
SUN-BLIND window-shade
SUNBURNT tanned; bronzed
SUNBURST dazzling gleam
SUNCRACK a fissure
SUNDERED parted; severed; broken
SUNDRIED dehydrated
SUNDRIES miscellanea; odds and ends; extras on bill or in scores
SUNLIGHT illumination from Helios
rl **SUNNITES** orthodox Moslems
SUNPRINT photograph
SUNPROOF fadeless
SUNSHADE a parasol
SUNSHINE solar illumination
SUNSHINY sunny
as **SUNSPOTS** regions of cool gas as dark patches
mn **SUNSTONE** feldspar
SUPERADD increase the total
SUPERBLY magnificently; gorgeously
pc **SUPER-EGO** conscience
ro **SUPERHET** (wireless oscillations)
rl **SUPERIOR** senior by rank; (larger, finer than); boss; head of a monastery
SUPERMAN fictional Herculean hero
SUPERNAL celestial; heavenly

SUPERTAX a gross imposition
SUPINATE bring palm upward
SUPINELY inertly; languidly
SUPPLANT displace by intrigue
SUPPLIAL provision; provenance
SUPPLIED bestowed; furnished; gave
SUPPLIER contributor; provider
SUPPOSAL supposition; conjecture
SUPPOSED assumed; opined; imagined
SUPPOSER surmiser; thinker; imaginer
SUPPRESS quell; check; smother
SURBASED (pedestal moulding)
SURCEASE cessation
bt **SURCULUS** a botanical sucker
SURENESS certainty; infallibility
SURETIES sponsors
SURFACED smoothed
zo **SURF-BIRD** plover; sandpiper
nt **SURF-BOAT** shallow-draught boat
zo **SURF-DUCK** the scoter
pc **SURGENCY** hypothesized personality trait
md **SURGICAL** chirurgical
zo **SURICATE** the meercat
SURMISAL surmise; assumption
SURMISED took for granted
SURMISER conjecturer; supposer
SURMOUNT overcome; surpass; scale
zo **SURMULOT** brown rat
SURNAMED having as family name
rl **SURPLICE** linen vestment
SURPRISE shock; bewilder; astound
lw **SURREBUT** rebut a rebuttal
pl **SURRENAL** above the kidneys
SURROUND encircle; hem; beset; loop
ma **SURSOLID** fifth power
SURVEYAL review; scrutiny; prospect
SURVEYED scrutinized; scanned
SURVEYOR inspector; land measurer
SURVIVAL an outliving; relic
SURVIVED outlasted; endured; outlived
SURVIVOR who lives through
SUSPENSE uncertainty; indecision
SUSPIRAL breathing-hole
SUSPIRED sighed
SUSURRUS whispering; muttering; rustling
SUZERAIN paramount ruler
SWABBING mopping
SWADDLED swathed; wrapped
rl **SWADDLER** a Methodist (nickname)
SWADESHI Indian boycott
SWAGGING sagging
SWAGSHOP where trash is sold
SWAINING lovemaking; courting
SWAINISH boorish; rustic
SWAMPING overwhelming; inundating
bt **SWAMP-OAK** semi-tropical tree
mn **SWAMP-ORE** bog-ore
SWAN-HERD tender of swans
SWANKING bragging
SWAN-LIKE as a swan
SWAN-MARK identification mark
bd **SWAN-NECK** curved; S-bend; handrail
zo **SWANNERY** nesting area, home for swan colony
SWANNING moving around aimlessly
SWAN-SHOT buck-shot
SWAN-SKIN soft flannel
SWAN-SONG last act or appearance
SWAPPING bartering
SWARDING turfing
SWARMING (bees, mosquitoes); (crowding)
SWASHING splashing
nv **SWASHWAY** navigable channel
SWASTIKA Nazi emblem; triskele
SWATHING wrapping; binding
SWATTING killing flies
SWEALING melting; singeing
SWEARING profaneness; avowing
SWEATILY laboriously
pt **SWEATING** toiling; extorting; perspiration; separation in paint; gloss
SWEAT-OUT plastic defect due to moisture
SWEEPING comprehensive; extensive
SWEEP-NET fishing gear
to **SWEEP-SAW** curved-cut saw
bt **SWEET-BAY** the tree laurel
bt **SWEET-GUM** a gum tree
bt **SWEETING** sweet apple; dearest one; beloved
SWEETISH rather sweet
SWEET-OIL olive oil
bt **SWEET-PEA** an attractive flower
bt **SWEET-SOP** an evergreen shrub
SWELLDOM fashionable world
SWELLING bombastic; dilating
SWELLISH foppish
SWELL-MOB thieving gang
SWERVING deviating; diverging
SWIFTEST fastest; fleetest
zo **SWIFTLET** (bird's nest soup)
SWIGGING quaffing; drinking
SWILLING rinsing; toping
SWIMMING waterborne mobility knack

SWIMSUIT bathing costume
SWINDLED defrauded; cheated
SWINDLER sharper; trickster
bt **SWINE-OAT** a coarse oat
vt **SWINE-POX** disease of pigs
SWINE-STY a pig-sty
SWINGING vibrating; dangling
SWINGLED flailed
SWINGMAN both guard and forward (baseball)
SWINKING drudging; moiling; toiling
SWIRLING twirling; gyrating; eddying
SWISHING birching; caning; chastising
SWISHING noise of winds, rushing water, dresses
rw **SWITCHED** changed choice, track; shunted
el, cp **SWITCHED** (-on); controlled (flow of electricity, traffic etc.)
SWITCHEL treacle beer
md **SWOONING** fainting; dizziness; a syncope
mu **SWOOPING** descending in a rush (tempo)
SWOPPING exchanging; bartering; (duplicates)
SWORD-ARM right arm
SWORD-CUT a wound
SWORD-LAW violence
SWOTTING studying hard
SYBARITE a voluptuary
SYBOTISM pig culture
bt **SYCAMINE** mulberry tree
bt **SYCAMORE** species of maple
bt **SYCONIUM** figlike fruit
mn **SYENITIC** (syenite)
SYLLABIC in syllables
SYLLABLE to utter
SYLLABUB sillabub; a drink; jelly sweetmeat or glass to hold it
SYLLABUS an abstract; summary; programme of education
SYLPHISH SYLPHINE, fairylike
SYMBATIC of partly-like polymorphism types
SYMBOLIC emblematic; representative
SYMMETRY harmony; regularity
SYMMORPH similar notion
SYMPATHY fellow-feeling; affinity
SYMPHILE guest species among insects
mu **SYMPHONY** unison of sound
zo **SYMPHYLA** an insect genus
cy **SYMPLAST** multinucleate cell variety
SYMPLOCE rhetorical repetition
SYNACRAL (common vertex)
md **SYNALGIA** sympathetic pain
zo **SYNANCIA** fish genus
zo **SYNAPSID** reptile skull condition
zo **SYNAPTIC** of nerve-cell contact
bl **SYNAPTON** model imitating living matter
SYNARCHY joint rule
SYNASTRY stellar coincidence
SYNCLINE geological basin
mu **SYNCOPAL SYNCOPIC**, syncopation rhythm
cy **SYNDESIS** fusion of chromosomes
SYNDETIC linking together
md **SYNDROME** concurrence; illness (AIDS)
md **SYNECHIA** an eye-disease
SYNEDRAL (angularity)
zo **SYNERGIC** working together
lw **SYNGRAPH** signed deed
md **SYNOCHAL** feverish
rl **SYNODIST** member, attender at Synod
SYNOMOSY sworn brotherhood
SYNONYME SYNONOMY, alternative word with similar meaning
SYNOPSIS abstract; short outline
SYNOPTIC comprehensive
md **SYNOVIAL** (synovia)
SYNTAXIS syntax; grammar; mode of thinking; expression
md **SYNTEXIS** emaciation
pc **SYNTONIA** reactiveness to environment, surroundings
mu **SYNTONIC** intense sharp
md **SYNTONIN** acid albumin
SYPHERED flush jointed
md **SYPHILIS** sex-transmitted venereal disease
rl **SYRIARCH** a chief priest
md **SYRIGMUS** noises in the ear
SYSTASIS political union
md **SYSTEMIC** pertaining to the system
SYSTOLIC contractive
SYZYGANT (quadratic function)
SZLACHTA Polish landowner

T

hd **TABARDER** a herald
mn **TABASHIR** mostly silica
tx **TABBINET** damask-like fabric
zo **TABBY-CAT** a mouser
tx **TABBYING** watered fabric process
md **TABITUDE** emaciation; atrophy
TABLEAUX theatrical pageants (Fr.)
TABLE-CUT flat-faced

TABLEDEX co-ordinate book index for computers
TABLEFUL filling a table
TABLEMAT plate underlay
ar **TABLINUM** room by atrium (Roman)
TABOOING prohibiting; banning
mu **TABORINE** tabor; tambourine
mu **TABORING** drumming
rl **TABORITE** extreme Hussite
tx **TABOURET** embroidery frame; drum shaped stool
cp **TABULATE** enumerate; classify; list; group totals for items
bt **TACAHOUT** a leaf gall
TAC-AU-TAC (fencing)
pt **TACHISME** spilling, smearing painting technique
el **TACITRON** type of thyratron
TACITURN mute; reticent; silent
TACKLING harnessing; dealing with; challenging (football)
pr **TACKMARK** dot(s) used in 'work and turn' system
TACTICAL strategic
TACTLESS insensitive; indiscreet
zo **TAENIDIA** thickenings of eudotrachea
TAENIOID ribbonlike
nt **TAFFRAIL** tatereel; stern-rail
ch **TAGILITE** copper phosphate
zo **TAGMOSIS** grouping of somites
TAIGLING entangling
TAILBACK retreating (Am. football)
TAILBACK long queue; dawdling cars on holiday
pr **TAILBAND** decorative back-cover band
TAIL-BOOM an aeroplane spar
TAILCOAT formal jacket
TAIL-EDGE lower edge
mu **TAILGATE** trombone technique
TAILINGS mining refuse
TAILLESS Manx; without end
TAILORED cut to figure
TAILRACE (mill stream)
TAILROPE guide-rope
TAINTING corrupting; sullying
TAINTURE taint; stain; blot
cp **TAKE-DOWN** dismantle prior to next job; hold after fall-back (wrestling)
TAKE-DOWN order to secretary; disrobe
TAKE-OVER acquire control
TAKER-OFF mimic; quantity surveyor
TAKINGLY captivatingly; winningly
cy **TALANDIC** of rhythmic changes in cell
rl **TALAPOIN** Buddhist monk
TALENTED accomplished; gifted
TALESMAN a juror
TALISMAN charm; amulet
TALKABLE conversable
ae, ro **TALK-DOWN** landing technique
TALLNESS height; loftiness
TALLOWED fattened; of candle wax
TALLOWER tallow-chandler
TALLYING recording; agreeing
TALLYMAN pedlar
rl **TALMUDIC** (the Talmud)
zo **TAMANDUA** **TAMANOIR**, arboreal ant-eater
bt **TAMARACK** American larch
bt **TAMARIND** tropical tree
bt **TAMARISK** evergreen shrub
TAMEABLE submissive; docile
TAMELESS intractable; wild
TAMENESS dullness; monotony
TAMPERED interfered; machinated
TAMPERER meddler; schemer; plotter
TANAISTE deputy premier (Irish)
TAN-BALLS (refuse bark)
TANGENCY **TANGENCE**, state of contact
TANGIBLE tactile; positive; corporeal
TANGIBLY palpably; obviously
TANGLING complicating; matting
TAN-HOUSE tan-bark store
lw **TANISTRY** Irish land tenure
le **TANNABLE** able to be cured
TANNADAR Indian policeman
TAN-STOVE used for tan-bark
ch **TANTALUM** metallic element
TANTALUS spirit-stand
zo **TANTICLE** stickleback
TANTRISM Indian doctrine
TANTRIST a devotee
TANZIMAT Turkish reform bill
TAPADERA leather stirrup guard
TAP-DANCE toe-tapping dance
TAPE-LINE tape measure
TAPERING slightly conical; pointed
TAPESTRY woven work
zo **TAPEWORM** a parasite
zo **TAPIROID** like the tapirs (S. America)
bt **TARA-FERN** bracken (NZ)
TAR-BLACK coal-tar product for earthed posts
TARBOOSH a fez; red hat (Moslem)
TARGETED aimed on target guns
rl **TARGUMIC** (Bible in Aramaic)
TARIFFED dutiable; taxed
tx **TARLATAN** muslin; tarletan
mu **TAROGATO** **TARAGOT**, Transylvanian clarinet

TARPEIAN (Roman rock)
bt **TARRAGON** savoury herb
TARRYING awaiting; loitering; halting
zo **TARSIPED** kangaroo-footed
zo **TARSIPES** small marsupial
ck **TARTARIC** wine incrustation; (-acid), sauce ingredient
ck **TARTARIN** carboxylic acid (food, medicines)
ch **TARTARUM** compound of above
TARTARUS sunless abyss
TARTNESS sharpness; piquancy
ch **TARTRATE** a tartar salt
TARTUFFE a hypocrite
ce **TARVIATE** of tar/stone surfacings
md **TAR-WATER** an infusion
TASKWORK piece-work
TASTABLE savoury; palatable
TASTE-BUD sensory bud on tongue
TASTEFUL discriminative; elegant
TATTERED in rags; rent
TATTLERY idle gossip
TATTLING chatting; prattling
TATTOOER TATTOOED, skin artist
TAUNTING deriding; flouting; reviling
TAUROCOL bull's glue
TAUTENED tightened; stretched
TAUTNESS strain; tenseness
TAVERNER inn-keeper
TAWDRILY gaudily; garishly; flashily
TAXATION imposition; levy; toll
TAXIARCH Greek commander
TAXIRANK cab queue
bt **TAXODIUM** swamp-cyprus
TAXOLOGY TAXONOMY, classification
TAXPAYER one liable for taxation
TEA-BOARD tea-tray
TEA-BREAK refreshment pause (industrial)
TEA-CADDY small tea box
TEA-CHEST box of tea
TEACHING instructing; enlightening; explaining
cp **TEACHING** hardware for storage; display, response
TEA-FIGHT a bun-worry
TEA-HOUSE oriental pleasure dome
TEAMSTER waggoner; drayman
TEAMWISE harnessed together
TEAMWORK cooperation
TEA-PARTY (Boston 1773)
TEA-PLANT source of tea
TEARDROP a tear
md **TEARDUCT** lachrymal duct
TEARLESS unfeeling
TEA-SPOON kitchen measurement
TEA-TABLE where tea is served
TEATHING fertilizing
TEA-TOWEL towel for drying dishes
TECHNICS doctrine of arts
zo **TECTARIA** shellfish
TECTONIC constructive
ar, gl **TECTONIC** of roofing, folds, faults
TEENAGER youngster
TEETHING dentition
TEETOTAL abstinence from alcohol; dry
TEETOTUM small top
pl **TEGUMENT** the skin
zo **TEGUMERE** portion of tegumant in somite
TELALGIA distant pain
TELAMONE carved male figure as support
zo **TELARIAN** web-spinner spider
bt **TELEBLEM** membrane of hyphae in agarics
TELECAST televised
TELECINE TV cine film projector
TELEFILM television film
TELEGONY hereditary influence
tc **TELEGRAM** a wire, cablegram message
TELEMARK ski turn on slope; paddle stroke (canoe)
bl **TELEOSIS** purposive development
TELESTIC ending
tv, tc **TELETEXT** graphics, documents sent by television system
TELETRON TV cathode ray tube
TELETYPE teleprint (Telex)
tv **TELEVIEW** watch television programmes
tv **TELEVISE** to broadcast
ar, bd **TELLTALE** revealer; indicator; earthquake indicator; glass in shifting wall; sneak; tin (squash rackets)
TELLURAL earthy
ch **TELLURIC** (tellurium)
TELONISM last letters of author's name; pseudonym
TELOOGOO Dravidian dialect
TELOTYPE printed telegram
TEMERITY rashness; audacity
TEMEROUS reckless; bold; foolhardy
TEMPERED toughened; moderated
cp **TEMPLATE** a pattern; a jig; similar pattern identifier
pl, md **TEMPORAL** secular; transient; of cortex area of the temples; of the head; of time
TEMPTING alluring; inveigling
TENACITY adhesiveness; cohesion

TENAILLE a rampart
TENANTED occupied; dwelt
TENANTRY the tenants
TENDANCE attendance; care; attention
TENDENCY bias; drift; inclination
TENDERED offered; estimated
TENDERLY leniently; gently; softly
rl **TENEBRAE** shades; R.C. evening service
TENEMENT a flat or house-block
TENESMUS ineffectual evacuation straining
TENONING mortising
to **TENON-SAW** metal-backed saw
mu **TENORIST** a tenor
mn **TENORITE** oxide of copper
md **TENOTOMY** tendon-cutting
TENSIBLE tensile; ductile
zo **TENTACLE** a feeler
TENTERED stretched
zo **TENTILLA** branches of a tentacle
TENTWORK embroidery
bt **TENTWORT** a fern
TEOCALLI Mexican temple
TEPEFIED warmed up
mn **TEPHRITE** andesite
TEPIDITY lukewarmness
TERAPHIM Hebrew idols
TERATISM being a foetal monstrosity
TERATOMA foetal tumour
ch **TEREBENE** (turpentine)
zo **TEREDINE** teredo; boring worm
zo **TERGETIC** dorsal
TERMATIC an artery
bt, md, tel, cp **TERMINAL** binding screw; oil-; air-; end of line; (illness); growing point
TERMINAL telephone; tele printer, (plug)
lw **TERMINER** a determination
rw **TERMINUS** the end of a line
TERMLESS boundless; openness
TERRACED having or being in terraces
zo **TERRAPIN** tortoise
bd **TERRAZZO** mosaic in cement; terrace
TERRIBLE formidable; dire; gruesome
TERRIBLY frightfully; awfully
TERRIFIC horrific; dreadful
TERTIARY third in order
TERTIATE triplicate
TERYLENE man-made cloth
mu **TERZETTO** a trio
TESSELLA TESSERAE, small tiles for paving
TESSERAL tesselated; tiled
TESSULAR like dice; cubes
lw **TESTABLE** can be proved; bequeathable
zo **TESTACEA** animals with shells
zo **TESTACEL** a little shell
lw **TESTAMUR** a certificate
lw **TESTATOR** will-maker; devisor
lw **TESTCASE** sample legal decision
pl **TESTICLE** male gonad
ch **TESTTUBE** laboratory vessel
TESTWISE by testing; test experience
md **TETANISE** cause spasms (tetany)
TETANOID convulsive
TETCHILY peevishly; testily
TETHERED restricted; tied; fastened
ch **TETRADIC** fourfold
TETRAGON quadrangle
ch **TETRALIN** organic solvent
rl **TETRAPLA** Bible in four versions
TETRAPOD four-footed
TETRARCH Roman governor
bt **TETRARCH** with 4 xylem strands
zo **TETRAXON** having 4 axes
pm **TETRONAL** hypnotic/sedative drug
TEUTONIC Germanic
TEXT-BOOK a manual
TEXT-HAND large script
tx, wv **TEXTRINE** textile
pr **TEXT-TYPE** type for bookprinting
TEXTUARY authoritative
rl **TEXTUIST** text reciter
bt **THALAMIA** layers of cells
pl **THALAMIC** of the brain
THALAMUS an inner room; brain
ch **THALLIUM** metallic element
rl **THANATOS** god of death (Gr.) (instinct)
THANEDOM thane's jurisdiction; earldom
THANKFUL grateful; beholden
THANKING acknowledging gratefully
THATCHED covered with straw
THATCHER straw-roof craftsman
rl **THEARCHY** theocracy; priestly government
THEIFORM like tea
THEMATIC dissertative
THEOCRAT divine ruler
THEODICY a philosophy
THEOGONY (genesis of the gods)
rl **THEOLOGY** divinity
THEORIES speculations; hypothesis
THEORIST conjecturer
THEORIZE postulate
THEOSOPH inspired person
THERBLIG division of movement
THEREFOR for that purpose
mu **THEREMIN** electronic instrument

THEREOUT therefrom
md **THERIACA** an opiate
THERMALS reflected solar heat; ascending air currents (gliding)
ps **THERMION** ion from incandescent matter
ch **THERMITE** incendiary mixture
THESPIAN of acting (trouper)
THEURGIC magical
THEWLESS weak; frail; feeble
ch **THIAMIDE** amide compound
THIAMINE vitamin B-1
ch **THIAZINE** heterocyclic compound
ch **THIAZOLE** pyridine-like liquid
THICKEST densest; closest
THICKISH rather thick
zo **THICKNEE** the stone curlew
THICKSET closely planted; heavily built (human)
THIEVERY larceny
THIEVING purloining; filching
THIEVISH sly; stealthy
THIGGING begging
cp **THIN FILM** glass-plate memory storage
THINGAMY thingumabob; whatsitsname
THINKING ruminating; cogitating
THINNESS attenuation; emaciation
THINNEST lankiest; leanest
THINNING reducing; diminishing
THINNISH meagre; spare
ch **THIO-ACID** hydroxyl-replaced acid
THIOCTIC lipoic acid
ch **THIOPHEN** coal-tar constituent
ch **THIOPHIL** with affinity for sulphur
ch **THIOUREA** thiocarbamide; bismuth reagent
lw **THIRLAGE** milling rights
THIRSTED craved; yearned; longed
THIRTEEN the baker's dozen
THISNESS individuality
md **THLIPSIS** compression
THOLE-PIN rowlock
rl **THOMEANS** Malabar Christians
THORACIC (thorax)
zo **THORNBUT** turbot
bt **THORNSET** beset with thorns
THOROUGH complete; perfect
THOUSAND M; mille
THRALDOM slavery; bondage
nt **THRANITE** trireme rower
zo **THRAPPLE** windpipe; thropple
THRASHED drubbed
zo **THRASHER** fox-shark; thrush
THREADED strung on a line; sewn
THREADEN made of thread
THREADER loom-shuttle worker
THREATEN menace; intimidate
bd **THREE-PLY** threefold; triple; treble; of wooden sheets
mu **THRENODY THRENODE**, lamentation for the dead (Fr.)
ag **THRESHED** beat out grain; (-out), discussed
THRESHEL a flail for harvesting
zo **THRESHER** mocking-bird
THRESTLE three-legged stool
THRIDACE lettuce juice
THRILLED agitated; stirred; excited
THRILLER a gripping story
THRIVING flourishing; prospering
THROBBED pulsated; beat; palpitated
md **THROMBIN** blood clotting enzyme
md **THROMBUS** blood-clot
THRONGED crowded; flocked
THRONING enthroning
zo **THROPPLE** windpipe; thrapple
zo **THROSTLE** missel thrush
THROTTLE garrote; strangle; stifle
THROWING casting; hurling; slinging
THROW-OUT rejected product
THRUMMED strummed
mu **THRUMMER** vamper
THRUSTED intruded; drove; pushed
THRUSTER reckless rider
THUDDING reverberating
THUGGERY THUGGISM, brutality; violence; criminal assault
THUMBING fingering
THUMB-NUT screwed by hand
THUMBPOT small flower pot
THUMPING enormous
THUNDERY gloomy; frowning
rl **THURIBLE** incense censer
rl **THURIFER** incense bearer
THURSDAY one of the weedays
THUSWISE like so
THWACKED thumped; belaboured
THWARTED frustrated; balked
THWARTER obstructionist
ch **THYROXIN** hormone; iodine containing amino acid
THYRSOID (Bacchus's ivied staff)
md **TIBIALIS** tibial muscle
TICK-BEAN horse bean
TICKETED labelled
TICKLING titillation of the body
TICKLISH sensitive to such touch; critical
bt **TICK-SEED** coreopsis
TICK-SHOP (goods on credit)
TICK-TACK signalling system (racing)
TICK-TICK TICK-TOCK, watch or clock

nt **TIDEGATE** **TIDE-LOCK**, dock
TIDELESS not rising/falling
TIDEMARK low or high water border
TIDEMILL sea-operated mill
TIDESMAN customs officer
TIDE-WAVE tidal wave
TIDINESS neatness; trimness
ga **TIE-BREAK** extra play for winning points; (sports finals, matches)
TIED-DOWN involved; restricted; busy
bt **TIGELLUM** first bud on a stem
bt **TIGELLUS** an internode
zo **TIGER-CAT** margay; ocelot
TIGERISH ferocious
TIGERISM voracity
TIGHT-WAD a miser
TILE-KILN tile factory
TILLABLE arable; cultivable
TILLERED produced offshoots
nt **TILT-BOAT** boat with roof; covered excursion boat, Thames
TILT-YARD jousting place
TIMBERED wooded
TIME-BALL time signal
TIME-BILL timetable
TIME-BOMB explodes by time-fuse
TIME-BOOK works record
TIME-CARD a register
TIME-FUSE time-fuze
TIMELESS untimely
TIME-WORK rate of pay
TIMEWORN decayed; weatherbeaten
TIMIDITY fearfulness; shyness
nt **TIMONEER** helmsman
TIMONIST misanthrope
mu **TIMOROSO** hesitatingly; timidly
TIMOROUS fearful; pusillanimous
md **TINCTURE** tinge; solution
bt **TINE-TARE** the vetch
TINEWALD **TYNEWALD**, Manx Parliament
TINGEING colouring
TINGLING thrilling
TINGLISH sensation
hr **TING-TANG** two-note clock
TINKERED botched
TINKERLY clumsily
TINKLING clinking
md **TINNITUS** ringing in the ears
TINPLATE covered in tin
TINSELLY tawdry
TINSMITH tin worker
mn **TINSTONE** cassiterite
mn **TINSTUFF** tin ore
TINTAMAR confused noise
TINTLESS colourless
pr **TIPPED-IN** inserted by use of gum
TIPPLING drinking to excess; toping; soaking
lw **TIPSTAFF** court officer
zo **TIPULARY** (crane-flies)
TIRELESS inexhaustible
TIRESOME tedious; fretful
TIRONIAN (Roman shorthand)
TISSUING interweaving soft material (paper)
TITANESS giantess
ch **TITANIAN** (titanium)
mn **TITANITE** sphene
rl **TITHABLE** subject to tithes
TITHONIC actinic
TITIVATE smarten oneself up to impress
pr **TITLE-CUT** title-page woodcut decoration
zo **TITMOUSE** a small bird
ch **TITRATED** solution added from burette
ga **TIT-TAT-TO** a game; criss-cross
TITTERED giggled
zo **TITTEREL** whimbrel; curlew
TITTERER sniggerer
TITTUPPY frisky; lively
TITUBANT stumbling
TITUBATE stagger
TITULARY nominal; titular
TIVERING marking sheep
ga **TLACHTLI** Mexican court game like baseball
zo **TOAD-FISH** the sapo
bt **TOAD-FLAX** snapdragon
bt **TOAD-PIPE** a horsetail
TOAD-SPIT cuckoo-spit
TOADYING fawning
TOADYISH sycophantic
TOADYISM obsequiousness
TOBOGGAN (toboggin; taboggin) long light sled for snow transport
md **TOCOLOGY** obstetrics
TODDLING strolling aimlessly
TOGETHER in unison
TOHU-BOHU desolation; confusion; chaos; (Heb.)
TOILETTE ceremonial wear (Fr.)
TOILLESS workless
TOILSOME arduous; laborious
TOILWORN fatigued; tired; weary
md **TOKOLOGY** tocology
bt **TOKONOMA** flower alcove in a house (Jap.)
TOLBOOTH a toll-booth
TOLERANT forbearing; liberal
TOLERATE suffer; brook
TOLEWARE japanning on tinplate (Amer.)

me **TOLL-DISH** (used in mills)
TOLLETAN of Toledo wares (swords) (steel)
TOLL-GATE high-road entry fees office
TOLTECAN early Mexican
TOMAHAWK war hatchet (of N. Am. Indians)
zo **TOMALLEY** lobster-liver
bt **TOMATOES** love apples
TOMBLESS no tomb
md **TOMENTUM** a downy covering
to **TOMMY-BAR** small lever
TOMMY-GUN a handy weapon
TOMMY-ROT balderdash; nonsense
zo **TOM-NODDY** puffin; a dolt
md **TOMOGRAM** X-ray photograph
TOMORROW the following day
TOMUNDAR Baluchi chief
mn **TONALITE** ingeous rock
mu **TONALITY** pitch
TONE-DEAF unmusical
TONELESS unmusical
nt **TONGKANG** ketch; lighter; (Singapore)
TONGUING barking; licking
md **TONICITY** healthiness; possessing tone
mu **TONOTOPY** concerning pitch of a tone
md **TONSILAR** (tonsils)
rl **TONSURED** clerical; shaven
bt **TOONWOOD** Indian red wood
TOOTHFUL a short drink
ar **TOOTHING** decorative indenting of bricks
md **TOOTH-KEY** forceps
mu **TOOTLING** playing the flute
TOPARCHY small state control
TOPAZINE (topaz)
TOP-BOOTS longish boots
ag **TOP-DRESS** to manure
TOP-HEAVY tipsy; ill-proportioned
TOP-LEVEL **TOPNOTCH**, excellent
TOP-LOFTY bombastic
ma, pc **TOPOLOGY** of distorted space; a child's outlook
TOPOLOGY an aid to memory
TOPONOMY **TOPONYMY**, topical terminology
zo **TOPOTYPE** specimen from original locality
TOPPLING falling
TOP-PROUD very proud
zo **TOP-SHELL** a mollusc
nt **TOPSIDES** above waterline; upper works of ship
TOP-STONE a finial

TORCHERE ornamental lampstand
TORCHING night fishing
md **TORCULAR** a tourniquet
TOREADOR bullfighter
TOREUTES an artist in metal
TOREUTIC chased metalwork
md **TORMINAL** colicky
mt **TORNADIC** (tornadoes); very stormy
zo **TORNARIA** larval form of balanoglossida
nt **TOROIDAL** like an anchor-ring
TOROSITY muscularity
zo **TOR-OUZEL** the ring-ousel
TORPIDLY apathetically; dully
TORQUATE collared
TORSHENT youngest child (USA)
ck **TORTILLA** maize cake; omelette (Sp.)
lw **TORTIOUS** injurious
zo **TORTOISE** terrapin
TORTUOSE **TORTUOUS**, twisted; winding; wreathed; deceitful
TORTURED agonized; racked
TORTURER tormentor
TORULOID **TORULOSE**, somewhat cylindrical
TOTALITY full amount; sum
ma **TOTALIZE** to tote; to add up
rl **TOTEMISM** of creatures depicting family or clan
TOTITIVE (no common factor)
TOTTERED reeled; staggered
TOUCHILY peevishly; petulantly
TOUCHING concerning; pathetic
TOUCHPAN priming pan
TOUGHEST most stubborn
TOUGHISH stiffish; leathery
TOURELLE slender tower
TOURNURE turn; contour; curver
TOUSLING ruffing; rumpling
TOWARDLY toward; docile; tractile
TOWERING soaring; mounting
TOWN-HALL council offices
TOWNLAND a township
TOWNLESS without a town
TOWNSHIP a municipality
TOWNSMAN urbanite
TOWN-TALK local gossip
md **TOXAEMIA** blood-poisoning
TOXICANT poisonous
TOXICITY poisonousness
TOYISHLY playfully
pl **TRACHEAL** **TRACHEAN**, (windpipe)
md **TRACHOMA** eye disease
mn **TRACHYTE** volcanic rock
TRACKAGE towing; traction
ce **TRACKING** spooring; trailing; liner of surface ways; horizontal progress during free fall (parachuting)

TRACKMAN (railroad track)
TRACKWAY path or open road
TRACTATE a treatise; a tract
TRACTILE ductile; tractable
TRACTION attraction; towage; hauling
TRACTIVE pulling
TRACTORY drawing; pulling
TRACTRIX geometrical curve
TRADEFUL commercial
TRADITOR traitor; quisling; renegade
TRADUCED defamed; slandered
TRADUCER calumniator; libeller
TRAGICAL calamitous; disastrous
zo **TRAGOPAN** Chinese pheasant
TRAGSITZ suspended alpine rescue stretcher (Ger.)
TRAILING hauling; dragging
TRAIL-NET a trawl
TRAINING drilling; schooling
rw **TRAIN-OIL** railway lubricant
TRAIPSED trudged to little purpose
TRAKENER cross country obstacle (steeple-chasing)
TRAMPING trudging; hiking
TRAMPLED trod under foot
TRAMPLER grape-treader
rw **TRAMROAD** tramway
pc **TRANCING** of semi-conscious; visions; ecstasy
TRANGRAM trinket; souvenir; knick-knack
TRANQUIL placid; calm; serene
TRANSACT negotiate; conduct; enact
bt **TRANSECT** belt of vegetation for study
ar, rl **TRANSEPT** cross-aisle; (church)
TRANSFER make over; exchange; send; move across
cp **TRANSFER** convey; copy; control; data; peripheral
TRANSFIX penetrate; perforate; impale
TRANSHIP change conveyance
TRANSIRE customs pass
TRANSMIT despatch; forward; remit; broadcast
cp **TRANSMIT** send data, information to other location
TRANSOME **TRANSOM**, cross beam; fanlight
TRANSUDE to sweat
tc **TRANSVAR** power-transfer coupler
ga **TRAP-BALL** an old game
TRAP-DOOR door in the floor
TRAPESED traipsèd; tramped
TRAPEZIA trapeziums
TRAP-FALL a trap
mn **TRAPPEAN** (traprock)
TRAPPING snaring
rl **TRAPPIST** Cistercian monk
mn **TRAPPOUS** like traprock
gl **TRAP-TUFA** **TRAP-TUFF**, igneous rock
TRASHERY rubbish; balderdash
TRASHILY in a rubbishy way
zo **TRASLING** freshwater perch
mu **TRAVERSA** **TRAVERSO**, transverse flute (It.)
TRAVERSE crossing or lateral movement; grid survey
TRAVERSE sideways or diagonal climb (mountaineering)
TRAVESTY a burlesque; parody; (of sex)
TRAWLING fishing towing a submerged net
ga **TRAY-TRIP** a draughts game
TREACLED (moth catching)
TREADING trampling; pacing; stepping
TREADLED **TREADLER**, pedalled; bicyclist
TREASURE preserve; hoard; garner
TREASURY money/gold office; repository
TREATING entertaining; dealing
TREATISE written discourse; essay
TREBLING doing 3-fold
TRECENTO 14th-century Italian art
TREE-CALF leather binding
zo **TREE-CRAB** (lives on coconuts)
zo **TREE-DOVE** Indian pigeon
bt **TREE-FERN** tropical fern
zo **TREE-FROG** many species
TREELESS lacking forest cover
TREE-NAIL long wooden pin
TREKKING migrating; hiking
mu **TREMANDO** tremulously
zo **TREMATIC** of gill-clefts
TREMBLED quivered; shook; quaked
TREMBLER vibrator; oscillator
bt **TREMLELA** jelly-like fungi
TRENCHED encroached; furrowed
TRENCHER wooden platter
TRENDING inclining; tending
md **TREPHINE** cutting tool
bl **TREPHONE** cell-breakdown substance
cy **TREPTION** environment-change response
TRESPASS sin; walk on others' land
TRESPOLO spindly three-legged table (It.)
hd **TRESSURE** heraldic border
tx **TREVETTE** loop-pile wire knife
TREWSMAN (wearing trews)
TRIADIST composer of triads

TRIALISM (body, soul and spirit)
TRIALITY threeness
ma, mu **TRIANGLE** flogging frame; three-sided figure; metal percussion
ar, rl **TRIAPSAL** church with three apses
TRIARCHY rule of three
TRIARIAN of the third rank
gl, mn **TRIASSIC** geological formation; era
cy **TRIASTER** mitobic figure
TRIAXIAL having three axes
ch **TRIAZOLE** heterocyclic compound
ch **TRIBASIC** with three hydrogen atoms
TRIBELET a small tribe
zo **TRIBONYX** genus of water-hens
TRIBRACH three short syllables
TRIBUNAL court of justice
TRIBUTED contributed
TRIBUTER piece-work miner
md **TRICHINA** parasitic worm
mn **TRICHITE** hairlike fibre
zo **TRICHODA** hairy infusoria
zo **TRICHOID** hairlike
md **TRICHOMA** hair disease
bt **TRICHOME** hairy outgrowth
mu **TRICHORD** three-stringed lyre
TRICKERY chicanery; deception
TRICKILY artfully; cunningly
TRICKING duping; gulling
TRICKLED oozed; percolated
TRICKLET small rill
TRICKSEY wily; pretty
TRICOLOUR flag of France
TRICORNE three-cornered hat
ga **TRICTRAC** variety of backgammon
TRICYCLE three-wheeled bicycle
zo **TRIDACNA** genus of molluscs
TRIFLING toying; trivial; paltry
TRIGAMMA wing-vein feature in lepidoptera
gn **TRIGENIC** controlled by three genes
TRIGGING stopping; skidding
zo **TRIGLOID** gurnard genus
TRIGLYPH Doric ornamentation
TRIGNESS trimness; neatness
ma **TRIGONAL TRIGONIC**, triangular
ma **TRIGONON** a triangle
TRIGRAPH a triphthong
TRILEMMA (three alternatives)
mu **TRILLING** quavering; warbling
TRILLION million^3 (GB) million^2 (USA)
bt **TRILLIUM** a lily genus
bt **TRILOBED** trilobate
nt **TRIMARAN** racing yacht between two outriggers
ch **TRIMERIC** of 3 times molecular weight
TRIMETER (versification)
ce **TRIMMERS** rib holes for structure
ck **TRIMMING** decorating; adjusting; extra delicacies; (barber)
TRIMNESS neatness; tidiness
TRIMURTI Hindu Trinity
zo **TRINGINE TRINGOID**, of sandpipers
TRINODAL treble-jointed
TRINQUET small covered court (pelota)
rl **TRIODION** Greek prayer-book
TRIOLEIN fatty oil
TRIP-BOOK (fishing records)
TRIPEMAN tripeseller
mn **TRIPHANE** spodumene
TRIPLANE an aeroplane
TRIPLING trebling
mn **TRIPLITE** a phosphate
cy **TRIPLOID** with triple chromosomes
TRIPODAL tripedal; three-footed
hd **TRIPPANT** heraldic trotting
TRIPPING lapsing; dancing; felling
TRIP-SLIP tram ticket (USA)
TRIPTANE trimethyl butane
TRIPTOTE having 3 cases only
rl **TRIPTYCH** painted screen
nt **TRIP-WIRE** obstacle; brake
TRISEMIC iambic
TRISKELE swastika
cy **TRISOMIC** of 3-chromosome type
TRISTFUL sorrowful; dejected; doleful
TRITICAL trite; common; hackneyed
TRITICUM wheat, etc.
TRIUMVIR one of three (Rome)
TRIUNITY trinity
TRIVALVE with three valves
TROCHAIC of **TROCHEE** (verse), long and short syllables
zo **TROCHITE** sea-urchin's joint
md **TROCHLEA** a cartilage
TROCHOID cycloid
pc **TROILISM** sexhibitionism
mn **TROILITE** nonmagnetic iron sulphide
TROLLING singing; spinning; towing metal bait (angling)
TROLLOPY slatternly
TROMBLON fire-arm support
mu **TROMBONE** a brass musical wind instrument with slide valve
zo **TROOPIAL** American starling
TROOPING collecting; parading
md **TROPHESY** indigestion
TROPHIES emblems of victory
TROPICAL figurative; fervid
ga **TROTTING** of horse- and sulky-racing
TROTTOIR side-walk (Fr.)
TROUBLED incommoded; vexed

TROUBLER disturber; pest
TROUNCED thrashed; castigated
zo **TROUPIAL** American song-bird
TROUSERS **TROWSERS**, hose; legwear
TROUTING fishing for trout
zo **TROUTLET** small trout
TROUVERE French lyric poet
TRUANTLY lazily; evasively
TRUCKAGE cost of conveyance
TRUCKING bartering; hawking; haulage
TRUCKLED cringed; yielded; stooped
TRUCKLER servile agent
TRUDGEON a swimming stroke
TRUDGING foot-slogging
TRUE-BLUE conservative partisan
TRUE-BORN **TRUE-BRED**, legitimate
bt **TRUE-LOVE** sweetheart; a herb
TRUENESS honesty; accuracy; veracity
TRUMPERY rubbish; trash; trifling
ga **TRUMPING** ruffing; (cards) bridge
bt **TRUNCATE** lop; shorten; reduce; prune
cp **TRUNCATE** suppress insignificant digits
TRUNDLED rolled; bowled; revolved
TRUNDLER barrow-mover; slow bowler
TRUNKFUL enough to fill a trunk
TRUNNION gun support
TRUSSING binding; fastening
TRUSTFUL confiding; trusty
TRUSTILY faithfully; staunchly
TRUSTING relying on; believing
md **TRYPTONE** pancreatic ferment
TRYSTING rendezvousing; meeting
TUBE-FORM tubular
md **TUBERCLE** tumour
bt **TUBEROSE** Mexican lily
bt **TUBEROUS** potato-like growth
TUBE-WELL artesian well
zo **TUBICOLE** caddis-worm
TUBIFORM tubular
zo **TUBIPORE** a coral
pp **TUB-SIZED** dipped and strengthened (handmade paper)
TUBULATE formed of tubes
TUB-WHEEL flat water-wheel
bt **TUCKAHOE** edible fungus
TUCKSHOP sweet-shop
zo **TUCOTUCO** small rodent
TUG-OF-WAR rope sport
ae **TUG-PLANE** gliders
zo **TUKUTUKU** tucotuco; rodent (SA)
TULA-WORK niello work
TUMBLING falling; tripping
TUMEFIED swollen; distended
TUMIDITY bombast; pomposity
TUMOURED distended; enlarged
TUMP-LINE carrying strap
TUMULATE make a barrow
TUMULOSE tumulous; many mounds
TUN-BELLY pot-belly
TUNELESS unharmonious; unmusical
ch **TUNGSTEN** same as wolfram
ch **TUNGSTIC** (tungsten)
zo **TUNICARY** ascidian; sea-squirt
zo **TUNICATE** coated; a mollusc
ro **TUNING-IN** adjusting to listen
TUNISIAN (Tunis)
TURANIAN family of languages
ch **TURANOSE** disaccharide
TURBANED wearing a turban
TURBIDLY disorderly; opaquely
md **TURBINAL** scroll-like bone
ae **TURBO-JET** gas engine
TURCOMAN **TURKOMAN**, Turk of Asia
TURF-CLAD grassy
TURF-MOSS boggy land
TURGIDLY in grossly swollen style
TURLOUGH shallow pool (Irish)
bt, ck **TURMERIC** yellow dye; hot spice; ingredient of curry
zo **TURNAGRA** thrush (NZ)
TURNCOAT renegade
TURNCOCK water-man
TURNDOWN fold down; reject
nt **TURNMARK** logline mark
ck **TURNOVER** a pasty; volume of sales; deliver; transfer
TURNOVER (leaf); generation and loss of cells; running with ball (basketball)
TURNPIKE toll-gate; a road
TURN-SICK giddy
TURN-SKIN a werewolf
bt **TURNSOLE** sunflower
TURNSPIT kitchen-boy
TURRETED having little towers
TUSSOCKY tufty
TUTELAGE guardianship; charge; care
TUTELARY protective
TUTORAGE instruction
TUTORESS governess
TUTORIAL educational
TUTORING teaching
TUTORISM education; coaching
TWADDLED gabbled
TWADDLER tattler; chatter-box
TWEAKING twisting
TWEEDLED fiddled
TWEELING twilling
to **TWEEZERS** forceps
pr **TWELVEMO** 4 times folded for 12 leaves

pr **TWENTYMO** paper folded into 20 leaves
TWIDDLED twisted
TWIDDLER thumb-twirler
TWIGGING understanding
TWILIGHT dusk
TWILLING weaving
pr **TWINBATH** 2-solution processing method
TWIN-BORN contemporaneous
TWINGING twitching
TWINKLED sparkled
TWINKLER a star
zo **TWINLING** twin lamb
tc **TWINPLEX** radio-telegraph system
pr **TWINWARE** paper-holding system for offset
TWIRLING revolving; whirling
TWISTING writhing; contorting
TWITCHED jerked; snatched
TWITCHER angle trowel; involuntary jerker
TWITTING upbraiding; taunting
TWO-EDGED double-cutting
TWO-FACED false; double-dealing
TWO-LAYER twin-ply paper/board
TWOPENNY cheap; worthless
el **TWO-PHASE** with 2 equal alternating voltages
TWO-PIECE costume; suit
TYCHONIC astronomic; (Tycho Brahe)
pl **TYMPANIC** like a drum; middle ear bone
md **TYMPANUM** eardrum
TYNEWALD Manx Parliament
TYPE-CAST single-character actor
TYPE-HIGH standard height
zo **TYPHLOPS** earthworms, etc.
mt **TYPHONIC** cyclonic
TYPIFIED exemplified; symbolized
TYPIFIER prototype
mn **TYPOLITE** fossil footstep
TYPOLOGY types and their classification
TYPORAMA facsimile
ch **TYRAMINE** amino-ethyl benzene
TYROCINY pupilage
TYROLEAN TYROLESE, of Tyrol (the Alps)
mn **TYROLITE** Tyrol sandstone
TYRONISM apprenticeship
ch **TYROSINE** precursor of amino acid
TYRRANIC despotic; autocratic
TYRTAEAN (warlike verse)
TZAREVNA TZARITSA, TSARINA, Empress of Russia

U

UBIQUITY omnipresence
UDOMETER rain gauge
UGLIFIED made hideous
UGLINESS repulsiveness; unsightliness
mn **UINTAITE** variety of natural asphalt
md **ULCERATE** cause or form an ulcer
ULTERIOR remote; hidden; indirect
ULTIMATE furthest; final; eventual
ULTIMITY last consequence
ULTRAISM extreme views
ULTRAIST extremist
ULULATED howled; yowled; lamented
bt **UMBELLAR** form of inflorescence
UMBONATE having a boss
UMBRATIC shadowy; shady; obscure
UMBRELLA a gamp; collapsible shade
zo **UMBRETTE** African heron
UMBRIERE vizor of helmet
UMPIRAGE arbitration; adjudication
UNABASED not degraded; unashamed
UNABATED undiminished; persistent
UNADORED unloved; unvenerated
UNAFRAID bold; valiant; undaunted
UNAIMING purposeless; random
UNALLIED alone; separate; isolated
UNAMAZED composed; unruffled
UNAMUSED not entertained; bored
UNARGUED not disputed
UNATONED not expiated
UNAVOWED unconfessed; secret
UNAWARES suddenly; unexpectedly
UNBACKED unaided; unassisted
UNBAGGED trouserless; let loose
UNBANDED disbanded; disembodied
UNBANNED permitted; unrestricted
UNBARBED unshaven; pointless
UNBARKED stripped of bark
UNBARRED unfastened; opened
UNBATHED untubbed
UNBEATEN untrodden; undefeated
UNBEDDED uprooted
UNBELIEF incredulity; scepticism
UNBENIGN malignant; malevolent
UNBEREFT not bereaved; unspoiled
UNBIASED impartial; unprejudiced
UNBIDDEN spontaneous; unsolicited
rl **UNBISHOP** deprive of a bishopric
UNBLAMED uncensured; unrebuked
UNBLOODY not cruel
UNBOILED raw
UNBOLTED unfastened; unbarred
UNBOUGHT not bribed; incorrupt
UNBOYISH sedate; unchildish

UNBRACED relaxed; unsupported
UNBREECH debag
UNBREWED pure; genuine
UNBRIBED not corrupt
UNBRIDLE free from restraint
UNBROKEN inviolate; continuous
UNBUCKLE unfasten; unclasp
UNBUNDLE unpack
UNBURDEN disclose; reveal
UNBURIED uninterred
UNBURNED uncharred
UNBURROW to ferret out
UNBUSIED free at that moment; unhurried
UNBUTTON unfasten a jacket etc.
UNCAGING releasing; liberating
UNCALLED not awakened
UNCAPPED his cap doffed
UNCARTED unloaded
UNCAUGHT still free
UNCHASTE impure; lewd
UNCHEERY dull; gloomy
UNCHEWED not masticated
UNCHIDED unrebuked
rl **UNCHURCH** excommunicate
UNCIATIM ounce by ounce
UNCIFORM hook-shaped
zo **UNCINATA** marine worms
UNCINATE hooked
UNCLENCH UNCLINCH, open the hand
nt **UNCLEWED** unwound
UNCLOSED open; ajar
UNCLOTHE undress
UNCLUTCH let go of something held
UNCLUTCH release the clutch of a car
UNCOILED unwound
UNCOMBED unkempt
UNCOMELY lacking grace
UNCOMMON odd; rare; strange
UNCOOPED set free
UNCORDED unbound
UNCORKED ready to pour
rw, el **UNCOUPLE** disconnect
rl **UNCOWLED** unveiled; dismonked
UNCTUOUS greasy; oily; fulsome
UNCULLED unpicked
UNCURBED licentious; loose; unbridled; unchecked
UNCURLED straightened
UNCURSED not execrated
UNDAMPED not put out, of fires
UNDASHED undaunted; undismayed
UNDEFIED unchallenged
UNDEFINE make indefinite
UNDENTED smooth
UNDERACT perform inadequately
lw **UNDER-AGE** not adult; immature
UNDERARM (bowling); underside of arm
UNDERBID offer less
UNDERBUY haggle the price downward
UNDERCUT tenderloin; buy below price
UNDERDID economized effort; below standard
UNDERDOG lower-class individual
UNDERFED starved of nourishment
UNDERLAP extend below
UNDERLAY foundation
lw **UNDERLET** sublet
UNDERLIE below the surface
nt **UNDERMAN** operate with insufficient crew
UNDERPAY remunerate inadequately
UNDERPIN support
UNDERSAY minimize essentials in report
UNDERTOW tidal current below surface
UNDEVOUT behaving irreligiously
UNDIMMED untarnished
pc **UNDINISM** urophilia; erotic effect of urine
UNDINTED undismayed by difficulties
UNDIPPED unbaptized; sheep uncleansed
UNDOCKED dogs, horses retaining their tails
nt **UNDOCKED** ships waiting to enter harbour
UNDULANT wavy, of the sea
UNDULATE UNDULOUS, of wavy movement; vibrate
UNEARNED free; gain without work
UNEASILY anxiously; nervously
UNELATED modestly content
UNENDING everlasting; ceaseless
UNENVIED viewed with complacency
UNERRING certain; sure; exact
UNESPIED not observed
UNEVENLY ruggedly; unequally
lw **UNEXEMPT** liable
UNEXPERT unskilled
UNFABLED of real true-life events
UNFADING everlasting; constant
UNFAIRLY dishonestly; falsely
UNFASTEN open; let loose
UNFAULTY free from blemish
UNFEARED not held in awe
UNFELLOW expel from a society
UNFENCED not enclosed; open
UNFETTER unchain; unshackle
UNFILIAL undutiful

UNFILLED empty
UNFILMED not photographed
UNFLOWER deflower (of virginity)
UNFLUENT tongue-tied
UNFOILED not baffled
UNFOLDED deployed; disclosed; unwrapped
UNFORCED freely agreed to; natural
UNFORGED not counterfeited
UNFORMED shapeless; not yet composed
UNFOUGHT uncontested
UNFOULED clean; unsullied
UNFRAMED of pictures; not 'set-up' by police, gangsters
UNFROZEN uncongealed
UNFRUGAL prodigal; lavish; wasteful
UNFUELED unfuelled
UNFUNDED floating; unmonied
UNFURLED displayed
UNGAINLY uncouth; clumsy
UNGEARED unharnessed; without gear system
UNGENTLE rude; rough
UNGIFTED without talent
UNGILDED plain
UNGILLED (free fish from net)
UNGIRDED beltless; unenclosed
UNGIVING rigid
UNGLAZED paneless; without window glass
UNGLOVED barehanded
UNGOWNED unrobed
UNGRACED awkward
UNGROUND not milled
zo **UNGUICAL** (snail, claw, hoof)
UNGUIDED unregulated
UNGUILTY innocent; unproven
zo **UNGULATA** hoofed mammals
zo **UNGULATE** having hoofs
UNGUMMED unstuck; not sealed
UNHACKED not notched
UNHANDED let go; released
UNHANGED not dependent; not executed
UNHARMED scatheless; immune
UNHASPED unlatched
UNHEATED cold; without heating
UNHEDGED hedgeless; without a border
UNHEEDED disregarded
UNHELPED unassisted
UNHEROIC timid; shrinking
UNHINGED unsettled
UNHIVING unhousing
UNHOODED bareheaded; (exposed)
UNHOOKED unfastened
UNHOOPED (casks and barrels)
UNHORNED uncuckolded
UNHORSED dismounted
UNIAURAL monaural; single ear
UNIAXIAL having a single axis
ch **UNIBASAL** having a single base
UNICYCLE acrobat's cycle
UNIFYING uniting; merging
bt **UNILOBAR UNILOBED**, having one lobe
UNIMBUED not saturated
UNIMODAL only one mode; single 'peak' effect
UNINURED not hardened
UNIONISM combination; alliance
UNIONIST confederate; conservative; (Ulster)
mn **UNIONITE** lime silicate
zo **UNIPOLAR** of one-process nerve cells
UNIQUELY peculiarly; exceptionally
UNIQUITY singularity
mu **UNISONAL** harmonious
UNITEDLY jointly; concertedly
UNITIZED treated as a unit
zo **UNIVALVE** a mollusc
UNIVERSE the world
UNIVOCAL unanimous
rw **UNJOINED** uncoupled; separated
UNJOYFUL dull; mirthless; downcast
UNJOYOUS gloomy; melancholy; glum
UNJUDGED awaiting verdict
UNJUSTLY prejudicially; unfairly
UNKINDLY unfriendly; harshly
UNLACING unloosing
UNLADING unloading
UNLAVISH sparse; frugal
UNLAWFUL illegal; illicit
UNLEARNT forgotten
UNLIKELY improbable; risky
UNLIMBER get into action
UNLINEAL not in succession
UNLOADED discharged
UNLOCKED open
UNLOOKED unheeded
UNLOOSED slackened
UNLOOSEN set free
UNLORDED not raised to peerage
UNLORDLY undignified
UNLOVING passionless
UNMANNED in absence of crew
UNMAPPED uncharted
UNMARKED unobserved
UNMARRED unsullied
UNMASKED exposed; unveiled
UNMELTED undissolved
UNMILKED fat-uddered
UNMILLED unground
UNMISSED good riddance

UNMOANED not lamented
UNMODISH out of fashion
UNMOVING motionless; impassive
UNMUDDLE coordinate
UNNEEDED superfluous
UNNERVED frightened
UNOPENED closed
UNPACKED taken out of wrappings
UNPACKER parcels, freight worker
UNPAIRED singly
UNPATHED trackless
UNPAWNED not pledged
UNPEELED with skin intact
UNPEGGED not stabilized
UNPENNED released
UNPICKED not selected
UNPLACED not in the first three
UNPOETIC prosaic
UNPOISED out of balance
UNPOSTED not advertised widely
UNPRICED without price-tag; unvalued
UNPRIEST de-frock (unfrock)
lw **UNPROVED** untested in law court
UNREAPED not harvested
UNREASON lack of sense
UNREELED unwound
UNREINED unbridled
UNREPAID not requited
UNRIDDLE solve; unravel; decipher
nt **UNRIGGED** dismantled; of sailing vessel
UNROLLED spread out
UNRUFFLE fail to disturb
UNSADDLE remove saddle from
UNSALTED without salt preservative
rl **UNSAYING** recanting
UNSEALED not yet closed; still open
UNSEATED unhorsed; fell off; expelled
UNSEEDED not sown; unselected (tennis)
UNSEEING blind
UNSEEMLY unbecoming
UNSETTLE unhinge; disturb
UNSEXUAL without sexual implications
UNSHADED exposed
UNSHAKEN unworried; undisturbed; firm
UNSHARED undivided
UNSHAVED not yet shaved
UNSHAVEN uncouth; of vagabond
UNSHELVE to act at once
UNSHROUD to unveil; to make public
UNSHRUNK unwashed as yet
UNSIFTED not yet sorted out
UNSINGED of the hair, unscorched
UNSLAKED unquenched (of lime)
ck **UNSMOKED** untreated; uncured
UNSMOKED cigar, cigarette unfinished
UNSMOOTH rough
UNSOAPED unwashed
pc **UNSOCIAL** shy; hermit-like; reserved
el **UNSOCKET** disconnect
UNSOILED still clean
UNSOLVED of enigma (puzzle) so far
UNSORTED not yet sorted
UNSOUGHT not looked for
UNSPIKED with barbs removed
UNSPOILT natural
UNSPOKEN agreed, but not mentioned
UNSPRUNG ready-set trap
UNSTABLE inconstant existence
UNSTATED not mentioned
UNSTAYED unrestrained
UNSTEADY vacillating
UNSTITCH unsew
UNSTORED not warehoused
UNSTRUNG remove strings
UNSTRUNG loosened; relaxed
UNSUCKED full, erect
UNSUITED unbecoming
UNSURELY of uncertainty
UNSWATHE unwrap (a small baby)
UNSWAYED unaffected by argument
UNTANGLE unravel confusion
UNTANNED not sunburnt (pale)
UNTAPPED problem not answered; discussed
UNTAPPED room free from listening microphone
ck **UNTASTED** new wine, cheese etc.
UNTAUGHT uninstructed; illiterate
UNTENDED neglected
UNTENDER of harsh manner
UNTESTED unproved
UNTETHER release; untie a knot
UNTHAWED still frozen
UNTHORNY smooth
UNTHREAD disentangle
UNTHRONE oust from royal rule
ga **UNTHROWN** still on horseback (rodeo)
UNTIDILY disorderly
UNTILLED left land fallow
UNTIMELY premature
lw **UNTINGED** uncoloured; innocent
UNTIRING unwearied
rl **UNTITHED** 10% tax not paid
UNTONGUE to extract the tongue; torture
UNTOWARD rude perverseness
UNTRACED no records found

UNTRUCED without truce
UNTRUSTY unfaithful
UNTUCKED half undressed
UNTUFTED hairless
UNTURFED expelled from horse racing
UNTURNED left untouched
UNTWINED not twisted together (rope)
UNVALUED worth uncalculated
UNVARIED monotonous
UNVEILED made open; disclosed
UNVEILER revealer
UNVENTED unuttered; unreleased
UNVERSED unskilled
UNVIZARD unhelm
UNVOICED not spoken; mute
UNWAITED unattended
UNWALLED not enclosed
UNWARILY rash; reckless
UNWARMED unheated
UNWARNED unadmonished
nt **UNWARPED** flat; original dry wood
UNWASHED dirty
UNWASTED made use of
UNWEANED suckling child
UNWEDDED unwed
UNWEEDED overgrown
UNWIELDY ponderous
UNWILFUL weakminded; docile
UNWILLED involuntary
UNWISDOM folly; fatuity
UNWISELY irrationally
UNWONTED unusual
UNWOODED treeless
UNWORDED silent
UNWORMED with worms removed
UNWORTHY undeserving
UNYOKING unharnessing; freeing
UPCAUGHT caught up
UPCOMING impending; ascending
UPHEAVAL earthquake; extreme change
UPHOLDER supporter
UPLIFTED elevated; exalted
UPPERCUT boxing blow
UPPER-TEN the aristocracy
UPRAISED lifted
UPRIDGED in ridges
UPRISING insurrection
UPROOTED eradicated
UPSTAIRS among the gentry
lw **UPSTAYED** upheld
UPSTREAM against the current
UPSTROKE alternates with downstroke
UPTHRUST upheaval
UPTOSSED upchucked
UPTURNED inverted
UPWAFTED borne aloft
UPWARDLY in ascending direction
mn **URALITIC** (uralite)
URBANISM changing to big-city styles
URBANITY suaveness; courteousness
URBANIZE make urban
bt **URCEOLUS** floral envelope
ch **URETHANE** ethyl carbamate
URGENTLY momentously; pressingly
UROBILIN bile/urine pigment
zo **UROCHORD** (sea-squirt)
zo **UROCHROA** humming-birds
zo **UROCISSA** Asiatic magpie
zo **URODAEUM** urinary duct in cloaca
zo **UROESTON** a tail bone
zo **UROMERIC** (tail-piece)
md **UROSCOPY** urine examination
zo **UROSTEGE** a snake's scale
zo **UROSTYLE** lengthy tail
zo **URSIFORM** like a bear
rl **URSULINE** a nun (St Ursula)
zo **URTICANT** irritating; stinging
URTICATE to sting; cause a rash
USEFULLY advantageously
USHERDOM schoolmastery
USHERING heralding; introducing
bt **USTILAGO** genus of fungi
USTULATE scorched
lw **USUFRUCT** temporary possession
USURIOUS at high interest
USURPING arrogating; assuming
UTILIZED employed; used
UTOPIAST (Utopia)
UTRIFORM bottle-shaped
UTTEREST furthest; remotest
UTTERING disclosing; issuing
UXORIOUS wife-loving

V

VACATING quitting; annulling
VACATION intermission; recess; holiday
md **VACCINAL** pertaining to vaccine
md **VACCINIA** cow-pox
VAGABOND VAGRANT, tramp; thief
rl **VAGANTES** itinerant clerics
VAGARIES whims; caprices; crotchets
ec **VAGILITY** power of movement
bt, pl **VAGINANT VAGINATE**, sheathing
bt **VAGINULA** sheath of seta in bryophyta
md **VAGOTOMY** division of vagus nerves
VAGRANCY itinerance of the homeless

VAINNESS vanity; conceit; inanity
VALENCED decorated; draped
tx **VALENTIA** woven material
bt **VALERIAN** all-heal; medicinal plant
VALETING personal attendance
rl **VALHALLA** palace of Norse gods
VALIANCE bravery; intrepidity
VALIANCY courageousness; chivalry
VALIDATE confirm; legalize
VALIDITY soundness; justness; aptness within limits
rl **VALKYRIE** Norse warrior angels
VALLANCY large wig
VALLATED cup-shaped; circumvallated
VALORIZE make a currency reform
VALOROUS intrepid; bold; heroic
VALUABLE precious; costly; expensive
VALUATOR appraiser; assessor
VALVELET small valve
VALVULAR containing valves
VAMBRACE arm-armour
VAMOOSED decamped; skedaddled
VAMPIRIC extortionate, of vampires
VAMPLATE hand-guard of lance
ch **VANADATE** vanadium salt
ch **VANADIUM** metallic element
ch **VANADOUS** of divalent vanadium
VANDALIC of Baltic raiders
VANDYKED indented; notched
VANGUARD forefront; front line
ck **VANILLIC** flavoured with vanilla
VANILLIN compound from vanilla pods
VANISHED disappeared; dissolved
VANISHER absconder
VANQUISH overpower; rout; subdue
VAPIDITY insipidity
VAPORIZE turn into gas
VAPOROSE unsubstantial; gaseous
VAPOROUS unreal; steamy
VAPOURED evaporated; peevish
VAPOURER boaster; vaunter; braggart
VAQUERIA cattle ranch
zo **VARANOID** lizardlike
mt **VARDARAC** mistral wind (Macedonia)
cp **VARIABLE** mutable; fickle; mercurial; (field)
VARIABLY changeably; fitfully
VARIANCE discord; strife; dispute
VARIANCE average of deviation squares
VARIANCE discrepancy; deviant human behaviour
VARIATED altered; variegated
VARIATIM variations; in different ways
zo **VARICORN** a horned beetle
md **VARICOSE VARICOUS**, permanently dilated (veins)
VARIETAL mutative; subgeneric
VARIFORM protean; diverse
md **VARIOLAR** pox-marked
VARIORUM commentated edition
el **VARISTOR** 2-electrode semi-conductor
VARLETRY the rabble; the crowd
rl **VARTABED** Armenian priest
md **VASALIUM** vascular tissue
md **VASCULAR** vessels; ducts, etc.
bt **VASCULUM** specimen-box
mn **VASELINE** petroleum jelly
md **VASIFORM** like a duct
VASSALED enslaved
VASSALRY bondage; feudal system
VASTNESS immensity; spaciousness
mn **VATERITE** polymorph of calcium carbonate
VATICIDE murder of a prophet
pp **VAT-SIZED** with sizing added to pulp
ar, bd **VAULTAGE** arched work
ar, bd **VAULTING** leaping; bounding; competition event (gymn.); cross-arched ceiling
VAUNTERY boastfulness; arrogance
VAUNTFUL ostentatious; swaggering
VAUNTING bragging; crowing
VAUNTLAY a dog in challenging mood
lw **VAVASORY** (land tenure)
VAVASOUR feudal tenant
md **VEALSKIN** a skin-disease
rl **VEDANTIC** (Hindu philosophy)
VEGETATE to sprout; (secluded life)
VEHEMENT impetuous; ardent
VEILLESS open to view; undisguised
bt **VEINLESS** lack of venation
VELARIUM awning; canopy
VELATION mystery; concealment
VELATURA picture glazing (It.)
VELLEITY volition; inclination
hd **VELLOPED** heraldic wattles
nt **VELOCERA** multi-rigged coaster (It.)
VELOCITY swiftness; rapidity; rate
el **VELODYNE** tachogenerator
ro **VELOGRID** a grid in a wireless valve
VELVERET ersatz velvet
VELVETED like velvet
VENALITY mercenariness; corruptness
bt, zo **VENATION** veins as a whole
VENATION hunting; pursuit of game

VENDETTA a blood feud; vengeance
VENDIBLE marketable; disposable
VENDIBLY saleably
VENEERED overlaid; disguised
VENENATE poisonous; poisoned; toxic
VENERATE esteem; respect; revere
md **VENEREAL** venusian; sexual diseases
VENETIAN (Venice)
VENGEFUL vindictive; retributive
VENIABLE pardonable
VENIALLY excusably; trivially
md **VENOMING** poisoning (snake bite)
VENOMOUS venemous; poisonous
VENOSITY full-bloodedness
VENOUSLY veined
go, gl **VENT-HOLE** blowhole; spouter
md **VENTOUSE** vacuum-traction birth
VENT-PLUG barrel-peg
VENTURED hazarded; dared
VENTURER speculator; adventurer
VENUSIAN pertaining to Venus, love goddess
VERACITY truth; truthfulness
VERANDAH covered balcony
ch **VERATRIC** hellebore extract
bt **VERATRUM** hellebore, etc.
VERBALLY orally; by word of mouth
VERBATIM word for word
VERBIAGE verbosity; prolixity
VERDANCY greenness
VERDERER forest-keeper
VERDITER green pigment
VERGENCE turning the eye
VERGENCY border; verge
hd **VERGETTE** heraldic pallet
VERIFIED confirmed; authenticated
VERIFIER corroborator
VERJUICE sourjuice
VERMINLY verminously
VERMOUTH wine flavoured with wormwood
VERNICLE miraculous imprint
VERONESE (Verona)
bt **VERONICA** speedwell plants
md **VERRUGAS** Peruvian skin disease
VERSABLE reversible
VERSELET **VERSICLE**, brief ode
pl **VERTEBRA** segment of the spine
VERTICAL upright; erect; perpendicular
VERTICES summits; apices; zeniths
bt **VERTICIL** a whorl
VESICANT blistering
VESICATE to blister
md **VESICULA** a pustule
VESPIARY wasp's nest
VESTIARY a wardrobe
rl **VESTMENT** garment; robe; dress
VESTUARY vestiary
VESTURAL (robe; clothing)
rl **VESTURER** vestment keeper
VESUVIAN fusee; fuzee
VEXATION affliction; torment; worry
zo **VEXILLAR** feathery
VEXILLUM a banner; Roman standard
VEXINGLY provokingly; annoyingly
me **VIAMETER** an odometer
rl **VIATICUM** Eucharist
VIBRATED quivered; oscillated
VIBRATOR a trembler; buzzer
el **VIBRATOR** device for producing A/C
VIBRISSA whisker; bristle
bt **VIBROGEN** cellular tissue
el **VIBRONIC** electronic vibrations
bt **VIBURNUM** guelder-rose
rl **VICARAGE** vicar's house
VICARIAL substituted
VICARIAN deputy
rl **VICARIUS** a vicar
rl **VICE-DEAN** a canon
VICE-KING regent; viceroy
VICENARY based on twenty
VICHYITE supporter of Vichy France
VICINAGE **VICINITY**, neighbourhood; proximity
VICTORIA a vehicle
VICTRESS woman conqueror; victrix
VICTUALS provisions; sustenance
VIDENDUM thing to be seen
VIDEOTIC addicted to media (TV)
VIETMINH Vietnam Communist
VIEWABLE able to be seen
VIEWLESS vistaless
VIEWSOME panoramic
VIGILANT circumspect; alert; wakeful
VIGNERON wine-grower (Fr.)
VIGNETTE character sketch
mu **VIGOROSO** forcibly
VIGOROUS lusty; powerful; virile
VIHYLITE plastic glass
VILENESS baseness; depravity; vice
VILIFIED slandered; defamed; decried
VILIFIER traducer; maligner
VILIPEND disparage; calumniate
VILLADOM suburban villas
VILLAGER dweller in village
VILLAINY depravity; fraud; rascality
vt **VILLITIS** coronet inflammation in horse
VINCIBLE conquerable; surmountable

VINCULUM bond of union; link; chain
VINE-CLAD covered with vines
VINE-GALL vine disease
zo **VINE-GRUB** a parasite
VINE-LAND grape acreage
bt **VINEYARD** grape plantation
VINOLOGY art of wine making
VINOSITY wine flavour
VINTAGER grape gatherer
VINTNERY the wine trade
VIOLABLE transgressive
VIOLATOR ravisher; debaucher
VIOLENCE brute force
zo **VIPERINE** venomous
VIPERISH malignant
VIPEROUS treacherous
VIREMENT bookkeeping transfer
mu **VIRGINAL** early form of spinet
VIRGINAL (spinster)
bt **VIRGINIA** tobacco; creeper
VIRIDIAN bluish-green colour
mn **VIRIDINE** green variety of andalusite
VIRIDITY verdure; greenness
VIRILISM male characteristics in woman
VIRILITY manhood; energy; manliness
md **VIROLOGY** virus diseases
VIRTUOSE expert in art
VIRTUOSO connoisseur; expert
VIRTUOUS upright; moral; chaste
VIRULENT bitter in enmity; toxic
zo **VISCACHA** pampas hare
md **VISCERAL** abdominal
VISCOUNT title of peerage
VISIGOTH Spanish Goth
VISIONAL illusory; chimerical
VISITANT guest; frequenter
VISITING inspecting; haunting; calling
VITALISM VITALIST, hypothetical vital principle
VITALITY vigour; life; energy
VITALIZE animate; quicken
VITELLIN a protein in egg
VITELLUS the yolk of an egg
VITIATED impaired; spoilt; debased
VITIATOR a pervert
zo **VITICIDE** a vine pest
md **VITILIGO** patchy skin depigmentation
VITREOUS glassy
VITULINE (veal)
VIVACITY sprightliness; liveliness
zo **VIVARIUM** small zoo
VIVA-VOCE orally
VIVIDITY vividness; clarity; lucidity
VIVIFIED quickened; enlivened
bt **VIVIPARY** manner of bud/seed production
md **VIVISECT** operate on the living
VIXENISH quarrelsome; snappish
VIZERATE viziership
mu **VOCALISE** wordless composition (Fr.)
mu **VOCALIST** singer
VOCALITY utterableness
VOCALIZE voice; articulate
VOCATION profession; calling; pursuit
VOCATIVE (invocation); a case
mn **VOGESITE** hornblende-lamprophyre
VOIDABLE able to be annulled
VOIDANCE evasion; annulment
VOIDNESS nullity; emptiness
mn **VOIGTITE** form of mica
VOLATILE lively; fickle; changeable; unstable
cp **VOLATILE** memory lost; without power
VOLCANIC eruptive
VOLITANT able to fly
VOLITION freewill; choice; purpose
VOLITIVE wishful
VOLLEYED (tennis)
VOLPLANE glider
VOLSUNGS Norse legendary leaders
VOLTAISM galvanism
mn **VOLTZITE** zinc sulphide
mn **VOLULITE** petrified shell
VOLUMIST an author
VOLUTION convolution; spiral
md **VOLVULUS** stoppage
VOMITING ejecting
md **VOMITION** sickness
VOMITIVE vomitory
md **VOMITORY** an emetic
VORACITY rapacity; greed
mu **VORSPIEL** prelude; overture (Ger.)
VORTEXES whirlpools; vortices
go **VORTICAL** eddies; maelstroms
VOTARESS lady devotee
VOTARIST adherent; votary; zealot
VOTIVELY by way of vow
VOUCHING warranting; backing
VOUSSOIR arch stone
VOWELISM use of vowels
VOWELIST user of vowels
VOWELLED with vowels
VRAICING gathering seaweed (Ch. Is.)
VULCANIC volcanic
VULGARLY commonly; boorishly
md **VULSELLA** forceps

W

WABBLING wobbling
WADDLING walking like a duck
WAFERING sealing a letter (early days)
WAGE-FUND (a theory)
WAGELESS unpaid
WAGERING betting; laying; staking
WAGE-WORK paid work
WAGGLING swaying
WAGGONER wagoner
WAGGONET wagonette
WAGONAGE cost of transport
WAGONFUL load
WAGONING carting
WAGON-LIT sleeping car (Fr.)
zo **WAHDEROO** langur monkey
WAILMENT lamentation
WAINBOTE timber for carts
WAINROPE cart-rope
WAINSCOT panelling
bt **WAIT-A-BIT** (various shrubs)
WAITRESS a female waiter
nt **WAKA-TAUA** Maori war canoe (New Zealand)
WAKENING rousing; stimulating
mu **WALDHORN** hunting horn (Ger.)
WALHALLA VALHALLA, palace of Norse gods
WALKABLE within walking distance
WALK-MILL hammer-mill (blacksmith)
WALK-OVER easy victory
zo **WALLAROO** large kangaroo
WALL-EYED glaring; fierce
WALL-GAME Eton football
nt **WALL-KNOT** Turk's head
bt **WALL-MOSS** stonecrop
zo **WALL-NEWT** lizard; gecko
WALLOPED WALLOPER, thrashed; slogger
WALLOWED WALLOWER, floundered in mud
bt **WALL-TREE** fruit tree against sunny garden wall
bt **WALL-WORT** dwarf-elder
WALOGLAS WEALDGLASS, green glass process (Ger.)
WALTZING dancing
WAMBLING rumbling
WANDERED strayed; roamed
WANDERER rambler; nomad
WANGLING winning by craft
WANTLESS fully satisfied; abundant
WANTONED frolicked
WANTONLY sportively; capriciously
WAPPENED tearful; beaten; wearied; done in
WAPPERED blinked
WARBLING gurgling; birdsong; trifling
WAR-DANCE tribal ceremony
WARDCORN castle guard
WARDENRY warden's district
WARDMOTE court of inquiry
WARDROBE clothes closet
nt **WARD-ROOM** mess-room
WARDSHIP guardianship
WARE-ROOM show-room
WARFARER combatant
WAR-FIELD battle-field
zo **WAR-HORSE** a charger
WARINESS alertness; craftiness
WARM-DOWN relaxing after exertion
WARMNESS warmth; ardour
WARPAINT battle make-up
WAR-PLANE fighting aircraft
WAR-PLUME plume de guerre
WARPROOF valorous
zo **WARRAGAL** the dingo dog (Australia)
WARRANTY authority
WARRENER warren keeper
WARTLESS smooth-skinned
bt **WARTWEED WARTWORT**, spurge used for curing warts
WAR-WEARY tired of fighting
WAR-WHOOP a war-cry
WASHABLE easily washed (clothes)
WASHBALL soap-ball
WASHBOWL washbasin
pt **WASH-COAT** pre-treatment primer
mn **WASH-DIRT** process
WASHLAND between river and flood
WASH-ROOM ablution room
WASTEFUL prodigal; improvident
WASTEWAY overflow weir; spillway
WATCHBOX sentry box
WATCHDOG guard (dog)
WATCHFUL vigilant; alert; wary
WATCHING wakefulness; vigil
WATCH-KEY antique implement
WATCHMAN a look-out; custodian
WATER BAR water or flood excluder
WATERAGE transport dues
WATER-BED with water-filled mattress
zo **WATER-BUG** various types
WATERCAN watering-can for plants
zo **WATER-DOG** water spaniel
zo **WATERFLY** aquatic insect
zo **WATER-FOX** the carp
WATER-GAS illuminating gas
WATER-GOD Neptune

zo **WATER-HEN** moorhen
WATER-ICE a confection
WATERING diluting; irrigating
WATERISH insipid; moist; damp
WATERLOG saturate
WATERMAN ferryman; turncock
bt **WATER-POA** species of grass
WATERPOT watering can
WATER-RAM hydraulic ram
zo **WATER-RAT** water vole
zo **WATER-RUG** water spaniel
WATER-TAP spigot
go **WATERWAY** a canal
me **WATT-HOUR** measure of work
WATTLING plaiting; hurdling
WAVEBAND group of wavelengths
WAVEFORM characteristic of radiowave
WAVELESS calm; undisturbed; serene
WAVELIKE undulating; rippling
WAVE-LINE stream-line
WAVE-LOAF a wave-offering
WAVERING tottering; vacillating
WAVEROUS fluctuating; unsteady
el **WAVETAIL** fall in voltage of a unidirectional impulse
WAVE-TRAP maritime hazard
el **WAVETRAP** interference reducer for radios
WAVEWORN of coastal rocks
WAVINESS wave-like line drawing
WAXCLOTH oil-cloth
WAXLIGHT a taper
WAX-PAPER stencil paper
bt **WAX-PLANT** honeywort
WAXWORKS an exhibition (wax statues)
mn **WAY-BOARD** thin stratum
bt **WAYBREAD** common plantain
WAYFARER traveller; pedestrian
WAYGOING departing
WAYGOOSE a printer's festivity
WAYLAYER interceptor; lurker
WAYLEAVE right of way
WAYMAKER a precursor
me **WAYMETER** pedometer
WAY-SHAFT engine shaft
bt **WAYTHORN** buckthorn
WEAKENED debilitated; enfeebled
WEAKENER enervator
WEAK-EYED needing glasses
WEAKLING delicate creature
WEAKNESS feebleness; frailty
WEANLING newly weaned
WEAPONED armed
WEARABLE fit to be worn
WEARIFUL wearisome; tedious
WEARYING tiring; fatiguing
WEED-HOOK garden tool
WEEDLESS well weeded
bd **WEEPHOLE** small drain hole for water
zo **WEEVILED** infested with weevils
lw **WEIGHAGE** a toll on laden trucks
WEIGHING balancing; pondering
WEIGHOUT prior to boxing, wrestling, (horse racing)
WEIGHTED given extra weight (horse racing)
mn **WEISSITE** iolite
WELCOMED greeted; hailed; saluted
WELCOMER polite host; receptionist
WELDABLE fusable
WELD-IRON wrought iron
eg **WELDMENT** welded assembly
WELLADAY alas; alackaday
WELLAWAY everything going splendidly
nt **WELL-BOAT** fishing boat
WELL-BORN of noble birth
WELL-BRED of good stock
WELLCURB ring of masonry
nt **WELL-DECK** space above cargo hold
WELLDOER a benefactor
WELL-HEAD source of a spring
ar, bd **WELL-HOLE** ventilation spaces
WELL-KEPT carefully tended
WELL-KNIT compact; sturdy
WELLNIGH nearly; almost
WELL-READ learned; scholarly
WELL-SEEN experienced; skilful
WELLSIAN (H. G. Wells)
WELL-TO-DO prosperous; affluent
WELL-WORN threadbare; shabby
WELSHING absconding; reneging
WELSHMAN a man of Wales
WELTERED wallowed; floundered
WEREGILD compensation for homicide
zo **WEREWOLF** a changeling
rl **WESLEYAN** (John Wesley)
WESTERLY in westward direction
WESTWARD toward the west
ar, rl **WESTWORK** W. end of Carolingian, Romanesque church
WET-NURSE breast-giver
WET-ON-WET short-interval spray-painting
WHACKING astounding; a beating
WHALEMAN Jonah
WHALE-OIL oil from blubber of whale
bt **WHANGEE** bamboo cane
WHANGING whacking; beating
WHARFAGE dock dues

WHARFING using a wharf (for cargoes)
nt **WHARFING WHARVES**, existence of jetties
WHATEVER anything which
zo **WHEATEAR** fallowfinch
zo **WHEAT-EEL** a wheat disease
zo **WHEAT-FLY** a pest
WHEEDLED coaxed; cajoled; inveigled
WHEEDLER sycophant; fawner; toady
WHEELAGE a toll
WHEELING cycling; turning; twirling
WHEELMAN cyclist
mn **WHEEL-ORE** bournonite
WHEEL-TAX carriage tax
WHEEZILY asthmatically
WHEEZING breathing heavily
WHELPING littering; mothering (dogs)
WHENEVER at any time that
WHEREOUT out of which
WHEREVER to whatever place
WHETTING sharpening
WHEY-FACE pale face
WHIFFING puffing
WHIFFLER prevaricator
WHIGGERY WHIGGISH, WHIGGISM, liberalism
zo **WHIMBREL** wimbrel; curlew
WHIMSIES notions; caprices; fancies
WHIM-WHAM a gadget
zo **WHINCHAT** singing bird
WHINNIED neighed
WHINNOCK a milk-pail
WHINYARD sword; dirk
WHIPCORD string; material
WHIPHAND advantage over; control
WHIPLASH crack of whip
WHIPPING lashing; castigating
WHIPSTER whippersnapper
WHIPTAIL slender tail
WHIRLBAT cestus
WHIRLING gyrating; rotating
WHIRRING spinning; twirling; turning
gl **WHISKERS** cats; minute single crystals
WHISKERY with whiskers, bristles
WHISKING brushing lightly
mu, nt **WHISTLED** piped; (by mouth); signalled attention
rw **WHISTLED** of steam locomotives, warning or starting
zo **WHISTLER** broken-winded horse
zo **WHITE-ANT** a termite
WHITE-ARM arme blanche
WHITE-BOY Irish white-shirt
WHITE-HOT hotter than red-hot
WHITE-LIE an evasion
WHITEMAN of European ancestry
WHITENED WHITENER, blanched; bleacher
WHITE-OUT open space in display texts
WHITE-OUT snowblindness; loss of orientation in arctic regions
WHITEPOT a confection
zo **WHITLING** sea trout; bull trout
WHITSOUR summer apple
WHITSTER a whitener
WHITTLED pared; cut; trimmed
WHITTLER reducer; trimmer (wood)
zo **WHITTRET** the weasel
WHIZZING speeding
WHODUNIT a crime novel
WHOMEVER whomsoever
WHOOPING yelling; hooting
WHOPPING beating; colossal
WHURRING a spinning sound
WICKEDLY evilly; atrociously
WICKERED chairs etc. made of osiers
WIDE-EYED afraid; gullible
pp **WIDELINE** vertical mark in papermaking
WIDENESS breadth; width
WIDENING extending; broadening
WIDOWING bereaving
WIELDING brandishing; plying
WIFEHOOD wivehood
WIFELESS unmarried
WIFELIKE wifely
WIG-BLOCK wigmaker's block
WIGGLING wriggling
WIGMAKER perukist
hd, zo **WILDBOAR** Richard III's badge; hog; swine
WILD-BORN not born indoors
zo **WILD-DUCK** mallard and others
WILD-FIRE sheet lightning
WILDFIRE wind-blown forest fire
zo **WILD-FOWL** untamed birds
WILD-LAND uncultivated soil
WILDNESS savageness; recklessness
WILD-WOOD forest
WILFULLY obstinately; deliberately
WILINESS craftiness; artfulness
mt **WILLIWAW** westerly blasting wind (Straits of Magellan)
bt **WILLOWED** full of willows
WIMBLING boring
WIMPLING rippling
WINCHMAN windlass operator
lw **WIND BILL** guarantee
mu **WIND-BAND** instrumental ensemble
WINDERED fanned; blown

lw **WINDFALL** fruit from trees; legacy
WIND-GALL puffy swelling
nl **WINDLASS** a winch; capstan
WINDLESS calm, still; winded (lungs)
WINDMILL wind-driven machine
WINDOWED fenestrated
WINDPIPE the access to lungs; trachea
nt **WIND-PUMP** small windmill
nt **WIND-ROSE** the nautical chart compass
bd **WINDSAIL** rotating ventilator funnel
WINDSCAB snow surface crust; skiing
WIND-SEED carried by the wind
nt **WINDWARD** toward the wind, (course)
WINE-CASK barrel for wine
WINELESS without wine
WINE-RACK wine-bottle storage unit
WINESKIN bag for wine
WINGBACK half back (Amer. football)
zo **WING-CASE** horny cover of wing (beetles)
zo **WINGLESS** flightless bird; apterous
WING-LOCK wrestlers' hold
ae **WINGOVER** aerobatic, gliding manoeuvre
nt **WING-SHOT** threatening, flying shot
ag **WINNOWED** sifted grain (threshed)
WINNOWER chaff remover
WINTERED hibernated
WINTERLY every winter; wintry
WIREDRAW wire-making process
WIRE-HEEL a foot disease
WIRELESS radio
pp **WIREMARK** horizontal mark in papermaking
WIREROPE tightrope; circus stay
pp **WIRESIDE** underside of paper
zo **WIRE-WORM** a centipede
pp **WIRE-WOVE** (glazed writing paper)
WIRINESS toughness
WISEACRE a simpleton
WISELING wiseacre
mn **WISERITE** manganese carbonate
WISHBONE merrythought; frame of racing cars; T formation (Amer. football)
WISH-WASH weak drink; dishwater; undrinkable
bt **WISTARIA** a climbing plant
bt **WITCH-ELM** variety of elm tree
WITCHERY fascination; sorcery
WITCHING enchanting; charming
WITHDRAW retire; recall; retract
WITHDREW retreated; departed
WITHERED faded; shrunk; drooped
bt **WITHE-ROD** American shrub
WITHHELD kept back; detained
WITHHOLD restrain; reserve
bt **WITHWIND** bindweed
WITTOLLY complacently
WIVEHOOD wifehood
WIVELESS wifeless
WIZARDLY magically
WIZARDRY sorcery; necromancy
WIZENING withering
WOAD-MILL dye-extracting mill
WOBEGONE woebegone; calamitous
WOEFULLY sorrowfully; tragically
zo **WOLF-FISH** catfish
WOLF-SKIN wolf pelt
WOMANISH effeminate
WOMMERAH stick for spear-throwing
WONDERED speculated; marvelled
WONDERER conjecturer; ponderer
WONDROUS marvellous; miraculous
WONTLESS unaccustomed; unused
ch **WOOD-ACID** acetic acid
bt **WOODBIND** **WOODBINE**, wild honeysuckle
zo **WOODBIRD** forest denizen
zo **WOODCHAT** shrike; woodpecker
mn **WOOD-COAL** charcoal; lignite
zo **WOODCOCK** bird allied to snipe
zo **WOOD-DOVE** stockdove
vt **WOOD-EVIL** cattle disease
WOOD-HOLE woodstore
zo **WOOD-IBIS** tantalus; stork
WOOD-KERN Irish outlaw
WOODLAND forest land
zo **WOODLARK** forest bird
WOODLESS treeless
zo **WOOD-LICE** wood-beetles
bt **WOOD-LILY** lily of the valley
nt **WOODLOCK** to stop
zo **WOOD-MITE** a beetle
lw **WOODMOTE** forest court
WOODNOTE bird call
mn **WOOD-OPAL** silicified wood
WOOD-PULP cellulose
mn **WOODROCK** asbestos
bt **WOODROOF** **WOODRUFF**, a plant
WOOD-SEAR **WOOD-SEER, WOOD-SERE**, insect; cuckoo-spit; season
WOOD-SHED store for wood
nt **WOODSKIN** Guyana canoe
WOODSMAN a woodcutter
WOOD-SOOT charcoal soot
zo **WOOD-TICK** death-watch beetle
bt **WOOD-VINE** clematis
zo **WOODWALE** **WOODWALL**, golden oriole; green woodpecker

WOODWARD forest keeper
mu **WOODWIND** section of orchestra
WOODWORK carpentry
zo **WOOD-WORM** a grub
zo **WOOD-WREN** willow-warbler
WOOINGLY enticingly
WOOLBALL roll of yarn
WOOLDING binding
WOOL-DYED dyed in the wool
WOOLFELL skin with wool on it
WOOL-MILL cloth factory
WOOLPACK 240 lb. of wool
WOOLSACK Lord Chancellor's seat
WOOLWARD wearing wool
tx **WOOLWORK** wool-embroidery
WORD-BOOK dictionary; vocabulary
WORDLESS at a loss to speak
WORDLESS without language; silent; dumb
WORD-PLAY punning; repartee
WORKABLE feasible
WORKADAY prosaic; ordinary
WORKBOOK duties of staff for the day
WORKCARD report on work, defects, results
WORKFOLK toilers
WORKGIRL female employee
pr **WORKMARK** title letter and catalogue number
WORKROOM crafts workplace
WORKSHOP tool workroom
WORM-BORE damage by worms to books, furniture
WORMCAST thrown by worms
WORMGEAR gear wheels, etc.
WORM-HOLE track of woodworm
zo **WORMLIKE** vermicular
bt **WORMSEED** santonica
bt **WORMWOOD** absinthe; vermouth
WORRICOW hobgoblin
WORRYING harassing; fretting; chafing
WORSENED deteriorated
WORSTING besting; defeating
WORTHILY deservedly; meritoriously
mn **WORTHITE** silica compound
WOUNDILY excessively; hurtful
WOUNDING injuring
WRACKFUL ruinous; destructive
WRACKING gathering seaweed
WRANGLED brawled; bickered
WRANGLER disputant
zo **WRANNOCK** the wren
WRAPPAGE a wrapper
WRAPPING enclosing; muffling
WRATHFUL irate; incensed; wroth
WRATHILY indignantly; furiously
WRAULING caterwauling
WREAKFUL revengeful; angry
WREAKING inflicting; punishing
WREATHED garlanded; festooned
WREATHEN entwined
WRECKAGE crash-debris
WRECKING sabotaging; destroying
WRENCHED twisted; strained; wrung
WRESTING extorting; forcing; usurped
WRESTLED strove; grappled
ga **WRESTLER** master of wrestling bouts
WRETCHED miserable; paltry; sorry
WRICKING spraining; straining
WRIGGLED squirmed
WRIGGLER shuffler
bt **WRIGHTIA** tropical climber
pc **WRINGING** twisting wrists; (emotional stress)
WRINGING squeezing out water (laundry)
WRINKLED furrowed; creased; rumpled
WRISTLET band for wrist-watch
WRIST-PIN connecting pin of bracelet
WRITE-OFF total loss (disaster) (insurance)
WRITHING snake-like wriggling; squirming
WRONGFUL injurious; unjust; unfair
WRONGING violating; maltreating
mn **WURTZITE** sulphide of zinc

X

ch **XANTHATE** a salt
XANTHEIN yellow colour
XANTHENE chemical dye
XANTHIAN from Xanthus
XANTHINE yellow dye
mn **XANTHITE** yellow idocrase
bt **XANTHIUM** a plant
md **XANTHOMA** skin disease
XANTHOUS yellowish
zo **XANTHURA** American jay
bt **XENOGAMY** cross-fertilization
mn **XENOLITE** aluminium silicate
zo **XENOPHYA** foreign particles
mn **XENOTIME** yttrium phosphate
zo **XENURINE** armadillo-like
md **XERANSIS** dryness
md **XERANTIC** exsiccant
ec **XEROCOLE** animal living in dry place
bt **XEROSERE** dry-land succession
XESTURGY process of polishing
XILINOUS of cotton

zo **XIPHIOID** like a swordfish
bt **XYLOCARP** hard woody fruit
XYLOIDIN starch/nitric acid explosive
XYLONITE form of celluloid
pr **XYLOTYPE** wood engraving; print

Y

YACHTING ice, ocean, or lake pastime
YAHOOING howling and yelping
YAMMERED lamented; whined
mn **YANOLITE** axinite
pr **YAPPEDGE** overlapping bookcover
gl, mo **YARDANGS** overhanging rock ridges (Central Asia)
me **YARDLAND** 30 acres (12 hectares)
YARDSMAN scorer (Canadian football)
me **YARDWAND** yardstick
zo **YARWHELP** bar-tailed godwit
YATAGHAN long Turkish dagger
zo **YEANLING** eanling; a lamb
YEAR-BOOK voluminous annual
zo **YEARLING** one year old animal
YEARLONG twelve months
YEARNFUL mournful; distressing
YEARNING longing; craving; desirous
zo **YELDRING YELDROCK**, yowley; yorling; yellow-bunting
YELLOWED dyed yellow
YEOMANLY loyally supportive
YEOMANRY smallholder; attendant of sovereign
YEOMANRY signaller; chartman (navy); territorial (army)
YIELDING submitting; affording; bearing
YODELLED sang in alpine voice
YOGEEISM abstract meditation
YOICKING chanting (Lapland style)
YOKELESS unbound; at liberty
YOKEMATE the other ox of the plough
YOKE-TOED pair-toed
zo **YOKOHOMA** a breed of fowls
YONDMOST farthest; uttermost
YOUNGEST most youthful
YOUNGISH somewhat juvenile
YOURSELF reflexive pronoun
YOUTHFUL boyish; puerile; fresh
ch **YTTERBIA** oxide of ytterbium
mn **YTTERITE** gadolinite
ch **YTTRIOUS** containing yttrium
YUGOSLAV Jugo-Slav (South Slav)
YULETIDE Christmas; Noel; winter solstice
YUZBASHI Captain of 100 men (Turk.)

Z

zo **ZALOPHUS** seal genus
mu **ZAMBOMBA** Spanish instrument
ZAMINDAR zemindar; tax-collector
mu **ZAMPOGNO** Italian bagpipe
ZANTIOTE native of Zante
mn **ZARATITE** nickel compound
mu **ZARZUELA** Spanish operetta
ZEALLESS slack; apathetic
ZEALOTRY fanaticism; fervour; ardour
nm **ZECCHINO** sequin (Venice)
ZEGIDINE silver drinking cup (Hung.)
ZELANIAN (New Zealand)
ZEMINDAR Indian tax collector
ZENITHAL culminating; crowning
mn **ZEOLITIC** (felspar)
ZEPPELIN airship
bt **ZERUMBET** East Indian drug
ZETICULA a small room
zo **ZIBELINE** like a sable
ar, rl **ZIGGURAT** Sumerian temple
bd, rl **ZIGGURAT** ancient Eg. stepped pyramid
ZINCKIFY cover with zinc
bt **ZINGIBER** ginger, etc.
ZINNOBER vermilion pigment
ZIONWARD to Jerusalem (temple Sion)
zo **ZIPHIOID** like a swordfish
mn **ZIRCONIA** zirconium oxide
bt **ZIZYPHUS** jujube tree
zo **ZOANTHUS** sea-anemone
as **ZODIACAL** of signs of the Zodiac
ZOETROPE early form of cinema
ZOIATRIA veterinary surgery
mo **ZOLOTNIK** Russian weight
bt **ZONATION** occurrence in bands
ZONELESS beltless
zo **ZOOBLAST** animal cell
ch **ZOOCHEMY** animal chemistry
zo **ZOOECIUM** wall/chamber of polyzoan individual
ZOOGENIC generative
md **ZOOGLOEA** colony of bacteria
md **ZOOGRAFT** grafting tissue
ZOOLATER animal worshipper
ZOOLATRY animal worship
mn **ZOOLITIC** (fossilized animals)
ZOOMANCY divination

ZOOMETRY animal mensuration
ZOOMORPH animal in decorative art
zo **ZOONITIC** articulated
ZOONOMIA animal physiology
zo **ZOOPHAGA** carnivorous animals
ZOOPHILY love of animals
zo **ZOOPHYTE** plantlike animal
md **ZOOSCOPY** seeing snakes, etc.
md **ZOOSPERM** male seed-cell
bt **ZOOSPORE** animated spore
md **ZOOTOMIC** (vivisection)
ZOOT-SUIT long coat and tight trousers
ZOPFSTIL pig-tail style (Ger.)
zo **ZOPILOTE** turkey-buzzard
ck **ZUCCHINI** green squash, marrow (It.)
ZUGZWANG compulsive move to disaster (chess)
ck **ZWIEBACK** biscuit rusk
mn **ZYGADITE** aluminium compound
md **ZYGODONT** (molar teeth)
cy **ZYGONEMA** zygotene phase of meiosis
cy **ZYGOTENE** 2nd stage of meiotic prophase
ZYMOLOGY study of fermentation and enzymes

PENGUIN ONLINE

News, reviews and previews of forthcoming books

read about your favourite authors

•

investigate over 12,000 titles

•

browse our online magazine

•

enter one of our literary quizzes

•

win some fantastic prizes in our competitions

•

e-mail us with your comments and book reviews

•

instantly order any Penguin book

'To be recommended without reservation ... a rich and rewarding online experience' *Internet Magazine*

www.penguin.com

READ MORE IN PENGUIN

In every corner of the world, on every subject under the sun, Penguin represents quality and variety – the very best in publishing today.

For complete information about books available from Penguin – including Puffins, Penguin Classics and Arkana – and how to order them, write to us at the appropriate address below. Please note that for copyright reasons the selection of books varies from country to country.

In the United Kingdom: Please write to *Dept. EP, Penguin Books Ltd, Bath Road, Harmondsworth, West Drayton, Middlesex UB7 0DA*

In the United States: Please write to *Consumer Services, Penguin Putnam Inc., 405 Murray Hill Parkway, East Rutherford, New Jersey 07073-2136.* VISA and MasterCard holders call 1-800-631-8571 to order Penguin titles

In Canada: Please write to *Penguin Books Canada Ltd, 10 Alcorn Avenue, Suite 300, Toronto, Ontario M4V 3B2*

In Australia: Please write to *Penguin Books Australia Ltd, 487 Maroondah Highway, Ringwood, Victoria 3134*

In New Zealand: Please write to *Penguin Books (NZ) Ltd, Private Bag 102902, North Shore Mail Centre, Auckland 10*

In India: Please write to *Penguin Books India Pvt Ltd, 11 Community Centre, Panchsheel Park, New Delhi 110017*

In the Netherlands: Please write to *Penguin Books Netherlands bv, Postbus 3507, NL-1001 AH Amsterdam*

In Germany: Please write to *Penguin Books Deutschland GmbH, Metzlerstrasse 26, 60594 Frankfurt am Main*

In Spain: Please write to *Penguin Books S. A., Bravo Murillo 19, 1°B, 28015 Madrid*

In Italy: Please write to *Penguin Italia s.r.l., Via Vittorio Emanuele 45/a, 20094 Corsico, Milano*

In France: Please write to *Penguin France, 12, Rue Prosper Ferradou, 31700 Blagnac*

In Japan: Please write to *Penguin Books Japan Ltd, Iidabashi KM-Bldg, 2-23-9 Koraku, Bunkyo-Ku, Tokyo 112-0004*

In South Africa: Please write to *Penguin Books South Africa (Pty) Ltd, P.O. Box 751093, Gardenview, 2047 Johannesburg*

READ MORE IN PENGUIN

LANGUAGE/LINGUISTICS

Language Play David Crystal

We all use language to communicate information, but it is language play which is truly central to our lives. Full of puns, groan-worthy gags and witty repartee, this book restores the fun to the study of language. It also demonstrates why all these things are essential elements of what makes us human.

Swearing Geoffrey Hughes

'A deliciously filthy trawl among taboo words across the ages and the globe' *Observer*. 'Erudite and entertaining' Penelope Lively, *Daily Telegraph*

The Language Instinct Stephen Pinker

'Dazzling . . . Pinker's big idea is that language is an instinct, as innate to us as flying is to geese . . . Words can hardly do justice to the superlative range and liveliness of Pinker's investigations' *Independent*. 'He does for language what David Attenborough does for animals, explaining difficult scientific concepts so easily that they are indeed absorbed as a transparent stream of words' John Gribbin

Mother Tongue Bill Bryson

'A delightful, amusing and provoking survey, a joyful celebration of our wonderful language, which is packed with curiosities and enlightenment on every page' *Sunday Express*. 'A gold mine of language-anecdote. A surprise on every page . . . enthralling' *Observer*

Longman Guide to English Usage
Sidney Greenbaum and Janet Whitcut

Containing 5000 entries compiled by leading authorities on modern English, this invaluable reference work clarifies every kind of usage problem, giving expert advice on points of grammar, meaning, style, spelling, pronunciation and punctuation.

READ MORE IN PENGUIN

REFERENCE

The Penguin Dictionary of Troublesome Words Bill Bryson

Why should you avoid discussing the *weather conditions*? Can a married woman be celibate? Why is it eccentric to talk about the aroma of a cowshed? A straightforward guide to the pitfalls and hotly disputed issues in standard written English.

Swearing Geoffrey Hughes

'A deliciously filthy trawl among taboo words across the ages and the globe' Valentine Cunningham, *Observer*, Books of the Year. 'Erudite and entertaining' Penelope Lively, *Daily Telegraph*, Books of the Year.

Medicines: A Guide for Everybody Peter Parish

Now in its seventh edition and completely revised and updated, this bestselling guide is written in ordinary language for the ordinary reader yet will prove indispensable to anyone involved in health care: nurses, pharmacists, opticians, social workers and doctors.

Media Law Geoffrey Robertson QC and Andrew Nichol

Crisp and authoritative surveys explain the up-to-date position on defamation, obscenity, official secrecy, copyright and confidentiality, contempt of court, the protection of privacy and much more.

The Penguin Careers Guide
Anna Alston and Anne Daniel; Consultant Editor: Ruth Miller

As the concept of a 'job for life' wanes, this guide encourages you to think broadly about occupational areas as well as describing day-to-day work and detailing the latest developments and qualifications such as NVQs. Special features include possibilities for working part-time and job-sharing, returning to work after a break and an assessment of the current position of women.

READ MORE IN PENGUIN

REFERENCE

The Penguin Dictionary of the Third Reich
James Taylor and Warren Shaw

This dictionary provides a full background to the rise of Nazism and the role of Germany in the Second World War. Among the areas covered are the major figures from Nazi politics, arts and industry, the German Resistance, the politics of race and the Nuremberg trials.

The Penguin Biographical Dictionary of Women

This stimulating, informative and entirely new Penguin dictionary of women from all over the world, through the ages, contains over 1,600 clear and concise biographies on major figures from politicians, saints and scientists to poets, film stars and writers.

Roget's Thesaurus of English Words and Phrases
Edited by Betty Kirkpatrick

This new edition of Roget's classic work, now brought up to date for the nineties, will increase anyone's command of the English language. Fully cross-referenced, it includes synonyms of every kind (formal or colloquial, idiomatic and figurative) for almost 900 headings. It is a must for writers and utterly fascinating for any English speaker.

The Penguin Dictionary of International Relations
Graham Evans and Jeffrey Newnham

International relations have undergone a revolution since the end of the Cold War. This new world disorder is fully reflected in this new Penguin dictionary, which is extensively cross-referenced with a select bibliography to aid further study.

The Penguin Guide to Synonyms and Related Words
S. I. Hayakawa

'More helpful than a thesaurus, more humane than a dictionary, the *Guide to Synonyms and Related Words* maps linguistic boundaries with precision, sensitivity to nuance and, on occasion, dry wit' *The Times Literary Supplement*

READ MORE IN PENGUIN

DICTIONARIES

Abbreviations
Ancient History
Archaeology
Architecture
Art and Artists
Astronomy
Biographical Dictionary of Women
Biology
Botany
Building
Business
Challenging Words
Chemistry
Civil Engineering
Classical Mythology
Computers
Contemporary American History
Curious and Interesting Geometry
Curious and Interesting Numbers
Curious and Interesting Words
Design and Designers
Economics
Eighteenth-Century History
Electronics
English and European History
English Idioms
Foreign Terms and Phrases
French
Geography
Geology
German
Historical Slang
Human Geography
Information Technology
International Finance
International Relations
Literary Terms and Literary Theory
Mathematics
Modern History 1789–1945
Modern Quotations
Music
Musical Performers
Nineteenth-Century World History
Philosophy
Physical Geography
Physics
Politics
Proverbs
Psychology
Quotations
Quotations from Shakespeare
Religions
Rhyming Dictionary
Russian
Saints
Science
Sociology
Spanish
Surnames
Symbols
Synonyms and Antonyms
Telecommunications
Theatre
The Third Reich
Third World Terms
Troublesome Words
Twentieth-Century History
Twentieth-Century Quotations